2 0 0 0
POET'S
MARKET

1,800 PLACES TO PUBLISH YOUR POETRY

EDITED BY

CHANTELLE BENTLEY

WRITER'S DIGEST BOOKS
CINCINNATI, OHIO

2.00

Important market listing information

- Listings are based on questionnaires and verified copy. They are not advertisements *nor* are markets necessarily endorsed by the editors of this book.
- Information in the listings comes directly from the publishers and is as accurate as possible, but publications and editors come and go, and poetry needs fluctuate between the publication date of this directory and the time you use it.
- *Poet's Market reserves the right to exclude any listing that does not meet its requirements.*

Complaint procedure

If you feel you have not been treated fairly by a listing in *Poet's Market*, we advise you to take the following steps:

- First try to contact the listing. Sometimes one phone call or a letter can quickly clear up the matter.
- Document all your correspondence with the listing. When you write to us with a complaint, provide the details of your submission, the date of your first contact with the listing and the nature of your subsequent correspondence.
- We will enter your letter into our files and attempt to contact the listing.
- The number and severity of complaints will be considered in our decision whether or not to delete the listing from the next edition.

If you are a poetry publisher and would like to be considered for a listing in the next edition of *Poet's Market*, send a SASE (or SAE and IRC) with your request for a questionnaire to *Poet's Market*—QR, 1507 Dana Ave., Cincinnati OH 45207. Questionnaires received after February 25, 2000, will be held for the 2002 edition.

Supervisory Editor: Barbara Kuroff
Managing Editor, Annuals Department: Cindy Laufenberg
Production Editor: Ian Bessler

Writer's Digest Books website: http://www.writersdigest.com

International Standard Serial Number 0883-5470
International Standard Book Number 0-89879-915-5

Attention Booksellers: This is an annual directory of F&W Publications. Return deadline for this edition is December 31, 2000.

Contents

From the Editor

Writing poetry is often compared to giving birth—from the conception of the idea to the delivery of the poem upon the page. The same can be said for editing and producing a book. In fact, the production of this edition of *Poet's Market* coincided with my second pregnancy; even their due dates—one to the printer, one to the hospital—were the same. And while editing *Poet's Market* caused me far fewer physical symptoms—aside from the occasional headache—I eagerly anticipated the final arrival date of both the baby and the book.

Updated and easier to use . . . Part of my excitement stems from the changes and new information we try to incorporate into each edition of *Poet's Market*. Take for instance the new article The "Quick-Start" Guide to Publishing. If you are a beginning poet or are new to submitting your work, this article provides a ten-step guide to locating and contacting poetry editors and publishers as well as suggestions for using this book to its maximum potential.

New indexes . . . Also new this year are the Book Publishers Index and the Openness to Submissions Index. The Book Publishers Index lists all publishers within *Poet's Market* who consider full-length poetry manuscripts, as opposed to only publishing chapbooks or a magazine. The Openness to Submissions Index organizes all poetry publishers, contests and awards according to their openness to unsolicited submissions.

The inside information on self-publishing . . . For those poets who want to bypass the submission process and publish their own work, we asked editor/publisher Alan Britt to provide the low-down on what poets need to know before hastening into self-publication. You will find his article, Self-publishing: understand the process before taking the plunge, on page 468.

Do's and don'ts for the greeting card market . . . As a rule, *Poet's Market* does not contain listings for greeting card publishers because this market is not typically open to poetry submissions. However, a common misconception exists that writing poetry and writing greeting cards are one and the same. To dispel that myth, Sandra Miller-Louden, author of *Write Well & Sell: Greeting Cards*, discusses what greeting card companies are seeking from freelance writers and how poets can adapt their writing to suit these needs. Her article begins on page 156.

The benefits of poetry readings . . . For even more information on the workings of the poetry field, we turned to author Daniel Grant to learn more about poetry readings. In his article The Value of Participating in Public Poetry Readings, beginning on page 5, Grant discusses how participating in poetry readings can help poets determine if a poem works and tells how readings may provide poets with another method for meeting editors and publishers.

Motivation to keep going . . . We also like to provide the readers of *Poet's Market* with the inspiration that will keep them writing and submitting work. Therefore in this edition, we have included nine Insider Report interviews with poets and editors who have a lot to say about the place poetry plays in their lives and the significance of publishing work. Our interviews include poets Errol Miller and Denise Duhamel, as well as poets/editors Brian Daldorph and Laura Qa.

And as a new baby brings joy as well as major adjustments, I hope the *2000 Poet's Market* provides you with the pleasure of seeing your work in print as well as the knowledge that poetry is a worthwhile pursuit that can change your life. So keep writing, keep submitting and, most of all, keep believing in yourself and your poetry.

Chantelle Bentley

poetsmarket@fwpubs.com

The "Quick-Start" Guide to Publishing Your Poetry

To make the most of *Poet's Market* you need to know how to use it. And with more than 600 pages of poetry publishing markets and resources, a poet could easily get lost amidst the plethora of information. But, fear not. This "quick-start" guide will help you wind your way through the pages of *Poet's Market*, as well as the poetry publishing process, and emerge with your dream accomplished—a published poem.

1. Read, read, read.

Read numerous literary journals and poetry collections to determine if your poetry compares favorably with work currently being published. If your poems are at least the same caliber as the ones you're reading, then move on to step two. If not, postpone submitting your work and spend your time polishing your poetry. Writing and reading the work of others are the best ways to improve craft.

For help with craft and critique of your work:
- You'll find Conference & Workshop listings beginning on page 508.
- You'll find Organizations, including poetry societies, on pages 527-544.

2. Analyze your poetry.

Determine the type of poetry you write to best target your submissions to markets most suitable to your work. Do you write haiku, free verse, prose poems, sonnets; political verse, nature poetry, poems about your locale, feminist poetry? There are magazines and presses seeking specialized work in each of these areas as well as numerous others.

For editors and publishers with specialized interests:
- You'll find the Subject Index beginning on page 576.
- You'll find the Glossary of Poetic Forms and Styles on page 554, which provides definitions for the various styles and forms of poetry found in the Subject Index.
- Also, look for the ◎ symbol before listing titles in the Publishers of Poetry and Contests & Awards sections.

3. Learn about the market.

Read writing-related magazines such as *Poets & Writers*, *Writer's Digest*, *The Writer* and others for interviews with poets and fiction writers, help with various aspects of writing and publishing, and reviews of small press magazines. Also, don't forget to utilize the Internet. There are numerous online journals geared specifically toward writers.

For additional writing-related publications:
- You'll find Publications of Interest on pages 545-550.
- You'll find Websites of Interest on page 551.

4. Find markets for your work.

There are a variety of ways to locate markets for poetry. The publication sections of bookstores and libraries are great places to discover new journals and magazines that might be open to your type of poetry. Read writing-related magazines and newsletters for information about new markets and publications seeking poetry submissions. Online journals often have links to the websites of other journals that may publish poetry. And last but certainly not least, read about magazines, presses and contest markets in the listings found here in *Poet's Market*.

For poetry-publishing possibilities:
- You'll find the Publishers of Poetry section beginning on page 15.

- You'll find Contest & Award listings on pages 478-504.
- Also, don't forget to utilize the indexes at the back of this book to help you target your poems to the right market.

5. Send for guidelines.

In the listings in this book, we try to include as much submission information as we can glean from editors and publishers. Over the course of the year, however, editors' expectations and needs may change. Therefore, it is best to request submission guidelines by sending a self-addressed stamped envelope (SASE). You can also check the websites of magazines and presses which usually contain a page with guideline information.

6. Begin your publishing efforts with journals and contests open to beginners.

If this is your first attempt at publishing your work, your best bet is to begin with local publications or with publications that you know are open to beginning poets. Then, after you have built a publication history, you can try the more prestigious and nationally distributed magazines. For publications and contests most open to beginners, look for the ◘ symbol preceding listing titles.

- Check the Openness to Submissions Index, on pages 560-565, for a list of magazines, presses and contests organized according to their openness to submissions. (◘ beginners; ◙ beginners and experienced; ◖ mostly experienced, few beginners; ◉ specialized)

7. Submit your poetry in a professional manner.

Take the time to show editors that you care about your work and are serious about publishing. By following a publication's submission guidelines and practicing standard submission etiquette, you can better ensure your chances that an editor will want to take the time to read your poems and consider them for publication. Remember, first impressions last, and a carelessly assembled submission packet can jeopardize your chances before your poems have had a chance to speak for themselves.

For help with preparing submissions:

- You'll find The *Poet's Market* Guide to Poetry Submission Etiquette article on page 8.
- Also, read the chapter on getting published in *The Poet's Companion: A Guide to the Pleasures of Writing Poetry* by Kim Addonizio and Dorianne Laux (W.W. Norton, 1997).

8. Keep track of your submissions.

Know when and where you have sent poems and how long you need to wait before expecting a reply. If an editor does not respond by the time indicated in his market listing or guidelines, wait a few more weeks and then follow up with a letter (and SASE) asking when the editor anticipates making a decision. If you still do not receive a reply from the editor within a reasonable amount of time, send a letter withdrawing your poems from consideration and move on to the next magazine on your list.

9. Learn from rejection.

Rejection is the hardest part of the publication process. Unfortunately, rejection happens to every writer and every writer needs to learn to deal with the negativity involved. On the other hand, rejection can be valuable when used as a teaching tool rather than a reason to doubt yourself and your work. If an editor offers suggestions with his or her rejection slip, take those comments into consideration. You don't have to automatically agree with an editor's opinion of your work. It may be that the editor has a different perspective on the piece than you do. Or, you may find that the editor's suggestions give you new insight into your work and help you improve your craft.

For more insight into how poetry editors think:

- You'll find interviews with editors Joyce Odam (page 294), Kathleen Iddings (page 390), Laura Qa (page 368), Brian Daldorph (page 106) and Stellasue Lee (page 352) in this edition of *Poet's Market*.

10. Don't give up.

The best advice for poets trying to get their poems published is be persistent and to always believe in themselves and their work. By continually reading other poets' work, constantly working on the craft of poetry and relentlessly submitting your work, you will eventually find that magazine or journal that's the perfect match for your poetry. And, *Poet's Market* will be here to help you every step of the way.

GUIDE TO LISTING FEATURES

Below you will find an example of the market listings contained in the Publishers of Poetry section. Also included are callouts identifying the various format features of the listings. (For an explanation of the symbols used, see the front and back covers of this book.)

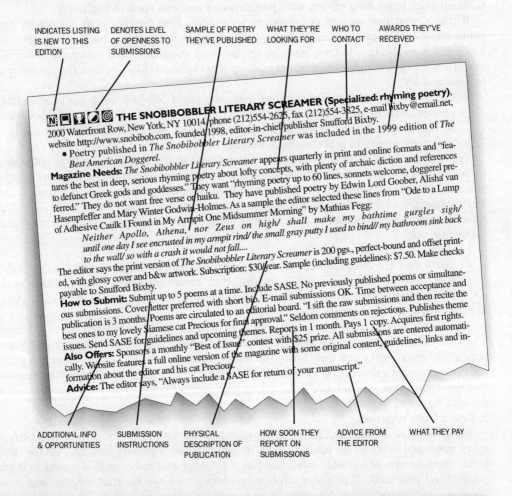

INDICATES LISTING IS NEW TO THIS EDITION

DENOTES LEVEL OF OPENNESS TO SUBMISSIONS

SAMPLE OF POETRY THEY'VE PUBLISHED

WHAT THEY'RE LOOKING FOR

WHO TO CONTACT

AWARDS THEY'VE RECEIVED

THE SNOBIBOBBLER LITERARY SCREAMER (Specialized: rhyming poetry), 2000 Waterfront Row, New York, NY 10014, phone (212)554-2625, fax (212)554-3825, e-mail bixby@email.net, website http://www.snobibob.com, founded 1998, editor-in-chief/publisher Snufford Bixby.
• Poetry published in *The Snobibobbler Literary Screamer* was included in the 1999 edition of *The Best American Doggerel.*
Magazine Needs: *The Snobibobbler Literary Screamer* appears quarterly in print and online formats and features the best in deep, serious rhyming poetry about lofty concepts, with plenty of archaic diction and references to defunct Greek gods and goddesses." They want "rhyming poetry up to 60 lines, sonnets welcome, doggerel preferred." They do not want free verse or haiku. They have published poetry by Edwin Lord Goober, Alisha van Hasenpfeffer and Mary Winter Godwin-Holmes. As a sample the editor selected these lines from "Ode to a Lump of Adhesive Caulk I Found in My Armpit One Midsummer Morning" by Mathias Fegg:
Neither Apollo, Athena, nor Zeus on high/ shall make my bathtime gurgles sigh/
until one day I see encrusted in my armpit rind/ the small gray putty I used to bind// my bathroom sink back
to the wall/ so with a crash it would not fall....
The editor says the print version of *The Snobibobbler Literary Screamer* is 200 pgs., perfect-bound and offset printed, with glossy cover and b&w artwork. Subscription: $30/year. Sample (including guidelines): $7.50. Make checks payable to Snufford Bixby.
How to Submit: Submit up to 5 poems at a time. Include SASE. No previously published poems or simultaneous submissions. Cover letter preferred with short bio. E-mail submissions OK. Time between acceptance and publication is 3 months. Poems are circulated to an editorial board. "I sift the raw submissions and then recite the best ones to my lovely Siamese cat Precious for final approval." Seldom comments on rejections. Publishes theme issues. Send SASE for guidelines and upcoming themes. Reports in 1 month. Pays 1 copy. Acquires first rights.
Also Offers: Sponsors a monthly "Best of Issue" contest with $25 prize. All submissions are entered automatically. Website features a full online version of the magazine with some original content, guidelines, links and information about the editor and his cat Precious.
Advice: The editor says, "Always include a SASE for return of your manuscript."

ADDITIONAL INFO & OPPORTUNITIES

SUBMISSION INSTRUCTIONS

PHYSICAL DESCRIPTION OF PUBLICATION

HOW SOON THEY REPORT ON SUBMISSIONS

ADVICE FROM THE EDITOR

WHAT THEY PAY

For More Information

If you are interested in writing for greeting card companies, *Writer's Market* (Writer's Digest Books) has a whole section dedicated to these companies, complete with contact names, addresses, phone numbers, needs and submission requirements. For poets who are also lyricists, *Songwriter's Market* (Writer's Digest Books) offers pages of opportunities in this field. Both books are available through your local library or bookstore, or can be ordered directly from the publisher by calling (800)289-0963.

The Value of Participating in Public Poetry Readings

BY DANIEL GRANT

Published and unpublished writers would seem to be much in demand these days. All over the country book signings and public readings regularly take place at bookstores, cafés, colleges and community centers, malls and theaters, even at saloons and auto repair shops. Most of these same venues have open-mike nights, when would-be writers may try out their work on an audience.

Book signings and readings are certainly a source of potential publicity as well as tired arms and voices. Perhaps the attention they may bring to a writer's work is their main purpose. Bookstores and publishers, of course, hope that a reading sells books, but no writer can make a living from readings. Writers themselves describe the value of hearing their words read aloud and the feel-good experience of going out into the world and watching as other people listen to them. However, only occasionally do writers recall any specific feedback from an audience other than smiles or bored looks during the reading or polite applause after it is over.

Meeting the marketplace

For some writers, the value of readings is in the hope they will be discovered by a literary agent or a publisher. "Readings are not primarily about the marketplace, but there is always the chance that someone important will hear your work," says Pat Schneider, a poet and director of Amherst Writers & Poets Press in Amherst, Massachusetts. Similarly, Allan Lefcowitz, founder and artistic director of The Writer's Center in Bethesda, Maryland, notes, "It does occasionally happen that someone in the audience is a small press editor or publisher who contacts the poet about sending in a manuscript." According to Karl Kirchwey, co-director of the Unterberg Poetry Center of the 92nd Street Y in New York City, "Readings serve the same function as a literary review, given the fact that poetry books are rarely reviewed by the print media. A reading makes poetry available to a wider audience, and it gives poets a platform. That may not translate into more sales of poetry books, but it can be a source of inspiration for both the audience and the poet."

Considering the distribution of many small press books and literary reviews is so limited, a writer of poetry or fiction may actually reach a larger audience through a series of readings than from the published work. In addition, readings frequently become a separate category on a writer's résumé, reflecting at least the writer's view that a career and work have been recognized in some way. Writers invited to a reading at a well-regarded institution such as the Unterberg Poetry Center are likely to highlight the event on a résumé.

Kirchwey notes that literary readings also provide an opportunity for writers, who otherwise may work in solitude, to meet other writers. Over time, writers offer each other support, informed critical feedback and possibly connections to publishers, literary reviews, teaching positions and other career opportunities. It is frequently the case at the 92nd Street Y and elsewhere that more

DANIEL GRANT *is the author of* The Writers' Resource Handbook *as well as* The Business of Being an Artist *and* The Fine Artist's Career Guide *(all published by Allworth Press). He is also a career consultant to writers and visual artists.*

than one writer is scheduled to speak at a reading. Just Buffalo Literary Center in Buffalo, New York, for example, pairs a nationally known writer with one who is local, increasing the size of the potential audience for the local writer. The pairing also enables the local writer to make a contact with an established writer who may help his career.

"Readings are a way of introducing your work to people who might otherwise never have read it," says poet Katha Pollitt. "Also, it's certainly a nice way to get out of the house. It's even better if you get paid and if you sell some books." Honoraria and the sale of books aside, the main benefit of a reading for Pollitt is to see how her poetry plays to an audience. "A line that seems to work when you wrote it down may not work when read out loud. At times, a line that struck me as very earnest and serious makes an audience break up in laughter and I'll wonder is it the line itself or the audience or the way I'm reading it."

Audience and sound

A reading may or may not be a welcome activity for a writer. But writing, many writers and sponsors of literary readings claim, is not entirely a private affair; and the oral tradition of reciting poetry establishes an important bond between writers and the audience. "Reading is honoring the music of the work," says Schneider. To others, a reading "presents work in a context it wasn't really intended for, saying aloud what was originally expected to be read silently," says novelist Russell Banks. Novelist Madison Smartt Bell says, "I think of a reading as a performance. To read well is an ability that is completely different than writing."

For instance, the eye may see alliteration in a different and less jarring way than the ear hears it. Speaking favorably of the oral presentation, Sam Hazo, a poet and director of the International Poetry Forum in Pittsburgh, Pennsylvania, notes that "something may look good on the page but when you actually say it, it sounds like there's a tennis ball in your mouth."

The way a work sounds when read aloud concerns a number of writers who worry some pieces are being written in order to be read, affecting both the language and the depth of ideas involved. "I don't like the idea of the reading as the central thing a poem is for," says Pollitt. "Readings may make poetry thinner by making poets shape their poems as humorous little stories, clever anecdotes. The complexity of language and complicated ideas don't work well in a reading, so they aren't part of the poetry. A Robert Lowell poem can be read aloud, and half of it goes over your head, but the poem is still a good one. Elizabeth Bishop, a wonderful poet, was shy and tended to read her work in a somber way, which didn't do much for the poem. Other poets may read their poems with a strong, sonorous delivery but, when you read the poem itself, it's very slight. I have looked at poems after hearing them in a reading and find there's not much there."

The problem may be inherent in literary readings. An audience comes not simply to watch a writer read from a piece of paper but to hear a kind of performance. And the more the readers perform, the greater the reaction they will receive from the audience—and it is to generate a response that writers read their work in the first place.

If a writer's intention is to elicit feedback about the work, a dramatic recitation is likely to increase the overall applause but may diminish the ability to determine audience reaction to specific lines or words. A less theatrical reading, on the other hand, may only produce restlessness on the part of an audience that expects the writer to "perform." The problem was identified by E. Jean Lanyon, poet laureate of Delaware since 1979, who states, "I've looked at some poems after hearing them in a theatrical reading and have been quite disappointed but, if the reading was blah, I'm probably not going to try to find the poem and read it on my own."

Perhaps the most extreme form of this emphasis on theatrical reading performances may be found in the "poetry slams" that take place around the country in which the audience is also implicitly invited to boo and cheer and express their sentiments as loudly and exuberantly as the readers.

Preparation and poise

Preparing to read aloud requires writers to pay attention to the sound of their voices as well as to their physical appearance. Doing a reading well—exciting an audience but not so much as to overwhelm its appreciation of the individual words and lines themselves—also takes considerable practice and a commitment to overcoming shyness and insecurity. "You have to aim for a zone between acting—which is misrepresenting the work because it is a text and not a performance—and the private voice," says Banks. "It's tricky."

Lanyon says that writers find their public voice through repeated readings, "learning to project, to look up from the book. They begin to understand that the voice of the poet gives the poem emphasis that is different than simply reading it on your own. After a while, the little downy sparrow changes into a peacock." Repeated readings not only improve a writer's self-confidence, she notes, but develop one's market. "The more times you read publicly, the more people are likely to know your work and want to buy it. People come up to me at the end of a reading wanting to buy something. I sell books at readings and, if I don't have any books with me, I'll run off some chapbooks in order to have something to sell."

Selling may be an awkward experience for writers at a reading. There is a different role they have when standing before people reading their work than when, afterwards, they take money and make change as vendors. Lanyon recommends that writers "bring a friend who can sit there and take the money. It's more comfortable, and the poet can chat with members of the audience and sign the books as at any other author signing."

Awkwardness may also ensue in determining what to write at a signing, Lanyon adds. "One's name may be sufficient, perhaps a generic 'Best Wishes' or 'Good Luck.' Otherwise, the writer may be asked to inscribe a greeting 'To Aunt Mary' or a more difficult name, requiring the book buyer to slowly spell the letters of the name. Writers need as much composure selling and signing their books as when they read from them."

The takeaway

Many writers learn not to expect anything more from a reading than the personal experience of speaking their lines to an audience. The people in attendance may sit in rapt attention or fidget, understand what is being read or not follow anything, buy books or not. Knowing how to read an audience—how seriously do I take the applause? Did the audience miss my point or did I not communicate well?—is not an exact science. Writers take away from a reading whatever they can. "A reading sells books and helps to expand your audience," Banks says. "Of course, what is called the 'conversion rate'—turning a reading into sales—is never a clear-cut matter."

"A reading makes poetry available to a wider audience, . . . That may not translate into more sales of poetry books, but it can be a source of inspiration for both the audience and the poet."

—*Karl Kirchwey*

The *Poet's Market* Guide to Poetry Submission Etiquette

BY CHANTELLE BENTLEY

If you're a beginning poet who has yet to submit work or a veteran poet who needs a refresher course on submission procedures, this article provides the basic information you'll need to successfully submit your poetry for publication.

Before we begin discussing how to prepare poems for submission, however, determine where you want to send your work. The "Quick-Start" Guide to Publishing Your Poetry, on page 2, provides beginning poets with ways to determine if their poetry is ready for submission and ideas on how to locate suitable markets. Experienced poets should utilize the six indexes at the back of this book or go straight to the listings to find their most promising markets. In either situation, our new Openness to Submissions Index, which lists magazines, presses and contests according to their openness to unsolicited manuscripts, will make your search for markets easier by quickly identifying those markets who are open to beginners and those markets who want only experienced poets.

Once you've decided where to send your work, you can then focus on proper presentation. In the following pages, you will find specifics about approaching magazines and presses, formatting poetry manuscripts, selling the rights to your work and preparing cover letters. You'll also find suggestions about what to do if you don't receive a reply from an editor about work submitted.

Reading and following these guidelines should help you decrease the occurrence of common submission mistakes as well as increase the number of acceptance letters flowing into your mailbox.

Approaching magazine markets

If you are submitting work to a quarterly newsletter, an online magazine or an annual poetry journal, poetry editors are primarily interested in seeing how you write. Therefore, a query letter is not necessary, but a sample of your work is. Usually three to five poems with a cover letter and self-addressed stamped envelope (SASE) is preferred by most editors.

Occasionally, editors will require poets to submit in a manner other than the traditional method just mentioned. Because of this, *Poet's Market*'s Publishers of Poetry section provides the most essential submission information in its listings. Also, it's a good idea to obtain writer's guidelines by sending a SASE or visiting a magazine's website prior to submitting.

In general, agents are not needed to submit poetry to magazines. Most agents do not handle poetry because it simply does not pay. (It's hard for an agent to earn commission when a poet is paid in contributor's copies.) And because the majority of book publishers who accept unsolicited poetry are small presses—paying a small honorarium or a percentage of the print run—poets are also best to handle their own book submissions, too.

Approaching book publishers

When submitting a full-length poetry manuscript for possible publication, most editors want to first receive a query with a few sample poems and a cover letter with brief bio and publication credits. However, there are those editors who prefer to receive the complete manuscript, especially if the editor publishes chapbooks and not full-length collections. (See the discussion of chapbook publishing on page 13 of this article.)

As with approaching magazines, the best route to take when preparing to submit a manuscript to a book publisher is to send a SASE for complete guidelines or visit the publisher's website.

Proper submission format for poetry manuscripts

For the most part, a standard format exists for poetry manuscript submissions. However, as we've previously mentioned, some editors' submission guidelines deviate from the norm. For those editors, we state their submission preferences within their listings. For all others, the following list will provide you with the information needed for presenting a professional manuscript. When in doubt, however, send a SASE to the journal or press and request their writer's guidelines or check their website. To receive information from publishers outside your own country, send a self-addressed envelope (SAE) with an International Reply Coupon (IRC).

For magazine submissions:
- Submit only three to five poems at one time, positioning your best poems on top. Most editors don't have time to read more than five poems but less than three doesn't provide them with a large enough sample of your work.
- Type or print (in a legible font, e.g., Times New Roman) one poem to a page, single-spaced with double spacing between stanzas. (The only exception here may be for haiku.) Leave at least a one-inch margin on all sides of the page. *Avoid handwriting your work.*
- Use white, 8½ × 11 bond paper, preferably 16 or 20 lb. weight. The paper should be heavy enough to withstand handling by several people.
- Include your name, address, phone number and e-mail address on separate lines, single-spaced, in the upper left or right corner of each poem. (If you write under a pseudonym, you must still use your legal name here.)
- The title of your poem should appear in all caps or initial caps about six lines underneath your contact information, centered or flush left. The poem should begin one line beneath the title.
- If a poem does carry over to a second sheet, list your name in the top left margin. Underneath your name include a key word from the poem's title, the page number and information on whether the lines at the top are a continuation of the same stanza or the start of a new one (e.g., SILENCE, page 2, continue stanza or begin new stanza).

For book submissions:
- When submitting a poetry collection to a book publisher, it's best to request guidelines, because press requirements vary from a query letter with a few sample poems to the entire manuscript.
- Use a separate cover sheet for your name, address, phone number and e-mail address. Center your book title and byline about halfway down the page. Then include your last name and page number in the top left margin of the first and each subsequent manuscript page.
- If a poem, or poems, in your collection carries over to a second sheet, remember to follow the instructions from the sixth bullet of **For magazine submissions** above.

For both magazine and book submissions:
- Proofread carefully. Even the shortest poem can contain typos that elude the eye of the poet all too familiar with the lines in front of her. Also, an occasional white-out is okay, but retype (or correct and reprint) poems with numerous typos.
- Fold manuscript, five pages and under, neatly into thirds (do not fold poems individually) and mail in a business-size (#10, 4⅛ × 9½) envelope. For a manuscript over five pages, fold in half and mail in a 6 × 9 envelope. Larger manuscripts will look best mailed flat in 9 × 12 or 10 × 13 envelopes.
- To ensure a response to your submission, you must enclose a SASE (or SAE and IRCs). You can use either a #9 (4 × 9) reply envelope or a #10 business-size envelope (fold into thirds if you are also using a #10 envelope to mail your manuscript).
- To have your manuscript returned, enclose a SASE the same size as the mailing envelope

with the same amount of postage. Another option is to send a disposable manuscript. However, you must tell the editor the manuscript is disposable and the SASE you've provided is for reply only. (NOTE: One IRC is needed for one ounce by surface mail or each half-ounce by airmail. And, three pages of poetry, a cover letter and a SASE can usually be mailed for one first-class stamp. The website, http://www.usps.gov/business/calcs.htm, calculates postage for both domestic and international destinations.)

Before sending disk or e-mail submissions . . .

- Verify that the editor accepts electronic submissions. You will find a list of publications and presses open to e-mail submissions on page 552 of this book. Also, openness to fax, disk or e-mail submissions is usually noted in market listings or in writer's guidelines.
- Check market listings or writer's guidelines for specific instructions for electronic submissions, including the format in which editors prefer to receive electronic submissions (i.e., MS Word, Word Perfect, ASCII, etc.).
- Always include a printed copy with any disk submission. For e-mail submissions, it's usually best to include poems in the body of the message rather than including them as an attachment.

Concerning rights

The Copyright Law states that writers selling to magazines are primarily offering one-time rights to their work—that is, the editor or publisher may only publish your poem once—unless you and the publisher agree otherwise (in writing). Therefore, if an editor requests something different, such as the right to also later publish the work in a retrospective anthology, and you are open to such an agreement, make sure the agreement is documented.

Following is a list of various rights. Be sure you know exactly what rights you are selling before you agree to the sale. For more information on rights, refer to the revised edition of *The Writer's Legal Guide* (Allworth Press, 1998).

- **Copyright** is the legal right to exclusive publication, sale or distribution of a literary work. Since the most recent Copyright Law went into effect in 1978, your "original works of authorship" are protected as soon as they are "fixed in a tangible form of expression." As the writer or creator of a written work, you can also include your name, date and the copyright symbol (©) on your poem to establish copyright. However, copyright notices are typically considered unnecessary and, in many editors' minds, signal the work of amateurs who are distrustful of editors and publishers. If you wish, you can register your copyright with the Copyright Office for a $20 fee. If paying $20 to register each of your poems is not feasible, you can register a group of poems with one form under one title for one $20 fee.

Obtain more information about copyright from the U.S. Copyright Office, Library of Congress, 101 Independence Ave. SE, Washington DC 20559. For answers to specific questions (but not legal advice), call the Copyright Public Information Office at (202)707-3000 weekdays between 8:30 a.m. and 5:00 p.m. (EST). Copyright forms can also be ordered at that same number or downloaded from the Library of Congress website at http://lcweb.loc.gov/copyright. The website also includes information on filling out the forms, general copyright information and links to copyright-related websites.

- **First Rights (a.k.a. First Serial Rights)**—This means the poet offers a journal or magazine the right to publish the poem for the first time in any periodical. All other rights to the material remain with the writer. It's important to note that first North American serial rights means the editor will be the first to publish your work in a U.S. or Canadian periodical. Your work can still be submitted to editors outside North America, or those open to reprint rights.

• **One-time Rights**—A periodical licensing one-time rights to a work (also known as simultaneous rights) buys the *nonexclusive* rights to publish the work once. That is, there is nothing to stop the poet from submitting the work to other publications at the same time. Simultaneous submissions would typically be to periodicals without overlapping audiences.

• **Second Serial (Reprint) Rights**—Editors and publishers seeking reprint rights are open to submissions of previously published work—provided you tell them when and where the work was previously published so they can properly credit the periodical in which your work first appeared. You'll notice many poetry collections list such "credits," often on the copyright page. In essence, they've acquired reprint rights.

• **All Rights**—Some publishers require poets to relinquish all rights, which means you cannot submit that particular work for publication anywhere else—not even as part of your own collection—unless you negotiate to get reprint rights returned to you. Before you agree to this type of arrangement, ask the editor whether he is willing to buy first rights instead of all rights. If not, you can simply write a letter withdrawing your work from consideration. Also, some editors will reassign rights to a writer after a given time, such as one year.

• **Electronic Rights**—These rights cover usage in a broad range of electronic media, from online magazines and databases to CD-ROM magazine anthologies and interactive games. The editor should specify in writing if—and which—electronic rights are being requested. The presumption is that unspecified rights are kept by the writer.

Because the issue of rights is so important, almost all editors and publishers will state (in their market listing or guidelines) what rights they acquire. And once your work is accepted for publication, a number of editors and publishers will ask you to sign an agreement which not only tells you what rights are being requested, but also asks you to certify that the poetry is your own.

Including a cover letter

Though the issue of cover letters is far less serious in nature than selling rights, poets still must determine the appropriateness of including cover letters with their submissions. Some experts in the field say cover letters are unnecessary and may even impede the publication process. And a few editors agree a cover letter has never caused them to accept or reject a manuscript. However, many editors indicate a desire for cover letters in their market listings and submission guidelines.

If you do include a cover letter with your poems, the following tips will help you compose a professional letter that allows you to personally present your work to editors.

☑ Keep it brief. Your cover letter should be no more than one page.

☑ Include your name, address, phone number and e-mail address.

☑ If an editor wants biographical information for the magazine's contributors page, add two to three lines about your job, interests, why you write poetry, etc. Editors like to know there are real people behind the submissions.

☑ Avoid praising your work in a cover letter. Let your poems speak for themselves.

☑ Include the titles (or first lines) of the poems you are submitting.

☑ Include a few (no more than five) of your most recent publishing credits. If you haven't published a poem yet, either note that you have no prior credits, don't mention publication credits at all, or don't include a cover letter (unless a cover letter is required, of course). Be aware that some editors are particularly interested in new writers and make special efforts to publish beginners' work.

☑ Demonstrate some familiarity with the magazine to which you're submitting: comment on a poem in the magazine you enjoyed, tell the editor why you chose to submit to their publication, give your opinion of the magazine. More than anything, editors like to know their contributors are also their readers.

☑ Address your submission to the correct contact person. Most of the publications and presses in this directory have a particular individual to whom you should direct your submissions. If no one is listed, however, check the publication's guidelines or the masthead of a recent copy. If you are still unable to locate a specific name, simply address your letter to "Poetry Editor."

☑ Use an acceptable business-style format for your letter and make sure it is error free.

☑ Keep in mind that editors are people, too. Be brief and professional, but also personable, in your cover letter. Remember, kindness goes a long way.

Waiting for a reply

Most editors and publishers indicate (in their market listings and submission guidelines) approximately how long you must wait before you can expect to receive a reply about your submission. If an editor does not specify when you will receive a report, it is generally expected to be within three months. Many times, however, the approximate date (or three-month benchmark) will come and go without a word from the editor or publisher.

What should you do when you haven't heard from an editor within the specified time period?

1. Wait another month, then send a note inquiring about the status of your submission. Note the titles of your poems and the date sent. Ask when the editor will be making a decision. Enclose a SASE or self-addressed, stamped postcard for the editor's reply.
2. If you still do not hear from the market, send a letter or postcard withdrawing your poems from consideration. Then submit your work elsewhere.
3. If you are desperate to learn the status of your submission, you may contact an editor by phone but keep the call brief and to the point. Remember, not only is time a valuable commodity for poets eager to get published, but also for those editors who divide their time between publishing a magazine, working full-time and maintaining family obligations.

Submitting previously published poems and simultaneous submissions

When you submit your poetry to magazine editors and publishers, they not only assume the work is original (that it is yours and nobody else's), but they also assume the work has not been previously published and is not under consideration elsewhere. Before submitting a poem that has already been published or simultaneously submitting work to more than one magazine, consider the following guidelines:

- Check market listings or submission guidelines to see if an editor or publisher is willing to consider previously published poems. Some editors are simply not open to such submissions. They want to be the first to publish new work—not the second. These editors are looking to acquire first rights to your poetry—not reprint rights.
- If an editor is open to previously published work, note in your cover letter where the particular poem(s) first appeared.
- In listings and guidelines, editors should also note their preferences in regard to simultaneous submissions (i.e., sending the same package of poems to several editors at the same

time). Most poets who engage in this practice believe a batch of three to five poems submitted to two or more editors has a better chance of resulting in acceptance.

- If you choose to submit your work simultaneously and an editor accepts one of your poems, you must contact the other editor(s) immediately and withdraw your work from consideration. Be mindful that this may annoy (or even anger) the other editor(s) still in the process of making a decision. And future submissions to these markets may no longer be welcome.
- Again, even if an editor is open to simultaneous submissions, note in your cover letter that you are simultaneously submitting your work.
- If you're just beginning to submit your work or are still perfecting your craft, you are likely to quickly collect numerous rejections by simultaneously submitting your work. That can be discouraging. You may want to avoid the shortcut and submit to publications one at a time. Then you can use any rejections received to hone your craft and improve your poem before sending it on to the next editor.

Publishing a collection of poems

Once you have gathered a fair number of publication credits in literary or small press magazines, you may want to begin thinking about book publication. Book publishers, by the way, expect some of the poems in your manuscript to be previously published. And, knowing the difficulty poets face in placing a collection, they are more accepting of the practice of simultaneous submissions. Often, publishing a chapbook is a good middle step between publishing in magazines and publishing a full-length book collection.

What is a chapbook?

A chapbook is a small volume of work, usually under 50 pages in length. As such a volume is less expensive to produce than a full-length book collection (which may range from 50 to over 100 pages), a chapbook is a safe way for a publisher to take a chance on a lesser-known poet. Most chapbooks are saddle-stapled with card covers. Some are photocopied publications. Others contain professionally printed pages. While chapbooks are seldom noted by reviewers or carried by bookstores, they are good items to sell after readings or through the mail. You'll discover that, in addition to some book publishers, a number of magazine publishers also publish chapbooks (for a complete list, refer to the Chapbook Publishers Index on page 556).

Whether you're planning to submit your work to either chapbook or book publishers, you should always examine sample copies of their previously published collections. This is not only the best way to familiarize yourself with the press's offerings, but also a good way to determine the quality of the product.

Publishing contracts for book manuscripts

Various publishing arrangements exist and greatly depend on the publisher with which you are dealing. Some, in fact, are more beneficial than others. Consider the following options carefully:

- **Standard publishing**—In a standard publishing contract, the publisher usually agrees to assume all production and promotion costs for your book. You receive a 10% royalty on the retail (or sometimes wholesale) price, though with some small presses you are paid a percentage of the press run instead. Such publishers only release a few poetry volumes each year.
- **Cooperative publishing**—This arrangement is exactly that: cooperative. Although the details of such contracts vary, they require some type of investment of either time or money on your part. Some require involvement in marketing. Others specify money for production costs. In any case, know what you're signing. While cooperative publishing is respected in the literary and small press world (and many such publishers can bring your work the attention it deserves), some vanity presses try to label themselves as "cooperative." True cooperative publishing, however, shares both the risks and the profits.

- **Self-publishing**—This option may be most appealing if your goal is to publish a small collection of your work to distribute at readings or to give to family and friends. It is also a good choice for those who prefer complete control over the creative process. In this scenario, you work hand-in-hand with a local printer and invent a name for your "press." Most importantly, you pay all the costs but own all the books and net all the proceeds from any sales (which you must generate). For details, read the article Self-publishing: understand the process before taking the plunge, on page 468 of the Publishers of Poetry section or *The Complete Guide to Self-Publishing* by Tom and Marilyn Ross (Writer's Digest Books).
- **Vanity/subsidy presses**—This is probably the least desirable option. Companies in this category usually advertise for manuscripts, lavishly praise your work, and ask for fees far in excess of costs (compare their figures to those of a local printer for a book of similar size, format and binding). These companies also make a habit of collectively advertising their books. That is, your work will simply receive a line along with 20 or so other books in an ad placed in the general media rather than a specific market. Worse yet, sometimes you own all copies of your book; sometimes you don't.

It's important to note that some anthology publications fall under "vanity/subsidy" publishing because you must pay a tidy sum to purchase the volume containing your work. If you have concerns about a particular publisher call the Poets & Writers Information Center at (212)226-3586. Calls are welcome weekdays from 11 a.m. to 3 p.m. (EST).

Tracking submissions

Once you begin submitting individual poems or manuscripts, you'll need to keep a record of all poetry submissions and correspondence with editors.

To track which poems you have submitted and where and when you submitted them, you should record such information as the title of each poem, the name of the magazine to which it was submitted, and the date your work was mailed. Also, note the date of each editor's reply, the outcome of your efforts, and any comments that may prove useful when you're next submitting to that market (such as changes in editors, reading periods or frequency of publication).

Keep current on changes and opportunities in poetry publishing

New markets are established all the time. Therefore, to keep up-to-date with new literary journals and small presses in between the yearly editions of *Poet's Market*, read such publications as *Poets & Writers Magazine* or *Writer's Digest*, both of which regularly contain information about new markets. Also, check out the Web, including our website www.writersdigest.com. Many websites for writers exist that list electronic and print publications seeking submissions. These websites may also provide direct links to those publications. (See Websites of Interest, on page 551, for a list of websites for poets seeking publication.)

The Markets
Publishers of Poetry

Containing everything from stapled newsletters published by individuals in kitchen-corner offices to perfect-bound, paperback collections produced in large suites by paid staffs, this section of *Poet's Market* provides a comprehensive look at those publishers listed within its nearly 500 pages. All the activities a publisher may conduct—whether it's publishing a quarterly magazine, maintaining a website, sponsoring a contest, or offering writing workshops—are represented within one listing to give you an overview of the publisher's operations. And for those few publishers with projects at different addresses, we've cross-referenced the listings so you still may be aware of all of a publisher's involvements.

Evaluating these publishers to determine which is right for you and your work is not an easy task—and, because our tastes and interests may differ from yours, this is something we cannot do for you. However, learning all you can about publishers and their operations is a huge step on the road toward publication. Therefore, within the following listings, we provide you with as much information as we can glean from editors and publishers—specialized interests, contact names, submission requirements, payment policies, awards received, etc.

To make the information you seek accessible and easy to locate, we include subheads using key terms in the listings to help you readily identify the type of information provided within a particular paragraph. For example, the subhead **Magazine Needs** indicates information about the type of poetry sought by a magazine or journal, a physical description of the publication and the amount of poetry received versus the amount of poetry published each year; the subhead **How to Submit** includes the magazine's submission requirements, reporting times and payment policies. For book publishers, the subheads **Book/Chapbook Needs** and **How to Submit** are used to separate their editorial needs and submission requirements. Sometimes, for very brief listings or for a listing with more than one magazine or book publishing operation, the subheads will be combined into one subhead (e.g., **Magazine Needs & How to Submit** or **Book/Chapbook Needs & How to Submit**).

The **Also Offers** subhead indicates information about contests, conferences, workshops, readings or organizations a publisher may either sponsor or be associated with. If a magazine also maintains a website, the contents of that website are noted under this subhead.

We believe letting editors speak for themselves is an excellent way for you to get an inside look at how a particular editor thinks or works. So, under the **Advice** subhead, most listings contain quotes from editors and publishers on their publishing philosophies, what types of poetry particularly interest them, any pet peeves or recurring problems they have in regard to submissions, or advice they have for poets about the poetry field or the submission process in general. You can learn much about publishers by what they choose to include in these brief statements. But, for even more insight into what makes publishers tick, read the editorial introductions included in most publications. Many editors use these first few pages of their journals to let readers know why they do what they do and exactly what kind of work they want.

LOCATE YOUR PERFECT MARKETS

The best way to approach this rather large section of information depends on what you are seeking. If you do not have a specific publisher in mind, dive right in and start reading through the listings. This will give you a good idea of what publishing opportunities are available and what types of markets exist.

However, if you are looking for a particular market, begin with the General Index. Let's say, for example, you've recently written a poem inspired by your experiences as a home healthcare nurse and you think a likely market for the poem might be *the Compleat Nurse*. You won't find *the Compleat Nurse* in this section alphabetized under C, however. The editor requested the listing be under the name of the publisher of the magazine, Dry Bones Press, and that's where you will find it. You might not have discovered that without looking in the General Index, where *the Compleat Nurse* is cross-referenced to Dry Bones Press.

The General Index also contains the names of publishers from the 1999 edition who are not included in this edition and, if known, the reasons for their absence. It also provides a way to find publishers who have changed names: though you will find a publication listed in this section under its new name, you can still find the previous name with the appropriate cross-reference in the General Index.

The Publishers of Poetry section contains 1,800 poetry publishing markets, includes 9 "Insider" interviews with editors and poets, 2 informative "Insider" articles, and showcases the covers of 9 diverse publications. Also worthy of mention are the roughly 300 new markets included in this edition—especially considering that new listings are often more receptive to submissions.

DISCOVER NEW LISTINGS

To locate this year's new listings, look for the new listing symbol (🆖) preceding the listing titles. As in years past, some new listings are publications that were in earlier editions of *Poet's Market* but not the previous one. We're happy to welcome back, for example, *Caveat Lector, First Time* (from East Sussex, England), *Mandrake Poetry Review* (from Poland), *Pikeville Review, Reflect* (publishing spiral poetry), *Sea Oats*; and (M)öthêr TØñgué Press and *White Wall Review* (both from Canada).

Other listings new to this edition are actually "new," that is, they are magazines or presses that began publishing in the last few years. These include *About Such Things, Barrow Street, Lonzie's Fried Chicken Literary Magazine, Pacific Enterprise Magazine, Rattapallax, The Rejected Quarterly*; and *Eternity* and *For Poetry.Com* (both web-based publications). Also new to this edition are Alden Enterprises and Synaesthesia Press, both publishers of chapbooks; Bear Star Press which publishes one to two paperbacks per year with one selected through a competition; and The People's Press and Perugia Press, both paperback publishers.

We would also like to welcome some of the new listings from outside the United States, including *Backwater Review, The Canadian Journal of Contemporary Literary Stuff* and Red Deer Press, all based in Canada; Barking Dog Books, from Mexico; *Monas Hieroglyphica* and *Plume Literary Magazine*, both published in the United Kingdom; and *Jejune: America Eats Its Young*, from the Czech Republic.

To quickly find those markets located outside the United States, look for the maple leaf symbol (🍁) before the titles of all listings from Canada and a globe symbol (🌐) before all international listings.

REFINE YOUR SEARCH FOR LOCAL AND SPECIALIZED MARKETS

One of the best ways for most poets to become a part of the literary scene is to start in their home territory. Therefore the Geographical Index, located in the back of this book, will quickly lead you to publishers with whom you have a lot in common because of either the state, region or country in which you currently live or from which you originate.

And to help poets with ties outside the United States more easily locate potential markets, we post listings from Australia, Canada, France and the United Kingdom under their own category heads in the Geographical Index. In addition, a variety of unrelated international listings are included under the category Other Countries.

For those who write specialized poetry—pertaining to a particular group or subject or poetry written in a particular form—refer to the Subject Index. This index lists publishers according to their specialties. For instance, under the heading Women/Feminism you will find a list of publishers who seek poetry written by women or focusing on issues of interest to women. Under the heading Form/Style you'll find publishers who want haiku as well as those who seek sonnets or experimental work.

DEFINE YOUR STYLE

Besides locating the publications whose interests match yours, you need to be sure your understanding of the subject matter and the editor's are the same. So, to help you be right on target with your submissions, we include a Glossary of Poetic Forms and Styles. This glossary defines the specific poetic forms and styles publishers are seeking. We have concentrated on providing definitions for those forms appearing most frequently in the Subject Index under the heading Forms/Styles. However, we have also provided definitions for many other forms not listed in the Subject Index, especially the less-known forms. For a more comprehensive list of terms, see *The Poetry Dictionary* by John Drury (Story Press, 1995) or the Glossary in *You Can Write Poetry* by Jeff Mock (Writer's Digest Books, 1998).

For any terms and abbreviations in the listings with which you are not familiar, see the Glossary of Listing Terms which follows the Glossary of Poetic Forms and Styles at the back of this book.

KEEP AN EYE ON THE DETAILS

Once you have selected the markets you feel match your interests and style, you must pay attention to submission details if you want your poetry to be given serious consideration. While a number of practices are considered standard, more and more editors are opting for variations. Thus, each year we ask editors and publishers to not only update the general information within their listings (such as reporting times and payment policies) but also to clarify specific submission details. (For a detailed discussion on preparing submissions, see *Poet's Guide: How to Publish and Perform Your Work* by Michael J. Bugeja [Story Line Press, 1995].)

For example, it is important to know if and when editors publish theme issues. While some editors develop all their issues around themes (see the Themes heading in the Subject Index for a list of these types of publications contained in *Poet's Market*), others only publish one or two theme issues a year (or even every few years). Of course, whenever an editor is reading for a theme issue, that's the type of work he or she wants to receive. If you send unrelated work, even if the editor does not normally publish theme-based material, your work will not be considered.

Once again we specifically asked editors to supply details about their upcoming themes and related deadlines. Though a number of editors were able to provide this information for 2000, many had not yet finalized their plans when we contacted them. To be sure your submission will be welcome, send a self-addressed, stamped envelope (SASE) to receive up-to-date information about themes, deadlines, and other submission guidelines.

For immediate identification of important changes to the contact information in *Poet's Market* listings, look for a check mark symbol (☑) preceding a listing's title. This symbol indicates a change in address, phone number, e-mail address or contact name from last year's edition. The dollar sign symbol ($) points out listings that pay a monetary amount, even if that amount is only $1. Editors also advertise contact information changes, upcoming themes and deadlines in the pages of such periodicals as *Writer's Digest*, *The Writer* and *Poets & Writers Magazine*. Checking these publications frequently, as well as the Market of the Day section of the Writer's

Digest website (www.writersdigest.com), will keep you current on submission needs.

SNAIL MAIL VERSUS E-MAIL

As you read the listings in this section—and we encourage you to review them all—you will notice an increasing amount of fax numbers and e-mail addresses. Be careful when contacting editors by these methods. While some actually encourage electronic submissions, most still prefer manuscripts be sent via regular mail with SASEs for reply or the return of your work. Many editors simply supply fax numbers and e-mail addresses to facilitate requests for guidelines or other information.

Determining the best method for submitting your work is tricky but critical, especially because submitting material in an undesired manner may jeopardize your chances of receiving a response or even being read. Within the listings themselves, we have noted preferences for and against electronic submissions. If a listing includes a fax number or e-mail address but does not state their submission preference, or requires a reading fee, the best method is to contact the publisher before submitting your poems to verify if an e-mail or fax submission is acceptable.

To further eliminate some of the guess work, a list of those markets open to e-mail submissions appears at the end of our Websites of Interest to Poets section at the back of this book. Also, we use the computer symbol (◼) to indicate online or electronic market listings. The appearance of this symbol before a listing's title should be a strong indicator of the editor's or publisher's openness to e-mail submissions.

DON'T FORGET THE REPLY ENVELOPE

For those listings not connected to the electronic world or for those requiring submissions be sent through the post, a reply envelope is, with few exceptions, an absolute necessity. Many publishers run their operations on shoe-string budgets and cannot afford to reply to every submission, query or request for information received. Including a SASE or SAE (self-addressed envelope) and IRCs (International Reply Coupons, for replies from countries outside your own) with all correspondence provides an easy way for overworked and underpaid editors to contact you.

And remember, if you want your manuscript returned, you must provide a SASE (or SAE and IRCs) large enough to contain your work and with sufficient postage. If it takes three stamps to mail material, it will take three stamps for the material to be returned—unless you are sending a disposable manuscript. But if you do not want your poems returned to you (that is, the manuscript can be discarded), the editor needs to be told the SASE is only for his or her response.

It's not surprising that editors, frustrated with receiving more and more manuscripts without SASEs, are creating policies in regard to such submissions. Many choose to include disclaimers stating that submissions without SASEs will not be acknowledged. However, some editors are not so kind; they discard submissions without SASEs before the material is even read. Other editors may require a minimal reading fee to cover postage costs. To get past this stickiest of spots in the poet/editor relationship, make a habit of sending a SASE (or SAE and IRCs) with all correspondence. Also, to make sure you are following other expected submission procedures, read (or reread) The *Poet's Market* Guide to Poetry Submission Etiquette, on page 8.

AWARDS AND HONORS

As another way of helping you evaluate publishers, we have also included information about awards and honors that have been bestowed on editors and publishers or their magazines and books. For instance, we continue to note which publications have had poetry selected for inclusion in recent volumes of *The Best American Poetry*, an annual anthology highlighting the best poetry published in periodicals during the previous year. (Listings with this information will have the trophy symbol (🏆), which indicates award-winning market listings, before their titles. The information itself will be set off by a bullet (●) near the beginning of the listing). As a different guest editor compiles the anthology every year, knowing which publications have work included, especially in a number of recent volumes, can provide insight into the type and quality of material used.

In addition, *The Best American Poetry* (published by Scribner, 1230 Avenue of the Americas, New York NY 10020, 800/223-2348) can help you develop a sense for trends in the field. The 1999 volume, by the way, is published at the same time as this edition of *Poet's Market*. So, when you are ready to read the poetry that has been selected from the publications listed here, check your nearest library or bookstore.

UNDERSTAND OPENNESS TO SUBMISSIONS SYMBOLS

Finally, all listings in this section include one or more "openness" symbols preceding their titles. These symbols, selected by editors and publishers, can help you determine the most appropriate markets for your poetry. (For details see The "Quick-Start" Guide to Publishing Your Poetry on page 2.) The openness to submissions symbols and their explanations are:

☐ **Publisher encourages beginning or unpublished poets to submit work for consideration and publishes new poets regularly.**

◔ **Publisher accepts quality work by beginning and established poets.**

◑ **Publisher seeks mostly experienced poets with previous publication credits, very few new poets; does not encourage beginners.**

◎ **Specialized publication encourages poets from a specific geographical area, age-group, gender, sexual orientation or ethnic background or accepts poems in specific forms or on specific themes.**

⊘ **Closed to unsolicited manuscripts.**

✔ ◑ **A SMALL GARLIC PRESS (ASGP); AGNIESZKA'S DOWRY (AGD)**, 5445 Sheridan #3003, Chicago IL 60640, e-mail asgp@enteract.com or marek@enteract.com or ketzle@aa.net, website http://www.enteract.com/~asgp/, founded 1995, co-editors Marek Lugowski, katrina grace craig and Amy L. Wray.
Magazine Needs: *Agnieszka's Dowry (AgD)*, is "a magazine published both in print and as a permanent Internet installation of poems and graphics, letters to Agnieszka, and a navigation in an interesting space, all conducive to fast and comfortable reading. No restrictions on form or type. We use contextual and juxtapositional tie-ins with other material in making choices, so visiting the online *AgD* is assumed to be part of any submission." Single copy: usually $3. Make checks payable to A Small Garlic Press.
How to Submit: Submit 5-10 poems at a time. E-mail submissions preferred—plain text only. "Please inform us of the status of publishing rights." Sometimes comments on rejections. Guidelines can be obtained via website. Reports online usually in 3-8 weeks. Pays 1 copy. Acquires one-time rights where applicable.
Book/Chapbook Needs & How to Submit: A Small Garlic Press (ASGP) publishes 2-7 chapbooks of poetry/year. Query with a full online ms, ASCII only.
Also Offers: "See our webpage for policies and submission guidelines. The press catalog and page of links to other markets and resources for poetry are maintained online at our website."

🌐 ◑ **AABYE; AABYE'S BABY**, (formerly *New Hope International*), 20 Werneth Ave., Gee Cross, Hyde, Cheshire SK14 5NL United Kingdom, e-mail newhope@iname.com, website http://www.nhi.clara.net/nhihome.htm, founded 1969 as Headland, 1980 as New Hope International, 1998 as Aabye, editor Gerald England.
Magazine Needs: *Aabye* publishes all types of poetry from traditional to avant-garde, from haiku to long poems, including collaborative poetry, translations (usually with the original), long poems, short poems, prose poems, haiku, englynion. They have published poetry by Bill Headdon, Joan Payne Kincaid, Anthony Lawrence, Ernest Slyman, Steve Sneyd and Neca Stoller. As a sample the editor selected these lines from "Out or Urban" by David A. Bishop:
> Come out of urban:/Come with me to the soil,/the flesh and blood of everything./Lie naked on bare
> earth and come

Aabye is 52 pgs., digest-sized, printed offset-litho from computer typesetting, saddle-stapled, with glossy cover using color artwork. Press run is 500 for 200 subscribers of which 20 are libraries. Subscription: £10 (£13 non-UK)/3 issues. Sample: £3.75 (£5 non-UK). Make checks payable to Gerald England. "Non-sterling cheques not accepted. Payment by International Giro (available from Post Offices worldwide), or currency notes to the sterling equivalent preferred."
How to Submit: Submit up to 6 poems at a time on separate sheets; put name and address on each sheet.

Include SASE (or SAE with IRCs) or submissions will not be considered. No simultaneous submissions. Cover letter required. Translations should include copy of original. "If you do not require the ms returned (and disposable mss are preferred, especially from overseas) please advise, but do note that an SAE or IRC is still required for reply." No e-mail submissions, "except by prior arrangement." Send SASE (or SAE with IRCs) or e-mail for guidelines. Reports usually within 1 month. Always sends prepublication galleys. Pays 1 copy. Acquires first British serial rights.

Book/Chapbook Needs & How to Submit: "Only writers with a body of work already published in periodicals should consider approaching us. Always query before submitting."

Also Offers: Website (http://www.nhi.clara.net/nhihome.htm) includes guidelines, information on books and magazines available for sale, samples of poetry published by *New Hope International* and links to other sites. A separate website (http://www.geocities.com/Athens/Oracle/1735) publishes reviews of books, magazines, audio material, PC software, videos of interest to all lovers of words, arts and music. All books sent are considered for review. The associated website *Aabye's Baby* (http://www.geocities.com/Paris/Cafe/9091) publishes poetry only electronically. Its content differs entirely from that published in the printed magazine *Aabye*. Poems not selected for *Aabye* may be considered for *Aabye's Baby*. Contributors may indicate when submitting whether or not they wish their work to be considered for website.

Advice: The editor advises, "Long lists of previous publications do not impress; perceptive, interesting, fresh writing indicative of a live, thinking person makes this job worthwhile."

🔿 THE AARDVARK ADVENTURER; THE ARMCHAIR AESTHETE; PICKLE GAS PRESS, 59 Vinal Ave., Rochester NY 14609, phone (716)342-6331, e-mail bypaul@netacc.net, website http://www.geocities.com/SoHo/Museum/1499/, founded 1996, editor Paul Agosto.

Magazine Needs: *The Aardvark Adventurer* is "a quarterly family-fun newsletter-style zine of humor, thought and verse. Very short stories (less than 500 words) are sometimes included." They prefer "light, humorous verse; any style; any 'family acceptable' subject matter; length limit 32 lines. Nothing obscene, overly forboding, no graphic gore or violence." They have published poetry by C. David Hay, Najwa Brax and Dennis Norville. As a sample the editor selected his poem "Squiggles and Doodles":

> wandering, pointless, meandering line/serving one purpose: to occupy time./without you i'm certain i'd probably find/i'd have to resort back to using my mind.

TAA is 6-12 pgs., 8½×14, photocopied and corner-stapled with some b&w graphics. They receive about 500 poems a year, accept approximately 40%. Press run is 100 for 100 subscribers. Single copy: $2; subscription: $6. Sample: $2. Make checks payable to Paul Agosto. "Subscription not required but subscribers given preference."

Magazine Needs: Also publishes *The Armchair Aesthete*, a quarterly digest-sized zine of "fiction and poetry of thoughtful, well-crafted concise works. Interested in more fiction submissions than poetry though." Line length for poetry is 30 maximum. The editor says *The Armchair Aesthete* is 30-40 pgs., 5½×8½, quality desktop-published, photocopied, gray cover, includes ads for other publications and writers' available chapbooks. Each issue usually contains 10-15 poems and 6-9 stories. They receive about 300 poems/year, accept 25-30%. Subscription: $12/year. Sample postpaid: $3. Make checks payable to Paul Agosto.

How to Submit: For both publications, previously published poems and simultaneous submissions OK, if indicated. Cover letter preferred. E-mail and disk submissions OK. Time between acceptance and publication is 1 year. Seldom comment on rejections. *The Aardvark Adventurer* occasionally publishes theme issues, but *The Armchair Aesthete* does not. For both, send SASE for guidelines. Report in 1-2 months. Pay 1 copy. Acquire one-time rights. The staff of *Aardvark* reviews books and chapbooks of poetry in 100 words. The staff of *Armchair* occasionally reviews chapbooks. Send books for review consideration.

Advice: "*The Aardvark Adventurer* is a perfect opportunity for the aspiring poet, a newsletter-style publication with a very playful format."

🔿 ABBEY; ABBEY CHEAPOCHAPBOOKS, 5360 Fallriver Row Court, Columbia MD 21044, e-mail greisman@aol.com, founded 1970, editor David Greisman.

Magazine Needs & How to Submit: *Abbey*, a quarterly, aims "to be a journal but to do it so informally that one wonders about my intent." They want "poetry that does for the mind what that first sip of Molson Ale does for the palate. No pornography or politics." They have published poetry and artwork by Richard Peabody, Vera Bergstrom, D.E. Steward, Carol Hamilton, Harry Calhoun, Wayne Hogan and Cheryl Townsend. It is 20-26 pgs., magazine-sized, photocopied. They publish about 150 of 1,000 poems received/year. Press run is 200. Subscription: $2. Sample: 50¢. Send SASE for guidelines. Reports in 1 month. Pays 1-2 copies.

Book/Chapbook Needs & How to Submit: *Abbey Cheapochapbooks* come out 1-2 times a year averaging 10-15 pgs. For chapbook consideration query with 4-6 samples, bio and list of publications. Reports in 2 months. Pays 25-50 copies.

Advice: The editor says he is "definitely seeing poetry from two schools—the nit'n'grit school and the textured/reflective school. I much prefer the latter."

🌐 🔿 🔿 ABIKO ANNUAL WITH JAMES JOYCE FW STUDIES (Specialized: translations), 8-1-8 Namiki, Abiko-shi, Chiba-ken 270-1165 Japan, phone/fax 011-81-471-84-7904, e-mail alp@db3.so-net.or.jp, founded 1988, founding editor Laurel Sicks.

Magazine Needs: *Abiko* is a literary-style annual journal "heavily influenced by James Joyce's *Finnegan's*

Wake. We publish all kinds, with an emphasis like Yeats's quote: 'Truth seen in passion is the substance of poetry!' We include originals and translations from Japanese and other languages." They have published poetry by Louise Kennelly, Christine J. Lee and Elizabeth Howkins. It is about 800 pgs., 15cm×20.5cm, perfect-bound with coated paper cover. Press run is 500 for 50 subscribers of which 10 are libraries. Sample: $35.

How to Submit: "See *Writer's Digest, Poets & Writers* and *AWP Chronicle* for details." Open to unsolicited reviews. Writers may also send books for review consideration.

Also Offers: Sponsors contests. Send SASE for guidelines.

Advice: The editor says, "Please remember U.S. postage does not work in Japan with SAEs! Send 2 International Reply coupons."

$ 🔘 ABORIGINAL SF (Specialized: science fiction), Box 2449, Woburn MA 01888-0849, founded 1986, editor Charles C. Ryan, appears quarterly.

Magazine Needs: "Poetry should be 1-2 pgs., double-spaced. Subject matter must be science fiction, science or space-related. No long poems, no fantasy." The magazine is 64 pgs., with 10 illustrations. Press run is 6,000, mostly subscriptions. Subscriptions for "special" writer's rate: $14/4 issues. Sample: $6.85.

How to Submit: No simultaneous submissions. Send SASE for guidelines. Reports in 2-3 months, no backlog. Always sends prepublication galleys. Pays $20/poem and 2 copies. Buys first North American serial rights. Reviews related books of poetry in 100-300 words.

🅽 🔘 ABOUT SUCH THINGS (Specialized: religious), 1701 Delancey St., Philadelphia PA 19103, phone (215)849-1583, e-mail aboutsuch@juno.com, website http://world.std.com/~pduggan/ast/astroot.html, founded 1996, managing editor Laurel W. Garver.

Magazine Needs: *AST* appears twice a year. "We seek to publish poetry, fiction and arts- and culture-related essays that reflect a Christian worldview and retain a sense of wonder about God. We seek contemporary voices that speak what is noble, true, excellent and praiseworthy—that can see the possibility of healing in the midst of brokenness." They want inspirational, nature, relationship themes; contemporary free verse; "work that appeals to the senses, fresh and original, makes a lasting impression." No erotica, occult, feminist, gay/lesbian, non-Christian religions, haiku, "anything resembling Helen Steiner Rice." They have published poetry by Rachel Toliver, Ben Ohmart, Michael Aleman and Philip Hughes. As a sample the editor selected these lines from "The Word" by Rachel Toliver:

> This I know and this I write;/sure in the unsure hand of faith:/He is robed and flung through the sky,/
> He has tender, broken hands./This is the thought of all my days,/the song which spins my world/and
> presses breath into my lungs.

AST is 28 pgs., magazine-sized, photocopied and saddle-stitched with 70 lb. text paper cover, includes grayscale original art and some clip art. They receive about 140 poems a year, accept approximately 20%. Press run is 400 for 40 subscribers, 150-200 shelf sales. Single copy: $3; subscription: $7/year. Sample: $3 plus $1.01 postage. "Purchase of a sample is highly recommended."

How to Submit: Submit up to 5 poems at a time. Line length for poetry is 4 minimum, 80 maximum. Previously published poems and simultaneous submissions OK. Cover letter preferred. Disk submissions OK. "Phone number is essential. This is how authors are contacted if accepted. One poem per page. SASE must be #10 envelope or larger with at least 2 stamps for returns." Reads submissions Spring—November through January 20; Autumn—May through July 20 only. Time between acceptance and publication is 3 months. Poems are circulated to an editorial board. "Poems are read with authors' names removed and a number assigned to them. Five or six evaluators critique each poem and score it based on set criteria. The group meets to discuss the poems, then final scores are turned in and tallied. Twelve to seventeen top poems are published." Often comments on rejections. Send SASE for guidelines or obtain via website. Reports in 1 year. Sometimes sends prepublication galleys. Pays 2 copies/accepted piece. Acquires one-time rights.

Also Offers: Website includes writing samples, art samples, submission guidelines, ordering information and contact information.

Advice: The editor says, "Poetry should be much more than prose broken into stanzas. If you aren't using vivid imagery, you need to read more."

✓ $ ▢ 🔘 ABOVE THE BRIDGE MAGAZINE; THIRD STONE PUBLISHING (Specialized: regional), P.O. Box 416, Marquette MI 49855, phone (906)494-2458, e-mail classen@mail.portup.com, website http://www.portup.com/above, founded 1985, poetry editor Sean MacManus.

Magazine Needs: *Above the Bridge* is a bimonthly magazine designed to reflect life and living in Michigan's Upper Peninsula. The editor says the magazine is 60 pgs., 8½×11, and includes line art and graphics. They receive about 200 poems a year, accept approximately 10%. Press run is 4,000 for 3,000 subscribers of which 50 are libraries. Single copy: $3.50; subscription: $18. Sample: $4.

How to Submit: Submit 2-3 poems at a time. Previously published poems and simultaneous submissions OK. Cover letter preferred. Often comments on rejections. Send SASE for guidelines. Reports in 4 months. Pays $5 and 2 copies. Acquires one-time rights. Staff reviews books of poetry only if author or topic is related to Michigan's Upper Peninsula. Send related books for review consideration.

⊘ ◯ ABRAXAS MAGAZINE; GHOST PONY PRESS, P.O. Box 260113, Madison WI 53726-0113, e-mail irmarkha@students.wisc.edu, website http://www.geocities.com/Paris/4614 or http://www.litline.org/html/ABRAXAS.html, *Abraxas* founded in 1968 by James Bertolino and Warren Woessner, Ghost Pony Press in 1980 by editor/publisher Ingrid Swanberg. Contact for both presses is Ingrid Swanberg.
Magazine Needs & How to Submit: *Abraxas* no longer considers unsolicited material, except as announced as projects arise. The editor is interested in poetry that is "contemporary lyric, concrete, experimental." Does not want to see "political posing; academic regurgitations." They have published poetry by William Stafford, Ivan Argüelles, Denise Levertov, César Vallejo and Andrea Moorhead. As a sample the editor selected these lines from "the silence of lascaux" by próspero saíz:

> in the silence of lascaux a wavering light is fading/outside the cave the bones of slaughter linger still/
> traces of mass killings beneath the cliffs of stone/yet far from the equine ossuary stubby ponies tumble/
> in the vanishing lines of the sacred terror of the horse . . .

Abraxas is up to 80 pgs. (160 pgs., double issues), 6×9, flat-spined (saddle-stitched with smaller issues), litho offset, with original art on its matte card cover, using "unusual graphics in text, original art and collages, concrete poetry, exchange ads only, letters from contributors, essays." It appears "irregularly, 4- to 9-month intervals or longer." Press run is 600 for 500 subscribers of which 150 are libraries. Subscription: $16/4 issues, $20/4 issues Canada, Mexico and overseas. Sample: $4 ($8 double issues). *Abraxas* will announce submission guidelines as projects arise. Pays 1 copy plus 40% discount on additional copies.
Book/Chapbook Needs & How to Submit: To submit to Ghost Pony Press, inquire with SASE plus 5-10 poems and cover letter. Previously published material OK for book publication by Ghost Pony Press. Editor sometimes comments briefly on rejections. Reports on queries in 1-3 months, mss in 3 months or longer "We currently have a considerable backlog of mss." Payment varies per project. Send SASE for catalog to buy samples. They have published three books of poetry by próspero saíz including *the bird of nothing & other poems*; 168 pgs., 7×10, sewn and wrapped binding, paperback available for $20 (signed and numbered edition is $35), as well as *Zen Concrete Ex Etc.*, by d.a. levy; 268 pgs., 8½×11, perfect bound, illustrated, paperback for $27.50.
Also Offers: Website includes writer's guidelines and submission dates; book prices; and links to the editor.
Advice: The editor says, "Ghost Pony Press is a small press publisher of poetry books; *Abraxas* is a literary journal publishing contemporary poetry, criticism and translations. Do not confuse these separate presses!"

Ⓝ $◯ ABUNDANCE—A HARVEST OF LIFE, LITERATURE AND ART; ABUNDANCE PRESS, 265 SW Port Saint Lucie Blvd., Suite 175, Port Saint Lucie FL 34984, phone (561)336-3793, fax (561)336-4176, e-mail slpbear@aol.com, website http://www.abundancepress.com, founded 1995, editor Anthony Watkins, online editor Suzanne Robinson, poetry editor Kevin McLaughlin.
Magazine Needs: *Abundance* is "a bimonthly literary magazine published and distributed throughout South Florida's Treasure Coast dedicated to promoting the arts in our community and, now, all over the world. We consider all submissions but can only use one or two poems or fiction pieces per month. We have no content requirements other than the work be well written and interesting in the opinion of our editors." The editors say *Abundance* is about 30 pgs., published in tabloid and online formats. They receive about 100 poems a year, accept approximately 15-20%. Press run is 6,000. Sample: $1 "to cover postage & handling." Make checks payable to Abundance Press.
How to Submit: Submit 3-4 typed poems at a time. Line length for poetry is 30 maximum. Previously published poems and simultaneous submissions OK. Cover letter preferred. E-mail submissions OK. "Make sure your name and address are on each page if you submit by snail-mail. If you are submitting work to multiple publications, we reserve the right to publish if you do not withdraw your submission in writing within 30 days of notice of intent to publish." Time between acceptance and publication is 2 months. Poems are circulated to an editorial board. "All editors read submissions being considered for publication." Seldom comments on rejections. Send SASE for guidelines or obtain via website. Reports in 1 month. Pays 3¢/word up to $25 (500 words). Also accepts work under a non-paid category. "Selecting paid or non-paid category does not decrease your chance of getting paid, it only increases your chance of getting published." Buys one-time rights plus reprint rights for "Best of" Collections. Reviews books and chapbooks of poetry in 500 words. Open to unsolicited reviews. Poets may also send books for review consideration.
Advice: The editors say, "While we are open to all forms of poetry and fiction, we publish only minimal amounts of rhyming, religious or humorous poetry. We are drawn to work that reflects the beauty of the life of the everyday man or woman."

⊕ ◯ ACID ANGEL, 35 Falkland St. (GFL), Glasgow, Scotland G12-9QZ, phone 44(0)41-221-1223, e-mail acidangel@acidity.globalnet.co.uk, first founded 1984, relaunched 1998, editor Dee Rimbaud.
Magazine Needs: *Acid Angel* is published "whenever there is enough cash in the kitty: usually once or twice per year. The magazine is innovative, leftfield, dynamic, visionary, spiritual, avant-garde, visceral and intelligent. Contributors should be the same. Poetry, Prose, Stories, Artwork, anything in two dimensions considered. Mostly UK writers and artists, but willing to consider worthwhile USA/Canada talent." They have published poetry by Ivor Cutler, Angela Death, Yoshi Ooshi, James Kelman, Alasdair Gray, Arthur Rimbaud, Edwin Morgan. As a sample they selected these lines from "Angel of Obscurity" by Eve Lilith Macrae:

> . . . could only dream/in road-movie monochrome,/in narcotic naiveté, imagining myself/descending

into the nirvana of pain/knowing nothing of how painful/pain can be; and now you are unreachable,/ beyond me, an angel of obscurity.

The editor says *AA* is 60 pgs., A4, lazer-printed and stapled with card cover, includes art and ads. They receive about 2,000 poems a year, accept approximately 5%. Press run is 1,000. Single copy: $15; subscription: $60. Make checks payable to Dee Rimbaud (U.S. purchasers should send cash or international money orders).

How to Submit: Submit 4-10 poems at a time with SAE and 2 IRCs. "Do not send original manuscripts as these cannot be returned." No previously published poems or simultaneous submissions. Cover letter required. "Information included is up to you." E-mail and disk submissions OK (Microsoft Word files). Reads submissions May 1 through December 31 only. Time between acceptance and publication is 6-18 months. Seldom comments on rejections. Criticism fee: $1 per poem. "Editor will red pen suggestions on poem. Payment in advance only." Reports in 1-3 months. "Be patient, I will reply to everyone eventually." Pays 1 copy. Reviews books of poetry and other magazines in 20-100 words. Open to unsolicited reviews. Poets may also send books for review consideration.

Also Offers: Publishes *Acid Angel Database,* "a listing of over 450 UK magazines. We can send on floppy or e-mail to you." Single copy: $13. "Website will be launched by 2000. E-mail for details."

Advice: The editor says, "If you have not yet found a magazine that truly excites your head, heart and spirit, then *Acid Angel* will probably be the mag that does it for you."

⚑ $◖ ACM (ANOTHER CHICAGO MAGAZINE); LEFT FIELD PRESS, 3709 N. Kenmore, Chicago IL 60613, founded 1977, poetry editor Barry Silesky.

• Work published in *ACM* has been included in *The Best American Poetry* (1992, 1994, 1995, 1996 and 1997) and *Pushcart Prize* anthologies.

Magazine Needs: *ACM* is a literary biannual, with emphasis on quality, experimental, politically aware prose, fiction, poetry, reviews, cross-genre work and essays. No religious verse. They have published prose and poetry by Albert Goldbarth, Michael McClure, Jack Anderson, Jerome Sala, Nance VanWinkel, Nadja Tesich, Wanda Coleman, Charles Simic and Diane Wakoski. As a sample the editor selected these lines by Dean Shavit:

> *Just the facts. Forgotten on purpose./This is our land. Yes, you said, "ours."/A gang of teenagers, too young for the army, too stupid for respect.*

Silesky says *ACM* is 220 pgs., digest-sized, offset with b&w art and ads. Editors appreciate traditional to experimental verse with an emphasis on message, especially poems with strong voices articulating social or political concerns. Circulation is 2,000 for 500 subscribers of which 100 are libraries. Subscription: $16/year. Sample: $8.

How to Submit: Submit 3-4 typed poems at a time. No previously published poems; simultaneous submissions OK. Reports in 2-3 months, has 3- to 6-month backlog. Sometimes sends prepublication galleys. Pays $5/page, "if funds permit," and 1 copy. Buys first serial rights. Reviews books of poetry in 250-800 words. Open to unsolicited reviews. Poets may also send books for review consideration.

Advice: The editor says, "Buy a copy—subscribe and support your own work."

✓ ◖ ◎ THE ACORN; EL DORADO WRITERS' GUILD (Specialized: regional), P.O. Box 1266, El Dorado CA 95623-1266, phone (530)621-1833, fax (530)621-3939, e-mail cje@foothill.net, founded 1993, poetry consultant Taylor Graham.

Magazine Needs: *the ACORN* is a quarterly journal of the Western Sierra, published by the El Dorado Writers' Guild, a nonprofit literary organization. It includes "fiction and nonfiction, history and reminiscence, story and legend, and poetry." They want poetry "up to 30 lines long, though we prefer shorter. Focus should be on western slope Sierra Nevada. No erotica, pornography or religious poetry." They have published poetry by Nancy Cherry, Joyce Odam and Edward C. Lynskey. As a sample the poetry consultant selected these lines from "Talking Water" by Blaine Hammond:

> *It has been the hawk/after it was a rat/eaten by the hawk. Listen!/It was your lover/after she breathed moist oxygen/once exhaled by the pine,/which gave its limbs a perch/to the hawk, breathed/carbon dioxide expiration.//It has passed through so many cells,/been alive so many times/without dying, by now/it has become aware./You should taste/its memory.*

The poetry consultant says *the ACORN* is 44 pgs., 5½×8½, offset-printed and saddle-stapled with light card cover. They receive about 400 poems a year, use approximately 15%. Press run is 200 for 110 subscribers. Subscription: $12. Sample: $3.

How to Submit: Submit 3-5 poems, neatly typed or printed, at a time. Previously published poems OK—indicate where published; however, no simultaneous submissions. E-mail submissions OK. Cover letter with short (75-word) bio and publication credits preferred. "Our issues favor topical items suitable for the season." Deadlines are February 1, May 1, August 1 and November 1. Time between acceptance and publication is 1 month. "Poetry consultant screens, then five editors score the poems for content, form and suitability." Graphics editor selects to fit space available." Often comments on rejections. Reports within 1 month after deadline. Pays 2 copies.

Also Offers: Sponsors annual contest. First prize $100, second prize $50, third prize $25. Entry fee: $7/3 poems, 40 lines maximum/poem. Deadline: June 15. All winning entries are published in the contest edition of *the ACORN*. Send SASE for complete rules.

Advice: The editor says, "If your poetry is about nature, be accurate with the species' names, colors, etc. If you describe a landscape, be sure it fits our region. Metered rhyming verse had better be precise. (We have an editor with an internal metronome!) Slant rhyme and free verse are welcome. Avoid trite phrases."

ACORN WHISTLE; ACORN WHISTLE PRESS, 907 Brewster Ave., Beloit WI 53511, e-mail burwellf @lib.beloit.edu, website http://www.acornwhistle.com, founded 1994, first issue published in spring 1995, editor Fred Burwell.
Magazine Needs: *Acorn Whistle* appears once or twice a year. "We seek writing that moves both heart and mind. We seek accessible poetry: narrative, lyrical, prose poem. No length requirements. We are not interested in experimental, religious, erotic or New Age work. We also publish fiction, memoir and personal essay." They have published poetry by Mary Legato Brownell, Wendy Taylor Carlisle, Daniel Smith and JoAnne McFarland. As a sample the editor selected these lines from "Splicing the Rope" by Sara DeLuca:
> There would be little rest for any crewman/on a 1950's haying day,/little respite from the growling
> tractors, hissing heat,/blue dust of stem and leaf baled tight,/the bite of twinestring,/sharp and throbbing
> through thick leather gloves.
The editor says *AW* is 75-100 pgs., 8½×11, staple-bound, using b&w photos and art, no ads. Press run is 500. Subscription: $14. Sample: $7.
How to Submit: Include SASE with all submissions. No previously published poems; simultaneous submissions OK. Often comments on rejections. Send SASE for guidelines. Reports in 3 months. Pays 2 copies. Acquires first North American serial rights.
Also Offers: Founded in 1998, Acorn Whistle Press has published *Songs From an Inland Sea*, a collection of poems by Sara DeLuca and another collection, *Stills*, by Joanne McFarland. Website includes guidelines, table of contents of each issue, photos of covers, sample poems and prose, reviews of magazines and books, information on Acorn Whistle Press and its books.
Advice: The editor says, "We publish no reviews, although we plan to mention publications by our past authors. We wish more writers would focus on material that matters to them, rather than trying to impress an audience of editors and teachers. We seek accessible writing for an audience that reads for pleasure and edification. We encourage a friendly, working relationship between editors and writers."

ACUMEN MAGAZINE; EMBER PRESS; THE LONG POEM GROUP NEWSLETTER, 6 The Mount, Higher Furzeham, Brixham, South Devon TQ5 8QY England, phone (01803)851098, press founded 1971, *Acumen* founded 1984, poetry editor Patricia Oxley. *The Long Poem Group Newsletter* founded 1995, editors William Oxley and Sebastian Barker.
Magazine Needs: *Ember Press* appears 3 times a year (in January, May and September) and is a "small press publisher of a general literary magazine with emphasis on good poetry." They want "well-crafted, high quality, imaginative poems showing a sense of form. No experimental verse of an obscene type." They have published poetry by Elizabeth Jennings, William Oxley, Gavin Ewart, D.J. Enright, Peter Porter, Kathleen Raine and R.S. Thomas. As a sample the editor selected this poem, "Learning A Language" by Danielle Hope:
> . . . And I walk to the sea/to look for messages in dunes/and sea-grass/but I find a tangle of red flowers
> I cannot identify./The sea shuffles/illegible scatters of sand.
Acumen is 100 pgs., A5, perfect-bound. "We aim to publish 120 poems out of 12,000 received." Press run is 650 for 400 subscribers of which 20 are libraries. Subscription: $35 surface/$40 air. Sample copy: $15.
How to Submit: Submit 5-6 poems at a time. No previously published poems; simultaneous submissions OK, if not to UK magazines. Reports in 1 month. Pays "by negotiation" and 1 copy. Staff reviews books of poetry in up to 300 words, single format or 600 words, multi-book. Send books for review consideration to Glyn Pursglove, 25 St. Albans Rd., Brynmill, Swansea, West Glamorgan SA2 0BP Wales.
Also Offers: Publishes *The Long Poem Group Newsletter* featuring short articles about long poems and reviews of books of long poems. Free for large SASE (or SAE with IRC).
Advice: Patricia Oxley advises, "Read *Acumen* carefully to see what kind of poetry we publish. Also read widely in many poetry magazines, and don't forget the poets of the past—they can still teach us a great deal."

ADASTRA PRESS, 16 Reservation Rd., Easthampton MA 01027-2536, founded 1980, publisher Gary Metras.
Book/Chapbook Needs: "Adastra is primarily a chapbook publisher using antique equipment and methods, i.e., hand-set type, letterpress printed, hand-sewn bindings. Any titles longer than chapbook length are by special arrangement and are from poets who have previously published a successful chapbook or two with Adastra.

MARKET CONDITIONS are constantly changing! If you're still using this book and it is 2001 or later, buy the newest edition of *Poet's Market* at your favorite bookstore or order directly from Writer's Digest Books (800)289-0963.

Editions are generally released with a flat-spine paper wrapper, and some titles have been bound in cloth. Editions are limited, ranging from 200-400 copy print runs. Some of the longer titles have gone into reprint and these are photo-offset and perfect-bound. Letterpress chapbooks by themselves are not reprinted as single titles. Once they go out of print, they are gone. Instead, I have released *The Adastra Reader, Collected Chapbooks, 1979-1986* (1987) and *The Adastra Reader II, collected Chapbooks, 1987-1992* (1999). These anthologies collect the first twelve chapbooks and the second twelve, respectively, and I am now planning the third series. I am biased against poems that rhyme and/or are religious in theme. Sequences and longish poems are always nice to present in a chapbook format. There are no guidelines other than these. Competition is keen. Less than .5% of submissions are accepted." Poets published include W.D. Ehrhart (*Beautiful Wreckage, New & Selected Poems*), Thomas Lux (*The Blind Swimmer: Selected Early Poems, 1970-1975*), Miriam Sagan (*Pocahontas Discovers America*) and Geoffrey Jacques (*Suspended Knowledge*). As a sample the editor selected these lines from "Neighbor" in *Leaving for a Year*, by Tom Sexton:

> Across a stubble field his old house/is an accordian played by wind,//A life of hauling lobster traps/ has worn him to the bone.//After dark we watch him carrying/a lamp from room to room//talking to shadows on the wall.

Two to four chapbooks are brought out each year. Sample chapbook: $5.

How to Submit: Send a complete chapbook ms of 12-18 pgs., double-spaced preferred, during the month of February. Notification of acceptance/rejection by April. "I choose 1 or 2 mss to publish the following year." Query with a sample of 5 poems from a chapbook ms in the Fall. "If I like what I see, I'll ask you to submit the chapbook ms in February. Always include an SASE." Time between acceptance and publication is 1-2 years. Payment is 10% of the print run in copies with a discount on additional copies.

ADOBE ABALONE; CONFECTION (Specialized: form/style); CALYPSO WINGS (Specialized: spirituality/inspirational), 6185 Magnolia Ave., Suite 131, Riverside CA 92506-2524, phone (909)359-1988, founded 1997, founding editor Sheryl Gregg, *adobe abalone* chief editor Charles Ardinger, *CONFECTION* chief editor Duane Dodson, *Calypso Wings* chief editor Marilyn Injeyan.

Magazine Needs: *adobe abalone* is a biannual publishing "free verse and prose that pluck the strings of our universal feelings and life issues." *CONFECTION* is a biannual publishing rhyming work only—"prove good poetry can still rhyme." *Calypso Wings* is an annual collection, appearing in October, of spiritual/inspirational poetry, all forms. The editor says *adobe abalone*, *CONFECTION* and *Calypso Wings* are about 20 pgs., 5½×8½, photocopied and saddle-stapled with color paper cover, includes art. They receive "hundreds of poems monthly." Subscription: $10/2 issues, $25/year for all three publications. Sample: $5. "Please specify publication."

How to Submit: For all publications, submit 5 poems at a time with reading fee and SASE. "Submissions without SASEs will be returned postage due." Previously published poems and simultaneous submissions OK. Reading fee: $5. Send SASE for guidelines. Reports in 1 week with SASE. Pays 3 copies. Acquires one-time rights.

Also Offers: Each publication sponsors an on-going chapbook contest. Entry fees: $10. Send SASE for details.

Advice: The editor says, "If you like rules—stick to them. If you find formality too fatiguing, abandon your weary wings to whatever wind awakens your whimsy. Write what you like to read or can't find. Forget what anyone else has told you—do your own thing and send it to us first."

ADRIFT (Specialized: ethnic), 46 E. First St., #3D, New York NY 10003, founded 1980, editor Thomas McGonigle.

Magazine Needs: The editor says, "The orientation of the magazine is Irish, Irish-American. I expect the reader-writer knows and goes beyond Yeats, Kavanagh, Joyce, O'Brien." The literary magazine is open to all kinds of submissions, but does not want to see "junk." They have published poetry by James Liddy, Thomas McCarthy, Francis Stuart and Gilbert Sorrentino. *Adrift* appears twice a year and is 32 pgs., magazine-sized, offset on heavy stock, saddle-stapled with matte paper cover. Circulation is 1,000 with 200 subscriptions, 50 of which are libraries. Single copy: $4; subscription: $8. Sample: $5. Make checks payable to T. McGonigle.

How to Submit: Simultaneous submissions OK. Magazine pays, rate varies; contributors receive 1 copy. Reviews books of poetry. Open to unsolicited reviews. Poets may also send books for review consideration.

ADVOCATE, PKA's PUBLICATION, 301A Rolling Hills Park, Prattsville NY 12468, phone (518)299-3103, founded 1987.

Magazine Needs: *Advocate* is a bimonthly advertiser-supported tabloid, 12,000 copies distributed free, using "original, previously unpublished works, such as feature stories, essays, 'think' pieces, letters to the editor, profiles, humor, fiction, poetry, puzzles, cartoons or line drawings." They want "nearly any kind of poetry, any length, but not religious or pornographic. Poetry ought to speak to people and not be so oblique as to have meaning only to the poet. If I had to be there to understand the poem, don't send it. Now looking for horse related poems, stories, drawings and photos." They accept approximately 25% of poems received. Sample: $4.

How to Submit: No previously published poems or simultaneous submissions. Time between acceptance and publication is an average of 4-6 months. Editor "occasionally" comments on rejections. Reports in 6-8 weeks. Pays 2 copies. Acquires first rights only.

Advice: The editor says, "All submissions and correspondence must be accompanied by a self-addressed, stamped envelope with sufficient postage."

AETHLON: THE JOURNAL OF SPORT LITERATURE (Specialized: sports/recreation), Dept. PM, English Dept., East Tennessee State University, Box 70270, Johnson City TN 37614-0270, founded 1983, general editor Don Johnson, Dean, Arts & Sciences, ETSU. Submit poems to poetry editor Robert W. Hamblin, Professor of English, Southeast Missouri State University, Cape Girardeau MO 63701.
Magazine Needs: *Aethlon* publishes a variety of sport-related literature, including scholarly articles, fiction, poetry and reviews; 6-10 poems/issue; two issues annually, fall and spring. Subject matter must be sports-related; no restrictions regarding form, length, style or purpose. They do not want to see "doggerel, cliché-ridden or oversentimental" poems. Poets published include Neal Bowers, Joseph Duemer, Robert Fink, Jan Mordenski, H.R. Stoneback and Don Welch. The magazine is 200 pgs., digest-sized, offsét printed, flat-spined, with illustrations and some ads. Circulation is 1,000 for 750 subscribers of which 250 are libraries. Subscription is included with membership ($40) in the Sport Literature Association. Sample: $15.
How to Submit: "Only typed mss with SASE considered." No simultaneous submissions. Submissions are reported on in 6-8 weeks and the backlog time is 6-12 months. Contributors receive 5 offprints and a copy of the issue in which their poem appears.

AFFAIR OF THE MIND: A LITERARY QUARTERLY, 8 Mare Lane, Commack NY 11725, phone (516)864-5135, founded 1997, editor Tracy Lyn Rottkamp, associate editor D. Henri Bormann, art director Catherine Kenney.
Magazine Needs: *AOTM* contains "literary, humor and narrative work; translations; exclusive interviews with prominent poets; and work focusing on relationships, psychological, personal, history, etc. Please SASE for subject themes." They have published poetry by David M. Wright, Ruth Wildes Schuler, Hugh Fox, Ward Kelley, Richard Alan Bunch and B.Z. Niditch. The editor says *AOTM* is 100-120 pgs., 9×12, desktop-published with glossy cover, includes art and ads. "We use the highest-quality paper, from Ivory Linen, 100% cotton fiber, Parchment, etc. Photographs of each contributor are accompanied by their biographical information in the 'Contributors Notes' section. Each issue is comprised of 2-4 parts, approximately 350 pgs. in all, so subscribers actually receive 20 issues per year including special Limited Editions." They receive over 6,000 poems a year, accept approximately 1%. Press run is 1,500 for 800 subscribers. Single copy: $8; subscription: $28. Make checks payable to Tracy Lyn Rottkamp.
How to Submit: Submit 3-10 poems at a time. No previously published poems or simultaneous submissions. "If we accept your poem and it is later published elsewhere, please credit its initial appearance in *Affair of the Mind*." Cover letter "essential." Time between acceptance and publication is 3-20 weeks. Poems are circulated to an editorial board. Always comments on rejections. Publishes theme issues occasionally. Send SASE for guidelines and upcoming themes. Reports in 1-2 weeks. Pays 1-3 copies. Acquires one-time rights. Staff reviews books and chapbooks of poetry and other magazines in a 20 pg. book review and advertising supplement that comes with each issue. Send books for review consideration.

AFRICAN VOICES (Specialized: ethnic), 270 W. 96th St., New York NY 10025, phone/fax (212)865-2982, founded 1992, poetry editor Layding Kalida.
Magazine Needs: *AV* is a quarterly "art and literary magazine that highlights the work of people of color. We publish ethnic literature and poetry on any subject. We do not wish to limit the reader or author." They have published poetry by Reg E. Gaines, Maya Angelou, Tony Medina and Louis Reyes Rivera. They receive about 100 submissions a year, accept approximately 30%. Press run is 20,000 for 5,000 subscribers of which 30 are libraries, 40% shelf sales. Single copy: $2; subscription: $12. Sample: $3.
How to Submit: Submit no more than 5 poems at any one time. Previously published poems and simultaneous submissions OK. Cover letter and SASE required. Seldom comments on rejections. Send SASE for guidelines. Reports in 6-8 weeks. Pays 5 copies. Acquires first or one-time rights. Reviews books of poetry in 500-1,000 words. Open to unsolicited reviews. Poets may also send books for review consideration, attn. Layding Kaliba.
Also Offers: Sponsors periodic poetry contests. Send SASE for details.
Advice: The editor says, "We strongly encourage new writers/poets to send in their work and not give up if their work is not accepted the first time. Accepted contributors are encouraged to subscribe."

AFRO-HISPANIC REVIEW (Specialized: ethnic), Romance Languages, #143 Arts & Sciences Bldg., University of Missouri, Columbia MO 65211, founded 1982, editors Marvin A. Lewis and Edward J. Mullen.
Magazine Needs: The *Review* appears twice a year, in the fall and spring, using some poetry related to Afro-Hispanic life and issues. They have published poetry by Cristina Rodriguez Cabral, Luz Argentina Chiriboga, Nancy Norejón and Marcelino Arozarena. Sample copy: $7.50.
How to Submit: Submit 2 poems at a time. "Prefer clean copy with accents." Reports in 6 weeks. Pays 3 copies. Reviews books of poetry in "about 500 words."

AFTER HOURS CLUB MAGAZINE, 5122 N. Oakley, Apt. 505, Chicago IL 60605, phone (773)334-0335, e-mail highpriority@juno.com or galaga@sie.edu, founded 1996, contact Ernesto Cano.
Magazine Needs: *After Hours Club* appears biweekly and contains poetry, short stories, prose and works of local artists and college students. They want "poetry about life, love, sadness, happiness. No racism or hate poetry." As a sample they selected these lines from "Father Time" by Lesley Ann Faoing:

> *How long a second lasts when time is void, how quickly death is upon us. Count your days, for when*

we grieve the clock stands still.
They say the magazine contains 4 pgs. of material and is desktop-published. Subscription: $5/year. Contributors are required to buy subscription.
How to Submit: Submit any number of poems at a time. Previously published poems and simultaneous submissions OK. Cover letter required. Reads submissions September 1 through April 30 only. Time between acceptance and publication is 2 weeks. Always comments on rejections. Publishes theme issues. Send SASE for guidelines and upcoming themes.
Also Offers: "The *After Hours Club Magazine* prints a collection of poems in a book in early May. The book includes all the *Club* favorites. Sold for $7."

AFTERTHOUGHTS; DEFIANCE! (Specialized: political, social issues), P.O. Box 23176, 380 Wellington St., London, Ontario N6A 5N9 Canada, founded 1994, editor Andreas Gripp.
● Please note that *Defiance!* is a new addition to this listing.
Magazine Needs: *Afterthoughts* seeks to publish "the highest quality English language verse available. Poems should be meaningful, highly imaginative and inspiringly original." They publish both new and established writers. Those published include Louis Gallo, Molly Peacock, Al Purdy, Ruth Daigon, Jack Rickard and Claire Litton. As a sample the editor selected the poem "Gauguin" by Peter Duncan:
    We think of you as an adored Adam/in his luxuriant Eden/but the truth was/you subsisted on macaroni and beans,/girls ran from/your open sores/and the blunt bishop spoke of the enemy/of God.
Afterthoughts is 120 pgs., digest-sized, offset printed and perfect-bound with quality cover stock and b&w illustrations and photos throughout. Press run is 500 for 80 subscribers including 15 libraries. Sample: $5. Make checks payable to *Afterthoughts*.
How to Submit: Send up to 7 poems, with the poet's name and address appearing on each work. Previously published poems and simultaneous submissions OK. Cover letter with brief bio preferred. "Please include an International Reply Coupon or $1 US with your SAE if you are submitting from the U.S. or overseas. U.S. stamps can't be used in return mail from Canada, and due to high postage costs, we are unable to reply to submissions lacking IRC or $1 US. SASE required for Canadian writers." Reports in 6 weeks. Pays 1 copy. "We reserve the right to reprint accepted poetry in future issues. Other than that, all rights revert back to the poet after publication."
Magazine Needs & How to Submit: The editor also publishes the triannual magazine, *Defiance!*, "a magazine presenting non-violent insurrectionist opinion that seeks to be a forum for radical social change. We include poetry that is political, socially conscious, and upholds the equality of all life." *Defiance!* is 44 pgs., 7×8½, saddle-stapled with quality cover stock. Single copy: $3. Make checks payable to *Afterthoughts*. Same submission guidelines as pertainable to *Afterthoughts*.
Advice: The editor says, "We are restructuring our publishing operations during 2000 and may only be able to put out one edition of *Afterthoughts*. Because of this, we will be forced to be very restrictive in what we can accept for publication. Therefore, send only your very, very best work."

AGNI, Boston University, 236 Bay State Rd., Boston MA 02215, phone (617)353-7135, fax (617)353-7136, e-mail agni@bu.edu, website http://www.webdelsol.com/agni, founded 1972, editors Askold Melnyczuk and Colette Kelso.
● Work published in *AGNI* has been included in *The Best American Poetry* (1992, 1993, 1994, 1995, 1997 and 1998) and *Pushcart Prize* anthologies.
Magazine Needs: *AGNI* is a biannual journal of poetry, fiction and essays "by both emerging and established writers. We publish quite a bit of poetry in forms as well as 'language' poetry, but we don't begin to try and place parameters on the 'kind of work' that *AGNI* selects." Editors seem to select readable, intelligent poetry—mostly lyric free verse (with some narrative and dramatic, too)—that somehow communicates tension or risk. They have published poetry by Adrienne Rich, Seamus Heaney, Maxine Scates, Rosanna Warren, Chinua Achebe and Ha Jin. *AGNI* is typeset, offset-printed and perfect-bound with about 40 poems featured in each issue. Circulation is 1,500 by subscription, mail order and bookstore sales. Subscription: $18. Sample: $9.
How to Submit: Submit 3 poems at a time. "No fancy fonts, gimmicks or preformatted reply cards. No work accepted via e-mail. Brief, sincere cover letters." No previously published poems; simultaneous submissions OK. Reads submissions October 1 through January 31 only. Mss received at other times will be returned unread. Reports in 2-5 months. Pays $10/page, $150 maximum, plus 2 copies and one-year subscription. Buys first serial rights.
Also Offers: *AGNI* also publishes Take Three, an annual series of work by three young poets in conjunction with Graywolf Press. Poets are chosen by *AGNI*'s editorial board. Website includes writer's guidelines, names of editors, poetry and interviews, plus information on back issues.

THE AGUILAR EXPRESSION (Specialized: social issues); EROS ERRANT (Specialized: love/romance/erotica), 1329 Gilmore Ave., Donora PA 15033, phone (724)379-8019, founded 1986, editor/publisher Xavier F. Aguilar.
Magazine Needs: *Aguilar Expression* appears 2 times/year. "In publishing poetry, I try to exhibit the unique reality that we too often take for granted and acquaint as medicre. We encourage poetics that deal with *now*, which our readers can relate to. We are particularly interested in poetry dealing with social issues." They have

published poetry by Martin Kich and Gail Ghai. As a sample the editor selected these lines from "The Water Truck" by Donna Taylor Burgess:

> *But pockets are as empty/As the taps/In a government day/And water has never been free.*

AE is 4-20 pgs., photocopied on 8½×11 sheets and corner stapled. They receive about 20-30 poems a month, use approximately 5-10 poems. Circulation is 300. Sample: $6. Make checks payable to *Aguilar Expression*.
How to Submit: "We insist that all writers send a SASE for writer's guidelines before submitting." Submit up to 3 poems at a time, 24-line limit, any topic/style. "Send copies; mss will not be returned." Cover letter, including writing background, and SASE for contact purposes, required with submissions. Reports in 2 months. Pays 1 copy. Open to unsolicited reviews.
Magazine Needs: *Eros Errant* appears 2 times/year (June and December) and publishes poetry, fiction and b&w line art. They want poems that "exhibit the sexual travels of various characters and situations—diversity is our call. All situations with adults considered. The more graphic the better. No fetish." As a sample the editor selected these lines from "Obsessed" by Corrine DeWinter:

> *I whispered to you,/told you secrets./I asked you to come,/to bring me stars,/to say my name.*

EE is 4-12 pgs., photocopied on 4¼×5½ sheets. Circulation is 100. Sample: $3. Make checks payable to *Aguilar Expression*.
How to Submit: Submit up to 5 poems at a time, 20-line limit/poem. "We ask that writers send a SASE for guidelines before submitting work." No simultaneous submissions; previously published poems OK. Pays 1 copy. Acquires one-time rights.

☑ ◎ AHSAHTA PRESS; COLD-DRILL; COLD-DRILL BOOKS; POETRY IN PUBLIC PLACES

(Specialized: regional), English Dept., Boise State University, Boise ID 83725, phone (208)426-1999, e-mail ttrusky@boisestate.edu, website http://www.boisestate.edu/english/ahsahta/index.html, editor Tom Trusky.
Magazine Needs: *cold-drill* publishes "primarily Boise State University students, faculty and staff, but will consider writings by Idahoans—or 'furriners.' " They do some of the most creative publishing in this country today, and it is worth buying a sample of *cold-drill* for $9 just to see what they're up to. This annual "has been selected as top undergraduate literary magazine in the U.S. by such important acronyms as CSPA, CCLM and UCDA." It comes in a box stuffed with various pamphlets, postcards, posters, a newspaper, even 3-D comics with glasses to read them by. No restrictions on types of poetry. Circulation is 400, including 100 subscribers, of which 20 are libraries.
How to Submit: "We read material throughout the year, notifying only those whose work we've accepted December 15 through January 1. Manuscripts should be photocopies with author's name and address on separate sheet. Simultaneous submissions OK. Pays 1 copy."
Book/Chapbook Needs: Ahsahta Press is a project to publish contemporary poetry of the American West. But, the editor says "Don't send paens to the pommel, Jesus in the sagebrush, haiku about the Eiffel Tower, 'nice' or 'sweet' poems." The work should "draw on the cultures, history, ecologies of the American West." They publish collections (45 pgs.) of individual poets in handsome flat-spined paperbacks with plain matte covers, with an appreciative introduction, at most 3/year. Occasionally they bring out an anthology of their authors on cassette. And they have published *Women Poets of the West*, an anthology (94 pgs.) with an introduction by Ann Stanford, and also *The Ahsahta Anthology* (277 pgs.). They have published poetry by Susan Deal, Leo Romero, David Baker, Linda Bierds, Philip St. Clair and Gretel Ehrlich. As a sample here are lines from Wyn Cooper's "Fun," in the collection *The Country of Here Below* (set to music, it is Sheryl Crow's Grammy-winning "All I Wanna Do"):

> *"All I want is to have a little fun/Before I die," says the man next to me/Out of nowhere, apropos of nothing. He says/His name is William but I'm sure he's Bill/Or Billy, Mac or Buddy: he's plain ugly to me,/And I wonder if he's ever had fun in his life.*

How to Submit: Submit only during their January 1 through March 31 reading period—a sample of 15 of your poems with SASE. Multiple and simultaneous submissions OK. They will report in about 2 months. If your sample is approved, a complete book ms is requested. If it is accepted, you get 25 copies of the 1st and 2nd printings and a 25% royalty commencing with the 3rd. They seldom comment on the samples, frequently on the mss. See their press samples and titles at their website and order a few books, if you don't find them in your library. "Old advice but true: Read what we publish before submitting. 75% of the submissions we receive should never have been sent to us. Save stamps, spirit and sweat."
Also Offers: They publish two 24-page chapbooks and one 75-page flat-spined paperback/year. Query about book publication. Poetry in Public Places is a series of 8 monthly posters/year "presenting the poets in Boise State University's creative students series and poets in BSU's Ahsahta Press poetry series." The posters are on coated stock. These, like all publications emanating from BSU, are elegantly done, with striking art.
Advice: "We want to publish a literary magazine that is exciting to read. We want more readers than just our contributors and their mothers. Our format and our content have allowed us to achieve those goals, so far."

☑ $ ◑ ◎ AIM MAGAZINE (Specialized: social issues, ethnic, political), P.O. Box 1174, Maywood

IL 60153, phone (773)874-6184, fax (206)543-2746, founded 1974, poetry editor Ruth Apilado.
Magazine Needs: *Aim* is a quarterly, "dedicated to racial harmony and peace." They use 3-4 poems ("poetry with social significance mainly"—average 32 lines) in each issue. They have published poetry by J. Douglas Studer, Wayne Dowdy and Maria DeGuzman. *Aim* is magazine-sized with glossy cover, circulation 10,000. They

receive about 30 submissions a year, use half. They have 3,000 subscribers of which 15 are libraries. Single copy: $3; subscription: $12. Sample: $4.

How to Submit: Simultaneous submissions OK. Send SASE for upcoming themes. Reports in 3-6 weeks. Pays $3/poem and 1 copy. You will not receive an acceptance slip: "We simply send payment and magazine copy."

Advice: The editor says, "Read the work of published poets."

⊕ $◖ AKROS PUBLICATIONS; ZED₂O MAGAZINE, 33 Lady Nairn Ave., Kirkcaldy, Fife KY1 2AW Scotland, United Kingdom, founded 1965, contact Duncan Glen.

Magazine Needs & How to Submit: *ZED₂O* is an annual poetry and arts magazine containing a "variety of special topics in each issue." They are open to all forms and length of poetry. The editor says *ZED₂O* is 48 pgs., 210×130mm. They accept approximately 10% of work received. Press run is 500. Single copy: £2.75. Make checks payable to Duncan Glen. Does not accept checks in US funds. Submit 6 poems at a time. No previously published poems or simultaneous submissions. Cover letter preferred. "Submit hard copy initially; disks welcomed after acceptance if compatible with IBM—high density. We get many submissions from USA and UK without SASE or SAE and IRCs." Time between acceptance and publication is 9 months. Always comments on rejections but "very briefly." Publishes theme issues. Guidelines included inside magazine. Reports monthly. Sometimes sends prepublication galleys. No payment. Acquires first United Kingdom publication rights.

Book/Chapbook Needs & How to Submit: Akros Publications is a poetry press—"often publishing Scottish poems." They publish 1 paperback and 6 chapbooks/year. Chapbooks (also called pamphlets in the U.K.) are 20 pgs., 210×130mm, offset litho printed. Replies to queries in 2 months maximum, to mss "quickly." Pays 10% royalties and/or 6 author's copies (out of a press run of 500). "No royalties given if chapbooks are by new poets." Send SAE and IRCs for catalog.

◖ ALABAMA LITERARY REVIEW, English Dept., Troy State University, Troy AL 36082, phone (334)670-3286, fax (334)670-3519, poetry editor Ed Hicks.

Magazine Needs: *ALR*, a biannual, wants contemporary poetry that is "imagistic—but in motion." Will look at anything, but does not want to see "lyrics sent as poetry. We want serious craft." They have published poetry by David Musgrove, R.T. Smith, Ed Peaco, Joanne M. Riley, Martha Payne, Edward Byrne and Katherine McCanless. The beautifully printed 100-page, 7×10 magazine, matte cover with art, b&w art and some colored pages inside, receives 300 submissions/year, uses 30, has a 2-month backlog. Sample: $5.

How to Submit: Submit 2-5 poems at a time. "SASE with appropriate postage is paramount." Simultaneous submissions OK. Reads submissions September 1 through July 31 only. Sometimes comments on rejections. Reports in 2-3 months. Sometimes sends prepublication galleys. Pays copies, sometimes honorarium. Acquires first rights. Open to unsolicited reviews. Poets may also send books for review consideration.

▼ ◖ ALASKA QUARTERLY REVIEW, University of Alaska Anchorage, 3211 Providence Dr., Anchorage AK 99508, phone/fax (907)786-6916, founded 1981, executive editor Ronald Spatz.

• Poetry published in *AQR* has been selected for inclusion in *The Best American Poetry 1996* and the *Pushcart Prize* anthologies.

Magazine Needs: "A journal devoted to contemporary literary art. We publish both traditional and experimental fiction, poetry, literary nonfiction and short plays." They have published poetry by Kim Addonizio, Tom Lux, Pattiann Rogers, John Balaban, Albert Goldbarth, Jane Hirshfeld, Billy Collins and Dorianne Laux. Editors seem to welcome all styles and forms of poetry with the most emphasis perhaps on voice and content that displays "risk," or intriguing ideas or situations. They publish two double-issues a year, each using between 25-50 pgs. of poetry. They receive up to 3,000 submissions a year, accept 40-60. Circulation is 2,200 for 500 subscribers of which 32 are libraries. Subscription: $8. Sample: $5.

How to Submit: Manuscripts are *not* read from May 15 through August 15. They take up to 4 months to report, sometimes longer during peak periods in late winter. Pay depends on funding. Acquires first North American serial rights. Guest poetry editors have included Stuart Dybek, Jane Hirshfield, Stuart Dischell, Maxine Kumin, Pattiann Rogers and Dorianne Laux.

◖ ◎ ALBATROSS; THE ANABIOSIS PRESS (Specialized: nature), P.O. Box 7787, North Port FL 34287-0787, phone (941)625-6342, founded 1985, editors Richard Smyth and Richard Brobst.

Magazine Needs: *Albatross* appears: "as soon as we have accepted enough quality poems to publish an issue. We consider the albatross to be a metaphor for an environment that must survive. This is not to say that we publish only environmental or nature poetry, but that we are biased toward such subject matters. We publish mostly free verse, 200 lines/poem maximum, and we prefer a narrative style, but again, this is not necessary. We do not want trite rhyming poetry which doesn't convey a deeply felt experience in a mature expression with words." They have published poetry by Simon Perchik, Lyn Lifshin, Daniel Comiskey, Mitchell LesCarbeau and E.G. Burrows. As a sample the editors selected these lines by Claire Hero:

> *I am with the women in my life,/learning their patterns,/trying to understand myself in them—/how I*
> *will stand at counters when/my back is curved, the way my/arms will look when the/skin goes slack . . .*

The magazine is 28-36 pgs., $5\frac{1}{2} \times 8\frac{1}{2}$, laser typeset with linen cover, some b&w drawings, and sometimes, in addition to the poetry, has an interview with a poet in each issue. Circulation is 300 for 75 subscribers of which

10 are libraries. Many complimentary copies are sent out to bookstores, poets and libraries. Subscription: $5/2 issues. Sample: $3.

How to Submit: Submit 3-5 poems at a time. "Poems should be typed single-spaced, with name and address in left corner and length in lines in right corner." No simultaneous submissions. Cover letter not required; "We do, however, need bio notes if published." Send SASE for guidelines. Reports in 4-6 months, has 6- to 12-month backlog. Pays 1 copy. Acquires all rights. Returns rights provided that "previous publication in *Albatross* is mentioned in all subsequent reprintings."

Also Offers: Holds a chapbook contest. Submit 20-24 pgs. of poetry, any theme, any style. Deadline is June 31 of each year. Include name, address and phone number on the title page. Charges $7 reading fee (check payable to Anabiosis Press). Winner receives $100 and 25 copies of his/her published chapbook. All entering receive a free copy of the winning chapbook. "The Anabiosis Press is a nonprofit, tax-exempt organization. Membership fee is $20/year."

Advice: The editors say, "We expect a poet to read as much contemporary poetry as possible."

N ▣ $□ ⊘ ALDEN ENTERPRISES; GRACIE PUBLICATIONS; POETIC VOICES MAGA-ZINE, P.O. Box 2068, Fairhope AL 36533-2068, e-mail gracieaml@aol.com or gtaldenent@aol.com, website http://members.aol.com/GTAldenEnt/GraciePubs.htm, founded 1997, executive editor (Alden Ent.) R.C. Travis, submissions editor (Poetic Voices) Ursula T. Gibson.

Magazine Needs: E-mailed to subscribers monthly, *Poetic Voices* is "informational and educational in content. Articles include feature interviews, columns on the mechanics of writing, questions on writing and publishing, information on organizations useful to poets, contest and award opportunities, publishing opportunities, workshops and conferences, book reviews and more. We are open to most forms, styles and subjects. No pornography, scatology, racial slurs or dehumanizing poems." They have published poetry by Lyn Lifshin. As a sample the editors selected these lines from "The Created" by Sue Scalf:

> From this rough clay/pounded upon the wheel,/from this body made of dirt, spinning/like a wind lifted
> in that turning,/he is making a porcelain,/fired in the kiln and glowing,/a vessel of intricate filligree/
> planned and wrought/before the world was made,/of our bones the bone-white/light, translucent.

PV is an electronic magazine containing 30-60 pgs. It can be accessed at http://members.aol.com/gracieami/arch.htm. They receive about 1,200 poems a year, accept approximately 10%. Circulation is "over 10,000 poets in 20 countries each month."

How to Submit: Submit up to 4 poems a month by e-mail, text in body of message, to UrsulaTG@aol.com. Previously published poems and simultaneous submissions OK. Cover letter preferred. Often comments on rejections. Send SASE for guidelines or obtain via website. Reports in 1-2 months. Sometimes sends prepublication galleys. Acquires one-time rights. Reviews books and chapbooks of poetry and other magazines in 200-500 words. Open to unsolicited reviews. Poets may also send books for review consideration to R.C. Travis at above address or e-mail gracieaml@aol.com.

Book/Chapbook Needs & How to Submit: Gracie Publications, a division of Alden Enterprises, seeks "to promote new and talented poets, and their work, via the publication of chapbooks of poetry. All styles of poetry are welcome. . . . We are open to new writers, look for variety and excellence, are open to concrete forms, traditional, and free verse as well as other varieties. We do accept religious theme poems." They publish 6-10 chapbooks/year. Chapbooks are usually 20-40 pgs., 8½ × 5½, laser printed and saddle-stitched with cardstock covers containing art. Submit ms containing 20-30 poems ("no epic poetry please"), typed and double spaced on 8½ × 11 paper. ("We ask that you also include a disk copy of your poetry saved in text format.") No e-mail submissions. Include cover letter with address and phone number. Poems must be original; simultaneous submissions and previously published poetry OK If noted. Reading fee: $10, must be included with submission. Make checks payable to Alden Enterprises. Reads submissions March 15 through September 15. Replies to queries in 1-2 months; to mss in 3-4 months. Pays royalties of 8-15% and 10 author's copies (out of a press run of 200). Order sample books or chapbooks by sending $5 to above address.

Also Offers: Sponsors WritersClub.com, the online community for writers. The website (www.writersclub.com) includes chats, genre newsletters, searchable agents and publishers database, courses, message boards, reviews, author interviews and horoscopes for writers. The Alden website includes writer's guidelines, books published, purpose and purchasing information on books.

Advice: The editor says, "Make sure you read and follow guidelines. Make sure your work is neatly presented. There is nothing worse than receiving messy work or work that does not conform to the guidelines."

N ○ ALEMBIC; TRISKELION PRESS; ALEMBIC ANNUAL POETRY CONTEST, P.O. Box 41009, Philadelphia PA 19127, phone (610)513-5373, e-mail alembic33@aol.com, founded 1998, editor L.P. Farrell.

Magazine Needs: *Alembic* is a "quarterly magazine of poetry, fiction and artwork dedicated to giving a venue for publication of new poets, writers and artists." They want "all kinds with exception to typewritten gymnastics, pornography, hate works, obscure works and forced rhymes. Also, no poems over 40 lines." The editor says *Alembic* is 50 pgs., 8½ × 11, photocopied and side-stapled with card cover with artwork, includes b&w drawings. They receive about 500 poems a year, accept approximately 40%. Press run is 200 for 60 subscribers. Subscription: $11. Sample: $3.50. Make checks payable to L.P. Farrell.

How to Submit: Submit 3 poems at a time. Line length for poetry is 40 maximum. No previously published poems or simultaneous submissions. Cover letter required. "For cover letters, we need a short biography, a statement that the work(s) are original and not previously published or a simultaneous submission." Time between acceptance and publication is 1 year. Often comments on rejections. "I always write a couple paragraphs of suggestions, but charge $10 per story and $2 per poem for editing advice and corrections." Send SASE for guidelines. Reports in 3 months. Pays 1 copy. Acquires first North American serial rights. Staff reviews books and chapbooks of poetry in 100 words, single book format. Send books for review consideration to L.P. Farrell. "Include cover letter."

Also Offers: Sponsors the Alembic Annual Poetry Contest. Awards $50 Grand Prize. Submit maximum of 3 unpublished poems in 1 envelope. Entry fee: $3/3 poems. Award issue published in October.

Advice: The editor says, "Get emotionally involved with your work. Always revise, revise and then revise again after letting your work sit between revisions. Take a chance and submit: rejection never killed anyone; getting published makes you feel very alive."

ALICE JAMES BOOKS; NEW ENGLAND/NEW YORK AWARD, BEATRICE HAWLEY AWARD, JANE KENYON CHAPBOOK AWARD (Specialized: regional, women, ethnic), University of Maine at Farmington, 98 Main St., Farmington ME 04938, phone/fax (207)778-7071, e-mail ajb@umf.maine.edu, website http://www.umf.maine.edu/~ajb, founded 1973.
• *The Art of the Lathe*, by B.H. Fairchild, was a finalist for the 1998 National Book Award for Poetry.
Book/Chapbook Needs: *Alice James Books* is "a nonprofit author's collective which only publishes poetry. Authors are primarily from the New England Area. We emphasize poetry by women, though we now seek poetry by any contemporary voice. We strongly encourage submissions by poets of color." They publish flat-spined paperbacks of high quality, both in production and contents, no children's poetry or light verse. They publish 3-4 books, 72 pgs., each year in editions of 1,000, paperbacks—no hardbacks. They have published poetry by Jane Kenyon, Jean Valentine and B.H. Fairchild.
How to Submit: "Each poet becomes a working member of the co-op with a two-year work commitment." That is, you have to live close enough to attend meetings and participate in the editorial and publishing process. Query first, but no need for samples: simply ask for dates of reading period, which is in early fall and winter. No phone queries. May contact by phone or fax for submission guidelines only. Send 2 copies of the ms. Simultaneous submissions OK, but "we would like to know when a manuscript is being submitted elsewhere." Reports in 3 months. Pays authors 100 paperback copies.
Also Offers: Offers Beatrice Hawley Award for poets who cannot meet the work requirement due to geographical restraints. Winners of the New England/New York competition become members of the collective with a two-year work commitment. Both competitions pay 100 copies. Beatrice Hawley Award winner also receives a cash award of $1,000. Also offers the Jane Kenyon Chapbook Award every 2 years. Send SASE for guidelines.

$ ALIVE NOW (Specialized: spirituality, themes); POCKETS (Specialized: religious, children, themes); DEVO'ZINE (Specialized: religious, youth, themes); WEAVINGS; THE UPPER ROOM, 1908 Grand Ave., P.O. Box 189, Nashville TN 37202, website http://www.upperroom.org. This publishing company brings out about 30 books a year and 5 magazines: *The Upper Room, Alive Now, Pockets, Devo'Zine* and *Weavings*. Of these, three use unsolicited poetry.
Magazine Needs & How to Submit: *Pockets, Devotional Magazine for Children*, which comes out 11 times/year, circulation 90,000, is for children 6-12, "offers stories, activities, prayers, poems—all geared to giving children a better understanding of themselves as children of God. Some of the material is not overtly religious but deals with situations, special seasons and holidays, and ecological concerns from a Christian perspective." It uses 3-4 pgs. of poetry/issue. Sample free with 7½×10½ SAE and 4 first-class stamps. Ordinarily 24-line limit on poetry. Send SASE for themes and guidelines. Pays $25-50.
Magazine Needs & How to Submit: *Alive Now*, editor George Graham, is a bimonthly, circulation 75,000, for a general Christian audience interested in reflection and meditation. They buy 30 poems a year, avant-garde and free verse. Submit 5 poems, 10-45 lines. Send SASE for themes and guidelines. Pays $25-50.
Magazine Needs & How to Submit: *Devo'Zine: Just for Teens*, is a bimonthly devotional magazine for youth ages 12-18, offers meditations, scripture, prayers, poems, stories, songs and feature articles to "aid youth in their prayer life, introduce them to spiritual disciplines, help them shape their concept of God, and encourage them in the life of discipleship." Ordinarily 20-line limit on poetry. Send SASE for theme and guidelines. Pays $20.
Also Offers: *The Upper Room* magazine does not accept poetry.

**FOR EXPLANATIONS OF THESE SYMBOLS,
SEE THE INSIDE FRONT AND BACK COVERS OF THIS BOOK.**

⬭ ◎ **ALLEGHENY REVIEW (Specialized: undergraduate students)**, Dept. PM, Box 32, Allegheny College, Meadville PA 16335, phone (814)332-4339, e-mail review@alleg.edu, website http://www.alleg.edu/Student/Organizations/AllegReviews, founded 1983, faculty advisor Sonya Jones.

Magazine Needs: "Each year *Allegheny Review* compiles and publishes a review of the nation's best undergraduate literature. It is entirely composed of and by college undergraduates and is nationally distributed both as a review and as a classroom text, particularly suited to creative writing courses." In the Fall of 1995, they added a section of essays on poetry and literature. (Submit 10-15 typed pgs., double-spaced.) "We will print poetry of appreciable literary merit on any topic, submitted by college undergraduates. No limitations except excessive length (2-3 pgs.) as we wish to represent as many authors as possible, although exceptions are made in areas of great quality and interest." They have published poetry by Eric Sanborn, Cheryl Connor, Rick Alley and Kristi Coulter. The *Review* appears in a 6×9, flat-spined, professionally-printed format, b&w photo on glossy card cover. Single copy: $5. Sample: $4 and 11×18 SASE.

How to Submit: Submit 3-5 poems, typed. Submissions should be accompanied by a letter "telling the college poet is attending, year of graduation, any background, goals and philosophies the author feels are pertinent to the work submitted." Reports 1-2 months following deadline. Poem judged best in the collection earns $50-75 honorarium.

Advice: "Ezra Pound gave the best advice: 'Make it new.' We're seeing far too much imitation; there's already been a Sylvia Plath, a Galway Kinnell. Don't be afraid to try new things. Be innovative. Also, traditional forms are coming 'back in style,' or so we hear. Experiment with them; write a villanelle, a sestina or a sonnet. And when you submit, please take enough pride in your work to do so professionally. Handwritten or poorly typed and proofed submissions definitely convey an impression—a negative one."

✓ ⬭ ⬭ **ALLIGATOR JUNIPER**, Prescott College, 220 Grove Ave., Prescott AZ 86301, phone (520)778-2090, ext. 2012, e-mail aj@prescott.edu, founded 1995, managing editor Melanie Bishop, poetry editor Sheila Sanderson.

Magazine Needs: *Alligator Juniper* is a contest publication appearing annually in May. "Aside from advertised theme issues, we publish work based only on artistic merit." They have published poetry by Elton Glaser and Fatima Lim-Wilson. The editors say *AJ* is approximately 200 pgs. with b&w photography. They receive about 1,200-1,500 poems a year, accept approximately 6-20 poems. Press run is 1,500 for 600 subscribers; 200 distributed free to other reputable journals, MFA programs and writers' colonies. Subscription: $12/2 years (2 issues). Sample: $7.50. "We publish one issue per year and it's always a contest, requiring a $10 fee which allows us to pay a $500 first prize in each category—fiction, poetry, creative nonfiction and photography. All entrants receive a copy of the next issue."

How to Submit: Submit up to 5 poems at a time with reading fee. No previously published poems; simultaneous submissions OK. Cover letter preferred. No e-mail or fax submissions. Reads submissions October 1 through December 15 only. "We read and select what we will publish from all the work submitted so far that calendar year." Reading fee: $10/entry (5 poems or 5 pages of poetry). Time between acceptance and publication is 3-5 months. "Finalists are selected inhouse and passed on to a different guest judge each year." Publishes theme issues occasionally. Send SASE for guidelines or obtain via e-mail or website. Reports in 3-7 months. Each year, one winner receives $500 plus 4 copies; all other poets whose work is selected for publication receive payment in copies only.

[N] ⬭ **ALLISON PRESS; STAR RISING MAGAZINE; STAR RISING PUBLISHERS**, P.O. Box 494, Mt. Shasta CA 96067, phone (530)926-5830, e-mail kmay@gurlmail.com, website http://www.homestead.com/starrisingpublishers, founded 1996, editor Kristen B. May, publisher Robin B. May.

Magazine Needs: *Star Rising Magazine* is published biannually and contains "all types of writing—poetry, short stories and articles." They want "poetry that speaks from experience and the heart. Be creative. No pornographic material." They have published poetry by Anna Laxague and Anmol Bhagchand. As a sample the editor selected these lines from "Heaven is Falling" by Matthew Donald Wetherby:

> Molding all within a fetish light/While the earth's very breath is transformed/Into but a shade of the
> universe,/Mocking mankind with an impotent fear,/Commanding all life to breathe of its tears;/Frown
> oh sulking stars, heaven is falling.

SRM is about 60 pgs., magazine-sized, photocopied and glued into a folder-like card cover, includes art/graphics and ads. They receive about 200 poems a year, accept approximately 60%. Press run is 500 for 200 subscribers of which 50 are libraries, 100 shelf sales; 50 distributed free to "hospitals, rest homes, etc." Subscription: $17.95/year, $35/2 years. Sample: $8.95. Make checks payable to Star Rising Publishers.

How to Submit: Submit 5 poems at a time. Previously published poems and simultaneous submissions OK. Cover letter preferred. E-mail submissions OK. Time between acceptance and publication is 4 months. Poems are circulated to an editorial board. Often comments on rejections. Send SASE for guidelines or obtain via e-mail or website. Reports in 1 month. Pays 1 copy, more copies available at wholesale cost. Acquires one-time rights. Reviews books of poetry in single book format. Open to unsolicited reviews. Poets may also send books for review consideration to Robin B. May, publisher.

Book/Chapbook Needs & How to Submit: Star Rising Publishers considers all types and forms of poetry. They publish 2 paperbacks/year. Books are usually 60-200 pgs., 5½×8½, offset printed and perfect-bound with cover stock, includes art/graphics.

How to Submit: Send complete ms with cover letter, list of credits and brief bio. Replies to queries in 1 month; to mss in 4 months. Pays royalties of 10-20% and 10 author's copies (out of a press run of 100). Order sample books by sending $10.

Also Offers: Sponsors annual poetry contest. Deadline: October 1. 1st Place, $200 plus a book of poetry published; 2nd Place, $100; 3rd Place, $50. All winners receive a one-year subscription to the magazine. First entry free, every other entry $1 per poem. Send SASE for details or visit website. Website includes guidelines, submissions, contest information, advertising, books, address and subscriptions. Allison Press publishes New Age, metaphysical and how-to titles.

Advice: The editor says, "Be creative and never limit your expression. Be open to new ideas and ways of writing. We like to see new writers. They usually receive first consideration."

$⬜ **ALMS HOUSE PRESS; WHEAT EAR**, P.O. Box 217, Pearl River NY 10965-0217, fax (914)735-5628, founded 1985, poetry editors Lorraine De Gennaro and Alana Sherman, publishes the biannual *Wheat Ear* and 3-4 chapbooks/perfect-bound books per year.

Magazine Needs & How to Submit: For *Wheat Ear* (formerly *The Alms House Journal*), submit 3-5 poems at a time with $5 reading fee. Include SASE. Pays 2 copies.

Book/Chapbook Needs: "We have no preferences with regard to style as long as the poetry is high caliber. We like to see previous publication in the small press, but we are open to new writers. We look for variety and excellence and are open to experimental forms as well as traditional forms. Any topics as long as the poems are not whiny or too depressing, pornographic or religious." They have published poetry by Karen Nelson and Don Schofield. As a sample the editors selected these lines of poetry:

> *moving my arms like giant/wings breathing/minerals and sand/inhaling you/an orange and black fan*

How to Submit: For chapbooks, submit 16- to 24-page ms with $15 reading fee; for longer collections, submit up to 50 pages with $25 reading fee. All mss must be typed with 1 poem/page. No previously published poems or simultaneous submissions. Reads submissions March 15 through June 15 and September 15 through December 15 only. Send SASE for guidelines or request via fax. Reports in 2-3 months. Press pays $25 plus 10 copies and 7% of all sales over first 100 books.

Also Offers: They sponsor a poetry reading series and offer a critical and editorial service for $50.

Advice: The editors say, "We treat every poem, every manuscript and every author with respect. We believe poetry should be well presented."

⬜ 📷 **ALPHA BEAT SOUP; ALPHA BEAT PRESS (Specialized: form/style)**, 31 Waterloo St., New Hope PA 18938-1210, phone (215)862-0299, founded 1987, poetry editor David Christy.

Magazine Needs: Appearing irregularly emulating the Beat literary tradition, *Alpha Beat Soup* is "an international poetry and arts journal featuring Beat, 'post-Beat independent' and modern writing." Christy says 25% of each issue is devoted to little known or previously unpublished poets. They have published works by Ana Christy, Ralph Haselmann, Ed Galing, Steve Richmond and A.D. Winans. As a sample the editor selected these lines by Joe Verrilli:

> *it's always the sensitive one/the vulnerable soul/sought out by the vultures/of this society.*

ABS is 50-75 pgs., 7×8½, photocopied from IBM laser printer, card cover offset, graphics included. They use 50% of the poetry received. Press run is 600 for 400 subscribers of which 11 are libraries. Single copy: $8; subscription: $15. Sample: $10.

How to Submit: Submit 3-6 poems at a time. Simultaneous submissions and previously published poems OK. Cover letter, including "an introduction to the poet's work," required. Editor comments on rejections "only on request." Send SASE for list of upcoming themes. Sometimes sends prepublication galleys. Pays 1 copy. Reviews books of poetry in approximately 700 words, multi-book format. Open to unsolicited reviews. Poets may also send books for review consideration.

Book/Chapbook Needs & How to Submit: Alpha Beat Press publishes chapbooks and supplements as well as a monthly broadside series featuring unknown poets. They offer cooperative publishing of chapbooks, "as a way to fund our press and also showcase the unknown poet." Write for details.

Also Offers: See the listings for *Bouillabaisse* and *Cokefish*.

◪ **AMARANTH**, P.O. Box 184, Trumbull CT 06611, founded 1995, editors Becky Rodia and Christopher Sanzeni.

Magazine Needs: *Amaranth* is a biannual poetry journal. The editors would like to see "formal and free verse with line-by-line energy, concrete imagery and a good sense of sound and rhythm. We especially enjoy prose poems and 'personal' poems—'personal' in the sense that we prefer portraits of people rather than landscapes and abstracts. We see too many poems which try to squeak by on a strong beginning, a good ending, or one interesting line; please send us poems which achieve more than that. Though there is no restriction on length as such, we discourage poems longer than two pages." They have published poetry by Charles H. Webb, Robert Clinton and Kim Addonizio. As a sample the editors selected these lines from "The Drowned" by Kristofer Nelson:

> *Just as sudden: bubbles, clear orbs/tumble upwards from the mouth of the woman/next to me, full of all the shuddering words//I could never bring myself to say. But I'm the one/who can't swim. So I keep to the roof, following her/thin path of air before it runs out of rope—*

Amaranth is 36-40 pgs., 5½×8½, professionally printed and saddle-stapled with glossy card cover with full-color artwork. They receive about 1,000 poems a year, accept approximately 5%. Press run is 1,000. Subscription: $10. Current sample (including guidelines): $6. Back issue: $4.

How to Submit: Submit 3-5 poems at a time, name and address on each. Include SASE. No previously published poems; simultaneous submissions OK, "but please notify us immediately if the work is accepted elsewhere." Cover letter preferred. Often comments on rejections. Send SASE for guidelines. Reports on rejections almost immediately; work held for 4-6 months is receiving serious consideration. Sometimes sends prepublication galleys. Pays 2 copies, additional copies available at a discount. Rights revert to authors upon publication. The editors review chapbooks and books in under 1,000 words, single format. Poets may send books for review consideration.

Also Offers: They also plan to run occasional contests. Watch the trade publications for announcements.

Advice: They add, " 'Amaranth' means 'flower which never fades' and we look for poems that are beautiful, but timeless, hardy, universal and human. We expect our contributors to be well-read in contemporary poetry and to be familiar with the literary publications available these days."

$ ⬤ ◎ AMELIA; CICADA; SPSM&H; THE AMELIA AWARDS (Specialized: form), 329 "E" St., Bakersfield CA 93304 or P.O. Box 2385, Bakersfield CA 93303, phone (805)323-4064, founded 1983, poetry editor Frederick A. Raborg, Jr.

Magazine Needs & How to Submit: *Amelia* is a quarterly magazine that publishes chapbooks as well. Central to its operations is a series of contests, most with entry fees, spaced evenly throughout the year, awarding more than $3,500 annually, but they publish many poets who have not entered the contests as well. Among poets published are Pattiann Rogers, Stuart Friebert, John Millett, David Ray, Larry Rubin, Charles Bukowski, Maxine Kumin, Charles Edward Eaton and Shuntaro Tanikawa. They are "receptive to all forms to 100 lines. We do not want to see the patently-religious or overtly-political. Erotica is fine; pornography, no." The digest-sized, flat-spined magazine is offset on high-quality paper and sometimes features an original four-color cover; its circulation is about 1,642, with 702 subscribers, of which 28 are libraries. Subscription: $30/year. Sample: $9.95. Submit 3-5 poems at a time. No simultaneous submissions except for entries to the annual Amelia Chapbook Award. Reports in 2-12 weeks, the latter if under serious consideration. Pays $2-25/poem plus 2 copies. "Almost always I try to comment." The editor says, "*Amelia* is not afraid of strong themes, but we do look for professional, polished work even in handwritten submissions. Poets should have something to say about matters other than the moon. We like to see strong traditional pieces as well as the contemporary and experimental. And neatness *does* count." Fred Raborg has done more than most other editors to ensure a wide range of styles and forms, from traditional European to Asian, from lyric to narrative. Typically he is swamped with submissions and so response times can exceed stated parameters. *Amelia* continues to place in outside surveys as a top market, because of editorial openness. Brief reviews are also featured.

Magazine Needs & How to Submit: *Cicada* is a quarterly magazine that publishes haiku, senryu and other Japanese forms, plus essays on the form—techniques and history—as well as fiction which in some way incorporates haiku or Japanese poetry in its plot, and reviews of books pertaining to Japan and its poetry or collections of haiku. Among poets published are Roger Ishii, H.F. Noyes, Knute Skinner, Katherine Machan Aal, Ryah Tumarkin Goodman and Ryokufu Ishizaki. They are receptive to experimental forms as well as the traditional. "Try to avoid still-life as haiku; strive for the *whole* of an emotion, whether minuscule or panoramic. Erotica is fine; the Japanese are great lovers of the erotic." The magazine is offset on high-quality paper. Circulation is 663, with 448 subscribers of which 27 are libraries. Subscription: $14/year. Sample: $4.95. Submit 3-10 haiku or poems. No simultaneous submissions. Reports in 2 weeks. No payment, except three "best of issue" poets each receive $10 on publication plus copy. "I try to make some comment on returned poems always."

Magazine Needs & How to Submit: *SPSM&H* is a quarterly magazine that publishes only sonnets, sonnet sequences, essays on the form—both technique and history—as well as romantic or Gothic fiction which, in some way, incorporates the form, and reviews of sonnet collections or collections containing a substantial number of sonnets. They are "receptive to experimental forms as well as the traditional, and appreciate wit when very good." Among poets published are Margaret Ryan, Harold Witt, Sharon E. Martin, Rhina P. Espaillat and Robert Wolfkill. Perhaps it may help to know the editor's favorite Shakespearean sonnet is #29, and he feels John Updike clarified the limits of experimentation with the form in his "Love Sonnet" from *Midpoint*. The magazine is offset on high-quality paper. Circulation is 602, for 409 subscribers and 26 libraries. Subscription: $14/year. Sample: $4.95. Submit 3-5 poems at a time. No simultaneous submissions. Reports in 2 weeks. No payment, except two "best of issue" poets each receive $14 on publication plus copy. "I always try to comment on returns."

Also Offers: The following annual contests have various entry fees: The Amelia Awards (six prizes of $200, $100, $50 plus three honorable mentions of $10 each); The Anna B. Janzen Prize for Romantic Poetry ($100, annual deadline January 2); The Bernice Jennings Traditional Poetry Award ($100, annual deadline January 2); The Georgie Starbuck Galbraith Light/Humorous Verse Prizes (six awards of $100, $50, $25 plus three honorable mentions of $5 each, annual deadline March 1); The Charles William Duke Longpoem Award ($100, annual deadline April 1); The Lucille Sandberg Haiku Awards (six awards of $100, $50, $25 plus three honorable mentions of $5 each, annual deadline April 1); The Grace Hines Narrative Poetry Award ($100, annual deadline May 1); The Amelia Chapbook Award ($250, book publication and 50 copies, annual deadline July 1); The Johanna B. Bourgoyne Poetry Prizes (six awards of $100, $50, $25, plus three honorable mentions of $5 each); The Douglas Manning Smith Epic/Heroic Poetry Prize ($100, annual deadline August 1); The Hildegarde Janzen

Prize for Oriental Forms of Poetry (six awards of $50, $30, $20 and three honorable mentions of $5 each, annual deadline September 1); The Eugene Smith Prize for Sonnets (six awards of $100, $50, $25 and three honorable mentions of $5 each); The A&C Limerick Prizes (six awards of $50, $30, $20 and three honorable mentions of $5 each); The Montegue Wade Lyric Poetry Prize ($100, annual deadline November 1).

$ ☑ AMERICA; FOLEY POETRY CONTEST, 106 W. 56th St., New York NY 10019, phone (212)581-4640, founded 1909, poetry editor Patrick Samway, S.J.

Magazine Needs: *America* is a weekly journal of opinion published by the Jesuits of North America. They primarily publish articles on religious, social, political and cultural themes. They are "looking for imaginative poetry of all kinds. We have no restrictions on form or subject matter, though we prefer to receive poems of 35 lines or less." They have published poetry by Paul Mariani, John Frederick Nims and Dabney Stuart. *America* is 36 pgs., magazine-sized, professionally printed on thin stock with thin paper cover. Circulation is 39,000. Subscription: $42. Sample: $2.25.

How to Submit: Send SASE for "excellent" guidelines. Reports in 2 weeks. Pays $1.40/line plus 2 copies.

Also Offers: The annual Foley Poetry Contest offers a prize of $500, usually in late winter. Send SASE for rules. "Poems for the Foley Contest should be submitted between January and April. Poems submitted for the Foley Contest between July and December will normally be returned unread."

Advice: The editor says, "*America* is committed to publishing quality poetry as it has done for the past 89 years. We encourage beginning and established poets to submit their poems to us."

☐ ◎ THE AMERICAN COWBOY POET MAGAZINE (Specialized: cowboy), Dept. PM, P.O. Box 326, Eagle ID 83616, phone (208)888-9838, fax (208)888-2986, e-mail acpm@cyberhighway.net, founded 1988 as *The American Cowboy Poet Newspaper*, magazine format in January 1991, publisher Rudy Gonzales, editor Rose Fitzgerald.

Magazine Needs: *ACPM* is a quarterly "about real cowboys" using "authentic cowboy poetry. Must be clean—entertaining. Submissions should avoid 'like topics.' We will not publish any more poems about Old Blackie dying, this old hat, if this pair of boots could talk, etc. We do not publish free verse poetry. Only traditional cowboy poetry with rhyme and meter." They also publish articles, including a "Featured Poet," stories of cowboy poetry gatherings, and news of coming events. Subscription: $12/year US, $15 Canada, $20 Overseas. Sample: $3.50.

How to Submit: Cover letter required with submissions. Send SASE for guidelines or request via e-mail. Editor always comments on rejections. Staff reviews related books and tapes of poetry. Send books and cowboy music tapes for review consideration.

◎ THE AMERICAN DISSIDENT (Specialized: political), 1837 Main St., Concord MA 01742, e-mail enmarge@juno.com, founded 1998, editor G. Tod Slone.

Magazine Needs: *AD* appears at least once a year to "provide an outlet for critics of America." They want "well-written dissident work (non-rhyming poetry and short 250-950 word essays) in English, French or Spanish. Submissions should be iconoclastic and anti-obfuscatory in nature and should criticize some aspect of the American scene, including poet laureates, assimilated beatnik and hippy radicals, poetry slams of theatricality, artistes non-engagés, impenetrable ivory towers, state and national cultural councils, literary prizes, millionaire politicos proclaiming themselves champions of the poor, teachers, professors and deans of hypocrisy, armchair Thoreaus, media whores, medicare-bilking doctors, boards of wealthy used-car-salesmen trustees, justice-indifferent lawyers, judges and other careerists, global human rapports, the democratic sham masking the plutocracy and, more generally, the veil of charade placed upon the void of the universe to keep the current oligarchical system operational and the wealthy power elite firmly entrenched in North America." The editor says *AD* is 56 pgs., digest-sized, offset printed and perfect-bound with card cover, includes b&w photos, ads. Press run is 200. Subscription: $10.

How to Submit: Submit 3 poems at a time. No previously published poems; simultaneous submissions OK. No e-mail submissions. "Include SASE and cover letter containing short bio (Manifest humility! Don't list 5,000 acceptances!), including affirmative action states (age, sex, religion, color), de-programing and personal dissident information and specific events that may have pushed you to shed the various national skins of indoctrination and stand apart from your friends and/or colleagues to howl against corruption." Time between acceptance and publication is 3-9 months. Seldom comments on rejections. Send SASE for guidelines. Reports in 2-3 months. Pays 1 copy. Acquires first North American serial rights. Reviews books and chapbooks of poetry and other magazines in 250 words, single book format. Open to unsolicited reviews. Poets may also send books for review consideration.

Advice: The editor says, "Do not submit work apt to be accepted by the multitudinous valentine and academic journals and presses that clog up the piping of the nation's bowels. *AD* is concerned about the overly successful indoctrination of the citizenry and inevitable eventuality of fascism. It is concerned that too many citizens have become clonified teamplayers, networkers and blind institutional patriots for whom loyalty (semper fi) has overwhelming priority over the truth. *AD* is interested in unique insights and ways of looking at the national infrastructure of hypocrisy, fraud and corruption, the glue that seems to be holding America together."

◎**AMERICAN INDIAN STUDIES CENTER; AMERICAN INDIAN CULTURE AND RESEARCH JOURNAL (Specialized: ethnic/nationality)**, 3220 Campbell Hall, Box 951548, UCLA, Los Angeles CA 90095-1548, phone (310)825-7315, fax (310)206-7060, e-mail aisc@UCLA.edu, website http://www.sscnet.UCL A.edu/esp/aisc/index.html, founded 1975.

Magazine Needs: The *American Indian Culture and Research Journal* is a quarterly which publishes new research and literature about American Indians. All work must have Native American content. The editor says the journal is 300 pgs., 5×9, perfect-bound. They receive about 50-70 poems a year, accept approximately 30. Press run is 1,200 for 1,000 subscribers of which 400 are libraries, 10 shelf sales. Subscription: $25 individual, $35 institution. Sample: $7.50. Make checks payable to Regents of the University of California.

How to Submit: Submit 5-6 poems at a time. No previously published poems or simultaneous submissions. Cover letter preferred. No fax or e-mail submissions. Time between acceptance and publication is 6 months. Poems are circulated to an editorial board. Often comments on rejections. Publishes theme issues. Reports in 2 months. Always sends prepublication galleys. Pays 1 copy.

Book/Chapbook Needs & How to Submit: The American Indian Studies Center also publishes 1-2 paperback books of poetry in their Native American Literature Series. They have published *The Light on the Tent Wall: A Bridging* by Mary TallMountain and *Old Shirts & New Skins* by Sherman Alexie. Pays author's copies and offers 40% discount on additional copies. Send SASE for a complete list of the center's publications.

◪**AMERICAN LITERARY REVIEW**, University of North Texas, P.O. Box 311307, Denton TX 76203-1307, phone (940)565-2755, website http://www.engl.unt.edu/alr, editor Lee Martin, poetry editors Bruce Bond and Austin Hummell.

Magazine Needs: *ALR* is a biannual publishing all forms and modes of poetry and fiction. "We are especially interested in originality, substance, imaginative power and lyric intensity." They have published poetry by Christopher Howell, David Citino, Laura Kasischke, Pattiann Rogers, Eric Punkey and David St. John. *ALR* is about 120 pgs., 6×9, attractively printed and perfect-bound with color card cover with photo. Subscription: $15/year, $28/2 years. Sample: $9 (US), $10 (elsewhere).

How to Submit: Submit up to 5 typewritten poems at a time. Cover letter with author's name, address, phone number and poem titles required. Reports in 2 months. Pays copies.

Also Offers: Sponsors a poetry contest in alternating years. Next contest will be in 2000. Send SASE for details.

◪ **$◪ AMERICAN POETRY REVIEW; JEROME J. SHESTACK PRIZES; JESSICA NOBEL MAXWELL MEMORIAL POETRY PRIZE**, Dept. PM, 1721 Walnut St., Philadelphia PA 19103, phone (215)496-0439, fax (215)569-0808, founded 1972.

● Poetry published here has also been included in the 1992, 1993, 1994, 1995, 1997 and 1998 volumes of *The Best American Poetry*.

Magazine Needs: *APR* is probably the most widely circulated (18,000 copies bimonthly) and best-known periodical devoted to poetry in the world. Poetry editors are Stephen Berg, David Bonanno and Arthur Vogelsang, and they have published most of the leading poets writing in English and many translations. The poets include Gerald Stern, Brenda Hillman, John Ashbery, Norman Dubie, Marvin Bell, Galway Kinnell, James Dickey, Lucille Clifton and Tess Gallagher. *APR* is a newsprint tabloid with 13,000 subscriptions, of which 1,000 are libraries. They receive about 10,000 submissions a year, accept approximately 200. This popular publication contains mostly free verse (some leaning to the avant-garde) with flashes of brilliance in every issue. Editors seem to put an emphasis on language and voice. Because *APR* is a tabloid, it can feature long poems (or ones with long line lengths) in an attractive format. Translations are also welcome. In all, this is a difficult market to crack because of the volume of submissions. Sample: $3.95.

How to Submit: No simultaneous submissions. Reports in 3 months, has 1- to 3-year backlog. Always sends prepublication galleys. Pays $1/line. The magazine is also a major resource for opinion, reviews, theory, news and ads pertaining to poetry.

Also Offers: Each year the editors award the Jerome J. Shestack Prizes, 2 prizes of $1,000 for the best poems, in their judgment, published in *APR*. Also sponsors the Jessica Nobel Maxwell Memorial Poetry Prize, $2,000 awarded annually to a younger poet whose work has appeared in *APR* during the preceding calendar year. The editors also sponsor the *APR*/Honickman First Book Prize in Poetry. Award is $3,000 and publication. Entry fee: $20. Mss must be postmarked by October 31. Send SASE for complete guidelines.

◪**AMERICAN POETS & POETRY**, P.O. Box 7692, Port St. Lucie FL 34985-7692, founded 1996, editor John DeStefano.

Magazine Needs: *American Poets & Poetry* is a national magazine of contemporary poetry which appears monthly, except July and August. They want "high-quality poetry by new and established writers. Individuality as well as skillful crafting with respect to the art must be evident in the framework of the poem. Nothing abstract or political." They have published poetry by Alfred Dorn, Norman Leer, H.R. Coursen, June Owens. *AP&P* is 24-36 pgs., 5½×8½, offset printed on quality paper and saddle-stapled with a white card cover printed in 2 colors. They receive about 3,000-3,500 mss a year, accept 25-30% and publish 30-35 poems in each issue. Press run is 375 for 225 subscribers. Subscription: $24.50/10 issues. Sample: $3.50. Make checks payable to John DeStefano.

How to Submit: Submit 3-5 poems at a time. No previously published poems; simultaneous submissions OK.

Cover letter with brief bio preferred. "High volume of submissions does not allow comments on rejections." Reports "usually within 15 days." Pays 1 copy.

☑ $ ◖ THE AMERICAN SCHOLAR, 1785 Massachusetts Ave., NW, 4th Floor, Washington DC 20036, phone (202)265-3808, founded 1932, poetry editor Robert Farnsworth, associate editor Sandra Costich.
Magazine Needs: *American Scholar* is an academic quarterly which uses about 5 poems/issue. "The usual length of our poems is 34 lines." The magazine has published poetry by John Updike, Philip Levine and Rita Dove. What little poetry is used in this high-prestige magazine is accomplished, intelligent and open (in terms of style and form). Study before submitting (sample: $6.95, guidelines available for SASE).
How to Submit: Submit up to 4 poems at a time; "no more for a careful reading. Poems should be typed, on one side of the paper, and each sheet should bear the name and address of the author and the name of the poem." Reports in 2 months. Always sends prepublication galleys. Pays $50/poem. Buys first rights only.

☑ ◎ AMERICAN TANKA (Specialized: form/style), P.O. Box 120-024, Staten Island NY 10312, e-mail editor@americantanka.org, website http://www.americantanka.org, founded 1996, contact editor.
Magazine Needs: *AT* appears twice a year (Spring and Fall) and is devoted to single English-language tanka. They want "concise and vivid language, good crafting, and echo of the original Japanese form." They do not want anything that is not tanka. They have published poetry by Sanford Goldstein, ai li, Jane Reichhold and George Swede. As a sample the editor included this tanka by Marianne Bluger:
> Headed back/from good-byes at the airport/I keep checking/in rear-view the sky/where your contrail lingers.

American Tanka is 65-85 pgs., 8½ × 5½, perfect-bound with glossy cover, b&w original drawings. Single copy: $8; subscription: $16. Sample: $8.
How to Submit: Submit 5 poems at a time. No previously published poems or simultaneous submissions. Electronic submissions OK. E-mail submissions OK. "Send submissions in the text of the e-mail." Submission deadlines: August 15 for Fall, February 15 for Spring. Send SASE for guidelines or see website. Reports in 4-6 weeks. Pays 1 copy. Acquires first North American serial rights.
Also Offers: Website includes guidelines, sample poems from issues, information about the tanka form and a tanka bibliography.
Advice: "The tanka form is rapidly growing in popularity in the West because of its emotional accessibility and because it is an exquisite way to capture a moment in one's life."

☒ $ ◖ THE AMERICAN VOICE, 332 W. Broadway, Louisville KY 40202, phone (502)562-0045, founded 1985, editor Frederick Smock.
• *The American Voice* has received an *Utne Reader* Alternative Press Award and has had work included in *The Best American Poetry* (1995 and 1996 volumes) and *Pushcart Prize* anthologies.
Magazine Needs: *TAV* is a literary quarterly publishing North and South American writers. They prefer free verse, avant-garde, in areas such as ethnic/nationality, gay/lesbian, translation, women/feminism and literary. They have published poetry by Olga Broumas, Wendell Berry, Barbara Kingsolver, Jane Kenyon and May Swenson. *TAV* is 140 pgs. of high-quality stock, elegantly printed and flat-spined with matte card cover. Press run is 2,000 for 1,000 subscribers of which 100 are libraries. Subscription: $15/year. Sample: $7.
How to Submit: No simultaneous submissions. Cover letter requested. Occasionally comments on rejections. Reports in 6 weeks, has a 3-month backlog. Pays $100/poem and 2 copies. (They pay $50 to translator of a poem.) Open to unsolicited reviews. Poets may also send books for review consideration.

☒ ◎ AMERICAN WRITING: A MAGAZINE; NIERIKA EDITIONS (Specialized: form/style), 4343 Manayunk Ave., Philadelphia PA 19128, founded 1990, editor Alexandra Grilikhes.
• Since *American Writing* began, 20 of the authors they have published won national awards after publication in the magazine.
Magazine Needs: *American Writing* appears twice a year using poetry that is "experimental and the voice of the loner, writing that takes risks with form, interested in the powers of intuition and states of being. No cerebral, academic poetry. Poets often try to make an experience 'literary' through language, instead of going back to the original experience and finding the original images. That is what we are interested in: the voice that speaks those images." They have published poetry by Ivan Argüelles, Antler, Eleanor Wilner, Diane Glancy and Margaret Holley. *AW* is 96 pgs., digest-sized, professionally printed and flat-spined with matte card cover. Press run is 1,000 for 350 subscribers. Subscription: $10. Sample: $6.
How to Submit: Submit 8 poems at a time. No previously published poems; simultaneous submissions OK. Guidelines on subscription form. Reports anywhere from 6 weeks to 6 months. Pays 2 copies/accepted submission group.
Advice: The editor says, "Many magazines print the work of the same authors (the big names) who often publish 'lesser' works that way. *AW* is interested in the work itself, its particular strength, energy and voice, not necessarily in the 'status' of the authors. We like to know *something* about the authors, however. We recommend reading a sample issue before just blindly submitting work."

THE AMETHYST REVIEW, 23 Riverside Ave., Truro, Nova Scotia B2N 4G2 Canada, phone (902)895-1345, e-mail amethyst@col.auracom.com, website http://www.col.auracom.com/~amethyst, founded 1992, editors Penny Ferguson and Lenora Steele.
Magazine Needs: *TAR* is a biannual publication of poetry, prose and black ink art. They want "quality, contemporary poetry to 200 lines. No bad rhyme and meter." They have published poetry by Joe Blades and Liliane Welch. As a sample the editors selected these lines from "Shade Garden of Your Bones" by Shawna Lemay:

> For me, it was not the rape itself/which leaves its trace on the body/the way espresso stains white
> linen/and on the heart which is soft and spongy and forgets/for me, it was not even the seven months
> trial,/but the sibille

TAR is 84 pgs., about 7×8½, perfect-bound with colored recycled paper cover and b&w art on the cover and inside. They receive 1,000 poems a year, accept approximately 4%. Press run is 175 for 125 subscribers of which 5 are libraries, 25 shelf sales. Single copy: $6 Canadian; subscription: $12 Canadian, $14 US. Sample (including guidelines): $4 Canadian, $6 US.
How to Submit: Submit 3-5 poems at a time. No previously published poems or simultaneous submissions. Cover letter preferred. No e-mail submissions; inquiries via e-mail OK. Send SASE (or SAE and IRC) for guidelines. "No American stamps please!" Reports in 6 months maximum, "usually in 1-2 months." Pays 1 copy. Acquires first North American serial rights. Occasionally reviews books of poetry published by contributors only.
Also Offers: They also sponsor an annual contest with a theme which changes each year. The contest fee is the cost of (and includes) a subscription. First prize is $100 Canadian. Send SASE (or SAE and IRC) for details after May. Website features writer's and contest guidelines, contest winners, samples of prose and poetry, editors' names, links, cover of current issue, people in current issue, etc.
Advice: The editors add, "Therapy is not always good poetry. The craft must be the important focus."

THE AMHERST REVIEW, Box 2172, Amherst College, P.O. Box 5000, Amherst MA 01002-5000, e-mail review@amherst.edu, editor-in-chief Justin Snider.
Magazine Needs: *The Amherst Review* is an annual literary magazine seeks quality submissions in fiction, poetry, nonfiction and photography/artwork. "All kinds of poetry welcome." The editor says *AR* is 50 pgs., 5×8, soft cover with photography, art and graphics. They receive 300-500 poems a year, accept around 10. Most copies are distributed free to Amherst students. Sample: $6. Make checks payable to *The Amherst Review*.
How to Submit: No previously published poems; simultaneous submissions OK. E-mail submissions OK. Reads submissions from September to March only. Magazine staff makes democratic decision. Seldom comments on rejections. Send SASE for guidelines. Reports in late March. Pays 1 copy.

$ THE AMICUS JOURNAL (Specialized: nature/rural/ecology), 40 W. 20th St., New York NY 10011, phone (212)727-4412, fax (212)727-1773, e-mail amicus@nrdc.org, website http://www.nrdc.org/eamicus/home.html, poetry editor Brian Swann.
Magazine Needs: The quarterly journal of the Natural Resources Defense Council, *Amicus* publishes about 15 poems a year and asks that submitted poetry be "rooted in nature" and no more than one ms page in length. They have published poetry by some of the best-known poets in the country, including Mary Oliver, Gary Snyder, Denise Levertov, Reg Saner, John Haines and Wendell Berry. As a sample the editor selected these lines from "Into the Light" by Pattiann Rogers:

> There may be some places the sun/never reaches—into the stamen/of a prairie primrose bud burned/
> and withered before blooming,/or into the eyes of a fetal/lamb killed before born. I suppose . . .

The Amicus Journal is 48 pgs., about 7½×10½, finely printed, saddle-stapled, on high quality paper with glossy cover, using art, photography and cartoons. Circulation is 400,000. Sample: $4.
How to Submit: "All submissions must be accompanied by a cover note (with notable prior publications) and self-addressed, stamped envelope. We prefer to receive submissions by mail, no fax or e-mail. However, poets can request information by e-mail." Pays $50/poem plus 1 copy and a year's subscription.
Also Offers: They publish *e-Amicus*, an online magazine.

ANACONDA PRESS; FUEL, P.O. Box 118028, Chicago IL 60611, e-mail alowry@tezcat.com, editor-in-chief Andy Lowry.
Magazine Needs: Currently publishes *fuel*, "a wiry publication seeking biting, concise poetry, art and fiction. We're looking for daring, eccentric works. No academia allowed!" As a sample the editor selected these lines from "A Child, Dead in Chicago" by Arthur Powers:

> In twenty countries hundreds of men/stop for a moment, look at the walls/around them, and a great
> machine stumbles/for an instant to a halt./By telex at night the messages come in,/tapping sympathy
> into a dark, empty room.

fuel is 44 pgs., digest-sized, offset printed, saddle-stapled with b&w art on card cover, art and ads inside. Subscription: $10/4 issues. Sample: $3.
How to Submit: Submit up to 6 poems at a time, include name, address and SASE. "Submissions sent sans SASE will not be acknowledged or returned." E-mail submissions OK. "Previously published poems are OK if not too terribly recent. Simultaneous submissions are frowned upon. We appreciate cover letters." Send SASE

"The cover sets the precedent for all that which is inside the journal," says editor-in-chief David Michaelsen about the Issue 24 cover of *Analecta*, an annual journal containing work by students at the University of Texas. "The cover complements the principle art piece produced by Annie Simpson, a fine arts student at the University of Texas. Our designer, Barry Stone, a University of Texas Fine Arts graduate student, chose the yellow color and placed the hazy text above the art piece. His job was to arrange Simpson's work on the cover in such a way that it would represent the journal. He created the hazy text area by layering excerpts from the four featured writers, forming a translucent composition of the text. In a very real sense, this cover hints at the best of what is inside the journal."

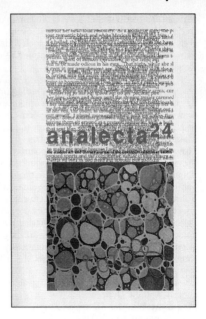

for guidelines and upcoming themes or request via e-mail. Reports in 3-4 weeks. Sometimes sends prepublication galleys. Pays 2 copies if published in 'zine.

ANALECTA (Specialized: students), Dept. PM, Liberal Arts Council, FAC 17, University of Texas, Austin TX 78712, phone (512)471-6563, fax (512)471-4518, e-mail analecta@www.dla.utexas.edu, website http://www.utexas.edu/cola/depts/lac/analecta.html, founded 1974, editor David Michaelsen.
Magazine Needs: *Analecta* is an annual of literary works and art by college/university students and graduate students chosen in an annual contest. No restrictions on type. Submissions cannot be returned. "Our purpose is to provide a forum for excellent student writing. Works must be previously unpublished." Published in the fall, it is a 150-page, digest-sized magazine, professionally printed and perfect-bound with glossy 4-color card cover, glossy plates for interior artwork in b&w. They receive about 800 submissions a year, accept approximately 40. Press run is 800 for 700 subscribers, 100 shelf sales. Sample: $7.50.
How to Submit: Limited to 5 submissions/writer. Entries must be typed; name should appear on cover sheet only. Send SASE for guidelines. Deadline is in mid-October. Prizes in each category. Pays 2 copies and $100 for each prize.
Also Offers: Website includes contest guidelines, links to other Austin literary organizations and brief description of *Analecta*.

ANAMNESIS PRESS; ANAMNESIS POETRY CHAPBOOK AWARD CONTEST, P.O. Box 51115, Palo Alto CA 94303, phone (415)255-8366, fax (415)255-3190, e-mail anamnesis@compuserve.com, website http://ourworld.compuserve.com/homepages/Anamnesis, founded 1990, publisher Keith Allen Daniels.
Book/Chapbook Needs: Primarily publishes chapbooks selected through its annual contest, though occasionally publishes a larger volume "to preserve poetry that might otherwise be forgotten. We wish to see poems of intellectual and emotional depth that give full rein to the imagination, whether free verse or formalist. Please don't send us trite, sappy, maudlin or 'inspirational' poetry." They have published poetry by Joe Haldeman, James Blish, David R. Bunch and Steven Utley. Chapbooks are 25-40 pgs., photo offset and saddle-stapled with 2-color covers.
How to Submit: For the Anamnesis Poetry Chapbook Award Contest, submit 20-30 pgs. of poetry with a cover letter, SASE and $15 entry fee postmarked by March 15. Previously published poems (if author provides acknowledgments) and simultaneous submissions OK. "Poets can request guidelines via fax and e-mail and obtain guidelines via our website, but we do not accept poetry submissions via e-mail or fax." Winners are selected in June. Prize: $1,000, an award certificate, publication and 20 copies of winning chapbook.
Advice: The publisher adds, "We encourage poets to purchase a sample chapbook for $6 before submitting, to get a feel for what we're looking for. We use free verse and well done formal poetry."

ANCIENT PATHS (Specialized: religious), 709 Coronado, P.O. Box 117, Harlingen TX 78550, founded 1998, editor Skylar Burris.
Magazine Needs: *Ancient Paths* is published biannually "to provide a forum for Christian writers in a journal

that can be distributed at cost. It contains poetry, short stories and drawings." They want "traditional forms or free verse; Christian images, issues, events or themes. No 'preachy' poetry or obtrusive rhyme; no stream of conscious or avant-garde work; no poetry that is not accessible." They have published poetry by Joseph F. Jamar, Pam Wynn and Ed Wier. As a sample the editor selected these lines from "Obstruction of Construction" by Roger Sedarat:

> *The carpenter nailed across the plank/And started crying. He didn't know why./He did not see, as each*
> *nail sank,/The carpenter nailed across the plank.*

AP is 20-23 pgs., 8½×11, photocopied and stapled with color cardstock cover, includes clip art and b&w drawings. They receive about 300 poems a year, accept approximately 15%. Press run is 250 for 50-100 orders and subscriptions; 150 distributed free to churches, libraries, individuals. Subscription: $9/2 years. Sample: $2.25. Make checks payable to Skylar Burris.

How to Submit: Submit up to 4 poems at a time. Line length for poetry is 70 maximum; 20-50 lines preferred. Previously published poems and simultaneous submissions OK. Disk submissions OK. Cover letter preferred. "Name, address and line count on first page. Save as text only if submitting on disk. Note if the poem is previously published and what rights (if any) were purchased." Reads submissions March 1 through July 1 and September 1 through January 1 only. Time between acceptance and publication is up to 6 months. Often comments on rejections. Send SASE for guidelines. Reports in "2-3 weeks if rejected, longer if being seriously considered." Pays 1 copy. Acquires first or one-time rights. Staff reviews other magazines in 50 words. "We publish submission guidelines for some other magazines if they submit them and qualify (i.e., other Christian lit journals)."

Also Offers: "All poems are automatically entered in a contest each issue. Three pieces of literature (poems or short stories) are selected. Prizes are $12, $7 and $4 plus an additional free copy of the journal."

N ⊕ ⊍ ANGEL EXHAUST, Flat 6, Avon Court, London N12 8HR United Kingdom, founded 1977, contact Andrew Duncan.

Magazine Needs: *AE* appears twice a year and publishes poetry and prose about poetry (95% British). They want "anything which staves off boredom and desperation even for a moment—poems about engineering, poems about shopping. No poems full of objects, psychotherapy, hypochondria, body parts. No conservative or religious poetry." They have published poetry by Denise Riley, Allen Fisher, Roy Fisher and Maggie O'Sullivan. As a sample the editor selected the poem "Tuist" by Helen Macdonald:

> *ah, how the hay smokes/into papaverous skies/as we address the heights of the C20th/in a poplin shirt,*
> *all declamatory and tired/with a suit that seals to rest these soft/& perfect metals.*

The editor says *AE* is 120 pgs., 6×9 with laminate cover and photos. They receive poems from about 100 poets a year, accept approximately 20%. Press run is 300 for 20 subscribers of which 3 are libraries. Subscription: $14. Sample: $10.

How to Submit: Submit 10 poems at a time. Previously published poems and simultaneous submissions OK. Cover letter preferred. Time between acceptance and publication is 6-12 months. Seldom comments on rejections. Publishes theme issues. Always sends prepublication galleys. Pays 1 copy. Reviews books of poetry in up to 6,000 words, single book format. Open to unsolicited reviews. Send books for review consideration.

Advice: "Poets should have an adequate theory of social agency."

○ ⊚ ANGEL NEWS MAGAZINE (Specialized: spirituality/inspirational, religious, themes), 519 W. Plantation Blvd., Lake Mary FL 32746-2530, phone (407)323-5037, e-mail dbaumbach@aol.com, founded 1980, publisher/editor Daphne C. Baumbach, membership chairman Jeanne Foley.

Magazine Needs: *Angel News* is a quarterly publication "devoted to the constant study and reflection of Angels. By sharing knowledge, it offers information on the nature and functions of Angels and Angelic beings." They want "angel poetry or stories mentioning God and Heaven; on eagles or roses; any length. Nothing vulgar." They have published poetry by Mary E. Matthews, Dottie Melton, Marcia Ann Kolovich and Melissa Deal Forsh. *Angel News* is 70 pgs., 8½×11, computer-generated then photocopied, flat-spined with paper cover, includes b&w graphics and photos, ads. Press run is 100. Single copy: $4.95; subscription: $16/year. Make checks payable to Daphne C. Baumbach.

How to Submit: Submit 4 poems at a time. Previously published poems and simultaneous submissions OK. Cover letter required. E-mail submissions OK. Time between acceptance and publication is 1 month. Always comments on rejections. Publishes theme issues. Send SASE for guidelines and upcoming themes. Reports in 1 month. Pays 1 copy the first time a poet is published then purchase is required to receive contributor's copy. Reviews books of poetry and other magazines, single book format. Poets may also send books for review consideration.

○ ANGELFLESH; ANGELFLESH PRESS, P.O. Box 141123, Grand Rapids MI 49514, founded 1994, editor Jim Buchanan.

FOR AN EXPLANATION of symbols used in this book, see the Key to Symbols on the front and back inside covers.

Magazine Needs: *Angelflesh* appears up to 3 times/year and publishes "today's best cutting-edge fiction, poetry and art." They want poetry that is "strong, real and gutsy, with vivid images, emotional and spiritual train wrecks. No taboos, no 'Hallmark' verse." They have published poetry by John Bennett, Elizabeth Florio, Catfish McDaris and E.A. Hilbert. As a sample the editor selected these lines from an untitled poem by Catfish McDaris:

> only the dead die young/(everyone's good when dead)//now i just wanna be/a catfish in the Pecos/or perhaps Paiute Sage/in a Ghost Dance shirt/with a new plan for Mt. Rushmore.

The editor says *Angelflesh* is 40-50 pgs., various sizes, photocopied and saddle-stitched. They receive about 1,000 poems a year, accept 2-5%. Press run is up to 500. Subscription: $10. Sample: $4.

How to Submit: Submit 3-5 poems at a time. Simultaneous submissions OK. Cover letter preferred. Time between acceptance and publication is 2-12 months. Seldom comments on rejections. Reports in around 1 month. "I will respond to submissions via e-mail if the poets do not need their material returned." Pays 1 copy.

Book/Chapbook Needs & How to Submit: Under Angelflesh Press the editor also publishes 1-2 perfect-bound paperback and 1-2 chapbooks/year. Chapbooks are usually 20-30 pgs., 5½×8, photocopied and saddle-stitched with some artwork. Replies in 1 month. Pay negotiable. Obtain a sample chapbook by sending $4.

☑ Ⓓ **ANHINGA PRESS; ANHINGA PRIZE**, P.O. Box 10595, Tallahassee FL 32302-0595, phone (850)521-9920, fax (850)442-6323, e-mail info@anhinga.org, website http://www.anhinga.org, founded 1972, poetry editors Rick Campbell and Van Brock.

Book/Chapbook Needs: The press publishes "books and anthologies of poetry. We want to see contemporary poetry which respects language. We're inclined toward poetry that is not obscure, that can be understood by any literate audience." They have published *The Secret History of Water* by Silvia Curbelo; and *Conversations During Sleep* by Michele Wolf (the 1997 Anhinga Prize winner).

How to Submit: Considers simultaneous submissions. Include SASE with all submissions.

Also Offers: The Anhinga Prize for poetry awards $2,000 and publication to a book-length manuscript each year. Send SASE for rules. Submissions accepted January 1 to March 31 only. Entry fee: $20. The contest has been judged by such distinguished poets as William Stafford, Louis Simpson, Henry Taylor, Hayden Carruth, Marvin Bell, Donald Hall and Joy Harjo. "Everything we do is on our website."

Ⓝ ◯ Ⓞ **ANNA'S JOURNAL (Specialized: childlessness issues)**, P.O. Box 341, Ellijay GA 30540, phone/fax (706)276-2309, e-mail annas@ellijay.com, founded 1995, editor Catherine Ward-Long.

Magazine Needs: *Anna's Journal* appears quarterly to offer "spiritual support for childless couples who for the most part have decided to stay that way." They want any type of poetry as long as it relates to childless issues. *AJ* is 8 pgs., 8½×11, neatly printed on colored paper and saddle-stapled, includes clip art and b&w photos. They receive about 10 poems a year, accept approximately 50%. Press run is 200 for 36 subscribers; 20 distributed free to churches, doctor's offices. Subscription: $14/1 year, $24/2 years. Sample: $4.

How to Submit: Submit 3 poems at a time. Previously published poems OK; no simultaneous submissions. E-mail submissions OK. Cover letter preferred. Time between acceptance and publication is 1-2 months. Publishes theme issues occasionally. Reports in 1-2 months. Pays 3 copies. Acquires first rights and reprint rights. Reviews books of poetry, single book format. Open to unsolicited reviews. Poets may also send books for review consideration.

Advice: The editor says, "Poetry must relate to childlessness issues. It helps if writer is childless."

◯ Ⓓ **ANTHOLOGY; INKWELL PRESS**, P.O. Box 4411, Mesa AZ 85211-4411, e-mail tavara@juno.com, website http://www.primenet.com/~inkwell, executive editor Sharon Skinner, publisher Bob Nelson.

Magazine Needs: *Anthology* appears every 2 months and intends to be "the best poetry, prose and art magazine." They want "poetry with clear conceit. Evocative as opposed to provocative. We do not dictate form or style but creative uses are always enjoyed. Graphic horror and pornography are not encouraged." They have published poetry by Paula Ashley and Carol Michalski. As a sample the editor selected these lines from "Laurel's Prayer" by Vivian V. Eyre, 3rd Place winner of the 1998 *Anthology* Poetry Contest:

> she writes/sacred sentiments/of urgency and grace/to a single strand of surnames/like a single strand of pearls.

Anthology is 28-32 pgs., 8½×11, printed on coated glossy paper, saddle-stitched with two-color cover, b&w drawings and clip art inside. Press run is 1,000 for 100 subscribers of which 2 are libraries, with 50-75 distributed free to local coffeehouses, beauty parlors, doctors' offices, etc. Single copy: $3.95; subscription: $17 (6 issues). Make checks payable to *Anthology*.

How to Submit: Submit up to 5 poems at a time with SASE. Previously published and simultaneous submissions OK. E-mail submissions OK in PC compatible format. "Please try not to send handwritten work." Time between acceptance and publication is 6-8 months. Send SASE for guidelines or obtain via e-mail or website. Reports in 10-12 weeks. Pays 1 copy. Acquires one-time rights.

Also Offers: Sponsors annual contest with cash and other prizes for both poetry and short stories. Entry fee: $1/poem required. Send SASE for guidelines. Website includes submission guidelines, sample poems, and listings of staff members, events and contest information.

Advice: "Send what you write, not what you think an editor wants to hear. And always remember that a rejection is seldom personal, it is just one step closer to a yes."

THE ANTHOLOGY OF NEW ENGLAND WRITERS; ROBERT PENN WARREN POETRY AWARDS (Specialized: form); NEW ENGLAND WRITERS/VERMONT POETS ASSOCIATION, P.O. Box 483, Windsor VT 05089, phone (802)674-2315, e-mail newvtpoet@juno.com, founded 1989, editor Frank Anthony, associate editor Susan Anthony.
Magazine Needs: *The Anthology of New England Writers* appears annually in November. All poems published in this annual are winners of their contest. They want "unpublished, original, free verse poetry only; 10-30 line limit." Open to *all* poets, not just New England. They have published poetry by Richard Eberhart, Rosanna Warren, David Kirby and Vivian Shipley. *Anthology* is 44 pgs., 5½×8½, professionally printed and perfect-bound with colored card cover, b&w illustrations. Press run is 400. Single copy: $3.95. Sample: $3. Make checks payable to New England Writers.
How to Submit: Submit 3-9 poems at a time with reading fee (1-3 poems: $6; 4-6 poems: $10; 7-9 poems: $15). Include 3×5 card with name, address and titles of poems. No previously published poems or simultaneous submissions. Reads submissions September through June 15 (post mark) only. SASE for guidelines optional; also may request via e-mail. Reports 6 weeks after June 15 deadline. Sometimes sends prepublication galleys. Pays 1 copy. All rights revert to author upon publication.
Also Offers: Sponsors an annual free verse contest with The Robert Penn Warren Poetry Awards. Awards $500 for first, $200 for second and $150 for third. They also award 10 Honorable Mentions, 10 Commendables and 10 Editor's Choice. Entry fee: $6/3 poems. Winners announced at the New England Writers Conference in July. All submissions are automatically entered in contest. The Vermont Poets Association was founded in 1986 "to encourage precision and ingenuity in the practice of writing and speaking, whatever the form and style." Currently has 400 members. Writing information free, critiques, consultation and advice on markets are included in the biannual newsletter, *NewScript*. Meetings are held several times a year. Membership dues: $9, $6 senior citizens and students. Send SASE for additional information. Also sponsors the annual New England Writers Conference with nationally known writers and editors involved with workshops, open mike readings and a writer's panel. 1999 date: July 24. Conference lasts one day and is "affordable," and open to the public.

$ ANTIETAM REVIEW (Specialized: regional), Washington County Arts Council, 41 S. Potomac St., Hagerstown MD 21740-5512, phone/fax (301)791-3132, founded 1982, poetry editor Crystal Brown.
Magazine Needs: *The Antietam Review* appears annually in June and looks for "well-crafted literary quality poems. We discourage inspirational verse, haiku, doggerel." Uses poets (natives or residents) from the states of Maryland, Pennsylvania, Virginia, West Virginia, Delaware and District of Columbia. Needs 25 poems/issue, up to 30 lines each. They have published poetry by Elisabeth Murawski, Mikia Leopold and Michael S. Glaser. As a sample the editor selected these lines from "Positive" by Cheryl Snell:
> Some moments have no clock and/The floating girl had her own agenda:/When she scrambled the
> cross of you against her birdy shoulders/She aimed straight for the darkening edge of stage.
AR is 64 pgs., 8½×11, saddle-stapled, glossy paper with glossy card cover and b&w photos throughout. Press run is 1,000. Sample: $3.15 back issue, $5.25 current.
How to Submit: Submit 5 typed poems at a time. "We prefer a cover letter stating other publications, although we encourage new and emerging writers. We do not accept previously published poems and reluctantly take simultaneous submissions." Do not submit mss from February through August. "We read from September 1 through February 1 annually." Send SASE for guidelines. Sends prepublication galleys, if requested. Pays between $15-25/poem, depending on funding, plus 2 copies. Buys first North American serial rights.
Also Offers: Sponsors a contest for natives or residents of DC, DE, MD, PA, VA and WV. Send SASE for details.

THE ANTIGONISH REVIEW, St. Francis Xavier University, P.O. Box 5000, Antigonish, Nova Scotia B2G 2W5 Canada, phone (902)867-3962, fax (902)867-5563, e-mail tar@stfx.ca, website http://www.antigonish.com/review, founded 1970, editor George Sanderson, poetry editor Peter Sanger.
Magazine Needs: *The Antigonish Review* appears quarterly and "tries to produce the kind of literary and visual mosaic that the modern sensibility requires or would respond to." They want poetry not over "80 lines, i.e., 2 pgs.; subject matter can be anything, the style is traditional, modern or post-modern limited by typographic resources. Purpose is not an issue." No "erotica, scatalogical verse, excessive propaganda toward a certain subject." They have published poetry by Andy Wainwright, W.J. Keith, Michael Hulse, Jean McNeil, M. Travis Lane and Douglas Lochhead. *TAR* is 150 pgs., 6×9, flat-spined with glossy card cover, offset printing, using "in-house graphics and cover art, no ads." They receive 2,500 submissions/year; accept 10%. Press run is 850 for 700 subscribers. Subscription: $20. Sample: $3.
How to Submit: Submit 5-10 poems at a time. No simultaneous submissions or previously published poems. Include SASE (or SAE and IRCs if outside Canada). Editor "sometimes" comments on rejections. Pays 2 copies.

$ THE ANTIOCH REVIEW, P.O. Box 148, Yellow Springs OH 45387, phone (937)767-6389, founded 1941, poetry editor Judith Hall.
● Work published in this review has also been included in *The Best American Poetry* (1995 and 1998 volumes) and *Pushcart Prize* anthologies.
Magazine Needs: *The Review* "is an independent quarterly of critical and creative thought . . . For well over 50 years, creative authors, poets and thinkers have found a friendly reception . . . regardless of formal reputation.

We get far more poetry than we can possibly accept, and the competition is keen. Here, where form and content are so inseparable and reaction is so personal, it is difficult to state requirements or limitations. Studying recent issues of *The Review* should be helpful. No 'light' or inspirational verse." They have published poetry by Ralph Angel, Jorie Graham, Jacqueline Osherow and Mark Strand. They receive about 3,000 submissions/year, publish 16 pages of poetry in each issue, and have about a 6-month backlog. Circulation is 5,000, of which 70% is through bookstores and newsstands. Large percentage of subscribers are libraries. Subscription: $35. Sample: $6.

How to Submit: Submit 3-6 poems at a time. No previously published poems. Reads submissions September 1 through May 1 only. Send SASE for guidelines. Reports in 6-8 weeks. Pays $10/published page plus 2 copies. Reviews books of poetry in 300 words, single format.

$ ◎ ANTIPODES (Specialized: regional), 8 Big Island, Warwick NY 10990, e-mail kane@vassar.edu, founded 1987, poetry editor Paul Kane.

Magazine Needs: *Antipodes* is a biannual of Australian poetry and fiction and criticism and reviews of Australian writing. They want work from Australian poets only. No restrictions as to form, length, subject matter or style. They have published poetry by A.D. Hope, Judith Wright and John Tranter. The editor says *Antipodes* is 180 pgs., 8½×11, perfect-bound, with graphics, ads and photos. They receive about 500 submissions a year, accept approximately 10%. Press run is 500 for 200 subscribers. Subscription: $20. Sample: $17.

How to Submit: Submit 3-5 poems at a time. No previously published poems or simultaneous submissions. Cover letter with bio note required. The editor says they "prefer submission of photocopies which do not have to be returned." Seldom comments on rejections. Reports in 2 months. Pays $20/poem plus 1 copy. Acquires first North American serial rights. Staff reviews books of poetry in 500-1,500 words. Send books for review consideration.

■ ◯ ◎ THE APOSTOLIC CRUSADE (Specialized: religious), P.O. Box 1724, La Mirada CA 90637, e-mail arg1296@aol.com, website http://members.aol.com/arg1296/index.html, founded 1992, editor/publisher Art Garcia.

Magazine Needs: *The Apostolic Crusade* is "a network resource information center for Catholics." They want "short, simple poems relating to spirituality and divine inspiration." The editor says, "Rather than being a bulletin, we provide an outlet for submissions sent through e-mail by forwarding the material to its respectful audience—it's rerouted to the cliental of *The Apostolic Crusade*."

How to Submit: Submit 1 poem via e-mail only. Include name and e-mail address on all submissions. Previously published poems and simultaneous submissions OK. "We like to receive cover letters explaining a little bit about the poet and the reasons for publication." Time between acceptance and publication is 1-6 months. No reply or return of rejections. Rather, the authors of the accepted poems simply receive the issues in which their poems are included. Pays 1 copy via e-mail.

◗ ◎ APPALACHIA; THE APPALACHIA POETRY PRIZE (Specialized: nature), 5 Joy St., Boston MA 02108, phone (617)523-0636, founded 1876, poetry editor Parkman Howe, editor-in-chief Sandy Stott.

Magazine Needs: *Appalachia* is a "semiannual journal of mountaineering and conservation which describes activities outdoors and asks questions of an ecological nature." They want poetry relating to the outdoors and nature—specifically weather, mountains, rivers, lakes, woods and animals. "No conquerors' odes." They have published poetry by Bruce Ducker, Warren Woessner, Lucille Day, Mary Oliver and Thomas Reiter. The editor says *Appalachia* is 160 pgs., 6×9, professionally printed with color cover, using photos, graphics and a few ads. They receive about 200 poems a year, use 10-15. Press run is 10,000. Subscription: $10/year. Sample: $5.

How to Submit: Submit up to 6 poems at a time. "We favor shorter poems—maximum of 36 lines usually." No previously published poems or simultaneous submissions. Cover letter required. Time between acceptance and publication is 1 year. Seldom comments on rejections. Send SASE for guidelines. Reports in 4-6 weeks. Pays 1 copy. Acquires first rights. Staff reviews "some" books of poetry in 200-400 words, usually single book format.

Also Offers: An annual award, The Appalachia Poetry Prize, given since 1972. Write for details.

Advice: The editor says, "Our readership is very well versed in the outdoors—mountains, rivers, lakes, animals. We look for poetry that helps readers see the natural world in fresh ways. No generalized accounts of the great outdoors."

◎ APPALACHIAN HERITAGE; THE DENNY C. PLATTNER AWARDS (Specialized: regional), Hutchins Library, Berea College, Berea KY 40404, phone (606)986-9341 ext. 5260, fax (606)986-9494, e-mail sidney_farr@berea.edu, founded 1973, editor Sidney Saylor Farr.

Magazine Needs: *AH* a literary quarterly with Southern Appalachian emphasis. The journal publishes several poems in each issue, and the editor wants to see "poems about people, places, the human condition, social issues, etc., with Southern Appalachian settings. No style restrictions but poems should have a maximum of 14 lines, prefer 8-10 lines." She does not want "blood and gore, hell-fire and damnation, or biased poetry about race or religion." She has published poetry by Jim Wayne Miller, James Still, George Ella Lyon and Robert Morgan. The flat-spined magazine is 6×9, professionally printed on white stock with b&w line drawings and photos, glossy white card cover with 4-color illustration. Issues we have scanned tended toward lyric free verse, emphasiz-

ing nature or situations set in nature, but the editor says they will use good poems of any subject and form. Sample copy: $6.
How to Submit: Submit 2-4 poems at a time, typed one to a page. No previously published poems; simultaneous submissions OK. Requires cover letter giving information about previous publications where poets have appeared. Electronic submissions OK. Publishes theme issues occasionally. Send SASE for upcoming themes or request via fax or e-mail. Reports in 2-4 weeks. Sometimes sends prepublication galleys. Pays 3 copies. Acquires first rights. Reviews books of poetry. Open to unsolicited reviews. Poets may also send books for review consideration.
Also Offers: The Denny C. Plattner Awards go to the authors of the best poetry, article or essay, or short fiction published in the four issues released within the preceding year. The award amount in each category is $200.

APROPOS (Specialized: subscribers), Ashley Manor, 450 Buttermilk Rd., Easton PA 18042, founded 1989, editor Ashley C. Anders.
Magazine Needs: *Apropos* publishes all poetry submitted by subscribers except that judged by the editor to be pornographic or in poor taste. $25 for 6-issue subscription. As a sample the editor selected her own poem "With Pen in Hand":

> With pen in hand I can confess/my innermost unhappiness,/or wonder in the things I see—/a newborn bird; a lovely tree.//This gift that God has given me/Allows my feelings to be free./With pen in hand I always say/whatever's on my mind each day.

Apropos is 90 pgs., digest-sized, plastic ring bound, with heavy stock cover, desktop-published. Sample: $3.
How to Submit: Submit 1 poem at a time. Line length for poetry is 40 maximum—50 characters/line. Editor prefers to receive sample of poetry prior to acceptance of subscription. Samples will not be returned. No simultaneous submissions; previously published poems OK. Send SASE for guidelines. All poems are judged by subscribers. Prizes for regular issues are $50, $25, $10 and $5.

ARACHNE, INC. (Specialized: rural), 2363 Page Rd., Kennedy NY 14747-9717, founded 1980, senior editor Susan L. Leach.
Book/Chapbook Needs: *Arachne* focuses on the work of "America's finest rural poets" and publishes 2 chapbooks/year (500 press run). They want "any style, as long as its theme is rural in nature. No purient subjects." Chapbooks are usually 30 pgs., staple-bound, #10 cover, no graphics.
How to Submit: Submit 7 poems at a time. No previously published poems or simultaneous submissions. Cover letter preferred. "Please include a SASE for return and correspondence." Reads submissions January and June only. Time between acceptance and publication is 6 months. Poems are circulated to an editorial board. "Poems selected initially by membership, presented to board for final decision." Seldom comments on rejections. Replies to queries and mss within 3 months. The editor says, "We will not consider any material of a sexually questionable nature. We remain a conservative press."

ARC: CANADA'S NATIONAL POETRY MAGAZINE; THE CONFEDERATION POETS PRIZE; POEM OF THE YEAR CONTEST, P.O. Box 7368, Station Vanier, Ottawa, Ontario K1L 9Z9 Canada, founded 1978, co-editors Rita Donovan and John Barton.
Magazine Needs: *Arc* is a biannual of poetry, poetry-related articles, interviews and book reviews. "Our tastes are eclectic. Our focus is Canadian, but we also publish writers from elsewhere." They have published poetry by Anne Szumigalski, Heather Spears, Robert Priest, Anne Michaels and Erin Mouré. *Arc* is 80-96 pgs., perfect-bound, with laminated 2-color cover, artwork and ads. They receive about 500 submissions a year, accept 40-50 poems. Press run is 750 for 350 subscribers. Single copy: $8.50 Canadian/Canada, $12 Canadian/US, $14 Canadian/overseas; subscription (4 issues): $32 Canadian/Canada, $32 Canadian/US, $36 Canadian/overseas. Cost of sample varies.
How to Submit: Submit 5-8 poems, single spaced, with name and address on each page. No previously published poems or simultaneous submissions. Cover letter required. Send SASE (or SAE and IRC) for guidelines and upcoming themes. Reports in 3-6 months. Pays $25 Canadian/page plus 2 copies. Buys first North American serial rights.
Also Offers: The Confederation Poets Prize is an annual award of $100 for the best poem published in *Arc* that year. *Arc* also sponsors a "Poem of the Year Contest." Awards first prize of $1,000, second prize of $750 and third prize of $500. Deadline in June.

ARC PUBLICATIONS, Nanholme Mill, Shaw Wood Rd., Todmorden, Lancashire OL14 6DA United Kingdom, phone (01706)812338, founded 1969, partners Tony Ward, Angela Jarman and Rosemary Jones.
Book/Chapbook Needs: ARC publishes 8 paperback books of poetry a year. They want "literary, literate, contemporary poetry. No religious or children's verse. We specialize not only in contemporary poetry of the U.K. but also in poetry written in English from across the world." They have published books of poetry by John Goodby (UK), Tomas Salamun (Slovenia), Robert Gray (Australia) and Tariq Latif (UK). Their books are 64-100 pgs., 5½×8½, offset litho and perfect-bound with card covers in 2-3 colors.
How to Submit: Query first with 10 sample poems and a cover letter with brief bio and publication credits. "No submissions replied to if there is no IRC." Previously published poems and simultaneous submissions OK. Mss are read by at least 2 editors before possible acceptance. Seldom comments on rejections. Replies to queries

in up to 4 months. Pays 7-10% royalties and 5 author's copies (out of a press run of 600). Send SASE (or SAE and IRCs) for current list to order samples.

Advice: They say, "Poets should have a body of work already published in magazines and journals, and should be acquainted with our list of books, before submitting."

N ⊘ **ARCTOS PRESS; HOBEAR PUBLICATIONS**, P.O. Box 401, Sausalito CA 94966-0401, phone (415)331-2503, e-mail runes@aol.com, founded 1997, editor CB Follett.

Book/Chapbook Needs: Arctos Press, under the imprint HoBear Publications, publishes 1-2 paperbacks each year. "We publish quality books and anthologies of poetry, usually theme-oriented, in runs of 1,000, paper cover, perfect-bound." They have published poetry by Robert Hass, Kay Ryan, Brenda Hillman and Jane Hirshfield. As a sample the editor selected these lines from "Every Day" by Ellery Akers:

> It is not impersonal, the world./Or strict. If she is awake to every stalk./If she can watch the hyacinths
> hammer their green beaks/through the ground.

How to Submit: "We do not accept unsolicited mss unless a current call has been posted in *Poets & Writers* and/or elsewhere, at which time up to 5 poems related to the theme should be sent." Previously published poems (if author holds the rights) and simultaneous submissions ("if we are kept informed.") OK.

Advice: "Our first title *Beside the Sleeping Maiden: Poets of Marin* has been very favorably reviewed."

⊘ ⊙ **ARJUNA LIBRARY PRESS; JOURNAL OF REGIONAL CRITICISM**, 1025 Garner St. D, Space 18, Colorado Springs CO 80905-1774, library founded 1963, press founded 1979, editor-in-chief Count Prof. Joseph A. Uphoff, Jr.

Magazine Needs: "The Arjuna Library Press is avant-garde, designed to endure the transient quarters and marginal funding of the literary phenomenon (as a tradition) while presenting a context for the development of current mathematical ideas in regard to theories of art, literature and performance; photocopy printing allows for very limited editions and irregular format. Quality is maintained as an artistic materialist practice." He publishes "surrealist prose poetry, visual poetry, dreamlike, short and long works; not obscene, profane (will criticize but not publish), unpolished work." He has published work by Tina M. Johnston and Andrew Ross. As a sample the editor selected these lines from "The Brook" by Lupe Sampayo:

> . . . Creating ripples. Clean water From the Highlands,/Weaving through Miniscule Ravines,/Hindered
> by Stones. A brook looking for A river,/Tadpoles, Leaves,/Minnow Desperately Following.

Journal of Regional Criticism is published on loose photocopied pages of collage, writing and criticism, appearing frequently in a varied format. Press run: 1 copy each. Reviews books of poetry "occasionally." Open to unsolicited reviews. Poets may also send books for review consideration. "Upon request will treat material as submitted for reprint, one-time rights."

Book/Chapbook Needs: Arjuna Library Press publishes 6-12 chapbooks/year, averaging 50 pgs. Sample: $2.50.

How to Submit: He is currently accepting one or two short poems, with a cover letter and SASE to be considered for publication.

Advice: The editor says, "Poets should be aware that literature has become a vast labyrinth in which the vision of the creative mind may be solitary. One can no longer depend upon an audience to entertain the storyteller. The writer may be left lonely in the presence of the creation which should, therefore, be entertainment in its own right if not for an audience then at least for the holder of the copyright."

N ⊚ **ARKANSAS REVIEW: A JOURNAL OF DELTA STUDIES (Specialized: regional)**, P.O. Box 1890, State University AR 72467-1890, phone (870)972-3043, fax (870)972-2795, e-mail delta@toltec.astate.edu, website http://www.clt.astate/arkreview, founded 1968 (as *Kansas Quarterly*), general editor William M. Clements, creative materials editor Norman E. Stafford.

Magazine Needs: Appearing 3 times a year, the *Arkansas Review* is "a regional studies journal devoted to the seven-state Mississippi River Delta. Interdisciplinary in scope, we publish academic articles, relevant creative material, interviews and reviews. Material must respond to or evoke the experiences and landscapes of the seven-state Mississippi River Delta (St. Louis to New Orleans)." They have published poetry by Errol Miller, Mary Kennan Herbert, Lora Dunetz and Mark DeFoe. As a sample the editors selected this untitled poem:

> On her good old stove, her hardy skillet/waits, iron sentinel guarding those grim days/when her food
> stuck to the field hand's ribs./Her stove is as yellow now as an old/wedding gown. It stands, perfuming
> the air/with the just aroma of Mr. Clean.

The editors say *AR* is 68 pgs., magazine-sized, photo offset printed, saddle-stitched with 4-color cover, includes photos, drawings and paintings. They receive about 500 poems a year, accept approximately 5%. Press run is 600 for 400 subscribers of which 300 are libraries, 20 shelf sales; 50 distributed free to contributors. Subscription: $20. Sample: $7.50. Make checks payable to ASU Foundation.

How to Submit: No limit on number of poems submitted at a time. No previously published poems or simultaneous submissions. Cover letter with SASE preferred. E-mail and disk submissions OK. Time between acceptance and publication is about 6 months. Poems are circulated to an editorial board. "The Creative Materials Editor makes the final decision based—in part—on recommendations from other readers." Often comments on rejections. Publishes theme issues occasionally. Send SASE for guidelines and upcoming themes. Reports in 4 months. Pays 5 copies. Acquires first rights. Staff reviews books and chapbooks of poetry in 500 words, single and multi-

book format. Send books for review consideration to William M. Clements. ("Inquire in advance.")
Also Offers: Website includes past table of contents, guidelines for contributors, list of editors.

N ⊕ **⦿ ARKTOS; MUSINGS OF A DRUNKEN POET**, P.O. Box 471, Bromley, Kent BR2 0WU England, founded 1999, editor Maxine.
Magazine Needs: *Musings of a Drunken Poet* is a quarterly newsletter designed "to support and encourage the underground literary scene by featuring aspiring writers, poetry, review, contacts, etc. Also aims to educate and inspire by profiling great writers and poets through the ages." They want work that is "thoughtful, intriguing, from the heart; words that inspire and strike deep. Both poetry and prose are considered. Influences include: Winterson, Rimbaud, T.S. Eliot, Jarman. No political or brash, in-yer-face anger." They have published poetry by Simon Brown and D. Michael McNamara. As a sample the editor selected these lines (poet unidentified):
> we pause, like silver, as if by magic./the will for words to stop . . . just for a second . . . so we can
> gather/the stillness in our hands and feel its weight./lighter than a feather and heavier than xenon.
The editor says *Musings* is 8-16 pgs., newsletter-sized, photocopied, spot color cover, includes photography. They receive about 150-200 poems a year, accept approximately 5-10%. Press run is 200-500. Sample is free with SASE or SAE and IRCs.
How to Submit: Submit 2-5 poems at a time. Previously published poems and simultaneous submissions OK. Cover letter preferred. Disk submissions OK. Time between acceptance and publication is 2-6 months. Seldom comments on rejections. Reports in 1 month. Sometimes sends prepublication galleys. Pays 5 copies. All rights to remain with author. Reviews books and chapbooks of poetry and other magazines. Open to unsolicited reviews. Poets may also send books for review consideration.
Also Offers: "Besides the newsletter, we publish individual poems/prose in the form of graphic flyers which are widely distributed within and beyond the underground literary scene. The aim is to make poetry accessible to as many people as possible, regardless of their poetic leanings. Zines are also planned in the near future."

N **⦿ ARNAZELLA**, Bellevue Community College, 3000 Landerholm Circle SE, Bellevue WA 98007-6484, phone (206)603-4032, e-mail arnazella@prostar.com, established 1979, advisor Woody West.
Magazine Needs: *Arnazella* is a literary annual, published in spring, using well-crafted poetry, no "jingles or greeting card" poetry. They have published poetry by Judith Skillman and Colleen McElroy. The editor describes this student publication (which uses work from off campus) as 75 pgs., 6×8, offset printed, using photos and drawings. Of 150-200 poems received/year they use about 20. Press run is 500 for 3 subscriptions, one of which is a library. Sample: $10.
How to Submit: Submit up to 3 poems. Deadline is usually at the end of December or early January. Send SASE for guidelines. Reports in 1-4 months. Pays 1 copy.

⊠ **⦿ ARSENAL PULP PRESS**, 103-1014 Homer St., Vancouver, British Columbia V6B 2W9 Canada, founded 1980, publishes 1 paperback book of poetry/year. They only publish the work of Canadian poets and are *currently not accepting any unsolicited mss.*

⊠ **⦿ ARSHILE; 96 TEARS PRESS**, P.O. Box 3749, Los Angeles CA 90078-3749, founded 1993, editor Mark Salerno.
   ● Poetry published in *Arshile* has also been included in *The Best American Poetry 1997.*
Magazine Needs: *Arshile* is a biannual "Magazine of the Arts," including poetry, fiction, drama, essays, reviews and interviews. They want poetry "that shows evidence of formal innovation." They have published poetry by Notley, Dorn, Moriarty, Ashbery, Koch, Guest, Baraka, Rakosi and Towle. As a sample the editor selected these lines from "Edges" by Robert Creeley:
> Particular, located, familiar in its presence/and reassuring. The end//of the seeming dream was simply/
> a walk down from the house through the field.
The editor says *Arshile* is 5½×8½, professionally printed and perfect-bound with 4-color cover and b&w art and ads inside. They receive about 2,500 poems a year, accept less than 10%. Press run is 1,500 for 100 subscribers of which 25% are libraries. Subscription: $18 for 2 issues. Sample: $10.
How to Submit: Submit 5-7 poems at a time. No previously published poems or simultaneous submissions. Reports in 3 months. Pays 2 copies. Rights revert to authors/artists.
Book/Chapbook Needs & How to Submit: 96 Tears Press "brings out small books (64 pgs.) of new writing by new and established authors." Query first with sample poems. Replies to queries in 1-3 months.
Advice: The editor says, "It's always best to have a look at a journal before submitting to it."

⦿ ART TIMES: A LITERARY JOURNAL AND RESOURCE FOR ALL THE ARTS, P.O. Box 730, Mount Marion NY 12456-0730, phone (914)246-6944, poetry editor Raymond J. Steiner.
Magazine Needs: *Art Times* is a monthly tabloid newspaper devoted to the arts. It focuses on cultural and creative articles and essays, but also publishes some poetry and fiction. The editor wants to see "poetry that strives to express genuine observation in unique language; poems no longer than 20 lines each." As a sample he selected these lines from "Satin" by Paul Camacho:
> an encounter with a noticed article,/the satin of a bias smile,/which causes the novice to speak/of no
> experience save his own:/what is beauty, but articulate bone?

Art Times is 16-24 pgs., newsprint, with reproductions of artwork, some photos, advertisement-supported. They receive 300-500 poems/month, use only 40-50/year. Circulation is 19,000, of which 5,000 are by request and subscriptions; most distribution is free through galleries, theatres, etc. Subscription: $15/year. Sample: $1 with 9 × 12 SASE with 3 first-class stamps.

How to Submit: Submit 4-5 typed poems at a time, up to 20 lines each. "All topics; all forms." Include SASE with all submissions. "Simultaneous submissions discouraged." They have an 18-month backlog. Send SASE for guidelines. Reports in 6 months. Pays 6 copies plus 1-year subscription.

$ 🔲 ◎ ARTFUL DODGE (Specialized: translations), Dept. of English, College of Wooster, Wooster OH 44691, founded 1979, poetry editor Daniel Bourne.

Magazine Needs: *AD* is an annual literary magazine that "takes a strong interest in poets who are continually testing what they can get away with successfully in regard to subject, perspective, language, etc., but who also show mastery of current American poetic techniques—its varied textures and its achievement in the illumination of the particular. What all this boils down to is that we require high craftsmanship as well as a vision that goes beyond one's own storm windows, grandmothers or sexual fantasies—to paraphrase Hayden Carruth. Poems can be on any subject, of any length, from any perspective, in any voice, but we don't want anything that does not connect with both the human and the aesthetic. Thus, we don't want cute, rococo surrealism, someone's warmed-up, left-over notion of an avant-garde that existed 10-100 years ago, or any last bastions of rhymed verse in the civilized world. On the other hand, we are interested in poems that utilize stylistic persuasions both old and new to good effect. We are not afraid of poems which try to deal with large social, political, historical, and even philosophical questions—especially if the poem emerges from one's own life experience and is not the result of armchair pontificating. We often offer encouragement to writers whose work we find promising, but *Artful Dodge* is more a journal for the already emerging writer than for the beginner looking for an easy place to publish. We also have a sustained commitment to translation, especially from Polish and other East European literatures, and we feel the interchange between the American and foreign works on our pages is of great interest to our readers. We also feature interviews with outstanding literary figures. They have published poetry by Gregory Orr, Julia Kasdorf, Denise Duhamel, Gary Gildner and John Haines. As a sample the editor selected these lines from "How It Was" by Jeff Gundy:

> . . . It was the last year of the old world, the last spring/of the old time, you don't believe me but
> watch it/or next thing you know you'll be carving sticks/by the scant fire and waiting for somebody to
> ask you,/hey grandpa, about all that, and nobody will.

The digest-sized, perfect-bound format is professionally printed, glossy cover, with art, ads. There are about 60-80 pgs. of poetry in each issue. They receive at least 2,000 poems/year, use 60. Press run is 1,000 for 100 subscribers of which 30 are libraries. Sample: $7 for current issue, $3 for others.

How to Submit: "No simultaneous submissions. Please limit submissions to 6 poems. Long poems may be of any length, but send only one at a time. We encourage translations, but we ask as well for original text and statement from translator that he/she has copyright clearance and permission of author." Reports in up to 6 months. Pays 2 copies, plus, currently, $5/page honorarium because of grants from Ohio Arts Council. Open to unsolicited reviews; "query first." Poets may also send books for review consideration; however, "there is no guarantee we can review them!"

🔲 ARTISAN, A JOURNAL OF CRAFT, P.O. Box 157, Wilmette IL 60091, e-mail artisanjnl@aol.com, website http://members.aol.com/artisanjnl, founded 1995, editor Joan Daugherty.

Magazine Needs: *artisan* is a quarterly publication based on the idea that "anyone who strives to express themselves with skill is an artist and artists of all kinds can learn from each other. We want poetry that is vital, fresh and true to life; evocative. Nothing trite, vague or pornographic." As a sample the editor selected these lines from "The Last Ode to Rain" by Ted Hazelgrove:

> The last act of love/On the last evening under a sad bridge/Where the old couple who refuse to sleep
> listen/for the last thunderclap//The last diminishing drops/Like a lazy argument between cousins

artisan is 36 pgs. (including cover), 8½ × 11, saddle-stitched with card stock cover, minimal graphics and ads. They receive about 450 poems a year, use approximately 10%. Press run is 400 for 100 subscribers, 100 distributed free to coffeehouses and local libraries. Subscription: $15. Sample: $4.50. Make checks payable to artisan, ink.

How to Submit: Submit 3-5 poems at a time. No previously published poems; no simultaneous submissions. E-mail submissions and queries OK (submit as part of message or attach files saved in ASCII text format only). Cover letter not necessary, however "if you send a cover letter, make it personal. We don't need to see any writing credentials; poems should stand on their own merit." Often comments on rejections. Send SASE for guidelines. Reports in 6-8 months. Pays 2 copies. Acquires first rights.

Also Offers: *artisan* sponsors an annual poetry contest. First prize is $150, second is $75. Prize winners and works meriting honorable mention are published in an upcoming issue. Entry fee is $5/poem. Postmark deadline: November 30. Send SASE for guidelines.

☑ 🔲 ARTWORD QUARTERLY; ARTWORD; ARTWORD CHAPBOOK CONTEST, 5273 Portland Ave., White Bear Lake MN 55110-2411, phone (651)426-7059, e-mail artword@wavefront.com, *ArtWord Quarterly* founded 1995, ArtWord founded 1994, editor/publisher Carol Robertshaw.

• Please note that the ArtWord Chapbook Contest is a new addition to this listing.

Magazine Needs: *ArtWord Quarterly* is interested in "voices that are rich in life experiences. The best poetry, in our opinion, gives readers an epiphanic encounter with the familiar. We consider any form, subject matter or style, but we are partial to poems that are image filled, metaphorical, and written with precision and depth. No false appendages, no useless joints, all parts in service to the whole. Please no self-absorbed, pornographic, lovelorn or suicide poems." They have published poetry by Chet Corey, Joe Paddock, Joyce Sutphen, K.A. Alma Peterson, Joyce Sidman and J.L. Kubicek. As a sample the editor selected these lines from "Everybody Knows" by Rosemary C. Hildebrandt:

> *That show-girl, Autumn, sashays/in on bustling gold-dark days, a burst burst/burst of rouge-blown frondescence, brassy/teasel and savory saxifrage. Forgivably/deceitful, as great beauty is. As time is.*

AQ is 40 pgs., 5½×8½, offset printed and saddle-stapled with 2-color glossy card cover. They receive about 2,000 poems a year, accept approximately 10%. Press run is 200 for 100 subscribers, 25 shelf sales and 5 libraries. Subscription: $15 (International: $20). Sample: $4. Back issues: $2 each.

How to Submit: Submit 3-5 poems at a time. No previously published poems or simultaneous submissions. Cover letter preferred. No e-mail submissions. "Name and address should appear on each page. No more than one poem per page, single-spaced, not to exceed 33 lines (including title, inscriptions, stanza breaks, etc.). Include brief bio, plus publication credits and SASE." Submission deadlines are March 1, June 1, September 1 and December 1. Time between acceptance and publication is 1 month or less. Seldom comments on rejections. Send SASE for guidelines. Reports in 1-3 months. Pays 1 copy. All rights revert to author upon publication.

Also Offers: ArtWord offers an annual chapbook competition. Submit 30-40 pages of original poetry with two title pages (name and address on first, title only on second; name must not appear anywhere else on mss), table of contents, acknowledgments, brief bio, $10 entry fee (includes copy of winning chapbook), and SASE for contest results (mss cannot be returned). Postmark deadline: May 1. Notification of results: November 1. Winner receives $50 and 50 copies. Send SASE for guidelines.

◙ ASCENT, Dept. of English, Concordia College, Moorhead MN 56562, e-mail olsen@gloria.cord.edu, founded 1975, editor W. Scott Olsen.

Magazine Needs: *Ascent* appears 3 times/year, using poetry that is "eclectic, shorter rather than longer." They have published poetry by Thomas Reiter, Michael Bugeja and Kathleen Lynch. As a sample the editor selected these lines from "Flat Country" by Mark Vinz:

> *Give me a landscape where the sky is huge/with scudding, booming clouds—no walls of trees/obscuring hovering hawks, except along/the riverbanks where cottonwood and willow/watch meandering currents, ox-bowed in/their own stubborn time.*

The editor describes *Ascent* as 64 pgs., 6×9, professionally printed and perfect-bound with matte card cover. They receive about 750 poems a year, accept approximately 5%. Press run is 900 for 250 subscribers of which 90 are libraries. Subscription: $9/year. Sample: $4.

How to Submit: Submit 3-6 poems at a time. Always sends prepublication galleys. Pays 2 copies.

Advice: The editor says, "Poems are rejected or accepted from 2-8 weeks, usually closer to 2 weeks. Acceptances are usually published within the year."

◙ SHERMAN ASHER PUBLISHING, P.O. Box 2853, Santa Fe NM 87504, phone (505)984-2686, fax (505)820-2744, e-mail 71277.2057@compuserve.com, website http://www.shermanasher.com, founded 1994, contact Judith Rafaela or Nancy Fay.

Book Needs: "We are dedicated to changing the world one book at a time, committed to the power of truth and the craft of language expressed by publishing fine poetry. We specialize in anthologies. We do *not* publish chapbooks." They publish 3-5 paperbacks/year. "Please see our current books as an example of what we look for in poetry. We enjoy well-crafted form. No rhymed doggerel, cowboy poetry or stiff academic work." They have published poetry by Marge Piercy, Galway Kinnell, Naomi Shihab Nye and Judyth Hill.

How to Submit: Submit 5 poems at a time with SASE only during calls for submissions. Previously published poems and simultaneous submissions OK. Cover letter preferred. No e-mail or fax submissions. "We specialize in anthologies and do not accept manuscripts for books. Also, we read submissions only during calls for submissions for our anthologies. Write for list with SASE." Time between acceptance and publication is 3-6 months. Poems are circulated to an editorial board. "Selection depends on the content/idea of the anthology and how well the poems fit together." Does not comment on rejections. Replies to queries in 6-8 weeks. Pays 1 copy per poem. Inquire for catalog or buy through local bookstores.

Also Offers: Website includes writer's guidelines, names of editors, poetry, interviews with authors and book ordering information.

Advice: "We do not take unsolicited manuscripts—only individual poems during our calls for submissions for

---

ALWAYS include a self-addressed, stamped envelope (SASE) when sending a ms or query to a publisher within your own country. When sending material to other countries, include a self-addressed envelope and International Reply Coupons (IRCs), available at many post offices.

our anthologies. Writers can check *Poets & Writers* magazine and other related magazines for these dates, or write us for a list. Enclose SASE."

ⓝ Ⓓ ASHEVILLE POETRY REVIEW, P.O. Box 7086, Asheville NC 28802, phone (828)298-5825, founded 1994, founder/managing editor Keith Flynn.
Magazine Needs: *APR* appears biannually. "We publish the best regional, national and international poems we can find. We publish translations, interviews, essays, historical perspectives and book reviews as well." They want "quality work with well-crafted ideas married to a dynamic style. Any subject matter is fit to be considered so long as the language is vivid with a clear sense of rhythm." They have published poetry by Robert Bly, Yevgeny Yevtushenko, Eavan Boland and Fred Chappell. The editor says *APR* is 160-180 pgs., 6×9, perfect-bound with laminated, full-color cover with b&w art inside. They receive about 1,200 poems a year, accept approximately 10-15%. Press run is 600-750. Subscription: $22.50/1 year, $43.50/2 years. Sample: $13. "We prefer poets purchase a sample copy prior to submitting."
How to Submit: Submit 3-5 poems at a time. No previously published poems; simultaneous submissions OK. Cover letter required. Include comprehensive bio, recent publishing credits and SASE. Submission deadlines: January 15 and July 15. Time between acceptance and publication is 3-5 months. Poems are circulated to an editorial board. Seldom comments on rejections. Publishes theme issues occasionally. Send SASE for guidelines and upcoming themes. Reports in 3-5 months. Pays 1 copy. Acquires all rights. Reviews books and chapbooks of poetry. Open to unsolicited reviews. Poets may also send books for review consideration.

Ⓓ ASIAN PACIFIC AMERICAN JOURNAL; ASIAN AMERICAN WRITERS' WORKSHOP (Specialized: ethnic/nationality, anthology), 37 St. Mark's Place #B, New York NY 10003, phone (212)228-6718, fax (212)228-7718, e-mail aaww@panix.com, website http://www.panix.com/~aaww, founded 1992, contact poetry editor.
Magazine Needs: The *APA Journal* is a biannual published by the AAWW, a not-for-profit organization. It is "dedicated to the best of contemporary Asian-American writing." They have published poetry by Arthur Sze, Mei-Mei Berssenbrugge and Sesshu Foster. *APA Journal* is 200 pgs., digest-sized, typeset and perfect-bound with 2-color cover and ads. They receive submissions from about 150 poets/year, accept about 30%. Press run is 1,500 for 400 subscribers of which 50 are libraries, 800 shelf sales. Single copy: $10; subscription/membership: $35; institutional membership: $50. Sample: $12.
How to Submit: Submit 4 copies of up to 10 pages of poetry, maximum of one poem per page. No previously published poems. Cover letter with phone and fax numbers and 1- to 4-sentence biographical statement required. Submissions on 3.5 Macintosh disk (or IBM, if necessary) plus hard copy requested. Deadlines are usually September 15 and February 15 for May 1 and October 1 issues, respectively. "We will work with authors who are promising." Send SASE for guidelines. Reports in 3-4 months. Pays 2 copies. Acquires one-time rights. In 1998, they published *Watermark: Vietnamese American Poetry & Prose* and *Black Lightning: Poetry in Progress*.
Also Offers: The AAWW offers creative writing workshops, a newsletter, a bookselling service, readings and fellowships to young Asian-American writers. Write for details. Website includes general workshop information, names of editors and submission guidelines.

Ⓓ ATLANTA REVIEW; POETRY 2000, P.O. Box 8248, Atlanta GA 31106, e-mail dveach@avetr.edu, website http://www.atlantareview.com, founded 1994, editor Daniel Veach.
Magazine Needs: *Atlanta Review* is a semiannual primarily devoted to poetry, but also featuring fiction, interviews, essays and fine art. They want "quality poetry of genuine human appeal." They have published poetry by Seamus Heaney, Derek Walcott, Maxine Kumin, Rachel Hadas, Charles Simic and Naomi Shihab Nye. As a sample the editor selected these lines from "Prayer for the Small Engine Repairman" by Charles W. Pratt:
> Let him come into our homes,/Let him discipline our children,/Console and counsel our mates,/Adjust the gap of our passions,/The mix of our humors: lay hands/On the small engine of our days/And make it again as new.

AR is 132 pgs., 6×9, professionally printed on acid-free paper and flat-spined with glossy color cover and b&w artwork. They receive about 10,000 poems a year, use about 1%. Press run is 4,000 for 700 subscribers of which 20 are libraries, 3,000 shelf sales. Single copy: $6; subscription: $10. Sample: $5.
How to Submit: No previously published poems. Issue deadlines are June 1 and December 1. Time between acceptance and publication is 3 months. Editors alternate as final issue editor. Seldom comments on rejections. Each spring issue has an International Feature Section. Send SASE for guidelines. Reports in 1 month. Pays 2 copies plus author's discounts. Acquires first North American serial rights.
Also Offers: *AR* also sponsors POETRY 2000, an annual international poetry competition. Prizes are $2,000, $500 and $250, plus 50 International Merit Awards. Winners are announced in leading literary publications. All entries are considered for publication in *Atlanta Review*. Entry fee is $5 for the first poem, $2 for each additional. No entry form or guidelines necessary. Send to POETRY 2000 at the above address. Postmark deadline: May 1, 2000. Website includes submission and contest guidelines, names of editors, poetry samples from several issues, and a free issue offer.
Advice: They say, "We are giving today's poets the international audience they truly deserve."

$ THE ATLANTIC MONTHLY, Dept. PM, 77 North Washington St., Boston MA 02114, phone (617)854-7700, website http://www.theatlantic.com, founded 1857, poetry editor Peter Davison, assistant poetry editor David Barber.
 • Poetry published here has been included in the 1992, 1993, 1995 and 1996 volumes of *The Best American Poetry.*
Magazine Needs: *The Atlantic Monthly* publishes 1-5 poems in each issue. Some of the most distinguished poetry in American literature has been published by this magazine, including work by William Matthews, Mary Oliver, Stanley Kunitz, Rodney Jones, May Swenson, Galway Kinnell, Philip Levine, Richard Wilbur, Tess Gallagher, Donald Hall and W.S. Merwin. The magazine has a circulation of 500,000, of which 5,800 are libraries. They receive some 35,000 poems/year, of which they use 35-40 and have a backlog of 6-12 months. Sample: $3.
How to Submit: Submit 3-5 poems with SASE. No simultaneous submissions. No fax or e-mail submissions. Publishes theme issues. Always sends prepublication galleys. Pays about $4/line. Buys first North American serial rights only.
Advice: Wants "to see poetry of the highest order; we do *not* want to see workshop rejects. Watch out for workshop uniformity. Beware of the present tense. Be yourself."

ATOM MIND; MOTHER ROAD PUBLICATIONS, P.O. Box 22068, Albuquerque NM 87154-2068, first founded 1968-70, reestablished 1992, editor Gregory Smith.
Magazine Needs: *Atom Mind* is a quarterly journal of "alternative literature, mostly influenced by the Beats, Steinbeck, John Fante and Bukowski. Narrative, free verse, 20-80 lines preferred, although length restrictions are not set in stone. No light verse, inspirational poetry, doggerel, 'moon-spoon-June' rhyming verse." They have published poetry by Lawrence Ferlinghetti, Charles Plymell and Wilma Elizabeth McDaniel. The editor says *AM* is 120 pgs., 8½×11, offset, with illustrations and photographs. They receive approximately 2,000 submissions annually, publish perhaps 5%. Press run is 1,000 for 750 subscribers of which 25 are libraries. Subscription: $20/4 issues. Sample: $6.
How to Submit: Prefers to consider submissions of 5-8 poems at a time, 20-80 lines each. Poems should be typed and single-spaced, with name and address on the first page. "Do not staple or otherwise bind your manuscript; a paper clip will suffice. Do not submit low-resolution dot-matrix computer printouts." Include SASE "large enough to hold your manuscript" with sufficient postage for return of materials. Previously published poems OK; no simultaneous submissions. No electronic submissions. Time between acceptance and publication is 8-12 months. "*Atom Mind* is very much a one-man operation; therefore, submissions are subject to the whims and personal biases of the editor only." Often comments on rejections. Send SASE for guidelines. Reports in 1-2 months. Pays copies, number varies. Acquires first or one-time rights.
Book/Chapbook Needs & How to Submit: "Book-length poetry manuscripts considered by invitation only." Mother Road Publications publishes 2 paperback and 2 hardback collections of poetry/year. Send SASE for catalog.

THE AUROREAN: A POETIC QUARTERLY; ENCIRCLE PUBLICATIONS, P.O. Box 219, Sagamore Beach MA 02562, phone/fax (508)833-0805 (call before faxing), press founded 1992, magazine founded 1995, editor Cynthia Brackett-Vincent.
Magazine Needs: *The Aurorean*, which appears in March, June, September and December, seeks to publish "poetry that is inspirational (but not religious), meditational or reflective of the Northeast. Strongly encouraged (but not limited to) topics: positiveness, recovery and nature. Maximum length: 38 lines. Typographical oddities are OK as long as it can be reproduced on our page. No hateful, overly religious or poetry that uses four-letter words for four-letter words' sake. Four-letter words are a rare necessity. Uses mostly free-verse; occasional rhyme; I am biased toward haiku and well-written humor. I use very little rhyme. I'm *always* in need of short (2-6 lines), seasonal poems. For seasonal poems, please note specific deadlines in our guidelines." They have published poetry by Rhoda Bandler, B.Z. Niditch, Peter Saunders and Nancy Means Wright. As a sample the editor selected this haiku by Carol Gursky:
     birches whispering/silver branches pleat the air/Autumn leaves descend
The Aurorean contains 29 pgs. of poetry, 4 pgs. of contributor's bios and separate insert page for subscription information and other market information, 5½×8½, professionally printed and saddle-stapled with 65 lb. cover, with papers and colors varying from season to season. Press run is 500. Single copy: $5 US, $6 international. Subscription: $17 US, $21 international. Make checks payable to Encircle Publications or *The Aurorean*.
How to Submit: Submit 3-5 poems at a time. No previously published poems or simultaneous submissions. No fax submissions. "Make it clear what you're submitting; notes on photocopies of something else you've been published in are not considered a submission, but are appreciated for my reading pleasure when sent. Type if possible; if not, write as clearly as possible." Cover letter strongly preferred (especially with first submission). Sometimes comments on rejections. Send SASE for guidelines. "I notify authors of receipt of manuscripts immediately and report on decisions in one week to three-and-a-half months maximum." Always sends prepublication galleys. Pays 3 copies/poem with an-up-to 50-word bio in the "Who's Who" section. Also features a "Poet-of-the-Quarter" each issue with publication of up to 3 poems and an extended bio (100 words). The "Poet-of-the-Quarter" receives 10 copies and a 1-year subscription.
Advice: The editor says, "Study *Poet's Market*. If possible, request a sample before you submit. Always have

a ms out there. Stop saying you want to be a writer. You are a writer if you write. Remember, editors are people too. What one editor rejects one day, another may jump at the next. Invest in small presses with samples. Invest in yourself with postage. Always include enough postage for the return/reply process!!! When sending requests and enclosing SASEs, just use common sense. For example, if requesting a sample copy and guidlines, no SASE is necessary as guidelines can be placed in with sample; if sending a submission and requesting guidelines (people do) two SASEs are needed if guidelines are expected before reply to manuscript. When in doubt, an extra first-class stamp or SASE is appreciated. Read more poetry than you write, and read your poetry out loud. Editors: I'm open to subscription and ad-swapping with other markets."

◎ AVOCET; AVOCET PRESS (Specialized: nature, spirituality), P.O. Box 8041, Calabasas CA 91372-8041, e-mail patricia.j.swenson@csun.edu, website http://www.csun.edu/~pjs44945/avocet.html, first issue published fall 1997, editor Patricia Swenson.
Magazine Needs: *Avocet* is a quarterly poetry journal "devoted to poets seeking to understand the beauty of nature and its interconnectedness with humanity." They want "poetry that shows man's interconnectedness with nature; discovering the Divine in nature." They do not want "poems that have rhyme or metrical schemes, cliché, abstraction and sexual overtones." The editor says *Avocet* is 30 pgs., 4¼×5½, professionally printed and saddle-stapled with card cover, some illustrations. Single copy: $2.50; subscription: $10. Make checks payable to Pat Swenson.
How to Submit: Submit up to 5 poems at a time. Previously published poems OK if acknowledged; no simultaneous submissions. Cover letter required including SASE. E-mail submissions OK with name, city, state and e-mail address. Time between acceptance and publication is 3-6 months. Reports in 4-6 weeks. Pays 1 copy.
Also Offers: Website includes writer's guidelines, editor's e-mail address, deadlines and sample poems.

◖ ◖ AXE FACTORY REVIEW; CYNIC PRESS, P.O. Box 40691, Philadelphia PA 19107, *Axe Factory* founded 1986, Cynic Press founded 1996, editor/publisher Joseph Farley.
● We highly recommend obtaining a sample before submitting as the editor has displayed, in his answers to our questionnaire, a quirky sense of humor.
Magazine Needs: *Axe Factory* is published 1-4 times/year and its purpose is to "spread the disease known as literature. The content is mostly poetry and essays. We now use short stories too." They want "eclectic work. Will look at anything but suggest potential contributors purchase a copy of magazine first to see what we're like. No greeting card verse." They have published poetry by Taylor Graham, A.D. Winans, Normal and Kimberly Brittingham. As a sample the editor selected these lines from "Starting Over" by Louis McKee:
> I kept the doll I found/in the yard, a Barbie with matted/blond hair and not a stitch/of clothing. A new
> wife,/I thought, and I proposed to her
Axe Factory is 20-40 pgs., 8½×11, saddle-stitched, neatly printed with light card cover. Press run is 100. Single copy: $8; subscription: $20 for 4 issues. Sample: $3 for old issue, $5 for recent. Make checks payable to Joseph Farley.
How to Submit: Submit up to 10 poems. Previously published poems "sometimes, but let me know up front"; simultaneous submissions OK. Cover letter preferred "but not a form letter, tell me about yourself." Often comments on rejections. Pays 1-2 copies. Reserves right to anthologize poems under Cynic Press; all other rights returned. Reviews books of poetry in 10-1,000 words. Open to unsolicited reviews. Poets may also send books for review consideration.
Book/Chapbook Needs & How to Submit: Cynic Press occasionally publishes chapbooks. Published *Yellow Flower Girl* by Xu Juan and *Under The Dogwood* by Joseph Barford. Send SASE for details before submitting.
Advice: The editor says, "Writing is a form of mental illness, spread by books, teachers, and the desire to communicate."

◖ BABYSUE, P.O. Box 8989, Atlanta GA 31106-8989, founded 1985, e-mail lmnop@babysue.com, website http://www.babysue.com, editor/publisher Don W. Seven.
Magazine Needs: *babysue* appears twice a year publishing obtuse humor for the extremely open-minded. "We are open to all styles, but prefer short poems." No restrictions. They have published poetry by Edward Mycue, Susan Andrews and Barry Bishop. The editor says *babysue* is 32 pgs., offset printed. "We print prose, poems and cartoons. We usually accept about 5% of what we receive." Subscription: $12 for 4 issues. Sample: $3.
How to Submit: Previously published poems and simultaneous submissions OK. Deadlines are March 30 and September 30 of each year. Seldom comments on rejections. Reports "immediately, if we are interested." Pays 1 copy. "We do occasionally review other magazines."
Advice: The editor adds, "We have received no awards, but we are very popular on the underground press circuit and sell our magazine all over the world."

ℕ ◖ BACCHAE PRESS; SOUTH JETTY BOOKS, No. 10 Sixth St., Astoria OR 97103, phone (503)325-7972, e-mail brown@pacific.com, founded 1992, publisher Dr. Robert Brown.
Book/Chapbook Needs: Under the imprints Bacchae Press and South Jetty Books, this press publishes poets who are in transition from smaller to larger publishers. They publish 2 paperbacks and 4 chapbooks/year. They want "high quality, literary poetry by poets who read and reflect. No greeting card verse." They have published

insider report

Persistence pays off for the "Woolworth Poet of America"

"The Rebel"

Today my son is confined to Vicksburg
and before him other soldiers
who wore the Gray.
The rumor is of soldiers killed in war.
Who in this world would know?
All night I have tossed and turned.
My son is confined to Vicksburg.

(reprinted by permission of the author)

Errol Miller and his wife, Mary Jo

He lives in Louisiana and is considered a Southern writer but has penned poems about New England. He has an M.A. but doesn't have a full-time job (he works on his writing fulltime). He's definitely on the fringe but has published over 25 books and thousands of poems in hundreds of journals. He rarely does readings but Dustbooks ranks him number nine among small press poets. His poetry is accessible to average readers but rich enough to appeal to academics. He speaks as softly as a sparrow but submits his poems with the precision and aggression of a hawk. He's Errol Miller, the self-proclaimed "Woolworth Poet of America—shopworn, dusty, on the shelf for awhile."

Miller began writing poetry in the late '60s, while a sports editor for his college paper. "I would write a few poems and put them in the paper, too. Eventually I found writing poems much more interesting and rewarding than writing about sports." So he put sports on the back page of his mind and poetry on the front.

It was in the Spring of 1972 when Miller seriously started to devote himself to becoming a poet. He says, "I had no formal training. I'd never taken a creative writing course or anything. I think I've always had this gift for writing but it took me a while to do something with it." Once he did recognize his gift, however, he wrote with a vengeance. He left his first marriage, lived in a cheap motel for a year, hung out in bars, and wrote about the ups and downs of lower-middle-class Southerners.

In 1978, however, Miller's attitude toward poetry changed. He says, "I had what you'd call a religious or spiritual conversion and I stopped writing. I thought writing was not compatible with being a spiritual person." So he put down the poetic pen for eight years, until 1986, when he realized his poetry could work in conjunction with his conversion. "Because my earlier work came from more hard living, I didn't think

I could write without living in and using those darker, down-and-out themes. That doesn't mean I'm totally getting away from those themes—I'm not and I don't want to, because I can identify with those who struggle. They're still fertile ground for my writing, but there are new perspectives and plenty of other themes as well."

Miller has been called "the aging poet of the aging South" and that doesn't really bother him. "I was born in 1939 in the rural South, so I guess that's true. I am a Southern writer, and I do feel connected to the tradition. There's a real sense of place in my work, and I like that. That doesn't mean I want to be pigeonholed as a writer who writes only about the South, but I don't mind being called a Southern writer. A lot of my stuff is about gain and loss. I've covered a bit of change in my life, and the South has undergone a lot of change in its life."

Poet Robert Creeley once said that with poetry, form is an extension of content. Miller agrees and thinks beginning poets need to keep that in mind. "Form and content are equally important," he says. "Your poem could be great and say a lot of good things, but if the line breaks are off and the poem doesn't look good on paper you're in trouble. A lot of people who write poetry think, 'I just got to write something but it doesn't matter how I put it down on paper,' and that's too bad. One of the major parts of revising is not only to revise your words and what you're saying but to revise the way the poem lays out and flows on the page." For Miller, a poet needs to spend as much time on the visual aspect of a poem—punctuation, line breaks and such—as with what the poem is trying to convey.

Perhaps one drawback Miller finds in being a poet is that poetry consumes his life: no matter what he does and where he goes, he sees an opportunity to write a poem or "gather" material. So he wonders if he uses all the different things, places and moments in his life as fodder for his writing—perhaps even at the expense of living. "The writing does consume so much of my life. I try to keep it in check, try to compartmentalize it a bit, but it's hard to let go of. It does consume me." A large part of that consumption is the time Miller spends organizing, preparing, submitting and marketing his work. "Oh, of course, this process takes most of my time. But that's part of being a poet."

There are two major reasons for Miller's success. First, he's very prolific—the poetry comes out fast and often, so he has a lot of material. Second, he works his tail off—"beating the bushes for markets," as he says. It's true; at any one time Miller has 400-500 submissions floating out to different journals. "I try to keep that high number of submissions pretty steady. If a batch of ten comes back, then I send ten more out."

Another key to Miller's poetic achievement is that he takes the business aspect of publishing seriously. "I try to do things with integrity. I always send a SASE with enough return postage. If an editor makes a suggestion about my work, I take it seriously. I'll rework the poem and resubmit it." Miller also tries to keep up with all the literary magazines he can, especially new ones. "As soon as I hear of a new magazine, I find out what it's about, see if I have any poems suitable for it, and submit a few of them. I'm always on the lookout for possibilities."

But what did Miller do when he initially tried to get published, before he had all these poems and a distinguished reputation? "I just got markets from wherever I could, and I'd submit my work, get rejected a lot, and once in a while get published." Miller also bought a lot of small press books and journals to get a sense of the business of small press publishing, and that really helped him. "As I began to develop a sense of the business, I began to perfect where to submit, what to submit, the caliber of the publication, its likes and dislikes, the positions of the editors, things like that. I learned to orient my work toward what the magazine publishes."

Although most people don't think writing poetry and networking go hand in hand, in Miller's case, they do. He doesn't network in the corporate sense of the word; he simply makes the most out of those he knows and meets. Here's an example of how networking has worked for Miller: Although he lives in Louisiana, Miller is from a small town in Alabama and his son is a chiropractor in a nearby town. Miller submitted some poetry to a new market in Alabama he had read about. The editor turned out to be one of his son's patients. She published Miller's poetry in her magazine, and his book, *The Evening of Seasons* (New Dawn Unlimited/Dancing Rabbit Press, 1998), was one of the first collections her press published. She proceeded to give Miller information about two other new magazines and presses in Birmingham, which published his work. One of these publishers referred him to a third press in the area, and that press published his work as well.

Even with all this success, most of Miller's submissions today are still cold submissions and he therefore follows the same rules everyone else does. "I typically send about five poems. I try to follow the magazine's guidelines. If a journal says send three to five poems with no cover letter, I always keep that in mind. I won't send ten poems because that shows I either didn't pay attention to their guidelines or ignored them. Editors want to be respected, and I've alienated some editors by sending too many poems."

Miller also never gives up. "Sometimes it takes me a number of years and submissions before I get published in a journal. I keep trying until an editor tells me never to send anything ever again. I still find myself getting published in journals that at one time wouldn't give me the time of day."

While it's been some time since the days when Miller published his first poems, he does have some good advice for those trying to break into poetry. "First, do it—write and make a commitment to write. Second, do something with what you write, which means not just showing it to your friends or hiding it in a drawer. Third, study as many journals and their market listings as you can. It's tough getting started but don't give up, because if you've got the talent and you send your stuff to appropriate places, it'll get published. Fourth, no matter how good you are, you've got to learn to live with rejection. Even the best hitters in baseball only get a hit two or three times out of ten. Rejection is part of the process. I still get rejection letters every day, but I get published, too. I would also encourage newer poets to submit to contests. That has helped me in the past, because winning a contest, however small, carries weight with editors."

If all this talk of preparation, research and rejection sounds demanding . . . well, it is. But one must make sacrifices to become a regularly published poet. "I spend about $2,000 a year on postage and supplies, and I don't make that back from the work, but it's still worth it." It's worth it because although Miller has not amassed great wealth, he has built a formidable literary career—something money can't buy and few people can boast. Says Miller, "My philosophy has been, 'build it and they will come.'" And it's working. "No, I'm not rich, and, yes, I still live low-key, but now that I've built this literary career people are coming to me, asking me to be a judge in a contest or a speaker at an event—so I'm getting recognized and paid at the same time." Not bad for the modest man from West Monroe, Louisiana.

—Don Prues

poetry by Hal Sirowitz, Bart Baxter and Karen Braucher. Books/chapbooks are usually 28/72 pgs., 5½×8½, offset printed, saddle-stitched/perfect-bound.
How to Submit: Query first with 5 sample poems and cover letter with brief bio and publication credits. Previously published poems and simultaneous submissions OK. Time between acceptance and publication is 6-12 months. Poems are circulated to an editorial board. Seldom comments on rejections. Replies to queries and ms in 2 months. Pays 25 author's copies. Order sample books or chapbooks by sending $5.
Also Offers: Sponsors the annual Bacchae Press Poetry Chapbook Contest. Winner(s) receive 25 copies of the chapbook, which is scheduled to be published in September. Submit 16-24 typed ms pages. No more than 1 poem/page. Deadline: April 15. Entry fee: $9, includes copy of the winning chapbook. "With your submission, include a brief bio, acknowledgements, and a SASE for return of your manuscript and/or contest results." Contest winners announced in June.

☑ ◐ ◑ **THE BACK PORCH; BURN BRIGHT PUBLICATIONS**, P.O. Box 376, Lawrenceburg IN 47025, phone (812)537-2903, fax (812)537-4812, founded 1997, publisher Timothy Burnett.
Magazine Needs: *"The Back Porch* is a quarterly journal which promotes art, poetry and photography with universality that appeals to every man." They want "poetry that is imaginative, real and strong. No 'Hallmark' verse or cutesy poetry; no forced rhyme." They have published poetry by Damniso Lopez, Simon Perchik, Virgie Suarez and Alexandra Beller. As a sample the publisher selected his poem "Coming Home":

> Up the tall wooden staircase and through the door/I close it softly, 'click'/Padded footfalls upon the
> long carpeted corridor/I feel a creaking in the aged wood beneath/There is a scent, your scent and it
> permeates the/Dimness/I smile/I am Home.

Back Porch is 75-80 pgs., 6×9, professionally printed and perfect-bound with glossy card stock cover, includes b&w art and photography, will consider ads. Press run is 500 for 100 subscribers of which 10 are libraries, 250 shelf sales. Single copy: $9.95; subscription: $30. Sample: $12.50. Make checks payable to Burn Bright Publications. They suggest potential contributors purchase a sample copy. Published authors are strongly encouraged to subscribe for 1 year.
How to Submit: Submit 3-5 poems at a time. Previously published poems and simultaneous submissions OK. Cover letter preferred. Reads submissions January 1 through October 1 only. Time between acceptance and publication is 4-6 months. "Acceptance at editors discretion only." Often comments on rejections. Written critiques available for $5/poem or short story. Send SASE for guidelines. Reports in 1 month. Pays 1 copy. Acquires one-time rights.

◎ **BACKSPACE: A QUEER POETS JOURNAL (Specialized: gay/lesbian)**, (formerly *Queer Poets Journal*), 25 Riverside Ave., Gloucester MA 01930-2552, e-mail bckspqpj@aol.com, managing editor Kim Smith.
Magazine Needs: *Backspace*, published 3 times a year, is a collection of queer poetry, provides a forum for gay/lesbian poets to share their work with their peers." They prefer gay and lesbian themes, but nothing more than 50 lines. The editor says *Backspace* is digest-sized, laser-printed and saddle-stitched. Single copy: $4; subscription: $8/year. Sample: $2. Make checks payable to Kim Smith.
How to Submit: Submit 8 poems at a time. E-mail and diskette submissions OK. No previously published poems; simultaneous submissions OK. Cover letter with brief bio (no more than 25 words) required. Send SASE for guidelines. Reports immediately. Pays 1 copy.

░ ♣ ◯ ◑ **BACKWATER REVIEW; HINTERLAND AWARD FOR POETRY**, P.O. Box 222, Station "B", Ottawa, Ontario K1P 6C4 Canada, e-mail backwaters@cybertap.com, website http://www.cybertap.

com/backwaters, founded 1996, editor L. Brent Robillard, assistant editor Caroline Bergeron.
Magazine Needs: *Backwater Review* appears 2 times a year and publishes poetry, fiction, reviews and interviews. "All forms and styles of poetry are encouraged. Emphasis is on craft." They have published poetry by Stephanie Bolster, Tim Bowling, Tony Cozier, D.C. Reid and John B. Lee. As a sample the editors selected these lines from "Upon the Diving Board, Precarious" by Jason Rama:
> the air meets the water/to form another dissolving line,/an eroding division/and yet, when the flesh
> encounters this frontier/it is the only truth

The editors say *BR* is 60 pgs., digest-sized, professionally printed and saddle-stitched with glossy cover, includes color photos/art, some ads. They receive about 1,000 poems a year, accept approximately 1-2%. Press run is 500 for 100 subscribers, 300 shelf sales. Single copy: $5; subscription: $10. Sample: $4.
How to Submit: Submit 5 poems at a time. No previously published poems or simultaneous submissions. Cover letter required. E-mail and disk submissions OK. "Send one poem per page typed and double-spaced on 8½×11 paper." Reads submissions February through August only. Time between acceptance and publication is 3-6 months. Seldom comments on rejections. Send SASE for guidelines. Reports in 3-6 months. Pays 2 copies. Acquires one-time rights. Staff reviews books of poetry in 300 words, single book format. Send books for review consideration to L. Brent Robillard, editor.
Also Offers: Sponsors the Hinterland Award for Poetry. Entry fee: $10, includes 1-year subscription. Submit up to 5 poems. Judging is blind. Include name, address and bio on a separate sheet. Winner receives $100 plus publication. Deadline: January 31. Website includes writer's guidelines, names of editors, poetry and reviews.
Advice: The editors say, "Tell the truth, the whole truth and nothing but the truth."

BAD POETRY QUARTERLY, P.O. Box 6319, London E11 2EP Great Britain, founded 1994, editor/publisher Gordon Smith, administrator Kathryn Holmes.
Magazine Needs: *BPQ* is a weekly publication open to all types of poetry. They have published poetry by Andrew Belsey, Maurice Tasnier, Coral Hull and Bethany Fowler. *BPQ* is 20 pgs., A5, photocopied and side-stapled with paper cover, includes cartoons/line drawings. They receive about 800 poems a year, accept approximately 50%. Subscription: £.99 plus £.60 p&h (outside UK). "All subscriptions must be in Sterling. Do not send cash or stamps."
How to Submit: Submit up to 4 poems at a time. No previously published poems or simultaneous submissions. Cover letter preferred. "Name and address on every sheet. One poem per sheet." Time between acceptance and publication varies. Seldom comments on rejections. Send SASE (or SAE and IRC) for guidelines. Pays 1 copy. Acquires one-time rights. Staff reviews books and chapbooks of poetry and other magazines in single and multi-book format. Send books for review consideration.

BADLANDS PRESS; SCORPION'S DREAMS (Specialized: science fiction/fantasy, horror), 304-314 Broadway Ave., Winnipeg, Manitoba R3C 0S5 Canada, e-mail valdron@escape.ca, founded 1993, editor Anna Boudreau.
Magazine Needs: *Scorpion's Dreams*, first published in Spring 1997, is dedicated to expanding Canadian horror, science fiction and fantasy. They want "no poems longer than 100 words; free verse on the subjects of horror, science fiction or fantasy. No bad, moody and self-depressing poetry." They have published poetry by Nancy Bennett and Uncle River. The editor says the format of *Scorpion's Dreams* is similar to a chapbook. Single copy: $6.
How to Submit: Submit 3 poems at a time. No previously published poems or simultaneous submissions. Cover letter required. Reads submissions March 15 through May 30. Time between acceptance and publication is 4 months. Often comments on rejections. Publishes theme issues. Send SASE for guidelines and upcoming themes. Reports in 1 month. Pays $5/poem. Buys "publishing rights only."
Book/Chapbook Needs & How to Submit: BadLands Press's purpose is "to explore undeveloped talent, and expand the appreciation of a neglected genre in literature." Books are formatted "to enhance the imagery of material." Query first with a few sample poems and a cover letter with brief bio and publication credits. Replies to queries in 4 months, to mss in 6 weeks. Pays $5 honorarium and 1 author's copy (out of a press run of 100).
Advice: The editor says, "Always proofread. Don't stop at a rejection, keep trying. Writers and books are poorly advertized by publishers. The same is true for small press, self-promotion is important. I welcome working with my contributors to promote their work in *Scorpion's Dreams*."

THE BALTIMORE REVIEW; BALTIMORE WRITER'S ALLIANCE, P.O. Box 410, Riderwood MD 21139, phone (410)377-5265, fax (410)377-4325, e-mail hdiehl@bcpl.net, website http://www.bcpl/~hdiehl, *BR* founded 1996, Baltimore Writers' Alliance founded 1980, editor Barbara Diehl.
Magazine Needs: *The Baltimore Review* appears 2 times a year (winter and summer) and showcases the "best short stories and poems of writers from the Baltimore area and beyond." They have no restrictions on poetry except they do not want to see "sentimental-mushy, loud or very abstract work; corny humor; poorly crafted or preachy poetry." They have published poetry by Lyn Lifshin, Julia Wendell, Barbara F. Lefcowitz and Simon Perchik. *BR* is 128 pgs., 6×9, offset lithography, perfect-bound with 10 pt. CS1 cover, back cover photo only. Publish 20-30 poems/issue. Press run is 1,000. Single copy: $7.95; subscription: $14/year (2 issues). Sample: $7. Make checks payable to Baltimore Writers' Alliance.

How to Submit: Submit up to 5 poems at a time. No previously published poems; simultaneous submissions OK. Cover letter preferred. No e-mail or fax submissions. Time between acceptance and publication is 1-6 months. "Poems and short stories are circulated to at least 2 reviewers." Sometimes comments on rejections. Send SASE for guidelines. Reports in 1-3 months. Pays 2 copies, reduced rate for additional copies.

Also Offers: The Baltimore Writers' Alliance is "a vital organization created to foster the professional growth of writers in the metro Baltimore area." The Alliance meets monthly and sponsors workshops, an annual conference, and an annual contest. It also publishes *Writers' Bloc*, a monthly newsletter for members. Write for details. Website includes writer's guidelines and distributor information.

◎ **BANGTALE INTERNATIONAL**, P.O. Box 83984, Phoenix AZ 85071-3984, e-mail bangtale@primenet. com, founded 1989, editor William Edward Dudley.

Magazine Needs & How to Submit: *Bangtale* appears twice a year. They want "poetry that is telling and doesn't complicate itself through evasive word salad but seeks understanding and gives emotion. Use quality in language that is humane, humorous, passionate, culturally forward and unexpected. Above all we encourage writing as an instrument that disentangles your thought process." They have published poetry by Mary Winters, Stephen R. Roberts, Lyn Lifshin and Thomas Dorsett. *Bangtale* is 50 pgs., digest-sized, offset printed and saddle-stapled, with glossy card cover and b&w art. Press run is 450. Subscription: $8. Sample: $5. E-mail submissions OK. Sometimes sends prepublication galleys. Pays 1 copy.

❀ ♟ ◑ ◐ ◎ **BARBARIAN PRESS (Specialized: translations)**, 12375 Ainsworth Rd., R.R. 8, Mission, British Columbia V2V 5X4 Canada, phone (604)826-8089, fax (604)826-8092, founded 1977, publisher Crispin and Jan Elsted.

• Barbarian Press won the 1998 Allvin Society Citation for Excellence in Book Design in Canada for their book *Rufinus: The Completed Poems*, translated by Robin Skelton.

Book/Chapbook Needs: "We publish poetry of many kinds, but favor strong lyric poetry and accomplished translation." They publish 1 hardback and 1-2 chapbooks/year. They want "strong lyric poetry, rhymed or unrhymed, but immaculate technique essential. Translations a strong interest. No Hallmark poems, feminist/racist polemics, satirical verse, parodies, hard-nosed cynicism." They have published poetry by Robert Bringhurst, Paula Gardiner, Rachel Norton and John Carroll. Chapbooks are usually 48 pgs., 6×9, letterpress printed, sewn binding with printed paper wraps, wood engravings if any art is used.

How to Submit: "We prefer at least a chapbook-length manuscript, i.e., 30-50 pages." Previously published poems OK; no simultaneous submissions. Cover letter required. Time between acceptance and publication varies, but at least 1 year. Seldom comments on rejections. Replies to queries in 2-4 months; to mss in 4-6 weeks. Pays in copies, 10% of press run.

✅ ◯ ◐ **BARBARIC YAWP; BONEWORLD PUBLISHING**, 3700 County Route 24, Russell NY 13684, phone (315)347-2609, founded 1996, co-editors John Berbrich and Nancy Berbrich.

Magazine Needs: *Barbaric Yawp*, appears quarterly, "publishing the best fiction, poetry and essays available"; encourages beginning writers. "We are not preachers of any particular poetic or literary school. We publish any type of quality material appropriate for our intelligent and wide-awake audience; all types considered, blank, free, found, concrete, traditional rhymed and metered forms. We do not want any pornography, gratuitous violence, or any whining, pissing or moaning." They have published poetry by Errol Miller, Mark Spitzer and Jade. As a sample the editors selected these lines from this untitled poem by J. Patrick:

> The shadow tosses in a mist of snow/Sparkling, now Ruby!/Hunter springs! Lunge after lunge!/His
> wide padded paws-feet race madly./Club held high as he approaches/The beast furiously wrestling
> against its fate . . .

The editors say *BY* is a 60-page booklet, stapled with 67 lb. cover, line drawings. They receive 1,000 poems a year, accept approximately 10%. Press run is 100 for 20 subscribers. Single copy: $4; subscription: $15/year for 4 issues. Sample: $3. Make checks payable to John Berbrich.

How to Submit: Submit up to 5 poems at a time, no more than 50 lines each, and include SASE. All types considered. Previously published poems and simultaneous submissions OK. One-page cover letter preferred, include a short publication history (if available) and a brief bio. No deadlines; reads year round. Time between acceptance and publication is 2-6 months. Often comments on rejections. Send SASE for guidelines. Reports in 1-2 months. Pays 1 copy. Acquires one-time rights.

Advice: The editors say, "We are primarily concerned with work that means something to the author but which is able to transcend the personal into the larger more universal realm. Send whatever is important to you. We will use yin and yang. We really like humor."

🄽 ⊕ ◎ **BARKING DOG BOOKS (Specialized: Expatriate life and travel in Baja, Mexico and Gen'ly)**, ℅ Centro de Mensajes, A.P. 48, Todos Santos, B.C.S. C.P. 23300 Mexico, founded 1996, editor Michael Mercer.

Book/Chapbook Needs: Barking Dog Books "promotes expatriate literature, especially in Baja and mainland Mexico." Books are usually 60-120 pgs., 5×8, offset printed and perfect-bound with matte stock cover, includes work by local artists.

How to Submit: Query first with a few sample poems and cover letter with brief bio and publication credits.

Previously published poems and simultaneous submissions OK. Often comments on rejections. Replies to queries in 1 month; to mss in 2 months. Order sample books by sending $12 US.

Advice: The editor quotes Malcolm Lowry, " 'Even bad poetry is better than life.' "

N ◐ BARROW STREET, P.O. Box 2017, Old Chelsea Station, New York NY 10113-2017, founded 1998, editors Andrea Carter Brown, Peter Covino, Ron Drummond, Lois Hirshkowitz, Melissa Hotchkiss.

Magazine Needs: *"Barrow Street*, a new poetry journal appearing in fall and spring, is dedicated to publishing award-winning, emerging, and previously undiscovered poets." They want "well-crafted poetry of the highest literary quality; open to all styles and forms." They have published poetry by Kim Addonizio, Brooks Haxton, Mark Jarman, Maureen Owen and Molly Peacock. As a sample the editors selected these lines from "The Voyage Out" by Yvette Christiansë:

> A pipe dropped, rolling on the deck—/we looked for the bird chucking/deep in its woody throat, thought/
> of trees, their shade across our bodies, not/a pipe dropped, rolling on the deck.

The editors say *BS* is 96-120 pgs., 6×9, professionally printed and perfect-bound with glossy cardstock cover with color and photography. They receive about 3,000 poems a year, accept approximately 3%. Press run is 1,000. Subscription: $12/1 year; $22/2 years. Sample: $7.

How to Submit: Submit up to 5 poems at a time. No previously published poems; simultaneous submissions OK (when notified). Cover letter with brief bio preferred. Reads submissions September 1 through June 15 only. Time between acceptance and publication is 3-6 months. Poems are circulated to an editorial board. Seldom comments on rejections. Publishes theme issues occasionally. Send SASE for guidelines and upcoming themes. Reports in 1-4 months. Always sends prepublication galleys. Pays 2 copies. Acquires first rights.

☑ ◯ ◐ BATHTUB GIN; PATHWISE PRESS, P.O. Box 2392, Bloomington IN 47402, e-mail charter@ bluemarble.net, website http://www.bluemarble.net/~charter/btgin.htm, founded 1997, co-editors Christopher Harter and Tom Maxedon.

Magazine Needs: *Bathtub Gin*, a biannual, is described by its editors as "an eclectic aesthetic . . . we want to keep you guessing what is on the next page." They want poetry that "takes a chance with language or paints a vivid picture with its imagery . . . has the kick of bathtub gin, which can be experimental or a sonnet. No trite rhymes . . . Bukowski wannabes (let the man rest) . . . confessional (nobody cares about your family but you)." They have published poetry by A.D. Winans, Laurel Speer, John Grey and Patrick McKinnon. As a sample the editor selected these lines from "The Water Horses" by John Gohmann:

> Whiskey had slit poetry's throat in a barfight/So painting was the only exorcism I could muster/And
> as I set out my oils and brushes,/Cubism seemed the logical tool/To pulverise two separate nightmares/
> Into a communal pile of rubble

BG is approximately 50 pgs., 8½×5½, laser-printed and saddle-stapled, 54 lb. cover stock cover, includes "eclectic" art. "We feature a 'News' section where people can list their books, presses, events, etc." They receive about 800 poems a year, accept approximately 10%. Press run is 160 for 30 subscribers, 60 shelf sales; 15 distributed free to reviewers, other editors. Subscription: $10. Sample: $6. Make checks payable to Christopher Harter.

How to Submit: Submit 4-6 poems at a time. Include SASE. Previously published poems and simultaneous submissions OK (include in text of message). Cover letter preferred. E-mail submissions OK. "Three to five line bio required if you are accepted for publication . . . if none [given], we make one up." Reads submissions July 1 through September 15 and January 1 through March 15 only. Time between acceptance and publication is 2-4 months. Often comments on rejections. Send SASE for guidelines. Reports in 1-2 months. Pays 1 copy. "We also sell extra copies to contributors at a discount, which they can give away or sell at full price. Reviews books and chapbooks of poetry and spoken word recordings. Open to unsolicited reviews. Poets may also send books for review consideration.

Book/Chapbook Needs & How to Submit: Pathwise Press's goal is to publish chapbooks, broadsides and "whatever else tickles us. Another part of our goal is to help create a network for writers/artists with a focus on distribution."

Also Offers: "We also publish a newsletter, *The Bent*, with reviews, ads and news items. Price is $1." Website includes guidelines, subscription and patronage info, outlets, links to small presses, resources and independent music labels.

Advice: The editors say, "The small presses/magazines are where it's at. They are willing to take chances on unknown and experimental writers and because of that they are publishing the most interesting work out there— have been for years."

◎ �� WILLIAM L. BAUHAN, PUBLISHER (Specialized: regional), P.O. Box 443, Old County Rd., Dublin NH 03444, phone (603)563-8020, fax (603)563-8026, founded 1959, editor William L. Bauhan, publishes poetry and art, especially New England regional books. *Currently accepts no unsolicited poetry.*

N ☑ ◯ BAY AREA POETS COALITION (BAPC); POETALK, P.O. Box 11435, Berkeley CA 94712-2435, e-mail poetalk@aol.com, founded 1974, direct submissions to Editorial Committee. Coalition sends bi-monthly poetry journal, *Poetalk*, to over 300 people. They also publish an annual anthology (21st—180 pgs., out in February 2000), giving one page to each member of BAPC (minimum 6 months) who has had work published in *Poetalk* during the previous year.

Magazine Needs: *Poetalk* publishes approximately 90 poets each issue. BAPC has 150 members, 70 subscribers, but *Poetalk* is open to all. No particular genre. Short poems (under 35 lines). "Rhyme must be well done." Membership: $15 for 12 months of *Poetalk*, copy of anthology and other privileges; extra outside US. Also offers a $50 patronage, which includes a subscription and anthology for another individual of your choice, and a $25 beneficiary/memorial, which includes membership plus subscription for friend. Subscriptions: $6/year. As a sample the editors selected this complete poem, "Moon" by Tim Nuveen:

> At least five thousand nights I've seen the moon/And with great benefit//And only just tonight I saw/
> The space between myself and it.

Poetalk is 24 pgs., 5½×8½, photocopied, saddle-stapled with heavy card cover. Send SASE with 55¢ postage for a free complimentary copy.

How to Submit: Submit up to 4 poems, typed and single-spaced, 35 lines maximum, with SASE, no more than twice a year. "Be sure and count blank lines, and add *two* for title and *two* for Author and the Address. *Too large is the number one reason for rejection.*" Simultaneous and previously published work OK, but must be noted. "All subject matter should be in good taste." No e-mail submissions. Response time is 2 weeks to 4 months. Pays 1 copy. Acquires one-time rights.

Also Offers: BAPC holds monthly readings, yearly contest, etc.; has mailing list open to local members. BAPC's annual contest, established in 1980, awards a $40 first prize, $25 second prize, $10 third prize, certificate for honorable mention, plus publication in and 1 copy of BAPC's annual anthology. Submissions must be unpublished. Submit 2 copies of up to 8 poems on any subject of 15-35 lines (blank lines count), with SASE for winners list. Include name, address and whether member or nonmember on 1 copy only. Entry fee: $1/poem for members. Submission period: October 1 through November 15, 2000. Winners will be announced by mail in January 2000. People from many states and countries have contributed to *Poetalk* or entered their annual contests. Send SASE in early September for contest guidelines.

Advice: The editors say, "We differ from many publishers in that we are very actively involved in working with the poets to make their poems publishable. We try to help people get to the point where we can publish their work, i.e., we make editorial comments on almost everything we reject. If you don't want suggested revisions you need to say so clearly in your cover letter."

BAY WINDOWS (Specialized: gay/lesbian), 631 Tremont St., Boston MA 02118, phone (617)266-6670 ext. 211, fax (617)266-5973, website http://www.baywindows.com, founded 1983, poetry editor Rudy Kikel.

Magazine Needs: *Bay Windows* is a weekly gay and lesbian newspaper published for the New England community, regularly using "short poems of interest to lesbians and gay men. Poetry that is 'experiential' seems to have a good chance with us, but we don't want poetry that just 'tells it like it is.' Our readership doesn't read poetry all the time. A primary consideration is giving pleasure. We'll overlook the poem's (and the poet's) tendency not to be informed by the latest poetic theory, if it does this: pleases. Pleases, in particular, by articulating common gay or lesbian experience, and by doing that with some attention to form. I've found that a lot of our choices were made because of a strong image strand. Humor is always welcome—and hard to provide with craft. Obliquity, obscurity? Probably not for us. We won't presume on our audience." They have published poetry by Judith Saunders, Mina Kumar, Tom Cole, Diane Adair and Dennis Rhodes. As a sample the editor selected these lines from "This Man" by Ron Mohring:

> With his breath/fogs my skin, then watches/his traces erase. I am a window/he sees into, a house in
> which/the lamps are coming on again

"We try to run four poems each month." They receive about 300 submissions/year, use 1 in 10, have a 3-month backlog. Press run is 13,000 for 700 subscribers of which 15 are libraries. Single copy: 50¢; subscription: $40. Sample: $3.

How to Submit: Submit 3-5 poems at a time, "up to 30 lines are ideal; include short biographical blurb and SASE. No submissions via e-mail, but poets may request info via e-mail." Fax submissions OK. Reports in 2-3 months. Pays 1 copy. Acquires first rights. Editor "often" comments on rejections. They review books of poetry in about 750 words—"Both single and omnibus reviews (the latter are longer)."

BAYBURY REVIEW (Specialized: regional), P.O. Box 462, Ephraim WI 54211, e-mail baybury@flash.net, founded 1997, editor Janet St. John.

Magazine Needs: *Baybury Review* appears annually and publishes "any style or form of poetry as long as it demonstrates attention to craft and fresh insight. While we advise Midwestern writers to submit work, we also welcome poems about, or from, anywhere in the world." They have published poetry by Susan Aizenberg, Mark Halperin, Lyn Lifshin and Susan Swartwout. As a sample the editor selected these lines from "Lost" by W.E. Butts:

OPENNESS TO SUBMISSIONS: ◻ beginners; ◑ beginners and experienced; ◐ mostly experienced, few beginners; ◎ specialized; ● closed to unsolicited mss.

> *You began with death. Your mother falling/in her seventh month, so you did not know/your stillborn*
> *brother. Your father, who had/your name, and never had enough money,/is now dark. Later, you learned*
> *how love dies,/gasping with the best intentions. Never mind . . .*

Baybury Review is 80-125 pgs., 5½×8½, professionally printed and flat-spined with glossy card cover, b&w graphics, accepts exchange ads. They receive about 450 poems a year, accept approximately 5%. Press run is 500. Subscription: $7.25 (includes postage). Sample: $6.

How to Submit: Submit 3-6 poems at a time. No previously published poems; simultaneous submissions OK. Cover letter preferred. "Manuscripts should be clearly typewritten and include author's name and address on each work. Please indicate simultaneous submissions in cover letter." Reads submissions June 1 through December 1 only. Time between acceptance and publication is 4-9 months. Poems are circulated to an editorial board. Often comments on rejections. "Editors may comment on manuscripts that have passed the first round." Reports in 1-2 months. Pays 2 copies. Acquires first North American serial rights. Reviews books of poetry in 350 words, single book format. Open to unsolicited reviews. Poets may also send books for review consideration.

Advice: The editor says, "We encourage submissions from emerging as well as established writers, but suggest that, before submitting, writers spend some time reading literary magazines to get a feel for where their work might belong."

◎ **BEACON (Specialized: regional)**, Southwestern Oregon Community College, 1988 Newmark Ave., Coos Bay OR 97420-2956, phone (541)888-7335, editor changes yearly.

Magazine Needs: *Beacon* is a small, college literary magazine that appears twice a year and publishes the work of local writers and artists. They want poetry only from those who have had their beginnings or currently reside in Southwestern Oregon. No specifications as to form, length, subject matter or style. "Submissions limited to five poems per term, prefer non-saga poems; one story per term, maximum 1,500 words." The editor says *Beacon* is 50-75 pgs., 5½×8, professionally printed with color cover and b&w art within; no ads. They receive about 400 poems a year, accept approximately 25%. Press run is 300, all shelf sales. Sample: $4.50.

How to Submit: No previously published poems or simultaneous submissions. Cover letter required. "Prefer short bio, SASE." Reads submissions December 1 through January 15 and March 1 through April 15 only. Time between acceptance and publication is 2 months. Seldom comments on rejections. Reports "on publication." Pays 1 copy. Acquires first rights.

Advice: The editor says, "We encourage poets to visit for readings and bring works to offer for sale. We do not compensate in any way for these readings. The purpose of our magazine is to heighten the value of literature in our community."

Ⓝ ◗ ◎ **BEACON STREET REVIEW (Specialized: graduate-level writers)**, 100 Beacon St., Emerson College, Boston MA 02116, e-mail c_hennessy@emerson.edu, founded 1986, editor Christopher Hennessy, poetry editor Robert Levine.

Magazine Needs: *BSR* appears biannually "to publish the best prose (fiction and nonfiction) and poetry we receive; to publish specifically the poetry that evidences the highest degree of creative talent and seriousness of effort and craft. Facile poetry that is not polished and crafted and poems that lack a strange sense of the 'idea' will not be ranked highly." They have published poetry by Charlotte Pence, John McKernan and Paul Berg. As a sample the editors selected these lines from "At Celilo" by Rochelle Cashdan:

> *Barges move/above buried rapids,//your camera follows/the sound of my voice.*

BSR is 96-104 pgs., 5½×8½, offset printed and perfect-bound with 4-color, matte finish cover with art/photo. They receive about 300 poems a year, accept approximately 10%. Press run is 800; 200 distributed free to Emerson College students. Subscription: $5/year (2 issues), $9/2 years (4 issues). Sample: $3.

How to Submit: Submit 3-5 poems at a time. No previously published poems; simultaneous submissions OK. Disk submissions OK. Cover letter required. "Poets should include three copies of each poem. The poet's name and address should not appear on those copies but should appear on the cover letter with all titles clearly listed." Reads submissions year round but responds only during early November and late March. Time between acceptance and publication is 2 months. Poems are circulated to an editorial board. "We have reading boards who read and rate all poems, submitting ranks and comments to a poetry editor. The poetry editor and the editor-in-chief confer with those ranks and comments in mind and then make final decisions." Send SASE for guidelines. Reports in 1-2 months. Pays 2 copies. Acquires first rights. Staff reviews of poetry in 250 words, single book format. Send books for review consideration to editor-in-chief.

Also Offers: Sponsors the Editor's Choice Awards. Selected by local established poets, the award gives a cash prize for the best poems published in *BSR* during the year.

$ ◎ **THE BEAR DELUXE (Specialized: nature/rural/ecology)**, P.O. Box 10342, Portland OR 97296-0342, phone (503)242-1047, fax (503)243-2645, e-mail bear@orlo.org, website http://www.orlo.org, founded 1993, editor Tom Webb, contact poetry editor.

• Note: *The Bear Deluxe* is published by Orlo, a nonprofit organization exploring environmental issues through the creative arts.

Magazine Needs: *Bear Deluxe*, formerly *Bear Essential*, is a quarterly that "provides a fresh voice amid often strident and polarized environmental discourse. Street-level, non-dogmatic and solution-oriented, *The Bear Deluxe* presents lively creative discussion to a diverse readership." They want poetry with "innovative environmental perspectives, not much longer than 50 lines. No rants." They have published poetry by Judith Barrington, Robert Michael Pyle, Mary Winters, Stephen Babcock, Carl Hanni and Derek Sheffield. As a sample the editor selected these lines from "Smoking" by Leanne Grabel:

> *I wonder what I/think's going to/happen if I/breathe only/air.*

The publication is 60 pgs., 11 × 14, newsprint with brown Kraft paper cover, saddle-stitched, with lots of original graphics and b&w photos. They receive about 400 poems a year, publish 20-30. Press run is 17,000 for 750 subscribers of which 10 are libraries, 16,000 distributed free on the streets of the Western US and beyond. Subscription: $6. Sample: $3. Make checks payable to Orlo.

How to Submit: Submit 3-5 poems at a time up to 50 lines each. Previously published poems and simultaneous submissions OK. E-mail and fax submissions OK; "no attachments." Poems are reviewed by a committee of 7-9 people. Publishes 1 theme issue/year. Send SASE for guidelines and upcoming themes. Reports in 6-8 weeks. Pays $10/poem, 5 copies (more if willing to distribute) and subscription. Buys first or one-time rights.

N $ ⊘ ◎ BEAR STAR PRESS; DOROTHY BRUNSMAN POETRY PRIZE (Specialized: regional), 185 Hollow Oak Dr., Cohasset CA 95973, phone (530)891-0360, founded 1996, publisher/editor Beth Spencer.

Book/Chapbook Needs: Bear Star Press accepts work by poets from Western and Pacific states. ("Those in Mountain or Pacific time zones.") "Bear Star is committed to publishing the best poetry it can attract. Each year it sponsors a contest open to poets from Western and Pacific states, although other eligibility requirements change depending on the composition of our list up to that point. Because the winner of our first competition was an established male poet, we limited our second competition to women who had not yet published a full-length collection. From time to time we add to our list other poets from our target area whose work we admire." They publish 1-2 paperbacks and occasionally chapbooks/year. They want "well-crafted poems. No restrictions as to form, subject matter, style or purpose." They have published poetry by George Keithley and Terri Drake. As a sample the publisher selected these lines from "Beeman" by Deborah Woodard:

> *Bitten near the mouth, he keeps/completely still under his burred coat./The bees have flung a leopard skin/over the shoulders of a strong man./And then intractable as ivy,/they dedicate themselves to hanging on,*

Books are usually 35-75 pgs., size varies, professionally printed and perfect-bound.

How to Submit: "Poets should enter our annual book competition. Other books are occasionally solicited by publisher, sometimes from among contestants who didn't win." Previously published poems and simultaneous submissions OK. "Prefer single-spaced manuscripts in plain font such as Times New Roman. SASE required for results. Manuscripts not returned but are recycled." Generally reads submissions August through November. Send SASE for current guidelines before submitting. Contest entry fee: $15. Time between acceptance and publication is 3-9 months. Poems are circulated to an editorial board. "I occasionally hire a judge. More recently I have taken on the judging with help from poets whose taste I trust." Seldom comments on rejections. Replies to queries regarding competitions in 1-2 weeks. Contest winner notified February 1 or before. Contest pays $500-1,000 and 50 author's copies (out of a press run of 500).

Advice: "Send your best work, consider its arrangement. A 'Wow' poem early on keeps me reading."

N ⊘ THE BEATNIK PACHYDERM, P.O. Box 161, Deadwood SD 57732, phone (605)578-1178, founded 1998, editor Tim Brennan, editor Randall K. Rogers.

Magazine Needs: *TBP* appears 3 times a year and publishes poems, prose, artwork, letters and short stories. They want "shorter poems; poems from social philosopher poets of the everyday life; humor, experimental, slice of life poems; Beat-influenced." As a sample they selected these lines from "Bank Job" by editor Tim Brennan:

> *I had this strange dream early this morning/it was about me four or five people I work with and Bing Crosby/we were successful bank robbers/celebrating a major bank job/my dreams aren't always like this/in this one Bing kept his clothes on*

TBP is 25-30 pgs., magazine-sized, photocopied, artwork contributions desired. They receive about 400 poems a year, accept approximately 20%. Press run is 250. Single copy: $5; subscription: $13. Make checks payable to Tim Brennan.

How to Submit: Submit up to 6 poems at a time. Line length for poetry is 60 maximum. Previously published poems and simultaneous submissions OK. Cover letter preferred. "Name and address on each page; include SASE." Time between acceptance and publication is 6 months. Poems are circulated to an editorial board of 3 editors. Often comments on rejections. Reports in 6 months. Pays 1 copy. Acquires one-time rights.

Advice: The editors say, "Enjoy writing, reflect, tell a unique or twisted observation."

⊘ ⊘ BEAUTY FOR ASHES POETRY REVIEW, 1000 Charles St., Mechanicsburg PA 17055-3944, e-mail beautyforashes@geocities.com, website http://www.geocities.com/paris/2729/, founded 1996, editor C.R. Cain.

Magazine Needs: *BFAPR* appears 3 times/year. "Our desire is to join the reader and the poet together; that they see the spiritual even when the mundane is always present. We consider free verse first but this does not mean abstract. We will consider well-written rhyme. No erotica, vulgar or profane poems. If 'I' or 'me' is used too often, consider sending your poems elsewhere. Better yet, rewrite it then submit here." They have published poetry by Linda Malnack, Doreen Zimmerman and Joy Dworkin. As a sample the editor selected these lines from "Prodigal Sons" by Charles Obaskahr:

> But there is not one life,/there are many;/a son feels the persistent burn,/of them rising/in places he
> can not name./He discovers the voice that speaks/when naked feet/find holy dust.

BFAPR is 40 pgs., digest-sized, desktop-published and saddle-stitched with card cover with pen & ink drawings. "We are interested in receiving artwork for future covers. We will also carry ads for chapbooks. Send SASE for details. They accept approximately 5% of poems received. Press run is 150 for 40 subscribers, 75-100 shelf sales. Subscription: $10. Sample: $4.

How to Submit: Submit up to 5 poems at a time. No previously published poems; simultaneous submissions OK if notified. Cover letter required including bio. E-mail submissions OK, no attachments. "Unfortunately, this option does not always allow for proper line breaks in the poems." Time between acceptance and publication is 3-6 months. Often comments on rejections. Send SASE for guidelines or obtain via website. Reports in 4-6 weeks, "occasionally longer." Pays 2 copies. Acquires first or one-time rights. "Some poems are held in archive at our website. After publication in print, poets may request their poem be removed from the website." Reviews books and chapbooks of poetry. Open to unsolicited reviews. Poets may also send books for review consideration.

Also Offers: Sponsors annual contest. Contest submissions are accepted from November 1 to February 15. Subject is open. Reading fee: $10 for up to 3 poems. First place: $100 and 1-year subscription. Website includes writer's guidelines, annual contest guidelines, sample poems from previous issues, editor's comments and bookstores that carry the journal.

Advice: The editor says, "Too many poets write but don't read poetry. And all too often poets go to open readings to read and not to listen. How can you hear a poem when the one you're holding is screaming to be read? Go to a reading empty handed, you will hear some uncommonly good works from others—and learn something. And lastly, never submit a poem you wrote last night or last week."

$◯ BEGGAR'S PRESS; THE LAMPLIGHT; RASKOLNIKOV'S CELLAR; BEGGAR'S REVIEW, 8110 N. 38th St., Omaha NE 68112-2018, phone (402)455-2615, founded 1977, editor Richard R. Carey.

Magazine Needs & How to Submit: *The Lamplight* is a semiannual (more frequent at times) publication of short stories, poetry, humor and unusual literary writings. "We are eclectic, but we like serious poetry, historically orientated. Positively no religious or sentimental poetry. No incomprehensible poetry." They have published poetry by Fredrick Zydek and John J. McKernan. As a sample the editor selected these lines (poet unidentified):

> Lord, why did you curse me with doubt!/I'm a shot discharged in a wood without trees,/like a scream
> that began as a shout./Never too far from famine or mire;/hunger and cold, and all creatures turn
> bold—/But, Lord, why did you give me desire!

The Lamplight is 40-60 pgs., 8½×11, offset printed and perfect-bound with 65 lb. cover stock. They receive about 600 poems a year, use approximately 10-15%. Press run is 500 for 300 subscribers of which 25 are libraries. Single copy: $9.50. Sample: $7 plus 9×12 SASE. No previously published poems; simultaneous submissions OK. Cover letter required—"must provide insight into the poet's characteristics. What makes this poet different from the mass of humanity?" Time between acceptance and publication is 4-12 months. Often comments on rejections. Also offers "complete appraisals and evaluations" for $4/standard sheet, double-spaced. Brochure available for SASE. Reports in 2-2½ months. Pays 2 copies plus discount on up to 5. Acquires first North American serial rights. *Raskolnikov's Cellar* is an irregular magazine of the same format, dimensions and terms as *The Lamplight*. However, it deals in "deeper psychologically-orientated stories and poetry. It is more selective and discriminating in what it publishes. Guidelines and brochures are an essential to consider this market." Send SASE and $1 for guidelines. Brochures require only SASE. *Beggar's Review* is 20-40 pgs., 8½×11, offset printed and saddle-stitched. It lists and reviews books, chapbooks and other magazines. "It also lists and reviews unpublished manuscripts: poetry, short stories, book-length, etc. Our purpose is to offer a vehicle for unpublished work of merit, as well as published material. We like to work with poets and authors who have potential but have not yet been recognized." Lengths of reviews range from a listing or mere caption to 1,000 words, "according to merit." Single copy: $6.

Book/Chapbook Needs & How to Submit: Beggar's Press also plans to publish 4-6 paperbacks/year—some on a subsidy basis. "In most cases, we select books which we publish on a royalty basis and promote ourselves. Borderline books only are author-subsidized." Query first with a few sample poems and a cover letter with brief bio and publication credits. "We also like to know how many books the author himself will be able to market to friends, associates, etc." Replies to queries in 1 month, to mss in 2½ months. Pays 10-15% royalties and 3 author's copies. Terms vary for subsidy publishing. "Depending on projected sales, the author pays from 20% to 60%."

Advice: The editor says, "Our purpose is to form a common bond with distinguished poets whose poetry is marketable and worthy. Poetry is difficult to market, thus we sometimes collaborate with the poet in publishing costs. But essentially, we look for poets with unique qualities of expression and who meet our uncustomary requirements. We prefer a royalty arrangement. Beggar's Press is different from most publishers. We are impressed with concrete poetry, which is without outlandish metaphors. Keep it simple but don't be afraid to use our language to the fullest. Read Poe, Burns and Byron. Then submit to us. There is still a place for lyrical poetry."

✓◯ BEHIND BARS, P.O. Box 1684, Fort Collins CO 80522-1684, founded 1996, editor-in-chief Stephanie Owen, contact poetry editor.

Magazine Needs: *Behind Bars* is a biannual "literary magazine of mostly poetry, fiction, essays, reviews and art based on quality by both known and undiscovered writers." They want "any subject, any length, in any voice but strong in image and emotion. We only want poets who are obsessed with their poetry to submit based on quality not bio information. No cliché-bound, worn-out language; no punctuation, no capital letters." They have published poetry by Martha Vertreace, Brian Beatty and Barbara Daniels. As a sample the editor selected these lines from "Like A Knife Into The Heart of Morpheus (for John Berryman)" by Joseph Allgren:

> *The leap provides the certainty of change,/and stops the chance some god will take/you while you*
> *dream. The sky, enameled, pure/and starless, flies back as you roll and, like/a knife into the heart of*
> *Morpheus,/descend toward the waking, the crack of ice.*

BB is 40-50 pgs., 5½×8½, professionally printed and saddle-stapled with colored card cover, b&w art and photos. They accept less than 5% of poetry received. Press run is 60-70, 50% shelf sales. Subscription: $6. Sample (including guidelines): $3. Make checks payable to Stephanie Owen.

How to Submit: Submit 3-5 poems at a time. No previously published poems or simultaneous submissions. Cover letter optional. "Make sure name and address are on every page; only interested in reading cover letters that are three lines or less." Reports in 2-3 months. Pays 1 copy. "All rights revert to the author upon publication."

BELHUE PRESS (Specialized: gay), 2501 Palisade Ave., Suite A1, Riverdale, Bronx NY 10463, e-mail belhuepress@earthlink.net, website http://www.perrybrass.com, founded 1990, editor Tom Laine.

Book/Chapbook Needs: A small press specializing in gay male poetry, publishing 3 paperbacks/year—no chapbooks. "We are especially interested in books that get out of the stock poetry market." They want "hard-edged, well-crafted, fun and often sexy poetry. No mushy, self pitying, confessional, boring, indulgent, teary or unrequited love poems—yuck! Poets must be willing to promote book through readings, mailers, etc." As a sample the editor included these lines from "Two Steppin' with Mr. Right," from *The Lover of My Soul*, by Perry Brass

> *He knotted his scarf/'bout my neck like a cowboy,/then pulled me to his mouth/for one last sweet taste./*
> *I held on to his tanned neck,/his chest and his biceps,/but he blew like the wind/to embrace his hard*
> *fate.*

"We have a $10 sample and guideline fee. Please send this before submitting any poetry. We have had to initiate this due to a deluge of bad, amateur, irrelevant submissions. After fee, we will give constructive criticism when necessary."

How to Submit: Query first with 6 pgs. of poetry and cover letter. Previously published poems and simultaneous submissions OK. Time between acceptance and publication is 1 year. Often comments on rejections. Will request criticism fees "if necessary." Replies to queries and submitted mss "fast." No payment information provided. Sample: $7.95.

Advice: "The only things we find offensive are stupid, dashed off, 'fortune cookie' poems that show no depth or awareness of poetry. We like poetry that, like good journalism, tells a story."

THE BELLINGHAM REVIEW; THE SIGNPOST PRESS; 49TH PARALLEL POETRY AWARD, M.S. 9053, Western Washington University, Bellingham WA 98225, website http://www.wwu.edu/~bhreview/, founded 1975, editor Robin Hemley.

Magazine Needs: *The Bellingham Review* appears twice a year, runs an annual poetry competition and publishes other books and chapbooks of poetry occasionally. "We want well-crafted poetry but are open to all styles," no specifications as to form. They have published poetry by David Shields, Tess Gallagher, Gary Soto, Jane Hirsh-field, Albert Goldbarth, R.T. Smith and Rebecca McClanahan. As a sample the editor selected these lines from "Sitting at Dusk in the Back Yard After the Mondrian Retrospective" by Charles Wright:

> *Form imposes, structure allows—/the slow destruction of form/So as to bring it back resheveled,*
> *reorganized,/Is the hard heart of the enterprise./Under its camouflage,/The light, relentless shill and*
> *cross-dresser, pools and deals./Inside its short skin, the darkness burns.*

The *Review* is 6×9, perfect-bound, with art and glossy cover. Each issue has about 60 pgs. of poetry. They have a circulation of 1,500 with 500 subscriptions. Subscription: $10/year, $19/2 years. Sample: $5. Make checks payable to The Western Foundation/*Bellingham Review*.

How to Submit: Submit 3-5 poems at a time with SASE. Simultaneous submissions OK with notification. Reads submissions October 1 through May 1 only. Send SASE for guidelines or obtain via website. Reports in 1-4 months. Pays 1 copy, a year's subscription plus monetary payment (if funding allows). Acquires first North American serial rights. Reviews books of poetry. Send books for review consideration also between October 1 and May 1.

Book/Chapbook Needs & How to Submit: Query about book publication before sending a ms.

Also Offers: The 49th Parallel Poetry Award, established in 1983, awards a $1,000 first prize, $250 second prize and $100 third prize, plus a year's subscription to the *Review*. Submissions must be unpublished and may be entered in other contests. Send any number of poems on any subject, in any form. The author's name must not appear on the ms. Enclose with each poem a 3×5 index card with the poem's title, first line of poem, author's name and address, phone/fax number, e-mail address (if any). Manuscripts will not be returned. Include SASE for winners list. Send SASE or visit website for guidelines. Entry fee: $5/poem. Submission period: October 1 through November 30. Most recent award winner was Suzanne Wise (1998). Judge was Heather McHugh. Winners will be announced in April. Copies of previous winning poems may be obtained by sending for a sample copy of the *Review*'s winners issue ($5 postpaid). Website features submission guidelines, contest guidelines, names of editors and staff, and selections from recent issue.

✓ ⊘ BELLOWING ARK; BELLOWING ARK PRESS, P.O. Box 55564, Shoreline WA 98155, phone (206)440-0791, founded 1984, editor Robert R. Ward.

Magazine Needs: *Bellowing Ark* is a bimonthly literary tabloid that "publishes only poetry which demonstrates in some way the proposition that existence has meaning or, to put it another way, that life is worth living. We have no strictures as to length, form or style; only that the work we publish is to our judgment life-affirming." They do not want "academic poetry, in any of its manifold forms." They have published poetry by Len Blanchard, Robert King, David Ross, Paula Milligan, Muriel Karr, Teresa Noelle Roberts and Elizabeth Biller Chapman. The paper is 32 pgs., tabloid-sized, printed on electrobright stock with b&w photos and line drawings. Circulation is 1,000, of which 275 are subscriptions and 500 are sold on newsstands. Subscription: $15/year. Sample: $3.

How to Submit: Submit 3-6 poems at a time. "Absolutely *no* simultaneous submissions." They reply to submissions in 2-12 weeks and publish within the next 1 or 2 issues. Occasionally they will criticize a ms if it seems to "display potential to become the kind of work we want." Sometimes sends prepublication galleys. Pays 2 copies. Reviews books of poetry. Send books for review consideration.

Book/Chapbook Needs & How to Submit: Bellowing Ark Press publishes collections of poetry by *invitation only*.

◻ ⊘ ◎ BELL'S LETTERS POET (Specialized: subscribers), P.O. Box 2187, Gulfport MS 39505-2187, founded 1956, publisher/editor Jim Bell.

Magazine Needs: *BL* is a quarterly which you must buy ($5/issue, $20 subscription) to be included. The editor says "many say they stop everything the day it arrives," and judging by the many letters from readers, that seems to be the case. Though there is no payment for poetry accepted, many patrons send awards of $5-20 to the poets whose work they especially like. Poems are "four to 20 lines in good taste." They have published poetry by Kimberly Courtright, Najwa Salam Brax, Margie Zimmerman and Winnie Mae Fitzpatrick. As a sample the editor selected these lines from "Mending Old Fences" by J.R. Libby:

> Remember how our kites of/Autumn never soared as high/As the fire of our pens. We could/Wring some
> potent verses out of/The turning leaves back then . . .

BL is about 64 pgs., digest-sized, photocopied on plain bond paper (including cover) and saddle-stitched. Sample (including guidelines): $5. "Send a poem (under 20 lines, in good taste) with your sample order and we will publish in our next issue."

How to Submit: Submit 4 poems a year. Ms must be typed. No simultaneous submissions. Previously published poems OK "if cleared by author with prior publisher." Accepted poems by subscribers go immediately into the next issue. Deadline for poetry submissions is 3 months prior to publication. Reviews books of poetry by subscribers in "one abbreviated paragraph." "The Ratings" is a competition in each issue. Readers are asked to vote on their favorite poems, and the "Top 40" are announced in the next issue, along with awards sent to the poets by patrons. *BL* also features a telephone exchange among poets and a birth-date listing.

Advice: The editor asks, "Tired of seeing no bylines this year? Subscription guarantees a byline in each issue."

✓ ⚲ ⊘ THE BELOIT POETRY JOURNAL; CHAD WALSH POETRY PRIZE, 24 Berry Cove Rd., Lamoine ME 04605-4617, phone (207)667-5598, e-mail sharkey@maine.edu (for information only), website http://www.bpj.org. founded 1950, editor Marion K. Stocking.

● Poetry published in *The Beloit Poetry Journal* has also been included in *The Best American Poetry* (1994 and 1996) and *Pushcart Prize* anthologies.

Magazine Needs: *The Beloit Poetry Journal* is a well-known, long-standing quarterly of quality poetry and reviews. "We publish the best poems we receive, without bias as to length, school, subject or form. It is our hope to discover the growing tip of poetry and to introduce new poets alongside established writers. We publish occasional chapbooks to diversify our offerings. These are almost never the work of one poet." They want "fresh, imaginative poetry, with a distinctive voice. We tend to prefer poems that make the reader share an experience rather than just read about it, and these we keep for up to three months, circulating them among our readers, and continuing to winnow for the best. At the quarterly meetings of the Editorial Board we read aloud all the surviving poems and put together an issue of the best we have." They have published poetry by Bei Dao, Molly Tenenbaum, Albert Goldbarth and Sherman Alexie. As a sample the editor selected an excerpt from the poem "Exactitude" by Hillel Schwartz:

> In Yale seminars exactitude keeps the dumb/from speaking; they know better than to say/what lies in
> the heart—but here the lay/of the grain must come to fortunate expression,/the tempering, the tuning,
> the turn of the pin/to fugue and quickness of pulse, the beat/of the blood.

The journal averages 48 pgs., 6×9, saddle-stapled, and attractively printed with tasteful art on the card cover. They have a circulation of 1,300 for 580 subscribers of which 328 are libraries. Sample (including guidelines): $4. Send SASE for guidelines alone.

How to Submit: Submit any time, without query, any legible form. No e-mail submissions. "No previously published poems or simultaneous submissions. Any length of ms, but most poets send what will go in a business envelope for one stamp. Don't send your life's work." Pays 3 copies. Acquires first serial rights. Staff reviews books by and about poets in an average of 500 words, usually single format. Send books for review consideration.

Also Offers: The journal awards the Chad Walsh Poetry Prize ($3,000 in 1998) to a poem or group of poems published in the calendar year. "Every poem published in 2000 will be considered for the 2000 prize." Website includes writer's guidelines, magazine history, names of editors, sample poems and table of contents of recent issues.
Advice: The editor says, "We'd like to see more strong, imaginative, experimental poetry; more poetry with a global vision; and more poetry with fresh, vigorous language."

BENEATH THE SURFACE, % The Dept. of English, Chester New Hall, McMaster University, Hamilton, Ontario L8S 4L9 Canada, founded 1911, editor changes yearly.
Magazine Needs: *BTS* is an annual using "top quality poetry/prose that achieves universality through individual expression." They want "quality poetry; any form; no restrictions." Also interested in short stories. They have published poetry by Janice Knapp and Jeffrey Donaldson. *BTS* is 30-50 pgs., professionally printed, saddle-stapled, with cover art, drawings and b&w photographs. They receive about 250 submissions/year, use approximately 10%. Press run is 75 for 8 subscribers of which 3 are libraries, 92 shelf sales. Subscription: $8/2 years. Sample: $4.
How to Submit: No previously published poems or simultaneous submissions. Submit poems with cover letter, including short bio and summary of previous publications, if any. Reads submissions September through April only. Pays 1 copy. Acquires first North American serial rights. Rarely reviews books of poetry, "though we do include literary essays when submitted." Reports in 8-10 months.

BENNETT & KITCHEL (Specialized: form), P.O. Box 4422, East Lansing MI 48826, phone (517)355-1707, founded 1989, editor William Whallon.
Book/Chapbook Needs: Publishes 1-2 hardbacks/year of "poetry of form and meaning. No free verse or blank verse." As an example of what he admires, the editor selected these lines by Anthony Lombardy:
> From recent fires surrounding groves are ashen,/Are like the Trojan women mad with thirst,/Who
> begged for water while the one accursed/Allowed the guards to fill her pool to splash in.
Sample: $4.
How to Submit: Submit 6 poems at a time. Simultaneous submissions and previously published poems OK if copyright is clear. Minimum volume for a book "might be 750 lines." Time between acceptance and publication is 9 months. Seldom comments on submissions. Reports in 2 weeks. Terms are "variable, negotiable."
Advice: The editor says, "To make a bad rhyme not from incompetence but willfully is like stubbing your toe on purpose."

$ BIBLE ADVOCATE (Specialized: religious), P.O. Box 33677, Denver CO 80233, e-mail cofgsd @denver.net, website http://www.baonline.org, founded 1863, associate editor Sherri Langton.
Magazine Needs: The *Bible Advocate*, published monthly, features "Christian content—to advocate the Bible and represent the church." They want "free verse, some traditional; 5-20 lines, with Christian/Bible themes." They do not want "avant garde poetry." The editor says *BA* is 24 pgs., 8¾×11⅞ with most poetry set up with 4-color art. They receive about 30-50 poems a year, accept 10-20. Press run varies for 12,500 subscribers with all distributed free.
How to Submit: Submit 5 poems at a time, 5-20 lines each. Previously published poems (with notification) and simultaneous submissions OK. E-mail submissions OK (ASCII files or Microsoft Word 5.0 or 6.0 files). "No fax or handwritten submissions, please." Cover letter preferred. Time between acceptance and publication is 3-12 months. "I read them first and reject those that won't work for us. I send good ones to editor for approval." Seldom comments on rejections. Publishes theme issues. Send SASE for guidelines. Reports in 1-2 months. Pays $10. Buys first, reprint and one-time rights.
Advice: The editor says, "Avoid trite, or forced rhyming. Be aware of the magazine's doctrinal views (send for doctrinal beliefs booklet)."

BIBLIOPHILOS, 200 Security Building, Fairmont WV 26554, phone (304)366-8107, fax (304)366-8461, founded 1981, editor Gerald J. Bobango.
Magazine Needs: "*Bibliophilos* is a quarterly academic journal, for the literati, illuminati, amantes artium, and those who love animals; scholastically oriented, for the liberal arts. Topics include fiction and nonfiction; literature and criticism, history, art, music, theology, philosophy, natural history, educational theory, contemporary issues and politics, sociology and economics. Published in English, French, German, Romanian." They want "traditional forms, rhyme is OK; also blank verse, free verse. Aim for concrete visual imagery, either in words or on the page. No inspirational verse, or anything that Ann Landers or Erma Bombeck would publish." They have published poetry by Belle Randall. As a sample the editor selected these lines from "Trademark" (poet unidentified):
> superimposed on a picture too faint to see,/printed in red in English and Chinese,/concludes: ". . .
> should not be poured out/until five minutes have passed/when the taste will come out/in its full glory."
Bibliophilos is 64 pgs., 5½×8, laser photography printed and saddle-stapled with light card, includes clip art and ads. They receive about 60 poems a year, accept approximately 33%. Press run is 200 for 100 subscribers. Subscription: $18/year. Sample: $5. Make checks payable to The Bibliophile.
How to Submit: Query first with SASE and $5 for sample and guidelines. Then, if invited, submit 3-5 poems

at a time. Previously published poems and simultaneous submissions OK. Cover letter with brief bio preferred. Time between acceptance and publication is 3 months. Often comments on rejections. Send SASE for guidelines. Reports in 2 weeks. Pays 5 copies. Acquires first North American serial rights. Staff reviews books and chapbooks of poetry in 750-1,000 words, single book format. Send books for review consideration.

Also Offers: Sponsors poetry contest. Send SASE for rules. 1st Prize $25 plus publication and offprints.

Advice: The editor says, "There is too much maudlin over-emotionalism and instant pop psychology in this touchy-feely world. We need some good traditional, hearty, Kiplingesque poetry that stirs, inspires, and hits you between the eyes. Also, we need more peristaltic belchings of crabbed organisms arguing that malls, 'feeling everyone's pain,' and building self-esteem as opposed to educating people, should all be extinguished as blights."

$ ◎ BILINGUAL REVIEW PRESS; BILINGUAL REVIEW/REVISTA BILINGÜE (Specialized: ethnic/Hispanic, bilingual/Spanish), Hispanic Research Center, Arizona State University, Box 872702, Tempe AZ 85287-2702, phone (602)965-3867, journal founded 1974, press in 1976, managing editor Karen Van Hooft.

Magazine Needs: "We are a small press publisher of U.S. Hispanic creative literature and of a journal containing poetry and short fiction in addition to scholarship." *BR/RB*, published 3 times/year, contains some poetry in most issues. "We publish poetry by and/or about U.S. Hispanics and U.S. Hispanic themes. We do not publish translations in our journal or literature about the experiences of Anglo-Americans in Latin America. We have published a couple of poetry volumes in bilingual format (Spanish/English) of important Mexican poets." They have published poetry by Alberto Ríos, Martín Espada, Judith Ortiz Cofer and Marjorie Agosín. The editor says the journal is 96 pgs., 7×10, offset printed and flat-spined, with 2-color cover. They use less than 10% of hundreds of submissions received each year. Press run is 1,000 for 700 subscribers. Subscriptions: $21 for individuals, $35 for institutions. Sample: $7 individuals/$12 institutions.

How to Submit: Submit "two copies, including ribbon original if possible, with loose stamps for return postage." Cover letter required. Pays 2 copies. Acquires all rights. Reviews books of US Hispanic literature only. Send books, Attn: Editor, for review consideration.

Book/Chapbook Needs & How to Submit: Bilingual Review Press publishes flat-spined paperback collections of poetry. For book submissions, inquire first with 4-5 sample poems, bio and publication credits. Pays $250 advance, 10% royalties and 10 copies. Over the years, books by this press have won 6 American Book Awards and 2 Western States Book Awards.

✓ $ ☑ BIRCH BROOK PRESS, P.O. Box 81, Delhi NY 13753, phone (212)353-3326, fax (607)746-7453, founded 1982, contact Tom Tolnay.

Book/Chapbook Needs: Birch Brook "is a letterpress book printer/typesetter/designer that uses monies from these activities to publish several titles of its own each year with cultural and literary interest." Publishes 4-6 paperbacks and/or hardbacks per year. The press specializes "mostly in anthologies with specific subject matter. BBP publishes one or two books by individuals with high-quality literary work, on a co-op basis." Books are "handset letterpress editions printed in our own shop." They have published *The Melancholy of Yorick* by Joel Chace; *Waiting On Pentecost* by Tom Smith; and *The Derelict Genius of Martin M* by Frank Fagan.

How to Submit: Query with a few sample poems or send the entire ms. "Include SASE with submissions." Occasionally comments on rejections. Authors may obtain sample books by sending for catalog. Pays from $5-20 for publication in anthology.

$ ◎ BIRD WATCHER'S DIGEST (Specialized: nature), P.O. Box 110, Marietta OH 45750, phone (740)373-5285, e-mail editor@birdwatchersdigest.com, website http://www.birdwatchersdigest.com, founded 1978, editor William H. Thompson, III.

Magazine Needs: *BWD*, a bimonthly, is "a specialized but promising market for poems of 'true literary merit' in which birds figure in some way, at least by allusion. *Bird Watcher's Digest*'s audience ranges from the backyard bird watcher to the very knowledgeable field birder. We are especially interested in fresh, engaging accounts of closely observed bird behavior and displays and of bird watching experiences and expeditions. We use articles on particular species; on attracting backyard birds; on photographing birds; on where to go to see birds; on sightings of rare species. We frequently run updates on endangered or threatened species as well as reports on recent ornithological research. We also use profiles of interesting people, humorous essays, and, infrequently, poetry and cartoons. We publish no pet bird stories." They have published poetry by Susan Rea, Nancy G. Westerfield, Suzanne Freemans and William D. Barney. They have up to 2 year's backlog and use 2-6 of the approximately 500 poems received each year. Sample: $3.99.

How to Submit: "Preferred: no more than 20 lines, 40 spaces, no more than 3 poems at a time, no queries." Reports in 2 months. Pays $25/poem.

Also Offers: Website includes writer's guidelines, photographer's guidelines, illustrator's guidelines, articles/poetry from magazine, FAQ, subscription pages and online store.

◐ ◎ BIRMINGHAM POETRY REVIEW (Specialized: translations), English Dept., University of Alabama at Birmingham, Birmingham AL 35294, phone (205)934-8573, website http://www.uab.edu/english/bpr, founded 1988, co-editors Robert Collins and Randy Blythe.

Magazine Needs: The review appears twice a year using poetry of "any style, form, length or subject. We are biased toward exploring the cutting edge of contemporary poetry. Style is secondary to the energy, the fire the poem possesses. We don't want poetry with cliché-bound, worn-out language." They have published poetry by Hague, Daley, McDonald, Richards, R.T. Smith and Miltner. They describe their magazine as 50 pgs., 6×9, offset printed, with b&w cover. Press run is 700 for 300 subscribers. Subscription: $4/year; $7/2 years. Sample: $2.

How to Submit: Submit 3-5 poems, "no more. No cover letters. We are impressed by good writing; we are unimpressed by publication credits." SASE required. No simultaneous or multiple submissions, and previously published poems only if they are translations. Editor sometimes comments on rejections. Send SASE for guidelines. Reports in 1-6 months. Pays 2 copies and one-year subscription.

Also Offers: Website includes guidelines, contents of current issue, submission guidelines, subscription information, list of editors and sample poems.

Advice: They say, "Advice to beginners: Read as much good contemporary poetry, national and international, as you can get your hands on. Then be persistent in finding your own voice."

THE BITTER OLEANDER; FRANCES LOCKE MEMORIAL AWARD (Specialized: translations), 4983 Tall Oaks Dr., Fayetteville NY 13066-9776, phone (315)637-3047, fax (315)637-5056, e-mail bones44@ix.netcom.com, founded 1974, editor/publisher Paul B. Roth.

Magazine Needs: *The Bitter Oleander* appears biannually, publishing "imaginative poetry; poetry in translation; serious language." They want "highly imaginative poetry whose language is serious. We prefer short poems of no more than 25 lines. We are not interested in very long poems and prefer not to receive poems about the common values and protests of society." They have published poetry by Robert Bly, Alan Britt, Duane Locke and Ray Gonzalez. *The Bitter Oleander* is 80-125 pgs., digest-sized, offset printed, perfect-bound with glossy 2-color cover, cover art and ads. They receive about 2,500 poems a year, accept approximately 4%. Press run is 1,500, 1,000 shelf sales. Single copy: $8; subscription: $15. Make checks payable to Bitter Oleander Press.

How to Submit: Submit up to 8 poems at a time with name and address on each page. No previously published poems or simultaneous submissions. No e-mail submissions. Cover letter preferred. Does not read mss during July. Time between acceptance and publication is 4-6 months. "All poems are read by the editor only and all decisions are made by this editor." Often comments on rejections. Reports within a month. Pays 1 copy.

Also Offers: Sponsors the Frances Locke Memorial Award, awarding $500 and publication. Submit any number of poems. Entry fee: $10/5 poems, $2 each additional poem. Open to submissions January 1 through June 15 only.

Advice: The editor says, "We simply want poetry that is imaginative and serious in its performance of language. So much flat-line poetry is written today that anyone reading one magazine or another cannot tell the difference."

BKMK PRESS, University House, University of Missouri-Kansas City, 5101 Rockhill Rd., Kansas City MO 64110-2499, phone (816)235-2558, fax (816)235-2611, founded 1971, associate editor Michelle Boisseau, managing editor Ben Furnish, director/executive editor James McKinley.

Book/Chapbook Needs: BkMk Press generally publishes 4-5 full-length paperbacks. The press seeks to publish "well-known and beginning poets fairly and equally." They have no specifications regarding form, length or subject matter but do not want to see "pretentious, unserious poetry." They have published books of poetry by Howard Schwartz and Neal Bowers. Their books are generally 64 pgs., 5½×8½, professionally printed and perfect-bound with laminated covers with art and photographs.

How to Submit: Query first with sample poems and a cover letter with brief bio and publication credits. Previously published poems and simultaneous submissions OK. Seldom comments on rejections. Replies to queries in 1 month, to mss in 2-6 months. Pays 10% royalties and 20 author's copies (out of a press run of 600). Call or write for catalog to order samples.

BLACK BEAR PUBLICATIONS; BLACK BEAR REVIEW (Specialized: social issues), 1916 Lincoln St., Croydon PA 19021-8026, email bbreview@aol.com, website http://members.aol.com/bbreview/index.htm, founded 1984, poetry and art editor Ave Jeanne, producer Ron Zettlemoyer.

Magazine Needs: *Black Bear Review* is a semiannual international literary and fine arts magazine that also publishes chapbooks and holds an annual poetry competition. "We like well-crafted poetry that mirrors real life—void of camouflage, energetic poetry, avant-garde, free verse and haiku which relate to the world today. We seldom publish the beginner, but will assist when time allows. No traditional poetry is used. The underlying theme of *BBR* is social and political, but the review is interested also in environmental, war/peace, ecological and minorities themes. We would like to receive more ideas on AIDS awareness, life styles and current political topics." They have published poetry by Livio Farallo, C.B. Follett, Louis McKee, Alan Kaufman and Harry Calhoun. As a sample the editor selected these lines from "Chorale" by Kevin Simmonds:

> all night, you half asleep/to the rumble of people/and cars on their way/to being somewhere/and you
> just hate the way/that has it over you

BBR is 64 pgs., digest-sized, perfect-bound, offset from typed copy on white stock, with line drawings, collages and woodcuts. Circulation is 500 for 300 subscribers of which 15 are libraries. Subscription: $12, $18 overseas. Sample: $6; back copies when available are $5.

How to Submit: Submit 5 poems at a time by e-mail only. "E-mail submissions are answered within a few days. Include snail mail address. No attached files please." Simultaneous submissions are not considered. Time between acceptance and publication is 6 months. Send SASE for guidelines. Reports in 2 weeks. Pays 1 copy.

Acquires first North American serial rights and electronic rights, "as work may appear on our website."

Book/Chapbook Needs & How to Submit: They publish 2 chapbooks/year. They have published *America* by A.D. Winans and *Rubato Jitter* by John Sullivan. Chapbook series requires a reading fee of $5, complete ms and cover letter. Send SASE for guidelines. For book publication, they require that "*BBR* has published the poet and is familiar with his/her work." Author receives one-half print run.

Also Offers: "Our yearly poetry competition offers cash awards to poets." Deadline: November 1. Send SASE for guidelines. Website features most recent issues, complete guidelines, links and current needs. "Our website is designed and maintained by Ave Jeanne and is updated regularly to meet the diverse needs of our readers."

Advice: They say, "We appreciate a friendly, brief cover letter. Tell us about the poet; omit degrees or any other pretentious dribble. All submissions are handled with objectivity and quite often rejected material is directed to another market. If you've not been published before, mention it. We are always interested in aiding those who support small press. We frequently suggest poets keep up with the current edition of *Poet's Market*. We make an effort to keep our readers informed and on top of the small press scene. Camera-ready ads are printed free of charge as a support to small press publishers. We also run an ad page on the Internet, "InterActions," for all interested poets and writers to advertise. We do suggest poets and artists read issues before submitting to absorb the flavor and save on wasted postage. Send your best!" The editors add, "Visit our applauded website. *Black Bear* will continue to print in our paperback format as well as art and poems online."

☑ $ ☺ **BLACK BELT PRESS**, P.O. Box 551, Montgomery AL 36101, website http://www.blackbeltpress.com, founded 1989, contact poetry editor.

Book/Chapbook Needs: Black Belt publishes literature, poetry, history and biography—"primarily examining the culture and history of the Deep South." They publish 1-2 poetry hardbacks/year. Their preferred subjects are the South, civil rights, women, ethnic minorities. No religious, romantic or pastoral work. As a sample the editor selected these lines from "Someone Will Go On Owing" by Andrew Glaze:

> For the first time in my life, I had neither shield nor friend,/no place, no enemy, no time./I crouched
> there counting the holes in my pockets./The wind was cold, there was no wall nor roof/nor any fire to
> keep me warm./I began to dance.

How to Submit: Query first. Previously published poems and simultaneous submissions OK. Time between acceptance and publication is 1-3 years. Poems are circulated to an editorial board. "They are reviewed by the in-house editors with final approval going to the editor-in-chief." Seldom comments on rejections. Replies to queries within 1 month, to mss within 6 months. Pays 5-15% royalties and 10 author's copies. For sample books "order from us or through bookstores (1-800-959-3245)."

☑ ◑ ◎ $ **BLACK BOUGH (Specialized: haiku)**, 188 Grove St. #1., Somerville NJ 08876, founded 1991, editor Chuck Easter.

Magazine Needs: *bb* is a triannual that publishes "haiku and related poetry that uses the Eastern form in the Western milieu." They want "haiku, senryu, tanka, haibun (in particular) and sequences. No academic essays or extremely long poems." They have published work by Michael Dylan Welch, Jim Kacian and Emily Romano. As a sample the editor selected this haiku by Larry Kimmel:

> a chickadee feeding/from my hand, the clutch/of tiny talons

bb is 30 pgs., digest-sized, professionally printed, saddle-stitched, with photos. They receive about 5,200 poems a year, use 5-10%. Press run is 200 for 100 subscribers. Subscription: $16.50. Sample: $6.

How to Submit: "Submit no more than 20 haiku; prefer several haiku/page." No previously published poems or simultaneous submissions. Time between acceptance and publication is 3-6 months. Comments on rejections "if requested." Reports in 6-10 weeks. Pays $1/verse, up to $4 for a long poem or haiku sequence. Buys first rights.

Also Offers: *black bough* books has published *Spirit Dance* by Chuck Easter and *Road Work* by Michael Ketchek. Send SASE for additional information.

◑ **BLACK BUZZARD PRESS; BLACK BUZZARD REVIEW; VISIONS—INTERNATIONAL, THE WORLD JOURNAL OF ILLUSTRATED POETRY; THE BLACK BUZZARD ILLUSTRATED POETRY CHAPBOOK SERIES; INTERNATIONAL—VISIONS POETRY SERIES**, 1007 Ficklen Rd., Fredericksburg VA 22405, founded 1979, poetry editor Bradley R. Strahan, associate editor Shirley G. Sullivan.

Magazine Needs: *Visions*, a digest-sized, saddle-stapled magazine finely printed on high-quality paper, appears 3 times a year, uses 56 pages of poetry in each issue. Circulation 800 with 400 subscribers of which 50 are libraries. Sample: $4. Current issue: $5.50. They receive *well* over 1,000 submissions each year, use 150, have a 3- to 18-month backlog. "*Visions* is international in both scope and content, publishing poets from all over the

---

USE THE GENERAL INDEX, located at the back of this book, to find the page number of a specific publisher. Also, publishers that were listed in last year's edition but not included in this edition are listed in the General Index with a notation explaining why they were omitted.

world and having readers in 48 U.S. states, Canada and 24 other countries." *Black Buzzard Review* is a "more or less annual informal journal, dedicated mostly to North American poets and entirely to original English-language poems. In *BBR*, we are taking a more wide-open stance on what we accept (including the slightly outrageous)." Sample: $4.50. Current issue: $5.50. It is 36 pgs., magazine-sized, side-stapled, with matte card cover.

How to Submit: Submit 3-6 poems at a time. "Poems must be readable (not faded or smudged) and not handwritten. We resent having to pay postage due, so use adequate postage! No more than six pages, please." No previously published poems or simultaneous submissions. Publishes theme issues. Send SASE for upcoming themes. Reports in 3 days to 3 weeks. Pays 1 copy or $5-10 "if we get a grant." Buys first North American serial rights. Staff reviews books of poetry in "up to two paragraphs." Send books for review consideration.

Book/Chapbook Needs & How to Submit: "We are an independent nonsubsidized press dedicated to publishing fine accessible poetry and translation (particularly from lesser-known languages such as Armenian, Gaelic, Urdu, Vietnamese, etc.) accompanied by original illustrations of high quality in an attractive format. We want to see work that is carefully crafted and exciting, that transfigures everyday experience or gives us a taste of something totally new; all styles except concrete and typographical 'poems.' Nothing purely sentimental. No self-indulgent breast beating. No sadism, sexism or bigotry. No unemotional pap. No copies of Robert Service or the like. Usually under 80 lines but will consider longer." They have published poetry by Ted Hughes, Michael Mott, Louis Simpson, Marilyn Hacker, James Dickey, Naomi Shihab Nye and Lawrence Ferlinghetti. To submit for the chapbook series, send samples (5-10 poems) and a brief cover letter "pertinent to artistic accomplishments." Reports in 3 days to 3 weeks. Pays in copies. Usually provides criticism. Send $4 for sample chapbook. They also publish the International-Visions Poetry Series. Send SASE for flyer describing titles and order information.

Advice: The editors add that in *Visions*, "We sometimes publish helpful advice about 'getting published' and the craft of poetry, and often discuss poets and the world of poetry on our editorial page."

N $ □ ◎ BLACK DIASPORA MAGAZINE; BLACK DIASPORA COMMUNICATIONS, LTD. (Specialized: ethnic/nationality), 298 Fifth Ave., 7th Floor, New York NY 10001, phone (212)268-8348, fax (212)268-8370, e-mail blakdias@earthlink.net, website http://www.blackdiaspora.net, founded 1979, managing editor Michelle Phipps, publisher Rene John-Sandy.

Magazine Needs: Published 7 times a year, *BDM* is a "general interest publication for African-Americans, Caribbeans, Africans, Hispanics. Covers general topics in all facets of their lives." They want "long and short poems—creatively done. Sonnets are good. They should all follow editorial guidelines. Be imaginative. No five-page poems." They have published poetry by Sabrina Smith and Annan Boodram. As a sample they selected these lines from "Altered Mind" by Barbara Grant-Richardson:

> We are the family of Black/America standing at the turning/point of life/Silently absorbed in a world/
> misunderstood by many./Where the human spirit and level/of admiration are steadily stripped of their
> luster.

They say *BDM* is 68-84 pgs., magazine-sized, flat-spined with glossy cover, includes photos and ads. They receive about 60 poems a year, accept approximately 100%. Press run is 50,000 for 250,000 subscribers. Single copy: $2.95; subscription: $15/year. Sample: $5.

How to Submit: Submit up to 2 poems at a time. Previously published poems OK; no simultaneous submissions. Cover letter preferred. Disk submissions OK. "Format should be in Word Perfect 5.1." Time between acceptance and publication is 3 months. Seldom comments on rejections. Publishes theme issues. Send SASE for guidelines and upcoming themes. Reports in 2-3 weeks. Pays $15. Buys first North American serial rights or one-time rights. Reviews books of poetry in 200-300 words, single book format. Open to unsolicited reviews. Poets may also send books for review consideration to Michelle Phipps.

Also Offers: Website includes a preview of the latest issue.

Advice: The editor says, "Please do not call editors. They're very busy and don't have time for all calls. Be patient. Make friends with editorial assistants and assistant editors."

✓ ▼ ◐ BLACK DIRT; MIDWEST FARMER'S MARKET, INC., Elgin Community College, 1700 Spartan Dr., Elgin IL 60123-7193, phone (847)888-7995, fax (847)888-7995, founded 1981, poetry editor Steve Sherrill.

● This publication has received numerous Illinois Arts Council Literary Awards and poetry published here has also been included in *The Best American Poetry 1996*.

Magazine Needs: *Black Dirt* is a biannual seeking high quality poems. They have published poetry by Kenneth Pobo, Kristy Nielsen, Allan Peterson, William Aiken, Brian Cochran and James Doyle. *BD* is 80-150 pgs., digest-sized, perfect-bound with card cover. They receive about 1,000 submissions/year, of which they use 40-50, have a 6-month backlog. Circulation 850 for 250 subscribers, of which 25 are libraries. Sample: $4.50 plus $1 p&h.

How to Submit: Submit 4-6 poems at a time, typed. No simultaneous submissions. Reads submissions September through November and March through May only. Reports in 1-2 months. Pays 2 copies plus 1-year subscription. Acquires one-time rights.

◐ BLACK MOON: POETRY OF IMAGINATION, 233 Northway Rd., Reisterstown MD 21136, fax (410)833-9362, founded 1994, contact Alan Britt.

Magazine Needs: *Black Moon* appears annually in January and publishes the "most imaginative, outspoken poetry available. Experimental poetry and essays welcome." They have published poetry by Colette Inez, Marjorie Agosín, Duane Locke, Louis Simpson, Paul B. Roth, Donald Ryburn and Silvia Scheibli. As a sample the editor selected these lines from "The Apache Harp" by Steve Barfield:

> Draping a twilight's blue limb/a ghost of a jade mountain lion/screams/trying to remove the moon/
> from his mouth.

Black Moon is about 224 pgs., 6×9, professionally printed and perfect-bound, with glossy card cover, ads. They accept 10% of work received. Press run is 4,000 for 200 subscribers of which 20 are libraries, 3,500 shelf sales. Single copy: $8.95. Sample: $10.70. "Read sample copy before submitting."

How to Submit: No previously published poems; simultaneous submissions OK. Cover letter preferred. Time between acceptance and publication is 6-12 months. "Some poems are accepted by various consultants for *Black Moon.*" Often comments on rejections. Reports in 1-3 months. Pays 1 copy. Does not acquire rights, however, "we would like to be recognized for having published the piece."

Advice: They say, "We would like to see more submissions that reflect political and social consciousness. Surreal, deep-image, immanentist poetry welcome."

◖ BLACK SPRING PRESS; BLACK SPRING REVIEW, 61-36 160th St., Flushing NY 11365, founded 1997, editor/publisher John Gallo.

Magazine Needs: *Black Spring Review* is published 2 times a year (June and December). "We are seeing poetry from two different camps: Those who use poetry as a form of expression and those who use poetry as a craft. We prefer poetry as expression. Don't be afraid to let it all hang out. Bleed all over the page. Make the reader feel what you feel. No 'Sword & Sorcery'/Hallmark type poems." They have published poetry by Linda La Porte, Ana Christy, A.D. Winans, Frank Lima, Raymond Mason and Catfish McDaris. As a sample the editor selected these lines from "Dada" by Laura Joy Lustig:

> best/painters/blind/poets—/mute.

The editor says *BSR* is approximately 80 pgs., 8½×5½, perfect-bound, cardstock cover. They receive about 300 poems a year, uses about 30%. Press run is 100 for 40 subscribers. Singly copy: $10; subscription: $20/year. Make checks payable to John Gallo.

How to Submit: Submit 5-6 poems at a time. Previously published poems and simultaneous submissions OK. Cover letter required. "Please ensure that name and address appears on each page." Time between acceptance and publication is about 3-6 months. Often comments on rejections. Send SASE for guidelines and upcoming themes. Reports in 2-4 weeks. Pays 1 copy.

Book/Chapbook Needs & How to Submit: Black Spring Press wants "strong, emotional writing that isn't afraid to be bold, hard and risky" and publishes 5 paperbacks and 2-4 chapbooks/year. "We also publish broadsides by individual poets." They have published *Bloody and Living* by Ed Galing, *Wounded Heart, Naked Soul* by Ralph Haselmann Jr., and *Suck Out the Marrow of Life* by Linda La Porte. Chapbooks are usually 40 pgs., 5½×8½, photocopied and saddle-stapled with card stock cover. Query first, with a few sample poems and a cover letter with brief bio and publication credits. *However, books and chapbooks are usually solicited.* "We do offer co-op publishing of books and chapbooks. Write for details." Replies to queries and mss in 2 weeks. Pays 35 author's copies (out of a press run of 100). Write to obtain sample books or chapbooks.

Advice: The editor says, "We are seeing a lot of strong writing from younger poets. We encourage younger poets to submit. Although we do publish any great writing from writers of all ages, we suggest you disregard the workshop mentality and follow your guts. Also, a lot of the current literary scene is too hung up on the subjective notion that 'good writing' comes out of the universities. The underground scene is a perfect antidote to this, but they too can have literary pretensions. Be true to yourself and be confident. Remember, editors are not gods."

⊘ BLACK THISTLE PRESS, 491 Broadway 6th Floor, New York NY 10012, phone (212)219-1898, fax (212)431-6044, e-mail bthistle@netcom.com, website http://www.blackthistlepress.com, founded 1990, publisher Ms. Hollis Melton. "We are no longer accepting submissions because we are not publishing new projects at this time."

◉ BLACK TIE PRESS, P.O. Box 440004, Houston TX 77244-0004, fax (713)789-5119, founded 1986, publisher and editor Peter Gravis.

Book/Chapbook Needs: "Black Tie Press is committed to publishing innovative, distinctive and engaging writing. We publish books; we are not a magazine or literary journal. We are not like the major Eastern presses, university presses or other small presses in poetic disposition. To get a feel for our publishing attitude, we urge you to buy one or more of our publications before submitting. Prefer the exotic, the surreal, the sensual—work that provokes, shocks . . . work that continues to resonate long after being read. Surprise us." They do not want "rhyme or fixed forms, unless remarkably well done. No nature, animal, religious, or pet themes." They have published poetry by Steve Wilson, Guy Beining, Laura Ryder, Donald Rawley, Harry Burrus and Jenny Kelly. As a sample the editor selected these lines from "Late November, Los Angeles" in *Steaming* by Donald Rawley:

> In this rubbed dusk,/the false fall sky/silvers itself/into a pale, nude witch,/a sun of mother's cologne,/
> and a neck of distanced chill

Sample: $8.

How to Submit: "We have work we want to publish, hence, unsolicited material is not encouraged. However, we will read and consider material from committed, serious writers as time permits. Query with four sample poems. Write, do not call about material. No reply without SASE." Cover letter with bio preferred. Reports in 2-6 weeks. Always sends prepublication galleys. Author receives percent of press run.

Advice: Peter Gravis says, "Too many writers are only interested in getting published and not interested in reading or supporting good writing. Black Tie hesitates to endorse a writer who does not, in turn, promote and patronize (by actual purchases) small press publications. Once Black Tie publishes a writer, we intend to remain with that artist."

✓ ⚑ $ ◎ **BLACK WARRIOR REVIEW**, P.O. Box 862936, Tuscaloosa AL 35486-0027, phone (205)348-4518, website http://www.sa.ua.edu/usm/bwr, founded 1974, poetry editor Susan Gaslee, editor Laura Didyk.

    ● Poetry published in *BWR* has been included in the 1993 and 1997 volumes of *The Best American Poetry*.

Magazine Needs: *BWR* is a semiannual review. They have published poetry by Billy Collins, D.C. Berry, Nicole Cooley and C.D. Wright. As a sample the editor selected these lines from "The Birth of a Saint" by Bob Hicok:

> *If there's a gun in her theory of Heaven it's unloaded,/pearl-handled, graced with the feel of flesh/*
> *extending from hand to steel, the confidence/of her palm radiating to the man . . .*

BWR is 200 pgs., 6×9. Circulation is 2,000. Sample: $8.

How to Submit: Submit 3-6 poems at a time. Simultaneous submissions OK if noted. No electronic submissions. Send SASE for guidelines. Reports in 1-4 months. Pays $30-45/poem plus 2 copies. Buys first rights. Reviews books of poetry in single or multi-book format. Open to unsolicited reviews. Poets may also send books for review consideration to Christopher Chambers, editor.

Also Offers: Awards one $500 prize annually to a poet whose work appeared in either the fall or spring issue. Website includes guidelines, names of editors, poetry, and subscription information.

Advice: The editor says, "We solicit a nationally-known poet for a chapbook section. The remainder of the issue is chosen from unsolicited submissions. Many of our poets have substantial publication credits, but our decision is based simply on the quality of the work submitted."

🌐 ✓ $ ◎ **BLACKWATER PRESS (Specialized: regional)**, P.O. Box 5115, Leicester LE2 8ZD Great Britain, phone +44 01 16 223 8703, founded 1996, contact Hilary Solanki.

Book/Chapbook Needs: Blackwater Press "aims to publish poets based in the United Kingdom who have established a reputation in journals, pamphlets, etc., but who have not yet had a full collection published." The press publishes 3-4 paperbacks/year. They have published poetry by David Grubb, Robert Hamberger and Ian Parks. Books are usually about 50 pgs., 21×15cm, professionally printed and perfect-bound with soft cover.

How to Submit: Submit "enough poems for a 50- to 60-page book. Previously published poems OK, if in journals/pamphlets; no simultaneous submissions. Cover letter required. Time between acceptance and publication is 1 year. Poems are circulated to an editorial board. Replies to queries in 1 month; to mss in 2 months. Pays 10% royalties and 6 author's copies (out of a press run of 750). Obtain sample books or chapbooks by purchasing from the press.

🌐 ◎ **BLAXLAND TAN; POETRY GROUPS REGISTER**, 12 Matthews Rd., Taunton, Somerset TA1 4NH United Kingdom, phone/fax (01823)324423, founded 1985, editor J.N. Jarrett.

Book/Chapbook Needs: Blaxland Tan annually publishes the *Poetry Groups Register: How to Run a Poetry Club*, "a national directory of British poetry groups and a source of information and advice on organizing poetry events, poetry competitions and running a lively poetry group. We also publish poems, both old and new." They want "poetry with a strong rhythm which may be slow or fast, heavy or light; need not follow traditional forms. Poems should be no more than 100 lines. Work on any subject matter or in any style—the poet's own. No concrete poetry or limericks; no poetry of a philosophical, didactic nature. No Christian poetry. Poetry for three voices particularly wanted." They have published poetry by Jack Cormack, Ray Hull and Sheila Vanderstay. As a sample the editor selected his poem "Moon":

> *Missing you/black-haired gull/moon silent sliding gull/white soft white soft bright/hair night-black*
> *around you/round face*

The directory is "to be enlarged but exact size not yet determined (nor price). Expected to be at least doubled [from 75 pgs.] and will be in paperback only. No more handmade issues." They receive about 100 poems a year, accept approximately 8%. Press run depends on number of orders received

How to Submit: Submit 6 poems at a time with SASE for return of materials. Previously published poems OK; no simultaneous submissions. Submissions via fax OK. Cover letter with "mention of some magazines that have published the poet's work" preferred. No handwritten mss. Time between acceptance and publication is 1 year. Seldom comments on rejections. Reports in 2 months. Pays 1 author's copy for each poem published and £25 for three-voice poems. The directory contains staff-written reviews of books and chapbooks of poetry and magazines in about 200 words, single book format. Send books for review consideration.

Advice: The editor says, "Read as much modern poetry as you write. Have at least as many stressed syllables in a line of poetry as unstressed. Try to incorporate all the five senses plus colour in your poetry. Keep adjectives to a minimum and avoid abstract words. Give detail, not generalisations."

◎ **BLIND BEGGAR PRESS; LAMPLIGHT EDITIONS; NEW RAIN (Specialized: ethnic, anthology, children)**, P.O. Box 437, Williamsbridge Station, Bronx NY 10467, phone/fax (914)683-6792, founded 1976, literary editor Gary Johnston, business manager C.D. Grant.
Book/Chapbook Needs: Publishes work "relevant to Black and Third World people, especially women." *New Rain* is an annual anthology of such work. They want to see "quality work that shows a concern for the human condition and the condition of the world—art for people sake." They have published work by Judy D. Simmons, A.H. Reynolds, Mariah Britton, Kurt Lampkin, Rashidah Ismaili, Jose L. Garza and Carletta Wilson. *New Rain* is a 60- to 200-page book, digest-sized, finely printed, saddle-stapled or perfect-bound, with simple art, card covers. Sample: $5. They also publish about 3 collections of poetry by individuals each year, 60-100 pgs., flat-spined paperback, glossy, color cover, good printing on good paper. Sample: $5.95.
How to Submit: For either the anthology or book publication, first send sample of 5-10 poems with cover letter including biographical background, philosophy and poetic principles. Considers simultaneous submissions. Reads submissions January 15 through September 1 only. Replies to queries in 3-4 weeks, to submissions in 2-3 months. Pays copies (the number depending on the print run). Acquires all rights. Returns them "unconditionally." Willing to work out individual terms for subsidy publication. Catalog available for SASE.
Also Offers: Lamplight Editions is a subsidiary that publishes "educational materials such as children's books, manuals, greeting cards with educational material in them, etc."

◻ **BLIND MAN'S RAINBOW**, P.O. Box 1557, Erie PA 16507-0557, founded 1993, editor Melody Sherosky.
Magazine Needs: *Blind Man's Rainbow* is a quarterly publication "whose focus is to create a diverse collection of quality poetry and art." They want "all forms of poetry (Beat, rhyme, free verse, haiku, etc.), though excessively long poems are less likely to be accepted. All subject matter accepted. We look for poetry that reaches inside, captures the feeling and mood of the author." They do not want "anything graphically sexual or violent." As a sample the editor selected these lines by Kyle Still:
> My love is Kemet/(rich, brown soil)/for your feelings,/thoughts, and/hands/to root themselves in,/as
> everyone else/walks on top of us/and says, "oh,/this could make/a lovely garden."
Blind Man's Rainbow is 20-24 pgs., 8½×11, photocopied and side-stapled, paper cover with art, line drawings inside. They receive about 750 poems a month. Subscription: $10 US, $14 foreign. Sample: $3 US, $4 foreign. Make checks payable to Melody Sherosky.
How to Submit: Submit 2-10 poems at a time with name and address on each poem. Include SASE. Previously published poems and simultaneous submissions OK, "but it is nice to let us know." Cover letter preferred. "Submissions only returned if requested and with adequate postage." Time between acceptance and publication is 1-6 months. Often comments on rejections. Send SASE for guidelines. Reports in 2-3 months. Pays 1 copy. Acquires one-time rights.

🅽 $ ◎ **BLINDSKILLS, INC.; DIALOGUE MAGAZINE (Specialized: blind or visually impaired)**, P.O. Box 5181, Salem OR 97304-0181, phone (800)860-4224 or (503)581-4224, fax (503)581-0178, e-mail blindskl@teleport.com, website http://www.teleport.com/~blindskl, founded 1963, editor Carol M. McCarl, assistant editor Richard L. Belgard.
Magazine Needs: *Dialogue*, a world of ideas for visually impaired people of all ages, appears quarterly and publishes "interviews of interest or assistance to newly blind and other visually impaired persons, examples of career and leisure experiences, fiction, humor and poetry. Material that is religious, controversial, political or contains explicit sex, is not acceptable. We are eager to find new poets. Our readers enjoy traditional forms of poetry such as blank verse and free verse. Submit one poem to a page, complete with title, date, name and address of author. Poems may mention a supreme being, but will not be accepted if their theme or nature is religious." *Dialogue* is published in four formats: braille, large print, 4-track cassette tape and IBM-compatible diskette. The large print format is about 150 pgs., 8½×11, neatly printed and spiral-bound with colored paper cover. Subscription (4 issues): $28 for legally blind readers, $40 for not legally blind readers. Sample: $6 for blind or visually impaired readers. "Please indicate preferred format."
How to Submit: Submit up to 5 poems at a time. Line length for poetry is 20 maximum. No previously published poems or simultaneous submissions. Disk submissions OK. "Material should be submitted on a low-density IBM-compatible diskette in WordPerfect format. Include a hard copy and a SASE if you would like your disk returned. If you do not have a computer, material may also be submitted in typed or brailled form." Receipt of ms acknowledged via postcards. SASE required for return of rejected material. Deadlines: January 1 (Spring issue), April 1 (Summer issue), July 1 (Fall issue), October 1 (Winter issue). Always comments on rejections. Send SASE for guidelines or obtain via website. Reports in 1-2 months. Pays $10-15 for poetry plus 1 copy. Buys all rights "with a generous reprint policy."

◙ **BLOOD AND FIRE REVIEW**, P.O. Box 89, Cassville GA 30123-0089, e-mail vgilreath@yahoo.com, founded 1996, editor Valerie Gilreath.
Magazine Needs: *Blood and Fire* is a biannual (November and May) and "provides an outlet for quality poetry and short fiction. Contains mostly poetry with usually one short story per issue." They want "poetry that speaks from experience, but is concise with a strong sense of imagery. No limit on length, subject matter or style." No epic poetry or sentimental Hallmark verse. They have published poetry by Mildred Greear and Anselm Brocki. As a sample the editor selected these lines from "My Mother at Seventy Nine" by Lyn Lifshin:

her dark eyes losing their/mahogany. Someone in the hollow/of her cheeks whispers the night/aid with an accent is a murderer,/a monster and she hisses her out/of the room, . . .

BFR is 40-50 pgs., digest-sized, attractively printed and saddle-stapled with 2- or 3-color card cover. No artwork. They receive about 1,300 poems a year, accept approximately 5%. Press run is 75 for 25 subscribers, 20-25 shelf sales. Subscription: $8.50. Sample: $4.50. Make checks payable to Valerie Gilreath, *BFR*.

How to Submit: Submit 5 poems at a time. Include SASE. "Submissions without a SASE will not read." No previously published poems; simultaneous submissions OK. Cover letter preferred, "include a bio that can be used if work is accepted. No electronic submissions." Time between acceptance and publication is "no longer than 7 months, usually sooner." Seldom comments on rejections. Send SASE for guidelines. Reports in 8-10 weeks. Pays 1 copy and a discount on additional copies. Acquires first rights.

Also Offers: Sponsors annual contest. 1st, 2nd and 3rd Place winners receive publication in May issue, 3 free issues and $50, $25 and $10 respectively. Reading fee: $5/3 poems, $3/1 poem. Line length for poems is 100 maximum. Mark envelope "Contest Entry." Send SASE for guidelines.

Advice: The editor says, "We use a lot of free verse, but we like to see forms as well when they are done right. Just send us your best. Also, we do provide guidelines, but my advice is just to go ahead and submit or buy a sample instead."

◐ ◎ BLUE COLLAR REVIEW; PARTISAN PRESS; WORKING PEOPLE'S POETRY COMPETI-TION (Specialized: political, social issues), P.O. Box 11417, Norfolk VA 23517, phone (757)627-0952, e-mail partisan@juno.com, *BCR* founded 1997, Partisan Press founded 1993, editor A. Markowitz, co-editor Mary Franke.

Magazine Needs: *Blue Collar Review* (*Journal of Progressive Working Class Literature*) is published quarterly and contains poetry, short stories and illustrations "reflecting the working class experience, a broad range from the personal to the societal. Our purpose is to promote and expand working class literature and an awareness of the connections between workers of all occupations. Also to inspire 'common' people's creativity and latent talent." They want "writing of high quality which reflects the working class experience from delicate internal awareness to the militant. We accept a broad range of style and focus—but are generally progressive, political/social. Nothing racist, sexist-misogynist, right wing or overly religious. No overly personal or confessional, abstract 'New Yorker' type poetry. No simple beginners rhyme or verse." They have published poetry by Katherine Arnoldi, Robert Edwards, Sonia Sanchez and Jay Griswold. As a sample the editor selected these lines from "Over There" by Robert Edwards:

> *And I want us to arise/and go now, together/leaving our chains in the sea,/laughing on our way to*
> *that place/we have hunted since the first money drew blood.//Sometimes you can see it from here,/in*
> *the darkest angry eyes.*

BCR is 46-60 pgs., 8½×5½, offset printed or photocopied and saddle-stitched with colored card cover, includes b&w photos and drawings, also includes literary and political ads. They receive hundreds of poems a year, accept approximately 30%. Press run is 350 for 200 subscribers of which 6 are libraries, 50 shelf sales. Subscription: $10/year. Sample: $5. Make checks payable to A. Markowitz (*BCR*).

How to Submit: Submit up to 4 poems at a time. Previously published poems and simultaneous submissions OK. No e-mail submissions. Cover letter preferred. "We prefer poems typed as they should be published with author's name on each poem." Time between acceptance and publication is 3-9 months. Poems are reviewed by editor and co-editor. Seldom comments on rejections. Reports in 3 months. Sometimes sends prepublication galleys. Pays 1-3 copies. Reviews books and chapbooks of poetry and other magazines in 750 words, single or multi-book format. Open to unsolicited reviews. Poets may also send books for review consideration.

Book/Chapbook Needs & How to Submit: Partisan Press looks for "poetry of power that reflects a working class consciousness and which moves us forward as a society. Must be good writing—not didactic screed." They publish 5 chapbooks/year. Chapbooks are usually 26-50 pgs., 5½×8½, offset printed and saddle-stitched with card or glossy colored cover. "Send 6-10 poems (minimum) for consideration, except for long narrative poetry—send what you have with cover letter and SASE." No requirements for consideration, "but being published in the *Blue Collar Review* or subscribing helps." Replies to queries in 1-2 months. Pays 40 author's copies (out of a press run of 100). Obtain sample chapbooks by sending $5/book with request.

Also Offers: Sponsors the Working People's Poetry Competition. Entry fee: $15 per entry. Prize: $100 and 1-year subscription. Deadline: May 1. Winner announced in Summer issue. "Include cover letter with entry and make check payable to A. Markowitz."

Advice: The editors say, "Don't be afraid to try. We want to encourage beginners. Read a variety of poetry and find your own voice. Write about reality, what moves you. There is a lot of posturing and stylistic cubbyholing in the literary scene—it's all just opinions, be honest, write from the guts and try not to get stuck in one pattern or style."

☑ ▣ ◐ BLUE INK PRESS, P.O. Box 21037, Columbus Circle Station, New York NY 10023, e-mail blueink@netzero.net, website http://www.Geocities.com/soho/nook/7285/index.html, founded 1996, publisher/editor Lisa Zuckerman.

Magazine Needs: *Blue Ink Press* is a webzine published annually in the spring. They want "poems that have a certain something, an unexplainable quality that makes them 'a poem.' Depressing, dark poetry OK." They do not want "rhyming poems, Hallmark sounding verse, book-length poems. No bird poems." They have published poetry by Phebe Davidson, Alan Elyshevitz, Alice Fogel, James Healy, Mary Beth Kosich, Mary McLaughlin Slechta, Anne Spollen and R.S. Nelson. As a sample, the editor selected these lines from "Rescuers" by James Healy:

> As the day grew on and we became practiced/In the ways of hiding and discovery/The numbers grew
> and you noticed/Not all starfish needed saving. Some were very/Content in tidal pools under stones
> patiently/Waiting for the inevitable return of the sea.

How to Submit: Submit any number of poems with SASE. "All poetry should be typed." Previously published poems not preferred. Simultaneous submissions OK. "Cover letters, although sometimes interesting, are not necessary." Seldom comments on rejections. Send SASE for guidelines. Reports in a few days to 1 year. Authors retain all rights to their work.

⬤ BLUE LIGHT PRESS; THE BLUE LIGHT POETRY PRIZE AND CHAPBOOK CONTEST, P.O. Box 642, Fairfield IA 52556, phone (515)472-7882, founded 1988, chief editor Diane Frank.
Book/Chapbook Needs: Publishes 2 paperbacks, 3 chapbooks/year. "We like poems that are imagistic, emotionally honest and uplifting, where the writer pushes through the imagery to a deeper level of insight and understanding. No rhymed poetry." They have published poetry by Rustin Larson, Viktor Tichy, Tom Centolella and Meg Fitz-Randolph. As a sample the editor selected these lines from "Seven Messages" from *Collecting Moon Coins* by Diane Averill:

> This letter may follow you/when you leave Russia for France/the way a peony petal floats a current,/
> or light from an exploding star travels/to Earth . . .

That book is 88 pgs., digest-sized, professionally printed and flat-spined with elegant matte card cover, includes woodcuts by Molly Bellman: $12 plus $1.50 p&h. They have also published 3 anthologies of Iowa poets.
How to Submit: Send SASE for submission deadlines. They have an editorial board, and "work in person with local poets, have an ongoing poetry workshop, give classes, and will edit/critique poems by mail—$30 for 4-5 poems."
Also Offers: Sponsors The Blue Light Poetry Prize and Chapbook Contest. "The winner will be published by Blue Light Press, receive a $100 honorarium and 50 copies of his or her book, which can be sold for $8 each, for a total of $500. We will also announce the winner in *Poets & Writers*." Submit ms of 10-24 pages, typed or printed with a laser or inkjet printer, between March 1, 1999 and May 1, 2000. Reading fee: $10. Make checks payable to Blue Light Press. Include SASE. No ms will be returned without a SASE. Winner will be announced on or before September 1, 2000, and the book will be published in November or December, 2000. Send SASE for more information.

✔ ⬤ ◎ BLUE MESA REVIEW (Specialized: themes), Dept. of English, Humanities Bldg. #217, University of New Mexico, Albuquerque NM 87131-1106, phone (505)277-6155, fax (505)277-5573, e-mail bluemesa@unm.edu, website http://www.unm.edu/~english/bluemesa/, founded 1989 by Rudolfo Anaya, managing editor Elise McHugh.
Magazine Needs: *Blue Mesa* is an annual review of poetry, short fiction, creative essays and book reviews. They want "all kinds of free, organic verse; poems of place encouraged. Limits: four poems or six pages of poetry; one story; one essay. We accept theoretical essays as well as fiction, poetry, nonfiction and book reviews." They have published poetry by Virgil Suarez, David Axelrod and Brian Swann. As a sample they selected these lines from "Que Milagro" by Melissa Flores:

> a poco piensas que you can hold/back the swelling tide with one hand/leading the pledge of allegiance
> with the other/then you believe/in the power la fuerza/of miracles

BMR is about 250 pgs., 6×9, professionally printed and flat-spined with glossy cover, photos and graphics. This hefty publication includes a number of long poems—several spanning 3 pages. They receive about 1,000 poems a year, accept 10% or less. Press run is 1,000 for 600 shelf sales. Single copy: $10. Sample: $12.
How to Submit: "Please submit two copies of everything with your name, address and telephone number on each page. Fax numbers and e-mail addresses are also appreciated." No previously published poems or simultaneous submissions. No electronic submissions. Cover letter required. Accepts mss from July 1 through October 1 only. Poems are then passed among readers and voted on. Publishes special theme sections. Send SASE for upcoming themes. Reports on mss by mid-December to mid-January. Pays 2 copies. Reviews books of poetry and fiction. Open to unsolicited reviews. Poets may also send books for review consideration.

$ ◎ BLUE MOUNTAIN ARTS, INC. (Specialized: greeting cards), Dept. PM, P.O. Box 1007, Boulder CO 80306-1007, e-mail bma@rmi.net, website http://www.bluemountainarts.com, founded 1971, contact editorial staff.
Book/Chapbook Needs: Blue Mountain Arts is a publisher of greeting cards, calendars, prints and mugs. They are looking for poems, prose and lyrics ("usually nonrhyming") appropriate for publication on greeting cards and in poetry anthologies. "Poems should reflect a message, feeling or sentiment that one person would want to share with another. We'd like to receive creative, original submissions about love relationships, family members, friendships, philosophies and any other aspect of life. Poems and writings for specific holidays (Christmas, Valentine's Day, etc.) and special occasions, such as graduation, anniversary and get well, are also considered. Only a small portion of the material we receive is selected each year and the review process can be lengthy, but be assured every manuscript is given serious consideration."

How to Submit: Submissions must be typewritten, 1 poem/page or sent via e-mail. Enclose SASE if you want your work returned. Simultaneous submissions "discouraged but OK with notification." Submit seasonal material at least 4 months in advance. Send SASE for guidelines or request via e-mail. Reports in 3-6 months. Pays $200/poem for the worldwide, exclusive right, $25/poem for one-time use in an anthology.

Advice: They advise, "We strongly suggest that you familiarize yourself with our products before submitting material, although we caution you not to study them too hard. We do not need more poems that sound like something we've already published. Overall, we're looking for poetry that expresses real emotions and feelings."

☑ ◯ **BLUE SATELLITE; THE SACRED BEVERAGE PRESS**, P.O. Box 10312, Burbank CA 91510-0312, fax (818)780-1912, e-mail sacredbev@aol.com, website http://www.sacredbeverage.com, founded 1994, editors/publishers Amélie Frank and Matthew Niblock.

 • In 1996 and 1998, *Blue Satellite* was voted "favorite SoCal literary magazine."

Magazine Needs: *Blue Satellite* appears twice a year (February and September) and "publishes the best quality poetry to support and promote new and returning talent." They want any style, subject matter or length. "If we see the word 'empower' in any form, we'll trash the manuscripts on the spot." They have published poetry by Diane DiPrima, Laurel Ann Bogen, Marc Olmsted, Ellyn Maybe, Scott Wannberg, Viggo Mortensen and S.A. Griffin. As a sample the editor selected this poem "Five Questions" by Jamie O'Halloran:

> There is a kiss behind the mirror./See its silver tongue?//There is a kiss under the pillow./See the
> smoke?

Blue Satellite is 60-100 pgs., 5½ × 8½, saddle-stitched with light card cover, graphics limited to cover title, no ads. They receive about 1,000 poems a year, accept approximately 5%. Press run is 250 for 25 subscribers of which 5 are libraries, 100 shelf sales; 50 distributed free to authors, reviewers. Subscription: $25 for 2 years. Sample: $7. Make checks payable to The Sacred Beverage Press.

How to Submit: Submit 5 poems at a time. No previously published poems or simultaneous submissions. "Please include name and address on each page." Cover letter preferred. "We ask for a SASE with mailed submissions and require a 25-word bio. If we publish an author's work and don't get a bio, we make one up!" E-mail and fax submissions OK. "Standard ASCII .txt files, please. OK to paste into body of e-mail, too." Reads submissions March 15 through July 15 for fall issues; October 15 through December 15 for spring issues. Time between acceptance and publication is 2 months. Always comments on rejections. Send SASE for guidelines or obtain via e-mail. Reports "as soon as publication reading date is set and can be announced in acceptance or rejection letter." Pays 1 copy. Acquires first North American serial rights.

Book/Chapbook Needs & How to Submit: The Sacred Beverage Press "publishes deserving (and often unrecognized) talents." They publish paperbacks and chapbooks on an occasional basis. They have published *Chasing Fires* by Jeanette Clough; *Mowing Fargo* by Rick Lupert; and *The Apocalyptic Kid* by Erica Erdman. Books are usually 100 pgs., trade size, offset-printed, perfect-bound with 2-color covers, illustrations and photos. "Queries are welcome in the form of sample poems (5 maximum), but we tend to approach authors whose work we have known for some time." Replies to queries and mss in 2-3 months. Pays 25 author's copies (out of a press run of about 300). "We don't have a typical press run." Obtain sample books or chapbooks by sending SASE for backlist.

◯ ◎ **THE BLUE SKUNK COMPANION (Specialized: regional)**, P.O. Box 8400, MSU 59, Mankato MN 56002-8400, phone (507)625-7176, founded 1994, co-editors Scott Welvaert and Evelyn Fielding.

Magazine Needs: *The Blue Skunk Companion* is the publication of The Blue Skunk Society, the official student organization of Mankato State University. *Blue Skunk* is a biannual publishing poetry, fiction, nonfiction, essays and art by emerging and veteran writers from Minnesota. They want "any length of poetry utilizing language that creates images inside the reader's head. We don't want poetry that overuses abstractions and 'poet's language.'" They have published poetry by Angelica Kauti, Leo Dangel, Susan Shulka and Jen Studer. As a sample the editor selected these lines from "Note Found Inside a Barrel" by Philip Dacey:

> But I will set that word,/that coffin-boat, floating/last home, upon some water/that will take it and its/
> voluble captain//up and down and around/some bend, a rudderless thing,/whirl it till language itself/
> dizzies, becomes its own/rapids, its own falls.

BSC is 35-45 pgs., 8½ × 11, attractively printed, saddle-stapled with glossy cover, b&w line art, sketches, drawings. They receive about 100 poems a year, accept approximately 20%. Press run is 500-1,000 for 100 subscribers of which 12 are libraries, 200 shelf sales. Single copy: $5; subscription: $9. Sample: $4. Make checks payable to The Blue Skunk Society Inc.

How to Submit: Submit 4-6 poems at a time. No previously published poems; simultaneous submissions OK. Cover letter required. Include name and address on each poem. Submission deadlines: June 1 (summer), December 1 (winter). Time between acceptance and publication is 6 months. Poems are circulated to an editorial board.

THE SUBJECT INDEX, located at the back of this book, can help you select markets for your work. It lists those publishers whose poetry interests are specialized ◎ .

"Our staff comments, critiques and votes on each piece of poetry and fiction." Always comments on rejections. Send SASE for guidelines. Reports in 1-2 months. Sometimes sends prepublication galleys. Pays 1 copy. Acquires first rights.

Advice: The editors say, "We like to see poetry and prose inspired by life, not other literature or styles/periods. The author's voice is best when it's a 'human being' and not a 'writer.'"

BLUE UNICORN, A TRIQUARTERLY OF POETRY; BLUE UNICORN POETRY CONTEST (Specialized: translations), 22 Avon Rd., Kensington CA 94707, phone (510)526-8439, founded 1977, poetry editors Ruth G. Iodice, Martha E. Bosworth and Fred Ostrander.

Magazine Needs: *Blue Unicorn* wants "well-crafted poetry of all kinds, in form or free verse, as well as expert translations on any subject matter. We shun the trite or inane, the soft-centered, the contrived poem. Shorter poems have more chance with us because of limited space." They have published poetry by James Applewhite, Kim Cushman, Charles Edward Eaton, Patrick Worth Gray, Joan LaBombard, James Schevill, John Tagliabue and Gail White. As a sample the editors selected this poem, "White Pages" by Charles Edward Eaton:

> What is more subtle than a book of white?—/All the passions written down in black, the print elite:/
> The wings are folded now, will not take flight.//We come at last to some pure sense of testament:/It is
> all in the book from early start to laggard finish,/All except some final thing you may have meant.//
> On the table, dahlias, pink and glorious, call for sequel./When the letter was folded, sealed, something
> was left out—/was it more than what was said or merely equal?

Blue Unicorn is "distinguished by its fastidious editing, both with regard to contents and format." It is 56 pgs., narrow digest-sized, finely printed, saddle-stapled, with some art. It features 40-50 poems in each issue, all styles, with the focus on excellence and accessibility. They receive over 35,000 submissions a year, use about 200, have a year's backlog. Sample: $5.

How to Submit: Submit 3-5 typed poems on 8½×11 paper. No simultaneous submissions or previously published poems. "Cover letter OK, but will not affect our selection." Send SASE for guidelines. Reports in 1-3 months (generally within 6 weeks), sometimes with personal comment. Pays 1 copy.

Also Offers: They sponsor an annual contest with small entry fee, with prizes of $150, $75, $50 and sometimes special awards, distinguished poets as judges, publication of 3 top poems and 6 honorable mentions in the magazine. Entry fee: $6 for first poem, $3 for others to a maximum of 5. Write for current guidelines. Criticism occasionally offered.

Advice: The editors add, "We would advise beginning poets to read and study poetry—both poets of the past and of the present; concentrate on technique; and discipline yourself by learning forms before trying to do without them. When your poem is crafted and ready for publication, study your markets and then send whatever of your work seems to be compatible with the magazine you are submitting to."

BLUE VIOLIN (Specialized: form/style), P.O. Box 1175, Humble TX 77347-1175, founded 1995, editor Mary Agnes Dalrymple.

Magazine Needs: *BV* is an annual publication of free verse poetry (month of publication varies). The editor wants "free verse poetry only, no longer than 60 lines. Shorter poems have a better chance of being accepted. I tend to select poems that are drawn from life experiences but will consider any well written poem. Send your best work. Submissions are read and considered year-round." As a sample the editor selected these lines from "Church Supper Marriage" by Jennifer B. MacPherson:

> We listen to the clock,/beating hope from the future/with its tiny hands,/rolling piecrusts/which all look
> the same.

Blue Violin is 40 pgs. (including cover), digest-sized, neatly printed and saddle-stapled with colored card cover and graphics done by the editor. She receives about 5,000 poems a year, accepts 30-40. Press run is 100-200. Subscription: $10. Sample: $5. "The purchase of a sample copy is helpful to the editor and to submitting poets who need to know if *Blue Violin* is a good market for their work."

How to Submit: Submit 3-7 poems at a time, typed 1 to a page, name and address on each. "Please include SASE with proper postage." Previously published poems and simultaneous submissions OK. Cover letter and letter-sized envelope preferred. Time between acceptance and publication is 6-12 months. Often comments on rejections. Reports in 2-4 weeks. "Poets who are accepted receive a free copy of the issue in which their poem appears. Patron donations are accepted (and greatly appreciated). Patrons receive a free copy and are named in subsequent issues. These funds help pay printing and postage costs."

BLUELINE (Specialized: regional), Dept. PM, English Dept., Potsdam College, Potsdam NY 13676, fax (315)267-2043, e-mail blueline@potsdam.edu, founded 1979, editor-in-chief Rick Henry, and an editorial board.

Magazine Needs: *Blueline* "is an annual literary magazine dedicated to prose and poetry about the Adirondacks and other regions similar in geography and spirit." They want "clear, concrete poetry pertinent to the countryside and its people. It must go beyond mere description, however. We prefer a realistic to a romantic view. We do not want to see sentimental or extremely experimental poetry." They usually use poems of 75 lines or fewer, though "occasionally we publish longer poems" on "nature in general, Adirondack Mountains in particular. Form may vary, can be traditional or contemporary." They have published poetry by Phillip Booth, George Drew, Eric Ormsby, L.M. Rosenberg, John Unterecker, Lloyd Van Brunt, Laurence Josephs, Maurice Kenny and Nancy L.

Nielsen. *Blueline* is 200 pgs., 6×9, with 90 pgs. of poetry in each issue. Circulation is 600. Sample copies: $4 for back issues.

How to Submit: Submit 3 poems at a time. Include short bio. No simultaneous submissions. Submit September 1 through November 30 only. Occasionally comments on rejections. Send SASE for guidelines or request via e-mail. Reports in 2-10 weeks. Pays 1 copy. Acquires first North American serial rights. Reviews books of poetry in 500-750 words, single or multi-book format.

Advice: "We are interested in both beginning and established poets whose poems evoke universal themes in nature and show human interaction with the natural world. We look for thoughtful craftsmanship rather than stylistic trickery."

☐ ◎ BLUSTER; BLUSTER JR. (Specialized: children/teen), P.O. Box 2639, Quincy MA 02269, e-mail sqirrel@ix.netcom.com, website http://www.tekntype.com/bluster, founded 1997, editors Ian Alexx, Paul D'Espinosa, Mike Dubson and Chris Pinney.

Magazine Needs: *Bluster* is published 2 times a year "to provide a forum for poets, essayists, short story writers, artists, etc. We do publish well known poets but are especially interested in publishing talented but unheralded writers. We have no formal writers' guidelines, but are more likely to publish poems which are two pages or less in length." No Hallmark verse. As for a sample poem the editors say, "We publish such a diversity of poetry that it would be impossible to give a representative sample." *Bluster* is 50 pgs., 8½×11, digitally published and flat-spined with card cover with b&w line drawing, includes b&w art. They receive several hundreds of poems a year, accept approximately 10%. Press run is hundreds for dozens of subscribers. Single copy: $5. Sample: $6.50.

How to Submit: Submit 3 poems at a time. Previously published poems and simultaneous submissions OK. Brief cover letter preferred. Time between acceptance and publication is 1 month. Poems are circulated to an editorial board. "All four editors read each submission and consequently make decisions based on discussion." Seldom comments on rejections. Publishes theme issues occasionally. Reports in 6-8 weeks. "We publish only twice annually, so please expect delays in response time." Pays 1 copy. Acquires one-time rights.

Also Offers: Publishes *Bluster Jr.*, a poetry journal exclusively for kids (ages 5-15).

Advice: The editor says, "The only trick is work."

Ⓜ BOA EDITIONS, LTD., 260 East Ave., Rochester NY 14604, phone (716)546-3410, e-mail boaedit@fronti ernet.net, founded 1976, poetry editor Thom Ward. They have published some of the major American poets, such as W.D. Snodgrass, John Logan, Isabella Gardner, Richard Wilbur and Lucille Clifton, and they publish introductions by major poets of those less well-known. For example, Gerald Stern wrote the foreword for Li-Young Lee's *Rose*. Send SASE for guidelines.

Ⓖ BOGG PUBLICATIONS; BOGG, 422 N. Cleveland St., Arlington VA 22201-1424, founded 1968, poetry editors John Elsberg (USA), George Cairncross (UK: 31 Belle Vue St., Filey, N. Yorkshire YO 14 9HU England) and Sheila Martindale (Canada: P.O. Box 23148, 380 Wellington St., London, Ontario NGA 5N9 Canada).

Magazine Needs: Appearing at least twice a year, *Bogg* is "a journal of contemporary writing with an Anglo-American slant. Its contents combines innovative American work with a range of writing from England and the Commonwealth. It includes poetry (to include prose poems and experimental/visual poems), very short fiction, interviews, essays on the small press scenes both in America and in England /the Commonwealth, reviews, review essays and line art. We also publish occasional free-for-postage pamphlets." The magazine uses a great deal of poetry in each issue (with several featured poets)—"poetry in all styles, with a healthy leavening of shorts (under ten lines). Prefer original voices." They accept all styles, all subject matter. "Some have even found the magazine's sense of play offensive. Overt religious and political poems have to have strong poetical merits—statement alone is not sufficient." *Bogg* started in England and in 1975 began including a supplement of American work; it now is published in the US and mixes US, Canadian, Australian and UK work with reviews of small press publications from all of those areas. They have published work by Robert Cooperman, Robert Peters, Richard Peabody and Miriam Sagan. As a sample the editors selected these lines from "Bondi Afternoons" by Australian poet Peter Bakowski:

> I hear children and seagulls squeal,/the clock leisurely licks its paws./There is rust and washing and
> tin chimneys./It's timeless, lazy, beautiful./An acoustic guitar and mist can still/break your heart.

It's about 68 pgs., typeset, saddle-stitched, in a 6×9 format that leaves enough white space to let each poem stand and breathe alone. There are about 50 pgs. of poetry/issue. They receive over 10,000 American poems/ year, use 100-150. Press run is 850 for 400 subscribers of which 20 are libraries. Single copy: $4.50; subscription: $12 for 3 issues. Sample: $3.50.

How to Submit: Submit 6 poems at a time. SASE required or material discarded ("no exceptions.") Prefer typewritten manuscripts, with author's name and address on each sheet. "We will reprint previously published material, but with a credit line to a previous publisher." No simultaneous submissions. Cover letters preferred. "They can help us get a 'feel' for the writer's intentions/slant." SASE required for return of ms. Send SASE for guidelines. Reports in 1 week. Pays 2 copies. Acquires one-time rights. Reviews books and chapbooks of poetry in 250 words, single book format. Open to unsolicited reviews. Poets may also send books to relevant editor (by region) for review consideration.

Book/Chapbook Needs & How to Submit: Their occasional pamphlets and chapbooks are by *invitation* *only*, the author receiving 25% of the print run, and you can get chapbook samples free for 6×9 SASE. "Better make it at least 2 ounces worth of postage."

Advice: John Elsberg advises, "Become familiar with a magazine before submitting to it. Long lists of previous credits irritate me. Short notes about how the writer has heard about *Bogg* or what he or she finds interesting or annoying in the magazine I read with some interest."

☑ $ 🖵 **BOMB MAGAZINE**, 594 Broadway, Suite 905, New York NY 10012, phone (212)431-3943, fax (212)431-5880, e-mail bomb@echonyc.com, website http://www.bombsite.com, founded 1981, senior editor Minna Proctor.

Magazine Needs: *Bomb* is a quarterly magazine that "encourages a dialogue among artists of various media. Experiments with form and language are encouraged. No limericks, inspirational verse, clever or greeting card styles." They have published poetry by Joe Osterhaus, Sidney Wade, David Mamet and Harold Pinter. *Bomb* is 116 pgs., perfect-bound with 4-color cover. "We receive about 100 manuscripts a month; we accept 2 or 3 every 4 months." Press run is 37,000 for 6,500 subscribers of which 1,000 are libraries. Single copy: $4.95; subscription: $18/year. Sample: $7.70.

How to Submit: No previously published poems; simultaneous submissions OK. Cover letter including name, address, telephone number and previous publications required. "Poetry should be legibly typed." Time between acceptance and publication is 4-6 months. Reports in 4 months. Pays $50. Buys first North American serial rights.

Ⓝ 🖵 **BOMBAY GIN**, The Naropa Institute, 2130 Arapahoe Ave., Boulder CO 80302, phone (303)546-3540, fax (303)546-5297, e-mail bgin@naropa.edu, website http://www.naropa.edu, founded 1974, contact the editor.

Magazine Needs: "*Bombay Gin* is the annual literary magazine of the Jack Kerouac School of Disembodied Poetics at The Naropa Institute. Produced and edited by MFA students, *Bombay Gin* publishes established poets and fiction writers alongside new writers. It has a special interest in works that push conventional literary boundaries." Recent issues have included works by Lawrence Ferlinghetti, Anne Waldman, Robert Creeley, Anselm Hollo and Eileen Myles. As a sample the editor selected these lines from "Ode to a perfect stranger and Greece" by Jeni Olin:

> too sad to wear the blue slip/tears blossomed in the highlands and on my cold feet/toenails blue in the
> dark as mandolin music/filtered through run-down apartments without bed springs

BG is 124 pgs., 6×9, professionally printed, perfect-bound with color card cover, includes art and photos. They receive about 300 poems a year, accept approximately 5%. Press run is 500, 400 shelf sales; 100 distributed free to contributors. Single copy: $10. Sample: $5.

How to Submit: "Submit 3-5 pages of poetry or 5-10 pages of prose/fiction (12 pt. Palatino or Times). Art may be submitted as slides, negatives or prints." No previously published poems or simultaneous submissions. Cover letter preferred. Disk submissions OK (Mac format). Reply with SASE only. Deadline: December 1. Submissions read December 15 through March 15. Send SASE for guidelines. Notification of acceptance/rejection: April 15. Pays 2 copies. Acquires one-time rights.

Also Offers: Website includes writer's guidelines, sample poems, readings and events.

🖵 **BORDERLANDS: TEXAS POETRY REVIEW**, % Austin Writer's League, 1501 W. Fifth St., Suite E-2, Austin TX 78703-5155, e-mail awl@eden.com, website http://www.fastair.com/borderlands, founded 1992.

Magazine Needs: *Borderlands* appears twice a year publishing "high-quality, outward-looking poetry by new and established poets, as well as brief reviews of poetry books and critical essays. Cosmopolitan in content, but particularly welcomes Texas and Southwest writers." They want "outward-looking poems that exhibit social, political, geographical, historical or spiritual awareness coupled with concise artistry. We also seek poems in two languages (one of which must be English), where the poet has written both versions. Please, no introspective work about the speaker's psyche, childhood or intimate relationships." They have published poetry by Walter McDonald, Charles Behlen, Marlys West, Naomi Shihab Nye, Lyn Lifshin and Edward Byrne. As a sample the editors selected these lines from "If There Were No Joy in This World" by Jill Alexander Essbaum:

> And if there were no joy, this thing/you love,/my body, would be just a body,/and flesh/and fear would
> suffice it, and you and I/would walk only close enough not/to touch . . .

Borderlands is 80-120 pgs., 5½×8½, offset, perfect-bound, with 4-color cover, art by local artists. They receive about 2,000 poems a year, use approximately 120. Press run is 1,000. Subscription: $17/year; $33/2 years. Sample: $10.

How to Submit: Submit 5 typed poems at a time. No previously published poems or simultaneous submissions. Include SASE (or SAE and IRCs) with sufficient postage to return poems and a response. Seldom comments on rejections. Reports in 4-6 months. Pays 1 copy. Acquires first rights. Reviews books of poetry in one page. Also uses 3- to 6-page essays on single poets and longer essays (3,500-word maximum) on contemporary poetry in some larger context (query first). Address poetry submissions to "Editors, *Borderlands*."

Also Offers: The Austin Writers' League is a state-wide group open to the general public. Founded in 1981, the purpose of the Austin Writers' League is "to provide a forum for information, support, and sharing among writers; to help members improve and market their writing skills; and to promote the interests of writers and the writing community." Currently has 1,600 members. Annual membership dues are $40. Send SASE for more information.

BORDERLINES; ANGLO-WELSH POETRY SOCIETY, Nant Y Brithyll, Llangynyw, Powys SY21 OJS United Kingdom, phone (01938)810263, founded 1977, editor Kevin Bamford, editor Dave Bingham. **Magazine Needs:** *Borderlines* is published biannually to encourage reading and writing of poetry. "We try to be open-minded and look at anything. We do not normally publish very long poems. Most poems fit on one page. No poems about poems; unshaped recitals of thoughts and/or feelings." They have published poetry by Peter Abbs, Mike Jenkins and Vuyelwa Carlin. As a sample we selected this poem, "fane" by Gigliola Millard:

> supine in the cathedral wood/summer light faint/through green-dark eaves/for the briefest of moments/
> out hands are still-/carved sinners reminded of repentant days

Borderlines is 40-48 pgs., 7 × 10, neatly printed and saddle-stapled with light card cover, art on cover only. They receive about 600 poems a year, accept approximately 16%. Press run is 200 for 100 subscribers of which 8 are libraries. Single copy: £1.50; subscription: £3, other EU countries £4, non-EU countries £5. Make checks payable to Anglo-Welsh Poetry Society.
How to Submit: Cover letter preferred. "Please write name and address on each poem sheet." Time between acceptance and publication is usually between 1-6 months. Seldom comments on rejections. Send SASE (or SAE and IRC) for guidelines. Reports in 1-6 weeks. Sometimes sends prepublication galleys. Pays 1 copy.
Also Offers: "The Anglo-Welsh Poetry Society is a group of people interested in the reading, writing and promotion of poetry, particularly in the Marches—the Anglo-Welsh border country. It is based in the border counties of Shropshire and Montgomeryshire, though there are members all over the country. A core group of members meets on the first Tuesday of the month at the Loggerheads pub in Shrewsbury. Other meetings such as readings, workshops, poetry parties are arranged at intervals over the course of the year. A monthly newsletter gives information of interest to members on events, publications, competitions and other news of the poetry world." Membership fee for AWPS is £5/year.

$ BORDIGHERA, INC.; VOICES IN ITALIAN AMERICANA; VIA FOLIOS; THE BOR-DIGHERA POETRY PRIZE; ANIELLO LAURI AWARD (Specialized: ethnic/nationality), P.O. Box 1374, Lafayette IN 47902-1374, phone (765)494-3839, fax (765)496-1700, e-mail tamburri@purdue.edu, founded 1990, editor Anthony Julian Tamburri.
Magazine Needs: *Voices in Italian Americana* (*VIA*) is "a semiannual literary and cultural review devoted to the dissemination of information concerning the contributions of and about Italian Americans to the cultural and art worlds of North America." They are open to all kinds of poetry. They have published poetry by Daniela Gioseffi, David Citino, Felix Stefanile and Dana Gioia. As a sample the editor selected these lines from "Coming To Know Empedokles" by Diane diPrima:

> A couple of millennia seems like a moment:/This song cd be planting rite of black Sicilians/in autumn
> fields behind a small house/the sounds / the colors as if/intervening greys & anglo stillness/had never
> entered.

The editor says *VIA* is about 250 pgs., 8½ × 5½, docutech printed, perfect-bound with glossy paper cover, includes art and ads. They receive about 150 poems a year, accept approximately 25%. Press run is 500 for 300 subscribers of which 50 are libraries, 50 shelf sales; 50 distributed free to contributors. Subscription: $20 individual; $15 student/senior citizen; $25 institutional; $30 foreign. Sample: $10. Make checks payable to Bordighera, Inc.
How to Submit: No previously published poems or simultaneous submissions. Cover letter required. E-mail and disk submissions OK. Reads submissions September 1 through June 30 only. Time between acceptance and publication is 3 months. Poems are circulated to an editorial board. Often comments on rejections. Publishes theme issues occasionally. Send SASE for guidelines. Reports in 4-6 weeks. Always sends prepublication galleys. Acquires all rights. Rights returned upon publication. "But in subsequent publications, poet must acknowledge first printing in *VIA*." Reviews books and chapbooks of poetry in 500-1,000 words, single book format. Open to unsolicited reviews. Poets may also send books for review consideration to Fred Gardaphé, Center for Italian Studies, State University of New York, Stony Brook NY 11794-3358.
Book/Chapbook Needs & How to Submit: Bordighera, under the imprint *VIA* Folios, publishes 5 titles/year with the print run for each paperback being 550. Books are usually 50-75 pgs., 8½ × 5½, docutech printed and perfect-bound with glossy paper cover and art. Query first, with a variety of sample poems and a cover letter with brief bio and publication credits. Replies to queries in 2 weeks; to mss in 4-6 weeks. Pays 10% royalties. Offers subsidy arrangements. Poets are required to subsidize 50% of publishing costs. "Author regains subsidy through sales with 50% royalties up to subvention paid, 10% thereafter."
Also Offers: Sponsors the Bordighera Poetry Prize, which awards book publication and $2,000, and the Aniello Lauri Award, which awards $150 plus publication in *Voices in Italian Americana*. Send SASE for contest rules.

BOREALIS PRESS; TECUMSEH PRESS LTD.; JOURNAL OF CANADIAN POETRY (Specialized: regional), Dept. PM, 9 Ashburn Dr., Nepean, Ontario K2E 6N4 Canada, phone (613)224-6837, fax (613)829-7783, e-mail borealis@istar.ca, founded 1972. They are presently not considering unsolicited submissions.
Also Offers: The *Journal* is an annual that publishes articles, reviews and criticism, not poetry. Sample: $15.95.

$ THE BOSTON PHOENIX: PHOENIX LITERARY SECTION (PLS), 126 Brookline Ave., Boston MA 02215, phone (617)536-5390, founded 1966, poetry editor Lloyd Schwartz.

● Poems published in this review have appeared in the 1992 and 1995 volumes of *The Best American Poetry*.

Magazine Needs: *TBP* is a monthly book review with one poem in almost every issue. Press run is 150,000. Single copy: $1.50.

How to Submit: Submit 1-3 poems at a time, under 50 lines each. "Please include cover letter and SASE." Reports in 1 month. Pays $50. Open to unsolicited reviews. Poets may also send books for review consideration to Susan Vollmar, book editor.

▼ $ ◙ BOSTON REVIEW, E53-407, MIT, 30 Wadsworth St., Cambridge MA 02139-4307, phone (617)253-3642, fax (617)252-1549, website http://www.polisci.mit.edu/BostonReview/, founded 1975, poetry editors Mary Jo Bang and Timothy Donnelly.

● Poetry published by this review has been included in *The Best American Poetry* (1993 and 1998 volumes).

Magazine Needs: *Boston Review* is a bimonthly tabloid format magazine of arts, culture and politics which uses about 25 poems a year, for which they receive about 2,500 submissions. "We are open to both traditional and experimental forms. What we value most is originality and a strong sense of voice." They have published poetry by Gilbert Sorrentino, Heather McHugh, John Yau, Brenda Hillman, Bill Knott and Lee Upton. Circulation is 20,000 nationally including subscriptions and newsstand sales. Single copy: $3; subscription: $15. Sample: $4.50.

How to Submit: Submit 3-5 poems at a time. Cover letter listing recent publications encouraged. Submissions and inquiries are accepted via regular mail only. They have a 6-12 month backlog. Reports in 1-3 months. Pays $40/poem plus 5 copies. Buys first serial rights. Reviews books of poetry. Only using *solicited* reviews. Publishers may send books for review consideration.

Also Offers: Sponsors an annual poetry contest. Awards publication and $1,000. Submit up to 5 unpublished poems, no more than 10 pgs. total, with postcard to acknowledge receipt. Deadline: June 15. Entry fee: $10. Send SASE for guidelines.

◙ BOTTOMFISH, De Anza College, 21250 Stevens Creek Blvd., Cupertino CA 95014, website http://laws.at c.fhda.edu/documents/bottomfish/bottomfish.html, founded 1976, editor David Denny.

Magazine Needs: This college-produced magazine appears annually in April. It has published poetry by Chitra Divakaruni, Robert Cooperman, Walter Griffin and Tom Clark. As a sample the editor selected these lines from "The Clumsy Contest" by Kurt Brown:

He was good. Real good. Mama fed him/vinegar and nettles while Papa pulled his punches—/only inches from the boy's lips—to insure/a life of stumbling and dropping things.

Bottomfish is 80 pgs., 7×8¼, well-printed on heavy stock with b&w graphics, perfect-bound. Circulation is 500, free to libraries, but $5/copy to individuals.

How to Submit: Submit 3-5 poems at a time. "Before submitting, writers are strongly urged to purchase a sample copy." Best submission times: September through December. Annual deadline: December 31. Reports in 1-6 months, depending on backlog. Include SASE for reply or return of materials. Pays 2 copies.

◯ ◎ BOUILLABAISSE (Specialized: form/style), % Alpha Beat Press, 31 Waterloo St., New Hope PA 18938-1210, phone (215)862-0299, founded 1991, editors Dave Christy and Ana Christy.

Magazine Needs: *Bouillabaisse* is a biannual using "poetry that reflects life and its ups and downs." They want "modern, Beat poetry; poetry from the streets of life—no limit. No rhythm, Christian or sweet poetry." They have published poetry by A.D. Winans, Daniel Crocker, Fielding Dawson, t.k. splake and Joseph Verrilli. As a sample the editors selected these lines by Wayne Wilkinson:

Victims of demented history./Awaiting what despite all/our rationalizing scares us silly,/This is the craziest reality of all!/The worst injustice. The final insult: Death

The editors say *Bouillabaisse* is 160 pgs., 8½×11, offset printed, saddle-stitched, with graphics. They receive 200 submissions a year, accept 40%. Press run is 500 for 350 subscribers of which 9 are libraries. Subscription: $17. Sample: $10.

How to Submit: Submit 5 poems at a time. Previously published poems and simultaneous submissions OK. Cover letter required. Always comments on rejections. Send SASE for guidelines and upcoming themes. Reports "immediately." Pays 1 copy. Reviews books of poetry in 250-500 words. Open to unsolicited reviews. Poets may also send books for review consideration.

Book/Chapbook Needs & How to Submit: They publish 2 paperbacks and 10 chapbooks/year. "We work with each individual on their project." Replies to queries "immediately," to mss within 3 weeks. Always sends prepublication galleys for chapbooks. Pays 1 copy.

Also Offers: See the listings for *Alpha Beat Soup* and *Cokefish*.

$ ◙ BOULEVARD, % editor Richard Burgin, 4579 Laclede Ave. #332, St. Louis MO 63108-2103, phone (314)361-2986, founded 1985.

Magazine Needs: *Boulevard* appears 3 times a year. "*Boulevard* strives to publish only the finest in fiction, poetry, and nonfiction (essays and interviews; we do not accept book reviews). While we frequently publish writers with previous credits, we are very interested in publishing less experienced or unpublished writers with exceptional promise. We've published everything from John Ashbery to Howard Moss to a wide variety of styles from new or lesser known poets. We're eclectic. Do not want to see poetry that is uninspired, formulaic, self-conscious, unoriginal, insipid." They have published poetry by Amy Clampitt, Molly Peacock, Jorie Graham and Mark Strand. *Boulevard* is 200 pgs., digest-sized, professionally printed, flat-spined, with glossy card cover. Their press run is 3,500 with 1,000 subscribers of which 200 are libraries. Subscription: $15. Sample: $8.

How to Submit: Submit up to 5 poems at a time. "Prefer name and number on each page. All submissions must include an SASE. Encourage cover letters but don't require them. Will consider simultaneous submissions but not previously published poems." Line length for poetry is 200 maximum. Reads submissions October 1 through April 1 only. Editor sometimes comments on rejections. Pays $25-250/poem, depending on length, plus 1 copy. Buys first-time publication and anthology rights. Open to unsolicited reviews.

Advice: Richard Burgin says, "Write from your heart as well as your head."

N ⊕ ◑ **BRANDO'S HAT; TARANTULA PUBLICATIONS**, 14 Vine St., Kersal, Salford, Manchester M7 3PG United Kingdom, phone (0161)792 4593, founded 1998, contact Sean Body.

Magazine Needs: *Brando's Hat* appears 3 times a year. They want "extremely high-quality poetry only. No restrictions on subject matter, form or style." They do not want "careless, unrhythmical, boring, unoriginal work—i.e., 90 percent of what we get." They have published poetry by Tony Curtis, Peter Sansom, Kevin Crossley-Holland and John Latham. As a sample they selected these lines from "Searching" by Gaia Holmes:

> *Night falls/like you slip into my head/I smell the scent of something late./You're curled into yourself/*
> *like paper when it burns/and a hundred black moths*

They say *Brando's Hat* is 42 pgs., A5, laser printed and saddle-stapled with color card cover. They receive about 1,300 poems a year, accept approximately 10%. Press run is 250 for 200 subscribers. Subscription: £13 Sterling. Sample: £5 Sterling. Make checks (Sterling only) payable to Tarantula Publications.

How to Submit: Submit 6 or more poems at a time. No previously published poems or simultaneous submissions. Cover letter required. "Cover letters should give brief (just a few lines) biographical details, publications, etc. Must include SAE with appropriate postage [or IRCs], otherwise discarded." Time between acceptance and publication is 3 months. Poems are circulated to an editorial board. "There are four editors (all poets). Decisions for publishing have to be unanimous." Seldom comments on rejections. Reports in 3 months or less. Pays 1 copy. Acquires first rights.

✿ ◎ **THE BREAD OF LIFE MAGAZINE (Specialized: religious)**, 209 Macnab St. N., P.O. Box 395, Hamilton, Ontario L8N 3H8 Canada, phone (905)529-4496, fax (905)529-5373, founded 1977, editor Fr. Peter Coughlin.

Magazine Needs: *The Bread of Life* is "a Catholic charismatic magazine, published bimonthly and designed to encourage spiritual growth in areas of renewal in the Catholic Church today." It includes articles, poetry and artwork. As a sample the editor selected these lines from "To Know His Love" by Margaret Larrivee:

> *In times when all is going well/on His great love we seldom dwell./It's only when we are laid low/His*
> *abundant love we start to know.//It comes in cards with loving words/get well wishes, written, heard./*
> *Calls and visits cheerfully bring/joy to my soul, my heart to sing.*

TBOL is 34 pgs., 8½×11, professionally printed and saddle-stapled with glossy paper cover, includes original artwork and photos. They receive about 50-60 poems a year, accept approximately 25%. Press run is 4,000 for subscribers only. "It's good if contributors are members of *The Bread of Life*."

How to Submit: Previously published poems and simultaneous submissions OK. Cover letter preferred. Publishes theme issues. Send SASE (or SAE with IRCs) for upcoming themes.

◑ ◎ **THE BRIAR CLIFF REVIEW (Specialized: regional)**, Briar Cliff College, 3303 Rebecca St., Sioux City IA 51104-2340, e-mail emmons@briar-cliff.edu, website http://www.briar-cliff.edu/administrative/publications/bccrevie/bcreview.htm, founded 1989, managing editor Tricia Currans-Sheehan, poetry editor Jeanne Emmons.

Magazine Needs: *The Briar Cliff Review*, appearing in April, is an attractive annual "eclectic literary and cultural magazine focusing on (but not limited to) Siouxland writers and subjects." They want "quality poetry with strong imagery; especially interested in regional, Midwestern content with tight, direct, well-wrought language. No allegorical emotional landscapes." They have published poetry by Diane Frank, Connie Wanek and Stephen Coyne. As a sample the editor selected these lines from "Sonnet to Sexual Tension" by Bill Rudolph:

> *Wasps hum above us, hovering like sin,/as though again returned from childhood springs./To this day*
> *I sit within this unease,/stirring my coffee while their jaundiced wings/spin in a whispering cloud.*

BCR is 64 pgs., 8½×11, professionally printed on 70 lb. matte paper, saddle-stapled, four-color cover on 10 pt. coated stock, b&w photos inside. They receive about 100 poems a year, accept 12. Press run is 500, all shelf sales. Sample: $9.

How to Submit: Submissions should be typewritten or letter quality, with author's name and address on the first page, with name on following pages. No previously published poems; simultaneous submissions OK. "We will assume that submissions are not simultaneous unless notified." Cover letter with short bio required. "No manuscripts returned without SASE." Reads submissions August 1 through November 1 only. Time between acceptance and publication is 5-6 months. Seldom comments on rejections. Reports in 6 months. Pays 2 copies. Acquires first serial rights.

The cover for the Spring issue of *The Briar Cliff Review* features the oil painting "Organizational Controls" by Karen Chesterman, a local artist from Sioux City, Iowa. According to editor Jeanne Emmons, the painting was selected for the cover because it intuitively echoed the magazine's aesthetic philosophy. "We like to encourage new and unpublished poets who can see the extraordinary in everyday life. The strong lines and contrasts of light and dark, and the combination of solid masses and semi-translucent areas, suggest a balance of the material and the spiritual, the ordinary and the luminous, that echoes the poetry and fiction inside." *The Briar Cliff Review* publishes about 20 poems in each issue, along with fine photos and artwork "to create unified and eye-appealing spreads."

BRICKHOUSE BOOKS, INC.; NEW POETS SERIES, INC./CHESTNUT HILLS PRESS; STONEWALL SERIES (Specialized, Stonewall only: gay/lesbian/bisexual), 541 Piccadilly Rd., Baltimore MD 21204, phone (410)828-0724, e-mail charriss@towson.edu, website http://www.towson.edu/~harriss/!bhbweds.ite/bhb.htm, founded 1970, editor/director Clarinda Harriss. NPS, along with Chestnut Hills Press and Stonewall, is now a division of BrickHouse Books.

Book/Chapbook Needs: BrickHouse and The New Poets Series, Inc. brings out first books by promising new poets. Poets who have previously had book-length mss published are not eligible. Prior publication in journals and anthologies is strongly encouraged. They want "excellent, fresh, nontrendy, literate, intelligent poems. Any form (including traditional), any style." BrickHouse Books and NPS pay 20 author's copies (out of a press run of 1,000), the sales proceeds going back into the corporation to finance the next volume. "BrickHouse has been successful in its effort to provide writers with a national distribution; in fact, The New Poets Series was named an Outstanding Small Press by the prestigious Pushcart Awards Committee, which judges some 5,000 small press publications annually." Chestnut Hills Press publishes author-subsidized books—"High quality work only, however. CHP has achieved a reputation for prestigious books, printing only the top 10% of mss CHP and NPS receive." CHP authors receive proceeds from sale of their books. The Stonewall series publishes work with a gay, lesbian or bisexual perspective. NPS/CHP has published books by Richard Fein, Donald Menaker and Gerald George. As a sample the editor selected these lines by Rane Arroyo from *The Naked Thief*:

> A Bloody Mary at midnight, my burning/mouth. You stand naked under the evening//star. I think of
> what prayer used to taste like/on my tongue. Neighbors' stereos throb on//our ceilings and floors.
> Something in me is/old tonight and needs attendance. You wish//to be captured by something, someone.
> Love,/I can't even haunt myself, tonight, tonight.

Brickhouse publishes 64-112 page works. Chapbooks: $8. Full-length books: $10.

How to Submit: Send a 50- to 55-page ms, $10 reading fee and cover letter giving publication credits and bio. Indicate if ms is to be considered for BrickHouse, NPS, CHP or Stonewall. Simultaneous submissions OK. No e-mail submissions. Cover letters should be very brief, businesslike and include an accurate list of published work. Editor sometimes comments briefly on rejections. Reports in 6 weeks to 1 year. Mss "are circulated to an editorial board of professional, publishing poets. BrickHouse is backlogged, but the best 10% of the mss it receives are automatically eligible for Chestnut Hills Press consideration," a subsidy arrangement. Send $5 and a 7×10 SASE for a sample volume.

Also Offers: Stonewall Series offers a chapbook contest whose winner is published by NPS. Send 20-30 poems with $20 entry fee, postmarked no later than August 15. Rane Arroyo's *The Naked Thief* is a recent Stonewall winner. Website features writer's guidelines, names of editors, list of in-print publications, plus sample poetry from individual books.

THE BRIDGE: A JOURNAL OF FICTION AND POETRY, 14050 Vernon St., Oak Park MI 48237, founded 1990, editor Jack Zucker, poetry editor Mitzi Alvin.

Magazine Needs: *The Bridge* appears twice a year using "exciting, largely mainstream poetry." They have published poetry by Ruth Whitman and Daniel Hughes. It is 160 pgs., digest-sized, perfect-bound. Press run is 700. Subscription: $13. Sample: $7.

How to Submit: Line length for poetry is 200 maximum. Poems are circulated to an editorial board. Three consider mss; decision made by editor and 1 special editor. Editor rarely comments at length on submissions.

Pays 2 copies. Acquires first rights. Reviews books of poetry and prose in 1-10 pgs.

BRIGHT HILL PRESS; NATIONAL POETRY BOOK COMPETITION; NATIONAL CHAP-BOOK COMPETITION, P.O. Box 193, Treadwell NY 13846, phone (607)746-7306, fax (607)746-7274, e-mail wordthurs@aol.com, founded 1992, director/editor-in-chief Bertha Rogers.
Book/Chapbook Needs: Bright Hill Press publishes 2-3 paperbacks and 1 chapbook/year through their competitions. They want "intelligent, well-crafted poetry—traditional or experimental." They have published *Blue Wolves* by Regina O'Melveny; *To Fit Your Heart into the Body* by Judith Neeld; and *Whatever Was Ripe* by William Jolliff. As a sample the director selected these lines from "The Branch" by Judith Neeld:
> This year the bud end turned/black: a thumbnail/flogged/for trusting the hammer./Useless/to paint the split./You've watched its joints go/dry, thickening/with ages-old lichen,/the knobs like signs:/queer-knuckled/angles.
Chapbooks are usually 24-36 pgs., 5½×8½, stapled-bound; full-length books are 48-64 pgs., 5½×8½, perfect-bound. Full-length poetry books: $12; chapbooks: $6; anthologies: $15-25.
How to Submit: Submit 48-64 pgs. including bio, table of contents and acknowledgments page. Poems may be previously published in journals or anthologies. No submissions via fax or e-mail. Mss will be judged blindly by nationally-known poet. Send SASE for complete guidelines. Entry fee: $15; $10 for Word Thursdays/Bright Hill Press members. Postmark deadline: September 15. Winner announced winter of the following year. Winner receives $500, publication and 25 copies. For the Chapbook Competition (poetry in odd-numbered years; fiction in even-numbered years), winner receives $100, publication and 25 copies. Submit 16-24 pgs. including bio, table of contents, acknowledgments page and title page. Poems may be previously published in journals or anthologies. Send SASE for complete guidelines. Entry fee: $9; $6 Word Thursday/Bright Hill Press members. Postmark deadline: May 31 of odd-numbered years. Winner announced in late fall. Obtain sample books or chapbooks by sending SASE for catalog.
Also Offers: Bright Hill Press also sponsors a large variety of activities throughout the year, including a bi-monthly reading series and an annual festival. Write for details.
Advice: The director says, "Revise, revise, revise! Read other poets to learn how good poetry is crafted."

$ BRILLIANT CORNERS: A JOURNAL OF JAZZ & LITERATURE (Specialized: jazz-related literature), Lycoming College, Williamsport PA 17701, phone (570)321-4279, fax (570)321-4090, e-mail feinstei@lycoming.edu, website http://www.lycoming.edu/dept/bc/bcvol1.html, founded 1996, editor Sascha Feinstein.
Magazine Needs: *Brilliant Corners*, a biannual, publishes jazz-related poetry, fiction and nonfiction. "We are open to length and form, but want work that is both passionate and well crafted—work worthy of our recent contributors. No sloppy hipster jargon or improvisatory nonsense." They have published poetry by Amiri Baraka, Jayne Cortez, Philip Levine, Colleen McElroy and Al Young. As a sample the editor selected these lines from "Rhythm Method" by Yusef Komunyakaa:
> If you can see blues/in the ocean, light & dark,/can feel worms ease through/a subterranean path/ beneath each footstep,/Baby, you got rhythm.
BC is 100 pgs., 6×9, commercially printed and perfect-bound with color card cover with original artwork, ads. They accept approximately 5% of work received. Press run is 1,800 for 200 subscribers. Subscription: $12. Sample: $7.
How to Submit: Submit 3-5 poems at a time. Previously published poems "very rarely, and only by well established poets"; no simultaneous submissions. Cover letter preferred. No e-mail or fax submissions. Reads submissions September 1 through May 15 only. Seldom comments on rejections. Reports in 2 months. Pays 2 copies. Acquires first North American serial rights. Staff reviews books of poetry. Poets may also send books for review consideration.

BRILLIANT STAR (Specialized: children, religious), Baha'i National Center, 1233 Central St., Evanston IL 60201.
Magazine Needs: *Brilliant Star* is a Baha'i bimonthly for children, appearing in a magazine-sized format. "Poems are always illustrated, so think about how your poem will look. Our readers are ages 6-12. Write for them not for yourself. We do not want to see Christmas themes in any form. If you are not familliar with the Baha'i Faith, research is encouraged." As a sample the editor selected these lines from "Which Wealth" by Susan Engle:
> Now do you think our king was sad?/No! Gold was gone, but he was glad./He'd found that love was irreplaceable/And gold, mere gold, was, well, erasable./Sometimes I wonder just how much/I would enjoy the golden touch./Would I have chosen, if I could/The gold for now, or love for good?
Sample: $3 with 9×12 SASE (sufficient postage for 5 oz.).
How to Submit: Objectives are printed in the masthead. Considers simultaneous submissions. Pays 2 copies.
Advice: The editor urges children who wish to write poetry to avoid "writing about tired subjects like 'dogs as friends' and being 'afraid of the dark.' Write about today's world in fun, exciting language. Write about a realistic fear—guns, drugs, the school dance, my ugly feet, will my parents divorce. Make your poem an engaging short story." This is also good advice for adults who wish to write children's poetry for this publication.

N ⊕ ◯ ◪ THE BROBDINGNAGIAN TIMES, 96 Albert Rd., Cork, Ireland, phone (21)311 227, founded 1996, editor Giovanni Malito.

Magazine Needs: *TBT* appears quarterly. "It's purpose and contents are international and eclectic. We wish to present a small sample of what is happening out there in the 'world' of poetry." They are open to all kinds of poetry of 40 lines or less. "Translations are very welcome. Not very partial to rhyming forms." They have published poetry by Miroslav Holub, Leonard Cirino, Albert Huffstickler and John Millet. It is 8 pgs., A3 sheet folded twice, photocopied from laser original. They receive about 200 poems a year, accept approximately 15-20%. Press run is 250 for 42 subscribers, variable shelf sales; 12 distributed free to writers' groups. Subscription: $4. Sample: $1 or postage. Make checks payable to Giovanni Malito.

How to Submit: Submit 4-8 poems at a time. Line length for poetry is 1 minimum, 40 maximum. Previously published poems and simultaneous submissions OK. Cover letter preferred. "SASE is required. If IRCs are not convenient then loose stamps for trade with Irish stamps are fine." Time between acceptance and publication is 1-3 weeks. Often comments on rejections. Publishes theme issues occasionally. Note: the theme issues appear as supplements. Send SASE for guidelines and upcoming themes. Reports in 1-3 months. Sometimes sends prepublication galleys. Pays 2 copies. Acquires one-time rights. Staff reviews books and chapbooks of poetry in 300-500 words, single book format. Send books for review consideration.

Book/Chapbook Needs & How to Submit: The Brobdingnagian Times Press is open to any type of prose and/or poetry and publishes 2-8 chapbooks/year. Chapbooks are usually "palmtop" in size, photocopied from laser original and side-stapled with slightly heavier stock colored paper, cover art only. "The palmtops are quite small. They may be one long poem (8 pages) or several (8-16) short poems (less than 6 lines) or something in between. Collections (unless haiku/senryu) must be more or less themed." Replies to queries in 1 week; to mss in 1-3 weeks. Pays 50 author's copies (out of a press run of 100). "Poets outside of Ireland are asked to cover the postage." Order sample chapbooks by sending 2 IRCs.

Also Offers: "We are also in the planning stages for a more substantial annual which is review and translations driven. The reviews are assigned and the translations appear with the originals. Each annual features two poets."

Advice: The editor says, "Nerve and verve and the willingness to edit: these are three qualities a poet must possess. Be lucid. Be imaginative. Be serious. Be funny too."

N BROODING HERON PRESS, Bookmonger Rd., Waldron Island WA 98297, founded 1984, co-publishers Sam and Sally Green.

Book/Chapbook Needs: Brooding Heron Press publishes 3 chapbooks/year. They have "no restriction other than excellence." They do not want "prose masquerading as poetry or poems written for form's sake." They have published poetry by Denise Levertov, James Laughlin and Gary Snyder.

How to Submit: "We're too backlogged to look at anything new until 2000." Query in late 1999 to determine when the press will be reading again. If open to submissions, submit complete ms of 16-20 poems; no query. Previously published poems OK; no simultaneous submissions. Cover letter required. Time between acceptance and publication varies. Seldom comments on rejections. Reports within 6 weeks. "We print 300 books per title, bound in paper and cloth. Payment is 10% of the press run. Author retains copyright." This press has received many awards for fine printing. Write for catalog to order samples.

$ ◯ ◪ BROWNOUT LABORATORIES, RD 2, Box 5, Little Falls NY 13365, founded 1994.

Book/Chapbook Needs: "Brownout Laboratories publishes works by the young intelligentsia. Though open to poetry submissions, we are not primarily a poetry (or even literary) press." They publish 1 poetry chapbook/year. "Unfortunately, we can only review poetry written in English, French, German, Spanish or Croatian/Bosnian." They have published poetry by Kurt Hemmer. Chapbooks are usually 5×8, photocopied with hand-sewn binding, 80 lb., 100% post-consumer recycled cover.

How to Submit: Previously published poems and simultaneous submissions OK. "We prefer to receive all submissions and correspondence on reused paper (or at least recycled paper printed on both sides)." Time between acceptance and publication is up to 2 months. Poems are circulated to an editorial board. Always comments on rejections. Replies to queries in up to 3 weeks; to mss in up to 1 month. Pays 20% royalties. Send SASE for a list of available publications.

Also Offers: Plans to compile an anthology of poetry and short literary pieces by women authors. Send query letter, samples and SASE for details.

◪ THE BROWNSTONE REVIEW, 335 Court St., #114, Brooklyn NY 11231, phone (718)788-6220, founded 1995, poetry editor Aaron Scharf.

Magazine Needs: *BR* appears twice a year. "We will consider poems of any length or style and addressing any theme. Formal poetry is encouraged, provided the form is used for a reason. Keep your language fresh and incantatory, your imagery vivid. No workshop poems, no greeting card verse." They have published poetry by Charles Edward Mann, Mary Kennan Herbert, John Lowery, Mark DeFoe, Elizabeth Florio and Nancy Berg. As a sample the editor selected these lines from "Renoir's Onions" by Jan Weiss:

> *He fell in love with women stacking grapes,/fell in love with all the women—young ones,/faces seamless*
> *as peaches,/and the old—gnarled like figs.//He was an outsider, drunk on the glory of it—/even death*
> *was grand—sheep from whom the guts were slit,/still hanging.//But it was the onion Renoir chose to*
> *immortalize,/the lowly onion,/abandoned on its table of simple wood,//long after the market was swept*

clean,/the voices gone.

The editor says *TBR* is 60 pgs., 7×8½, side-stapled. They receive 750-1,000 poems/year, use 30-40. Press run is 200. Single copy: $5; subscription: $10. Make checks payable to Dawson Publishing.

How to Submit: Submit 3-5 poems at a time. No previously published poems; simultaneous submissions OK. Cover letter preferred. Seldom comments on rejections. Send SASE for guidelines. Reports within 4-12 weeks. Pays 2 copies.

Advice: The editor says, "Strive to create the poetic state in others, rather than living it yourself."

◯ BRUNSWICK PUBLISHING CORPORATION, 1386 Lawrenceville Plank Rd., Lawrenceville VA 23868, phone (804)848-3865, fax (804)848-0607, e-mail brunspub@jnent.com, founded 1978, poetry editor Dr. Walter J. Raymond.

Book/Chapbook Needs: Brunswick is a partial subsidy publisher. Books are digest-sized, flat-spined, neatly printed, glossy cover with photo. Send SASE for catalog to order samples and "Statement of Philosophy and Purpose," which explains terms. That Statement says: "We publish books because that is what we like to do. Every new book published is like a new baby, an object of joy! We do not attempt to unduly influence the reading public as to the value of our publications, but we simply let the readers decide that themselves. We refrain from the artificial beefing up of values that are not there. . . . We are not competitors in the publishing world, but offer what we believe is a needed service. We strongly believe that in an open society every person who has something of value to say and wants to say it should have the chance and opportunity to do so."

How to Submit: Query with 3-5 samples. Response in 2 weeks with SASE. If invited, submit double-spaced, typed ms. Reports in 3-4 weeks, reading fee only if you request written evaluation. Always sends prepublication galleys. Poet pays 50-80% of cost, gets same percentage of profits for market-tester edition of 500-1,000, advertised by leaflets mailed to reviewers, libraries, book buyers and bookstores.

[N] ◯ BUDDHA EYES; INFINATE HIWAY, 1077 Brite Lane, Potect TX 78065, phone/fax (830)276-8387, founded 1998, editor/publisher Leticia Coward.

Magazine Needs: *Buddha Eyes* appears 2 times a year and publishes "fiery, beat, underground and street poetry. Anthing exciting, wild, fresh and alive. Any length. No rhyming, sweet, religious or children's poetry. Nothing boring." Editor says *BE* is 8½×11, desktop-published and side-stapled. Single copy: $3; subscription: $6. Sample: $5. Make checks payable to Leticia Coward.

How to Submit: Submit 5 poems at a time (with $3 reading fee). No previously published poems or simultaneous submissions. Cover letter required. "Prefer only mailed submissions with friendly cover letter." Time between acceptance and publication is 6 months. Always comments on rejections. Send SASE for guidelines. Reports in 1-3 months. Pays 1 copy. Acquires first rights.

Also Offers: Publishes *Infinate Hiway* which contains plays, prose and stories.

◢ ◎ BUFFALO BONES (Specialized: regional), Evergreen Poets & Writers, P.O. Box 714, Evergreen CO 80437, founded 1994, contact editors (editorial staff rotates).

Magazine Needs: *Buffalo Bones* appears 4 times/year, is a nonprofit publication containing "nothing elitist. Poems by known and unknown poets stand side by side. We look for high quality. Open to Western states only!" They want "any form of poetry, 40-line limit, strong imagery, narratives with a new twist, and a bit of fun once in awhile. No profanity, graphic/sexual, or woe-is-me poems." They have published poetry by Robert Cooperman, Judith Herschemeyer, Donna Park, Carolyn Campbell and Lyn Lifshin. *BB* is 50 pgs., digest-sized, nicely printed on quality paper. Sample: $5. Make checks payable to Evergreen Poets & Writers.

How to Submit: Submit 3 poems with a $5 reading fee. "Poems are not returned." Previously published poems and simultaneous submissions OK. Reads submissions September 1 through June 1. Poems are circulated to an editorial board. "We have a rotating editorship in order to ensure variety and a fresh look in every issue." Send SASE for guidelines. Reports in 3 months. Pays 1 copy.

Advice: The editors say, "Every poem gets attention from several readers. There are many fine poems—so little space. Our editorial staff rotates for each issue, therefore, try us again."

☑ $◯ BUFFALO SPREE MAGAZINE, 5678 Main St., Williamsville NY 14221, founded 1967, poetry editor Rachel Slaughter.

Magazine Needs: *BSM* is the quarterly regional magazine of western New York. It has a controlled circulation (21,000) in the Buffalo area, mostly distributed free (with 3,000 subscriptions, of which 25 are libraries). Its glossy pages feature general-interest articles about local culture, fiction and poetry contributed nationally. It receives about 300 poetry submissions/year and uses about 25, which have ranged from work by Robert Hass and Carl Dennis to first publications by younger poets. They use 2-3 poems/issue, these are selected 3-6 months prior to publication. Sample: $2.95 plus postage.

How to Submit: Submit up to 6 poems at a time. "The practical maximum [length] is one page of single-spaced typing; however, some longer poems will be considered if they are extremely good. We don't use haiku or other very short forms." Considers simultaneous submissions with notification. Reports in up to 4 months. Pays $25/poem on publication.

$ ▨ ◎ BUGLE, JOURNAL OF ELK AND THE HUNT (Specialized: animals, nature/rural/ecology, conservation, sports/recreation), Rocky Mountain Elk Foundation, P.O. Box 8249, Missoula MT 59807-8249, phone (406)523-4570, fax (406)523-4550, e-mail bugle@rmef.org, website http://www.rmef.org, founded 1984, editorial assistant Lee Cromrich.

Magazine Needs: *Bugle* is the bimonthly publication of the nonprofit Rocky Mountain Elk Foundation, whose mission is to ensure the future of elk, other wildlife and their habitat. "The goal of *Bugle* is to advance this mission by presenting original, critical thinking about wildlife conservation, elk ecology and hunting." They want "high quality poems that explore the realm of elk, the 'why' of hunting, or celebrate the hunting experience as a whole. Prefer one page. Free verse, cowboy poetry, etc., OK. No 'Hallmark' poetry." *Bugle* is 130 pgs., 8½×11, professionally printed on coated stock and saddle stitched with full-color glossy cover containing photos, illustrations, ads. They receive about 20 poems a year, accept approximately 30%. Press run is 195,000 for 110,000 subscribers, 85,000 shelf sales. Subscription: $30 membership fee. Sample: $4.95. Make checks payable to Rocky Mountain Elk Foundation.

How to Submit: "Poets may submit as many poems as they'd like at a time." Simultaneous submissions OK. Cover letter preferred. E-mail, fax and disk submissions OK. Time between acceptance and publication varies. "Poems are screened by editorial assistant first, those accepted then passed to editorial staff for review and comment, final decision based on their comments. We will evaluate your poem based on content, quality and our needs for the coming year." Rarely comments on rejections. Publishes special sections. Themes for September 1999 and November 1999 are "Camps (Elk)" and "Horses and Mules," respectively. Send SASE for guidelines and upcoming themes. Reports in 3 months. Pays $100/poem plus 3 copies. Acquires first North American serial rights. Staff reviews other magazines.

Advice: They say, "Although poetry has appeared periodically in *Bugle* over the years, it has never been a high priority for us, nor have we solicited it. A lack of high-quality work and poetry appropriate for the focus of the magazine has kept us from making it a regular feature. However, we've decided to attempt to give verse a permanent home in the magazine. . . . Reading a few issues of *Bugle* prior to submitting will give you a better sense of the style and content of the magazine. The Rocky Mountain Elk Foundation is a nonprofit conservation organization committed to putting membership dollars into protecting elk habitat. So we appreciate, and still receive, donated work. However, if you would like to be paid for your work, our rate is $100 a poem, paid on acceptance. Should your poem appear in *Bugle*, you will receive three complimentary copies of the issue."

$ ◻ BUTTON MAGAZINE; THIMBLE PRESS; BUTTON 2000 POETRY CONTEST, P.O. Box 26, Lunenburg MA 01462, e-mail buttonx26@aol.com, founded 1993, poetry editor D.E. Bell.

● Please note that the Button 2000 Poetry Contest is a new addition to this listing.

Magazine Needs: *Button* "is New England's tiniest magazine of fiction, poetry and gracious living." They want "poetry about the quiet surprises in life, not sentimental, and true moments carefully preserved. Brevity counts." They have published poetry by William Corbett, David Barber and Amanda Powell. As a sample the editor selected these lines from "Town Dump" by Brendan Galvin:

> Muddle and rummage, and men/with a special talent for it. Take Tilton/for starters, drawing on/his
> White Mule gloves/so slow he won't have to/help you unload

Button appears twice a year and is 30 pgs., 4¼×5½, saddle-stitched, card stock 4-color cover with illustrations that incorporate one or more buttons. Press run is 1,200 for more than 500 subscribers; 750 shelf sales. Subscription: $5/2 years, $25/lifetime. Sample: $2.

How to Submit: Submit up to 3 poems at a time. No previously published poems. Cover letter required. Time between acceptance and publication is 3-6 months. Poems are circulated to an editorial board. Often comments on rejections. Send SASE for guidelines or request via e-mail. Reports in 3-4 months. Pays honorarium, 2-year subscription and author's copies. Acquires first North American serial rights.

Also Offers: Sponsors the Button 2000 Poetry Contest. Submit poems on any topic, 25 lines or fewer, with SASE. Entry fee: $10/2 poems ($5 for each additional poem). Deadline: December 31, 1999. Awards $100 and publication. Send SASE for guidelines.

Advice: The editor says, "*Button* was started so that a century from now when people read it they'll say, 'Gee, what a wonderful time to have lived. I wish I lived back then.' Our likes include wit and humanity, intelligence and eccentricity. Button tries to reflect a world one would *want* to live in."

$ ◎ BYLINE MAGAZINE; BYLINE LITERARY AWARDS (Specialized: writing), P.O. Box 130596, Edmond OK 73013-0001, phone (405)348-5591, e-mail bylinemp@aol.com, website http://www.bylinemag.com, founded 1981, poetry editor Sandra Soli, editor Marcia Preston.

Magazine Needs: *ByLine* is a magazine for the encouragement of writers and poets, using 8-10 poems/issue about writers or writing. As a sample the editor selected these lines from "Revise, Revise" by L.G. Mason:

> there will be a version/left in autumn/like a darkened lantern/swinging on a limb,/like a poem/surviving
> a man:/let anyone/find in it what he can.

ByLine is magazine-sized, professionally printed, with illustrations, cartoons and ads. They have more than 3,000 subscriptions and receive about 2,500 poetry submissions/year, of which they use about 100. Subscription: $22. Sample: $4.

How to Submit: Submit up to 3 poems at a time, no reprints. Send SASE for guidelines. Reports within 6 weeks. Pays $10/poem ($5 for poems 5 lines or fewer). Buys first North American serial rights.

Also Offers: Sponsors up to 20 poetry contests, including a chapbook competition open to anyone. Send #10 SASE for details. Also sponsors the ByLine Literary Awards. Prize: $250. Subscribers only. Send SASE for guidelines. Website features guidelines, contest listings, subscription info and sample column or article from magazine.

Advice: Marcia Preston advises, "We are happy to work with new writers, but please read a few samples to get an idea of our style. We would like to see more serious poetry about the creative experience (as it concerns writing)."

N **CADENCE; TENTH STREET PRESS**, 300 W. 10th St., Morris MN 56267, founded 1999, editor Heather Timmerman.

Magazine Needs: "*Cadence* is a new quarterly magazine devoted entirely to poetry." They want "poetry that is clear and insightful. Precise, lyrical language is more important than any particular form or style." The editor says *Cadence* is 8½×7, laser printed and saddle-stapled with glossy card cover, includes b&w photography. Subscription: $15. Sample: $5. Make checks payable to Tenth Street Press.

How to Submit: Submit 5-7 poems at a time. Previously published poems and simultaneous submissions OK. Cover letter preferred. "Enclose a brief cover letter with some information about yourself and your writing credentials, if any. *Cadence* welcomes new writers, and your work will not be screened out for lack of publishing experience. Enclose a SASE with sufficient postage to return your work." Time between acceptance and publication is 6 months. Seldom comments on rejections. Send SASE for guidelines. Reports in 2 months. Always sends prepublication galleys. Pays 3 copies. Acquires one-time rights.

Book/Chapbook Needs & How to Submit: Tenth Street Press publishes 2 chapbooks per year through its biannual chapbook contest. Chapbooks are usually 24-30 pgs., 8½×5½, laser printed and saddle-stapled with glossy or matte card cover, may include b&w photographs. "Chapbook style is determined by the author's preference." Contest entries may be previously published or unpublished and may be entered in other contests. No limit on entries, but each must be accompanied by entry fee. Entry fee: $12 for 20-24 poems. Make checks payable to Tenth Street Press. Deadlines: February 1 and August 1. Contest entries are not returned. Winners notified within 1 month. Awards $200 plus 50 author's copies. Each entrant will receive a copy of the winning chapbook. Order sample chapbooks by sending $5.

Also Offers: *Cadence* also sponsors quarterly and annual poetry contests for individual poems. Guidelines for these contests are similar to the chapbook contest. The Quarterly Poetry Contest awards $100 and publication in *Cadence*. Entry fee: $5/3 poems. Deadlines: March 15, June 15, September 15 and December 15. The Annual Poetry Contest awards $300 and publication in *Cadence*. Entry fee: $10/3poems. Deadline: November 1. "All contest entries will be considered for publication in *Cadence*."

THE CAFÉ REVIEW, c/o Yes Books, 20 Danforth St., Portland ME 04101, e-mail all@seegerlake.com, website http://www.cafereview.com, founded 1989, editor-in-chief Steve Luttrell.

Magazine Needs: *Café Review* is a quarterly which has grown out of open poetry readings held at a Portland cafe. The editors say they aim "to print the best work we can!" They want "free verse, 'beat' inspired and fresh. Nothing clichéd." They have published poetry by Charles Bukowski, Robert Creeley, Janet Hamill and Diane Wakoski. *The Review* is 70-80 pgs., 5½×8½, professionally printed and perfect-bound with card cover, b&w art, no ads. They receive over 1,000 submissions a year, accept approximately 15%. Press run is 500 for 70 subscribers of which 10 are libraries, 75-100 shelf sales. Subscription: $25. Sample: $6.

How to Submit: No previously published poems or simultaneous submissions. Cover letter with brief bio required. "Poems only may be sent via e-mail. All other requests should be sent via U.S. mail. We usually respond with a form letter indicating acceptance or rejection of work, seldom with additional comments." Reports in 2-4 months. Pays 1 copy.

Book/Chapbook Needs: They also publish 1-2 chapbooks/year.

CALDER PUBLICATIONS LTD.; WHITEHURST & CLARKE BOOK FULFILLMENT CO. (NYC); ASSOCIATION CALDER, 126 Cornwall Rd., London SE1 8TQ England, phone 0171-633-0599, publisher John Calder, is a literary book publisher. On their list are Samuel Beckett, Breyten Breytenbach, Erich Fried, Paul Eluard, Pier Paolo Passolini and Howard Barker. "We do not read for the public," says John Calder, and *he wants no unsolicited mss.* "Any communication which requires a response should be sent with a SAE."

CALYX, A JOURNAL OF ART & LITERATURE BY WOMEN (Specialized: women, lesbian, multicultural); CALYX BOOKS, P.O. Box B, Corvallis OR 97339-0539, phone (541)753-9384, fax (541)753-0515, e-mail calyx@proaxis.com, founded 1976, senior editor B. McFarland.

Magazine Needs: *Calyx* is a journal edited by a collective editorial board, publishes poetry, prose, art, book reviews and interviews by and about women. They want "excellently crafted poetry that also has excellent content." They have published poetry by Maurya Simon, Robin Morgan, Carole Boston Weatherford and Eleanor Wilner. As a sample the editor selected these lines from "Transparent Woman" by Donna Henderson:

> in the basement of the science museum,/half-lit, naked and marvelous with her perfect/posture, lucite
> arms straight and slightly apart,/palms turned toward us like the Blessed Virgin's,/helplessly
> welcoming.

Calyx appears 3 times every 18 months and is 6×8, handsomely printed on heavy paper, flat-spined, glossy

color cover, 128 pgs., of which 50-60 are poetry. Poems tend to be lyric free verse that makes strong use of image and symbol melding unobtrusively with voice and theme. Single copy: $9.50. Sample: $11.50.
How to Submit: *Calyx* is open to submissions October 1 through December 15 only. Mss received when not open to reading will be returned unread. Send up to 6 poems with SASE and short bio. "We accept copies in good condition and clearly readable. We focus on new writing, but occasionally publish a previously published piece." Simultaneous submissions OK, "if kept up-to-date on publication." Send SASE or e-mail for guidelines. Reports in 2-6 months. Pays 1 copy/poem and subscription. Open to unsolicited reviews. Poets may also send books for review consideration.
Book/Chapbook Needs & How to Submit: Calyx Books publishes 1 book of poetry a year. All work published is by women. Recently published: *Details of Flesh* by Cortney Davis. Open for submissions August 1 through September 10 and January 1 through March 1. Send SASE or e-mail for guidelines.
Advice: They say, "Read the publication and be familiar with what we have published."

⬤ CAMELLIA; CAMELLIA PRESS INC., P.O. Box 40438, Washington DC 20016-0438, editor Tomer Inbar, associate editor Beth Stevens.
Magazine Needs: *Camellia* is published biannually as a fold-out magazine/poster "available for free in New York City, the San Francisco/Oakland Bay area, Seattle, Ithaca, D.C., Northern Virginia and Baltimore, or by sending 2 first-class stamps. We publish poetry in the W.C. Williams tradition. The poetry of things, moment and sharpness. We encourage young writers and like to work with the writers who publish with us. Our main goal is to get the poetry out. We do not want to see poetry where the poem is subordinate to the poet or poetry where the noise of the poetic overshadows the voice. We look for poetry that is honest and sharp and unburdened." *Camellia*'s exact dimensions, the theme for a given issue and the mix of poetry and other art will be determined on an issue by issue basis. "We will keep the basic graphic design consistent with the style we have used for the past seven years, however we will be inviting guest designers to work with that design, bringing something new to each issue. We will continue to publish special project issues from time to time using various formats and mediums." They receive approximately 300-350 poems/issue and publish about 20. Press run is 1,000-2,000. Subscription: $5/year, $7 overseas. Sample: 2 first-class stamps.
How to Submit: Submit 8 poems at a time. Simultaneous submissions and previously published poems OK. "Cover letters are helpful, but shouldn't go overboard. Sometimes the cover letters are more interesting than the poetry received." Reports "ASAP." Pays 2 copies. Editor comments on submissions "if asked for or if I want to see more but am not satisfied with the poems sent."
Book/Chapbook Needs & How to Submit: A chapbook of poems by Jerry Mirskin, entitled *Picture A Gate Hanging Open And Let That Gate Be The Sun*, is available for $5 from Camellia Press Inc. Also available is a poster of poetry, photographs and design using poems from the first 6 years of *Camellia*. They send prepublication galleys only for chapbooks.

🍁 ⬤ ◎ CANADIAN DIMENSION: THE MAGAZINE FOR PEOPLE WHO WANT TO CHANGE THE WORLD (Specialized: political), 2B-91 Albert St., Winnipeg, Manitoba R3B 1G5 Canada, phone (204)957-1519, fax (204)943-4617, e-mail info@canadiandimension.mb.ca, website http://www.canadiand imension.mb.ca/cd/index.html, founded 1964, editorial contact George Harris.
Magazine Needs: *Canadian Dimension* appears 6 times/year, using "short poems on labour, women, native, gay/lesbian and other issues. Nothing more than one page." They have published poetry by Tom Wayman and Milton Acorn. It is 48-56 pgs., magazine-sized, slick, professionally printed, with glossy paper cover. Press run is 3,500 for 2,500 subscribers of which 800 are libraries, 1,000 shelf sales. Subscription: $34.50 US ($24.50 Canadian). Sample: $2.
How to Submit: Submit up to 5 poems at a time. Previously published poems are unlikely to be accepted. Simultaneous submissions OK, if notified. Editor comments on submissions "rarely." Publishes theme issues. Send SASE (or SAE and IRC) for upcoming themes. Reviews books of poetry in 750-1,200 words, single or multi-book format.
Advice: They say, "We are broadly political—that is, not narrowly sloganeering, but profoundly sensitive to the connections between words and the state of the world. Topics can be personal as well as political. Also, American writers are reminded to include Canadian return postage or its equivalent in reply coupons, etc."

🅽 🍁 ⬤ THE CANADIAN JOURNAL OF CONTEMPORARY LITERARY STUFF, P.O. Box 53106, Ottawa, Ontario K1N 1C5 Canada, e-mail grunge@achilles.net, founded 1997, editor Grant Wilkins, editor Tamara Fairchild.
Magazine Needs: *CJOCLS* appears 2-4 times a year and aims "to make Canadian literature interesting to read, interesting to read about, accessible and fun." They want "fresh, literate poetry written in a unique voice. Poetry that actually says something. No insipid, banal pieces about broken hearts. No landscapes or navel gazing about writing." They have published poetry by Bill Bissett, Stan Rogal, Sharon H. Nelson and Catherine Jenkins. As a sample we selected these lines from "where are you from, really?" by Sumana Sen-Bagchee:

> they call this time of year, fall/yet, these aged planes and sycamores/lining the Embankment walk/have
> neither turned colour/nor dropped their leaves/as they are supposed to—/today's soothing sunlight/is
> the colour of pernod/spilling onto the pavement/where we wade through pigeons,/pass other strollers,
> the odd dove//the sun on our spines/tingling down to our palms//(we keep them tightfisted in pockets)/

*words flutter from him/random, like pigeons/his fresh English face, eager/where are you from, really,/
I've been wondering . . .*

The editors say it is 40 pgs., magazine-sized, saddle-stapled with b&w plus third color cover, includes b&w photos and ads. They receive about 400 poems a year, accept approximately 5%. Press run is 1,000. Single copy: $4.75; subscription: $16. Sample: $6.50. Make checks payable to *CJOCLS*.

How to Submit: Submit 5 or more poems at a time. No previously published poems or simultaneous submissions. Cover letter and SASE required. E-mail and disk submissions OK. Time between acceptance and publication is 3 months. Poems are circulated to an editorial board. "We are two editors in two separate cities. We both get a copy of submissions for an issue. We each go through submissions on our own, then get together and compare notes." Seldom comments on rejections. Send SASE (or SAE and IRC) for guidelines or obtain via e-mail. Reports in 4-8 months. Pays 5 copies. Acquires first rights. Reviews books and chapbooks of poetry in 300-500 words. Open to unsolicited reviews. Poets may also send books for review consideration.

Advice: The editors say, "We're also looking for fiction, articles, interviews, cartoons, art and photos."

CANADIAN LITERATURE (Specialized: regional), 167-1855 West Mall, University of British Columbia, Vancouver, British Columbia V6T 1Z2 Canada, phone (604)822-2780, fax (604)822-5504, website http://www.cdn-lit.ubc.ca, founded 1959, editor E.M. Kröller.

Magazine Needs: *CL* is a quarterly review which publishes poetry by Canadian poets. "No limits on form. Less room for long poems." They have published poetry by Atwood, Ondaatje, Layton and Bringhurst. As a sample the editor selected these lines from "Forerunners" by Elizabeth Brewster:

> *Before the king comes, he sends messengers./Tyrant or liberator, which is he?/How judge the message
> that the postman brings?/Promise or threat? true? false? ambiguous?/Loveletter or a summons to a
> trial?*

Each issue is professionally printed, digest-sized, flat-spined, with 175-200 pgs., of which about 10 are poetry. They receive 100-300 submissions/year, use 10-12. Circulation is 1,200, two-thirds of which are libraries. Sample for the cover price: $15 Canadian plus postage and GST.

How to Submit: No simultaneous submissions or reprints. Cover letter and SASE (or SAE and IRC) required. Reports within the month. "Accepted poems must be available on diskette." *CL* retains full copyright. Reviews books of poetry in 500-1,000 words.

CANADIAN WOMAN STUDIES (Specialized: women), 212 Founders College, York University, 4700 Keele St., North York, Ontario M3J 1P3 Canada, phone (416)736-5356, fax (416)736-5765, e-mail cwscf@yorku.ca, website http://www.yorku.ca/org/cwscf/home.html, founded 1978, literary editor Marlene Kadar.

Magazine Needs: *CWS* appears quarterly and focuses on "women's studies; experiential and academic articles, poetry, book reviews and artwork." They want poetry "exploring women's lives/perspectives. No long poems (i.e., more than 50 lines)." They have published poetry by Libby Scheier, Patience Wheatley and Lyn Lifshin. The editor says *CWS* is about 152 pgs., magazine-sized, offset printed and perfect-bound with full color cover, includes art and ads. They receive about 400 poems a year, accept approximately 15%. Press run is 4,000 for 1,500 subscribers of which 500 are libraries, 1,000 shelf sales; 250 distributed free to women's groups. Single copy: $8; subscription: $30 plus $2.10 gst/year. Sample: $11.45.

How to Submit: Submit 5 poems at a time. No previously published poems or simultaneous submissions. Cover letter required. E-mail submissions OK. "SASE (or SAE and IRC) appreciated, bio note must accompany submission." Time between acceptance and publication is 5 months. Publishes theme issues. Reports in 5 months. Pays 1 copy. "Poets maintain copyright of their work at all times." Reviews books and chapbooks of poetry in 750 words, single and multi-book format. Open to unsolicited reviews. Poets may also send books for review consideration to Fran Beer, book review editor.

Also Offers: Website includes tables of contents, policies, order information, guidelines for submissions and calls for papers.

CANADIAN WRITER'S JOURNAL (Specialized: writing), White Mountain Publications, Box 5180, New Liskeard, Ontario P0J 1P0 Canada, phone (705)647-5424, fax (705)647-8366, e-mail wmpub@ntl.sympatico.ca, website http://www.nt.net/~cwj/index.htm, owner Deborah Ranchuk.

Magazine Needs: *CWJ* is a small quarterly, publishing mainly short "how-to" articles of interest to writers at all levels. They use a few "short poems or portions thereof as part of 'how-to' articles relating to the writing of poetry and occasional short poems with tie-in to the writing theme." Subscription: $15/year, $25/2 years. Sample: $5.

THE CHAPBOOK INDEX, located at the back of this book, lists those publishers who consider chapbook mss. A chapbook, a small volume of work (usually under 50 pages), is often a good middle step between magazine and book publication.

How to Submit: Submit up to 5 poems (identify each form). Include SASE ("U.S. postage accepted; do not affix to envelope"). No previously published poems. E-mail and fax submissions OK. "Include inside text of message, not as attachment. Send hard copy and SASE if accepted." Token payment. Pays $2-5 and 1 copy/ poem.

Also Offers: The magazine runs an annual poetry competition with closing date May 31. Send SASE for current rules or check on website. Website includes writer's guidelines, names of editors and indexes of past issues.

⬛ THE CAPE ROCK, Dept. of English, Southeast Missouri State University, Cape Girardeau MO 63701, phone (314)651-2500, founded 1964, editor Dr. Harvey Hecht.

Magazine Needs: *Cape Rock* appears twice yearly and consists of poetry and photography. "No restrictions on subjects or forms. Our criterion for selection is the quality of the work. We prefer poems under 70 lines; no long poems or books; no sentimental, didactic or cute poems." They have published poetry by Stephen Dunning, Joyce Odam, Judith Phillips Neeld, Lyn Lifshin, Virginia Brady Young, Gary Pacernick and Laurel Speer. *Cape Rock* is a 64-page, handsomely printed, flat-spined, digest-sized magazine. Circulation is about 500 for 200 subscribers of which half are libraries. Single copy: $5; subscription: $7/year. Sample: $4.

How to Submit: Submit 3-7 poems at a time. Do not submit mss in May, June or July. Send SASE for guidelines. They have a 2- to 8-month backlog and report in 1-3 months. Pays 2 copies.

Also Offers: They also offer a $200 prize for the best poem in each issue and $100 for featured photography.

⬛ ✔ $⬤ THE CAPILANO REVIEW, 2055 Purcell Way, North Vancouver, British Columbia V7J 3H5 Canada, phone (604)984-1712, fax (604)990-7837, e-mail tcr@capcollege.bc.ca, website http://www.capcollege. bc.ca/dept/TCR/tcr.html, founded 1972, editor Robert Sherrin.

Magazine Needs: *The Capilano Review* is a literary and visual media review appearing 3 times/year. They want "avant-garde, experimental, previously unpublished work, poetry of sustained intelligence and imagination. We are interested in poetry that is new in concept and in execution." They have published poetry by Erin Mouré, Michael Crummey and Lea Littlewolfe. *TCR* comes in a handsome digest-sized format, 115 pgs., flat-spined, finely printed, semi-glossy stock with a glossy full-color card cover. Circulation is 1,000. Sample: $9 prepaid.

How to Submit: Submit 5-6 poems, minimum, at a time with SASE (or SAE and IRC). Do not submit mss during June and July. No simultaneous submissions. No e-mail or disk submissions. Reports in up to 5 months. Pays $50-200, subscription, plus 2 copies. Buys first North American serial rights.

Also Offers: Website includes guidelines, excerpts, subscription info, etc.

Advice: The editor says, "*TCR* receives several manuscripts each week; unfortunately the majority of them are simply inappropriate for the magazine. The best advice we can offer is to research carefully before you submit."

✔ $⬜ ◎ CAPPER'S (Specialized: nature, inspirational, humor, senior citizen), 1503 SW 42nd St., Topeka KS 66609-1265, phone (785)274-4300, website http://www.cappers.com, founded 1879, editor Ann Crahan.

Magazine Needs: *Capper's* is a biweekly tabloid (newsprint) going to 240,000 mail subscribers, mostly small-town and rural families. Uses 6-8 poems in each issue. They want short poems (4-10 lines preferred, lines of one-column width) "relating to everyday situations, nature, inspirational, humorous. Most poems used in *Capper's* are upbeat in tone and offer the reader a bit of humor, joy, enthusiasm or encouragement." They have published poetry by Elizabeth Searle Lamb, Robert Brimm, Margaret Wiedyke, Helena K. Stefanski, Sheryl L. Nelms and Claire Puneky. Send $1.95 for sample. Not available on newsstand.

How to Submit: Submit 5-6 poems at a time, 14-16 lines. No simultaneous submissions. No e-mail or fax submissions. Returns mss with SASE. Publishes seasonal theme issues. Send SASE for upcoming themes. Reports in 2-3 months. Pays $10-15/poem. Additional payment of $5 if poem is used on website. Buys one-time rights.

Advice: The editor says, "Poems chosen are upbeat, sometimes humorous, always easily understood. Short poems of this type fit our format best."

✔ ◎ THE CARIBBEAN WRITER (Specialized: regional); THE DAILY NEWS PRIZE; THE CHARLOTTE AND ISIDOR PAIEWONSKY PRIZE; THE UNA MARSON PRIZE; THE MARGUE- RITE COBB MCKAY PRIZE, University of the Virgin Islands, RR 02, P.O. Box 10,000, Kingshill, St. Croix, USVI 00850, phone (340)692-4152, fax (340)692-4026, e-mail ewaters@uvi.edu or qmars@uvi.edu, website http://www.uvi.edu/CaribbeanWriter/, founded 1987, editor Dr. Erika Waters, contact submissions editor.

Magazine Needs: *The Caribbean Writer* is an annual literary magazine, appearing in June, with a Caribbean focus. The Caribbean must be central to the literary work or the work must reflect a Caribbean heritage, experience or perspective. They have published poetry by Derek Walcott, Kamau Brathwaite and Opal Palmer Odisa. The magazine is 250 pgs., 6×9, handsomely printed on heavy stock, perfect-bound, with glossy card cover, using advertising and b&w art by Caribbean artists. Press run is 1,000. Single copy: $10 plus $1.50 postage; subscrip- tion: $18/2 years. Sample: $5 plus $1.50 postage. Send SASE for guidelines. (Note: Postage to and from the Virgin Islands is the same as within the US.)

How to Submit: Submit up to 5 poems. No previously published poems; simultaneous submissions OK. Submissions by e-mail OK. No fax submissions. Blind submissions only: name, address, phone number and title of ms should appear in cover letter along with brief bio. Title only on ms. Deadline is September 30 of each year. The annual appears in the spring. Pays 2 copies. Acquires first North American serial rights. Reviews books of poetry and fiction in 500 words. Open to unsolicited reviews. Poets may also send books for review consideration.

Also Offers: The magazine annually awards The Daily News Prize ($300) for the best poem or poems, The Una Marson Prize to a Caribbean author ($500), The Marguerite Cobb McKay Prize to a Virgin Island author ($100) and The Charlotte and Isidor Paiewonsky Prize ($200) for first-time publication. Website includes work from previous issues and current issue, along with biographies and photos of contributors.

CARLETON ARTS REVIEW, Box 78, 18th Floor, Davidson Dunton Tower, Carleton University, Ottawa, Ontario K1S 5B6 Canada, phone (613)228-1479, founded 1982, co-ordinating editor Jason McDonald.
Magazine Needs: *Carleton Arts Review* is a 60-page semiannual publishing poetry, prose, visual art (b&w) and reviews. "All kinds of poetry accepted and encouraged." They have published poetry by Stan Rogal, Brian Burke, Calvin White and Alan Packwood. They receive 200-300 poems a year, publish about 10%. Press run is 300 for 50 subscribers most of which are libraries, 150 shelf sales. Subscription: $8. Sample: $4.
How to Submit: No previously published poems or simultaneous submissions. "Please include a short biography and list of publications plus a SASE or SAE and IRC." Always comments on rejections. Reports in 1-2 months. Pays 2 copies.

THE CAROLINA QUARTERLY; THE CHARLES B. WOOD AWARD, CB #3520 Greenlaw Hall, University of North Carolina, Chapel Hill NC 27599-3520, phone (919)962-0244, e-mail cquarter@unc.edu, website http://www.unc.edu/student/orgs/cquarter, founded 1948, poetry editor Al Benthall.
Magazine Needs: *Carolina Quarterly* appears 3 times a year publishing fiction, poetry, reviews, nonfiction and graphic art. They have no specifications regarding form, length, subject matter or style of poetry. They also consider translations of work originally written in languages other than English. They have published poetry by Denise Levertov, Richard Wilbur, Robert Morgan, Eamon Grennan and Charles Wright. *TCQ* is about 90 pgs., 6×9, professionally printed and perfect-bound with one-color matte card cover, a few graphics and ads. They receive about 6,000 poems a year, accept less than 1%. Press run is 1,500 for 200 library subscriptions and various shelf sales. Subscription: $12, $15 (institution). Sample: $5.
How to Submit: No previously published poems or simultaneous submissions. SASE required. Poems are circulated to an editorial board. "Manuscripts that make it to the meeting of the full poetry staff are discussed by all. Poems are accepted by majority consensus." Seldom comments on rejections. Reports in 4 months. "Poets are welcome to write or phone about their submission's status, but please wait about four months before doing so." Pays 4 copies. Acquires first rights. Reviews books of poetry. Poets may also send books for review consideration (attn: Editor).
Also Offers: The Charles B. Wood Award for Distinguished Writing is given to the author of the best poem or short story published in each volume of *The Carolina Quarterly.* Only those writers *without* major publications are considered and the winner receives $500. Website includes the history of the publication, subscription information, writer's guidelines, contents of current issue and index to poetry and fiction from 1948-present.

CAROLINA WREN PRESS (Specialized: women, ethnic, gay/lesbian, social issues), 120 Morris St., Durham NC 27701, phone (919)560-2738, e-mail carolinawrenpress@compuserve.com, founded 1976.
Book/Chapbook Needs: Publishes 1 book/year, "primarily women and minorities, though men and majorities also welcome." They have published poetry by Jaki Shelton Green, Mary Kratt and Steven Blaski.
How to Submit: They currently are not accepting any unsolicited mss. Send 9½×12 SASE for catalog (include postage for 3 ounces).
Also Offers: "We are launching our new North American Poetry Chapbook Series with George Elliott Clarke's *Gold Indigoes.*"

CARPE LAUREATE DIEM; MIDDLE GEORGIA ASSOCIATION OF WORDSMITHS AND ARTISTS, 3063 Stokes Store Rd., Forsyth GA 31029, e-mail laureate@rose.net, website http://home.rose.net/~heidiho/, founded 1995, hard copy editor Emily Worthington, electronic editor Heidi Pehrson.
Magazine Needs: *Carpe Laureate Diem* is published quarterly to "encourage new/unpublished writers and artists and to bring poetry and art to people who don't usually see new poets and artists." They want "poetry you feel passionately about. No graphic, erotica/pornography; no harsh profanity (remember children contribute and read)." They have published poetry by Mike Catalano, Kent Clair Chamberlain, John Grey and Daniel Green. As a sample the editor selected this poem, "Grace," by Tim Scannell:

> the Supreme Court/decided 9:0/that poetry was "utterly/without redeeming social/importance," so/I began writing full-time

CLD is 24 pgs. (printed on 1 side only), 8½×11, photocopied and corner-stapled, includes b&w line drawings. They receive about 400 poems a year, accept approximately 90%. Press run is 400 for 50 subscribers; the rest distributed free to area businesses. Subscription: $8. Sample: $3. Make checks payable to Emily Worthington.
How to Submit: Submit 3 poems at a time. Previously published poems OK; no simultaneous submissions. "Cover letters are appreciated and will make a difference in the way we perceive your submission." E-mail submissions OK, prefer MS Publisher, Word Perfect or Microsoft Office formats. "One poem to a page, typed preferred—must be legible if handwritten." Time between acceptance and publication is 3-6 months. Often comments on rejections. Publishes theme issues occasionally. Send SASE for guidelines and upcoming themes

or obtain via e-mail. Reports in 2 months. Sometimes sends prepublication galleys. Pays 1 copy (extra copies available at reduced rate). Acquires one-time rights. Reviews books and chapbooks of poetry and other magazines. Open to unsolicited reviews. Poets may also send books for review consideration.

Also Offers: Each issue features a Readers' Choice contest in three categories—adult writer, young writer and artist. "Person with the most reader votes wins a prize. Prize is usually writing- or art-related such as books, handheld recorders or pencil sets."

Advice: The editors say, "Please be patient with us, sometimes we are slow because we have an extremely small staff."

◐ ◎ CATAMOUNT PRESS; COTYLEDON (Specialized: anthology), 2519 Roland Rd. SW, Huntsville AL 35805-4147, founded 1992, editor Georgette Perry.

Magazine Needs: *Cotyledon*, founded in 1997, published 4 times a year is a miniature magazine. They want poems up to 8 lines. Nature and the environment are favorite subjects, but a variety of subject matter is needed. Poets published include Kurt Brown, Christopher Presfield, Kaye Bache-Snyder and Kennette H. Wilkes. It is 16 pgs., 3½×4¼, photocopied, saddle-stapled, with bond cover and b&w art.

How to Submit: Submit 3-6 poems at a time with cover letter and SASE. Previously published poems OK if identified as such. Publishes theme issues. Send three unattached first-class stamps for a sample *Cotyledon* and guidelines for any contest, chapbook or anthology planned. Reports in 1 month. Pays copies.

Book/Chapbook Needs & How to Submit: Catamount Press publishes one to two 5½×8½ chapbooks or anthologies/year. Poets who have had poems in *Cotyledon* have a better chance of acceptance. As a sample the editor selected "Cicada" from William J. Wilson's chapbook *Haiku for All Seasons:*

> For whom this plainsong?/in the hills there are no/processions with torches.

Ⓝ ◐ THE CATBIRD SEAT; CAT POEM CONTEST, P.O. Box 506, Tolland CT 06084-0506, founded 1997, editor/publisher Nancy Purnell.

Magazine Needs: Appearing 3 times a year, *The Catbird Seat* is "a seasonal poetry and fiction 'zine about nature, the forces of the universe and humankind's ambivalent relationship with all of it." They want "free verse, experimental poetry; dark, unusual, surreal, science fiction, but also some positive work—celebration of nature, supernatural forces and humanity. Also would like to see seasonal poetry. No rhyme, light verse, X-rated work; TV or movie-type conventional horror poetry." They have published poetry by John Grey, Nancy Bennett and W. Gregory Stewart. As a sample the editor selected these lines from "Drinking the Light" by Charlee Jacob:

> Zen cat rests beside her thoughts,/separated by the history of whiskers./Stretched long in the heat,/
> summer sun creating vitamin D,/she then licks the warm fur,/A form of drinking the light/and a method
> of self-invention.

TCS is 72 pgs., digest-sized, desktop published/laser printed and saddle-stapled with colored paper cover, includes b&w drawings and exchange with other 'zines. They receive about 1,200 poems a year, accept approximately 30%. Press run is 150 for 25 subscribers, 45 shelf sales; 80 distributed free to contributors, exchanges, reviews. Subscription: $13 US, $14 Canada, $18 overseas. Sample: $4.50 US and Canada, $6 overseas. Make checks payable to Nancy Purnell.

How to Submit: Submit 5-7 poems at a time. Line length for poetry is 30 maximum ("prefer, but will read longer"). No previously published poems or simultaneous submissions. Cover letter preferred. Time between acceptance and publication is 1-9 months. Seldom comments on rejections. Publishes theme issues occasionally. Send SASE for guidelines. Reports in 2-6 weeks. Sometimes sends prepublication galleys. Pays 1 copy. Acquires first North American serial rights. Staff reviews chapbooks of poetry and other magazines in single book format. Send books for review consideration.

Also Offers: Sponsors the Cat Poem Contest in each issue. Poems should be 30 lines or less. No rhyme or light verse. Winner receives 10 first-class (letter) stamps plus 1 copy of issue. A few runners-up receive 5 first-class (letter) stamps plus 1 copy of issue. Deadlines: January 1, May 1 and September 1. Send SASE for return of poems and notification of winner.

Advice: The editor says, "We want to see original, thought-provoking poetry."

Ⓝ ◔ CAVEAT LECTOR, 400 Hyde St., Apt. 606, San Francisco CA 94109-7445, phone (415)928-7431, founded 1989, editors Christopher Bernard, James Bybee and Andrew Towne.

Magazine Needs: Appearing 2 times/year, "*Caveat Lector* is devoted to the arts and to cultural and philosophical commentary. We publish visual art and music as well as literary and theoretical texts. We are looking for accomplished poems, something that resonates in the mind long after the reader has laid the poem aside. We want work that has authenticity of emotion and high craft, whether raw or polished, that rings true—if humorous, actually funny, or at least witty. Classical to experimental. 500-line limit." They have published poetry by Mary Winters, Taylor Graham, Nathan Whiting, Lee Chilcote, among others. As a sample the editor selected these lines from "To A Friend Who Has Not Written," by Christopher Hewitt:

> You must have some news./I do. The asters bloomed. There's/still no rain./Oh and I go often to/A place
> I found/Where leaves are letters falling/All of which I've written.//How I exhaust myself/Catching
> them!

The editors say *CL* is 36-64 pgs., 11×4¼, photocopied and saddle-stitched with b&w card cover. They receive about 600-800 poems a year, accept less than 2%. Press run is 300 for 30 subscribers, 200 shelf sales. Single copy: $2.50; subscription: $10/4 issues. Sample: $3.

How to Submit: Submit up to 6 short poems (up to 50 lines each), 3 medium length poems (51-100 lines), or 1 long poem (100 to 500 lines) at a time "on any subject, in any style, as long as the work is authentic in feeling and appropriately crafted." Place name, address, and (optional) telephone number on each page. Include SASE, cover letter, and brief bio (30 words or less). Simultaneous submissions OK, "but please inform us." Time between acceptance and publication is 1 year. Sometimes comments on rejections. Reports in 1 month. Pays 5 copies. Acquires first publication rights.

Advice: Christopher Bernard says, "The two rules of writing are: 1. Rewrite it again. 2. Rewrite it again. The writing level of most of our submissions is pleasingly high. A rejection by us is not always a criticism of the work, and we try to provide comments to our more promising submitters."

N ☺ **CAYO, REFLECTIONS OF LIFE IN THE KEYS (Specialized: regional)**, P.O. Box 4516, Key West FL 33041, founded 1994, poetry editor Kirby Congdon.

Magazine Needs: *Cayo* is a quarterly regional literary magazine focusing on the Florida Keys. The editor says *Cayo* is 40 pgs., magazine-sized, offset printed and saddle-stitched with self-cover, includes photography. They receive about 100 poems a year, accept approximately 20%. Press run is 1,000 for 100 subscribers, 400 shelf sales; 500 distributed free to sponsors/contributors. Single copy: $3; subscription: $16. Sample: $4.

How to Submit: Submit 3 poems at a time. Previously published poems and simultaneous submissions OK. Disk submissions OK. SASE required. Time between acceptance and publication is 3-6 months. Poems are circulated to an editorial board; "from poetry editor for review by editor/publisher." Often comments on rejections. Reports in 3 months. Pays 2 copies. Acquires one-time rights.

$ ☺ **CC MOTORCYCLE NEWS MAGAZINE (Specialized: sports/recreation)**, P.O. Box 808, Nyack NY 10960-0808, phone (914)353-MOTO, fax (914)353-5240, e-mail moto-mag@aol.com, website http://www.moto-mag.com, founded 1990.

Magazine Needs: *CCMNM* is a monthly containing regional motorcycle news and features. They want motorcycle-related poetry. They say *CCMNM* is tabloid-sized and printed on newsprint. Circulation of 50,000; distributed from Washington DC to Boston MA. Sample: $3. Make checks payable to Motomag Corp.

How to Submit: Submit up to 5 poems at a time. Previously published poems and simultaneous submissions OK. Cover letter required including SASE. Time between acceptance and publication is 1-4 months. Often comments on rejections. Publishes theme issues. Send SASE for guidelines and upcoming themes. Reports in 1 month. Pays $10-25. Buys one-time regional rights.

$ ◻ **CEDAR HILL PUBLICATIONS; CEDAR HILL REVIEW**, 3722 Hwy. 8 West, Mena AR 71953, phone (501)394-7029, founded 1996, managing editor Gloria Doyle, senior editor Christopher Presfield, poetry editor Maggie Jaffe, editorial assistants David Goyette and Thom Hofman.

Magazine Needs: *Cedar Hill Review* is "eclectic in its taste (formal and free verse) but favors contemporary themes and engaged poetry. Nothing racist, sexist or anti-environment." They have published poetry by Hayden Carruth, Leonard Cirino, Yannis Ritsos, Sharon Doubiago, Adrian C. Louis, Virgil Suarez, Sara Saper Gauldin, Joanne Lowery, Michael McIrvin and Jon Forrest Glade. As a sample the editor selected these lines from "Conversation in the Kitchen at 3 a.m." by J. Mills:

> *This is what I know about love/my father said/then he leaned forward/kissed my tense face/and left the room.*

CHR is 64 pgs., 5½×8½, professionally printed and perfect-bound with laminated cover, includes cover art. They receive about 2,000 poems a year, accept approximately 10%. Press run is 300 for 200 subscribers of which 10 are libraries; 50 distributed free to institutions. Single copy: $6; subscription: $15. Sample: $4. Make checks payable to Cedar Hill Publications.

How to Submit: Submit 5 poems at a time, September through May, to Maggie Jaffe at 3438 Villa Terrace, San Diego CA 92104-3424, (619)294-4924, e-mail mjaffe@mail.sdsu.edu. Previously published poems and simultaneous submissions OK. Cover letter required. Reports in 3-6 months. Acquires all or one-time rights. Returns rights upon publication. Reviews books of poetry and occasionally other journals.

Book/Chapbook Needs & How to Submit: Cedar Hill Publications "seeks to publish the best sound North America has to offer." They publish 10 paperbacks and 2 chapbooks/year. Books are usually 64-80 pgs., 5½×8½, professionally printed and perfect-bound with laminated cover with art. "Must appear in *Cedar Hill Review* for book consideration." Replies to queries and mss in 1 month.

⊕ ✓ **$** ◻ **CENCRASTUS; CURLY SNAKE PUBLISHING**, Unit One, Abbeymount Telhbase, Easter Rd., Edinburgh EH8 8EJ Scotland, phone/fax (0044)131 661 5687, e-mail cencrastus@dial.pipex.com, founded 1979, editor Raymond Ross, managing editor Richard Moore.

Magazine Needs: *Cencrastus* appears 3 times/year and contains literature, arts, affairs—Scottish and international. They want any form or style of poetry on any subject. They have published poetry by Iain Crichton Smith, Edwin Morgan, Dennis O'Donnell and Jim C. Wilson. As a sample the editors selected these lines from "A Calvinist Narrowly Avoids Pleasure" by Bill Duncan:

> *Trying so hard to nearly not enjoy the feelings/but the pleasure and the calm are almost beyond my*

control/then you touch me/and my back straightens/like a cat stroked the wrong way

The editors say *Cencrastus* is 44 pgs., A4. They receive about 300 poems a year, accept approximately 10%. Press run is 1,000 for 600 subscribers of which 50 are libraries, 300 shelf sales; 10 distributed free to small publishers. Single copy: £2.25; subscription: £12, £15 overseas. Sample: £2.50.

How to Submit: No previously published poems; simultaneous submissions OK. Cover letter preferred. E-mail and disk submissions OK. Seldom comments on rejections. Publishes theme issues occasionally. Reports in 8-10 weeks. Pays £10-40. Acquires first rights. Reviews books of poetry in 500-1,500 words, single or multi-book format. Open to unsolicited reviews. Poets may also send books for review consideration.

Book/Chapbook Needs & How to Submit: "Curly Snake Publishing has published so far only one poetry book (*Two Clocks Ticking* by Dennis O'Donnell), but anything worth publishing will be considered." Prefer poets to be published in magazine first. Replies to queries and mss in 10-12 weeks. Pays 7-10% royalties. Obtain sample books by sending £5.95.

THE CENTENNIAL REVIEW, 312 Linton Hall, Michigan State University, East Lansing MI 48824-1044, phone (517)355-1905, fax (517)432-1858, e-mail cenrev@pilot.msu.edu, website http://www.pilot.msu.edu/user/cenrev, founded 1957, editor R.K. Meiners.

Magazine Needs: *The Centennial Review* appears 3 times/year. They want "that sort of poem which, however personal, bears implications for communal experience." They have published poetry by David Citino, Jon Silkin and Dimitris Tsaloumas. It is 240 pgs., 6×9, desktop-published, perfect-bound, with 3-color cover, art, graphics and ads. They receive about 500 poems a year, accept about 2%. Press run is 1,000 for 800 subscribers. Subscription: $12/year. Sample: $6.

How to Submit: Submit 5 poems at a time. No previously published poems or simultaneous submissions. Seldom comments on rejections. Publishes theme issues. Send SASE for guidelines and upcoming themes or request via e-mail or fax. Reports in about 2 months. Pays 2 copies plus 1-year subscription. Acquires all rights. Returns rights "when asked by authors for reprinting."

CENTER PRESS; MASTERS AWARDS, Box 16452, Encino CA 91416-6452, e-mail news7@letterbox.com, website http://www.concentric.net/~medianet/index.html, founded 1980, editor Gabriella Stone.

Book/Chapbook Needs & How to Submit: Center Press is "a small press presently publishing 6-7 works per year including poetry, photojournals, calendars, novels, etc. We look for quality, freshness and that touch of genius." In poetry, "we want to see verve, natural rhythms, discipline, impact, etc. We are flexible but verbosity, triteness and saccharine make us cringe. *We now read and publish only mss accepted from the Masters Award.*" They have published books by Bebe Oberon, Walter Calder, Exene Vida, Carlos Castenada and Sandra Gilbert. As a sample the editor selected these lines from "The Patriot" by Scott Alejandro Sonders:

> *Underwire bras/and other implements/of torture, are remnants of the Inquisition./It would be best to set/the breast free to hang, as a proud silk flag/on a windless day.*

Their tastes are for poets such as Adrienne Rich, Li-Young Lee, Charles Bukowski and Czeslaw Milosz. "We have strong liaisons with the entertainment industry and like to see material that is media-oriented and au courant."

Also Offers: "We sponsor the Masters Awards, established in 1981, including a $1,000 grand prize annually plus each winner (and the five runners-up in poetry) will be published in a clothbound edition and distributed to selected university and public libraries, news mediums, etc. There is a one-time only $15 administration and reading fee per entrant. Submit a maximum of five poems or song lyric pages (no tapes) totaling no more than 150 lines. Any poetic style or genre is acceptable, but a clear and fresh voice, discipline, natural rhythm and a certain individuality should be evident. Further application and details available with a #10 SASE."

Advice: The editor says, "Please study what we publish before you consider submitting."

CHACHALACA POETRY REVIEW, English Dept., UT-Brownsville, Brownsville TX 78521, phone (956)544-8239, fax (956)544-8988, e-mail mlewis@utb1.utb.edu, founded 1997, contact Marty Lewis.

Magazine Needs: *CPR* is "published once or twice a year, depending on number of submissions. We are looking for thematic substance and crafted lines in the poetry we publish. That doesn't often mean standard stanza pattern or any particular style, but there should be some connection between form and content. We don't accept poems with skinny, three syllable lines, intrusive rhymes, arbitrary line breaks, random indentation, or center justification just because the PC can do it. No haikus or prose poems. Because of space limitations, we usually can't use poems of more than 60 lines." As a sample the editor selected these lines from "What to Do with Hands" by Anne Giles Rimbey:

> *My pain lets down like milk and whitens our tea./I am trying to tell you what my father/said: Understanding is not black or white but/surface with typography. Equal heights reached/here or there. I shape hands in a hill over/teapots like I am conjuring. Or praying.*

Chachalaca is 50-100 pgs., professionally printed and perfect-bound with no ads. Press run is 500 with 200 distributed free to libraries, 100 shelf sales. Single copy: $8. Sample: $4.

How to Submit: Submit 5-10 poems at a time. Include SASE. No previously published poems; simultaneous submissions OK "if you alert us." Cover letter with short bio preferred. Time between acceptance and publication varies. Poems are circulated to an editorial board of 3 readers. Seldom comments on rejections. Reports in 2 months or more. Pays 2 copies. Buys all rights. Returns rights.

Advice: They say, "*Chachalaca* is fairly new, but its editors are experienced and the journal is well supported."

☑ ◯ **CHAFF**, 4400 Shamrock, Unit 1A, McHenry IL 60050, e-mail jordan5450@aol.com, founded 1996, first issue 1997, editor Jordan Taylor Young.
Magazine Needs: *Chaff* is a semiannual publication "dedicated to the Lord, for the express purpose of reaching out to a lost and hurting world, as well as uniting Christian poets through the publication of their work." They want "free verse poetry—rhyme and meter only if exceptional quality—romance, nature, aging, friendship, family life and humor. Nothing satanic, obscene, violent, sensual, erotic or homosexual." As a sample the editor selected this poem, "Miracle," by Patricia Rourke:
> *I burn with multi-colored fire, I rush with my one ounce of faith, my one molecule of word, through the heart of whatever mountain needs moving.*
Chaff is 20-30 pgs., 5½×8, laser-printed and stapled. Press run is 50-100. Poetry may be complemented by appropriate photographs, illustrations or scripture. In addition, *Chaff* includes a "Featured Poet" segment, consisting of a short bio and photograph.
How to Submit: Submit no more than 5 poems at a time with $2/poem reading fee. Make checks payable to Jordan Taylor Young, editor. Previously published poems and simultaneous submissions OK. Cover letter and SASE required. E-mail submissions OK. Reports in 3-4 weeks. Pays 2 copies, 3 copies to Featured Poet.
Advice: The editor says, "Often poets are not recognized for their artistry, separated like chaff from wheat. The name *Chaff* stems from my deep conviction that we are like chaff, and separated from God we can do nothing. We intend to provide a stronger link to self, helping new and aspiring poets to find their own voices through the publication of their work. 'For where your treasure is, there will your heart be also.' (Matthew 6:21)."

🍁 ☑ ◯ ◑ ◎ **CHALLENGER INTERNATIONAL; MCNAUGHTON EDITIONS (Specialized: teen/young adult)**, 440 McNaughton Ave., McNaughton Center, Quesnel, British Columbia V2J 3K8 Canada, phone (250)991-5567, e-mail lukivdan@hotmail.com, founded 1978, editor Dan Lukiv.
Magazine Needs: *Challenger international*, a literary quarterly, contains poetry, short fiction, novel excerpts, and black pen drawings. The editor says he is open to "any type of work, especially by teenagers (*Ci*'s mandate: to encourage young writers, and to publish their work alongside established writers), providing it is not pornographic, profane, or overly abstract." He has published poetry from Canada, the US and Columbia. As a sample the editor selected "The Thinker" one of his poems:
> *A toothless old man/Drinks cold coffee/Alone./He scratches his scalp—/Dandruff floats in his coffee,/ Like snow-flecks./He wonders—//But soon only his coffee/Matters*
Ci is about 20 pgs., 8½×11, photocopied and side-stapled. Press run is 100. The journal is distributed free to McNaughton Center-secondary alternate-students.
How to Submit: Previously published poems and simultaneous submissions OK. Cover letter required with list of credits, if any. E-mail submissions OK. Sometimes comments on rejections. "No SASE (or SAE and IRC) means submission goes into the garbage. Sometimes we edit to save the poet rejection." Reports in 4 months. Pays 1 copy.
Book/Chapbook Needs & How to Submit: McNaughton Editions publishes chapbooks of work by authors featured in *Ci*. Pays 3 copies. Copyright remains with authors. They have published *Dear Teacher*, by Dawn Willey. Distribution of free copies through the Quesnel Library.
Advice: The editor says, "We like poems that make sense."

◑ **CHANCE MAGAZINE**, 3929 S. Fifth St., Louisville KY 40214, phone (502)375-0871, founded 1992, editor Robert L. Penick.
Magazine Needs: *Chance Magazine*, a biannual, "provides an outlet for the Van Gogh's and Hart Crane's of this world, fosters community and encourages growth between artists." They want "anything daring but not pretentious, sincere but not schmaltzy. Take off your clothes and show me your scars." They have published poetry by Thomas Michael McDade, Norman Olson, Cliff Wieck and Anna Wilson. As a sample the editor selected this poem, "All The Good Ones" by Mark Senkus:
> *Go for guys/That make them feel/Safe/Secure/Meanwhile I scare/Myself*
Chance is 32 pgs., digest-sized, photocopied and saddle-stapled with light card cover, includes b&w line drawings. They accept approximately 10% of the poems received each year. Press run is 200 for 105 subscribers; 50 distributed free to reviewers and contributors. Subscription: $4. Sample: $2. Make checks payable to Robert L. Penick.
How to Submit: Submit any number of poems at a time. Previously published poems OK (if noted); no simultaneous submissions. Cover letter preferred. "It is strongly recommended that poets sample the mag before submitting." Time between acceptance and publication is 4 months. Often comments on rejections. Reports in

---

🍁 ⊕ **SENDING TO A COUNTRY** other than your own? Be sure to send International Reply Coupons (IRCs) instead of stamps for replies or return of your manuscript.

3 weeks. Sometimes sends prepublication galleys. Pays 1 copy. Rights remain with poets. Staff reviews books and chapbooks of poetry and other magazines in 100 words. Open to unsolicited reviews. Send books for review consideration.

Advice: The editor says, "Learn a trade!"

⊕ $ ◎ **CHAPMAN (Specialized: ethnic); CHAPMAN PRESS**, 4 Broughton Place, Edinburgh EH1 3RX Scotland, phone (0131)557-2207, fax (0131)556-9565, founded 1970, editor Joy Hendry.

Magazine Needs: "*Chapman* magazine is controversial, influential, outspoken and intelligent. Founded in 1970, it has become a dynamic force in Scottish culture covering theatre, politics, language and the arts. Our highly-respected forum for poetry, fiction, criticism, review and debate makes it essential reading for anyone interested in contemporary Scotland. *Chapman* publishes the best in Scottish writing—new work by well-known Scottish writers in the context of lucid critical discussion. With our strong commitment to the future, we energetically promote new writers, new ideas and new approaches." They have published poetry and fiction by Alasdair Gray, Liz Lochhead, Sorley MacLean, T.S. Law, Edwin Morgan, Willa Muir, Tom Scott and Una Flett. As a sample the editor selected these lines from Judy Steel's poem "For Nicole Boulanger" who, Steel says, "was born in the same year as my daughter and died in the Lockerbie air disaster of 1988":

> *You died amongst these rolling Border hills:/The same our daughters played and rode and walked in -/*
> *They make a nursery fit to shape and mould/A spirit swift as water, free as air.//But you, west-winging*
> *through the Christmas dark/Found them no playground but a mortuary -/Your young life poised for*
> *flight to woman's years/Destroyed as wantonly as moorland game.*

Chapman appears 4 times a year in a 6×9, perfect-bound format, 104 pgs., professionally printed in small type on matte stock with glossy card cover, art in 2 colors. Press run is 2,000 for 900 subscribers of which 200 are libraries. They receive "thousands" of poetry submissions/year, use about 200, have a 4- to 6-month backlog. Sample: £4 (overseas).

How to Submit: Cover letter required. No simultaneous submissions. Reports "as soon as possible." Always sends prepublication galleys. Pays £8/page plus 1 copy. Staff reviews books of poetry. Send books for review consideration.

Book/Chapbook Needs: Chapman Press is currently not accepting submissions.

Advice: The editor says poets should not "try to court approval by writing poems especially to suit what they perceive as the nature of the magazine. They usually get it wrong and write badly." Also, they are interested in receiving poetry dealing with women's issues and feminism.

$ ◒ **THE CHARITON REVIEW**, Truman State University, Kirksville MO 63501, phone (816)785-4499, founded 1975, editor Jim Barnes.

Magazine Needs: *The Chariton Review* began in 1975 as a twice yearly literary magazine and in 1978 added the activities of the press (now defunct). The poetry published in the magazine is, according to the editor, "open and closed forms—traditional, experimental, mainstream. We do not consider verse, only poetry in its highest sense, whatever that may be. The sentimental and the inspirational are not poetry for us. Also, no more 'relativism': short stories and poetry centered around relatives." They have published poetry by Michael Spence, Neil Myers, Sam Maio, Andrea Budy, Charles Edward Eaton, Wayne Dodd and J'laine Robnolt. There are 40-50 pages of poetry in each issue of the *Review*, a 6×9, flat-spined magazine of over 100 pages, professionally printed, glossy cover with photographs. Circulation is about 600 for 400 subscribers of which 100 are libraries. They receive 8,000-10,000 submissions/year, of which they use 35-50, with never more than a 6-month backlog. Subscription: $9/1 year, $15/2 years. Sample: $5.

How to Submit: Submit 5-7 poems at a time, typescript single-spaced. No simultaneous submissions. Do *not* write for guidelines. Response times here are quick, and accepted poems often appear within a few issues of notification. Always sends prepublication galleys. Pays $5/printed page. Buys first North American serial rights. Contributors are expected to subscribe or buy copies. Open to unsolicited reviews. Poets may also send books for review consideration.

☑ $ ◒ **THE CHATTAHOOCHEE REVIEW**, Georgia Perimeter College, 2101 Womack Rd., Dunwoody GA 30338, phone (770)551-3019, website http://www.dc.peachnet.edu/~twadley/cr/index.htm, founded 1980, editor-in-chief Lawrence Hetrick, poetry editors (Mr.) Collie Owens and Steven Beauchamp.

Magazine Needs: *The Chattahoochee Review* is a quarterly of poetry, short fiction, essays, reviews and interviews, published by Georgia Perimeter College. "We publish a number of Southern writers, but *CR* is not by design a regional magazine. All themes, forms and styles are considered as long as they impact the whole person: heart, mind, intuition, and imagination." They have published poetry by Joanne Childers, Robert Dana, Mildred Greear, Rosemary Daniell and John Frederick Nims. *The Review* is 140 pgs., 6×9, professionally printed on cream stock with b&w reproductions of artwork, flat-spined, with one-color card cover. Recent issues feature a wide range of forms and styles augmenting prose selections. Circulation is 1,250, of which 300 are complimentary copies sent to editors and "miscellaneous VIPs." Subscription: $16/year. Sample: $6.

How to Submit: Writers should send 1 copy of each poem and a cover letter with bio material. No simultaneous submissions. Time between acceptance and publication is 3-4 months. Publishes theme issues. Send SASE for guidelines and upcoming themes. Queries will be answered in 1-2 weeks. Reports in 3 months. Pays $50/poem and 2 copies. Acquires first rights. Staff reviews books of poetry and short fiction in 1,500 words, single or multi-book format. Send books for review consideration.

■ $ ⊍ ◎ CHELSEA; CHELSEA AWARD COMPETITION (Specialized: translations), P.O. Box 773, Cooper Station, New York NY 10276-0773, founded 1958, editor Richard Foerster, senior associate editor Alfredo de Palchi, associate editor Andrea Lockett.

● Work published in *Chelsea* has been included in the 1993, 1994, 1995, 1997 and 1998 volumes of *The Best American Poetry.*

Magazine Needs: *Chelsea* is a long-established, high quality literary biannual, appearing in June and December, that aims to promote intercultural communication. "We look for intelligence and sophisticated technique in both experimental and traditional forms. We are also interested in translations of contemporary poets. Although our tastes are eclectic, we lean toward the cosmopolitan avant-garde. We would like to see more poetry by writers of color. Do not want to see 'inspirational' verse, pornography or poems that rhyme merely for the sake of rhyme." They have published poetry by Timothy Liu, Ruth Stone, Lisel Mueller, Karen Volkman, Carl Phillips and Brenda Shaughnessy. As an example of "the kind of attention to language and imagery" wanted for *Chelsea*, the editor selected these lines from "The Eye-mote" by Sylvia Plath, which first appeared in *Chelsea* in 1960:

> What I want back is what I was/Before the bed, before the knife,/Before the brooch-pin and the salve/
> Fixed me in this parenthesis;/Horses fluent in the wind,/A place, a time gone out of mind.

Chelsea is 192-240 pgs., 6×9, perfect-bound, offset printed, full-color cover art on card cover, occasional photos, ads. Circulation is 1,800 for 900 subscribers of which 200 are libraries. Subscription: $13 domestic, $16 foreign. Sample: $7.

How to Submit: Submissions of 5-7 pgs. of poetry are ideal; long poems should not exceed 10 pgs.; must be typed; include brief bio. No previously published poems or simultaneous submissions. "We try to comment favorably on above-average mss; otherwise, we do not have time to provide critiques." Reports within 3 months. Always sends prepublication galleys. Pays $20/page and 2 copies. Buys first North American serial rights and one-time nonexclusive reprint rights.

Also Offers: Sponsors the annual Chelsea Award Competition (deadline December 15), $1,000 for poetry. Guidelines available by SASE to P.O. Box 1040, York Beach ME 03910.

Advice: Editor Richard Foerster comments: "Beginners should realize editors of little magazines are always overworked and that it is necessary haste and not a lack of concern or compassion that makes rejections seem coldly impersonal."

⊍ ◎ CHICAGO REVIEW (Specialized: translations), 5801 S. Kenwood, Chicago IL 60637-1794, phone/fax (773)702-0887, e-mail org_crev@orgmail.uchicago.edu, website http://www.humanities.uchicago.edu/humanities/review/, founded 1946, poetry editor Devin Johnston.

Magazine Needs: "We publish high quality poetry. About 20% of the work we select is unsolicited; the remainder is solicited from poets whose work we admire. Translations are welcome, but please include a statement of permission from the original publisher if work is not in the public domain." They have published poets as diverse as Alice Fulton, Yusef Komunyakaa, Turner Cassity, Nathaniel Mackey, August Kleinzahler, Meena Alexander and Anne Carson. Circulation is 2,800. Sample: $6.

How to Submit: Queries and guideline requests may be sent/requested via fax and e-mail. No electronic submissions. Reports in 3 months, longer in some cases. Sometimes sends prepublication galleys. Pays 3 copies and one-volume subscription. Occasionally reviews books of poetry. Open to unsolicited reviews.

N ◎ CHICORY BLUE PRESS (Specialized: women, senior citizens), 795 East St. N., Goshen CT 06756, phone (860)491-2271, fax (860)491-8619, founded 1988, publisher Sondra Zeidenstein.

Book Needs: Publishes 1 book/year. The press focuses on women poets past 60 and has published poetry by Honor Moore, Joan Swift and Nelly Wong.

How to Submit: Submit 5-7 poems and cover letter with "a brief introduction of self and work." Replies to queries and mss (if invited) in 3 months. Seldom comments on rejections. Pays royalties. Obtain sample books by ordering from the press.

✓ ○ CHILDREN, CHURCHES AND DADDIES; SCARS PUBLICATIONS, 8830 W. 120th Place, Palos Park IL 60464, e-mail ccandd96@aol.com, website http://members.aol.com/scarspub/scars.html, founded 1993, editor and publisher Janet Kuypers.

Magazine Needs: *Children, Churches and Daddies (the unreligious, non-family oriented literary magazine)* is published "monthly or bimonthly depending on year and contains news, humor, poetry, prose and essays. We accept poetry of almost any genre, but we're not keen on rhyme for rhyme's sake, and we're not keen on religious poems (look at our current issue for a better idea of what we're like). We do accept longer works, but within two pages for an individual poem is appreciated. We don't go for racist, sexist (therefore we're not into pornography either), or homophobic stuff." They have published poetry by Paul Weimmann, Cheryl Townsend, C Ra McGuirt and Ray Heinrich. As a sample we selected these lines from the publisher's own poem "Scars 1997":

> I wear my scars like badges./These deep marks show through from under my skin/like war paint on
> an Apache chief./Decorated with feathers, the skins of his prey.

The publisher says the print version of *CCAD* is about 100 pgs., 8×11, photocopied and saddle-stitched, cover, includes art and ads. They receive hundreds of poems a year, accept approximately 40%. Press run "depends." Sample: $4. Make checks payable to Janet Kuypers.

How to Submit: Prefers electronic submissions. Submit via e-mail or mail floppy disk with ASCII text or Macintosh disk. Previously published poems and simultaneous submissions OK. Time between acceptance and publication is 2 weeks. Seldom comments on rejections. Send SASE for guidelines or obtain via e-mail or website. Reports in 2 weeks.

Also Offers: Scars Publications sponsors 2 contests—a chapbook contest and a book contest. Write or e-mail for information. Website includes writer's guidelines, names of editors, poetry, interviews. "The website is a more comprehensive view of what *CC&D* does. All the information, including issues, is there."

○ ☑ **CHIRON REVIEW; CHIRON BOOKS; CHIRON REVIEW POETRY CONTEST; KINDRED SPIRIT PRESS**, 702 N. Prairie, St. John KS 67576-1516, phone (316)549-6156 or (316)786-4955, e-mail chironreview@webtv.net, website http://www.geocities.com/SoHo/Nook/1748/, founded 1982 as *The Kindred Spirit*, editor Michael Hathaway, assistant editor Jane Hathaway, contributing editor (poetry) Gerald Locklin.

Magazine Needs: *Chiron Review* is a quarterly tabloid using photographs of featured writers. No taboos. They have published poetry by Charles Bukowski, Marge Piercy, Katherine Hageland and Donald Raymond Pollock. As a sample the editor selected this complete poem, "We All Need Folderol" by Walt Phillips:

> i call my wife bug and biddypoo/we are all guilty of something like this/hemingway talked baby talk
> to his wives/god calls the universe boomypie

Each issue is 24-48 pgs. and "contains dozens of poems." Their press run is about 1,000. Sample: $4 ($8 overseas or institutions).

How to Submit: Submit 3-6 poems at a time, "typed or printed legibly." No simultaneous submissions or previously published poems. No submissions via e-mail. Very seldom publishes theme issues. Send SASE for guidelines and upcoming themes. Reports in 2-8 weeks. Pays 1 copy. Acquires first-time rights. Reviews books of poetry in 500-700 words. Open to unsolicited reviews. Poets may also send books for review consideration.

Book/Chapbook Needs & How to Submit: For book publication submit complete ms. They publish 1-3 chapbooks/year, flat-spined, professionally printed, paying 25% of press run of 100-200 copies.

Also Offers: Their annual poetry contest offers awards of $100 plus 1-page feature in Winter issue, $50, and 5 free subscriptions and a Chiron Press book. Entry fee: $5/poet. Website includes guidelines, sample poems, contest information, news and notes, and Personal Publishing Program information. They feature their Personal Publishing Program under the Kindred Spirit Press imprint. "Through special arrangements with a highly specialized printer, we can offer extremely short run publishing at unbelievably low prices." Send SASE for information.

$ ☑ ◎ **THE CHRISTIAN CENTURY (Specialized: religious, social issues)**, Dept. PM, 407 S. Dearborn St., Chicago IL 60605, phone (312)427-5380, fax (312)427-1302, website http://www.ChristianCentury.com, founded 1884, named *The Christian Century* 1900, founded again 1908, joined by *New Christian* 1970, poetry editor Jill Peláez Baumgaertner.

Magazine Needs: This "ecumenical weekly" is a liberal, sophisticated journal of news, articles of opinion and reviews from a generally Christian point-of-view, using approximately 1 poem/issue, not necessarily on religious themes but in keeping with the literate tone of the magazine. They want "poems that are not statements but experiences, that do not talk about the world, but show it. We want to publish poems that are grounded in images and that reveal an awareness of the sounds of language and the forms of poetry even when the poems are written in free verse." They do not want "pietistic or sentimental doggerel." They have published poetry by Jeanne Murray Walker, Ida Fasel, Kathleen Norris, Luci Shaw, J. Barrie Shepherd and Wendell Berry. As a sample the editor selected this poem, "Rapture" by Ashley Mace Havird:

> In a straight-backed pew/on the balcony's front row,/I keep my distance./Still, the sunburst/of red-hot
> gladiolus,/fireball mums,/spikes me blind. . . .

The journal is magazine-sized, printed on quality newsprint, using b&w art, cartoons and ads, about 30 pgs., saddle-stapled. Sample: $3.

How to Submit: Submit poems of up to 20 lines, typed and double-spaced, 1 poem/page. Include your name, address and phone number on the first page of each poem. "Prefer shorter poems." No simultaneous submissions. Submissions without SASE or SAE and IRCs will not be returned. Pays usually $20/poem plus 1 copy and discount on additional copies. Acquires all rights. Inquire about reprint permission. Reviews books of poetry in 300-400 words, single format; 400-500 words, multi-book format.

Ⓝ ☑ **THE CHRISTIAN SCIENCE MONITOR**, The Home Forum Page, 1 Norway St., Boston MA 02115, website http://www.csmonitor.com, founded 1908, poetry editor Elizabeth Lund.

Magazine Needs: *CSM* is an international daily newspaper. Poetry used regularly in The Home Forum. They want "finely crafted poems that celebrate the extraordinary in the ordinary. Seasonal material always needed. Especially interested in poems about life in the city. No violence, sensuality or racism. Poems about illness, death or suffering are not a good fit. Short work preferred." They have published work by Diana der-Hovanessian, Lyn Lifshin and Vivian Shipley. As a sample the editor included these lines from "Doing Nothing" by Michael T. Young:

> It rains and hardens into ice./Clear, rippling streamers streak the windows./Trees drip with slim,
> transparent nails./One abstinate car passes/ignorant of the changing streetlight.

How to Submit: Submit up to 5 poems at a time, single-spaced. SASE must be included. "No submissions via fax or e-mail, please." No previously published poems or simultaneous submissions. Usually reports within 1-2 months. Pays varying rates, upon publication.

Also Offers: Website includes all of the daily paper, a complete archive (back to 1980), and interviews with authors including Peter Davison, Alice Quinn and Judson Hale.

⬚ ⊘ ◎ **CHRISTIANITY AND THE ARTS (Specialized: religious)**, P.O. Box 118088, Chicago IL 60611, phone (312)642-8606, fax (312)266-7719, e-mail chrnarts@aol.com, founded 1994, editor/publisher Marci Whitney-Schenck, poetry editor Robert Klein Engler (and submissions should go directly to him at 901 S. Plymouth Ct., Apt. 1801, Chicago IL 60605).

Magazine Needs: *Christianity and the Arts* is a quarterly magazine designed "to celebrate the revelation of God through the arts and to encourage excellent Christian artistic expression." They want poetry of "excellence—open to all styles—with a Christian viewpoint." They have published poetry by William Preston, Paul Barkman, Judith Deem Dupree and Carl Winderl. It is 64 pgs., 8½×11, professionally printed on coated stock and saddle-stapled, with b&w and color photos. They accept 20% of the poetry received. Press run is 5,000 for 3,500 subscribers, 700 shelf sales. Single copy: $5; subscription: $21. Sample: $7.

How to Submit: Simultaneous submissions OK. Time between acceptance and publication is 6 months. Publishes theme issues. Send SASE for upcoming themes. Reports within 2 weeks. Always sends prepublication galleys. Pays 2 copies. Acquires first or one-time rights.

Advice: The editor says, "We wish to support the efforts of Christian poets, however we get more poetry than any other type of writing. We can't publish everyone's wonderful efforts but we do try to include as many poems as possible, especially when the poems concern our themes. Many submissions read more like prayers than poems. We are looking for quality verse."

🄽 ◎ **CHRONICLES OF DISORDER (Specialized: themes)**, 20 Edie Rd., Saratoga Springs NY 12866, founded 1996, editor Thomas Christian.

Magazine Needs: Published biannually, each issue of *COD* is based on a theme—poetry, prose, art influenced by that theme. "Understand this quote from Antonin Artaud: 'If there is one hellish, accursed thing in our time, it is our artistic dallying with form, instead of being like victims burnt at the stake, signaling through the flames.' " They have published poetry by Thurston Moore, Ron Whitehead, Arthur Winfield Knight and G.J. Bassett. As a sample the editor selected these lines from his poem "Daimonswey":

> The poet sings. She is Sikelianos./Our spears are twisted. Mangled./A churchbell bangs/A string of
> gongs/the Laconian bitches howl

The editor says *COD* is 48 pgs., digest-sized, photocopied and stapled with cardstock cover, includes photography and art sketches. They receive about 150 poems a year, accept approximately 20%. Press run is 500 for 50 subscribers of which 10 are libraries, 300 shelf sales; 100 distributed free to review publications. Single copy: $2.95. Sample: $4. Make checks payable to Thomas Christian.

How to Submit: Submit 4 poems at a time with SASE. Previously published poems and simultaneous submissions OK. Cover letter preferred. "Tell a bit of yourself." Time between acceptance and publication is 3-12 months. Seldom comments on rejections. Send SASE for guidelines and upcoming themes. Reports in 1 month. Sometimes sends prepublication galleys. Pays 2 copies.

Advice: The editor says, "Be in love with your life. Realize that existence is a gift; a temporary window of opportunity in time; a lusting. Find the language as your expression."

💲 ⊘ ◎ **CHRYSALIS READER (Specialized: spirituality, themes)**, Rt. 1 Box 184, Dillwyn VA 23936-9616, fax (804)983-1074, founded 1985, poetry editor Robert F. Lawson, editor Carol S. Lawson,

Magazine Needs: *Chrysalis Reader* is published by the Swedenborg Foundation as a "contribution to the search for spiritual wisdom." It appears intermittently and is now a "book series that draws upon diverse traditions to engage thought on questions that challenge inquiring minds using literate and scholarly fiction, essays and poetry." They want poetry that is "spiritually related and focused on the particular issue's theme. Nothing overly religious or sophomoric." They have published work by Jan Frazier, Linda Pastan, Julia Randall, Robert Bly, Peter Bethanis and Tom O'Grady. As a sample the editor selected these lines from "The Only Love That Lasts" by Kate Gleason:

> I want to grow alike/in the grand tradition of great marriages,/want our faces to wrinkle like wax
> paper/that's been used and smoothed and used again.

CR is 192 pgs., 7×10, professionally printed on archival paper and perfect-bound with coated cover stock, illustrations and photos. They receive about 1,000 poems a year, use 2-5%. Press run is 3,500. Sample: $10.

How to Submit: Submit no more than 5 poems at one time. No previously published poems or simultaneous submissions. Time between acceptance and publication is typically 18 months. Send SASE for themes and guidelines. Upcoming themes are Ages and Education. Reports in 2-3 months. Always sends prepublication galleys. Pays $25 and 3 copies. Buys first-time rights. "We expect to be credited for reprints after permission is given."

Advice: The editor says, "Be professional. Editorial suggestions are offered in the spirit of all good literature."

N Ⓞ **CIDER PRESS REVIEW; CIDER PRESS REVIEW POETRY CALENDAR**, P.O. Box 881914, San Diego CA 92168, e-mail editor@PoetryCalendar.com, website http://www.PoetryCalendar.com, founded 1997, co-editors Caron Andregg and Robert Wynne.

Magazine Needs: *Cider Press Review* appears twice a year and features "the best new work from contemporary poets." They want "thoughtful, well-crafted poems with vivid language and strong images. We prefer poems that have something to say. We would like to see more well-written humor. No didactic, inspirational, greeting-card verse; therapy or religious doggerel." They have published poetry by Michael McNeilley, Michael Estabrook, Larry Colker and Laurel Ann Bogen. As a sample the editors selected these lines from "Why My Father Smoked" by Jennifer Lesh:

> Just before he'd shake/open a newspaper and block me from sight,/he'd blow me a ring, two, three,
> fat/as hoopskirts, and as these dissolved/into my laughter, my father/would slide slowly into silence/
> of important words and men.

The editors say *CPR* is 120 pgs., digest-sized, offset printed and perfect-bound with 2-color coated card cover. They receive about 1,500 poems a year, accept approximately 3%. Press run is 1,000. Subscription: $20/3 issues. Sample: $10.

How to Submit: Submit up to 5 poems at a time. No previously published poems; simultaneous submissions OK. Cover letter with short bio preferred. "Please include two SASEs. Poets whose work is accepted will be expected to provide a copy of the poem on disk. Do not send unsolicited disk submissions." Time between acceptance and publication is 6-10 months. Poems are circulated to an editorial board. Seldom comments on rejections. Obtain guidelines via website. Reports in 2-6 months. Pays 1 copy. Acquires first North American serial rights.

Also Offers: They also publish the annual *Poetry Calendar*. "The *Poetry Calendar* is the original poetry anthology/datebook and features a week-at-a-glance organizing page accompanied by a new poem each week." Send up to 5 poems, 30 lines maximum. Deadline: April 30. See website for details.

$ Ⓞ **CIMARRON REVIEW**, 205 Morrill Hall, Oklahoma State University, Stillwater OK 74078-0135, phone (405)744-9476, founded 1967, poetry editors Doug Martin, Mark Cox, Lisa Lewis, James Cooper and Todd Fuller.

Magazine Needs: *Cimarron* is a quarterly literary journal. "We take pride in our eclecticism. We like evocative poetry (lyric or narrative) controlled by a strong voice. No sing-song verse. No quaint prairie verse. No restrictions as to subject matter. We look for poems whose surfaces and structures risk uncertainty and which display energy, texture, intelligence, and intense investment." Among poets they have published are Dorothy Barresi, Cesare Pauese, Mark Doty, Tess Gallagher, David Rivard and Albert Goldbarth. This magazine, 100-150 pgs., 6×9, perfect-bound, boasts a handsome design, including a color cover and attractive printing. Poems lean toward free verse, lyric and narrative, although all forms and styles seem welcome. There are 15-25 pages of poetry in each issue. Circulation is 500 of which most are libraries. Single copy: $5; subscription: $16/year ($20 Canada), $45/3 years ($55 Canada), plus $2.50 for all international subscriptions.

How to Submit: Submit 3-5 poems, name and address on each, typed single- or double-spaced. No simultaneous submissions. Send SASE for upcoming themes. Reports within 3 months. Pays $15 for each poem published, 1 copy and a subscription. Buys all rights. "Permission for a reprinting is granted upon request." Reviews books of poetry in 500-900 words, single book format, occasionally multi-book. All reviews are assigned.

✓ Ⓞ **THE CINCINNATI POETS' COLLECTIVE**, 634 Linden, Newport KY 41071, founded 1988, editor Rebecca M. Weigold.

Magazine Needs: *TCPC* is a poetry magazine accepting only well-crafted poems, and wants more poetry concerning political issues with conservative themes. No rhyme or greeting card verse; no cartoons or artwork, "no sexually explicit or violent content that is gratuitous in nature." Published irregularly. *TCPC* is digest-sized, saddle-stapled. Circulation is approximately 150.

How to Submit: Submit up to 5 camera-ready poems per submission period. SASE required for consideration. No previously published poems. Simultaneous submissions OK, if noted. Submissions accepted October 1 through April 1 only. Reports in 4-6 months. Pays 1 copy.

Advice: The editor says, "Do not send anything outside the submission period. Please submit only completely polished work. I am backlogged with submissions so do not hurriedly send me your rough drafts. Reporting time may take longer than usual."

Ⓜ **CITY LIGHTS BOOKS**, 261 Columbus Ave., San Francisco CA 94133, phone (415)362-1901, founded 1955, edited by Lawrence Ferlinghetti and Nancy J. Peters.

Book/Chapbook Needs & How to Submit: City Lights Books is a paperback house that achieved prominence with the publication of Allen Ginsberg's *Howl* and other poetry of the "Beat" school. They publish "poetry, fiction, philosophy, political and social history." Simultaneous submissions OK. "All submissions must include SASE." Reports in 2 months. Payment varies.

N **Y** Ⓞ **CLACKAMAS LITERARY REVIEW; WILLAMETTE AWARD**, 19600 South Molalla Ave., Oregon City OR 97045, phone (503)657-6958 ext. 2520, website http://www.clackamas.cc.or.us/cir, founded 1997, editors Jeff Knorr and Tim Schell.

• The *Clackamas Literary Review* received the Community College Humanities Association's Best New Magazine Award.

Magazine Needs: "The *Clackamas Literary Review* is a nationally distributed magazine that publishes quality literature. It is an annual magazine produced at Clackamas Community College under the direction of the English Department. *CLR* promotes the work of emerging writers and established writers of fiction, poetry, and creative nonfiction." They consider all quality poetry. They have published poetry by Beckian Fritz Goldberg, Walt McDonald, Paul Berg, Amanda Coffey and Pamela Rice Porter. The editors say *CLR* is 150-200 pgs., 6×9, paperback. They receive about 1,800 poems a year, accept approximately 5%. Press run is 1,500 for 400 subscribers of which 20 are libraries, 420 shelf sales; 211 distributed free to graduate programs. Single copy: $6; subscription: $10/1 year, $20/2 years. Sample: $3. Make checks payable to *CLR*.

How to Submit: Submit 4 poems at a time. No previously published poems; simultaneous submissions OK. "Please inform us if your submitted work is accepted elsewhere." Cover letter with bio and SASE required. Reads submissions September 1 through June 1 only. Time between acceptance and publication is 2-6 months. Poems are circulated to an editorial board. Seldom comments on rejections. Send SASE for guidelines or obtain via website. Reports in 3-4 months. Acquires first North American serial rights.

Also Offers: Sponsors Willamette Award for fiction and poetry. The winning prize in each category is $500. Send no more than 6 poems or 1 story to *CLR* by September 1. Entry fee: $10. "Each contestant will receive a copy of the journal. Follow our general submission guidelines for submitting work and remember that if you wish return of the manuscript or notification you must enclose a SASE. All work submitted to the contest will also be considered for inclusion in the journal." Judges for upcoming contests will be announced.

Advice: The editors say, "Always submit your best work."

■ ○ ◎ **THE CLAREMONT REVIEW (Specialized: teens/young adults)**, 4980 Wesley Rd., Victoria, British Columbia V8Y 1Y9 Canada, phone (250)658-5221, fax (250)658-5387, e-mail review@claremont.victoria.bc.ca, website http://206.12.151.253, founded 1991.

Magazine Needs: *The Claremont Review* is a biannual review which publishes poetry and fiction written by those ages 13 to 19. Each fall issue also includes an interview with a prominent Canadian writer. They want "vital, modern poetry with a strong voice and living language. We prefer works that reveal something of the human condition. No clichéd language nor copies of 18th and 19th century work." They have published poetry by Jen Wright, Erin Egan and Max Rosenblum. As a sample the editors selected these lines from "The Last Room" by Jen Wright:

> These men study death./They say it is congestive heart failure,/brain hemorrhage, invasive tumor./But
> that's not what you showed me/one child's day/after we found a robin, frozen, on the porch.

The Claremont Review is 110 pgs., 6×9, professionally printed and perfect-bound with an attractive color cover. They receive 600-800 poems a year, publish 120. Press run is 700 for 200 subscribers of which 50 are libraries, 250 shelf sales. Subscription: $12/year, $20/2 years. Sample: $6.

How to Submit: Submit poems typed one to a page with author's name at the top of each. No previously published poems; simultaneous submissions OK. E-mail submissions OK. Cover letter with brief bio required. Reads submissions September through June only. Always comments on rejections. Send SASE (or SAE and IRC) for guidelines. Reports in 2-6 weeks (excluding July and August). Pays 1 copy and funds when grants allow it. Acquires first North American serial rights.

Advice: The editors say "We strongly urge potential contributors to read back issues of *The Claremont Review*. That is the best way for you to learn what we are looking for."

✓ ◎ **THE CLASSICAL OUTLOOK (Specialized: translations, classics, Latin)**, Classics Dept., Park Hall, University of Georgia, Athens GA 30602-6203, phone (706)542-9257, fax (706)542-8503, e-mail mricks@arches.uga.edu, founded 1924, editor Prof. Richard LaFleur, poetry editors Prof. David Middleton (original English verse) and David Slavitt (translations and original Latin verse).

Magazine Needs: *The Classical Outlook* "is an internationally circulated quarterly journal (4,200 subscriptions, of which 250 are libraries) for high school and college Latin and Classics teachers, published by the American Classical League." They invite submissions of "original poems in English on classical themes, verse translations from Greek and Roman authors, and original Latin poems. Submissions should, as a rule, be written in traditional poetic forms and should demonstrate skill in the use of meter, diction and rhyme if rhyme is employed. Original poems should be more than mere exercise pieces or the poetry of nostalgia. Translations should be accompanied by a photocopy of the original Greek or Latin text. Latin originals should be accompanied by a literal English rendering of the text. Submissions should not exceed 50 lines." They have published work by Sarah Ruden. As a sample the editors selected these lines from "Gaia" by R.H. Morrison:

> Or does she store for them, as in a void,/seeds of the fruit of some unripe abyss/that we call future?

THE OPENNESS TO SUBMISSIONS INDEX at the back of this book lists all publishers in this section by how open they are to submissions.

> *With that patient gait/through silvered darknesses and golden joys/we go from the emblazoned to the*
> *hidden/as once, out of the hidden, Gaia came.*

There are 2-3 magazine-sized pgs. of poetry in each issue, and they use 20% of the approximately 350 submissions they receive each year. They have a 12- to 18-month backlog, 4-month lead time. Single copy: $10.

How to Submit: Submit 2 anonymous copies, double-spaced, no more than 5 poems at a time. No previously published or simultaneous submissions. "Please include a floppy disk containing work, if possible. Also, please identify the name and version number of word-processing package used." Poetry is refereed by poetry editors. Send SASE for guidelines or request via e-mail or fax. Reports in 6-9 months. Pays 2 copies. Sample copies are available from the American Classical League, Miami University, Oxford OH 45056 for $10. Reviews books of poetry "if the poetry is sufficiently classical in nature."

Advice: The editors add, "Since our policy is to have poetry evaluated anonymously, names and addresses on poems, etc., just make work at this end. Cover letters are not forwarded to the poetry editors. Also, we never knowingly publish any works which have been or will be published elsewhere."

$ ◎ CLEANING BUSINESS MAGAZINE; CLEANING CONSULTANT SERVICES, INC. (Specialized: cleaning, self-employment), P.O. Box 1273, Seattle WA 98111, phone (206)622-4241, fax (206)622-6876, e-mail wgriffin@cleaningconsultant.com, website http://www.cleaningconsultants.com, founded 1976, poetry editor William R. Griffin.

Magazine Needs: *CBM* is "a monthly magazine for cleaning and maintenance professionals" and uses some poetry relating to their interests. "To be considered for publication in *Cleaning Business*, submit poetry that relates to our specific audience—cleaning and self-employment." He has published poetry by Don Wilson, Phoebe Bosche, Trudie Mercer and Joe Keppler. The editor says it is 100 pgs., 8½×11, offset litho printed, using ads, art and graphics. They receive about 50 poems a year, use approximately 10. Press run is 5,000 for 3,000 subscribers of which 100 are libraries, 500 shelf sales. Single copy: $5; subscription: $20. Sample: $3.

How to Submit: No previously published poems; simultaneous submissions OK. Send SASE and $3 for guidelines. Pays $5-10 plus 1 copy.

Advice: The poetry editor suggests, "Poets identify a specific market and work to build a readership that can be tapped again and again over a period of years with new books. Also write to a specific audience that has a mutual interest. We buy poetry about cleaning, but seldom receive anything our subscribers would want to read."

✓ ◐ ◎ CLEVELAND STATE UNIVERSITY POETRY CENTER; CSU POETRY SERIES; CLEVELAND POETS SERIES; CSU POETRY CENTER PRIZE (Specialized: regional), 1983 E. 24 St., Cleveland OH 44115-2440, phone (216)687-3986, or toll-free (888)278-6473, fax (216)687-6943, e-mail poetrycenter@popmail.csuohio.edu, website http://www.ims.csuohio.edu/poetry/poetrycenter.html, coordinator Rita Grabowski, editors Dave Evett, Bonnie Jacobson, Ted Lardner, Ruth Schwartz and Leonard Trawick. The Poetry Center was founded in 1962, first publications in 1971.

Book/Chapbook Needs: The Poetry Center publishes the CSU Poetry Series for poets in general and the Cleveland Poets Series for Ohio poets. "Open to many kinds of form, length, subject matter, style and purpose. Should be well-crafted, clearly of professional quality, ultimately serious (even when humorous). No light verse, devotional verse or verse in which rhyme and meter seem to be of major importance." They have published poetry by David Breskin, Jared Carter, Beckian Fritz Goldberg, Tim Seibles and Judith Vollmer. As a sample the editors selected these lines from "Swept With an Enormous Sadness" from *Hyena* by Jan Freeman:

> *The afternoon dropped like a concrete mass/but the boxwood held me safely./The moth balanced on*
> *your fingertip/then slowly crossed to mine./I sleep remembering your palm cupped up;/the days pass*
> *more in dream than waking.*

Books are chosen for publication from the entries to the CSU Poetry Center Prize contest. (Write and send $1 for catalog of Poetry Center books.) Postmark deadline: February 1. Entry fee: $20. The winner receives $1,000 and publication. They publish some other entrants in the Poetry Series, providing 50 copies (out of a press run of 1,000) and $300 lump sum. The Cleveland Poets Series (for Ohio poets) offers 100 copies of a press run of 600.

How to Submit: To submit for all series, send ms between November 1 and February 1 only. Reports on all submissions for the year by the end of July. No e-mail submissions. Mss should be for books of 50-100 pgs., pages numbered, poet's name, address and phone number on cover sheet, clearly typed. Poems may have been previously published (listed on an acknowledgment page). Simultaneous submissions OK, if notified and "poet keeps us informed of change in status." Send e-mail or SASE for guidelines.

Also Offers: The Center also publishes other volumes of poetry, including chapbooks (20-50 pgs.), with a $15 reading fee for each submission (except for Ohio residents, who can submit without the fee). Chapbook submissions are not eligible for the $1,000 prize.

◎ THE CLIMBING ART (Specialized: sports/recreation), 6390 E. Floyd Dr., Denver CO 80222, phone/fax (303)757-0541, e-mail rmorrow@dnur.uswest.net, founded 1986, editor Ron Morrow.

Magazine Needs: *The Climbing Art* is a biannual journal "read mainly by mountain enthusiasts who appreciate good writing about mountains and mountaineering. We are open to all forms and lengths. The only requirement is that the work be fresh, well-written and in some way of interest to those who love the mountains." They have published poetry by Terry Gifford, Allison Hunter, Paul Willis, Denise K. Simon and Barry Govenor. *TCA* is

160 pgs., digest-sized, professionally printed on heavy stock with glossy card cover. They use 12-20 poems/issue, receive 50 submissions/month. Press run is 1,500 for 700 subscribers of which 10 are libraries, 500 shelf sales. Subscription: $18. Sample: $4.

How to Submit: Simultaneous submissions and previously published poems OK. Reports in 6 months. Sometimes sends prepublication galleys. Pays 2 copies and subscription. Acquires one-time rights. Reviews books of poetry only if they concern mountains. Open to unsolicited reviews.

⊠ ⊕ ◎ CLÓ IAR-CHONNACHTA (Specialized: bilingual/foreign language), Indreabhán, Co. Galway, Ireland, phone (091)593307, fax (091)593362, e-mail cic@iol.ie, website http://www.wombat.ie/cic, founded 1985, contact Deirdre O'Toole.

Book/Chapbook Needs: Publishes paperback books of Irish language poetry, one of which is selected through a competition. They have published collections of poetry by Cathal Ó Searcaigh, Nuala Ni Dhomhnaill and Gabriel Rosenstock.

How to Submit: Query with 20 sample poems and a cover letter with brief bio and publication credits. Mss are read by an editorial panel. Often comments on rejections. No payment information provided. The poetry competition offers a £5,000 first prize in addition to publication. Deadline: December 1. Send SASE (or SAE and IRC) for details.

⊠ $ ◎ ⊘ CLUBHOUSE; YOUR STORY HOUR (Specialized: children, teens), P.O. Box 15, Berrien Springs MI 49103, phone (616)471-3701, website http://www.yourstoryhour.com, poetry editor Krista Phillips-Hainey.

Magazine Needs: The publication is printed in conjunction with the Your Story Hour radio program, founded 1949, which is designed to teach the Bible and moral life to children. The magazine, *Clubhouse*, started with that title in 1982, but as *Good Deeder*, its original name, it began publication in 1951. The editor says, "We do like humor or mood pieces. Don't like mushy-sweet 'Christian' poetry. We don't have space for long poems. Best—16 lines or under." They have published poetry by Lillian M. Fisher, Audrey Osofsky, Sharon K. Motzko, Bruce Bash and Craig Peters. *Clubhouse*, published monthly, is 20 pgs. The magazine has a circulation of 500, all for subscribers of which maybe 5 are libraries. Subscription: $5/year. Sample cost: 3 oz. postage.

How to Submit: They are closed to submissions until 2001. Simultaneous submissions OK. The "evaluation sheet" for returned mss gives reasons for acceptance or rejection. Writer's guidelines available for SASE. Pays about $12 for poems under 24 lines plus 2 copies. Negotiates rights.

Also Offers: Website includes general information about *Your Story Hour*, current newsletter and the current issue of *Clubhouse*.

⊠ ⊻ $ ⃞ ◎ CLUBHOUSE JR. (Specialized: children, religious), 8605 Explorer Dr., Colorado Springs CO 80920, phone (719)531-3400, fax (719)531-3499, founded 1988, associate editor Kim Washburn, editor Jesse Florea.

• *Clubhouse Jr.* won the Evangelical Press Association Award for Youth Publication.

Magazine Needs: *Clubhouse Jr.* is a monthly magazine published by Focus on the Family for 4-8 year olds. They want short poems—less than 100 words. "Poetry should have a strong message that supports traditional values. No cute, but pointless work." As a sample the editors selected this poem, "My Friend," by Mary Ryer:

> If I'm feeling very sad/And don't know what to do./If I'm feeling all alone/Or angry through and
> through./I really shouldn't worry/Or sit alone and cry./I always have a friend to help./Jesus is nearby.

Clubhouse Jr. is 16-20 pgs., magazine-sized, web printed on glossy paper and saddle-stapled with 4-color paper cover, includes 4-color art. Press run is about 90,000 for 85,000 subscribers; 500 distributed free. Single copy: $1.25; subscription: $12/year. Sample: $1 with SASE. Make checks payable to Focus on the Family.

How to Submit: Submit up to 5 poems at a time. No previously published poems; simultaneous submissions OK. Cover letter preferred. Time between acceptance and publication is 4-12 months. Seldom comments on rejections. Publishes theme issues occasionally. Send SASE for guidelines. Reports in 6-8 weeks. Pays $40-100. Acquires first rights.

⊘ CLUTCH, 147 Coleridge St., San Francisco CA 94110, e-mail dan@igc.apc.org, founded 1991, editors Dan Hodge and Oberc.

Magazine Needs: *Clutch* is an irregular (1 or 2 issues/year) "alternative/underground literary review." They want "poetry which explores or reveals an edge, societal edges especially. Take chances. Academic, overly-studied poems are not considered." They have published poetry by Charles Bukowski, Lorri Jackson, Todd Moore and Robert Peters. As a sample the editors selected these lines from "1492" by Mitchel Cohen:

> and the syringe is the size of a lover, O yes!/and the kisses, and the bodies,/and the fleshy zipless
> hallucinations/that pass for lovers/are no cure, no cure at all . . .

The editors describe *Clutch* as 60-70 pgs., approximately 5½×8½. "Printing, binding and graphics vary with each issue. We receive approximately 400-500 unsolicited submissions a year, but we accept less than 10% of unsolicited material. The majority of material is solicited." Press run is 200-500 for 40 subscribers of which 6 are libraries, approximately 70 shelf sales. Subscription: $5/issue for as many future issues as specified. Sample: $5. Make checks payable to Dan Hodge.

How to Submit: Simultaneous submissions OK. Cover letter required. Seldom comments on rejections. Reports

in 1-6 months. Pays 1 copy. Rights revert to authors. "Open to publishing reviews of books/magazines from underground press." Poets may also send books for review consideration.
Advice: The editors say, "Length isn't as important as impact, and I have yet to find a subject that was truly dangerous in its own right. If this doesn't clear things up, buy an issue and get a feel for what we like . . . just don't send a bunch of poems about kitties and butterflies."

COAL CITY REVIEW, English Dept., University of Kansas, Lawrence KS 66045, e-mail briandal@eagle.cc.ukans.edu, founded 1989, editor Brian Daldorph.
Magazine Needs: *CCR* is an annual publication of poetry, short stories, reviews and interviews—"the best material I can find." As for poetry, the editor quotes Pound: " 'Make it new.' " They do not want to see "experimental poetry, doggerel, five-finger exercises or beginner's verse." They have published poetry by Taylor Graham, David Ray, Gary Lechliter and Elliot Richman. As a sample the editor selected these lines from "My Monster" by Jim Mikoley:
> I could see that last day coming/like a twister down the highway.//When it hit,/I grabbed the pistol,/
> took my monster out back.//I kissed him on the head,/set him facing/toward the forest//As he started
> for the trees,/I raised the gun/and cleared my haunted skull out.
CCR is 80 pgs., 5½×8½, professionally printed on recycled paper and perfect-bound with light, colored card cover. They accept approximately 5% of the material received. Press run is 200 for 50 subscribers of which 5 are libraries. Subscription: $10. Sample: $5.
How to Submit: Submit 6 poems at a time. Accepts previously published poems occasionally; prefers not to receive simultaneous submissions. "Please do not send list of prior publications." Seldom comments on rejections. Send SASE for guidelines. Reports in 1-3 months. Pays 1 copy. Reviews books of poetry in 300-1,000 words, mostly single format. Open to unsolicited reviews. Poets may also send books for review consideration.
Book/Chapbook Needs & How to Submit: *CCR* also publishes occasional chapbooks as issues of the magazine but does not accept unsolicited chapbook submissions. Their most recent chapbook is *Under a Flare-lit Sky: Vietnam Poems* by John Musgrave.
Advice: The editor says, "Care more (much more) about writing than publication. If you're good enough, you'll publish."

COCHRAN'S CORNER (Specialized: subscribers), 1003 Tyler Court, Waldorf MD 20602-2964, phone (301)870-1664, founded 1985, executive editor Jeanie Saunders, poetry editor Billye Keene.
Magazine Needs: *Cochran's Corner* is a "family type" quarterly open to beginners, preferring poems of 20 lines or less. You have to be a subscriber to submit. "Any subject or style (except porn)." They have published poetry by Jean B. York, Brian Duthins, C.J. Villiano and Annette Shaw. As a sample the editor selected this poem, "Journey," (poet unidentified):
> You take me to places/Within myself/Where I have never been—/foreign places/Timidly I follow you
> through/Subterranian chambers/And/Undiscovered essences/to the/mainstream/that/is/I
CC is 58 pgs., desktop-published, saddle-stapled, with matte card cover. Press run is 500. Subscription: $20. Sample: $5 plus SASE.
How to Submit: Submit 5 poems at a time. Simultaneous submissions and previously published poems OK. Send SASE for guidelines. Reports in average of 3 months. Pays 2 copies. Acquires first or one-time rights. Reviews books of poetry. Send books for review consideration.
Also Offers: Sponsors contests in March and July; $5 entry fee for unlimited poems "if sent in the same envelope. We provide criticism if requested at the rate of $1 per page."
Advice: The editor says, "Write from the heart, but don't forget your readers. You must work to find the exact words that mirror your feelings, so the reader can share your feelings."

COFFEE HOUSE PRESS, 27 N. Fourth St., Suite 400, Minneapolis MN 55401, phone (612)338-0125, founded 1984, managing editor Chris Fischbach.
● Coffee House Press books have won numerous honors and awards. As an example, *The Book of Medicines* by Linda Hogan won the Colorado Book Award for Poetry and the Lannan Foundation Literary Fellowship.
Book/Chapbook Needs: The press publishes 12 books/year, 4-5 of which are poetry. They want poetry that is "challenging and lively; influenced by the Beats, the NY School or Black Mountain." They have published poetry collections by Victor Hernandez Cruz, Anne Waldman and Paul Metcalf.
How to Submit: Submit 8-12 poems at a time. Previously published poems OK. Cover letter and vita required. "Please include a SASE for our reply and/or the return of your ms." Seldom comments on rejections. Replies to queries in 1 month, to mss in 6 months. Always sends prepublication galleys. Send SASE for catalog to order sample. No phone calls.

COKEFISH; COKEFISH PRESS, 31 Waterloo St., New Hope PA 18938-1210, phone (215)862-0299, founded 1990, editor Ana Christy.
● Also see the listings for *Alpha Beat Soup* and *Bouillabaisse*.
Magazine Needs: *Cokefish* is an irregular journal with an entry fee of $1/3 poems. "I want to see work that has passion behind it, from the traditional to the avant-garde, provocative to discreet, trivial to the significant. I

am interested in social issues, alternative, avant-garde, erotica and humor for people with nothing to hide." They have published poetry by Dan Buck, Margaret Crocker, Kevin Hibshman, Joe Rochette and Wayne Wilkinson. As a sample the editor selected these lines by Joan Reid:

I have seen death face to face/webs of memory/that wreathes the heart/grey as hair migrating

Cokefish is 60 pgs., side-stapled on heavy paper with a cover printed on both sides on colored photocopy paper. They accept 30% of mss received. Press run is 300 for 150 subscribers. Subscription: $15. Sample: $4.

How to Submit: Submit 5-7 poems at a time. Note entry fee: $1/3 poems, additional $1 for additional poems. Simultaneous submissions and previously published poems OK. Cover letter "explaining why the poet chose *Cokefish*" required. Send SASE for guidelines and upcoming themes. Reports in 1 week. Sometimes sends prepublication galleys. Pays 1 copy.

Book/Chapbook Needs & How to Submit: "We publish a mostly poetry broadside and will work with poets on publishing their chapbooks and audiotapes through Cokefish Press. Manuscript length up to 40 pages— $5 reading fee." Cokefish Press also publishes cooperative chapbooks. Write for details.

Advice: The editor advises, "Spread the word; don't let your poems sit and vegetate in a drawer. Send me stuff that will make my hair stand up on end."

☑ ◑ **COLD MOUNTAIN REVIEW**, English Dept., Appalachian State University, Boone NC 28608, phone (828)262-3078, editor Deanna Shelor.

Magazine Needs: *CMR* is published twice a year by graduate students in the English Department at Appalachian State University and features poetry, short fiction, b&w line drawings and photographs. They have no specifications regarding form, subject matter or style of poetry. "Works longer than 15 pages in length are discouraged." They have published poetry by Charles Frazier, Donald Seachrist, Deanne Bayer, Carol Frith and Saleem Peeradina. As a sample the editors selected these lines from "Metamorphosis" by Louise Till:

your breath permeating the earth./I heard your soft sigh, looked out my window/To see nothing left but the strands of your hair/swaying through the plants/And the tips of your breasts/Sprouting

The editor says *CMR* is about 72 pgs., 6×9, neatly printed with 1 poem/page (or 2-page spread), saddle-stitched, with light card stock cover. They publish about 10% of the submissions received. For sample, send SASE or make donation to ASU Cold Mountain Review.

How to Submit: No simultaneous or previously published submissions. "Please include short biographical sketch, with name, address and phone/e-mail number on each poem." Reads submissions August 25 through November 15 and January 10 through March 15 only. Send SASE for guidelines. Pays 3 copies.

☑ ◑ ◎ **COLLAGES & BRICOLAGES, THE JOURNAL OF INTERNATIONAL WRITING (Specialized: translations, feminist, political, social issues, themes)**, P.O. Box 360, Shippenville PA 16254, founded in 1986, editor Marie-José Fortis.

Magazine Needs: *C&B* is a "small literary magazine with a strong penchant for literary, feminist, avant-garde work. Strongly encourages poets and fiction writers, as well as essayists, whether English-speaking or foreign. (Note: Writers sending their work in a foreign language must have their mss accompanied by an English translation.) As a sample the editor selected these lines from "Anna Citrino":

But the women here are not silent/It may still be a man's world in Kuwait, yet/a moon sits atop/every pinnacle minaret,/the sun pierced point/counter balanced/with a round moon dome.

The annual is 130-160 pgs., magazine-sized, perfect bound with card cover. They accept 7% of 900 poetry submissions/year. Press run is 800. Sample: $10 (postage not included for orders outside the U.S.), $5 for back issue.

How to Submit: Submit up to 5 poems at a time, no more (only 1 piece if poem is several pages long). Poems submitted without SASE will neither be read nor returned. Reads submissions August 15 through November 30 only. Publishes theme issues. Send SASE for upcoming themes. Reports in 1-3 months. Always sends prepublication galleys. Pays 2 copies with 50% off additional copies. Acquires first rights (rights revert to author after publication).

Advice: "It is recommended that potential contributors order a copy, so as to know what kind of work is desirable. We understand that nobody's budget is unlimited, but remember that most lit mags' back issues are half price. Be considerate to editors, as many of them work on a voluntary basis and sacrifice much time and energy to encourage writers. And please, use a SASE that is at least 9½×4"." Marie-José Fortis says, "Show me that you write as if nothing else mattered."

☒ $ ◑ **COLORADO REVIEW; COLORADO PRIZE FOR POETRY**, Dept. of English, Colorado State University, Ft. Collins CO 80523, phone (970)491-5449, e-mail creview@vines.colostate.edu, website http://www.colostate.edu/Depts/English/pubs/colrev/colrev.htm, founded 1955 as *Colorado State Review*, resurrected 1967 under "New Series" rubric, renamed *Colorado Review* 1985, editor David Milofsky, poetry editors Jorie Graham and Donald Revell.

● Poetry published in *Colorado Review* has been included in the 1993, 1994, 1995, 1996 and 1997 volumes of *The Best American Poetry*.

Magazine Needs: *Colorado Review* is a journal of contemporary literature which appears twice annually; it combines short fiction, poetry, interviews with articles about significant contemporary poets and writers, articles on literature, culture and the arts and reviews of recent works of the literary imagination. They have published

insider report

Penetrating the riddle of history with poetry

Aristotle once said, "The artistic representation of history is a more scientific and serious pursuit than the exact writing of history. For the art of letters goes to the heart of things, whereas the factual report merely collocates details." For Brian Daldorph, editor, university professor and author of the two-part poem cycle *The Holocaust and Hiroshima: Poems* (Mid-American Press, 1997), finding the poetic thread he sought in the massive edifice of Second World War history required that he somehow connect with the individual humanity of both the perpetrators and the victims, those with direct experience of history.

Brian Daldorph

The confounding, horrific nature of the Holocaust exerted a special gravity upon Daldorph's muse and initially drove his search to find this human connection. "For as long as I could remember, it was a subject I found enormously engaging. The Holocaust seemed like such a monstrosity that it was something I felt compelled to understand."

The inspirational floodgates opened when he read a newspaper article on the infamous Nazi SS Doctor Josef Mengele. "The first poem I wrote was about the doctor who examines Mengele for racial purity, which is something the Germans had to prove if they were to join the Nazi S.S. I wrote the poem from the doctor's point of view, and it was a breakthrough for me. I had found a way to write about the subject that hadn't really been done before—to bring it down from the kind of gross scale we most often discuss it on to the level of the people actually involved, to try to see it through their eyes."

The character of Josef Mengele, while central to the poems, presented a special riddle to Daldorph as a writer. Mengele stands at the center of the first cycle of poems, and his specter casts a long shadow over the proceedings, but he is seen and heard only through the recollections of an orbiting cast of voices. Daldorph says, "I knew when I started writing these poems that Mengele would be at the center of them. However, they're all in the different voices of the people surrounding him. I did try to write poems from Mengele's point of view, but I

BRIAN DALDORPH

Poet and Editor
Founded: Coal City Review
Recent Title: The Holocaust and Hiroshima: Poems (Mid-American Press)

just couldn't get it. So, in the end, he was really the black hole of the collection. He's at the center, but he never speaks apart from reported speech in some of the poems. That wasn't a deliberate move; but I just found I couldn't get his voice. I couldn't really understand him." Mengele's essence as a human being ultimately resists Daldorph's efforts as a poet to capture him, and his phantom hovers just beyond reach, forever unknowable. By the end of the cycle, Mengele vanishes into the projections and memories of his victims and post-war pursuers.

"Cold"

My bones are still cold
from that winter night two drunk Nazis
crashed into our hut, and,
for sport, chose
Jews to march outside
and roll in the snow, naked.
The Nazis' laughter kept them warm,
until they'd had enough
and let the skin and bones Jews
back into the hut.
My bones are still cold from that night
and will always be cold,
though I was not one of the chosen.

(originally published in *The Holocaust and Hiroshima: Poems*; reprinted by permission of the author)

The second cycle of poems explores the atomic bombing of Hiroshima, and represents a shift to a more conscious writing strategy. "In 1994, I was a visiting professor in Japan, and the city where I taught was fairly close to Hiroshima. Going to Japan was the key to writing those poems; also being close enough to Hiroshima that I could spend a lot of time there and speak to survivors of the bombing. But I feel that sequence of poems was much more deliberate. I set out from the beginning to write them and I went to places where I thought I would be able to write."

When asked about the amount of research and sheer concentration required to write a long cycle of poems about historical events, Daldorph says, "To be able to write about those kinds of topics, you just have to know more, and that involves research. I knew that in order to write those poems convincingly I needed to do that research, because they were about topics I was not really close to, and I needed to get closer by doing this kind of background work."

Even with the success of this poem cycle under his belt, Daldorph is quick to point out that a great deal of preparation and research won't always lead to successful poetry. "I do think you take a chance when doing something like this. I did write another long sequence of poems and spent probably two years doing research, and, after all of that, it's not a sequence of poems that I think worked. So, obviously, you make a big investment, and you're not always going to get out of it what you want."

As a corollary, he emphasizes the importance of the initial poetic vision to the eventual success or failure of his writing. "I think that with both of the poem sequences in *The Holocaust and Hiroshima* I was enormously interested in the subjects and felt very much compelled to do the writing, and perhaps that made the poems work in the end. If I hadn't had that initial impulse and real belief in what I was doing, then I don't think I could have done it. So, I don't think I could write about many topics, even if I spent five years researching them. I think I have to have the initial drive and belief in what I'm doing, and some kind of poetic inspiration for it to work."

Following inspiration also led Daldorph to cross over into the realm of publishing, when he founded *Coal City Review* in 1989. "I'd been involved with small press publishing for a number of years, and I found that a lot of very fine work came through my hands from a lot of different sources—from friends who were writing, from students of mine, and from various workshops I was involved with. The sort of work I was seeing was as good as anything I was reading in other publications. I guess what I wanted to do was to have a way of collecting this work and publishing it and trying to establish some sort of writing community. So, it really started from the poems that were coming into my hands that I thought deserved to be published and read by as wide an audience as possible. I've been publishing the *Coal City Review* for about ten years and the journal is fairly well known in the publishing world. Now, I get submissions from all over the United States and from all over the world."

As both a published poet and an editor, Daldorph straddles the line between the creative impulse and the critical faculty. For many writers, the intermeshing of the two can lead to deadlock and creative paralysis, but when asked about the relationship of his muse to his inner critic, Daldorph is confident about his ability to navigate the narrow way in between. "For the most part I'm able to keep those pretty separate, but I try to have a broader view as an editor than I do as a writer. I don't just try to publish poems that are like my own; I try to look at poems I never could have written and I never will write. In fact, I think I try to be as broad as possible in my interest in other people's poems. Although sometimes I come across a poem I really wish I could have written, because it just says something I would so much like to have said in that particular way."

However, as a writer, Daldorph works steadily to find his own way of speaking through poetry. One aspect of the process he finds valuable and recommends to other poets is participating in poetry readings. He finds that reading a poem out loud in front of an audience hones his sense of the language as sound and reveals the overall shape of the poem with greater clarity. "It does give you a good sense of when a poem is finished, and sometimes you know after you've read at a poetry reading that you've got it exactly right. Sometimes you just hear the words coming together. I've certainly had that experience on many occasions. It's an immediate sort of response. You'll read a new poem and people will tell you afterwards that they liked it or they didn't understand it. A poetry reading is a great opportunity to have that kind of immediate feedback."

Daldorph holds an M.A. in Creative Writing from Illinois State University and believes such training can be very useful to a poet who is self-motivated enough to make the most of a structured learning situation. He feels the discipline of writing in fixed forms has since been especially valuable to him as a poet. "I seldom write in fixed forms anymore, but I think my training and apprenticeship have made me a better writer. I think it really heightened my sensitivity to language. It's hard work. People want to take a shortcut to saying whatever it is they want to say. They don't want to take the time to learn the craft, thinking they can get at something immediately. Some people can, but I think for the vast majority of us, it's really important to learn what poetry is and what it can do and work very hard on getting some basic forms down. I think that frees you up to be able to write in your own way."

Daldorph is quick to point out that at the end of the day, the most important motivation for a poet should be the joy of the writing process itself. "You must care about that, even before publication or having anybody read the poems. You have to care most of all about the writing itself. If you make that the focus, then anything else that happens is just an addition, just a kind of added blessing."

—Ian Bessler

poetry by Mark Strand, Mary Jo Bang and W.S. Merwin. *CR* is about 180 pgs., 6×9, professionally printed and perfect-bound with glossy card cover. Circulation is 1,500 for 300 subscribers of which 100 are libraries. They receive about 6,000 submissions a year, use approximately 2%. Subscription: $18/year. Sample: $10.
How to Submit: Submit about 5 poems at a time. Submissions must include SASE or e-mail address for response. No previously published poems or simultaneous submissions. No electronic or e-mail submissions. Reads submissions September 1 through May 1 only. Reports in 6-8 weeks. Pays $5/printed page for poetry. Buys first North American serial rights. Reviews books of poetry, both single and multi-book format. Poets may also send books for review consideration.
Also Offers: Also sponsors the annual Colorado Prize for Poetry, established in 1995, offering an honorarium of $1,500. Complete book must be unpublished. Submit a book-length ms on any subject in any form. Send SASE for guidelines. Entry fee: $20. Deadline: January 11. Most recent award winner was Michael White (1998). Judge was Mark Strand. Winner will be announced in May. Website includes writer's guidelines, list of editorial staff, subscription guidelines and Colorado Prize for Poetry guidelines.

COLUMBIA: A JOURNAL OF LITERATURE AND ART, 415 Dodge Hall, Columbia University, New York NY 10027, phone (212)854-4216, e-mail arts-litjournal@columbia.edu, website http://www.columbia.edu/cu/arts/writing/columbiajournal/columbiafr.html, founded 1977, editors Dave King and Nova Suma, poetry editor Gabe Fried.
Magazine Needs: *Columbia* appears semiannually and "will consider any poem that understands the tradition from which it was found." They have published poetry by Mark Pansot, Marie Howe, Linda Gregg and Tony Hoagland. As a sample the editor selected these lines from "On a Mandarin Inscription" by David Yezz:

> I have no Chinese; yet how these calligraphs/do articulate the spattered flight of swans,/or pines
> tortured by sleet on mountain paths./Beside this columned hand, along a pond,/an introspective couple
> walks in clothes/blazoned with ceremony.

The editor says *Columbia* is 180 pgs., 6×9, offset printed with notch binding, matte cover, includes art and ads. They receive about 2,000 poems a year, accept approximately 2%. Press run is 1,500 for 100 subscribers of which 30 are libraries. Single copy: $8. Make checks payable to *Columbia Journal*.
How to Submit: Submit 4 poems at a time. No previously published poems; simultaneous submissions OK, when noted. Cover letter preferred. Reads submissions September 1 through May 1 only. Poems are circulated to an editorial board. Seldom comments on rejections. Send SASE for guidelines. "Solicits theme section for each issue. Send SASE for subject and guidelines prior to submitting." Recent themes include Film and Writing; Reinventing Fairy Tales, Myth and Legends; and Beyond Sportswriting: Spectatorship, Exhaustion, Competition. Reports in 6 months. Pays 2 copies. Acquires first North American serial rights.
Also Offers: Sponsors annual contest with an award of $250. Open to submissions January 1 though March 1.

Entry fee: $12. Submit no more than 6 poems/entry. All entrants receive a copy of the issue publishing the winners.

✓ ◎ **COMMON THREADS; OHIO HIGH SCHOOL POETRY CONTESTS; OHIO POETRY ASSOCIATION (Specialized: membership, students)**, 3520 State Route 56, Mechanicsburg OH 43044, founded 1928, editor Amy Jo Zook. Ohio Poetry Association (Amy Renee Daniel, treasurer, 161 Crestview Lane, Tiffin OH 44883), is a state poetry society open to members from outside the state, an affiliate of the National Federation of State Poetry Societies.
Magazine Needs: *Common Threads* is their poetry magazine, appearing twice a year. Only members of OPA may submit poems. They do not want to see poetry which is highly sentimental, overly morbid or porn—and nothing over 40 lines. "We use beginners' poetry, but would like it to be good, tight, revised. In short, not first drafts. Too much is sentimental or prosy when it could be passionate or lyric. We'd like poems to make us think as well as feel something." They have published poetry by Yvonne Hardenbrook, Betsy Kennedy, Rose Ann Spaith and Dalene Workman Stull. As a sample the editor selected these lines from "In Dubiis" by Timothy Russell:

> . . . as the boy practices the limited part/for tenor sax of a popular theme/for the twentieth time tonight./
> He's had it perfect for two days./Warped images dance in the bell/of the boy's polished instrument:/
> his father sitting like a gargoyle/on the wooden steps, wiping his eye.

The magazine is 52 pgs., digest-sized, computer typeset, with matte card cover. "Ours is a forum for our members, and we do use reprints, so new members can get a look at what is going well in more general magazines." Annual dues including *Common Threads*: $15. Senior (over 65): $12. Single copies: $2.
How to Submit: Previously published poems OK, if "author is upfront about them. All rights revert to poet after publication."
Also Offers: Ohio Poetry Association (formerly Verse Writers' Guild of Ohio) sponsors an annual contest for unpublished poems written by high school students in Ohio with categories of traditional, modern, and several other categories. March deadline, with 3 money awards in each category. For contest information write Ohio Poetry Association, % Elouise Postle, 4761 Willow Lane, Lebanon OH 45036. "Also, we have a quarterly contest open to all poets, entry fee, two money awards and publication. Write to Janeen Lepp, president, 1798 Sawgrass Dr., Reynoldsburg OH 43068 (#10 SASE) for dates and themes."

$ ✉ ◎ **COMMONWEAL (Specialized: religious)**, 475 Riverside Dr., New York NY 10115, fax (212)662-4183, website http://www.commonwealmagazine.org, poetry editor Rosemary Deen.
Magazine Needs: *Commonweal* appears every 2 weeks, circulation 20,000, is a general-interest magazine for college-educated readers by Catholics. Prefers serious, witty, well-written poems of up to 75 lines. Does not publish inspirational poems. As a sample the editor selected these lines from "One is One," a sonnet by Marie Ponsot:

> Heart, you bully, you punk, I'm wrecked, I'm shocked/stiff. You? you still try to rule the world—though/
> I've got you: identified, starving, locked/in a cage you will not leave alive . . .

Subscription: $44. Sample: $3.
How to Submit: Considers simultaneous submissions. Reads submissions September 1 through June 30 only. Pays 50¢ a line plus 2 copies. Buys all rights. Returns rights when requested by the author. Reviews books of poetry in 750-1,000 words, single or multi-book format.
Also Offers: Website include writer's guidelines, names of editors, poetry, interviews, samples from current issue, and back issues with table of contents.

✓ ◎ **COMMUNITIES (Specialized: intentional community living)**, 290 McEntire Rd., Tuyon NC 28782, phone/fax (828)863-4425, e-mail communities@ic.org, website http://www.ic.org/, founded 1972, editor Diana Christian.
Magazine Needs: *Communities* is a "quarterly publication on intentional communities and cooperative living," occasionally using poetry relevant to those topics. It is 80 pgs., magazine-sized, professionally printed on recycled white stock with 2-color glossy paper cover, saddle-stapled. Sample: $6.
How to Submit: Submit any number of poems at a time. SASE required. Previously published poems and simultaneous submissions OK. E-mail submissions OK. Publishes theme issues. Send SASE for upcoming themes. Pays 4 copies and subscription. They also publish the *Communities Directory*.
Advice: The editor says, "Poets rarely 'get' who we are and what our publication is about, so I reject good poems for wrong content. We're about cooperation and intentional community living."

Ⓝ 🌐 $ ▢ ◪ ◎ **COMMUNITY OF POETS PRESS; PAMPHLET POETS; POEMS BY POST; COMMUNITY OF POETS; PARCHMENT POETS (Specialized: innovative work with community and organizational focus)**, Hatfield Cottage, Chilham, Kent CT4 8DP England, e-mail bennetta@cpoetspress.f reeserve.co.uk, founded 1994, editor Philip Bennetta, artistic director Susan Bennetta.
Magazine Needs: *Community of Poets* is an "international quarterly where creative and innovative work of any genre is sought and published. New voices from all communities are especially welcome and encouraged." No "well worn cliché rhyming." They have published poetry by Ruth Padel, Dr. Bill Petty, William Hazel and Dr. M.P.A. Sheaffer. As a sample the editor selected these lines from "Stiletto" by Dawn Gorman:

> *Here it's the hawthorn/strings everything together,/farms and houses the nodes in a network/from*
> *Dundalk to Castlebear./There's hardly a football beside the hedge/that isn't accounted for later/over*
> *a pint, the post office counter/or wet gravestones after Mass.*

The editor says *COP* is 36 pgs., magazine-sized, stapled with quality card embossed cover, original artwork on cover. They receive about 250 poems a year, accept approximately 50%. Press run is 200 for 100 subscribers of which 8 are libraries, 20 shelf sales; 15 distributed free to contributors. Single copy: $5; subscription: $16 (4 issues). Make checks payable to Community of Poets Press.
How to Submit: Submit 3 typed poems at a time with SAE and IRC. Line length for poetry is 30 maximum. No previously published poems or simultaneous submissions. Cover letter required. E-mail submissions OK. Time between acceptance and publication is 3 months. Seldom comments on rejections. Publishes theme issues occasionally. Send SASE for guidelines. Reports in 1 month. Sometimes sends prepublication galleys. Pays 1 copy. Copyright remains with poet.
Book/Chapbook Needs & How to Submit: The Community of Poets Press publishes poetry under the imprints Pamphlet Poets and Parchment Poets. "We prefer to publish material we have published examples of in our magazine." They publish 1 hardback and 8 chapbooks/year. Books are usually 36 pgs., A5, hand-sewn binding, quality card cover, original art/printmaking.
How to Submit: "We prefer to get to know the work of a poet via contributions to our magazine *Community of Poets*." Replies to queries in 1 month. Pays royalties of 3-5% plus 10 author's copies. 50% of books are author-subsidy published each year. "Limited Edition of 100 books—£300 author subsidy or Limited Edition 100 books—author handles sales in partnership and takes 5% of sales, we stand cost of production." Order sample books by sending cheque for $8 to Community of Poets Press.

■ ◎ **A COMPANION IN ZEOR (Specialized: science fiction/fantasy)**, 307 Ashland Ave., Egg Harbor Township NJ 08234-5568, phone (609)645-6938, fax (609)645-8084, e mail klitman323@aol.com or karenlitman @juno.com, website http://www.simegen.com/CZ, founded 1978, editor Karen Litman.
Magazine Needs: *A Companion in Zeor* is a science fiction/fantasy fanzine appearing irregularly on the Internet. Material used is now limited to creations based solely on works (universes) of Jacqueline Lichtenberg. No other submission types considered. Prefer nothing obscene. Homosexuality not acceptable unless very relevant to the piece. Prefer a 'clean' publication image."
How to Submit: Cover letter preferred with submissions; note whether to return or dispose of rejected mss. E-mail and faxed submissions OK. Send SASE for guidelines. Sometimes sends prepublication galleys. Pays 1 copy, "but can negotiate." Acquires first rights. "Always willing to work with authors or poets to help in improving their work." Reviews books of poetry. Open to unsolicited reviews. Poets may also send books for review consideration.
Also Offers: Website includes submission guidelines, excerpts from past issues, and current issues.

◯ **COMPASS ROSE**, White Pines College, 40 Chester St., Chester NH 03036, phone (603)887-4401, fax (603)887-1777, website http://www.whitepinescollege.org, founded 1995, co-editors Pat Parnell and Mary White-head.
Magazine Needs: *Compass Rose* is a biennial publication that contains fiction, nonfiction and poetry, b&w art and photography. "Our purpose is to provide a venue for talent and originality to beginning and experienced writers and artists." They want "strong, original voice, fresh images, accessible, a new point of view on the familiar. No overly sentimental work, forced rhyme, superficial thinking or clichéd style." They have published poetry by Dolores Kendrick, Donald Murray, Erica Funkhouser and Charles Pratt. As a sample the editor selected these lines from "Give Heed and Heat to the Heroic" by John Tagliabue:

> *Would that we could on cold or grim or grey days/all be kind; the kind/that Emerson would cheer;*
> *and Whitman shaking the/flakes of snow from his white beard/says: "Here is the hospitality which*
> *forever indicates heroes."*

CR is 60 pgs., 8½×11, offset printed and saddle-stitched, cover stock with b&w graphic, includes b&w art and photographs. They receive about 500 poems a year, accept approximately 30-35%. Press run is 500, 200 shelf sales; 200 distributed free to contributors, students and friends of the college. Sample: $5. Make checks payable to White Pines College.
How to Submit: Submit 5-6 poems at a time. Previously published poems and simultaneous submissions OK "by special arrangement with the editors." Cover letter with bio preferred. "If poetry is accepted for publication, we ask the poet to send it to us on 3.5 computer disk (if possible)." Submission deadline: June 1, 2000. Time between acceptance and publication is 6 months. Poems are circulated to an editorial board. "All work is read by two editors. A third faculty member reads if the editors can't reach consensus." Often comments on rejections. Send SASE for guidelines. Reports in 3 months. Sometimes sends prepublication galleys. Pays 1 copy. Acquires first rights.
Advice: The editors say, "Let your work out of the desk drawer! Join a writer's group for feedback and creative stimulation. Revise, polish, study your market, and submit. This is a great time for poetry!"

☑ ◎ **THE COMSTOCK REVIEW; COMSTOCK WRITERS' GROUP INC.; MURIEL CRAFT BAILEY MEMORIAL PRIZE**, 4958 St. John Dr., Syracuse NY 13215, phone (315)488-8077, e-mail kniles1@t weny.rr.com, founded 1987 as *Poetpourri*, published by the Comstock Writers' Group, Inc., coordinator Kathleen Bryce Niles.

Magazine Needs: *CR* appears biannually. They use "well-written free and traditional verse. No obscene, obscure, patently religious or greeting card verse." They have published poetry by Gayle Elen Harvey, Susan Terris, Katharyn Howd Machan, Robert Cooperman and Philip Dacey. As a sample they selected these lines from "The Hopeful Dialectic of Marriage" by Georgia A. Popoff:

> Some dreams I've yet to sleep/my way into: an intimation of husband,/the secrets the hairs on our thighs,/world whisper to each other/beneath the cool breath of sheets as we/drift into our singular syllables of starlight

The Comstock Review is about 100 pgs., digest-sized, professionally printed, perfect-bound. Circulation is 600. Subscription: $15/year; $8/issue. Sample: $6.

How to Submit: Submit 3-6 poems at a time, name and address on each page, unpublished poems only. Cover letter with short bio preferred. Poems are read January 1 through February 28 and July 1 through August 31 only. Poems are held until next reading period for consideration. Editors sometimes comment on returned submissions. Pays 1 copy. Acquires first North American serial rights.

Also Offers: They offer the Muriel Craft Bailey Memorial Prize yearly with $1,000 1st Prize, $200 2nd Prize, $100 3rd Prize, honorable mentions, publication of all finalists. Entry fee: $3/poem. 40-line limit.

CONCHO RIVER REVIEW; FORT CONCHO MUSEUM PRESS, P.O. Box 10894, Angelo State University, San Angelo TX 76909, phone (915)942-2273, fax (915)942-2155, e-mail james.moore@angelo.edu, website http://www.angelo.edu, founded 1984, editor James A. Moore, poetry editor Jerry Bradley.

Magazine Needs: *Concho River Review* is a literary journal published twice a year. "Prefer shorter poems, few long poems accepted; particularly looking for poems with distinctive imagery and imaginative forms and rhythms. The first test of a poem will be its imagery." Short reviews of new volumes of poetry are also published. *CRR* is 120-138 pgs., digest-sized, professionally printed and flat-spined, with matte card cover. They use 35-40 of 600-800 poems received/year. Press run is 300 for about 200 subscribers of which 10 are libraries. Subscription: $14. Sample: $5.

How to Submit: "Please submit 3-5 poems at a time. Use regular legal-sized envelopes—no big brown envelopes; no replies without SASE. Type must be letter-perfect, sharp enough to be computer scanned." Reports in 1-2 months. Pays 1 copy. Acquires first rights.

Also Offers: Website includes writer's guidelines and names of editors.

Advice: The editor says, "We're always looking for good, strong work—from both well-known poets and those who have never been published before."

CONCRETE ABSTRACT; THE ABSTRACT CONCRETE, % Will Lennertz, Santiago Canyon College, 8045 E. Chapman Ave., Orange CA 92669-4512, e-mail concreteabstract@hotmail.com, founded 1998, editor Will Lennertz.

Magazine Needs: *The Concrete Abstract* is updated bimonthly at http://www.members.tripod.com/concreteabstract "to publish online the best poetry we can find. Clarity, precision and concrete details are highly valued. Subject matter and form are open. We publish poetry with a strong sense of the physical world and an emphasis on the tangible materials we encounter every day. No obtuse, abstract, senseless word play." They have published poetry by Erik Brown, Bug and The Latin Dragon. As a sample the editor selected these lines from "The Big Muddy" by Diane Thomas:

> My friend the river never fit their mold, either/He'd carry their barges and pleasure boats, then/Reclaim a field that once had been his or hold/A swimmer too close, not giving up what he took.

They receive about 2,500 poems a year, accept approximately 7-10%.

Magazine Needs: *The Abstract Concrete* is updated quarterly at http://www.members.tripod.com/abstractconcrete "to publish experimental word-art, poetry, poem-art collisions. The journal explores the mystery of language and art." They receive about 1,500 poems a year, accept approximately 10%. *The Abstract Concrete* is the inverse function of the *Concrete Abstract* (its sister publication). Submissions sent to one magazine will be considered for the other."

How to Submit: For both online publications, submit 3-5 poems at a time. No previously published poems or simultaneous submissions. Cover letter preferred. E-mail submissions OK. "Prefer e-mail submissions to concreteabstract@hotmail.com. Cut and paste poetry into e-mail. Also accepts fiction and art. Jpeg and gif formats for art submissions." Time between acceptance and publication is 2 months. Seldom comments on rejections. Obtain guidelines via website. Reports in 2-3 months. Acquires first rights. For both, staff reviews books and chapbooks of poetry and other magazines in 300-500 words, single and multi-book format. Send books for review consideration.

Advice: The editor says, "Send some poems. See what happens. Rejection is not a personal issue. This labor of love is ruled by the editor's tastes. Try me a few times and realize I am going by my vision of poetry. Yours may just clash with mine. So be it. I am not evaluating your worth as a writer."

CONDUIT, 510 Eighth Ave. NE, Minneapolis MN 55413, e-mail conduit@bitstream.net, founded 1993, editors William D. Waltz and Brett Astor.

Magazine Needs: *Conduit* is a triquarterly designed "to explore language, art, life without ulterior motives; to publish work that is 'essential.' " They want "lively, honest poetry that is attuned to language." They have published poetry by Russell Edson, Campbell McGrath, Michael Burkard, Dean Young and Dara Wier. *Conduit* is 60 pgs., 4¼×11, neatly printed on recycled paper and perfect bound with matte card cover and art. They receive about 3,000 poems a year, publish about 150. Press run is 1,000-1,200 for 300 subscribers, 100-400 shelf sales. Subscription: $15. Sample: $5.

How to Submit: Submit 3-5 poems at a time. No previously published work. Time between acceptance and publication is 6-12 months. Seldom comments on rejections. Send SASE for guidelines or request via e-mail. Reports in 6-10 weeks. Pays 3 copies. Rights revert to authors upon publication. Reviews books of poetry in 500 words. Open to unsolicited reviews. Poets may also send books for review consideration.

Advice: The editors say, "*Conduit* is dedicated to the work of poets and artists who wear the stains of a life lived and whose edges are neither affected nor accidental. *Conduit* will grow and evolve, but one thing will remain constant: quality writing that risks annihilation."

CONFLUENCE; OHIO VALLEY LITERARY GROUP, P.O. Box 336, Belpre OH 45714, phone (304)422-3112, e-mail dbprather@prodigy.net, founded 1983 as *Gambit*, 1989 as *Confluence*, poetry editors James Scott Bond and David B. Prather.

Magazine Needs: *Confluence* is an annual "credible platform for established/emerging authors and outstanding student work. This literary magazine is published at Marietta College, Marietta, Ohio, and was named to represent the merging of the Ohio and Muskingum Rivers as well as the collaboration of the Ohio Valley Literary Group with Marietta College." They have published poetry by Daniel Bourne, Walt McDonald, Pamela Kircher and Richard Hague. *Confluence* is 80-100 pgs., digest-sized, professionally printed and perfect-bound with full color, coated card cover and b&w graphics. They receive 2,500-5,000 submissions a year, accept approximately 2%. Press run is 500 for 300 subscribers of which 10 are libraries, about 150 shelf sales. Single copy: $5. Sample: $4 plus $1.25 postage.

How to Submit: Submit 5-7 poems with SASE. No previously published poems or simultaneous submissions. Cover letter with brief bio required. E-mail submissions OK. Reads submissions September 1 through March 1 only. Time between acceptance and publication is 6 months. Seldom comments on rejections. Send SASE for guidelines or request via e-mail. Reports in 2-8 weeks. Pays 1-3 copies. Returns rights upon publication.

CONFLUENCE PRESS (Specialized: regional), Lewis-Clark State College, Lewiston ID 83501, phone (208)799-2336, founded 1975, poetry editor James R. Hepworth.
- "We have received four Western States Book Awards and two awards from The Pacific Northwest Booksellers within the last decade."

Book/Chapbook Needs: Confluence is an "independent publisher of fiction, poetry, creative nonfiction and literary scholarship. We are open to formal poetry as well as free verse. No rhymed doggerel, 'light verse,' 'performance poetry,' 'street poetry,' etc. We prefer to publish work by poets who live and work in the northwestern United States." They have published poetry by John Daniel, Greg Keeler, Nancy Mairs and Sherry Rind. They print about 2 books a year.

How to Submit: "Please query before submitting manuscript." Query with 6 sample poems, bio and list of publications. Replies to queries in 6 weeks. Pays $100-500 advance and 10% royalties plus copies. Buys all rights. Returns rights if book goes out of print. Send SASE for catalog to order samples.

CONFRONTATION MAGAZINE, English Dept., C.W. Post Campus of Long Island University, Brookville NY 11548-0570, phone (516)299-2720, fax (516)299-2735, founded 1968, editor-in-chief Martin Tucker.

Magazine Needs: *CM* is "a semiannual literary journal with interest in all forms. Our only criterion is high literary merit. We think of our audience as an educated, lay group of intelligent readers. We prefer lyric poems. Length generally should be kept to two pages. No sentimental verse." They have published poetry by Karl Shapiro, T. Alan Broughton, David Ignatow, Philip Appleman, Jane Mayhall and Joseph Brodsky. *Confrontation* is 250 pgs., digest-sized, professionally printed, flat-spined, with a circulation of about 2,000. They receive about 1,200 submissions/year, publish 150, have a 6- to 12-month backlog. Subscription: $10/year. Sample: $3.

How to Submit: Submit no more than 10 pgs., clear copy. No previously published poems. Do not submit mss June through August. "Prefer single submissions." Publishes theme issues. Send SASE for upcoming themes. Reports in 6-8 weeks. Sometimes sends prepublication galleys. Pays $5-50 and copy of magazine. Staff reviews books of poetry. Send books for review consideration.

Also Offers: Basically a magazine, they do on occasion publish "book" issues or "anthologies." Their most recent "occasional book" is *Clown at Wall*, stories and drawings by Ken Bernard.

THE BOOK PUBLISHERS INDEX, located at the back of this book, lists those publishers who consider full-length book collections.

🌀 $💿 CONJUNCTIONS, Dept. PM, Bard College, Annandale-on-Hudson NY 12504, phone (914)758-1539, fax (914)758-2660, e-mail conjunctions@bard.edu, website http://www.conjunctions.com, founded 1981, managing editor Michael Bergstein, editor Bradford Morrow.
  • Poetry published in *Conjunctions* has also been included in *The Best American Poetry 1998*.
Magazine Needs: *Conjunctions* is an elegant journal appearing twice a year, using work that is "stylistically innovative. Potential contributors should be familiar with the poetry published in the journal." They have published poetry by John Ashbery, Robert Kelly, Charles Stein, Michael Palmer, Ann Lauterbach and Fanny Howe. This publication is distributed by Consortium. It is 350 pgs., 6×9, flat-spined, professionally printed. Poems compete with prose, with more pages devoted to the latter. Press run is 5,500 for 1,000 subscribers of which 250 are libraries. Subscription: $18. Sample: $15. Pays $100-175 plus 2 copies.
Also Offers: Website includes current and past texts, art, subscription and back issue information.

$💿 THE CONNECTICUT POETRY REVIEW, P.O. Box 818, Stonington CT 06378, founded 1981, poetry editors J. Claire White and Harley More.
Magazine Needs: *CPR* is a "small press annual magazine. We look for poetry of quality which is both genuine and original in content. No specifications except length: 10-40 lines." They have published such poets as John Updike, Robert Peters, Diane Wakoski and Marge Piercy. Each issue seems to feature a poet. As a sample the editors selected these lines from "Massasoit, An Epic" by James Wm. Chichetto:
> *Not far from Nemasket, Massasoit/Arose from a reef blistered with dark-stained/Waves. Trees nearby*
> *sucking blood from their roots/Sweetened the mouth of the air.*
The flat-spined, large digest-sized journal is "printed letterpress by hand on a Hacker Hand Press from Monotype Bembo." Most of the 45-60 pgs. are poetry, but they also have reviews. They receive over 1,500 submissions a year, use about 20, have a 3-month backlog. Press run is 400 for 80 subscribers of which 35 are libraries. Sample: $3.50.
How to Submit: Reports in 3 months. Pays $5/poem plus 1 copy.
Advice: The editors advise, "Study traditional and modern styles. Study poets of the past. Attend poetry readings and write. Practice on your own."

🌀 💿 CONNECTICUT REVIEW, Southern Community State University, 501 Crescent St., New Haven CT 06473, phone (203)392-6737, founded 1968, editor Dr. Vivian Shipley. Send submissions to: Dr. Vivian Shipley, 34 Old Orchard Rd., North Haven CT 06473.
  • Poetry published in this review has been included in *The Best American Poetry 1998* and 1998 Pushcart Prizes, *XXIII*.
Magazine Needs: *CR*, published biannually, contains essays, poetry, articles, fiction and color artwork. They have published poetry by Margot Schilpp, Ron Wallace, Colette Inez, David Citino, Marge Piercy, Mark Jarman and Walt McDonald. *Connecticut Review* is 176 pgs., digest-sized, offset printed, perfect bound, with glossy 4-color cover and 8-color interior art. They receive about 2,500 poems a year, accept approximately 5%. Press run

"Connecticut Review is open to poems that unite the heart and mind with a fresh vision," says editor Dr. Vivian Shipley. "The cover and interior art in this Fall issue of *CR* is all fractal art. The issue demonstrates *Connecticut Review*'s interest in exploring all forms of creative expression and dedication to trying new ways of expressing the different ways the creative spirit can manifest itself." The cover art, titled "Excess," is by artist Carlos Ginzburg. He says, "The schema that art is using today is fractal because the paradigm of the culture at large reflects the tendencies of hermetic dynamic behavior. This comes to us from our overall condition, from the state of our unconscious, from the architecture of our cities, and from the physical and emotional landscape within which we find ourselves."

is 3,000 of which 400 are libraries, with 1,000 distributed free to Connecticut State libraries and high schools. Sample: $6. Make checks payable to Connecticut State University.

How to Submit: Submit 3-5 typed poems at a time, 2 copies of each with name, address and phone in the upper left-hand corner on 8½×11 paper with SASE for return only. Publishes theme issues. Send SASE for guidelines and upcoming themes. Pays 2 copies. Acquires first or one-time rights.

☑ ◙ **CONNECTICUT RIVER REVIEW; BRODINE CONTEST; WINCHELL CONTEST; LYNN DECARO HIGH SCHOOL COMPETITION; CONNECTICUT POETRY SOCIETY,** P.O. Box 185, Ansonia CT 06401-0185, founded 1978, editor Kevin Carey.

Magazine Needs: *CRR* appears biannually. They are looking for "original, honest, diverse, vital, well-crafted poetry; any form, any subject. Translations and long poems accepted." They have published poetry by Jana Harris, Lewis K. Parker, Alyce Miller, Walt McDonald and Miguel Torga. As a sample the editor selected these lines from "Bicycler's Sonnet" by Fileman Waitts:

> On pedals I have climbed as steep as spires,/have sweated fiercely in the glaring noon;/and coasted
> straight down into sunset fires/to hang my handlebars upon the moon.

The editor says *CRR* is attractively printed, digest-sized and contains about 40 pgs. of poetry, has a circulation of about 500 with 175 subscriptions of which 5% are libraries. They receive about 2,000 submissions a year, use approximately 80. Subscription: $12. Sample: $6.

How to Submit: Submit up to 3 poems at a time. Include SASE for return of mss. Cover letter with current bio appreciated. "SASE must be sufficient for additional communication. SASE with insufficient postage will not be returned." No previously published poems or simultaneous submissions. Guidelines available with SASE. Reports in 4-6 weeks. Pays 1 copy. International submissions must be accompanied by a minimum of 2 IRCs.

Also Offers: The Brodine Contest has a $2 entry fee/poem and 3 cash awards plus publication in the *Connecticut River Review*. Entries must be postmarked between May 1 and July 31. The Winchell Contest has a $2 entry fee/ poem and 3 cash awards plus publication in the *Connecticut River Review*. Entries must be postmarked between October 1 and December 31. The Lynn DeCaro Competition for Connecticut high school students only has no entry fee and 3 cash prizes plus publication in the *Connecticut River Review*. Entries must be postmarked between September 1 and February 27. Connecticut Poetry Society (203 Hanover Rd., Newtown CT 06470, president Faith Vicinanza) was founded in 1974 to encourage the art of poetry. State-wide organization open to all who are interested in poetry. Affiliated with the National Federation of State Poetry Societies. Currently has 150 members. Sponsors conferences, workshops. Publishes *Poets at Work*, for members only, appearing irregularly; and *Newsletter*, a bimonthly publication, also available to nonmembers for SASE. Members or nationally known writers give readings that are open to the public. Sponsors open-mike readings. Membership dues are $20/year. Members meet monthly. Send SASE for additional information.

☒ ⊕ $□ **CONNECTIONS, THE LITERARY SCENE IN THE SOUTH EAST,** 13, Wave Crest, Whitstable, Kent CT5 1EH United Kingdom, editor Narissa Knights.

Magazine Needs: *Connections* is a quarterly magazine. "Just producing its sixteenth issue, it aims to encourage new writers and provides an outlet for aspiring writers to see their work alongside articles, reviews and critiques from professionals. Each issue carries three or four poems and at least one short story." *Connections* is 28 pgs., A4, printed on coated paper and saddle-stapled with 2-color glossy cover, includes b&w photos. Press run is 350. Single copy: £4 (10 IRCs); subscription: £12 (17 IRCs).

How to Submit: Submit up to 6 poems at a time. "Nothing longer than those which will fit on a single page of A4." Reports in 6-24 weeks. Pays £5.

☒ $□ ◙ **CONTEMPORARY VERSE 2; THE LENA CHARTRAND AWARD,** P.O. Box 3062, Winnipeg, Manitoba R3C 4E5 Canada, phone (204)949-1365, fax (204)942-1555, founded 1975, contact Janine Tschuncky.

Magazine Needs: *CV2* appears quarterly. "We publish poetry, prose, essays, interviews, reviews and art by women and men." They want "writing which in its diversity represents a range of social and cultural experience, with a particular focus on the experience of women." They have published poetry by Di Brandt, Gail Scott and Claire Harris. As a sample the editor selected these lines from "Sometimes" by Beth Goobie:

> Sometimes the girl is covered in butterflies, a flock/rises from her bones, hovers as the winged molecules
> of her skin.

CV2 is 76 pgs., 6×9, with cover art, inside art, exchange ads. They receive about 800-1,000 poems a year, accept approximately 160. Press run is 700 for 480 subscribers of which 50 are libraries, 130 shelf sales; 80 distributed free at readings and events. Subscription: $23.98. Sample: $7.

How to Submit: Submit 4-6 poems at a time. No previously published poems or simultaneous submissions. Fax submissions OK, "as long as poets send a SASE by mail." Cover letter required with a 3-line bio and SASE. Time between acceptance and publication is 6 weeks. Poems are circulated to an editorial board. Poems go to the editorial collective; usually 3 out of 6 editors work on an issue and make those decisions. Often comments on rejections. Publishes theme issues. Send SASE (or SAE and IRC) for guidelines and upcoming themes. Reports in 4-6 weeks. Always sends prepublication galleys. Pays $20/poem. Reviews books and chapbooks in 800 words. Open to unsolicited reviews. Poets may also send books for review consideration.

Also Offers: Sponsors 2 annual contests, and administers The Lena Chartrand Award recognizing the outstanding

work of one poet over the year. The award is around $300/year.
Advice: The editor says, "Familiarize yourself with the publication you are submitting to."

◙ **COPPER CANYON PRESS; HAYDEN CARRUTH AWARD**, P.O. Box 271, Port Townsend WA 98368, phone (360)385-4925, fax (360)385-4985, e-mail cprcanyn@olympus.net, website http://www.ccpress.org, founded 1972, editor Sam Hamill.
Book/Chapbook Needs: Copper Canyon publishes books of poetry. They have published books of poetry by Lucille Clifton, Hayden Carruth, Carolyn Kizer, Olga Broumas and Jim Harrison. As a sample, the editor selected these lines from "Comice" in *Below Cold Moutain* by Joseph Stroud:

> I think of Issa often these days, his poems about the loneliness/of fleas, watermelons becoming frogs
> to escape from thieves./Moon in solstice, snowfall under the earth, I dream of a pure life./Issa said of
> his child, She smooths the wrinkles from my heart./Yes, it's a dewdrop world. Inside the pear there's
> a paradise/we will never know, our only hint the sweetness of its taste.

How to Submit: Query first with sample poems and cover letter with brief bio and publication credits. Include SASE. No queries via e-mail or fax. Replies to queries and mss (if invited) in 1 month. Time between acceptance and publication is 2 years. Write for catalog to order samples.
Also Offers: Copper Canyon Press publishes 1 volume of poetry each year by a new or emerging poet through its Hayden Carruth Award. "For the purpose of this award an emerging poet is defined as a poet who has published not more than two books." Winning poet receives a book contract with Copper Canyon Press and $1,000. Send SASE for contest guidelines.

☑ $ ◎ **CORNERSTONE (Specialized: religious)**, Jesus People USA, 939 W. Wilson, Chicago IL 60640-5706, phone (773)561-2450 ext. 2080, website http://www.cornerstonemag.com, poetry editor Curt Mortimer.
Magazine Needs: *Cornerstone* is a mass-circulation (40,000), free publication appearing 2-4 times/year, directed at young adults (20-35), covering "contemporary issues in the light of Evangelical Christianity." They use avant-garde, free verse, haiku, light verse, rarely traditional—"no limits except for epic poetry. (We've not got the room.)" As a sample the editor selected these lines by Beth Wagler:

> she lies like a young man's tie thin and pressed/holding her own hand/open-mouthed/baby robin-like/
> waiting for Bigness to drop in/something that'll make her strong enough to fly

They buy 10-25 poems/year, use 1-2 pgs./issue, and have a 6- to 9-month backlog. Sample free with 9×12 envelope and 5 first-class stamps. "Do not send SASE for response. We will not reply unless we accept the poem(s). We will not return submitted materials."
How to Submit: Submit maximum of 5 poems at a time. Cover letter required. Send SASE for guidelines. Pays 6 copies and $10 for poems having 1-15 lines, $25 for poems having 16 lines or more. Buys first or one-time rights. Open to unsolicited reviews. Poets may also send books for review consideration.

◙ **CORONA**, Dept. of History and Philosophy, Montana State University, Bozeman MT 59717, phone (406)994-5200, founded 1979, poetry editors Lynda and Michael Sexson.
Magazine Needs: *Corona* "is an interdisciplinary occasional journal bringing together reflections from those who stand on the edges of their disciplines; those who sense that insight is located not in things but in relationships; those who have deep sense of playfulness; and those who believe that the imagination is involved in what we know." In regard to poetry they want "no sentimental greeting cards; no slap-dash." They have published poetry by Wendy Battin, William Irwin Thompson, Frederick Turner and James Dickey. The journal is 125-140 pgs., perfect-bound, professionally printed. They use about 20-25 pgs. of poetry/issue. Press run is 2,000. Sample: $7.
How to Submit: Submit any number of pages. No simultaneous submissions. Reports in 1 week to 9 months. Payment is "nominal" plus 2 copies.
Advice: The editors advise, "Today's poet survives only by the generous spirits of small press publishers. Read and support the publishers of contemporary artists by subscribing to the journals and magazines you admire."

▣ ◙ **THE CORTLAND REVIEW**, 5941 Arlington Blvd., Arlington VA 22203, e-mail spalding@cortlandreview.com, website http://www.cortlandreview.com, founded 1997, editor-in-chief J.M. Spalding, co-editor Guy Shahar.
Magazine Needs: *The Cortland Review* is a quarterly online literary magazine. They want "the best poetry regardless of source or form." They are also interested in receiving translations. They have published poetry by Charles Simic, Thomas Lux, Neal Bowers, Lloyd Schwartz and R.T. Smith. As a sample the editor selected these lines from "The Kindnesses of Bad Neighbors" by Neal Bowers:

> Whenever they absolutely must discharge a gun/in celebration or anger or simple idleness,/they try to
> aim low so the bullet won't carry;/and none of the fires they've set/by accident with cigarettes or
> overloaded outlets/has ever spread beyond their walls

How to Submit: Submit 3-5 poems at a time. No previously published poems or simultaneous submissions. Cover letter required. E-mail submissions preferred. "Word format or as text in e-mail." Time between acceptance and publication is 1-5 months. "Poetry submissions read by J.M. Spalding, fiction by Guy Shahar." Seldom comments on rejections. Obtain guidelines via e-mail. Always sends prepublication galleys. Acquires first rights.

Staff reviews books and chapbooks of poetry and other magazines in 100 words, multi-book format. Send books for review consideration to J.M. Spalding.
Also Offers: Website includes recommended sites page and interviews with "some of today's finest poets and writers."

⚑ ◯ ◎ COSMIC TREND; PARA*PHRASE (Specialized: themes, love/romance/erotica), Sheridan Mall Box 47014, Mississauga, Ontario L5K 2R2 Canada, founded 1984, Cosmic Trend poetry editor George Le Grand, *PARA*phrase editor Tedy Asponsen.
Magazine Needs: *PARA*phrase—Newsletter of Cosmic Trend (irregular: 2-3 times a year)—publishes "poetry related to our major anthologies advertised here." Sample: $6.
Book Needs: Cosmic Trend annually publishes 1 anthology with narrated music cassettes of "New Age, and Post-New-Age, sensual and mind-expanding short material of any style, but preferably unrhymed; also: humorous, unusual or zany entries (including graphics) with deeper meaning. We ignore epics, run-of-a-mill romantic and political material. Would like to publish more free verse." They have published poetry by Heather Fraser and Joanna Nealon. As a sample the editor selected these lines by Joanna Nealon:
> Why incarcerate a star in a tower of bone,/A ray of sun/Behind barricades of blood,/A moonbeam/In a fathomless moat of hormones?/And then, why give the piece of sky no peace?

How to Submit: For both Cosmic Trend and *PARA*phrase, submit up to 10 poems at a time with name and address on each sheet. Submission fee: $1 for each 2 poems submitted, plus $1 for postage. Minimum fee is $2 plus postage. ("No U.S. postal stamps, please.") They will consider simultaneous submissions and previously published poems "with accompanied disclosure and references." Publishes theme issues. Theme for Summer 2000 and 2001 are "Beyond Dimensions of Truth" (deadline: November 15, 1999) and "Tomorrows Seem Forever" (deadline: November 15, 2000), respectively. Send $1 for guidelines and upcoming themes or $6 for sample publication, guidelines and upcoming themes. Response time is usually less than 3 weeks. Editor "often" comments on submissions. Does not pay for poetry. However, poets may purchase a discounted copy of the publication in which their work appears. Rights revert to authors upon publication. Poets may also send books for review consideration, attn. Tedy Asponsen.
Also Offers: Cosmic Trend publishes electronic music cassette tapes in addition to their poetry/music anthology accompaniments.
Advice: They say, "Share your adventure of poetry beyond the usual presentation! Cosmic Trend can choose your poems for narration with music and inclusion into our cassette accompaniments to our illustrated anthologies."

⚑ $ ◐ ◎ COTEAU BOOKS; THUNDER CREEK PUBLISHING CO-OP (Specialized: regional, children), 401-2206 Dewdney Ave. #401, Regina, Saskatchewan S4R 1H3 Canada, phone (306)777-0170, fax (306)522-5152, e-mail coteau@coteau.unibase.com, website http://coteau.unibase.com/index.htm, founded 1975, publisher Geoffrey Ursell, managing editor Nik L. Burton.
Book/Chapbook Needs: Coteau is a "small literary press that publishes poetry, fiction, drama, anthologies, criticism, young adult novels—by Canadian writers only." They have published poetry by Susan Andrews Grace, Jim Smith, Barbara Nickel and William Robertson as well as 2 anthologies of Saskatchewan poetry. As a sample they selected these lines from "Our Sullen Art" in *On Glassy Wings* by Anne Szumigalski:
> the language of poetry has something to do/with the open mouth the tongue that jumps/up and down like a child on a shed roof calling/ha ha and who's the dirty rascal now?/the same boy sent to his room for punishment/leans from his window listening for animals/far away in the woods strains his ears to catch/even the slightest sound of rage but nothing howls/even the hoot of owls in the dusk is gentle

"We publish theme anthologies occasionally."
How to Submit: Writers should submit 30-50 poems "and indication of whole ms," typed with at least 12 point type; simultaneous and American submissions not accepted. Cover letter required; include publishing credits and bio and SASE (or SAE and IRC) for return of ms. E-mail submissions OK (send as .txt file attachments). No fax submissions. Queries will be answered in 2-3 weeks and mss reported on in 3-4 months. Always sends prepublication galleys. Authors receive 10% royalty and 10 copies. Their catalog is free for 9×12 SASE (or SAE and IRC), and sample copies can be ordered from it.
Advice: The editor says, "Generally, poets should have a number of publishing credits, single poems or series, in literary magazines and anthologies before submitting a manuscript."

Ⓝ ◐ ◎ COTTONWOOD; COTTONWOOD PRESS (Specialized: regional), 400 Kansas Union-Box J, University of Kansas, Lawrence KS 66045, phone (913)864-3777, e-mail cottonwd@falcon.cc.ukans.edu, website http://www.falcon.cc.ukans.edu/~cottonwd, founded 1965, poetry editor Philip Wedge.
Magazine Needs: For *Cottonwood* they are looking for "strong narrative or sensory impact, non-derivative, not 'literary,' not 'academic.' Emphasis on Midwest, but publishes the best poetry received regardless of region. Poems should be 60 lines or fewer, on daily experience, *perception.*" They have published poetry by Rita Dove, Denise Low, Gloria Vando, Walter Griffin and Patricia Traxler. As a sample the editors selected these lines from "The World Remade" by Lyn Plath:
> Sunlight becomes a room in the city,/an angle of windows, a bar of gold on the floor./In a white vase on a table in the corner/flowers open, pulling the day into themselves,/into the rush and flutter of

yellow petals/the way one body draws another body into itself.
The magazine, published 2 times/year, is 112 pgs., 6×9, flat-spined, printed from computer offset, with photos, using 10-15 pages of poetry in each issue. They receive about 3,000 submissions/year, use about 30, have a maximum of 1-year backlog. They have a circulation of 500-600, with 150 subscribers of which 75 are libraries. Single copy: $8.50. Sample: $5.
How to Submit: Submit up to 5 pgs. of poetry at a time. No simultaneous submissions. Sometimes provides criticism on rejected mss. Reports in 2-5 months. Pays 1 copy.
Book/Chapbook Needs & How to Submit: The press "is auxiliary to *Cottonwood Magazine* and publishes material by authors in the region. Material is usually solicited." The press published *Violence and Grace* by Michael L. Johnson and *Midwestern Buildings* by Victor Contoski.
Advice: The editors advise, "Read the little magazines and send to ones you like."

N ○ COUNTRY FOLK, HC 77, Box 608, Pittsburgh MO 65724, phone/fax (417)993-5944, founded 1994, editor Susan Salaki.
Magazine Needs: "*Country Folk* is a quarterly magazine written for, by and about people living in country and rural areas. We publish poetry that reflects the serenity and peace of mind one feels when living close to nature. We also like humorous poetry. We do not want to see poetry with images of violence or meanness." They have published poetry by Goldena Trolinger of Hermitage MO and Reed Shook of Zion IL. As a sample the editor selected these lines from "Our Small Town" by Bev Boucher:

> *Friendly and warm, where I was born,/I like my small country town./No traffic light, or gangs that*
> *fight,/that pleases me, somehow.*

The editor says *CF* is 40 pgs., magazine-sized, web offset printed, 2-color cover, includes "photos of country people" and ads. They receive about 100 poems a year, accept approximately 10%. Press run is 2,000 for 500 subscribers. Single copy: $2.50; subscription: $10/4 issues. Sample: $4.
How to Submit: Submit up to 3 poems at a time. Line length for poetry is 8 minimum, 30 maximum. Previously published poems and simultaneous submissions OK. Cover letter preferred. "Include SASE if you want your poetry returned." Time between acceptance and publication is 2 months. Seldom comments on rejections. Publishes theme issues occasionally. Send SASE for guidelines. Pays 1 copy. Acquires one-time rights. Staff reviews other magazines in 500 words, single book format.
Advice: The editor says, "We strongly suggest poets read a copy of *Country Folk* to get a flavor for what we like. Your poetry may be outstanding work but if you mail it to the wrong magazine for review it will get rejected. Know your market. It's the least you can do for your poetry. Without exception, most of the poems we read could be improved with additional revisions. Yet we find that poets usually decline to revise when asked to do so because they feel it was an inspirational work and should not be tampered with. At that point, we must either reject the work, which we often do, or publish it 'as is' because it's the best we have been able to find, a sad conclusion but true."

$ ◎ COUNTRY WOMAN; REIMAN PUBLICATIONS (Specialized: women, humor), P.O. Box 643, Milwaukee WI 53201, founded 1970, managing editor Kathy Pohl.
Magazine Needs: *Country Woman* "is a bimonthly magazine dedicated to the lives and interests of country women. Those who are both involved in farming and ranching and those who love country life. In some ways, it is very similar to many women's general interest magazines, and yet its subject matter is closely tied in with rural living and the very unique lives of country women. We like short (4-5 stanzas, 16-20 lines) traditional rhyming poems that reflect on a season. No experimental poetry or free verse. Poetry will not be considered unless it rhymes. Always looking for poems that focus on the seasons. We don't want rural putdowns, poems that stereotype country women, etc. All poetry must be positive and upbeat. Our poems are fairly simple, yet elegant. They often accompany a high-quality photograph." They have published poetry by Hilda Sanderson, Edith E. Cutting and Ericka Northrop. *CW* is 68 pgs., magazine-sized, printed on glossy paper with much color photography. They receive about 1,200 submissions of poetry/year, use 40-50 (unless they publish an anthology). One of their anthologies, *Cattails and Meadowlarks: Poems from the Country*, is 90 pgs., saddle-stapled with high-quality color photography on the glossy card cover, poems in large, professional type with many b&w photo illustrations. Their backlog is 1 month to 3 years. Subscription: $16.98/year. Sample: $2.
How to Submit: Submit up to 6 poems at a time. Photocopy OK if stated not a simultaneous submission. Reports in 2-3 months. Pays $10-25/poem plus 1 copy. Buys first rights (generally) or reprint rights (sometimes).
Also Offers: They hold various contests for subscribers only.
Advice: The editor says, "We're always welcoming submissions, but any poem that does not have traditional rhythm and rhyme is automatically passed over."

○ COVER MAGAZINE, P.O. Box 1215, Cooper Station, New York NY 10276, phone (212)673-1152, website http://www.covermag.com, founded 1986, editor/publisher Jeffrey C. Wright, poetry editor Lita Hornick.
Magazine Needs: *Cover* is a "broad-based arts monthly covering all the arts in every issue, a 64-page magazine sold on newsstands and in select bookstores nationwide." They want "shorter poems—2-24 lines generally, modern, favoring new romantic work. Nothing stodgy or simplistic." They have published poetry by John Ashbery, Lawrence Ferlinghetti, Allen Ginsberg, Robert Creeley and Molly Peacock. *Cover* tries "to reach a cutting-edge/front-line audience in touch with the creative fields." They receive about 1,000 poems a year, accept

approximately 50. Entirely supported by subscriptions, sales and ads. Press run is 20,000 for 3,400 subscribers of which 20 are libraries, 4,000 shelf sales. Subscription: $18/2 years. Sample: $5.
How to Submit: Submit 4 poems with cover letter. Time between acceptance and publication is 4-6 months. Editor often comments on submissions. Send SASE for upcoming themes. Reports in 4 months. Pays nothing, not even a copy. Open to unsolicited reviews. Poets may also send books for review consideration.
Also Offers: Offers annual poetry contest, for subscribers only.

◻ ⬖ ◎ **COYOTE CHRONICLES: NOTES FROM THE SOUTHWEST (Specialized: political, regional)**, 222 W. Brown Rd., Suite #9, Mesa AZ 85201, founded 1993, editor Jody Namio.
Magazine Needs: *Coyote Chronicles* is the "biannual literary journal of a small press publisher of fiction, poetry, nonfiction and scholarly publications." The editor wants "poetry with emphasis on progressive political themes and ideas, ecology etc. No religious, fantasy or 'scenery' poetry." She has published poetry by Norman German, John Grey, Mark Maire and Richard Davignon. *CC* is 80 pgs., 8½×11, professionally printed on recycled paper, saddle-stitched. *Coyote Chronicles* will also appear on a limited scale on the Internet as an e-zine." They accept 10-15% of 1,000 poems received a year. Subscription: $12. Sample: $4.
How to Submit: Guidelines available for SASE. They consider simultaneous submissions and previously published poems. Submit with cover letter and bio. "Backlog of submissions at this time." Editor sometimes comments on rejections, "more substantial critiques on request." Reports in 6-8 weeks. Pays 5 copies. "Contributors encouraged to buy additional copies."
Book/Chapbook Needs & How to Submit: Publishes several chapbooks a year averaging 64 pgs. For chapbook consideration either query or send ms with cover letter and bio. Reports in 12-14 weeks. "Large backlog at this time, but we welcome all submissions." Payment "varies with author." Send SASE for catalog to buy samples. They also offer limited subsidy publishing services offered to selected authors.

CRAB CREEK REVIEW (Specialized: themes), 7265 S. 128th St., Seattle WA 98178, e-mail ccr@drizzle.com, website http://www.drizzle.com/~ccr, founded 1983, editorial collective Kimberly Allison, Harris Levinson, Laura Sinai and Terri Stone.
Magazine Needs: Published biannually, *CCR* publishes "an eclectic mix of energetic poems, free or formal, and more interested in powerful imagery than obscure literary allusion. Wit? Yes. Punch? Sure. Toast dry? No thank you. Translations are welcome—please submit with a copy of the poem in its original language, if possible." They have published poetry by Yehuda Amichai, Naomi Shihab Nye, David Lee, Linda Casebeer and Kevin Miller. The editor says *CCR* is an 80 to 100-page, perfect-bound paperback. Subscription: $10 (2 issues). Sample: $5.
How to Submit: Submit up to 5 poems at a time. Include SASE ("without one we will not consider the work"). Reports in 2-4 months. Pays 2 copies. Send SASE for guidelines.
Also Offers: Occasional contests and theme issues.

◼ $◪ **CRAB ORCHARD REVIEW; CRAB ORCHARD AWARD SERIES IN POETRY**, English Dept., Faner Hall, Southern Illinois University at Carbondale, Carbondale IL 62901-4503, website http://www.siu.edu/~crborchd, founded 1995, poetry editor Allison Joseph, managing editor Jon C. Tribble, editor-in-chief Richard Peterson.
 • *Crab Orchard Review* received a 1998 Literary Award from the Illinois Arts Council.
Magazine Needs: The *Crab Orchard Review* appears biannually in May and December. "We are a general interest literary journal publishing poetry, fiction, creative nonfiction, interviews, book reviews and novel excerpts." They want all styles and forms from traditional to experimental. No greeting card verse; literary poetry only. They have published poetry by Leslie Adrienne Miller, William Olsen, R.T. Smith and Patricia Spears Jones. In response to our request for sample lines of poetry the editors say, "We'd prefer not to, since no one excerpt can convey the breadth of poetry we'd like to receive." *COR* is 200 pgs., 5½×8½, professionally printed and perfect-bound with photos, usually glossy card cover containing b&w photo. They receive about 1,200 poems a year, accept approximately 10%. Each issue usually includes 35-40 poems. Press run is 1,200 for 850 subscribers of which 60 are libraries, 300 shelf sales; 50 distributed free to exchange with other journals. Subscription: $10. Sample: $6.
How to Submit: Submit up to 5 poems at a time. No previously published poems; simultaneous submissions OK with notification. Cover letter preferred. "Indicate stanza breaks on poems of more than one page." Reads submissions April to October for our Spring/Summer special issue, November to April for regular, non-thematic Fall/Winter issue. Time between acceptance and publication is 6-12 months. Poems are circulated to an editorial board. "Poems that are under serious consideration are discussed and decided on by the editor-in-chief, managing editor, and poetry editor." Seldom comments on rejections. Publishes theme issues. Theme for Spring/Summer 2000 issue is "The World of Music, The Music of the World." Deadline: October 15, 1999. Send SASE for guidelines and upcoming themes or obtain via website. Reports in 3-5 months. Pays $5/page, $50 minimum plus 2 copies and 1 year's subscription. Buys first North American serial rights. Staff reviews books of poetry in 500-700 words, single book format. Send books for review consideration to managing editor Jon C. Tribble.
Also Offers: Sponsors the Crab Orchard Award Series in Poetry. The publisher of the books will be Southern Illinois University Press. The competition is open from October 1 to November 15 for US citizens and permanent residents. "The Crab Orchard Award Series in Poetry, launched in 1997, is committed to publishing two book-

length manuscripts each year. We also run an annual fiction/nonfiction contest." Books are usually 50-70 pgs., 9×6, perfect-bound with color paper covers. Entry fee: $20/submission. 1st and 2nd Prize winners each receive a publication contract with Southern Illinois University Press. In addition, the 1st Prize winner will be awarded a $2,000 prize and $1,000 as an honorarium for a reading at Southern Illinois University at Carbondale; also, the 2nd Prize winner will receive $1,000 as an honorarium for a reading at Southern Illinois University at Carbondale. Both readings will follow the publication of the poets' collections by Southern Illinois University Press. Recent winners were Denise Duhamel's *The Star Spangled Banner* and Richard Cecil's *In Search of the Great Dead*. Send SASE for details. Website includes guidelines, list of contributors, contest requirements and results, editors' biographies and calls for submissions.

N ▣ ◑ CRANIA, A LITERARY/ARTS MAGAZINE, e-mail editor@crania.com, website http://www. crania.com, founded 1997.
Magazine Needs: *Crania* is an online publication appearing 3 times a year and publishing literary art—poetry, fiction, essays and reviews. They want "poetry with high attention to craft. No religious, New Age/spiritual or inspirational work." They have published poetry by Amy Gerstler, Janet Holmes, Michael Chitwood and Richard Garcia. They receive about 100 poems a year, accept approximately 10%.
How to Submit: Submit 3 poems at a time. Line length for poetry is 40 maximum. No previously published poems; simultaneous submissions only. Cover letter preferred. E-mail submissions only. "All poems must be submitted by e-mail to poetry@crania.com." Time between acceptance and publication is 3 months. Seldom comments on rejections. Obtain guidelines via e-mail or website. Reports in 3 months. Sometimes sends prepublication galleys. Acquires first rights. Reviews books and chapbooks of poetry in 750 words. Open to unsolicited reviews. Poets may also send books for review consideration to *Crania*, 1072 Palms Blvd., Venice CA 90291.

✓ ♉ ◑ CREAM CITY REVIEW, P.O. Box 413, Dept. of English, University of Wisconsin at Milwaukee, Milwaukee WI 53201, phone (414)229-4708, website http://www.edu:80/Dept/English/CCR, editor Kate Ranft, poetry editors Laura Micciche and Karen Howland.
 ● Poetry published in this review has been included in the 1996 and 1997 volumes of *The Best American Poetry*.
Magazine Needs: *Cream City Review* is a nationally distributed literary magazine published twice a year by the university's Creative Writing Program. "We seek to publish all forms of writing, from traditional to experimental. We strive to produce issues which are challenging, diverse and of lasting quality. We are not interested in sexist, homophobic, racist or formulaic writings." They have published poetry by Audre Lorde, Marge Piercy, May Sarton, Philip Dacey, Amiri Baraka, Tess Gallagher, Cathy Song, Mary Oliver and Philip Levine. They do not include sample lines of poetry; "We prefer not to bias our contributors. We strive for variety—vitality!" *CCR* is averaging 200 pgs., $5\frac{1}{2} \times 8\frac{1}{2}$, perfect-bound, with full-color cover on 70 lb. paper. Press run is 1,000 for 450 subscribers of which 40 are libraries. Single copy: $7; subscription: $12/1 year, $21/2 years. Sample: $5.
How to Submit: "Include SASE when submitting and please submit no more than five poems at a time." Simultaneous submissions OK when notified. "Please include a few lines about your publication history and other information you think of interest." Reads submissions September 1 through April 30 only. Editors sometimes comment on rejections. Send SASE for guidelines. Reports in 4 months. Payment includes choice of 2 copies or 1-year subscription. Buys first rights. Reviews books of poetry in 1-2 pgs. Open to unsolicited reviews. Poets may also send books to the poetry editors for review consideration.
Also Offers: Sponsors an annual contest for poems under 100 lines. Submit 3-5 poems/entry. Entry fee: $10. Awards $100 plus publication and one-year subscription for first place; publication and one-year subscription for second through fifth place. Website includes submission guidelines; publication index—a list of contributors, their submitted (published) essays, poems, fiction and the volume # in which their piece appears; publication/magazine overview and history; complete list of staff.

◑ ◑ CREATIVE JUICES; FORESTLAND PUBLICATIONS, 423 N. Burnham Highway, Canterbury CT 06331, e-mail forestland.powell@gte.net, website http://www.geocities.com/Soho/atrium/1782, founded 1989 (Forestland Publications), editor Geraldine Hempstead Powell.
Magazine Needs: *Creative Juices*, published bimonthly, features poetry, arts, photos, "something to inspire everyone's creative juices." They want "any style or subject, 50 lines or less." They do not want pornography. They receive about 100-1,000 poems a year, accept approximately 350. Press run is 100 for 65 subscribers, 30 shelf sales. Single copy: $3; subscription: $18 (6 issues). Sample: $1.50. Make checks payable to Geraldine Powell.
How to Submit: Submit 3-5 poems at a time. Previously published poems (with credits) and simultaneous submissions OK. E-mail submissions OK. Cover letter preferred. Time between acceptance and publication is 1-3 months. Submissions reviewed by editor. Often comments on rejections. Publishes theme issues. Send SASE or visit website for guidelines and upcoming themes. Reports in 1-4 weeks. Sometimes sends prepublication galleys. Pays 1 or more copies. Acquires first North American serial or one-time rights. Always returns rights. Reviews books of poetry. Open to unsolicited reviews. Poets may also send books for review consideration.
Book/Chapbook Needs & How to Submit: Forestland Publications publishes 3 chapbooks/year. Chapbooks are usually 5×7, 20 pgs. Query first with sample poems and cover letter with brief bio and publication credits. Replies to queries in 1 week, to mss in 1 month. Obtain sample chapbooks by sending SASE. "Beginning in

1999, non-subscribers [to *Creative Juices*] should remit a $10 reading fee for chapbook submissions."

⭕ ◎ **CREATIVE WITH WORDS PUBLICATIONS (C.W.W.); SPOOFING (Specialized: themes); WE ARE WRITERS, TOO (Specialized: children); THE ECLECTICS (Specialized: adults)**, P.O. Box 223226, Carmel CA 93922, fax (408)655-8627, e-mail cwwpub@usa.net, founded 1975, poetry editor Brigitta Geltrich.

Magazine Needs: *C.W.W.* offers criticism for a fee. It focuses "on furthering folkloristic tall tales and such; creative writing abilities in children (poetry, prose, language art); creative writing in adults (poetry and prose)." The editors publish on a wide range of themes relating to human studies and the environment that influence human behaviors. $5 reading fee/poem, includes a critical analysis. The publications are anthologies of children's poetry, prose and language art; anthologies of 'special-interest groups' poetry and prose; *Spoofing: An Anthology of Folkloristic Yarns and Such*; and anthologies with announced themes (nature, animals, love, travel, etc.). "Do not want to see: too mushy; too religious; too didactic; expressing dislike for fellow men; political; pornographic; death and murder poetry." Send SASE for guidelines and upcoming themes. They have published poetry by Emma J. Blanch, Brittany Hendricks, Grace Rasmussen, Alexandra Paull and Hillary Dingee. As a sample the editor selected these lines by Mandeep Sandhu:

> I wish people could become whatever they want,/Whatever they wish would come true./I wish I could
> be invisible/To see the wonderlands of the world.

Spoofing! and *We are Writers, Too!* are low-budget publications, photocopied from typescript, saddle-stapled, card covers with cartoon-like art. Samples: $8-12 plus p&h. Single copy: $9-12, depending on length; subscription: 12 issues for $60; 6 issues for $36; 3 issues for $21. Libraries and schools receive 10% discount. Make checks payable to Brigitta Ludgate.

How to Submit: Submit poems of 20 lines or less, 46 character maximum line length, poems geared to specific audience and subject matter. No simultaneous submissions or previously published poems. No fax submissions. "Query with sample poems (one poem/page, name and address on each), short personal biography, other publications, poetic goals, where you read about us, for what publication and/or event you are submitting. Also include SASE for response." Queries via fax OK. They have "no conditions for publication, but C.W.W. is dependent on author/poet support by purchase of a copy or copies of publication." They offer a 20% reduction on any copy purchased.

Also Offers: Sponsors "Best of the Month" contest, awards publication certificate and 1 copy. Contests on the website with prizes.

Advice: The editor advises, "Trend is proficiency. Poets should research topic; know audience for whom they write; check topic for appeal to specific audience; should not write for the sake of rhyme, rather for the sake of imagery and being creative with the language. Feeling should be expressed (but no mushiness). Topic and words should be chosen carefully; brevity should be employed; and author should proofread for spelling and grammar. We would like to receive more positive and clean, family-type poetry."

⭕ **CREATIVITY UNLIMITED PRESS®; ANNUAL CREATIVITY UNLIMITED PRESS® POETRY COMPETITION**, 30819 Casilina, Rancho Palos Verdes CA 90275, e-mail sstockwell@earthlink.net, founded 1978, editor Shelley Stockwell.

Book/Chapbook Needs: Creativity Unlimited® publishes annually a collection of poetry submitted to their contest, $5 fee for 1-5 poems; prizes of $50, $35 and $25 and possible publication. Deadline: December 31. "Clever spontaneous overflows of rich emotion, humor and delightful language encouraged. No inaccessible, verbose, esoteric, obscure poetry. Limit three pgs. per poem, double-spaced, one side of page." They also accept submissions for book publication.

How to Submit: "Poems previously published will be accepted provided writer has maintained copyright and notifies us." E-mail submissions OK. They often use poems as chapter introductions in self-help books. Always comments on rejections. Publishes theme issues. Send SASE for upcoming themes. Sometimes sends prepublication galleys. Pays 2 copies.

Advice: The editor says, "We are interested in receiving more humorous poetry."

🏆 $ ◎ **CRICKET; SPIDER, THE MAGAZINE FOR CHILDREN; LADYBUG, THE MAGAZINE FOR YOUNG CHILDREN; BABYBUG, THE LISTENING AND LOOKING MAGAZINE FOR INFANTS AND TODDLERS (Specialized: children); CICADA (Specialized: teens)**, P.O. Box 300, Peru IL 61354-0300, *Cricket* founded 1973, *Ladybug* founded 1990, *Spider* founded 1994, *Babybug* founded 1995, *Cicada* founded 1998, editor-in-chief Marianne Carus.

• *Cricket* has received Parents' Choice Awards every year since 1986. *Ladybug*, launched in 1990, has received Parents' Choice Awards every year since 1991.

MARKETS THAT WERE listed in the 1999 edition of *Poet's Market* but do not appear this year are listed in the General Index with a notation explaining why they were omitted.

Magazine Needs: *Cricket* (for ages 9-14) is a monthly, circulation 78,000, using "serious, humorous, nonsense rhymes" for children and young adults. They do not want "forced or trite rhyming or imagery that doesn't hang together to create a unified whole." They sometimes use previously published work. *Cricket* is 64 pgs., 8 × 10, saddle-stapled, with color cover and full-color illustrations inside. *Ladybug*, also monthly, circulation 140,000, is similar in format and requirements but is aimed at younger children (ages 2-6). *Spider*, also monthly, circulation 92,000, is for children ages 6-9. Format and requirements similar to *Cricket* and *Ladybug*. *Cicada*, appearing bimonthly, is a new magazine for ages 14 and up publishing "short stories, poems, and first-person essays written for teens and young adults." They want "serious or humorous poetry; rhymed or free verse." *Cicada* is 128 pgs., 5½ × 8½, perfect-bound with full-color cover and b&w illustrations. Subscription: $32.97/6 issues. *Babybug*, published at 6-week intervals, circulation 50,000, is a read-aloud magazine for ages 6 months to 2 years; premier issue published January 1995. It is 24 pgs., 6¼ × 7, printed on cardstock with nontoxic glued spine and full-color illustrations. The magazines receive over 1,200 submissions/month, use 25-30, and have up to a 2-year backlog. Sample of *Cricket*, *Ladybug*, *Spider* or *Babybug*: $5; sample of *Cicada*: $8.50.

How to Submit: Do not query. Submit no more than 5 poems—up to 50 lines (2 pgs. max.) for *Cricket*; up to 20 lines for *Spider* and *Ladybug*, up to 25 lines for *Cicada*, up to 8 lines for *Babybug*, no restrictions on form. Guidelines available for SASE. Reports in 3-4 months. Payment for all is up to $3/line and 2 copies. "All submissions are automatically considered for all five magazines."

Also Offers: *Cricket* and *Spider* hold poetry contests every third month. *Cricket* accepts entries from readers of all ages; *Spider* from readers ages 10 and under. Current contest themes and rules appear in each issue.

▓ ◎ CROSS & QUILL, THE CHRISTIAN WRITERS NEWSLETTER (Specialized: religious); CHRISTIAN WRITERS FELLOWSHIP INTERNATIONAL, 1624 Jefferson Davis Rd., Clinton SC 29325-6401, phone (864)697-6035, e-mail cwfi@aol.com, website http://members.aol.com/cwfi/writers.htm, founded 1976, editor/publisher Sandy Brooks.

Magazine Needs: *Cross & Quill* is a bimonthly newsletter published "to encourage and equip Christians in publishing at all experience levels." They want traditional, free verse, blank verse and rhymed verse. Nothing longer than 12 lines. They have published poetry by Fannie Houck, Mary Sayler, Leona Choy and Jane Lippy. As a sample the editor selected these lines (poet unidentified):

> Pen of Heaven/write to me/words of what the Master sees./Pen from Heaven/speak to me/oracles of
> sweet simplicity./Take my laughter, take my pain/and write for me as heaven's gain

The editor says *C&Q* is 12 pgs., newsletter-sized, desktop-published, folded/loose, b&w cover, includes computer-generated art and ads. They receive about 100 poems a year, accept approximately 1%. Press run is over 1,000. Single copy: $4; subscription: $20/year. Sample (including guidelines): $2. Make checks payable to CWFI.

How to Submit: Submit 3 poems at a time. Line length for poetry is 12 maximum. Previously published poems OK; no simultaneous submissions. "We will accept electronic submissions upon request. If previously published, tell me where and when it was published." Reads submissions January through December only. Time between acceptance and publication is 3-6 months. Usually comments on rejections. Send SASE for guidelines or obtain via e-mail. Reports in 2 weeks. Pays 3 copies. Acquires first or reprint rights. Reviews books and chapbooks of poetry, "only as it applies to writing poetry."

Also Offers: "We provide critiques, online writers group, help with contracts, publicity for member books, connections with writers and groups near them." Website includes publicity for member books, links for writers, information about CWFI and sample articles.

Advice: The editor says, "We lean toward informational materials rather than personal experience."

◖ ◎ CROSS-CULTURAL COMMUNICATIONS; CROSS-CULTURAL REVIEW OF WORLD LITERATURE AND ART IN SOUND, PRINT, AND MOTION; CROSS-CULTURAL MONTHLY; CROSS-CULTURAL REVIEW CHAPBOOK ANTHOLOGY; INTERNATIONAL WRITERS SERIES (Specialized: translations, bilingual), 239 Wynsum Ave., Merrick NY 11566-4725, phone (516)868-5635, fax (516)379-1901, founded 1971, Stanley H. and Bebe Barkan.

Magazine Needs & How to Submit: *Cross-Cultural Monthly* focuses on bilingual poetry and prose. Subscription (12 issues/editions): $50. Sample postpaid: $7.50. Pays 1 copy.

Book/Chapbook Needs & How to Submit: *CCR* began as a series of chapbooks (6-12 a year) of collections of poetry translated from various languages and continues as the Holocaust, Women Writers, Latin American Writers, African Heritage, Asian Heritage, Italian Heritage, International Artists, Art & Poetry, Jewish, Israeli, Yiddish, Cajun, Dutch, Finnish, Swedish, Scandinavian, Turkish, and Long Island and Brooklyn Writers Chapbook Series (with a number of other permutations in the offing)—issued simultaneously in palm-sized and regular paperback and cloth-binding editions and boxed and canned editions, as well as audiocassette and videocassette. Cross-Cultural International Writers Series, focusing on leading poets from various countries, includes titles by Leo Vroman (Holland) and Pablo Neruda (Chile). As a sample the editor selected the beginning of a poem by Rainer Maria Rilke, as translated by Stephen Mitchell:

> She was no longer that woman with blue eyes/who once had echoed through the poet's songs,/no
> longer the wide couch's scent and island,/and that man's property no longer.//She was already loosened
> like long hair,/poured out like fallen rain,/shared like a limitless supply.

That's from the bilingual limited poetry and art edition, *Orpheus. Eurydice. Hermes: Notations on a Landscape*, published in 1996. It is 35 pgs., 10½ × 13½, smythe-sewn cloth. Sample chapbook: $10. All submissions should be preceded by a query letter with SASE. Send SASE for guidelines. Pays 10% of print run.

Also Offers: CCC continues to produce the International Festival of Poetry, Writing and Translation with the International Poets and Writers Literary Arts Week in New York. CCC won the Poor Richards Award "for a quarter century of high-quality publishing," presented by The Small Press Center in New York.

⬤ ◐ **CRUCIBLE; SAM RAGAN PRIZE**, Barton College, College Station, Wilson NC 27893, phone (919)399-6456, founded 1964, editor Terrence L. Grimes.

Magazine Needs: The *Crucible* is an annual using "poetry that demonstrates originality and integrity of crafts-manship as well as thought. Traditional metrical and rhyming poems are difficult to bring off in modern poetry. The best poetry is written out of deeply felt experience which has been crafted into pleasing form. No very long narratives." They have published poetry by Robert Grey, R.T. Smith and Anthony S. Abbott. It is 100 pgs., 6×9, professionally printed on high-quality paper with matte card cover. Press run is 500 for 300 subscribers of which 100 are libraries, 200 shelf sales. Sample: $6.

How to Submit: Submit 5 poems at a time between Christmas and mid-April only. No previously published poems or simultaneous submissions. Reports in 4 months or less. "We require three unsigned copies of the manuscript and a short biography including a list of publications, in case we decide to publish the work."

Also Offers: Send SASE for guidelines for contests (prizes of $150 and $100), and the Sam Ragan Prize ($150) in honor of the former Poet Laureate of North Carolina.

Advice: Editor leans toward free verse with attention paid particularly to image, line, stanza and voice. However, he does not want to see poetry that is "forced."

⬤ ◎ **CUMBERLAND POETRY REVIEW; THE ROBERT PENN WARREN POETRY PRIZE (Spe-cialized: translations)**, Dept. PM, P.O. Box 120128, Acklen Station, Nashville TN 37212, founded 1981.

Magazine Needs: *CPR* is a biannual journal presenting poets of diverse origins to a widespread audience. "Our aim is to support the poet's effort to keep up the language. We accept special responsibility for reminding American readers that not all excellent poems in English are being written by U.S. citizens. We have published such poets as Debra Marquart, Richard Tillinghast, Rachel Hadas and Yves Bonnefoy (in translation)." *CPR* is 75-100 pgs., 6×9, flat-spined. Circulation is 500. Sample: $9.

How to Submit: Send poetry, translations or poetry criticism with SASE or SAE with IRC. Submit up to 6 poems at a time. No previously published poems. "We accept, but do not like to receive simultaneous submis-sions." Cover letter with brief bio required. Reports in 6 months. Pays 2 copies. Acquires first rights. Returns rights "on request of author providing he acknowledges original publication in our magazine."

Also Offers: They award The Robert Penn Warren Poetry Prize annually. Winners receive $500, $300 and $200 and publication in the review. For contest guidelines, send SASE.

⬤ **CURIO**, 81 Pondfield Rd., Suite 264, Bronxville NY 10708, phone (914)961-8649, fax (914)779-4033, e-mail genm20b@prodigy.com, founded 1996, editor Mickey Z.

Magazine Needs: Published quarterly, "*Curio* is best described as a salon—a place people come to exchange ideas and promote the artistic spirit. We publish three-four poems per issue so chances are very slim for publica-tion. All types of poetry are reviewed." They have published poetry by Elizabeth Wurtzel, the author of *Prozac Nation*, and model Antonio Sabato, Jr. As a sample we selected this poem, "Disney Land," by Yussef El Guindi:

> Black is a disney land for/liberal white/With these provisions:/The school must be guarded/and the
> house shut tight./Otherwise:/Black is a park on/a seamless night.

Curio is 84-100 pgs., 8⅜×10½, professionally printed in 4 color on glossy paper, saddle-stitched, 4-color color cover, includes art, photos and ads. They receive about 200 poems a year, accept approximately 10%. Press run is 100,000. Single copy: $3.50.

How to Submit: Submit 1 poem at a time. Previously published poems OK, "but only for fringe section"; no simultaneous submissions. Cover letter undesired. "We read poetry the first week of each month." Time between acceptance and publication is 3 months. Poems are circulated to an editorial board. "The editor picks five to six poems and the entire staff picks the final three." Publishes theme issues. Send SASE for guidelines and upcoming themes. Reports in 2 months. Sometimes sends prepublication galleys. Pays 2 copies. Acquires first rights. Reviews books of poetry and other magazines in 300 words. Open to unsolicited reviews. Send books for review consideration.

🌐 ⬤ ◎ **CURRENT ACCOUNTS; WILDERSWOOD PRESS (Specialized: membership); BANK STREET WRITERS COMPETITION**, 16-18 Mill Lane, Horwich, Bolton, Lancashire BL6 6AT England, phone/fax (01204)669858, e-mail 100417.3722@compuserve.com, founded 1994, editor Rod Riesco.

Magazine Needs: *Current Accounts* is a biannual publishing poetry, fiction and nonfiction by members of Bank Street Writers and other contributors. They are open to all types of poetry; maximum 100 lines. They have published poetry by Pat Winslow, M.R. Peacocke and Gerald England. As a sample the editor selected these lines from "The Artillery Inn (Topsham Road, 1972)" by Mike Elam:

> Darts thud steadily/into the buckled tuft at twelve o'clock./At the counter Alice orders,/rotates the
> wedding band/no broader than the ring that marks/the bull's eye's final dart and cheer.

CA is 24-44 pgs., A5, photocopied and saddle-stapled, card cover with b&w photo or artwork. They receive about 40 poems a year, accept approximately 20%. Press run is 40 for 2 subscribers, 30 shelf sales; 4 distributed free to competition winners. Subscription: UK £3. Sample: UK £1.50. Make checks payable to Bank Street Writers (sterling checks only). "No requirements, although some space is reserved for members."

How to Submit: Submit up to 6 poems at a time. Previously published poems OK; no simultaneous submissions. Cover letter required. E-mail submissions OK. Time between acceptance and publication is 6 months. Seldom comments on rejections. Reports in 1 month. Pays 1 copy. Acquires first rights. Reviews books and chapbooks of poetry and other magazines in 100-1,000 words, single book format. Open to unsolicited reviews. Poets may also send books for review consideration.

Book/Chapbook Needs & How to Submit: Wilderwood Press publishes "poetry/prose that appeals to the publisher." They publish 1 chapbook/year. Chapbooks are usually 30-40 pgs., A5, photocopied and saddle-stapled with cover containing various graphics. Query first, with a few sample poems and a cover letter with brief bio and publication credits. "Send SAE and IRCs for return of manuscripts." Replies to queries and mss in 1 month. Payment is negotiable.

Also Offers: Sponsors the annual Bank Street Writers Poetry and Short Story Competition. Submit poems up to 40 lines, any subject or style. Deadline: October 31. Entry fee: £1/poem. Send SAE and IRC for entry form. Also, the Bank Street Writers meets once a month and offers workshops, guest speakers and other activities. Write for details.

⊘ ◎ CURRICULUM VITAE LITERARY SUPPLEMENT; SIMPSON PUBLICATIONS (Specialized: themes), Grove City Factory Store, P.O. Box 1309, Grove City PA 16127, e-mail simpub@hotmail.com, website http://www.geocities.com/soho/cafe/2550, founded 1995, editor Amy Dittman.

Magazine Needs: *Curriculum Vitae Literary Supplement* appears quarterly. "*CVLS* is a thematic zine, but quality work is always welcome whether or not it applies to our current theme. We'd like to see more metrical work, especially more translations, and well-crafted narrative free verse is always welcome. However, we do not want to see rambling Bukowski-esque free verse or poetry that overly relies on sentimentality. We are a relatively new publication and focus on unknown poets." As a sample the editor selected these lines from "Faye's Loose Hair" by Andy Krackow:

> Grandma called you Susan,/But Mom I named you Faye/To my ninth grade classmates/Because it was romantic and I wanted you/To be a movie star with a murderous man.

The editor says *CVLS* is 40 pgs., digest-sized, photocopied and saddle-stitched with a 2-color card stock cover. They receive about 500 poems a year, accept about 75. Press run is 1,000 for 300 subscribers of which 7 are libraries, 200 shelf sales. Subscription: $6 (4 issues). Sample: $4.

How to Submit: Submit 3 poems at a time. "Submissions without a SASE cannot be acknowledged due to postage costs." Previously published poems and simultaneous submissions OK. Cover letter "to give us an idea of who you are" preferred. E-mail submissions OK. Time between acceptance and publication is 8 months. Poetry is circulated between 3 board members. Often comments on rejections. Publishes theme issues. Send SASE for guidelines and upcoming themes or request via e-mail. Reports within a month. Pays 2 copies plus 1-year subscription.

Book/Chapbook Needs & How to Submit: Simpson Publications also publishes about 5 chapbooks a year. Interested poets should query.

Also Offers: "We are currently looking for poets who would like to be part of our Poetry Postcard series." Interested writers should query to The *CVLS* Poetry Postcard Project at the above address for more information. Website includes writer's guidelines, masthead, standards and practices and a condensed version of the magazine.

⊘ CUTBANK; THE RICHARD HUGO MEMORIAL POETRY AWARD, English Dept., University of Montana, Missoula MT 59812, phone (406)243-6156, e-mail cutbank@selway.umt.edu, website http://www.umt.edu/cutbank, founded 1973, contact poetry editor.

Magazine Needs: *Cutbank* is a biannual literary magazine which publishes regional, national and international poetry, fiction, reviews, interviews and artwork. They have published poetry by Jane Miller, Sheryl Noethe, Nance Van Winckel and Jane Hirshfield. There are about 100 pgs. in each issue, 25 pgs. of poetry. Circulation is 400 for 250 subscribers of which 30% are libraries. Single copy: $6.95; subscription: $12/2 issues. Sample: $4.

How to Submit: Submit 3-5 poems at a time, single-spaced with SASE. Simultaneous submissions discouraged but accepted with notification. "We accept submissions from August 15 through March 15 only. Deadlines: Fall issue, November 15; Spring issue, March 15." Send SASE for guidelines or request via e-mail. Reports in 2 months. Pays 2 copies. All rights return to author upon publication.

Also Offers: It also offers 2 annual awards for best poem and piece of fiction published in the magazine, The Richard Hugo Memorial Poetry Award and The A.B. Guthrie, Jr. Short Fiction Award. Winners are announced in the spring issue. Website includes "pretty much the whole magazine."

Ⓝ ▣ $⊘ CYBER OASIS, e-mail eide491@earthlink.net, website http://people.delphi.com/eide491/oasis.html, founded 1996, contact David Eide.

Magazine Needs: *Cyber Oasis* is a monthly online journal containing poems, stories, personal essays, articles for writers and commentary. "The purpose is two-fold. Number one is to publish excellent writing and number two is to explore the web for all the best writing and literary venues. Not only does *Cyber Oasis* publish original material but it investigates the web each month to deliver the very best material it can find." They want "poetry that has an active consciousness and has artistic intention. Open on form, length, subject matter, style, purpose, etc. It must deliver the active consciousness and artistic intention. No sing song stuff, fluff stuff, those who write poems without real artistic intent because they haven't given the idea a thought." They have published poetry by Libby Hart (Australia), John Horvath, Jeff Crooke and Prakash. As for the format of *Cyber Oasis*, Mr. Eide says "I'm trying to find the right style for the Web. I was inspired by the literary magazine phenomena but find the Web to be a new medium. One that is terrific for poetry." They receive "hundreds" of poems a year, accept approximately 15%.

How to Submit: Submit 5 poems at a time. Previously published poems OK; no simultaneous submissions. E-mail and disk submissions OK. "Try to include submission in ASCII plain-text in body of e-mail message." Time between acceptance and publication is 2-3 months. "If I know I don't want it I'll turn it back that day. If there is something there that warrants further reading I'll put it into a review folder. As the day of publication approaches I'll get the review folder out and start to eliminate stuff. If I eliminate something that I like I'll put it into next month's folder. Then I come down to a chosen few. One or two I pick for publication, the others I schedule for another month. I then notify the writer of acceptance, I notify the others that I want to publish their poems later and give them updates on that." Often, but not always, comments on rejections. Obtain guidelines via e-mail or website. Reports in 3-4 weeks. Pays $10/poem. Buys first, first North American serial, one time and reprint rights.

Advice: Mr. Eide says, "Seek to improve the writing; take poetry seriously, treat it as an art and it will treat you well."

◻ ◎ **CYCLE PRESS; INTERIM BOOKS; CAYO MAGAZINE (Specialized: regional)**, 715 Baker's Lane, Key West FL 33040, founded 1968, contact Kirby Congdon.

Magazine Needs & How to Submit: *Cayo* appears biannually and "uses regionally oriented material, but literary quality is our original motivation. We look for material pertinent to the Florida Keys." Submit 3 poems at a time. Previously published poems and simultaneous submissions OK. Cover letter preferred. Reads submissions July through August and October through April only. Poems are circulated to an editorial board. "The poetry editor finalizes his choices with the publisher and editor-in-chief." Often comments on rejections.

Book/Chapbook Needs: Cycle Press and Interim Books publish poems that are "contemporary in experience and thought. We concentrate on single poems, rather than more elaborate projects, for the author to distribute as he sees fit—usually in numbered copies of 50 to 300 copies." They want "provocative, uncertain queries; seeking resolutions rather than asserting solutions. No nineteenth century platitudes." As a sample Mr. Congdon selected these lines from his poem "Discus Thrower":

His figure, cut in silhouette/with no excess expended/not stint in measure,/takes its careful aim.

Books are usually 6-12 pgs., 5×8, computer-generated with hand-sewn binding, paper jackets, some photos.

How to Submit: Submit 3 poems at a time. Simultaneous submissions OK. Cover letter preferred. "If spelling, punctuation and grammer are secondary concerns to the author. I feel the ideas and experience have to be secondary too." Time between acceptance and publication is 1 year. Often comments on rejections. "No requirements except a feeling of rapport with the author's stance."

$ ◎ **DAGGER OF THE MIND; K'YI-LIH PRODUCTIONS; BREACH ENTERPRISES (Specialized: science fiction/fantasy, horror)**, 1317 Hookridge Dr., El Paso TX 79925-7808, phone (915)591-0541, founded 1989, executive editor Arthur William Lloyd Breach.

Magazine Needs: The editor wants "poetry that stirs the senses and emotions. Make the words dance and sing, bring out the fire in the human soul. Show flair and fashion. No four-letter words, nothing pornographic, vulgar, blasphemous, obscene and nothing generally in bad taste. *DOTM* is devoted to *quality* horror." They have published poetry by Jessica Amanda Salmonson. The quarterly *DOTM* is magazine-sized, saddle-stapled, with high glossy covers. They receive about 300-450 poems a year, use approximately 75. Press run is 4,000-5,000. Subscription: $8/half year, $16/year. Sample: $3.50 with 5 first-class postage stamps.

How to Submit: "Send in batches of ten. I will consider simultaneous submissions only if told in advance that they are such. Include cover letter with publication credits, a very brief bio and kinds of styles written. Length is open as is style. Be creative and try to reflect something about the human condition. Show me something that reflects what is going on in the world. Be sensitive but not mushy. Be intelligent not sophomoric. Don't try to carbon copy any famous poet. You lead the way—don't follow. I don't like the trend toward blood and gore and obscenity. Report back in six months." Publishes theme issues. Send SASE for guidelines. Pays $1-5/poem plus 1 copy. Buys first North American serial rights and reprint rights. The editor will evaluate work and review books of poetry for a fee, depending on length and quantity. Send books for review consideration.

Advice: He says, "I'm planning an anthology of Lovecraftian related material. The paperback will be predominantly Cthulhu Mythos fiction, but I do intend to publish some poetry."

⌧ ⊕ ◻ ◎ **DANDELION ARTS MAGAZINE; FERN PUBLICATIONS (Specialized: membership/subscription)**, 24 Frosty Hollow, East Hunsbury, Northants NN4 0SY England, founded 1975, editor/publisher Mrs. Jacqueline Gonzalez-Marina M.A.

● Fern Publications subsidizes costs for their books, paying no royalties.

Magazine Needs: *Dandelion Arts Magazine*, published biannually, is "a platform for new and established poets to be read throughout the world." They want poetry "not longer than 35-40 lines. Modern but not wild." They do not want "bad language poetry, religious or political, nor offensive to any group of people in the world." They have published poetry by Andrew Duncan, Donald Ward, Andrew Pye, John Brander and Diane Moore. As a sample the editor selected these lines from her own poem:

> . . . The human spirit without a planned path/to follow, is a sad landscape,/only grass and weeds, and nothing more/to expect.

The editor says *Dandelion* is 25 pgs., A4, thermal binding with b&w illustrations, original cover design, some ads. They receive about 200-300 poems a year, accept approximately 15%. Press run is up to 1,000 for 100 subscribers of which 10% are libraries, some distributed free to chosen organizations. Single copy: £9; subscription: £18. Sample: £10. Make checks payable to J. Gonzalez-Marina.

How to Submit: Poets must become member-subscribers of *Dandelion Arts Magazine* and poetry club in order to be published. Submit 4-6 poems at a time. No previously published poems; simultaneous submissions OK. Cover letter required. "Poems must be typed out clearly and ready for publication, if possible, accompanied by a SAE or postal order to cover the cost of postage for the reply. Reads submissions preferably March through May and September through November, but there are no restrictions. Time between acceptance and publication is 4-6 months. "The poems are read by the editor when they arrive and a decision is taken straight away." Seldom comments on rejections. Send SASE (or SAE and IRC) for guidelines. Reports "straight away." Reviews books of poetry. Open to unsolicited reviews. Poets may also send books for review consideration.

Also Offers: *Dandelion* includes information on poetry competitions and events.

Book/Chapbook Needs & How to Submit: Fern Publications is a subsidy press of artistic, poetic and historical books and publishes 2 paperbacks/year. Books are usually 50-80 pgs., A5 or A4, "thermal bound" or hand finished. Query first with 6-10 poems. Requires authors to subscribe to *Dandelion Arts Magazine*. Replies to queries and mss in 1-2 weeks. "All publications are published at a minimum cost agreed beforehand and paid in advance."

Advice: The editor says "Consider a theme from all angles and to explore all the possibilities, never forgetting grammar! Stay away from religious or political or offensive issues."

$ 🖊 JOHN DANIEL AND COMPANY, PUBLISHER; FITHIAN PRESS, a division of Daniel & Daniel, Publishers, Inc., P.O. Box 21922, Santa Barbara CA 93121-1922, phone (805)962-1780, fax (805)962-8835, e-mail dandd@danielpublishing.com, website http://www.danielpublishing.com/, founded 1980, reestablished 1985.

Book/Chapbook Needs: John Daniel, a general small press publisher, specializes in literature, both prose and poetry. "Book-length mss of any form or subject matter will be considered, but we do not want to see pornographic, libelous, illegal or sloppily written poetry." He has published *Cleopatra in the Night*, by Bruce Feld; *Cow'sleap: A Nightbook*, by Tom Smith; and *Sustenance*, by Sheila Bender. As a sample John Daniel selected these lines from "To His Guitar" from the book *After the Serpent's Word*, by Francis Fike:

> In you, laid in the case, I see/An image of a mortal me/Whom someday friends will lay/Silent into a box, and pray./And I pray now;/Lord, on that day,/Lift me from darkness: on me play/Your music of eternity.

He publishes about 4 flat-spined poetry paperbacks, averaging 80 pgs., each year. Press runs average between 500-1,000. For free catalog of either imprint, send #10 SASE.

How to Submit: Send 12 sample poems and bio. Reports on queries in 2 weeks, on mss in 2 months. Simultaneous submissions OK. No fax or e-mail submissions. Always sends prepublication galleys. Pays 10% royalties of net receipts. Buys English-language book rights. Returns rights upon termination of contract.

Also Offers: Fithian Press books (50% of his publishing) are subsidized, the author paying production costs and receiving royalties of 60% of net receipts. Books and rights are the property of the author, but publisher agrees to warehouse and distribute for one year if desired.

Advice: John Daniel advises, "We receive over five thousand unsolicited manuscripts and query letters a year. We publish only a few books a year, of which fewer than half were received unsolicited. Obviously the odds are not with you. For this reason we encourage you to send out multiple submissions and we do no expect you to tie up your chances while waiting for our response. Also, poetry does not make money, alas. It is a labor of love for both publisher and writer. But if the love is there, the rewards are great."

$ 🖊 ◎ DARK REGIONS (Specialized: horror, science fiction/fantasy), P.O. Box 6301, Concord CA 94524, phone (510)254-7442, e-mail isedmorey@aol.com, founded 1985, poetry editor Bobbi Sinha-Morey.

Magazine Needs: *Dark Regions* is a quarterly magazine "dedicated to putting out an on-time quality product that will entertain as well as make the reader think. We publish weird fantasy and horror and occasionally weird science fiction. Our magazine is intended for mature readers. We want inventive tales that push the boundaries of originality and invention. We dislike overused themes like Friday the 13th, Conan and invaders from Mars." They want "dark fantasy, disturbing horror, vampires, gothicism, psychological verse, magic and wonder. For horror poetry, make it eerie and tantalizing. Use plenty of imagery and be passionate about your writing. Use your imagination and make your work fly. More fantasy!" Free verse and traditional verse. They have published poetry by Bruce Boston, Ann K. Schwader and Nancy Bennett. As a sample the editor selected these lines from "Punchline" by Scott Urban:

> After the flesh wears away./everyone shares the same ivory grin./Is that because we finally get the joke?

Dark Regions is 64-80 pgs., 5½ × 8½, offset printed and saddle-stapled with full color cover. They receive about 100 poems a year, accept approximately 25%. Press run is 1,000 for 300 subscribers of which 50 are libraries, 500 shelf sales; 150 distributed free to reviewers, writers, poets, advertising. Single copy: $3.95; subscription: $13. Make checks payable to Dark Regions Press.

How to Submit: Submit 4 poems at a time, either single-spaced or double-spaced, 1 poem/page. Line length for poetry is 35 maximum. Previously published poems OK; no simultaneous submissions. Cover letter preferred. "I take care of all poetry submissions and respond personally to each one." Often comments on rejections. Publishes theme issues occasionally. Send SASE for guidelines and upcoming themes. Reports in 2-3 weeks. Always sends prepublication galleys. Pays $5-10/poem plus 1 copy. Acquires first North American serial rights.

N ▣ $ ◯ DEAD END STREET PUBLICATIONS, LLC, 813 Third St., Hoquiam WA 98550, phone/fax (310)301-1818, e-mail webmaster@deadendstreet.com, website http://deadendstreet.com, founded 1997, director of submissions John Rutledge, director of publications Ivan Black.

Book/Chapbook Needs: Dead End Street Publications publishes electronic collections of poetry and seeks "cutting edge authors who represent the world's dead end streets." They have published poetry by Circe, Larry Jaffe, and Von Enemy. As a sample they offer their mission statement:
> *It must be known/that where I have been,/has both things to despise/and knowledge to lend.*

How to Submit: "We request complete collections so the depth and experience of the poet can be adequately judged." No previously published poems; simultaneous submissions OK. Cover letter required. "We prefer electronic submissions (disk and e-mail) in MS Word." Time between acceptance and publication is 6 months. Poems are circulated to an editorial board. Seldom comments on rejections. "Complete submission guidelines provided on company website." Replies to queries in 1 month. Pays royalties of 10% minimum, 40% maximum and 10 author's copies. Obtain sample books via website.

◯ ◎ DEAD FUN (Specialized: horror), P.O. Box 752, Royal Oak MI 48068-0752, founded 1997 as *Dead Fun*, editoress Kelli.

Magazine Needs: *Dead Fun* appears 2 times a year and is a "gothic horror zine with a sense of humor. Includes interviews, poetry, art, photography, editorials, fun, spooky stuff; ads, clip-art, etc." They prefer "gothic horror-related, religious/sacrilegious material." They do not want poetry that is "political, flowery." They have published poetry by David Sanders, Ben Wilensky and Rod Walker. As a sample the editor selected these lines from "Hope" by Cynthia Ruth Lewis:
> *I claw the dirt with fevered hands;/it yields fast to my demands/and alters not my desperate plans/to*
> *reach you in your crypt. . . .//At last ensconced in your abyss,/to snatch you close in mortal bliss/I*
> *slowly kneel and gently kiss/the smile of hope upon your lips*

Dead Fun is about 50 pgs., digest-sized, photocopied and stapled with color cardstock cover, includes pen and ink drawings, charcoal art, photography and ads for zines, bands, photography, "anything relative." Accept approximately 50% of poetry submitted. Sample: $3 plus 4 first-class stamps or IRC. Make money orders payable to Kelli or send well-concealed cash.

How to Submit: Submit up to 3 poems at a time. Previously published poems and simultaneous submissions OK. Cover letter strongly preferred. Time between acceptance and publication up to 6 months. Always comments on rejections. Send SASE for guidelines. Reports in 6 weeks. Pays 1 copy. Staff reviews books of poetry in approximately 40 words. Send books for review consideration.

N ◖ ◉ DEBUT REVIEW, P.O. Box 414071, Kansas City MO 64141-4071, founded 1999, editor M.L. Acksonj.

Magazine Needs: *Debut Review* appears annually to "showcase the work of a select few talented poets. We are looking for poetry of the highest order in traditional form or free verse. We prize the voice that demonstrates both objectivity and control. Wit is fine, but nothing overly humorous, trite, or unpolished." Because *Debut Review* is a brand new publication the editor says its first edition will be "somewhere between 25-30 pages, printed in a somewhat informal manner (stapled or folded) but highly professsional. After two or three issues, the review will be perfect-bound by a printer, and presented to contributors and libraries." Samples will not be available until after the first year of publication.

How to Submit: Submit 7-10 poems at a time. No previously published poems or simultaneous submissions. Cover letter required. Mss should be double-spaced with name and address in upper right-hand corner of each page. Reads submissions January through March only. Time between acceptance and publication is 8 months. Always comments on rejections. Send SASE for guidelines. Reports in 2-3 weeks. Pays 2 copies. Acquires one-time rights.

Advice: The editor says, "As our title suggests, we are looking to showcase the work of emerging poets, although this is probably not the place for beginners. We are interested in poets who have honed their craft, but have not yet had a collection of poems published. We request that poets write for guidelines before submittting."

N $ ◉ DEEMAR COMMUNICATIONS, 6325-9 Falls of Neuse Rd., Suite 320, Raleigh NC 27615, phone (919)870-6423, e-mail deemar@aol.com, website http://www.deemarcommunications.com, founded 1995, owner Diane Tait.

Book/Chapbook Needs: "DeeMar Communications is a woman-owned publishing house with a social conscience. We strive to promote poets with great potential." They publish 1 paperback/year. They want "poetry with some social/historical significance. No romance, erotica." They have published poetry by Neca Stoller and Andrew Malekoff. Books are usually 50-80 pgs., 5½×8½, offset printed and perfect-bound with 2-color covers.
How to Submit: Query first with 3-6 sample poems and cover letter with brief bio and publication credits. Previously published poems OK; no simultaneous submissions. "Poets should visit our website for complete guidelines." Reads submissions January 1 through April 1 only. Time between acceptance and publication is 1 year. Often comments on rejections. Replies to queries in 2 weeks; to mss in 1 month. Pays royalties of 10% and 10 author's copies. Order sample books via website.
Advice: The editor says, "We ask that poets be willing to work closely with the owner in all phases of production and marketing."

DEFINED PROVIDENCE; DEFINED PROVIDENCE PRESS, P.O. Box 16143, Rumford RI 02916, e-mail defprov@aol.com, website http://members.aol.com/defprov, founded 1992, editor Gary J. Whitehead. For the year 2000, *Defined Providence* will publish its annual volume in the form of a single book of poetry, chosen in open competition. Postmark deadline: June 30. The author of the winning 64-120 page ms will receive a prize of $1,000 and 100 copies of a perfect-bound, professionally printed book, selling in paperback for $8. Submissions will be accepted starting January 1. A distinguished poet will judge the competition. For more details, visit the *Defined Providence* website or send a SASE.

$ DENVER QUARTERLY; LYNDA HULL POETRY AWARD, Dept. of English, University of Denver, Denver CO 80208, phone (303)871-2892, fax (303)871-2853, founded 1965, editor Bin Ramke.
● Poetry published here has also been included in the 1992, 1997 and 1998 volumes of *The Best American Poetry*.
Magazine Needs: *DQ* is a quarterly literary journal that publishes fiction, poems, book reviews and essays. There are no restrictions on the type of poetry wanted. Poems here focus on language and lean toward the avant-garde. Length is open, with some long poems and sequences also featured. Translations are also published. They have published poetry by John Ashbery, Jorie Graham, Arthur Sze and Paul Hoover. *Denver Quarterly* is about 130 pgs., 6×9, handsomely printed on buff stock and perfect-bound with 2-color matte card cover. Press run is 1,600 for 700 subscribers of which 300 are libraries, approximately 700 shelf sales. Subscription: $20/year to individuals and $24 to institutions. Sample: $6.
How to Submit: Submit 3-5 poems at a time. Include SASE. Simultaneous submissions discouraged. Do not submit between May 15 and September 15 each year. Publishes theme issues. Send SASE for guidelines and upcoming themes. Reports in 2-3 months. "Will request diskette upon acceptance." Pays 2 copies and $5/page. Reviews books of poetry.
Also Offers: The Lynda Hull Poetry Award of $500 is awarded annually for the best poem published in a volume year. All poems published in the *Denver Quarterly* are automatically entered.

DESCANSO LITERARY JOURNAL, P.O. Box 20066, Seattle WA 98102, e-mail goyozura@earthlink.net, website http://home.earthlink.net/~goyozura, founded 1996, editor Gregory Zura.
Magazine Needs: *Descanso Literary Journal* is a biannual focusing on the "exploration of different issues facing Americans and people of the world through contemporary poetry, fiction and art. One topic is covered per issue." They want "contemporary and honest work; any length, subject matter or style; verse or prose. No overly romantic or gothic style." They have published poetry by Joan Fiset and Noel Franklin. The editor says *DLJ* is 58-64 pgs., 5½×8½, offset printed and saddle-stitched with 4-color cover stock, includes cover photo and photos throughout magazine, b&w ads (3-4 per issue). They receive about 300 poems a year, accept approximately 10%. Press run is 1,000 for 350 subscribers, 300 shelf sales; 50 distributed free to advertisers and contributors. Single copy: $7; subscription: $20/4 issues. Sample: $8.
How to Submit: Submit 5 poems at a time, do not exceed 5 printed pages for any 1 poem. No previously published poems or simultaneous submissions. Cover letter required—"must include brief biography with previous publishing credits." E-mail (plain text or Word attachment) and disk submissions OK. "Name and address must be included on each piece." Time between acceptance and publication is 1 month. Poems are circulated to an editorial board. "Read and discussed by a board of three people." Seldom comments on rejections. Publishes theme issues. Send SASE for guidelines and upcoming themes. Reports in 1 month. Pays 2 copies. Acquires first rights.
Also Offers: Website includes writer's guidelines, ordering information, poetry and photos from past issues, performance information and resource links.

$ **DESCANT (Specialized: regional)**, Box 314, Station P, Toronto, Ontario M5S 2S8 Canada, phone (416)593-2557, founded 1970, editor-in-chief Karen Mulhallen.

Magazine Needs: *Descant* is "a quarterly journal of the arts committed to being the finest in Canada. While our focus is primarily on Canadian writing we have published writers from around the world." Some of the poets they have published are Lorna Crozier, Eric Ormsby and Jan Zwicky. *Descant* is 140 pgs., over-sized digest format, elegantly printed and illustrated on heavy paper, flat-spined with colored, glossy cover. They receive 1,200 unsolicited submissions/year, of which they use less than 10, with a 2-year backlog. Circulation is 1,200. Sample: $8.

How to Submit: Submit typed ms of no more than 6 poems, name and address on first page and last name on each subsequent page. Include SASE with Canadian stamps or SAE and IRCs. No previously published poems or simultaneous submissions. Send SASE (or SAE and IRC) for guidelines and upcoming themes. Reports within 4 months. Pays "approximately $100." Buys first rights.

Advice: Karen Mulhallen says, "The best advice is to know the magazine you are submitting to. Choose your markets carefully."

DESCANT: FORT WORTH'S JOURNAL OF POETRY AND FICTION, English Dept., Box 297270, Texas Christian University, Fort Worth TX 76129, phone (817)921-7240, fax (817)921-7722, e-mail descant@tcu.edu, founded 1956, editor Neil Easterbrook.

Magazine Needs: *Descant* appears twice a year. They want "well-crafted poems of interest. No restrictions as to subject matter or forms. We usually accept poems 40 lines or fewer but sometimes longer poems." It is 80 pgs., 6×9, professionally printed and saddle-stapled with matte card cover. Poems in issues we read tended to be lyric free verse under 50 lines with short line lengths (for added tension). "We publish 30-40 pgs. of poetry per year. We receive probably 4,000-5,000 poems annually." Their press run is 500 for 350 subscribers. Single copy: $6; volume: $12, $18 outside US. Sample: $4.

How to Submit: No simultaneous submissions. Reads submissions September through May only. Reports in 6 weeks. Pays 2 copies.

DESPERATE ACT, P.O. Box 1081, Pittsford NY 14534, e-mail desact@aol.com, founded 1995, editors Gary Wiener and Steve Engel.

Magazine Needs: *Desperate Act* appears 2 times a year and "focuses on art as something that we do not merely for enjoyment, college credit, fame or tenure, but because we are driven to do it—to keep ourselves sane perhaps. We favor regional writers but will consider good work from anywhere. Any style or content is acceptable so long as the work comes from the writer's inner impulses—some real need—and not from a M.F.A. program. We favor material that is witty, ironic, clever and original. We believe that a poem should 'mean' as well as 'be.' No rhymed or sentimental verse; Hallmark verse; L-A-N-G-U-A-G-E or meaningless poetry." They have published poetry by Thom Ward, William Heyen, Wendy Low and Sejal Shah. As a sample the editors selected these lines from "Bloodletting" by Mary Ann Satter:

> I know my life is leaking slowly/into the plastic bag:/I feel my heart pump steadily/as though the blood
> were taking/its usual route/and not this slick-tubed side-trip.

DA is 60-100 pgs., digest-sized, desktop-published and flat-spined with 4-color card cover, includes line art and photos. They receive about 200 poems a year, accept approximately 10%. Press run is 200 for 20 subscribers of which 5 are libraries, 100 shelf sales. Subscription: $10/2 issues, $20/4 issues. Sample: $5.

How to Submit: Submit 3-5 poems at a time. No previously published poems; simultaneous submissions OK if informed. Cover letter preferred. E-mail (any format) and disk submissions OK. "However, we do not necessarily send rejections through e-mail. That is, e-mail contributors should not expect a response." Time between acceptance and publication is 6-12 months. Poems are circulated to an editorial board. "Interns, contributing editors and head editors read and recommend pieces." Publishes theme issues occasionally. Send SASE for guidelines and upcoming themes. Reports in 1-6 months. Pays 1 copy. Acquires first North American serial rights.

Advice: The editors say, "Our ideal writer has a handful of previous acceptances and several hundred rejections, yet continues to toil away at the craft, convinced that just around the corner . . . are several hundred more rejections. Residence in a garret and/or nose rings are not mandatory, but a rejection slip from *The Iowa Review* is a big plus. Submissions need not be written in blood."

DEVIL BLOSSOMS, P.O. Box 5122, Seabrook NJ 08302-3511, founded 1997, editor John C. Erianne.

Magazine Needs: *Devil Blossoms* appears irregularly, 1-2 times/year, "to publish poetry in which the words show the scars of real life. Sensual poetry that's occasionally ugly. I'd rather read a poem that makes me sick than a poem without meaning." They want poetry that is "darkly comical, ironic, visceral, horrific; or any tidbit of human experience that moves me." They do not want religious greetings, 'I'm-so-happy-to-be-alive' tree poetry. They have published poetry by Faulkner Fox, George Held and Mark Read. As a sample the editor selected these lines from "The Big News" by Karl Wachter:

> A serpent is waiting/beneath the sewer drain/winged angels are asked/for change and the darkness/in
> a god's eyes is mistaken/for dirt.

Devil Blossoms is 24 pgs., 8½×11, saddle-stapled, with a matte-card cover and ink drawings (cover only). They receive about 1,500 poems a year, accept approximately 2-3%. Press run is 500, 200 shelf sales. Single copy: $3; subscription: $8. Make checks payable to John C. Erianne.

How to Submit: Submit 2-5 poems at a time. Simultaneous submissions OK. Cover letter preferred. Time between acceptance and publication is 3-6 months. "I promptly read submissions, divide them into a 'no' and a 'maybe' pile. Then I read the 'maybes' again." Seldom comments on rejections. Send SASE for guidelines. Reports in 2-5 weeks. Pays 1 copy. Acquires first rights.

Advice: The editor says, "Write from love; don't expect love in return, don't take rejection personally and don't let anyone stop you."

☑ ◐ THE DEVIL'S MILLHOPPER PRESS; THE DEVIL'S MILLHOPPER; KUDZU POETRY CONTEST; TDM PRESS POETRY CHAPBOOK CONTEST, English Dept., Box 26, University of South Carolina at Aiken, 471 University Parkway, Aiken SC 29801-6309, phone/fax (803)641-3239, e-mail gardner@vm.sc.edu, founded 1976, editor Stephen Gardner.

Magazine Needs: The press publishes 1 magazine issue of *The Devil's Millhopper* each year and 1 chapbook, winner of annual competition. They want to see any kind of poetry, except pornography or political propaganda, up to 100 lines. They have published poetry by Susan Ludvigson, Ann Darr, Lynne H. deCourcy, Ricardo Pau-Llosa, Dorothy Barresi and Richard Frost. The magazine is 32-48 pgs., digest-sized, printed on good stock and saddle-stapled with card cover and uses beautiful b&w original drawings inside and on the cover. The print run of *Devil's Millhopper* is 500. The annual chapbook has a print run of 600, going to 375 subscribers of which 20 are libraries. Sample: $4. Make checks payable to The Devil's Millhopper Press.

How to Submit: Submit 5-6 poems at a time. Send regular, non-contest submissions September and October only. They want name and address on every page of submissions; simultaneous submissions acceptable. Sometimes the editor comments on rejected mss. Reports usually in 2 months from end of submission period. Sometimes sends prepublication galleys. Pays 2 copies. Acquires first North American serial and reprint rights. Rights revert to author upon publication.

Also Offers: Send SASE for their annual Kudzu Poetry Contest rules (prizes of $150, $100 and $50, $3/poem entry fee), TDM Press Poetry Chapbook Contest rules, and guidelines for magazine submissions. Send Kudzu Contest submissions September 1 to October 31; TDM Press Poetry Chapbook Chapbook Contest submissions January 1 to February 28. Chapbook competition requires $10 reading fee (which includes a one-year subscription). Pays $50 plus 50 copies.

Advice: The editor advises, "There is no substitute for reading a lot and writing a lot or for seeking out tough criticism from others who are doing the same."

Ⓝ ◐ ◎ DIAL BOOKS FOR YOUNG READERS (Specialized: children), 345 Hudson St., New York NY 10014.

Book/Chapbook Needs & How to Submit: Publishes some illustrated books of poetry for children. "Poetry should be fairly straight forward." They have published poetry by J. Patrick Lewis and Nikki Grimes. Do not submit unsolicited mss. Query first with sample poems and cover letter with brief bio and publication credits. SASE required with all correspondence. No previously published poems; simultaneous submissions OK. Send queries to Attn: Submissions. Replies to queries in 2-4 months. Payment varies.

Ⓝ ⊕ ◯ DIAL 174 MAGAZINE, 21 Mill Rd., Watlington, King's Lynn, Norfolk PE33 0HH United Kingdom, phone 01553-811949, e-mail apoet@globalnet.co.uk, website http://www.users.global.co.uk/~apoet, founded 1989, editor/publisher Joseph Hemmings.

Magazine Needs: *Dial 174* is "essentially a quarterly poetry magazine. We also publish articles, illustrated works, stories, travelogues and readers' letters. It is our editorial policy to give new and experienced poets/writers alike the chance to present their work . . . overseas submissions are welcome." They are open to poetry of any form or style, or on any subject matter. However, "no pornographic or otherwise unacceptable decency." They have published poetry by Tobias Hill, Barry Tebb, Dan Pugh, John Light and Patricia Batstone. *Dial 174* is about 60 pgs., 5½×8½, neatly printed and saddle-stapled with glossy, color card cover, includes illustrations. They receive "thousands" of poems a year, accept "hundreds." Press run is 400 for 400 subscribers. Subscription: $20 plus postage. Sample: $5. "Non-subscribers work is accepted, . . . but precedence goes to those who enable the magazine to continue."

How to Submit: Submit 6 poems at a time. No previously published poems; simultaneous submissions OK. Cover letter required, with bio "if you are so inclined." E-mail and disk submissions OK. "We send out an information pack and publishing guidelines to all newcomers. All submissions require a SAE. Submissions abroad require two IRCs for letter reply." Often comments on rejections. Send SASE for guidelines or obtain via e-mail or website. Reports "ASAP (usually by return post)." Sometimes sends prepublication galleys. Copyright remains with author. Staff reviews books and chapbooks of poetry and other magazines, single book format. Poets may also send books for review consideration.

Also Offers: Anthology publishing service offered to subscribers. Send SAE and IRCs for details.

☑ ◐ JAMES DICKEY NEWSLETTER, 1753 Dyson Dr., Atlanta GA 30307, fax (404)373-2989, e-mail joycepair@mindspring.com. founded 1984, editor Joyce M. Pair.

Magazine Needs: *JDN* is a biannual newsletter devoted to critical articles/studies of James Dickey's works/

biography and bibliography. They "publish a few poems of high quality. No poems lacking form or meter or grammatical correctness." They have published poetry by Laurence Lieberman and Linda Roth. It is 30 pgs. of ordinary paper, neatly offset (back and front), with a card back-cover, stapled top left corner. The newsletter is published in the fall and spring. Subscription to individuals: $12/year (includes membership in the James Dickey Society), $14 to institutions in the US; outside the US send $14/year individuals, $15.50 institutions. Sample available for $3.50 postage.
How to Submit: Contributors should follow MLA style and standard ms form, sending 1 copy, double-spaced. Cover letter required. Fax submissions OK. "However, if a poet wants written comments/suggestions line by line, then mail ms with SASE." Pays 3 copies. Acquires first rights. Reviews "only works on Dickey or that include Dickey." Open to unsolicited reviews.
Advice: The editor's advice is: "Acquire more knowledge of literary history, metaphor, symbolism and grammar, and, to be safe, the poet should read a couple of our issues."

THE DIDACTIC, 11702 Webercrest, Houston TX 77048, founded 1993, editor Charlie Mainze.
Magazine Needs: *The Didactic* is a monthly publishing "only, only didactic poetry. That is the only specification. Some satire might be acceptable as long as it is didactic." The editor is still experimenting with the format of the magazine.
How to Submit: Previously published poems and simultaneous submissions OK. Time between acceptance and publication is about a year. "Once it is determined that the piece is of self-evident quality and is also didactic, it is grouped with similar or contrasting pieces. This may cause a lag time for publication." Reports "as quickly as possible." Pay is "nominal." Buys one-time rights. Considering a general review section, only using staff-written reviews. Poets may send books for review consideration.

DIG., A JOURNAL OF POETRY, ETC.; WAYWARD ARMADILLO PRESS, #2-95 Tyndall Ave., Toronto, Ontario M6K 2G1 Canada, phone (416)536-9460, e-mail digjen@interlog.com, founded 1997, editor/publisher j.a. LoveGrove.
Magazine Needs: Appearing 3 times a year, *dig.* is "an independent literary magazine committed to the development of contemporary writing, as well as handmade paper and book art." They prefer writing with challenge, innovation, attitude. Nothing cliché, sexist, racist, homophobic, inspirational or boring. They have published poetry by John Barlow, Louise Bak, Rob Mclennan and Jay Millar. The editor says *dig.* is 35-40 pgs., magazine-sized, photocopied and hand-stitched with hand-stamped covers on various handmade papers, includes b&w graphics, 1-5 ads/issue. They receive about 300 poems a year, accept approximately 20%. Press run is 200 for 15 subscribers, 150 shelf sales; 25 distributed free to contributors, reviewers. Single copy: $5; subscription: $12/3 issues. Sample: $4. Make checks payable to j.a. LoveGrove.
How to Submit: Submit 4-6 poems at a time. No previously published poems; simultaneous submissions OK. Cover letter with brief bio and SASE preferred. E-mail and disk submissions OK. Time between acceptance and publication is 1-6 months. Seldom comments on rejections. Publishes theme issues occasionally. Send SASE for guidelines and upcoming themes or obtain via e-mail. Reports in 1-6 weeks. Sometimes sends prepublication galleys. Pays 2 copies. Rights remain with author. Staff reviews books and chapbooks of poetry in 750 words, single book format. Send books for review consideration.
Book/Chapbook Needs & How to Submit: wayward armadillo press is expanding into publishing chapbooks. Query first with a few sample poems and cover letter with brief bio and publication credits. Replies to queries in 1 month.

DIM GRAY BAR PRESS, 600 W. 111th St., New York NY 10025, phone (212)866-4465, e-mail ordinarymind@erols.com, founded 1989, publisher Barry Magid.
Book/Chapbook Needs: Dim Gray Bar Press publishes letterpress limited editions marketed to the rare book/fine printing trade. They publish 1-2 hardbacks and 1-2 chapbooks/year. They have no restrictions regarding form or style. They have published poetry by William Matthews and James Laughlin. As a sample the publisher selected this poem "Favrile" by Mark Doty:
> Don't we need a word/for the luster/of things which insist/on the fact they're made,/which announce/
> their maker's bravura?
Books are letterpress printed and hand bound, both cloth and wrapper covers, include commissioned illustrations.
How to Submit: Submit 3-6 poems at a time. Previously published poems and simultaneous submissions OK. Cover letter preferred. E-mail submissions OK. Time between acceptance and publication is 6-9 months. "Almost (but not all) manuscripts are solicited by the publisher from established authors whose first editions are considered collectible by the rare book market." Seldom comments on rejections. Replies to queries and mss in 1-2 months. Pays $100 honorarium or 5-10 author's copies (out of a press run of 100).
Also Offers: The press has printed/designed winning chapbooks in the Center for Book Arts Poetry Chapbook Competition series. Send SASE for guidelines to CBA, 626 Broadway, New York NY 10012.

DIRIGIBLE (Specialized: form/style, avant-garde, translations), 101 Cottage St., New Haven CT 06511, e-mail dirigibl@javanet.com, founded 1994, co-editors David Todd and Cynthia Conrad.
Magazine Needs: "*Dirigible* is a quarterly avant-garde journal of language art which publishes prose, poetry, selective reviews, translations, and hybrid genres. We seek language-centered poetry, controlled experiments,

fiction that is postmodern, paraliterary, nonlinear or subjective, and work that breaks with genre, convention or form. Hybrid forms of writing and essays on aesthetics, poetics, reader experience and writing processes are also of interest to us. No social issues, no inspirational, scatological or emotional work; no exhibitionism." They have published poetry by Sheila E. Murphy, W.B. Keckler, Simon Perchik, Ron Padgett, Richard Kostelanetz, Scott Keeney and Dennis Holt. As a sample the editor selected these lines from "Weights and Measures" by Morgan Avery Sispoidis:

> I hold your steadfastness/like a spirit level/to keep a balance that/does not fall/to guide me past the
> worn down chairs/away from spoon-faces and kitchen knives/and things that linger in thin curtains/
> sharp and white like razor blades.

Dirigible is 40-48 pgs., 4¼×7, photocopied, saddle-stapled with buff card cover, in-house graphics; "will swap ads with similar publications." They accept approximately 10% of poems received each year. Press run is 500-800, 60% shelf sales. Subscription: $7/year. Sample: $2. Make checks payable to David Todd.

How to Submit: Submit up to 8 poems at a time. No previously published poems or simultaneous submissions. No e-mail submissions. Cover letter preferred. Time between acceptance and publication is 1-3 months. Reports in 1-3 months. Pays 2 copies. Acquires first rights. Staff reviews books of poetry—"selective reviews; length and type vary."

Advice: The editors say, "We are interested in a phenomenological lyricism which recreates the texture and logic of interior experience. We are grinding an aesthetic ax and acceptance is dependent upon our editorial vision."

DISSIDENT EDITIONS (Specialized: non-anecdotal, dissident, metaphysical verse), 71 Ballyculter Rd., Down Patrick, Northern Ireland BT30 7BD United Kingdom, website http://www.gmtnet.co.uk/indigo/dissiden/, founded 1994, editor Frederik Wolff.

Book/Chapbook Needs: Dissident Editions publishes 2 paperbacks/year plus pamphlets. They want "short metaphysical, dissident, anticapitalist, antimaterialist verse with punch and/or zap, and/or humor. High quality work with individuality." As a sample the editor selected these lines from "Beyond the form" in *Dispatches from the War against the World* by Anthony Weir:

> Beyond the form/of growls or barks/& all things mauled, devoured or bitten,/the sheerest poetry is
> composed by dogs,/the most shimmering symphonies by sharks./The finest human poetry, says the
> worm,/is not just unpublished, but unwritten.

Books are usually A5, perfect-bound or stapled.

How to Submit: "Submit no more than ten poems, no biography or other irrelevance, by regular mail." Time between acceptance and publication is 6 months. Always comments on rejections. Replies to queries and mss in 2 weeks. Obtain samples of books or chapbooks by ordering through booksellers or directly from press.

Advice: When queried about the current literary scene, the editor said, "What current literary scene? There are only self-therapists and ego-wavers!"

THE DISTILLERY, Motlow State Community College, P.O. Box 88100, Tullahoma TN 37388-8100, phone (931)393-1700, fax (931)393-1761, founded 1994, editor Niles Reddick.

Magazine Needs: *The Distillery* appears twice a year and publishes "the highest quality poetry, fiction and criticism. We are looking for poetry that pays careful attention to line, voice and image. We like poems that take emotional risks without giving in to easy sentimentality or staged cynicism." They have published poetry by Walter McDonald, Thomas Rabbitt, Stella Nesanovich and H.R. Coursen. As a sample the editor selected these lines from "Morning Etude: Gustav Williams" by Neal Kirchner:

> Today/he is the oat in harvest time, the bead-leafed head of grain/that shakes itself in cardiac wind/
> for the harvester to clip its angry growth

Distillery is 88 pgs., digest-sized, professionally printed on matte paper, perfect-bound, color cover, b&w photography. They receive about 600 poems a year, accept approximately 5%. Press run is 500. Subscription: $12/year (2 issues). Sample: $6.

How to Submit: Submit 4-6 poems at a time with SASE. No previously published poems; simultaneous submissions OK "if poet informs us immediately of acceptance elsewhere." Cover letter preferred. Reads submissions August 15 through May 15 only. Time between acceptance and publication is 6-12 months. Poems are circulated to an editorial board. "Poems are read by three preliminary readers then passed to the poetry editor." Seldom comments on rejections. Send SASE for guidelines. Reports in 2-3 months. Pays 2 copies. Acquires first North American serial rights.

Advice: "Too much poetry we see looks rushed. Take your time and get it right. We are also seeing too many therapy sessions disguised as poetry. Some things should be kept in the family."

DIXIE PHOENIX, 3888 N. 30th St., Arlington VA 22207, e-mail srimichel@delphi.com, website http://www.concentric.net/~yamyak/DixiePhoenix/Frontporch.html, founded 1992, co-editor Michael Munson.

Magazine Needs: *Dixie Phoenix* is "a home-grown literary magazine featuring short stories, travel essays, poetry, history, spirituality, reviews, recipes, etc." They want "anything from free verse to sonnet in style, spiritual (your own definition) and/or sincere in subject matter; confessional to transcendentalist. No profanity or violence; no shock poetry in general." They have published poetry by Erroll Miller and Verna Doberty. As a sample the editor selected these lines from "The Would-Be Buddies" by Edward Mycue:

nor a secret sting nor a single source/for light. You won't go against the/grain. To open the grain you have to/continue the assault on summer, assault/the seasons, senses, force the glistening/hasp, confront what still could grow again.

The editor says *DP* is 40-60 pgs., 5½×8½, photocopied and stapled with 20-60 lb. color paper cover, includes photocopied graphics and trades ads. They receive about 90-100 poems a year, accept approximately 3-4%. Press run is 500 for 30 subscribers of which 5-10 are libraries. Subscription: $8/4 issues. Sample: $2. Make checks payable to Michael Munson. Potential contributors are encouraged to buy sample copy.

How to Submit: Submit up to 5 poems at a time. Previously published poems and simultaneous submissions OK. Cover letter preferred. E-mail and disk (ASCII only) submissions OK. Reads submissions August 1 through November 1 for winter issue, January 1 through June 1 for summer issue. Time between acceptance and publication is 6 months. Seldom comments on rejections. Publishes theme issues occasionally. Send SASE for guidelines. Reports in 4 months. Pays 3 copies. Acquires one-time rights. Staff reviews books and chapbooks of poetry and other magazines in 200-700 words. Send books for review consideration.

Advice: The editor says, "Develop your own style, don't copy or adhere to others. We value sincerity over shock value."

DOC(K)S; EDITIONS NEPE (Specialized: bilingual/foreign language), Le Moulin de Ventabren, 13122 Ventabren, France.

Magazine Needs: *Doc(k)s* uses "concrete, visual, sound poetry; performance; mail-art; metaphysical poetry." They have published work by J.F. Bory, Nani Balestrini, Bernard Heidsieck, James Koller, Julien Blaine, Philippa Castellin and Franco Beltrametti. The magazine *Doc(k)s* is published 4 times a year and has a circulation of 1,100, of which 150 are subscriptions. It is an elegantly produced volume of over 300 pgs., 7×10, flat-spined, using heavy paper and glossy full-color card covers. Most of it is in French. "We cannot quote a sample, because concrete poetry, a cross between poetry and graphic art, requires the visual image to be reproduced."

How to Submit: There are no specifications for submissions. Pays 5 copies.

Book/Chapbook Needs: Editions Nepe publishes collections of poetry, mostly in French.

DOGGEREL; INSPECTOR J. LEE POETRY CONTEST, 312 S. 16th Ave., Hattiesburg MS 39401, phone (601)583-7422, e-mail hrozelle@ocean.st.usm.edu, founded 1994, editor Hugh E.L. Rozelle.

Magazine Needs: *Doggerel* is a biannual journal designed "to publish poetry with a limp. We also take short prose, reviews, photos, cartoons, etc." They have published poetry by Philip Heldrich, Angela Ball, Mark Cox and Sue Walker. As a sample the editor selected these lines from "Hitch Hiker" by Wayne Sheldrake:

When you pass,/I search for the vocabulary/of black magic. I drive needles/made of my middle finger into the/voo doo doll of your asphalt heart.

Doggerel is 30-50 pgs., 6½×8½ (folded 8½×11), printed by "the cheapest method possible," saddle-stapled with glossy card cover containing b&w photo or art. They receive about 250 poems a year, accept approximately 20%. Press run is 150. Subscription: $8. Sample: $4. Make checks payable to Hugh E.L. Rozelle.

How to Submit: Submit 3-5 poems at a time. Previously published poems OK; no simultaneous submissions. Mac disk submissions OK. Time between acceptance and publication is 6 months. Poems are circulated to an editorial board. Seldom comments on rejections. Send SASE for guidelines. Reports in 3 months. Sometimes sends prepublication galleys. Pays 1 copy. Acquires all rights. Returns rights after publication Reviews books and chapbooks of poetry and other magazines in 250 words. Open to unsolicited reviews. Poets may also send books for review consideration.

Also Offers: Sponsors the Inspector J. Lee Poetry Contest. 1st Prize: $100. Reading fee: $1. No restrictions on matter or style. Send query for deadline info.

DOLPHIN-MOON PRESS; SIGNATURES (Specialized: regional), P.O. Box 22262, Baltimore MD 21203, founded 1973, president James Taylor.

Book/Chapbook Needs: Dolphin-Moon is "a limited-edition (500-1,000 copies) press which emphasizes quality work (regardless of style), often published in unusual/'radical' format." The writer is usually allowed a strong voice in the look/feel of the final piece. "We've published magazines, anthologies, chapbooks, pamphlets, perfect-bound paperbacks, records, audio cassettes and comic books. All styles are read and considered, but the work should show a strong spirit and voice. Although we like the feel of 'well-crafted' work, craft for its own sake won't meet our standards either." They have published work by Teller, Michael Weaver, John Strausbaugh, Josephine Jacobsen and William Burroughs. Send SASE for catalog and purchase samples or send $15 for their 'sampler' (which they guarantee to be up to $25 worth of their publications).

How to Submit: To submit, first send sample of 6-10 pgs. of poetry and a brief cover letter. Replies to query or to submission of whole work (if invited) in 2-4 weeks. Always sends prepublication galleys. Pays in author's copies, negotiable, though usually 10% of the run. Acquires first edition rights.

Advice: "Our future plans are to continue as we have since 1973, publishing the best work we can by local, up-and-coming and nationally recognized writers—in a quality package."

DOUBLEBUNNY PRESS; OMNIVORE, P.O. Box 3094, Worcester MA 01613, e-mail bunnyx2@earthlink.net, editor-in-chief Sou Macmillan.

Magazine Needs: *Omnivore*, published 4 times/year, features regular and guest columns, Slam column, poetry, fiction, b&w art and photos and the occasional puzzle. They want "free verse, 1-2 pages/work. We are excited by interesting/unorthodox use of the page, including concrete poetry, though will consider new twists on the old canons. Haikus are cool too. No classic style or canon-bound. No Hallmark cards, please." They have published poetry by Gayle Danley, Lea Deschenes and Patricia Smith. *Omnivore* is 24 pgs., 11×17, offset, staple-bound with b&w graphics and photos, occasional ads. They receive about 200 poems a year, accept approximately 50%. Press run is 100-400 for 103 subscribers of which 2 are libraries; 10-20 distributed free "to people we hope will submit work." Single copy: $3; subscription: $10. Sample: $5. Make checks payable to S. Macmillan.

How to Submit: Submit up to 4 poems at a time with name and address on each page. Previously published poems and simultaneous submissions OK. Cover letter preferred. Time between acceptance and publication is 2 months. Poems are circulated to an editorial board where "we sit around and read 'em, pass 'em around." Often comments on rejections. Publishes theme issues. Send SASE for guidelines. Reports in 1-2 months. Sometimes sends prepublication galleys. Pays 5 copies. Reviews books of poetry and other magazines in 50-1,500 words, multi-book format. Open to unsolicited reviews. Poets may also send books for review consideration.

Book/Chapbook Needs & How to Submit: doublebunny press specializes in "living writers, preferably authors who tour, authors who stray from the classical canons yet remain intelligible," publishes 3 paperbacks, 1 hardback and 6 chapbooks/year. Chapbooks are usually up to 36 pgs., 8½×5 or 8½×7, some double, "flip" books; paperbacks up to 50 pgs., 8½×5½ or 5½×4¼, all hand bound by glue press or stitching; hardcover up to 200 pgs., 8½×7, hand stitched and bound. Hand-bounds are in small runs (50-200). Query first, include literary résumé. Prefers a publication in *Omnivore* first. Replies to queries in 3 months, to mss in 5 months. Pay is "negotiable as runs are small."

N ⊕ ○ ⊘ DRAGON HEART PRESS; LIVING POETS ONLINE POETRY JOURNAL, 11 Menin Rd., Allestree, Derby, Derbyshire DE22 2NL England, e-mail dragonheart@compuserve.com, website http://dougal.derby.ac.uk/lpoets, founded 1985, executive editor Mr. S. Woodward.

Magazine Needs: *Living Poets* is an online showcase for poetry. They want "crafted poetry with strong imagery. No constrained rhyming structures." As a sample the editor selected these lines from his poem "Shades of 1870":

> The elegant lead lines in sweeping jesture/Frame the head/of one seen only in a vision.//This is the
> dread sovereign/Blake has seen/whose temple afire/Drain all colour from the world

They receive about 400 poems a year, accept approximately 20%. Sample (printed): $10. Make checks payable to S. Woodward.

How to Submit: Submit 3 poems at a time. Previously published poems and simultaneous submissions OK. Cover letter with bio and publication credits preferred. Time between acceptance and publication is 1-2 months. Often comments on rejections. Publishes theme issues. Send SASE for guidelines or obtain via e-mail or website. Reports in 1 month. Pays 1 copy. Reviews books and chapbooks of poetry or other magazines in single book format. Open to unsolicited reviews. Poets may also send books for review consideration to Review Editor, Dragon Heart Press.

Also Offers: Sponsors annual poetry competition. Deadline: December 31. Send SAE (or SAE and IRC) for details.

■ ◎ DRAIGEYE (Specialized: psychic/occult, magick), P.O. Box 5511, Pasadena CA 91117, phone (626)584-0008, e-mail draigeye@earthlink.net, website http://home.earthlink.net/~draigeye, founded 1996, editor Capella.

Magazine Needs: *Draigeye* is a monthly website "intended as a forum of expression for diverse magical, Pagan and Wiccan concerns, issues, facts, fantasy and opinion." They want "occult, magick, wicca, metaphysical and druidical work. No Christian fundamentalist poetry or channeled material. Check out website for sample."

How to Submit: Submit 5 poems at a time. Previously published poems and simultaneous submissions OK. E-mail submissions OK. Cover letter required. May submit on 5.25 disk, MSDOS ASCII format. Seldom comments on rejections. Publishes theme issues. Send hard copy submissions to the address above.

○ ◎ DREAM INTERNATIONAL QUARTERLY (Specialized: dreams), 809 W. Maple St., Champaign IL 61820-2810, founded 1981, senior poetry editor Carmen M. Pursifull.

Magazine Needs: "Poetry must be dream-inspired and/or dream-related. This can be interpreted loosely, even to the extent of dealing with the transitory as a theme. Nothing written expressly or primarily to advance a political or religious ideology. We have published everything from neo-Romantic sonnets to stream-of-consciousness, ala 'the Beat Generation.' " They have published poetry by Ursula Le Guin, Errol Miller, Dr. Dimitri Mihalas and Kathy Youmans. As a sample the editor selected these lines from her poem "Hostage":

> Terror swallows light/& browndreams follow/a crooked cane/down a crooked lane/where a road toad
> squats/waiting for somnambulists/summoned to a party.

DIQ is 120-150 pgs., 8½×11, with vellum cover and drawings. They receive 300 poems a year, accept about 30. Press run is 300 for 20 subscribers. Subscription: $50 for 1 year. Sample: $13.

How to Submit: Submit up to 5 typed poems at a time. Previously published poems and simultaneous submissions OK. Cover letter including publication history, if any. "As poetry submissions go through the hands of two readers, poets should enclose one additional first-class stamp, along with the standard SASE." Do not submit mss in September or October. Time between acceptance and publication is 1-2 years. Comments on rejections if requested. Send large SASE with 2 first-class stamps plus $1 for guidelines. Reports in 1-2 weeks. Sometimes sends prepublication galleys. Pays 1 copy, "less postage. Postage/handling for contributor's copy costs $3." Also, from time to time, "exceptionally fine work has been deemed to merit a complimentary subscription." Acquires first North American serial or nonexclusive reprint rights.

Advice: The editor says, "We consider all types of poetry from blank verse to sonnets, from shape poems to haiku. However, nothing will turn me off more quickly on a submission than 'sing-song' greeting card style verse. Be very careful with rhyming poetry."

N **©** **THE DRIFTWOOD REVIEW (Specialized: regional)**, P.O. Box 700, Linden MI 48451-0700, e-mail driftwdmi@aol.com, founded 1996, poetry editor Jeff Vande Zande.

Magazine Needs: "An annual publication, *The Driftwood Review* strives to publish the best poetry and fiction being written by Michigan writers—known and unknown. We consider any style, but are particularly fond of poetry that conveys meaning through image. Rhyming poetry stands a poor chance. Give up the ghost; rhyme is dead—good riddance." They have published poetry by Daniel James Sundahl, Anca Vlasopolos, Terry Blackhawk and Joe Sheltraw. As a sample the editor selected these lines from "Tattooed" by Matthew Echelberger:

> I remember when he bought me a speed bag/for Christmas and made the red leather sing,/his sinew
> and muscle straining/against the anchor tattooed on his forearm

TDR is 100-125 pgs., digest-sized, professionally printed and perfect-bound with glossy card cover containing b&w artwork. They receive about 500 poems a year, accept approximately 5-7%. Press run is 200 for 75 subscribers. Subscription: $6.

How to Submit: Submit 3-5 poems at a time. No previously published poems or simultaneous submissions. Cover letter preferred. "Cover letter should include a brief bio suitable for contributors notes. No SASE? No reply." Reads submissions January 1 through October 1 only. Time between acceptance and publication is 9 months. Seldom comments on rejections. "Will comment on work that's almost there." Reports in 2-3 months. Pays 1 copy. Acquires first North American serial rights. Staff reviews chapbooks of poetry by Michigan writers only in 500 words, single book format. Send chapbooks for review consideration.

Also Offers: Sponsors a Reader's Choice Award. "Our readers vote by e-mail and the winner receives a cash award.'

Advice: The editor says, "There are too many writers and not enough readers."

■ **○** **THE DRINKIN' BUDDY MAGAZINE**, P.O. Box 720608, San Jose CA 95172, phone (408)397-8226, e-mail kc@drinkinbuddy.com, website www.drinkinbuddy.com, founded 1994, contact Poetry Dept.

Magazine Needs: *The Drinkin' Buddy Magazine*, published weekly online, is "a magazine for art and words." They want "shorter, concise work." They receive about 50 poems a year, "use what we can."

How to Submit: Previously published poems and simultaneous submissions OK. Cover letter preferred. Prefers e-mail or disk submissions but will accept paper submissions. For disk submissions, send 3.5 Mac or IBM format disk with poems in DOS/ASCII text along with a printout/copy of the work on paper. For e-mail submissions, include text file or Word document. Time between acceptance and publication "depends on when we can use it." Seldom comments on rejections. Acquires first North American serial or one-time rights. Reviews books of poetry. Open to unsolicited reviews. Poets may also send books for review consideration.

○ **©** **DRY BONES PRESS; THE COMPLEAT NURSE (Specialized: nursing)**, P.O. Box 640345, San Francisco CA 94164, phone (415)292-7371, website http://www.drybones.com, founded 1992 (Dry Bones Press), editor/publisher Jim Rankin, RN, MSN.

Magazine Needs: *the Compleat Nurse*, a monthly newsletter, "is a voice of independent nursing featuring matters of interest to nurses—a very broad range, indeed." They have published poetry by James Snydal. *the Compleat Nurse* is 4 pgs., 8½×11, desktop-published, folded with clip art; occasionally published as an anthology. They receive about 10-20 poems a year, "accept most, if in our range." Press run is 500-1,000 with all distributed free. Sample for SASE.

How to Submit: Submit 2-3 poems at a time. Previously published poems and simultaneous submissions OK. Cover letter preferred. Time between acceptance and publication "varies greatly; 1 month to 2 years." Poems are selected by editor with consideration of space availability. Always comments on rejections. Reports "within 30 days." Sometimes sends prepublication galleys. Pays 4 copies. Acquires "one-time rights, plus right to include in anthology." Reviews books or chapbooks of poetry. Open to unsolicited reviews. Poets may also send books for review consideration.

Book/Chapbook Needs & How to Submit: Dry Bones Press seeks "to encourage nurses, or just do things we like, or want to take a flyer on." Publishes 1-3 paperbacks and 2-3 chapbooks/year. Books are usually 5½×8½, offset, stapled or "fine wire-O" bound with glossy, b&w cover. Replies to queries and mss in 1 month. Pays 10 author's copies.

N. ⊘ THE DRY CREEK REVIEW, Aims Community College, Loveland Center, 104 E. Fourth, Loveland CO 80537, founded 1990, faculty advisor Tony Park.

Magazine Needs: *TDCR* is an annual. "We accept creative nonfiction, fiction, translations and quality poetry." They are open to all forms/styles. "We want poems built around vivid imagery, rich language and risk. We do not want to see the abstract based on the insignificant." They have published poetry by Carolyn Forché, Joy Harjo, Bill Tremblay and Veronica Patterson. As a sample the editor selected these lines from "Driving Home After Spanish Class" by Jane Oakley:

> Dark as the inside of a wolf's mouth/Tenses of verbs flood my brain/The bruja empties a bucket of
> water/on the windshield/Estuvo lloviendo/It was raining.

The editors say *Dry Creek Review* is 120-140 pgs., 6×9, professionally printed and flat-spined with glossy card cover. They receive 500-600 poems a year, accept 5-15%. Press run is 1,000, all distributed free.

How to Submit: No previously published poems; simultaneous submissions OK. Poems are circulated to an editorial board. Seldom comments on rejections. Reports in 3-6 months. Pays 2 copies. Rights revert to author on publication. Open to unsolicited reviews. Poets may also send books for review consideration.

⊘ DUSTY DOG PRESS, 202 W. Hermosa Dr., #B201, Tempe AZ 85282, phone (602)755-8831, founded 1990, editor/publisher John Pierce.

Book/Chapbook Needs & How to Submit: *Dusty Dog Press* publishes 1-2 chapbooks of poetry per year by invitation only, usually by poet Simon Perchik.

○ ◎ DWAN (Specialized: gay/lesbian/bisexual, translations, bilingual/foreign language), Box 411, Swarthmore PA 19081-0411, e-mail dsmith3@swarthmore.edu, founded 1993, editor Donny Smith.

Magazine Needs: Published every 2 to 3 months, *Dwan* is a "queer poetry zine; some prose; some issues devoted to a single poet or a single theme ('Jesus' or 'Mom and Dad,' for instance)." The editor wants "poetry exploring gender, sexuality, sex roles, identity, queer politics, etc. Heterosexuals usually welcome." They have published poetry by Maureen Daniels, Carlos Schröder and Susana Cattaneo. As a sample the editor selected these lines from "want some" by Melanie Hemphill:

> stare like a child/at her mouth and her hands/tracing and retracing/the contours of her body/enchanted
> by/what I cannot have

Dwan is 20 pgs., 5½×8½, photocopied on plain white paper, and stapled. They receive 400-500 pgs. of poetry/year, accept less than 10%. Press run is 100. Sample available for $2 (free to prisoners).

How to Submit: Submit 5-15 poems typed. Previously published poems and simultaneous submissions OK. E-mail submissions OK, "no attachments." Cover letter required. Time between acceptance and publication is 6-18 months. Often comments on rejections. Send SASE for upcoming themes. Reports in 1-3 months. Pays copies. The editor reviews books, chapbooks and magazines usually in 25-150 words. Send books for review consideration.

Advice: The editor says, "Our guidelines: Queer. Legible. You decide what that means."

○ ⊘ ◎ EAGLE'S FLIGHT; EAGLE'S FLIGHT BOOKS (Specialized: translations), P.O. Box 465, Granite OK 73547, phone (580)535-2452, founded 1989, editor/publisher Shyamkant Kulkarni.

Magazine Needs: *EF* is a quarterly "platform for poets and short story writers—new and struggling to come forward." They want "well-crafted literary quality poetry, any subject, any form, including translations. Translations should have permission of original poets." They have published poetry by Robert O. Schulz, Amrita Kulkarni and Kim Klemm. As a sample the editor selected these lines from "Midnight" by Camille E. Torok:

> Midnight calls, I respond./The force of nature beckons/me from constraint. Dawn is a lifetime away/
> and the darkness lasts forever.

Eagle's Flight is 8-12 pgs., 7×8½, printed on colored paper and saddle-stapled, including simple art, few ads. They receive about 200 poems/year, accept 10%. Press run is 200 for 100 subscribers. Subscription: $5. Sample: $1.25.

How to Submit: Submit up to 5 poems at a time, no more than 21 lines each. No previously published poems or simultaneous submissions. Cover letter required; include short bio, up to 4 lines. Reads submissions January 1 through June 30 only. Time between acceptance and publication is 1-3 years. Seldom comments on rejections. "All material accepted for publication is subject to editing according to our editorial needs." Send SASE for guidelines. Reports in 2-3 months. Pays 1 copy. Acquires first publication rights. Reviews books of poetry in 250-750 words, single format.

Advice: The editor says, "We expect poets to be familiar with our publication and our expectations and our limitations. To be a subscriber is one way of doing this. Everybody wants to write poems and, in his heart, is a poet. Success lies in getting ahead of commonplace poetry. To do this one has to read, to be honest, unashamed and cherish decent values of life in his heart. Then success is just on the corner of the next block."

◎ **EARTH'S DAUGHTERS: A FEMINIST ARTS PERIODICAL (Specialized: women/feminism, themes)**, P.O. Box 41, Central Park Station, Buffalo NY 14215, website http://home.att.net/~colvard/, founded 1971.

Magazine Needs: The "literary periodical with strong feminist emphasis" appears 3 times a year, irregularly spaced. Its "format varies. Most issues are flat-spined, digest-sized issues of approximately 60 pgs. We also publish chapbooks, magazine-sized and tabloid-sized issues. Past issues have included broadsheets, calendars, scrolls and one which could be assembled into a box." Poetry can be "up to 40 lines (rare exceptions for exceptional work), free form, experimental—we like unusual work. All must be strong, supportive of women in all their diversity. We like work by new writers, but expect it to be well-crafted. We want to see work of technical skill and artistic intensity. We rarely publish work in classical form, and we never publish rhyme or greeting card verse." They have published poetry by Christine Cassidy, Diane di Prima, Janine Pommy Vaga, Joseph Bruchak, Lyn Lifshin, Susan Fantl Spivack, "and many fine 'unknown' poets, writers and artists." They publish poetry by men if it is supportive of women. As a sample the editor selected "Sweet Dream" by Tori Gallagher:

> I woke from dreaming the smooth arctic/wasteland of your skin which I have haunted/slowly, again
> and again. The cliffs/of your face soared above me, the sea/washing green to blue in your/tropic
> eyes . . .

"Our purpose is to publish work that otherwise might never be printed, either because it is unusual, or because the writer is not well known." Subscription: $14/3 issues for individuals; $22 for institutions. Sample: $5.

How to Submit: Simultaneous submissions OK. "Per each issue, authors are limited to a total of 150 lines of poetry, prose or a combination of the two. Submissions in excess of these limits will be returned unread. Business-size envelope is preferred, and use sufficient postage—we do not accept mail with postage due." Send SASE for guidelines. Some issues have themes, which are available for SASE after March of each year. Length of reporting time is atrociously long if ms is being seriously considered for publication, otherwise within 3 weeks. Pays 2 copies and reduced prices on further copies. Editor comments "whenever we have time to do so—we want to encourage new writers."

Also Offers: Website includes writers guidelines, upcoming topics, history of *ED*, etc.

Advice: The collective says: "Once you have submitted work, please be patient. We only hold work we are seriously considering for publications, and it can be up to a year between acceptance and publication. If you must contact us (change of address, notification that a simultaneous submission has been accepted elsewhere), be sure to state the issue theme, the title(s) of your work and enclose SASE."

☐ ◎ **EASTERN CARIBBEAN INSTITUTE (Specialized: regional)**, P.O. Box 1338, Frederiksted, U.S. Virgin Islands 00841, phone (340)692-4109, fax (340)772-3463, e-mail sjonesh@gecko.uvi.edu, founded 1982, editor S.B. Jones-Hendrickson, editorial contact Cora Christian.

Book/Chapbook Needs: *Eastern Caribbean Institute* is a "small press publisher" especially interested in poetry of the Caribbean and Eastern Caribbean. As a sample the editor included these lines from "We'll Understand Why" in *A Walk Through My Mind* by Meredith Warner-Phipps:

> Sometimes our lives are filled with sorrow,/How we grown and how we cry/But in spite of our tears
> and anguish/One of these days we'll understand why.

Their books are softcover, averaging 60 pgs. Sample copies available for purchase.

How to Submit: Submit 5 sample poems and cover letter with bio and previous publications. Simultaneous submissions and previously published poems OK. Reads submissions January to May only. Reports in 1 month. Pays 50 copies.

Advice: The editor says, "In our part of the world, poetry is moving on a new level. People who are interested in regional poetry should keep an eye on the Caribbean region."

✓ ◎ **ECKERD COLLEGE REVIEW**, Eckerd College, 4200 54th Ave. S., St. Petersburg FL 33711, phone (727)864-7859, e-mail siren@eckerd.edu, founded 1993.

Magazine Needs: Appearing annually in March, *Eckerd College Review* is the nationally-distributed literary magazine of Eckerd College which publishes high quality poetry, fiction and color and b&w artwork. "We want to see poems of a wide range of content, length and tone from poets who pay particular attention to craft (particularly line, stanza and voice). Nothing sentimental or cliché, nor poems that are needlessly obscure or Beat." They have published poetry by Kathryn Stripling Byer, Fred Chappell and R.T. Smith. As a sample the editor selected these lines from "Postscript" by Simeon Berry:

> This light/that falls away, from the mud in the bricks,//from the street of crushed shell, from everything/
> that is involuntary in your body, this light//will fall away forever.

The editor says *ECR* is 100 pgs., perfect-bound with full-color cover and art. "We receive 800-900 poems a year and usually accept 1%." Press run is 1,400 for 800 shelf sales. Sample: $6.

How to Submit: Submit 3-5 poems at a time. Line length for poetry is 75 maximum. No previously published poems or simultaneous submissions. Cover letter with short bio and SASE required. Reads submissions September 1 through January only. Postmark deadline: January 15. Seldom comments on rejections. Send SASE for guidelines. Reports in 6 weeks. Pays 2 copies. Acquires first rights. Staff reviews books of poetry and fiction in 900 words, single format. Send books for review consideration.

Advice: The editor says, "Editors favor authors who have studied other poets as well as their craft."

N ⚑ $ ◐ ◎ ÉCRITS DES FORGES; ESTUAIRE; ARCADE; EXIT (Specialized: foreign language, women), 1497 Laviolette, Trois-Rivières, Québec G9A 5G4 Canada, phone (819)379-9813, fax (819)376-0774, e-mail ecrits.desforges@aiqnet.com, founded 1971, président Gaston Bellemare, directrice générale Maryse Baribeau.

Magazine Needs: Écrits des Forges publishes 3 poetry journals each year: *Estuaire* appears 5 times a year and wants poetry from well-known poets; *Exit* appears 4 times a year and wants poetry from beginning poets; and *Arcade* appears 3 times a year and wants poetry from women only. All three publications only accept work in French. They want poetry that is "authentic and original as a signature." "We have published poetry from more than a thousand poets coming from most of the francophone's countries: André Romus (Belgium), Amadou Lamine Sall (Sénégal), Nicole Brossard, Claudine Bertrand, Denise Brassard, Tony Tremblay and Jean-Paul Daoust (Québec)." As a sample they selected these lines from "La peau fragile du ciel" by Bernard Pozier:

> l'infini défait ses gris hérités de la pluie/dans la brume laiteuse du soir/et l'on tente de distinguer la
> plage le ciel et l'océan/en flottant dans ce néant/et c'est comme essayer enfin de savoir/s'il est plus
> facile de faire parler le poème/ou bien faire taire la mer

The 3 journals are 88-108 pgs., 5½×8, perfect-bound with art on cover, includes ads from poetry publishers. They receive more than 1,000 poems a year, accept less than 5%. Press run for *Estuaire* is 750 for 450 subscribers of which 250 are libraries. Press run for *Arcade* is 650 for 375 subscribers of which 260 are libraries. Press run for *Exit* is 500 for 110 subscribers of which 235 are libraries. Subscription for *Estuaire* is $45 plus p&h; for *Arcade* is $27 plus p&h; for *Exit* is $36 plus p&h. Samples: $10 each. For *Exit* make checks payable to Éditions Gaz Moutarde. For *Estuaire* and *Arcade*, make checks payable to the respective publication.

How to Submit: Submit 10 poems at a time. No previously published poems or simultaneous submissions. "We make decisions on submissions in February, May, September and December." Time between acceptance and publication is 3-12 months. Poems are circulated to an editorial board. "Nine persons read the submissions and send their recommendations to the editorial board." *Arcade* publishes theme issues. Upcoming themes are listed in the journal. Obtain guidelines via e-mail. Reports in 3-5 months. Pays "10% of the market price based on number of copies sold." Buys all rights for 1 year. Retains rights to reprint in anthology for 10 years. Staff reviews books and chapbooks of poetry and other magazines on 1 page, double-spaced, single book format. Send books for review consideration.

Book/Chapbook Needs & How to Submit: Écrits des Forges inc. publishes poetry only—40-50 paperbacks/year. Books are usually 80-88 pgs., 5½×8, perfect-bound with 2-color cover with art. Query first with a few sample poems and cover letter with brief bio and publication credits. Replies to queries in 3-6 months. Pays royalties of 10-20%, advance of 50% maximum, and 25 author's copies. Order sample books by writing or faxing.

Also Offers: Sponsors the International Poetry Festival. "250 poets from 30 countries based on the 5 continents read their poems over 10-day period in 70 different cafés, bars, restaurants, etc. 30,000 persons attend. All in French." For more information, see website: http://www.aiqnet.com/fiptr.

N ⚑ $ ◐ ECW PRESS, 2120 Queen St. E., Suite 200, Toronto, Ontario M4E 1E2 Canada, phone (416)694-3348, fax (416)698-9906, e-mail ecw@sympatico.ca, website http://www.ecw.ca/press, founded 1979, literary editor Michael Holmes.

Book/Chapbook Needs: ECW Press publishes 4 paperbacks/year. They want interesting—structurally challenging poetry. No greeting card doggerel. They have published poetry by Robert Priest, Sky Gilbert, David McGimpsey and Libby Scheier. Books are usually 96-150 pgs., 5×8, perfect-bound with full color covers.

How to Submit: Query first with a few sample poems and cover letter with brief bio and publication credits. Then, when requested, submit 10 poems at a time. Previously published poems and simultaneous submissions OK. Cover letter required. Time between acceptance and publication is 12-18 months. Seldom comments on rejections. Replies to queries in 2 weeks; to mss in 2 months. Pays royalties of 10% plus advance of $200 and 20 author's copies (out of a press run of 750). Order sample books by sending $12.

N ◯ ◎ EDGAR: DIGESTED VERSE (Specialized: macabre), 486 Essex Ave., Bloomfield NJ 07003, e-mail dragoons5@aol.com, founded 1999, editor John Picinich, associate editor Victoria Picinich.

Magazine Needs: *EDGAR* is a "quarterly eclectic collection of the darkly bizarre, erotic, offbeat and quirky." They want "horror, gothic, surreal, science fiction. Go for the jugular, but give the reader something to chew over." They do not want "prose poems; werewolf and vampire verse; sappy sweet stuff." They have published poetry by John Grey, Charlee Jacob and Nancy Bennett. As a sample the editors selected these lines from "Even More Frightened" by William P. Robertson:

> Sleet-smeared ghosts/strangle in the slipstream./They gurgle, gasp & groan/as they boil the sky black./
> Dire is their distress./Even more frightened are we.

The editors say *EDGAR* is 24-28 pgs., digest-sized, offset printed and saddle-stapled with b&w card cover with illustrations. They receive about 220 poems a year, accept approximately 40%. Press run is 125 for 50 subscribers, 30 shelf sales; 6 distributed free to reviewers. Subscription: $10. Sample: $2.50. Make checks payable to John Picinich.

How to Submit: Submit up to 3 poems at a time. No previously published poems or simultaneous submissions. E-mail submissions OK. Cover letter required. "For e-mail submissions, do not send poem as an attached file; keep within the body of the e-mail message along with street and e-mail addresses. Snail mail submissions must have a SASE. Also, tell me a little bit about yourself in the cover letter." Time between acceptance and publication is 3-6 months. Always comments on rejections. Send SASE for guidelines. Reports in 3-4 weeks. Pays 1 copy. Acquires first North American serial rights.

Advice: The editors say, "We recommend poets send SASE for guidelines and buy a sample copy. Each issue runs one or two Poe-ish poems and one or two food poems. Do not force your rhymes. We run mostly free verse. Poems of 30 lines or less have a good chance of getting accepted."

THE EDGE CITY REVIEW, 10912 Harpers Square Court, Reston VA 20191, fax (703)716-5752, e-mail terryp17@aol.com, website http://www.edge-city.com, founded 1991, editor T.L. Ponick.

Magazine Needs: *The Edge City Review* appears 3 times a year and "publishes poetry, fiction, criticism and book reviews for a combined lay and academic audience—iconoclastic, conservative and not hospitable to left-wing crusaders." They want poetry in traditional forms (sonnets, ballads, rhyme), narrative, satire; quality verse. No free verse; no greeting card verse. They have published poetry by Dana Gioia, Alexander Theroux, Jared Carter, M.A. Schaffner and Alfred Dorn. As a sample the editor selected this sonnet by Peter Russell:

> I own the freehold of my small estate/I am my sole and only mortgagee./Stranger! Look carefully at
> the well hung gate/That's closed between us—I Have the only key./My walls are skull and skin, my
> earth's my mind—/My gate, the eyes you never see behind.

ECR is 48-52 pgs., 8½×11, neatly printed and saddle-stitched with 80 lb. colored stock cover, only occasionally includes ads. They receive about 250 poems a year, accept approximately 15%. Press run is 535 for 305 subscribers of which 25 are libraries, 75 shelf sales; 130 distributed free for promotional purposes. Sample: $5.50.

How to Submit: No previously published poems; simultaneous submissions OK "if so indicated." Cover letter preferred. E-mail and disk submissions OK. "Disk submissions can be Mac or PC, Word or WordPerfect preferred. For e-mail, send poems in the body of the message or include as an ASCII attachment." Do not submit mss in December. Time between acceptance and publication is 6 months. Poems are circulated to an editorial board. "Poetry editor makes first cut, final selections based on consensus." Seldom comments on rejections. Reports in 4 months. Pays 2 copies. Acquires first North American serial rights. Staff reviews books of poetry and other magazines in 800-1,000 words, single book format. Send books for review consideration.

Also Offers: Website includes reprints from hardcopy magazine, book reviews, poetry, commentary, Washington, DC theater and music reviews.

Advice: The editor says, "We are sometimes exasperated with the inappropriateness of submissions to our magazine. We are open to formal poetry only, and simply do not want to see free verse. We strongly encourage purchase of a sample copy."

EDGEWISE PRESS, INC., 24 Fifth Ave., #224, New York NY 10011, website http://www.angelfire.com/ Giz/edgewisebooks. Currently accepts no unsolicited poetry.

EIDOS MAGAZINE: SEXUAL FREEDOM & EROTIC ENTERTAINMENT FOR WOMEN, MEN & COUPLES (Specialized: erotica, women), P.O. Box 96, Boston MA 02137-0096, phone (617)262-0096, fax (617)364-0096, e-mail eidos@eidos.org, website http://www.eidos.org, founded 1982, poetry editor Brenda Loew.

Magazine Needs: "Our press publishes erotic literature, photography and artwork. Our purpose is to provide an alternative to women's images and male images and sexuality depicted in mainstream publications like *Playboy*, *Penthouse*, *Playgirl*, etc. We provide a forum for the discussion and examination of two highly personalized dimensions of human sexuality: desire and satisfaction. We do not want to see angry poetry or poetry that is demeaning to either men or women. We like experimental, avant-garde material that makes a personal, political, cultural statement about sensu-sexuality." They have published poetry by Jeff N. Foster, Tracy L. Sturgill and Antler. As a sample we selected this poem, "Source Mythology," by John Hulse:

> When I was young someone told me/that to really please a woman/I had to learn how to balance a
> nickel/on the tip of my tongue.

Eidos is 40 pgs., 8½×11, professionally printed with b&w photography and art. They receive hundreds of poems/ year, use about 100. Readership is 12,000. Subscription: $25 for 4 issues. Sample: $7.

How to Submit: Only accepts sexually-explicit material. Length for poetry is 1-page maximum, format flexible. Must be 18 or over; age statement required. Camera-ready, "scannable" poems preferred, but not required. No previously published poems; simultaneous submissions OK. "Poets must submit their work via regular 'snail' mail. No faxes or e-mail submissions accepted." Do not send computer disks. Publishes bio information as space permits. Comment or criticism provided as often as possible. Send SASE for guidelines. Reports in 1 month. Pays 1 copy. Acquires first North American serial rights. Open to unsolicited reviews. Send books for review consideration.

Also Offers: Website features names of publisher, editor and webmaster; interviews; articles and essays; poetry and photos. The *Eidos* website was selected as the "Playboy Online Pick of the Day."

Advice: The editor advises, "There is so much poetry submitted for consideration that a rejection can sometimes mean a poet's timing was poor. We let poets know if the submission was appropriate for our publication and suggest they resubmit at a later date. Keep writing, keep submitting, keep a positive attitude."

■ ○ ◐ **1812; NEW WRITING AWARDS**, P.O. Box 1812, Amherst NY 14226, e-mail box1812@aol.c om, website http://www.newwriting.com/1812.html, founded 1993, editors Richard Lynch, Rick Lupert and Sam Meade.

Magazine Needs: *1812* is an annual electronic, literary arts publication appearing in February. They want "material with a bang." They receive about 1,000 poems a year, accept 1-3%.

How to Submit: Previously published poems OK; no simultaneous submissions. Cover letter required. E-mail submissions OK; "do not use attached files. Submit poems in the body of the e-mail only." Time between acceptance and publication is 6-12 months. Sometimes comments on rejections. Send SASE for guidelines. Payment is "arranged." Buys one-time rights. Open to unsolicited reviews.

Also Offers: Sponsors New Writing Awards with $3,000 in prizes plus publication. "See http://www.newwriting. com/contest.html for more information." Entry fee: $10. Send SASE or visit website for forms and guidelines. Website has complete magazine contents, including poetry, stories, artwork and music.

$ ◎ **THE EIGHTH MOUNTAIN PRESS (Specialized: women/feminism)**, 624 SE 29th Ave., Portland OR 97214, founded 1985, editor Ruth Gundle.

Book/Chapbook Needs: Eighth Mountain is a "small press publisher of literary works by women." They have published poetry by Lucinda Roy, Maureen Seaton, Irena Klepfisz, Almitra David, Judith Barrington and Elizabeth Woody. They publish 1 book of poetry averaging 128 pgs., every other year. "Our books are handsomely designed and printed on acid-free paper in both quality trade paperbacks and library editions." Initial press run for poetry is 2,500.

How to Submit: "We expect to receive a query letter along with a few poems. A résumé of published work, if any, should be included. Work should be typed, double-spaced, and with your name on each page. If you want to know if your work has been received, enclose a separate, stamped postcard." Reports within 6 weeks. SASE (#10 envelope) must be included for response. "Full postage must be included if return of the work submitted is desired." Pays 7-8% royalties. Buys all rights. Returns rights if book goes out of print.

◐ ◎ **EKPHRASIS (Specialized: ekphrastic verse); FRITH PRESS; OPEN POETRY CHAPBOOK COMPETITION**, P.O. Box 161236, Sacramento CA 95816-1236, *Ekphrasis* founded Summer 1997, Frith Press 1995, editors Laverne Frith and Carol Frith.

• Martha Modena Vertreace's "Smokeless Flame" was winner of the 1998 Open Poetry Chapbook Competition.

Magazine Needs: *Ekphrasis* is a biannual "outlet for the growing body of poetry focusing on individual works from any artistic genre." They want "poetry whose main content is based on individual works from any artistic genre. Poetry should transcend mere description. Form open. No poetry without ekphrastic focus. No poorly crafted work. No archaic language." They nominate for Pushcart Prize: Best of the Small Press editions. They have published poetry by Rhina Espaillat, William Greenway, Joseph Stanton, Susan Spilecki, Simon Perchik, Robert Sargent and Stephanie Strickland. *Ekphrasis* is 40-50 pgs., digest-sized, photocopied and saddle-stapled with matte cover. Subscription: $12/year. Sample: $6. Make checks payable to Laverne Frith.

How to Submit: Submit up to 7 poems at a time with SASE. Accepts previously published poems "occasionally, must be credited"; no simultaneous submissions. Cover letter required including short bio with representative credits and phone number. Time between acceptance and publication is up to 1 year. Seldom comments on rejections. Send SASE for guidelines. Reports in 2-16 weeks. Pays 1 copy. Acquires first North American serial or one-time rights.

Book/Chapbook Needs & How to Submit: Frith Press publishes well-crafted poems—all subjects and forms considered—through their annual Open Poetry Chapbook Competition. Submit 14-22 pages of poetry with $8 reading fee. Include cover sheet with poet's name, address and phone number. Previously published poems must be credited. No simultaneous submissions. Deadline: October 31. Winner receives $100, publication and 50 copies of their chapbook.

Advice: The editors say, "With the focus on ekphrastic verse, we are bringing attention to the interconnections between various artistic genres and dramatizing the importance and universality of language. Study in the humanities is essential background preparation for the understanding of these interrelations."

Ⓝ ◐ **ELM: A JOURNAL OF CONTEMPORARY POETRY**, 1928 Chapel St., Third Floor, New Haven CT 06515, founded 1995, editor Mark Horosky.

Magazine Needs: *Elm* is published biannually. "A single copy of *Elm* costs no more than one dollar. By making the journal accessible to everyone, the editors hope to emphasize the importance of poetry in our contemporary life." They want contemporary poetry and have no restrictions as to form or style. "Because of our limited space, epic poems are difficult to accommodate." They have published poetry by Mark Strand, Charles Fort, Leo Connelan and Jeff Mock. As a sample the editor selected these lines from "The Hours of the Five Fingers" by Brad Richard:

> At dawn, my moon-spawned thumb rises, pale and/bulbous from the rich earth of its slumber . . .

Elm is 25-35 pgs., 5½×8½, photocopied and saddle-stapled with light card cover containing b&w photo. They accept approximately 10% of poems received a year. Press run is 300-500. Single copy: $1.

How to Submit: Submit 3-5 poems at a time. No previously published poems or simultaneous submissions. Cover letter preferred. "Brief bios read with interest; more so than a 'laundry list' of publication credits." Time between acceptance and publication is about 6 months. Seldom comments on rejections. Send SASE for guidelines. Reports in 1-3 months. Pays 1-2 copies, "depending on press run." Acquires first rights.

⊘ EMOTIONS LITERARY MAGAZINE; WINGS OF DAWN ANNUAL POETRY CONTEST, 17216 Saticoy St., PMB 370, Van Nuys CA 91406, phone/fax (818)345-9759, e-mail wingsbooks@aol.com, website http://members.aol.com/PoetWings/Emotions.html, founded 1997, editor-in-chief Lupi Basil.

Magazine Needs: Appearing 6 times a year, *Emotions*, *"where the pen meets the heart,"* welcomes "good quality work from talented writers as they share their thoughts and emotions in their own unique style and form." They want "all styles and topics as long as they are good quality and in good taste, and not degrading to the human spirit. Each line in the poem should not exceed 65 characters in length, including spaces. We also consider fiction, short stories, essays and articles if they are between 1,000-2,000 words." They have published poetry by award-winning novelist Ben Bova, C. David Hay, Dave Taub, k.t. Frankovich, G. Elton Warrick and David Graves. The editor says *Emotions* is 40-44 pgs., 8½×11, printed on 60 lb. good quality paper and saddle-stapled with glossy cover, includes b&w photos and artwork, ads. They receive about 1,500 poems a year, accept approximately 15%. Press run is 500 for 50% subscribers. Single copy (including guidelines): $3.99 US, $5 international; subscription: $22/year US, $35/year international. Make checks payable to Wings of Dawn Publishing Co.

How to Submit: Submit 3 poems at a time. Previously published poems OK (sometimes); no simultaneous submissions unless previously notified. Cover letter with 50-word bio required. E-mail submissions OK, if mailing address and bio included. Time between acceptance and publication is 2-4 months. Sometimes comments on rejections. Send SASE for guidelines or obtain via e-mail or website. Reports in 2-4 months. Pays 1 copy. Acquires first North American serial or one-time rights.

Also Offers: Sponsors Wings of Dawn Annual Poetry Contest: 1st Prize-$100, 2nd Prize-$75, 3rd Prize-$25, 4th Prize-1-year subscription to magazine. Fee: $5/3 poems per submission.

⊘ EMPLOI PLUS; DGR PUBLICATION, 1256 Principale N. St. #203, L'Annonciation, Quebec J0T 1T0 Canada, phone (819)275-3293, founded 1988 (DGR Publication), 1990 (*Emploi Plus*), publisher Daniel G. Reid.

Magazine Needs: *Emploi Plus*, published irregularly, features poems and articles in French or English. They have published poetry by Robert Ott. *Emploi Plus* is 12 pgs., 7×8½, photocopied, stapled, with b&w drawings and pictures, no ads. Press run is 500 for 400 subscribers; 100 distributed free to friends and relatives. Sample: $10. Make checks payable to Daniel Reid.

How to Submit: *They do not accept unsolicited submissions.*

Ⓝ ⊘ EMRYS JOURNAL, P.O. Box 8813, Greenville SC 29604, founded 1982, editor Jeanine Halva-Neubauer.

Magazine Needs: *Emrys Journal* is an annual appearing in April. They want "the accessible poem over the fashionably sophisticated, the touching dramatic or narrative poem over the elaborately meditative, the humorous poem over the ponderously significant, the modest poem over the showily learned." They have published poetry by Jan Bailey, Gil Allen and Cecile Goding. As a sample the editor selected the first stanza from "Motor without a Boat" by Mary Matthews:

> An enormously wealthy oil company/had thousands of things to sell and so/they took their things to
> an enormously/barren lot where no wildflowers or/weeds would grow and where the prints/of a working
> man's shoes left no impression.

EJ is up to 120 pgs., 6×9, handsomely printed, flat-spined. Press run is 400 for 250 subscribers of which 10 are libraries. "About 10 poems are selected for inclusion." Single copy: $13.28.

How to Submit: Submit up to 5 poems. "No individual poem may exceed three pages. Include phone number, fax and/or e-mail, if desired." Reads submissions August 1 through December 1. Reports in about 2 months. Send SASE for guidelines. Pays 5 copies.

Ⓝ ◎ THE EMSHOCK LETTER (Specialized: subscribers), Randall Flat Rd., P.O. Box 411, Troy ID 83871-0411, phone (208)835-4902, founded 1977, editor Steve Erickson.

Magazine Needs: *The Emshock Letter* appears 3-12 times/year, occasionally with poetry and other writings by subscribers. It is "a philosophical, metaphysical, sometimes poetic expression of ideas and events. It covers a wide range of subjects and represents a free-style form of expressive relation. It is a newsletter quite unlike any other." The editor describes it as 5-7 pgs., magazine-sized, photocopied from typescript on colored paper. Subscription: $25.

How to Submit: "Poets (who are subscribers) should submit poetry which contains some meaning, preferably centering on a philosophic theme and preferably 50 lines or less. Any good poetry (submitted by a subscriber) will be considered for inclusion and will receive a personal reply by the editor, whether or not submitted material is published in *The Emshock Letter.* Editor will promptly discard any and all material submitted by nonsubscribers. Poets must become subscribers prior to submitting any material!" Reviews books of poetry only if written by subscribers.

ENDEMONIADA FANZINE; EROTIKA-X FANZINE (Specialized: left-hand path/satanic/occult), 3018 Heath Ave. #27C, Bronx NY 10463, founded 1993, editor Elena León (Lucifera), co-editor Maria Paulino (Xastur), co-editor Mercedes Paulino (Jeda).

Magazine Needs: *Endemoniada Fanzine* appears 2-4 times a year "to expose female underground bands, performers and artists. Also deals with the left-hand path (satanism/occult) and bands (black metal, Gothic, industrial, punk)." They want "strong-willed, satanic, erotic, poems of torture and agony, praising beauty. One poem per person with name and address. Form and length unrestricted. No Christian poetry." They have published poetry by Lucifera, Cary Webb, John Kapshaw and Joey Jabor. As a sample the editor selected these lines from an untitled poem by Mabus:

> But deliver us from the flaccid bosom of the Christ/For everything is thy kingdom/And the power &
> the glory therein forever & ever/Nema/We look for the destruction of the Earth/And the torment of thy
> world to come.

EF is 50-90 pgs., 8½×11, photocopied and side-stapled, color paper cover, includes b&w line drawings and photos, ads. They receive about 20 poems a year, accept all. Press run is 150-200 for 150-200 subscribers. Single copy: $3 (US), $4 World. Sample (including guidelines): $3. Make checks payable to Maria Paulino (Xastur).

How to Submit: Submit 1 poem at a time. Previously published poems OK; no simultaneous submissions. Cover letter undesired. Time between acceptance and publication is 6-8 months. Always sends prepublication galleys. "We do not pay for poetry, submitter can either pay for a copy (full price), ask to pay half price or send 6 first-class stamps to receive copy of issue." Staff reviews books of poetry and other magazines. Send books for review consideration.

ENGLISH JOURNAL, Dept. of English, Youngstown State University, Youngstown OH 44555, phone (330)742-3415, fax (330)742-2304, e-mail whgreenway@msn.com, website http://www.ysu.edu, founded 1912, poetry editor William Greenway.

Magazine Needs: The *English Journal* is a magazine "for high school English teachers, with articles mostly on pedagogy." They want poetry of any style/form under 40 lines. They have published poetry by Elton Glaser and Philip Dacey. The editor says *EJ* is 150 pgs., perfect-bound with glossy cover, includes photos and ads. Distributed to 55,000 library subscribers. Single copy: $6.25; subscription: $20/year.

How to Submit: Submit 5 poems at a time. No previously published poems or simultaneous submissions. Cover letter preferred. E-mail and fax submissions OK. Reads submissions September through May only. Time between acceptance and publication is 6 months. Often comments on rejections. Publishes theme issues occasionally. Guidelines available in magazine or obtain via e-mail or website. Reports in 1 month. Pays 2 copies. Acquires first North American serial rights.

ENTERZONE, 1440 Broadway, Suite 920, Oakland CA 94612, phone/fax (510)451-4964, e-mail query@ezone.org, website http://ezone.org/ez/, founded 1994, poetry editor Freeman Ng.

Magazine Needs: *Enterzone* is a quarterly online publication containing writing, art and new media. They want concrete poetry. No vague poetry. They have published poetry by Janan Platt, David Hunter Sutherland and Cort Day. They receive about 80 poems a year, accept approximately 10%.

How to Submit: Submit 1 poem at a time. Previously published poems and simultaneous submissions OK. Cover letter required. E-mail and disk submissions OK. "Please query first by e-mail." Time between acceptance and publication is 6-9 months. Often comments on rejections. Publishes theme issues occasionally. Obtain guidelines via e-mail. Reports in 2 months. Acquires one-time rights. Reviews books and chapbooks of poetry in 1,500 words, single book format. Open to unsolicited reviews. Poets may also send books for review consideration.

EPICENTER, P.O. Box 367, Riverside CA 92502, website http://www.geocities.com/Athens/Delphi/2884, founded 1994.

Magazine Needs: *Epicenter* is a biannual poetry and short story forum open to all styles. "*Epicenter* is looking for ground-breaking poetry and short stories from new and established writers. No angst-ridden, sentimental or earthquake poetry. We are not adverse to graphic images if the work is well presented and contains literary merit." They have published poetry by Lon Risley, Max Berkovitz, Stan Nemeth and Vicki Solheid. *Epicenter* is 24 pgs., digest-sized and saddle-stapled with semi-glossy paper cover and b&w graphics. They receive about 1,000 submissions a year, use approximately 5%. Press run is 400 for 250 shelf sales. Single copy: $3. Sample: $3.50. Make checks payable to Rowena Silver.

How to Submit: Submit up to 5 poems. Include SASE with sufficient postage for return of materials. Previously published poems and simultaneous submissions OK. Seldom comments on rejections. Send SASE for guidelines. Pays 1 copy. Acquires one-time and electronic rights.

$ ☑ EPOCH; BAXTER HATHAWAY PRIZE, 251 Goldwin Smith, Cornell University, Ithaca NY 14853, phone (607)255-3385, founded 1947.
Magazine Needs: *Epoch* has a distinguished and long record of publishing exceptionally fine poetry and fiction. They have published work by such poets as Ashbery, Ammons, Eshleman, Wanda Coleman, Molly Peacock, Robert Vander Molen and Alvin Aubert. The magazine appears 3 times/year in a 6×9, professionally printed, flat-spined format with glossy color cover, 128 pgs., which goes to 1,000 subscribers. They use less than 1% of the many submissions they receive each year, have a 2- to 12-month backlog. Mostly lyric free verse, with emphasis on voice and varying content and length, appears here (and, occasionally, avant-garde or "open" styles)—some of it quite powerful. Sample: $5.
How to Submit: "We don't read unsolicited mss between April 15 and September 15." Reports in 2 months. Occasionally provides criticism on mss. Pays $5-10/page. Buys first serial rights.
Also Offers: The annual Baxter Hathaway prize of $1,000 is awarded for a long poem or, in alternate years, a novella. At this time, however, the Baxter Hathaway Prize has been temporarily suspended.
Advice: The editor advises, "I think it's extremely important for poets to read other poets. I think it's also very important for poets to read the magazines that they want to publish in. Directories are not enough."

☑ $ ◻ ◎ EQUILIBRIUM¹⁰; EAGLE PUBLISHING PRODUCTIONS (Specialized: equilibrium), 7111 W. Alameda Ave., L248, Lakewood CO 80226, e-mail equilibrium10@compuserve.com, website http://ourworld.compuserve.com/homepages/equilibrium10, founded 1982, publisher Gary A. Eagle.
Magazine Needs: "We publish everything and I mean everything dealing with equilibrium: balance, opposites, pairs, equality, opposite and equal reactions, etc." They are open to "all types, lengths and styles. Very lenient!" on themes given above. The following sample is from "The Supposition of Opposition" by Caral Davis:

>   *The sun rises, just to fall./It's all for one and one for all./It rains on the rich and on the poor,/The rich*
>   *get richer and the poor get poorer./Winter withers summer away, only to revive/another day.*

The quarterly is photocopied on pocket-edition 4¼×8½ sheets of various colors, about 70 pgs., saddle-stapled with glossy b&w paper cover, using many photos, drawings and cartoons throughout. One page is devoted to "Poems," each with an illustration. Circulation is 10,000. Single copy: $4. Sample: $4 plus 5 first-class stamps.
How to Submit: Backlog 1-6 months. "We prefer to hold in files until needed!" Editor sometimes comments on rejections. E-mail submissions OK. Reports in 3 months. Pays $50 and up plus 1 copy.
Also Offers: Website includes a statement of the magazine's philosophy, links and articles.
Advice: The publisher says, "We prefer for poets to keep a photocopy and send us the original for our files. They may be handwritten if you wish for your poem printed as such. It is best for the poet (even youngsters) to include art, pictures, etc., too. Letter and queries arriving at our office will become the property of our company and material may and will be published 'as-is.'"

◖ ERATICA, HALF A BUBBLE OFF PLUMB, P.O. Box 936, Wayne MI 48184-0936, phone (734)467-1920, e-mail loonfether@aol.com, founded 1996, editor Elizabeth MacKenzie Hebron, editor William J. Emerson III.
Magazine Needs: *Eratica* appears quarterly and "seeks out and offers sanctuary for the excellent, the eccentric, and the homeless works of genius." They want "well crafted poetry in any form, length, subject or style. We prefer the more visual, tactile work that elicits a gut-level emotional response. Nothing poorly written, full of clichés, adjectives, etc." They have published poetry by Errol Miller, David Chorlton, Barbara F. Lefcowitz and Alan Catlin. As a sample the editors selected these lines from "Definitions days before her death, for Victoria" by Cynthia Harper:

>   *Death is a pin/a tiny hole/we slip through/when the wind/kidnaps our songs.*

Eratica is 64 pgs., 8½×11, offset-printed and saddle-stitched with 2-color semi-gloss cover, includes graphics and ads. They receive about 600 poems a year, accept approximately 5-10%. Press run is 500 for 50 subscribers, 150 shelf sales; 15 distributed free to reviewers. Subscription: $18. Sample (including guidelines): $5.95.
How to Submit: Submit 6 poems at a time. Previously published poems and simultaneous submissions OK. Cover letter with brief bio preferred. E-mail submissions OK, include in the body of e-mail message. "*Eratica* uses a Macintosh system with Adobe PageMaker 6.0 and ClarisWorks 4.0. Any electronic submissions may be requested via hard copy if the attachment can't be opened." Time between acceptance and publication is 3-6 months. Poems are circulated to an editorial board. "All manuscripts are prescreened by three editors. Then they are read by a staff of five editors and discussed." Seldom comments on rejections. Send SASE for guidelines or obtain via e-mail. Reports in 2-3 months. Pays 2 copies. Acquires one-time rights.
Advice: The editors say, "We believe in the portable printed word—hard copy magazines and books. We are looking for the unusual yet well-written; that which will not fit neatly into mainstream literary magazines."

◖ ETCETERA, P.O. Box 8543, New Haven CT 06531, e-mail iedit4you@aol.com, founded 1995, editor Mindi Englart.
Magazine Needs: *Etcetera* is a biannual journal of "art, literature and ideas designed to encourage creative thought, action and risk-taking." They want "avant-garde work, linguistics, word play and experimental poetry;

humor, thought-provoking and deep work. No rhyming (in most cases) or traditional poetry." They have published poetry by John M. Bennett, Albert Huffstickler, Michael Estabrook, Sheila E. Murphy and Richard Kostelanetz. As a sample the editor selected these lines from "When America Starts Seeping" by David Todd:

> When America starts seeping/into my skin I quickly shake myself/like a wet dog and run/into another state of mind.

Etcetera is 28 pgs., 5½ × 8½, offset printed and staple-bound with b&w art and photography. They receive about 550 poems a year, accept approximately 50. Press run is 500 for about 300 subscribers, about 50 shelf sales; about 150 distributed free "to those who wouldn't/couldn't get it otherwise." Sample: $3.

How to Submit: Submit 2-3 poems at a time. Include SASE. Previously published poems and simultaneous submissions OK. Cover letter preferred. "Please include 30-word biography with all submissions." E-mail submissions OK (include submissions in body of message). Time between acceptance and publication is 1-5 months. Sometimes comments on rejections. Send SASE for guidelines or request via e-mail. Reports final acceptance/rejections in April (for June issue) and October (for December issue). Sometimes sends prepublication galleys. Pays 1 copy plus a 1-year subscription. Staff reviews chapbooks of poetry and other magazines. Send books for review consideration.

N 回 $ ◻ ⊘ ETERNITY, THE ONLINE JOURNAL OF THE SPECULATIVE IMAGINATION; ETERNITY PRESS; PULP ETERNITY, P.O. Box 930068, Norcross GA 30003, phone/fax (770)222-4751, e-mail pulpeternity@hotmail.com, website http://www.pulpeternity.com, founded 1997, senior editor Steve Algieri.

Magazine Needs: *Eternity* is a monthly web journal that includes all types of genre fiction and poetry. They are open to all style and lengths. "We prefer poetry with an element of the fantastic, romantic or mysterious." They have published poetry by W. Gregory Stewart, Corrine DeWinter, Robert Kleinengler and James S. Dorr. They receive about 1,000 poems a year, accept 4-6%.

How to Submit: Submit no more than 3 poems at a time. No previously published poems or simultaneous submissions. Cover letter required. E-mail and disk submissions OK. "Text-only e-mail submissions." Time between acceptance and publication is 6 months. Often comments on rejections. Publishes theme issues occasionally. Send SASE for guidelines and upcoming themes or obtain via website. Reports in 2 months. Pays $2. Buys first rights.

Book/Chapbook Needs & How to Submit: Eternity Press publishes genre poetry: science fiction, fantastic, horrific, mysterious, romantic, erotica. Query first with a few sample poems and cover letter with brief bio and publication credits. Replies to queries in 1 week; to mss in 2 months.

Also Offers: Sponsors occasional online and chapbook contests. See website or send SASE for guidelines and upcoming themes. Also publishes *Pulp Eternity*, a journal of speculative fiction, mystery and fantastic romance. Website includes contests, guidelines, editors and poetry.

Advice: The editor says, "We like cutting edge poetry and themes. Erotic poetry OK."

N ⊘ ETHEREAL GREEN, 720 Ann St., East Lansing MI 48823, founded 1996, contact Sarah Hencsie.

Magazine Needs: *EG*, published quarterly, strives "to feed readers unknown talent. Contains poetry, art and articles." They want "the avant-garde, spiritual and the unknown. Poems should be less than 40 lines." They do not want "children's, ethnic or edited poems." They have published poetry by Drew Cloone. As a sample the editor selected these lines by Jaime Morrison:

> Because it's raining . . . you're/falling from the sky, from/your soul being drained . . .

Ms. Hencsie says *Ethereal Green* is 30-70 pgs., approximately 6 × 8, with cover art. They receive hundreds of poems a year, accept approximately 50%. Press run is 250 for about 70 subscribers, 60% shelf sales. Subscription: $27. Sample: $7. Make checks payable to Sarah C. Hencsie.

How to Submit: Submit 3-7 printed or typed poems at a time. Previously published poems and simultaneous submissions OK. Cover letter preferred. Time between acceptance and publication is 3-7 months. Poems are circulated to an editorial board with "poems edited twice; once by publisher and again by select editors on board." Always comments on rejections. Send SASE for guidelines and upcoming themes. Reports within 1 month. Sometimes sends prepublication galleys. Pays 2 copies. Acquires first North American serial or one-time rights. Open to unsolicited reviews.

⊕ ⊘ ◎ EUROPEAN JUDAISM (Specialized: religious, ethnic), Kent House, Rutland Gardens, London SW7 1BX England, founded 1966, poetry editor Ruth Fainlight.

Magazine Needs: *European Judaism* is a "twice-yearly magazine with emphasis on European Jewish theology/philosophy/literature/history, with some poetry in every issue. It should preferably be short and have some relevance to matters of Jewish interest." They have published poetry by Linda Pastan, Elaine Feinstein, Daniel Weissbort and Dannie Abse. As a sample the editor selected these lines from a poem by Michael Heller:

> I took silence into time, marking the absence/of our late vocabularies in their conspirings,/these new mythologies, as they fell from on high//through our skies and through our roofs/scouring the mind as cosmic rays leave/traceries in the cool white lime of tunnels.

It is a glossy, elegant, 6 × 9, flat-spined magazine, rarely art or graphics, 110 pgs. They have a press run of 950, about 50% of which goes to subscribers (few libraries). Subscription: $27.

How to Submit: Submit 3-4 poems at a time. No material dealt with or returned if not accompanied by SASE (or SAE with IRCs). "We cannot use American stamps. Also, I prefer unpublished poems, but poems from published books are acceptable." Cover letter required. Pays 1 copy.

$ ☑ ◎ EVANGEL; LIGHT AND LIFE COMMUNICATIONS (Specialized: religious), P.O. Box 535002, Indianapolis IN 46253-5002, founded 1897, editor J. Innes.

Magazine Needs: *Evangel* is a weekly adult Sunday school paper. "Devotional in nature, it lifts up Christ as the source of salvation and hope. The mission of *Evangel* is to increase the reader's understanding of the nature and character of God and the nature of a life lived for Christ. Material that fits this mission that isn't more than one page will be considered." No rhyming work. *Evangel* is 8 pgs., 5½×8½ (2 8½×11 sheets folded), printed in 4 color and unbound with photos and graphics used. They accept approximately 5% of poetry received. Press run is approximately 20,000 for 19,000 subscribers. Subscription: $1.85/quarter (13 weeks).

How to Submit: Submit 3 poems at a time. Simultaneous submissions OK. Cover letter preferred. Seldom comments on rejections. Send #10 SASE for guidelines Reports in 4-6 weeks. Pays $10 plus 2 copies on publication. Buys one-time rights.

Advice: The editor says, "Poetry is used primarily as filler. Send for sample and guidelines to better understand what and who the audience is."

◪ $ ◪ ◎ EVENT (Specialized: themes), Douglas College, P.O. Box 2503, New Westminster, British Columbia V3L 5B2 Canada, founded 1971, editor Calvin Wharton.

Magazine Needs: *Event* appears 3 times/year and is "a literary magazine publishing high-quality contemporary poetry, short stories and reviews. In poetry, we tend to appreciate the narrative and sometimes the confessional modes. In any case, we are eclectic and always open to content that invites involvement. We publish mostly Canadian writers." They have published poetry by Tom Wayman, Lorna Crozier and Tim Bowling. *Event* is 140 pgs., 6×9, finely printed and flat-spined with glossy cover. Press run is 1,000 for 700 subscribers of which 50 are libraries. Sample: $8.

How to Submit: Submit 5 poems at a time. No previously published poems. Brief cover letter with publication credits required. Include SASE or SAE and IRCs. "Tell us if you'd prefer your manuscript to be recycled rather than returned." Time between acceptance and publication is within 1 year. Comments on some rejections. Reports in 3-4 months. Pays honorarium. Buys first North American serial rights.

◪ THE EVER DANCING MUSE; WHO WHO WHO PUBLISHING, P.O. Box 7751, East Rutherford NJ 07073-1624, website http://members.aol.com/Jac63/index.html, founded 1993, editor John Chorazy.

Magazine Needs: *TEDM* is a "semiannual collection of poetry and short prose, publishing fine work in a small press format." The editor wants "poems that speak of reality bathed in the sublime and surreal, 'feminine' in sensibility but not necessarily in gender, poems that dig deep into personal and universal themes of dreams, intimacy and goddess archetypes, poems of grave consequence and inspiration, poems that can whisper as well as scream. Poems of very short length (including haiku), up to two typed pages. Not using much rhyming poetry. Submit poems that you care deeply about, and want me to care about as well as the readers." They have published poetry by Errol Miller, George C. Harvilla and Sheryl Morang Holmberg. As a sample the editor selected these lines from "mother/daughter" by Melanie Hemphill:

> i think of my life/my mother's life/and how we are locked together/in violence and silence/how we
> share the patterns/the worst part of being women/quieted by a fist/or a shove/or a word

The Ever Dancing Muse is 20 pgs., 5½×8½, saddle-stapled with light card cover. Press run is 150 for 50 subscribers. Subscription: $13 for 3 issues. Sample: $5.

How to Submit: Submit up to 5 poems, no longer than 2 typed pages each, and include SASE with sufficient postage to return ms. Previously published poems and simultaneous submissions OK, "if stated as such, and author holds the rights to the work." No e-mail submissions. Cover letters "are interesting and appreciated but not required." Seldom comments on rejections. Send SASE or e-mail for guidelines. Reports in 3-6 months. Time between acceptance and publication is 6-8 months. Pays 2 copies. Acquires one-time rights.

Also Offers: The press has started a "broadside" series with the publication of Oliver Hydon's poem "Samsara," and will continue to consider poems for future broadsides.

◎ EXIT 13 (Specialized: geography/travel), % Tom Plante, P.O. Box 423, Fanwood NJ 07023-1162, phone (908)889-5298, e-mail plante@bellatlantic.net, founded 1987, editor Tom Plante.

Magazine Needs: *Exit 13* is a "contemporary poetry annual" using poetry that is "short, to the point, with a sense of geography." They have published poetry by Charles Plymell, Errol Miller, Mary Grow, Varese Layzer and Ken Smith. As a sample the editor selected these lines by Askold Skalsky:

> We saw egrets by the exit ramps,/tigers lazing on small islands/guarded by pines and the purple waters/
> of amusement parks. The brave/innuendos of love went unanswered.

Exit 13, #8, was 64 pgs. Press run is 300. Sample: $6.50.

How to Submit: They accept simultaneous submissions and previously published poems. Send SASE for guidelines. Reports in 4 months. Pays 1 copy. Acquires one-time and possible anthology rights. Staff reviews books of poetry and magazines in a "Publications Received" column, using 25-30 words/listing. Send books for review consideration.

Advice: The editor advises, "Write about what you know. Study geography. *Exit 13* looks for adventure. Every state, region and ecosystem is welcome. Send a snapshot of an 'Exit 13' road sign and receive a free copy of the issue in which it appears."

⊌ ◎ EXPEDITION PRESS (Specialized: love, religious), 411 Stanwood St., Apt. E, Kalamazoo MI 49006-4543, phone (616)382-6823, publisher Bruce W. White.

Book/Chapbook Needs: Expedition Press publishes chapbooks of love poems and religious poems. "I dislike violence." He likes to see "experimental, fresh new approaches, interesting spatial relationships, as well as quality artwork. I dislike political diatribes." He has published poetry by J. Kline Hobbs, Robin Reish, Todd Zimmerman, Margaret Tyler, Martin Cohen and C. VanAllsburg. As a sample the publisher selected these lines from "Central Park" by Margaret Tyler:

> . . . . By the zoo, maids push patriarchs in wheelchairs./They nod like the shadows, dapple grey and dancing./The monkey strikes the hour on the Delacourte clock./Brass animals glide in stately circles and then stop.

How to Submit: Submit typed ms of 20-30 pgs. and cover letter with brief bio. No previously published poems or simultaneous submissions. Ms on cassette OK. Reports in 1 month. Sometimes sends prepublication galleys. Pays 100 copies. Bruce White provides "much" criticism on rejected mss.

⊙ EXPLORATIONS; EXPLORATIONS AWARD FOR LITERATURE, UAS, 11120 Glacier Highway, Juneau AK 99801-8761, e-mail jfamp@uas.alaska.edu, founded 1980, editor Professor Art Petersen.

Magazine Needs: Explorations is the literary magazine of the University of Alaska Southeast and appears annually in July. "The editors respond favorably to 'language really spoken by men and women.' Standard form and innovation are encouraged as well as appropriate and fresh aspects of imagery (allusion, metaphor, simile, symbol . . .)." Explorations is digest-sized, nicely printed and saddle-stapled, with front and back cover illustration in one color. The editors tend to go for smaller-length poems (with small line breaks for tension) and often print two on a page—mostly lyric free verse with a focus on voice. Sample: $5.

How to Submit: An entry/reading fee is required: $6 for 1 or 2 poems (60 lines/poem maximum), $2/poem for 3-5 poems (5 maximum, no more than 60 lines each); those paying reader/contest entry fees receive a copy of the publication. Checks should be made payable to "UAS Explorations." Mss must be typed with name, address, and 3- to 4-line biography on the back of each first page. Simultaneous submissions OK. Submit January through May 15 only. Mss are not returned. Send SASE for guidelines or request via e-mail. Reports in July. Pays 2 copies. Acquires one-time rights.

Also Offers: Sponsors the Explorations Award for Literature. First place (for a poem or short story): $1,000; second place (for best work in a genre different from first place winner): $500; and third place for poetry: $100. Submit up to 5 poems, no more than 60 lines each. Entry fee: $6 for 1-2 poems, $3/poem for 3-5 poems. Judge for 1999 contest was Richard Dauenhauer. Send SASE for guidelines.

⊙ FAT TUESDAY, 560 Manada Gap Rd., Grantville PA 17028, phone (717)469-7159, e-mail harvesthome-fattuesday@desupernet.net, founded 1981, editor-in-chief F.M. Cotolo, other editors Kristen Cotolo and Lionel Stevroid.

Magazine Needs: Fat Tuesday publishes irregularly as "a Mardi Gras of literary, visual and audio treats featuring voices, singing, shouting, sighing and shining, expressing the relevant to irreverent." They want "prose poems, poems of irreverence, gems from the gut. Particularly interested in hard-hitting 'autofiction.' " They have published poetry by Mark Cramer, Mary Lee Gowland, Patrick Kelly, Gerald Locklin and Julia Solis, as well as material by unknown authors. The magazine is up to 60 pgs., typeset (large type, heavy paper), saddle-stapled, card covers, usually chapbook style (sometimes magazine-sized, unbound) with cartoons, black line art and ads. Circulation is 1,000/year with poetry on 80% of the pages. They receive hundreds of submissions each year, use 3-5%, have a 3- to 5-month backlog "but usually try to respond with personal, not form, letters." "In 1998 Fat Tuesday was presented in a different format with the production of a stereo audio cassette edition. Fat Tuesday's Cool Noise features readings, music, collage and songs, all in the spirit of Fat's printed versions. Other Cool Noise editions will follow. Fat solicits artists who wish to have their material produced professionally in audio form. Call the editors about terms and prices on how you can release a stereo audio cassette entirely of your own material. Fat soon hopes to release Seven Squared, by Frank Cotolo and is looking for other audio projects. In-print magazines will still be produced as planned." All editions are $5, postage paid.

How to Submit: Submit any number of poems at a time. No previously published poems or simultaneous submissions. "Cover letters are fine, the more amusing the better." Reports in 1-2 weeks. Pays 1 copy. Rights revert to author after publication.

Advice: The editors say, "Be yourself. Use your own voice. We don't care about trends, we listen for unique and individual voices. We rely on sales to subsidize all projects so writers should be sensitive to this hard truth and buy sample editions."

⊌ ⊙ FAULTLINE, P.O. Box 599-4960, Irvine CA 92716-4960, phone (714)824-6712, founded 1991.

● Poetry published by this journal has also been selected for inclusion in a Pushcart Prize anthology.

Magazine Needs: Faultline is an annual journal of art and literature occasionally edited by guest editors and published at the University of California, Irvine. "We are looking for top, top quality poetry from poets who are obviously acquainted with contemporary poetry." They have published poetry by Thomas Lux, Heather McHugh and Sabina Grogan. As a sample we selected the opening lines of "Gravediggers" by Linda Thomas:

> *At first I am sure/the sea once covered our backyard./With each spadeful of dirt/come cones and sea*
> *slippers,/the dry dishes of scallops and jackknives,/and I am sure/this neglected plot of hard clay/once*
> *served as the ocean floor.*

Faultline is approximately 120 pgs., 6×9, professionally printed on 60 lb. paper, perfect-bound with 80 lb. cover stock and featuring color and b&w art and photos. They receive about 1,500 poems a year, accept approximately 5%. Press run is 500 for 50 subscribers, 175 shelf sales. Single copy: $7. Sample: $5.

How to Submit: Submit up to 5 poems at a time. Simultaneous submissions OK. Cover letter preferred. Do not include name and address on ms to assist anonymous judging. Reads submissions September 15 to March 1 only. Poems are selected by a board of up to 6 readers. Seldom comments on rejections. Send SASE for guidelines. Reports in 3 months. Always sends prepublication galleys. Pays 2 copies. Buys first or one-time rights.

⬤ FAUQUIER POETRY JOURNAL, P.O. Box 68, Bealeton VA 22712-0068, founded 1994, managing editor D. Clement.

Magazine Needs: *Fauquier Poetry Journal* is a quarterly that contains poetry, poetry commentary, editorials, contest announcements and book reviews. They want "fresh, creative, well-crafted poetry, any style. Due to format, longer poems over 40 lines are not often used. Do not want overly sentimental or religious themes, overdone subjects, or overly obscure work." They have published poetry by Sean Brendan-Brown, B.R. Culbertson, Maura Ramer, Steve Carter, Nancy Ryan and Marilyn Injeyan. As a sample the editor selected these lines from "Winter's Edge" by Daniel Green:

> *Condensing fog weaves skeins of beads/in tassels hanging from my hat brim./I walk through my own*
> *exhaled vapors/mixed in the pre-dawn mist, as though/afloat upon a clouded sense of boundless/space;*
> *sounds muffled to a sibilant whisper . . .*

FPJ is 40-50 pgs., digest-sized, laser-printed on plain white paper and saddle-stapled with bright colored paper cover. Press run is more than 300 for 100 subscribers, including libraries. Subscription: $20. Sample: $5.

How to Submit: The editor encourages subscriptions by requiring a reading fee for nonsubscribers ($5 for 1-5 poems only per month); no reading fee for subscribers. Submit up to 5 poems with name and address in the upper left corner of each page and include SASE. Simultaneous submissions OK. Accepts previously published poems. Sometimes comments on rejections. Send SASE for guidelines and upcoming themes. Reports in 2-6 weeks. Offers Editor's Choice Awards of $5-25 for the best entries in each issue. Pays 1 copy to remainder of published poets. Acquires one-time rights.

Also Offers: They sponsor quarterly poetry contests, explained in the journal. Entry fee: $5. Prizes range from $15-75, and winners are published in the following issue. In addition to poetry, *FPJ* occasionally prints articles by guest columnists. Articles should deal with some aspect of poetry, the writing experience, reactions to particular poems or poets, the mechanics (how to), etc. No reading fee, no guidelines other than word limit (around 1,000 words). "Pretty much anything goes as long as it's interesting and well-written." Pays 2¢/word.

Advice: The editor says, "Let us see a variety in your submission; what one editor likes, another won't. Send a range of work that illustrates the breadth and depth of your talent; this helps us decide if there's something we like. We encourage submissions from anyone who is writing mature, well-crafted poetry."

⬛◯◎ FEATHER BOOKS; THE POETRY CHURCH MAGAZINE; CHRISTIAN HYMNS & SONGS (Specialized: religious), Fairview, Old Coppice, Lyth Bank, Shrewsbury, Shropshire SY3 0BW United Kingdom, phone/fax (01763)872177, e-mail john@feather.com, website http://www.poetry-church.com or www.feather-books.com. Feather Books founded 1982, *Poetry Church Magazine* founded 1996, contact Rev. John Waddington-Feather.

Magazine Needs: *The Poetry Church Magazine* appears quarterly and contains Christian poetry and prayers. They want "Christian or good religious poetry—usually around 20 lines, but will accept longer." They do not want "unreadable blasphemy." They have published poetry by M.A.B. Jones, Joan Smith, Bruce James, Idris Caffrey and Walter Nash. *TPCM* is 40 pgs., digest-sized, photocopied, saddle-stapled with laminated cover and b&w cover art. They receive about 1,000 poems a year, accept approximately 500. Press run is 1,000 for 400 subscribers of which 10 are libraries. Single copy free; subscription: £7 ($15 US). Sample: $5. Make checks payable to Feather Books. Payment can also be made through website.

How to Submit: Submit 2 typed poems at a time. Previously published poems and simultaneous submissions OK. Cover letter preferred with information about the poet. All work must be submitted by mail with SASE (or SAE and IRC). Time between acceptance and publication is 4 months. "The editor does a preliminary reading;

FOR EXPLANATIONS OF THESE SYMBOLS,
SEE THE INSIDE FRONT AND BACK COVERS OF THIS BOOK.

then seeks the advice of colleagues about uncertain poems." Always comments on rejections. Send SASE (or SAE and IRC) for guidelines or request via e-mail or fax. Reports within a week. Pays 1 copy. Poets retain copyright.

Book/Chapbook Needs & How to Submit: Feather Books publishes the Feather Books Poetry Series, books of Christian poetry and prayers. Books are usually photocopied and saddle-stapled with laminated covers. "Poets' works are selected for publication in collections of around 20 poems in our Feather Books Poetry Series. We do not insist, but most poets pay for small run-offs of their work, e.g., around 50-100 copies for which we charge $200 per fifty. If they can't afford it, but are good poets, we stand the cost. We expect poets to read our *Poetry Church Magazine* to get some idea of our standards." Pays 5% royalty "where we sell copies of poetry" or 1 author's copy (out of a press run of 50) "if we pay cost."

Also Offers: Feather Books also publishes *Christian Hymns & Songs*, a quarterly supplement by Grundy and Feather. And, each fall, selected poems that have been published throughout the year in *Poetry Church Magazine* appear in *The Poetry Church Anthology*, the leading Christian poetry anthology used in churches and schools.

Advice: The editor says, "We find it better for poets to master rhyme and rhythm before trying free verse. Many poets seem to think that if they write 'down' a page they're writing poetry, when all they're doing is writing prose in a different format."

FEMINIST STUDIES (Specialized: women/feminism), % Dept. of Women's Studies, University of Maryland, College Park MD 20742, phone (301)405-7415, fax (301)314-9190, e-mail femstud@umail.umd.edu, website http://www.inform.umd.edu/femstud, founded 1969, poetry editor Alicia Ostriker.

Magazine Needs: *Feminist Studies* "welcomes a variety of work that focuses on women's experience, on gender as a category of analysis, and that furthers feminist theory and consciousness." They have published poetry by Janice Mirikitani, Paula Gunn Allen, Cherrie Moraga, Audre Lorde, Valerie Fox and Diane Glancy. The elegantly printed, flat-spined, 250-page paperback appears 3 times a year in an edition of 8,000, goes to 7,000 subscribers, of which 1,500 are libraries. There are 4-10 pgs. of poetry in each issue. Sample: $12.

How to Submit: No simultaneous submissions; will only consider previously published poems under special circumstances. Manuscripts are reviewed twice a year, in May and December. Deadlines are May 1 and December 1. Authors will receive notice of the board's decision by June 30 and January 30. Always sends prepublication galleys. Pays 2 copies. Commissions reviews of books of poetry. Poets may send books to Claire G. Moses for review consideration.

FEMINIST VOICES (Specialized: women/feminism, lesbian), P.O. Box 853, Madison WI 53701-0853, phone (608)251-9268, founded 1987, poetry editor Xanda.

Magazine Needs: *Feminist Voices* is a feminist news journal appearing 10 times a year. "We welcome creative work from all women and all feminist perspectives for 'And So She Said.' Written work can include poetry, journal entries, and short stories, and should usually not exceed three double-spaced typewritten pages; exceptions are possible, though. Work can be handwritten if you don't have a typewriter or computer, or on IBM-compatible disk if you do have a computer, or on audio tape. Art work should be work that will reproduce well in black and white; we can work from originals, color or black and white photos, or slides. All contributions should include your name (although any work can be printed anonymously), address, phone number, and a very brief biographical statement. If you can also include a self-addressed, stamped envelope that'd be much appreciated." *FV* is a 12- to 16-page newspaper containing art and ads. Press run is 7,000.

How to Submit: Submit "as many poems as you like." Previously published poems and simultaneous submissions OK. Cover letter preferred. Disk submissions OK. Time between acceptance and publication varies. Seldom comments on rejections. Publishes theme issues. Pays 1-year subscription. Rights belong to writer. Reviews books and chapbooks of poetry in single book format. Poets may also send books for review consideration.

FENICE BROADSHEETS; NEW BROOM PRIVATE PRESS, 78 Cambridge St., Leicester LE 3 0JP England, founded 1968, poetry editor Cynthia A. Savage (assumed the press after Toni Savage's death in 1994).

Book/Chapbook Needs: Publishes chapbooks, pamphlets and broadsheets on a small Adana Horizontal Hand Press. The editor wants poetry which is "descriptive—not too introvert or modern, not erotica or concrete, up to 12 lines (for the sheets). Also some personal background of the poet." Published poets include Jack Woolgar, Paul Humphrey and Alix Weisz. As a sample the editor selected this poem, "Dartmoor Pony," by Edward Murch (Fenice Broadsheet No. 34):

> The November sun, spring-warm, is very low/And casts around this pony, in a golden glow,/An aureole
> of mystic morning light,/That makes him seem like Pegasus just landed from the night.

The broadsheets are letterpress printed on tinted paper (about 5×8) with graphics. "Some sheets are hand coloured."

How to Submit: Submit no more than 3 poems with cover letter giving "personal background and feelings." Poet receives 20-30 copies. Broadsheets are given away in streets, hospitals and leisure groups. "This is a hobby and strictly part-time, production is therefore erratic." *Fenice Broadsheets* may be obtained by sending adequate postage (IRCs), approximately $1.50 for 5 or more sheets.

THE FIDDLEHEAD (Specialized: regional, students), Campus House, University of New Brunswick, P.O. Box 4400, Fredericton, New Brunswick E3B 5A3 Canada, founded 1945, poetry editors Ross Leckie, Julie Dennison and Eric Hall.

Magazine Needs: From its beginning in 1945 as a local little magazine devoted mainly to student writers, the magazine retains an interest in poets of the Atlantic region and in young poets but prints poetry from everywhere. It is open to excellent work of every kind, looking always for vitality, freshness and surprise. They have published poetry by James Gurley and Thomas O'Grady. As a sample, the editors selected these lines by Al Moritz:

> As if you erased the city where the house/where I was born was standing. As if I/had gone away a
> minute, just to see what lies beyond,/as if anything does, and you swept away my path/with your broom
> and rubbed it out/with your wheels, crisscrossing it into chaos

The Fiddlehead is a handsomely printed, 6×9, flat-spined paperback (120 pgs.) with b&w graphics, colored cover, paintings by New Brunswick artists. They use less than 10% of submissions. Circulation is 1,000. Subscription: $20/year plus $6 postage (US). Sample: $7 (US).

How to Submit: Submit 3-10 poems at a time. No simultaneous submissions. For reply or return of ms, send SAE with Canadian stamps, IRCs or cash. Reporting time is 2-6 months, backlog 6-18 months. Pay is $10-12/ printed page. Reviews books of poetry by Canadian authors mainly.

FIELD; FIELD TRANSLATION SERIES; FIELD POETRY PRIZE; FIELD POETRY SERIES; OBERLIN COLLEGE PRESS (Specialized: translations), Rice Hall, Oberlin College, Oberlin OH 44074, phone (440)775-8408, fax (440)775-8124, e-mail oc.press@oberlin.edu, website http://www.oberlin.edu/~ocpress, founded 1969, editors David Young, Alberta Turner, David Walker, Martha Collins and Pamela Alexander.

• Work published in *Field* has also been included in the 1992, 1993, 1994, 1995 and 1998 volumes of *The Best American Poetry.*

Magazine Needs: *Field* is a literary journal appearing twice a year with "emphasis on poetry, translations and essays by poets." They want the "best possible" poetry. They have published poetry by Marianne Boruch, Miroslav Holub, Charles Simic and Sandra McPherson. The handsomely printed, digest-sized journal is flat-spined, has 100 pgs., rag stock with glossy card color cover. Although most poems fall under the lyrical free verse category, you'll find narratives and formal work here on occasion, much of it sensual, visually appealing and resonant. Circulation is 2,500, with 800 library subscriptions. Subscription: $14/year, $24/2 years. Sample: $7.

How to Submit: Submit up to 5 poems at a time. Cover letters preferred. Reads submissions year-round. No previously published poems, simultaneous submissions, e-mail or disk submissions. Seldom comments on rejections. Reports in 1 month. Time between acceptance and publication is 1-6 months. Always sends prepublication galleys. Pays $15-20/page plus 2 copies. Staff reviews books of poetry. Poets and publishers may send books for review consideration.

Book/Chapbook Needs & How to Submit: They publish books of translations in the Field Translation Series, averaging 150 pgs., flat-spined and hardcover editions. Query regarding translations. Pays 7½-10% royalties with some advance and 10 author's copies. They also have a Field Poetry Series. They have published *Ill Lit* by Franz Wright; *A Saturday Night at the Flying Dog* by Marcia Sorthwick. This series is by invitation only. Write for catalog to buy samples.

Also Offers: Sponsors the *Field* Poetry Prize, the winning ms will be published in their poetry series and receive $1,000 award. Submit mss of 50-80 pgs. with a $22 reading fee in May only. Contest guidelines available for SASE. Website includes information on all publications, including excerpts and ordering information.

FILLING STATION, P.O. Box 22135, Bankers Hall, Calgary, Alberta T2P 4J5 Canada, phone (403)234-0336 or (403)252-8185, fax (403)234-7463, e-mail cfthomps@cadvision.com or housepre@cadvision.com, founded 1993, co-managing editor Derek Beaulieu.

Magazine Needs: Appearing 3 times/year (February, June and October), *filling Station* is a magazine of contemporary writing featuring poetry, fiction, interviews, reviews and other literary news. "We are looking for all forms of contemporary writing. No specific objections to any style." They have published poetry by Fred Wah, Larissa Lai and Paula Tatarunis. As a sample the editor selected these lines from "Breath Ghazal 53" by Douglas Barbour:

> To say it all You need big lungs./That heavy intake then a slow rush.

fS is 56 pgs., 8½×11, saddle-stapled with card cover and includes photos, artwork and ads. They receive about 100 submissions for each issue, accept approximately 10%. Press run is 500 for 100 subscribers, 250 shelf sales. Subscription: $15/1 year, $30/2 years. Sample: $6.

How to Submit: Submit typed poems with name and address on each page. No previously published poems; simultaneous submissions OK. Fax and e-mail submissions OK (include mailing address). Cover letter required. Deadlines are November 15, March 15 and July 15. Seldom comments on rejections. Send SASE (or SAE with IRC) for guidelines. Reports in 3 months. Pays 1-year subscription. Acquires first North American and second reprint rights. Reviews books of poetry in both single and multi-book format. Open to unsolicited reviews. Poets may also send books for review consideration.

Advice: Here's what the collective has to say about *filling Station* and the philosophy behind this publication: "You stop between these 'fixed' points on the map to get an injection of something new, something fresh that's going to get you from point to point. . . . We want to be a kind of connection between polarities: a link. We'll publish any poem or story that offers a challenge: to the mind, to the page, to writers and readers."

✔ ◐ **FINE MADNESS**, P.O. Box 31138, Seattle WA 98103-1138, website http://www.scn.org/arts/finemadness, founded 1982, editors Sean Bentley, John Malek, David Brewster, Anne Pitkin and Alan Wald.
Magazine Needs: *Fine Madness* aims to publish 3 issues every 2 years (a new issue roughly every 8 months). They want "contemporary poetry of any form and subject. We look for the highest quality of thought, language and imagery. We look for the mark of the individual: unique ideas and presentation; careful, humorous, sympathetic. No careless poetry, greeting card poetry, poetry that 10,000 other people could have written." They have published poetry by Pattiann Rogers, Albert Goldbarth and Caroline Knox. As a sample we selected these lines from "Sugar" by Alan Ridenour:

> The piñata explodes like a beehive./Amid the sound of clubs,/its candy is trampled into diamonds/
> while paper crowns are whirled through/blind rage and love of chocolate.

Fine Madness is 64 pgs., digest-sized, offset printed and perfect-bound with color card cover. They accept about 40 of 1,500 poems received each year. Their press run is 1,000 for 100 subscribers of which 10 are libraries. Subscription: $9. Sample: $4.
How to Submit: Submit 2-5 poems, preferably originals, not photocopies, 1 poem/page. No previously published poems or simultaneous submissions. Send SASE for guidelines. Reports in 4 months. Pays 1 copy plus subscription.
Also Offers: Website includes guidelines, subscription and back issue information and samples of work published.
Advice: Editor Sean Bentley says, "If you don't read poetry, don't send us any."

N ⊕ ◖ **FIRE**, Field Cottage, Old Whitehill, Tackley, Kidlington, Oxfordshire OX5 3AB United Kingdom, founded 1994, editor Jeremy Hilton.
Magazine Needs: *Fire* appears quarterly "to publish little-known, unfashionable or new writers alongside better known ones." They want "experimental, unfashionable, demotic work; longer work encouraged." No rhyming verse. They have published poetry by Donna Hilbert, B.Z. Niditch, Carlyle Reedy, Allen Fisher, Gael Turnbull and David Hart. The editor says *Fire* is 150 pgs., A5. They receive about 400 poems a year, accept approximately 35%. Press run is 250 for 180 subscribers of which 20 are libraries. Single copy: £4, add £1 postage Europe, £2 postage overseas. Subscription (3 issues): £7, add £2 postage Europe, £4 postage overseas.
How to Submit: Previously published poems OK; no simultaneous submissions. Cover letter preferred. Disk submissions OK. Time between acceptance and publication "varies enormously." Often comments on rejections. Send SASE for guidelines. Reports in 2 months. Sometimes sends prepublication galleys, "but rarely to overseas contributors." Pays 2 copies.

$ ◎ **FIREBRAND BOOKS (Specialized: feminist, lesbian, ethnic)**, 141 The Commons, Ithaca NY 14850, phone (607)272-0000, website http://www.firebrandbooks.com, founded 1984, editor/publisher Nancy K. Bereano.
Book/Chapbook Needs: Firebrand "is a feminist and lesbian publishing company committed to producing quality work in multiple genres by ethnically diverse women." They publish both quality trade paperbacks and hardbacks. Books are usually 94 pgs., flat-spined, elegantly printed on heavy stock with a glossy color card cover, a photo of the author on the back.
How to Submit: Simultaneous submissions acceptable with notification. Replies to queries within 2 weeks, to mss within 1 month. Pays royalties. Send for catalog to buy samples.

⊕ ✔ ◐ **FIREWATER PRESS INC.; VARIOUS ARTISTS; WORKING TITLES**, 34, Northleare, Long Ashton, Bristol BS41 9HT United Kingdom, founded 1989, contact editor Tony Lewis-Jones for *Various Artists* and editor Claire Williamson for *Working Titles*.
Magazine Needs: Both *Various Artists* and *Working Titles* appear annually and intend "to encourage good accessible poetry by new and established writers. *Working Titles* also has a brief to encourage women's writing." They want any format/style "so long as the work is not anti-minority. Prefer short poems (up to 40 lines)." They have published poetry by Sophie Hannah, Robert Etty, Michael Daugherty and Martha Holroyd. As a sample, editor Tony Lewis-Jones selected his own haiku:

> Mist on the river/Skies are as fickle/As love, as snow.

The editors say *VA* is approximately 30 pgs., A5, saddle-stitched with graphics; *WT* is approximately 30 pgs., A5, saddle-stitched. Both publications accept 10% of poems received a year (2,000 for *VA*, 1,500 for *WT*). Press runs are 250 for 100 subscribers of which 10 are libraries. Single copy: $5; subscription: $10. Sample: $3. Make checks payable to A. Lewis-Jones (they prefer currency from the US).
How to Submit: Submit 6 poems at a time. No previously published poems or simultaneous submissions. Cover letter preferred. Time between acceptance and publication is 1-12 months. Always comments on rejections. Send SASE (or SAE and IRC) for guidelines. *VA* reports in 2 weeks; *WT* in less. Pays 2 copies. Returns rights upon publication. Staff reviews books of poetry. Send books for review consideration.
Also Offers: Firewater Press also sponsors a number of awards for poets working in the United Kingdom.
Advice: The editors say, "Write from the heart, don't compromise and keep trying. If you're good enough,

you'll make it."

$◎ FIREWEED: A FEMINIST QUARTERLY (Specialized: women), P.O. Box 279, Station B, Toronto, Ontario M5T 2W2 Canada, founded 1978, contact editorial collective.
Magazine Needs: *Fireweed*, edited by the Fireweed editorial/collective, is a feminist journal of writing, politics, art and culture that "especially welcomes contributions by women of color, working-class women, native women, lesbians and women with disabilities." As a sample they selected the opening lines of "Remembering My Voice" by Treena Kortje:
> Today the baby discovers sound under water./It is my own voice she recognizes,/how it reached her
> once through soft folds of skin,/to the swell in my belly where she began
Fireweed is 88 pgs., 6¾×9¾, professionally printed and perfect-bound with 3- or 4-color glossy cover, includes b&w art. Press run is 1,500. Subscription: $22 individuals, $35 institutions in Canada; $30 individuals, $45 institutions in US. Sample: $5-15 (double issues), Canadian or US funds.
How to Submit: Submit up to 5 poems, single-spaced. Simultaneous submissions OK. Send cover letter with brief bio and publication credits, if any. Publishes theme issues. Send SASE (or SAE and IRC) for upcoming themes. Reports in 6-12 months. "Please include SAE and IRC for reply." Pays $30 for first printed page, $10 for remaining full or partial printed page and 2 copies.

◎ FIREWEED: POETRY OF WESTERN OREGON (Specialized: regional), 2917 NE 13th, Portland OR 97212, phone/fax (503)460-9063, e-mail jazzpo@iccom.com, founded 1989.
Magazine Needs: *Fireweed* is a quarterly publishing the work of poets living in Western Oregon or having close connections to the region. However, poems need not be regional in subject; any theme, subject, length or form is acceptable. They have published poetry by Stephanie Van Horn, James Grabill, Paulann Peters and Lex Runciman. As a sample they selected these lines from "Memory for a City Dweller" by Michael Spurlin:
> Recall this day when the world/spoke its center in you,/when a glacier's movement into water/was the
> rapid motion of earth/and your eye roved around/the world's stillness, bounded/by mountain, river
> and open range.
Fireweed is 44 pgs., digest-sized, laser printed and saddle-stapled with card cover. "We receive several hundred poems and publish about ¼ or ⅕ of them." Press run is 250 for 180 subscribers of which 20 are libraries, 25 shelf sales. Subscription: $10. Sample: $2.50.
How to Submit: Submit 3-5 poems at a time, name and address on each page. No previously published poems; simultaneous submissions OK. Cover letter with brief bio required. Often comments on rejections. They do not publish guidelines for poets but will answer inquiries with SASE. Reports in 2-4 months. Pays 2 copies. Acquires first North American serial rights. Reviews books of poetry by Oregon poets in 500-750 words, single format. Open to unsolicited reviews. Oregon poets may also send books for review consideration.
Advice: They add, "Try to examine a copy before submitting."

◎ FIRM NONCOMMITTAL: AN INTERNATIONAL JOURNAL OF WHIMSY (Specialized: humor), 5 Vonda Ave., North York, Ontario M2N 5E6 Canada, e-mail firmnon@idirect.com (queries only), website http://webhome.idirect.com/~firmnon, founded 1995, editor Brian Pastoor, assistant editor Vince Cicchine.
Magazine Needs: *FN* is an annual forum, published in August, for international light verse and humorous, short fiction and nonfiction. "Short poems under 40 lines are preferred, in all forms and styles from visual to villanelle. There is a morass of morose writing out there. We seek writers who find the sunshine in the saturnine, who 'take the utmost trouble to find the right thing to say and then say it with the utmost levity'—G.B. Shaw." They have published "levity" by bill bissett (Canada), K.V. Skene (England), Michael Shuval (Israel) and haiku by Francine Porad (U.S.). *Firm Noncommittal* is 40-48 pgs., 6¼×8¼, professionally printed and perfect-bound with matte card cover, using mirthful, b&w art. They accept "nearly 10%" of the submissions received. Circulation is 100 and growing, "thanks to support from *Krax* and other light-minded magazines." Sample: $5 (Canadian funds). Make checks payable to Brian Pastoor.
How to Submit: Submit up to 6 poems in *May or June only*. Previously published poems OK; no simultaneous submissions. Cover letter required; include a brief bio, "preferably under 50 words, preferably factual. Unless of edificial genius, mss without SASE or SAE and IRCs will be binned (sorry)." Often comments on rejections. Send SASE (or SAE and IRCs) for guidelines. Reports in 2 months. Pays 1 copy.
Advice: Brian Pastoor says, "While we do admit a bias to the ironist here, we shy away from satire that is too heavy. We're after light, perspicuous writing that reveals a quickness of mind about the spiritual or mundane (all themes universal), writing that is characterized by imagination, ingenuity and/or self-conscious verbal artifice. Tom Robbins, as always, put it best: 'Those who fail to see the whimsy of things will experience rigor mortis before death.' "

◢ FIRST CLASS; FOUR-SEP PUBLICATIONS, P.O. Box 12434, Milwaukee WI 53212, website http://www.execpc.com/~chrifton, founded 1994, editor Christopher M.
Magazine Needs: *First Class* appears 3-4 times/year and "publishes excellent/odd writing for intelligent/creative readers." They want "short post-modern poems, also short fiction." No traditional work. They have published poetry by Bennett, Locklin, Fitzsimmons, Splake, Catlin and Huffstickler. *FC* is 46-48 pgs., 8½×11,

printed, saddle-stitched with colored cover. They receive about 600 poems a year, accept approximately 30. Press run is 200-400. Sample (including guidelines): $5 or mini version $1. Make checks payable to Christopher Meyer.
How to Submit: Submit 5 poems at a time. Previously published poems and simultaneous submissions OK. Cover letter preferred. Time between acceptance and publication is 2-4 months. Often comments on rejections. Reports in 2-3 weeks. Pays in 1 copy. Acquires one-time rights. Reviews books of poetry. Open to unsolicited reviews. Poets may also send books for review consideration.
Also Offers: Chapbook production available. Website includes guidelines, recent books and chapbooks, current issue information, etc.
Advice: The editor says, "Belt out a good, short, thought-provoking, graphic, uncommon piece."

N 🌐 ◎ **FIRST OFFENSE (Specialized: form/style)**, Syring, Stodmarsh, Canterbury, Kent CT3 4BA England, founded 1985, contact Tim Fletcher.
Magazine Needs: *First Offense* is published 1-2 times a year. "The magazine is for contemporary poetry and is not traditional, but is received by most ground-breaking poets." They want "contemporary, language and experimental poetry and articles. No traditional work." Mr. Fletcher says *FO* is photocopied. "So we need well typed manuscripts, word processed." Press run is 300. Subscription: £2.50 plus 75¢ p&h. Make checks payable to Tim Fletcher.
How to Submit: No previously published poems. "No reply without SASE or SAE and IRC." Reviews books and chapbooks of poetry and other magazines.
Advice: Mr. Fletcher says, "Buy a copy before submitting for research so as not to waste everyone's time."

N ◯ ◯ **FIRST STEP PRESS; STEPPING STONES MAGAZINE: A LITERARY MAGAZINE FOR INNOVATIVE ART; CRIMSON RIVERS**, P.O. Box 902, Norristown PA 19404-0902, founded 1996, editor/publisher Michael D. Ross, Sr.
Magazine Needs: "*Stepping Stones Magazine* is published quarterly to showcase established talent as well as the aspiring poet; to provide a means of helping poets with their craft." They want any style, any length, any genre "so long as it's good." No first drafts. They have published poetry by Harvey Stanbrough, Kimberly Brittingham, William J. Middleton and Kimberly Courtright. *SSM* is 60 pgs., 5½ × 8½, photocopied and saddle-stapled with cardstock cover, includes b&w clip art. They receive about 720 poems a year, accept approximately 30%. Press run is 300 for 100 subscribers; 100 distributed free to coffeehouses. Single copy: $5; subscription: $15. Sample: $3. Make checks payable to Michael D. Ross, Sr.
How to Submit: Submit 7 poems at a time. Previously published poems and simultaneous submissions OK. Cover letter preferred. Disk submissions in ASCII, WordPerfect or MSWord formats OK. Time between acceptance and publication is up to 1 year. Always comments on rejections. Send SASE for guidelines. Reports in 2-4 weeks. Always sends prepublication galleys. Pays 1 copy. Acquires first or one-time rights. Reviews books and chapbooks of poetry and other magazines in 250-500 words, single book format. Open to unsolicited reviews. Poets may also send books for review consideration.
Also Offers: Publishes *Crimson Rivers*, a yearly anthology of splatter punk poetry and short fiction. "This publication will provide a forum for those wishing to express the darkness that resides in the deepest regions of the soul. Here, there are no limits, no boundaries, there is no turning back." For poetry, send 1-30 poems "any style is fine, so long as it can chill the marrow in the reader's bones. Poems about unseen fears are especially desired." Also sponsors contests. Send SASE for details.
Advice: The editor says, "There are no proven methods for success, the best thing to do is to keep writing and believe in your work because if you can't—nobody else will."

N $ 📧 **FIRST THINGS**, 156 Fifth Ave., Suite 400, New York NY 10010, phone (212)627-1985, fax (212)627-2184, e-mail ft@firstthings.com, website http://www.firstthings.com, founded 1990, contact poetry editor.
Magazine Needs: *FT* contains "social commentary with a special interest in issues of religion and public life: ethics, law, education, mores, politics." They have published poetry by Marjorie Maddox, Laurance Wieder, Luci Shaw and Atar Hadari. *FT* is 64-84 pgs., magazine-sized, web offset printed and perfect-bound with 80 lb. text paper cover, includes display and classified ads. They receive about 500 poems a year, accept approximately 5%. Subscription: $29/year.
How to Submit: Line length for poetry is 40 maximum. No previously published poems or simultaneous submissions. Cover letter preferred. Time between acceptance and publication is 2-8 months. Publishes theme issues occasionally. Reports in 1-3 weeks. Pays $50 plus 2 copies.

N 🌐 ◯ ◯ **FIRST TIME; NATIONAL HASTINGS POETRY COMPETITION**, Burdett Cottage, 4 Burdett Place, George St., Hastings, East Sussex TN34 3ED England, phone/fax 01424 428855, founded 1981, editor Josephine Austin.
Magazine Needs: The biannual magazine is open to "all kinds of poetry—our magazine goes right across the board—which is why it is one of the most popular in Great Britain." As a sample the editor selected these lines from "Why a Poet?" by R.M. Griffiths:

> *Of all types of people/and all their differences in depth,/the poet is the deepest,/Or is it just the most vacuous?*

The digest-sized magazine, 24 pgs., saddle-stapled, contains several poems on each page, in a variety of small type styles, on lightweight stock, b&w photographs of editor and 1 author, glossy one-color card cover. Subscription: $13. Sample: $2 plus postage. "Please send dollars."

How to Submit: Submit 10 poems with name and address of poet on each. Poems submitted must not exceed 30 lines. No previously published poems. Cover letter required. Time between acceptance and publication is up to 2 months. "Although we can no longer offer a free copy as payment, we can offer one at a discounted price of $3."

Also Offers: The annual National Hastings Poetry Competition for poets 18 and older offers awards of £150, £75 and £50, £2/poem entry fee.

Advice: The editor advises, "Keep on 'pushing your poetry.' If one editor rejects you then study the market and decide which is the correct one for you. Try to type your own manuscripts as longhand is difficult to read and doesn't give a professional impression. Always date your poetry — ©1997 and sign it. Follow your way of writing, don't be a pale imitation of someone else—sooner or later styles change and you will either catch up or be ahead."

⬤ **FISH DRUM**, P.O. Box 966, Murray Hill Station, New York NY 10156, founded in 1988 by Robert Winson (1959-1995), editor Suzi Winson.

Magazine Needs: *Fish Drum* is a literary magazine appearing once a year. They want "West Coast poetry, the exuberant, talky, often elliptical and abstract 'continuous nerve movie' that follows the working of the mind and has a relationship to the world and the reader. Philip Whalen's work, for example, and much of *Calafia, The California Poetry*, edited by Ishmael Reed. Also magical-tribal-incantatory poems, exemplified by the future/primitive *Technicians of the Sacred*, ed. Rothenberg. *Fish Drum* has a soft spot for schmoozy, emotional, imagistic stuff. Literate, personal material that sings and surprises, OK?" They have published poetry by Philip Whalen, Arthur Sze, Nathaniel Tarn, Alice Notley, John Brandi, Steve Richmond, Jessica Hagedorn and Leo Romero. As a sample the editor selected these lines from "Glossolalia" by Kate Bremer:

> Everywhere I look I see amino acids on the ground./When I close my eyes, I see molecules and pieces
> of Sanskrit:/I hear syllables and alphabets.

FD is approximately 80 pgs., professionally printed, perfect-bound. Press run is 2,000 for subscribers, libraries and shelf sales. Subscription: $24/4 issues.

How to Submit: Publishes theme issues. Sends prepublication galleys. Pays 2 copies. Acquires first serial rights. Reviews books or chapbooks of poetry in long essays and/or capsule reviews. Open to unsolicited reviews. Poets may also send books for review consideration.

Advice: The editor says, "We're looking for prose, fiction, essays, what-have-you, and artwork, scores, cartoons, etc.—just send it along. We are also interested in poetry, prose and translations concerning the practice of Zen. We publish chapbooks, but solicit these from our authors." She also adds, "It is my intention to complete Robert's work and to honor his memory by continuing to publish *FishDrum*."

⬤ **5 AM**, 1109 Milton Ave., Pittsburgh PA 15218, founded 1987, editors Ed Ochester and Judith Vollmer.

Magazine Needs: *5 AM* is a poetry publication that appears twice a year. They are open in regard to form, length, subject matter and style. However, they do not want poetry that is "religious or naive rhymes." They have published poetry by Rita Dove, Edward Field, Jesse Lee Kercheval, Billy Collins, Alicia Ostriker and Alberto Rios. *5 AM* is a 24-page, offset tabloid. They receive about 3,000 poems a year, use approximately 2%. Press run is 1,000 for 550 subscribers of which 22 are libraries, about 300 shelf sales. Subscription: $12/4 issues. Sample: $4.

How to Submit: No previously published poems or simultaneous submissions. Seldom comments on rejections. Reports within 2 months. Pays 2 copies. Acquires first rights.

$⬤ **FIVE POINTS; JAMES DICKEY PRIZE FOR POETRY**, Georgia State University, University Plaza, Atlanta GA 30303-3083, phone (404)651-0071, fax (404)651-1710, website http://www.gsu.edu/~wwweng/fivepoints/, founded 1996, managing editor Megan Sexton.

Magazine Needs: *Five Points* appears 3 times a year and "publishes quality poetry, fiction, nonfiction, interviews and art by established and emerging writers." They want "poetry of high quality which shows evidence of an original voice and imagination." They have published poetry by Charles Wright, Kate Daniels and Philip Levine. As a sample the editor selected these lines from "Talc" by Jane Hirschfield:

> When you phoned I was far, and sleeping,/but they brought me the message and I ran,/I ran to the
> phone where you were,/You were speaking, we two were speaking,/When I ran back to the room I no
> longer/knew we would speak again.

Five Points is about 200 pgs., 6½×9, professionally printed and perfect-bound with 4-color card cover, includes b&w photos and ads. They receive about 1,000 poems a year, accept approximately 10%. Press run is 2,000 for about 500 subscribers of which 10% are libraries, 40% shelf sales. Single copy: $6. Sample: $5.

How to Submit: Submit no more than 5 poems at a time. No previously published poems or simultaneous submissions. Cover letter preferred. Reads submissions September 1 through May 30 only. Time between acceptance and publication is 1-3 months. Poems are circulated to an editorial board. "First reader culls poems then send them to the final reader." Seldom comments on rejections. Publishes theme issues occasionally. Send SASE for guidelines and upcoming themes. Reports in 1-3 months. Always sends prepublication galleys. Pays $50/poem plus 2 copies and 1-year subscription. Acquires first North American serial rights.

Also Offers: Sponsors the James Dickey Prize for Poetry which awards $1,000 and publication in the Spring issue. Reading fee: $10/3-5 poems of any length. Fee includes 1-year subscription. Deadline: November 30.

FLAMBARD, Stable Cottage, East Fourstones, Hexham NE47 5DX England, phone +44 1434 674360, fax +44 1434 674178, founded 1990, contact Peter Lewis.

Book/Chapbook Needs: Flambard "is particularly sympathetic to new or neglected writers from the North of England, and is keen to nourish developing talent." But open to all. They publish 5 paperbacks/year. Books are usually 64 pgs., 234×156mm, disk to plate printing, limp-sewn binding, 4-color cover, art work sometimes included.

How to Submit: "Books only considered." Submit at least 15 poems at a time. Previously published poems and simultaneous submissions OK. Cover letter required. "If accepted, we expect the text on a disk we can read." Time between acceptance and publication is 12-15 months. Often comments on rejections. Replies to queries and mss in 1 month. Pays honorarium and 6 author's copies. Obtain samples of books or chapbooks "by direct mail purchase or through shops."

Advice: Peter Lewis says, "Not much point thinking about book publication until a reasonable level of magazine publication has been achieved."

FLAMING ARROWS, County Sligo VEC, Riverside, Sligo, Ireland, phone (+353)7145844, fax (+353)7143093, website http://www.artspark.com/home/sligovec, founded 1989, editor Leo Regan, A.E.O.

Magazine Needs: *Flaming Arrows*, published annually in January, features poetry, prose, interviews, graphics and photographs. They want "cogent, lucid, coherent, technically precise poetry. Poems of the spirit, mystical, metaphysical but sensuous, tactile and immediate to the senses." They do not want "loose rambling emotional release." They have published poetry by Sydney Bernard Smith, Medbh McGuckian, James Liddy and Ciaran O'Driscoll. As a sample the editor selected these lines from "The Summons" by Peter Van Belle:

> Sacred hawk, descend from your heights,/star clenched in beak, your eyes, my diamonds,/your mind,
> a twine of steel./From this roof I speak to you,/holding one foot over the abyss./I relish the dizziness.

Flaming Arrows is 80-102 pgs., A5, offset printed, perfect-bound or saddle-stapled, with 2-color cover stock, and b&w interior photos and graphics used in conjunction with the written work. They receive about 500 poems a year, accept 6%. Press run is 500 for 150 subscribers of which 30 are libraries, 180 shelf sales; 100 distributed free to writer's groups, contributors, literary events. Sample: $6. Make checks payable to Co. Sligo VEC.

How to Submit: Submit 5 poems "typed, A4, in 10 or 12 pt. for scanning or discs for Word 7 in Windows 95." Previously published poems and simultaneous submissions OK. Cover letter required. Time between acceptance and publication is 10 months. Reports in 3 months. Pays 1 copy, additional copies at cost. They receive financial assistance from the Arts Council of Ireland.

Advice: The editor says, "Inspection of previous issues, especially 2, 3, 5 or 6 will inform prospective contributors of style and standard required."

FLARESTACK PUBLISHING; OBSESSED WITH PIPEWORK, Redditch Library, 15 Market Place, Redditch, Worcestershire B98 8AR England, phone (01527)63291, fax (01527)68571, e-mail flare.stack@virgin.net or redditchlib@worcestershire.gov.uk, founded 1995, editor Charles Johnson.

Magazine Needs: *Obsessed with Pipework* appears quarterly. "We are very keen to publish strong new voices—'new poems to surprise and delight' with somewhat of a high-wire aspect. We are looking for original, exploratory poems—positive, authentic, oblique maybe—delighting in image and in the dance of words on the page." They do not want "the predictable, the unfresh, the rhyme-led; the clever, the sure-of-itself. No formless outpourings, please." They have published poetry by David Hart, Jennifer Compton, Susan Wicks and Vuyelwa Carlin. As a sample the editor selected these lines from "Fixtures and Fittings" by Dianne Neoh:

> That summer/we folded up the contents of our lives/and placed them into boxes./Even I became of use/
> sanctioning the closure of the dolls house/and removal of toys.

The editor says *OWP* is 49 pgs., A5, photocopied and stapled with card cover, ads "by arrangement." They receive about 1,500 poems a year, accept approximately 10%. Press run is 70-100. Single copy: £3.50; subscription: £12. Sample: £2 if available. Make checks payable to Flarestack Publishing.

How to Submit: Submit maximum of 6 poems at a time. No previously published poems or simultaneous submissions. Cover letter preferred. E-mail and disk submissions OK. "If sending by e-mail, send a maximum 3 poems in the body of the message, as attached files may become lost or corrupted." Time between acceptance and publication is 4 months maximum. Often comments on rejections. Send SASE for guidelines or request via fax or obtain via e-mail. Reports in 1 month. Pays 1 copy. Acquires first rights.

Book/Chapbook Needs & How to Submit: Flarestack Publishing ("talent to burn") aims to "find an audience for new poets, so beginners are welcome, but the work has to be strong and clear." They publish 12 chapbooks/year. Chapbooks are usually 12-50 pgs., A5, photocopied and stapled with card cover, uses some line drawings.

How to Submit: Query first with a few sample poems and cover letter with brief bio and publication credits. "Normally we expect a few previous magazine acceptances, but no previous collection publication." Replies to queries in 3 weeks; to mss in 2 months. Pays royalties of 25% plus 6 author's copies (out of a press run of 50-100). Order sample chapbooks by sending £3.50.

Advice: The editor says, "Most beginning poets show little evidence of reading poetry before writing it! Join a poetry workshop. For chapbook publishing, we are looking for coherent first collections that take risks, make leaps, come clean, walk naked as by real people."

N ◯ ◐ FLINT HILLS REVIEW, Division of English, Box 4019, Emporia State University, Emporia KS 66801, phone (316)341-5216, fax (316)341-5547, e-mail heldricp@emporia.edu or webbamy@emporia.edu, website http://www.emporia.edu/fhr, founded 1995, editors Phil Heldrich and Amy Sage Webb.

Magazine Needs: Published annually in June, *Flint Hills Review* is "a regionally focused journal presenting writers of national distinction alongside burgeoning authors." They are open to all forms except "rhyming, sentimental or gratuitous verse." They have published poetry by E. Ethelbert Miller, Elizabeth Dodd, Vivian Shipley and Gwendolyn Brooks. *FHR* is about 100 pgs., digest-sized, offset printed and perfect-bound with glossy card cover with b&w photo, also includes b&w photos. They receive about 2,000 poems a year, accept approximately 5%. Single copy: $5.50.

How to Submit: Submit 3-5 poems at a time. No previously published poems; simultaneous submissions OK. Disk submissions OK. Cover letter with SASE required. Reads submissions January through March only. Time between acceptance and publication is about 1 year. Seldom comments on rejections. Publishes theme issues occasionally. Send SASE for guidelines and upcoming themes. Pays 1 copy. Acquires first rights.

Also Offers: Sponsors the annual Bluestem Press Award. See listing in the Contests & Awards section of this book. Website includes guidelines, samples, "a comprehensive web presence."

Advice: The editors say, "Subscribe for examples of what we publish, understand our guidelines and see our website."

◎ FLOATING BRIDGE PRESS (Specialized: regional), P.O. Box 18814, Seattle WA 98118, website http://www.scn.org/arts/floatingbridge, founded 1994.

Book/Chapbook Needs: The press publishes chapbooks and anthologies by Washington state poets, selected through an annual contest. They have published chapbooks by Nance Van Winckel, Joannie Kervran, Molly Tenenbaum and Donna Waidtlow. In 1997 they began publishing *Pontoon*, an annual anthology featuring the work of Washington state poets. That anthology is 74 pgs., digest-sized, offset-printed and perfect-bound with matte cardstock cover. For a sample chapbook or anthology, send $6.

How to Submit: For consideration, Washington poets (only) should submit a chapbook ms of 20-24 pgs. of poetry with $10 reading fee and SASE (for results only). The usual reading period is November 1 to February 15. Previously published individual poems and simultaneous submissions OK. Author's name must not appear on the ms; include a separate page with title, name, address, telephone number and acknowledgments of any previous publication. Mss are judged anonymously and will not be returned. In addition to publication, the winner receives $500 (minimum), 50 copies and a reading in the Seattle area. All entrants receive a copy of the winning chapbook. All entrants will be considered for inclusion in *Pontoon*, a poetry anthology. Send SASE for complete guidelines or visit website.

✓ ◐ THE FLORIDA REVIEW, Dept. of English, University of Central Florida, Box 25000, Orlando FL 32816, phone (407)823-2038, website http://pegasus.cc.ucf.edu/~english/floridareview/home.htm, founded 1972, editor Russ Kesler.

Magazine Needs: *FR* is a "literary biannual with emphasis on short fiction and poetry." They want "poems filled with real things, real people and emotions, poems that might conceivably advance our knowledge of the human heart." They have published poetry by Knute Skinner, Elton Glaser, Silvia Curbelo and Walter McDonald. It is 128 pgs., professionally printed, flat-spined, with glossy card cover. Press run is 1,000 for 500 subscribers of which 50 are libraries, 300 shelf sales. Subscription: $10. Sample: $6.

How to Submit: Submit no more than 6 poems at a time. No correspondence, including mss, will be read or acknowledged unless accompanied by a SASE. Simultaneous submissions OK. Editor comments on submissions "occasionally." Send SASE for guidelines. Reports in 1-3 months. Always sends prepublication galleys. Pays 3 copies, small honorarium occasionally available. Acquires all rights. Returns rights "upon publication, when requested." Reviews books of poetry in 1,500 words, single format; 2,500-3,000 words, multi-book format. Send books for review consideration.

Also Offers: Website includes contents of past issues, information about Editors' Awards competition and submission guidelines.

Advice: The editor says they would like more formal verse.

◐ FLYWAY, A LITERARY REVIEW, 206 Ross Hall, Iowa State University, Ames IA 50011-1201, fax (515)294-6814, e-mail flyway@iastate.edu, founded 1961, editor Debra Marquart.

Magazine Needs: Appearing 3 times a year, *Flyway* "is one of the best literary magazines for the money; it is packed with some of the most readable poems being published today—all styles and forms, lengths and subjects." The editor shuns elite-sounding free verse with obscure meanings and pretty-sounding formal verse with obvious meanings. It is 112 pgs., 6×9, professionally printed and perfect-bound with matte card cover with color. Circulation is 600 for 400 subscribers of which 100 are libraries. Subscription: $24. Sample: $8.

insider report

Poetry does not equal success when writing for greeting cards

BY SANDRA MILLER-LOUDEN

So, you're a poet. You write poetry and you'd like to have your poems published somewhere besides photocopied journals that pay in copies. You walk past a greeting card store and it hits you—this would be the perfect venue for your poems to finally find a huge audience. Right? Wrong.

Greeting card companies do not want, nor do they accept, poetry from freelance writers. How the misconception began that greeting card writing equals poetry—and why this fallacy stubbornly endures—isn't hard to figure out. Writers—or for that matter, nonwriters—have a collective, generic memory of the greeting cards they bought—and received—through decades of personal occasions and national holidays. They remember the physical appearance of the card—the stiff paper, the French fold, the embossing, the deckled edge. When they think of artwork, they see flowers and hearts and hearts and flowers, a fleur-de-lis or two and maybe a cute puppy or kitten thrown in for good measure.

The strongest recollection, however, is the one concerning the words. (Not surprisingly either; you pick up a greeting card for the artwork, but you buy it for the message.) Greeting card verse is, in most minds, defined as a rhyming poem, done in iambic pentameter, with the number of lines divisible by four. In other words, something that often sounds like recycled Dr. Seuss with sappy overtones.

"Now wait a minute," I can hear you saying, "I just walked into a store last week and bought one of those cards you described for my Aunt Ellie. There was a whole rack full of them." Which is precisely why the greeting-card-writing-equals-poetry equation stubbornly persists. In my 14 years as a freelance writer, many of those years spent teaching both "live" and cyberspace students how to write for greeting cards, the most frequent comment I get is: "How can I write cards? I don't write poetry."

Let's start by dispelling this myth. True, you see poetry—defined here as an arrangement of words written in rhymed, metered form—in today's greeting cards. But for the most part, poetry in greeting cards is the domain of the "Big Three" in the greeting card industry: Hallmark, founded in 1910; American Greetings, founded 1906; and

---

SANDRA MILLER-LOUDEN *is the author of* Write Well & Sell: Greeting Cards *(Jam-Packed Press, 1998) and is a regular contributor/columnist to* Greetings Today, *the official magazine of the Greeting Card Association. She also teaches a greeting card course through the Writer's Club University on the Internet (www.writersclub.com). For more information on her book, write to P.O. Box 9701, Pittsburgh PA 15229 or e-mail her at FelshamLdy@aol.com.*

Gibson Greetings, the oldest, founded in 1850. When these companies want traditional poetry for their cards, they usually turn to one of two sources—either their enormous databases filled with poems or their inhouse writing staff. They simply don't shell out freelance cash for stuff they already have—or can generate—on premises.

Which brings us immediately to a second related myth: that Hallmark, American Greetings and Gibson Greetings are the only card companies out there. When I teach or lecture at conferences, I always ask my audience to give me company names. The dialogue goes something like this: *Hallmark*. Okay, next. *Um, Shoebox*. That's a division of Hallmark. Next. *American Greetings*. Fine. Who else? *Carlton*. That's a division of American Greetings. What else?

Occasionally, but not always, someone will come up with Blue Mountain Arts. After that, silence. Well, because we're here to dispel myths, let's dump another. There are between 900-1,200 card companies in the U.S. and Canada, depending upon whose estimates you accept. Those run the gamut from the Big Three to the mom-and-pop operations on the dining room table.

However, in between those two extremes are a multitude of midsize companies. How and why they came into being, as well as the exciting, creative inroads they continually make is another article in itself. For our purposes here, you need only remember this: Midsize companies want and need your freelance work. What they don't want or need is your rhymed, metered poetry.

So, what *do* you write for today's greeting card market?

Let's find out by going in through the back door. First, how do we redefine what constitutes poetry? According to Nancy Bogen, professor of English and author of *How to Write Poetry* (Simon & Schuster Macmillan, 1994), "It is sometimes said that a poet's audience is him- or herself; readers are subsequent eavesdroppers." If you agree with this statement, you've already messed up as far as greeting card writing goes. The style—or as we in the card industry prefer, the voice—of a greeting card is just the opposite. What Professor Bogen is talking about can best be described in four words: *Poetry is about me*.

However, greeting card writing is from *me-to-you*. As I define this concept, me-to-you is the most basic, vital core of all greeting card writing reflecting why people buy our product.

Professor Bogen then goes on to distinguish between traditional verse with its rhythms, meters and external objective rules and free or "unshackled" verse which "has laws unto itself with no set rhythm or meter or sound pattern." And here, even though Bogen is still implying the *about me* factor, if we look at her second designation and apply it to greeting cards with its inherent me-to-you flavor, we've been given the magic key that opens the freelance card-writing door. Second only to the humorous caption, contemporary prose (what others in the industry like to term as "conventional prose" or "serious social expression") is what editors look for, use, and more to the point, pay for.

Let's look at some examples. The following, a woman-to-woman friendship caption comes from Carlton Cards' line *Today I Thought of You.*

Outside: *When we were girls,*
They told us to look for love
and hope for romance
and think about kids
and get a good job.
They never mentioned,
"Oh yes,
and you'll need a best friend
and she's gonna make
everything so much
better."

Inside: *You really do, you know.*
Because you really know me.
I am so grateful
for our friendship.

A Father's Day card, written by RosaLinda Buchner Graziano, comes from Renaissance Greeting Cards, Inc.

I: *On this special day,*
I'm filled with love and admiration
when I think of all the things
you say and do that make
you such an exceptional father
and such an extraordinary man.

I just wanted to let you know
how much I love you and
how happy I am for all that we share.

Happy Father's Day

Finally, this Louie Nominee (the greeting card industry's highest award), designed and written by Joanne Fink, and published by Renaissance Greeting Cards, Inc. reads:

O: *On Our Anniversary*
I Promise To Share With You
In Times Of Joy As In Times Of Trouble—
To Talk And To Listen—
To Honor And To Appreciate You—
To Provide For And Support You
In Trust And In Love.

Together, let us create a home that expresses our individuality and our love for each other

I: *I love you very much.*
Happy Anniversary!

What did you notice about those verses? Even though the lines don't rhyme, nor do they have a strict, constructed meter, there is still a definite rhythm or cadence to them. They sound conversational, as if one person is talking to another. They all carry a lot of personal pronouns—I, you, me, we, us, our. In other words, *me-to-you*.

According to Linda Jackman, product development assistant to Renaissance Greeting Cards, about 70 percent of all unsolicited, freelance submissions are in poetry form and out of these, about half use rhyme. Yet, in their entire line of cards, Renaissance only publishes about 5 percent traditional rhymed, metered poetry, as opposed to 80 percent soft, conversational prose like we read above. (The other 15 percent is humor—again, still with that personal, conversational voice.) These numbers speak for themselves.

In addition, Jackman says the successful greeting card writer studies and knows her market. "Study the card line of the company you're interested in submitting your material to. Send for the company's submission guidelines." Jackman also advises that right after *me-to-you*, you remember another set of three little words: *Timing is everything*. "Often potentially acceptable verses are returned due to the timing of the submission. February 1st is not the optimal time to send a Valentine's Day verse submission packet." [For those seeking more information on the submission requirements of greeting card companies, *Writer's Market* (Writer's Digest Books) has a whole section dedicated to these companies.]

To this point, I've only told you what you shouldn't write for today's cards. If you want to learn—not what to write but rather how to think so your natural talent and creativity will burgeon on its own—here are some suggestions:

- Study the card racks and spinners out there; yes, even the traditional rhymed, metered poetry. Concentrate, however, on the contemporary prose we talked about. Note the me-to-you element in every card you examine.
- Read books which go into detail on craft as well as other elements of successful freelance writing for today's greeting card markets. Two such books are my book *Write Well & Sell: Greeting Cards* (Jam-Packed Press, 1998) and Karen Ann Moore's *You Can Write Greeting Cards* (Writer's Digest Books, 1999).
- Take courses, on the Internet and through workshops, until that particular *me-to-you* voice of greeting card writing becomes second nature.

Do one of these, all or none. Just please, don't write rhymed, metered poetry for today's card companies and expect it to sell.

How to Submit: Submit 4-6 poems at a time. Cover letter preferred. "We do not read mss between the end of May and mid-August." May be contacted by fax or e-mail, but "work should come by mail." Reports in 4-6 weeks (often sooner). Pays 1 copy. Acquires first rights.
Also Offers: Sponsors an annual award for poetry, fiction and nonfiction. Offers $500 prize for poetry and fiction, $300 for nonfiction. Send SASE for details.

☑ ◻ ◪ **FOOTPRINTS; WRITER'S WORKS CHAPBOOKS**, 604 Crabill Rd., Toutle WA 98649, phone (360)274-4372, founded 1998, editor Larry Stewart.
Magazine Needs: *Footprints* appears quarterly and is "a forum for poets and writers containing poetry and short stories." They want "quality poetry. Shorter poems are preferred, but, if a long poem says a lot, we will be interested." No "vulgar or suggestive language. Quality works can be produced without sexually explicit

scenes. Controversial political opinions are to be avoided. Then there is religion. Leave out references to denominations, specific doctrines or people." They have published poetry by Dolores Malaschak, Ezra Cardiff and Virginia Cole Veal. As a sample the editor selected these lines from his poem "Of Chance Encounters":

> Among the peaks of Olympia, heavy were the snows,/ in the days when the winter kept our souls imprisoned./ It was the time of our great longing, our reaching out/ to touch each other, to explore the regions of our youth;/ the uncharted wilderness—like this improbable place,/chosen, by our parents, to put down roots . . .

The editor says *Footprints* is 40-50 pgs., 8½×11, offset printed and saddle-stapled with glossy color cover and b&w and color illustrations. Press run is 100 for 54 subscribers of which 15 are libraries. Single copy: $7.50; subscription: $19.50. Sample: $6. Make checks payable to Larry Stewart.
How to Submit: Submit up to 10 poems at a time. Previously published poems OK; no simultaneous submissions. Cover letter preferred. Time between acceptance and publication is 1-3 months. Often comments on rejections. Send SASE for guidelines. Reports in 3 weeks. Pays 1 copy. Acquires first rights. Reviews chapbooks of poetry. Poets may send books for review consideration.
Book/Chapbook Needs & How to Submit: Writer's Works Chapbooks publishes chapbooks of 24-40 pgs., digest-sized, offset printed and saddle-stapled. Query first with a few sample poems and cover letter with brief bio and publication credits. Replies to queries in 4 weeks, to mss in 2 months. Pays 10% royalties. "Expect poet to subsidize cost! Help in sales!"

N ◼ ◷ FOR POETRY.COM, e-mail editors@forpoetry.com, website http://www.forpoetry.com, founded March 1999, editor Jackie Marcus.
Magazine Needs: *For Poetry.Com* is a web magazine with daily updates. "We wish to promote new and emerging poets, with or without MFAs. We will be publishing established poets, but our primary interest is in publishing excellent poetry, prose, essays, reviews, paintings and photography. We are interested in lyric poetry, vivid imagery, open form, natural landscape, philosophical themes but not at the expense of honesty and passion: model examples: Robert Hass, James Wright, Charles Wright's *The Other Side of the River*, Montale, Neruda, Levertov and Karen Fish. No city punk, corny sentimental fluff or academic workshop imitations." They have published poetry by Brenda Hillman, Jane Hirshfield and Wayne Dodd. As a sample the editor selected these lines from "Elegy" by Joseph Duemer:

> Wind lifts the curtains/in an empty room./I'm somewhere else—/a line storm moving up from the Gulf/ meaning a downpour in Tennessee./Like all the weather—a blessing & a curse.

"We receive lots of submissions and are very selective about acceptances, but we will always try to send a note back on rejections."
How to Submit: Submit no more than 2 poems at a time. No previously published poems; simultaneous submissions OK. Cover letter preferred. Accepts e-mail submissions only. Reads submissions September through May only. Time between acceptance and publication is 2-6 weeks. Poems are circulated to an editorial board. "We'll read all submissions and then decide together on the poems we'll publish." Comments on rejections "as often as possible." Obtain guidelines via website. Reports in 1-2 weeks. Reviews books and chapbooks of poetry and other magazines in 800 words. Open to unsolicited reviews.
Advice: The editor says, "As my friend Kevin Hull said, 'Get used to solitude and rejection.' Sit on your poems for several months or more. Time is your best critic."

☑ ◷ FORKLIFT, OHIO: A JOURNAL OF POETRY, COOKING & LIGHT INDUSTRIAL SAFETY, P.O. Box 19650, Cincinnati OH 45219-0650, e-mail hubcap@one.net, website http://w3.one.net/~hubcap, founded 1994, editor Matt Hart, editor Eric Appleby.
Magazine Needs: *Forklift, Ohio* is a biannual journal seeking "language that does work." They want "poems, recipes, light industrial safety tips; also artwork, essays and short stories. No literal, natural or political work; nothing 'experimental,' spiritual, erotic or gothic." They have published poetry by Terri Ford, Cornelius Eady, Nancy Bonnell-Kangas and Forrest Griffen. As a sample the editor selected these lines from "BP Station Employee Restroom, 2 a.m." by Terri Ford:

> Here are some words/we use toward love: Crush Flame./Arrow. Torch. Fallen. I//fell. Maintain eye/ contact with each incoming//person. Greet them. Hi.

Forklift is 30-40 pgs., uses eclectic artwork, ads on back page only. A recent issue was bound with a bolt and sandpaper. They receive about 300 poems a year, accept approximately 15%. Press run is 300; distributed free in Cincinnati and across the US and to other journals. Single copy: $3 plus SASE; subscription: $12/4 issues. Sample for SASE. Make checks payable to Eric Appleby.
How to Submit: Submit 3-5 poems at a time, 1 poem/page. No previously published poems; simultaneous submissions OK. Cover letter preferred with brief bio. E-mail submissions OK, "plain text, MS Word." Time between

---

FOR AN EXPLANATION of symbols used in this book, see the Key to Symbols on the front and back inside covers.

acceptance and publication is 1 month. Poems are circulated to an editorial board—"two editors, occasional guest editor." Often comments on rejections. Send SASE for guidelines. Reports in 6 months. Pays 2 copies. Staff reviews books and chapbooks of poetry and other magazines in 30 words. Send books for review consideration.

Also Offers: Forklift Press has also released broadsheets, chapbooks and cassette recordings of selected poets who have been published in *Forklift, Ohio*. Website includes back issues, submission guidelines and recipes from the *Forklift, Ohio* test kitchen.

Advice: The editors say, "Request a sample before submitting and include SASE for response from editors."

THE FORMALIST; HOWARD NEMEROV SONNET AWARD (Specialized: form, translations), 320 Hunter Dr., Evansville IN 47711, founded 1990, editor William Baer.

Magazine Needs: *The Formalist*, appears twice a year, "dedicated to contemporary *metrical* poetry written in the great tradition of English-language verse." We're looking for well-crafted poetry in a contemporary idiom which uses meter and the full range of traditional poetic conventions in vigorous and interesting ways. We're especially interested in sonnets, couplets, tercets, ballads, the French forms, etc. We're not, however, interested in haiku (or syllabic verse of any kind) or sestinas. Only rarely do we accept a poem over 2 pages, and we have no interest in any type of erotica, blasphemy, vulgarity or racism. Finally, like all editors, we suggest that those wishing to submit to *The Formalist* become familiar with the journal beforehand. We are also interested in metrical translations of the poetry of major, formalist, non-English poets—from the ancient Greeks to the present. They have published poetry by Richard Wilbur, Donald Justice, Mona Van Duyn, Derek Walcott, John Updike, Maxine Kumin, James Merrill, Karl Shapiro, X.J. Kennedy, May Swenson, W.S. Merwin, W.D. Snodgrass and Louis Simpson. As a sample the editor selected the opening stanza from "The Amateurs of Heaven" by Howard Nemerov:

> Two lovers to a midnight meadow came/High in the hills, to lie there hand in hand/Like effigies and look up at the stars,/The never-setting ones set in the North/To circle the Pole in idiot majesty,/And wonder what was given them to wonder.

The Formalist is 128 pgs., digest-sized, offset printed on bond paper and perfect-bound with colored card cover. Subscription: $12/year; $22/2 years (add $3/year for foreign subscription). Sample: $6.50.

How to Submit: Submit 3-5 poems at a time. No simultaneous submissions, previously published work, or disk submissions. A brief cover letter is recommended and a SASE is necessary for a reply and return of ms. Reports within 2 months. Pays 2 copies. Acquires first North American serial rights.

Also Offers: The Howard Nemerov Sonnet Award offers $1,000 and publication in *The Formalist* for the best unpublished sonnet. The final judge for 1999 was Wendy Cope. Entry fee: $3/sonnet. Postmark deadline: June 15. Send SASE for guidelines. See also the contest listing for the World Order of Narrative and Formalist Poets. Contestants must subscribe to *The Formalist* to enter.

$ FORUM (Specialized: erotic poetry), Northern & Shell Tower, City Harbour, London E14 9GL England, phone (0171)308 5090, fax (0171)308 5075, founded 1967, editor Elizabeth Coldwell.

Magazine Needs: Appearing 13 times a year, *Forum* is "a magazine which deals with all aspects of human sexuality." Poetry has to be short (16 lines maximum) and erotic in nature. The editor says *Forum* is 196 pgs. and magazine-sized. They receive about 200 poems a year, accept approximately 5%. Press run is 40,000 for 100 subscribers; 35,000 distributed free. Single copy: £3.60.

How to Submit: Submit 1 poem at a time. No previously published poems or simultaneous submissions. Cover letter preferred. Pays £10/poem. Buys one-time rights. Staff reviews books of erotic poetry. Send books for review consideration.

4*9*1 NEO-IMMANENTIST*IMAGINATION (Specialized: neo-immanentist/sursymbolist), P.O. Box 91212, Lakeland FL 33804-1212, phone/fax (941)607-9100, e-mail stompdncr@aol.com, website http://www.4*9*1.com, founded 1997, editor Donald Ryburn, third assistant editor Norris Benjamin.

Magazine Needs: *4*9*1 Neo-Immanentist*Imagination* appears annually and publishes neo-immanentist/sursymbolist poetry, art, photography, essays and interviews. They want "poetry that deifies the radical singularity of the concrete particular and the unique reception and transformation of the personal consciousness. No academic poetry, limited and fallacious language, the egotistical sublime." They have published poetry by Lind Call, Duane Locke and Anna Blake. As a sample the editor selected this poem by Damniso Lopez:

> Did these words/come from a priest wearing a slough hat like a comedian/standing on a corner with a tincup and shouting to crows/from a school teacher with chalky fingers/talking about the skillful throwing of hand grenades in WWI/while thinking of apple pie and crystal glasses/from an ancestor who believed the sun moved around the earth/and in the shooting of spinning pidgeons/when I speak I feel I've betrayed myself.

The editor say it is about 150 pgs., magazine-sized, professionally printed and perfect-bound with cardstock cover, includes art/graphics. They receive about 1,000 poems a year, accept approximately 1%. Press run is 2,000, 1,500 shelf sales; 500 distributed free. Single copy: $9.95.

How to Submit: Submit 3-6 poems at a time. Previously published poems and simultaneous submissions OK. Cover letter with picture and SASE preferred. E-mail, disk and CD-ROM submissions OK. "Would like to hear the poets own words not some standard format." Time between acceptance and publication varies. Poems are circulated to an editorial board. "All poems given two complete circles through 'The Tampa Group' and discussed in an open meeting." Often comments on rejections. Send SASE for guidelines. Reporting time varies. Payment varies. Acquires first or one-time rights. Reviews books and chapbooks of poetry and other magazines. Open to unsolicited reviews. Poets may also send books for review consideration.

Book/Chapbook Needs & How to Submit: The editor also publishes 1 paperback and 4-6 chapbooks/year by "generally unknown writers who we feel deserve to be published." Books/chapbooks are usually 44-150 pgs., 5×7, professionally printed and perfect-bound with cardstock covers, using art/graphics. Query first with a few sample poems and cover letter with brief bio and publication credits.

Also Offers: Sponsors a series of creative projects. Also publishes the "Undisputed Duane Locke Chapbook Series." Write for details or visit the website.

◯ FOX CRY REVIEW, University of Wisconsin-Fox Valley, 1478 Midway Rd., P.O. Box 8002, Menasha WI 54952-8002, phone (920)832-2600, e-mail lmills@uwc.edu, founded 1974, editor Laurel Mills.

Magazine Needs: *Fox Cry Review* is a literary annual, published in August, using poems of any length or style, include brief bio, deadline February 15. They have published poetry by David Graham, Doug Flaherty, Daniel J. Weeks, Carol Hamilton and Estella Lauter. As a sample the editor selected these lines from "Let the Words of My Mouth" by Beverly Voldseth:

> We take comfort in these lines/that wait on our tongues—/to be rolled out to bank tellers//neighbors
> we pass on the street/strangers in the post office./What little boredoms our lives//are made up of, how
> they stand/in the mouth like truth.

Fox Cry is 86 pgs., digest-sized, professionally printed and perfect-bound with light card cover with b&w illustration, also contains b&w illustrations. Their press run is 300. Single copy: $6 plus $1 postage.

How to Submit: Submit maximum of 3 poems from September 1 through February 15 only. Include SASE. "Include name, address and phone number on each poem." No previously published poems. Request guidelines via e-mail. Pays 1 copy.

$ ◯ ◎ FRANK: AN INTERNATIONAL JOURNAL OF CONTEMPORARY WRITING AND ART (Specialized: form, translations), 32 rue Edouard Vaillant, 93100 Montreuil France, phone (33)(1)48596658, fax (33)(1)48596668, e-mail david@paris-anglo.com, website http://www.paris-anglo.com/frank, founded 1983, editor David Applefield.

Magazine Needs: *Frank* is a literary semiannual that "encourages work of seriousness and high quality which falls often between existing genres. Looks favorably at true internationalism and stands firm against ethnocentric values. Likes translations. Publishes foreign dossier in each issue. Very eclectic." There are no subject specifications, but the magazine "discourages sentimentalism and easy, false surrealism. Although we're in Paris, most Paris-poems are too thin for us. Length is open." They have published poetry by C.K. Williams, Michael Anania, Jim Morrison, Raymond Carver, Tomas Tranströmer, James Laughlin, Breytenbach, Michaux, Gennadi Aigi, W.S. Merwin, Edmond Jabes, John Berger, and many lesser known poets. The journal is 224 pgs., digest-sized, flat-spined and offset in b&w with color cover and photos, drawings and ads. Circulation is 4,000 of which 2,000 are bookstore sales and subscriptions. Subscription: $38 (individuals), $60 (institutions) for 4 issues. Sample: $10 airmail from Paris.

How to Submit: Queries via e-mail OK. Guidelines and upcoming themes available for SAE and IRCs. Poems must be previously unpublished. The editor often provides some criticism on rejected mss. Submissions are reported on in 3 months, publication is in 3-6 months. Pay is $5/printed page and 2 copies. Editor organizes readings in US and Europe for *Frank* contributors. "All submissions after June 1999 will automatically be entered into *Frank*'s poetry contest, with $1,000 being offered in prize money, plus publication in the journal and online. All submissions must be accompanied by an entry fee of $20 for up to three poems and $5 for each additional poem. Win or lose, all contestant poets will receive a one-year subscription (2 issues) to *Frank*. This new policy helps enable the journal to respond and publish with a more regular schedule. Checks or money orders should be made out to Frank Association."

Also Offers: Website includes full online version of the magazine and ordering information.

Advice: He says, "Send only what you feel is fresh, original, and provocative in either theme or form. Work of craft that also has political and social impact is encouraged."

◯ FREE LUNCH, P.O. Box 7647, Laguna Niguel CA 92607-7647, founded 1988, editor Ron Offen.

Magazine Needs: *Free Lunch* is a "poetry journal interested in publishing the whole spectrum of what is currently being produced by American poets. Occasionally offers a 'Reprise Series' in which an overlooked American poet is reexamined and presented. Among those who have been featured are Kenneth Patchen, Maxwell Bodenheim, Stephen Vincent Benet, Kenneth Fearing and Lola Ridge. Also features a 'Mentor Series,' in which an established poet introduces a new, unestablished poet. Mentors have included Maxine Kumin, Billy Collins, Lucille Clifton, Kenneth Koch, Carolyn Forché, Wanda Coleman, Lyn Lifshin and Robert Mezey. Especially interested in experimental work and work by unestablished poets. Hope to provide all serious poets living in the US with a free subscription. For details on free subscription send SASE. No restriction on form, length, subject matter, style, purpose. Don't want cutsie, syrupy, sentimental, preachy religious or aggressively 'uplifting' verse. No aversion to form, rhyme." Poets published include Neal Bowers, Thomas Carper, Jared Carter, Billy Collins, D. Nurkse, Marge Piercy and Lila Zeiger. As a sample the editor selected this poem, "Handful," by Cathy Song:

> Like scooping water by the handful/out of a lake,/you write a poem,/contain it, gaze/into the small/
> cup of your hand./While you admire/what feels cold and impossibly/clear, unlike anything/you've ever

held before,/you still did not get it./Into the momentary displacement/left by the dipping of your hand/ flows more.

FL, published 2-3 times a year, is 32-40 pgs., digest-sized, attractively printed and designed, saddle-stapled, featuring free verse that shows attention to craft with well-knowns and newcomers alongside each other. Press run is 1,200 for 1,000 free subscriptions and 200 paid of which 15 are libraries. Subscription: $12 ($15 foreign). Sample: $5 ($6 foreign).

How to Submit: "Submissions must be limited to three poems and are considered only between September 1 and May 31. Submissions sent at other times will be returned unread. Although a cover letter is not mandatory, I like them. I especially want to know if a poet is previously unpublished, as I like to work with new poets." Simultaneous submissions OK. Editor comments on rejections and tries to return submissions in 2 months. Occasionally publishes theme issues. Send SASE for guidelines. Pays 1 copy plus subscription.

Advice: The editor quotes Archibald MacLeish, " 'A poem should not mean/ But be.' I have become increasingly leery of the ego-centered lyric that revels in some past wrong, good-old-boy nostalgia, or unfocused ecstatic experience. Poetry is concerned primarily with language, rhythm and sound; fashions and trends are transitory and to be eschewed; perfecting one's work is often more important than publishing it."

⬜ 🎯 **FRISSON: DISCONCERTING VERSE; SKULL JOB PRODUCTIONS (Specialized: form/ style)**, 1012 Pleasant Dale Dr., Wilmington NC 28412-7617, founded 1995, editor Scott H. Urban.

Magazine Needs: *frisson: disconcerting verse*, published quarterly, "presents poetry that is disturbing, haunting, macabre, yet subtle—poetry that attempts to elicit 'frisson.' " They want "poetry that takes readers past the edge of comfort and into disturbing realms of experience. Poems should attempt to elicit the delicate sensation of 'frisson.' Any form or length, although shorter poems stand better chance." They do not want "light verse, romantic verse, inspirational verse, humorous verse." They have published poetry by Tom Piccirilli, Wendy Rathbone, Lee Ballentine and Steve Sneyd. As a sample the editor selected these lines from "Arabesque" by Richard Geyer:

> *death is sweeter than a kiss,/a blooming rose/or waves of bliss./there is no veil to be pierced,/just a lantern/and a wish.*

frisson is 16-20 pgs., digest-sized, photocopied, saddle-stapled with cardstock cover, original artwork on cover and in interior with limited ads. They receive about 150-200 poems a year, accept approximately 10-15%. Press run is 100 for 50 subscribers, with 15 distributed free to reviewers. Subscription: $8. Sample: $2. Make checks payable to Scott H. Urban.

How to Submit: Submit 4-10 poems at a time in standard poem ms format. "Shorter ones (50 lines or less) stand a better chance of acceptance." No previously published poems; simultaneous submissions OK. No e-mail submissions. Cover letter preferred. Time between acceptance and publication is 3-5 months. Poems chosen "solely according to editor's personal taste—how well each individual poem is applicable to the concept of 'disconcerting verse.' " Often comments on rejections. Send SASE for guidelines. Reports within a week. Sometimes sends prepublication galleys. Pays 2 copies or "short" subscription. Acquires first North American serial rights. There is no review column as such, although editor recommends material in the introductory 'Foreshadowings' article. Send books for review consideration.

Advice: The editor advises, "Open others' perceptions to that shadowy, half-glimpsed world that you as a poet are aware lurks just at the edge of each dream. . . ."

🌐 ✅ 🅾 **FROGMORE PAPERS; FROGMORE POETRY PRIZE**, 18 Nevill Rd., Lewes, East Sussex BN7 1PF England, founded 1983, poetry editor Jeremy Page.

Magazine Needs: *Frogmore Papers* is a biannual literary magazine with emphasis on new poetry and short stories. "Quality is generally the only criterion, although pressure of space means very long work (over 100 lines) is unlikely to be published." They have published poetry by Carole Satyamurti, John Mole, Linda France, Elizabeth Garrett, John Harvey and John Latham. As a sample the editor selected these lines by Tobias Hill:

> *if I stand just here, just right/and look up, I can see the rain/coming, and light on aeroplanes/high and certain, crossing time zones.*

The magazine is 42 pgs., saddle-stapled with matte card cover, photocopied in photoreduced typescript. They accept 3% of the poetry received. Their press run is 300 for 120 subscribers. Subscription: £7 ($20). Sample: £2 ($5). (US payments should be made in cash, not check.)

How to Submit: Submit 5-6 poems at a time. Considers simultaneous submissions. Editor rarely comments on rejections. Reports in 3-6 months. Pays 1 copy. Staff reviews books of poetry in 2-3 sentences, single book format. Send books for review consideration to Sophie Hannah, reviews editor, Flat 3, Dryden House, 16A Newton Road, Cambridge CB2 2AL England.

Also Offers: Sponsors the annual Frogmore Poetry Prize. Write for information.

Advice: The editor says, "My advice to people starting to write poetry would be: Read as many recognized modern poets as you can and don't be afraid to experiment."

🎯 **FROGPOND: INTERNATIONAL HAIKU JOURNAL; HAIKU SOCIETY OF AMERICA; HAIKU SOCIETY OF AMERICA AWARDS/CONTESTS (Specialized: form/style, translation)**, % Japan Society, 333 E. 47th St., New York NY 10017, e-mail redmoon@shentel.net, website http://www.octet.com/ ~hsa/, founded 1978, editor Jim Kacian (send submissions to him at P.O. Box 2461, Winchester VA 22604-1661).

Magazine Needs: *Frogpond* is the international journal of the Haiku Society of America and is published triannually. They want "contemporary English-language haiku, ranging from 1-4 lines or in a visual arrangement, focusing on a moment keenly perceived and crisply conveyed, using clear images and non-poetic language." They also accept "related forms: senryu, sequences, linked poems, and haibun. It welcomes translations of any of these forms." As a sample the editor selected these poems by John Martone and Carol Conti-Entin:

> thunder/the/sleeping//child's/cry/just//as/far/off/—John Martone//midnight sprinkle/leaf by leaf the timbre/of summer/—Carol Conti-Entin

Frogpond is 96 pgs., 5½×8½, perfect-bound, and has 40 pgs. of poetry. They receive about 20,000 submissions/ year and use about 600. *Frogpond* goes to 750 subscribers, of which 15 are libraries, as well as to over a dozen foreign countries. Sample back issues: $10 (biannual issues of 1992, 1993); $7 (issues of 1997, 1997); $5 (quarterly issues). Make checks payable to Haiku Society of America.

How to Submit: Submit 5-10 poems, with 5 poems per 8½×11 sheet, with SASE. (Send submissions to Jim Kacian at address mentioned above.) No single poems. No simultaneous submissions. E-mail submissions OK. Send SASE for submission guidelines and information on the HSA. Reports "usually" in 3 weeks or less. Pays $1/accepted item. Poetry reviews usually 1,000 words or less. Open to unsolicited reviews. "Authors are urged to send their books for review consideration."

Also Offers: The *Supplement* publishes longer essays, articles and reviews from quarterly meetings and other haiku gatherings. It is 96 pgs., 5½×8½, perfect-bound. The *HSA Newsletter*, edited by Charles Trumbull, appears 6 times a year and contains reports of the HSA Quarterly meetings, regional activities, news of upcoming events, results of contests, publications activities and other information. A "best of issue" prize is awarded for each issue through a gift from the Museum of Haiku Literature, located in Tokyo. The Society also sponsors The Harold G. Henderson Haiku Award Contest, the Gerald Brady Senryu Award Contest, The Bernard Lionel Einhand Memorial Renku Contest, The Nicholas A. Virgilio Memorial Haiku Competition for High School Students and the Merit Book Awards for outstanding books in the haiku field.

Advice: The editor says, "Submissions to *Frogpond* are accepted from both members and nonmembers, although familiarity with the magazine will aid writers in discovering what it publishes."

☑ **FUGUE**, Brink Hall, Room 200, University of Idaho, Moscow ID 83844-1102, website http://www.uidaho. edu/LS/Eng/Fugue, founded 1989.

Magazine Needs: *Fugue* is a biannual literary digest of the University of Idaho. They have "no limits" on type of poetry. "We're not interested in trite or quaint verse. Nothing self-indulgent or overly metaphoric to the point of being obscure." They have published poetry by Raymond Federman and Stephen Dann. As a sample the editor selected these lines from "The Burned Diary" by Sharon Olds:

> . . . And when the dawn came up/on the black water of the house, they found it/by the side of her bed,
> its pages scorched,/a layer of them arched, the corners curled up/like the tips of wings, a messenger/
> from the other world, the solitary heart.

The editor says *Fugue* is 80 pgs., digest-sized, perfect-bound. They receive approximately 400 poems/semester, use 5-10 poems/issue. Press run is 250 plus an electronic version on the World Wide Web. Sample: $5.

How to Submit: No previously published poems or simultaneous submissions. Submit with #10 SASE or submission will not be considered. No e-mail submissions. Reads submissions September 1 through May 1 only. Time between acceptance and publication is up to 1 year. "Submissions are reviewed by staff members and chosen by consensus with final approval by the editorial board. No major changes are made to a manuscript without author approval." Reports in 1-3 months. Pays at least 1 copy and honorarium. Buys first North American serial rights.

Also Offers: Website includes writer's guidelines, names of editors, poetry samples and cover art.

Advice: The editor says, "Proper manuscript format and submission etiquette are expected; submissions without proper SASE will not be read or held on file."

☑ ◯ ◎ **FULL MOON PRESS; THE DANCING ROSE (Specialized: anthology, love/romance/ erotica)**, P.O. Box 809, New London CT 06320, phone (860)448-1606, e-mail fulmnpress@aol.com. founded 1996, editor David D. Baker.

Magazine Needs: "*The Dancing Rose* is an annual publication, appearing in October, for all fans of romance, both in poetry and fiction. Our anthology is one you would purchase for a romantic friend, a bride, or avid romance reader." They want "poetry of 32 lines maximum; free form verse, but well written sonnets or rhymed verse OK. No pornography or overtly sentimental drivel. Poetry which conveys romantic or sensual passion. Our goal is to reintroduce the art of romantic love." They have published poetry by Tamara Lea Baker, Judith D. Harris and Justin A. Powers. As a sample the editor selected this untitled poem by Lenore Ambergis:

> In the sultry heat/our bodies play./He wants my happiness/Above all else./My God . . . he loves me.

The editor says *TDR* is 80-100 pgs., magazine-sized, perfect-bound with full color cover, and pre-Raphaelite art. They receive about 500 poems a year, accept approximately 10-15%. Press run is 500-1,000 (depending on sales). Single copy: $10 ($7 for included poets). Sample: $8.50. Make checks payable to Full Moon Press.

How to Submit: Submit up to 3 poems with $5 reading fee. Previously published poems OK; no simultaneous submissions. Cover letter undesired—"unless poet wishes to cite publication credits. Include e-mail address if poet would like to be informed by electronic mail." No e-mail submissions. "May e-mail for guidelines." Accepts submissions year round, usually read between January and June. Time between acceptance and publication "can be long, but we usually notify of acceptance in 3-6 months." Seldom comments on rejections. Send SASE for guidelines. Pays 1 copy. Acquires first or one-time rights.

Book/Chapbook Needs & How to Submit: "We usually publish one hardcover a year by invitation only and to a waiting audience. We offer a limited chapbook service to interested poets. They have published *The Erotic Soul* by Lenore Ambergis. For information about chapbook services, send cover letter, sample poems, and SASE."

Advice: The editor says, "Write what you love. Write with passion. Write what you would like to read. Submit, submit and submit some more."

N $○ THE FUNNY PAPER; F/J WRITERS SERVICE, P.O. Box 22557, Kansas City MO 64113-0557, e-mail felix22557@msn.com, website http://angelfire.com/biz/funnypaper, founded 1985, editor F.H. Fellhauer.

Magazine Needs: *The Funny Paper* appears 4 times a year "to provide readership, help and the opportunity to write for money to budding authors/poets/humanists of all ages." They want "light verse; space limited; humor always welcome. No tomes, heavy, dismal, trite work." As a sample we selected this poem, "Farewell" by Betty R. Cevoli:

> Roughly grasping at my fingers,/They pull at my tee-shirt/My arms scratched as I/clutch them//Bright,
> sunny orange with/dark hills and valleys/covering their skin.//Roadmaps—promising tender,/juicy, rich
> flavor—/The last canteloupes of summer.

The Funny Paper is 10 pgs., 8½ × 11, photocopied on colored paper and unbound, includes clip art and cartoons. They receive about 300 poems a year, accept approximately 15-20%. Single copy: $2. Make checks payable to F/J Writers Service.

How to Submit: Submit 1-2 poems at a time. Previously published poems and simultaneous submissions OK. E-mail and disk submissions OK. "We encourage beginners; handwritten poems OK. SASE a must or no return." Seldom comments on rejections. Publishes contest theme issues regularly. Send SASE for guidelines and upcoming themes or obtain via website. Pays $5-25/published poem. Acquires one-time rights.

Also Offers: Sponsors contests with $100 prize. Send SASE for guidelines or visit website. Website includes guidelines, jokes, descriptive page.

Advice: "When trying for $100 prize, take us seriously. The competition is fierce."

N ◑ FUTURE TENSE PRESS, P.O. Box 42416, Portland OR 97242, e-mail futuret@teleport.com, website http://www.teleport.com/~futuret, founded 1990, publisher/editor Kevin Sampsell.

Book/Chapbook Needs: Future Tense Press publishes "some poetry by unique poets, but mostly fiction that displays edge and style and craft." They publish 1 paperback and 4-6 chapbooks/year. The publisher wants "bold, brave, challenging work. I like funny, sexy, experimental and rule breaking writing. Mostly short fiction, some poetry. Nothing too political or sentimental or workshop dull. No Hallmark or rhyming verse either." They have published poetry by Brandon Freels, Richard Meltzer and Carl Miller Daniels. As a sample the publisher selected these lines from "Independence" by Verlena Orr:

> She trains like a prizefighter,/Drinks brewer's yeast and orange juice./Children follow her to breakfast,/
> try to please her. One calls her mom.

Books are usually 36 pgs., 4¼ × 5½, with either cardstock cover or "something unique."

How to Submit: Submit 4 poems or 2 stories at a time. Previously published poems and simultaneous submissions OK. Cover letter required. "E-mail query with bio if you like before submitting work." Time between acceptance and publication is 8 months. Often comments on rejections. Replies to queries in 2 weeks; to mss in 2 months. Pays 30 author's copies (out of a press run of about 200). "Other payment negotiable." 25% of books are author-subsidy published each year. "If an author can help with money it will probably be helpful in speeding up the publication." Order sample books or chapbooks by sending a $5 check to Kevin Sampsell.

N ◎ FUTURIFIC (Specialized: optimistic poems of the future), Futurific Inc., Foundation for Optimism, 305 Madison Ave., New York NY 10165, phone/fax (212)297-0502, e-mail keytonyc@aol.com, founded 1977, publisher Balint Szent-Miklosy.

Magazine Needs: *Futurific* is a monthly magazine published to "improve our understanding of the future and show our readers the direction of development. Optimistic only." The publisher says it is 32 pgs., 8½ × 11, glossy cover, includes b&w art. They receive about 12 poems a year, accept approximately 1%. Press run is 10,000. Single copy: $15; subscription: $70/year individual, $140/year institutional. Sample: $10.

How to Submit: Previously published poems and simultaneous submissions OK. Disk submissions OK (PC compatible disks in WordPerfect 5.0, 5.1 or 5.2.) Time between acceptance and publication is 1 month. Send SASE for guidelines or obtain via e-mail. Reports in 1 month. Pays 5 copies. Acquires one-time rights. Reviews

ALWAYS include a self-addressed, stamped envelope (SASE) when sending a ms or query to a publisher within your own country. When sending material to other countries, include a self-addressed envelope and International Reply Coupons (IRCs), available at many post offices.

other magazines in single and multi-book format. Open to unsolicited reviews. Send magazines for review consideration.

[N] G.W. REVIEW, Marvin Center Box 20, 800 21st St. NW, Washington DC 20052, fax (202)994-6102, e-mail jsw@gwu.edu or gwreview@gwu.edu, founded 1980, editor-in-chief Julie Will.

Magazine Needs: *G.W. Review* appears twice a year publishing unconventional, solid work and some translations. The magazine is published for distribution to the George Washington University community, the Washington D.C. metropolitan area and an increasing number of national subscribers. They have published poetry by Ann Caston, Jane Shore, Maxine Clair, E. Ethelbert Miller and Linda Pastan. As a sample the editor selected these lines from "On Muranowska Street" by Myra Sklarew:

> I have always loved particulars: the angels/bearing a martyr's palm, the way the hair/of the
> worshippers forms waves or/filaments, the flowers embroidered/on your sleeve.

It is 64 pgs., perfect-bound with b&w illustration or photo on the cover. They receive about 3,300 poems a year and accept 20-30. Their annual press run averages 4,000 copies. Subscription: $9/year, $16/2 years. Sample: $4.50.

How to Submit: Submit up to 5 poems at a time. They consider simultaneous submissions but not previously published poems. E-mail and fax submissions OK (send e-mail submissions to the jsw@gwu.edu address only). Cover letter, including list of enclosures, recent publications and phone number, required. The staff does not read manuscripts from May 15 through August 15. Editor sometimes comments on rejections when the staff likes the work but thinks it needs to be revised. Reports in 1-3 months. Pays 5 copies.

[globe] [copyright] GAIRM; GAIRM PUBLICATIONS (Specialized: ethnic, foreign language), 29 Waterloo St., Glasgow G2 6BZ Scotland, phone/fax (0141)221-1971, editor Derick Thomson, founded 1952.

Magazine Needs: *Gairm* is a quarterly that uses modern/cosmopolitan and traditional/folk verse in Scottish Gaelic only. It has published the work of all significant Scottish Gaelic poets, and much poetry translated from European languages. An anthology of such translations, *European Poetry in Gaelic*, is available for £7.50 or $15. A recent collection is Derick Thomson's *Meall Garbh/The Rugged Mountain*, £7.50 or $15. *Gairm* is 96 pgs., digest-sized, flat-spined with coated card cover. Circulation is 1,000. Sample: $3.50.

How to Submit: Submit 3-4 poems at a time, Gaelic only. Staff reviews books of poetry in 500-700 words, single format; 100 words, multi-book format. Occasionally invites reviews. Send books for review consideration. All of the publications of the press are in Scottish Gaelic. Catalog available.

[globe] [M] GALAXY PRESS, 71 Recreation St., Tweed Heads N.S.W., 2485 Australia, phone (07)5536-1997, founded 1978, editor Lance Banbury.

Book/Chapbook Needs: Galaxy Press publishes "high seriousness about the opportunities of culture at the latter end of the twentieth century, including personal or experimental responses." They publish 2-3 paperbacks/year. They want "poetry equally concerned with form and content. No formalistic verse concerned only with genre or blank verse." They have published work by Henry Baker and Sam Stone. As a sample the editor selected these lines from Stone's "The Church's one foundation":

> She waits the consummation/Of peace for evermore . . .

Books are usually 16-20 pgs., 15×21cm, offset/lithograph printed, glossy color card cover, includes art. Press run is 100-150.

How to Submit: Previously published poems and simultaneous submissions OK. Cover letter preferred. Often comments on rejections. Replies to queries in 2 weeks. Obtain sample books or chapbooks by "written request."

Advice: The editor says, "The current literary scene is receiving unprecedented help from global technology and other kinds of writing and therefore needs to be aware of its blessings and erudite in advancing within at the same time that it defends them."

[M] GARGOYLE MAGAZINE; PAYCOCK PRESS, % Atticus Books, 1508 U St. NW, Washington DC 20009, phone/fax (202)667-8148, e-mail atticus@radix.net, website http://www.atticusbooks.com, founded 1976, co-editors Richard Peabody, Lucinda Ebersole and Maja Prausnitz.

Magazine Needs: *Gargoyle Magazine* appears annually "to publish the best literary magazine we can. We generally run short one page poems. We like wit, imagery, killer lines. Not big on rhymed verse or language school." They have published poetry by Nicole Blackman, Wayne Koestenbaum and Jeremy Reed. As a sample the editors selected these lines from "Abortion Elegy: What I Know About Her" by Rose Solari:

> There are times I can see her face as if/she were here, as if she had lived—hair darker/than yours or
> mine, your cheeks, my mouth./She stands over my bed as she did almost/a full year before we knew of
> her, or runs/through the living room, both hands spread,/chasing a shadow.

The editors say *Gargoyle* is 365 pgs., 6×9, offset printed and perfect-bound, color cover, includes photos, artwork and ads. Accept approximately 10% of the poems received each year. Press run is 3,000. Subscription: $20 for 2; $25 to institutions. Sample: $10. Make checks payable to Atticus Books. "We have a London editor and international distribution through Bernhard DeBier, Airlift Book Co. and Perigo Distribution."

How to Submit: Submit 5 poems at a time. Simultaneous submissions OK. E-mail and disk submissions OK in Microsoft Word or WordPerfect format. Reads submissions March through Labor Day only. Time between acceptance and publication is 4-5 months. Poems are circulated to an editorial board. "The three editors make some concessions but generally concur." Often comments on rejections. Reports in 2 months. Always sends prepublication galleys. Pays 1 copy and ½ off additional copies. Acquires first rights

Book/Chapbook Needs & How to Submit: Paycock Press has published 9-10 books since 1976. However, they are not currently seeking mss.

GARNET, P.O. Box 655, Hampden-Sydney VA 23943, phone (804)223-6462, e-mail somervillen@hsc. edu, website http://www.hsc.edu, founded 1937, editor Nate Somerville.

Magazine Needs: *Garnet* is a semiannual journal of literature and the creative arts published by Hampden-Sydney College. "We like to see most anything—forms, free verse, light verse. Poems must, of course, be of the highest quality. No trash. No erotica, juvenile, religious or romantic work." They have published poetry by Craig Challender, Jaroslav Seifert, Grace Simpson and Louis Simpson. As a sample the editor selected these lines from "Who Knows" by Richard Stern:

> *Such the enzymes that decayed/the sugars of life and laid/him youthful in the ground, amazed, decayed.*

Garnet is 80-100 pgs., 6×9, professionally printed, perfect-bound with glossy card cover, photography and art included. They receive about 500 poems a year, accept approximately 5-10%. Press run is 1,000 for 400 subscribers of which 20 are libraries, 100-200 shelf sales; about 500 distributed free to students, professors, alumni and contributors. Single copy: $3.95; subscription: $6. Sample: $5.

How to Submit: Submit no more than 3 poems at a time, "two page limit to any poetry." No previously published poems; simultaneous submissions OK. Cover letter required. "Include name, address and phone number on ms; include 50-word bio; electronic submissions accepted—contact editor for details." Time between acceptance and publication is 6-8 months. Poems are circulated to an editorial board. Often comments on rejections. Send SASE for guidelines and upcoming themes or request via e-mail. Reports in 6-8 weeks. Sometimes sends prepublication galleys. Pays 1 copy. Acquires one-time rights. Reviews books or chapbooks in 1,000-2,000 words, single book format. Open to unsolicited reviews. Poets may also send books for review consideration.

Also Offers: Sponsors several contests awarding a total of $1,000. All submissions are automatically eligible.

Advice: The editor says, "We have published both beginners and Pulitzer Prize recipients. We're not looking for names; we're looking for outstanding poetry. Show us you care for your work."

A GATHERING OF THE TRIBES; FLY BY NIGHT PRESS, P.O. Box 20693, New York NY 10009, phone (212)674-3778, e-mail tribes@interport.net, website http://www.tribes.org, founded 1991, managing editor Steve Cannon.

Magazine Needs: *A Gathering of the Tribes*, published biannually, "showcases established and emerging poets, writers, artists and forums." They want poetry 30 lines maximum. They do not want "third-rate poetry." They have published poetry by Jayne Cortez, Nikki Giovanni, Victor Cruz and Kimiko Hahn. The editor says *A Gathering of the Tribes* is 89 pgs., 8×10, glossy cover, with ads in back pages. They receive about 600 poems a year, accept approximately 5%. Press run is 2,000 for 100 subscribers of which 10 are libraries, 100 shelf sales; 200 distributed free. Subscription: $30. Sample: $15.

How to Submit: Submit 3 poems at a time. Previously published poems and simultaneous submissions OK. Cover letter preferred. No e-mail submissions. Time between acceptance and publication is 3 months. Always comments on rejections. Send SASE for guidelines. Reports immediately. Always sends prepublication galleys. Pays 1 copy. Staff reviews books of poetry or other magazines. Send books for review consideration.

Book/Chapbook Needs & How to Submit: Fly By Night Press is a subsidy press publishing "excellence in poetry from a diverse perspective (topics of the author's choosing)." Books are usually 70 pgs., 5½×7½. Replies to queries in 3 months. Pays 12-15% royalties and 500 author's copies (out of a press run of 1,000). Offers subsidy arrangements: Fly By Night Press puts up 50% fee, author puts up 50% and sells their half. Obtain sample books by writing to the above address.

Also Offers: Sponsors annual poetry contest. Deadline is in April. Send up to 3 poems, no poem to exceed 30 lines with a $10 entry fee. 1st Place prize of $500 and publication.

Advice: The editor says, "We believe the United States should celebrate its diversity from a global perspective. *Tribes* tries to achieve the same through excellence in the arts."

GAZELLE PUBLICATIONS, 11650 Red Bud Trail, Berrien Springs MI 49106, phone (616)471-4717 or (800)650-5076 (orders only), e-mail kivu@juno.com, website http://www.hoofprint.com, founded 1976, editor Ted Wade, is a publisher for home schools and compatible markets including books of verse for children but is not currently considering unsolicited manuscripts. Obtain guidelines via e-mail.

GECKO, P.O. Box 25021, Lexington KY 40524, phone (606)271-4028, founded 1998, editor Rebecca Lu Kiernan.

Magazine Needs: Published annually, *Gecko* "is an ambitious literary journal desirous of showcasing exciting new talent as well as established writers. A featured writer is chosen for each issue. All writers submitting will be treated with respect! Give me vivid imagery; make me feel like I am in the work, not outside looking in. Make me laugh, cry, pound my fists. Say it in a fresh, new way that no one else could have expressed. Knock me out!" The editor does not wish to see "anything degrading to women. Also no haiku, no rhyme and please, God, no limerick! Please don't put a gecko in your work just for me." They have published poetry by Bright

Majikay, Grant Logan Jambors, Chaney Keblusek and Hiro Yamauchi. As a sample the editor selected these lines from her poem "Intrepid Vagina":

> *Does my desire unnerve you?/Unblinking, lips parted/my breath/condensating in your ear/down on my haunches/like a jaguar/muscled for the strike./Are you happier to hunt me/over a half scrubbed toilet/in yellow gloves,/pinned hair/woefully accommodating you/like wet, underfoot grass?*

Gecko is 32-40 pgs., 5½×8½, professionally printed and flat-spined, color card cover with art/graphics. They receive about 500 poems a year, accept under 10%. Press run is 200 for 120 subscribers; 80 distributed free to writers, libraries, media, colleges.
How to Submit: Submit 3-5 poems at a time. Line length for poetry is 12 minimum, 42 maximum. No previously published poems; simultaneous submissions OK. Cover letter required. "Writers must enclose SASE." Reads submissions year-round, slow during summer months. Time between acceptance and publication is 3-10 months. Seldom comments on rejections. Reports in 2-16 weeks. Pays 1 copy. Acquires first North American serial rights.
Advice: The editor says, "I choose the best of the best. If I must reject, don't give up until you have been rejected by every appropriate listing in *Poet's Market*. If you have any talent, I promise you someone will discover it."

GENERATOR; GENERATOR PRESS, 3503 Virginia Ave., Cleveland OH 44109, phone (216)351-9406, founded 1987, editor John Byrum.
Magazine Needs: *Generator* is an annual magazine "devoted to the presentation of all types of experimental poetry, focusing on language poetry and 'concrete' or visual poetic modes."
Book/Chapbook Needs: Generator Press also publishes the Generator Press chapbook series. Approximately 1 new title/year.
How to Submit: They are currently not accepting unsolicited manuscripts for either the magazine or chapbook publication.

GEORGE & MERTIE'S PLACE: ROOMS WITH A VIEW, P.O. Box 10335, Spokane WA 99209-1335, phone (509)325-3738, founded 1995, editors George Thomas and Mertie Duncan.
Magazine Needs: Appearing monthly except for January, *GMP* is "a Spokane home for wayward literature, a monthly journal of opinion and imagination or any realm between. We are open to any form but our limited format prohibits long poetry." They have published poetry by Simon Perchik and Eric Howard. As a sample the editors selected these lines from "Why I Don't Vote" by Geoff Peterson:

> *Some columnist said it best./He said remember the shiny boys and girls/who courted your vote/to be president/when you were horny and failing math/and too crazy to drive a car? . . .*

GMP is a 4- to 8-page, 8½×11, "micromagazine," printed (unbound) on colored paper with b&w graphics. In addition to poetry it may contain essays, short short stories, letters, opinions and "tidbits with a twist." Press run is 100 for 40 subscribers, 20 shelf sales. Subscription: $15/year. Sample: $2.
How to Submit: Submit 3-5 poems at a time. No previously published poems or simultaneous submissions. Cover letter preferred, "but not a long list of credits; we're looking for historical comments to personalize your submission." Time between acceptance and publication is 3 months. Comments on rejections. Reports in 1-2 months. Pays 1¢/word ($2 minimum) and 1 copy. A $25 "The Dick Diver Best of Issue" prize is awarded each month; poetry, fiction and essays compete.
Advice: They say, "Be always drunken, with wine, with poetry or with virtue—as you will—but be always drunken."

GEORGETOWN REVIEW, P.O. Box 6309, Southern Station, Hattiesburg MS 39406-6309, website http://www.georgetownreview.com, founded 1992, poetry editor Marvyn Petrucci.
Magazine Needs: *GR* is a biannual literary journal publishing fiction and poetry in separate print and online editions—no criticism or reviews. They want "honest, quality work; not interested in tricks." They have published poetry by Fred Chappell, John Tagliabue, Vivian Shipley, Elton Glaser, X.J. Kennedy, Richard Garcia, Lyn Lifshin and Alan Feldman. *GR* is 200-250 pgs., 5½×8½, perfect-bound, with heavy stock cover with art. They receive about 1,000 mss a year, "take maybe 10%." Press run is 1,000. Subscription: $15/year. Sample: $8.
How to Submit: Submit no more than 5 poems at a time, name and address on each page. No previously published poems; simultaneous submissions OK. No electronic submissions for print issue. Reads submissions September 1 through May 1 only. Poems are read by at least 3 readers. Sometimes comments on rejections. Reports in 2-4 months. Always sends prepublication galleys. Pays 2 copies. Acquires all rights. Returns rights provided "our name is mentioned in any reprint."
Also Offers: Sponsors annual poetry contest. $500 1st Prize; runners-up receive publication and subscription. Entry fee: $5 for first poem, $2 each additional poem. Deadline: October 1. Winner and runners-up announced in fall issue. Website includes special online edition with its own contest and submission guidelines (poetry for the online edition must be submitted electronically to poetry@georgetownreview.com—no paper submissions).

THE GEORGIA REVIEW, The University of Georgia, Athens GA 30602-9009, phone (706)542-3481, website http://www.uga.edu/garev, founded 1947, editor Stanley W. Lindberg, associate editor Stephen Corey, assistant editor Janet Wondra.

Magazine Needs: *Georgia Review* appears quarterly. "We seek the very best work we can find, whether by Nobel laureates and Pulitzer Prize-winners or by little-known (or even previously unpublished) writers. All manuscripts receive serious, careful attention." They have published poetry by Rita Dove, Stephen Dunn, Philip Levine and Pattiann Rogers. "We have featured first-ever publications by many new voices over the years, but encourage all potential contributors to become familiar with past offerings before submitting." As a sample the editor selected these lines from "Waste" by Kay Ryan:

> Not even waste/is inviolate./The day misspent/the love misplaced/has inside it/the seed of redemption./
> Nothing is exempt/from resurrection

GR is 208 pgs., 7 × 10, professionally printed, flat-spined with glossy card cover. They use 60-70 poems a year, less than one-half of one percent of those received. Circulation is 6,000. Subscription: $18/year. Sample: $6.
How to Submit: Submit 3-5 poems at a time. No simultaneous submissions. Rarely uses translations. No submissions accepted during June, July and August. Publishes theme issues occasionally. Reports in 2-3 months. Always sends prepublication galleys. Pays $3/line, 1-year subscription and a copy of issue in which work appears. Buys first North American serial rights. Reviews books of poetry. "Our poetry reviews range from 500-word 'Book Briefs' on single volumes to 5,000-word essay reviews on multiple volumes."
Also Offers: Website includes writer's guidelines, names of the *GR* staff, subscription and advertising information, and samples of work published in *The Review*.
Advice: The editor says, "Needless to say, competition is extremely tough. All styles and forms are welcome, but response times can be slow during peak periods in the fall and late spring."

◑ ◎ GERBIL: A QUEER CULTURE ZINE; GERBIL PRESS (Specialized: gay/lesbian/bisexual), P.O. Box 10692, Rochester NY 14610, phone (716)262-3966, e-mail gerbilzine@aol.com, website http://www.mu lticom.org/gerbil/gerbil.htm, founded 1994, editors Tony Leuzzi and Brad Pease.
Magazine Needs: *Gerbil* is a quarterly designed to provide "an open forum for lesbian/gay-identified writers and artists to express themselves and their work." They seek poetry with gay/lesbian content but are not limited to that. They are "open to all forms as long as the poetic voice is honest and clear. We look for lively, personal material of literary merit. No angst, pointless experimentation or abstraction." They have published poetry by Dave Trinidad, Beth Bailey, Deb Owen, Glenn Sheldon and Ken Pobo. As a sample the editors selected these lines from "French Lessons" by Darrel Borque:

> he will feel the world plumb/to his toes/he will feel it course through/the top of his head/scramble back
> inside him/go straight for the trapdoor/at the back of his throat

Gerbil is 28 pgs., about 7½ × 9½, offset and saddle-stitched with coated paper cover and b&w photos and graphics and lots of spot color inside. They receive about 750 poems a year, accept about 20. Press run is 3,000 for 100 subscribers, 1,000 shelf sales. Subscription: $10/4 issues. Sample: $3.
How to Submit: Submit 3-5 poems at a time. No previously published poems. "Friendly" cover letter preferred. Disk submissions (for Mac) welcome. E-mail submissions OK. Time between acceptance and publication is up to 1 year. Always comments on rejections. Publishes theme issues occasionally. Reports usually in 3-5 months. Pays 2 copies. Acquires first rights. Reviews books of poetry and other magazines. Open to unsolicited reviews. Poets may also send books for review consideration.
Also Offers: Occasionally sponsors poetry contests; watch website or zine for details. Gerbil Press also occasionally publishes chapbooks on a cooperative basis. They usually work with poets who first published in the magazine, and their publishing arrangements vary based on the writer and project.
Advice: As for the zine, they say, "If you're a beginning writer, don't be afraid to submit work! We publish a wide range of work of literary merit."

🅽 ◯ ◑ ◎ GERTRUDE: A JOURNAL OF VOICE & VISION (Specialized: gay/lesbian/bisexual/ transgender), P.O. Box 270814, Fort Collins CO 80527-0814, founded 1998, founding editor Eric Delehoy, art editor Ronda Stone.
Magazine Needs: "Published two times a year, *Gertrude* is a literary journal showcasing the voices and visions of the gay, lesbian, bisexual, transgendered and straight-supportive community. Provides a positive, nonpornographic forum free of ads. Open to all forms and subjects, we'd like to see positive poetry." They do not want "bitter ex-love poetry, five-minute poetry or Hallmark verse; steer clear of work that portrays gays as victims." They have published poetry by Deanna Kern Ludwin, Miriam R. Sachs Martin and Jennifer Dick. As a sample the editor selected these lines from "PMS" by Elisabeth Tyler James:

> Last month/in my hormonal rage/I sold my dog and ate/the paint off the walls

The editor says *Gertrude* is 36-48 pgs., digest-sized, professionally printed and saddle-stitched with glossy cardstock cover, includes b&w art/photography. They receive about 160 poems a year, accept 8-10%. Press run is 500 for about 100 subscribers, 250 shelf sales; 50 distributed free to gay/lesbian/bisexual/transgender organizations. Single copy: $4.95; subscription: $8/year. Sample: $4.95 plus $1.50 postage.
How to Submit: Submit 3-5 poems at a time. Previously published poems OK; no simultaneous submissions. Cover letter preferred. Include previous publication credits, short bio and SASE. Time between acceptance and publication is 1-2 months. Poems are circulated to an editorial board. "Three editors apply initial rating system to determine final selections. Final selections are re-read by all editors." Seldom comments on rejections. Publishes theme issues occasionally. Send SASE for guidelines. Reports in 2-3 months. Pays 1 copy plus discount on additional copies. All rights revert to authors upon publication.

Also Offers: Sponsors Editors' Choice Awards in poetry, fiction and art. They also invite contributors to an annual contributors' reading.

Advice: The editors say, "Write for yourself, not for publication. In this you find your voice and produce your best."

■ $◨ THE GETTYSBURG REVIEW, Gettysburg College, Gettysburg PA 17325, phone (717)337-6770, founded 1988, editor Peter Stitt.

● Work appearing in *The Gettysburg Review* has been included in *The Best American Poetry* (1993, 1994, 1995, 1997 and 1998) and *Pushcart Prize* anthologies. As for the editor, Peter Stitt won the first PEN/Nora Magid Award for Editorial Excellence.

Magazine Needs: *TGR* is a multidisciplinary literary quarterly considering "well-written poems of all kinds." They have published poetry by Rita Dove, Donald Hall, Susan Ludvigson, Pattiann Rogers, Charles Wright and Paul Zimmer. As a sample the editor selected these lines by Thomas Rabbitt:

> My father nods again and does not speak./This is Boston. He is thirty-six. The war is over./The good
> times have begun. And yet, overhead,/Floating in the oaks above Hyde Park, there is/This blimp, round
> as a breast, gray as death,/Slow as a mortgage, going nowhere overhead.

They accept 1-2% of submissions received. Press run is 4,500 for 2,700 subscriptions. Sample: $7.

How to Submit: Submit 3-5 poems at a time, with SASE. No previously published poems or simultaneous submissions. Cover letter preferred. Reads submissions September through May only. Publishes theme issues occasionally. Response times can be slow during heavy submission periods, especially in the late fall. Pays 1 copy plus subscription plus $2/line. Essay-reviews are featured in each issue. Open to unsolicited essay-reviews. Poets may also send books for review consideration.

◧ GINGER HILL, c/o English Dept., Room 314, Spotts World Cultures Building, Slippery Rock University, Slippery Rock PA 16057, founded 1963.

Magazine Needs: *Ginger Hill* is an annual literary magazine using "academic poetry, with preference for excellent free verse, but all forms considered. No greeting card verse, no sentimentality, no self-serving or didactic verse." They have published poetry by Carla Uzelac, Bill Cantry, Lyn Lifshin and Mary Winters. It is digest-sized, "varies in format and layout every year," perfect-bound, with 2,000 distributed free.

How to Submit: Submit 3 poems at a time in duplicate. "One copy should have your name and address; leave the second copy blank for blind jurying." Line length for poetry is 57 maximum. No previously published poems. Submissions must be postmarked on or before December 1 of each year. Send SASE for guidelines. Pays 1 copy.

Advice: They say, "We choose about 5-10% of all submissions. Excellence is stressed. Be sure that your form is in keeping with the general principles of prosody, and if you must have regular rhyme, fit this to the subject matter, and not the subject matter to the type of form that you choose. Good poetry is not forced."

$◯ ◪ ◎ GLB PUBLISHERS (Specialized: gay/lesbian/bisexual), P.O. Box 78212, San Francisco CA 94107-8212, phone (415)621-8307, e-mail glbpubs@aol.com, website http://www.glbpubs.com, founded 1990, associate editor John Hanley.

Book/Chapbook Needs: "We are a cooperative publisher founded for gay, lesbian and bisexual writers. Authors share cost of printing and promotion but have much control over cover design, typefaces, general appearance." They publish 2-4 paperbacks and 1-2 hardbacks/year. They want "book-length collections from gay, lesbian or bisexual writers. Nothing antagonistic to gay, lesbian or bisexual life-styles." They have published poetry by Robert Peters, Paul Genega, Thomas Cashet and Winthrop Smith.

How to Submit: Request author guidelines before submission. E-mail submissions OK—"WordPerfect or PDF (format is important)." Previously published poems OK; no simultaneous submissions. Cover letter required. "Author should explain intention for poems and expectations for sales of books." Often comments on rejections. Replies to queries in 10 days, to mss in 1 month. Always sends prepublication galleys. Pays 15-25% royalties and 20 author's copies. Check bookstores for samples.

Also Offers: Website includes poetry excerpts, the Authors Showcase (an online publication for 6-week periods for a fee) and author bios.

◯ ◎ A GLEEFUL PRESS!; IMPS IN THE INKWELL (Specialized: themes), P.O. Box 6724, Minneapolis MN 55406, e-mail jewel@gleeful.com, website http://www.gleeful.com/press (a gleeful press!) http://www.gleeful.com/hellespont (*imps in the inkwell*), a gleeful press! founded 1995, *imps* founded 1997, publisher/editrix jewel.

Magazine Needs: *imps in the inkwell* is a quarterly zine of "poetry, fiction, friction, comix and miscellaneous oddities. We look for poetry with sass, verve and fire; pieces that bite back!" *imps* is 60-80 pgs., 5½×8½, photocopied and stapled. Press run is approximately 200. Single copy: $2. Make checks payable to J. Brown-Micko.

How to Submit: Previously published poems and simultaneous submissions OK. Cover letter preferred. E-mail submissions OK. Seldom comments on rejections. Publishes theme issues. Obtain guidelines and upcoming themes via e-mail, website or SASE. Reports "within 3 months, often sooner." Pays 2 copies.

Book/Chapbook Needs & How to Submit: a gleeful press! publishes "unique, limited-run hardbound books of poetry and fiction." However, they do not accept unsolicited manuscripts.

☑ **DAVID R. GODINE, PUBLISHER**, 9 Hamilton Place, Boston MA 02108, website http://www.godine.c om. They say, "Our poetry program is completely filled through 2000, and we do not accept any unsolicited materials."

☑ $☐ ◎ **GOLDEN ISIS MAGAZINE; GOLDEN ISIS PRESS; PAGAN POETS SOCIETY (Specialized: pagan/wiccan)**, P.O. Box 4263, Chatsworth CA 91313, founded 1980, editor Gerina Dunwich.
Magazine Needs: "*Golden Isis* is a biannual New Age/Neo-Pagan journal of Goddess-oriented poetry, Pagan art, Wiccan news and announcements, reviews, networking services, witchy recipes, ritual outlines and ads. Positive magick for solitaries and covens of all traditions, and a literary forum in which individuals from around the world can share poetic visions and their special love for the Goddess and Horned God. Occult, Egyptian, mystical haiku and magickal chants are published. We are also interested in New Age spiritual poetry and astrological verses. All styles considered; under 60 lines preferred. We do not want to see pornographic, Satanic, sexist or racist material." They have published poetry by Lee Prosser, Reed Dunwich, Sheryl J. Miller and Anne Wilson. As a sample the editor selected these lines from "Transformation (A Circle Prayer)" by Gerina Dunwich:
> Learn, learn, the magick of the Earth,/the spiral dance of life,/the cauldron of re-birth./Yearn, yearn,
> for the old forgotten days;/return, return to our ancient Pagan ways.
The newsletter is about 10 pgs., desktop published. International circulation is 5,000. Single copy: $5; subscription: $10/year.
How to Submit: Submit 1 poem/page, typed single-spaced, name and address on upper left corner and the number of lines on upper right corner. No limit on number of poems submitted. Previously published poems and simultaneous submissions OK. Occasionally comments on rejected material. Reports within 2-3 weeks. Pays $10 per poem to current subscribers and members of the Pagan Poets Society, $5 per poem to all others. All rights revert to author upon publication. Reviews books of poetry, "length varies." Open to unsolicited reviews. Poets may also send books for review consideration.
Book/Chapbook Needs & How to Submit: Golden Isis Press currently accepts mss for chapbook publication. Send complete ms and $5 reading fee. "Make checks payable to Golden Isis. We offer a small advance, ten free copies of the published work, and 10% royalty on every copy sold for as long as the book is in print."
Also Offers: "Golden Isis is affiliated with the Pagan Poets Society—a distinguished Literary Circle for both publishers and writers of Pagan poetry. The Society sponsors an annual poetry contest offering cash prizes (determined by amount of entry fees received) and autographed books by Miss Dunwich. For more information and registration form, send SASE."

▧ ⊘ ◎ **GOOSE LANE EDITIONS (Specialized: regional)**, 469 King St., Fredericton, New Brunswick E3B 1E5 Canada, phone (506)450-4251, acquisitions editor L. Boone, founded 1956.
Book/Chapbook Needs: Goose Lane is a small press publishing Canadian fiction, poetry and literary history. Writers should be advised that Goose Lane considers mss by Canadian poets only. They receive approximately 400 mss/year, publish 10-15 books yearly, 2 of these being poetry collections. Writers published include Douglas Lochhead and Gary Geddes.
How to Submit: They are not currently reading submissions. "Call to inquire whether we are reading submissions." Always sends prepublication galleys. Authors may receive royalty of up to 10% of retail sale price on all copies sold. Copies available to author at 40% discount.

$◎ **GOSPEL PUBLISHING HOUSE; LIVE; TAKE FIVE; DISCOVERY TRAILS (Specialized: religious, children/teens)**, The General Council of the Assemblies of God, 1445 Boonville Ave., Springfield MO 65802-1894, phone (417)831-8000 ext. 4290, fax (417)862-7566.
Magazine Needs & How to Submit: Gospel Publishing House produces the Spirit of Praise Bulletin Series. Poems accepted for back cover of bulletins. For more information, call or write to Promotions. *Live* is a weekly for adults in Assemblies of God Sunday schools, circulation 125,000. Traditional free and blank verse, 12-20 lines. "Please do not send more than three poems at one time." Submit seasonal material 1 year in advance; do not mention Santa Claus, Halloween or Easter bunnies. Sample copy and writer's guidelines for 7×10 SAE and 2 first-class stamps. Pays $35 or $65/poem on acceptance. Buys first and/or second rights. *Take Five* is a youth devotional accepting poetry written by teens. Poetry should be typed, double-spaced, and must include the teen's name, complete address, church and age. Pays $15 upon acceptance. *Discovery Trails* (formerly *Junior Trails*) is a weekly tabloid covering religious fiction and biographical, historical and scientific articles with a spiritual emphasis for boys and girls ages 10-11, circulation 38,000. Buys 10-15 poems/year. Free verse and light verse. Submit seasonal/holiday material 15 months in advance. Simultaneous and previously published submissions OK. Sample copy and writer's guidelines for #10 SASE. Reports in 2-4 weeks. Pays $5-10 on acceptance. Buys first and/or second rights.
Advice: "We like poems showing contemporary children positively facing today's world. For all our publications, submit not more than one to two poems at a time."

☐ ⊘ ◎ **GOTTA WRITE NETWORK LITMAG; MAREN PUBLICATIONS (Specialized)**, 515 E. Thacker, Hoffman Estates IL 60194, phone/fax (847)882-8054 (nights only), e-mail netera@aol.com, founded 1988, editor/publisher Denise Fleischer.
Magazine Needs: GWN features "contemporary poetry, articles, short stories and market listings. *GWN* now

spans 40 states, Canada, England and Japan. Half of the magazine is devoted to science fiction and fantasy in a section called 'Sci-Fi Galleria.' A short checklist of what I look for in all poems and stories would be: drawing the reader into the protagonist's life from the beginning; presenting a poem's message through powerful imagery and sensory details; and language that is fresh and dynamic. I prefer free verse. Would also like to receive experimental, multicultural, feminist, humor, contemporary and translations. The poetry I publish expresses today's society with a tell-it-like-it-is voice. Contributors dive into subjects where others turn away. They speak of rape, suicide, the lives of Native Americans, the Holocaust and the sign of the times." *Gotta Write* has published poetry by Debbi McIntyre, Priscilla Wichrowski, Tim DiVita and Mariana Berner. As a sample the editor has selected the poem "I am the daughter of Crazy Horse and Black Buffalo Woman" by Raven:

> *I came from that mad morning/dash across Yellowstone Country,/I came from the loins of that strange/*
> *man sprang from the belly of that/woman "warm and good as May/earth," I am the love that blood/*
> *could not kill the love that no/bullets could end . . .*

The semiannual is 48-76 pgs., magazine-sized, desktop-published, saddle-stapled. "*Gotta Write Network* subscribers receive more than a magazine. In subscribing, they become part of a support group of both beginners and established poets. Readers are from all walks of life. I'm striving to give beginners a positive starting point (as well as promote the work of established writers and editors) and to encourage them to venture beyond rejection slips and writer's block. Publication can be a reality if you have determination and talent. There are over a thousand U.S. litmags waiting for submissions. So take your manuscripts out of your desk and submit them today!" Subscription: $12.75. Sample: $5.

How to Submit: Submit up to 5 poems at a time. Name and address on each page. No previously published poems or simultaneous submissions. Fax and e-mail submissions OK (no attachments). Include a cover letter and SASE. "No SASE, no response!" Accepts poetry submissions via fax "at night" or via e-mail "any hour." Reports in 2-4 months. Sometimes sends prepublication galleys. Pays 1 copy, offers second copy at a discount. Acquires first North American serial rights. Pays $10 for assigned by-mail interviews with established big press authors and small press editors.

Advice: The editor says, "Write the way you feel the words. Don't let others mold you into another poet's style. Poetry is about personal imagery that needs to be shared with others."

✔ ◯ ◪ **GRAFFITI RAG; GRAFFITI RAG POETRY AWARD; HELEN YOUNG/LINDA ASHEAR PRIZE**, 422 E. 72nd St., #36A, New York NY 10021, phone (212)737-8846, e-mail hayan.charara@worldnet.att. net, founded 1995, editor Hayan Charara, co-editor Erik Fahren Kopf, west coast editor Bayla Winters.

Magazine Needs: *Graffiti Rag*, published annually, is a "poetry journal that seeks to publish work of well-known and gifted unknown poets on the urban experience." They want "poetry of the highest quality that brings a unique perspective on the shifting and limitless themes of urban life—economic, ethnic, intellectual, political, sexual." They have published poetry by Khaled Mattawa, Catherine Bowman, Wang Ping, Jim Daniels and Chase Twichell. As a sample the editor selected these lines from "A Last Look Back" by Chase Twichell:

> *So strange, to inhabit a space/and then leave it vacant, standing open.//Each change in me is a stone*
> *step/beneath the blur of snow./In spring the sharp edges cut through.//When I look back, I see my*
> *former selves,/numerous as the trees.*

Graffiti Rag is approximately 96 pgs., 6×9, perfect-bound, professionally printed with a colored matte cover. They receive about 900-1,500 poems a year, accept less than 10%. Press run is 750, 400 shelf sales. Single copy: $9.95; subscription: $9.95 plus $1.50 p&h. Sample issue: $7.95 plus $1.50 p&h.

How to Submit: Submit 3-5 poems at a time. No previously published poems or simultaneous submissions. Cover letter preferred. Time between acceptance and publication varies. Poems are circulated to an editorial board. "Guest editor (usually poets) assist in editorial process. Final decisions are made by main editor, Charara." Often comments on rejections. Send SASE for guidelines. Reports in 2-16 weeks. Pays 1 copy. Acquires first North American serial or one-time rights.

Also Offers: Sponsors the annual Graffiti Rag Poetry Award. Submit 3-5 unpublished poems from February 1 through June 30. Enclose reading fee of $10 (check or money order) and a SASE. Winning poet is featured in the anthology and receives cash award of $1,000. Also sponsors the Helen Young/Linda Ashear Prize for poets between the ages 14-19. No entry fee. Submit 3-5 poems with SASE. 1st Prize: $250 plus publication; 2nd Prize: $150 plus publication; and 3rd Prize: $100 plus publication.

Advice: The editor says, "Read literary journals to better gauge their 'likes.' "

🍁 ◪ **GRAFFITO, THE POETRY POSTER**, Dept. of English, Dept. PM, University of Ottawa, Ottawa, Ontario K1N 6N5 Canada, fax (613)738-1929, e-mail graffito@uottawa.ca, website http://www.webapps.com/ graffito, founded 1994, managing editor b stephen harding.

Magazine Needs: *graffito* is a monthly poster/zine. They want any style of poetry, maximum 32 lines. They have published poetry by R.M. Vaughan, George Elliot Clark, Michael Dennis, John B. Lee and Susan McMaster. *graffito* is an 11×17 sheet of colored paper folded in half to allow for a front cover and back cover containing reviews. Press run is 250; half distributed free within the local area of Ottawa. Subscription: $12 in Canada, $20 in US. Sample: $1. Make checks payable to b stephen harding.

How to Submit: Submit 5-8 poems at a time. Previously published poems OK "only in special cases;" no simultaneous submissions. Cover letter preferred. Reads submissions the 15th of every month. Time between acceptance and publication is 3-4 months. "We have a guest editor who is responsible for the content of their issues. However, final approval rests with the managing editor." Often comments on rejections. Send SASE (or SAE and IRC) for guidelines or obtain via website. Reports in 3-4 months. Pays 3 copies. "We review books and chapbooks with preference for chapbooks." Poets may also send books for review consideration.

GRAIN; SHORT GRAIN CONTEST, Box 1154, Regina, Saskatchewan S4P 3B4 Canada, phone (306)244-2828, fax (306)244-0255, e-mail grain.mag@sk.sympatico.ca, website http://www.skwriter.com, founded 1973, editor Elizabeth Philips, poetry editor Séan Virgo.
Magazine Needs: "*Grain*, a literary quarterly, strives for artistic excellence and seeks poetry that is well-crafted, imaginatively stimulating, distinctly original." *Grain* is 128-144 pgs., digest-sized, professionally printed. Press run is 1,500 for 1,100 subscribers of which 100 are libraries. They receive about 1,200 submissions of poetry/year, use 80-140 poems. Subscription: $26.95/1 year, $39.95/2 years, for international subscriptions provide $4 postage for 1 year, $8 postage for 2 years in US dollars. Sample: $6.95 plus IRC.
How to Submit: Submit up to 8 poems, typed on 8½ × 11 paper, single-spaced, one side only. No previously published poems or simultaneous submissions. Cover letter required. Include "the number of poems submitted, address (with postal or zip code) and phone number. Submissions accepted by regular post only. No e-mail submissions." Reads submissions August through May only. Send SASE (or SAE and IRC) for guidelines or request via e-mail or website. Reports in 3 months. "Response by e-mail if address provided (ms recycled). Then IRCs or SASE not required." Pays over $30/poem plus 2 copies. Buys first North American serial rights.
Also Offers: Holds an annual Short Grain Contest. Entries are either prose poems (a lyric poem written as a prose paragraph or paragraphs in 500 words or less), dramatic monologues (also 500 words or less) or postcard stories (also 500 words or less). Also sponsors the Long Grain of Truth contest for nonfiction and creative prose (5,000 words or less). Prizes for short categories are $400 first, $250 second, $150 third; long category, $600 first, $300 second, $200 third, also honorable mentions. All winners and honorable mentions receive regular payment for publication in *Grain*. Entry fee of $22 allows up to two entries in the same category, and includes a 1-year subscription. Additional entries are $5 each. "U.S. and international entrants send fees in U.S. funds ($22 for two entries in one category plus $4 to help cover postage)." Entries are normally accepted between September 1 and January 31. Website includes contest winners, submission guidelines, sample work from current issue, back issues available, contest rules, information on editors and mandate.
Advice: The editor comments, "Only work of the highest literary quality is accepted. Read several back issues."

GRAND STREET, 214 Sullivan St., 6C, New York NY 10012, phone (212)533-2944, fax (212)533-2737, poetry editor Michael Schmidt.
● Work published in *Grand Street* has been included in the 1992, 1993, 1994, 1995 and 1997 volumes of *The Best American Poetry*.
Magazine Needs: *Grand Street* is a quarterly magazine publishing poetry, fiction, nonfiction and art. "We have no writer's guidelines, but publish the most original poetry we can find—encompassing quality writing from all schools." They have published poetry by John Ashbery, Nicholas Christopher, Fanny Howe, Robert Kelly, August Kleinzahler and Charles Simic. Sample: $15.
How to Submit: Submit 5 poems at a time. Publishes theme issues. Send SASE for list of upcoming themes. Reports in 2 months.

GRASSLANDS REVIEW, P.O. Box 626, Berea OH 44017, e-mail lkennelly@aol.com, website http://members.aol.com/GLReview/index.html, founded 1989, editor Laura B. Kennelly.
Magazine Needs: *Grasslands Review* is a biannual magazine "to encourage beginning writers and to give adult creative writing students experience in editing fiction and poetry; using any type of poetry; shorter poems stand best chance." They have published poetry by Cynthia Roth, Bennett Rader, Georgia Tiffany, Catherine Jervey, Janice Pang and Heather Elko. As a sample the editor selected these lines from "Parts in Love" by William Freedman:

> Who is to say/parts of bodies cannot love?/Sauce for the heart,/they might have said as wisely,/is sauce for the pancreas or spine.

GR is 80 pgs., digest-sized, professionally printed, photocopied, saddle-stapled with card cover. They accept 60-70 of 500 submissions received. Press run is 300. Subscription (2 issues): $10 for individuals, $20 institutions. Sample: $4.
How to Submit: Submit only during October and March, no more than 5 poems at a time. No previously published poems or simultaneous submissions. No e-mail submissions. Short cover letter preferred. Send #10

OPENNESS TO SUBMISSIONS: ◻ beginners; ◪ beginners and experienced; ◕ mostly experienced, few beginners; ◉ specialized; ◙ closed to unsolicited mss.

SASE for response. Editor comments on submissions "sometimes." Reports in 3-4 months. Sometimes sends prepublication galleys. Pays 1 copy.

Also Offers: Sponsors annual Editors' Prize Contest. Prize: $100 and publication. Deadline: March 31. Entry fee: $12 for 5 poems, $1/poem extra for entries over 5 poems. Entry fee includes 1-year subscription. Send SASE for reply. Website includes writer's guidelines and information on contests.

GRAVITY PRESSES; NOW HERE NOWHERE; VOICES ON THE WIND, 27030 Havelock, Dearborn Heights MI 48127-3639, phone (313)563-4683, e-mail MikeB5000@yahoo.com, website http://www.bignet.net/~blank/gravity/gphome.html, founded 1998, publisher Michael J. Barney, editor Paul Kingston.

Magazine Needs: *NOW HERE NOWHERE* is a quarterly magazine publishing "the best poetry and short prose (fiction and nonfiction) that we can find. We are primarily a poetry magazine but will publish one to two prose pieces per issue. We have no restrictions or requirements as to form, content, length, etc. We publish what we like and what we think is good. No greeting card verse or song lyrics (unless by Leonard Cohen and Tom Waits)." They have published poetry by John Carle, Laurence W. Thomas, C.C. Russell and T. Kilgore Splake. As a sample the editor selected these lines from "Communication" by Patti Couture:

> Sometimes my words seemed carved/with the dull clumsy chisels barely scratching/the granite air/I
> long for sharp clean edges/to cut precisely/deep through the silent stone

NOW HERE NOWHERE is 48-52 pgs., 6¾×8½, offset printed or photocopied, saddle-stapled with glossy card cover, includes b&w illustrations. They receive about 500 poems a year, accept approximately 30%. Press run is 100 for 10 subscribers, 85 shelf sales. Single copy: $5.50; subscription: $20/4 issues. Sample: $6. Make checks payable to Gravity Presses.

How to Submit: Submit 5 poems at a time. No previously published poems; simultaneous submissions OK. Disk submissions OK. Cover letter preferred. "SASEs should accompany all submissions." Time between acceptance and publication is 6-12 months. Poems are circulated to an editorial board. "All work is seen by at least two editors (of four) and must be accepted by at least two editors. Controversies are settled by the editor-in-chief with no appeals." Seldom comments on rejections. Publishes theme issues occasionally. Send SASE for guidelines and upcoming themes. Reports in 3-6 months. Sometimes sends prepublication galleys. Pays $3-5/issue plus 1 copy. Buys first North American serial rights.

Book/Chapbook Needs & How to Submit: Gravity Presses seeks to "publish the best work we can find for the broadest audience we can." They publish 3-5 chapbooks per year, plus 1 anthology titled *Voices on the Wind*. Chapbooks are usually 64-76 pgs., 8½×7, offset printed or photocopied, saddle-stapled with glossy card-stock cover, includes art/illustrations "if appropriate."

How to Submit: Query first with 5 sample poems and cover letter with brief bio and publication credits. Replies to queries in 6-12 months. Pays 200 author's copies (out of a press run of 250). Obtain sample chapbooks by sending "requests to our address."

Advice: The editors say, "The only advice we have for beginners is to write well and submit fearlessly and unrelentingly."

GREEN BEAN PRESS, P.O. Box 237, Canal Street Station, New York NY 10013, phone/fax (718)302-1955, e-mail gbpress@earthlink.net, website http://www.earthlink.net/~gbpress, founded 1993, editor Ian Griffin.

● Their journal, *Brouhaha*, is no longer being published.

Book/Chapbook Needs: Green Bean Press publishes 1-2 chapbooks and 1-2 full-length books/year. Chapbooks are usually 20-30 pgs., priced $3-5, no graphics, occasional cover art, "but each one is different." Average press run is 125. "Chapbook arrangements consist of payment in copies only." Full-length books can range from 78-300 pgs., usually 5½×8½, list prices $10-20, catalog available upon request. No unsolicited mss are read for full-length books. Average press run is 600.

How to Submit: Query first, with 5-10 sample poems and cover letter with brief bio and publication credits by mail, fax or e-mail. "Not the entire manuscript, please." Replies to queries and mss in 1 month. Pays 35% author's copies (out of a press run of "whatever.") "Each arrangement is different. Some authors have helped with costs, others have not."

GREEN HILLS LITERARY LANTERN, P.O. Box 375, Trenton MO 64683, phone (660)359-3948 ext. 324, fax (660)359-3202, e-mail jsmith@mail.ncmc.cc.mo.us, editors Jack Smith and Ken Reger, poetry editor Joe Benevento.

Magazine Needs: *Green Hills* is the annual journal of North Central Missouri College and the North Central Missouri Writer's Guild and is open to short fiction and poetry of "exceptional quality." They want "the best poetry, in any style, preferably understandable. There are no restrictions on subject matter, though pornography and gratuitous violence will not be accepted. Obscurity for its own sake is also frowned upon. Both free and formal verse forms are fine, though we publish more free verse overall. No haiku, limericks or anything over three pages." They have published poetry by R. Nikolas Macioci, Mary Winters, Jim Thomas and Sofia M. Starnes. As a sample the editor selected these lines from "Addison Street" by David Wright:

> A small, rounded woman sits next to me. She is gumming sunflower seeds/Her lips close and click like
> the clasps on a purse. She makes a comic/face, like my infant daughter/tasting peaches for the first
> time. We stop, just past Wrigley Field, old, green/and empty.

Green Hills is 160-170 pgs., 6×9, professionally printed and perfect-bound with glossy, 4-color cover. They

receive work by more than 200 poets a year and publish 2-3 poems by about 10% of the poets submitting—less than 10% of all poetry received. Press run is 500. Sample: $7.
How to Submit: Send submissions to Joe Benevento, Truman State University, Division of Language and Literature, McClain Hall 310, 100 E. Normal, Kirksville MO 63501-4221. Submit 3-7 poems at a time, typed, 1 poem/page. No previously published poems; simultaneous submissions OK but not preferred. No fax or e-mail submissions. Cover letter with list of publications preferred. Often comments on rejections. Send SASE for guidelines or request via e-mail. Reports in 3-4 months. Always sends prepublication galleys. Pays 2 copies. Acquires one-time rights.
Advice: The editor says, "Read the best poetry and be willing to learn from what you encounter. A genuine attempt is made to publish the best poems available, no matter who the writer. First time poets, well-established poets, and those in-between, all can and have found a place in the *GHLL*. We try to supply feedback, particularly to those we seek to encourage."

GREEN MOUNTAINS REVIEW, Johnson State College, Johnson VT 05656, phone (802)635-1350, fax (802)635-1294, e-mail gmr@badger.jsc.vsc.edu, founded 1975, poetry editor Neil Shepard.
• Poetry published in *GMR* has been selected for inclusion in *The Best American Poetry* (1994 and 1997) and *Pushcart Prize* anthologies.
Magazine Needs: *Green Mountains Review* appears twice a year and includes poetry (and other writing) by well-known authors and promising newcomers. "We publish quality work, formal or free verse, realistic or surrealistic, narrative-based or language poetry." They have published poetry by Alice Fulton, Yusef Komunyakaa, Mary Oliver, Robert Pinsky, James Tate, Carol Muske and Elizabeth Spires. *GMR* is digest-sized, flat-spined, 150-200 pgs. Of 2,000 submissions they publish 30 authors. Press run is 1,800 for 200 subscribers of which 30 are libraries. Subscription: $14/year. Sample back issue: $5; current issue $8.50.
How to Submit: Submit no more than 5 poems at a time. Simultaneous submissions OK. Reads submissions September 1 through May 1 only. Editor sometimes comments on rejection slip. Publishes theme issues. Send SASE for guidelines and upcoming themes. Reports in 2-3 months. Pays 1 copy plus 1-year subscription. Acquires first North American serial rights. Send books for review consideration.

GREEN'S MAGAZINE, P.O. Box 3236, Regina, Saskatchewan S4P 3H1 Canada, founded 1972, editor David Green.
Magazine Needs: *Green's Magazine* is a literary quarterly with a balanced diet of short fiction and poetry. They publish "free/blank verse examining emotions or situations." They do not want greeting card jingles or pale imitations of the masters. They have published poetry by Walter Kuchinsky, Robert Cooperman, Mary Balazs, Rod Farmer and Robert Tener. As a sample the editor selected these lines from "Accessory Girl" by Wendy Bacon:
> Fashion is oxygen/neglecting to accessorise/is like forgetting to breathe . . .//Without your matching
> necklace/and hair ribbon you're telling/the world you hit the snooze/button one too many times
The magazine is 92 pgs., digest-sized, typeset on buff stock with line drawings, matte card cover, saddle-stapled. Circulation is 300. Subscription: $15. Sample: $5.
How to Submit: Submit 4-6 poems at a time. The editor prefers typescript, complete originals. No simultaneous submissions. "If © used, poet must give permission to use and state clearly the work is unpublished." Time between acceptance and publication is usually 3 months. Comments are usually provided on rejected mss. Send SASE (or SAE and IRCs) for guidelines. Reports in 2 months. Pays 2 copies. Acquires first North American serial rights. Occasionally reviews books of poetry in "up to 150-200 words." Send books for review consideration.
Advice: The editor says, "Would-be contributors are urged to study the magazine first."

THE GREENSBORO REVIEW; GREENSBORO REVIEW LITERARY AWARDS, English Dept., Room 134, McIver Bldg., University of North Carolina, P.O. Box 26170, Greensboro NC 27402, phone (336)334-5459, fax (336)334-3281, e-mail jlclark@uncg.edu, website http://www.uncg.edu/eng/mfa, founded 1966, editor Jim Clark.
Magazine Needs: *TGR* appears twice yearly and showcases well-made verse in all styles and forms, though shorter poems (under 50 lines) seem preferred. They have published poetry by Brendan Galvin, Michael McFee, Adrienne Su and David Rivard. As a sample the poetry editor selected these lines from "Wanting A Divorce" by Rynn Williams:
> A door grows too large/for the delicate memory/of its doorjamb . . . The asphalt is so soft/my heel
> sinks/as it might into flesh.
The magazine is 120 pgs., digest-sized, professionally printed and flat-spined with colored matte cover. Uses about 25 pgs. of poetry in each issue, about 1.5% of the 2,000 submissions received for each issue. Press run is 1,000 for 300 subscribers of which 100 are libraries. Subscription: $10. Sample: $5.
How to Submit: "Submissions (no more than five poems) must arrive by September 15 to be considered for the Spring issue (acceptances in December) and February 15 to be considered for the Fall issue (acceptances in May). Manuscripts arriving after those dates will be held for consideration with the next issue." No simultaneous submissions. No fax or e-mail submissions. Cover letter not required but helpful. Include number of poems submitted. Reports in 2-4 months. Always sends prepublication galleys. Pays 3 copies. Acquires first North American serial rights.

Also Offers: They sponsor an open competition for *The Greensboro Review* Literary Awards, $250 for both poetry and fiction each year. Deadline: September 15. Send SASE for guidelines. Website includes writer's guidelines, subscription information and literary award information.

☑ ◌ **GSU REVIEW; GSU REVIEW ANNUAL WRITING CONTEST**, Georgia State University, Campus Box 1894, Atlanta GA 30303, phone (404)651-4804, fax (404)651-1710, e-mail mnewcome@mindspring.com, website http://www.gsu.edu, founded 1980, poetry editor Katie Chaple, editor Michelle Newcome.
Magazine Needs: *GSU Review* is a biannual literary magazine publishing fiction, poetry and photography. They want "original voices searching to rise above the ordinary. No subject or form biases." They do not want pornography or Hallmark verse. They have published poetry by Bert Hedin, Gary Sange and Dana Littlepage Smith. The editors say *GSU Review* is 112 pgs. Press run is 2,500 for 500 subscribers, 600 shelf sales; 500 distributed free to students. Single copy: $5; subscription: $8. Sample: $3.
How to Submit: Submit 3 poems at a time. No previously published poems; simultaneous submissions OK. Cover letter with 3- to 4-line bio preferred. Disk submissions OK, both Mac and DOS. Time between acceptance and publication is 3 months. Seldom comments on rejections. Send SASE for guidelines. Reports in 4 weeks. Pays 1 copy.
Also Offers: Sponsors the *GSU Review* Annual Writing Contest, an annual award of $1,000 for the best poem; copy of issue to all who submit. Submissions must be previously published and may be entered in other contests. Submit up to 3 poems on any subject or in any form. "Specify 'poetry' on outside envelope." Send SASE for guidelines. Inquiries via fax and e-mail OK. Postmark deadline: January 31. Competition receives 200 entries. Past judges include Sharon Olds, Jane Hirschfield and Phil Levine. Winner will be announced in the Spring issue.
Advice: The editor says, "Avoid cliched and sentimental writing but as all advice is filled with paradox—write from the heart. We look for a smooth union of form and content."

▨ ◎ **GUERNICA EDITIONS INC.; ESSENTIAL POET SERIES, PROSE SERIES, DRAMA SE-RIES; INTERNATIONAL WRITERS** (Specialized: regional, translations, ethnic/nationality), P.O. Box 117, Toronto, Ontario M5S 2S6 Canada, fax (416)657-8885, website http://ourworld.compuserve.com/Home pages/Guernica, founded 1978, poetry editor Antonio D'Alfonso.
Book/Chapbook Needs: "We wish to bring together the different and often divergent voices that exist in Canada and the U.S. We are interested in translations. We are mostly interested in poetry and essays on pluriculturalism." They have published work by Mary Melfi, Fulvio Caccia, Claude Peloquin (Canada), Peter Carravetta, Tonino Guerra (US); and Maria Luzi (Italy).
How to Submit: Query with 1-2 pgs. of samples. Send SASE (Canadian stamps only) or SAE and IRCs for catalog.
Advice: The editor comments, "We are interested in promoting a pluricultural view of literature by bridging languages and cultures. Besides our specialization in international translation."

◪ **GULF STREAM MAGAZINE**, English Dept., Florida International University, North Miami Campus, North Miami FL 33181, phone (305)919-5599, founded 1989, editor Lynne Barrett, associate editors Michael Plummer and Lissette Mendez-Delaney.
Magazine Needs: *Gulf Stream* is the biannual literary magazine associated with the creative writing program at FIU. They want "poetry of any style and subject matter as long as it is of high literary quality." They have published poetry by Gerald Costanzo, Naomi Shihab Nye, Jill Bialosky and Catherine Bowman. The handsome magazine is 96 pgs., digest-sized, flat-spined, printed on quality stock with glossy card cover. They accept less than 10% of poetry received. Press run is 750. Subscription: $7.50. Sample: $4.
How to Submit: Submit no more than 5 poems and include cover letter. Simultaneous submissions OK (with notification in cover letter). Reads submissions September 15 through April 30 only. Editor comments on submissions "if we feel we can be helpful." Publishes theme issues. Send SASE for guidelines. Reports in 2-3 months. Pays 2 copies and 2 subscriptions. Acquires first North American serial rights.

◪ ◎ **HABERSHAM REVIEW** (Specialized: regional), P.O. Box 10, Demorest GA 30535, fax (706)776-2811, e-mail swhited@piedmont.edu, founded 1991, poetry editor Dr. Stephen R. Whited.
Magazine Needs: *Habersham Review* is a biannual, general interest, regional journal published by Piedmont College. "While we are interested in publishing regional poets, we will publish a good poem no matter where the poet lives. We accept all styles, and we prefer a range of subject matter." They have published poetry by Judson Mitcham, R.T. Smith, William Miller and James Baker Hall. As a sample we selected these lines from "When I Survey the Wondrous Cross" by David Bottoms:

> *A heavy odor of flowers/rode the fans,/and I sat with my bare feet dangling over a bench./Light from*
> *an open window fell across the face/of a brown guitar, dust twisting like worms in that light,/as the*
> *pail of water/slid across the splintered floor.*

HR is about 100 pgs., 6×9, perfect-bound, offset, with color art and photographs on the cover, some b&w art and photographs inside, and ads. It receives 250 poems a year, accepts 25. Press run is 1,000 for 300 subscribers of which 10% are libraries, 50-100 shelf sales. Subscription: $12. Sample: $6. Make checks payable to Piedmont College.

How to Submit: Submit up to 5 poems at a time. No previously published poems or simultaneous submissions. Cover letter preferred. Time between acceptance and publication is 1-2 years, "in some cases." Send SASE for guidelines. Reports in 3-6 months. Pays 5 copies. Acquires first rights. Requires acknowledgment if reprinted elsewhere. Staff reviews books of poetry in 200-500 words, single or multi-book format. Send books for review consideration.

HAIGHT ASHBURY LITERARY JOURNAL (Specialized: social issues, themes), 558 Joost Ave., San Francisco CA 94127, founded 1979-1980, editors Indigo Hotchkiss, Alice Rogoff and Conyus.
Magazine Needs: *Haight Ashbury* is a newsprint tabloid that appears 1-3 times/year. They use "all forms including haiku. Subject matter sometimes political, but open to all subjects. Poems of background—prison, minority experience—often published, as well as poems of protest and of Central America. Few rhymes." They have published poetry by Molly Fisk, Laura del Fuego, Dancing Bear, Lee Herrick, Janice King and Laura Beausoleil. As a sample the editors selected these lines from "in the lines" by Tia Blassingame:
> color boys and girls/leaves the trees in flower/triggers the metal from which year olds drop/drug addict
> babes born on/crack open their skulls/on the ground/color boys and girls/does not become men and
> women

The tabloid has a photo of its featured poet on the cover, uses graphics, ads, 16 pgs., circulation 2,000-3,000. $35 for a lifetime subscription, which includes 3 back issues. Subscription: $12/4 issues. Sample: $3.
How to Submit: Submit up to 6 poems. "Please type one poem to a page, put name and address on every page and include SASE." No previously published poems. Each issue changes its theme and emphasis. Send SASE for guidelines and upcoming themes. Upcoming themes include "Homelessness," "Jazz Poetry" and "Spirituality." Reports in 2-4 months. Pays 3 copies, small amount to featured writers. Rights revert to author. An anthology of past issues, *This Far Together*, is available for $15.

HANDSHAKE; THE EIGHT HAND GANG (Specialized: science fiction), 5 Cross Farm, Station Rd., Padgate, Warrington, Cheshire WA2 OQG United Kingdom, founded 1992, contact J.F. Haines.
Magazine Needs: *Handshake*, published irregularly, "is a newsletter for science fiction poets. It has evolved into being one side of news and information and one side of poetry." They want "science fiction/fantasy poetry of all styles. Prefer short poems." They do not want "epics or foul language." They have published poetry by Margaret B. Simon, Fleming A. Calder and Jacqueline Jones. As a sample the editor selected these lines from "A Home in Space" by Jacqueline Jones:
> Blueish splinters and a lightning beauty/Saw us through the orbits throat on earth

Handshake is 1 sheet of A4 paper, photocopied with ads. They receive about 50 poems a year, accept approximately 50%. Press run is 60 for 30 subscribers of which 5 are libraries. Subscription: SAE with IRC. Sample: SAE with IRC.
How to Submit: Submit 2-3 poems, typed and camera-ready. No previously published poems or simultaneous submissions. Cover letter preferred. Time between acceptance and publication varies. Editor selects "whatever takes my fancy and is of suitable length." Seldom comments on rejections. Publishes theme issues. Reports ASAP. Pays 1 copy. Acquires first rights. Staff reviews books or chapbooks of poetry or other magazines of very short length. Send books for review consideration.
Also Offers: *Handshake* is also the newsletter for The Eight Hand Gang, an organization for British science fiction poets, established in 1991. They currently have 60 members. Information about the organization is found in their newsletter.

HANDSHAKE EDITIONS; CASSETTE GAZETTE, Atelier A2, 83 rue de la Tombe Issoire, Paris, France 75014, phone 33-1-4327-1767, fax 33-1-4320-4195, e-mail jim_haynes@wanadoo.fr, founded 1979.
Magazine Needs & How to Submit: *Cassette Gazette* is an audiocassette issued "from time to time. We are interested in poetry dealing with political/social issues and women/feminism themes." Poets published include Ted Joans, Yianna Katsoulos, Judith Malina, Elaine Cohen, Amanda Hoover, Jayne Cortez, Roy Williamson and Mary Guggenheim. Single copy: $10 plus postage. Pays in copies.
Book/Chapbook Needs & How to Submit: Handshake Editions does not accept unsolicited mss for book publication. New Book: *Just Say "No" to Family Values* by David Day.
Advice: Jim Haynes, publisher, says, "I prefer to deal face to face."

HANGING LOOSE PRESS; HANGING LOOSE (Specialized: teens/students), 231 Wyckoff St., Brooklyn NY 11217, founded 1966, poetry editors Robert Hershon, Dick Lourie, Mark Pawlak and Ron Schreiber.
● Poetry published in *Hanging Loose* has been included in the 1993, 1995, 1996 and 1997 volumes of *The Best American Poetry*.
Magazine Needs: *Hanging Loose* appears 3 times/year. The magazine has published poetry by Sherman Alexie, Paul Violi, Donna Brook, Kimiko Hahn, Ron Overton, Jack Anderson and Frances Phillips. *Hanging Loose* is 120 pgs., flat-spined, offset on heavy stock with a 2-color glossy card cover. One section contains poems by high-school-age poets. The editor says it "concentrates on the work of new writers." Sample: $9.
How to Submit: Submit 4-6 "excellent, energetic" poems. No simultaneous submissions. "Would-be contributors should read the magazine first." Reports in 1-12 weeks. Pays small fee and 3 copies.

Book/Chapbook Needs & How to Submit: Hanging Loose Press does not accept unsolicited book mss or artwork.

🌐 ◐ **HANGMAN BOOKS**, 11 Boundary Rd., Chatham, Kent ME4 6TS England, founded 1982, editor Jack Ketch, poetry editor Kyra De Coninck.

Book/Chapbook Needs: Hangman publishes selected books of poetry on a cooperative basis. They want "personal" poetry, "underground" writing, "none rhyming, none political, bla bla bla." They have published poetry by Chris Broderick and Dan Melchior. As a sample the editor selected these lines from "dead funny" by Billy Childish from his book, *Big Hart and Balls*:

> and with every poem i rite/my fame grows/another nail in my coffin/people feel embarrassed for me/
> everything i utter becomes a cliche//when oh when the people ask/will billy shut up?

How to Submit: When submitting a ms, send sufficient IRCs for return. Editor always sends prepublication galleys. 60% of press run belongs to poet.

[N] **$** ◐ **HANOVER PRESS, LTD.; THE UNDERWOOD REVIEW**, P.O. Box 596, Newtown CT 06470-0596, phone (203)426-3388, fax (203)426-3398, e-mail faithv@aol.com, website http://www.hanoverpress .com, founded 1994, editor Faith Vicinanza, editor Linda Claire Yuhas.

Magazine Needs: *The Underwood Review* biannually publishes poetry, short stories, essays, reviews and b&w artwork including photographs. They want "cutting-edge fiction, poetry and art. We are not afraid of hard issues, love humor, prefer personal experience over nature poetry. We want poetry that is strong, gutsy, vivid images, erotica accepted. No religious poems; no 'Hallmark' verse." They have published poetry by Patricia Smith ("Queen of Performance Poetry"), Marc Smith ("father of slam poetry") and Michael Brown. As a sample the editor selected these lines from "Mommy's Hubby" by Leo Connellan (Poet Laureate of Connecticut):

> Yes, it's Fisk tellin' you split./Imagine it, Fisk tellin' you leave!/Because now I'm Mommy's Hubby and
> we've got our coffins/picked out/plots and perpetual flowers.

TUR is 120-144 pgs., 6×9, offset printed and perfect-bound with card cover with computer graphics, photos, etc. They receive about 600 poems a year, accept approximately 10%. Press run is 1,000. Subscription: $24. Sample: $13. Make checks payable to Hanover Press, Ltd./Faith Vicinanza.

How to Submit: Submit up to 6 poems at a time. No previously published poems; simultaneous submissions OK. Cover letter with short bio (up to 60 words) preferred. E-mail and disk submissions OK. Reads and responds to submissions twice a year—January/February and June/July. Time between acceptance and publication is 1-6 months. Send SASE for guidelines. Reports in 3-5 months. Pays 2 copies. Acquires one-time rights. Reviews books and chapbooks of poetry and other magazines in 500 words, single book format. Open to unsolicited reviews. Poets may also send books for review consideration.

Book/Chapbook Needs & How to Submit: Hanover Press, Ltd. seeks "to provide talented writers with the opportunity to get published and readers with the opportunity to experience extraordinary poetry." They publish 5 paperbacks/year. Books are usually 6×9, offset printed and perfect-bound with various covers, include art/ graphics. Query first with a few sample poems and cover letter with brief bio and publication credits. Replies to queries in 2 months; to mss in 6 months. Pays royalties of 3-7% or 100 author's copies (out of a press run of 1,000). Order sample books by sending $11.

Ø **HARCOURT, INC.; HB CHILDREN'S BOOKS; GULLIVER BOOKS; BROWNDEER PRESS; SILVER WHISTLE**, 525 B St., Suite 1900, San Diego CA 92101, phone (619)231-6616. HB Children's Books, Gulliver Books, Browndeer Press and Silver Whistle publish hardback and trade paperback books for children. They do not accept unsolicited material.

◐ ◎ **HARD ROW TO HOE; MISTY HILL PRESS (Specialized: nature/rural/ecology)**, P.O. Box 541-I, Healdsburg CA 95448, phone (707)433-9786, editor Joe E. Armstrong.

Magazine Needs: *Hard Row to Hoe,* taken over from Seven Buffaloes Press in 1987, is a "book review newsletter of literature from rural America with a section reserved for short stories (about 2,000 words) and poetry featuring unpublished authors. The subject matter must apply to rural America including nature and environmental subjects. Poems of 30 lines or less given preference, but no arbitrary limit. No style limits. Do not want any subject matter not related to rural subjects." As a sample the editor selected these lines from "Draw Your Delicate Heart" by Tracy Anne Wagers:

> Every time I see thunder/heads pushing the sky up and out/of our city ways, crowding/forward to
> promise noise or/a little rain, a longing, a fever enters/me slowly, through the heart/like a fence post
> piercing the ground

HRTH is 12 pgs., magazine-sized, side-stapled, appearing 3 times a year, 3 pgs. reserved for short stories and poetry. Press run is 300. Subscription: $7/year. Sample: $2.

How to Submit: Submit 3-4 poems at a time. No simultaneous submissions. Previously published poems OK only if published in local or university papers. Send SASE for guidelines. Editor comments on rejections "if I think the quality warrants." Pays 2 copies. Acquires one-time rights. Reviews books of poetry in 600-700 words. Open to unsolicited reviews. Poets may also send books for review consideration.

$ THE HARPWEAVER; BROCK UNIVERSITY PRESS; CANADIAN AUTHORS ASSO-CIATION PRIZE FOR POETRY, Dept. of English, 500 Glenridge Ave., St. Catharines, Ontario L2S 3A1 Canada, phone (905)688-5550 ext. 3469, fax (905)688-5550 ext. 4492, e-mail harpweav@spartan.ac.BrockU.ca, founded 1996. Contact editor.

Magazine Needs: *"the Harpweaver* annually publishes the creative work of emerging and established artists. We want poetry embodying the best words in the best order. This poetry is always consistent with innovation in form and content. No racist, homophobic or misogynistic verse." They have published poetry by Kristin Andrychuk, Joe Blade and John Rives. As a sample the editors selected these lines from "The Horologist" by Chris Yurkoski (which won *Harpweaver*'s 1997 Canadian Authors Association Prize for Poetry):

> In the Beginning:/there is everything at once/and a host angels gyre/from a fount of numbers that/spit
> away forever./God takes a breath:

Harpweaver is 75-100 pgs., 5½×8½, offset printed and perfect-bound with card cover, includes artwork. They receive about 200 poems a year, accept approximately 8-10%. Press run is 300. Subscription: $6. Sample: $4.

How to Submit: Submit up to 12 poems at a time. No previously published poems or simultaneous submissions. Cover letter required. E-mail and disk submissions OK. Reads submissions March through May only. Time between acceptance and publication is 2 months. Poems are circulated to an editorial board—"student board to faculty editor to journal editors." Often comments on rejections. Send SASE for guidelines or request via fax or e-mail. Reports in 2-3 months. Pays $10. Reviews books and chapbooks of poetry in 5,000 words, single book format. Open to unsolicited reviews. Poets may also send books for review consideration.

Also Offers: Sponsors the Canadian Authors Association Prize for Poetry, a cash award of $50 given "to the author of the poem that our judges consider to be the most noteworthy among the many fine poems *the Harpweaver* has the opportunity to publish in its one yearly issue."

THE HARVARD ADVOCATE (Specialized: university affiliation), 21 South St., Cambridge MA 02138, phone (617)495-0737, fax (617)496-9740, e-mail soudavar@fas.harvard.edu/~advocate, website http://www.hcs.harvard.edu/~advocate, founded 1866, president Saadi Soudavar.

Magazine Needs: *The Harvard Advocate* is a quarterly literary and arts review, circulation 4,000, that publishes poetry, fiction and art only by undergraduate and graduate students currently enrolled at Harvard University. Sample: $5.

How to Submit: In submitting state your exact relationship to Harvard. Submissions should be typed and single-sided. Use only 10 point or larger font. No previously published work. E-mail submissions OK. "Submissions are considered anonymously; write the title of your poem, your name, class, address, telephone number, and e-mail address on an index card. Place the index card inside an envelope and seal it. Upon the envelope write only the title of your work. Use a paper clip to attach the envelope to your manuscript." Does not pay. Reviews books, including poetry.

Also Offers: Website includes full magazine text as well as submission policies and the magazine's history.

HAWAII PACIFIC REVIEW, 1060 Bishop St., Honolulu HI 96813, phone (808)544-1107, fax (808)544-0862, e-mail hpreview@hpu.edu, founded 1986, poetry editor Patrice Wilson, fiction editor Catherine Sustana.

Magazine Needs: *HPR* is an annual literary journal appearing in September. They want "quality poetry, short fiction and personal essays from writers worldwide. Our journal seeks to promote a world view that celebrates a variety of cultural themes, beliefs, values and viewpoints. We wish to further the growth of artistic vision and talent by encouraging sophisticated and innovative poetic and narrative techniques." They have published poetry by Robert Cooperman and Mary Kay Rummel. *HPR* is 80-120 pgs., 6×9, professionally printed on quality paper, perfect-bound, with coated card cover; each issue features original artwork. They receive 800-1,000 poems a year, accept 30-40. Press run is approximately 1,000 for 200 shelf sales. Single copy: $7. Sample: $5.

How to Submit: Submit up to 5 poems, maximum 100 lines each. 1 submission/issue. "No handwritten manuscripts." No previously published poems; simultaneous submissions OK with notification. No e-mail submissions. Cover letter with 5-line professional bio including prior publications required. Seldom comments on rejections. Send SASE for guidelines or request via e-mail. Reports within 3 months. Pays 2 copies. Acquires first North American serial rights.

Advice: The editor says, "We'd like to receive more experimental verse. Good poetry is eye-opening; it investigates the unfamiliar or reveals the spectacular in the ordinary. Good poetry does more than simply express the poet's feelings; it provides both insight and unexpected beauty."

USE THE GENERAL INDEX, located at the back of this book, to find the page number of a specific publisher. Also, publishers that were listed in last year's edition but not included in this edition are listed in the General Index with a notation explaining why they were omitted.

N ⃝ **HAWAI'I REVIEW**, 1733 Donaghho Rd., Honolulu HI 96822, founded 1973, poetry editor Lisa Kanae, editor Kyle Koza.
Magazine Needs: *Hawai'i Review* is a biannual literary journal. "We publish high quality poetry, fiction, nonfiction and some visual art." They want "mostly free verse; all topics as long as they are interesting, provocative, insightful and skillfully crafted. No rhymed verse, traditional forms, or concrete poems. Please, no self-indulgent or incomprehensible poems, or song lyrics." They have published poetry by Colette Inez, Juliet Kono, Samrat Upadhyay and Lois-Ann Yamanaka. The editors say *HR* is 150-250 pgs., digest-sized, web offset printed and perfect-bound with coated card stock cover. They receive about 1,000 poems a year, accept approximately 5%. Press run is 1,000 for 200 subscribers of which 100 are libraries, 75 shelf sales. Subscription: $20. Sample: $10. Make checks payable to University of Hawaii.
How to Submit: Submit 5 typed poems at a time. No previously published poems; simultaneous submissions OK. Cover letter preferred. Disk submissions OK. "SASE required for response." Poems are circulated to an editorial board. Seldom comments on rejections. Publishes theme issues occasionally. Send SASE for guidelines and upcoming themes. Reports in 3 months. Always sends prepublication galleys. Pays 4 copies. Acquires first North American serial rights.

⃝ **HAYDEN'S FERRY REVIEW**, Box 871502, Arizona State University, Tempe AZ 85287-1502, phone (602)965-1243, founded 1986.
Magazine Needs: *Hayden's Ferry* is a handsome literary magazine appearing twice a year. They have published poetry by Dennis Schmitz, Raymond Carver, Maura Stanton, Ai, and David St. John. *HFR* is 6×9, 120 pgs., flat-spined with glossy card cover. Press run is 1,300 for 200 subscribers of which 30 are libraries, 800 shelf sales. They accept about 3% of 5,000 submissions annually. Subscription: $10. Sample: $6.
How to Submit: "No specifications other than limit in number (six) and no simultaneous submissions. We would like a brief bio for contributor's note included." Submissions circulated to two poetry editors. Editor comments on submissions "often." Send SASE for guidelines. Reports in 8-10 weeks of deadlines. Deadlines: February 28 for Spring/Summer issue; September 30 for Fall/Winter. Sends contributors galley proofs. Pays 2 copies.

N ⃝ ⃝ **HAYPENNY PRESS; IPSISSIMA VERBA (THE VERY WORDS) (Specialized: poetry written in first-person singular)**, 32 Forest St., New Britain CT 06052, e-mail ipsiverba@aol.com, founded 1989 (press), 1991 (magazine), editor/publisher P.D. Jordan.
Magazine Needs: *ipsissima verba (the very words)* appears twice yearly, with special issues, and publishes fiction and poetry in the first person. They want poetry of "any length, topic, format, etc., as long as it's written in first person." They have published poetry by Laurel Speer, Ron Watson and the late Joe Singer. As a sample the editor selected this poem by Tony Lewis-Jones:
> I kept no photographs of you; I wanted/to erase you from my life, my memory./Impossible I've realized,
> for now/Some nights you appear to me in dreams
The editor says *ipsissima verba* is about 65 pgs., magazine-sized, offset and digitally printed, binding varies (usually glue), cover varies, includes illustrations or photos and ads. They receive about 200 poems a year, accept approximately 30%. Subscription: $15. Sample: $8. Make checks payable to P.D. Jordan.
How to Submit: Submit up to 5 poems at a time. Previously published poems OK; no simultaneous submissions. Cover letter preferred. "All submissions, correspondence, etc., must include SASE." Time between acceptance and publication averages 3 months. Seldom comments on rejections. Publishes theme issues occasionally. Send SASE for guidelines and upcoming themes. Reports in 1 month (on average). Pays 2 copies. Acquires one-time rights. Staff reviews books and chapbooks of poetry and other magazines, multi-book format. "Sometimes only a 'Top Picks' list depending on space and reviewer's time." Send books for review consideration.
Also Offers: The editor says, "We will be sponsoring contests (probably with entry fees) in the future. We also will be going to a cash payment format for published submissions."

$ ⃝ ⃝ **THE HEARTLANDS TODAY (Specialized: regional, themes)**, Firelands College, 901 Rye Beach Rd., Huron OH 44839, phone (419)433-5560, fax (419)433-9696, founded 1990, editors Deb Benko and David Shevin.
Magazine Needs: *The Heartlands Today* is an annual publication of the Firelands Writing Center at Firelands College. They want work by Midwestern writers about the Midwest Heartlands, "writing and photography that is set in the Midwest today and deals revealingly and creatively with the issues we face—good writing and art that documents our lives." Each issue has a specific theme. They have published poetry by Alberta Turner, Chris Llewellyn and Lawrence Ferlinghetti. The editors describe it as 160 pgs., 6×9, perfect-bound with 20 b&w photos. They accept 10-20% of the poetry received. Press run is 850-900. Single copy: $8.50. Sample: $5.
How to Submit: Submit up to 5 poems at a time. Simultaneous submissions OK. Cover letter with brief bio required. Reads submissions January 1 to July 1 only. Often comments on rejections. Send SASE for guidelines and upcoming themes. Reports in 2 months once reading period begins. Pays $10 and 2 copies. Buys first or second rights.

⃝ ⃝ **HEAVEN BONE MAGAZINE; HEAVEN BONE PRESS; HEAVEN BONE PRESS INTERNATIONAL CHAPBOOK COMPETITION (Specialized: spiritual, nature/rural/ecology)**, P.O. Box 486,

Chester NY 10918, phone (914)469-9018, e-mail poetsteve@compuserve.com, founded 1986, poetry editor Steve Hirsch.

Magazine Needs: *Heaven Bone* publishes poetry, fiction, essays and reviews with "an emphasis on spiritual, metaphysical, surrealist, experimental, esoteric and ecological concerns." They have published poetry and fiction by Charles Bukowski, Marge Piercy, Kirpal Gordon, Diane di Prima and Michael McClure. As a sample the editor selected these lines from "Message of Hope" by G. Sutton Breiding:

> *The screech owl's call/Is vertical: a tower/Rippling in the mist,/A door of oracles/Hung between night/*
> *And dawn that opens/And shuts softly/In the white places/Of sleep.*

Heaven Bone is approximately 96 pgs., magazine-sized, saddle-stapled, using b&w art, photos and ads, on recycled bond stock with glossy 4-color recycled card cover. They receive 700-1,000 poems a year, accept 18-30. Press run is 2,000. Sample: $8.

How to Submit: Submit 3-10 poems at a time. "I will not read submissions without SASEs." Simultaneous submissions and previously published poems OK, "if notified." Time between acceptance and publication is up to 1 year. Occasionally publishes theme issues. Send SASE for upcoming themes. Reports in 2 weeks to 6 months. Sometimes sends prepublication galleys. Pays 2 copies. Acquires first North American serial rights. Reviews books of poetry. Open to unsolicited reviews. Poets may also send books for review consideration.

Also Offers: The press sponsors the biannual Heaven Bone Press International Chapbook Competition which awards $100 plus publication to an original, unpublished poetry ms of 30 pgs. or less. Reading fee $10. Send SASE for guidelines.

Advice: Editor advises, "Please be familiar with the magazine before sending mss. We receive too much religious verse. Break free of common 'poetic' limitations and speak freely with no contrivances. No forced end-line rhyming please. Channel the muse and music without being an obstacle to the poem."

HEIST MAGAZINE (Specialized: men), P.O. Box 2, Newcastle University Union, Callaghan NSW 2308 Australia, e-mail matthew@mockfrog.com, website http://www.mockfrog.com/heist, founded 1998, submissions editor Matt Ward.

Magazine Needs: *Heist Magazine* appears bimonthly and "aims to encourage men to write and get themselves published. *Heist* is mostly short fiction, with a section devoted to quality poetry." They want poetry of any form (except haiku) and any theme. "We take both amusing and serious work. No haiku, no cut-and-paste surrealist poems. No 'revenge' on my ex-girlfriend/wife poems." They have published poetry by Timothy Hodor, Austria; Robert Dunn, New York; and Frank Finney, Thailand. They receive about 50 poetry submissions a year, accept approximately 50%. Press run is 1,000 for 100 subscribers, 700 shelf sales; 200 distributed free to contributors and various Australian writing societies. Single copy: $2.50 AUS, $1.50 US; subscription: $5 AUS, $10 US. Sample (including postage): $2.50. Those outside Australia should send cash only.

How to Submit: Submit 6 poems at a time. No previously published poems or simultaneous submissions. Disk submissions OK (PC or Mac). Cover letter required. "Poems should be single-spaced. Also, include a floppy disk saved in Word or Word Perfect or Clarisworks; IRCs and cover letter." Time between acceptance and publication is 4 months. Seldom comments on rejections. Send SASE for guidelines or obtain guidelines via e-mail or website. Reports in 3 months. Pays 1 copy. Acquires first Australian rights.

Advice: The editor says, "Be brave in what you write, but do not take yourself too seriously. If your poetry is serious, throw in one or two amusing, satirical poems as well."

HELIKON PRESS, 120 W. 71st St., New York NY 10023, founded 1972, poetry editors Robin Prising and William Leo Coakley, "try to publish the best contemporary poetry in the tradition of English verse. We read (and listen to) poetry and ask poets to build a collection around particular poems. We print fine editions illustrated by good artists. Unfortunately we cannot encourage submissions."

HELIOTROPE, P.O. Box 9517, Spokane WA 99209-9517, e-mail gribneal@on-ramp.ior.com, founded 1996, editors George Thomas, Jan Stever, Iris Gribble-Neal and Thomas Gribble.

Magazine Needs: *Heliotrope*, published annually in January, is "an outlet for poetry, fiction, prose and criticism." They want "poetry of any form, length, subject matter, style or purpose with no restrictions." They have published poetry by James Grabill, Jon Fischer and Kris Christensen. The editor says *Heliotrope* is 100 pgs., $5\frac{1}{2} \times 8\frac{1}{2}$, offset printed, perfect-bound with card stock cover with art. Press run is 200, all shelf sales. Subscription: $6. Make checks payable to George Thomas/*Heliotrope*.

How to Submit: Submit 5 poems at a time. No previously published poems or simultaneous submissions. Cover letter preferred. E-mail submissions OK. Reads submissions June 21 through September 21 only. Poems are circulated to an editorial board. Seldom comments on rejections. Send SASE for guidelines. Reports in 1 month. Sometimes sends prepublication galleys. Pays 1 copy.

Advice: The editors say, "We are open to all writers."

HELLAS: A JOURNAL OF POETRY AND THE HUMANITIES; THE HELLAS AWARD; THE ALDINE PRESS, LTD.; THE NEW CLASSICISTS (Specialized: form), 304 S. Tyson Ave., Glenside PA 19038, phone (215)884-1086, e-mail harnett@aldinepress.com, website http://www.aldinepress.com, founded 1988, editor Gerald Harnett.

Magazine Needs: *Hellas* is a semiannual published by Aldine Press that wants poetry of "any kind but especially poems in meter. We prize elegance and formality in verse, but specifically encourage poetry of the utmost boldness and innovation, so long as it is not willfully obscurantist; no ignorant, illiterate, meaningless free verse or political poems. If we don't understand it, we don't print it. On the other hand, we don't want obvious, easy, clichéd or sentimental verse." They have published poetry by Hadas, Steele, Moore, Bowers, Conquest, Gioia and many others. *Hellas* is 172 pgs., 6×9, flat-spined, offset printed, using b&w art. Press run is 1,000. Subscription: $16/year, $28/2 years. Sample: $9.

How to Submit: Submit 3-5 poems at a time. No simultaneous submissions or previously published poems. No e-mail submissions. Editor comments on rejections "happily if requested." Send SASE for guidelines. Reports in 3-4 months. Pays 1 copy. Acquires first North American serial rights.

Also Offers: The *Hellas* Award ($100) is open to *Hellas* subscribers only and is awarded annually to the finest poem entered in the contest. Poems may be submitted to both *Hellas* and the contest simultaneously at any time throughout the year, but the annual deadline is December 31. Winner is published in spring issue of *Hellas*. Enclose SASE if submission is to be returned. In addition, they sponsor the *Hellas* readings, held at various locations in Philadelphia, New York and elsewhere. Send SASE for guidelines.

Advice: Their flyer says, "*Hellas* is a lively and provocative assault on a century of modernist barbarism in the arts. A unique, Miltonic wedding of *paideia* and *poiesis*, engaging scholarship and original poetry, *Hellas* has become the forum of a remarkable new generation of poets, critics and theorists committed to the renovation of the art of our time . . . Meter is especially welcome, as well as rhymed and stanzaic verse. We judge a poem by its verbal artifice and its truth. Lines should not end arbitrarily, diction should be precise: We suggest that such principles can appear 'limiting' only to an impoverished imagination. To the contrary, we encourage any conceivable boldness and innovation, so long as it is executed with discipline and is not a masquerade for self-indulgent obscurantism. . . . We do not print poems about Nicaragua, whales or an author's body parts. We do specifically welcome submissions from newer authors."

⊘ HELLP!; HELLP! PRESS, P.O. Box 38, Farmingdale NJ 07727, founded 1997, editors Joe Musso and Rick Silvani.

Magazine Needs: *HELLP!* appears at least 4 times a year and includes poetry, fiction, interviews, drawings and articles. "The purpose of *HELLP!* is to give freedom of expression yet another forum. Everyone needs a little *HELLP!*." They want "edgy, thought-provoking work with depth—challenge us. Send your best." They have published poetry by Koon Woon, Richard Quatrone, Catfish McDaris, Bill Lambdin and Richard Houff. *HELLP!* is 40-48 pgs., 5½×8½, photocopied on white or colored paper and saddle-stapled with paper cover, b&w drawings, includes ads. They receive a lot of poems, accept "what we like." Press run is 150 for 25 subscribers. Subscription: $20, includes issues of three and one chapbook. Sample: $3. Make checks payable to Joe Musso

How to Submit: Submit a few pieces at a time. Previously published poems and simultaneous submissions OK, if notified. Cover letter preferred. Time between acceptance and publication is 1-2 months. Often comments on rejections. Send SASE for guidelines. Reports quickly. Pays 1 copy.

Book/Chapbook Needs & How to Submit: "At HELLP! Press, we're publishing edgy, eye-popping work." They publish about 5 chapbooks/year. Chapbooks are usually 20-48 pgs., 5½×8½, photocopied and saddle-stapled with card stock cover, includes b&w drawings. *By invitation only.*

Also Offers: "We also publish *Three*, which features two writers and one artist in each issue. At a slim 12 pages, it is a taut, easy-to-circulate forum spot-lighting several pieces at a time, by an individual, allowing a more comprehensive display of one's creative output." Sample: $1 and one first-class stamp. Included in subscription to *HELLP!*

Advice: The editors say, "Support the underground literary scene whenever and wherever possible, and most important, don't eat yellow snow."

$ ◎ HERALD PRESS; PURPOSE; STORY FRIENDS; ON THE LINE; WITH; CHRISTIAN LIVING (Specialized: religious, children), 616 Walnut Ave., Scottdale PA 15683-1999, phone (724)887-8500. Send submissions or queries directly to the editor of the specific magazine at address indicated.

Magazine Needs & How to Submit: *Herald Press*, the official publisher for the Mennonite Church in North America, seeks also to serve a broad Christian audience. Each of the magazines listed has different specifications, and the editor of each should be queried for more exact information. *Purpose*, editor James E. Horsch, a "religious young adult/adult monthly in weekly parts," circulation 13,000, its focus: "action oriented, discipleship living." It is 5⅜×8⅜, with two-color printing throughout. They buy appropriate poetry up to 12 lines. *Purpose* uses 3-4 poems/week, receives about 2,000/year of which they use 150, has a 10- to 12-week backlog. Send SASE for guidelines and free sample. Mss should be typewritten, double-spaced, one side of sheet only. Simultaneous submissions OK. Reports in 6-8 weeks. Pays $7.50-20/poem plus 2 copies. *On the Line*, edited by Mary C. Meyer, a monthly religious magazine, for children 9-14, "that reinforces Christian values," circulation 6,000. Sample free with SASE. Wants poems 3-24 lines. Submit poems "each typed on a separate 8½×11 sheet." Simultaneous submissions and previously published poems OK. Reports in 1 month. Pays $10-25/poem plus 2 copies. *Story Friends*, edited by Rose Mary Stutzman, is for children 4-9, a "monthly magazine that reinforces Christian values," circulation 6,500, uses poems 3-12 lines. Send SASE for guidelines/sample copy. Pays $10. *With*, Editorial Team, Box 347, Newton KS 67114, phone (316)238-5100, is for "senior highs, ages 15-18," focusing on empowering youth to radically commit to a personal relationship with Jesus Christ, and to share

God's good news through word and actions." Circulation 4,000, uses a limited amount of poetry. Poems should be 4-50 lines. Pays $10-25. *Christian Living*, edited by Levi Miller, published 8 times/year, is "for people and faith today," uses poems up to 30 lines. They have published poetry by Julia Kasdorf. As a sample the editor selected these lines from "Sometimes Hope" by Jean Janzen:

> *But sometimes hope/is a black ghost/in a fantastic twist,/an old dream that flickers/in the wind.*

The editor says *Christian Living* is 28-44 pgs., 8 × 10, 1-3 color with photos and artwork. They receive about 75 poems a year, accept approximately 15-20. Press run is 4,000 for 4,000 subscribers of which 8-10 are libraries, 10-20 shelf sales; 100-300 distributed free. Single copy: $3.10; subscription: $21.95. Sample: $2.50. Make checks payable to *Christian Living*. Submit 3-5 poems at a time. Previously published poems and simultaneous submissions OK. Cover letter preferred with information about previous publications. Time between acceptance and publication is 2-14 months. Seldom comments on rejections. Publishes theme issues. Send SASE for guidelines. Reports in 1-6 months. Pays $1/line plus 2 copies. Buys first or one-time rights. Staff reviews books or chapbooks of poetry in 200-800 words. Poets may also send books for review consideration.

THE HERB NETWORK (Specialized: herbs), P.O. Box 12937, Albuquerque NM 87195, fax (505)452-8615, e-mail herbnetmom@aol.com, website http://www.herbnetwork.com, founded 1995, editor Kathleen O'Mara.

Magazine Needs: *The Herb Network* is a quarterly newsletter of information for herbal enthusiasts. They want poetry related to herbs or plants—real or folklore. Short poems to 250 words. They have published poetry by Nancy L'enz and Anne Wilson. As a sample the editor selected "Dandelions" by Elizabeth Willis DeHuff:

> *Slim little girls with green flounced dresses,/Dandelions stand with yellow shaggy hair./Soon they grow to gray haired ladies,/Whose locks sail away through the air./Ashamed of their baldness, each of these dears,/Fringes a cap which she always wears.*

The newsletter is 16 pgs., 8½ × 11, neatly printed on plain white paper with a few b&w graphics. The issue we received included recipes, information about herbs used by midwives, an article focusing on lavender, book reviews and classified ads. Press run is 5,500 for 5,000 subscribers. Subscription: $35/year.

How to Submit: "Contact first with short query before submitting material." Submit up to 3 poems at a time, typed double-spaced, one poem/page, name and address on each. Line length for poems is 25 maximum. Previously published poems and simultaneous submissions OK. Submissions via fax and e-mail OK. Cover letter preferred. Send e-mail or SASE for guidelines. Reports in 3-6 months. Sometimes sends prepublication galleys. Pays with 1 copy and 2 tearsheets and by barter, offering free advertisements or copies or $1-5 as budget allows. Acquires first or one-time rights.

Also Offers: Website includes writer's guidelines, membership information, articles and an interview with the editor.

HEY, LISTEN!; SEAWEED SIDESHOW CIRCUS, 3820 Miami Rd., Apt. 3, Cincinnati OH 45227, phone (513)271-2214, e-mail sscircus@aol.com, website http://hometown.aol.com/SSCircus/sscweb.html, founded 1994, editor Andrew Wright Milam.

Magazine Needs: *Hey, listen!* is an annual "small press magazine created to bring personal response back into publishing." They are open to all poetry, except rhyme. They have published poetry by Jim Daniels, Susan Firer, James Liddy and Sarah Fox. As a sample the editor selected these lines from "he found being in love/more difficult than driving/52 hours home" by Erich Ebert:

> *no one wants to be sad/from saying "in 52 hours I'll be home."/especially since we should be/asking someone "Do the leaves change/when I touch your skin?"*

The editor says *Hey, listen!* is 30 pgs., magazine-sized, photocopied and saddle-stapled with cardstock cover. They receive about 50-100 poems a year, accept approximately 20-30%. Press run is 100. Subscription: $5/2 years. Sample: $2. Make checks payable to Seaweed Sideshow Circus.

How to Submit: Submit 3-5 poems at a time. No previously published poems or simultaneous submissions. Cover letter preferred. E-mail submissions OK. Include SASE and name and address on each page. Time between acceptance and publication is 1-2 months. Often comments on rejections. Send SASE for guidelines. Reports in 1-2 months. Pays 1 copy. Rights revert to author upon publication.

Book/Chapbook Needs & How to Submit: Seaweed Sideshow Circus is "a place for young or new poets to publish a chapbook." They publish 1 chapbook/year. Chapbooks are usually 30 pgs., 8½ × 5½, photocopied and saddle-stapled with cardstock cover. Send 5-10 sample poems and cover letter with bio and credits. Replies to queries in 1-3 weeks; to mss in 2-3 months. Pays royalties of 50% plus 10 author's copies (out of a press run of 100). Order sample chapbooks by sending $6.

THE HIGGINSVILLE READER; THE HIGGINSVILLE WRITERS, P.O. Box 141, Three Bridges NJ 08887, phone (609)924-2842, e-mail hgvreader@yahoo.com, founded 1990, editors Eileen Fisher, Frank Magalhaes, Kathe Palka.

Magazine Needs: *The Higginsville Reader* is a "quarterly litmag for a general adult audience. *HR* prints poetry, short fiction and essays; also b&w artwork and photographs." They want "work rich in imaginative language. We are open to all forms and styles, accept both very short poems and longer works and are always more concerned with quality than name. We do not want poems that wander without aim, overt sentimentality, assaultive negativism." They have published poetry by Taylor Graham, David Chorlton, D.E. Steward and Joanne Lowery. As a sample the editor selected this poem "In Our Likeness" by Ed Orr:

> *Imagine a wind that bends the silver maple/half to the ground so that it looks like a willow/with all*
> *its green hair tossed over its head,/whipping in waves like seaweed. Well, it's/a little like that when he*
> *tries to shake/the last drops from his penis like a man.*

HR is 16 pgs., 7 × 8½, laser-printed, unbound, b&w artwork and photography inside only—no cover art. They receive about 750-1,000 poems a year, accept approximately 8-10%. Press run is 100-150 for 100 subscribers. Subscription: $5/year. Sample (including guidelines): $1.50. Make checks payable to The Higginsville Writers. **How to Submit:** Submit 3-6 poems at a time. Previously published poems ("but prefer new work") and simultaneous submissions (if advised and notified) OK. E-mail submissions OK. Time between acceptance and publication is 6-12 months. Poems are circulated to an editorial board. "Two editors (out of three) must agree on a piece for it to be accepted." Seldom comments on rejections. Send SASE for guidelines or obtain via e-mail. Reports in 2 months. Pays 1 copy. Acquires one-time rights.

$ ◎ HIGH PLAINS PRESS (Specialized: regional), P.O. Box 123, Glendo WY 82213, phone (307)735-4370, fax (307)735-4590, founded 1985, poetry editor Nancy Curtis.
Book/Chapbook Needs: High Plains considers books of poetry "specifically relating to Wyoming and the West, particularly poetry based on historical people/events or nature. We're mainly a publisher of historical nonfiction, but do publish one book of poetry every year." They have published poetry by Charles Levendosky, Robert Roripaugh and Jane Candia Coleman. As a sample the editor selected these lines from "Gathering Mint" from the book *Glass-eyed Paint in the Rain* by Laurie Wagner Buyer:

> *He returned at dusk, drunk on solitude, singing/in time with the gelding's rocky trot,/moccasined feet*
> *wet with mud,/the burlap bag he tossed me/stuffed full of mint/from the beaver slough.*

How to Submit: Query first with 3 sample poems (from a 50-poem ms). Reports in 2 months. Time between acceptance and publication is 18-24 months. Always sends prepublication galleys. Pays 10% of sales. Buys first rights. Catalog available on request; sample books: $5.

☑ ☒ $ ◎ HIGH/COO PRESS; MAYFLY (Specialized: form), 4634 Hale Dr., Decatur IL 62526, phone (217)877-2966, e-mail brooksbooks@q-com.com, website http://www.family-net.net/~brooksbooks, founded 1976, editors Randy and Shirley Brooks.
● Their books have received the Haiku Society of America Merit Awards.
Magazine Needs: High/Coo is a small press publishing nothing but haiku in English. "We publish haiku poemcards, minichapbooks, anthologies and a bibliography of haiku publications in addition to paperbacks and cloth editions and the magazine *Mayfly*, evoking emotions from contemporary experience. We are not interested in orientalism nor Japanese imitations." They want "well-crafted haiku, with sensual images honed like a carved jewel, to evoke an immediate emotional response as well as a long-lasting, often spiritual, resonance in the imagination of the reader." They publish no poetry except haiku. They have published haiku by Virgil Hutton, Lee Gurga and Wally Swist. *Mayfly* is 16 pgs., 3½ × 5, professionally printed on high-quality stock, saddle-stapled, one haiku/page. It appears in January and August. They publish 32 of an estimated 1,800 submissions. Subscription: $8. Sample: $4; or send $17 (Illinois residents add 7½% tax) for the *Midwest Haiku Anthology* which includes the work of 54 haiku poets. A Macintosh computer disk of haiku-related stacks is available for $10.
How to Submit: Submit no more than 5 haiku/issue. No previously published poems or simultaneous submissions. E-mail submissions OK. Deadlines are March 15 and October 15. Send SASE for guidelines. Pays $5/poem; no copies.
Book/Chapbook Needs & How to Submit: High/Coo Press considers mss "by invitation only."
Also Offers: Website includes sample poetry, book reviews, featured haiku writers and online collections.
Advice: Randy Brooks says, "Publishing poetry is a joyous work of love. We publish to share those moments of insight contained in evocative haiku. We aren't in it for fame, gain or name. We publish to serve an enthusiastic readership."

◎ HIGHLIGHTS FOR CHILDREN (Specialized: children), 803 Church St., Honesdale PA 18431, phone (570)253-1080, founded 1946, contact Marileta Robinson.
Magazine Needs: *Highlights* appears every month using poetry for children ages 2-12. They want "meaningful and/or fun poems accessible to children of all ages. Welcome light, humorous verse. Rarely publish a poem longer than 16 lines, most are shorter. No poetry that is unintelligible to children, poems containing sex, violence or unmitigated pessimism." Note: Although *Highlights* is a monthly magazine, they only publish 6-10 poems a year. They have published poetry by Bobbi Katz, Myra Cohn Livingston and Carl Sandburg. As a sample the editor selected "Instead of Buying You a Valentine, I Looked Out My Kitchen Window" by Barbara Crooker:

> *In February, trees are bare,/snowflakes lace the frosted air/and make the ground a clean white sheet/*
> *of paper, scrawled by tiny feet/of juncoes, titmice, chickadees,/who write their names with practiced*
> *ease,/and on a branch of snowy pine,/two cardinals sit—a valentine.*

It is generally 42 pgs., magazine-sized, full-color throughout. They receive about 300 submissions/year, accept 6-10. Press run is 3.3 million for approximately 2.8 million subscribers. Subscription: $29.64/year (reduced rates for multiple years).

How to Submit: Submit typed ms with very brief cover letter. Please indicate if simultaneous submission. Editor comments on submissions "occasionally, if ms has merit or author seems to have potential for our market." Reports "generally within 1 month." Always sends prepublication galleys. Payment: "money varies" plus 2 copies. Buys all rights.

Advice: The editor says, "We are always open to submissions of poetry not previously published. However, we purchase a very limited amount of such material. We may use the verse as 'filler,' or illustrate the verse with a full-page piece of art. Please note that we do not buy material from anyone under 16 years old."

N: ⊕ ◎ HILLTOP PRESS (Specialized: science fiction), 4 Nowell Place, Almondbury, Huddersfield, West Yorkshire HD5 8PB England, website (online catalog) http://www.bbr-online.com/catalogue, founded 1966, editor Steve Sneyd.

Book/Chapbook Needs: Hilltop publishes "mainly science fiction poetry nowadays." Publications include *Star-Spangled Shadows* and *Kin To the Far Beyond*, between the two publications they cover poetry in US SFanzines from the 1930s to 1990s, including A-Z of writers/publications and poem extracts; and Fierce Far Suns—Proto-SF&SF Poetry in America: the 1750s to 1960s. As a sample the editor selected these lines from the book *Ape Into Pleiades*, poems by pioneering American woman SF poet Lilith Lorraine:

> *A slim wave breaking/on no coast whatever/While the moon drops like manna/and the stars flow into the mind*

Hilltop titles are distributed in the USA by the New Science Fiction Alliance. For full list of UK publications NSFA distributes, send SAE/IRC to A. Marsden, 31192 Paseo Amapola, San Juan Capistrano CA 92675-2227.

How to Submit: Does not accept unsolicited mss. Query (with SAE/IRC) with proposals for relevant projects.

Advice: "My advice for beginning poets is (a) persist—don't let any one editor discourage you. 'In poetry's house are many mansions,' what one publication hates another may love; (b) be prepared for long delays between acceptance and appearance of work—the small press is mostly self-financed and part time, so don't expect it to be more efficient than commercial publishers; (c) *always* keep a copy of everything you send out, put your name and address on *everything* you send and *always* include adequately stamped SAE."

⊕ $⊘ ◎ HIPPOPOTAMUS PRESS (Specialized: form); OUTPOSTS POETRY QUARTERLY; OUTPOSTS ANNUAL POETRY COMPETITION, 22 Whitewell Rd., Frome, Somerset BA11 4EL England, phone/fax 01373-466653, *Outposts* founded 1943, Hippopotamus Press founded 1974, poetry editor Roland John.

Magazine Needs: "*Outposts* is a general poetry magazine that welcomes all work either from the recognized or the unknown poet. The Hippopotamus Press is specialized, with an affinity with Modernism. No Typewriter, Concrete, Surrealism." They have published in *OPQ* poetry by John Heath-Stubbs, Peter Dale and Elizabeth Jennings. *Outposts* is 70-100 pgs., digest-sized, flat-spined, litho printed, in professionally set small type, using ads. Of 60,000 poems received he uses about 300. Press run is 3,000 for 2,800 subscribers of which 10% are libraries, 2% of circulation through shelf sales. Subscription: $32. Sample: $8.

How to Submit: Submit 5 poems at a time. "IRCs must accompany U.S. submissions." Simultaneous submissions and previously published poems OK. Cover letter required. Reports in 2 weeks plus post time. Sometimes sends prepublication galleys. Pays $8/poem plus 1 copy. Copyright remains with author. Staff reviews books of poetry in 200 words for "Books Received" page. Also uses full essays up to 4,000 words. Send books for review consideration, attn. M. Pargitter.

Book/Chapbook Needs & How to Submit: Hippopotamus Press publishes 6 books a year, averaging 80 pgs. For book publication query with sample poems. Simultaneous submissions and previously published poems OK. Reports in 6 weeks. Pays 10% royalties plus 20 paper copies, 6 cloth. Send for book catalog to buy samples.

Also Offers: The magazine also holds an annual poetry competition.

■ ◐ ⊘ HIRAM POETRY REVIEW, P.O. Box 162, Hiram OH 44234, founded 1967, poetry editor Hale Chatfield.

Magazine Needs: *HPR* is an annual publication appearing in September. "We favor new talent—and except for one issue every three to four years, read only unsolicited mss." They are interested in "all kinds of high quality poetry" and have published poetry by Grace Butcher, David Citino, Michael Finley, Peter Wild, Jim Daniels, Peter Klappert and Harold Witt. *Hiram Poetry Review* is now a multimedia CD-Rom for Windows or Macintosh computers. The CD-Rom is enclosed in a 6×9 binder with printed supplement of poetry text. Circulation is 400 for 300 subscriptions of which 150 are libraries. They receive about 7,000 submissions/year, use 30, have up to a 6-month backlog. Although most poems appearing here tend to be lyric and narrative free verse under 50 lines, exceptions occur (a few longer, sequence or formal works can be found in each issue). Single copy: $15; subscription: $15. Sample (of printed back issues): $5.

How to Submit: "Send 2-4 fresh, neat copies of your best poems. We scan poetry text electronically, directly from the typed manuscripts." No simultaneous submissions. Reports in 2-6 months. Pays 2 copies plus 1-year subscription. Acquires first North American serial rights; returns rights upon publication. Reviews books of poetry in single or multi-book format, no set length. Send books for review consideration.

N: ⊕ $⊘ HOBO POETRY & HAIKU MAGAZINE; HOBO PUBLISHERS, INC., P.O. Box 166, Hazelbrook NSW 2779 Australia, founded 1993, editor Dane Thwaites.

Magazine Needs: *Hobo* appears quarterly and publishes "poems, haiku, articles and reviews relating to both. All kinds of poetry considered. Very rigorous standards are applied." They have published poetry by Eric Beach and Colleen Burke. As a sample the editor selected these lines from "postcards from lounge lizard isle" by Joanne Burns:

> interior decoration runs through her fingertips/like a frisson through a thigh, the way a design/concept
> flows through the whole envelope of an/apartment, loft style, art deco, or harbourside/high rise, the
> way lift out self enhancement runs/through the glossy print of a lifestyle magazine . . .

Hobo is 68 pgs., digest-sized, offset printed and saddle-stapled with paper cover. They receive about 4,000 poems a year, accept approximately 2%. Press run is 750. Subscription: $20 AUS/$30 US/$25 NZ. Sample: $5.50 AUS/$7 others. Make checks payable to Inkstream.

How to Submit: Submit up to 6 poems at a time. No previously published poems or simultaneous submissions. Cover letter preferred. SASE (or SAE and IRC) required. Time between acceptance and publication is about 6 weeks. Often comments on rejections. Send SASE for guidelines. Reports in 6 weeks on average. Sometimes sends prepublication galleys. Pays $12/page. Buys one-time rights. Staff reviews books and chapbooks of poetry and other magazines, single book format. Open to unsolicited reviews. Poets may also send books for review consideration.

Also Offers: Sponsors an annual haiku competition. Send for entry form. 1999 deadline was April 15. First prize: $400.

N $ ◻ ◎ HODGEPODGE SHORT STORIES & POETRY (Specialized: subscribers), P.O. Box 6003, Springfield MO 65801, e-mail fictionpub@aol.com, founded 1994, editor Vera Jane Goodin.

Magazine Needs: *Hodgepodge* appears quarterly to "provide a showcase for new as well as established poets and authors; to promote writing and offer encouragement." They are open to all kinds of poetry. They have published poetry by Delphine LeDoux and Tom Padgett. As a sample the editor selected these lines from "Freeing Flame" by M.D. LeDoux:

> Silken starlight shimmerfire/silver moonset haze/windlace plaiting filigree/playful spiritblaze

The editor says *Hodgepodge* is a 24- to 32-page chapbook, photocopied and saddle-stitched with self cover, includes clip art. They receive about 100 poems a year, accept approximately 50%. Press run is about 100 for about 100 subscribers. Single copy: $3; subscription: $10. Sample: $1. Make checks payable to Goodin Communications. "Potential contributors either need to purchase a copy or be annual subscribers."

How to Submit: Submit up to 4 poems at a time. Previously published poems and simultaneous submissions OK. SASE required for return of poems. Time between acceptance and publication is 1 week. Seldom comments on rejections. Publishes theme issues occasionally. Send SASE for guidelines and upcoming themes. Reports in 2 months. Pays $1/poem. Acquires one-time rights. Staff reviews books and chapbooks of poetry and other magazines in 250 words, single and multi-book format. Send books for review consideration to Review Editor.

Also Offers: Sponsors a Best-of-the-Year Contest. Any poem published in *Hodgepodge* is eligible for the contest. 1st Place $30, 2nd Place $15, 3rd Place free subscription. Also awards honorable mentions and certificates. "Judging is done by staff, but readers are asked for input." Also co-sponsors the annual Poetry From Planet Pissantium International Contest. Send SASE for details.

◑ ◎ HOLIDAY HOUSE, INC. (Specialized: children), 425 Madison Ave., New York NY 10017, founded 1936, associate editor Lisa Hopp, editor-in-chief Regina Griffin, is a trade children's book house. They have published hardcover books for children by Myra Cohn Livingston. They publish 1 poetry book a year averaging 32 pages. The editor says, "the acceptance of complete book manuscripts of high-quality children's poetry is limited." Send a query with SASE before submitting.

$ ◻ THE HOLLINS CRITIC, P.O. Box 9538, Hollins College, Roanoke VA 24020-1538, phone (540)362-6275, website http://www.hollins.edu/academics/critic, founded 1964, editor R.H.W. Dillard.

Magazine Needs: *THC*, appears 5 times/year, publishing critical essays, poetry and book reviews. They use a few short poems in each issue, interesting in form, content or both. They have published poetry by John Engels, Lyn Lifshin, George Garrett, Dara Wier. As a sample the editor selected these lines from "Carving the Salmon" by John Engels:

> And then it is recognizable, a fish,/and ready for finishing. It quivers//a little at the skew chisel, flinches/
> at the spoonbit. With the straight gouge/I give it eyes, and with the veiner, gills,//and it leaps a little
> in my hand.

The Hollins Critic is 24 pgs., magazine-sized. Circulation is 500. Subscription: $6/year ($7.50 outside US). Sample: $1.50.

How to Submit: Submit up to 5 poems, must be typewritten, to Cathryn Hankla, poetry editor. Cover letter preferred. Reports in 6 weeks (slower in the summer). Pays $25/poem plus 5 copies.

✓ $ ◻ HOME TIMES, 3676 Collins Dr. #12, West Palm Beach FL 33406, phone (561)439-3509, founded 1988, editor/publisher Dennis Lombard.

Magazine Needs: *Home Times* is a monthly "independent, conservative, pro-Christian, pro-Jewish," 24-page newsprint tabloid of local, national and world news and views, including information in the areas of home and family, arts and entertainment, and religion. *HT* tries not to moralize but to just be positive and Biblical in perspective. Our goal is to publish godly viewpoints in the marketplace, and to counteract the culturally elite of media and politics who reject Judao-Christian values, traditional American values, true history, and faith in God." They want poetry that is "humorous or spiritual—not 'religious'; for a general audience. Prefer traditional or light verse up to 16 lines." They receive about 200 poems a year, accept 1-2%. Press run is 5,000. Single copy: $1. Samples: $3 for 3 current issues.

How to Submit: Submit 3 poems at a time. Previously published poems and simultaneous submissions OK. Time between acceptance and publication is 1-6 months. Sometimes comments on rejections. Send SASE for guidelines. Reports in 2-4 weeks. Pays $5 "generally"; a 6-month subscription, if requested. Buys one-time rights.

Advice: The editor says, "*Home Times* is very different! Please read guidelines and sample issues." Also, the editor has written a 12-chapter report for new writers entitled "101 Reasons Why I Reject Your Mss"—which is "an effective training course for new freelancers, easy to understand and written with lots of humor."

$ ◎ HOPSCOTCH: THE MAGAZINE FOR GIRLS; BOYS' QUEST (Specialized: children), P.O. Box 164, Bluffton OH 45817-0164, phone (419)358-4610, founded 1989, editor Marilyn B. Edwards.
Magazine Needs: *Hopscotch* is a bimonthly magazine for girls 6-12. "In need of short traditional poems for various holidays and seasons. (Limit to 21 lines if possible, 700-1,000 words.) However, we do not want Halloween-related material. Nothing abstract, experimental." The few poems in this children's magazine occasionally address the audience, challenging young girls to pursue their dreams. To see how, order a sample copy (or check one out at the library) because it is too easy for poets who write children's verse to forget that each magazine targets a specific theme . . . in a specific way. They have published poetry by Lois Grambling, Judy Nichols, Leila Dornak, Judith Harkham Semas and Maggie McGee. The editor describes *Hopscotch* as "full-color cover, 50 pgs. of 2-color inside, 7×9, saddle-stapled." They use about 30-35 of some 2,000 poems received/year. Press run is 16,000 for 10,000 subscribers of which 7,000 are libraries, 200 to inquiring schools and libraries, 2,000 shelf sales. Subscription: $17.95. Sample: $3.95, $4.95 outside US.
How to Submit: Submit 3-6 poems/submission. Cover letter preferred; include experience and where published. Publishes theme issues. Send SASE for upcoming themes. Themes include Babysitting (October/November 1999), Winter (December 1999/January 2000), Tea Parties (February/March 2000), Mothers (April/May 2000), Friends (June/July 2000), Bugs (August/September 2000) and Rabbits (October/November 2000). Reports in 2-4 weeks. Pays $10-40. Buys first North American serial rights.
Magazine Needs & How to Submit: They also publish *Boys' Quest*, a bimonthly magazine for boys 6-13. Similar in format to *Hopscotch*, the magazine premiered in June/July 1995. Upcoming themes include: States (December 1999/January 2000), Helping Others (February/March 2000), Pets (April/May 2000), Summertime (June/July 2000), Astronomy (August/September 2000) and Unique & Unusual (October/November 2000). Send SASE for details. Sample: $3.95, $4.95 outside US.

⊕ ◯ HORIZON, Stationsstraat 232A, 1770 Liedekerke, Belgium, founded 1985, editor Johnny Haelterman.
Magazine Needs & How to Submit: *Horizon*, published annually in December, is a "cultural magazine with prose and illustrations, in Dutch and a few pages in English." Preference is given to "poems with punctuation, metre and rhyme but that is not a hard and fast rule. If a poem is not published after a year, it means that it couldn't be used. *Horizon* takes poems only as a filler." They have published poetry by Giovanni Malito, Joy R. King and Bernard Frank. The editor says *Horizon* is 29.7×21cm, "reprographic," saddle-stapled with color cover. They receive about 100 poems (in English), used about 10. Press run is 120. Single copy: $10. Pays 1 copy.

$ ◯ HOUGHTON MIFFLIN CO., 222 Berkeley St., Boston MA 02116, founded 1850.
Book/Chapbook Needs: Houghton Mifflin is a high-prestige trade publisher that puts out both hardcover and paperback books. They have published poetry books by Donald Hall, May Swenson, Rodney Jones, Geoffrey Hill, Galway Kinnell, Thomas Lux, Erica Funkhouser, William Matthews, Margaret Atwood, Linda Gregerson, Mary Oliver and Andrew Hudgins.
How to Submit: *Poetry submission is by invitation only* and they are not seeking new poets at present. Always sends prepublication galleys. Authors are paid 10% royalties on hardcover books, 6% royalties on paperbacks (minimum), $1,000 advance and 12 author's copies.

◤ ✓ $ ◯ ◎ HOUSE OF ANANSI PRESS (Specialized: regional), 34 Lesmill Rd., Toronto, Ontario M3B 2T6 Canada, phone (416)445-3333, fax (416)445-5967, e-mail info@anansi.ca, website http://www.anansi.ca, founded 1967, publisher Martha Sharpe, editorial assistant Adrienne Leahey.
Book/Chapbook Needs: House of Anansi publishes literary fiction and poetry by Canadian writers. "We seek

THE SUBJECT INDEX, located at the back of this book, can help you select markets for your work. It lists those publishers whose poetry interests are specialized ◎ .

to balance the list between well-known and emerging writers, with an interest in writing by Canadians of all backgrounds. We publish Canadian poetry only, and poets must have a substantial publication record—if not in books, then definitely in journals and magazines of repute. No children's poetry and no poetry by previously unpublished poets." They have published *Power Politics* by Margaret Atwood and *More Watery Still* by Patricia Young. As a sample they selected these lines from "The Ecstasy of Skeptics" in the book *The Ecstasy of Skeptics* by Steven Heighton:

> *This tongue/is a moment of moistened dust, it must learn/to turn the grit of old books/into hydrogen, and burn/The dust of the muscles must burn/down the blood-fuse of the sinews, . . .*

Their books are generally 96-144 pgs., trade paperback with French sleeves, a matte finish cover and full-color cover art.

How to Submit: Canadian poets should query first with 10 sample poems (typed double-spaced) and a cover letter with brief bio and publication credits. Previously published poems and simultaneous submissions OK. Poems are circulated to an editorial board. Often comments on rejections. Replies to queries within 3 months, to mss (if invited) within 4 months. Pays 8-10% royalties, a $500 advance and 10 author's copies (out of a press run of 1,000).

Advice: To learn more about their titles, check their website or write to the press directly for a catalog. They say, "We strongly advise poets to build up a publishing résumé by submitting poems to reputable magazines and journals. This indicates three important things to us: One, that he or she is becoming a part of the Canadian poetry community; two, that he or she is building up a readership through magazine subscribers; and three, it establishes credibility in his or her work. There is a great deal of competition for only three or four spots on our list each year—which always includes works by poets we have previously published."

HQ POETRY MAGAZINE (THE HAIKU QUARTERLY); THE DAY DREAM PRESS, 39 Exmouth St., Kingshill, Swindon, Wiltshire SN1 3PU England, phone 01793-523927, founded 1990, editor Kevin Bailey.

Magazine Needs: *HQ* is "a platform from which new and established poets can speak and/or experiment with new forms and ideas." They want "any poetry of good quality." They have published poetry by Peter Redgrove, Alan Brownjohn, James Kirkup and Cid Corman. The editor says *HQ* is 48-64 pgs., A5, perfect-bound with art, ads and reviews. They accept approximately 5% of poetry received. Press run is 500-600 for 500 subscribers of which 30 are libraries. Subscription: £10 UK, £13 foreign. Sample: £2.70.

How to Submit: No previously published poems or simultaneous submissions. Cover letter and SASE (or SAE and IRCs) required. Time between acceptance and publication is 3-6 months. Often comments on rejections. Reports "as time allows." Pays 1 copy. Reviews books of poetry in about 1,000 words, single book format. Open to unsolicited reviews. Poets may also send books for review consideration.

Also Offers: Sponsors "Piccadilly Poets" in London, a "Live Poet's Society" based in Bath, Somerset England.

HU (HONEST ULSTERMAN) (Specialized: regional), 49 Main St., Greyabbey, County Down BT22 2NF United Kingdom, founded 1968, editor Tom Clyde.

Magazine Needs: *HU* is a literary magazine appearing 3-4 times a year using "technically competent poetry and prose and book reviews. Special reference to Northern Irish and Irish literature. Lively, humorous, adventurous, outspoken." They have published poetry by Seamus Heaney, Paul Muldoon, Gavin Ewart, Craig Raine, Fleur Adcock and Medbh McGuckian. As a sample the editor selected these lines from "Badger With Ursa Minor" by Frankie McGurk:

> *You can see this fire in a badger's eyes,/it blazes in the white of his mask./The pole star is in his nose./ With a bouncing gait/he moves through space/in the vast and fertile/galaxy of a field.*

HU is 128 pgs., A5 (digest-sized), photolithographic, phototypeset, perfect-bound with photographs and line drawings and loose, inserted ads with an "occasional color cover." Press run is 1,000 for 350 subscribers. Subscription: $30. Sample: $10.

How to Submit: "Potential contributors are strongly advised to read the magazine before submitting their work." Submit 6 poems at a time. Editor comments on submissions "occasionally." Publishes theme issues. Send SAE and IRCs for upcoming themes. Pays "a nominal fee" plus 2 copies. Reviews books of literary and cultural interest in 500-1,000 words, single or multi-book format. Open to unsolicited reviews. Poets may also send books for review consideration.

Also Offers: They also publish occasional poetry pamphlets, and a separate index ($15).

HUBBUB, VI GALE AWARD; ADRIENNE LEE AWARD, 5344 SE 38th Ave., Portland OR 97202, founded 1983, editors L. Steinman and J. Shugrue.

Magazine Needs: Appearing once a year (in July/August), *Hubbub* is designed "to feature a multitude of voices from interesting contemporary American poets. We look for poems that are well-crafted, with something to say. We have no single style, subject or length requirement and, in particular, will consider long poems. No light verse." They have published poetry by Madeline DeFrees, Cecil Giscombe, Carolyn Kizer, Primus St. John, Shara McCallum and Alice Fulton. The editors describe *Hubbub* as 60-65 pgs., 5½×8½, offset printed and perfect-bound, cover art only, usually no ads. They receive about 1,200 submissions/year, use approximately 2%. Press run is 350 for 100 subscribers of which 12 are libraries, about 150 shelf sales. Subscription: $5/year. Sample: $3.35 (back issues), $5 (current issue).

How to Submit: Submit 3-6 typed poems (no more than 6) with SASE. No previously published poems or simultaneous submissions. Send SASE for guidelines. Reports in 2-4 months. Pays 2 copies. Acquires first North American serial rights. "We review two to four poetry books a year in short (three-page) reviews; all reviews are solicited. We do, however, list books received/recommended." Send books for consideration.
Also Offers: Outside judges choose poems from each volume for two awards: Vi Gale Award ($100) and Adrienne Lee Award ($50). There are no special submission procedures or entry fees involved.

☑ $☑ THE HUDSON REVIEW, 684 Park Ave., New York NY 10021, contact poetry editor.
• Work published in this review has been included in the 1993, 1994, 1997 and 1998 volumes of *The Best American Poetry*.
Magazine Needs: *The Hudson Review* is a high-quality, flat-spined quarterly of 176 pgs., considered one of the most prestigious and influential journals in the nation. Editors welcome all styles and forms. However, competition is extraordinarily keen, especially since poems compete with prose. Subscription: $28 ($32 foreign)/ 1 year, institutions $34 ($38 foreign)/1 year. Sample: $8.
How to Submit: Nonsubscribers may submit poems between April 1 and July 31 only. "Simultaneous submissions are returned unread." Reports in 6-8 weeks. Always sends prepublication galleys. Pays 2 copies and 50¢/ line.

☑ ◎ THE HUMAN QUEST (Specialized: political), 4300 NW 23rd Ave., Box 203, Gainesville FL 32614-7050, editor Edna Ruth Johnson.
Magazine Needs & How to Submit: *Human Quest* is a "humanistic bimonthly dealing with society's problems, especially peace. We use practically no poetry." It is magazine-sized and appears 6 times a year. Circulation is 10,000, of which 1,000 go for library subscriptions. Send for free sample. Pays copies.

◎ HUNGER MAGAZINE; HUNGER PRESS, P.O. Box 505, Rosendale NY 12472, phone (914)658-9273, fax (914)658-7044 (5**), e-mail hungermag@aol.com, founded 1997, publisher/editor J.J. Blickstein, assistant editor Susan McKechnie.
Magazine Needs: *Hunger Magazine* is an international zine based in the Hudson Valley and appears 2 times a year (January, May and September). "*Hunger* publishes mostly poetry but will accept some short fiction, essays, translations, cover art drawings and book reviews. Although there are no school/stylistic limitations, our main focus is on language-image experimentation with an edge. We publish no names for prestige and most of our issues are dedicated to emerging talent. Well known poets do grace our pages to illuminate possibilities. No dead kitty elegies; Beat impersonators; Hallmark cards; 'I'm not sure if I can write poems'. All rhymers better be very, very good. We have published poetry by Amiri Baraka, Paul Celan, Charles Bernstein, Robert Kelly, Ray Bremser, Andy Clausen, Simon Perchik, Anne Gorrick and Steve Hirsch. *Hunger* is 52-80 pgs., magazine-sized, saddle-stitched with glossy full-color card cover, uses original artworks and drawings. They receive about 1,300 poems a year, accept approximately 10%. Press run is 250-500. Single issue: $7, $10 (foreign); subscription: $14, $20 foreign. Back issue: $7. Chapbooks: $5. Make checks payable to Hunger Magazine & Press.
How to Submit: Submit 3-10 poems at a time. No previously published poems; simultaneous submissions OK, if notified. Brief cover letter with SASE preferred. E-mail submissions and queries OK. No attachments. "Manuscripts without SASEs will be recycled. Please proof your work and clearly indicate stanza breaks." Time between acceptance and publication is 1-6 months. Full critiques available for $1 per page/poem (10 pages maximum). Reports in 2-8 weeks. Sends prepublication galleys upon request. Pays 1-3 copies. "If invited to be a featured poet we pay a small honorarium and copies." Acquires first North American serial rights.
Also Offers: Sponsors a chapbook contest. Reading fee: $10. Accepting original mss, 25 pgs. maximum between January and May only. Chapbooks are 5½×8½, photocopied, saddle-stitched with full color card stock cover. Pays $25-50 and at least 20% of press run. Send SASE or e-mail for guidelines. Chapbooks from Richard Rizzi (*the monkey in his body; the highest paid gun in America*) and Susan G. McKechnie (*The Sailor Poems*) are available for $4.
Advice: The editors say, "Read, read, read."

◖ ◎ THE HUNTED NEWS; THE SUBOURBON PRESS, P.O. Box 9101, Warwick RI 02889, phone (401)826-7307, e-mail mikekwood@prodigy.com, founded 1990, editor Mike Wood.
Magazine Needs: *The Hunted News* is an annual "designed to find good writers and give them one more outlet to get their voices heard." As for poetry, the editor says, "The poems that need to be written are those that need to be read." They do not want to see "the poetry that does not need to be written or which is written only to get a reaction or congratulate the poet." The editor says *THN* is 25-30 pgs., 8½×11, photocopied, unstapled. "I receive over 200 poems per month and accept perhaps 10%." Press run is 150-200. Sample free with SASE.
How to Submit: Previously published poems OK; no simultaneous submissions. E-mail submissions OK. Always comments on rejections. Publishes theme issues. Send SASE for guidelines and upcoming themes. Reports in 1 month. Pays 2-5 copies, more on request. "I review current chapbooks and other magazines and do other random reviews of books, music, etc. Word count varies."
Advice: The editor says, "I receive mostly beginner's poetry that attempts to be too philosophical, without much experience to back up statements, or self-impressed 'radical' poems by poets who assume that I will publish them because they are beyond criticism. I would like poets to send work whose point lies in language and

economy and in experience, not in trite final lines, or worse, in the arrogant cover letter."

HURRICANE ALICE (Specialized: feminist), Dept. of English, Rhode Island College, Providence RI 02908, e-mail mreddy@grog.ric.edu, founded 1983, contact Joan Dagle.

Magazine Needs: *Hurricane Alice* is a quarterly feminist review. Poems should be "infused by a feminist sensibility (whether the poet is female or male)." They have published poetry by Alice Walker, Ellen Bass, Patricia Hampl, Nellie Wong, Edith Kur and Barbara Hendryson. As a sample the editor selected these lines from "The Gift" by Marjorie Roemer:

> I would give you my right hand/My mother always said/Too many times/As if she really wanted to/As
> if she needed to.

The magazine is a "12-page folio with plenty of graphics." Press run is 500-1,000, of which 350 are subscriptions and about 50 go to libraries. Subscription: $12 (or $10 low-income). Sample: $2.50.

How to Submit: Considers simultaneous submissions. Time between acceptance and publication is 3-6 months. Send SASE for upcoming themes. Reports in 3-4 months. Pays 6 copies. Reviews books of poetry.

ICON; HART CRANE AWARD, Kent State University-Trumbull, 4314 Mahoning Ave., NW, Warren OH 44483-1998, phone (330)847-0571, e-mail lynchm@trumbull.kent.edu, website http://www.trumbull.kent.edu/icon.html/, founded 1966.

Magazine Needs: *Icon* is a biannual, "eclectic" literary and art magazine. "We prefer short lyric poems, although all forms are considered. Originality and innovation are appreciated. Sentimental or angst-ridden poems should send themselves elsewhere." They have published poetry by Gay Brewer and William Greenway. The editor says *Icon* is 48-60 pgs., saddle-stapled with color photos and graphics. They receive 1,200 poems a year, publish about 90. Press run is 500 for 75 subscribers of which 15 are libraries, 400 distributed free to Kent State students. Single copy: $3; subscription: $6.

How to Submit: Submit up to 5 poems at a time. No previously published poems; simultaneous submissions OK. Cover letter preferred. Reads submissions September 15 through April 15 only. Poems are circulated to an editorial board. Reports in 2-6 months. Pays 1 copy.

Also Offers: They also offer the Hart Crane Award, an annual poetry award of $100. The winner is published in the spring issue. Send SASE for details.

THE ICONOCLAST, 1675 Amazon Rd., Mohegan Lake NY 10547-1804, founded 1992, editor/publisher Phil Wagner.

Magazine Needs: *The Iconoclast* is a general interest literary publication appearing 8 times/year. They want "poems that have something to say—the more levels the better. Nothing sentimental, obscure or self-absorbed. Try for originality; if not in thought, than expression. No greeting card verse or noble religious sentiments. Look for the unusual in the usual, parallels in opposites, the capturing of what is unique or often unnoticed in an ordinary, or extraordinary moment. What makes us human—and the resultant glories and agonies. Our poetry is accessible to a thoughtful reading public." *The Iconoclast* is 32 pgs., journal-sized, photo offset on #45 white wove paper, with b&w art, graphics, photos and ads. They receive about 2,000 poems a year, use 3%. Press run is 2,000 for 310 subscribers. Subscription: $13 for 8 issues. Sample: $2.

How to Submit: Submit 3-4 poems at a time. Previously published poems and simultaneous submissions OK, when noted, though they say "previously published and simultaneous submissions must be demonstrably better than others. No simultaneous publication!" Time between acceptance and publication is 4-12 months. Sometimes comments on rejections. Reports in 1 month. Pays 1 copy per published page or poem, 40% discount on extras. Acquires one-time rights. Reviews books of poetry in 250 words, single format.

Advice: The editor says, "Within a year we should be able to offer at least subscribers $2-15 per poem, for first rights, in addition to the above. Check future issues for announcement."

$ ☑ IDEALS MAGAZINE; IDEALS PUBLICATIONS INC., P.O. Box 305300, Nashville TN 37230, phone (615)333-0478, founded 1944, editor Michelle Prater Burke.

Magazine Needs: *Ideals Magazine* appears 6 times/year and publishes "light poetry and short articles with a nostalgic theme. Issues are seasonally oriented." They want "traditional forms and subjects, such as home, family, nature, holidays, patriotic. No limericks, erotica, haiku." They have published poetry by Edna Jaques, Edgar A. Guest and Patience Strong. The editor says *Ideals* is 88 pgs., 8½×11, perfect-bound with 4-color glossy cover, old-fashioned artwork, no ads. They receive about 2,000 poems a year, accept approximately 5%. Press run is 200,000 for 180,000 subscribers of which 6,000 are libraries, 40,000 shelf sales. Single copy: $5.95; subscription: $19.95. Sample: $4. Make checks payable to Ideals Publications Inc.

How to Submit: Submit 10 poems at a time. Previously published poems and simultaneous submissions OK. Cover letter preferred. Publishes theme issues. "Send seasonal material 8 months prior." Send SASE for guidelines. Reports in 6-8 weeks. Pays $10/poem and 1 copy. Buys one-time rights.

THE IDIOT (Specialized: humor), 1706 S. Bedford St., Los Angeles CA 90035, e-mail purple-hayes@juno.com, founded 1993, editor Sam Hayes.

Magazine Needs: *The Idiot* is a biannual humor magazine. "We mostly use fiction, articles and cartoons, but will use anything funny, including poetry. Nothing pretentious. We are a magazine of dark comedy. Death, dismemberment, and the Talmud are all subjects of comedy. Nothing is sacred. But it needs to be funny, which brings us to . . . Laughs! I don't want whimsical, I don't want amusing, I don't want some fanciful anecdote about childhood. I mean belly laughs, laughing out loud, fall on the floor funny. If it's cute, give it to your sweetheart or your puppy dog. Length doesn't matter, but most comedy is like soup. It's an appetizer, not a meal. Short is often better. Bizarre, obscure, and/or literary references are often appreciated but not necessary." They have published poetry by Joe Deasy, Moho Greene and Brian Campbell. As a sample the editor selected these lines from "Untitled" by Brian Campbell:

> Armenia the hungry, Armenia/the short/you yearn for yummy semi-solid foodstuffs./Moloch! Moloch!
> Schlomo and Schecky!

The Idiot is 48 pgs., 5½×8½, professionally printed and staple-bound with glossy cover. They receive about 100 submissions a year, accept 3-4. Press run is 300. Single copy: $4. Sample: $5.

How to Submit: Previously published poems and simultaneous submissions OK. E-mail submissions OK. Seldom comments on rejections. Reports in 2-6 months. Pays 1 copy. Acquires one-time rights.

Advice: The editor says, "If it ain't funny, don't send it! I mean it! We're talkin' belly laughs, damn it!"

◐ ILLUMINATIONS, AN INTERNATIONAL MAGAZINE OF CONTEMPORARY WRITING, % Dept. of English, College of Charleston, 66 George St., Charleston SC 29424-0001, phone (843)953-1993, fax (843)953-3180, e-mail lewiss@cofc.edu, website http://www.cofc.edu/~lewis/illums.html, founded 1982, editor Simon Lewis.

Magazine Needs: *Illuminations* is published annually "to provide a forum for new writers alongside already established ones." They are open as to form and style. Do not want to see anything "bland or formally clunky." They have published poetry by Peter Porter, Michael Hamburger, Geri Doran and Anne Born. As a sample the editor selected these lines from "For Stephen Spender" by Louis Bourne:

> Old romantic, imprisoned in your speech,/Steeled in a world racing to its doom,/We've taken in the
> news from your compass-points./You've given us some signs that still can teach.

Illuminations is 48-60 pgs., 8×5, offset printed and perfect-bound with 2-color card cover, includes photos and engravings. They receive about 1,500 poems a year, accept approximately 5%. Press run is 500. Subscription: $20 for 3 issues. Sample: $10.

How to Submit: Submit up to 6 poems at a time. No previously published poems or simultaneous submissions. E-mail and fax submissions OK. Brief cover letter preferred. Time between acceptance and publication "depends on when received. Can be up to a year." Publishes theme issues occasionally. Obtain guidelines via e-mail. Reports within 2 months. Pays 2 copies plus one subsequent issue. Acquires all rights. Returns rights on request.

☑ $ ◖ ◎ IMAGE: A JOURNAL OF ARTS & RELIGION (Specialized: religious), P.O. Box 674, Kennett Square PA 19348, phone (302)652-8279, e-mail gwolfe@compuserve.com, website http://www.imagejou rnal.org, founded 1989, publisher Gregory Wolfe.

Magazine Needs: *Image*, published quarterly, "explores and illustrates the relationship between faith and art through world-class fiction, poetry, essays, visual art, and other arts." They want "poems that grapple with religious faith, usually Judeo-Christian." They have published poetry by Philip Levine, Edward Hirsch, Denise Levertov and Annie Dillard. As a sample we selected these lines from "Receptionism" by Marjorie Maddox:

> Does our kneeling/bring him down/again, from the wood,/unhinge his stone,/trumpet for ourselves/our
> catalytic salvation?

Image is 136 pgs., 10×7, perfect-bound, acid free paper with glossy 4-color cover, averages 10 pgs. of 4-color art/issue (including ads). They receive about 800 poems a year, accept approximately 2%. They have 3,000 subscribers of which 100 are libraries. Subscription: $30. Sample: $10.

How to Submit: Submit up to 4 poems at a time. No previously published poems. Cover letter preferred. No e-mail submissions. Time between acceptance and publication is 1 year. Reports in 3 months. Always sends prepublication galleys. Pays 4 copies plus a variable honorarium. Acquires first North American serial rights. Reviews books of poetry in 1,000-1,300 words, single or multi-book format. Open to unsolicited reviews. Poets may also send books for review consideration.

⊕ $ ◖ ◎ IMAGO: NEW WRITING (Specialized: regional), School of Media & Journalism, Q.U.T., GPO Box 2434, Brisbane 4001 Queensland, Australia, fax (07)3864-1810, founded 1988.

Magazine Needs: *Imago*, appears three times a year, publishing "the best Australian writing, placing particular emphasis on Queensland writing and culture, but also welcoming submissions from overseas. Poems preferably short—up to about 50 lines, most from 12-25 lines. Our main criterion is good writing." They have published poetry by Tom Shapcott, Peter Rose and Philip Hammial. *Imago* is 160 pgs., digest-sized, with glossy card cover. They accept about 10% of 500 poems from about 150 writers. Press run is 1,000 for 450 subscribers of which 36 are libraries. Subscription: $A21 in Australia; $A28, overseas (airmail). Sample: $A9.50.

How to Submit: Submit 6-8 poems at a time. "A brief biography (few lines) of the writer accompanying the submission saves time if the work is accepted. We have a Notes on Contributors column." Comments on rejections if requested. Reports in 1-6 months. Never sends prepublication galleys "unless specifically asked for by contributor." Pays $A30-40 plus 1 copy. Buys first Australian serial rights. Reviews books of poetry in 600 words— "usually commissioned. Unsolicited reviews would have to be of books relevant to *Imago* (Queensland or writing)." Send books for review consideration.

◻ ◪ ◎ **IMPLOSION PRESS; IMPETUS** (Specialized: erotica, women), 4975 Comanche Trail, Stow OH 44224-1217, phone/fax (216)688-5210, e-mail impetus@aol.com, founded 1984, poetry editor Cheryl Townsend.

Magazine Needs: Publishes *Impetus*, a "somewhat" quarterly literary magazine, chapbooks and special issues. The editor would like to see "strong social protest with raw emotion. No topic is taboo. Material should be straight from the gut, uncensored and real. Absolutely no nature poetry or rhyme for the sake of rhyme, oriental, or 'Kissy, kissy I love you' poems. Any length as long as it works. All subjects OK, providing it isn't too rank. *Impetus* is now publishing annual erotica and all-female issues. Material should reflect these themes." They have published poetry by Ron Androla, Kurt Nimmo, Lyn Lifshin and Lonnie Sherman. The magazine varies in size and is photocopied from typescript, saddle-stapled. Press run is about 1,000, with 300 subscriptions. Subscription: $15 for 4 issues; $20 for 4 issues plus chapbooks. Sample: $5; make checks payable to Implosion Press.

How to Submit: Submit 3-8 poems at a time. The editor says, "I prefer shorter, to-the-point work." Include name and address on each page. Previously published work OK if it is noted when and where. "I always like a cover letter that tells me how the poet found out about my magazine." E-mail submissions OK. Generally a 5-month backlog. Send SASE for guidelines. Usually reports within 4 months. Pays 1 copy. Acquires first or one-time rights. In her comments on rejections, the editor usually refers poets to other magazines she feels would appreciate the work more. Reviews books of poetry. Open to unsolicited reviews. Poets may also send books for review consideration.

Also Offers: Implosion Press hosts "The Impecunious Poetry Project" with nationwide readings.

Advice: The editor says, "Bear with the small press. We're working as best as we can and usually harder. We can only do so much at a time. Support the small presses!"

◻ **IMPROVIJAZZATION NATION**, 5308 65th Ave., SE, Lacey WA 98513, phone (360)456-1683, fax (360)456-8982, e-mail rotcod@olywa.net, website http://www.olywa.net/rotcod, founded 1991, editor Dick Metcalf.

Magazine Needs: *Improvijazzation Nation* is a quarterly "devoted to networking; prime focus is tape/music reviews, includes quite a bit of poetry." They want "experimental, visual impact and non-establishment poetry, no more than 15 lines. No hearts and flowers, shallow, epic." They have published poetry by John M. Bennett, Joan Payne Kincaid and Anthony Lucero. The editor says *IN* is 20 pgs., 8½ × 11, photocopied, no binding. They receive 50-100 poems a year, use approximately 50%. Press run is 100. Single copy: $2.25; subscription: $8 for 4 issues. Sample: $2.50.

How to Submit: Submit 3 poems at a time. Previously published poems and simultaneous submissions OK. "Fax OK, e-mail is better." Often comments on rejections. Reports within a week or two. "No payment, no contributor's copies, no tearsheets; poets must buy the issue their work appears in. The one exception is that any contributor who furnishes a valid e-mail address will receive an ASCII copy of the entire magazine, if requested." Reviews books of poetry. Also accepts short essays/commentary on the use of networking to void commercial music markets, as well as material of interest to musical/artist improvisors.

$ ◎ **IN THE FAMILY** (Specialized: gay/lesbian/bisexual), P.O. Box 5387, Takoma Park MD 20913, phone (301)270-4771, fax (301)270-4660, e-mail lmarkowitz@aol.com, website http://www.inthefamily.com, founded 1995, fiction editor Helena Lipstadt.

Magazine Needs: *In the Family* is a quarterly "therapy magazine exploring clinical issues for queer people and their families." We're open to anything but it must refer to a gay/lesbian/bisexual theme. No long autobiography. No limericks." They have published poetry by Michael Montlack, Douglas Martin, Alden Reimonenq and Susan Landers. As a sample the editor selected these lines from "Haiku" by Shoshana T. Daniel:

> Smoke and whiskey sours,/whatever it takes to make/your mouth taste like hers./Idiot splashes/grown
> dumb with her absence. Blue/pool no orange koi./Thumbs shoved under rind/you split the orange.
> Your hands/sting me everywhere

The editor says *In the Family* is 32 pgs., 8½ × 11, offset printed and saddle-stitched with 2-color cover, includes art and ads. They receive about 50 poems a year, accept approximately 10%. Press run is 10,000 for 8,000 subscribers of which 10% are libraries, 5% shelf sales; 10% distributed free to direct mail promos. Subscription: $22. Sample: $5.50. Make checks payable to ITF.

How to Submit: Submit 5 poems at a time. No previously published poems; simultaneous submissions OK. Cover letter required. E-mail submissions OK. "Do not attach document. Paste poems into e-mail text." Time between acceptance and publication is 3-4 months. Poems are circulated to an editorial board. "Fiction editor makes recommendations." Publishes theme issues. Reports in 2 months. Always sends prepublication galleys. Pays $25 and 5 copies. Acquires first rights. Reviews books of poetry in 1,000 words, multi-book format. Open to unsolicited reviews. Poets may also send books for review consideration to attn. Wayne Scott.

THE GEOGRAPHICAL INDEX, located at the back of this book, can help you discover the publishers in your region. Publishers often favor poets (and work) from their own areas.

☑ ◯ ◐ ◎ **IN THE GROVE (Specialized: regional)**, P.O. Box 16195, Fresno CA 93755, phone (559)442-4600 ext. 8105, fax (559)265-5756, e-mail inthegrove@rocketmail.com, founded 1996, editor Lee Herrick, poetry editor Optimism One.

Magazine Needs: *In the Grove* appears 3 times/year and publishes "short fiction, essays and poetry by new and established writers born or currently living in the Central Valley and throughout California." They want "poetry of all forms and subject matter, no more than three pages in length (each). We seek the originality, distinct voice and craftsmanship of a poem. No greeting card verse or forced rhyme. Be fresh. Take a risk." They have published poetry by Timothy Lin, Amy Ugematsu and Renny Christopher. As a sample the editor selected these lines from "Husk Girl" by M. Jennings:

> *because when that one slip occurs/as it did/when* we were *tumbled out as* we was/like a weed through
> the dust of my marionette mouth/I knew what they was thinking/that I'd proved em right

The editors say *ITG* is 80-100 pgs., 5½×8½, photocopied and perfect-bound with heavy card stock cover, 4-5 pgs. of ads. They receive about 500 poems a year, accept approximately 10%. Press run is 150 for 50 subscribers, 75 shelf sales; 25 distributed free to contributors, colleagues. Subscription: $16. Sample: $6.

How to Submit: Submit 3-5 poems at a time. Previously published poems and simultaneous submissions OK. Cover letter preferred. Time between acceptance and publication is 2-4 months. "Poetry editor reads all submissions and makes recommendations to editor, who makes final decisions." Seldom comments on rejections. Send SASE for guidelines. Reports in 1-3 months. Pays 1 copy. Acquires first or one-time rights. Rights return to poets upon publication.

☑ ◯ **IN THE SPIRIT OF THE BUFFALO**, Media Menagerie, 233 N. 48th St., Suite MBE 151, Lincoln NE 68504, e-mail netpro@inetnebr.com, founded 1996 by Mark A. Reece, publisher/editor Keith P. Stiencke.

Magazine Needs: *In the Spirit of the Buffalo* is published quarterly to "provide forum for poets and authors of all experience levels to be a positive influence for social awareness and change through creative personal expression." They want "poetry that awakens social consciousness while still being positive in tone. Motivational, inspirational, and spiritual writing is highly acceptable. No poetry that promotes racism; no hate poetry; pornographic content is not acceptable." *ITSOTB* is 12-20 pgs., 5½×8½, photocopied from DTP output, includes artwork and graphics. Under the ownership of Mr. Reece, *ITSOTB* received about 250 poems a year, accepted approximately 25%. Press run is 150 for 25 subscribers with extra copies distributed free to coffeehouses. Subscription: $12. Sample: $3. Make checks payable to Opportunity Assistance. "Subscription is highly encouraged but not required. Subscribers get discounts on additional copies."

How to Submit: Submit 3 poems at a time. Previously published poems OK; no simultaneous submissions. Cover letter preferred. "Electronic submissions are welcome. E-mail is best or may attach text files. Cover letter may include a very brief bio and be no more than one page." Time between acceptance and publication is 3-6 months. Seldom comments on rejections. Reports in 2-16 weeks. Pays 1 copy and/or free publicity (your bio and address printed upon request). Acquires one-time rights. Open to unsolicited reviews. Poets may also send books for review consideration.

Advice: The editor says, "Proofread, again and again. Order samples and subscriptions to see examples of what we accept. Support the magazines you want to be published in. We sometimes will recommend to poets other sources to publish their work."

Ⓝ ↙ $ ◯ ◎ **IN 2 PRINT MAGAZINE (Specialized: children/teen/young adult, regional)**, P.O. Box 102, Port Colborne, Ontario L3K 5V7 Canada, phone (905)834-1539, fax (905)834-1540, founded 1994, publisher Jean Baird.

Magazine Needs: *In 2 Print*, a national forum for emerging artists, is a quarterly, award-winning, glossy color magazine which promotes and showcases the creativity of young Canadians: the magazine publishes original works by young adults ages 12-21 including poetry, short stories, plays, painting, photography, computer art and cartoons. *In 2 Print* also publishes an eclectic array of interviews and reviews of books, music and theatre." They are open to all forms and styles. "No mush, no gush! No class assignments or work produced to please teachers." As a sample we selected these lines from "angelfish" by Amelinda Berube:

> i cast my nets every day,/trying so desperately to capture you,/stars in a winter sky//ever remote, you
> are also fire/in a hearth i left so long ago to stand/here where everything is gray as ice/sea sky ropes/
> whose bite leaves blood on my hands//every day my nets come back/empty—

In 2 Print is 48 pgs., magazine-sized, web offset printed and saddle-stitched with color paper cover, includes b&w and color photos and artwork, ads. They receive about 5,000 poems a year, accept approximately 1%. Press run is 25,000 for 9,000 subscribers of which 300 are libraries, 2,000 shelf sales; balance distributed free to schools, qualified lists. Sample: $4.

How to Submit: Submit 4 poems at a time with SASE (or SAE and IRC). No previously published poems or simultaneous submissions. Cover letter with brief bio required. "Submissions can only be made by the author, artist or photographer. While the magazine is delighted by all the teachers and educators who encourage their students to submit work for publication, the submission must be made by the creator(s) of the work. Bulk submissions from teachers or schools are not accepted." Time between acceptance and publication is 4 months. Poems are circulated to an editorial board. "Peer review to short-list. Short-list goes to six of Canada's finest poets—including Susan Musgrave, Christopher Dewdney, Lorna Crozier, Patrick Lane—for final recommendation." Send SASE (or SAE and IRC) for guidelines. Reports in 3-4 months. Sometimes sends prepublication galleys. Pays $50. Buys first rights. Reviews books and chapbooks of poetry and other magazines in 500-1,200 words. Open to unsolicited reviews. Poets may also send books for review consideration.

Advice: The publisher says, "Great writers are great readers."

$ ☐ ◎ INDIAN HERITAGE PUBLISHING; INDIAN HERITAGE COUNCIL QUARTERLY; NATIVE AMERICAN POETRY ANTHOLOGY (Specialized: ethnic/nationality); P.O. Box 2302, Morristown TN 37816, phone (423)581-4448, founded 1986, CEO Louis Hooban.

Magazine Needs: *Indian Heritage Council Quarterly* devotes 1 issue to poetry with a Native American theme. They want "any type of poetry relating to Native Americans, their beliefs or Mother Earth." They do not want "doggerel." They have published poetry by Running Buffalo and Angela Evening Star Dempsey. As a sample the editor selected these lines from his poem "the Pow-wow":

> And listen! You can/hear it/as the drum beats tune in/to the heartbeats of/Mother Earth/giving birth
> to life/in the center/of the Dance Circle.

IHCQ is 6 pgs., 5½×8½ (8½×11 folded sheet with 5½×8½ insert), photocopied. They receive about 300 poems a year, accept approximately 30%. Press run and number of subscribers vary, 50% shelf sales; 50 distributed free to Indian reservations. Subscription: $10. Sample: "negotiable." Make checks payable to Indian Heritage Council.

How to Submit: Submit up to 3 poems at a time. Previously published poems (author must own rights only) and simultaneous submissions OK. Cover letter required. Time between acceptance and publication is 3 months to 1 year. Poems are circulated to an editorial board. "Our editorial board decides on all publications." Seldom comments on rejections. Charges criticism fees "depending on negotiations." Publishes theme issues. Send SASE for guidelines and upcoming themes. Reports within 3 weeks. Pay is negotiable. Acquires one-time rights. Staff reviews books or chapbooks of poetry or other magazines. Send books for review consideration.

Book/Chapbook Needs & How to Submit: Indian Heritage Publishing publishes chapbooks of Native American themes and/or Native American poets. Format of chapbooks varies. Query first, with a few sample poems and cover letter with brief bio and publication credits. Replies to queries within 3 weeks, varies for mss. Pays 33-50% royalties. Offers subsidy arrangements that vary by negotiations, number of poems, etc. For sample chapbooks, write to the above address.

Also Offers: Sponsors a contest for their anthology, "if approved by our editorial board. Submissions are on an individual basis—always provide a SASE."

Advice: The editor says, "Any poet interested in Native American themes or any Native American poet expressing poems of any theme is invited to submit to us. If you have strong feelings for Native American people, culture, religion or ideas, express yourself through your poetry and let us help you get published."

☑ $ ◐ INDIANA REVIEW, Indiana University, 1020 E. Kirkwood, Bloomington IN 47405-7103, phone (812)855-3439, website http://www.indiana.edu/~inreview/, founded 1982, editor Brian Leung.

● Poetry published in *IR* has been selected for inclusion in the 1996 and 1997 volumes of *The Best American Poetry*.

Magazine Needs: *Indiana Review* is a biannual of prose, poetry and visual art. "We look for an intelligent sense of form and language, and admire poems of risk, ambition and scope. We'll consider all types of poems— free verse, traditional, experimental. Reading a sample issue is the best way to determine if *IR* is a potential home for your work. Any subject matter is acceptable if it is written well." They have published poetry by Philip Levine, Taslimā Nāsreen, Campbell McGrath, Charles Simic, Mark Strand and Alberto Rios. The magazine uses about 40-60 pgs. of poetry in each issue (6×9, flat-spined, 160 pages, color matte cover, professional printing). They receive about 6,000 submissions a year, use approximately 60. The magazine has 500 subscriptions. Sample: $8.

How to Submit: Submit 4-6 poems at a time, do not send more than 8-10 pages of poetry per submission. No electronic submissions. Pays $5/page ($10 minimum/poem), plus 2 copies and remainder of year's subscription. Buys first North American serial rights only. "We try to respond to manuscripts in 2-3 months. Reading time is often slower during summer and holiday months." Brief book reviews are also featured. Send books for review consideration.

Ⓝ $ ◪ ◑ INDIGENOUS FICTION, P.O. Box 2078, Redmond WA 98073-2078, e-mail deckr@earthlink.net (no e-mail submissions), founded 1998, publisher/managing editor Sherry Decker.

Magazine Needs: *Indigenous Fiction* appears 2 times a year and publishes "literary mainstream and genre fiction and poetry to provide a market for accomplished writers of 'unusual' or cross-genre fiction and poetry. We prefer poems that tell at least a story or part of a story; usually serious poems but have accepted two amusing 'spoof' type submissions. We do not want poetry that is so obscure and 'high literary' no one except the poet knows what it's about." They have published poetry by Errol Miller, James S. Dorr, Margo Solod and Holly Day. As a sample the publisher selected these lines from "The Chupacabra" by Scott Francis:

> Water-light and/rippling up the wet tangled nighttime branches, we clothe each other in our/naked
> cries. Hooking scarlets from the dark, our horns become the fires of our/cries. We're gorging on blood-
> thick petals. It has begun to rain, each drop's/touch flaming us more and more alive. Alone, we coo,
> far from the/stench called men

The publisher says *IF* is 64-84 pgs., digest-sized, digitally published and saddle-stitched with full color 30-60 lb. cover, includes drawings/watercolors/ink. They receive about 650 poems a year, accept approximately 2%. Press run is 300 for 75 subscribers, 50 shelf sales; 25 distributed free to critics/reviewers. Subscription: $11. Sample: $6. Make checks payable to Sherry Decker.

How to Submit: Submit 5 poems at a time. Previously published poems and simultaneous submissions OK. Cover letter preferred. "Listing credits will get my attention but will not sell me your work. Do not explain your work in your cover letter. Even though we accept previously published work, we accept very little of it. Must be truly exceptional." Time between acceptance and publication is up to 6 months. Seldom comments on rejections. Send SASE for guidelines or request via e-mail. Reports in 2 weeks. Pays $5/poem. Buys first North American serial rights or one-time rights for reprints. "Contributor's copies are provided for work of at least 1,500 words. All contributors are qualified to purchase copies at the discounted rate, as explained in contract."

N **$** **○** **◙** **INKLINGS**, 1650 Washington St., Denver CO 80203, phone (303)861-8517, fax (303)861-0659, e-mail inklings@paradoxpub.com, website http://www.paradoxpub.com, founded 1994, poetry submissions editor Susan Adams Kauffman.

Magazine Needs: *Inklings* is "a bimonthly literary magazine and arts discussion bridging classic literature and art with popular culture in the spirit of the Inklings of Oxford: C.S. Lewis, J.R.R. Tolkien, Charles Williams and friends. *Inklings* exists as a vital catalyst to encourage honest dialogue and affecting stories relating from the common human experience—by writers who approach their craft truthfully irrespective of their religion, nationality, race or political worldview. *Inklings* publishes poetry, essays, reviews, interviews and fiction of lasting merit, honestly written with depth of plot, characterization and meaning, with thoughtful insight into the human condition." They want "serious poetry, free verse, sonnet, haiku and traditional work that corresponds with quarterly themes or addresses the universal human experience. We tend not to publish poetry that is tritely religious." They have published poetry by Luci Shaw, Albert Haley and Jon Trott. As a sample the editor selected these lines from "A Leaf Landing in a Well" by Walt McDonald:

> *Rock, club, fistful of mud, something to fling/and swing again, again, until flat prose/lies battered, abstractions crushed, bleeding,/cheap rhymes scattered like rubies. Venus rose/dripping and blissful from the foam*

Inklings is up to 64 pgs., magazine-sized, professionally printed on 4-color glossy paper and saddle-stapled with 4-color glossy paper cover, includes b&w photos and ads. They receive about 200 poems a year, accept approximately 20%. Press run is 10,000 for 3,500 subscribers; the remaining 6,500 go to libraries and complimentary copies distributed mostly in Colorado. Subscription: $19.95/year (6 issues), $35.95/2 years (12 issues). Sample: $5.

How to Submit: Submit up to 10 poems at a time. Line length for poetry is 2 minimum, 100 maximum. No previously published poems or simultaneous submissions. Cover letter required. E-mail (preferred) and disk submissions OK. "Please enclose SASE [with regular mail submissions] and any background information that would be helpful." Time between acceptance and publication is up to 1 year. Poems are circulated to an editorial board. "All poems are handled by the poetry submissions editor who selects intial 6-8 poems for an issue and then involves other editors in final selection process." Often comments on rejections. Publishes theme issues. Send SASE for guidelines and upcoming themes or obtain via website. Reports in 2-3 months. Pays $25/poem. Buys first North American serial rights or one-time rights. Reviews books and chapbooks of poetry in 300 words. Open to unsolicited reviews. Poets may also send books for review consideration.

Also Offers: Sponsors regular poetry contests with cash awards. Contests advertised in *Inklings* or call or write to *Inklings* for details. Website includes writer's guidelines, names of editors, poetry, book reviews, articles, fiction and upcoming events.

Advice: The editor says, "Read poems that have already been accepted by *Inklings*. We are looking for fresh, original (as opposed to clichéd or trite) work. Most of the poetry we publish is free verse.

○ **◎** **INKSLINGER (Specialized: subscription); ONE VOICE**, 8661 Prairie Rd. NW, Washington Court House OH 43160-9490, founded 1993, publisher/editor Nancy E. Martindale.

Magazine Needs: *Inkslinger* appears 3 times/year (in March, July and November) to "provide an additional market for poets and to further the poetic arts." They want poetry from subscribers only. Any subject, any format, no longer than 20 lines. "No porn or erotica. Also no translations or foreign language poetry." They have published poetry by Chris F. Hensler, Ben Stivers, Jerry Hoff and Jennifer Fennell. As a sample the editor selected these lines from "Cross And Cross Again" by Jerry Hoff:

> *If/a swastika/is costumed in mistletoe,/will its guise survive the surprise—of its/breathless kisses?*

Inkslinger is 20 pgs., 4¼ × 5½, photocopied and saddle-stapled with colored paper cover. They receive 200-300 poems a year, accept 54 or more if short in length. Subscription (including *One Voice*): $12/year, $23/2 years, $35/3 years. Sample: $4 (*Inkslinger* and *One Voice*; for a copy of *One Voice* only, send SASE).

How to Submit: "Purchase of a one-year subscription is required to submit at present time." Send no more than 10 poems at a time. Previously published poems OK if author still owns copyright; no simultaneous submissions. Time between acceptance and publication is 1 month. "Poems arriving too late for one issue will be held for the next issue's consideration. Poems are judged according to imagery, style, creativity, originality and sincerity (5 points each). Poems with most points are accepted. One(s) with the highest is named 'Editor's Choice' and poet receives $10." Seldom comments on rejections. Send SASE for guidelines. Reports in 5 months maximum. Poets retain all rights.

Also Offers: *One Voice*, a supplement to *Inkslinger*, is a 4-page flyer featuring the work of a single poet in each issue. Submit 3-7 poems, no longer than 20 lines each, with $3 (flat) reading fee (waived for *Inkslinger* subscribers) and SASE for returns. Name and address on each page. Include brief bio of 75 words or less. Pays 25 loose copies. Make checks payable to Nancy E. Martindale. *One Voice* is open to nonsubscribers, unlike *Inkslinger*.

Advice: The editor says, "Novices and experienced poets welcome. We're small, but open. Always read guidelines first. We're forced to return a large number of manuscripts unread because poets submit without subscribing or sending reading fee. Please note that the size of our publications has decreased and that line length requirements have changed. We're still publishing the same number of poems (or more) now that they're shorter."

N ☐ ◑ THE INKWELL., % C.S. McDowell, 5455 Timber Creek Place Dr. #404, Houston TX 77084, founded 1999, contact C.S. McDowell.

Magazine Needs: *The Inkwell.* appears 3-4 times a year and "strives to discover and expose talent, new or old. A love of literature and a firm belief that practically nothing is stronger than the written word is my bread and butter. All forms and styles of poetry are accepted, from 1-100 lines. Also, prose and short fiction up to 1,000 words are included in each issue. The editor tends to stray towards well-worded, sound poetry with rhyme included, whether irregular or traditional. Free verse, haiku and all other forms are of equal importance, though. No forced rhyme. 'Tender skies at twilight', etc., tend to sour one's stomach. Nature and the environment are of significance to us all, but when writing on the subject try not to neuter it. Erotica may be stimulating, but please, all you ex-porn stars, exhibit your wares elsewhere." The editor says the journal is 15-30 pgs., digest-sized, high-quality print and saddle-stapled with cardstock or heavy weight paper cover with b&w illustration. "As this is a new magazine, I hope to receive 300-500 pieces a year of which 15-25% will be accepted." Press run is 250-1,000, "depending on funding and submissions received." Sample: 50¢ (for postage).

How to Submit: Submit up to 5 pieces at a time (poetry, prose and short fiction). Line length for poetry is 1 minimum, 100 maximum. Previously published poems and simultaneous submissions OK. Cover letter "not mandatory, but appreciated. If cover letter is included, please send a few words about oneself, life, interests (brief bio)." Include SASE for reply or return. Reading fees: $1/piece. Make checks payable to C.S. McDowell. "Currently seeking public funding. If accepted and supported, reading fees will be abolished." Time between acceptance and publication varies. "The author should be notified of their acceptance within 6-8 weeks. Actual publication may be from 3-6 months." Always comments on rejections. "As a writer, I have often tired of the dreaded Form Letter Rejection. As an editor, I will always personally respond to my rejections with criticism and reason. The aforementioned reading fee covers any criticism fee there may be." Send SASE for guidelines. Reports in 6-8 weeks. Pays 1 copy. If response is large enough, a "Best of Each Issue" cash prize (around $10-25) may be awarded. All rights remain with the author.

Also Offers: "If funding remains supportive, *The Inkwell.* will enter a piece of work or chapbook (with the author's blessing) into one or more national contests. Also, *The Inkwell.* is interested in producing 4-6 chapbooks/year. The reading fee for these is $20, of which 50% is returned if the manuscript is rejected." Follow same submission guidelines as given for the journal. Chapbook runs will be 100, of which 10 are paid to the author. The remaining 90 will be sold at $2 each, of which 50% returns to the author. Those remaining after 1 year will be given free to libraries and/or bookstores.

Advice: Mr. McDowell says, "Authors, if you are satisfied with your work, send it in. If not, stop a stranger on the street and recite to them. If a crowd gathers and applauds, send it in. If they walk on by, send it in. Develop a thick skin, and believe in your words. As a final note, remember that the written word is one of the most extraordinary powers in the known universe. Write your words and thoughts, revise them, taste them. Good craftsmanship is better than a Georgia Peach . . . in some circles."

◑ INNER VOICES (Specialized: prisoners), P.O. Box 4500 #219, Bloomington IN 46226, e-mail eviltwin @macconnect.com, website http://www.indy.net/~eviltwin, founded 1995, editor C.N. Williams.

Magazine Needs: *Inner Voices*, published biannually, is a "monograph of prison literature." They want "any form, subject or style. We try for balance and eclecticism. It doesn't have to be about prison or crime. Energy, sincerity and originality are often as important as polish." *Inner Voices* is 50 pgs., 5½ × 8½, photocopied, saddle-stapled with medium card cover, graphic art accepted, occasional color, trade ads with closely related organizations or businesses. They receive about 150 poems a year, use approximately 20. Press run is 200 for 30 subscribers, 30 shelf sales. Subscription: $8 ($5 for prisoners). Sample: $4.

How to Submit: Authors must be prisoners (or occasionally their loved-ones or ex-prisoners). Submit up to 10 poems at a time. Previously published poems OK; no simultaneous submissions. Cover letter preferred with a brief bio or personal statement of about 100 words. E-mail submissions OK. Time between acceptance and publication varies. Poems are circulated to an editorial board. Seldom comments on rejections. Theme issues possible in the future. Send SASE for guidelines. Reports "be patient." Pays 2 copies. Acquires first North American serial or one-time rights. Reviews books of prison poetry or journals. Open to unsolicited reviews. Poets may also send books for review consideration.

Also Offers: Website includes links to prison resources, information and bibliography on prison literature, the overflow of *IV* submissions, subscription information, new writers, etc.

N $ ◎ INNOVATIVE PUBLISHING CONCEPTS; RYTHM BOOKS (Specialized: ethnic, health concerns, women, overcoming adversity), 6908 E. Oak St., Scottsdale AZ 85257, phone/fax (602)947-

8386, e-mail innov8iv@nov8.com, website http://www.nov8.com, founded 1997, publisher/editor Nubia Levon.
Book/Chapbook Needs: Under the imprint Rythm Books, Innovative Publishing Concepts publishes 2 paper-backs/year. They want "poetry, 20 lines or less, dealing with life changes and self-improvement. Also accepts articles on health/mental health/career. No adult/erotic work." They also look for work on African-American issues and work by women. They have published poetry by Catherine Valdez. As a sample the publisher selected these lines (poet unidentified):

> At the crossroads of my life/My dream is to seek and find/All through the years, I lived in a child's
> mind/My existence depended on someone else, not mine.

Books are usually 80 pgs., 5½×8½, web-sheet fed printed and perfect-bound, 4-color glossy 10 pt. cover, includes 4-color art.
How to Submit: Query first with 5 sample poems and cover letter with brief bio and publication credits. Line length for poetry is 15 minimum, 20 maximum. No previously published poems; simultaneous submissions OK. Cover letter preferred. E-mail and disk submissions OK. Send SASE with brief bio of author and publication credits. Reads submissions February 15 through March 15, June 15 through July 15 and October 15 through November 15 only. Reading fees: $5/submission. Time between acceptance and publication is 6 months. Often comments on rejections. Replies to queries and mss in 3 months. Pays royalties of 8-10% and 50 author's copies (out of a press run of 5,000). Order sample books by sending $10.
Also Offers: Website includes current publications and author profiles.

○ ◎ **INSECTS ARE PEOPLE TWO; PUFF 'N' STUFF PRODUCTIONS (Specialized)**, P.O. Box 146486, Chicago IL 60614-6400, phone (773)772-8686, founded 1989, publisher H.R. Felgenhauer.
Magazine Needs: *Insects* is an infrequent publication focusing solely on "poems about insects doing people things and people doing insect things." They have published poetry by Bruce Boston, Steve Sneyd, Paul Wiene-man and Lyn Lifshin. *Insects* is 8½×11, stapled down the side, with card cover, b&w art and graphics. Press run is 400. Sample: $5.
How to Submit: Previously published poems and simultaneous submissions OK. Often comments on rejections. Reports "immediately." Pay varies. Open to unsolicited reviews. Send books for review consideration.
Book/Chapbook Needs & How to Submit: Puff 'N' Stuff Productions publishes 1 chapbook/year. Replies to queries and mss in 10 days. Pay is negotiable.
Advice: H.R. Felgenhauer says, "Hit me with your best shot. Never give up—editors have tunnel-vision. The *BEST* mags you almost *NEVER* even hear about. Don't believe reviews. Write for yourself. Prepare for failure, not success."

○ ◐ **INTERBANG; BERTYE PRESS, INC.**, P.O. Box 1574, Venice CA 90294, phone (310)450-6372, e-mail editors@interbang.net, website http://www.interbang.net, founded 1995, editor Heather Hoffman.
Magazine Needs: *Interbang*, published quarterly, is "Dedicated to Perfection in the Art of Writing." They want "enticing poetry of any length on any subject. Although we do not have strict standards regarding substance, texture, or structure, your craft, in tandem with your subject matter, should elicit a strong response in the reader: love, hate, shock, sorrow, revulsion, you name it. Write your name, address and phone number of each page of your submission." They have published poetry by Rob Lipton, David Centorbi and Jessica Pompei. As a sample the editor selected these lines from "Clutter Can Manipulate So Much Wisdom" by David Centorbi:

> The sidewalk holds nothing but wandering bodies,/life cycles without preparation./Believing in
> annihilation/means looking into their eyes.//So, dislocating myself/becomes the easiest response./
> Leaving the sidewalk is no longer walking,/but just another way of seeing.

Interbang is 30 pgs., 7½×8½, offset printed and saddle-stitched with colored card stock cover, includes line art and photos. They receive about 500 poems a year, accept approximately 50%. Press run is 2,000 for 100 subscrib-ers of which 10 are libraries, 20 shelf sales; 40 distributed free to other magazines, the rest distributed free at coffeehouses and bookstores in L.A. Subscription: $8. Sample: $2. Make checks payable to Heather Hoffman.
How to Submit: Submit 5-15 poems at a time. Previously published poems and simultaneous submissions OK. E-mail and disk submissions OK. "See website for information on e-mail submissions." Comments on rejections on request. Send SASE for *Interbang Writer's Guide* or obtain via e-mail (writersguide@interbang.net) or website. Reports in 6 months. Always sends prepublication galleys. Pays 5 copies. Reviews chapbooks of poetry and other magazines in 350-400 words, single book format. Open to unsolicited reviews. Poets may also send books for review consideration.

◐ **INTERIM**, Dept. of English 5034, University of Nevada—Las Vegas, Las Vegas NV 89154, phone (702)895-3458, founded in Seattle, 1944-55, revived 1986, editors James Hazen, Claudia Keelan and Timothy Erwin, English editor John Heath-Stubbs.
● Member CLMP, New York. Indexed in *Index of American Periodical Verse*.
Magazine Needs: *Interim* is an annual magazine, publishing the best poetry and short fiction it can find, no specific demands in form, new and established writers. They have published poetry by Walter McDonald, Faye George, Stephen Stepanchev and Mary Winters. As a sample the editor selected these lines from "A Photograph" by Maurice Lindsay:

> . . . Acres of the heart/lay unexplored behind that photo-smile/happiness, satisfactions, failures, halts/
> that tolerant age has learnt to reconcile./As wonder cadences its dying fall/old photograph, I turn you

to the wall.

Interim is 100 pgs., 6×9, professionally printed and perfect-bound with coated card cover. Press run is 600. Individual subscription: $7/year, $12/2 years, $15/3 years; libraries: $14/year. Sample copy: $5.

How to Submit: Submit 3-5 poems at a time, SASE and brief biographical note. No simultaneous submissions. Reports in 3 months. Pays 2 copies and a 2-year subscription. Acquires first serial rights. Poems may be reprinted elsewhere with a permission line noting publication in *Interim*.

✔ ▣ $◻ **INTERLINK BBS**, P.O. Box 2757, Springfield IL 62708-2757, phone (217)753-2471, fax (217)753-5573, e-mail info@interlink-bbs.com, website http://interlink-bbs.com, founded 1995, system administrator Rachel Link.

Magazine Needs: *InterLink BBS* is a weekly web page. "The purpose is entertainment. We want anything interesting, unusual or thought provoking. We especially like fun poetry. No trash. If you wouldn't read it, don't send it to us. Don't send us your English assignments." As a sample the editor selected these lines from "Final Scrimmage" by Sparrow:

> *Jesus was born at half-time/In the great Football game of history./That's why we're all dressed as linebackers now:/Prepare for the Final Scrimmage!*

They receive about 10 poems a year, accept approximately 50%.

How to Submit: Submit up to 5 poems at a time. Previously published poems and simultaneous submissions OK. Cover letter preferred. E-mail and disk submissions OK. "Since we publish on the Web, we need to know how the author would like the poem(s) to appear on our menu." Time between acceptance and publication is 1 week. Often comments on rejections. Publishes theme issues occasionally. Obtain guidelines and upcoming themes via e-mail or website. Reports in 1 week. Pays $0-50. Buys first rights.

Advice: Jay Link says, "Since we operate on a visual medium, including pictures or graphics greatly improves your odds of acceptance. We like fun poems, not long, somber, moody pieces about your depression. Cheer up! Also, we would be willing to run a regular column, if someone wanted to do that, and if we liked the idea."

◪ ◎ **INTERNATIONAL POETRY REVIEW (Specialized: translations)**, Dept. of Romance Languages, UNC-Greensboro, Greensboro NC 27412, phone (336)334-5655, fax (336)334-5358, e-mail kmather@un cg.edu, website http://www.uncg.edu/rom/ipr, founded 1975, editor Kathleen Mather.

Magazine Needs: *IPR* is a biannual primarily publishing translations of contemporary poetry with corresponding originals (published on facing pages) as well as original poetry in English. They have published work by Jasha Kessler, Lyn Lifshin, Pureza Canelo, Jaime Sabines and Fred Chappell. *IPR* is 100 pgs., 5½×8½, professionally printed and perfect-bound with 2-3 color cover. "We accept 5% of original poetry in English and about 30% of translations submitted." Press run is 500 for 250 subscribers of which 100 are libraries. Subscription: $10 individuals, $15 institutions. Sample: $5.

How to Submit: Submit no more than 5 pages of poetry. No previously published poems; simultaneous submissions OK. Seldom comments on rejections. Publishes theme issues. Send SASE for guidelines and upcoming themes. Reports in 2-6 months. Pays 1 copy. All rights revert to authors and translators. Occasionally reviews books of poetry. Open to unsolicited reviews. Poets may also send books for review consideration.

Advice: The editor says, "We strongly encourage contributors to subscribe. We prefer poetry in English to have an international or cross-cultural theme."

◪ ◎ **INTERNATIONAL QUARTERLY; CROSSING BOUNDARIES CONTEST (Specialized: translations)**, P.O. Box 10521, Tallahassee FL 32302-0521, phone (904)224-5078, fax (904)224-5127, e-mail vbrock@mailer.fsu.edu, website http://www.mailer.fsu.edu/~vbrock/, founded 1993, editor-in-chief Van K. Brock.

Magazine Needs: "We welcome outstanding writing in all genres, in original English and in translation, quality work that transcends cultural givens. No one-dimensional views of people or place, work that is amateurish or lacks complexity. Poetry in translation appears in original and in English." They are also interested in work addressing international concerns. They have published work by S'aadi Yusuf, Bei Dao and Juan Gelman. As a sample the editor selected these lines by Anna Akhmatova, translated by Judith Hemschemeyer:

> *I came here without a child, without a knapsack,/Without so much as a walking stick,/Accompanied only by the ringing voice/Of yearning.*

IQ is 128-216 pgs., 7½×10, offset printed, perfect-bound, with full-color artwork on the coated card cover and an 8-page, 4-color insert. They receive about 800 mss/year, accept a quarter. Press run is 3,000 for 1,000 shelf sales. Single copy: $10; subscription: $30/year. Sample: $6.

How to Submit: Submit up to 8 poems, name on each. No previously published poems; simultaneous submissions OK. Cover letter welcomed. Accepts submissions, requests for information, or any sort of query via phone, fax or e-mail. Time between acceptance and publication is 3-9 months. Poems go from multiple readers to poetry editor to editorial board and editor-in-chief. Often comments on rejections. Publishes theme issues. Send SASE for upcoming themes or request via e-mail. Reports within 4 months. Pays 2 copies plus 1-year subscription. Acquires first serial rights. Reviews books of poetry. Open to unsolicited reviews; query first. Poets may also send books for review consideration.

Also Offers: Sponsors an annual contest called Crossing Boundaries. Awards $1,000 in each of 2 categories: poetry, fiction, nonfiction and "Crossing Boundaries. Translations are also eligible." Send SASE for guidelines.

Advice: The editor says, "Writers who have not published elsewhere are welcome to submit, but rarely have the polish necessary to be published in *IQ*."

⊞ ⬛ ◎ **INTERPRETER'S HOUSE; BEDFORD OPEN POETRY COMPETITION (Specialized: regional)**, 10 Farrell Rd., Wootton, Bedfordshire MK43 9DU United Kingdom, founded 1996, contact Merryn Williams.

Magazine Needs: *IH* appears 3 times/year (February, June, October) and publishes short stories and poetry. "We are particularly open to writers from our area. They want "good poetry (and short stories), not too long. No Christmas-card verse or incomprehensible poetry." They have published poetry by Dannie Abse, Tony Curtis, Pauline Stainer and R.S. Thomas. As a sample the editor selected these lines from "Metrics" by R.S. Thomas:

> There should be no/introit into a poem.//The listener should come/to and realize/verse has been going
> on/for some time. . . .

Merryn Williams says *IH* is 74 pgs., A5 with attractive cover design. They receive about 1,000 poems a year, accept approximately 10%. Press run is 300 for 150 subscribers. Subscription: £8.50. Sample: £2.50 plus 38 p.

How to Submit: Submit 5 poems at a time. No previously published poems or simultaneous submissions. Cover letter preferred. Time between acceptance and publication is 2 weeks to 8 months. Often comments on rejections. Send SASE (or SAE and IRC) for guidelines. Reports "fast." Pays 1 copy.

Also Offers: Sponsors the Bedford Open Poetry Competition. Send SAE and IRC for details.

$ ◎ ⬛ **INTERTEXT (Specialized: translations)**, 2633 E. 17th Ave., Anchorage AK 99508-3207, founded 1982, editor Sharon Ann Jaeger.

Book/Chapbook Needs & How to Submit: Intertext publishes "full-length collections by poets of demonstrated achievement" electronically, in on-demand editions, and is "devoted to producing lasting works in every sense. We specialize in poetry, translations and short works in the fine arts and literary criticism." In 1999-2000 we will not be reading unsolicited material.

◎ **INTRO (Specialized: students)**, AWP, Tallwood House, MS 1E3, George Mason University, Fairfax VA 22030, website http://www.gmu.edu/departments/awp, founded 1970, publications manager David Sherwin.

• See Associated Writing Programs in the Organizations section of this book.

Magazine Needs & How to Submit: Students in college writing programs belonging to AWP may submit to this consortium of magazines publishing student poetry, fiction and plays. They are open as to the type of poetry submitted except they do not want "non-literary, haiku, etc." As to poets they have published, they say, "In our history, we've introduced Dara Wier, Carolyn Forché, Greg Pope, Norman Dubie and others." Circulation is 9,500. All work must be submitted by the writing program. Programs nominate *Intro* works in the fall. Ask the director of your writing program for more information.

☑ ◯ **INVERTED-A, INC.; INVERTED-A HORN**, 900 Monarch Way, Northport AL 35473-2663, founded 1977, editors Amnon Katz and Aya Katz.

Magazine Needs: *Inverted-A Horn* is an irregular periodical, usually 9 pages, magazine-sized, offset printed; circulation is 300. The editors do not want to see anything "modern, formless, existentialist." As a sample the editor selected these lines by Esther Beatrice Cameron:

> when I hear folk, not speaking their own minds/but tamely seconding a wether's bell/that clanks
> somewhere ahead to lead the blind,/though at whose bidding nobody can tell,/. . . //methinks I know
> why truth cannot be found/unless by those who seek it underground.

How to Submit: Simultaneous submissions OK. Replies to queries in 1 month, to mss in 4 months. Pays 1 copy plus a 40% discount on additional copies. Samples: SASE with postage for 2 ounces (subject to availability).

Book/Chapbook Needs & How to Submit: Inverted-A Inc. is a very small press that evolved from publishing technical manuals for other products. "Our interests center on freedom, justice and honor." They publish 1 chapbook/year.

Advice: The editor says, "I strongly recommend that would-be contributors avail themselves of this opportunity to explore what we are looking for. Most of the submissions we receive do not come close."

⊞ ⬛ **IOTA**, 67 Hady Crescent, Chesterfield, Derbyshire S41 0EB Great Britain, phone 01246-276532, founded 1988, editor David Holliday.

Magazine Needs: *Iota* is a quarterly wanting "any style and subject; no specific limitations as to length, though, obviously, the shorter a poem is, the easier it is to get it in, which means that poems over 40 lines can still get in if they seem good enough. No concrete poetry (no facilities) or self-indulgent logorrhea." They have published poetry by Joseph M. Farley, Peter Hinchcliffe, Elizabeth Howkins, Matthew Mead and Ra Page. As a sample the editor selected this poem, "Nighthawk" by Anne Lewis-Smith:

> Nighthawk cuts the dark/with pointed wings/swoops swift and deep/through frost-spiked trees/fades
> fast as dreams.

Iota is 44 pgs., professionally printed and saddle-stapled with light colored card cover. They publish about 250 of 5,000 poems received. Their press run is 400 with 200 subscribers of which 6 are libraries. Subscription: $15 (£8). Sample: $2 (£1) "but sometimes sent free."

How to Submit: Submit 4-6 poems at a time. The editor prefers name and address on each poem, typed, "but provided it's legible, am happy to accept anything." Simultaneous submissions OK, but previously published poems "only if outstanding." First report in 1-3 weeks (unless production of the next issue takes precedence) but final acceptance/rejection may take up to a year. Pays 2 copies. Acquires first British serial rights only. Editor usually comments on rejections, "but detailed comment only when time allows and the poem warrants it." Reviews books of poetry in about 200 words, single or multi-book format. Open to unsolicited reviews. Poets may also send books for review consideration.

Advice: He says, "I am after crafted verse that says something; self-indulgent word-spinning is out. All editors have their blind spots; the only advice I can offer a beginning poet is to find a sympathetic editor (and you will only do that by seeing their magazines) and not to be discouraged by initial lack of success. Keep plugging!"

$ ☯ THE IOWA REVIEW; THE TIM McGINNIS AWARD, 308 EPB, University of Iowa, Iowa City IA 52242, phone (319)335-0462, e-mail iowa-review@uiowa.edu, website http://www.iowa.edu/~iareview, founded 1970, editors David Hamilton and Mary Hussmann, contact poetry editor.

● Poetry published in *The Iowa Review* has also been included in the 1992, 1993, 1994, 1995, 1996 and 1997 volumes of *The Best American Poetry* and the *Pushcart Prize* anthology for 1994 and 1995.

Magazine Needs: *IR* appears 3 times/year and publishes fiction, poetry, essays, reviews, interviews and autobiographical sketches. The editors say, "We simply look for poems that at the time we read and choose, we admire. No specifications as to form, length, style, subject matter or purpose. There are around 40 pgs. of poetry in each issue and we like to give several pages to a single poet. Though we print work from established writers, we're always delighted when we discover new talent." *IR* is 200 pgs., professionally printed, flat-spined. They receive about 5,000 submissions/year, use about 100. Press run is 1,200-1,300 with 1,000 subscribers of which about half are libraries. Subscription: $18. Sample: $6.

How to Submit: Submit 3-6 poems at a time. No e-mail submissions. Cover letter (with title of work and genre) and SASE required. Reads submissions September 1 through January 31 "or until we fill our next volume year's issues." Time between acceptance and publication is "around a year. Sometimes people hit at the right time and come out in a few months." Occasionally comments on rejections or offers suggestions on accepted poems. Reports in 1-4 months. Pays $1/line, 2-3 copies and a 1-year subscription. Buys first North American serial rights, non-exclusive anthology rights and non-exclusive electronic rights.

Also Offers: Sponsors The Tim McGinnis Award. "The award, in the amount of $500, is given irregularly to authors of work with a light or humorous touch. We have no separate category of submissions to be considered alone for this award. Instead, any essay, story, or poem we publish which is charged with a distinctly comic vision will automatically come under consideration for the McGinnis Award." Website includes excerpts, download guidelines, table of contents, etc.

◖ ◎ IRIS: A JOURNAL ABOUT WOMEN (Specialized: translations, women/feminism), Women's Center, Box 323, HSC, University of Virginia, Charlottesville VA 22908, founded 1980, poetry editor Margo Andrea Figgins.

Magazine Needs: *Iris* is a semiannual magazine that "focuses on issues concerning women worldwide. It features quality poetry, prose and artwork—mainly by women, but will also accept work by men if it illuminates some aspect of a woman's reality. It also publishes translations. Form and length are unspecified. The poetry staff consists of experienced poets with a diversity of tastes who are looking for new and original language in well-crafted poems." Poets who have appeared in *Iris* include Sharon Olds, Elaine Terranova, Mary Oliver, Lisel Mueller, Linda Pastan, Naomi Shihab Nye, Liliana Ursu and Gregory Orr. As a sample the editor selected these lines from "The Lost Daughter" by Susan Imhof:

> Seven years dead and still she grows,/copper hair a strange fin/rippling through the furnace of desert
> noon,/your dream of oil spills:/birds descending/on the airstream, wings/tucked, legs unfolded to meet/
> their reflections before/the black gold swallows them,/wing tips rising a brief moment toward heaven/
> through the shimmering heat, a slow/explosion of blue flame. . . .

Iris is 82 pgs., magazine-sized, professionally printed on heavy, glossy stock, saddle-stapled with a full-color glossy card cover, using graphics and photos. Press run is over 3,000 for about 50 library subscriptions, 1,000 shelf sales. Single copy: $5; subscription: $9/year; $17/2 years. Sample: $6.50.

How to Submit: Submit up to 5 poems at a time. Simultaneous submissions are discouraged. Name, address, phone number should be listed on every poem. Cover letter should include list of poems submitted and a brief bio. Reports in 3-6 months. Pays 1 copy and subscription. Acquires first rights.

Advice: The editor says, "Because *Iris* is a feminist magazine, it receives a lot of poetry focusing on the political experience of coming to consciousness. The editor is interested in *all* aspects of the reality of women's lives and, because many poems are on similar topics, freshness of imagery and style are even more important."

◎ ITALIAN AMERICANA; JOHN CIARDI AWARD (Specialized: ethnic), URI/CCE, 80 Washington St., Providence RI 02903-1803, phone (401)277-5306, fax (401)277-5100, website http://www.uri.edu/prov/ital ian/italian.html, founded 1974, editor Carol Bonomo Albright, poetry editor Dana Gioia.

Magazine Needs: *IA* appears twice a year using 16-20 poems of "no more than three pgs. No trite nostalgia; no poems about grandparents." They have published poetry by Mary Jo Salter and Joy Parini. It is 150-200 pgs., 7×9, professionally printed and flat-spined with glossy card cover. Press run is 1,000 for 900 subscribers of which 175 are libraries, 175 shelf sales. Singly copy: $10; subscription: $20. Sample: $6.

How to Submit: Submit 3 poems at a time. No previously published poems or simultaneous submissions. Cover letter not required "but helpful." Name on first page of ms only. Do not submit poetry in July, August or September. Occasionally comments on rejections. Reports in 4-6 weeks. Acquires first rights. Reviews books of poetry in 600 words, multi-book format. Poets may send books for review consideration to Prof. John Paul Russo, English Dept., University of Miami, Coral Gables FL 33124.

Also Offers: Along with the National Italian American Foundation, *IA* co-sponsors the annual $1,000 John Ciardi Award for Lifetime Contribution to Poetry. *IA* also presents $500 fiction or memoir award annually; and $1,000 in history prizes. Website includes writer's guidelines, names of editors, poetry, historical articles and fiction.

Advice: The editor says, "Single copies of poems for submissions are sufficient."

$ ☺ ITALICA PRESS (Specialized: bilingual/foreign language), 595 Main St., #605, New York NY 10044-0047, phone (212)935-4230, fax (212)838-7812, e-mail italica@aol.com, founded 1985, publishers Eileen Gardiner and Ronald G. Musto.

Book/Chapbook Needs: Italica is a small press publisher of English translations of Italian works in Smyth-sewn paperbacks, averaging 175 pgs. They have published *Guido Cavalcanti, The Complete Poems*, a dual-language (English/Italian) book with English translation and introduction by Marc Cirigliano, and *Women Poets of the Italian Renaissance*, a dual-language anthology, edited by Laura Anna Stortoni and translated by Laura Anna Stortoni and Mary Prentice Lillie.

How to Submit: Query with 10 sample translations of medieval and Renaissance Italian poets. Include cover letter, bio and list of publications. Simultaneous submissions OK, but translation should not be "totally" previously published. No submissions via fax or e-mail; however, queries via fax or e-mail are OK. Reports on queries in 3 weeks, on mss in 3 months. Always sends prepublication galleys. Pays 7-15% royalties plus 10 author's copies. Buys English language rights. Sometimes comments on rejections.

○ ◑ JACK MACKEREL MAGAZINE; ROWHOUSE PRESS, P.O. Box 23134, Seattle WA 98102-0434, founded 1992, editor Greg Bachar.

Magazine Needs: *Jack Mackerel*, published quarterly, features poetry, fiction and art. They have published poetry by Brett Astor, William D. Waltz and Heather Hayes. *Jack Mackerel* is 40-60 pgs., 5½×8½, printed on bond paper, with glossy card cover stock, b&w illustrations and photos. Press run is 1,000. Subscription: $12. Sample: $5. Make checks payable to Greg Bachar.

How to Submit: No previously published poems or simultaneous submissions. Cover letter preferred. Poems are circulated to an editorial board. Seldom comments on rejections. Reports in 2-4 weeks. Pays with copies. Staff reviews chapbooks, books and magazines of poetry. Send books for review consideration.

Book/Chapbook Needs & How to Submit: Send SASE for information on Rowhouse Press or to obtain sample book.

Ⓝ ◖ JANUS, A JOURNAL OF POETRY; COLLINGS HOUSE PRESS, 815 Knorr St., Philadelphia PA 19111, editors Scott Jermyn and David Livewell.

Magazine Needs: *Janus* appears semiannually in the spring and fall. The editor says, "We seek well-crafted verse in forms that are necessary to the content. Both metrical and free verse are considered." They have published poetry by Fred Chappell, Rachel Hadas, Seamus Heaney, X.J. Kennedy, Thomas Kinsella, Edwin Morgan and Louis Simpson. *Janus* is 72 pgs., 5½×8½, neatly printed and saddle-stapled, with colored card cover and b&w graphics. They receive approximately 1,000 poetry submissions a year, accept about 12. Press run is 700. Subscription: $12/3 issues, $15 for institutions. Sample: $5.

How to Submit: Submit 3-5 poems at a time. "Submissions cannot be returned." Include SASE for response. No previously published poems or simultaneous submissions. Cover letter and short bio required. Seldom comments on rejections. Reports in 2-3 months. Pays in copies. "We review books of poetry and other books of literary merit." Open to unsolicited reviews and essays provided "they are serious and relevant to contemporary poetry."

Advice: The editor says, "We do not want to discourage submissions, but since we publish so few unsolicited poems, it is important that authors submit their very best work. In particular, we do not see enough attention paid to the intricacies of meter and form."

THE CHAPBOOK INDEX, located at the back of this book, lists those publishers who consider chapbook mss. A chapbook, a small volume of work (usually under 50 pages), is often a good middle step between magazine and book publication.

☑ $◎ **JAPANOPHILE (Specialized: form, ethnic)**, P.O. Box 7977, Ann Arbor MI 48107, phone (734)930-1553, e-mail susanlapp@aol.com or jpnhand@japanophile.com, website http://www.japanophile.com, founded 1974, editor Susan A. Lapp, poetry editor Ashby Kinch.

Magazine Needs: *Japanophile* is a literary quarterly about Japanese culture (not just in Japan). Issues include articles, photos, art, a short story and poetry. They want haiku or other Japanese forms ("they need not be about Japanese culture") or any form if the subject is about Japan, Japanese culture or American-Japanese relations. (Note: Karate and ikebana in the US are examples of Japanese culture.) They have published poetry by Renee Leopold, Nancy Corson Carter, Jean Jorgensen, Mimi Walter Hinman and reprints of Bashō. As a sample the editor selected this haiku (poet unidentified):

> *first snowstorm/our old cat rediscovers/the warm airduct*

There are 10-15 pgs. of poetry in each issue (digest-sized, about 58 pgs., saddle-stapled). They have a circulation of 800 with 200 subscriptions of which 30 are libraries. They receive about 500 submissions a year, use 70, have a 2-month backlog. Sample: $4.

How to Submit: Summer is the best time to submit. E-mail and fax submissions OK. Cover letter required; include brief bio and credits if any. Send SASE for guidelines and upcoming themes or request via e-mail. Reports in 2 months. Pays $3 for haiku and up to $15 for longer poems. Open to unsolicited reviews. Poets may also send books for review consideration, attn. Ashby Kinch.

Book/Chapbook Needs & How to Submit: They also publish books under the Japanophile imprint, but so far only one has been of poetry. Query with samples and cover letter (about 1 pg.) giving publishing credits, bio.

Also Offers: Website includes guidelines, information on the magazine and brief blurbs on the editors.

Advice: The editor says, "This quarterly is out as each season begins. Poems that name or suggest a season, and are received two or three months before the season, get a good look."

◐ ◎ **JAVELINA PRESS (Specialized: women, regional)**, P.O. Box 42131, Tucson AZ 85733-2131, founded 1995, editor Caitlin L. Gannon.

Book/Chapbook Needs: Javelina Press is interested in fiction and poetry by women, primarily representing the Southwestern US and publishes 1-2 paperbacks/year. They have published poetry by Judith McDaniel, Antonia Quintana Pigno, Jacqueline Moody and Maria Teresa Garcia.

How to Submit: Poetry mss accepted only in response to calls for submissions. "Calls for submissions are published in national and regional journals and newspapers." When responding to calls for submissions, previously published poems and simultaneous submissions OK. Cover letter required. Time between acceptance and publication is 6 weeks. Seldom comments on rejections. Replies to queries in 3 weeks, to mss (if invited) in 2 months.

⟦N⟧ ⊕ ◯ **JEJUNE: AMERICA EATS ITS YOUNG**, P.O. Box 85, Prague 1, 11001 Czech Republic, founded 1993, contact managing editor.

Magazine Needs: *JEJUNE: america eats its young* appears biannually and publishes "poetry, fiction and socio-political articles on Central Europe and the globalization of culture from the undeclared empire of the USA: zest for life vs. consumerism." They want "intense poetry. No high flautin' pretentious work." They have published poetry by Jack Hirschman, Jules Mann and Ed Mycue. As a sample they selected these lines from a poem by Eileen Myles:

> . . . *born speechless and female in America. I'm talking to you. A world turning in the sun. . . . active*
> *citizenry. To love, in a word.*

They say *JEJUNE* is 60 pgs., offset printed and perfect-bound, includes drawings, photos and collages, ads. They receive about 400 poems a year, accept approximately 10%. Press run is 500. Subscription: $20. Sample: $5. Make checks payable to Vincent Farnsworth.

How to Submit: Submit 4 poems at a time. Previously published poems and simultaneous submissions OK. Time between acceptance and publication is 1-2 months. Seldom comments on rejections. Reports in 1-2 months. Sometimes sends prepublication galleys. Pays in copies. Staff reviews books of poetry and other magazines in 200 words. Send books for review consideration.

Also Offers: *JEJUNE* organizes poetry readings for poets visiting Prague. In the past, they have arranged readings for Craig Denton, Jules Mann, Andrei Codrescu and Dave Brinks.

Advice: They offer, "Creeley: 'Words depend upon us for their existence.' Tom Clark: 'Internet Surfer(ing) waves of useless information.' Eileen Myles: 'Wield the language of world finance.' "

⊕ ◯ ◎ **JEWISH AFFAIRS (Specialized: ethnic)**, P.O. Box 87557, Houghton 2082, Johannesburg, South Africa, phone (27)(11)486-1434, fax (27)(11)646-4940, e-mail 071jos@muse.arts.wits.ac.za, founded 1941, executive editor professor Joseph Sherman.

Magazine Needs: *Jewish Affairs* is a "quarterly journal of Jewish interest containing scholarly essays on all aspects of Jewish history, culture, thought and religion." All poetry is welcome; poetry with Jewish themes or subject matter especially so. We do not accept previously published material." They have published poetry by Sinclair Beiles, Lionel Abrahams and Frieda Freeman. *JA* is 84 pgs., A4, perfect-bound, professionally printed with glossy 4-color cover, cover art, and b&w and color ads. They receive about 100 poems a year, accept approximately 20%. Press run is 2,000 for 1,500 subscribers of which 100 are libraries. Subscription: $40. Sample (including guidelines): $10. Make checks payable to South African Jewish Board of Deputies.

How to Submit: No previously published poems or simultaneous submissions. E-mail submissions OK. Cover letter required. Time between acceptance and publication is 6-8 months. Poems are circulated to an editorial board. "Poems are considered by two members of the editorial board before being accepted." Publishes theme issues. Write for list of upcoming themes. Reports within 2 months. Acquires first rights. Requests acknowledgement of first publication in *Jewish Affairs*. Reviews books of poetry in up to 2,500 words depending on significance of the book." Open to unsolicited reviews. Poets may also send books for review consideration. Pays 2 copies and 1 set of tearsheets.
Advice: Note: South Africa does not use IRCs. Therefore, *JA* cannot return submissions. A letter will be sent if work is accepted. The editor says, "We welcome all submissions, especially from poets never published before."

JEWISH CURRENTS (Specialized: themes, religious), 22 E. 17th St., Suite 601, New York NY 10003-1919, phone/fax (212)924-5740, founded 1946, editor Morris U. Schappes.
Magazine Needs: *Jewish Currents* is a magazine appearing 11 times a year that publishes articles, reviews, fiction and poetry pertaining to Jewish subjects or presenting a Jewish point of view on an issue of interest, including translations from the Yiddish and Hebrew (original texts should be submitted with translations). The editor says it is 48 pgs., 5×8, offset, saddle-stapled. Press run is 2,500 for 2,100 subscribers of which about 10% are libraries. Subscription: $30/year. Sample: $3.
How to Submit: Submit 1 poem at a time, typed, double-spaced, with SASE. Include brief bio. No previously published poems or simultaneous submissions. Fax submissions OK. Cover letter required. Publishes theme issues. Deadlines for themes are 6 months in advance. Time between acceptance and publication is 2 years. Seldom comments on rejections. Reports in 6-12 months. Always sends prepublication galleys. Pays 6 copies plus 1-year subscription. Reviews books of poetry.

JEWISH SPECTATOR (Specialized: religious), 9107 Wilshire Blvd., Beverly Hills CA 90210, e-mail isdev@aol.com, founded 1935, literary editor Avi Davis.
Magazine Needs: *Jewish Spectator* is a 68-page Judaic scholarly quarterly that welcomes poetry on Jewish themes. They have published poetry by Rodger Kamenetz, Louis Daniel Brodsky, Barbara Brent Brower, Lynn Levin and Robert Deluty. Subscribers: 1,400.
How to Submit: Cover letter with brief bio (2-3 lines) required. Reports in 6 weeks. Returns mss only with SASE. Pays 2 copies. Open to unsolicited reviews. Poets may also send books for review consideration.

$ JEWISH WOMEN'S LITERARY ANNUAL; JEWISH WOMEN'S RESOURCE CENTER (Specialized: ethnic, women), 9 E. 69th St., New York NY 10021, phone (212)751-9223, fax (212)935-3523, founded 1994, editor Henny Wenkart.
Magazine Needs: *JWLA* appears annually in April and publishes poetry and fiction by Jewish women. They want "poems by Jewish women on any topic, but of the highest literary quality." They have published poetry by Alicia Ostriker, Savina Teuba, Grace Herman, Enid Dame, Marge Piercy and Lesléa Newman. As a sample the editor selected these lines from "A Yiddish Poet in Winter" by Layle Silbert:
> in this winter of my life/I invent two children/scampering in snow/nourished on remains/of my past
> they say/we'll be alive for you/may they burst into a spill/of my dimming language/with last stories/of
> Vilna/take what is left/in my memory/tramped by war exile/finish children/before my winter ends
The annual is 160 pgs., 6×9, perfect-bound with a laminated card cover, b&w art and photos inside. They receive about 500 poems a year, publish approximately 15%. Press run is 1,500 for 480 subscribers. Subscription: $18/ 3 issues. Sample: $7.50.
How to Submit: No previously published poems. No fax submissions. Poems are circulated to an editorial board. Often comments on rejections. Reports in 3-5 months. Pays 3 copies plus a small honorarium. Rights remain with the poet.
Book/Chapbook Needs & How to Submit: The Jewish Women's Resource Center holds a monthly workshop, sponsors occasional readings and also publishes a few books of poetry. "We select only 1 or 2 manuscripts a year out of about 20 submitted. But although authors then receive editing help and publicity, they bear the cost of production. Members of the workshop we conduct and poets published in our annual receive first attention."
Advice: The editor says, "It would be helpful, but not essential, if poets would send for a sample copy of our annual before submitting."

THE JOHNS HOPKINS UNIVERSITY PRESS, 2715 N. Charles St., Baltimore MD 21218, website http://www.press.jhu.edu, founded 1878. "One of the largest American university presses, Johns Hopkins is a publisher mainly of scholarly books and journals. We do, however, publish short fiction and poetry in the series Johns Hopkins: Poetry and Fiction, edited by John Irwin. Unsolicited submissions are not considered."

JONES AV.; OEL PRESS, 88 Dagmar Ave., Toronto, Ontario M4M 1W1 Canada, phone (416)461-8739, e-mail oel@interlog.com, website http://utl2.library.utoronto.ca/~kaszuba/jones_av/index.html, founded 1994, editor/publisher Paul Schwartz.
Magazine Needs: *Jones Av.* is published quarterly and contains "poems from the lyric to the ash can; starting poets and award winners." They want poems "up to 30 lines mostly, concise in thought and image. Prose poems

sometimes. Rhymed poetry is very difficult to do well these days, it better be good." They have published poetry by Allan Brown, Lyn Lifshin, Michael Estabrook and Peter Bakowski. As a sample the editor selected this poem, "the red apple" by Claudia K. Grinnell:

> the red apple/sliced in/two redeems/spilling flesh/surrenders/to fingertips/inviting deep/ascension when/halves meet

Jones Av. is 24 pgs., 5½×8½, photocopied and saddle-stapled with card cover, uses b&w graphics. They receive about 300 poems a year, accept approximately 40-50%. Press run is 100 for 40 subscribers. Subscription: $8. Sample: $2. Make checks payable to Paul Schwartz

How to Submit: Submit 5-8 poems at a time. No previously published poems or simultaneous submissions. Cover letter required. E-mail and disk submissions OK. Time between acceptance and publication is 6-9 months. Often comments on rejections. Publishes theme issues occasionally. Send SASE (or SAE or IRC) for guidelines or obtain via e-mail or website. Remember, US stamps cannot be used in Canada. Reports in 3 months. Pays 1 copy. Acquires first rights. Staff reviews books and chapbooks of poetry and other magazines in 50-75 words, multi-book format. Poets may also send books for review consideration.

$ ☑ THE JOURNAL, Dept. of English, Ohio State University, 164 W. 17th Ave., Columbus OH 43210, phone (614)292-4076, fax (614)292-7816, e-mail thejournal05@postbox.acs.ohio-state.edu, website http://www.cohums.ohio-state.edu/english/journals/the_journal/, founded 1972, co-editors Kathy Fagan and Michelle Herman.
   ● Also see the listing for Ohio State University Press/*The Journal* Award in Poetry in this section.

Magazine Needs: *The Journal* appears twice yearly with reviews, essays, quality fiction and poetry. "We're open to all forms; we tend to favor work that gives evidence of a mature and sophisticated sense of the language." They have published poetry by Brigit Kelly, Lucia Perillo, Timothy Liu and Heather McHugh. *The Journal* is 6×9, professionally printed on heavy stock, 128-144 pgs., of which about 60 in each issue are devoted to poetry. They receive about 4,000 submissions a year, use approximately 200, and have a 3- to 6-month backlog. Press run is 1,900. Subscription: $12. Sample: $7.

How to Submit: No submissions via fax. On occasion editor comments on rejections. Pays 2 copies and an honorarium of $25-50 when funds are available. Acquires all rights. Returns rights on publication. Reviews books of poetry.

Advice: Contributing editor David Citino says, "However else poets train or educate themselves, they must do what they can to know our language. Too much of the writing we see indicates poets do not in many cases develop a feel for the possibilities of language, and do not pay attention to craft. Poets should not be in a rush to publish—until they are ready."

◎ JOURNAL OF AFRICAN TRAVEL-WRITING (Specialized), P.O. Box 346, Chapel Hill NC 27514, website http://www.unc.edu/~ottotwo, founded 1996, contact poetry editor.

Magazine Needs: *JATW*, published biannually, "presents and explores past and contemporary accounts of African travel." They want "poetry touching on any aspect of African travel. Translations are also welcome." Published poets include José Craveirinha, Theresa Sengova, Charles Hood and Sonia Gomez. As a sample the editor selected these lines from "Warthog Music" by Lynn Veach Sadler:

> Who cannot believe there is a God/has not the Kenyan warthog seen,/for in the delicacy of its going—/ gossamer strings plucked by divining being.

JATW is 96 pgs., 7×10, professionally printed, perfect-bound, coated stock cover with cover and illustrative art, ads. Press run is 600. Subscription: $10. Sample: $6.

How to Submit: Submit up to 6 poems at a time. Include SASE. No previously published poems; simultaneous submissions OK. Cover letter preferred. Time between acceptance and publication is 3-12 months. "The poetry editor usually makes these selections." Often comments on rejections. Send SASE for guidelines. Publishes theme issues. Upcoming themes include Travel by Africans Outside Africa. Deadline: September 30, 1999. Reports in 2-6 weeks. Always sends prepublication galleys. Pays 5 copies. Acquires first international publication rights. Reviews books, chapbooks or magazines of poetry. Open to unsolicited reviews. Poets may also send books for review consideration.

Also Offers: Website includes submission guidelines, poetry, reviews, articles and interviews.

☑ $ ◎ JOURNAL OF ASIAN MARTIAL ARTS (Specialized: sports/recreation), 821 W. 24th St., Erie PA 16502-2523, phone (814)455-9517, fax (814)526-5262, e-mail info@goviamedia.com, website http://www.goviamedia.com, founded 1991, editor-in-chief Michael A. DeMarco.

Magazine Needs: *JAMA* is a quarterly "comprehensive journal on Asian martial arts with high standards and academic approach." They want poetry about Asian martial arts and Asian martial art history/culture. They have no restrictions provided the poet has a feel for, and good understanding of, the subject. They don't want poetry showing a narrow view. "We look for a variety of styles from an interdisciplinary approach." As a sample the editor selected these lines from "Cloudburst" by R.E. Mitchell, Jr.:

> When a person strikes another/Is he hurting the other or himself . . ./Is he angry with another/Or with his own shortcomings?//Whether you are killed by flood or lightning,/A storm is still a storm.

The journal is 124 pgs., 8½×11, professionally printed on coated stock and perfect-bound with soft cover, b&w illustrations, computer and hand art and ads. Press run is 12,000 for 1,500 subscribers of which 50 are libraries, the rest mainly shelf sales. Single copy: $9.75; subscription: $32/year, $55/2 years. Sample: $10.

How to Submit: Previously published poems OK; no simultaneous submissions. E-mail submissions OK. Cover letter required. Often comments on rejections. Send SASE for guidelines or request via e-mail or fax. Reports in 1-2 months. Sometimes sends prepublication galleys. Pays $1-100 and/or 1-5 copies on publication. Buys first world and reprint rights. Reviews books of poetry "if they have some connection to Asian martial arts; length is open." Open to unsolicited reviews. Poets may also send books for review consideration.
Advice: The editor adds, "We offer a unique medium for serious poetry dealing with Asian martial arts. Any style is welcome if there is quality in thought and writing."

⊕ ⏻ ◎ JOURNAL OF CONTEMPORARY ANGLO-SCANDINAVIAN POETRY; ORIGINAL PLUS (Specialized: translations), 11 Heatherton Park, Bradford on Tone, Taunton, Somerset TA4 1EU England, phone 01823 461725, founded 1994, contact Sam Smith.
Magazine Needs: *JoCA-SP*, published biannually, features English poetry or English translations of Scandinavian poems and interviews with Scandinavian poets. They want "new poetry howsoever it comes, translations from Scandinavian and original English language poems." They do not want "staid, generalized, all form no content." They have published poetry by Tomas Tranströmer, Staffan Söderblom, Olav H. Hauge and Alexis Lykiard. As a sample the editor selected these lines from "We Too Are Laymen, Said the Waves" by Werner Aspenström, translated by Robin Fulton:

> Two nights in a row setting out from Stavanger/I made my way on foot over the Atlantic/between icebergs and oil-rigs/to the accompaniment/of excited conversations with the waves/who comforted me saying:/"We too are laymen."

JoCA SP is 60-70 pgs., A5, offset printed, perfect-bound with CS1 cover stock. They receive about 1,000 poems a year, accept approximately 5%. Press run is 100-150 for 70 subscribers of which 12 are libraries. Single copy: £6; subscription: £11. Sample: £2 or £3 (sterling). Make checks payable to Sam Smith.
How to Submit: Submit up to 6 poems. Previously published poems and simultaneous submissions OK. Cover letter preferred. "Please send hard copy submissions with 2 IRCs." Time between acceptance and publication is 6-8 months. Often comments on rejections. Send SASE (or SAE and IRC) for guidelines. Reports in 2-4 weeks. Always sends prepublication galleys. Pays 1 copy.
Also Offers: In 1997, original plus began publishing collections of poetry. They have published books by Don Ammons, Idris Caffrey and RG Bishop. Send SASE (or SAE and IRC) for details.

⏻ ◎ JOURNAL OF NEW JERSEY POETS (Specialized: regional), English Dept., County College of Morris, 214 Center Grove Rd., Randolph NJ 07869-2086, phone (973)328-5471, fax (973)328-5425, e-mail szulauf@ccm.edu, website http://www.garden.net/users/swaa/JrnlNJPoets.html, founded 1976, editor Sander Zulauf.
Magazine Needs: This biannual periodical uses poetry from current or former residents of New Jersey. They want "serious work that is regional in origin but universal in scope." They do not want "sentimental, greeting card verse." They have published poetry by Amiri Baraka, X.J. Kennedy, Brigit Pegeen Kelly, Kenneth Burke, Gerald Stern, Renée and Ted Weiss, and Rachel Hadas. As a sample the editor selected these lines from "Anniversary" by Peter Murphy:

> The world we live in is two worlds—/one clings to the other/the way a pencil wraps around its lead./ Its mark begins to make sense/only after the skin has been grazed/by the passing of sharp blades.

JNJP is published in summer and winter and is digest-sized, offset printed, with an average of 64 pgs. Press run is 900. Subscription: $10/2 issues, $16/4 issues; institutions: $12/2 issues, $20/4 issues; students/senior citizens: $10/4 issues. Sample: $5.
How to Submit: There are "no limitations" on submissions; SASE required. E-mail and fax submissions OK. Electronic submissions will not be returned. Reports in 6-12 months. Time between acceptance and publication is within 1 year. Pays 2 copies/published poem. Acquires first North American serial rights. Only using solicited reviews. Send books for review consideration.
Also Offers: Website includes cover picture of latest issue, names of editors and links to the editors.

⏻ ◎ JOURNAL OF THE AMERICAN MEDICAL ASSOCIATION (JAMA) (Specialized: health concerns, themes), 515 N. State, Chicago IL 60610, phone (312)464-2417, fax (312)464-5824, e-mail charlene_breedlove@ama_assn.org (for queries only), founded 1883, associate editor Charlene Breedlove.
Magazine Needs: *JAMA* has a "Poetry and Medicine" column and publishes poetry "in some way related to a medical experience, whether from the point-of-view of a health care worker or patient, or simply an observer. No unskilled poetry." They have published poetry by Aimée Grunberger, Floyd Skloot and Walt McDonald. As a sample the editor selected these lines from "Spleen (No. 78)" by Paula Tatarunis:

> Ennui is small and has a child-proof lid./Its skull collapses on each new-born thought./Its belt's cinched far beyond the tightest fit./Its life's in acronym on microdot.

JAMA is magazine-sized, flat-spined, with a glossy paper cover, has 360,000 subscribers of which 369 are libraries. They accept about 7% of 750 poems received/year. Subscription: $66. Sample free. "No SASE needed."
How to Submit: No previously published poems; simultaneous submissions OK, if identified. "I always appreciate inclusion of a brief cover letter with, at minimum, the author's name and address clearly printed. Mention of other publications and special biographical notes are always of interest." Fax submissions OK. "Poems sent via fax will be responded to by postal service." Publishes theme issues. Theme issues include

cancer, heart disease, violence, medical education, health promotion, obesity and aging/longevity. "However, we would rather that poems relate obliquely to the theme." Pays 1 copy, more by request. "We ask for a signed copyright release, but publication elsewhere is always granted free of charge."

Ⓝ $ 🖂 THE JOYFUL WOMAN; JOYFUL CHRISTIAN MINISTRIES, P.O. Box 90028, Chattanooga TN 37412, phone (706)866-5522, fax (706)866-2432, e-mail joyfulcmi@aol.com, website http://www.joyfulwoman.org, founded 1978, editor/executive director Joy Martin, assistant editor Joanna Rice.
Magazine Needs: *Joyful Woman* appears bimonthly "for and about Bible-believing women who want God's best." They want poetry "to encourage Christian women." They have published poetry by Jessie Sandberg. *TJW* is 32 pgs., magazine-sized, professionally printed on glossy paper and saddle-stapled, 4-color glossy paper cover, includes b&w and color photos. They receive about 10-20 poems a year, accept small percentage. Press run is 6,000 for 4,300 subscribers. Sample: $3.50 plus postage.
How to Submit: Previously published poems and simultaneous submissions OK. Cover letter preferred. E-mail and disk submissions OK. Time between acceptance and publication is 6-12 months. Seldom comments on rejections. Publishes theme issues. Send SASE for guidelines. Reports in 6 weeks. Pays $15-20 plus 5 copies. Acquires one-time rights.

🖂 JUNCTION PRESS, P.O. Box 40537, San Diego CA 92164, founded 1991, publisher Mark Weiss.
Book/Chapbook Needs: Junction Press aims to publish "overlooked non-mainstream poetry." The press publishes 2 paperback books of poetry a year. They want "modern or postmodern formally innovative work, any form or length. No academic, Iowa school or formal poetry." They have published poetry by Armand Schwerner, Susie Mee, Richard Elman, José Kozer and Mervyn Taylor. They say their books are typically 72-96 pgs., 5½×8½, offset printed and perfect-bound with coated covers with graphics.
How to Submit: Query first with 10-15 pgs. of poetry and a cover letter (bio unnecessary). Previously published poems OK; no simultaneous submissions. Often comments on rejections. Replies to queries in 6 months, to mss (if invited) "immediately." Pays 100 copies (out of a press run of 1,000).
Advice: The publisher says, "While I don't dismiss the possibility of finding a second Rimbaud, please note that all of my authors have been in their 50s and have written and published for many years."

Ⓝ 🖥 ◯ 🖂 📷 JUPITER'S FREEDOM (Specialized: science fiction/fantasy, horror, surreal), P.O. Box 110217, Palm Bay FL 32911-0217, e-mail J5FM@hotmail.com, website http://members.xoom.com/J5FM, founded 1998, editor Christine Smalldone.
Magazine Needs: *Jupiter's Freedom* is a quarterly online journal featuring fiction, poetry, art and articles. The editor is looking for "works which span the regions of science fiction—from speculative fiction to horror, fantasy and works of the surreal. I want poetry with edge, style and innovative thinking; with the ability to paint a visual landscape and go in new directions. Nothing sweet and sappy. I don't mind happy endings, just do them in an interesting way." As a sample we selected these lines from "A Bed Time Story" by Cs:

> I stand in silence, mezmerized by the story that/unfolds before my eyes. Like a child's fairy tale/being
> read by its mother, who sits at the edge of/our bed and subdues our eyes into sleep./Only to awaken
> in the midst of rest with fears of/dragons and monsters running in the dark places.

They receive about 100 poems a year, accept 50-60%. They also have a printed version of *Jupiter's Freedom*. The editor says it is 8½×11, desktop-published, brass fastened, 70 lb. card cover, includes b&w and color art. Subscription: $18/year. Sample: $5.
How to Submit: Submit 1-3 poems at a time. Previously published poems OK; no simultaneous submissions. E-mail and disk submissions OK. Cover letter preferred. Time between acceptance and publication is 1-2 months. Often comments on rejections. Send SASE for guidelines and specifications on electronic or disk submissions or request via e-mail. Reports in 1-3 weeks. Pays 1 copy and "3.5 inch floppy (no Mac)."
Advice: The editor says, "Remember, the longer it is the better it must be. Please try to stay away from overused and abused genre stereotypes such as vampire redemption, time travel, dragons, fairies, or robots gone mad. We don't accept any submissions having to do with sex, racism, sexism, overly gory (just for the sake of it) or anything that demeans, slanders or belittles anyone or anything. Be yourself and your own voice. Dare to be bold and different, take chances. Learn from others, but don't be like others. Break the mold and break it hard if you have to."

◯ JUS WRITE; IZOLA BIRD PUBLICATIONS, P.O. Box 574, South Bend IN 46624, founded 1994.
Magazine Needs: *Jus Write* appears 2 times a year in the Spring and Fall. "We want to help new poets get published. We know how discouraging the market can be. We are interested in receiving work from African American writers. No form; no poems over 20 lines long. No racial or sexual exploitative work." They have published poetry by Derrick Nelson and Hudson Bey. As a sample they selected these lines from "dark embrace" by Fred Goodall:

> I want to hold you softly in the night/and watch the moon light bathe your/sable cheeks/only you can
> appease/my appetite./I hunger for each work your body speaks/I often dream you on a rainy day./
> Making love to me beneath the dark sky/Drowning my soul with the music you play

Jus Write is 20 pgs., 8½×11, photocopied, saddle-stapled with paper cover, includes photos and ads. They receive about 100 poems a year, accept approximately 50%. Press run is 1,000, 50% shelf sales. Single copy:

$5.50/issue for subscribers. Sample: $6.50. Make checks payable to Izola Bird Publications. "We encourage writers to become subscribers."

How to Submit: Submit 4 poems at a time. No previously published poems or simultaneous submissions. Brief cover letter preferred. Send large SASE for return of ms. Time between acceptance and publication is 1 month. Always comments on rejections. Criticism fee: $50. Send SASE and $3.75 for guidelines. Sometimes sends prepublication galleys.

Also Offers: "We sponsor a poetry contest in which poem and author will be published in Spring and Fall issue, also in two local newspapers, *The Communicator* and *Expression*. We also send a news release to author's local newspaper. The fee is $15, $10 for writers already published by us." Write for details.

K.T. PUBLICATIONS; THE THIRD HALF; KITE BOOKS; KITE MODERN POETS; KITE YOUNG WRITERS, 16 Fane Close, Stamford, Lincolnshire PE9 1HG England, phone (01780)754193, founded 1987, editor Kevin Troop.

Magazine Needs: *The Third Half* is a literary magazine published irregularly. It contains "free-flowing and free-thinking material on most subjects." They are "open to all ideas and suggestions. No badly written or obscene scribbling." As a sample we selected this poem, "Without Words," by Isabel Cortan:

> a savage sound,/sharp crack of a man's hand/across a woman's chin//a ritual sound,/her weeping in
> the dark/burying her love

TTH is over 100 pgs., A5, neatly printed and perfect-bound with glossy card cover, includes line drawings and occasionally ads. They receive about 3,000 poems a year, accept approximately 20%. Press run is 100-500. Single copy: £5.50 in UK. Sample: £10 overseas. Make checks payable to K.T. Publications.

How to Submit: Submit 6 poems at a time. No previously published poems. Cover letter preferred. Time between acceptance and publication "depends on the work and circumstances." Seldom comments on rejections. Publishes theme issues occasionally. Reports in 1-2 weeks. Always sends prepublication galleys. Pays 1-6 copies. "Copyright belongs to the poets/authors throughout."

Book/Chapbook Needs & How to Submit: Under K.T. Publications and Kite Books, they publish 6 paperbacks and 6 chapbooks/year of poetry, short stories and books for children—"at as high a standard as humanly possible." Books are usually 50-60 pgs., A5, perfect-bound with glossy cover, and art ("always looking for more.") Query first, with up to 6 sample poems and a cover letter with brief bio and publication credits. "Also include suitable SAE—so that I do not end up paying return postage every time."

Also Offers: Offers a "reading and friendly help service to writers." Write for details.

Advice: The editor says, "Be patient—and never give up writing."

KAIMANA: LITERARY ARTS HAWAII; HAWAII LITERARY ARTS COUNCIL (Specialized: regional), P.O. Box 11213, Honolulu HI 96828, founded 1974, editor Tony Quagliano.

● Poets in *Kaimana* have received the Pushcart Prize, the Hawaii Award for Literature and the Cades Award.

Magazine Needs: *Kaimana*, an annual, is the magazine of the Hawaii Literary Arts Council. Poems with "some Pacific reference are preferred—Asia, Polynesia, Hawaii—but not exclusively." They have published poetry by Howard Nemerov, John Yau, Reuben Tam, Reuel Denney, Tony Friedson, Lyn Lifshin, Haunani-Kay Trask, Anne Waldman and Joe Stanton. *Kaimana* is 64-76 pgs., 7½ × 10, saddle-stapled, with high-quality printing. Press run is 1,000 for 600 subscribers of which 200 are libraries. Subscription: $12. Sample: $10.

How to Submit: Cover letter with submissions preferred. Sometimes comments on rejections. Reports with "reasonable dispatch." Pays 2 copies.

Advice: The editor says, "Hawaii gets a lot of 'travelling regionalists,' visiting writers with inevitably superficial observations. We also get superb visiting observers who are careful craftsmen anywhere. *Kaimana* is interested in the latter, to complement our own best Hawaii writers."

$ KALEIDOSCOPE: INTERNATIONAL MAGAZINE OF LITERATURE, FINE ARTS, AND DISABILITY (Specialized: disability themes), 701 S. Main St., Akron OH 44311-1019, phone (330)762-9755, fax (330)762-0912, founded 1979, senior editor Gail Willmott, editor-in-chief Dr. Darshan C. Perusek.

Magazine Needs: *Kaleidoscope* is based at United Disability Services, a nonprofit agency. Poetry should deal with the experience of disability but not limited to that when the writer has a disability. "*Kaleidoscope* is interested in high-quality poetry with vivid, believable images and evocative language. Works should not use stereotyping, patronizing or offending language about disability." They have published poetry by Sheryl L. Nelms. As a sample the editors selected these lines from "Burro" by Marc Hudson:

> Along a rutted path,/up among prickly pears/and spindly cholla,/I pause—/unseen, in the valley,/a dog
> barks,/a canyon wren/tries her wistful tremolo.

SENDING TO A COUNTRY other than your own? Be sure to send International Reply Coupons (IRCs) instead of stamps for replies or return of your manuscript.

Kaleidoscope is 64 pgs., 8½×11, professionally printed and saddle-stitched with 4-color semigloss card cover, b&w art inside. Circulation is 1,500, including libraries, social service agencies, health-care professionals, universities and individual subscribers. Single copy: $5; subscription: $9 individual, $14 agency. Sample: $4.
How to Submit: Submit up to 5 poems at a time. Send photocopies with SASE for return of work. Previously published poems and simultaneous submissions OK, "as long as we are notified in both instances." Fax submissions OK. Cover letter required. All submissions must be accompanied by an autobiographical sketch. Deadlines: March and August 1. Publishes theme issues. Send SASE for upcoming themes. Themes for 1999 were "For Our Parents With Disabilities" and "Disability and the Created Environment." Reports in 3 weeks; acceptance or rejection may take 6 months. Pays $10 plus 2 copies. Rights return to author upon publication. Staff reviews books of poetry. Send books for review consideration to Gail Willmott, senior editor.

$ ◎ KALLIOPE, A JOURNAL OF WOMEN'S LITERATURE & ART (Specialized: women, translations, themes); SUE SANIEL ELKIND POETRY CONTEST, 3939 Roosevelt Blvd., Jacksonville FL 32205, phone (904)381-3511, website http://www.fccj.org/kalliope/kalliope.htm, founded 1978, editor Mary Sue Koeppel.
Magazine Needs: *Kalliope* is a literary/visual arts journal published by Florida Community College at Jacksonville; the emphasis is on women writers and artists. The editors say, "We like the idea of poetry as a sort of artesian well—there's one meaning that's clear on the surface and another deeper meaning that comes welling up from underneath. We'd like to see more poetry from Black, Hispanic and Native American women. Nothing sexist, racist, conventionally sentimental. We will have one special theme issue each year. Write for specific guidelines." Poets published include Denise Levertov, Marge Piercy, Martha M. Vertreace, Karen Subach, Maxine Kumin and Tess Gallagher. As a sample the editor selected the following lines by Melanie Richards:

> With dried orange rind,/fragrant sage, and a blue//branch of coral, I seal/this package full of artifacts//
> in case the wild horses/all vanish from the earth,//or the red throat of the hummingbird/lies to us about
> summer;

Kalliope calls itself "a journal of women's literature and art" and publishes fiction, interviews, drama and visual art in addition to poetry. The magazine, which appears 3 times/year, is 7¼×8¼, flat-spined, handsomely printed on white stock, glossy card cover and b&w photographs of works of art. Average number of pages is 80. Press run is 1,500 for 400-500 subscribers of which 100 are libraries, 800 shelf sales. Subscription: $14.95/year or $24.95/2 years. Sample: $7.
How to Submit: Submit poems in batches of 3-5 with brief bio note, phone number and address. No previously published poems. Reads submissions September through April only. SASE required. Because all submissions are read by several members of the editing staff, response time is usually 3-4 months. Publication will be within 6 months. Criticism is provided "when time permits and the author has requested it." Send SASE for guidelines and upcoming themes. Usually pays $10 or subscription. Acquires first publication rights. Reviews books of poetry, "but we prefer groups of books in one review." Open to unsolicited reviews. Poets may also send books for review consideration.
Also Offers: They sponsor the Sue Saniel Elkind Poetry Contest. 1st Prize: $1,000; runners up published in

KARAMU

THE CONTEST ISSUE

"We asked artist Joanna Sklan Key to read the works we were publishing for the contest issue," says *Karamu* editor Olga Abella. "She created the collage with the first place poetry winner in mind, Barbara Cooker's 'Climbing the Eiffel Tower at Night.' In the collage there is a feeling of movement upward towards the flying horse, Pegasus, and this reflects the writing in the magazine. Many of the works suggest change or growth or difference." Abella adds, " 'Karamu' is a word and an idea. The word is African, the idea is universal. 'Karamu' means the meeting place, the center of the village life, where men (and women) bring their families, their problems, their challenges, their schemes, and thrust them into the commonweal. Here individuals stand forth from their fellows in their personal offerings: (her) song, his skill, (her) plan, his project. Here also (they) listen and ponder, borrow and barter the offerings of others . . ."

Kalliope. Deadline: November 1. Send SASE for details. Website includes writer's guidelines, names of editors, poetry contest guidelines, back issues list, table of contents of recent issues, "Lollipops, Lizards and Literature," special events, poetry.
Advice: The editor says, "*Kalliope* is a carefully stitched patchwork of how women feel, what they experience, and what they have come to know and understand about their lives . . . a collection of visions from or about women all over the world. Send for a sample copy, to see what appeals to us, or better yet, subscribe! We have increased our circulation and with a grant can pay our contributors a bit."

KARAMU, Dept. of English, Eastern Illinois University, Charleston IL 61920, founded 1966, co-editors Olga Abella and Lauren Smith.
   • *Karamu* has received grants from the Illinois Arts Council and has won recognition and money awards in the IAC Literary Awards competition.
Magazine Needs: *Karamu* is an annual, usually published by May, whose "goal is to provide a forum for the best contemporary poetry and fiction that comes our way. We especially like to print the works of new writers. We like to see poetry that shows a good sense of what's being done with poetry currently. We like poetry that builds around real experiences, real images and real characters and that avoids abstraction, overt philosophizing and fuzzy pontifications. In terms of form, we prefer well-structured free verse, poetry with an inner, sub-surface structure as opposed to, let's say, the surface structure of rhymed quatrains. We have definite preferences in terms of style and form, but no such preferences in terms of length or subject matter. Purpose, however, is another thing. We don't have much interest in the openly didactic poem. If the poet wants to preach against or for some political or religious viewpoint, the preaching shouldn't be so strident that it overwhelms the poem. The poem should first be a poem." They have published poetry by Allison Joseph, Katharine Howd Machan and Joanne Mokosh Riley. As a sample the editor selected these lines from "Climbing the Eiffel Tower at Night" by Barbara Crooker:
> *flood-lit, so the traceries of girder and beam/seem even more insubstantial, a conjurer's vision,/an airy web spun out of light. It's a pyramid of X's,/row on row of kisses curving up to the sky,/meeting at the vanishing point, where all things come/together.*
The format is 120 pgs., 5×8, matte cover, handsomely printed (narrow margins), attractive b&w art. They receive submissions from about 500 poets each year, use 40-50 poems. Sometimes about a year—between acceptance and publication. Press run is 350 for 300 subscribers of which 15 are libraries. Sample: $7.50.
How to Submit: Poems—in batches of no more than 5—may be submitted to Olga Abella or Lauren Smith. "We don't much care for simultaneous submissions. We read September 1 through May 1 only, for fastest decision submit February through April. Poets should not bother to query. We critique a few of the better poems. We want the poet to consider our comments and then submit new work." Publishes occasional theme issues. Send SASE for upcoming themes. Pays 1 copy. Acquires first serial rights.
Advice: The editor says, "Follow the standard advice: Know your market. Read contemporary poetry and the magazines you want to be published in. Be patient."

KATYDID BOOKS, 1 Balsa Rd., Santa Fe NM 87505, founded 1973, editors/publishers Karen Hargreaves-Fitzsimmons and Thomas Fitzsimmons.
Book/Chapbook Needs & How to Submit: Katydid Books publishes 3 paperbacks and 3 hardbacks/year. "We publish two series of poetry: Asian Poetry in Translation (distributed by University of Hawaii Press) and American Poets." They are currently not accepting submissions.

KAWABATA PRESS; SEPIA POETRY MAGAZINE (Specialized: anthology), Knill Cross House, Millbrook, Torpoint, Cornwall, United Kingdom, founded 1977, poetry editor Colin David Webb.
Magazine Needs: *Sepia Poetry Magazine* publishes "nontraditional poetry, prose and artwork (line only), open to all original and well thought-out work. I dislike rhymes, traditional poems and 'genre' stories. I want original and thought-provoking material." *Sepia* is published 3 times/year in an inexpensively produced, 32-page, digest-sized, saddle-stapled format, photoreduced from typescript, with narrow margins and bizarre drawings. They receive 500 submissions a year, use approximately 50. Press run is 150 for 75 subscribers of which 5-6 are libraries. Subscription: £2 ($5) a year. Sample: 75p. ($2).
How to Submit: Submit 6 poems at a time, typed. Prefers not to use previously published poems. Simultaneous submissions OK. "Letter with poems is polite." Reports in 3 weeks. Pays 1 copy. Reviews books of poetry in 50-100 words. Open to unsolicited reviews. Poets may also send books for review consideration.
Book/Chapbook Needs & How to Submit: Under the imprint of Kawabata Press, Colin Webb also publishes anthologies and collections. However, publication of these has been temporarily suspended. Query with 6-10 poems and "maybe a brief outline of intent. Currently fewer chapbooks are being published." Poet gets 50% of profits (after cost of printing is covered) and 5 copies. A book catalog of Kawabata Press publications is on the back of *Sepia*, for ordering copies.
Advice: The editor always comments on rejections and advises, "Strike out everything that sounds like a cliché. Don't try any tricks. Work at it, have a feeling for what you write, don't send 'exercise' pieces. Believe in what you send."

◎ **KELSEY REVIEW (Specialized: regional)**, Mercer County Community College, P.O. Box B, Trenton NJ 08690, phone (609)586-4800, fax (609)586-2318, e-mail kelsey.review@mccc.edu, website http://www.mccc.edu, founded 1988, editor-in-chief Robin Schore.

Magazine Needs: *KR* is an annual published in September by Mercer County Community College. It serves as "an outlet for literary talent of people living and working in Mercer County, New Jersey only." They have no specifications as to form, length, subject matter or style, but do not want to see poetry about "kittens and puppies." As a sample the editor selected this poem "Why I Like Newark, New Jersey" by Valerie L. Ezar:

> *Because on one too hot summer/afternoon when I walked to my car,/parked on a lot cleared of houses,/ littered with glass, a girl in tight yellow/satin pulled the cigarette from her mouth,/said,* Your perfume smells pretty./What's it called? *Her eyes were soft/breezes through fields of corn./Truth seemed important./*Coeur de Joie, *I said.*

Kelsey Review is about 60 glossy pgs., 7 × 11, with paper cover and line drawings; no ads. They receive about 60 submissions a year, accept 6-10. Press run is 2,000. All distributed free to contributors, area libraries, bookstores and schools.

How to Submit: Submit up to 6 poems at a time, typed. No previously published poems or simultaneous submissions. Deadline: May 1. Always comments on rejections. May request information via e-mail. Reports in June of each year. Pays 5 copies. All rights revert to authors.

Also Offers: Website includes address, deadlines, encouragement and announced publication.

◑ ◎ **THE KERF (Specialized: nature/ecology)**, College of the Redwoods, 883 W. Washington Blvd., Crescent City CA 95531, founded 1995, editor Ken Letko.

Magazine Needs: *The Kerf*, annually published, features "poetry that speaks to the environment and humanity." They want "poetry that exhibits an environmental consciousness." They have published poetry by Ruth Daigon, Meg Files, James Grabill and George Keithley. As a sample the editor selected these lines from "The Stones" by Janine Canan:

> *Along the beach, stones/exposed by the retreating tide/greet me like friends from long ago./And I bend to gather eggs/mounds, ovals, crescents/smoothed by life in the tumbling sea.*

The Kerf is 40 pgs., 8½ × 5½, printed via Docutech, saddle-stitched with CS2 cover stock. They receive about 2,000 poems a year, accept approximately 1-3%. Press run is 400, 150 shelf sales; 100 distributed free to contributors and writing centers. Sample: $5. Make checks payable to College of the Redwoods.

How to Submit: Submit up to 5 poems (up to 7 pgs.) at a time. No previously published poems; simultaneous submissions OK. Reads submissions January 15 through March 31 only. Time between acceptance and publication is 3 months. Poems are circulated to an editorial board. "Our editors debate (argue for or against) the inclusion of each manuscript." Seldom comments on rejections. Send SASE for guidelines. Reports in 1-2 months. Sometimes sends prepublication galleys. Pays 1-2 copies. Acquires first North American serial rights.

◎ **KEY SATCH(EL); QUALE PRESS (Specialized: form/style)**, P.O. Box 363, Haydenville MA 01039-0363, e-mail central@quale.com, website http://www.qusle.com/ks/kshome.html, founded 1997, director Gian Lombardo.

Magazine Needs: *Key Satch(el)* is a quarterly magazine focusing on prose poetry. They want "prose poems with imaginative imagery or unexpected usage of language. NO verse." They have published poetry by Russell Edson, Joseph Torra, Peter Johnson and Morton Marcus. *Key Satch(el)* is 24 pgs., 5½ × 8½, photocopied and saddle-stapled with b&w card cover with art. They receive about 400 poems a year, accept approximately 25-30%. Press run is 225. Subscription: $10/year. Sample (including guidelines): $3.

How to Submit: Submit 5-8 poems at a time. Rarely accepts previously published poems; simultaneous submissions OK. Cover letter preferred. E-mail submissions OK. Send MS Word attached file. "Please note if it is a simultaneous submission; if previously published, please note where and when the work was published." Time between acceptance and publication is 1-9 months. Reports in 2 days to 2 months. Sometimes sends prepublication galleys. Pays 2 copies. Acquires first North American serial or one-time rights.

▣ ◑ **KIMERA: A JOURNAL OF FINE WRITING**, 1316 Hollis, Spokane WA 99201, e-mail kimera@js.spokane.wa.us, website http://www.js.spokane.wa.us/kimera/, founded 1996, publisher Jan Strever.

Magazine Needs: *Kimera* is a biannual online journal (appears yearly in hard copy) and "attempts to address John Locke's challenge—'where is the head with no chimeras.' " They want poetry that "attempts to 'capture the soul in motion.' No flabby poems." They have published poetry by Wendy Battin, Colin Morton and N. Palmer Hall. They accept approximately 10% of poems/year. Press run is 300 for 200 subscribers. Single copy: $7; subscription: $14. Sample: $7.

How to Submit: Submit 3-6 poems at a time. No previously published poems; simultaneous submissions OK. Cover letter required. E-mail submissions in ASCII text OK. Poems are circulated to an editorial board. Seldom comments on rejections. Obtain guidelines via website. Reports in 3 months. Pays 1 copy. Acquires first rights.

⊕ ◎ ◑ **KINGFISHER PUBLICATIONS PLC (Specialized: anthologies, children)**, New Penderel House, 283-288 High Holborn, London WC1V 7HZ United Kingdom, phone (0171)903-9999, fax (0171)242-4979.

Book/Chapbook Needs & How to Submit: Kingfisher Publications Plc publishes very little poetry. "We currently have six titles in print, anthologies of verse for children either on particular themes or for particular age-groups, compiled by leading British poets. Because our anthologies are compiled by outside editors, we do not accept unsolicited poetry."

✪ **KINGS ESTATE PRESS**, 870 Kings Estate Rd., St. Augustine FL 32086-5033, phone (800)249-7485, founded 1993, publisher Ruth Moon Kempher.
Book/Chapbook Needs & How to Submit: "Publishes the best contemporary poetry available; all books are illustrated." They publish about 3 paperbacks/year. "Currently overstocked, not accepting submissions until after the year 2000."

✔ ✪ **KIOSK**, 306 Clemens Hall, SUNY, Buffalo NY 14260, phone (716)645-2578, founded 1985, poetry editor Loren Goodman, fiction editor Kevin Grauke.
Magazine Needs: *Kiosk* is an annual literary magazine using poetry of "any length, any style, especially experimental." They have published poetry by Robert Creeley, Carl Dennis, Colette Inez, Jon Anderson and Charles Bernstein. The editor describes *Kiosk* as flat-spined, digest-sized. They receive about 1,000 poems a year, accept approximately 40. Subscription: $6. Sample: $5. Make checks payable to SUNY at Buffalo.
How to Submit: Submit poems in batches of 5. No simultaneous submissions. Cover letter not required, "but we suggest one be included." Reads submissions September 1 through March 1 only. Reports within 4 months. Pays in copies.

N $ ▢ ✪ **THE KIT-CAT REVIEW; THE KIT-CAT REVIEW ANNUAL POETRY AWARD**, 244 Halstead Ave., Harrison NY 10528-3611, phone (914)835-4833, founded 1998, editor Claudia Fletcher.
Magazine Needs: *The Kit-Cat Review* appears quarterly and is "named after the 18th century Kit-Cat Club whose members included Addison, Steele, Congreve, Vanbrugh, Garth, etc. Purpose: to promote/discover excellence and originality." They want quality work—traditional, modern, experimental. They have published poetry by Romola Robb Allrud, Harriet Zinnes, Louis Phillips and Romania's Nobel Prize nominee Marin Sorescu. As a sample the editor selected these lines from "Poet's Day Off" by Mary Kennan Herbert:

> *sleep till the rooster/has left for work/read the morning paper very slowly/sip coffee in a desultory*
> *way/imagine ostrich plumes languidly/fanning a breeze just for me*

The editor says the *Review* is 75 pgs., 5½×8½, laser printed/photocopied, saddle-stitched with colored card cover, includes b&w illustrations. They expect to receive about 1,000 poems a year. Press run is 500 for 100 subscribers. Subscription: $25. Sample: $7. Make checks payable to Claudia Fletcher.
How to Submit: Submit any number of poems at a time. Previously published poems and simultaneous submissions OK. "Cover letter should contain relevant bio." Time between acceptance and publication is 2 months. Send SASE for guidelines. Reports within 2 months. Pays up to $100 a poem and 2 copies. Buys first or one-time rights.
Also Offers: Sponsors The Kit-Cat Review Annual Poetry Award of $1,000.

✪ **ALFRED A. KNOPF**, 201 E. 50th St., New York NY 10022, poetry editor Harry Ford. Over the years Knopf has been one of the most important and distinguished publishers of poetry in the United States. "The list is closed to new submissions at this time."

▢ ◎ **KOJA (Specialized: form/style)**, 7314 21st Ave. #6E, Brooklyn NY 11204, e-mail mikekoja@aol.com, website http://www.monkeyfish.com/koja, founded 1996, editor Michael Magazinnik.
Magazine Needs: *Koja* is published annually and "interested in experimental poetry but also publishes experimental prose and b&w artwork." They want "visual/concrete poetry, avant-garde poetry and experimental poetry. No religious or classical work." They have published poetry by Eileen Myles, Raymond Federman, Richard Kostelanetz and Bruce Andrews. The editor says *Koja* is 64 pgs., 8½×11, various printing and binding methods, glossy color cover. They receive about 300 poems a year, accept approximately 10%. Press run is 300 for 30 subscribers of which 5 are libraries, 200 shelf sales; 50 distributed free to contributors/reviewers. Subscription: $14. Sample: $7. Make checks payable to Michael Magazinnik.
How to Submit: Submit up to 10 poems at a time. No previously published poems or simultaneous submissions. Cover letter preferred. E-mail submissions OK in ASCII text or .jpg files. Time between acceptance and publication is 1-8 months. Seldom comments on rejections. Reports in 3-4 months. Pays 1 copy. Acquires first North American serial rights.

N ⊕ ✪ **KONFLUENCE; KONFLUENCE PRESS**, Bath House, Bath Rd., Nailsworth, Stroud, Gloucestershire 9L6 0JB United Kingdom, phone (01453)835896, founded 1998, editor Mark Floyer.
Magazine Needs: *Konfluence* is "an annual platform for poetry—mainly from the west country, United Kingdom, but accept anything from across the United Kingdom and the globe if it is suitable." They are "open to a wide variety of poetry. It must have a content/form equation which is successfully true unto itself. No stream of consciousness ranting! We want to see some craft." As a sample the editor selected these lines from his poem "Circle Line":

> *Slumped across his seat (a Madame/Tussaud's escapee!) he circles/Marble Arch, Baker street,/round*
> *and round and round he must/re-cycle flesh to wax, devolve-/dissolve at last to powdered dust.*

The editor says *Konfluence* is 50 pgs., magazine-sized, printed and staple bound with cardboard cover. They accept approximately 10% of poems received. Press run is 100, 50% shelf sales; 50% distributed free to contributors. Single copy: $6. Make checks payable to Konfluence Press.
How to Submit: Submit 6 poems at a time. Line length for poetry is 10 minimum, 80 maximum. Previously published poems and simultaneous submissions OK. Cover letter preferred. Time between acceptance and publication is 6 months. Often comments on rejections. Publishes theme issues occasionally. Reports in 1 month. Pays 1 copy.
Advice: The editor says, "Do send your material in! This is an 'open' publishing venture. No rules—just quality content at the editor's whim/judgement."

⊘ **KONOCTI BOOKS**, 23311 County Rd. 88, Winters CA 95694, phone (530)662-3364, founded 1973, editor/publisher Noel Peattie, publishes poetry by invitation only.

✔ ◯ ◎ **KOSHKOVICH PRESS; SEPULCHRE (Specialized: horror/dark fantasy)**, P.O. Box 429, Fort Meade MD 20755-0429, phone (301)490-1081, e-mail vannar@bigfoot.com, website http://members.aol.com/sepulchr97, founded 1997, editor Scot H.P. Drew.
● Koshkovich Press no longer publishes *MonkeySpank*.
Magazine Needs: *Sepulchre*, published quarterly, is "devoted to bringing new writers of dark fantasy and imaginative horror out into the sunlight of the small press literary scene. The best writers are often wrongly entombed in obscurity solely because their works have yet to be exhumed. *Sepulchre* is the result of opening that tomb and releasing those creative wraiths upon unsuspecting readers." They want "scary, dark, disturbing poetry in any form or length. I'll look at pretty much anything (keeping the aforementioned in mind)." They do not want "excessive violence, gratuitous sex, plotless snippets that read like scenes culled from B horror movies, urban/gangsta horror, or anything overtly humorous (a little dark humor is great, though)." They have published poetry by Douglas M. Stokes, Cindy Main and Karen R. Porter. As a sample the editor selected these lines from "terminal" by Tiffany Auxier:
> these are not tears./my breath/in the body bag/has condensed./it drips/onto pale eyes.
Sepulchre is 30-40 pgs., digest-sized, computer-printed and saddle-stapled with 67 lb. card stock cover, uses b&w clip art and photos. They receive about 50 poems a year, accept approximately 25%. Press run is 50 for 10 subscribers. Subscription: $10, foreign $13. Sample: $3, foreign $4. Make checks payable to Scot Drew.
How to Submit: Submit up to 5 poems at a time. Previously published poems and simultaneous submissions OK. Include SASE for reply. "Try to send a disposable copy of manuscript." Cover letter preferred, include bio of up to 5 lines. No e-mail submissions. Queries via e-mail OK. Time between acceptance and publication is 6 months. Often comments on rejections. Send SASE for guidelines. Reports in 1 month. Pays 1 copy. Acquires first North American serial or one-time rights.
Also Offers: Website includes writer's guidelines, names of writers and poems in the current issue and links to writers' websites.

🌐 ⊘ ◎ **KRAX (Specialized: humor); RUMP BOOKLETS**, 63 Dixon Lane, Leeds, Yorkshire LS12 4RR England, founded 1971, poetry editor Andy Robson.
Magazine Needs: *Krax* appears twice yearly, and publishes contemporary poetry from Britain and America. They want poetry which is "light-hearted and witty; original ideas. Undesired: haiku, religious or topical politics." 2,000 words maximum. All forms and styles considered. They have published poetry by Julia Darling, Bernard Young and Barry Tebb. As a sample the editor selected these lines from "Please Don't Make Me Take My Clothes Off" by Mandy Precious:
> I'm a handful, a tankful,/a reason to be thankful/that the deep end of the pool was designed./If you get
> the urge to run from these hips/We can always switch out the lights/or better, just kiss on the lips.
Krax is 6×8, 56 pgs. of which 30 are poetry, saddle-stapled, offset printed with b&w cartoons and graphics. They receive up to 1,000 submissions a year of which they use approximately 6%, have a 2- to 3-year backlog. Single copy: £3.50 ($7); subscription: £10 ($20). Sample: $1 (75p).
How to Submit: "Submit maximum of six pieces. Writer's name on same sheet as poem. Sorry, we cannot accept material on disk. SASE or SAE with IRC encouraged but not vital." No previously published poems or simultaneous submissions. Brief cover letter preferred. Reports within 2 months. Pays 1 copy. Reviews books of poetry (brief, individual comments; no outside reviews). Send books for review consideration.
Book/Chapbook Needs & How to Submit: *Currently not accepting unsolicited mss.* Rump Booklets publishes 1-2 chapbooks/year. Chapbooks are usually 16 pgs., 3×4 and offset printed. Replies to queries in 2-3 weeks, to mss in 2-3 weeks. Pays 60 author's copies.
Advice: The editor says, "Before sending your poems, always add your address to the piece—we can't always place everyone's pseudonym."

◯ ⊘ **KUMQUAT MERINGUE; PENUMBRA PRESS**, P.O. Box 736, Pine Island MN 55963, phone (507)367-4430, e-mail moodyriver@aol.com, website http://www.geostar.com/kumquatcastle, founded 1990, editor Christian Nelson.
Magazine Needs: *Kumquat Meringue* appears on an irregular basis, using "mostly shorter poetry about the small details of life, especially the quirky side of love and sex. We want those things other magazines find just

too quirky. Not interested in rhyming, meaning of life or high-flown poetry." The magazine is "dedicated to the memory of Richard Brautigan." They have published works by Gina Bergamino, T. Kilgore Splake, Antler, Monica Kershner, Lynne Douglass and Ianthe Brautigan. As a sample the editor selected these lines from "Leaping Lizards" by Emile Luria:

> After we made love . . . Kate said,/"You're so weird, really,/Even weirder than I thought."/And I thought, could she taste the salt,/Feel the sea lapping on my back?/I went to sleep wondering/About dinosaurs and lungfish/And the deepest reaches of the sea

KM is 40-48 pgs., digest-sized, "professionally designed with professional typography and nicely printed." Press run is 600 for 250 subscribers. Subscription: $10/3 issues. Sample: $5.

How to Submit: "We like cover letters but prefer to read things about who you are, rather than your long list of publishing credits. Previously published and simultaneous submissions are OK, but please let us know." Often comments on submissions. "Please don't forget your SASE or you'll never hear back from us. E-mail address is for 'hello, praise, complaints, threats and questions' only." Send SASE for guidelines. Usually reports in 3 months. Pays 1 copy. Acquires one-time rights.

Also Offers: "Our website includes guidelines and all information about *Kumquat Meringue* and our other projects."

Advice: The editor advises, "Read *Kumquat Meringue* and anything by Richard Brautigan to get a feel for what we want, but don't copy Richard Brautigan, and don't copy those who have copied him. We just want that same feel. We also have a definite weakness for poems written 'to' or 'for' Richard Brautigan. Reviewers have called our publication iconoclastic, post-hip, post-beat, post-antipostmodern; and our poetry, carefully crafted imagery. When you get discouraged, write some more. Don't give up. Eventually your poems will find a home. We're very open to unpublished writers, and a high percentage of our writers had never been published anywhere before they submitted here."

KUUMBA (Specialized: ethnic, gay/lesbian, love/romance/erotica), Box 83912, Los Angeles CA 90083-0912, phone (310)410-0808, fax (310)410-9250, e-mail newsroom@blk.com, website http://www.blk.com, founded 1991, editor Reginald Harris.

Magazine Needs: *Kuumba* is a biannual poetry journal of the black lesbian and gay community. They want subject matter related to black lesbian and gay concerns. "Among the experiences of interest are: coming out, interacting with family and/or community, substance abuse, political activism, oral histories, AIDS and intimate relationships." They do not want to see "gay-only subjects that have no black content, or black-only subjects with no gay content." They have published poetry by Robert Earl Penn Jr., Sharon Bridgforth, Mistinguette and Assotto Saint. As a sample we selected these lines from "The Sweetest Taboo" (for Gene) by Richard D. Gore:

> Forbidden,/But I loved you anyway/Dark, smouldering, and sweet/Luminous Black skin and Sloe-eyes . . .

Kuumba is 48 pgs., 8½×11, offset and saddle-stitched, with b&w cover drawing and ads. They receive approximately 500 poems a year, accept approximately 25%. Press run is 3,000 for 750 subscribers of which 25 are libraries, 2,000 shelf sales. Subscription: $7.50/year. Sample: $4.50. Make checks payable to BLK Publishing Company.

How to Submit: Submit 3 poems at a time. No previously published poems; simultaneous submissions OK, if notified. Cover letter preferred. Fax and e-mail submissions OK, no attachments. Seldom comments on rejections. Send SASE for guidelines or obtain via e-mail or website. Reports in 6 weeks. Pays 4 copies. Acquires first North American serial rights and right to anthologize.

Advice: The editors add, "Named for one of the Nguzo Saba (Seven Principles) which are celebrated at Kwanzaa, Kuumba means creativity." This poetry journal is not only dedicated to the celebration of the lives and experiences of black lesbians and gay men, but it is also intended to encourage new and experienced writers to develop their poetic craft.

LA JOLLA POET'S PRESS; NATIONAL POETRY BOOK SERIES; SAN DIEGO POET'S PRESS; AMERICAN BOOK SERIES, P.O. Box 8638, La Jolla CA 92038, editor/publisher Kathleen Iddings.

Book Needs & How to Submit: La Jolla Poet's Press and San Diego Poet's Press are nonprofit presses that publish only poets who "have published widely and/or won poetry awards. No beginners here." They have published 35 individual poet's books and 5 poetry anthologies featuring poetry by Allen Ginsberg, Carolyn Kizer, Galway Kinnell, Tess Gallagher, Robert Pinsky and Carolyn Forche. As a sample the editor included these lines from "Breakfast" in *Spare Change* by Kevin Pilkington:

> You take a seat/at a table/in a diner on Third/and order breakfast/. . . You pour cream in your coffee/ and by mistake/stir in the color of a woman you forgot/then gulp it down/to forget her all over again./ When the waiter brings a refill,/you keep it black/to make sure/you'll want to drink/instead of kiss.

The editor says most books are approximately 100 pgs., 5½×8½, perfect-bound, with laminated covers. Sample: $10.

LACTUCA (Specialized: translations), 159 Jewett Ave., Jersey City NJ 07304-2003, phone/fax (201)451-5411, e-mail lactuca@mindspring.com, website http://www.mindspring.com/~lactuca, founded 1986, editor/publisher Mike Selender.

Magazine Needs: *Lactuca* appears up to once a year. "Our bias is toward work with a strong sense of place, a strong sense of experience, a quiet dignity and an honest emotional depth. Dark and disturbing writings are preferred over safer material. No haiku, poems about writing poems, poems using the poem as an image, light poems or self-indulgent poems. Readability is crucial. We publish poetry that readily transposes between the spoken word and printed page. First English language translations are welcome provided that the translator has obtained the approval of the author." They have published poetry by Sherman Alexie, Joe Cardillo, Christy Beatty and Kathleen ten Haken. *Lactuca* will resume publication with a new format: 200 pgs., perfect-bound. Sample back issues: $4. Make checks payable to Stone Buzzard Press.

How to Submit: "*Lactuca* is currently dormant. Query to find out if we're accepting new submissions. Unsolicited manuscripts will not be responded to promptly." Queries accepted via e-mail. Submit 4-5 poems at a time. No previously published material or simultaneous submissions. "We comment on rejections when we can. However the volume of mail we receive limits this." Always sends prepublication galleys. Pays 1-2 copies. Acquires first rights. Reviews books of poetry. Open to unsolicited reviews. Poets may also send books for review consideration.

Advice: He says, "The purpose of *Lactuca* is to be a small literary magazine publishing high-quality poetry, fiction and b&w drawings. Much of our circulation goes to contributors' copies and exchange copies with other literary magazines. *Lactuca* is not for poets expecting large circulation. Poets appearing here will find themselves in the company of other good writers."

⚫ THE LAIRE, INC., P.O. Box 5524, Ft. Oglethorpe GA 30742, fax (706)858-1071, e-mail GHSD51D@prodi gy.com, founded 1995, editor Kim Abston.

Magazine Needs: *the LAIRE* is a bimonthly "newsletter for poets and poetry lovers, dedicated to bringing to our readers quality poetry, and related subject matter which is both creatively and/or socially aware. Open to all forms of poetry, provided it is well executed, both creatively and technically. Poetry may be of any length or subject, but we tend to prefer poems that are 40 lines or less and socially and/or politically aware." As a sample the editor selected these lines from a poem by Gregory Fiorini:

> In that line of neglect stand revolutionaries/portable to their cause/of wings sans feathers/among debris/and all other ways akimbo

the LAIRE is 8 pgs., 8½×11, photocopied, corner-stapled with line drawings and clip art. They receive about 1,500 poems a year, accept approximately 9%. Press run is 1,000 for 300-400 subscribers of which 50 are libraries, 400 shelf sales; 100 distributed free to schools, prisons, etc. Subscription: $10. Sample: $2.

How to Submit: Submit 5 poems at a time. No previously published poems or simultaneous submissions. Cover letter preferred. E-mail and disk submissions OK. "Author's name, address, and telephone number must appear on each page. One poem per page. We accept 1.44meg IBM formatted floppy disk submissions, provided name, address, and phone are on label. Nothing returned without SASE." Time between acceptance and publication is 1-6 months. Poems are circulated to an editorial board. "Poems are reviewed by the editorial board with the editor having final approval." Seldom comments on rejections. Publishes theme issues occasionally. Send SASE for guidelines. Reports in 1-2 months. Pays 1 copy. Reviews books and chapbooks of poetry and other magazines in 150-200 words, single or multi-book format. Open to unsolicited reviews. Poets may also send books for review consideration.

Also Offers: Sponsors poetry contests. Send SASE for details. They also accept article submissions on any subject related to poetry, including critiques, biographies, book reviews, and F.Y.I. pieces.

🌐 ✅ $◎ LANDFALL: NEW ZEALAND ARTS AND LETTERS (Specialized: regional), University of Otago Press, P.O. Box 56, Dunedin, New Zealand, phone 0064 3 479 8807, fax 0064 3 479 8385, e-mail university.press@stonebow.otago.ac.nz, founded 1947, originally published by Caxton Press, then by Oxford University Press, now published by University of Otago Press, editor Chris Price.

Magazine Needs: *Landfall* appears twice a year (in May and November). They say, "Apart from occasional commissioned features on aspects of international literature, *Landfall* focuses primarily on New Zealand literature and arts. It publishes new fiction, poetry, commentary, and interviews with New Zealand artists and writers, and reviews of New Zealand books." Single issue: NZ $21.95; subscription: $39.95 NZ for 2 issues for New Zealand subscribers, $30 A for Australian subscribers, $30 US for other overseas subscribers.

How to Submit: Submissions must be typed and include SASE. "Once accepted, contributions should if possible also be submitted on disk." No e-mail submissions. Publishes theme issues. Send SASE for upcoming themes and guidelines. Pays (for poetry) $15 NZ/printed page and 1 copy. New Zealand poets should write for further information.

THE OPENNESS TO SUBMISSIONS INDEX at the back of this book lists all publishers in this section by how open they are to submissions.

⊕ ◻ ◎ **LAPWING PUBLICATIONS (Specialized: ethnic/nationality)**, 1 Ballysillan Dr., Belfast BT14 8HQ United Kingdom, phone/fax (01232)391240, founded 1989, director/editor Dennis Greig, director/editor Rene Greig.

Book/Chapbook Needs: Lapwing publishes "emerging Irish poets and poets domiciled in Ireland, plus the new work of a suitable size by established Irish writers." They publish 6-10 chapbooks/year. They want poetry of all kinds. But, "no crass political, racist, sexist propaganda even of a positive or 'pc' tenor." They have published poetry by Robert Greacen, James Simmons, Padraig Fiacc, Jack Holland and Desmond O'Grady. As a sample the editor selected these lines from "The Only Emperor" by Robert Greacen:

> *I knock, I knock/I challenge the silence./Knock! Knock! Knock!/I open the door into the room.*

Chapbooks are usually 44-52 pgs., A5, Docutech printed and saddle-stitched with colored card cover, includes occasional line art.

How to Submit: "Submit 6 poems in the first instance, depending on these, an invitation to submit more may follow." No previously published poems; simultaneous submissions OK. Cover letter required. Poems are circulated to an editorial board. "All submissions receive a first reading. If these poems have minor errors or faults, the writer is advised. If poor quality, the poems are returned. Those 'passing' first reading are retained and a letter of conditional offer is sent." Often comments on rejections. Replies to queries in 1 month; to mss in 2 months. Pays 25 author's copies (out of a press run of 250).

Advice: The editors say, "Due to limited resources, material will be processed well in advance of any estimated publishing date. All accepted material is strictly conditional on resources available, no favoritism. The Irish domestic market is small, the culture is hierarchical, poet/personality culture predominates, literary democracy is limited."

◻ **THE LAUREATE LETTER CHAPBOOK; WRITERS GAZETTE; TROUVERE COMPANY**, 899 Williamson Trail, Eclectic AL 36024-6131, e-mail bren666@aol.com, founded 1993, editor Brenda Williamson.

Magazine Needs: *The Laureate Letter Chapbook* is an annually published newsletter open to submissions of poetry. They want "simple, easy-to-understand poems which stretch the mind to remember their lives, the hopes of others and the dreams that exist amongst us. Any form, 20 lines maximum. All poems must be titled. No jibberish or extremely mushy garbage." As a sample the editor selected the poem "Nightsong" by Denny E. Marshall:

> *Her lips were like silk sheets/wrapped loosely around my mind/Aboard a magic carpet/With our hearts*
> *intertwined.*

LLC is 32 pgs., 5½×8½. They receive 1,500-2,000 poems a year, accept 25%. Press run is 500. Single copy: $3.95.

How to Submit: Submit 3 or more poems at a time. Previously published poems and simultaneous submissions OK. E-mail submissions OK. Time between acceptance and publication is 1-3 months. Send SASE for guidelines. Reports in 1-4 weeks "most of the time." No pay in cash or copies, but no fee required for publication. Acquires one-time rights. "There is also an Editor's Choice Award—one poet per issue is selected Trouvere's Poet Laureate of the Year and will be notified prior to publication to submit a bio. The award will be 2 copies of the chapbook and $25."

Magazine Needs: They also publish *Writers Gazette*. Founded in 1980, the publication appears 4 times/year and is designed "for writers, by writers, about writing." It includes poetry, fiction, nonfiction, art, cartoons, occasional photos, market listings, contest information and news on related writing subjects. They want poems of "any style, subject or length, but prefer short verses of under 24 lines. Always looking for shorter poems of 4-12 lines. New writers are always encouraged and regularly published, even children." They have published poetry by Julian Cooksey III, Gerald Zipper, Robert W. Keller and Jan Brevet. As a sample the editor selected these lines from "Creative Canvas" by Cynthia Faye Hatten:

> *She's got fire in her fingers/ember heated in her bones/standing unassembled/where the earth unites*
> *the sky/she carves the longest silence/where the carving violet splatters/dripping ink beneath her nails.*

WG is approximately 28 pgs., 8½×11, center stapled, with some ads. They receive 2,000 poems a year, accept 10%. Press run is 2,500 for 1,000 subscribers. Subscription: $18. Sample: $5.

How to Submit: Previously published poems and simultaneous submissions OK. E-mail submissions OK, "but remember to include your real name and mailing address." Include short bio. Sometimes comments on rejections. Send SASE for guidelines. Reports in 1 month. No pay in cash or copies. Acquires one-time rights. Reviews books and chapbooks of poetry. Send books for review consideration.

Also Offers: They also publish 3 annual series, Poetry of Love, All Hallow's Eve and Christmas Magic. Each series is open to poetry submissions. Send SASE for details.

Advice: The editor says, "I read everything that crosses my desk and reply as soon as possible. Be creative and unusual. Don't query—send entire manuscripts. Also, we check for SASE before ever considering poems. If authors cannot consider sending SASE, we cannot consider their work. I look for originality, but also style. Maybe you write avant-garde and are adventurous, maybe you like blank verse or free verse or you're just a poetaster, that is, to some opinionated people your poetry lacks quality. Never the less I like it all if it truly moves me to tears or laughter and is a product of the writers own feelings."

⚫ **LAUREL REVIEW; GREENTOWER PRESS**, Dept. of English, Northwest Missouri State University, Maryville MO 64468, phone (816)562-1265, founded 1960, co-editors William Trowbridge, David Slater, Beth Richards and Catie Rosemurgy.

Magazine Needs: *LR* is a literary journal appearing twice a year using "poetry fiction, and creative nonfiction of the highest literary quality." They have published poetry by Patricia Goedicke, Paul Zimmer, Miller Williams, Albert Goldbarth, David Citino and Nancy Willard. As a sample the editors selected these lines from "Wheel" by Jim Simmerman:

> *Don't fall in love before you've made the wheel/your study. See how it crushes and churns/unsullied on to the next disaster./See how it burns like the hoop an animal/learns to leap through for its supper. Study/the heart and its demolition derby.*

This handsome journal (128 pgs., 6×9) features excellent poems—usually more than 20 each issue—in all styles and forms. Press run is 900 for 500 subscribers of which 53 are libraries, 100 shelf sales. Subscription: $8/year. Sample: $6.

How to Submit: Submit 4 poems at a time. No previously published poems or simultaneous submissions. Reads submissions September 1 through May 31 only. Editor "does not usually" comment on submissions. Reports in 1 week to 4 months. Always sends prepublication galleys. Pays 2 copies plus 1-year subscription. Rights revert to author upon publication.

◻ ◎ **LAURELS; WEST VIRGINIA POETRY SOCIETY (Specialized: membership)**, Rt. 2, Box 13, Ripley WV 25271, e-mail mbush814@aol.com, founded 1996, editor Jim Bush.

Magazine Needs: *Laurels* is the quarterly journal of the West Virginia Poetry Society containing 95% poetry/5% art. Only considers work from WVPS members. They want traditional forms and good free verse. "If it's over 100 lines it must be very, very good. No porn, foul language, shape poems; no 'broken prose.' " They have published poetry by Ernie O'Dell, Ann Gasser and Mary Barnes. The editor says *Laurels* is 50 pgs., digest-sized, photocopied and saddle-stapled with paper cover, some pen-and-ink art, no ads. They receive about 1,000 poems a year, accept approximately 50%. Press run is 200 for 150 subscribers. Membership: $10. Sample: $4. Make checks payable to the West Virginia Poetry Society for a subscription, to Jim Bush for a sample.

How to Submit: Requires contributors be members. For membership in WVPS, send $10 to Larry Bloomfield, 617-A Boggs Run Rd., Benwood WV 26031. Submit 4-5 poems at a time. Previously published poems and simultaneous submissions OK. Cover letter preferred including brief bio. E-mail submissions OK. Time between acceptance and publication is 3-12 months. Always comments on rejections. Send SASE for guidelines. Reports "next day, usually." Sometimes sends prepublication galleys. Pays 1 copy. Acquires one-time rights. Staff briefly reviews 3-4 books a year if author is a member. Send books for review consideration.

Also Offers: Sponsors a 35-category annual contest for members. Entry fee: no fee to current WVPS members or K-12 students, $1/poem for nonmembers, maximum of $12 for 12 or more categories. Send SASE for guidelines.

Advice: The editor says, "Our purpose is to encourage and aid amateur poets who believe that words can be used to communicate meaning and to create beauty."

✅ $ ◻ ◎ **THE LEADING EDGE (Specialized: science fiction/fantasy)**, 3163 JKHB, Provo UT 84602, e-mail tle@byu.edu (correspondence only, no submissions), website http://tle.clubs.byu.edu, editor-in-chief Loralee Leavitt.

Magazine Needs: *The Leading Edge* is a magazine appearing 2 times a year. They want "high quality poetry reflecting both literary value and popular appeal and dealing with science fiction and fantasy. We accept traditional science fiction and fantasy poetry, but we like innovative stuff. No graphic sex, violence or profanity." They have published poetry by Michael Collings, Tracy Ray, Susan Spilecki and Bob Cook. As a sample the editor selected this poem, "The Spectra of Galaxies (A Zen Joke)," by Alyce Wilson:

> *A man with a telescope/reduces the universe/to one red-shifted line/on a piece of graph paper.//Folds it in his pocket, forgets it.//On laundry day, he cleans/galaxies out of the lint filter./And at last, he understands.*

The editor describes the magazine as 120 pgs., 6×9, using art. They accept about 15 out of 150 poems received/year. Press run is 400, going to 100 subscribers (10 of them libraries) and 300 shelf sales. Single copy: $3.95; subscription: $11.85. Sample: $4.50.

How to Submit: Submit 1 or more poems with name and address at the top of each page. No simultaneous submissions or previously published poems. Cover sheet with name, address, phone number, length of poem, title and type of poem preferred. Send SASE for guidelines. Reports in 3-4 months. Always sends prepublication galleys. Pays $10 for the first 1-4 typeset pages, $4.50 for each additional page; plus 2 contributor's copies. Buys first North American serial rights.

Advice: The editor says, "Poetry is given equal standing with fiction and is not treated as filler, but as art."

Ⓝ ◻ **LEAPINGS LITERARY MAGAZINE; LEAPINGS PRESS**, 2455 Pinercrest Dr., Santa Rosa CA 95403, fax (707)568-7531, e-mail 72144.3133@compuserve.com, website http://home.inreach.com/editserv/leapings.html, founded 1998, editor S.A. Warner.

Magazine Needs: *Leapings* is a semiannual literary magazine that publishes essays, book reviews, b&w artwork, literary and genre fiction, and poetry. They are "open to any form, but prefer shorter verse. No rhymed for rhyming sake; no pornography." They have published poetry by Kit Knight. As a sample we selected these lines from "Her love in a widened margin" by G.E. Coggshall:

> *She rises at five a.m. unrebuked/for her nightgown's raveled hem. Each day/wrinkles like skin. The corners of her/wallpaper curl away from the plaster.//Her hindsight is clouded from cataracts,/yet she believes in all her layered-up/experience, her brick-and-mortar regrets.*

The editor says *Leapings* is 35-50 pgs., digest-sized, laserjet printed and saddle-stapled with cardstock cover, uses b&w graphics. They receive about 1,000 poems a year, accept approximately 10%. Press run is 200 for 25 subscribers of which 5 are libraries, about 50 shelf sales. Single copy: $6; subscription: $10/year. Sample: $5. Make checks payable to S.A. Warner.

How to Submit: Submit up to 6 poems at a time. No previously published poems or simultaneous submissions. Cover letter preferred. E-mail (poetry only) and disk submissions OK. "Poetry manuscripts may be submitted single-spaced and e-mailed." SASE with sufficient postage required for return of ms sent via regular mail. Time between acceptance and publication is 6 months. Often comments on rejections. Send SASE for guidelines or obtain via e-mail or website. Reports in 2 months. Pays 2 copies. Acquires first rights. Reviews books and chapbooks of poetry and other magazines in 300 words, single book format. Open to unsolicited reviews. Poets may also send books for review consideration.

Also Offers: *Leapings* sponsors an annual poetry competition to "encourage poets, and to recognize and reward excellence. Any poet residing in the U.S. is eligible to submit manuscripts." The competition has 3 categories: general, diversity of cultures and residents of the Pacific Coast states. Submit no more than 6 poems total. Entry fee: $5 for the first poem, $1 for each additional poem up to a maximum of six poems. Awards: $25 for 1st Place, $15 for 2nd Place, $10 for 3rd Place, plus publication. Postmark deadline: May 1. Awards announced by June 1. Send SASE for details or visit website. Website includes writer's guidelines, competition guidelines, subscription information and online featured poem.

THE LEDGE, 78-44 80th St., Glendale NY 11385, founded 1988, editor-in-chief/publisher Timothy Monaghan, co-editors George Held and Laura M. Corrado.

Magazine Needs: "We publish the best poems we receive. We seek poems with purpose, poems we can empathize with, powerful poems. Excellence is the ultimate criterion." Contributors include Sherman Alexie, Terri Brown-Davidson, Tony Gloeggler, Barry Seiler, Hal Sirowitz and Brooke Wiese. As a sample the editor-in-chief selected these lines from "Crossed Lines" by Elton Glaser:

> *If you were at hand, and the night warm,/And all the crossed lines clear,/Would we undo Newton and confuse the physical,//Proving that two bodies can enclose/The same space at the same time,/As in that hybrid gift, that tourist curio//Where the Midwest finds itself/Suddenly at sea: a sand dollar/Set in the smooth belly of a buckeye burl.*

The Ledge is 128 pgs., digest-sized, typeset and perfect-bound with b&w glossy cover. They accept 5% of poetry submissions. Press run is 1,000, including 400 subscribers. Single copy: $7; subscription: $12/2 issues, $22/4 issues or $30/6 issues.

How to Submit: Submit 3-5 poems at a time. Include SASE. No previously published work. Simultaneous submissions OK. Reads submissions September through May only. Reports in 4-6 months. Pays 2 copies. Acquires one-time rights.

Also Offers: *The Ledge* sponsors an annual poetry chapbook contest, as well as an annual poetry contest. Send SASE for details.

Advice: Timothy Monaghan says: "I believe the best poems appeal to the widest audience and consider *The Ledge* a truly democratic publication in that regard."

LEFT CURVE (Specialized: social issues), P.O. Box 472, Oakland CA 94604-0472, phone (510)763-7193, e-mail leftcurv@wco.com, website http://ncal.verio.com/~leftcurv, founded 1974, editor Csaba Polony.

Magazine Needs: *Left Curve* appears "irregularly, about every ten months." They want poetry that is "critical culture, social, political, 'post-modern,' not purely formal, too self-centered, poetry that doesn't address in sufficient depth today's problems." They have published poetry by Devorah Major, W.K. Buckley and Seamus Carraher. As a sample the editor selected these lines by Christos Tsiokas:

> *The great God money has dominion all over this globe. West, East. North,/South. Air, fire, water, earth. I could walk this planet, roam the last desert,/sail the lost sea searching for my Authentic Man. And find instead/Only Narcissus gazing into my reflection.*

Left Curve is 136 pgs., 8½×11, offset printed, perfect-bound with Durosheen cover, photos and ads. Press run is 2,000 for 200 subscribers; 50 are libraries, 1,500 shelf sales. Subscription: $25/3 issues (individuals). Sample: $8.

How to Submit: Submit up to 5 poems at a time. Cover letter stating "why you are submitting" required. Publishes theme issues. Send SASE for guidelines and upcoming themes. Reports in 3-6 months. Pays 3 copies. Open to unsolicited reviews. Poets may also send books for review consideration.

Also Offers: Website includes a statement of the editorial position, recent issues, poetry, guidelines and contact information.

■ $ 🗐 ◎ **LIBIDO: THE JOURNAL OF SEX AND SEXUALITY (Specialized: erotica, humor, gay/lesbian/bisexual)**, P.O. Box 146721, Chicago IL 60614-6721, phone (773)275-0842, fax (773)275-0752, e-mail rune@mcs.com, founded 1988, editors Marianna Beck and Jack Hafferkamp.

Magazine Needs: *Libido* is published 4 times/year. "Form, length and style are open. We want poetry of any and all styles as long as it is erotic and/or erotically humorous. We make a distinction between erotica and pornography. We want wit, not dirty words." They have published poetry by Chocolate Waters, Gordon Massman and Atar Hadari. *Libido* is 88 pgs., digest-sized, professionally printed, flat-spined, with 2-color varnished card cover. They accept about 2% of poetry received. Press run is 9,500 for 3,500 subscribers, 3,500 shelf sales and 1,500 single issues by mail. Subscription: $30 in US, $40 in Canada and Mexico (US funds), $50 in Europe and $60 elsewhere. Sample: $8.

How to Submit: Submit 2-3 poems at a time. Cover letter including "a one-sentence bio for contributors' page" required with submission. "Please, no handwritten mss and do not submit via fax or e-mail." Reports in 4-6 months. Pays $10-25 plus 1 copy. Send books for review consideration "only if the primary focus is love/eroticism."

◻ **LIBRA PUBLISHERS, INC.**, 3089C Clairemont Dr., Suite 383, San Diego CA 92117, phone/fax (619)571-1414, poetry editor William Kroll.

Book/Chapbook Needs: Publishes two professional journals, *Adolescence* and *Family Therapy*, plus books, primarily in the behaviorial sciences but also some general nonfiction, fiction and poetry. "At first we published books of poetry on a standard royalty basis, paying 10% of the retail price to the authors. Although at times we were successful in selling enough copies to at least break even, we found that we could no longer afford to publish poetry on this basis. Now, unless we fall madly in love with a particular collection, we offer professional services to assist the author in self-publishing." They have published books of poetry by Martin Rosner, William Blackwell, John Travers Moore and C. Margaret Hall.

How to Submit: Prefers complete ms but accepts query with 6 sample poems, publishing credits and bio. Replies to query in 2 days, to submissions in 2-3 weeks. Mss should be double-spaced. Sometimes sends prepublication galleys. Send 9×12 SASE for catalog. Sample books may be purchased on a returnable basis.

✓ ◻ **THE LICKING RIVER REVIEW**, Dept. of Literature and Language, Northern Kentucky University, Highland Heights KY 41099, founded 1991, faculty advisor Andrew Miller, mail submissions to poetry editor.

Magazine Needs: *TLRR* is an annual designed "to showcase the best writing by Northern Kentucky University students alongside work by new or established writers from the region or elsewhere." They have no specifications regarding form, subject matter or style of poetry. "No long poems (maximum 60 lines)." They have published poetry by Frederick Zydek, Helene Pilibosian and Tony Whedon. The review is 96 pgs., 7×10, offset printed on recycled paper and perfect-bound with a 16-page artwork inset (all art solicited). They accept 5% of the poetry received. Press run is 1,500. Sample: $5.

How to Submit: Submit up to 4 poems at a time. No previously published poems, no multiple or simultaneous submissions. Reads submissions September through December only. Poems are circulated to an editorial board. Reports in up to 6 months. Pays in copies. Rights revert to author. Requests acknowledgment if poem is later reprinted.

◻ **LIFTOUTS MAGAZINE; PRELUDIUM PUBLISHERS**, Dept. PM, 1414 S. Third St., Suite 102, Minneapolis MN 55454, fax (612)305-0655, founded 1971, poetry editor Barry Casselman, is a "publisher of experimental literary work and work of new writers in translation from other languages." Currently not accepting unsolicited material. *Liftouts* appears irregularly.

◻ **LIGHT**, Box 7500, Chicago IL 60680, founded 1992, editor John Mella.

Magazine Needs: *Light* is a quarterly of "light and occasional verse, satire, wordplay, puzzles, cartoons and line art." They do not want "greeting card verse, cloying or sentimental verse." The editor says *Light* is 64 pgs., perfect-bound, including art and graphics. Single copy: $5; subscription: $16. Sample: $4.

How to Submit: Submit 1 poem on a page with name, address, poem title and page number on each page. No previously published poems or simultaneous submissions. Seldom comments on rejections. Publishes theme issues. Send #10 SASE for guidelines. Reports in 3 months or less. Always sends prepublication galleys. Pays 2 copies to domestic contributors, 1 copy to foreign contributors. Open to unsolicited reviews; query first. Poets may also send books for review consideration.

✓ ◻ **LILITH**, P.O. Box 27071, Akron OH 44319, e-mail ad778@acorn.net, founded 1997, editor/publisher Raven.

Magazine Needs: *Lilith*, published monthly, is " 'no holds barred'—will publish just about everything, cartoons, comments, jokes, drawings; an open forum with a dark, bent and slightly twisted sense of humor. We will print anything, giving new poets a chance to see their work published." As a sample the editor selected this poem by DKD:

> Nightwalkers unite,/come and welcome in our time./Arise from your shadowed beds,/walk while the
> others sleep their/slumbered rest—/for this is our hour . . ./Children of the night.

Lilith is 10-14 pgs., 8½×11, photocopied and corner-stapled, includes cartoons. Press run is 150. Send SASE for sample

How to Submit: Previously published poems and simultaneous submissions OK. E-mail submissions OK. "If they want a copy of the issue with their poetry, they need to send a SASE." Time between acceptance and publication is 3 weeks. Publishes theme issues occasionally (holidays).

⊚ LILITH MAGAZINE (Specialized: women, ethnic), 250 W. 57th St., Suite 2432, New York NY 10107, phone (212)757-0818, fax (212)757-5705, e-mail lilithmag@aol.com, website http://www.lilithmag.com, founded in 1976, editor-in-chief Susan Weidman Schneider.

Magazine Needs: *Lilith* "is an independent magazine with a Jewish feminist perspective" which uses poetry by Jewish women "about the Jewish woman's experience. Generally we use short rather than long poems. Run four poems/year. Do not want to see poetry on other subjects." They have published poetry by Irena Klepfisz, Lyn Lifshin, Marcia Falk and Adrienne Rich. It is 48 pgs., magazine-sized, glossy. "We use colors. Covers are very attractive and professional-looking (one has won an award). Generous amount of art. It appears 4 times a year, circulation about 10,000, about 6,000 subscriptions." Subscription: $18 for 4 issues. Sample: $5.

How to Submit: Send up to 3 poems at a time; advise if simultaneous submission. Editor "sometimes" comments on rejections. Send SASE for guidelines.

Advice: "(1) Read a copy of the publication before you submit your work. (2) Be realistic if you are a beginner. The competition is *severe*, so don't start to send out your work until you've written for a few years. (3) Short cover letters only. Copy should be neatly typed and proofread for typos and spelling errors."

◑ ⊚ LILLIPUT REVIEW (Specialized: form), 282 Main St., Pittsburgh PA 15201-2807, founded 1989, editor Don Wentworth.

Magazine Needs: *Lilliput* is a tiny (4½×3.6 or 3½×4¼), 12- to 16-page magazine, appearing irregularly and using poems in any style or form no longer than 10 lines. They have published poetry by Albert Huffstickler, Lonnie Sherman, Lyn Lifshin and Linda Zeiser. As a sample the editor selected this poem by John Harter:

> *I TURN ON THE LIGHT AND LEAVE*

LR is laser-printed on colored paper and stapled. Press run is 250. Sample: $1 or SASE. Make checks payable to Don Wentworth.

How to Submit: Submit up to 3 poems at a time. Currently, every fourth issue is a broadside featuring the work of one particular poet. Send SASE for guidelines. Reports within 2-3 months. Pays 2 copies/poem. Acquires first rights. Editor comments on submissions "occasionally—always try to establish human contact."

Book/Chapbook Needs & How to Submit: Started the Modest Proposal Chapbook Series in 1994, publishing 1 chapbook/year, 18-24 pgs. in length. Chapbook submissions are by invitation only. Query with standard SASE. Sample chapbook: $3. Chapbook publications include *The Kingdom of Loose Board & Rusted Nail* by Christien Gholson.

Advice: The editor says, "A note above my desk reads 'Clarity & resonance, not necessarily in that order.' The perfect poem for *LR* is simple in style and language and elusive/allusive in meaning and philosophy. *LR* is open to all short poems in approach and theme, including any of the short Eastern forms, traditional or otherwise."

⦂ ◯ ◑ LIMESTONE CIRCLE, P.O. Box 178484, San Diego CA 92177-8484, e-mail renjef@earthlink.net, founded 1998, editor Renee Carter Hall.

Magazine Needs: *Limestone Circle* appears quarterly. "We publish artistic, accessible poetry with an emphasis on free verse, but we attempt to cover a range of styles, levels and voices. We are a market for both new and experienced poets to share their craft in a quality format. Free verse is preferred, but we will read formal, experimental, Oriental, etc., in hopes of publishing a variety of quality poetry. No greeting card verse; also, we are generally not an erotica publication and will definitely not consider pornography." They have published poetry by Fred Longworth and Walt Phillips. As a sample the editor selected these lines from "Love Poem At 4 AM" by Rayn Roberts:

> *He holds me so close we dream the same dream./But I cannot sleep/while I remember/a dream of driving down a back road in the dark/hoping for collision, a head-on in his arms.*

LC is 30-40 pgs., 8½×5½, photocopied and saddle-stapled or comb-bound with matte cardstock cover, includes b&w artwork and photos. They receive about 300 poems a year, accept approximately 30%. Press run is 100 for 30 subscribers, 20 shelf sales. Single copy: $4; subscription: $10/1 year (4 issues). Sample: $2. Make checks payable to Renee Carter Hall. "We prefer that poets send SASE or e-mail for guidelines before submitting."

How to Submit: Submit 3-5 poems at a time. Line length for poetry is 3 minimum, 40 maximum ("for best chance; these aren't rigid limits"). No previously published poems or simultaneous submissions. Cover letter preferred. E-mail submissions OK, "provided they are in the body of the message, not as attached files. There will be no replies without SASEs. Submit poems typed with name and address on each page. Any concrete poetry submitted must be camera-ready. (Please do not send concrete poetry via e-mail.)" Time between acceptance and publication is 1-4 months. Often comments on rejections. Send SASE for guidelines or obtain via e-mail. Reports in 2-8 weeks for postal submissions; usually within 1 week for e-mail submissions. Pays 2 copies. Acquires first rights.

Also Offers: "Also seeking b&w artwork and photos; terms and payment the same as for poetry submissions. For artwork, please send good-quality, uncreased copies; we will request originals if needed. Please indicate whether you want art or photos returned and include a properly-sized SASE with adequate postage."

Advice: The editor says, "Send us the work you like, not what you think we'll like. Remember that any editor's decision is only one person's opinion, and that persistence is most often the key to getting published."

◗ LIMITED EDITIONS PRESS; ART: MAG, P.O. Box 70896, Las Vegas NV 89170, phone (702)734-8121, founded 1982, editor Peter Magliocco.

Magazine Needs: They "have become, due to economic and other factors, more limited to a select audience of poets as well as readers. We seek to expel the superficiality of our factitious culture, in all its drive-thru, junk-food-brain, commercial-ridden extravagance—and stylize a magazine of hard-line aesthetics, where truth and beauty meet on a vector not shallowly drawn. Conforming to this outlook is an operational policy of seeking poetry from solicited poets primarily, though unsolicited submissions will be read, considered and perhaps used infrequently. Sought from the chosen is a creative use of poetic styles, systems and emotional morphologies other than banally constricting." They have published poetry by David P. Kozinski, Ken Smith, Bill Chown, Belinda Subraman and T. Kilgore Splake. As a sample the editor selected these lines from "Heidegger and Kristeva" by Ken Smith:

> Last night, I think I made a poem in sleeping/that I've spent today trying to recall./It comes at me in images, without words./There's a heron stalking the edge of a pond/raising and lowering its reedy legs/ with a mime's cautious deliberation . . .

ART: MAG, appearing in 1-2 large issues of 100 copies/year, is limited to a few poets. Subscription: $10. Sample: $5 or more. Make checks payable to Peter Magliocco.

How to Submit: Submit 5 poems at a time with SASE. "Submissions should be neat and use consistent style format (except experimental work). Cover letters are optional." No previously published poems; simultaneous submissions OK. Sometimes comments on rejections. Publishes theme issues. Send SASE for guidelines and upcoming themes. Reports within 3 months. Pays 1 copy. Acquires first rights. Staff occasionally reviews books of poetry. Send books for review consideration.

Book/Chapbook Needs & How to Submit: The press also occasionally publishes chapbooks (such as *Neo-Runes*, by Alan Catlin). Query before submitting.

Advice: The editor says, "The mag is seeking a futuristic aestheticism where the barriers of fact and fiction meet, where inner- and outer-space converge in the realm of poetic consciousness in order to create a more productively viable relationship to the coming 'cyberology' of the 21st century."

◖ LINES N' RHYMES, 5604 Harmeson Dr., Anderson IN 46013, phone (765)642-1239, founded 1989, editor Pearl Clark.

Magazine Needs: *Lines N' Rhymes* appears every other month using "some 4-line poetry, most between 12-20 lines. I like poems concerning life, belief in God's guidance, especially seasonal/holiday poetry. Nothing pornographic or occult." They have published poetry by Ainsley Jo Phillips, C. David Hay, Rosina Clifford, Evalyn Torrant and Pearl Wilshaw. As a sample the editor selected these lines from "Deliverance" by Jane F. Hutto:

> The weather's been cold/And our groceries are few,/The pickup won't start;/Our rent's overdue.

It is photocopied on 3 legal-sized colored sheets. Press run is 70, 3-5 shelf sales. Subscription: $7/6 issues. Sample: $2.

How to Submit: Submit 3 poems at a time. "A brief cover letter is OK but not essential. I receive 170 poems/year—accept 30%. I pay nothing for poetry used. I award 'Editor's Choice' to two poets/issue at $2. I give preference to subscribers. However, I sometimes use poetry from non-subscribers." Previously published poems and simultaneous submissions OK.

Also Offers: The editor holds a contest for limericks each September with 3 prizes of $5 each, free to subscribers, $2 fee to nonsubscribers.

⊕ ◖ LINKS; KERNOW POETS PRESS, Bude Haven, 18 Frankfield Rise, Tunbridge Wells TN2 5LF United Kingdom, founded 1992, editor Bill Headdon.

Magazine Needs: *Links* is published biannually in April and October and contains good quality poetry and reviews. They want "contemporary, strong poetry; must relate to the 'real' world; up to 80 lines. No chopped-up prose; no bleeding heart first-person confessions; no mock Shelley." They have published poetry by Gross, Bartlett and Shuttle. As a sample the editor selected these lines from "Masterpiece" by Barbara Daniels:

> I am a transparent woman,/My lover looks through me,/into a collaged landscape,/where any man can see/tamed hills and perfect pastures,/ego ego running free.

The editor says *Links* is up to 32 pgs., A5, photocopied and saddle-stitched with card cover. They receive about 1,000 poems a year, accept approximately 7%. Press run is 200 for 100 subscribers of which 5 are libraries, 30 shelf sales. Subscription: £4, £7.50/2 years, outside UK add £1. Sample (with guidelines): £2 (£3 outside UK).

How to Submit: Submit 5-6 poems at a time. No previously published poems or simultaneous submissions. Fax and e-mail submissions OK. Cover letter preferred. "No long bios or list of previous publications." Time between acceptance and publication is 1-6 months. Seldom comments on rejections. Send SASE for guidelines. Reports in 2 weeks. Pays 1 copy. Acquires first rights. Reviews books and chapbooks of poetry and other magazines in 100-200 words, single or multi-book format. Open to unsolicited reviews. Poets may also send books for review consideration.

⊕ ◐ **LINQ**, c/o English Dept., James Cook University, Townsville, Queensland 4811 Australia, phone (077)815097 or (07)47 814451, fax (07)47 815655, e-mail jcu.linq@jcu.edu.au, website http://www.jcu.edu.au/dept/English/tville/index.html, founded 1971, editors Dr. Greg Manning and Dr. Gina Mercer.
Magazine Needs: *LiNQ* is a 100-page biannual that "aims to publish works of a high literary standard, encompassing a wide and varied range of interest." They do not want to see "overtly naive and self-consciously subjective poetry." They have published poetry by Mark O'Connor, Alison Croggon, Aileen Kelly, Eve Stafford and Rebecca Edwards. As a sample they selected these lines from "Sign Me In" by Peter Porter:
> The private truth I kept within/Grew as a cancer undisclosed,/My books were bound in my dead skin,/
> My patent brilliances opposed/The ordinariness of life: I said/I'll show up brighter when I'm dead.

They receive about 250 poems a year, use approximately 20/edition. Press run is 350 for 160 subscribers of which 30 are libraries, 180 shelf sales. Single copy: $10 (within Australia), $15 (overseas); subscription: $20 individual (within Australia), $25 institution (within Australia), $30 overseas (for individual and institution). Since the journal is published in May and October, all subscriptions are due by November 1. Sample back issue: $6 (Australian).
How to Submit: Poems must be typed, 1/page, and contain title, page number and writer's name and address. No previously published poems; simultaneous submissions OK. Cover letter with brief bio required. Submissions via fax or e-mail OK. Submission deadlines: September 30 (May edition) and April 30 (October edition). Send SASE (or SAE and 3 IRCs) for return of work. Author retains copyright.
Advice: The editors say, "*LiNQ* aims for a broadly-based sympathetic approach to creative work, particularly from new and young Australian writers."

$ ◐ **LINTEL**, 24 Blake Lane, Middletown NY 10940, phone (212)674-4901, founded 1977, poetry editor Walter James Miller.
Book/Chapbook Needs: "We publish poetry and innovative fiction of types ignored by commercial presses. We consider any poetry except conventional, traditional, cliché, greeting card types, i.e., we consider any artistic poetry." We have published poetry by Sue Saniel Elkind, Samuel Exler, Adrienne Wolfert, Edmund Pennant, and Nathan Teitel. "Typical of our work" is Teitel's book, *In Time of Tide*, 64 pgs., digest-sized, professionally printed in bold type, flat-spined, hard cover stamped in gold, jacket with art and author's photo on back.
How to Submit: Query with 5 sample poems. Reads submissions January and August only. "We reply to the query within a month, to the ms (if invited) in 2 months." We consider simultaneous submissions if so marked and if the writer agrees to notify us of acceptance elsewhere." Ms should be typed. Always sends prepublication galleys. Pays royalties after all costs are met and 100 copies. Buys all rights. Offers usual subsidiary rights: 50%/50%. To see samples, send SASE for catalog and ask for "trial rate" (50%).
Advice: The editor says, "Form follows function! We accept any excellent poem whose form—be it sonnet or free verse—suits the content and the theme. We like our poets to have a good publishing record in literary magazines, before they begin to think of a book."

◐ **LIPS**, Box 1345, Montclair NJ 07042, founded 1981, poetry editor Laura Boss.
Magazine Needs: *Lips* "is a quality poetry magazine that is published twice a year and takes pleasure in publishing previously unpublished poets as well as the most established voices in contemporary poetry. We look for quality work: the strongest work of a poet; work that moves the reader; poems take risks that work. We prefer clarity in the work rather than the abstract. Poems longer than six pages present a space problem." They have published poetry by Gregory Corso, Richard Kostelanetz, Lyn Lifshin, Marge Piercy, Warren Woessner, Nicholas Christopher, David Ignatow and Ishmael Reed. As a sample the editor selected these lines from "The Dark" by Ruth Stone:
> In the dark of the moon/under the shadow of our local hydrogen fluff,/I look out of my worn eyes/and
> see the bright new Pleiades/My sister lies in a box/in a New England graveyard.

Lips is 70 pgs. (average), digest-sized, flat-spined. They receive about 8,000 submissions/year, use less than 1%, have a 6-month backlog. Circulation is 1,000 for 200 subscriptions, approximately 100 are libraries. Sample: $6. Occasional double issues are $10.
How to Submit: Poems should be submitted between September and March only, 6 pgs., typed, no query necessary. She tries to respond in 1 month but has gotten backlogged at times. Sometimes sends prepublication galleys. Pays 1 copy. Acquires first rights. Send SASE for guidelines.
Advice: Her advice to poets is, "Remember the 2 T's: Talent *and* Tenacity."

☑ ◐ **THE LISTENING EYE**, Kent State Geauga Campus, 14111 Claridon-Troy Rd., Burton OH 44021, phone (440)286-3840, e-mail hy151@cleveland.freenet.com, website http://www.geocities.com/Athens/3716, founded 1970 for student work, 1990 as national publication, editor Grace Butcher, assistant editors Jim Wohlken and Joanne Speidel.

THE BOOK PUBLISHERS INDEX, located at the back of this book, lists those publishers who consider full-length book collections.

Magazine Needs: *TLE* is an annual publication, appearing in late summer/early fall, of poetry, short fiction, creative nonfiction and art that welcomes both new and established poets and writers. They want "high literary quality poetry. Prefer shorter poems (less than two pages) but will consider longer if space allows. Any subject, any style. No trite images or predictable rhyme." They have published poetry by Walter McDonald, Timothy Russell, Ann Menebroker and John Knoepfle. As a sample the editor selected these lines from "Casualties" by Dean Blehert:

> *Some conversations are like sending my best men/on suicide missions.//Afterwards I must write hurtful letters/to their Greek, Latin, Sanskrit,/Hebrew and Old English parents,/and I just don't know what to say.*

The Listening Eye is 52-60 pgs., 5½×8½, professionally printed and saddle-stapled with card stock cover with b&w art. They receive about 200 poems a year, accept approximately 5%. Press run is 300. Single copy: $4. Sample: $4.50. Make checks payable to Kent State University.

How to Submit: Submit up to 4 poems at a time, typed, single-spaced, 1 poem/page, name and address in upper left-hand corner of each page, with SASE for return of work. Previously published poems occasionally accepted; no simultaneous submissions. Cover letter preferred. No e-mail submissions. Reads submissions January 1 through April 15 only. Time between acceptance and publication is 4-6 months. Poems are circulated to the editor and 2 assistant editors who read and evaluate work separately, then meet for final decisions. Occasionally comments on rejections. Send SASE for guidelines or obtain via e-mail or website. Reports in 3 months. Pays 2 copies. Acquires first or one-time rights. Also awards $30 to the best sports poem in each issue.

Advice: The editor says, "I look for tight lines that don't sound like prose, unexpected images or juxtapositions; the unusual use of language, noticeable relationships of sounds; a twist in viewpoint, an ordinary idea in extraordinary language, an amazing and complex idea simply stated, play on words and with words, an obvious love of language. Poets need to read the 'Big 3'—cummings, Thomas, Hopkins—to see the limits to which language can be taken. Then read the 'Big 2'—Dickinson to see how simultaneously tight, terse, and universal a poem can be, and Whitman to see how sprawling, cosmic and personal. Then read everything you can find that's being published in literary magazines today and see how your work compares to all of the above."

◐ LITERAL LATTÉ; LITERAL LATTÉ POETRY AWARDS, 61 E. Eighth St., Suite 240, New York NY 10003, phone (212)260-5532, e-mail litlatte@aol.com, website http://www.literal-latte.com, founded 1994, editor Jenine Gordon Bockman, contact Lisa Erdman.

Magazine Needs: *Literal Latté* is a bimonthly tabloid of "pure prose, poetry and art," distributed free in coffeehouses and bookstores in New York City, and by subscription. They are "open to all styles of poetry—quality is the determining factor." They have published poetry by Allen Ginsberg, Carol Muske and John Updike. As a sample we selected these lines from "What The Screech Owl Knows" by John Sokol, 1st Place winner of the annual *Literal Latté* Poetry Awards:

> *That, here, in the woods/of western Pennsylvania,/life burgeons by the hour/while death rides a pig;/ that larvae open like popcorn/and everything living/feasts on last year's detritus; . . .*

LL is 24-28 pgs., 11×17, neatly printed on newsprint and unbound with b&w art, graphics and ads. They receive about 3,000 poems a year, accept approximately 1%. Press run is 25,000 for distribution in over 200 bookstores and coffeehouses in New York City and nationwide. Subscription: $11. Sample: $3.

How to Submit: No previously published poems; simultaneous submissions OK. Cover letter with bio and SASE required. E-mail submissions OK. "No attachments." Time between acceptance and publication is 6 months. Often comments on rejections. Send SASE for guidelines or request via e-mail. Reports in 2-3 months. Pays 10 copies and 3 subscriptions (2 gift subscriptions in author's name). All rights return to author upon publication.

Also Offers: They also sponsor the *Literal Latté* Poetry Awards, an annual contest for previously unpublished work. Offers $500 in awards and publication. Entry fee: $10 for 6 poems (or buy a subscription and the entry fee for 6 poems is included). A past contest was judged by Carol Muske. Send SASE for current details. Website includes excerpts, guidelines, information on events and contests.

◻ ◎ LITERARY FOCUS POETRY PUBLICATIONS; ANTHOLOGY OF CONTEMPORARY POETRY; INTERNATIONAL POETRY CONTESTS: FALL CONCOURS, SPRING CONCOURS, SUMMER CONCOURS (Specialized: anthology), P.O. Box 36242, Houston TX 77236-6242, phone/fax (281)568-8780, e-mail dprince1@swbell.net, website http://www.literaryfocus.com, founded 1988, editor-in-chief Adrian A. Davieson.

Magazine Needs: Purchase of anthology may be required of poets accepted for publication. Literary Focus publishes anthologies compiled in contests, 3 times/year, with prizes of $200, $100 and $50, plus "Distinguished Mention" and "Honorable Mention." "Contemporary poetry with no restriction on themes. 20-line limit. No abusive, anti-social poetry." As a sample we selected these lines from the editor's own poem "My Deep Fears":

> *Out came the fears of yester-years/Eroding my very being. As I looked/The stream of tears cascaded my/Cheeks, reminding me the journey/Was not over.//Only yesterday I thought of my arrival/At shore, but now I know it was just a/Mirage, that to be thus is nothing but/To be safely thus!*

The digest-sized anthologies are either flat-spined or saddle-stapled, 70 pgs., typeset.

How to Submit: Submit maximum submission 15 poems, minimum three poems. Previously published poems and simultaneous submissions OK. E-mail submissions OK. "In order to evaluate serious entries, a $5 entry fee is required for the first three poems. Poems are evaluated on an individual basis by a panel of five editors chaired by editor-in-chief. Poets are notified of acceptance two weeks after deadlines." Send SASE for guidelines or obtain via website. Pays up to 5 copies. Reviews books of poetry.

⊘ THE LITERARY REVIEW: AN INTERNATIONAL JOURNAL OF CONTEMPORARY WRIT-ING, Fairleigh Dickinson University, 285 Madison Ave., Madison NJ 07940, phone/fax (973)443-8564, e-mail tlr@fdu.edu, website http://www.webdelsol.com/tlr/, founded 1957, editor-in-chief Walter Cummins.
Magazine Needs: *The Literary Review*, a quarterly, seeks "work by new and established poets which reflects a sensitivity to literary standards and the poetic form." No specifications as to form, length, style, subject matter or purpose. They have published poetry by Elizabeth Murawski, David B. Prather, Barbara F. Lefcowitz and Charles Wyatt. The magazine is 128 pgs., 6×9, professionally printed and flat-spined with glossy color cover, using 20-50 pgs. of poetry in each issue. Press run is 2,500 with 900 subscriptions of which one-third are overseas. They receive about 1,200 submissions a year, use approximately 100-150, have a 6- to 12-month backlog. Sample: $5, request a "general issue."
How to Submit: Submit up to 5 poems at a time, clear typed. Simultaneous submissions OK. Do not submit during the summer months of June, July and August. At times the editor comments on rejections. Publishes theme issues. Send SASE for upcoming themes or request via e-mail. Reports in 2-3 months. Always sends prepublication galleys. Pays 2 copies. Acquires first rights. Reviews books of poetry in 500 words, single book format. Open to unsolicited reviews. Poets may also send books for review consideration.
Advice: They advise, "Read a general issue of the magazine carefully before submitting."

⊘ ◎ LITERATURE AND BELIEF (Specialized: religious), 3076-E Jesse Knight Humanities Building, Brigham Young University, Provo UT 84602, phone (801)378-3073, fax (801)378-8724, e-mail cracrftr@email.b yu.edu, founded 1981, editors Richard H. Cracroft and John J. Murphy, poetry editor Lance Larsen.
Magazine Needs: *Literature and Belief* is the "biannual journal of the Center for the Study of Christian Values in Literature." It uses "carefully crafted, affirmation poetry in the Judeo-Christian tradition." They have published poetry by Ted Hughes, Donnel Hunter, Leslie Norris, Susan Elizabeth Howe and Lance Larsen. As a sample the editor selected these lines from "Cycle" by Cyd Adams:

> *The air bears the heaviness/of creation's spawning,/for Christ has borne the dogwood/to scale the last escarpment/so a risen sun can silver/the cobalt sky.*

It is handsomely printed and flat-spined. Single copy: $5 US, $7 outside US.
How to Submit: Submit 3-4 poems at a time. No previously published poems. Response within 6 weeks. Publishes theme issues. Send SASE for upcoming themes. Pays 5 copies and 10 "offprints."
Also Offers: The center also publishes religious monographs, most *Toward the Solitary Star*, selected poems by Östen Sjöstrand. Our "Values in Literature" monograph series invites queries for scholarly studies of authors or works which combine fine literature and religious values and faith in God. Currently in progress: "Willa Cather and Religion" and "The York Cycle of Morality Plays"; in print: Bruce L. Edwards, C.S. Lewis *A Rhetoric of Reaching*.

ᴺ ⊘ LITRAG, P.O. Box 21066, Seattle WA 98111, e-mail litrag@hotmail.com, website http://www.litrag.c om, founded 1997, editor Derrick Hachey, co-editor AJ Rathbun.
Magazine Needs: *LitRag* appears 3 times a year. "We strive to publish high-quality poetry, fiction and art from established and up-and-coming writers and visual artists. We look for poetry that is strong in both image and intelligence, and we admit to no thematic bias. We do not want poetry from writers who do not actually read books of contemporary poetry." They have published poetry by Ed Skoog, Barbara F. Lefowitz and Derick Burlson. As a sample the editor selected this poem, "What Dying Might Be Like For You," by Kathleen McCarthy:

> *Now, a man rumbles through the house asking, Where's/my oboe?, as he tosses pillows aside that land/ with the soft thud of a bird/confused into a window. But this can't be/right. Where's the transcendence/ in chaos?*

The editors say *LitRag* is 40 pgs., magazine-sized, laser printed and staple bound, screenprint cover, includes photos, ink drawings and illustrations. They receive about 4,000 poems a year, accept approximately 1%. Press run is 500 for 150 subscribers, 50 shelf sales; 150 distributed free to random people. Subscription: $12/4 issues. Sample: $3.
How to Submit: Submit 3 poems at a time. No previously published poems; simultaneous submissions OK. Cover letter preferred. E-mail and disk submissions OK. "We require a SASE." Time between acceptance and publication is 3 months. Poems are circulated to an editorial board. "One original reader who makes the initial decision to submit it to the editorial board, which makes the final decision." Seldom comments on rejections. Send SASE for guidelines or obtain via e-mail or website. Reports in 6 weeks. Sometimes sends prepublication galleys. Pays "commemorative gift" and 2 copies. Acquires first North American serial rights. Reviews books and chapbooks of poetry and other magazines in 300 words, single book format. Open to unsolicited reviews. Poets may also send books for review consideration.
Also Offers: Website features back issues, guidelines, editors, art and information on current issues, availability and upcoming events. "We host release parties for each issue."

◨ ◙ **THE LITTLE MAGAZINE**, S.U.N.Y. Albany, English Dept., 1400 Washington Ave., Albany NY 12222, phone (518)442-4398, e-mail litmag@csc.albany.edu, website http://www.albany.edu/~litmag, founded 1965, editor Dimitri Anastasopoulos, editor Christina Milletti.

Magazine Needs: "Since 1965, *The Little Magazine* has been a literary journal devoted to publishing fiction and poetry in experimental forms. In 1995, we embraced our own mission: we moved to the web and CD-ROM in order to explore and exploit the nexus of opportunities that now exist between literature and media, how literature, in effect, can benefit from emerging technologies. Above all, we remain devoted to work of strong artistic merit which pushes its own limits; to forms which writers and artists are just starting to take advantage. *The Little Magazine* publishes online biannually, and every two years collects the best of the web issues along with new material on a CD-ROM for distribution to libraries and bookstores." They want "innovative, experimental, stylish work—above all, poetry and fiction that has been written for or can be adapted to a hypertext or web environment." They have published poetry by Charles Bernstein, Nathaniel Mackey, Juliana Spahr and Richard Kostelanetz. Press run for CD-ROM is 2,000. Sample of CD-ROM: $15.

How to Submit: Previously published poems and simultaneous submissions OK. Cover letter preferred. Poets are encouraged to submit via e-mail or on disk (either MAC or PC). Reads submissions September through May only. Time between acceptance and publication is 3 months. Poems are circulated to an editorial board. Seldom comments on rejections. Publishes theme issues. Send SASE for guidelines and upcoming themes. Reports in 2 months. Pays 1 copy. Acquires first North American serial or one-time rights. They rarely do reviews, however, poets may send books for review consideration.

Advice: The editors say, "We're looking for writers bridging media between poetry or prose and emerging multimedia technologies—but we always want good work in any form, from the traditional to avant-garde."

◨ ⊕ ◗ ◙ **LOCHS MAGAZINE; WORLD PUBLISHING; THE INDEPENDENT PRESS; KIMBO PUBLISHING**, Kimbo International, P.O. Box 12412, London SW18 5SG United Kingdom, founded 1996, publisher/editor Rafaël Kimberley-Bowen.

Magazine Needs: *Lochs* is a quarterly "comedy publication, aiming to cover a maximum of different genres of comedy." They want humorous and short poems and limericks. "Nothing too long or too serious (i.e., not light-hearted enough)." They have published poetry by Neil K. Henderson, Tony Lake, Jan O'Hansen and Brian Pastdor. As a sample the publisher selected this poem "The Ballad of a Clumsy Nurse and an Intensive Care Patient" by Dave Bryan:

> *Drip/Drip/Trip/Rip/Rip*

The publisher says *Lochs* is 30-40 pgs., magazine-sized, staple bound, black and red on blue cover with picture and text, includes b&w photos, cartoons, drawings. They receive about 100 poems a year, accept approximately 10%. Press run is 400 for 150 subscribers, 50 shelf sales. Single copy: $2; subscription: $10/6 issues. Sample: $1. Make checks payable to Kimbo International.

How to Submit: Submit up to 5 poems at a time. Line length for poetry is 20 maximum. Previously published poems and simultaneous submissions OK. Cover letter preferred. Disk submissions OK. "Bio appreciated, SAE/IRC as well." Time between acceptance and publication is up to 6 months. Always comments on rejections. Publishes theme issues occasionally. Send SASE (or SAE and IRC) for guidelines. Reports in up to 4 months. Pays 1-3 copies. Acquires one-time rights. Reviews books and chapbooks of poetry and other magazines in 50-250 words, single book format. Open to unsolicited reviews. Poets may also send books for review consideration.

Also Offers: "We will be launching a nationwide (UK) student magazine. Anyone interested in participating in any aspect of the venture should contact publisher R. Kimberley-Bowen."

◨ ⊕ $ ◙ **LONDON MAGAZINE**, 30 Thurloe Place, London SW7 England, founded 1954, poetry editor Alan Ross.

Magazine Needs: *LM* is a literary and art monthly using poetry "the best of its kind." Editors seem open to all styles and forms, including well-made formal works. Some of the best poems in England appear here. It is a 6×8½, perfect-bound, elegant-looking magazine, with card cover, averaging about 150 pages and appearing six times/year. They accept about 150 of 2,000 poems received each year. Press run is 5,000 for 2,000 subscribers. Subscription: £28.50 or $67. Sample: £4.75.

How to Submit: Cover letter required. Reports "very soon." Pays £20/page. Buys first British serial rights. Reviews books of poetry in up to 1,200 words. Open to unsolicited reviews. Poets may also send books for review consideration.

Advice: Alan Ross says, "Quality is our only criterion."

◗ ◙ **LONE STARS MAGAZINE; "SONGBOOK" POETRY CONTEST**, 4219 Flinthill, San Antonio TX 78230, founded 1992, editor/publisher Milo Rosebud.

Magazine Needs: *Lone Stars*, published 3 times/year, features "contemporary poetry." They want poetry that holds a continuous line of thought. No profanity. They have published poetry by Ralph E. Martin, Sheila Roark and Lisamarie Leto. As a sample the editor selected these lines from "Let Life Decide" by Terry Lee:

> *A midnight rainbow, a tear never cried, words spoken in silence: a light that does not shine.*

Lone Stars is 25 pgs., 8½×11, photocopied, with some hand-written poems, saddle-stapled, bound with tape, includes clip art. Press run is 200 for 100 subscribers of which 3 are libraries. Single copy: $5; subscription: $15. Sample: $4.50.

How to Submit: Submit 3-5 poems at a time with "the form typed the way you want it in print." Charges reading fee of $1 per poem. Previously published poems and simultaneous submissions OK. Cover letter preferred. Time between acceptance and publication is 2 months. Publishes theme issues. Send SASE for guidelines and upcoming themes. Reports within 3 months. Acquires one-time rights.
Also Offers: Sponsors annual "Songbook" (song-lyric poems) Poetry Contest. Send SASE for details.

◉ LONE WILLOW PRESS, P.O. Box 31647, Omaha NE 68131-0647, e-mail lonewillowpress@hotmail.com, founded 1993, editor Dale Champy.
Book/Chapbook Needs: Publishes 2-3 chapbooks/year. "We publish chapbooks on single themes and are open to all themes. The only requirement is excellence. However, we do not want to see doggerel or greeting card verse." They have published *Cave Poems* by Marjorie Power and *Things Like This Happen All the Time* by Eric Hoffman. That book is 20 pgs., digest-sized, neatly printed on gray paper and saddle-stapled with a light, gray card stock cover.
How to Submit: Query first with 5 sample poems and cover letter with brief bio and publication credits. Previously published poems OK; no simultaneous submissions. E-mail submissions OK. Time between acceptance and publication is 6 months. Seldom comments on rejections. Send SASE for guidelines. Replies to queries in 1 month, to mss (if invited) in 2-3 months. Pays 25 author's copies. "We also pay a small royalty if the book goes into a second printing." For a sample chapbook, send $7.95 in check or money order.
Advice: The editor says, "If you don't know the work of Roethke, DeFrees and Hugo, don't bother sending work our way. We work with no more than two poets at a time."

◎ LONG ISLAND QUARTERLY (Specialized: regional), P.O. Box 114, Northport NY 11768, founded 1990, editor/publisher George Wallace.
Magazine Needs: *Long Island Quarterly* uses poetry (mostly lyric free verse) by people on or from Long Island. "Surprise us with fresh language. No conventional imagery, self-indulgent confessionalism, compulsive article-droppers." They have published poetry by Edmund Pennant and David Ignatow. As a sample the editor selected this poem, "The Willow," by William Heyen:

> Crazy Horse counted the leaves of willows along the river./He realized one leaf for each buffalo,/&
> the leaves just now appearing in the Moon of Tender Grass/were calves being born. If he could keep
> the trees/from the whites, the herds would seed themselves./He watched the buffalo leaves for long, &
> long,/how their colors wavered dark & light in the running wind./If he could keep his rootedness within
> this dream,/he could shade his people to the end of time.

LIQ is 28 pgs., digest-sized, professionally printed on quality stock and saddle-stapled with matte card cover. Press run is 250 for 150 subscribers of which 15 are libraries, 50-75 shelf sales. Subscription: $15. Sample: $4.
How to Submit: Submit 3 poems at a time. Name and address on each page. Cover letter including connection to Long Island region required. Submissions without SASE are not returned. Responds in 3 months. Sometimes sends prepublication galleys. Pays 1 copy.
Advice: The editor advises: "(1) Go beyond yourself; (2) Don't be afraid to fictionalize; (3) Don't write your autobiography—if you are worth it, maybe someone else will."

◙ LONG ISLANDER; WALT'S CORNER, 322 Main St., Huntington NY 11743, phone (516)427-7000, fax (516)427-5820, founded 1838 by Walt Whitman, poetry editor George Wallace.
Magazine Needs: *Long Islander* is a weekly newspaper, 25,000 circulation, using unrhymed poetry up to 20 lines "grounded in personal/social matrix; no haiku, inspirational." They have published poetry by David Ignatow, David Axelrod and R.B. Weber. It is "48 pgs., newsprint." They receive about 1,000 poems a year, use approximately 52. Subscription: $18. Sample: $2.50.
How to Submit: Submit 3 poems at a time. Simultaneous submissions OK. "Cover letter should be simple, not effusive. SASE missing? Then we won't reply or return copy." Editor "normally" comments on rejections. Pays 1 copy. Staff reviews books of poetry. Send books for review consideration.

◉ LONG SHOT, P.O. Box 6238, Hoboken NJ 07030, e-mail dshot@mindspring.com, website http://www.longshot.org, founded 1982, edited by Danny Shot, Nancy Mercado, Andy Clausen, David Stack and Ernie Hilbert.
Magazine Needs: Published biannually, *Long Shot* is, they say, "writing from the real world." They have published poetry by Wanda Coleman, Gregory Corso, Jayne Cortez, Diane diPrima, Amiri Baraka, Reg E. Gaines and June Jordan. As a sample the editors selected these lines from "For My Comrades" by Cheryl Boyce Taylor:

> rage is an aphrodisiac/i ride your fear/like an oversized cock/be afraid/this is a warning/i will not be
> silent

Long Shot is 192 pgs., professionally printed and flat-spined with glossy card cover using b&w photos, drawings and cartoons. Press run is 2,000. Subscription: $24/2 years (4 issues). Sample: $8.
How to Submit: No previously published poems; simultaneous submissions OK. Reports in 2 months. Pays 2 copies.
Also Offers: They have published *The Original Buckwheat* by Reg E. Gaines and *Sermons from the Smell of a Carcass Condemned to Begging* by Tony Medina. Send SASE for details.
Advice: Unlike other publishers, Danny Shot says they receive "too many requests for writer's guidelines. Just send the poems."

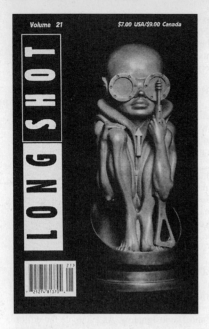

Volume 21 $7.00 USA/$9.00 Canada

LONG SHOT

The bronze sculpture featured on the Volume 21 cover of *Long Shot* is "Birth-Machine Baby/9 mm Giger" by Swiss surrealist artist H.R. Giger, photographed by Dana Frank. H.R. Giger is internationally known for his strange and fantastic artwork rendered in his unique "biomechanical" style. (Giger designed the alien for the movie *Alien*.) "We like covers that are eye-catching," says *Long Shot*'s publisher and editor-in-chief Danny Shot. "While we pride ourselves on choosing scintillating artwork and extremely readable prose, poetry is our reason for being. Poetry is the heart and soul and genitalia of our magazine." Based in Hoboken, New Jersey, *Long Shot* appears twice a year and is 192 pages, professionally printed and flat-spined with glossy card cover using black and white photos, drawings and cartoons.

N ◯ ◎ LONZIE'S FRIED CHICKEN™ LITERARY MAGAZINE; SOUTHERN ESCARPMENT CO. (Specialized: regional), P.O. Box 189, Lynn NC 28750, website http://www.lonziesfriedchicken.com, founded 1998, editor E.H. Goree.

Magazine Needs: *Lonzie's Fried Chicken™* is "a journal of accessible southern fiction and poetry—an opportunity for writers and poets to show their stuff and satisfy readers. Our focus is well-written short fiction, self-contained novel excerpts, and poetry with a feel for the South. We welcome the best contemporary, mainstream, and historical work by published and unpublished poets and writers." They have published poetry by Gwendoline Fortune, Errol Miller, Patricia Johnson, C.C. Wharton and Sallie Page. As a sample we selected this haiku, "Dog Barks As Car Stops," by Karen Wade:

> Dog barks as car stops/Silence ends with jingling keys/Doors close, steps echo/Sigh with an exhalation/
> Waiting wife closes her eyes

LFC is about 100 pgs., digest-sized, offset printed and perfect-bound with light card cover containing b&w photo, ads. They receive over 500 poems a year, accept approximately 10%. Press run is 1,000 for about 200 subscribers, 500 shelf sales; 100 distributed free to newspapers, reviewers and contributors. Single copy: $8.95; subscription: $12.95/year, $23.95/2 years. Sample (including guidelines): $9.95.

How to Submit: Submit up to 3 poems at a time. Line length for poetry is 40 maximum. No previously published poems; simultaneous submissions OK. Cover letter preferred. Time between acceptance and publication is up to 5 months. Poems are circulated to an editorial board. Seldom comments on rejections. Send SASE for return or reply. Reports in 3 months or less. Pays 3 copies. Acquires first rights and one-time anthology rights.

Also Offers: Website includes guidelines, contributors, list of bookstores and order form.

Advice: The editor says, "We enjoy publishing subtle, accessible southern fiction and poetry. Not interested in essays, bleak, or 'too quaint' (i.e., we're from the south an' we eat grits, love sweet 'tater pie, etc.') pieces."

$ ◉ LOOM PRESS, P.O. Box 1394, Lowell MA 01853-1394, founded 1978, editor/publisher Paul Marion.

Book/Chapbook Needs: Loom Press is a small press publisher of books with an emphasis on publishing poets from New England. Poets published include Marie Louise St. Onge, Susan April, Michael Casey and Eric Linder. Books are usually perfect-bound, 6×9, with an average page count of 64. Sample: $10.

How to Submit: Writers should query first for book publication, sending cover letter, credits, 5 sample poems and bio. "Do not send book-length mss." Queries will be answered in 2 months, mss reported on in 3 months. Simultaneous submissions will be considered. Time between acceptance and publication is 18-24 months. The editor comments on mss "when time allows." Always sends prepublication galleys. Pays royalties of 10%, plus 5% of print run.

Advice: The editor says, "We are especially interested in poems that address issues related to place, nature, history and cultural identity."

◖ ◎ LOONFEATHER; LOONFEATHER PRESS (Specialized: regional), P.O. Box 1212, Bemidji MN 56619-1212, phone (218)751-4869, founded 1979, poetry editors Betty Rossi, Mark Christensen and Gail Rixen.

Magazine Needs & How to Submit: The literary magazine *Loonfeather* appears 2 times a year, "primarily but not exclusively for Minnesota writers. Prefer short poems of not over 42 lines, accepts some traditional forms if well done, no generalizations on worn-out topics." They have published poetry by Spencer Reece, Joyce Penchansky, Thom Ward and Mary Winters. As a sample the editors selected these lines from "The Owl" by Malcolm Moos:

> Who was it that I saw moving through the language of the rain?/Was it my grandmother, lingering?/
> Something heard and forgotten, deep in the forest of my body,/something I am always trying to
> remember . . . .

Loonfeather is 48 pgs., 5½ × 8½, saddle-stapled, professionally printed in small type with matte card cover, using b&w art and ads. Single copy current issue: $5; back issues: $2.50, subscription: $8.50/year. Pays 2 copies.
Book/Chapbook Needs & How to Submit: Loonfeather Press publishes a limited number of quality poetry books. They published *Feast* by Carol Ann Russell, *Faith in Ice Time* by Mark Christensen and *Notes of an Ancient Chinese Poet* by Philip Dacey. Query with 2-3 sample poems, cover letter and previous publications. Replies to queries in 6 months. Time between acceptance and publication is 1-1½ years. Pays 10% royalties.

Ⓜ LOS, 150 N. Catalina St., No. 2, Los Angeles CA 90004, founded 1991, editors Virginia M. Geoffrey, I.B. Scrood, P.N. Bouts and M. Peel.
Magazine Needs: *Los,* published 4 times a year, features poetry. They have published poetry by Ed Orr, Peter Layton and James S. Proffitt. As a sample the editor selected these lines from "festina ne timeas" by C. Mulrooney:

> Roderick and Belacqua/figure the delay//and here is this poor fool/who slaps his pack of cigarettes/
> reflexively after a rock concert

The editors say *Los* is 5 × 8½ and saddle-stapled. Press run is 100 for 25 subscribers; 15 distributed free to local bookstores. Sample: $2. Make checks payable to Heather J. Lowe.
How to Submit: Submit any number of poems at a time. Previously published poems and simultaneous submissions OK. Time between acceptance and publication is up to 6 months. Reports in 1-2 weeks. Pays 1 copy.

$Ⓜ LOTHROP, LEE & SHEPARD BOOKS, 1350 Avenue of the Americas, New York NY 10019, phone (212)261-6641, fax (212)261-6648, website http://www.williammorrow.com, founded 1904, editor-in-chief Susan Pearson. Publishes 30 hardback children's books/year. Submissions by published poets or through agents only. "We do not accept unsolicited mss. No fax submissions." Reports in 2 months. Pays advance against royalties.

◎ LOTUS PRESS, INC.; NAOMI LONG MADGETT POETRY AWARD (Specialized: ethnic), P.O. Box 21607, Detroit MI 48221, phone (313)861-1280, fax (313)861-4740, founded 1972, editor Naomi Long Madgett.
Book/Chapbook Needs & How to Submit: "We occasionally publish sets of poster-poems on related subjects, including 'The Fullness of Earth' and 'Hymns Are My Prayers.' However, we are already committed through 1999 on book publications except for award-winning manuscripts." Query about status for 2000.
Also Offers: They sponsor the Naomi Long Madgett Poetry Award. The award goes to a ms by an African-American poet. "Under the new guidelines, poets who have already had a book published by Lotus Press are ineligible. However, inclusion in a Lotus Press anthology, such as *Adam of Ifé: Black Women in Praise of Black Men*, does not disqualify them. Those who have worked over a period of years at developing their craft will have the best chance for consideration. The work of novices is not likely to be selected. Poems submitted by another person, anthologies, or collaborations by more than one poet are not eligible." Awards $500 and publication by Lotus Press, Inc. Submit 3 complete copies of approximately 60-80 pages of poetry, exclusive of a table of contents or other introductory material, with a $15 reading fee. Any number of poems in the collection may be previously published individually in newspapers, magazines, journals or anthologies. Do not include author's name on any page of the ms. Include with each copy a cover sheet with the title of the collection only and no other information. Also enclose a sheet with the title of the ms, author's name, address, phone and brief statement, signed, indicating all the poems are original and uncollected and the author is an American of African descent. Mss will not be returned. Include a stamped, self-addressed postcard for acknowledgement of receipt. Submission period: February 1 through April 1. Winners will be announced no later than July 1. Send SASE for more information.

☑ ◑ ◎ LOUISIANA LITERATURE; LOUISIANA LITERATURE PRIZE FOR POETRY (Specialized: regional), SLU-792, Southeastern Louisiana University, Hammond LA 70402, phone (504)549-5022, fax (504)549-5021, e-mail lalit@selu.edu, editor Jack Bedell.
Magazine Needs: *Louisiana Literature* appears twice a year. They say they "receive mss year round although we work through submissions more slowly in summer. We consider creative work from anyone though we strive to showcase our state's talent. We appreciate poetry that shows firm control and craft, is sophisticated yet accessible to a broad readership. We don't use highly experimental work." They have published poetry by Claire Bateman, Kate Daniels, Elton Glaser, Gray Jacobik, Al Maginnes, Vivian Shipley, Richard Katrovas, D.C. Berry and Judy Longley. As a sample the editor selected these lines from "Notre Dame" by Alison T. Gray:

> Today Grandmama is as wide as Paris/and engulfs the city like smoke./She is looking for you, sister./
> You think for a moment it's raining.//but it's a trick of the dead: how/in certain light smoke can seem
> water. . . .

The magazine is 150 pgs., 6¾×9¾, flat-spined, handsomely printed on heavy matte stock with matte card cover. Single copies: $5 for individuals; subscription: $10 for individuals, $12.50 for institutions.

How to Submit: Submit up to 5 poems at a time. Send cover letter, including bio to use in the event of acceptance. No simultaneous submissions. Enclose SASE specifying whether work is to be returned or discarded. No submissions via fax. Publishes theme issues. Send SASE for details. Sometimes sends prepublication galleys. Pays 2 copies. Open to unsolicited reviews. Send books for review consideration; include cover letter.

Also Offers: The Louisiana Literature Prize for Poetry offers a $400 award. Send SASE for guidelines.

Advice: The editor says, "It's important to us that the poets we publish be in control of their creations. Too much of what we see seems arbitrary."

N ○ ◎ THE LOUISIANA REVIEW (Specialized: regional), Division of Liberal Arts, Louisiana State University at Eunice, P.O. Box 1129, Eunice LA 70535, e-mail mgage@lsue.edu, founded 1999, editors Dr. Maura Gage and Ms. Barbara Deger.

Magazine Needs: *The Louisiana Review* appears annually. "We wish to offer Louisiana residents a place to showcase their most beautiful, poignant pieces. Others may submit Louisiana-related poems. We want to publish the highest-quality poetry we can get. We like imagery, metaphor and craft, but we do not wish to have sing-song rhymes, abstract, religious or overly sentimental work." They have published poetry by Sandra Meek, David Middleton and Stella Nesanovich. As a sample the editor selected these lines from "Crabcakes" by Catharine Savage Brosman:

> It all brings back/one summer evening on a Texas beach./We swam, dried off, and found a seafood
> shack,/ate raw oysters, crabs, and something fried,/and washed them down with beer, then drove away,/
> our other hunger still unsatisfied.

The editor says *TLR* is 44-64 pgs. "depending on number of excellent poems received," magazine-sized, professionally printed and saddle-stapled with glossy cover, includes 15 photographs/artwork. They receive about 200-500 poems a year, accept 30-40 poems. Press run is 300-600.

How to Submit: Submit 5 poems at a time. Previously published poems OK. E-mail and disk (Word) submissions OK. Cover letter preferred. "Send typed poems with SASE, include name and address on each poem. If including a cover letter, please tell us your association with Louisiana: live there, frequent visitor, used to live there." Reads submissions January 1 through March 31 only. Time between acceptance and publication is up to 8 months. Poems are circulated to an editorial board. "Our board 'votes' yes or no, may request revision of a 'close' submission; it is done democratically." Seldom comments on rejections. Reports in 4-5 months. Sometimes sends prepublication galleys. Pays 1-2 copies. "Poets retain the rights to their works."

Advice: The editors say, "Be true to yourself as a writer. Hard work will reap its own rewards."

⊘ LOUISIANA STATE UNIVERSITY PRESS, P.O. Box 25053, Baton Rouge LA 70894-5053, phone (504)388-6294, fax (504)388-6461, founded 1935, poetry editor L.E. Phillabaum, is a highly respected publisher of collections by poets such as Lisel Mueller, Margaret Gibson, Fred Chappell, Marilyn Nelson and Henry Taylor. Currently not accepting poetry submissions; "fully committed through 2001."

✔ ◑ ◎ THE LOUISVILLE REVIEW (Specialized: children/teen), Dept. PM, Dept. of Humanities, Spalding University, 851 S. Fourth St., Louisville KY 40203, phone (502)585-9911 ext. 231, founded 1976, editors Sena Jeter Naslund and David Garrison.

Magazine Needs: *The Louisville Review* appears twice a year. They use any kind of poetry except translations, and they have a section of children's poetry (grades K-12). They have published poetry by Richard Jackson, David Ray, Jeffrey Skinner, Maura Stanton, Richard Cecil, Roger Weingarten and Greg Pape. *TLR* is 100 pgs., flat-spined, 6×9. They receive about 700 submissions a year, accept approximately 10%. Sample: $6.

How to Submit: "We look for the striking metaphor, unusual imagery and fresh language. Submissions are read by three readers; time to publication is two to three months. Poetry by children must include permission of parent to publish if accepted." Pays 1 copy.

✔ ◑ THE LOWELL REVIEW, 3075 Harness Dr., Florissant MO 63033-3711, e-mail rita@etext.org, website http://www.etext.org/Zines/Lowell_Review, founded 1994, managing editor Rita Chapman.

Magazine Needs: *The Lowell Review*, published annually in August, features "poetry, fiction, essays with special emphasis on issues surrounding post-industrial life." They want "anything—even genre work—if it is well done." They do not want "greeting card poetry, angst-ridden nihilism, gratuitous vulgarity." They have published poetry by Lola Haskins, Jim Daniels, William Greenway and Nancy Means Wright. As a sample the editor selected these lines from "Husking" by James Magorian:

> Stumbling over stories,/the dry stalks a stairway winding/away from words,/how the ear was grabbed,
> hooked,/shucked in one flowing motion,/and tossed, rows of garden teeth bared

The Lowell Review is 135 pgs., 5½×8, perfect-bound with b&w glossy cover, cover art and ads. They receive about 200 poems a year, accept approximately 10%. Press run is 500 for 15 subscribers of which 4 are libraries, 100 shelf sales; 100 distributed free as back issues to other presses, etc. Single copy: $7; subscription: $7. Sample: $5. Make checks payable to IK Press.

How to Submit: Submit up to 3 poems at a time. No previously published poems; simultaneous submissions OK. Cover letter preferred. E-mail submissions accepted in ASCII text. Reads submissions January through May only. "Please submit only once per reading period unless otherwise invited." Time between acceptance and publication is 6 months. "We reject what we don't like, forward 'maybes' to the other. Decisions are made from combined 'maybe' piles with both having input, but Ms. Dickeman-Nelson has final say." Seldom comments on rejections. Send SASE for guidelines. Reports in 2-24 weeks. Sometimes sends prepublication galleys. Pays 1 copy. Acquires first North American serial rights.

Also Offers: Website includes submission guidelines and general information, current themes, selections from each issue, plus links to other work by the writers where applicable.

Advice: The editor says, "I do not believe there is anything better than the slush pile to gauge what is going on in poetry today. Every year, without fail, we see themes emerge from the random chaos in the mailbox that mirror those of society in general. These themes do not often survive editors to manifest themselves in the small press at large."

⊘ **LOW-TECH PRESS**, 30-73 47th St., Long Island City NY 11103, founded 1981, editor Ron Kolm. "We only publish solicited mss."

◯ **LUCID MOON**, 67 Norma Rd., Hampton NJ 08827, founded 1997, e-mail lucidmoon@worldnet.att.net, editor Ralph Haselmann Jr.
- "Ralph Haselmann Jr. was named Editor of the Year by *Cedar Hill Review* and called the hardest working editor in the small press."

Magazine Needs: *Lucid Moon*, published monthly, aims "to publish lively, moving, humorous poems and to keep the magazine in the public eye." Also includes essays, articles and chapbook reviews. They want "post Beat, independent, modern poetry—no restrictions." They have published poetry by Antler, Lyn Lifshin, Gerald Locklin, Catfish McDaris, Tony Moffeit and Charles Plymell. As a sample the editor selected these lines from his poem "Lucid Moon":
> *Traveling across America in all its terrible beauty, hitchhiking through history/the miles of highways*
> *and open roads a typewriter ribbon of future stories we could tell . . .*

Lucid Moon is 160 pgs., 8½×11, photocopied, side-stapled with some hand-written poems, cartoons and line drawings. They receive about 5,000 poems a year, accept approximately 50%. Press run is 100 for 85 subscribers. Single copy: $10. Make checks payable to Ralph Haselman Jr.

How to Submit: "Contributors are encouraged to buy a subscription." Submit up to 6 poems at a time, must be "photocopy ready." Previously published poems and simultaneous submissions OK. Cover letter with 3- to 6-sentence bio and SASE required. Time between acceptance and publication is 5-6 months. "I choose poems that are honest and moving in some way. Humor is good." Reports same day. Rights revert to author upon publication. Poets may send poetry chapbooks, audio tape cassettes and broadsides for possible review.

Advice: The editor advises, "Read other poets and back issues of *Lucid Moon* to get a feel for the style wanted. Send poems you are proud of."

⊘ **THE LUCID STONE**, P.O. Box 940, Scottsdale AZ 85252-0940, founded 1994, managing editor Pauline Mounsey.

Magazine Needs: *The Lucid Stone* is a quarterly publishing "quality poetry and a small amount of quality artwork. We focus on poetry with complimentary artwork." They want "unpublished quality poetry of any style and length. We are interested in poetry in the full poetic range, including formal, traditional and experimental poems." Nothing trite or didactic. They have published poetry by Lucille Lang Day, Rupert M. Loydell, RD Savage and Janet St. John. As a sample the editor selected these lines from "Stress Won't Wait for a License" by Will Inman:
> *some waves do not take to being dived into head-on/undertow switches and snags like a giant squid/*
> *fury sometimes sees better blind/old friends and safe kitchens won't be taken for granted/plumbers*
> *will cage the tide at a certain cost*

LS is 56-72 pgs., 7×8½, offset printed and saddle-stitched with 80 lb. Tahoe dull cover with one halftone of artwork, 5-7 b&w pieces of artwork and photography, no ads. They receive about 5,000 poems a year, accept less than 200. Press run is 250-300 for 125 subscribers. Subscription: $16/4 issues. Sample: $6.

How to Submit: Submit 3-5 poems at a time. No previously published poems or simultaneous submissions. Cover letter preferred including "short personal biographical sketch other than the usual vita. No manuscripts or art will be returned nor queries answered unless accompanied by an SASE with adequate postage." Time between acceptance and publication is 1-6 months. Poems are circulated to an editorial board. "We have a staff of readers who individually review a group of approximately 50 poems at a time." Seldom comments on rejections. Send SASE for guidelines. Reports in 1-4 months. Pays 1 copy. Acquires first rights.

Advice: The editor says, "We look for fresh language and use of images."

MARKETS THAT WERE listed in the 1999 edition of *Poet's Market* but do not appear this year are listed in the General Index with a notation explaining why they were omitted.

✓ $☑ **LUCIDITY; BEAR HOUSE PUBLISHING**, 398 Mundell Rd., Eureka Springs AR 72631-9505, phone (501)253-9351, e-mail tbadger@ipa.net, website http://www.ipa.net/~tbadger, founded 1985, editor Ted O. Badger.

Magazine Needs: *Lucidity* is a quarterly of poetry. Submission fee required—$1/poem for "juried" selection by a panel of judges or $2/poem to compete for cash awards of $15, $10 and $5. Other winners paid in both cash and in copies. They also publish 10 pgs. of Succint Verse—poems of 12 lines or less—in most issues. "We expect them to be pithy and significant and there is no reading/entry fee if sent along with Cash Award or Juried poems. Just think of all poetic forms that are 12 lines or less: the cinquain, limerick, etheree, haiku, senryu, lune, etc., not to mention quatrain, triolet and couplets." In addition, the editor invites a few guest contributors to submit to each issue. Contributors are encouraged to subscribe or buy a copy of the magazine. The magazine is called *Lucidity* because, the editor says, "I have felt that too many publications of verse lean to obscurity." They are "open as to form, 36-line limit due to format. No restriction on subject matter except that something definitive be given to the reader. We look for poetry that is life-related and has clarity and substance." Purpose: "We dedicate our journal to publishing those poets who express their thoughts, feelings and impressions about the human scene with clarity and substance. We are open to poetry dealing with the good, bad and ugly . . . if done with finesse and style." He does not want "religious, nature or vulgar poems." Published poets include Kathleen Moore Joiner, Helen Lehmann, Joye S. Giroux, Kathleen Spivack and Patricia G. Rourke. As a sample of the type of verse sought, the editor offers these lines by Sharon W. Flynn:

> *Deep in my heart/I knew the reason love died:/it was Father Time/and unrelenting pride.*

The magazine is 76 pgs., digest-sized, photocopied from typescript and saddle-stapled with matte card cover. They publish about 54 poems in each issue. Press run is 350 for 220 subscribers. Subscription: $11. Sample (including guidelines): $2.75.

How to Submit: Submit 3-5 poems at a time. Simultaneous submissions OK. No e-mail submissions. Time between acceptance and publication is 4 months. Send SASE for guidelines or request via e-mail. Reports in 3-4 months. Pays 1 copy plus "cash." Buys one-time rights.

Book/Chapbook Needs & How to Submit: Bear House Press is a self-publishing arrangement by which poets can pay to have booklets published in the same format as *Lucidity,* prices beginning at 100 copies of 32 pgs. for $256. Publishes 10 chapbooks/year.

Also Offers: Sponsors the Lucidity Poets' Ozark Retreat, a 3-day retreat held during the month of April. (See listing in Conferences and Workshops section.)

Advice: The editor says, "Small press journals offer the best opportunity to most poets for publication."

Ⓝ $☑ **LUMMOX PRESS; LUMMOX JOURNAL; DUFUS!**, P.O. Box 5301, San Pedro CA 90733-5301, e-mail lumoxraindog@earthlink.net, website http://home.earthlink.net/~lumoxraindog, founded 1994 (press), 1996 (journal), editor/publisher Raindog.

Magazine Needs: *Lummox Journal* appears monthly and "explores the creative process through interviews, articles and commentary." The editor wants "genuine and authentic poetry that makes me think 'uh huh!'—socially conscious, heartfelt, honest, insightful, experimental. No angst-ridden confessional poetry; no pretentious, pompous, racist and/or sexist work." They have published poetry by Gerald Lockling, Fred Voss, S.A. Griffin and Joan Jobe Smith. As a sample the editor selected these lines from "Indian Summer" by Lyn Lifshin:

> *after the too early/October snow bending/trees to splitting/after I wrapped/in blackness/alone, no lights*

The editor says *LJ* is 16 pgs., digest-sized, photocopied and saddle-stitched with 24 lb. paper cover, includes art and ads. They receive about 100 poems a year, accept approximately 5-10%. Press run is 150 for 75 subscribers, 25 shelf sales; 25 distributed free to reviews/trades. Subscription: $20/12 issues. Sample: $2. Make checks payable to *Lummox Journal.*

How to Submit: Submit 3-5 poems at a time. Previously published poems and simultaneous submissions OK. Cover letter with bio preferred. E-mail and disk (PC compatible) submissions OK. Reads submissions January through July for the Lummox Press/Dufus!; year round for the journal. Reading fees: $5/submission. Time between acceptance and publication is 3-6 months. Seldom comments on rejections. Criticism fees: $10 to critique, $25 to advise, $50 to tutor. Publishes theme issues. Send SASE for guidelines or obtain via e-mail. Reports in 2 weeks. Always sends prepublication galleys. Pays 1 copy. Acquires first or one-time rights. Reviews books and chapbooks of poetry and other magazines in 50-100 words, single or multi-book format. Open to unsolicited reviews. Poets may also send books for review consideration.

Book/Chapbook Needs & How to Submit: Lummox Press publishes avant-garde and concrete poetry under the imprint Dufus! "We are creating limited edition, hand crafted artifacts that are testiments to the book as an art form." They publish 1-2 paperbacks and 2-3 chapbooks/year. Books are usually 24-72 pgs., digest-sized, photocopied/offset printed, saddle-stitched/perfect-bound. Query first with a few sample poems and cover letter with brief bio and publication credits. Reading fee: $5/submission. Replies to queries in 1 month; to mss in 2-3 weeks. Pays royalties of 40-60% plus 20 author's copies (out of a press run of 200). Offers subsidy arrangements for the cost of printing and distribution plus ISBN #, $1.50 to $2 per book (e.g., 100 copies = $150 to $200). Send check for $10 to Lummox for sample package or $2 for *Lummox Journal.*

Ⓞ **LUNA BISONTE PRODS; LOST AND FOUND TIMES (Specialized: style)**, 137 Leland Ave., Columbus OH 43214-7505, founded 1967, poetry editor John M. Bennett.

Magazine Needs: May be the zaniest phenomenon in central Ohio. John M. Bennett is a publisher (and practitioner) of experimental and avant-garde writing, sometimes sexually explicit, and art in a bewildering array of formats including the magazine, *Lost and Found Times*, postcard series, posters, chapbooks, pamphlets, labels and audiocassette tapes. You can get a sampling of Luna Bisonte Prods for $10. Numerous reviewers have commented on the bizarre *Lost and Found Times*, "reminiscent of several West Coast dada magazines"; "This exciting magazine is recommended only for the most daring souls"; "truly demented"; "Insults . . . the past 3,000 years of literature"; "revolution where it counts, in the dangerous depths of the imagination," etc. Bennett wants to see "unusual poetry, naive poetry, surrealism, experimental, visual poetry, collaborations—no poetry workshop or academic pabulum." He has published poetry by J. Berry, J. Leftwich, S.S. Nash, Peter Garick, S.E. Murphy and B. Heman. As a sample the editor selected these lines from a poem by Al Ackerman:

> *Besides so involved with them lice cakes you saw the bug's/leg retract saw ink like cream inside your socks saw a "dirty face"/in pelts of sky*

The digest-sized, 52-page magazine, photoreduced typescript and wild graphics, matte card cover with graphics, has a circulation of 350 with 75 subscribers of which 30 are libraries. Subscription: $25 for 5 numbers. Sample: $6.

How to Submit: Submit anytime—preferably camera-ready (but this is not required). Reports in 1-2 days. Pays copies. All rights revert to authors upon publication. Staff reviews books of poetry. Send books for review consideration.

Book/Chapbook Needs & How to Submit: Luna Bisonte also will consider book submissions: query with samples and cover letter (but "keep it brief"). Chapbook publishing usually depends on grants or other subsidies and is usually by solicitation. He will also consider subsidy arrangements on negotiable terms.

Advice: The editor says, "I would like to see more experimental and avant-garde material in Spanish and Portuguese, or in mixtures of languages."

N O **LUNA NEGRA**, Box 26, % Office of Campus Life/Student Activities or English Dept., Kent State University, Kent OH 44242, phone (330)672-2676, website http://www.studentmedia/lunanegra.kent.edu, editor K.M. Biller.

Magazine Needs: *Luna Negra* is a student-run, biannual literary and art magazine of the KSU main campus, open to all forms of poetry and prose. The editor says it is 36-42 pgs., 7½×7½, with art and photography throughout. They receive 400-450 poems a year, accept 40 or 50. Press run is 2,000, most distributed to KSU students. Sample: $3.

How to Submit: Submit up to 3 poems at a time with $5 reading fee. Line length for poetry is 100 maximum. Also accepts prose up to 1,000 words. Simultaneous submissions OK. Reads submissions September 1 through March 30 only. Reports in 3 months. "All rights revert to author immediately after publication."

O **LUNGFULL! MAGAZINE**, 126 E. Fourth St., #2, New York NY 10003, e-mail lungfull@interport.net, founded 1994, website http://www.interport.net/~lungfull, editor/publisher Brendan Lorber.

• *LUNGFULL!* was the recipient of a multi-year grant from the New York State Council for the Arts.

Magazine Needs: *LUNGFULL!*, published biannually, prints "the rough draft of each poem, in addition to the final so that the reader can see the creative process from start to finish." They want "any style as long as its urgent, immediate, playful, probing, showing great thought while remaining vivid and grounded. Poems should be as interesting as conversation." They do not want "empty poetic abstractions." They have published poetry by Alice Notley, Allen Ginsberg, Lorenzo Thomas, Tracie Morris, Hal Sirowitz, Sparrow, Bob Holman and Richard Kostelanetz. As a sample the editor selected this poem, "Jung and Restless: A Waitress Dreaming on Ernest Borgnines Birthday," by Julie Reid:

> *Your hair is combed differently than you ever wore it and a man in gray and/green with his hands up inside the working of a clock flirts lightly with the woman/beside him who's applying pink lotion from a travel size bottle to her hands./The woman ahead of you lifts her hair off her neck so you can read her tattoo . . ./She says 'To the maximum 36 . . . emotions, add umbrellas, bent and broken . . ./Add anticipation and dread, which . . . are both forms of dread . . .*

LUNGFULL! is 140 pgs., 8½×7, offset printed, perfect-bound, desktop-published, glossy 2 color cover with lots of illustrations and photos and a few small press ads. They receive about 500 poems a year, accept approximately 10%. Press run is 800 for 50 subscribers, 650 shelf sales; 100 distributed free to contributors. Single copy: $5.95; subscription: $23.80/4 issues, $11.90/2 issues. Sample: $7.50. Make checks payable to Brendan Lorber.

How to Submit: "We recommend you get a copy before submitting." Submit up to 6 poems at a time. Previously published poems and simultaneous submissions (with notification) OK. "However, other material will be considered first and stands a much greater chance of publication." Cover letter preferred. E-mail submissions OK. "We prefer hard copy by USPS—but e-submissions can be made in the body of the e-mail itself or in a file saved as text." Time between acceptance and publication is 1-6 months. "The editor looks at each piece for its own merit and for how well it'll fit into the specific issue being planned based on other accepted work." Obtain guidelines via e-mail. Reports in 1-4 months. Pays 2 copies.

Also Offers: "Each copy of *LUNGFULL! Magazine* now contains two short poems, usually from a series of six, printed on stickers—they can be removed from the magazine and placed on any flat surface to make it a little less flat. Innovatively designed and printed in black & white, previous stickers have had work by Sparrow

insider report

Capturing a generation in poetry

A new generation of poets is taking shape. Born between the early 1960s and early 1980s, these poets are members of the post-Baby Boom "cohort" (to use the demographer's term) called Generation X. Media attention to Generation X over the past five years has resulted in a familiar, even stereotypical portrait, but it is still useful to list some of its main aspects.

Denise Duhamel

It is a group that came of age in a time of pessimism, including the shadows of Vietnam, Watergate, and the Iranian hostage crisis. It is a group for whom popular culture is nearly synonymous with high culture. It is a group more accustomed than older generations to dramatic and rapid changes—economic, political, personal—which partly explains why the ephemerality of popular culture is so influential on them.

Denise Duhamel has emerged as a poet whose work captures many of the concerns of Generation X. She has emerged quickly, publishing five full-length collections since 1993, all with small and university presses. Duhamel makes witty, ironic, sometimes funny and sometimes wrenching poems out of her generation's experience. She examines sexuality, gender relations, popular culture, familial issues and broader historical issues in a vigorous, breezy free-verse line. One of her collections, *Kinky* (Orchises Press, 1997), explores all these subjects through the lens of one of popular culture's most familiar figures—Barbie. Another collection, *The Star-Spangled Banner* (SIU Press, 1999), takes a look at such American institutions as the movie *Grease*, the '70s self-help book *When I Say No I Feel Guilty*, and television shows such as *The Patty Duke Show*, *Oprah* and *Roseanne*.

Duhamel's interest in popular culture dates back a long way. "I've always been obsessed with popular culture," she says. "Like Rosie O'Donnell, I can recite TV commercials and theme songs from the '70s with almost total recall. As a kid, I'm sure my obsession with *The Brady Bunch* had to do with escapism from a not-always-happy home life."

DENISE DUHAMEL

Poet
Recent Title: The Star-Spangled
  Banner (SIU Press)

Given this obsession, it's not surprising that popular culture has found its way into Duhamel's work. "I see pop culture as a natural metaphor for everyday life and a lot of the 'isms.' For example, when

I wrote the poems in *Kinky*, it seemed to me Barbie was a perfect vehicle for the frustration surrounding feminist expression—Barbie always smiles, even when she's being gnawed on; she literally can't stand on her own two feet. I'm lucky to be writing at a time when pop culture is seen as an acceptable subject for poetry."

As Duhamel notes, her interest in popular culture also coincides with a strong interest in feminism. "I became a feminist in sixth grade when our teacher brought in her 45 [r.p.m. record] of Helen Reddy's 'I Am Woman' and taught us (boys and girls alike) all the words. 'I'm still an embryo, with a long long way to go,' as Helen says/sings. I totally identified with that song because (of all things) I'd wanted to become an altar boy that year (I was a strong Catholic back then) and I couldn't because I was a girl.

"The first contemporary poetry book I read was Kathleen Spivack's *The Jane Poems*. Her work really opened me up subject matter-wise, as she enlarged what it was OK to write about. So, Helen Reddy and Kathleen Spivack, I guess, gave me the courage to just go for it, even though writing about women's issues can make you feel very vulnerable. I never think about being a feminist or anything like that when I write. It's just that feminist teachings are a big part of my belief system and voice and that's bound to come out in my work."

Duhamel's interest in feminism and popular culture are exemplified in the title poem of her third collection, *Girl Soldier* (Garden Street Press, 1996):

> The girl soldier wears lipstick,
> wisps of hair falling from her bun,
> her eyelashes as long and dark as spider legs.
> She undoes her top buttons, not really enough
> to show cleavage, but her army insists
> on a sprig of collarbone
> as a reminder that she is dainty.
> She holds her gun like a hair dryer
> or a kitchen appliance she loves
> but, until recently, had taken for granted.
> The ocean waves crash behind her—
> the enemy boats glistening in the sun
> along with her hat-pin and the metal crowns
> on the lapels of her jacket.
> She is proud to be part of the Defense Force
> is the lie the picture is telling,
> as blatant as the old lie that all women love to iron
> or live in the suburbs
> as long as they have the right products.
> How big these falsehoods are, how many seas they span.
> If they have to be girl soldiers at all,
> shouldn't they fight for girl things?

To get them out of girl ghettos,
to shed them of their pink collar jobs
and the hoods that hide their faces
in so many places in the world?
To get a girl's perspective on religions?
To overthrow offices and put girls
in charge of governments?
But girls have been brainwashed they're safest
using their oppression as protection.
With their heels and hose
like big heavy shells on their backs,
they rely on jokes about girls not getting hit,
about girls who wear glasses.
They're told alone they'd be naked and squashy,
just ready for soup. But when they're reminded
this is not true, girls feel a deep strength
that has something to do with the earth.
Vaginas from all countries make peace—
the root of the word literally meaning sheath,
a resting place for men and their swords.

Although Duhamel's work is frequently humorous, in this poem her irony becomes darker. Based on a photograph titled "Girl Soldier of the Israel Defense Force," the poem suggests that women remain confined to the margins of power, as the still prevalent idea of woman as "girl" indicates. What would a military of women, in real power, look like? Certainly not the "girl soldier" of the book's title.

Born in 1961, Duhamel actually straddles the generation gap between Baby Boomers and Generation Xers, because there's some disagreement about the exact point when Generation X begins. She notices the conflict in her work, but feels closer to Generation X. "Because I was born in 1961, I am sort of the Grandma of Generation Xers. It's sort of like being born on the cusp between astrology signs. I have poems in the anthology *Boomer Girls: American Women Poets Come of Age* as well as *Hyper Age Magazine*, a magazine specifically for Generation X writers. I think, in very general terms, I identify more with the work of Xers because they are more playful, less serious in tone. Though I love and teach *No More Masks* (An Anthology of 20th-Century American Women's Poetry, HarperCollins, 1993), I wish it had a few more belly laughs in it. But I also can see very clearly how the Boomers paved the way for Generation Xers in terms of subject matter."

Duhamel makes her living chiefly from writing, reading her work at universities and part-time teaching. "I have taught fulltime in the past, but now I adjunct mostly. I supplement my income with lots of readings. I probably do about ten or more paid readings a year, as well as many more unpaid ones. It's sort of like being a freelance 'reader.' Unlike many poets, I really enjoy giving readings. I'm a frustrated actress, a ham (my sister says I put the 'ham' in Duhamel.)"

Such a life gives Duhamel ample time to write, and her prolific publication—five books in six years—is the result. She says writing every day is as difficult a job as any other, however. "Because I grew up in a working class family, I take that working class sensibility to my writing. I get up and write whether I feel like it or not, whether I produce anything good that day or not. I feel like writing is my job, as well as my love," Duhamel says. "I do have dry spells in that what I write is not any good or doesn't get sent out, but I don't have dry spells in which the page stays blank. I write right through my dry spells."
—*Kevin Walzer*

and Mike Topp. Upcoming stickers will include poems by Julie Reid, Donna Cartelli, Joe Maynard and Jeremy Sharpe, among others."

Advice: The editor advises, "Don't just read books, mark them up, write between the lines, make your own cover, transcribe the pages you love and burn the originals, get paper cuts kissing it, massage its spine, use only the words from the book you're reading in your speech, or none of them."

THE LUTHERAN DIGEST (Specialized: religious, inspirational), P.O. Box 4250, Hopkins MN 55343, phone (612)933-2820, fax (612)933-5708, founded 1953, editor David Tank.

Magazine Needs: *The Lutheran Digest* appears quarterly "to entertain and encourage believers and to subtly persuade non-believers to embrace the Christian faith. We publish short poems (24 lines or less) that will fit in a single column of the magazine. Most are inspirational, but that doesn't necessarily mean religious. No avant-garde poetry or work longer than 25 lines." They have published poetry by Kathleen A. Cain, William Beyer, Margaret Peterson, Florence Berg and Erma Boetkher. As a sample we selected these lines from "Easter Has Arrived" by Kathleen A. Cain:

> Sun rays streak across the rugged/mountains in the east,/Sweet warblings of the finch, wren and/
> cardinal break through the morning peace./All of God's creation arrayed in its/spring beauty begins
> to unfold,/The desert is a bright splash of purple verbena and/daisies of orange and gold.

TLD is 72 pgs., digest-sized, offset printed and saddle-stitched with 4-color paper cover, includes b&w photos and illustrations, local ads to cover cost of distribution. They receive about 200 poems a year, accept approximately 20%. Press run is 140,000; 139,000 distributed free to Lutheran churches. Subscription: $22/2 years. Sample: $3.

How to Submit: Submit 3 poems at a time. Line length for poetry is 30 maximum. Previously published poems and simultaneous submissions OK. Cover letter preferred. "Include SASE if return is desired." Time between acceptance and publication is 3-9 months. Poems are circulated to an editorial board. "Selected by editor and reviewed by publication panel." Send SASE for guidelines. Reports in 3 months. Pays credit and 1 copy. Acquires one-time rights.

Advice: The editor says, "Poems should be short and appeal to senior citizens. We also look for poems that can be sung to traditional Lutheran hymns."

LUZ EN ARTE Y LITERATURA; CARPETAS DE POESÍA LUZ; CARPETAS DE POESÍA LUZ BILINGÜE; LUZ BILINGUAL PUBLISHING, INC. (Specialized: translations, bilingual/spanish), P.O. Box 571062, Tarzana CA 91357-1062, phone (818)907-1454, founded 1991, director Veronica Miranda.

Magazine Needs: *Luz en Arte y Literatura*, published annually is an "international bilingual magazine with the purpose to promote art and literature throughout U.S.A. and foreign countries." They want "Latin American literature, poetry translation from Spanish to English and English to Spanish." They have published poetry by Luis Benitez, Alima Galliano, Martha Cerda and Eduardo Liendo. As a sample the editor selected these lines from "El silencia del viento" by Juan Miguel Asensi:

> El escritorio/la mosca en el tintero/zapatos negros//and translated by Kirk Anderson:/*The writing*
> *table/the fly in the inkpot/little black shoes*

Luz en Arte y Literatura is 100-200 pgs., 8½×6½, professionally printed, perfect-bound, CS1 cover stock with art, photos and ads. They receive about 1,000 poems a year, accept approximately 10%. Press run is 1,000 for 500 subscribers of which 300 are libraries, 200 shelf sales; 300 distributed free to reviewers, collaborators, cultural institutions. Single copy: $19; subscription: $25. Sample: $8. Make checks payable to Luz Bilingual Publishing, Inc.

How to Submit: Submit up to 10 poems at a time. Previously published poems and simultaneous submissions OK. Cover letter required with curriculum vitae. Time between acceptance and publication is 6-12 months. Poems are circulated to an editorial board. "There is a preselection a year before publication and a final selection upon publication." Publishes theme issues. Send SASE for guidelines and upcoming themes. Reports in 6-12 months. Pays 1 copy. Staff reviews books or chapbooks of poetry or other magazines in 1-3 pages. Send books for review consideration.

Book/Chapbook Needs & How to Submit: Luz Bilingual Publishing, Inc., publishes poetry translations: Spanish/English, English/Spanish and Spanish poetry in the form of poetry folders as the result of 2 annual poetry contests, Carpetas de Poesía Luz and Carpetas de Poesía Luz Bilingüe. Send SASE for entry form and guidelines. Entry fee: $10. Deadline for entry, February 15. Winners will be announced in *Luz en Arte y Literatura*, the works will be published in the spring and distributed with the magazine and made available to the public. The translator and/or author will receive a free magazine subscription. Poetry folders are 20-40 pgs., 9×7½, professionally printed. Replies to queries and mss in 3-6 months. Pays author's copies. For sample books or chapbooks, write to the above address.

■ ◎ **LYNX, A JOURNAL FOR LINKING POETS; AHA BOOKS; INTERNATIONAL TANKA SPLENDOR AWARD (Specialized: form)**, P.O. Box 1250, Gualala CA 95445, e-mail ahabooks@mcn.org, website http://www.faximum.com/aha!poetry, founded as *APA-Renga* in 1986, later the name was changed to *Lynx* "to link an endangered species of poetry with an endangered animal and to inspire the traditional wit of renga," says Jane Reichhold, who co-edits the publication with Werner Reichhold.

Magazine Needs: *Lynx*, published 3 times/year (February, June and October) "is based on the ancient craft of renga, linked verse with origins in Zen and Japanese culture, and now publishes both renga and tanka. A renga is a non-narrative series of linked images as a group effort. Tanka is the most popular poetry form in Japan and the oldest continued form." As a sample the editor selected this poem by Sanford Goldstein:

> heaven and earth,/I do remember/the long long delicate/contradictions/of done, not done

Lynx is 90 pgs., 4½×11, neatly printed and comb-bound with card cover. It also publishes essays, book reviews, articles, interviews, experimental linked forms, linked prose, art, commentaries and "whatever encourages poets to link ideas." They currently have 300 subscribers. Subscription: $20 US and Canada, $25 overseas surface mail, $33 overseas air mail. Sample (including guidelines): $6. Make checks payable to AHA Books.

How to Submit: Submit 1 renga and/or 6-10 tanka at a time. *Lynx* encourages submissions by those experienced and experimenting with collaborative forms. Subscribers participate in ongoing renga, start trends and otherwise determine the content. All submissions should include a brief bio with the title of the work. E-mail submissions are welcome. E-mail information requests are welcome, however, poets need to include an address as info is sent via regular mail. "I send a packet of info too large to attach to e-mail." Most information is available on the website. "Please send us copies that do not need to be returned." Include SASE for reply. Editor responds to all who submit. Reports in 1 week.

Book/Chapbook Needs & How to Submit: AHA Books publishes online books. Access through the above website (click on "read online books") or at http://www.faximum.com/aha.d/onlinebk.htm.

Also Offers: The press also sponsors the International Tanka Splendor Award. Winning entries will be published in *Tanka Splendor*. Deadline: September 30. Send SASE for details.

☑ $☐ ◿ **LYNX EYE; SCRIBBLEFEST LITERARY GROUP**, 1880 Hill Dr., Los Angeles CA 90041-1244, phone (323)550-8522, fax (323)550-8243, founded 1994, co-editors Pam McCully and Kathryn Morrison.

Magazine Needs: *Lynx Eye* is the quarterly publication of the ScribbleFest Literary Group, an organization dedicated to the development and promotion of the literary arts. *Lynx Eye* is "dedicated to showcasing visionary writers and artists, particularly new voices." Each issue contains a special feature called Presenting, in which an unpublished writer of prose or poetry makes his/her print debut. They have no specifications regarding form, subject matter or style of poetry. They have published poetry by Ed Skoog, Margery Snyder and A.D. Winans. As a sample the editors selected these lines from "Bird Repair" by Leland Stoney:

> The breeze comes gasping through the porous walls./Atop an orange crate dressed for surgery,/an
> anguished sparrow seizes the distraction,/freeing its wing from a makeshift splint—/a popsicle stick
> and someone's brother's shoelace.

Lynx Eye is about 120 pgs., 5½×8½, perfect-bound with b&w artwork. They receive about 2,000 poetry submissions a year and have space for about 75. Press run is 500 for 250 subscribers, 200 shelf sales. Subscription: $25/year. Sample: $7.95. Make checks payable to ScribbleFest Literary Group.

How to Submit: Submissions must be typed and include phone number, address, and an SASE. No previously published poems; simultaneous submissions OK. Name, address and phone number on each piece. Always comments on rejections. Send SASE for guidelines. Reports in 2-3 months. Pays $10/piece and 3 copies. Buys first North American serial rights.

◿ **THE LYRIC**, 307 Dunton Dr. SW, Blacksburg VA 24060-5127, founded 1921 ("the oldest magazine in North America in continuous publication devoted to the publication of traditional poetry"), poetry editor Leslie Mellichamp.

Magazine Needs: *The Lyric* uses about 55 poems each quarterly issue. "We use rhymed verse in traditional forms, for the most part, with an occasional piece of blank or free verse. Forty lines or so is usually our limit. Our themes are varied, ranging from religious ecstasy to humor to raw grief, but we feel no compulsion to shock, embitter or confound our readers. We also avoid poems about contemporary political or social problems—grief but not grievances, as Frost put it. Frost is helpful in other ways: If yours is more than a lover's quarrel with life, we're not your best market. And most of our poems are accessible on first or second reading. Frost again: Don't hide too far away." They have published poetry by Vito Victor, Tom Riley, Michael J. Bugeja, Rhina P. Espaillat, Richard Moore, Barbara Loots, Alfred Dorn, Avis Kunca Kubick, Gail White, Neill Megaw and Maureen Cannon. As a sample the editor selected these lines from "Moth To Your Lamp" by Muriel Marshall:

> *In the calm burning of your love/frets wither and fall from me,/burned clean in the cool flame of/your unflickering tranquility.*

The Lyric is 32 pgs., digest-sized, professionally printed with varied typography, matte card cover. It has a circulation of 700 of which 200 go to libraries. They receive about 5,000 submissions a year, use approximately 220, have an average 6-month backlog. Subscription: $12 US, $14 Canada and other countries (in US funds only). Sample: $3.

How to Submit: Submit up to 5 poems at a time. No previously published poems or translations; simultaneous submissions OK. "Cover letters often helpful, but not required." Send SASE for guidelines. Reports in 2 months (average). Pays 1 copy, and all contributors are eligible for quarterly and annual prizes totaling $750.

Advice: Leslie Mellichamp comments, "Our raison d'être has been the encouragement of form, music, rhyme and accessibility in poetry. As we witness the growing dissatisfaction with the modernist movement that ignores these things, we are proud to have provided an alternative for 75 years that helps keep the roots of poetry alive."

◎ **M.I.P. COMPANY (Specialized: foreign language, erotica)**, P.O. Box 27484, Minneapolis MN 55427, phone (612)546-7578, fax (612)544-6077, e-mail mp@mipco.com, website http://www.mipco.com, founded in 1984, contact Michael Peltsman.

Book/Chapbook Needs & How to Submit: M.I.P. Company publishes 3 paperbacks/year. They only publish Russian erotic poetry and prose written in Russian. They have published poetry collections by Mikhail Armalinsky and Aleksey Shelvakh. No previously published poems; simultaneous submissions OK. Replies to queries in 1 month. Seldom comments on rejections.

✓ ◙ **THE MACGUFFIN; NATIONAL POET HUNT**, Schoolcraft College, 18600 Haggerty Rd., Livonia MI 48152-2696, phone (734)462-4400 ext. 5292, e-mail alindenb@schoolcrft.cc.mi.us, website http://www.schoo lcraft.cc.mi.us, founded 1983, editor Arthur Lindenberg.

Magazine Needs: *"The MacGuffin* is a literary magazine which appears three times each year, in April, June and November. We publish the best poetry, fiction, nonfiction and artwork we find. We have no thematic or stylistic biases. We look for well-crafted poetry. Long poems should not exceed 300 lines. Avoid pornography, trite and sloppy poetry. We do not publish haiku, concrete or light verse." They have published poetry by Patricia Hooper, Jim Daniels and Gary Gildner. *The MacGuffin* is 160 pgs., digest-sized, professionally printed on heavy buff stock, with matte card cover, flat-spined, with b&w illustrations and photos. Press run is 600 for 215 subscribers and the rest are local newsstand sales, contributor copies and distribution to college offices. Single copy: $6; subscription: $15. Sample: $5.50.

How to Submit: "The editorial staff is grateful to consider unsolicited manuscripts and graphics." Submit up to 5 poems at a time of no more than 300 lines; poems should be typewritten. "We discourage simultaneous submissions." Prefers submissions to be sent through the mail. Publishes theme issues. Send SASE for guidelines and upcoming themes or request via fax or e-mail. Reports in 10-12 weeks; publication backlog is 6 months. Pays 2 copies, "occasional money or prizes."

Also Offers: Also sponsors the National Poet Hunt, established in 1996, offering annual awards of $500 1st Prize, $250 2nd Prize, $100 3rd Prize, 3 honorable mentions and publication. Submissions may be entered in other contests. Submit 5 typed poems on any subject in any form. Put name and address on separate 3 × 5 index card only. Send SASE for guidelines. Entry fee: $15/5 poems. Deadline: May 31. Judge for 1998 contest was Gerald Stern. Winners will be announced June 30, and in *Poets and Writers* in the fall. Website includes writer's guidelines, names of editors, current/upcoming contest information.

Advice: The editor says, "We will always comment on 'near misses.' Writing is a search, and it is a journey. Don't become sidetracked. Don't become discouraged. Keep looking. Keep traveling. Keep writing."

◙ **MAD POETS REVIEW; MAD POETS REVIEW POETRY COMPETITION; MAD POETS SO-CIETY**, P.O. Box 1248, Media PA 19063-8248, founded 1987, editor Eileen M. D'Angelo, associate editor Camelia Nocella.

Magazine Needs: *Mad Poets Review* is published annually in September/October. "Our primary purpose is to promote thought-provoking, moving poetry, and encourage beginning poets. We don't care if you have a 'name' or a publishing history, if your poetry is well-crafted." They are "anxious for work with 'joie de vivre' that startles and inspires." No restrictions on subject, form or style. "We are not interested in porn or obscenities used for the sake of shock value." They have published poetry by Lisa DeVuonc, Emiliano Martin, Janet Sadler and Richard Bank. As a sample the editor selected these lines from "Planning the Trip from Connecticut" by Glenn D. Barnes:

> *Even so, I will learn to live/without the deep touch of your eyes/I will learn to leave/the smooth creams and lobsters,/the sudden thunders of geese/on gray fall mornings,/the velvet bee's summer hum.*

MPR is about 70 pgs., digest-sized, attractively printed and perfect-bound with textured card cover. They receive about 400-600 poems a year, use approximately 50-60. Press run is 200. Sample: $9.50. Make checks payable to either Mad Poets Society or *Mad Poets Review*.

How to Submit: Submit 6 poems at a time. "Poems without an SASE with adequate postage will not be returned or acknowledged." Previously published poems and simultaneous submissions OK. Cover letter preferred. "Mark envelope 'contest' or 'magazine.'" Reads submissions January 1 through June 1 only. Time between acceptance and publication is 7-8 months. Often comments on rejections. Reports in 2-3 months. Pays 1 copy. Acquires one-time rights.

Also Offers: Sponsors the annual *Mad Poets Review* Poetry Competition. "All themes and styles of poetry are welcome, no line limit, previously unpublished work only. Send SASE for complete contest guidelines. Winners published in *MPR*. Cash prizes awarded—amount depends on number of entries. "The Mad Poets Society is an active organization in Pennsylvania. We run six poetry series; have monthly meetings for members for critique and club business; coordinate a children's contest through Del. Co. School system; run an annual poetry festival the first Sunday in October; sponsor Mad Poets Bonfires for local poets and musicians; publish an annual literary calendar and newsletters that offer the most comprehensive listing available anywhere in the tri-state area. We send quarterly newsletters to members, as well as PA Poetry Society news covering state and national events." Membership fee: $20.

Advice: The editor says, "It is advised that if someone is going to submit they see what kind of poetry we publish. We sometimes receive poetry that is totally inappropriate of our mag and it is obvious the poet does not know *MPR*."

MAD RIVER PRESS, State Road, Richmond MA 01254, phone (413)698-3184, founded 1986, editor Barry Sternlieb. Mad River publishes 1 broadside and 2 chapbooks/year, "all types of poetry, no bias," but none unsolicited.

THE MADISON REVIEW; PHYLLIS SMART YOUNG PRIZE IN POETRY, Dept. of English, 7123 Helen C. White Hall, University of Wisconsin, 600 N. Park St., Madison WI 53706, phone (608)263-0566, founded 1978, poetry editor Erin Hanusa.

Magazine Needs: *TMR* wants poems that are "smart and tight, that fulfill their own propositions. Spare us: religious or patriotic dogma and light verse." They have published work by Lise Goett, David Citino, Anne Caston, Lisa Steinman and Richard Tillinghast. *The Madison Review* is published in August and February, with 15-20 poems selected from a pool of 750. Sample: $2.50.

How to Submit: Submit up to 6 poems at a time. No simultaneous submissions. Usually reports in 4 months, may be longer in summer. Pays 2 copies.

Also Offers: The Phyllis Smart Young Prize in Poetry is for $500 and publication in *TMR*, for "the best group of three unpublished poems submitted by a single author, any form." Send SASE for rules before submitting for prize or see announcement for guidelines in *AWP* or *Poets & Writers* magazines. Submissions must arrive during September—winner announced December 15. Competition receives about 300 entries a year.

Advice: The editor says, "Contributors: Know your market! Read before, during and after writing. Treat your poems *better* than job applications!"

MAELSTROM, P.O. Box 7, Tranquility NJ 07879, e-mail imaelstrom@aol.com, website http://www.geociti es.com/~readmaelstrom, founded 1997, editor Christine L. Reed, art editor Mike Satterthwaite.

Magazine Needs: *Maelstrom*, a bimonthly, "tries to be a volatile storm of talents throwing together art, poetry, short fiction, comedy and tragedy." They want any kind of poetry, "humor appreciated. No pornography." They have published poetry by Grace Cavalieri, Simon Perchik, Barbara Lefcowitz and Edgar Silex. As a sample the editor selected this poem, "Two Love Tanka" by Karen Garrison:

> Bisexual snails/make easy love with both selves/soak the earth with warm/butter, melt in the sauce
> pan/of salty tongue . . . just like you.

Maelstrom is 40-50 pgs., 7×8½, laser printed or photocopied, saddle-stitched with glossy paper cover, includes b&w art. They receive about 600 poems a year, accept approximately 20%. Press run is 1,500 for 100 subscribers; 200 distributed free to libraries, bookstores, colleges. Single copy: $4; subscription: $20. Sample: $3.

How to Submit: Submit up to 4 poems at a time. Previously published poems and simultaneous submissions OK. Cover letter preferred. Include name and address on every page. Send sufficient SASE for return of work. E-mail submissions OK "in the body of the e-mail message. Please do not send attached files." Time between acceptance and publication is 1-3 months. Seldom comments on rejections. Obtain guidelines via e-mail. Reports in 1 month. Pays 1 copy. Acquires first North American serial or one-time rights. Staff reviews chapbooks of poetry and other magazines in 500 words, single book format. Send books for review consideration. "Materials cannot be returned."

Also Offers: "Our award winning website includes samples of past publications, writer's guidelines, editors bios and samples of some regular features."

THE MAGAZINE, University of Warwick, Continuing Education Dept., Coventry CV4 7AL United Kingdom, phone 44+(1203)523-831, founded 1995, editor Sally Russell.

Magazine Needs: Appearing 2 times a year, *The Magazine* is "published as part of the Creative Writing Program of the Continuing Education Dept., University of Warwick but open to all. Purpose is to provide a high quality forum for student work." They want "well-crafted work. We publish all sorts, eclectic subjects but tasteful. No verse, trite love poems, sloppy thought/execution, weak imagery." They have published poetry by

Peter Easter, Joanna Watson, John Alcock and Tim Armstrong. As a sample the editor selected these lines from "Parable for a Doomed Youth" by Raymond K. Avery:

> The sad-eyed Christ outside the phone box/Asks what it is you want this time/Are you looking for love/
> Or just someone else to hurt you/Then he hands you a shroud/From the pile he keeps by the door

The Magazine is about 50 pgs., offset printed and saddle-stapled with 2-color card cover. Press run is 200 for students, local bookstores and others. Sample: £4. Make checks in pound sterling only to University of Warwick.
How to Submit: Submit 4 poems at a time. No previously published poems; simultaneous submissions OK. Cover letter is "usually helpful if brief. I like a brief bio in the cover letter—2-3 lines—saves trouble getting it later if poems are accepted." Reads submissions January 1 through March 1 and mid-May through end of August. Time between acceptance and publication is 2-3 months. Sometimes comments on rejections, "brief comments." Reports in 2 months. Pays 1 copy. Authors retain rights.
Advice: The editor says, "Don't forget the SASE. Don't send a huge wad of poems. Do send clean readable copy. We have published poets from Ireland, Australia, U.S., Scotland and England. We are open to new writers but we expect high quality and professional submissions."

$ ◎ THE MAGAZINE OF SPECULATIVE POETRY (Specialized: science fiction), P.O. Box 564, Beloit WI 53512, founded 1984, editor Roger Dutcher.
Magazine Needs: *MSP* is an irregularly published magazine that features "the best new speculative poetry. We are especially interested in narrative form, but interested in variety of styles, open to any form, length (within reason). We're looking for the best of the new poetry utilizing the ideas, imagery and approaches developed by speculative fiction and will welcome experimental techniques as well as the fresh employment of traditional forms." They have published poetry by Terry A. Garey, Bruce Boston and Steve Rasnic-Tem. As a sample Roger Dutcher selected these lines from "Braids of Glass" by Michael Bishop:

> We step onto a plain of braided glass,/which rattles on its topographic loom/Like a million shattered
> vials of valium/Spilling everywhere the stench of emptiness.

MSP is 24-28 pgs., digest-sized, offset printed, saddle-stapled with matte card cover. They accept less than 5% of some 500 poems received/year. Press run is 100-200, going to nearly 100 subscribers. Subscription: $11. Sample: $3.50.
How to Submit: Submit 3 poems at a time, double-spaced. No previously published poems or simultaneous submissions. "We like cover letters but they aren't necessary. We like to see where you heard of us; the names of the poems submitted; a statement if the poetry ms is disposable; a big enough SASE; and if you've been published, some recent places." Editor comments on rejections "on occasion." Send SASE for guidelines. Reports in 1-2 months. Pays 3¢/word, minimum $3, maximum $25, plus copy. Buys first North American serial rights. Reviews books of speculative poetry. Query on unsolicited reviews. Send speculative poetry books for review consideration.

🌐 🗌 ◐ MAGMA POETRY MAGAZINE, 43 Keslake Rd., London NW6 6DH United Kingdom, e-mail magma@dcs.qmw.ac.uk, website http://www.dcs.qmw.ac.uk/~timk/Magma, founded 1994, editorial secretary David Boll.
Magazine Needs: *Magma* appears 3 times a year and contains "modern poetry, reviews and interviews with poets." They want poetry that is "modern in idiom and shortish (two pages maximum). Nothing sentimental or old fashioned." They have published poetry by Thom Gunn, Diane di Prima and Selima Hill. Mr. Boll says *Magma* is 168 pgs., 8½×6, photocopied and stapled, includes b&w illustrations. They receive about 200 poems a year, accept approximately 30%. Press run is about 500. Subscription: £8/year. Sample: £3. "Add postage per copy; UK: £0.50; Europe: £0.75; Far East/Pacific Rim: £1.50; rest of world, including USA: £1.30." Make checks payable to Stukeley Press. For subscriptions contact Helen Nicholson, distribution secretary, 82 St. James's Dr., London SW17 7RR.
How to Submit: Submit up to 6 poems at a time. Previously published poems and simultaneous submissions OK. Cover letter preferred. E-mail submissions OK (ASCII only, no attachments). Reads submissions September through November and February through July only. Time between acceptance and publication is maximum 3 months. Poems are circulated to an editorial board. "Each issue has an editor who submits his/her selections to a board for final approval. Editor's selection very rarely changed." Publishes theme issues occasionally. Reports in 4 months. Always sends prepublication galleys. Pays 1 copy.
Also Offers: "We hold a public reading in London three times a year, to coincide with each new issue, and poets in the issue are invited to read." Website includes contact details, information about *Magma* and its policies and method of operating, as well as some examples of sumissions (poetry and prose—i.e., interviews/reviews) for recent issues.

Ⓝ 🌐 🗌 ◐ MAGPIE'S NEST, 176 Stoney Lane, Sparkhill, Birmingham B12 8AN United Kingdom, founded 1979, contact Mr. Bal Saini.
Magazine Needs: The *Magpie's Nest* appears quarterly and publishes "cutting-edge, modern poetry and fiction which deals with the human condition. No love poetry or self-obsessed work." As a sample Mr. Saini selected this poem (poet unidentified):

> There is something adhesive/about the first parent singular/Loose/images stick to her/where she lives
> in the shadow/of the absent father

They receive about 200 poems a year, accept approximately 25%. Press run is 200 for 150 subscribers, 50 shelf sales. Single copy: $2.50; subscription: $12.50. Sample: $3.

How to Submit: Submit 4 poems at a time. Line length for poetry is 10 minimum, 40 maximum. Previously published poems and simultaneous submissions OK. Cover letter preferred. "Keep copies of poems submitted as poems which are not used are binned." Reads submissions September 1 through June 30 only. Time between acceptance and publication is 3 months. Seldom comments on rejections. Publishes theme issues occasionally. Reports in 3 months. Pays 1 copy. Reviews books of poetry and other magazines in 200 words, single book format. Open to unsolicited reviews. Poets may also send books for review consideration.

Also Offers: "For a fee I am willing to act as literary agent for American poets by submitting their poems to British magazines. This will save American poets postage as well as the hassle of finding out which British magazines are suitable for their poems. Please send SASE (or SAE and IRC) for further details."

Advice: Mr. Saini says, "It's recommended that a sample copy be read before submission."

◎ MAIL CALL JOURNAL (Specialized: American Civil War); DISTANT FRONTIER PRESS, P.O. Box 5031, Dept. P1, South Hackensack NJ 07606, phone (201)296-0419, e-mail mcj@historyonline.net, website http://www.historyonline.net, founded 1990, managing editor Anna Pansini.

Magazine Needs: *MCJ* is published 6 times/year with the purpose of "keeping the spirit of the Civil War soldier alive." They want poetry with unique Civil War themes in first or third person. As a sample the editor selected these lines from "Colors" by Jim Boring:

> *"Now," he said/And the boys fell down/Down fell the blue and the gray/Down fell the stars/From the noble stripes/Down from the proud blue bars.*

Mail Call Journal is 8 pgs., 8½ × 11, offset printed on colored paper and corner stapled. They receive about 100 poems a year, accept approximately 10. Subscription: $24.95/year. Sample: $5.

How to Submit: "We prefer contributors order a writer's packet for $5 which includes submission guidelines and a sample copy before submitting, but it is not required." Previously published poems and simultaneous submissions OK. Cover letter optional. "If poet is a descendant of a Civil War soldier or a member of any Civil War organizations, please provide details for publication." Time between acceptance and publication is 6-12 months. Often comments on rejections. Send SASE for guidelines or request via e-mail. Reports in 6-12 months. Pays 2 copies.

Book/Chapbook Needs & How to Submit: Distant Frontier Press publishes book excerpts, narratives, diary entries, poems and editorial think pieces. Send SASE for details.

Also Offers: Sponsors a biannual history poetry competition, established in 1997. Awards 3 prizes of "publication on website plus percentage of proceeds." Submissions may be entered in other contests. Two categories—American Civil War and general history. Indicate whether the poem is fictional or non-fictional. Entry fee: $5/category (3 poems). Deadlines: September 15 (for Fall), March 15 (for Spring).

Advice: The editor says, "Don't make a Civil War movie into a poem. Write with feeling from your heart."

◪◎ MAIN STREET RAG POETRY JOURNAL; INDEPENDENCE BOULEVARD (Specialized: regional), P.O. Box 25331, Charlotte NC 28229-5331, phone (704)535-1918, e-mail mainstrag@mindspring.com, website http://www.MainStreetRag.com, founded 1996, publisher/editor M. Scott Douglass.

Magazine Needs: *Main Street Rag*, published quarterly, aims "to bring poetry back to the main streets and living rooms of America." They want "any style, any subject, with emphasis on grittier material (open raincoats and unnecessary foul language are not grit, they're stupid)." They do not want "poetry containing derogatory language directed toward race, religion, gender or sexual orientation. Pissing off politicians, corporations, religious zealots and lawyers is acceptable and in fact, encouraged." They have published poetry by Robert Cooperman, Adrian C. Louis, Leslie Ann McIlroy, Jo Nelson and A.D. Winans. As a sample the editor selected these lines from "An Hour of Freedom Clear as Light" by Mbembe Milton Smith:

> *the stars that night/were cool, bright deaths,/impossibly themselves,/self-endowed/expostulating/ beyond any empires or equations/our enemies could ever erect, . . .*

The editor says *MSR* is at least 72 pgs., digest-sized, saddle-stapled with 100 lb. stock glossy cover, photos, art and ads. They receive about 3,000 poems a year, accept approximately 300. Press run is 500 for 200 subscribers. Subscription: $15. Sample: $5. "Sampling recommended."

How to Submit: Submit 6 pages of poetry at a time. No previously published poems or simultaneous submissions. No e-mail submissions. Cover letter preferred with a brief bio "about the poet, not their credits." Has backlog of 6-12 months. Send SASE for guidelines. Reports in 3-6 weeks. Pays 1 copy and contributor's discount for the issue in which they appear. Acquires one-time rights.

Magazine Needs & How to Submit: *Independence Boulevard* is "a free monthly regional tabloid—residents of NC, SC, GA, TN, VA are eligible for publication. Full color cover and centerfold featuring local visual artists.

Our goal here is to create a 'coffee-table friendly' publication financed by advertising (not grants) so we can provide our contributors with a larger audience, pay them, and help to remove government from the 'funding of the ARTS' debate." Publishes poetry, short stories, essays, creative nonfiction, arts-related articles, cartoons, graphic images, photography. They have published poetry by Anthony Abbott, Ann Campanella, Don Mager and Diana Pinckney. As a sample the editor selected these lines from "Smithsonian Riff" by R.T. Smith (editor of *Shenandoah*):

> When they banished the buffalo/from the nickel in favor of Jefferson/and the silhouette of Montecello,/ where did the great herds go?/In stampede their cleft hooves could/alter the landscape, their wallows/ were bare as landing sites for aliens.

Press run is 10,000, distributed predominantly in Charlotte/Western NC region. Subscription: $24. Samples (several): $2. "Sampling recommended." No previously published poems or simultaneous submissions. No e-mail submissions. Reports in 3-6 weeks. Pays cash (varies by amount of advertising).

Also Offers: Website includes subscription information, submission guidelines, editorial from current issue, poetry teasers from current and next issue, online advertising section, chapbook vanity publishing services, and *Main Street Rag* merchandising.

Advice: The editor says, "Rejection is an obstacle in the road—nothing personal—just drive around it. Always drive around it."

N ⊕ $ ⊚ MAKING WAVES (Specialized: translations, ethnic/nationality), P.O. Box 226, Guildford, Surrey GU1 4NW United Kingdom, phone/fax +44 1483 835891, e-mail makingwaves@msn.com, founded 1986, editor Anthony Selbourne.

Book/Chapbook Needs: Making Waves publishes 2 paperbacks/year of translation from the Nordic/Arctic regions and minority cultures/natives. Traveling exhibitions of illustrated work accompany the books. They do not want "poetry of a general racist, sexist or extremist nature or immature writing." They have published poetry by Anita Erdrezze, Inghilda Tapio and Jim Barnes. Books are usually 70 pgs., 8½×5¾, offset with 2- to 3-color cover and mixed media illustrations.

How to Submit: Query first with 10 sample poems and cover letter with brief bio, publication credits and proposed illustrations and artists if applicable. Previously published poems OK; no simultaneous submissions. Fax and e-mail submissions OK. Time between acceptance and publication is 6 months. Poems are circulated to an editorial board. Send SASE (or SAE with IRC) for guidelines and upcoming themes. Replies to queries and mss in 2-3 weeks. Pays $500-1,000 honorarium and 20 author's copies (out of a press run of 500.) Obtain samples of books by writing to the above address.

⊙ ⊚ MALAFEMMINA PRESS; LA BELLA FIGURA (Specialized: ethnic), 4211 Fort Hamilton Pkwy., Brooklyn NY 11219-1237, founded 1988, editor Rose Romano.

Magazine Needs: *La Bella Figura* is published quarterly and contains "poetry by Italian-Americans concerning Italian-American history, culture and issues." They want poetry "on the history, culture and concerns of Italian-Americans. No stereotypes." They have published poetry by Jennifer Lagier, Barbara Crooker, Grace Cavalieri and Eileen Spinelli. The editor says *LBF* is 20 pgs., 5½×8½, offset printed and stapled with paper cover. They receive about 100 poems a year, accept approximately 50%. Press run is 200 for 150 subscribers of which 27 are libraries. Subscription: $8. Sample: $2. Make checks payable to Rose Romano. "Must be Italian-American and proud of it."

How to Submit: Submit 3-5 poems at a time. Previously published poems OK; no simultaneous submissions. Cover letter preferred. Time between acceptance and publication is 3 months. Seldom comments on rejections. Publishes theme issues occasionally. Reports in 3-4 weeks. Pays 3 copies. Acquires first or one-time rights. Reviews books and chapbooks of poetry in 200 words, single book format. Open to unsolicited reviews. Poets may also send books for review consideration.

Book/Chapbook Needs & How to Submit: Malafemmina Press publishes 3 chapbooks/year of poetry "by and about Italian-Americans to promote awareness of our culture." Chapbooks are usually 20 pgs., 5½×8½, offset printed and saddle-stapled with paper cover. Query first, with a few sample poems and a cover letter with brief bio and publication credits. Replies to queries and mss in 3-4 months. Pays 50 author's copies (out of a press run of 200) plus 50% discount. Obtain sample books or chapbooks by sending inquiry. "Malafemmina Press will be moving to Italy soon, to publish bilingual English/Italian poetry chapbooks. Write now to be put on mailing list."

⊙ MAMA YAMA MAGAZINE; MAMA YAMA PRODUCTIONS AND PUBLICATIONS, P.O. Box 4881, Palos Verdes CA 90274, e-mail mamayama@juno.com, founded 1997, editors Cat Spydell, Teri Renner and Toby Estler.

Magazine Needs: Appearing annually on the Spring Equinox, *Mama Yama Magazine* "offers art and poetry and commentary on a wide range of topics, from the environment to the poetry scene. We like to publish thought-provoking, interesting poetry and art. One-and-a-half pages or less most likely to be published. No time for rhyme (unless you excel at it). Nothing cutsie, crass, vulgar or sexist." They have published poetry by Stephen Kessler, Gerald Locklin, Hayley Mitchell and David Hernandez. As a sample they selected these lines from "Norman, Oklahoma" by editor Cat Spydell:

> All this in a rear-view mirror:/The sun seeps into the Rockies/consuming crags with orange light;/a

flash, and in an instant,/silhouette.
The editors say *MYM* is 40-75 pgs., 8½×11, printed with soy ink and staple-bound with slick color cover, includes b&w photography and art, 2 pages of ads in back. They receive about 100-300 poems a year, accept approximately 40%. Press run is 750, 90% shelf sales; 10% distributed free to libraries, coffeehouses, etc. Single copy: $5 plus $1.50 p&h. Make checks payable to Cat Spydell.
How to Submit: Submit 3-7 poems at a time. Previously published poems OK; no simultaneous submissions. Cover letter required. "Name and address and title of poem in upper right-hand corner of each page. Pages numbered if longer than one sheet; 1 of 2, 2 of 2, etc. Also, paper clip entire submission. And of course, send SASE." Reads submissions October 1 through January 15 only. Time between acceptance and publication is 6 months, "not including October 1 through January 15." Poems are circulated to an editorial board. "Three editors review each poem with a ✔, −, + system and comments. Then a meeting confirms final decision." Often comments on rejections. Publishes theme issues occasionally. Send SASE for guidelines and upcoming themes or obtain via e-mail. Reports in 1-3 months. Pays 1 copy. Acquires first or one-time rights. Reviews books and chapbooks of poetry and other magazines in 200-500 words. Open to unsolicited reviews. Poets may also send books for review consideration to Cat Spydell. $3 reading fee for review material.
Also Offers: Sponsors an annual writer's contest. Deadline: September 15. Fee: $3. Prize: $25 plus 2-page feature including photo, bio, and publication of winning entry. Previously unpublished work only. Mama Yama Productions and Publications is a non-profit organization dedicated to bringing environmental and social issues to the public eye via the written word and film.
Advice: The editors say, "*Mama Yama* is nourishment for your head. Get some!"

MAMMOTH BOOKS; MAMMOTH PRESS INC., 7 South Juniata St., DuBois PA 15801, e-mail mammothbooks@hotmail.com, founded 1997, editor Antonio Vallone.
Book/Chapbook Needs: MAMMOTH books, an imprint of MAMMOTH press inc., publishes 1-6 paperbacks/year of creative nonfiction, fiction and poetry through annual competitions. "We are open to all types of literary poetry." They have published poetry by Liz Rosenberg, Philip Terman, Cynthia Hogue and John Stigall. Books are usually 5×7, offset printed and perfect-bound, covers vary (1-4 color), include art.
How to Submit: Send mss to contest. Not currently reading outside of contests. For poetry mss, submit a collection of poems or a single long poem. Translations are accepted. "Manuscripts as a whole must not have been previously published. Some or all of each manuscript may have appeared in periodicals, chapbooks, anthologies, or other venues. These must be identified. Authors are responsible for securing permissions." Simultaneous submissions OK. No e-mail submissions. Poetry mss should be single-spaced, no more than 1 poem/page. Reads submissions September 1 through February 28/29. Entry fee: $20. Make checks payable to MAMMOTH press inc. Time between acceptance and publication is 1 year. Poems are circulated to an editorial board. "Finalists will be chosen by the staff of MAMMOTH press inc. and an outside editorial board and/or guest editor. Manuscripts will be selected based on merit only." Seldom comments on rejections. Winner receives $750 advance against royalties ("if the number of contest entries generates at least $750"), a standard royalty contract, and publication in a first edition of at least 500 copies in a trade paperback format. Other finalist manuscripts may be selected for publication and offered a standard royalty contract and publication of at least 500 trade paperback copies. Finalists will be announced within 6 months from the end of each submission period. MAMMOTH press inc. reserves the right not to award a prize if no entries are deemed suitable. Send SASE for complete rules. Order sample books by sending for information to their mailing address or e-mail.
Advice: The editor says, "Read: literary magazines, good books of poetry (both old and new) and magazines and books seemingly unconnected to poetry. Don't learn about the world by watching TV. Go out into it, too!"

MANDRAKE POETRY REVIEW; THE MANDRAKE PRESS (Specialized: translations), ul. Wielkiej Niedźwiedzicy 35/8, Gliwice 44-117 Poland, phone 48-32-234-40-75, e-mail mandrake@pol box.com, website http://www.angelfire.com/pe/TheMandrakePress, or Box 792, Larkspur CA 94977-0792, founded 1993 in New York, European editor Leo Yankevich, North American editor David Castleman.
Magazine Needs: *MPR* appears at least twice a year. The editors say, "We will look at anything, but accept very little." They have published poetry by Michael Daugherty, George Held, Hugh Fox, Errol Miller, Simon Perchik and Joan Peternel. As a sample the editor selected these lines from "By A Philosopher's Tomb" by Cornel (Adam) Lengyel:

> *How may one thank in fitting terms the maker/of new and taller windows for the soul?/I turn my*
> *transient eyes without and see/the world's great ghostly wheels of change reduce/our mortal home to*
> *essences eternal—/the terror and the grandeur, all within.*

Mandrake Poetry Review is 76-150 pgs., A5, offset printed and flat-spined with glossy white card cover. The editors say they accept about 2% of the poetry received. Press run is 500 for 100 subscribers from 3 continents. Single copy: $5 (by airmail); subscription: $20/2 years. Make checks payable to David Castleman at the California address.
How to Submit: Submit up to 7 poems at a time. "Send only copies of your poems, as we do not return poems with our reply." Previously published poems and simultaneous submissions OK. Cover letter preferred. E-mail submissions OK. "Please send e-mail submissions in an attached file (MS Word 6.0 format)." Reports in 1-2 months. Pays 2 copies "sometimes more." All rights revert to author. "Poets are encouraged to send their books for review consideration to David Castleman at the above address. All editors and publishers whose books/

chapbooks are selected for review will receive one copy of the issue in which the review appears. We publish 50-100 reviews yearly."
Also Offers: Website includes magazine in its entirety.

☑ ◙ **MANGROVE**, University of Miami, Dept. of English, P.O. Box 248145, Coral Gables FL 33124-4632, founded 1994, contact poetry editors.
Magazine Needs: *Mangrove*, published annually in May, is a "high quality literary magazine." They want "high quality poetry of no more than five pgs. No restrictions on form. We seek to showcase a dynamic mix of styles and themes in every issue." They do not want "children's poetry." They have published poetry by Denise Duhamel, Joseph Millar, Jamaica Kincaid, Campbell McGrath and Jim Daniels. The editor says *Mangrove* is 125 pgs., perfect-bound with a colored cover. They receive about 1,000 poems a year, accept approximately 4%. Press run is 500 for 200 subscribers of which 30 are libraries, 100 shelf sales; 35 distributed free to contributors. Sample: $6. Make checks payable to *Mangrove*/Dept. of English.
How to Submit: Submit up to 5 poems at a time. Include SASE. No previously published poems; simultaneous submissions OK. Cover letter preferred. No fax or electronic submissions. Reads submissions postmarked from August 1 through December 1 only. "Manuscripts sent at other times may be returned unread or held until the following year. We respond, generally, from December through March." Send SASE for guidelines. Pays 2 copies and ⅓ discount on additional copies. Acquires first North American serial rights. All rights revert to authors upon publication.

◙ ◎ **THE MANHATTAN REVIEW (Specialized: translations)**, 440 Riverside Dr., Apt. 45, New York NY 10027, phone (212)932-1854, founded 1980, poetry editor Philip Fried.
Magazine Needs: *The Manhattan Review* "publishes American writers and foreign writers with something valuable to offer the American scene. We like to think of poetry as a powerful discipline engaged with many other fields. We want to see ambitious work. Interested in both lyric and narrative. Not interested in mawkish, sentimental poetry. We select high-quality work from a number of different countries, including the U.S." They have published poetry by Zbigniew Herbert, D. Nurkse, Penelope Shuttle and Peter Redgrove. The *MR* is now "an annual with ambitions to be semiannual." The magazine is 64 pgs., digest-sized, professionally printed with glossy card cover, photos and graphics. Press run is 500 for 400 subscribers of which 250 are libraries. It is also distributed by Bernhard DeBoer, Inc. They receive about 300 submissions a year, use few ("but I do read everything submitted carefully and with an open mind"). "I return submissions as promptly as possible." Single copy: $5; subscription: $10. Sample: $6.25 with 6×9 envelope.
How to Submit: Submit 3-5 pgs. of poems at a time. No simultaneous submissions. Cover letter with short bio and publications required. Editor sometimes comments "but don't count on it." Reports in 10-12 weeks if possible. Pays copies. Staff reviews books of poetry. Send books for review consideration.
Advice: Philip Fried says, "Don't be swayed by fads. Search for your own voice. Support other poets whose work you respect and enjoy. Be persistent. Keep aware of poetry being written in other countries."

◙ **MANKATO POETRY REVIEW**, Box 53, English Dept., Mankato State, Mankato MN 56001, phone (507)389-5511, e-mail roger.sheffer@mankato.msus.edu, founded 1984, editor Roger Sheffer.
Magazine Needs: *MPR* is a semiannual magazine that is "open to all forms and themes, though we seldom print 'concrete poetry,' religious, or sentimental verse. We frequently publish first-time poets." They have published poetry by Edward Micus and Walter Griffin. The magazine is 30 pgs., 5×8, typeset on 60 lb. paper, saddle-stapled with buff matte card cover printed in one color. It appears usually in May and December and has a circulation of 200. Subscription: $5/year. Sample: $2.50.
How to Submit: Submit up to 6 poems at a time. Line length for poetry is 60 maximum. "Please include biographical note on separate sheet. Poems not accompanied by SASE will not be returned." However, do not submit mss in summer (May through August). No previously published poems or simultaneous submissions. Cover letter required. Send SASE for guidelines. Deadlines are April 15 (May issue) and November 15 (December issue). Reports in about 2 months; "We accept only what we can publish in next issue." Pays 2 copies.
Advice: The editor says, "We're interested in looking at longer poems—up to 60 lines, with great depth of detail relating to place (landscape, townscape)."

◙ $◙ **MĀNOA: A PACIFIC JOURNAL OF INTERNATIONAL WRITING**, 1733 Donaghho Rd., Honolulu HI 96822, fax (808)956-7808, e-mail mjournal-l@hawaii.edu, website http://www2.hawaii.edu/uhpr ess/Journals/MA/MAHome.html (publication) and http://www2.hawaii.edu/mjournal (editorial office), founded 1989, poetry editor Frank Stewart.
● Poetry published in *Mānoa* has also been selected for inclusion in the 1995 and 1996 volumes of *The Best American Poetry*.
Magazine Needs: *Mānoa* appears twice a year. "We are a general interest literary magazine, open to all forms and styles. We are not for the beginning writer, no matter what style. We are not interested in Pacific exotica." They have published poetry by Arthur Sze, Linda Hogan and John Haines. It is 240 pgs., 7×10, offset printed, flat-spined using art and graphics. They receive about 3,000 poems a year, accept approximately 2%. Press run is 2,000 for 1,000 subscribers of which 30 are libraries, 700 shelf sales. Subscription: $22/year. Sample: $10.
How to Submit: Query by mail or e-mail. Submit 3-5 poems at a time. Send SASE for guidelines. Reports in

6 weeks. Always sends prepublication galleys. Pay "competitive" plus 2 copies. Seldom comments on rejections. They review current books and chapbooks of poetry. Open to unsolicited reviews. Poets may also send books for review consideration, attn. reviews editor.

Also Offers: Website includes writer's guidelines, names of editors, short fiction and poetry, RealAudio readings by authors, lists of back issues and future issues, subscription info, author index and awards received.

Advice: The editor says, "We welcome the opportunity to read poetry from throughout the country. We are not a regional journal, but we do feature work from the Pacific and Asia, especially in our reviews and essays. We are not interested in genre or formalist writing for its own sake, or picturesque impressions of the region."

THE MARLBORO REVIEW; MARLBORO PRIZE FOR POETRY, P.O. Box 243, Marlboro VT 05344, website http://www.marlbororeview.com, founded 1995, editor Ellen Dudley, poetry editor Ruth Anderson Barnett.

• "We have won a Pushcart Prize every year since we began publishing."

Magazine Needs: *The Marlboro Review*, published biannually, is a "literary magazine containing poetry, fiction, essays, reviews and translations." They want long poems. They do not want greeting card verse. They have published poetry by William Matthews, Jean Valentine, Bill Knott and Chana Bloch. The *MR* is 80-112 pgs., 6×9, offset printed and perfect-bound with laminated colored cover and ads. They receive about 1,000 poems a year, accept approximately 7%. Press run is 1,000 for 350 subscribers of which 25 are libraries, 300 shelf sales; 50-70 distributed free to writers and institutions. Single copy: $8; subscription: $16. Sample: $8.75.

How to Submit: Submit up to 5 typed, near letter quality or better poems at a time with SASE. No previously published poems; simultaneous submissions OK "if we are notified." Send SASE for guidelines. Reports in up to 3 months. Sometimes sends prepublication galleys. Pays 2 copies. Acquires all rights. Returns rights on publication. Reviews books of poetry in 500-1,000 words, single book format. Open to unsolicited reviews. Poets may also send books for review consideration.

Also Offers: Sponsors the Marlboro Prize for Poetry. Awards a $1,000 honorarium and publication. Submit $10 reading fee for up to 5 poems. Deadline: December 31, 1999. Include name on cover letter only, not on ms. All entrants receive the Marlboro Prize issue and are considered for publication.

MARYLAND POETRY REVIEW; MICHAEL EGAN MEMORIAL CONTEST; MARYLAND STATE POETRY AND LITERARY SOCIETY, P.O. Drawer H, Catonsville MD 21228, website http://members.aol.com/mdstpoetry, founded 1985, edited by Rosemary Klein.

Magazine Needs: The *Maryland Poetry Review* "is interested in promoting the literary arts in Maryland as well as nationally and internationally. We are interested in strong, thoughtful poetry with a slight bias to free verse. All submissions are read carefully. *MPR* is open to good poets who have not published extensively as well as to those who have." They have published poetry by Josephine Jacobsen, Richard Jackson, Gary Finke and Walter McDonald. As a sample the editor selected these lines from "Domestic Rhythm: A Pantoum" by Georgia Kreiger:

> Let us sip tea together, our knees touching/Under the oak table whose legs you carved/To crouch like
> the daunting legs of lions;/You always loved the thundering themes of nature.

MPR is 75 pgs., 7×11, professionally printed in small type on quality eggshell stock, perfect-bound with a glossy color cover. Current issue: $12; back issue: $8.

How to Submit: Submit up to 5 poems at a time with brief bio. No simultaneous submissions. "We read submissions only in January, April and September but accept all year." Publishes theme issues. Theme for the year 2000: Art & Technology. Send SASE for guidelines and upcoming themes. Reports in 3-6 months. Pays 1 copy. Staff reviews books of poetry. Send books for review consideration, attn. Hugh Burgess.

Also Offers: MSPLS sponsors the Michael Egan Memorial Contest for poetry of any length. Entry fee: $3/poem, $12/5 poems. Contest runs from July 1 through October 28 only. Cash prizes of $100, $50 and $25 and magazine publication. Also sponsors an annual chapbook contest. Prize includes $100 and 50 copies of winning ms. Submit mss between 20-30 pgs. Entry fee: $10/ms. Contest runs from January to June. Winners notified by Christmas. Send SASE for guidelines. Website features writer's guidelines, names of editors, poetry samples and is "a changing, interactive site."

MARYMARK PRESS (Specialized: form/style), 45-08 Old Millstone Dr., East Windsor NJ 08520, phone (609)443-0646, founded 1994, editor/publisher Mark Sonnenfeld.

Book/Chapbook Needs: Marymark Press's goal is "to feature and promote experimental poets. I will most likely be publishing only broadsides and samplers; no books at this time. I want to see experimental poetry of the outer fringe. Make up words, sounds, whatever, but say something you thought never could be explained. Disregard rules if need be." No traditional, rhyming or spiritual verse; no predictable styles. As a sample the editor selected his poem, "3-7," from the broadside, *With Conceptual Mistakes By*:

> It's to me image 222/Thought it is good/appropriate chant (semi-coma)/I so suppose, smoke, dust, oil,
> mist, etc./monday with clinical fabrics/OUT-the side a ha-street free, or gone, or barely

How to Submit: Submit 3 poems at a time. Previously published poems and simultaneous submissions OK. Cover letter preferred. "Copies should be clean, crisp and camera-ready. I do not have the means to accept electronic submissions. A SASE should accompany all submissions, and a telephone number if at all possible." Time between acceptance and publication is 2 months. Seldom comments on rejections. Replies to queries and mss in 1-2 months. Pays 1-20 author's copies (out of a press run of 200-300). May offer subsidy arrangements. "I am new at this. And so it all depends upon my financial situation at the time. Yes, I might ask the author to subsidize the cost. It could be worth their while. I have good connections in the small press." Order sample publications by sending a 6×9 SAE. "There is no charge for samples."

Advice: The editor says, "My advice is to find your writing voice, then go with it. Never give up trying to get published. A good alternative is to self-publish, then distribute anywhere and everywhere."

☑ 🌂 $☑ **THE MASSACHUSETTS REVIEW**, South College, University of Massachusetts, Amherst MA 01003, phone (413)545-2689, fax (413)577-0740, e-mail massrev@external.umass.edu, founded 1959, poetry editors Paul Jenkins, Anne Halley and Martín Espada.

● Work published in this review has been included in the 1995 and 1997 volumes of *The Best American Poetry.*

Magazine Needs: Mostly free verse, all lengths and topics, appears here, with emphasis in recent issues on non-narrative modes. An interesting feature: Editors run poems with long-line lengths in smaller type, to fit on the page without typographical interruption (as in other journals). They have published poetry by Tony Hoagland, Marilyn Hacker and Juan Felipe Herrera. As a sample the editor selected these lines from "What They Did" by Vern Rutsala:

> What they decided to do was so hard/we marvelled at their courage./It was like trying to tie knots/
> with two fingers inside a matchbox/the way surgeons do, practicing./Like that only much harder.

The Massachusetts Review is 308 pgs., 6×9, offset printed on bond paper, perfect-bound with 4-color card cover and 4-color pages of art. They receive about 2,500 poems a year, use about 50. Press run is 1,600 for 1,100-1,200 subscribers of which 1,000 are libraries, the rest for shelf sales. Subscription: $18 (US), $30 outside US, $24 for libraries. Sample: $7.

How to Submit: No simultaneous submissions or previously published poems. Read submissions October 1 through June 1 only. Send SASE for guidelines. Reports in 6 weeks. Pays minimum of $10, or 35¢/line, plus 2 copies.

Also Offers: Website includes guidelines, names of editors, table of contents for recent issues and excerpts from work in the latest issue.

ℕ 🌀 ◎ **MATRIARCH'S WAY, JOURNAL OF FEMALE SUPREMACY; ARTEMIS CREATIONS** **(Specialized: women/feminism)**, 3395-2J Nostrand Ave., Brooklyn NY 11229, phone (718)648-8215, e-mail artemispub@aol.com, founded 1994, editor S. Oliveira.

Magazine Needs: *Matriarch's Way* is a quarterly "matriarchal feminist" publication. They want "powerful fem" poetry. The editor says *MW* is 125-200 pgs., digest-sized, offset printed and perfect-bound, includes art. Single copy: $8.50 US, $14.50 overseas; subscription: $30 US, $36 overseas. Sample: $8.50. Make checks payable to Artemis Creations.

How to Submit: Previously published poems and simultaneous submissions OK. Time between acceptance and publication is 1 week. Comments on rejections. Publishes theme issues occasionally. Send SASE for guidelines and upcoming themes. Reports in 1 week. Sometimes sends prepublication galleys. "Book reviews needed." Open to unsolicited reviews.

🌐 ◗ **MATTOID**, School of Literary & Communication Studies, Deakin University, Geelong, Victoria, Australia 3217, fax (052)272484, founded 1977, contact Dr. Brian Edwards.

Magazine Needs: *Mattoid* appears 2 or 3 times/year. "No special requirements but interesting complexity, quality, experimentation. No naive rhyming verse." They have published poetry by Lauris Edmond, Kevin Hart and Judith Rodriguez. It is 200 pgs., flat-spined with 2-color cover. They receive about 800 poems a year, publish 10-15%. Press run is 650 for 400 subscribers of which 10 are libraries, 50-100 shelf sales. Sample: $15 overseas.

How to Submit: Publishes theme issues. Send SASE (or SAE and IRC) for upcoming themes. Reports in 2-3 months. Pays 1 copy. Reviews books of poetry in 1,000-2,000 words, single book format.

$◎ **MATURE YEARS (Specialized: senior citizen, religious)**, P.O. Box 801, 201 Eighth Ave. S., Nashville TN 37202, phone (615)749-6292, fax (615)749-6512, e-mail mcrepsey@umpublishing.org, founded 1954, editor Marvin W. Cropsey.

Magazine Needs: *Mature Years* is a quarterly. "The magazine's purpose is to help persons understand and use the resources of Christian faith in dealing with specific opportunities and problems related to aging. Poems are usually limited to 16 lines and may, or may not, be overtly religious. Poems should not poke fun at older adults, but may take a humorous look at them. Avoid sentimentality and saccharine. If using rhymes and meter, make sure they are accurate." *MY* is 112 pgs., magazine-sized, perfect-bound, with full-color glossy paper cover. Circulation is 70,000. Sample: $5.

How to Submit: Line length for poetry is 16 lines of up to 50 characters maximum. E-mail and fax submissions OK. Submit seasonal and nature poems for spring during December through February; for summer, March through May; for fall, June through August; and for winter, September through November. Send SASE for guidelines. Reports in 2 months; sometimes a year's delay before publication. Pays $1/line upon acceptance.

$ ◎ MEADOWBROOK PRESS (Specialized: anthologies, children, humor), 5451 Smetana Dr., Minnetonka MN 55343, founded 1975, contact children's poetry editor.

Book/Chapbook Needs: Meadowbrook Press publishes one anthology a year as part of a series of funny poetry books for children. They want humorous poems aimed at children ages 6-12. "Poems should be fun, light and refreshing. We're looking for new, hilarious, contemporary voices in children's poetry that kids can relate to." They have published poetry by Shel Silverstein, Jack Prelutsky, Jeff Moss and Bruce Lansky. Anthologies have included *Kids Pick the Funniest Poems*; *A Bad Case of the Giggles*; and *Miles of Smiles*.

How to Submit: "Send your best work." Submit 1 poem to a page, name and address on each. Line length for poetry is 45 maximum. Include SASE with each submission. Previously published poems and simultaneous submissions OK. Cover letter required "just to know where the poet found us." Time between acceptance and publication is 1-2 years. Poems are tested in front of grade school students before being published. Send SASE for guidelines. Pays $50-100/poem plus 1 copy.

◎ MEDICINAL PURPOSES LITERARY REVIEW; MARILYN K. PRESCOTT MEMORIAL POETRY CONTEST; POET TO POET, INC., 86-37 120th St., #2D, Richmond Hill NY 11418, phone (718)776-8853 or (718)847-2150, e-mail scarptp@worldnet.att, website http://wsite.com/poettopoet, founded 1994, executive editor Robert Dunn, managing editor Thomas M. Catterson, associate editor Leigh Harrison.

Magazine Needs: *Medicinal Purposes* appears 3 times/year and wants "virtually any sort of quality poetry (3 poems, up to 60 lines/poem). Please, no pornography, gratuitous violence or hate mongering." They have published poetry by D.H. Melhem, X.J. Kennedy, Rhina P. Espaillat, Chocolate Waters and George Dickerson. *Medicinal Purposes* is 64 pgs., 8½×5½ (landscape format), professionally printed and perfect-bound with card stock cover with b&w illustration, b&w illustrations also inside. They receive 1,200 poems a year, accept 10%. Press run is 1,000 for 270 subscribers of which 6 are libraries, 30% shelf sales. Subscription: $16/year. Sample: $6. Make checks payable to Poet to Poet.

How to Submit: Submit 3 poems at a time, up to 60 lines per poem, typed with SASE. E-mail submissions OK (1 poem per electronic page). No previously published poems or simultaneous submissions. Cover letter preferred. Time between acceptance and publication is 4-16 months. Often comments on rejections. Send SASE for guidelines or obtain via e-mail or website. Reports in 3 months. Always sends prepublication galleys. Pays 2 copies. Acquires first rights.

Also Offers: They produce a poetry/folk music public access cable show called "Poet to Poet." They also sponsor an annual poetry contest, 1st Prize $100. Submit 3 poems of 6-16 lines each with a $5 entry fee by May 15. Winners will be published in the year's end issue. Also administers The Marilyn K. Prescott Memorial Poetry Contest. Send SASE for details. Website includes guidelines, TV schedules, live events (open mics, etc.) and sample writings.

Advice: The editors say, "Poetry cannot be created out of a vacuum. Read the work of others, listen to performances, and most important—Get A Life! Do Things! If you get struck by lightning, then share the light. Only then do you stand a chance of finding your own voice."

◻ ◿ ◎ MEDIPHORS (Specialized: health concerns), P.O. Box 327, Bloomsburg PA 17815-0327, e-mail mediphor@ptd.net, website http://www.mediphors.org, founded 1992, editor Eugene D. Radice, M.D.

Magazine Needs: *Mediphors* is a biannual literary journal of the health professions that publishes literary work in medicine and health, including poetry, short story, humor, essay, drawing, art/photography. They want "fresh insights into illness and those caregivers with the burden and joy of working in the fields of medicine and health. Optimism in the face of adversity and overwhelming sorrow. The day-to-day feelings of healthcare workers in diverse settings from hospitals in cities to war zones in military hot spots." *Mediphors* is 72 pgs., 8½×11, offset printed and saddle-stapled with color cover and b&w art, graphics and photos throughout. They receive about 2,000 poetry submissions a year, accept approximately 100. Press run is 1,200 for 300 subscribers of which 20 are libraries, 450 shelf sales. Single copy: $6.95; subscription: $15. Sample: $6.

How to Submit: Submit "2 copies of each poem that we can keep; 6 poems maximum, 30 lines each. We do not accept previously published poems or simultaneous submissions, and it is upsetting to find out that this has occurred when we accept a poem." Cover letter not required "but helpful." No e-mail submissions. Time between acceptance and publication is 10-12 months. Seldom comments on rejections. Send SASE for guidelines. Reports in 1-3 months. Pays 2 copies. "We require authors to sign a very tight contract for first North American serial rights that makes them legally responsible for plagiarism, libel, copyright infringement, etc."

Also Offers: Website includes writer's guidelines, sample poems, essays and short stories, letters to the editor, cover and contents, editorials, art, photographs and staff listing/editors.

TO RECEIVE REGULAR TIPS AND UPDATES about writing and Writer's Digest publications via e-mail, send an e-mail with SUBSCRIBE NEWSLETTER in the body of the message to newsletter-request@writersdigest.com, or sign up online at www.writersdigest.com.

Advice: The editor says, "Our goal is to place in print as many new authors as possible, particularly those working within the health/medical fields (such as doctors, nurses, technologists, therapists, etc.). We encourage unsolicited manuscripts."

✔ ◎ **MEDUSA'S HAIRDO**, P.O. Box 358, Catlettsburg KY 41129-0358, e-mail bevymoore@yahoo.com, website http://sac.uky.edu/~bymoor0/medusa/mh.htm, founded 1994, contact Beverly Moore.
Magazine Needs: *Medusa's Hairdo* appears biannually, and is a "literary zine, specifically not dealing with classical myth but rather work that represents the 'mythology' of our generation." They want "poems no longer than one page. We publish a wide range of poetry." They do not want "humorous poetry or sex/violence." They have published poetry by Gary Every and Lyn Lifshin. As a sample the editor selected these lines from "The Tale of a Rock" by Mary Winters:
> I was a bully, a conqueror, a captor/I sneered: I want you lovely/in my dark dank airless room
The editor says *Medusa's Hairdo* is 30 pgs., 8½×11, with b&w art and ads. They receive about 200 poems a year, accept approximately 5%. Press run is 50 for 25 subscribers. Subscription: $8.70. Sample: $4.50. Make checks payable to Beverly Moore. "Purchase of a sample copy strongly encouraged."
How to Submit: Submit up to 6 poems at a time. Previously published poems and simultaneous submissions OK. Cover letter required. E-mail submissions and queries preferred. Reads submissions May 1 through August 1; November 20 through November 30; and March 1 through March 15 only. Time between acceptance and publication is 6 months. Often comments on rejections. Send SASE for guidelines or obtain via e-mail or website. Reports in 1 month. Pays 1 copy. Buys first North American serial rights.
Also Offers: Website includes "virtual sample copy", guidelines, news, publication schedule, writers' aids, links, mailing list, etc.
Advice: The editor says, "Beginners are welcome to try us though our acceptance rate is very low. Let us know in the cover letter that you are a beginner."

✄ $ ◎ ◎ **MEKLER & DEAHL, PUBLISHERS; UNFINISHED MONUMENT PRESS; HAMILTON HAIKU PRESS (Specialized: form); THE ACORN-RUKEYSER CHAPBOOK CONTEST; THE SANDBURG-LIVESAY ANTHOLOGY CONTEST; HERB BARRETT AWARD**, 237 Prospect St. S., Hamilton, Ontario L8M 2Z6 Canada, phone (905)312-1779, fax (905)312-8285, e-mail meklerdeahl@globalserve.net, founded 1978 (Unfinished Monument Press), 1983 (Hamilton Haiku Press), managing partner James Deahl.
Book/Chapbook Needs: Unfinished Monument Press and Hamilton Haiku Press, with their 2 imprints UnMon Northland (in Canada), UnMon America (in the USA), publish 3 paperbacks and 6 chapbooks/year with 1 chapbook and 2 anthologies published as the result of contests. They want "for Unfinished Monument Press: people's poetry; for Hamilton Haiku Press: haiku." They do not want "racist or sexist poetry." They have published poetry by Linda Rogers and Ronnie R. Brown. As a sample the editor selected these lines from "The Hands" by Milton Acorn:
> Why man, those hands, dyed/earth and tobacco brown, tough/as an old alligator suitcase, fissured/a dozen extra ways, have/a grip all courtesy, a touch/delicate and sure as a young woman's.
Books are usually 32-128 pgs., 6×9, offset printed with art and/or graphics.
How to Submit: "Always query first with 5 sample poems." Previously published poems and simultaneous submissions OK. "We like e-mail submissions." Fax submissions OK. Cover letter required. "U.S. poets may use our Pittsburgh address: Mekler & Deahl, Publishers, P.O. Box 4279, Pittsburgh PA 15203." Has backlog of 3-4 years. Time between acceptance and publication "varies greatly." "I publish what I like and what I think will sell." Seldom comments on rejections. Replies to queries in 6 months, to mss in 1 month. Pays 10-12% royalties and 10-20 author's copies (out of a press run of 500-1,000). Obtain sample books or chapbooks by writing to the above address.
Also Offers: Sponsors The Acorn-Rukeyser Chapbook Contest, awarding 1 prize of $100 (US), publication and 50 copies. Runner-Up receives $100 (US). Submissions may be entered in other contests. Submit a poetry ms of up to 30 pgs., poems must be within the People's Poetry tradition, as exemplified by the work of Milton Acorn and Muriel Rukeyser. Send SASE for guidelines. Entry fees: $10 (US). All entrants receive a copy of the winning chapbook. Postmark deadline: September 30. Winner will be notified in January. Also sponsors The Sandburg-Livesay Anthology Contest, awarding a $200 1st Prize and publication; a $100 (US) 2nd Prize and anthology publication; a $50 (US) 3rd Prize and anthology publication; and anthology publication for other prizes. Submit up to 10 poems of up to 70 lines; poems must be within the People's Poetry tradition, as exemplified by the work of Carl Sandburg and Dorothy Livesay. Send SASE for guidelines. Entry fees: $12 (US). All entrants receive a copy of the anthology. Postmark deadline: October 31. Winners will be notified in January. Also sponsors the Herb Barrett Award for short poetry in the haiku tradition, awarding publication and a $150 1st Prize; a $100 2nd Prize; a $50 3rd Prize; and anthology publication for other prizes. Winning poems will be published in an anthology. "What is most important is that each haiku be a concise image of life." Send SASE for guidelines. Entry fees: $10 (US). "Up to 10 poems may be submitted per entry." Postmark deadline: November 30.

◎ **MELLEN POETRY PRESS**, P.O. Box 450, Lewiston NY 14092-0450, phone (716)754-2266, fax (716)754-4056, e-mail mellen@wzrd.com, founded 1973, poetry editor Patricia Schultz.
Book/Chapbook Needs: Mellen Poetry Press is a scholarly press. "We do not have access to large chain bookstores for distribution, but depend on direct sales and independent bookstores." They pay 5 copies, no

royalties. "We require no author subsidies. However, we encourage our authors to seek grants from Councils for the Arts and other foundations because these add to the reputation of the volume." They want "original integrated work—living unity of poems, preferably unpublished, encompassable in one reading." They have published poetry by W.R. Elton and Albert Cook. Their books are 64 pgs., 6×9, softcover binding, no graphics. Price: $14.95.

How to Submit: Submit 30-60 sample poems with cover letter including bio and publications. "We do not print until we receive at least 50 prepaid orders. Successful marketing of poetry books depends on the author's active involvement. We send out up to 15 free review copies to journals or newspapers, the names of which may be suggested by the author. An author may (but is not required to) purchase books to make up the needed 50 prepublication sales."

Advice: The editor says, "We seek to publish volumes unified in mood, tone, theme."

MEMBRANE (III), 4213 12th St. NE, Washington DC 20017-3818, founded 1995, editor Nigel Hinshelwood.

Magazine Needs: *Membrane* appears biannually and contains "poetry, fiction, memoir, and visual art." They want innovative poetry. They have published poetry by Cynthia Tedesco, Eileen Tabios and Mark Wallace. *Membrane* is 150 pgs., 7×10, offset printed and perfect-bound with laminated card cover, includes photography and drawings. They receive about 500 poems a year, accept approximately 5%. Press run is 500 for 75 subscribers of which 6 are libraries, 40 shelf sales; 200 distributed free to the reading public, writers, editors. Single copy: $10; subscription: $25/3 issues. Sample: $5 (issue #2 only).

How to Submit: No previously published poems or simultaneous submissions. Disk submissions OK. Reads submissions September through April only. Time between acceptance and publication is about 1 year. Reports in 2-3 months. Always sends prepublication galleys. Pays 3-5 copies. Acquires all rights. Returns rights upon publication.

$ THE MENNONITE (Specialized: religious), P.O. Box 347, Newton KS 67114-0347, phone (316)283-5100, fax (316)283-0454, e-mail gordonh@gcmc.org, website http://www.themennonite.org, founded 1885, associate editor Gordon Houser.

Magazine Needs: *The Mennonite* is published weekly and wants "Christian poetry—usually free verse, not too long, with multiple layers of meaning. No sing-song rhymes or poems that merely describe or try to teach a lesson." They have published poetry by Jean Janzen and Julia Kasdorf. As a sample we selected these lines from "The matchbox" by Suzanne Lawrence:

> *The empty matchbox/looks like an empty cradle.//Since Frieda died,/I will always have emptiness.//*
> *This fall I hear the children/pass our farm to school.//They belong to others,/but have some claim on*
> *me.//I fill matchboxes with candy,/a trinket, a new hankie,//peppernuts, and when I have enough,/wrap*
> *them for the Christmas program.//I will walk the mile/and a half under the stars.*

The editor says *Mennonite* is 16-24 pgs., 8½×11, 2-color cover, includes art and ads. They receive about 100 poems a year, accept approximately 10%. Press run is 22,500 for 22,000 subscribers. Single copy: $1.25; subscription: $34.95. Sample: $1.

How to Submit: Submit up to 4 poems at a time. Previously published poems and simultaneous submissions OK. Cover letter preferred. E-mail submissions OK. Time between acceptance and publication is 1-2 months. Seldom comments on rejections. Publishes theme issues occasionally. Send SASE for guidelines and upcoming themes. Reports in 1-2 weeks. Pays $25-50 plus 2 copies. Buys first or one-time rights.

$ MERLYN'S PEN: FICTION ESSAYS AND POEMS BY AMERICA'S TEENS, GRADES 6-12 (Specialized: students, young adults), Dept. PM, Box 1058, East Greenwich RI 02818, phone (401)885-5175, fax (401)885-5222, e-mail merlinspen@aol.com, website http://www.merlinspen.com, founded 1985, editor R. Jim Stahl.

Magazine Needs & How to Submit: *MP* appears annually and is 100 pgs., magazine-sized, professionally printed with matte finish paper, color cover. Press run is 5,000 for 4,000 subscribers of which 2,000 are libraries. Subscription: $29, plus 10% shipping. Send SASE or visit website for guidelines. Reports in 9 weeks. Pays 3 copies plus $20-200/piece.

MESECHABE: THE JOURNAL OF SURRE(GION)ALISM, 1539 Crete St., New Orleans LA 70119-3006, phone (504)944-4823, e-mail daf09@gnofn.org, founded 1988, editor Dennis Formento.

Magazine Needs: *Mesechabe*, published annually, exists "to surre(gion)alize the earth." They want "poetry seriously committed to changing the language, the world, or both. Poetry addressing eternal themes: ecology, anarchism, culture and politics; traditional indigenous and alternative culture; jazz, the blues and the Mississippi Delta region." They do not want "poetry by poets who don't read the publications they submit to." They have published poetry by John Sinclair, Eileen Myles, Robert Creeley, Dave Shortt and A. di Michele. *Mesechabe* is 24 pgs., 8½×11, saddle-stapled with b&w photos, collages, computer graphics and drawings. They accept approximately 5% of poems received. Press run is 700 for 200 subscribers, 250-400 shelf sales; 50 distributed free to writers, friends and artists. Subscription: $20 individual, $30 institution. Sample: $5.

How to Submit: Submit 5-10 poems at a time. No previously published poems; simultaneous submissions OK. Cover letter required. Time between acceptance and publication is "unpredictable." Always comments on rejections. Publishes theme issues. Send SASE for guidelines and upcoming themes. Reports in 2-6 weeks. Sometimes sends prepublication galleys. Pays 2 copies. Staff reviews books in 200-700 words. Send books for review consideration.

⬤ ◪ **MESSAGES FROM THE HEART**, P.O. Box 64840, Tucson AZ 85728, phone (520)577-0588, fax (520)529-9657, e-mail lbsmith@theriver.com, founded 1993, editor Lauren B. Smith.
Magazine Needs: *MFTH*, published quarterly, offers "writings, specifically letters (letters, journal entries, poems, essays), which nurture understanding between people." They want "poems no more than 800 words, accessible to mainstream readers, which contain an element of hope." They do not want "explicit sexuality, hopelessness, 'cute.' " They have published poetry by Sheila Bender, David Citino, John Levy and W.H. Auden. As a sample the editor selected these lines from "Blessings" by Sheila O'Connor:
> You have taught me to taste the world again,/swallow the dry snow,/smell the surprise of the January
> sun./You, my small scientists of beauty,/recover the wonder of life/in your open, astonished hands.

Messages From the Heart is 20 pgs., 4¼×10½, offset printed, saddle-stapled with medium card cover. They receive about 500-600 poems a year, accept approximately 2-4%. Press run is 600 for 300 subscribers; 50 distributed free for public relations. Subscription: $13. Sample: $4.
How to Submit: Submit up to 6 poems at a time with SASE. Previously published poems and simultaneous submissions OK. Cover letter preferred. Time between acceptance and publication is 1 year. Poems are circulated to an editorial board. "Poems are selected by one editor and then reviewed by two others." Seldom comments on rejections. Publishes theme issues. Send SASE for guidelines. Reports in 1-3 weeks. Pays 3 copies. Acquires one-time rights. "We review books about letter writing in 300-600 words." Open to unsolicited reviews. Poets may also send books for review consideration "only if about or including letters."

⃞ ◐ **THE METROPOLITAN REVIEW**, P.O. Box 26470, San Francisco CA 94126-6470, e-mail metrorev @metroreview.com, website http://www.metroreview.com, founded 1996, editor Mary Claire Ray, associate editor-poetry Deborah Ager.
Magazine Needs: "*TMR* is a biannual of poetry, fiction, essays, art, book reviews and dialogues between writers. We publish strong work of any form. We like to see well-crafted work. Translations are acceptable." They have published poetry by Sidney Wade, Chard deNiord, Rachel Hadas and William Logan. The editor says *TMR* is 28-32 pgs., magazine-sized, professionally printed on quality stock and side-stapled with matte cover with art, includes photography and mixed media, ads. They receive about 200 poems a year, accept approximately 5-8%. Single copy: $6; subscription: $10. Sample: $4.
How to Submit: Submit 3-6 poems at a time. No previously published poems; simultaneous submissions OK. Cover letter preferred. E-mail submissions OK. "We prefer notice of simultaneous submissions. Clean, legible copies of poems. Include SASE." Time between acceptance and publication is 2-4 months. Seldom comments on rejections. Publishes theme issues occasionally. Send SASE for guidelines and upcoming themes or obtain via e-mail or website. Reports in 2-4 months. Pays 2 copies; extra issues are $2. Reviews books of poetry and other magazines in 500-1,200 words, single and multi-book format. Open to unsolicited reviews. Poets may also send books for review consideration to Deborah Ager, associate editor.
Also Offers: Website includes submission guidelines, list of past contributor's bios, poetry recordings, interviews, sample poems, links to other writing-related websites.
Advice: The editors say, "We suggest perusing a copy of *TMR* before submitting work in order to gain a sense of what we publish."

$ ◙ **MIAMI UNIVERSITY PRESS**, English Dept., Miami University, Oxford OH 45056, phone (513)529-5110, website http://www.muohio.edu/mupress/pcatalog/pdf, founded 1992, editor James Reiss.
Book/Chapbook Needs: Publishes 2 books/year in paperback and cloth editions. They want "book manuscripts by poets who have already published at least one full-length book of poems." They have published poetry by Ralph Angel, Judith Baumel, Steve Orlen and Hugh Seidman. Recent titles include *Brilliant Windows* by Larry Kramer, Spring 1998; *After a Spell* by Nance Van Winckel, Fall 1998; *Kingdom Come* by Jim Simmerman, Spring 1999; and *Dark Summer* by Molly Bendall, Fall 1999. All 4 of these books lists for $11.95 (paper) and $19.95 (cloth).
How to Submit: Time between acceptance and publication is 1-2 years. Sometimes comments on rejections. Replies to queries and mss vary. Pays 10% royalties and 10 author's copies (out of a press run of 1,000). For sample books, purchase in bookstores or order from Pathway Book Service (800)345-6665.

▣ $◙ **MICHIGAN QUARTERLY REVIEW**, Dept. PM, 3032 Rackham Bldg., University of Michigan, Ann Arbor MI 48109, phone (734)764-9265, e-mail michigan.quarterly.review@umich.edu, website http://www.u mich.edu/~mqr, founded 1962, editor-in-chief Laurence Goldstein.
  ● Poetry published in the *Michigan Quarterly Review* was also selected for inclusion in the 1992, 1994, 1995 and 1998 volumes of *The Best American Poetry.*
Magazine Needs: *MQR* is "an interdisciplinary, general interest academic journal that publishes mainly essays and reviews on subjects of cultural and literary interest." They use all kinds of poetry except light verse. No specifications as to form, length, style, subject matter or purpose. They have published poetry by Susan Hahn,

William Heyen, Joan Murray and Yusef Komunyakaa. As a sample the editor selected these lines from "Bill Evans" by Bruce Bond:

> *What is dissonance, he thought, if not/a seam in the body, a sweet dread./So when you lean into the sound and through,/the mind is a pupil floating in its eye,/descending into an unlit hallway.*

The *MQR* is 160 pgs., 6×9, flat-spined, professionally printed with glossy card cover, b&w photos and art. They receive about 1,400 submissions a year, use approximately 30, have a 1-year backlog. Circulation is 2,000, with 1,200 subscribers of which half are libraries. Single copy: $5; subscription: $18. Sample: $2.50 plus 2 first-class stamps.

How to Submit: They prefer typed mss. No previously published poems or simultaneous submissions. Cover letter preferred; "it puts a human face on the manuscript. A few sentences of biography is all I want, nothing lengthy or defensive." Publishes theme issues. Theme for fall of 2000 is "Culture's Borders, Nature's Spaces" (title tentative), an issue on human habitations and the environment. Reports in 4-6 weeks. Always sends prepublication galleys. Pays $8-12/page. Buys first rights only. Reviews books of poetry. "All reviews are commissioned."

Also Offers: Website includes information about the current and forthcoming issues, and about special issues of the past; also subscription information.

Advice: Laurence Goldstein says, "There is no substitute for omnivorous reading and careful study of poets past and present, as well as reading in new and old areas of knowledge. Attention to technique, especially to rhythm and patterns of imagery, is vital."

$🖊 MICHIGAN STATE UNIVERSITY PRESS; LOTUS POETRY SERIES, 1405 S. Harrison Rd., 25 Manly Miles Bldg., East Lansing MI 48823-5202, phone (517)355-9543, fax (800)678-2120, e-mail msupress@pilot.msu.edu, website http://pilot.msu.edu/unit/msupress, founded 1947, acquisitions editor Martha Bates.

Book/Chapbook Needs: Michigan State University Press publishes 4-6 paperbacks/year. "We publish poetry of literary quality, with an emphasis on poets living and writing in Michigan." Books are usually 80-125 pgs., 6×9.

How to Submit: Send 5-10 sample poems and brief cover letter. Include SASE "large enough to hold all materials you wish returned." Replies to queries in about 2 months, to mss in 2 years. Pays royalties and author's copies.

Ⓝ $🖊 🖊 ◎ THE MID-AMERICA PRESS, INC.; THE MID-AMERICA POETRY REVIEW; THE MID-AMERICA PRESS WRITING AWARD COMPETITION (Specialized: regional), P.O. Box 575, Warrensburg MO 64093-0575, e-mail rnjones@iland.net, press founded 1976, editor Robert C. Jones.

Magazine Needs: *Mid-America Poetry Review* appears 3 times a year and publishes "well-crafted poetry primarily from—but not limited to—poets living in Missouri, Illinois, Arkansas, Oklahoma, Kansas, Nebraska and Iowa. We are open to all styles and forms; what we look for is well-crafted poetry by writers who know both what they are doing and why. We have a prejudice against work with content that is primarily self-indulgent, confessional or overly private." They have published poetry by Brian Daldorph and Ceclie M. Franking Wu. As a sample the editor selected these lines from "Across the Winter Distance" by Greg Field:

> *Across the winter distance I come to you/through those icy amplitudes/to bring bad news:/There is nothing that keeps us whole./Though you thought the hundreds of blackbirds/rising from this field might be salvation/I have seen them gather to rise again and again.*

The editor says the *Review* is 16-32 pgs., digest-sized, offset printed and saddle-stapled with matte-paper cover. They receive about 1,000 poems a year, accept approximately 20%. Press run is 500. Single copy: $2.50; subscription: $10/2 years. Sample: $3. Make checks payable to The Mid-America Press, Inc.

How to Submit: Submit 3-5 poems at a time. No previously published poems or simultaneous submissions. Cover letter preferred. "Type submissions, single- or double-spaced, on 8½×11 white paper; name, address, telephone number and e-mail address (if available) in top left or right corner. Keep copy of your manuscript—unused submissions will be recycled; send SASE for response. One-page cover letter (if included) should list items to be considered; contain brief paragraphs of information about author and previous publications." Time between acceptance and publication is 1-5 months. Often comments on rejections. Publishes theme issues occasionally. Send SASE for guidelines. Reports in 1-4 weeks. Sometimes sends prepublication galleys. Pays $5/poem and 2 copies. Buys first North American serial rights. Staff reviews books of poetry. Send books for review consideration.

Book/Chapbook Needs & How to Submit: "*At present—with the exception of entries for the competition—the Press is not reading unsolicited book-length poetry manuscripts.*" The Mid-America Press, Inc. was founded "to encourage the creation and appreciation of creative writing." They publish 4-6 paperbacks per year with 1 book selected through The Mid-America Press Writing Award Competition. "The competition is limited to 48- to 148-page poetry mss by poets living in Missouri, Arkansas, Oklahoma, Kansas, Nebraska, Iowa or Illinois. Mss must be unpublished in book form." Reading fee: $20. Send SASE for deadline and entry guidelines. Obtain sample books by sending $13.95

$🖊 ◎ MID-AMERICAN REVIEW; JAMES WRIGHT PRIZE FOR POETRY (Specialized: translations), Dept. of English, Bowling Green State University, Bowling Green OH 43403, phone (419)372-2725, founded 1980, editor-in-chief George Looney, poetry editor David Hawkins.

Magazine Needs: *Mid-American Review* appears twice a year. "Poetry should emanate from strong, evocative images; use fresh, interesting language; and have a consistent sense of voice. Each line must carry the poem, and an individual vision should be evident. We encourage new as well as established writers. There is no length limit." They have published poetry by Stephen Dunn, Susan Ludvigson, Albert Goldbarth, Naomi Shihab Nye, Richard Jackson,and Frankie Paino. The review is 160 pgs., offset printed and flat-spined with laminated card cover using full-color artwork. They receive over 2,000 mss a year, use approximately 40-50 poems. Press run is 1,000. Single copy: $7; subscription: $12. Sample: $5.

How to Submit: Submit up to 6 poems at a time. Reads submissions September 1 through May 30 only. Send SASE for guidelines. Sometimes sends prepublication galleys. Pays $10/printed page when possible plus 2 copies. Rights revert to authors on publication. Reviews books of poetry. Open to unsolicited reviews.

Also Offers: They also publish chapbooks in translation and award the James Wright Prize for Poetry. "To be considered for the prize, send $10 fee and three poems addressed to the James Wright Prize, or write for complete guidelines."

MIDDLE EAST REPORT (Specialized: regional, ethnic, themes), 1500 Massachusetts Ave. NW, Suite 119, Washington DC 20005, phone (202)223-3677, website http://www.merip.org, founded 1971, editor Laurie King-Irani.

Magazine Needs: *MER* is "a magazine on contemporary political, economic, cultural and social developments in the Middle East and North Africa and U.S. policy toward the region. We occasionally publish poetry that addresses political or social issues of Middle Eastern peoples. Preference given to poets from the region or Western poets who have spent extensive time in the region." They have published poetry by Dan Almagor (Israeli) and Etel Adnan (Lebanese). It is 48 pgs., magazine-sized, saddle-stapled, professionally printed on matte finish stock with glossy paper cover, 4 issues/year. Press run is 7,500. Subscription: $32. Sample: $6 domestic; $8 airmail overseas.

How to Submit: Simultaneous submissions and previously published poems OK. Editor sometimes comments on submissions. Reports in 6-8 weeks. Pays 3 copies.

Advice: The editor says, "We key poetry to the theme of a particular issue. Could be as long as 6 months between acceptance and publication."

$ MIDSTREAM: A MONTHLY ZIONIST REVIEW (Specialized: ethnic), 110 E. 59th St., New York NY 10022, phone (212)339-6040, editor Joel Carmichael.

Magazine Needs: *Midstream* is an international journal appearing 7 times a year. They want short poems with Jewish themes or atmosphere. They have published poetry by Yehuda Amichai, James Reiss, Abraham Sutzkever, Liz Rosenberg and John Hollander. The magazine is 48 pgs., approximately 8½×11, saddle-stapled with colored card cover. Each issue includes 4 to 5 poems (which tend to be short, lyric and freestyle expressing seminal symbolism of Jewish history and Scripture). They receive about 300 submissions a year, use approximately 5-10%. Circulation is 10,000. Single copy: $3; subscription: $21.

How to Submit: Submit 3 poems at a time. Publishes theme issues. Reports in 6 months. Pays $25/poem. Buys first rights.

$ MIDWEST POETRY REVIEW, P.O. Box 20236, Atlanta GA 30325-0236, phone (404)350-0714, fax (404)352-8417, founded 1980, editor/publisher John K. Ottley, Jr.

Magazine Needs: *MPR* is a quarterly, with no other support than subscriptions, contest entry fees and an occasional advertisement. They are looking for "quality, accessible verse. Great imagery with powerful adjectives and verbs. Poetry that opens the door to the author's feelings through sensory descriptions. We are attempting to encourage the cause of poetry by purchasing the best of modern poetry. No jingly verses or limericks. Any subject is considered, if handled with skill and taste. No pornography. Nothing which arrives without SASE is read or gets reply. We are open to new poets, but they must show talent to get in." They have published poetry by Helene Barker, B.R. Culbertson, Junette Fabian, Glenna Holloway, Bettie Sellers, Clarence Socwell, Donna Jean Tennis, Joan Vistain and Mary Zachmeyer. As a sample the editor selected these lines from "Sandhill Cranes" by Helene Barker:

> Through binoculars you can see them dance/in pairs: one leaps, spreads wings/in a seven foot span, floats down/like a practiced parachutist, lands,/grabs dirt in his beak, tosses it/over his shoulder, a good luck salt, jumps again./It's astonishing, but a little sad, such stumbling/for love. What else/can they do? We all make ourselves/such fools to reach out to another.

MPR is 40 pgs., professionally printed in Univers type, digest-sized, saddle-stapled with matte card cover. Subscription: $20. Sample: $5.78 (when available).

How to Submit: Submit up to 5 poems at a time, 1 poem/page. Line length for poetry is 40 maximum. No previously published poems or simultaneous submissions. No bios or credit lists. Fax submissions OK. Send SASE and $1 for guidelines. "We will critique up to 10 of your poems at a time." Criticism fee: $10 plus SASE. Reports in 3-4 weeks. Pays $5/poem. Buys first rights.

Also Offers: They have varied contests in each issue, with prizes ranging from $10-250, with "unbiased, non-staff judges for all competitions." Contests have entry fees. Send SASE for details. A 20-point self-analysis survey to assist poets in analyzing their own work is offered free to new subscribers.

◯ **THE MIDWEST QUARTERLY**, Pittsburg State University, Pittsburg KS 66762, phone (316)235-4689, fax (316)235-4686, e-mail smeats@pittstate.edu (queries only, no submissions), founded 1959, poetry editor Stephen Meats.

Magazine Needs: *Midwest Quarterly* "publishes articles on any subject of contemporary interest, particularly literary criticism, political science, philosophy, education, biography and sociology, and each issue contains a section of poetry usually 15 poems in length. I am interested in well-crafted, though not necessarily traditional poems that explore the inter-relationship of the human and natural worlds in bold, surrealistic images of a writer's imaginative, mystical experience. Sixty lines or less (occasionally longer if exceptional)." They have published poetry by Ronald Wallace, Fleda Brown Jackson, Lyn Lifshin, Jeanne Murray Walker and William Kloefkorn. The magazine is 130 pgs., digest-sized, professionally printed and flat-spined with matte cover. Press run is 650 for 600 subscribers of which 500 are libraries. They receive about 4,000 poems a year, use approximately 60. "My plan is to publish all acceptances within 1 year." Subscription: $12. Sample: $3.

How to Submit: Mss should be typed with poet's name on each page, 10 poems or fewer. No previously published poems; simultaneous submissions OK. Publishes theme issues occasionally. Send SASE for guidelines and upcoming themes or request via fax or e-mail. Reports in 2 months, usually sooner. "Submissions without SASE cannot be acknowledged." Pays 3 copies. Acquires first serial rights. Editor comments on rejections "if the poet or poems seem particularly promising." Reviews books of poetry by *MQ* published poets only.

Advice: The editor says, "Keep writing; read as much contemporary poetry as you can lay your hands on; don't let the discouragement of rejection keep you from sending your work out to editors."

◎ ◯ **MIDWEST VILLAGES & VOICES (Specialized: regional)**, P.O. Box 40214, St. Paul MN 55104, phone (612)822-6878, founded 1979.

Book/Chapbook Needs & How to Submit: MVV is a cultural organization and small press publisher of Midwestern poetry and prose. "We encourage and support Midwestern writers and artists. However, at this time submissions are accepted by invitation only. Unsolicited submissions are not accepted."

✓ ◎ **MIDWIFERY TODAY (Specialized: childbirth)**, P.O. Box 2672, Eugene OR 97402-0223, phone (541)344-7438, fax (541)344-1422, e-mail midwifery@aol.com, founded 1986, editor Jan Tritten, poetry editor Denise Wallace.

Magazine Needs: *Midwifery Today* is a quarterly that "provides a voice for midwives and childbirth educators. We are a midwifery magazine. Subject must be birth or profession related." They do not want poetry that is "off subject or puts down the subject." *MT* is 75 pgs., 8½×11, offset printed, saddle-stapled, with glossy card cover with b&w photos and b&w artwork photos, and ads inside. They use about 1 poem/issue. Press run is 5,000 for 3,000 subscribers, 1,000 shelf sales. Subscription: $50. Sample: $10.

How to Submit: No previously published poems or simultaneous submissions. Fax and e-mail submissions OK. Cover letter required. Time between acceptance and publication is 1-2 years. Seldom comments on rejections. Publishes theme issues. Send SASE for guidelines and upcoming themes. Reports in 6 months. Pays 2 copies. Acquires first rights.

Advice: The editor says, "With our publication *please* stay on the subject."

✓ ◯ **MILKWEED EDITIONS**, 430 First Ave. N., Suite 668, Minneapolis MN 55401-1743, phone (612)332-3192, website http://www.milkweed.org, founded 1979, poetry editor Emilie Buchwald.

Book/Chapbook Needs: One to two collections published annually. One to two poetry anthologies published each year. Unsolicited mss are only accepted from writers who have previously published a book-length collection of poetry or a minimum of 6 poems in commercial or literary journals. One of the leading literary presses in the country, Milkweed publishes some of the best poets composing today in well-made, attractively designed collections. Published books of poetry include: *Eating Bread and Honey* by Pattiann Rogers; and *Verse and Universe: Poems about Science and Mathematics* edited by Kurt Brown.

How to Submit: Submit 90- to 200-page ms with SAS return bookmailer (or the ms will not be returned). Include SAS postcard for notification of ms arrival. Indicate in cover letter if ms is to be recycled. Unsolicited mss read in January and June; please include return postage. Send submissions to Poetry Readers. Send SASE for guidelines. Reports in 1-6 months. Catalog available on request, with $1.50 in postage.

Also Offers: Website includes writer's guidelines, catalog, info on publishing programs and "e-verse."

Ⓝ ◯ ◎ **JOHN MILTON MAGAZINE; DISCOVERY MAGAZINE (Specialized: children/teen, religious, visual impairment)**, John Milton Society for the Blind, 475 Riverside Dr., Room 455, New York NY 10115, phone (212)870-3335, fax (212)870-3229, e-mail order@jmsblind.org, website http://www.jmsblind.org, founded 1928, executive director Darcy Quigley.

Magazine Needs: The *John Milton Magazine* is "a quarterly digest of more than 50 Christian periodicals, produced in large print (20 point) and sent free to visually impaired adults." The executive director says *JMM* is 24 pgs., tabloid-sized, contains clip art. They receive about 30 poems a year, accept approximately 15%. Press run is 5,188 for 3,776 subscribers. Subscription is free.

Magazine Needs: *Discovery* is "a quarterly Braille magazine for blind youth (ages 8-18). Articles selected and reprinted from over 20 Christian and secular periodicals for youth." The executive director says *Discovery* is 44 Braille pgs. They receive about 50 poems a year, accept approximately 15%. Press run is 2,041 for 1,878 subscribers. Subscription is free (only available in Braille).

How to Submit: For both publications, they want "Christian themes and holidays (not exclusive), seasonal poems, subjects of interest and encouragement to blind and visually impaired persons." Submit up to 5 poems at a time. Line length for poetry is 5 minimum, 30 maximum. Previously published poems and simultaneous submissions OK. Cover letter preferred. E-mail and disk submissions OK. "Please enclose a SASE with regular mail submissions." Time between acceptance and publication is 3-6 months. Seldom comments on rejections. Publishes theme issues. Send SASE for guidelines. Reports in 3 months. *JMM* pays 1-3 copies. *Discovery* pays 1 Braille copy. Acquires one-time or reprint rights.

Also Offers: Website includes writer's guidelines, publications brochure, history of society, staff names, board of directors' names.

Advice: They say, "Review list of magazines we typically reprint from (available with writer's guidelines). The bulk of our material is reprinted from other periodicals."

☑ ◎ MIND IN MOTION: A MAGAZINE OF POETRY AND SHORT PROSE (II), P.O. Box 1701, Bishop CA 93515, founded 1985, editor Céleste Goyer.

Magazine Needs: *Mind In Motion* is a quarterly wanting poetry of "15-60 lines. Explosive, provocative. Images not clichéd but directly conveyant of the point of the poem. Use of free association particularly desired. We encourage free verse, keeping in mind the essential elements of rhythm and rhyme. Traditional forms are acceptable if within length restrictions. Meaning should be implicit, as in the styles of Blake, Poe, Coleridge, Stephen Crane, Emily Dickinson, Leonard Cohen. Not interested in sentimentality, emotionalism, simplistic nature worship, explicit references. *MIM* is known for thoughtful poetry that explores the timeless themes of philosophy and human nature." The editor has published poetry by Robert E. Brimhall, Michael Swofford, Wayne Hogan, Marty Walsh and Ruth Harrison. As a sample the editor selected these lines from "A Quiet Eulogy" by Jason Clanton:

> At this spot/a quiet eulogy/was said/for those who/were born with nothing/and returned to earth/ likewise

MIM is 54 pgs., digest-sized, saddle-stapled, photocopied from photoreduced typescript with a heavy matte cover with b&w photos. Of approximately 2,400 poems/year the editor accepts about 200. Press run is 525 for 350 subscribers. Subscription: $14 (overseas $18). Sample: $3.50 (overseas: $4.50).

How to Submit: Submit 6 poems at a time. No previously published poems; simultaneous submissions OK, if notified. "Please have name and address on each poem. We also use dates of composition; it would help if these were provided with submissions." Editor usually comments on rejected mss. Send SASE for guidelines. Reports in 1-6 weeks. Pays 1 copy. Magazine is copyrighted; all rights revert to author.

Advice: The editor says, "Please do not submit further material until your last submission has been responded to. Please be patient and don't overwhelm me."

◎ MIND MATTERS REVIEW, 2040 Polk St., #234, San Francisco CA 94109, founded 1988, phone (415)775-4545, e-mail openbook@earthlink.com, website http://www.home.earthlink.net/~openbook, editor Carrie Drake, poetry editor Bunny Williams (and submissions should be sent directly to her at 158-21 78th Ave., Flushing NY 11366).

Magazine Needs: *Mind Matters Review* is a "literary annual with emphasis on use of science as a tool for responsible organization of information; analysis of the role of language in consciousness, knowledge and intelligence; and social criticism particularly of metaphysics. Also includes book reviews, poetry, short stories, art and essays." They want "short poems for fillers." They have published poetry by Russell Eisenmann and Robert L. Brimm. As a sample the editor selected these lines by an anonymous poet:

> Poetic wisdom is one thing/But it is only in prose/That truth has sting./After all, it is the sound effect/ Which poets are after/Not the sober reality.

MMR is magazine-sized, desktop-published, includes graphics, sketches, b&w photos. Subscription: $10 US, $15 foreign. Sample: $3.50.

How to Submit: Poets are encouraged to buy a copy before submitting. Submit 3 poems at a time. E-mail submissions OK. No simultaneous submissions; previously published poems OK. Cover letter required; include publishing credits and note if submissions have been previously published or accepted for publication elsewhere. Publishes theme issues. Send SASE for guidelines and upcoming themes. Sometimes sends prepublication galleys. Pays 1 copy.

☑ ◎ ◎ MIND PURGE, NT Box 305471, Denton TX 76203, e-mail jivan@anet-dfw.com, founded 1994, editor Jason Hensel.

Magazine Needs: *Mind Purge* is a biannual literary and art magazine appearing in April and October that

---

publishes poetry, short fiction, one-act plays, short screenplays, essays, book reviews and art. They want poetry that is "well-crafted, insightful, imagistic. No specifications as to form, length, subject matter or style. However no greeting card verse, hackneyed themes or poetry that says nothing or goes nowhere." They have published poetry by Lyn Lifshin, Danny Daniels, Wayne Hogan, B.Z. Niditch and Ryan G. Van Cleave. As a sample the editors selected these lines from "The Last Days Of" by Holly Day:

> *Harvest. Cultivation. The words fall alien and pleasing/from our lips, songs of summers past/of a*
> *people long since dead. Practice. The round gearshift cupped/smooth in your confused palm. The wide*
> *flat pedals creak/with rust beneath your sandaled feet. Someday/the machines will work again./*
> *Someday, it will rain.*

Mind Purge is 36-52 pgs., 7 × 8½, neatly printed and saddle-stapled with matte card stock cover with b&w photo and b&w photos inside. They receive about 100 poems a year, accept approximately 10%. Press run is 100 for 10 subscribers. Subscription: $10. Sample: $4. Make checks payable to Jason Hensel.

How to Submit: Submit up to 5 poems or 10 pages at a time, name and address on each page. No previously published poems or simultaneous submissions. Cover letter preferred. E-mail submissions OK, no attachments. Seldom comments on rejections. Reports within 3 months. Pays 1 copy. Reviews books of poetry in 200 words, single book format. Open to unsolicited reviews. Poets may also send books for review consideration.

Advice: Jason Hensel says: "Don't give up, just keep submitting. And read, not only poetry, but everything you can get your hands on."

✓ ◑ **THE MINNESOTA REVIEW: A JOURNAL OF COMMITTED WRITING**, English Dept., University of Missouri-Columbia, 110 Tate Hall, Columbia MO 65211, founded 1960, editor Jeffrey Williams.

Magazine Needs: *TMR* is a biannual literary magazine wanting "poetry which explores some aspect of social or political issues and/or the nature of relationships. No nature poems, and no lyric poetry without the above focus." *TMR* is about 200 pgs., digest-sized, flat-spined, with b&w glossy card cover and art. Press run is 1,500 for 800 subscribers. Subscription: $12 to individuals, $36 to institutions. Sample: $7.50.

How to Submit: Address submissions to "Poetry Editor" (not to a specific editor). Cover letter including "brief intro with address" preferred. SASE with sufficient postage required for return of mss. Publishes theme issues. Send SASE for upcoming themes. Reports in 2-4 months. Pays 2 copies. Acquires all rights. Returns rights upon request. Reviews books of poetry in single or multi-book format. Open to unsolicited reviews.

✓ ○ ◎ **MINORITY LITERARY EXPO (Specialized: membership, minorities)**, 317 Third Ave. SW, Apt. 2E, Birmingham AL 35211, phone (205)297-9658, e-mail poochie@uab.edu, founded 1990, editor/publisher Kervin Fondren.

Magazine Needs & How to Submit: *MLE* is an annual literary professional publication featuring minority poets, novices and professionals. "Organization membership open to all minority poets nationally. I want poems from minority poets that are holistic and wholesome, less than 24 lines each, no vulgar or hate poetry accepted, any style, any form, any subject matter. Poetry that expresses holistic views and philosophies is very acceptable. Literary value is emphasized. Selected poets receive financial awards, certificates, honorable mentions, critiques and special poetic honors." No fee is charged for inclusion. As a sample the editor selected his poem "It's Lonely at the Top":

> *No Man Can/Reach the Top of the Mountain/With Hate, Greed and Despair.//Because in Reaching the*
> *Top/He Soon Will Find Out that/he is the only one There.*

Single copy: $14.95. Send SASE for guidelines and upcoming themes. Pays 1 copy. E-mail submissions OK. "Send edited copy, no more than one page via e-mail."

Also Offers: They also sponsor an annual poetry chapbook contest and an annual "Analyze the Poem" contest. Send SASE for details.

Advice: The editor says, "We seek novices and unpublished poets to breathe the new life every poetry organization needs."

$ ◎ **THE MIRACULOUS MEDAL (Specialized: religious)**, 475 E. Chelten Ave., Philadelphia PA 19144-5785, phone (215)848-1010, founded 1928, editor Rev. William J. O'Brien, C.M.

Magazine Needs: *MM* is a religious quarterly. "Poetry should reflect solid Catholic doctrine and experience. Any subject matter is acceptable, provided it does not contradict the teachings of the Roman Catholic Church. Poetry must have a religious theme, preferably about the Blessed Virgin Mary." They have published poetry by Gladys McKee. The editor describes it as 32 pgs., digest-sized, saddle-stapled, 2-color inside and cover, no ads. *The Miraculous Medal* is used as a promotional piece and is sent to all clients of the Central Association of the Miraculous Medal. Circulation is 250,000.

How to Submit: Sample and guidelines free for postage. Line length for poetry is 20 maximum, double-spaced. No simultaneous submissions or previously published poems. Reports in 6 months to 3 years. Pays 50¢ and up/line, on acceptance. Buys first North American rights.

$ ◖ **MISSISSIPPI MUD**, 7119 Santa Fe Ave., Dallas TX 75223, founded 1973, editor Joel Weinstein.

Magazine Needs: *Mississippi Mud*, published irregularly, features fiction, poetry and artwork which "portray life in America as the 20th century crashes and burns." As for poetry they want "smart, contemporary themes and forms, free verse preferred." They do not want "anything stodgy, pathetic or moralistic; the self-consciously pretty or clever; purely formal exercises." They have published poetry by Tino Villanueva, Diane Averill and Simon Perchik. *MM* is 96 pgs., 7¾×10, perfect-bound, with 4-color glossy paper cover, full-page graphics and display ads. They receive 100-200 poems a year, accept less than 10%. Press run is 1,500 for 150 subscribers of which 16 are libraries, 1,000 shelf sales; about 200 distributed free to galleries, museums and critical media. Subscription: $12/2 issues. Sample: $6.

How to Submit: Submit up to 6 poems at a time. No previously published poems; simultaneous submissions OK. Time between acceptance and publication is a year or more. Seldom comments on rejections. Reports in 4-6 months. Pays $25 and 2 copies. Buys first North American serial rights.

■ MISSISSIPPI REVIEW, University of Southern Mississippi, Box 5144, Hattiesburg MS 39406-5144, phone (601)266-4321, fax (601)266-5757, e-mail fb@netdoor.com, website http://www.sushi.st.usm.edu\mrw, editor Frederick Barthelme, managing editor Rie Fortenberry.

Magazine Needs & How to Submit: Literary publication for those interested in contemporary literature. Poems differ in style, length and form, but all have craft in common (along with intriguing content). Sample: $8. Query first, via mail, e-mail or their website. Does not read manuscripts in summer. Pays 3 copies. Sponsors contests. Send SASE for guidelines.

$■ MISSOURI REVIEW; TOM MCAFEE DISCOVERY FEATURE; LARRY LEVIS EDITORS' PRIZE CONTEST IN POETRY, 1507 Hillcrest Hall, University of Missouri, Columbia MO 65211, phone (573)882-4474, fax (573)884-4671, e-mail moreview@showme.missouri.edu, website http://www.missourirevie w.org, founded 1978, poetry editor Greg Michalson, general editor Speer Morgan.

Magazine Needs: *Missouri Review* is 6×9, 208 pgs., and appears 3 times/year, publishing poetry features only—6-12 pages for each of 3 to 5 poets/issue. "By devoting more editorial space to each poet, *MR* provides a fuller look at the work of some of the best writers composing today." They have published poetry by Michael Pettit, David Clewell, Tina Chang and Robert Gibb. Sample: $7.

How to Submit: Submit 6-12 poems at a time. No previously published poems or simultaneous submissions. Reports in 8-10 weeks. Sometimes sends prepublication galleys. Pays $125-250/feature. Buys all rights. Returns rights "after publication, without charge, at the request of the authors." Staff reviews books of poetry.

Also Offers: Awards the Tom McAfee Discovery Feature once or twice a year to an outstanding young poet who has not yet published a book; poets are selected from regular submissions at the discretion of the editors. Also offers the Larry Levis Editors' Prize Contest in Poetry. Deadline: October 15. $1,500 1st Prize and publication. Three finalists named in addition. Write for details. Website includes guidelines, staff photos, poetry, interviews and discussion forum.

Advice: The editors add, "We think we have enhanced the quality of our poetry section and increased our reader interest in this section. We remain dedicated to publishing at least one younger or emerging poet in every issue."

$◎ MKASHEF ENTERPRISES; PRISONERS OF THE NIGHT (Specialized: psychic/occult, science fiction/fantasy, horror, erotica); POETIC LICENSE, P.O. Box 688, Yucca Valley CA 92286-0688, e-mail alayne@inetworld.net, founded 1987, poetry editor Alayne Gelfand.

● No longer sponsors the Night Visions contest or the Monumental Moments Chapbook Contest.

Magazine Needs: *Prisoners of the Night*, focusing on vampire erotica, uses poetry that is "erotic, unique, less horrific and more romantic, non-pornographic, original visions of the vampire." They have published poetry by Charlee Jacob, Tippi Blevins, Bobbi Sinaha-Morey, Elizabeth Wein, Della Van Hise and Wendy Rathbone. As a sample the editor selected these lines from "Bone-Birds" by Johnnah Kincaid:

> The bone-whiteness of my molding hands/ignites the fire which propels you/out into the nyght,/out into Time,/only to reTurn to me,/the sculpture come/to capture the creator's heart.

POTN is 70-90 pgs., digest-sized beginning with issue #11 (1999), saddle-stapled or perfect-bound with artful cover, produced by high-speed photocopying. Most poems are illustrated. It appears annually, usually in August. They receive about 300 poems a year, accept approximately 10-20. It has an initial press run of 3,000, but each issue is kept in print. Sample: $15 each (for #1-4), $12 (#5), $9.95 each (#6-9), $7.95 (#10).

How to Submit: Beginning in September 1999, she will be accepting submissions for the 2000 issue. Send SASE for guidelines. When *POTN* is open to submissions, submit up to 6 poems at a time. No simultaneous submissions or previously published poems, "unless they've only appeared in your own chapbook." Editor sometimes comments on rejections. Reports "within 1 month." Pays $5/poem plus 1 copy. Buys first serial rights. *POTN* wants unusual visions of the vampire, not stereotypical characterizations.

Also Offers: Also sponsors Poetic License, a biannual poetry contest awarding $500 1st Prize, $100 2nd Prize and $50 3rd Prize, plus publication in anthology and 2 copies. Five honorable mentions receive 1 copy; other poems of exceptional interest will also be included in the anthology. Send SASE for themes and deadlines. Submit any number of poems, any style, of up to 50 lines/poem. Include name, address and phone on each poem. Enclose an SASE, for notification of winners. "Judges prefer original, accessible and unforced works." No entry fee.

Advice: The editor says, "Be original! Find new ways of saying things, explore the infinite possibilities of words and images. Do not rely on stereotypical visions of the vampire; the use of clichés is the quickest road to rejection. I'm not looking for your typical 'count' or 'countess,' no loners in ruined castles. I'm looking for the unusual image and sharp word usage, I want you to make my heart race with both the structure and subject of your poem. Non-rhyming, unstructured poems much preferred."

⬛ **MM REVIEW; MUTANT MULE; FINISHING LINE PRESS; NEW WOMEN'S VOICES CHAP-BOOK SERIES**, P.O. Box 1016, Cincinnati OH 45201-1016, e-mail FinishingL@aol.com, website http://membe rs.aol.com/FinishingL/index.html, founded 1998, editor C.J. Morrison.

Magazine Needs: *MM Review* is a biannual literary arts magazine publishing mostly poetry, but also short stories, short drama, essays and, sometimes, reviews. "We hope to discover new talent." They want "quality verse. We are open to any style or form, but prefer free verse." They have published poetry by Errol Miller, Dennis Saleh, Mark McCloskey, Rane Arroyo and Alexandra Grilikhes. As a sample the editor selected these lines from "Feeling Fireworks" by Leah Maines:

>Fireflowers bloom/in the warm summer air/your hand/unaware/brushes my breast

The editor says *MM Review* is 40 pgs., digest-sized, laser-printed and saddle-stapled with glossy cover, includes b&w photos. They receive about 1,000 poems a year, accept approximately 4%. Press run is 500 for 300 subscribers. Single copy: $6; subscription: $10. Sample: $5. Make checks payable to Finishing Line Press.

How to Submit: Submit up to 3 poems at a time. Include SASE. No previously published poems; simultaneous submissions OK. Brief cover letter with 50- to 75-word bio required, include past publication credits. Time between acceptance and publication is 6 months. Poems are circulated to an editorial board. Often comments on rejections. Publishes theme issues occasionally. Send SASE for guidelines. Reports in 3-4 months. Sometimes sends prepublication galleys. Pays 1 copy. Acquires all rights. Returns rights upon publication. Staff reviews books and chapbooks of poetry in 200 words, multi-book format. Send books for review consideration to Finishing Line Press.

Book/Chapbook Needs & How to Submit: Finishing Line Press seeks to "discover new talent" and through their New Women's Voices Series publishes 2 chapbooks/year by women who have not previously published a book or chapbook of poetry. Chapbooks are usually 25-30 pgs., digest-sized, laser-printed and saddle-stapled with card cover with textured matte wrapper, includes b&w photos. Submit ms of 16-24 pgs. with cover letter, bio, acknowledgements and $10 reading fee. Replies to queries in 3-4 weeks, to mss in 3-4 months. Pays 50 author's copies (out of a press run of 300). "Sales profits, if any, go to publish the next new poet." Obtain sample chapbooks by sending $5.

Advice: The editor says, "We are very open to new talent. If the poetry is great, we will consider it for a chapbook."

◻◙ **MÖBIUS**, P.O. Box 7544, Talleyville DE 19803-0544, founded 1982, editor Jean Hull Herman.

Magazine Needs: *Möbius* is published twice a year, at Memorial Day and Thanksgiving. The editor looks for "the informed mind responding to the challenges of reality and the expression of the imagination in poetry that demonstrates intelligence and wit. Poets should say significant, passionate things about the larger world outside themselves, using all the resources of the English language. Preference is given to poetry that pleases the ear as well as the intellect and soul; strong preference will be shown for work that is fine, structured, layered, as opposed to untitled, unpunctuated jottings. General topics include usage of language and the forms of poetry; the great philosophical questions; romance; relationships; war; science and technology; and humor (editor has a weakness for humorous lines). Poetry from all 50 states, Canada, countries in South America, in Europe, in Asia, Australia and Japan has been printed." They have published poetry by Ace Boggess, Ward Kelley and Ryan G. Van Cleave. As a sample the editor selected these lines from her poem "Ague Of Enlightenment" by Alan Reynolds:

>It's hard to remember/our goal/is to drain the swamp/—to train/the tunnel-end light/of Brownian
>motion/onto David Hume's/unhealthy and/"complex idea"/that spontaneous/experience/is a good
>thing/—when I'm/up to miasma/in alligators.

Möbius is 60-80 pgs., magazine-sized, professionally printed, saddle-stapled with matte card cover. Subscription: $14/year. Sample: $8.

How to Submit: Submit up to 3 poems at a time, typed, name and address on each poem, 1 submission/issue. No electronic submissions. Submissions read year-round. Reports in 2 months. Comments on all rejections. Pays 1 copy. Send SASE for guidelines.

💲◙ **MODERN HAIKU; FOUR HIGH SCHOOL SENIOR SCHOLARSHIPS (Specialized: form, students)**, P.O. Box 1752, Madison WI 53701-1752, phone (608)233-2738, founded 1969, poetry editor Robert Spiess.

Magazine Needs: *Modern Haiku* appears 3 times/year in February, June and October and "is the foremost international journal of English language haiku and criticism. We are devoted to publishing only the very best haiku being written and also publish articles on haiku and have the most complete review section of haiku books. Issues average 92 pages." They want "contemporary haiku in English (including translations into English) that incorporate the traditional aesthetics of the haiku genre, but which may be innovative as to subject matter, mode of approach or angle of perception, and form of expression. Haiku, senryu and haibun only. No tanka or other forms." They have published haiku by Randy Brooks, A.C. Missias, Lee Gurga and Yu Chang. As a sample the editor included this haiku by Joyce Currier:

>spinal cord unit:/each patient's iron halo/glints in the moonlight

The digest-sized magazine appears 3 times/year, printed on heavy quality stock with cover illustrations especially painted for each issue by the staff artist. They receive about 12,000-14,000 submissions a year, use approximately 800. There are over 260 poems in each issue. Circulation is 675. Subscription: $17.75. Sample: $6.

How to Submit: Submit on "any size sheets, any number of haiku on a sheet; but name and address on each sheet." Include SASE. No previously published haiku or simultaneous submissions. Send SASE for guidelines. Reports in 2 weeks. Pays $1/haiku (but no contributor's copy). Buys first North American serial rights. Staff reviews books of haiku in 350-1,000 words, single book format. Send books for review consideration.

Also Offers: They offer 4 annual scholarships for the best haiku by high school seniors. Scholarships range from $200-500 (total $1,400). Deadline is mid-March. Send SASE for rules. Also offers two $50 Best of Issue awards.

Advice: The editor says, "Haiku achieve their effect of felt-depth, insight and intuition through juxtaposition of perceived entities, not through intellective comment or abstract words."

$ ⬤ ◎ MODERN POETRY IN TRANSLATION (Specialized: translations), King's College London, Strand, London WC2 R2LS United Kingdom, phone (171)873-2360, fax (171)873-2415, website: http://www.kcl.ac.uk/mpt/, founded 1965 (original series), 1992 (new series), advisory and managing editor Professor Norma Rinsler, editor Daniel Weissbort.

Magazine Needs: *MPT*, published biannually, features "translations of poems from any language into English, and essays on translation (practice rather than theory). Our aim is to further international cultural understanding and exchange and to awaken interest in poetry." They want "only translations from any language into English—'modern' refers to translation (which should be unpublished), not to original." They do not want "self-translation by those not familiar with English; work by translators who are not poets or not familiar with a range of works in the original language rarely succeed (unless they work with original authors)." *MPT* averages 240 pgs., 5⅝ × 8½, offset printed, perfect-bound with illustrated 2-color cover on scanchip board, matte laminated. Accept approximately 50% of the poems they receive. Press run is 500 for 350 subscribers of which 50% are libraries, 50 shelf sales. Single copy: £10 (UK/EU); £12 (foreign). Subscriptions (2 issues): £20 (UK/EU); £24 (foreign), inc. surface mail (airmail extra). Sample: £7.50. Make checks payable to King's College London (*MPT*).

How to Submit: Submit 5-6 poems at a time "unless very long, in which case 1 or 2". Disk submissions (in Word) preferred. Originals should accompany translation. No previously published poems or simultaneous submissions. Cover letter required. No fax submissions. Time between acceptance and publication is 3-9 months. The editor and managing/advisory editor discuss submissions and consult individual members of advisory board if expertise required. Often comments on rejections. Publishes theme issues. Send SASE (or SAE and IRC) for upcoming themes. Reports "as soon as possible—within weeks." Sometimes sends prepublication galleys. Pays £12/poem or £15/page plus 1 copy to translator, 1 for original author. "Copyright on selection as printed—general rights remain with contributors." Features reviews of poetry books often commissioned from experts in the field. Poets may also send books for review consideration (translations only).

⬤ MOJO RISIN' MAGAZINE; JOSH SAMUELS BIANNUAL POETRY COMPETITION, P.O. Box 268451, Chicago IL 60626-8451, founded 1995, editor Ms. Josh Samuels.

Magazine Needs: *mojo risin'* published quarterly, features "poetry, prose, short stories and some sort of contest in each issue." She wants "any form or style." She does not want "incest, racism, blatant sex or anything written for shock value." She has published poetry by Alan Catlin, normal and Albert Huffstickler. As a sample the editor selected these lines from "Hustler" by B.Z. Niditch:

> your tongue/is ready/you jump/into the car/it's 2 AM/your legs/bend backwards

mojo risin' is 32 pgs., 8½ × 11, photocopied, saddle-stapled or spiraled, with colored paper cover and b&w artwork. She receives about 300 poems a year, accepts ⅓. Press run is 300 for 200 subscribers. Subscription: $20. Sample: $7.

How to Submit: Subscription not required for acceptance. Submit 3-5 poems (2 pages maximum) at a time. No previously published poems or simultaneous submissions. Cover letter preferred. Time between acceptance and publication is 1-3 months. The editor is solely responsible for all aspects of editing and publishing. Send SASE for guidelines. Reports within 10 days. Acquires first North American serial rights.

Also Offers: Sponsors the Josh Samuels Biannual Poetry Competition. 1st Place: $100; 2nd Place: $75; 3rd Place $50. Entry fee: $10/5 poems maximum. Any form, style or subject. No previously published poems or simultaneous submissions. Mss not returned. Deadlines: May 31 and November 30. Submissions read March through May and September through November only. Winners published and paid in February and August. Send SASE for guidelines.

Ⓝ ⬤ ◯ MONAS HIEROGLYPHICA, 58 Seymour Rd., Hadleigh, Benfleet, Essex SS7 2HL United Kingdom, founded 1994, contact Mr. Jamie Spracklen.

Magazine Needs: *MH* appears quarterly and "supports the Gothic music movement, but aims to provide an eclectic mix of material." For their poetry needs they say, "Send for sample copy and see." No racist or sexist work. They have published poetry by Sean Russell Friend and Steve Sneyd. As a sample Mr. Spracklen selected this poem, "The Passing of Life & Death," by S.R. Friend:

> Come, join the game of death;/My sweet black butterfly:/There is only cloud where/The fire should be,
> sun where/We should love the moon.

The editor says *MH* is 30 pgs., magazine-sized, photocopied and stapled with paper cover, includes art/graphics

and ads. They receive about 100 poems a year, accept approximately 25%. Press run is 100 for 50 subscribers. Single copy: $3; subscription: $12. Sample: $2. Make checks payable to Jamie Spracklen.
How to Submit: Submit 3 poems at a time. Line length for poetry is 60 maximum. No previously published poems; simultaneous submissions OK. Cover letter required. "Poems must be typed on size A4 paper and in English." Time between acceptance and publication is 3 months. Seldom comments on rejections. Publishes theme issues occasionally. Send SASE for guidelines and upcoming themes. Reports in 2 weeks. Pays 1 copy. "Rights stay with author." Reviews books and chapbooks of poetry and other magazines in 20 words, multi-book format. Open to unsolicited reviews. Poets may also send books for review consideration.

N **□** **Ø** **MONKEY FLOWER: SANTIAGO CANYON COLLEGE REVIEW**, % Will Lennertz, 8045 E. Chapman Ave., Orange CA 92669-4512, phone (714)564-4781, e-mail themonkeyflower@hotmail.com, website http://www.members.tripod.com/monkeyflower, founded 1999, faculty advisor Will Lennertz.
Magazine Needs: *Monkey Flower* is a "biannual online literary magazine dedicated to publishing the best literature and art we can." They are open in form and subject matter. "Our desire is to publish quality poetry, fiction and art. No doggerel or greeting card verse." They receive about 1,500 poems a year, accept approximately 7-10%.
How to Submit: Submit 3-5 poems at a time. No previously published poems or simultaneous submissions. Cover letter preferred. E-mail submissions OK. "Cut and paste poems, fiction and nonfiction into e-mail submissions." Reads submissions August through December and February through May. Time between acceptance and publication is 2 months. Poems are circulated to an editorial board. "Collectively editors reach the decision to publish poetry, fiction, nonfiction and art." Seldom comments on rejections. Obtain guidelines via e-mail or website. Reports in 2 months. Acquires first North American serial rights. Staff reviews books and chapbooks of poetry and other magazines in 300-500 words, single or multi-book format. Send books for review consideration.
Also Offers: Website includes poetry, guidelines, fiction, nonfiction and art.
Advice: Mr. Lennertz says, "We are open to a great variety of poetry. Try us."

N **ϒ** **◎** **Ø** **(m)ÖTHÊR TØÑGUÉ PRESS (Specialized: regional)**, 290 Fulford-Ganges Rd., Salt Spring Island, British Columbia V8K 2K6 Canada, founded 1990, editor/publisher Mona Fertig.
Book/Chapbook Needs: "Private literary press. Specializing in beautiful chapbooks of poetry and prose, broadsides and book art. Limited and signed editions. Large letterpress printing studio. Custom die-cuts, lino cuts, debossing. Catalog available."
How to Submit: No unsolicited mss.

Ø **MOUNT OLIVE COLLEGE PRESS; MOUNT OLIVE REVIEW; LEE WITTE POETRY CONTEST**, 634 Henderson St., Mount Olive NC 28365, phone (919)658-2502, founded 1987 (*Mount Olive Review*), 1990 (Mount Olive College Press), editor Dr. Pepper Worthington.
Magazine Needs: *Mount Olive Review*, features "literary criticism, poetry, short stories, essays and book reviews." They want "modern poetry." The editor says *Mount Olive Review* is 7½×10. They receive about 2,000 poems a year, accept approximately 8%. Press run is 1,000. Single copy: $25. Make checks payable to Mount Olive College Press.
How to Submit: Submit 6 poems at a time. No previously published poems or simultaneous submissions. Cover letter preferred. Time between acceptance and publication varies. Poems are circulated to an editorial board. Seldom comments on rejections. Publishes theme issues. Send SASE for guidelines and upcoming themes. Reports in 3 months. Sometimes sends prepublication galleys. Acquires first rights. Reviews books and chapbooks of poetry and other magazines. Open to unsolicited reviews. Poets may also send books for review consideration.
Book/Chapbook Needs & How to Submit: Mount Olive Press publishes 2 books/year and sponsors the Lee Witte Poetry Contest. Write to above address for guidelines. Books are usually 5½×8. Submit 12 sample poems. Replies to queries and mss in 3 months. Obtain sample books by writing to the above address.

Ø **MOVING PARTS PRESS**, 10699 Empire Grade, Santa Cruz CA 95060-9474, phone (408)427-2271, fax (408)458-2810, e-mail frice@movingparts.com, website http://www.movingparts.com, founded 1977, poetry editor Felicia Rice. They do not accept unsolicited mss.

$ **◎** **MURDEROUS INTENT (Specialized: mystery)**, Madison Publishing Company, P.O. Box 5947, Vancouver WA 98668-5947, phone (360)695-9004, e-mail madison@teleport.com, website http://www.murderousintent.com, founded 1994, editor Margo Power.
Magazine Needs: *MI* is a quarterly magazine of mystery and suspense using mystery-related poetry, limericks and such as fillers. The editor says all poetry (including humorous verse) must be mystery-related and must easily entertain. They do not want poetry with "deep, convoluted meaning" and the shorter the work, the better. "Four-liners are always good though we occasionally buy a longer, ballad-type poem—always mystery-related." The editor says *Murderous Intent* is 64 pgs., 8½×11, saddle-stapled, with 2-color cover and b&w interior including art, graphics and ads. Press run is 5,500, 85% shelf sales. Single copy: $5.95; subscription: $20. Sample: $7.19. Make checks payable to Madison Publishing Company.

How to Submit: Submit 6-10 poems at a time. No previously published poems or simultaneous submissions. E-mail submissions only; no fax or snail mail submissions. Send poetry in body of e-mail message. Occasionally comments on rejections. Pays $2. Buys first or one-time rights.

 **MUSE JOURNAL; THE ANNUAL LOVE POEM AWARD**, 226 Lisgar St., Toronto, Ontario M6J 3G7 Canada, e-mail love@musejournal.com, website http://www.musejournal.com, founded 1990, editor-in-chief Manny Goncalves.

Magazine Needs: *Muse Journal* is "a quarterly online literary magazine of the arts." They have published poetry by Linda Stitt, Giovanni Malito, Ronnie Brown and Joe Blades. They receive about 1,500 poems a year, accept approximately 10%.

How to Submit: Submit 3 poems at a time. Line length for poetry is 60 maximum. No previously published poems or simultaneous submissions. E-mail submissions OK. Cover letter preferred. "Poets may only submit online (not by mail)." Time between acceptance and publication is 1 month. Poems are circulated to an editorial board. "Poems are read by at least two editors." Seldom comments on rejections. Charges a criticism fee, "if criticism is requested." Publishes theme issues occasionally. Obtain guidelines via website. Reports in 2 months. Acquires one-time rights. Reviews books of poetry. Open to unsolicited reviews. Poets may also send books for review consideration.

Also Offers: Website includes all "pertinent" information, including information about The Annual Love Poem Award.

MUSE OF FIRE, 21 Kruse Rd., Port Angeles WA 98362-8900, founded 1994, editor/publisher Tim Scannell.

Magazine Needs: *Muse Of Fire* appears at least 15 times/year "when the editor receives a score of worthy poems." "All forms welcome: lyric, fixed, narrative, etc. No taboos. Craftsmanship is the only requirement." As a sample the editor chose this poem "JJ" (poet unidentified):

> *Bless you, John James Audubon/in those lean years keeping on/with the rainbow of your brush/of feathered worlds—miraculous.*

Muse Of Fire is 6 pgs., 8½×11, unbound with b&w clip art. Press run is 50. Sample available for $1 and #10 SASE.

How to Submit: Previously published poems and simultaneous submissions OK. Cover letter required. Sometimes comments on rejections. Reports in 1 week. Pays 1 copy. Acquires one-time rights.

Advice: The editor says, "There are nine musae and so nine grand areas for poetry. Write in all nine areas, in every traditional and untraditional form! Remember, words become a poem only after 8 to 12 revisions."

MUSE PORTFOLIO, 419 Southwick Rd., Q72, Westfield MA 01085-4800, founded 1992, editor Joe Balgassi.

Magazine Needs: Appearing annually in February, *Muse Portfolio* is a "casual magazine for sincere, eloquent, earnest writers who crave forum to share work with others." They want poetry of "any structure, formal or free, 15 lines maximum. Poetry with writing themes welcome. No forced rhymes, nothing profane. We also publish short stories. They have published poetry by Shirley Alger, Charles Pierre and Jill Hammer. As a sample the editor selected these lines from "Life" by Rachel Squires:

> *Mom's hair has been grey/for at least ten years/She's not old, but her/hands are papery.*

Muse Portfolio is 40 pgs., 5½×8½, saddle-stapled, printed on 20 lb. paper with heavier stock cover, b&w artwork, occasional ads. They receive about 500 poems a year, accept approximately 2%. Press run is 150 for 100 subscribers. Subscription: $5. Sample: $3.

How to Submit: Submit up to 3 poems at a time. "Submit only in odd-numbered months." Previously published poems and simultaneous submissions OK. Cover letter required. "Include a biographical paragraph—need not list published credits if author prefers to write something else." Seldom comments on rejections. Reports in 3-6 months. Pays 1 copy. Acquires one-time rights.

Advice: The editor says, "Please remember to include a SASE with submissions."

MUSE'S KISS WEBZINE, P.O. Box 703, Attn: L.S. Bush, Lenoir NC 28645, e-mail museskiss@aol.com, website http://members.aol.com/museskiss, founded 1998, publisher L.S. Bush, editor Alex Reeves.

Magazine Needs: "*Muse's Kiss* is a free webzine by writers and poets for writers and poets. It contains experimental and traditional poetry and short stories. We will consider general fiction, science fiction, historical

---

**FOR EXPLANATIONS OF THESE SYMBOLS,
SEE THE INSIDE FRONT AND BACK COVERS OF THIS BOOK.**

fiction, and mystery for short stories and anything except erotica for poetry. Please do not send nonfiction, religious, romance, gay/lesbian, children's stories or anything explicit. We're interested in printing new and beginning writers and poets. *Muse's Kiss* will publish as much or as little on a regular basis depending on the number of submissions we receive." They have published poetry by William C. Burns, Jr., Chuck Pool and Brett Auten. As a sample the editor selected these lines from "The Airplane" by Lauran Tyler:

> *Overhead compartments are for storing stuff: bags, books and unwanted loves./Stand back—don't get too close, in case the compartments erupt into smoke./Wheels rattle as they move along carpeted hallways—/bringing with them decadent delights of freeze-dried food, peanuts and liquids laden with ice.*

They receive about 150 poems a year, accept approximately 50%. Sample: $3 (for offline version). Make checks payable to L.S. Bush.

How to Submit: Submit 3 poems at a time via e-mail. Line length for poetry is 18 minimum, 30 maximum. No previously published poems or simultaneous submissions. Cover letter with brief bio and publishing credits preferred. "Poems must be typed in body of e-mail—no attachments. If you prefer, you may submit offline by sending your poems and a cover letter. If you submit offline, there is a reading fee of $2 for up to 3 poems. Please e-mail museskiss@aol.com for offline submission details." Time between acceptance and publication is 3 months. Obtain guidelines via website. Reports in 3 months. Acquires one-time rights. Staff reviews books and chapbooks of poetry and other magazines in 100 words, multi-book format. Send books for review consideration to L.S. Bush.

Also Offers: Sponsors annual poetry contests. 1st Prize: $10 plus publication. 2nd Prize: $5 plus publication. Entry fee: $5 for up to 5 poems. Deadline: January 1. Winners announced in March. Note: Contest entries only accepted by regular mail. Website includes monthly issues, submission guidelines, subscription and advertising information.

Advice: "*Muse's Kiss* is devoted to publishing all types of poetry and short stories except we do not print explicit material. We wish to help new writers and poets get a start and to see their work online in print. There is no charge for anyone to view our webzine issues. There is no charge to writers or poets for publication. So send your friends, family, etc. to our webzine to see your work!"

THE MUSING PLACE (Specialized: poets with a history of mental illness), 2700 N. Lakeview, Chicago IL 60614, phone (773)281-3800 ext. 2470, fax (773)281-8790, e-mail lkrinsky@thn.thresholds.org, founded 1986, editor Heidi Kronenberg.

Magazine Needs: *The Musing Place* is an annual magazine "written and published by people with a history of mental illness. All kinds and forms of poetry are welcome." The editor says *TMP* is 32 pgs., 8½ × 11, typeset and stapled with art also produced by people with a history of mental illness. They receive about 300 poems/year, publish about 40. Press run is 1,000. Single copy: $3.

How to Submit: No previously published poems; simultaneous submissions OK. Cover letter required. "Poets must prove and explain their history of mental illness." Fax submissions OK. Time between acceptance and publication is 6-12 months. "The board reviews submissions and chooses those that fit into each issue." Seldom comments on rejections. Reports within 6 months. Pays 1 copy (additional copies at a discount).

$ MYSTERY TIME (Specialized: mystery, humor); RHYME TIME (Specialized: subscribers); SPRING FANTASY; WOMEN IN THE ARTS; WOMEN IN THE ARTS SPRING FANTASY CONTEST, P.O. Box 2907, Decatur IL 62524, fax (217)763-3311, e-mail jagusch@novanet1.com, *Mystery Time* and *Rhyme Time* founded 1983, *Spring Fantasy* and Women in the Arts founded 1994, poetry editor and vice president Linda Hutton.

Magazine Needs & How to Submit: *Mystery Time* is a semiannual containing 3-4 pages of humorous poems about mysteries and mystery writers in each issue. As a sample the editor selected the poem "Kernel of Truth" by Linda Bosson:

> *Twelve ears of corn/Were found terribly torn./"It would seem," said Inspector Miller,/"He who did these deeds/Had a grudge against seeds/And turned into a cereal killer."*

Mystery Time is 44 pgs., digest-sized, stapled with heavy stock cover. They receive up to 15 submissions a year, use approximately 4-6. Circulation is 100. Sample: $4. Submit 3 poems at a time, up to 16 lines, "typed in proper format with SASE." Previously published poems OK. No fax or e-mail submissions. Does not read mss in December. Guidelines available for #10 SASE. Pays $5 on acceptance.

Magazine Needs & How to Submit: *Rhyme Time*, is a quarterly newsletter publishing only the work of subscribers. No length limit or style restriction. Subscription: $24. Sample: $4. Cash prize of $10 awarded to the best poem in each issue. No fax or e-mail submissions.

Magazine Needs: *Spring Fantasy* is "an annual collection of artwork, poetry, fiction, personal essays and photography on any theme appearing in May." They are open to all types of poetry ("except shaped"), up to 100 lines. They have published poetry by Betty Lou Hebert, Vera Koppler, Marian Ford Park and Diane L. Schirf. As a sample they selected these lines from "The Secret Sky" by Evelynn Merilatt Boal:

> *That secret overhead, which we call sky;/the vast infinity of stellar space,/extends beyond the search of human eye.*

Spring Fantasy is about 60 pgs., photocopied and spiral-comb bound. They receive 25-30 poems a year, accept approximately 50%. Press run is 100. Sample: $6. Make checks payable to Women In the Arts.

"We selected this cover by Karen Olsen Murley, a professional free-lance graphic artist, because it typifies our image—a pleasant, relaxing reading session with no worries to intrude," says *Mystery Time* editor Linda Hutton. "Also, we tend to concentrate on women protagonists, and I wanted a woman on the cover." *Mystery Time* features half a dozen poems on the topic of mystery writers or suspenseful themes. Hutton says, "And while we do use poems as occasional page-fillers, other poems have an entire page to themselves." *Mystery Time*, published in Decatur, Illinois, is 44 pages, digest-sized and stapled with heavy stock cover.

How to Submit: Submit 4 poems at a time with SASE. Previously published poems and simultaneous submissions OK. No fax or e-mail submissions. Do not submit mss in December. Time between acceptance and publication is 3-4 months. "A committee of Women In the Arts members chooses poems for publication." Often comments on rejections. Send SASE for guidelines. Reports in 1-2 months. Pays 1 copy plus 20% discount on additional copies. Acquires one-time rights.

Also Offers: Sponsors an annual poetry contest that awards a $25 cash prize for the best poem in any style or length. Submit typed poem with SASE. No entry fee; one entry/person. Deadline: November 1. Sponsors annual Women in the Arts Spring Fantasy Contest. 1st Prize: $30; 2nd Prize: $25; and 3rd Prize: $15. Submit up to 5 poems, up to 32 lines each, on any topic, in any form, no name or address on entry, include cover sheet. Entry fee: $2/poem. Make checks payable to Women in the Arts. Deadline: November 15. Send SASE for guidelines. "WITA is a group of 60 women who share and encourage creative ideas through art, literature, music, crafts, dance, photography, etc. Most of our members live in Illinois; those out-of-state send their work for critique by pen-palling. Follow the rules carefully; half the entries are disqualified for some infraction."

Advice: They say, "Always send for guidelines before submitting."

✓ ◐ ◎ **THE MYTHIC CIRCLE; THE MYTHOPOEIC SOCIETY (Specialized: fantasy)**, 54322 US Hwy. 275, Glenwood IA 51534, e-mail mythiccircle@hotmail.com, website http://home.earthlink.net/mythsoc/mythcir.html, editor Gwenyth Hood and co-editor Trent Walters.

Magazine Needs: *The Mythic Circle* is a "writer's workshop in print," appearing 2-3 times a year, publishing fantasy short stories and poems. They want "poetry that's mythopoeic, interpreted as broadly as possible—whether traditional, modern, or fairy tale—anything with the mark of new." They have published poetry by Angelee Anderson. They receive 100 poetry submissions/year, accept 10%. Press run is 230 for 200 subscribers. Subscription: $18/year for non-members; $13/year for members. Sample: $6.50.

How to Submit: No previously published poems or simultaneous submissions. E-mail submissions OK. Time between acceptance and publication is 6-12 months. Seldom comments on rejections. Send SASE for guidelines. Reports in 2-4 months. Pays 1 copy for 3 poems.

Advice: The editor says, "Subscribers are heavily favored, since they provide the critical review which our authors need in their letters of comment. Avoid archaic use of English. Poetry requires the current language but ideas as old as humankind. Put rhyme and meter in consistent patterns or break them for a reason. Read the poem aloud: is it pleasing? Subtlety and understatement are a poet's most powerful tools. Shock has lost its shock."

◐ ◎ **NADA PRESS; BIG SCREAM (Specialized: form/style)**, 2782 Dixie SW, Grandville MI 49418, phone (616)531-1442, founded 1974, poetry editor David Cope.

Magazine Needs: *Big Scream* appears annually and is "a brief anthology of mostly 'unknown' poets. We are promoting a continuation of objectivist tradition begun by Williams and Reznikoff. We want objectivist-based short works; some surrealism; basically short, tight work that shows clarity of perception and care in its making." They have published poetry by Antler, Richard Kostelanetz, Andy Clausen, Allen Ginsberg, John Steinbeck, Jr., Jim Cohn and Marcia Arrieta. *Big Scream* is 35 pgs., magazine-sized, xerograph on 60 lb. paper, side-stapled, "sent gratis to a select group of poets and editors." They receive "several hundred (not sure)" unsolicited submissions a year, use "very few." Press run is 100. Subscription to institutions: $6/year. Sample: $6.

How to Submit: Submit after July. Send 10 pgs. No cover letter. "If poetry interests me, I will ask the proper questions of the poet." Simultaneous submissions OK. Comments on rejections "if requested and ms warrants it." Reports in 1-14 days. Sometimes sends prepublication galleys. Pays as many copies as requested, within reason.

Advice: The editor says: "Read Pound's essay, 'A Retrospect,' then Reznikoff and Williams; follow through the Beats and NY School, especially Denby & Berrigan, and you have our approach to writing well in hand. I expect to be publishing *Big Scream* regularly ten years from now, same basic format."

○ ◐ NANNY FANNY; FELICITY PRESS, 2524 Stockbridge Dr. #15, Indianapolis IN 46268-2670, e-mail nightpoet@prodigy.net, founded 1998, editor Lou Hertz, assistant editor Alex DeBonis.

Magazine Needs: *Nanny Fanny* appears 3 times/year and "publishes poetry accessible by the common person, but of high quality. Some artwork wanted (b&w line art); may expand to include commentary, reviews and contests." They want "external, extroverted observations and character studies. Happy or sad, rhyme or not, okay. Formal poetry discouraged. Prefer 30 lines or less. No internalized, self-pitying poetry. Nothing under 8 lines or over 30 unless exceptional. No pornography, extremes of violence or language. No political poems." They have published poetry by Errol Miller, Ella J. Cuancara and John Grey. As a sample the editor selected these lines from "She Is Like Jazz" by Gary Jurechka:

> She is like jazz/with playful rhythms &/sensual saxophone sighs,/a deep bass heart beat &/love
> overflowing dreamy eyes/she is like jazz

The editor says *NF* is 32 pgs., 5½×8½, laser-printed and side-stapled with colored 67 lb. cover, includes cover art and some b&w line drawings inside. They receive about 500 poems a year, accept approximately 15%. Press run is 100 for 25 subscribers; 40 distributed free to contributors, etc. Subscription: $9/3 issues. Sample: $3.50. Make checks payable to Lou Hertz.

How to Submit: Submit 3-8 poems at a time, 1 poem/page with name and address on each. Previously published poems OK; no simultaneous submissions. No e-mail submissions. Cover letter with brief bio preferred. Disk submissions OK. Time between acceptance and publication is 1-6 months. Sometimes comments on rejections. Publishes theme issues occasionally. Send SASE or e-mail for guidelines. Reports in 2-8 weeks. Sends prepublication galleys on request. Pays 1 copy, more at a discount. Acquires one-time rights.

Book/Chapbook Needs: Felicity Press is not currently open for submissions.

Advice: The editor says, "I want good quality poetry that the average person will be able to understand and enjoy. Let's use poetic imagery to draw them in, not scare them away."

◖ NASSAU REVIEW, English Dept., Nassau Community College, Garden City NY 11530-6793, phone (516)572-7792, founded 1964, managing editor Dr. Paul A. Doyle.

Magazine Needs: *Nassau Review* is an annual "creative and research vehicle for Nassau College faculty and the faculty of other colleges." They want "serious, intellectual poetry of any form or style. No light verse or satiric verse." Submissions from adults only. "No college students; graduate students acceptable. Want only poems of high quality." They have published poetry by Patti Tana, Dick Allen, Louis Phillips, David Heyen and Simon Perchik. *NR* is about 190 pgs., digest-sized, flat-spined. They receive over 1,500 poems a year, use approximately 20-25. Press run is 1,200 for about 1,200 subscribers of which 300 are libraries. Sample free.

How to Submit: Submit only 3 poems per yearly issue. No previously published poems or simultaneous submissions. Reads submissions November 1 through March 1 only. Reports in 3-8 months. Pays copies.

Also Offers: They sponsor occasional contests with $200 poetry award. Deadline: March 31.

Advice: The editor says, "Each year we are more and more overwhelmed by the number of poems submitted, but most are of an amateur quality."

$ ◖ THE NATION; "DISCOVERY"/THE NATION POETRY CONTEST, 72 Fifth Ave., New York NY 10011, founded 1865, poetry editor Grace Schulman.

Magazine Needs & How to Submit: *The Nation*'s only requirement for poetry is "excellence," which can be inferred from the list of poets they have published: Marianne Moore, Robert Lowell, W.S. Merwin, Maxine Kumin, Donald Justice, James Merrill, Richard Howard, May Swenson, Amy Clampitt, Edward Hirsch and Charles Simic. Pays $1/line, not to exceed 35 lines, plus 1 copy.

Also Offers: The magazine co-sponsors the Lenore Marshall Prize for Poetry which is an annual award of $10,000 for an outstanding book of poems published in the US in each year. For details, write to the Academy of American Poets, 584 Broadway, #1208, New York NY 10012. They also co-sponsor the "Discovery"/*The Nation* Poetry Contest ($200 each plus a reading at The Poetry Center, 1395 Lexington Ave., New York NY 10128. Deadline: mid-February. Send SASE for application).

$ ◐ ◎ NATIONAL ENQUIRER (Specialized: humor), Lantana FL 33464, filler editor Kathy Martin.

Magazine Needs: *NE* is a weekly tabloid which uses short poems, most of them humorous and traditional rhyming verse. "We want poetry with a message or reflection on the human condition or everyday life. Avoid sending obscure or 'arty' poetry or poetry for art's sake. Also looking for philosophical and inspirational material. Submit seasonal/holiday material at least three months in advance. No poetry over eight lines will be accepted."

How to Submit: Submit up to 5 poems at a time. Requires cover letter from first-time submitters; include name, address, social security and phone numbers. "Do not send SASE; filler material will not be returned." Pays $25 after publication; original material only. Buys first rights.

◐ NATIONAL FORUM: THE PHI KAPPA PHI JOURNAL, 129 Quad Center, Mell St., Auburn University, Auburn AL 36849-5306, phone (334)844-5200, e-mail kaetzjp@mail.auburn.edu, website http://www.auburn.edu/academic/societies/phi_kappa_phi/natforum.html, founded 1915, editor James P. Kaetz.

Magazine Needs: *National Forum* is the quarterly publication of Phi Kappa Phi using quality poetry. *NF* is 48 pgs., magazine-sized, professionally printed, saddle-stapled, with full-color paper cover and two-color interior. They receive about 300 poems a year, accept approximately 20. Press run is 120,000 for 117,000 subscribers of which 300 are libraries. Subscription: $25.

How to Submit: Submit 3-5 short (one page) poems at a time, including a biographical sketch with recent publications. E-mail submissions OK. Reads submissions approximately every 3 months. Reports in about 4 months. Pays 10 copies.

ℕ ◯ ◎ NATIVE TONGUE; NATIVE TONGUE PRESS (Specialized: ethnic), P.O. Box 822, Eufaula AL 36072-0822, phone (334)616-7722, founded 1998, submissions editor Anthony Canada.

Magazine Needs: *Native Tongue* is published bimonthly "to keep the voices and history of the black poet historic, and expand an audience for new black poets." They want poetry "on or about the African-American experience. Open to all forms, subject matter, styles or purpose. Interested in poems which emphasize but are not limited to cultural issues, the exploration of self-esteem and personal empowerment, and the exploration of the direction of African-American people. No submissions that do not deal with the African-American experience." As a sample the editor selected these lines from his poem "society's child":

> late nite lust on rooftops/society's child conceived/bewildered, beleagured/black bastard/preteen
> mother's screams/social service slaves/sing the welfare blues

NT is 1-4 pgs., 8½×11 sheets, 3-column format, stapled. They receive about 150 poems a year, accept approximately 85%. Press run is 200 for 55 subscribers, 45 shelf sales; 100 distributed free to the public, colleges, poetry groups. Subscription: $9. Sample: $2. Make checks payable to Anthony G. Canada.

How to Submit: Submit up to 5 poems at a time. Previously published poems and simultaneous submissions OK. Cover letter required. "In cover letter include basic poet information—name, address, occupation, experience, previous publishings, books, etc." SASE required for return of submitted poems. Time between acceptance and publication is 2 months. Poems are circulated to an editorial board. "Submissions reviewed by board; published pieces selected by committee." Often comments on rejections. Reports in 2 months. Pays 10 copies. Acquires one-time rights. Reviews books and chapbooks of poetry in 200 words, single book format. Open to unsolicited reviews. Poets may also send books for review consideration.

Advice: The editor says, "The aim and goal of this newsletter is to open up to a wider audience the poetic voices of our many talented brothers and sisters. The African-American community has always had a historic and rich poetic legacy. We at *Native Tongue* wish to continue and expand upon this great tradition of African-American poets. So brothers and sisters take pen to paper, and continue to make our history historic. Let your voices by heard!"

$◎ NATURALLY: NUDE RECREATION FOR ALL AGES; EVENTS UNLIMITED PUBLISHING CO. (Specialized), P.O. Box 317, Newfoundland NJ 07435-0317, phone (973)697-3552, fax (973)697-8313, e-mail naturally@nac.net, website http://www.internaturally.com, founded 1981, editor/publisher Bern Loibl.

Magazine Needs: *Naturally* is a quarterly magazine devoted to family nudism and naturism. They want poetry about the naturalness of the human body and nature, any length. As a sample the editor selected these lines from "On a Woman who is Busy Deliberating her Liberation" by Wolfgang Somary:

> I bet: you wouldn't dare yet/to walk bare in the wet/glare of the moon/or just for fun/under the sun/in
> the nudeness of noon—

Naturally is 60 pgs., 8½×11, printed on glossy paper and saddle-stitched with full-color photos throughout. They receive about 30 poems a year, use 5-10. Press run is 16,000 for 6,500 subscribers, 8,500 shelf sales. Single copy: $6.50; subscription: $21.95. Sample: $9.

How to Submit: Previously published poems and simultaneous submissions OK. E-mail and fax submissions OK. "Name and address must be submitted with e-mail." Often comments on rejections. Send SASE for guidelines or obtain via e-mail. Reports in 2 months. Pays $20 and 1 copy. Buys first North American serial or one-time rights.

Book/Chapbook Needs & How to Submit: Events Unlimited Publishing Co. is planning a poetry/photography book. Poems must have a natural/nudism theme. Write for more information.

$◎ NAZARENE INTERNATIONAL HEADQUARTERS; STANDARD; LISTEN; HOLINESS TODAY (Specialized: religious, children), 6401 The Paseo, Kansas City MO 64131, phone (816)333-7000.

Magazine Needs & How to Submit: Each of the magazines published by the Nazarenes has a separate editor, focus and audience. *Standard*, circulation 177,000, is a weekly inspirational "story paper" with Christian leisure reading for adults. Send SASE for free sample and guidelines. Uses 2 poems each week. Submit maximum of 5 poems, no more than 50 lines each. Pays 25¢ a line. For *Listen* and *Holiness Today*, write individually for guidelines and samples.

⬤ **NEBO: A LITERARY JOURNAL**, English Dept., Arkansas Tech University, Russellville AR 72801-2222, phone (501)968-0256, website http://www.atu.edu/acad/schools/lfa/english/nebo.html, founded 1982, poetry editor Michael Ritchie.

Magazine Needs: *Nebo* appears in May and December. Regarding poetry they say, "We accept all kinds, all styles, all subject matters and will publish a longer poem if it is outstanding. We are especially interested in formal poetry." They have published poetry by Jack Butler, Turner Cassity, Wyatt Prunty, Charles Martin, Julia Randall and Brenda Hillman. *Nebo* is 50-70 pgs., digest-sized, professionally printed on quality matte stock with matte card cover. Press run "varies." Sample: $6.

How to Submit: Submit 3-5 poems at a time. Simultaneous submissions OK. "Please no offbeat colors." Cover letter with bio material and recent publications required. Do not submit mss between May 1 and August 15. Editor comments on rejections "if the work has merit but requires revision and resubmission; we do all we can to help." Reports at the end of November and February respectively. Pays 1 copy. Staff reviews books of poetry. Send books for review consideration.

✓ ⬤ **THE NEBRASKA REVIEW; TNR AWARDS**, Creative Writing Program, FA, University of Nebraska, Omaha NE 68182-0324, phone (402)554-3159, fax (402)554-3436, founded 1973, fiction and managing editor James Reed, poetry editor Susan Aizenberg.

Magazine Needs: *The Nebraska Review* is a semiannual literary magazine publishing fiction and poetry with occasional essays. The editors want "lyric poetry from 10-200 lines, preference being for under 100 lines. Subject matter is unimportant, as long as it has some. Poets should have mastered form, meaning poems should have form, not simply 'demonstrate' it." They don't want to see "concrete, inspirational, didactic or merely political poetry." They have published poetry by Erin Belieu, Michael Bugeja, Stuart Dybek and Carl Phillips. As a sample the editors selected these lines from "Crickets" by Pamela Stewart:

> In every small place the eye, toe, or caught breath turns,/crickets are singing. From that shin/just
> above the ground they fling an edge of sound/straight through what's left of wilderness./It swings out
> across the trees and yards,/up to the warm sills of September.

The magazine is 60 pgs., 6×9, nicely printed and flat-spined with glossy card cover. It is a publication of the Writer's Workshop at the University of Nebraska. Press run is 500 for 380 subscribers of which 85 are libraries. Single copy: $6; subscription: $11/year. Sample: $3.50.

How to Submit: Submit 4-6 poems at a time. "Clean typed copy strongly preferred." Reads open submissions January 1 through April 15 only. Reports in 3-4 months. Time between acceptance and publication is 3-12 months. Pays 2 copies and 1-year subscription. Acquires first North American serial rights.

Also Offers: Submissions for The Nebraska Review Awards are read from September 1 through November 30 only. The TNR Awards of $500 each in poetry and fiction are published in the spring issue. Entry fee: $9, includes discounted subscription. You can enter as many times as desired. Deadline: November 30.

Advice: The editor says, "Your first allegiance is to the poem. Publishing will come in time, but it will always be less than you feel you deserve. Therefore, don't look to publication as a reward for writing well; it has no relationship."

⬤ **NEDGE**, P.O. Box 2321, Providence RI 02906, website http://wings.buffalo.edu/epc/mags/nedge, founded 1994, co-editors Henry Gould and Janet Sullivan.

Magazine Needs: *Nedge* is a biannual published by The Poetry Mission, a nonprofit arts organization. It includes poetry, fiction, reviews and essays. They want work that "exhibits originality, talent, sincerity, skill and inspiration." The purpose of *Nedge* is "to aim toward a Rhode Island literary standard, both local and international in scope." Circulation is 300. Subscription: $12/2 issues. Sample: $6.

How to Submit: No simultaneous submissions. SASE required. Reports in 2-3 months. Pays 1 copy.

⬤ **NEGATIVE CAPABILITY; NEGATIVE CAPABILITY PRESS; EVE OF ST. AGNES COMPETITION**, 62 Ridgelawn Dr. E., Mobile AL 36608-2465, fax (334)344-8478, e-mail negcap@datasync.com, founded 1981, poetry editor Sue Walker.

Magazine Needs: *Negative Capability* is a biannual of verse, fiction, commentary, music and art. They want both contemporary and traditional poetry. "Quality has its own specifications—length and form." They have published poetry by John Brugaletta, Marge Piercy, John Updike, Pat Schneider, Vivian Shipley and Diana Der Hovanessian. As a sample Sue Walker selected these lines from "Don't Look At The Moon" by Pat Schneider:

> You talk to your daughter//You listen./You can hear the green plant growing/in the sunlight in her
> window.//She is packing her bags to go./All that you know is not enough.

The editor says, "Reaching irritably after a few facts will not describe *Negative Capability*. Read it to know what quality goes to form creative achievement. Shakespeare had negative capability, do you?" This journal has indeed achieved a major prominence on our literary scene. It is an elegantly printed, flat-spined, digest-sized format of 200 pgs., glossy card color cover with art, circulation 1,000. About 60 pgs. of each issue are devoted to poetry. They receive about 1,200 unsolicited submissions a year, use approximately 350. Single copy: $5; subscription: $15. Sample: $5.

How to Submit: Submit 3-5 poems at a time. Fax and e-mail submissions OK. Reads submissions September 1 through May 30 only. Send SASE for guidelines and upcoming themes. Reports in 6-8 weeks. Pays 1 copy. Acquires first rights. Reviews books of poetry.

Book/Chapbook Needs & How to Submit: Negative Capability Press publishes broadsides, chapbooks, perfect-bound paperbacks and hardbacks. Recent titles include *Little Dragons*, by Michael Bugeja and *The Mouse Whole*, by Richard Moore. For book publication, query with 10-12 samples and "brief letter with major publications, significant contributions, awards. We like to know a person as well as their poem." Replies to queries in 3-4 weeks, to submissions (if invited) in 6-8 weeks. Payment arranged with authors. Editor sometimes comments on rejections.

Also Offers: They offer an annual Eve of St. Agnes Competition with major poets as judges. Send SASE for details.

Advice: The editor says, "Poets should keep abreast of current books, know who the contemporary poets are and learn from them. Reading stimulates the muse."

○ ☑ **THE NEOVICTORIAN/COCHLEA**, P.O. Box 55164, Madison WI 53705, e-mail eacam@execpc.com, founded 1995, editor Esther Cameron.

Magazine Needs: *N/C* appears biannually and "seeks to promote a poetry of introspection, dialogue and social concern." They want "poetry of beauty and integrity with emotional and intellectual depth, commitment to subject matter as well as language, and the courage to ignore fashion. Welcome: well-crafted formal verse, social comment, love poems, philosophical/religious poems, poems reflecting dialogue with other writers (in particular: responses to the work of Paul Celan)." They have published poetry by Ida Fasel, Mark Halperin, Richard Moore, Carolyn Stoloff and Martha Modena Vertreace. As a sample the editor selected these lines from "Roots" by Rose Rosberg:

> the groping tendrils find their way/around the stones which lie between/and block their words, blindly cling,/wordless to each other sing//how nerves of all the kindred meet/beneath the surface, reaching forth

N/C is 28-32 pgs., 8×11, photocopied and saddle-stapled with cardstock cover, occasional graphics, no ads. They receive about 900 poems a year, accept approximately 180. Press run is 250 for 30 subscribers, 20 shelf sales; 100 distributed free to friends, 10-15 to reviewers. Single copy: $6; subscription: $10.

How to Submit: Submit 3-5 poems at a time. Previously published poems and simultaneous submissions OK. Cover letter "not necessary. Poets whose work is accepted will be asked for titles of books available, to be published in the magazine." Time between acceptance and publication is 6-12 months. Often comments on rejections. Does not offer guidelines because "the tradition is the only 'guideline.' We do encourage contributors to write for a sample." Reports in 3-8 weeks. Pays 2 copies. Acquires first rights. *N/C* publishes the addresses of poets who would welcome correspondence.

Advice: The editor says, "Like all our social functioning, poetry today suffers from a loss of community, which translates into a lack of real intimacy with the reader. Poets can work against this trend by remaining in touch with the poetry of past generations and by forming relationships in which poetry can be employed as the language of friendship. Publication should be an afterthought."

○ ☑ **NERVE COWBOY; LIQUID PAPER PRESS**, P.O. Box 4973, Austin TX 78765, website http://www.eden.com/~JWHAGINS/nervecowboy.html, founded 1995, co-editors Joseph Shields and Jerry Hagins.

Magazine Needs: *Nerve Cowboy* is a biannual literary journal featuring contemporary poetry, short fiction and b&w drawings. The editors are "open to all forms, styles and subject matter preferring writing that speaks directly, and minimizes literary devices. We want to see poetry of experience and passion which can find that raw nerve and ride it." They have published poetry by Serena Fusek, Ron Androla, Belinda Subraman, Albert Huffstickler, Paul Agostino, Maggie Jaffe, Joan Jobe Smith and Gerald Locklin. As a sample the editors selected these lines from "The Good Lord Giveth and the Good Lord Taketh Away (Life in the Big City)" by Mark Weber:

> The same day that/I gloriously found a quarter in the gutter/I stuck it into a parking meter/which had its red flag frozen/for all eternity

Nerve Cowboy is 64 pgs., 7×8½, attractively printed and saddle-stapled with matte card cover with b&w cover art. They currently accept 5-10% of the submissions received. Press run is 250 for 85 subscribers. Subscription: $14/4 issues. Sample: $4.

How to Submit: Submit 3-5 poems at a time, name on each page. Previously published poems with notification OK; no simultaneous submissions. Informal cover letter with bio credits preferred. Seldom comments on rejections. Send SASE for guidelines. Reports in 6-8 weeks. Pays 1 copy. Acquires first or one-time rights.

Book/Chapbook Needs & How to Submit: Liquid Paper Press publishes 3-4 chapbooks/year but will not be accepting unsolicited chapbook mss in the foreseeable future. Only chapbook contest winners and solicited mss will be published in the next couple of years. For information on *Nerve Cowboy*'s annual chapbook contest, please send a SASE. Deadline is January 15 of each year. Entry fee: $10. Cash prizes and publication for 1st and 2nd place finishers. Chapbooks are 24-40 pgs., 5½×8½, photocopied with some b&w artwork. Recent winners include Belinda Subraman, Thomas Michael McDade and Susanne R. Bowers. Publications include *Grappling* by Susanne R. Bowers; and *The Back East Poems* by Gerald Locklin. Send SASE for a list of available titles.

● **NEW COLLAGE MAGAZINE**, 5700 N. Tamiami Trail, Sarasota FL 34243-2197, phone (941)359-5605, founded 1970, poetry editor A. McA. Miller.

Magazine Needs: *New CollAge* provides "a forum for contemporary poets, both known and undiscovered. We are partial to fresh slants on traditional prosodies and poetry with clear focus and clear imagery. No greeting card verse." They have published poetry by Peter Meinke, Yvonne Sapia, Lola Haskins, J.P. White, Peter Klappert, Peter Wild, Stephen Corey and Malcolm Glass. The magazine appears 2 times a year, 28-32 pgs. of poetry in each issue. Circulation is 500 with 200 subscribers of which 30 are libraries. They receive about 5,000 poems a year, use approximately 90. Subscription: $6. Sample: $2.

How to Submit: Submit 3-5 poems at a time. "We prefer poems shorter than five single-spaced pages." No simultaneous submissions. "September through April is the best submission time for response to poems." Publishes theme issues. Send SASE for upcoming themes. Reports in 6 weeks. Pays 2 copies. Editor sometimes comments on rejections. "We review books and chapbooks in 1,000-2,000 words."

Advice: Editor "Mac" Miller advises, "Sending a ms already marked 'copyright' is absurd and unprofessional. Mss may be marked 'first North American serials only,' though this is unnecessary. Also, quality is the only standard. Get a sample issue to see our taste."

N **$** ● **THE NEW CRITERION**, The Foundation for Cultural Review, Inc., 850 Seventh Ave., New York NY 10019, poetry editor Robert Richman.

   ● Poetry published in this review was selected for inclusion in the 1992 and 1994 volumes of *The Best American Poetry*.

Magazine Needs: *New Criterion* is a monthly (except July and August) review of ideas and the arts, which uses poetry of high literary quality. They have published poetry by Donald Justice, Andrew Hudgins, Elizabeth Spires and Herbert Morris. It is 90 pgs., 7 × 10, flat-spined. Poems here truly are open, with structured free verse and formal works. Sample: $4.75.

How to Submit: Cover letter required with submissions. Reports in 2-3 months. Pays $2.50/line ($75 minimum).

Advice: The editor says, "To have an idea of who we are or what we stand for, poets should consult back issues."

● **NEW DELTA REVIEW; THE EYSTER PRIZE**, English Dept., Louisiana State University, Baton Rouge LA 70803-5001, phone (225)388-4079, website http://www.lsu.edu:80/guests/wwwndr, contact poetry editor.

Magazine Needs: They "publish works of quality, many of them by young writers who are building their reputations." They have published poetry by Ann F. Walker, George Looney and Doug Martin. *NDR* appears twice a year, 90-120 pgs., 6 × 9, flat-spined, typeset and printed on quality stock with matte card cover with art. Press run is 500 for 100 subscribers of which 20 are libraries; the rest are for shelf sales. Subscription: $10. Sample: $6. Back issue: $4. Make checks payable to *New Delta Review*.

How to Submit: Submit up to 5 poems "and specify on the outside of the envelope that you are submitting poetry." No previously published poems. Cover letter with author's name, address, phone number, social security number and biographical information required. Include SASE for reply and return of work. Poetry editor sometimes comments on rejections, often suggesting possible revisions. Reports in 3-4 months. Pays 2 copies. Acquires first North American serial rights. Reviews books of poetry in no more than 2,000 words, single or multi-book format. Poets may also send books to poetry editor for review consideration.

Also Offers: The Eyster Prize of $50 is awarded to the best story and best poem in each issue. Website includes guidelines, names of editors and examples of work from the latest issue.

Advice: The editor says, "Make sure two things are present in your poems: do the heart work and attend to craft."

M **$** ● **NEW ENGLAND REVIEW**, Middlebury College, Middlebury VT 05753, phone (802)443-5075, fax (802)443-2088, e-mail nereview@mail.middlebury.edu, website http://www.middlebury.edu/~nereview/, founded 1978, editor Stephen Donadio.

   ● Work published in this review was included in the 1992, 1993, 1994 and 1998 volumes of *The Best American Poetry*.

Magazine Needs: *New England Review* is a prestigious, nationally distributed literary quarterly, 180 pgs., 7 × 10, flat-spined, elegant make-up and printing on heavy stock, glossy cover with art. Receives 3,000-4,000 poetry submissions/year, uses 70-80 poems/year, has a 3-6 month backlog between time of acceptance and publication. The editors urge poets to read a few copies of the magazine before submitting work. They have published poetry by Henri Cole, Debora Greger, Brigit Pegeen Kelly, J.D. McClatchy, Rosanna Warren and Charles Wright. Subscription: $23. Sample: $7.

How to Submit: Submit up to 6 poems at a time. Address submissions to Poetry Editor. No previously published poems. "Brief cover letters are useful. All submissions by mail. Questions by e-mail OK." Reads submissions September 1 through May 31 only. Response time is 10-12 weeks. Always sends prepublication galleys. Pays $10/page, $20 minimum, plus 2 copies. Also features essay-reviews. Send books for review consideration.

Also Offers: Website includes guidelines, editorial staff, sample poetry from current and recent issues, ordering information and secure online ordering.

☑ **$☐ ◎ NEW ERA MAGAZINE (Specialized: religious, teen/young adult)**, 50 E. North Temple St., Salt Lake City UT 84150-3225, phone (801)240-2951, fax (801)240-5997, founded 1971, managing editor Larry Hiller.

Magazine Needs: *New Era* appears monthly and is an "official publication for youth of The Church of Jesus Christ of Latter-day Saints; it contains feature stories, photo stories, fiction, news, etc." They want "short verse in any form, particularly traditional—must pertain to teenage LDS audience (religious and teenage themes). No sing-songy doggerel, gushy love poems or forced rhymes." *New Era* is 52 pgs., approximately 8×10½, 4-color offset printed, saddle-stitched, quality stock, top-notch art and graphics, no ads. They receive 200-300 submissions a year, accept approximately 2-5%. Press run is 226,000 for 205,000 subscribers, 10,000 shelf sales. Single copy: $1.50; subscription: $8/year. Sample: $1.50 plus postage.

How to Submit: Send up to 5 poems at one time. No previously published poems or simultaneous submissions. Time between acceptance and publication is a year or longer. "We publish one poem each month next to our photo of the month." Sometimes comments on rejections. Publishes 1-2 theme issues each year, one of which is geographically themed (LDS youth in one country). Theme deadlines are 6 months minimum to 1 year in advance. Send SASE, fax or e-mail for guidelines and upcoming themes. Reports in 6-8 weeks. Sometimes sends prepublication galleys. Pays $10 minimum. "LDS church retains rights to publish again in church publications—all other rights returned."

Also Offers: They also offer an annual contest—including poetry—for active members of the LDS church between ages 12-23. Poetry entries should consist of one entry of 6-10 different original poems (none of which exceeds 50 lines) reflecting LDS values. Deadline: January. Winners receive either a partial scholarship to BYU or Ricks College or a cash award. Send SASE for rules.

Advice: The editor says, "Study the magazine before submitting. We're a great market for beginners, but you must understand Mormons to write well for us. Just because a subject is noble or inspirational doesn't mean the poetry automatically is noble or inspirational. Pay attention to the craft of writing. Poetry is more than just writing down your thoughts about an inspirational subject. Poetry needs to communicate easily and be readily understood—it's too easy to mistake esoteric expression for true insight."

◢ ◎ **NEW ISSUES PRESS; NEW ISSUES PRESS POETRY SERIES; NEW ISSUES PRESS POETRY PRIZE; THE GREEN ROSE PRIZE IN POETRY (Specialized: regional)**, Dept. of English, Western Michigan University, Kalamazoo MI 49008-5092, phone (616)387-2592, fax (616)387-2562, e-mail herbert.scott@wmich.edu, website http://www.wmich.edu/english/fac/nipps, founded 1996, editor Herbert Scott.

Book/Chapbook Needs: New Issues Press publishes 3-6 first books of poetry per year, one through its annual New Issues Poetry Prize. Additional mss will be selected from those submitted to the competition for publication in the series. "A national judge selects the prize winner and recommends other manuscripts. The editors decide on the other books considering the judge's recommendation, but are not bound by it." Past judges include Chase Twichell, Philip Levine and Marianne Boruch. The editor says books are published on acid free paper in editions of 1,500.

How to Submit: Open to "US residents writing in English and US citizens living abroad who have not previously published a full-length collection of poems in an edition of 500 or more copies." Submit 48- to 72-page ms with 1-paragraph bio, publication credits (if any) and $12 reading fee. No e-mail or fax submissions. Reads submissions June 1 through November 30 only. Send SASE for complete guidelines. Winner will be notified the following April. Winner receives $1,000 plus publication of manuscript. "We offer 33⅓% discounts on our books to competition entrants."

Also Offers: New Issues Press also sponsors a new competition, The Green Rose Prize in Poetry. Award is $1,000 and publication for a book of poems by an established poet who has published one or more full-length collections of poetry. Reading fee: $20/ms. Mss accepted May 1 through September 30. Winner announced in January. Send SASE for complete guidelines or obtain via website.

Advice: The editor says, "Our belief is that there are more good poets writing than ever before. Our mission is to give some of the best of these a forum. Also, our books have been reviewed in *Publishers Weekly*, *Booklist*, and the *Library Journal*. New Issues books are advertised in *Poetry*, *Poets & Writers*, *APR*, *American Poet*, *The Bloomsbury Review*, etc."

◢ ◎ **THE NEW LAUREL REVIEW (Specialized: translations)**, 828 Lesseps St., New Orleans LA 70117, phone (504)947-6001, founded 1971, editor Lee Meitzen Grue, poetry editor Lenny Emmanuel.

Magazine Needs: *The New Laurel Review* "is an annual independent nonprofit literary magazine dedicated to fine art. Each issue contains poetry, translations, literary essays, reviews of small press books, and visual art." They want "poetry with strong, accurate imagery. We have no particular preference in style. We try to be eclectic. We're looking for original work, without hackneyed phrases or tired thinking." They have published poetry by Jared Carter, Kalamu Ya Salaam, Melody Davis, Sue Walker and Keith Cartwright. The *Review* is 6×9, laser printed, 115 pgs., original art on cover, accepts 30 poems out of 300 mss received. It has a circulation of 500. Single copy: $10 individuals, $12 institutions. Sample (back issue): $8.

How to Submit: Submit 3-5 poems with SASE and a short note with previous publications. No simultaneous submissions. Reads submissions September 1 through May 30 only. Guidelines for SASE. Reports on submissions in 3 months, publishes in 8-10 months. Pays contributor's copies. Acquires first rights. Reviews books of poetry in 1,000 words, single or multi-book format.

Advice: The editor advises, "Read our magazine before submitting poetry."

$ **NEW LETTERS; NEW LETTERS POETRY PRIZE**, University of Missouri-Kansas City, Kansas City MO 64110, phone (816)235-1168, fax (816)235-2611, founded 1934 as *University Review*, became *New Letters* in 1971, managing editor Bob Stewart, editor James McKinley.

● Work published in *New Letters* appeared in the 1992 and 1997 volumes of *The Best American Poetry*.

Magazine Needs: *New Letters* "is dedicated to publishing the best short fiction, best contemporary poetry, literary articles, photography and artwork by both established writers and new talents." They want "contemporary writing of all types—free verse poetry preferred, short works are more likely to be accepted than very long ones." They have published poetry by Joyce Carol Oates, Amiri Baraka, Nancy Willard, Margaret Randall, Gary Gildner and Trish Reeves. The 6×9, flat-spined, professionally printed quarterly, glossy 2-color cover with art, uses about 40-45 (of 120) pgs. of poetry in each issue. Circulation is 2,500 with 1,800 subscriptions of which about 40% are libraries. They receive about 7,000 submissions a year, use less than 1%, have a 6-month backlog. Poems appear in a variety of styles exhibiting a high degree of craft and universality of theme (rare in many journals). Subscription: $17. Sample: $5.

How to Submit: Send no more than 6 poems at a time. No previously published poems or simultaneous submissions. Short cover letter preferred. "We strongly prefer original typescripts and we don't read between May 15 and October 15. No query needed." Reports in 4-10 weeks. Pays a small fee plus 2 copies. Occasionally James McKinley comments on rejections.

Also Offers: The New Letters Poetry Prize of $750 is given annually for a group of 3-6 poems, entry fee $10 (check payable to New Letters Literary Awards). Send SASE for entry guidelines. Deadline: May 15. They also publish occasional anthologies, selected and edited by McKinley.

N **🌐** **○** **NEW LONDON WRITERS**, 31 Thicket Rd., Averly, London SE20 8DB United Kingdom, phone (0181)778 2813, e-mail newlonrite@aol.com, founded 1998, editor Alice Wickham.

Magazine Needs: *New London Writers* biannually publishes "new and experimental work by daring new writers." They want "daring, forward looking, provocative, erotic work. No racist or sexist poems." They have published poetry by S. Lucas, M. Fitzgerald, J. Jackson and Estill Pollock. The editor says *NLW* is 20 pgs., magazine-sized, Docutech printed and staple-bound with b&w cover with photo. They receive about 600 poems a year, accept approximately 50%. Press run is 100 for 70 subscribers, 10 shelf sales; 20 distributed free to publishers and agents. Subscription: $30. Sample: $5.50. Make checks payable to Alice Wickham.

How to Submit: Submit 2 poems at a time. Previously published poems and simultaneous submissions OK. Cover letter preferred. E-mail and disk submissions OK. Time between acceptance and publication is 2 months. Poems are circulated to an editorial board. "Poems seen by up to five readers. Feedback offered; decision made by editor." Criticism fee: $20/2 poems, "if comments requested." Obtain guidelines via e-mail. Reports in 2 months. Acquires one-time rights. Staff reviews books of poetry in 1,000 words. Poets may also send books for review consideration.

Advice: The editor says, "Be as provocative as possible but avoid cliché or 'shock value.' A lot of dreary material passes this way. Think about craft, style, content; read good poets."

○ **THE NEW MIRAGE QUARTERLY; GOOD SAMARITAN PRESS; THE MIRAGE AWARD**, P.O. Box 803282, Santa Clarita CA 91380, phone/fax (213)383-3447, e-mail adorxyz@aol.com, founded 1996, editor Jovita Ador Lee, publisher Jerome Vallens Brooke.

Magazine Needs: *The New Mirage Quarterly* contains poetry and reviews. They want all types of poetry. As a sample the editor selected this poem, "Mirage" (poet unidentified):

> Layers of false illusion lie,/Veils of lies that bind and tie./Choice returns; hope shall remain/Love returns, and love shall remain.

The editors say *TNMQ* is 12 pgs., 5½×8½, photocopied and stapled with bond paper cover, includes clip art and ads. They receive about 90 poems a year, accept approximately 80%. Press run is 90 for 20 subscribers, 10 shelf sales; 20 distributed free to general public. Subscription: $26. Sample: $7. Make checks payable to Good Samaritan Press.

How to Submit: Submit up to 3 poems at a time. Previously published poems and simultaneous submissions OK. Cover letter preferred. E-mail and disk submissions OK. Reads submissions March 1 through December 1 only. Time between acceptance and publication is 6 weeks. Often comments on rejections. Reports in 6 weeks. Pays 2 copies. Acquires all rights. Returns rights upon publication. Reviews books and chapbooks of poetry and other magazines in 200-300 words, single book format. Open to unsolicited reviews. Send books for review consideration.

Book/Chapbook Needs & How to Submit: Good Samaritan Press publishes an annual poetry anthology.

FOR AN EXPLANATION of symbols used in this book, see the Key to Symbols on the front and back inside covers.

The anthology is 50-100 pgs., 5½×8½, photocopied and perfect-bound, hard cover with art prints. Poets must first appear in *The New Mirage Quarterly*. Replies in 6 weeks.
Also Offers: Sponsors The Mirage Award, an annual award to a poet included in the magazine.

N ◎ ⊘ NEW NATIVE PRESS (Specialized: translations), P.O. Box 661, Cullowhee NC 28723, phone (828)293-9237, founded 1979, publisher Thomas Rain Crowe.
Book/Chapbook Needs: New Native Press has "selectively narrowed its range of contemporary 20th century literature to become an exclusive publisher of writers in marginalized and endangered languages. All books published are bilingual translations from original languages into English." They publish on average 2 paperbacks/year. Their last 4 titles have included poetry by Philip Daughtry (Geordie); Danielle Truscott (Cornish-American); and Gaelic, Welsh, Breton, Cornish and Manx poets in an all-Celtic language anthology of contemporary poets from Scotland, Ireland, Wales, Brittany, Cornwall and Isle of Man entitled *Writing The Wind: A Celtic Resurgence (The New Celtic Poetry)*. Books are sold by distributors in four foreign countries and in the US by library vendors and Small Press Distribution. Books are typically 80 pgs., offset printed and perfect-bound with glossy 120 lb. stock with professionally-designed color cover.
How to Submit: Not currently accepting submissions. For specialized translations only—authors should query first with 10 sample poems and cover letter with bio and publication credits. Previously published poems and simultaneous submissions OK. Time between acceptance and publication is 6-12 months. Always comments on rejections. Reports in 2 weeks. Pays copies, "amount varies with author and title."
Advice: The publisher says, "We are still looking for work indicative of rare talent—unique and original voices using language experimentally and symbolically, if not subversively."

N ▢ ◯ ◎ NEW ORLEANS POETRY FORUM; GRIS-GRIS PRESS; DESIRE STREET (Specialized: membership), 257 Bonnabel Blvd., Metairie LA 70005-3738, phone (504)833-0641, fax (504)834-2005, poetry forum founded 1971, press and magazine founded 1994, president Andrea S. Gereighty, editor Barbara J. Sahm.
Magazine Needs: *Desire Street* is the quarterly electronic magazine of the New Orleans Poetry Forum. "The Forum, a non-profit entity, has as its chief purpose the development of poets and contemporary poetry in the New Orleans area. To this end, it conducts a weekly workshop in which original poems are presented and critiqued according to an established protocol which assures a non-judgmental and non-argumentative atmosphere. A second aim of the NOPF is to foster awareness and support for poetry in the New Orleans area through readings, publicity, and community activities. Promotion is emphasized in order to increase acceptance and support for contemporary poetry." They want "modern poetry on any topic—1 page only. No rhyming verse; no porn, obscenity or child molestation themes." They have published poetry by Herman Baxter, Yusef Komunyakaa, Beverly Matherne and Yevgeny Yevtushenko. As a sample we selected these lines from "Bottled Mosaic" by Rebecca Morris:

> *Swirls of turbulent blue/Depression spread across the canvas/Words travel around the edges/Never*
> *touching empty spaces//Shadows/Created by a single harsh stroke/Splashes of red/And anger enter the*
> *picture.//The color of whisky fills gaps/Blends the whole to a blur*

DS is 8-10 pgs., desktop-published, downloaded photocopied and distributed, uses clip art. They receive about 550 poems a year, accept approximately 10%. Press run is 200 hard copies for 200 subscribers. Single copy: $3; subscription: $12/year. Sample (including guidelines): $5. Make checks payable to New Orleans Poetry Forum.
How to Submit: Submit 2 poems at a time, 10 poem limit/year. Line length for poetry is one 8½×11 page only. Previously published poems OK; no simultaneous submissions. Cover letter required. Disk submissions OK, in ASCII or MS Dos text. Membership in the New Orleans Poetry Forum is required before submitting work. Annual fee: $25, includes 4 issues of *Desire Street*, 52 3-hour workshops and 1 year's free critique of up to 10 poems. Time between acceptance and publication is up to 1 year. Poems are circulated to an editorial board. "First, poems are read by Andrea Gereighty. Then, poems are read by a board of five poets." Comments on rejections. Publishes theme issues occasionally. Reports in 1 year. Pays 10 copies. Acquires one-time rights.
Also Offers: The Forum conducts weekly workshops on Wednesday nights at the Broadmoor Library. They also conduct workshops at schools and in prisons. Send SASE for details.

◐ NEW ORLEANS POETRY JOURNAL PRESS, 2131 General Pershing St., New Orleans LA 70115, phone (504)891-3458, founded 1956, publisher/editor Maxine Cassin, co-editor Charles deGravelles.
Book/Chapbook Needs: "We prefer to publish relatively new and/or little-known poets of unusual promise or those inexplicably neglected." They do not want to see "cliché or doggerel, anything incomprehensible or too derivative, or workshop exercises. First-rate lyric poetry preferred (not necessarily in traditional forms)." They have published books by Vassar Miller, Everette Maddox, Charles Black, Malaika Favorite, Raeburn Miller and Martha McFerren.
How to Submit: Query first. They do not accept unsolicited submissions for chapbooks, which are flat-spined paperbacks. Unsolicited mss will not be returned. The editors report on queries in 2-3 months, mss in the same time period, if solicited. Simultaneous submissions will possibly be accepted. Sometimes sends prepublication galleys. Pays copies, usually 50-100. The press does not subsidy publish at present and does not offer grants or awards.
Advice: For aspiring poets, Ms. Cassin quotes the advice Borges received from his father: "1) Read as much

as possible! 2) Write only when you must, and 3) Don't rush into print!" As a small press editor and publisher, she urges poets to read instructions in *Poet's Market* listings with utmost care! She says, "No poetry should be sent without querying first! Publishers are concerned about expenses unnecessarily incurred in mailing manuscripts. *Telephoning is not encouraged.*"

NEW ORLEANS REVIEW, Box 195, Loyola University, New Orleans LA 70118, phone (504)865-2295, fax (504)865-2294, e-mail noreview@loyno.edu, founded 1968, editor Ralph Adamo.
Magazine Needs: *New Orleans Review* publishes "lyric poetry of all types, fiction that is strongly voiced and essays." They have published poetry by Jack Gilbert, Rodney Jones, Besmilr Brigham and Moira Crone. It is 120-200 pgs., perfect-bound, elegantly printed with glossy card cover. Circulation is 1,700. Sample: $10.
How to Submit: Submit 3-6 poems at a time. No previously published work. Brief cover letter preferred. Publishes some theme issues. Send SASE for upcoming themes. Reports in 3 months. Pays 5 copies. Acquires first North American serial rights.

THE NEW PRESS LITERARY QUARTERLY; THE NEW PRESS POETRY CONTEST, 65-39 108th St., Suite E-6, Forest Hills NY11375, phone (718)459-6807, founded 1984, poetry editor Victoria Figuereda.
Magazine Needs: *TNPLQ* is a quarterly magazine using poems "less than 100 lines, accessible, imaginative. No doggerel, sentimentality." They include a multilingual section for poetry. They want poems in Spanish, Italian, Portuguese, Japanese, Chinese, Russian, Hungarian, German, Icelandic and French, accompanied by their English versions/translations. Each poem must list the author's and translator's names and addresses. They have published poetry by Allen Ginsberg, Lawrence Ferlinghetti, Louise Jaffe, Mary Winters, D.H. Melhem, Les Bridges and Gina Bergamino. It is 32-48 pgs., magazine-sized, desktop-published, with glossy cover, saddle-stapled. They receive 500-1,000 poems a year, accept approximately 10%. Press run is 2,000 for 350 subscribers. Subscription: $15/year, $29/2 years (add $5/year for overseas). Sample: $5.50. "Payable by check or money order in U.S. funds only."
How to Submit: Submit no more than 6 poems at a time. Nonsubscribers are required to pay a reading fee of $2 (1-3 poems) or $4 (4-6 poems). "Include name and address on the top of each page." Publishes theme issues. Send SASE for upcoming themes. Reports in 4 months. Always sends prepublication galleys. Pays 2 copies. Acquires first-time rights.
Also Offers: The New Press Poetry Contest is annual, deadline is July 1, entry fee of $5 for up to 3 poems or 100 lines, has prizes of $100, $75 and five 2-year subscriptions. They also sponsor poetry readings in Brooklyn and Manhattan. Send SASE for details.

$ THE NEW RENAISSANCE (Specialized: translations, bilingual), 26 Heath Rd. #11, Arlington MA 02474-3645, e-mail wmichaud@gwi.net, founded 1968, editor-in-chief Louise T. Reynolds, poetry editor Frank Finale.
Magazine Needs: *the new renaissance* is "intended for the 'renaissance' person—the generalist, not the special-ist. Publishes the best new writing and translations and offers a forum for articles on political, sociological topics; features established as well as emerging visual artists and writers, and highlights reviews of small press. Open to a variety of styles, including traditional." They have published poetry by Jane Mayhall, Daniel Tobin, Ralph Salisbury, Ann Struthers, and translations of de Andrade (by A. Levitin) and Ivan Davidkor (by Lisa Lupin-Kopf). As a sample the editor selected these lines from "Shepherd of Rivers" by Ivan Davidkov, translated from Bulgarian by Lisa Sapinkopf with Georgi Belev:

> Who will wind the clock of the forest/with rain's tiny key?/Evenings, the cuckoo will re-emerge/as if projected by a tiny silver coil between the branches./And if she cries out, what will she awaken—/the river, the hunters' shots, our rainfilled footsteps?//Already it's too late to pray for the vanished song.

tnr is 144-186 pgs., 6×9, flat-spined, professionally printed on heavy stock, glossy, color cover, using 24-40 pgs. of poetry in each issue. They receive about 670 poetry submissions a year, use 22-35 have about a 1½- to 2-year backlog. Usual press run is 1,500 for 710 subscribers of which approximately 132 are libraries. Subscrip-tions: $26/3 issues US, $28 Canada, $30 all others. "A 3-issue subscription covers 18-22 months."
How to Submit: "Until January 1, 2000, we are accepting only bilingual translations." Submit 3-6 poems at a time, "unless a long poem—then one." No previously published poems "unless magazine's circulation was under 250"; simultaneous submissions OK, if notified. No e-mail submissions. "All poetry submissions are tied to our Awards Program for best poetry published in a three-issue volume. Entry fee: $15 for nonsubscribers, $10 for subscribers, for which they receive the following: two back issues or a recent issue or an extension of their subscription. Submissions without entry fee are *returned unread.*" Send SASE for guidelines. Reports in 3-5 months. Pays $18-26, more for the occasional longer poem, plus 1 copy/poem. Buys all rights. Returns rights provided *tnr* retains rights for any *tnr* collection. Reviews books of poetry. The Awards Program gives 3 awards of $250, $125 and $50, with 3 Honorable Mentions of $20.
Advice: The editor says, "Poets should read, read and write. Our range is from traditionalist poetry to post-modern, occasionally experimental, and street poetry. We also like the occasional 'light' poem and, of course, have an emphasis on translations. We're especially interested in the individual voice. If you query us about anything, please include a SASE. We can't answer unless there is one."

$ **THE NEW REPUBLIC**, 1220 19th St. NW, Washington DC 20036, phone (202)331-7494, founded 1914, poetry editor Mark Strand.
- Poetry published in *The New Republic* has also been included in the 1993, 1994, 1995, 1997 and 1998 volumes of *The Best American Poetry*.

Magazine Needs & How to Submit: *The New Republic*, a weekly journal of opinion, is magazine-sized, printed on slick paper, 42 pgs., saddle-stapled with 4-color cover. Subscription: $69.97/year. Sample: $3.50. Include SASE with submissions. Always sends prepublication galleys. Pays $100/poem.

NEW RIVERS PRESS; MINNESOTA VOICES PROJECT; HEADWATERS LITERARY COMPETITION (Specialized: regional, translations), 420 N. Fifth St., Suite 910, Minneapolis MN 55401, phone (800)339-2011, fax (612)339-9047, e-mail newrivpr@mtn.org, website http://www.mtn.org/newrivpr, founded 1968, contact managing editor.

Book/Chapbook Needs: Publishes collections of poetry, novels or novellas, translations of contemporary literature, collections of short fiction. Write for free catalog or send SASE for guidelines/inquiries. New and emerging authors living in Minnesota are eligible for the Minnesota Voices Project.

How to Submit: Book-length mss of poetry, short fiction, novellas or familiar essays are all accepted. No e-mail submissions. Send SASE for entry form and guidelines. Winning authors receive a stipend of $500 plus publication by New Rivers.

Also Offers: "The Headwaters Literary Competition is open to residents of the Dakotas, Iowa, Illinois, Wisconsin and Michigan, and is not limited to new and emerging writers. There is a $10 reading fee. Our website describes current and backlist titles and contests."

A NEW SONG: THE POETRY OF GOD'S PEOPLE; NEW SONG PRESS; NEW SONG CHAPBOOK COMPETITION (Specialized: spirituality), P.O. Box 629, W.B.B., Dayton OH 45409-0629, phone (937)294-4552, e-mail nsongpress@aol.com, founded 1995, editor/publisher Susan Jelus.

Magazine Needs: *A New Song* is published 2 times a year, in June and December, and "exhibits contemporary American poetry that speaks to endeavors of faith and enriches the spiritual lives of its readers. Includes poetry that takes a fresh approach and uses contemporary, natural language." They want "free verse that addresses spiritual life through a wide-range of topics and vivid imagery. No rhyming, sing-song, old-fashioned 'religious' poetry; or difficult-to-follow poetry." They have published poetry by Claude Wilkinson, Janet McCann, Herbert W. Martin and John Grey. As a sample the editor selected these lines from "From a Seat Among Thousands at Cincinnati's Festival" by William J. Vernon:

> Before the music started, he appeared./Although his oddness grabbed us, no/one yelled, or laughed,
> or said a thing./His clothing fit as if his flesh/had peeled off, hanging loose. We turned/to watch the
> river, lapping stones/

ANS is 40-50 pgs., 5½×8½, usually Docutech or offset printed, saddle-stitched, cardstock cover, photo or artwork on cover. They receive about 600 poems a year, accept approximately 20%. Press run is 300 for 150 subscribers, 100 shelf sales; 50-75 distributed free to reviewers, bookstores, editors, professors, pastors. Single copy: $5; subscription: $10. Sample back issue: $3. Make checks payable to New Song Press.

How to Submit: Submit 3-5 poems at a time with short bio and SASE. No previously published poems or simultaneous submissions. E-mail submissions OK, "up to 2 poems only and must have a mailing address and bio." Send SASE with regular mail submissions. Time between acceptance and publication is 6-12 months. Poems are circulated to an editorial board. Often comments on rejections, "brief comments only." Publishes theme issues occasionally. Send SASE for guidelines. Reports in 3 months. Pays 1 copy. Acquires first North American serial rights. Sometimes reviews books of poetry in 750-1,000 words, single book format. Open to unsolicited reviews. Poets may also send books for review consideration.

Book/Chapbook Needs & How to Submit: New Song Press's goals are "to help develop a genre of contemporary spiritual poetry." They publish 1-2 chapbooks per year. Chapbooks are usually 20-40 pgs., 5½×8½, usually Docutech printed, sometimes offset printed color cover, saddle-stitched, cardstock cover, include art/graphics. Query first, with a few sample poems and a cover letter with brief bio and publication credits. Replies to queries in 3 months; to mss in 6 months. Payment varies.

Also Offers: Sponsors annual chapbook contest. Prize: $200 plus copies. Deadline: November 30th and 2 runners-up also recognized.

$ **THE NEW WRITER; THE NEW WRITER POETRY PRIZES**, P.O. Box 60, Cranbrook TN17 2ZR England, phone 01580 212626, fax 01580 212041, website http://freespace.virgin.net/ignotus.press/index.html, founded 1996, poetry editor Abi Hughes-Edwards.

Magazine Needs: Published 10 times a year, "*The New Writer* is the magazine you've been hoping to find. It's *different* and it's aimed at writers with a serious intent; who want to develop their writing to meet the high expectations of today's editors. The team at *The New Writer* are committed to working with their readers to increase the chances of publication. That's why masses of useful information and plenty of feedback is provided. More than that, we let you know about the current state of the market with the best in contemporary fiction and cutting-edge poetry backed up by searching articles and in-depth features in every issue. We are interested in short fiction, 2,000 words max.; subscribers' only; short and long unpublished poems, provided they are original and undeniably brilliant; articles that demonstrate a grasp of contemporary writing and current editorial/publishing policies; news of writers' circles, new publications, competitions, courses, workshops, etc." The poetry editor says submitted poems "must keep my heart beating. I don't have any problems with length/form but anything over two pages (150 lines) needs to be brilliant. Cutting edge shouldn't mean inaccessible. No recent disasters—they date. No my baby/doggie poems; no God poems that sound like hymns, dum-dum rhymes or comic rhymes (best left at the pub). *New Writer* is 48 pgs., A4, professionally printed and saddle-stapled with paper cover, includes clipart and b&w photos. Press run is 1,500 for 1,350 subscribers; 50 distributed free to publishers, agents. Single copy: £2.95; subscription: £42.50 in US. Sample: £4.25.

How to Submit: Submit up to 6 poems at a time. Previously published poems OK. Time between acceptance and publication is up to 6 months. Often comments on rejections. Offers criticism service: £12/6 poems. Send SASE (or SAE and IRC) for guidelines. Pays £3 voucher plus 1 copy. Buys first British serial rights. Reviews books and chapbooks of poetry and other magazines. Open to unsolicited reviews. Poets may also send books for review consideration.

Also Offers: Sponsors The New Writer Poetry Prizes. An annual prize, "open to all poets writing in the English language, who are invited to submit an original, previously unpublished poem or collection of six to ten poems. Up to 25 prizes will be presented as well as publication for the prize-winning poets in an anthology plus the chance for a further 10 shortlisted poets to see their work published in *The New Writer* during the year." Write for contest rules.

$ ◻ ◖ ◎ NEW WRITER'S MAGAZINE (Specialized: humor, writing), P.O. Box 5976, Sarasota FL 34277-5976, phone (941)953-7903, e-mail newriters@aol.com, website http://www.newriters.com, founded 1986, editor George J. Haborak.

Magazine Needs: *New Writer's Magazine* is a bimonthly magazine "for aspiring writers, and professional ones as well, to exchange ideas and working experiences." They are open to free verse, light verse and traditional, 8-20 lines, reflecting upon the writing lifestyle. "Humorous slant on writing life especially welcomed." They do not want poems about "love, personal problems, abstract ideas or fantasy." *NWM* is 28 pgs., 8½×11, offset printed, saddle-stapled, with glossy paper cover, b&w photos and ads. They receive about 300 poems a year, accept approximately 10%. Press run is 5,000. Subscription: $15/year, $25/2 years. Sample: $3.

How to Submit: Submit up to 3 poems at a time. No previously published poems or simultaneous submissions. Time between acceptance and publication is up to 1 year. Send SASE for guidelines or request via e-mail. No e-mail submissions. Reports in 1-2 months. Pays $5/poem. Buys first North American serial rights. Each issue of this magazine also includes an interview with a recognized author, articles on writing and the writing life, tips and markets.

◖ NEW YORK QUARTERLY, P.O. Box 693, Old Chelsea Station, New York NY 10113, founded 1969, poetry editor William Packard.

Magazine Needs: *New York Quarterly* appears 3 times/year. They seek to publish "a cross-section of the best of contemporary American poetry" and, indeed, have a record of publishing many of the best and most diverse of poets, including W.D. Snodgrass, Gregory Corso, James Dickey and Judson Jerome. It appears in a 6×9, flat-spined format, thick, elegantly printed, glossy color cover. Subscription: $15.

How to Submit: Submit 3-5 poems at a time with your name and address; include SASE. Simultaneous submissions OK with notification. Reports within 2 weeks. Pays copies.

☑ ☒ $ ◖ ◎ THE NEW YORKER (Specialized: translations, humor), 20 W. 43rd St., New York NY 10036, founded 1925, contact poetry editor.

• Poems appearing in *The New Yorker* have also been selected for inclusion in the 1992, 1993, 1994, 1995, 1996, 1997 and 1998 volumes of *The Best American Poetry*.

Magazine Needs: *The New Yorker*, circulation 800,000, uses poetry of the highest quality (including translations). Sample: $3 (available on newsstands).

How to Submit: Mss are not read during the summer. Replies in 10-12 weeks. Pays top rates.

◖ NEW ZOO POETRY REVIEW; SUNKEN MEADOWS PRESS, P.O. Box 36760, Richmond VA 23235, founded 1997, editor Angela Vogel.

Magazine Needs: *New Zoo Poetry Review* is published every 9 months and "tends to publish free verse in well-crafted lyric and narrative forms. Our goal is to publish established poets alongside lesser-known poets of great promise. We want to showcase poets at various stages of their literary careers. *NZPR* wants serious, intellectual poetry of any form, length or style. Rhyming poetry only if exceptional. No light verse, song lyrics or greeting card copy. If you are not reading the best of contemporary poetry, then *NZPR* is not for you." They have published poetry by Heather McHugh, William Greenway, Anita Endrezze and Martha Collins. As a sample the editor selected these lines from "Planning the Garden" by Richard Gilmore Loftus:

> *Like the photo of a mail order bride,/the seed catalogue describes/what will be needed/in the ensuing weeks:/a fit and proper bed/laid out east to west,/a vessel of tendered water,/a strong sun to part the veil of trees.*

The editor says *NZPR* is 30 pgs., digest-sized, professionally printed and saddle-stapled with heavy stock, glossy cover with b&w photography. They receive about 2,000 poems a year, accept approximately 5%. Press run is 200. Subscription: $7 for 2 consecutive issues. Sample: $4.

How to Submit: Submit 3-5 poems at a time. No previously published poems; simultaneous submissions OK. Cover letter with brief bio required. Seldom comments on rejections. Reports in 1-2 months. Pays 1 copy. Acquires first North American serial rights.
Advice: The editor says, "It's not enough to report something that happened to you. A great poem involves the reader in its experience. It surprises us with fresh language."

○ **NEWSLETTER INAGO**, P.O. Box 26244, Tucson AZ 85726-6244, phone (520)294-7031, founded 1979, poetry editor Del Reitz.
Magazine Needs: *NI* is a monthly newsletter. "Free verse and short narrative poetry preferred although other forms will be read. Rhymed poetry must be truly exceptional (nonforced) for consideration. Due to format, 'epic' and monothematic poetry will not be considered. Cause specific, political or religious poetry stands little chance of consideration. A wide range of short poetry, showing the poet's preferably eclectic perspective is best for *NI*. No haiku, please." They have published poetry by Rives Holder, Richard Alan Bunch, Andrea M. Grant, Rich Kenney, Mike Krischik, Jennifer Singleton and Askold Skalsky. As a sample the editor selected these lines from "Amoeba Amoeba" by Helen Buckingham:
> nothing like spending time/tending amoeba . . ./whilst deep in the forest/your tyger/is turning blue
NI is 4-5 pgs., corner-stapled. Press run is approximately 200 for that many subscriptions. No price is given for the newsletter, but the editor suggests a donation of $3.50 an issue or $17.50 annually ($3.50 and $21 Canada, £8 and £21 UK). Make checks payable to Del Reitz.
How to Submit: Submit 10-15 poems at a time. "Poetry should be submitted in the format in which the poet wants it to appear, and cover letters are always a good idea." Simultaneous submissions and previously published poems OK. Sometimes comments on rejections. Send SASE for guidelines. Reports ASAP (usually within 2 weeks). Pays 4 copies.

○ **NEXUS**, WO16A Student Union, Wright State University, Dayton OH 45435, phone (937)775-5533, founded 1967, editor Larry Sawyer.
Magazine Needs: "*Nexus* is a student operated magazine of mainstream and street poetry; also essays on environmental and political issues. We're looking for truthful, direct poetry. Open to poets anywhere. We look for contemporary, imaginative work." *Nexus* appears 3 times a year—fall, winter and spring, using about 40 pgs. of poetry (of 80-96) in each issue. They receive about 1,000 submissions a year, use approximately 30-50. Circulation is 1,000. For a sample, send a 10×15 SAE with 5 first-class stamps and $5.
How to Submit: Submit 4-6 pgs. of poetry with bio. Reads submissions September through May only. Simultaneous submissions OK, "but due to short response time we want to be told it's a simultaneous submission." Editor sometimes comments on rejections. Send SASE for guidelines. Reports in 15-20 weeks except summer months. Pays 2 copies. Acquires first rights.

○ ◎ **NIGHT ROSES** (Specialized: teen/young adult, love/romance, nature, students, women/feminism), P.O. Box 393, Prospect Heights IL 60070-0393, phone (847)392-2435, founded 1986, poetry editor Allen T. Billy.
Magazine Needs: *Night Roses*, appears 2-4 times/year. They want "poems about dance, bells, clocks, nature, ghost images of past or future, romance and flowers (roses, wildflowers, violets, etc.). We look for women/feminism themes for our *Cocktail Shakers* series. Do not want poems with raw language." They have published poetry by Emma J. Blanch, M. Riesa Clark, Joan Payne Kincaid, Lyn Lifshin and Alice Rogoff. As a sample the editor selected these lines from "secret light" by Cathy Drinkwater Better:
> she looked into his eyes/and saw all of eternity/staring back at her/with the face of an enchanter
Night Roses is 44 pgs., saddle-stapled, photocopied from typescript on offset paper with tinted matte card cover. Press run is 200-300. Subscription: $10/3 issues. Sample: $4.
How to Submit: Submit up to 8 poems at a time with #10 SASE. "Desire author's name and address in top left corner on all sheets of ms. If previously published—an acknowledgment must be provided by author with it." No simultaneous submissions; some previously published poems used. "I prefer submissions between March and September only." Reports in 1-4 months. "Material is accepted for current issue and two in progress." Sometimes sends prepublication galleys. Pays 1 copy. Acquires first or reprint rights. Staff reviews books of poetry. Send books for review consideration.
Advice: The editor says, "We are more interested in items that would be of interest to our teen and women readers and to our readership in the fields of dance, art and creative learning. We are interested in positive motives in this area."

○ **NIGHTSUN**, Dept. of English, Frostburg State University, Frostburg MD 21532, phone (301)687-4221, Fax (301)687-3099, founded 1981, co-editors Brad Barkley, Barbara Hurd and Karen Zealand.

Magazine Needs: *Nightsun* is a literary annual of poetry, fiction and interviews. They want "highest-quality poetry." Subject matter open. Publishes mostly free verse. Prefers poems not much longer than 40 lines. Not interested in "sentimental, obvious poetry." They have published poetry by Maxine Kumin, Marge Piercy, Bruce Jacobs and Wendy Bishop. Interviews include Lucille Clifton, Sharon Olds, Carol Frost, Roland Flint and W.D. Snodgrass. As a sample the editor selected these lines from "What the White Horse Said" by Grace Butcher:

> We had to be dream horses,/blue with the moon, black against snow/while you were gone. Never real./
> We were as lucky as horses in a painting./Our colors didn't matter.

Nightsun is 68 pgs., 6×9, printed on 100% recycled paper and perfect-bound with card cover, b&w print on front. This attractive journal features well-known poets alongside relative newcomers. They accept about 1% of poetry received. Subscription/sample: $6.50.

How to Submit: Submit 3-5 poems at a time. No simultaneous submissions. Do not submit mss during summer months. Reports within 3-6 months. Pays 2 copies. Acquires first rights. "Contributors encouraged to subscribe."

◘◑◕ NIMROD: INTERNATIONAL JOURNAL OF CONTEMPORARY POETRY AND FIC-TION; RUTH G. HARDMAN AWARD: PABLO NERUDA PRIZE FOR POETRY, University of Tulsa, 600 S. College, Tulsa OK 74104-3189, phone (918)631-3080, fax (918)631-3033, e-mail ringoldfl@centum.utulsa.edu, website http://www.utulsa.edu/nimrod/, founded 1956, editor-in-chief Francine Ringold.

• Poetry published in *Nimrod* has been included in *The Best American Poetry 1995*.

Magazine Needs: *Nimrod* "is an active 'little magazine,' part of the movement in American letters which has been essential to the development of modern literature. *Nimrod* publishes 2 issues/year, an awards issue in the fall featuring the prize winners of their national competition and a thematic issue each spring." They want "vigorous writing that is neither wholly of the academy nor the streets, typed mss." They have published poetry by Linda Watanabe McFerrin, Janet Holmes and George O'Connell. The journal is 160 pgs., 6×9, flat-spined, full-color glossy cover, professionally printed on coated stock with b&w photos and art, uses 50-90 pgs. of poetry in each issue. Poems in non-award issues range from formal to freestyle with several translations. They receive about 2,000 submissions a year, accept approximately 1%, have a 3- to 6-month backlog. Press run is 3,500 of which 200 are public and university libraries. Subscription: $17.50/year inside USA; $19 outside. Sample: $10. Specific back issues available.

How to Submit: Submit 5-10 poems at a time. Request submission guidelines via e-mail or with SASE. Publishes theme issues. Send SASE for upcoming themes. Responds in 4-6 weeks. Pays 2 copies plus reduced cost on additional copies. "Poets should be aware that during the months that the Ruth Hardman Awards Competition is being conducted, reporting time on non-contest manuscripts will be longer."

Also Offers: Send business-sized SASE for guidelines and rules for the Ruth G. Hardman Award: Pablo Neruda Prize for Poetry ($2,000 and $1,000 prizes). Entries accepted January 1 through April 30 each year. The $20 entry fee includes 2 issues. Also sponsors the Nimrod Writers' Workshop, a 1-day workshop held annually in October. Cost is $30. Send SASE for brochure and registration form. Website includes writer's guidelines, names of editors, contest rules, subscription information and excerpts of published poetry.

◘◑◎ 96 INC MAGAZINE; BRUCE P. ROSSLEY LITERARY AWARDS (Specialized: re-gional), P.O. Box 15559, Boston MA 02215, founded 1992, editors Julie Anderson, Vera Gold and Nancy Mehegan.

Magazine Needs: *96 Inc* is an annual literary magazine appearing in May that focuses on new voices, "connect-ing the beginner to the established, a training center for the process of publication." They want all forms and styles of poetry, though "shorter is better." They have published poetry by Ace Boggess, Stephen Cushman, Stephanie Kaplan Cohen and Barbara A. Rouillard. As a sample the editors selected this poem by John Tsoumas:

> when I write/I think of the trees/who gave their lives/for what I write on//it helps me to/concentrate

96 Inc is 38-50 pgs., 8½×11, saddle-stapled with coated card cover and b&w photos and graphics. They receive around 2,000 submissions a year, accept approximately 5%. Press run is 3,000 for 500 subscribers of which 50 are libraries, 1,500 shelf sales. Single copy: $4; subscription: $13. Sample: $5.50.

How to Submit: No previously published poems; simultaneous submissions OK. Time between acceptance and publication is 1 year or longer. Poems are circulated to an editorial board. Send SASE for guidelines. Reports in 6 months. Pays 4 copies, subscription and modest fee (when funds are available). Copyright reverts to author 2 months after publication. Occasionally, staff reviews books of poetry. Send books for review consideration, attn: Andrew Dawson.

Also Offers: The Bruce P. Rossley Literary Awards are given to previously under-recognized writers (of poetry or fiction) in New England. Writers can be nominated by anyone familiar with their work. Send SASE for further information.

ALWAYS include a self-addressed, stamped envelope (SASE) when sending a ms or query to a publisher within your own country. When sending material to other countries, include a self-addressed envelope and International Reply Coupons (IRCs), available at many post offices.

Advice: The editors add, "*96 Inc* is an artists' collaborative and a local resource. It often provides venues and hosts readings in addition to publishing a magazine."

N̄ ◎ ◑ NINETY-SIX PRESS (Specialized: regional), Furman University, Greenville SC 29613-0438, phone (864)294-3156, fax (864)294-2224, e-mail bill.rogers@furman.edu, website http://www.furman.edu/~wrog ers/96Press/HOME.htm, founded 1991, editors William Rogers and Gilbert Allen.
Book/Chapbook Needs & How to Submit: Publishes 1-2 paperback books of poetry/year. "The name of the press is derived from the old name for the area around Greenville, South Carolina—the Ninety-Six District. The name suggests our interest in the writers, readers and culture of the region." Books are usually 58 pgs., 6×9, professionally printed and perfect-bound with coated stock cover. For a sample, send $10. "We currently accept submissions by invitation only. At some point in the future, however, we hope to be able to encourage submissions by widely published poets who live in South Carolina."

✓ ◯ ◑ NITE-WRITER'S INTERNATIONAL LITERARY ARTS JOURNAL, 137 Pointview Rd. #300, Pittsburgh PA 15227-3131, phone (412)885-3798, e-mail nitewritez@aol.com, founded 1993, executive editor/publisher John A. Thompson Sr., associate editor Bree Ann Orner.
Magazine Needs: A quarterly open to beginners as well as professionals, *Nite-Writer's* is " 'dedicated to the emotional intellectual' with a creative perception of life." They want strong imagery and accept free verse, avant-garde poetry, haiku and senryu. Open to length and subject matter. No porn or violence. They have published poetry by Lyn Lifshin, Rose Marie Hunold, Peter Vetrano, Carol Frances Brown and Richard King Perkins II. As a sample the editors selected this poem, "Love Child," by Dianne Borsenik:
> make incense from the flower/dance naked in the light/weave a blanket/fringed with stars/to cover you
> at night/breathe kisses to the morning/braid songs into your hair/blow wishes on the feathered/spores
> that surf the curls of air/and if a storm should hurt you/pour honey on the pain/chase the clouds and
> catch them/then laugh/and drink the rain
The editors say the journal is 30-50 pgs., 8½×11, laser-printed, stock cover with sleeve, some graphics and artwork. They receive about 1,000 poems a year, use approximately 10-15%. Press run is about 100 for more than 60 subscribers of which 10 are libraries. Single copy: $6; subscription: $20. Sample (when available): $4.
How to Submit: Previously published poems and simultaneous submissions OK. Cover letter preferred. "Give brief bio, state where you heard of us, state if material has been previously published and where. Always enclose SASE if you seek reply and return of your material." Time between acceptance and publication is within 1 year. Always comments on rejections. Send SASE for guidelines. Reports in 2-4 weeks.
Advice: The editors say, "Don't be afraid to submit your material. Take rejection as advice—study your market. Create your own style and voice, then be heard. 'I am a creator, a name beneath words' (from my poem, 'unidentified-Identified')."

◑ NO EXIT, P.O. Box 454, South Bend IN 46624-0454, e-mail no_exit@usa.net, founded 1994, editor Mike Amato.
Magazine Needs: *No Exit* is a quarterly forum "for the experimental as well as traditional excellence." The editor says he wants "poetry that takes chances in form or content. Form, length, subject matter and style are open. No poetry that's unsure of why it was written. Particularly interested in long (not long-winded poems)." They have published poetry by Paul Weinman, Simon Perchik and Anthony Redisi. *NE* is 32 pgs., saddle-stapled, digest-sized, card cover with art. They accept 10-15% of the submissions received. Press run is less than 500 for 65 subscribers of which 6 are libraries. Subscription: $12. Sample: $4.
How to Submit: Submit up to 5 poems ("send more if compelled, but I will stop reading after the fifth"), 1 poem/page on 8½×11 paper. "No handwritten work, misspellings, colored paper, multiple type faces, typos, long-winded cover letters and lists of publication credits." No previously published poems; simultaneous submissions OK. No e-mail submissions. Time between acceptance and publication can vary from 1 month to 1 year. Sometimes comments on rejections, "if the poem strikes me as worth saving. No themes. But spring issues are devoted to a single poet. Interested writers should submit 24 pgs. of work. Don't bother unless of highest caliber." Send SASE for guidelines. Reports in 1-3 months. Pays 1 copy plus 4-issue subscription. Acquires first North American serial rights plus right to reprint once in an anthology. Reviews books of poetry. "Also looking for articles, critical in nature, on poetry/poets." Open to unsolicited reviews. Poets may also send books for review consideration.
Advice: The editor says, "Presentation means something; namely, that you care about what you do. Don't take criticism, when offered, personally. I'll work with you if I see something solid to focus on."

◯ ◎ NOCTURNAL LYRIC, JOURNAL OF THE BIZARRE (Specialized: horror), P.O. Box 115, San Pedro CA 90733-0115, phone (310)519-9220, e-mail nlyric@webtv.net, website http://www.angelfire.com/ ca/nocturnallyric, founded 1987, editor Susan Moon.
Magazine Needs: *Nocturnal Lyric* is a quarterly journal "featuring bizarre fiction and poetry, primarily by new writers." They want "poems dealing with the bizarre: fantasy, death, morbidity, horror, gore, etc. Any length. No 'boring poetry.' " They have published poetry by Donnie Nichols, Jennifer Berry and Irving Cross. *NL* is 40 pgs., digest-sized, photocopied, saddle-stapled, with trade ads and staff artwork. They receive about 200 poems

a year, use approximately 35%. Press run is 400 for 40 subscribers. Subscription: $10. Sample: $3, $2 for back issues; $4 for non-US addresses. Make checks payable to Susan Moon.

How to Submit: Submit up to 4 poems at a time. Previously published poems and simultaneous submissions OK. No e-mail submissions. Seldom comments on rejections. Reports in 4-6 months. Pays 50¢ "discount on subscription" coupons. Acquires one-time rights.

Advice: The editor says, "Please send us something really wild and intense!"

✓ ◐ NOMAD'S CHOIR, % Meander, 30-15 Hobart St. F4H, Woodside NY 11377, founded 1989, editor Joshua Meander.

Magazine Needs: *Nomad's Choir* is a quarterly. "Subjects wanted: love poems, protest poems, mystical poems, nature poems, poems of humanity, poems with solutions to world problems and inner conflict. 9-30 lines, poems with hope. Simple words, careful phrasing. Free verse, rhymed poems, sonnets, half-page parables, myths and legends, song lyrics. No curse words in poems, little or no name-dropping, no naming of consumer products, no two-page poems, no humor, no bias writing, no poems untitled." They have published poetry by Brenda Charles, Joseph Gourdji, Dorothy Wheeler and Jeff Swan. *Nomad's Choir* is 10 pgs., 8½×11, typeset and saddle-stapled with 3 poems/page. They receive about 150 poems a year, use approximately 50. Press run is 400; all distributed free. Subscription: $5. Sample: $1.25. Make checks payable to Joshua Meander.

How to Submit: Reports in 6-8 weeks. Pays 1 copy. Publishes theme issues. Send SASE for guidelines and upcoming themes.

Advice: The editor says, "Stick to your guns; however, keep in mind that an editor may be able to correct a minor flaw in your poem. Accept only minor adjustments. Go to many open poetry readings. Respect the masters. Read and listen to other poets on the current scene. Make pen pals. Start your own poetry journal. Do it all out of pure love."

▼ $ ◐ NORTH AMERICAN REVIEW, University of Northern Iowa, Cedar Falls IA 50614, phone (319)273-6455, fax (319)273-6455, e-mail nar@uni.edu, website http://www.webdelsol.com/NorthAmReview/NAR, founded 1815, poetry editor Peter Cooley.

● Work published in the *North American Review* has been included in the 1992, 1995, 1996 and 1997 volumes of *The Best American Poetry*.

Magazine Needs: *NAR* is a slick magazine-sized bimonthly of general interest, 48 pgs. average, saddle-stapled, professionally printed with glossy full-color paper cover, publishing poetry of the highest quality. They have published poetry by Francine Sterle, Cynthia Hogue and Marvin Bell. They receive about 15,000 poems a year, use approximately 20-30. Press run is 6,400 for 2,200 subscribers of which 1,100 are libraries, some 2,800 newsstand or bookstore sales. Subscription: $18. Sample: $5.

How to Submit: Include SASE. No simultaneous submissions or previously published poems. Fax and e-mail submissions OK. Time between acceptance and publication is up to 1 year. Send SASE for guidelines. Reports in 1-3 months. Always sends prepublication galleys. Pays 50¢/line and 2 copies. Buys first North American serial rights only. Returns rights after publication.

Ⓝ $ ◎ NORTH CAROLINA LITERARY REVIEW (Specialized: regional), English Dept., East Carolina University, Greenville NC 27858-4353, phone (252)328-1537, fax (252)328-4889, e-mail bauerm@mail.ecu .edu, founded 1992, editor Margaret Bauer.

Magazine Needs: *NCLR* is "an annual publication that contains articles and other works about North Carolina topics or by North Carolina authors." They want "poetry by writers currently living in North Carolina, those who have lived in North Carolina or those using North Carolina for subject matter." They have published poetry by Betty Adcock, James Applewhite and A.R. Ammons. The editor says *NCLR* is 200 pgs. and magazine-sized. They receive about 40-50 submissions a year, accept approximately 20%. Press run is 1,000 for 500 subscribers of which 150 are libraries, 100 shelf sales; 50 distributed free to contributors. Subscription: $20/2 years, $36/4 years. Sample: $10-12.

How to Submit: Submit 3-5 poems at a time. Previously published poems OK. Cover letter required. E-mail and disk submissions OK. "Submit 2 copies and include SASE or e-mail address for response." Reads submissions August 1 through April 30 only. Time between acceptance and publication is up to 1 year. Often comments on rejections. Publishes theme issues. Send SASE for guidelines and upcoming themes. Reports in 2 months. Sometimes sends prepublication galleys. Pays $25-50 plus 1-2 copies. Buys first or one-time rights. Reviews books of poetry in 2,000 words, multi-book format. Open to unsolicited reviews. Poets may also send books for review consideration.

◐ NORTH DAKOTA QUARTERLY, Box 7209, University of North Dakota, Grand Forks ND 58202-7209, founded 1910, poetry editor Jay Meek.

Magazine Needs: *North Dakota Quarterly* is a literary quarterly published by the University of North Dakota that includes material in the arts and humanities—essays, fiction, interviews, poems and visual art. "We want to see poetry that reflects an understanding not only of the difficulties of the craft, but of the vitality and tact that each poem calls into play." They have published poetry by Edward Kleinschmidt, Alane Rollings and Robert Wrigley. The poetry editor says *NDQ* is 6×9, about 200 pgs., perfect-bound, professionally designed and often printed with full-color artwork on a white card cover. You can find almost every kind of poem here—avant-garde to traditional. Typically the work of about 5 poets is included in each issue. Press run is 850 for 650 subscribers. Subscription: $25/year. Sample: $8.

How to Submit: Submit 5 poems at a time, typed, double-spaced. No previously published poems or simultaneous submissions. Time between acceptance and publication varies. Reports in 4-6 weeks. Always sends prepublication galleys. Pays 1 copy.

NORTHEAST; JUNIPER PRESS; JUNIPER BOOKS; THE WILLIAM N. JUDSON SERIES OF CONTEMPORARY AMERICAN POETRY; CHICKADEE; INLAND SEA SERIES; GIFTS OF THE PRESS (Specialized: form), 1310 Shorewood Dr., La Crosse WI 54601, founded 1962, poetry editors John Judson and Joanne Judson.
- "Poets we have published won The Pulitzer Prize, The Posner Poetry Prize, and one of our books was named to The Ten Most Notable Books of the year by the Wisconsin Library Association."

Magazine Needs & How to Submit: *Northeast* is an annual little magazine appearing in January. The editors say *Northeast* is digest-sized and saddle-stapled. Subscription: $33/year ($38 for institutions), "which brings you 1 issue of the magazine and the Juniper Books, Chickadees, WNJ Books and some gifts of the press, a total of about 3-5 items." (Or send SASE for catalog to order individual items; orders can be placed by calling the Order Dept. at (207)778-3454. Sample: $3.) No submissions by fax or e-mail. Reports in 2-4 months. Pays 2 copies.

Book/Chapbook Needs & How to Submit: Juniper Press does not accept unsolicited book/chapbook mss.

Advice: The editors say, "Please read us before sending mss. It will aid in your selection of materials to send. If you don't like what we do, please don't submit."

NORTHEAST ARTS MAGAZINE, P.O. Box 94, Kittery ME 03904, founded 1990, publisher/editor Mr. Leigh Donaldson.

Magazine Needs: *NEAM* is a biannual using poetry that is "honest, clear, with a love of expression through simple language, under 30 lines. Care for words and craftsmanship are appreciated." They have published poetry by S.P. Lutrell, Eliot Richman, Elizabeth R. Curry and Alisa Aran. *NEAM* is 32 or more pgs., digest-sized, professionally printed with 1-color coated card cover. They accept 20-25% of submissions. Press run is 500-1,000 for 150 subscribers of which half are libraries, 50 to arts organizations. An updated arts information section and feature articles are included. Subscription: $10. Sample: $4.50.

How to Submit: Reads submissions September 1 through February 28 only. "A short bio is helpful." Send SASE for guidelines. Reports in 2-3 months. Pays 2 copies. Acquires first North American serial rights.

NORTHEAST CORRIDOR (Specialized: regional), English Dept., Beaver College, Glenside PA 19038, phone (215)947-6732, founded 1993, contact Janna King.

Magazine Needs: *Northeast Corridor* is published semiannually. Ms. King dislikes "obscurity and sloppy estimations buried in pseudo-intellectualism. She wants poetry that employs brilliance of language to trigger and convey genuine emotion. In the end, the poem must be about the reader, or it is not effective." They have published poetry by Ted Kooser, Dana Gioia, Charity Hume and Stephen Dobyns. The editor says *NC* is 120-180 pgs., 6×8, perfect-bound, with color cover. They receive about 500 poems a year, use approximately 30-40. Press run is 1,000 for 200 subscribers of which 5 are libraries, 700 shelf sales; a few distributed free to contributors and donors. Single copy: $7; subscription: $20. Sample: $6.

How to Submit: Submit 3-5 poems with name and address on each page/poem. No previously published poems; simultaneous submissions OK. Cover letter preferred. Reads submissions September through May only. Time between acceptance and publication is 9 months. Poems are circulated to an editorial board. Often comments on rejections. Publishes theme issues. Send SASE for guidelines and upcoming themes. Reports in 3-4 months. Always sends prepublication galleys. Pays $10/poem plus 2 copies. Buys first rights. Occasionally sponsors contest issues.

THE NORTHERN CENTINEL (Specialized: nature/ecology/environment, ethics, legal/jurisprudence, political, social issues), e-mail Northern.Centinel@valley.net, website http://www.Centinel.org, founded 1788, poetry editors Ellen Rachlin and Lucie Aidinoff.

Magazine Needs: *The Northern Centinel* is an online publication focusing on "political/cultural essays and analyses on matters of national interest." They publish 12-24 poems annually. They have published poetry by Molly Peacock, Allen Ginsberg and Martin Tucker.

How to Submit: No previously published poems; simultaneous submissions OK. All submissions by e-mail only. Time between acceptance and publication is up to a year. Seldom comments on rejections. Reports within 4 months. Pays $10.

NORTHERN STARS MAGAZINE, N17285 Co. Rd. 400, Powers MI 49874, website http://members/aol.com/WriterNet/NorthStar.html or http://users/aol.com/WriterNet/, founded 1997, editor Beverly Kleikamp.

Magazine Needs: *Northern Stars* is published bimonthly and "welcomes submissions of fiction, nonfiction and poetry on any subject or style. The main requirement is good clean family reading material. Nothing you can't read to your child or your mother. No smut or filth." They have published poetry by Ella Dillon, Terri

Warden, Gary Edwards and Paul Agosto. As a sample the editor selected these lines from "Widow's Thoughts" by Terri Warden:

> *You told me I should not/Grieve. I should build/My life anew. How can I/Do as you suggest, when/My*
> *whole life was you?*

NS is 32 pgs., 8½×11, photocopied and saddle-stapled with paper cover, may include b&w line drawings. "Send SASE for subscription information." Sample: $4. Make checks payable to Beverly Kleikamp or *Northern Stars Magazine*.

How to Submit: Submit up to 10 poems at a time, no more than 25 lines each. Previously published poems and simultaneous submissions OK. Cover letter preferred. "Manuscripts must be typed—please do not submit handwritten material." Often comments on rejections. Publishes theme issues occasionally. "Once a year I plan to feature a state(s) as a vacation theme. Included in this issue will be various highlights and stories related to the chosen state. Pieces can be on vacation spots, sights, general information, or fiction stories with some tie to that state or area. Poems will still cover any subject." Pays either tearsheets or copy of *NS*. All rights return to authors on publication.

Also Offers: Sponsors monthly alternating issues contest for poetry and fiction/nonfiction (i.e., poetry contest in March-April issue, fiction/nonfiction in May-June). Reading fee: $2.50/poem for non-subscribers, $1/poem for subscribers. Deadline: 25th of month preceding publication. Publishes an annual chapbook of contest winners and honorable mentions.

◪ NORTHWEST REVIEW, 369 PLC, University of Oregon, Eugene OR 97403, phone (503)346-3957, founded 1957, poetry editor John Witte.

Magazine Needs: They are "seeking excellence in whatever form we can find it" and use "all types" of poetry. They have published poetry by Alan Dugan, Olga Broumas and Richard Eberhart. *NR*, a 6×9, flat-spined magazine, appears 3 times/year and uses 25-40 pgs. of poetry in each issue. They receive about 3,500 submissions a year, use approximately 4%, have up to a 4-month backlog. Press run is 1,300 for 1,200 subscribers of which half are libraries. Sample: $4.

How to Submit: Submit 6-8 poems clearly reproduced. No simultaneous submissions. The editor comments "whenever possible" on rejections. Send SASE for guidelines. Reports in 8-10 weeks. Pays 3 copies.

Advice: The editor advises poets to "persist."

✓ $ ◪ NORTHWOODS PRESS, THE POET'S PRESS; NORTHWOODS JOURNAL, A MAGA-ZINE FOR WRITERS; C.A.L. (CONSERVATORY OF AMERICAN LETTERS), P.O. Box 298, Thomaston ME 04861-0298, phone (207)354-0998, fax (207)354-8953, e-mail cal@ime.net, Northwoods Press founded 1972, *Northwoods Journal* 1993, editor Robert Olmsted.

Magazine Needs & How to Submit: *Northwoods Journal* is a quarterly literary magazine. "The journal is interested in all poets who feel they have something to say and who work to say it well. We have no interest in closet poets, or credit seekers. All poets seeking an audience, working to improve their craft and determined to 'get it right' are welcome here. Please request submission guidelines before submitting." *Northwoods* is about 40 pgs., digest-sized, desktop-published, flat-spined with matte card cover with b&w illustration. Subscription: $12.50/year. Sample: $5.50. Reading fee: $1.50/poem for nonmembers of C.A.L., 50¢/poem for members. One free read per year when joining or renewing membership in C.A.L. "Submission must accompany membership order." Send SASE for guidelines. Deadlines are the 1st of April, July, October and January for seasonal publication. Reports within 2 weeks after deadline, sometimes sooner. Pays $4/page, average, on acceptance.

Book Needs & How to Submit: "For book-length poetry manuscripts, submit to Northwoods Press. Our program is designed for the excellent *working poet* who has a following which is likely to create sales of $3,000 or more. Without at least that much of a following and at least that level of sales, no book can be published. Send SASE for our 15 pt. poetry program. Please do not submit manuscripts until you have read our guidelines." Northwoods Press will pay a minimum of $250 advance on contracting a book. The editors "rarely" comment on rejections, but they offer commentary for a fee, though they "strongly recommend *against* it."

Advice: The editors say, "Poetry must be non-trite, non-didactic. It must never bounce. Rhyme, if used at all, should be subtle. One phrase should tune the ear in preparation for the next. They should flow and create an emotional response."

⊕ ◪ ◎ NORTHWORDS; NORTHWORDS ANNUAL OPEN POETRY COMPETITION (Specialized: regional), The Stable, Long Rd., Avoch, Ross-Shire Scotland IV9 8QR United Kingdom, founded 1991, editor Angus Dunn.

Magazine Needs: Published 3 times a year, *Northwords* is "a literary journal focusing on material relevant to the North of Scotland, the geographical North generally, fiction (short) and poetry." They do not want "vague New Age poetry; philosophical poetry without physical referents. No trite sentiments in rhyme or otherwise." They have published poetry by Gael Turnbull, Sheena Blackhall, Tom Pow and Raymond Friel. As a sample the editor selected these lines from "Burnt River" by Betty Munnoch:

> *Return at dawn./Touch ancient rocks worn smooth/and smell the heavy orchid-bearing mulch/of*
> *northern woods. Listen to the lost soul cry of loons,/looking can come later. Slip into peat brown water/*
> *and swim the warming shallows to cooler deeps.*

The editor says *Northwords* is 36 pgs., A4, saddle-stitched with soft cover, illustrations often used. They receive about 500 poems a year, accept approximately 10%. Press run is 500 for 200 subscribers of which 10 are libraries, 180 shelf sales. Subscription: £10.50. Sample: £3 pounds sterling (international money order preferred if overseas).

How to Submit: Submit 4-6 poems at a time. No previously published poems or simultaneous submissions. Cover letter required. Reads submissions the first week of each month only. Time between acceptance and publication is 4 months. Poems are circulated to an editorial board. "All submissions are read by the editorial board, who advise acceptance or rejection. Final decision rests with the editor." Seldom comments on rejections. Reports in 2 months. Pays 1 copy and a small fee. Acquires first rights. Reviews books and chapbooks of poetry in 500-1,200 words, single and multi-book format. Open to unsolicited reviews. Poets may also send books for review consideration to Moira Forsyth, reviews ed., Northwords, Treetops, 25 Woodlands Rd., Dingwall, Ross-Shire 1V15 9LJ UK.

Also Offers: Sponsors the Northwords Annual Open Poetry Competition. 1st Prize £250; 2nd Prize £100; 3rd Prize £50. Entry fee: £2/poem. Deadline: July 31. Send SAE and IRC for contest rules.

☑ ◉ **W.W. NORTON & COMPANY, INC.**, 500 Fifth Ave., New York NY 10110, founded 1925, contact poetry editor.

Book/Chapbook Needs: W.W. Norton is a well-known commercial trade publishing house that publishes only original work in both hardcover and paperback. They want "quality literary poetry"; no "light or inspirational verse." They have published books by Rita Dove, Adrienne Rich, A.R. Ammons, Stanley Kunitz and Gerald Stein. W.W. Norton publishes approximately 10 books of poetry each year with an average page count of 64. They are published in cloth and flat-spined paperbacks, attractively printed, with 2-color glossy card covers.

How to Submit: Query first. No simultaneous submissions. Norton will consider only poets whose work has been published in quality literary magazines. Poems are circulated to an editorial board. Seldom comments on rejections. They report on queries in 6-8 weeks and mss in 4 months.

◉ **NOSTALGIA: A SENTIMENTAL STATE OF MIND**, P.O. Box 2224, Orangeburg SC 29116, website http://www.nospub.com, founded 1986, poetry editor Connie Lakey Martin.

Magazine Needs: *Nostalgia* appears spring and fall using "content at whim of poet, style open, prefer modern prose, but short poems, never longer than one page, no profanity, no ballads." *Nostalgia* is 24 pgs., digest-sized, offset typescript, saddle-stapled, with matte card cover. Press run is 1,000. Subscription: $8. Sample: $5.

How to Submit: "Most poems selected from contest." There are contests in each issue with award of $200 and publication for outstanding poem, publication and $25 for Honorable Mentions. Entry fee of $5 reserves future edition, covers 3 entries. Include SASE and put name and address on each poem. Deadlines: June 30 and December 31 each year. No previously published poems or simultaneous submissions. Guidelines available for SASE. Sometimes sends prepublication galleys. All rights revert to author upon publication.

Also Offers: Website includes updates on awards, deadlines and general guidelines for submission and contests.

Advice: Connie Martin says, "I offer criticism to most rejected poems, but I suggest sampling before submitting."

🖳 ◉ **NOTRE DAME REVIEW**, Dept. of English, University of Notre Dame, 356 O'Shaughnessy Hall, Notre Dame IN 46556-5639, phone (219)631-6952, fax (219)631-4268, e-mail english.ndreview.1@nd.edu, web-site http://www.nd.edu/~ndr/review.htm, founded 1994, poetry editor John Matthias.

Magazine Needs: *NDR* is "a biannual eclectic magazine of the best poetry and fiction." They are open to all types of poetry. They have published poetry by Ken Smith, Robert Creeley and Denise Levertov. As a sample the editor selected these lines from "The Watchman at Mycenae" by Seamus Heaney:

> *Some people wept, and not for sorrow-joy/That the king had armed and upped and sailed for Troy,/*
> *But inside me life struck sound in a gong/That killing-fest, the life-warm and world wrong/It brought*
> *to pass still argued and endured*

The editor says *NDR* is 170 pgs., magazine-sized, perfect-bound with 4-color glossy cover, includes art/graphics and ads. They receive about 4 poems a year, accept approximately 10%. Press run is 2,000 for 500 subscribers of which 150 are libraries, 1,000 shelf sales; 350 distributed free to contributors, assistants, etc. Single copy: $8; subscription: $15/year. Sample: $6. "Read magazine before submitting."

How to Submit: Submit 3-5 poems at a time. No previously published poems; simultaneous submissions OK. Cover letter required. Reads submissions September through May only. Time between acceptance and publication is 3 months. Seldom comments on rejections. Publishes theme issues. Obtain guidelines and upcoming themes via website. Reports in 3 months. Always sends prepublication galleys. Pays 2 copies. Acquires first rights. Staff reviews books of poetry in 500 words, single and multi-book format. Poets may also send books for review consideration.

Also Offers: Sponsors the Ernest Sandben Prize for Poetry, a book contest open to poets with at least one other book publication. Send SASE for details. Website includes writer's guidelines, names of editors, poetry and interviews.

◎ **NOVA EXPRESS (Specialized: science fiction/fantasy, horror)**, P.O. Box 27231, Austin TX 78755, e-mail lawrence@bga.com, website http://www.delphi.com/sflit/NovaExpress, founded 1987, editor Lawrence Person.

Magazine Needs: *Nova Express* appears "irregularly (at least once a year) with coverage of cutting edge science fiction, fantasy and horror literature, with an emphasis on post-cyperpunk and slipstream.'' They want ''poetry relating to literature of the fantastic in some way.'' They have published poetry by Alison Wimsatt. The editor says *Nova Express* is 48 pgs., 8½ × 11, stapled, desktop-published with b&w graphics and line art. They receive about 20-30 poems a year, use approximately 1-2. Press run is 750 for 200 subscribers, 200 shelf sales; 200-300 distributed free to science fiction industry professionals. Subscription: $12. Sample: $4.

How to Submit: Submit up to 5 poems at a time. No previously published poems or simultaneous submissions. Cover letter preferred. E-mail submissions preferred, ''they get the quickest response.'' Time between acceptance and publication is 3 months. Often comment on rejections. Publishes theme issues. Send SASE for guidelines or obtain via e-mail. Reports in 1-3 months. Sometimes sends prepublication galleys. Pays 2-4 copies plus subscription. Acquires one-time rights.

Advice: The editor says, ''We are not interested in any poetry outside the science fiction/fantasy/horror genre. *Nova Express* is read widely and well regarded by genre professionals.''

$ **NOW & THEN (Specialized: regional, themes)**, ETSU, P.O. Box 70556, Johnson City TN 37614-0556, phone (423)439-5348, fax (423)439-6340, e-mail woodsidj@etsu.edu, website http://www.cass.etsu. edu/n&t/N&T.htm, founded 1984, editor-in-chief Jane Woodside, poetry editor Linda Parsons.

Magazine Needs: *Now & Then* is a regional magazine that covers Appalachian issues and culture. It contains fiction, poetry, articles, interviews, essays, memoirs, reviews, photos and drawings. The editor specifically wants poetry related to the region. ''Each issue focuses on one aspect of life in the Appalachian region (anywhere hilly from Northern Mississippi on up to Southern New York). Previous theme issues have featured women, religion, blacks, Cherokees, the environment, music, the region's future and veterans. We want genuine, well-crafted voices, not sentimentalized stereotypes.'' They have published poetry by Fred Chappell, Rita Quillen, Michael Chitwood, Jim Wayne Miller and George Ella Lyon. *Now & Then* appears 3 times/year and is 42 pgs., magazine-sized, saddle-stapled, professionally printed, with matte card cover. Its press run is 1,250-1,500 for 900 members of the Center for Appalachian Studies and Services, of which 100 are libraries. They accept 6-10 poems an issue. Center membership is $20; the magazine is one of the membership benefits. Sample: $7.50 postage.

How to Submit: They will consider simultaneous submissions; they occasionally use previously published poems. Submit up to 5 poems, with SASE and cover letter including ''a few lines about yourself for a contributor's note and whether the work has been published or accepted elsewhere.'' Put name, address and phone number on every poem. No e-mail submissions. Deadlines: March 1, July 1 and November 1. Publishes theme issues. Upcoming themes include ''Museums & Archives'' (deadline November 1), ''Appalachian Accents'' (deadline March 1) and ''Rivers & Valleys'' (deadline July 1). Send SASE for guidelines and upcoming themes or obtain via website. Editor prefers fax or e-mail to phone calls. Reports in 4-6 months. Sends prepublication galleys. Pays $10/poem plus 2 copies. Acquires all rights. Reviews books of poetry in 750 words. Open to unsolicited reviews. Send poetry directly to poetry editor Linda Parsons Marion, 2909 Fountain Park Blvd., Knoxville TN 37917. E-mail for correspondence lpmarion@utk.edu. Poets may also send books for review consideration to Sandy Ballard, book review editor, Dept. of English, Carson-Newman College, Box 2059, Jefferson City TN 37760, e-mail ballard@cncacc.cn.edu.

NUTHOUSE; TWIN RIVERS PRESS (Specialized: humor), P.O. Box 119, Ellenton FL 34222, website http://members.aol.com/Nuthous499/index.html, press founded 1989, magazine founded 1993, editor Ludwig Von Quirk.

Magazine Needs: *Nuthouse*, ''amusements by and for delightfully diseased minds,'' appears every 6 weeks using humor of all kinds, including homespun and political. They simply want ''humorous verse; virtually all genres considered.'' They have published poetry by Holly Day, Daveed Garstenstein-Ross and Don Webb. The editor says *Nuthouse* is 12 pgs., digest-sized and photocopied from desktop-published originals. They receive about 500 poems a year, accept approximately 100. Press run is 100 for 50 subscribers. Subscription: $5/5 issues. Sample: $1.

How to Submit: Previously published poems and simultaneous submissions OK. Time between acceptance and publication is 6-12 months. Often comments on rejections. Reports within 1 month. Pays 1 copy/poem. Acquires one-time rights.

O!!ZONE (Specialized: visual poetry, photography, collage), 1266 Fountain View, Houston TX 77057-2204, phone (713)784-2802, fax (713)789-5119, e-mail hgburrus@msn.com, founded 1993, editor/publisher Harry Burrus.

Magazine Needs: *O!!Zone* is ''an international literary-art zine featuring visual poetry, travel pieces, interviews, haiku, manifestos, and art. We are particularly intrigued by poets who also do photography (or draw or paint). We also do broadsides, publish small, modest saddle-stitched collections, and will consider book-length collections (on a collaborative basis) *as time and dinero permits*.'' They want visual poetry and collage. ''I am interested in discovery and self-transcendence.'' No academic, traditional or rhyming poetry. They have published poetry by Demitry Babcuko, Willi Melnikov, Laura Ryder and Joel Lipman. The editor did not offer sample lines of poetry because he says, ''*O!!Zone* needs to be seen.'' The editor says *O!!Zone* is 80 pgs., 8½ × 5½, desktop-published, loaded with graphics. ''Write for a catalog listing our titles. Our *Vispo 96: O!!Zone Looks at International Visual Poetry* ($20) and *O!!Zone 97, International Visual Poetry* ($13) and *O!!Zone 98* ($15) are three anthologies that cover what's going on in international visual poetry.''

How to Submit: Submit 3-6 poems at a time. No previously published poems or simultaneous submissions. No fax submissions. "Submissions of visual poetry via snail mail; textual poems may come by e-mail." Cover letter preferred. They have a large backlog, "but always open to surprises." Seldom comments on rejections. Send SASE for guidelines. Reports "soon." Pays 1-2 copies..

◻ ◎ **THE OAK (Specialized: fantasy, soft horror, mystery); THE ACORN (Specialized: children); THE GRAY SQUIRREL (Specialized: senior citizens); THE SHEPHERD (Specialized: inspirational)**, 1530 Seventh St., Rock Island IL 61201, phone (309)788-3980, poetry editor Betty Mowery.
Magazine Needs & How to Submit: *The Oak*, founded 1990, is a "publication for writers with poetry and fiction." They want poetry of "no more than 35 lines and fiction of no more than 500 words." No restrictions as to types and style, but no pornography. Also takes fantasy and soft horror." *The Oak* appears quarterly. Founded 1991, *The Gray Squirrel* is now included in *The Oak* and takes poetry of no more than 35 lines only from poets 60 years of age and up. They take more than half of about 100 poems received each year. Press run is 250, with 10 going to libraries. Subscription: $10. Sample: $3. Make all checks payable to *The Oak*. Submit 5 poems at a time. Simultaneous submissions and previously published poems OK. Reports in 1 week. *"The Oak* does not pay in dollars or copies but you need not purchase to be published." Acquires first or second rights. *The Oak* holds several contests. Send SASE for guidelines.
Magazine Needs & How to Submit: *The Acorn*, founded 1988, is a "newsletter for young authors and teachers or anyone else interested in our young authors. Takes mss from kids K-12th grades. Poetry no more than 35 lines. It also takes fiction of no more than 500 words." It appears 4 times/year and "we take well over half of submitted mss." Press run is 100, with 6 going to libraries. Subscription: $10. Sample: $3. Make all checks payable to *The Oak*. Submit 5 poems at a time. Simultaneous submissions and previously published poems OK. Reports in 1 week. *"The Acorn* does not pay in dollars or copies but you need not purchase to be published." Acquires first or second rights. Young authors, submitting to *The Acorn*, should put either age or grade on manuscripts. *The Shepherd*, founded 1996, is a quarterly publishing inspirational poetry from all ages. Poems may be up to 35 lines. "We want something with a message but not preachy." Subscription: $10. Sample: $3.
Also Offers: Sponsors numerous contests. Send SASE for guidelines.
Advice: Editor Betty Mowery advises, "Beginning poets should submit again as quickly as possible if rejected. Study the market: don't submit blind. Always include a SASE or rejected manuscripts will not be returned. Please make checks for *all* publications payable to *The Oak*."

☑ $ ◻ **OASIS**, P.O. Box 626, Largo FL 33779-0626, phone (727)449-2186, e-mail oasislit@aol.com, website http://www.litline.org, founded 1992, editor Neal Storrs.
Magazine Needs: *Oasis* is a quarterly forum for high quality literary prose and poetry written almost exclusively by freelancers. Usually contains 7 prose pieces and the work of 6-7 poets. They want "to see original poetry of stylistic beauty. Prefer free verse with a distinct, subtle music. No superficial sentimentality, old-fashioned rhymes or rhythms." They have published poetry by Carolyn Stoloff, Fredrick Zydek and Kim Bridgford. As a sample the editor selected these lines from "The Lightning Speech of Birds" by Corrinne DeWinter:

> But now I must comply, twisting away from the clawed/lovers, shrinking from the familiar habits/of
> all three wives who have built cities and spires/under my skin/from the expectant crucifixions on the
> shoulder of the roads,/from the blessed damned on Venus' blushing sands.

Oasis is about 75 pgs., 7×10, attractively printed on heavy book paper, perfect-bound with medium-weight card cover, no art. They receive about 2,000 poems a year, accept approximately 2%. Press run is 300 for 90 subscribers of which 5 are libraries. Subscription: $20/year. Sample: $7.50.
How to Submit: Submit any number of poems. Rarely accepts previously published poems; simultaneous submissions OK. E-mail submissions OK. Cover letter preferred. Time between acceptance and publication is 4 months. Seldom comments on rejections. Send SASE for guidelines. Reports "the same or following day more than 99% of the time." Sometimes sends prepublication galleys. Pays 1 copy and $5/poem. Buys first or one-time rights.

$ ◎ **OBLATES (Specialized: religious, spirituality/inspirational)**, Missionary Association of Mary Immaculate, 9480 N. De Mazenod Dr., Belleville IL 62223-1160, phone (618)398-7640, ext. 3333, editor Christine Portell, mss editor Mary Mohrman.
Magazine Needs: *Oblates* is a bimonthly magazine circulating free to 500,000 benefactors. "We use well-written, perceptive traditional verse, average 16 lines. Avoid heavy allusions. We prefer a reverent, inspirational tone, but not overly 'sectarian and scriptural' in content." They have published poetry by Jean Conder Soule, Carlton J. Duncan and Jeanette M. Land. *Oblates* is 20 pgs., digest-sized, saddle-stapled, using color inside and on the cover. Sample and guidelines for SAE and 2 first-class stamps.
How to Submit: Submit up to 2 poems at a time. Considers simultaneous submissions. Time between acceptance and publication "is usually within 1 to 2 years." Editor comments "occasionally, but always when ms 'just missed or when a writer shows promise.' " Reports within 4-6 weeks. Pays $30 plus 3 copies. Buys first North American serial rights.
Advice: The editor says, "We are a small publication very open to mss from authors—beginners and professionals. We do, however, demand professional quality work. Poets need to study our publication, and to send no more

than one or two poems at a time. Content must be relevant to our older audience to inspire and motivate in a positive manner."

$ 🕊 ◎ OCEAN VIEW BOOKS (Specialized: form/style, science fiction), P.O. Box 102650, Denver CO 80250, founded 1981, editor Lee Ballentine.
Book/Chapbook Needs: Ocean View Books publishes "books of poetry by poets influenced by surrealism and/or science fiction." They publish 2 paperbacks and 2 hardbacks/year. No "confessional/predictable, self-referential poems." They have published poetry by Anselm Hollo, Janet Hamill and Tom Disch. Books are usually 100 pgs., 5½×8½ or 6×9, offset printed and perfect-bound with 4-color card cover, includes art. "Our books are distinctive in style and format. Interested poets should order a sample book for $5 (in the US) for an idea of our focus before submitting."
How to Submit: Submit 5 poems at a time. Previously published poems and simultaneous submissions OK. Cover letter preferred. Time between acceptance and publication is 1-3 years. "If our editors recommend publication, we may circulate manuscripts to distinguished outside readers for an additional opinion." Replies to queries in 6 months. Pays $100 honorarium and a number of author's copies (out of a press run of 500). "Terms vary per project."
Advice: The editor says, "In 15 years, we have published about 40 books—most consisted of previously published poems from good journals. A poet's 'career' must be well-established before undertaking a book."

Ⓝ 🖳 ◑ OCTAVO; THE ALSOP REVIEW, e-mail wasserman@alsopreview.com, website http://www.alsopreview.com/, founded 1998, editor Jamie Wasserman, founder Jaimes Alsop.
Magazine Needs: *Octavo* is a monthly Web publication and "contains 8 poems/stories per issue. It aims to merge the print and Web world, to bring established print writers to the Web and highlight those writers whose reputations are still word-of-mouth." They want "well-crafted verse with a strong voice. No pornography; overtly religious work, greeting card verse or sloppy writing." They have published poetry by Dorianne Laux, Kim Addonizio, Lola Haskins and Peter Johnson. As a sample the editors selected these lines from "Medievalism" by Ronald Donn:

> And the great theme is great/because you run from it,/in this world like water,/like skin—rush over
> muscle,/settle at the bottom into/the shape of a man.

They receive about 1,000 poems a year, accept approximately 2%.
How to Submit: Submit 3-5 poems at a time. No previously published poems; simultaneous submissions OK. Cover letter preferred. "Submissions may only be sent via e-mail." Time between acceptance and publication is 1 month. Seldom comments on rejections. Obtain guidelines via e-mail. Reports in 1 month. Acquires first rights.
Also Offers: "*Octavo* is a monthly magazine of the *Alsop Review*, a website that showcases literary works by some of today's premiere writers, including Carolyn Kizer, Barry Spacks, Kim Addonizio and Dorianne Laux."
Advice: The editors say, "The Web is rapidly becoming the new medium of choice for some of today's top writers. Take Internet submissions seriously and support the online literary community by exploring the myriad of sites out there."

◑ ODIN'S EYE, 400 Taylor Ave. #104, Renton WA 98055, phone (206)772-7446, e-mail odineye@yahoo.com, founded 1998, editor Jonathan Shipley, arts editor Marie Shipley.
Magazine Needs: *Odin's Eye* appears 4-5 times a year. "We are dedicated to the art of poetry. We are looking for any poem that will make us laugh, make us cry, make us think. We like all poetry as long as it's good. Shorter pieces have a better chance because of the format. We're also looking for scannable b&w artwork. We want what you're proud of." They have published poetry by B.Z. Niditch, Dan Hasso and Rebecca Hammer. As a sample the editor selected his poem "A Room With A View":

> I looked out the window towards/obsidian nights not expecting to/see anyone. But she stepped in/and
> we did a tango before she/left where the moon still hung.

The editor says *Odin's Eye* is about 10-20 pgs., 5½×8½, photocopied and stapled with b&w or color card stock cover, includes b&w, camera-ready art. Accept approximately 75% of poems received a year. Subscription: $12. Sample (including guidelines): $3. Make checks payable to Jonathan Shipley.
How to Submit: Submit 2-5 poems at a time. Previously published poems and simultaneous submissions OK. No e-mail submissions. Cover letter preferred. "We would appreciate a cover letter so we know the poet behind the poetry." Time between acceptance and publication is 2-6 months. Always comments on rejections. Reports in 1-4 weeks. Pays 1 copy. Acquires first or one-time rights. Reviews books and chapbooks of poetry and other magazines in 50-100 words. Open to unsolicited reviews. Poets may also send books for review consideration.
Advice: The editor says, "Horace once said, 'You will have written exceptionally well if, by skillful arrangements of words, you have made an ordinary one seem original.' Be original. Don't be afraid. Poetry is about passions."

OPENNESS TO SUBMISSIONS: ◑ beginners; ◐ beginners and experienced; 🕊 mostly experienced, few beginners; ◎ specialized; ◑ closed to unsolicited mss.

Write about what you love. Write passionately. Write not because you want to write, write because you have to."

$ ◎ OF UNICORNS AND SPACE STATIONS (Specialized: science fiction/fantasy), P.O. Box 97, Bountiful UT 84011-0097, e-mail gene@genedavis.com, website http://www.genedavis.com/magazine, founded 1994, editor Gene Davis.
Magazine Needs: *OUASS*, published biannually, features science fiction/fantasy literature. "Material written in traditional fixed forms are given preference. Poetry of only a scientific slant or that only uses science fiction/ fantasy imagery will be considered." As a sample the editor selected these lines from "Sick Satellite" by John Grey:
> *its orbit decays/like flesh and bone,/even in space*
OUASS is 60 pgs., digest-sized, digital press, saddle-stitched with "spot color" illustrated card cover. They receive about 200 poems a year, accept approximately 2%. Press run is 100 for 100 subscribers; 2-3 distributed free to convention organizers and critics. Subscription: $16/4 issues. Sample: $4. Make checks payable to Gene Davis.
How to Submit: Submit 3 poems, with name and address on each page. "Manuscripts should be paper-clipped, never stapled." Previously published poems OK; no simultaneous submissions. "No electronic submissions are read." Cover letter preferred. "If sending fixed form poetry, mention what form you used in your cover letter. Editors pulling 16-hour shifts don't always spot poem types at 1 a.m." Time between acceptance and publication is 6-9 months. Poems are circulated to an editorial board of 2 editors. "Both have veto power over every piece." Seldom comments on rejections. Send SASE for guidelines. Reports in 2-3 months. Pays 1 copy and "$5 flat rate for poetry." Acquires one-time rights.

✓ ◎ OFF THE ROCKS (Specialized: gay/lesbian), 921 West Argyle #1 West, Chicago IL 60640, e-mail offtherock@aol.com, website http://www.newtownwriters.org/, founded 1980, president (Newtown Writers) Randy Gresham, editor (*Off The Rocks*) Larry Lesperance.
Magazine Needs: *Off The Rocks*, a publication of Newtown Writers, is an annual and publishes poetry focused on gay/lesbian subjects. They want "all forms, 30 lines or less." They have published poetry by Robert Klein Engler, Adrian Ford, Gerald Wozek and Judy McCormick. As a sample the editor selected these lines from "Door Colmel" (poet unidentified):
> *You rang my bell/later on we lay/in the light of the alien t.v./at 5:00/alone I heard the self-same note/ float in my dream . . .*
The editor says *OTR* is about 50 pgs., 8×11, staple-bound with art/graphics, no ads. They receive about 100 poems a year, accept approximately 20%. Press run is 1,000, almost all shelf sales. Single copy: $5. Sample: $2. Make checks payable to Newtown Writers, Inc.
How to Submit: Submit 5 poems at a time. Previously published poems and simultaneous submissions OK. Cover letter preferred including bio and list of previously published work. Time between acceptance and publication is 1 year. Poems are circulated to an editorial board. "There is discussion of poem's merits, debate, rebuttal, then voting on poems to be published." Often comments on rejections. Obtain guidelines via e-mail or website. Reports in 3 months. Sometimes sends prepublication galleys. Pays 2 copies.

◯ ◪ OFFERINGS, P.O. Box 1667, Lebanon MO 65536-1667, founded 1994, editor Velvet Fackeldey.
Magazine Needs: *Offerings* is a poetry quarterly. "We accept traditional and free verse from established and new poets, as well as students. Prefer poems of less than 30 lines. No erotica." They have published poetry by Michael Estabrook, Kent Braithwaite, Jocelyne Kamerer and Robert Hentz. As a sample the editor selected these lines from "Reading" by Eric Colburn:
> *Some Memories/are better left in mothballs//Stored away/in boxes stashed in closets,/the dust not disturbed.//Or in the basement/damp from cement floors,/mice droppings on the lid*
Offerings is 50-60 pgs., digest-sized, neatly printed (one poem to a page) and saddle-stapled with paper cover. They receive about 500 poems a year, accept approximately 25%. Press run is 100 for 75 subscribers, 25 shelf sales. Single copy: $5; subscription: $16. Sample: $3.
How to Submit: Submit typed poems with name and address on each page. Students should also include grade level. SASE required. No simultaneous submissions. Seldom comments on rejections. Send SASE for guidelines. Reports in 1 week. All rights revert to author after publication.
Advice: The editor says, "We are unable to offer payment at this time (not even copies) but hope to be able to do so in the future. We welcome beginning poets."

◯ ◎ OFFICE NUMBER ONE (Specialized: form), 1708 S. Congress Ave., Austin TX 78704, e-mail onocdingus@aol.com, founded 1988, editor Carlos B. Dingus.
Magazine Needs: Appearing 2-4 times/year, *ONO* is a "humorous, satirical zine of news information and events from parallel and alternate realities." In addition to stories, they want limericks, 3-5-3 or 5-7-5 haiku and rhymed/metered quatrains. "Poems should be short (2-12 lines) and make a point. No long rambling poetry about suffering and pathos. Poetry should be technically perfect." As for a sample, the editor says, "No one poem provides a fair sample." *ONO* is 12 pgs., 8½×11, computer set in 10 pt. type, saddle-stitched, with graphics and ads. They use about 20 poems a year. Press run is 2,000 for 75 subscribers, 50 shelf sales; 1,600 distributed free locally. Single copy: $1.85; subscription: $8.82/6 issues. Sample: $2.

How to Submit: Submit up to 5 pgs. of poetry at a time. Previously published poems and simultaneous submissions OK. E-mail submissions OK. "Will comment on rejections if comment is requested." Publishes theme issues occasionally. Send SASE for guidelines and upcoming themes or request via e-mail. Reports in 1-2 months. Pays "23¢" and 1 copy. Buys "one-time use, and use in any *ONO* anthology."

Advice: The editor says, "Say something that a person can use to change his life."

☑ $◑ **THE OHIO REVIEW; OHIO REVIEW BOOKS**, 344 Scott Quad, Ohio University, Athens OH 45701-2979, phone (740)593-1900, website http://www-as.phy.ohiou.edu/Departments/English/Ohioreview/OR.html, founded 1971, editor Wayne Dodd.

Magazine Needs: *The Ohio Review* appears 2 times/year and attempts "to publish the best in contemporary poetry, fiction and reviews" in the *Review* and in chapbooks, flat-spined paperbacks and hardback books. "Only criterion is excellence." They have published poems by W.S. Merwin, Jane Miller, Bin Ramke, Mary Oliver, Charles Wright, David St. John and Rosmarie Waldrop. *The Ohio Review* is professionally printed, flat-spined format of 200 pgs., 4-color glossy cover with art, circulation 3,000, featuring about 28 poets/issue. Receives about 3,000 submissions a year, uses approximately 1% of them. Subscription: $16. Sample: $6.

How to Submit: Include SASE with submissions and type name and address on each page of ms. Reads submissions September 15 through May 30 only. Editor sometimes comments on rejections. Send SASE for guidelines. Reports in 1 month. Always sends prepublication galleys. Pays $1/line for poems and $5/page for prose plus 2 copies. Buys first North American serial rights. Reviews books of poetry in 5-10 pgs., single or multi-book format. Send books to Review Editor for review consideration.

Book/Chapbook Needs & How to Submit: They are not currently accepting unsolicited submissions of book mss. Query with publication credits, bio.

☑ ◑ **OHIO STATE UNIVERSITY PRESS/THE JOURNAL AWARD IN POETRY**, 1070 Carmack Rd., Columbus OH 43210-1002, phone (614)292-6930, fax (614)292-2065, e-mail ohiostatepress@osu.edu, website http://www.ohiostatepress.org, poetry editor David Citino.

Book/Chapbook Needs & How to Submit: Each year *The Journal* (see listing also in this section) selects for publication by Ohio State University Press one full-length (at least 48 pgs.) book ms submitted during September, typed, double-spaced, $20 handling fee (payable to OSU). They have published *Heroic Measures* by David Bergman and *Troubled Lovers in History* by Albert Goldbarth. Send SASE for confirmation of ms receipt. Mss will not be returned. Some or all of the poems in the collection may have appeared in periodicals, chapbooks or anthologies, but must be identified. Along with publication, *The Journal* Award in Poetry pays $1,000 cash prize. Each entrant receives a subscription (2 issues) to *The Journal*.

Ⓝ ◯ ◑ ◉ **OHIO TEACHERS WRITE (Specialized: work by teachers)**, English Dept., Youngstown State University, One University Plaza, Youngstown OH 44555-1001, phone (330)742-3421, fax (330)742-2304, e-mail htmccrac@cc.ysu.edu, founded 1995, *OTW* 1999 editor H. Thomas McCracken.

Magazine Needs: *Ohio Teachers Write* is published "to provide an annual collection of fine literature, to encourage teachers to compose literary works along with their students, and to provide Ohioans a window into the world of teaching." They want poems on any subject and in any style. Nothing X-rated. They have published poetry by Lou Suarez and Kathleen Burgess. As a sample the editor selected these lines from "fraternity summer" by Bill Newby:

> things in profusion/clothing that had multiplied in floor piles and on chairs/desk tops buried beneath
> last week's programs and yesterday's messages/and a wounded couch saved from a salvation suicide/
> waiting for one last couple to couple

OTW is 48 pgs., 8½ × 11, offset printed and flat-spined with cardstock cover, includes original drawings, photos. They receive about 100 poems a year, accept approximately 30%. Press run is 2,000. Subscription: $6. Sample: $4. Make checks payable to Ohio Council of Teachers of English Language Arts. "Contributors must be in-training, active or retired Ohio teachers."

How to Submit: Submit 2 poems at a time, maximum. No previously published poems or simultaneous submissions. E-mail and disk submissions OK. "Please mail six copies and a SASE." Submissions must be received by April 1 for publication each October. Time between acceptance and publication is 6 months. Poems are circulated to an editorial board. "Members of an editorial board read work independently and then confer together to select work for publication." Seldom comments on rejections. Send SASE for guidelines. Reports in June or July. Pays 2 copies. Acquires first rights..

Advice: "*Ohio Teachers Write* is a ready vehicle for Ohio teachers to share their creative writing with the teaching community and others. Submission also prepares teachers to better help students with the challenges of writing and publication."

🔊 ☑ $◉ **ON SPEC: MORE THAN JUST SCIENCE FICTION (Specialized: regional, science fiction/fantasy, horror)**, P.O. Box 4727, Edmonton, Alberta T6E 5G6 Canada, e-mail onspec@earthling.net, website http://www.icomm.ca/onspec/, founded 1989, poetry editor Barry Hammond.

Magazine Needs: *On Spec* is a quarterly featuring Canadian science fiction writers and artists. They want work by Canadian poets only and only science fiction/speculative poetry; 100 lines maximum. They have published poetry by Sandra Kasturi and Alice Major. As a sample the editor selected these lines from "Wild Things" by Eileen Kernaghan:

> *you can sing small songs to soothe them/make them soft and secret beds to lie in//still you will wake in winter dawns/to find them crouched upon your pillow/their sharp claws unravelling/the frayed edges of your dreams*

On Spec is 112 pgs., digest-sized, offset printed on recycled paper and perfect-bound with color cover, b&w art and ads inside. They receive about 100 poems a year, accept approximately 5%. Press run is 1,750 for 800 subscribers of which 10 are libraries, 600 shelf sales. Single copy: $4.95; subscription: $19.95 (both in Canadian funds). Sample: $6.

How to Submit: Submit up to 5 poems of up to 100 lines at a time with SASE (or SAE and IRC). No previously published poems or simultaneous submissions. No submissions via fax or e-mail. Cover letter with poem titles and 2-sentence bio required. Deadlines: February 28, May 31, August 31 and November 30. Reports in 4 months maximum. Time between acceptance and publication is 6 months. Usually comments on rejections. Publishes theme issues. Send SASE for guidelines and upcoming themes or check website. Pays $20/poem and 1 copy, pays on acceptance. Acquires first North American serial rights.

Also Offers: Website includes writer's guidelines, names and bios of editors, past editorials, excerpts from back issues, links for writers and announcements.

◐ ONE TRICK PONY; BANSHEE PRESS, P.O. Box 11186, Philadelphia PA 19136, phone (215)331-7389, founded 1997, editor Louis McKee.

Magazine Needs: *One Trick Pony* is published biannually and contains "poetry and poetry related reviews and essays (for reviews, essays, interviews, etc.—please query)." No limitations. They have published poetry by William Heyen, Naomi Shihab Nye, Denise Duhamel and Michael Waters. The editor says *OTP* is 60 pgs., 4¼ × 5½, offset printed and stapled, glossy cover with art. They receive about 750 poems a year, accept approximately 10%. Press run is 400 for over 150 subscribers of which 12 are libraries, 150 shelf sales. Single copy: $5; subscription: $10/3 issues. Sample: $4. Make checks payable to Louis McKee.

How to Submit: Submit 3-6 poems at a time. No previously published poems; simultaneous submissions OK. Reports in 2-4 weeks. Pays 2 copies. Acquires first rights. Reviews books and chapbooks of poetry. Open to unsolicited reviews. Poets may also send books for review consideration.

Book/Chapbook Needs: Banshee Press publishes 1 chapbook/year. Chapbooks are *by invitation only.*

Ⓝ ◐ THE ONSET REVIEW, P.O. Box 3157, Wareham MA 02571, phone/fax (508)291-1188, e-mail pizzo @mediaone.net, website http://www.word-studio.com/the-onset-review, founded 1994, editors Susan Pizzolato and Scott Withiam.

Magazine Needs: *The Onset Review* is published biannually "to showcase the best new writing by new and published poets and writers." They are "interested in poetry that takes risks, experiments with language and provokes the imagination. No obviously rhymed poems, early drafts or work unsure of voice; no clichéd imagery." They have published poetry by Carole Simmons Oles, Mark Cox, Martha Collins and Joyce Peseroff. The editors say *TOR* is 76-150 pgs., magazine-sized, offset printed and perfect-bound with cover photo and b&w photos and line drawings inside. They receive about 1,000 poems a year, accept approximately 10%. Press run is 1,000.

How to Submit: Submit 2-6 poems at a time. No previously published poems; simultaneous submissions OK. Disk submissions OK. Cover letter with bio notes preferred. Time between acceptance and publication is 2 months. Occasionally comments on rejections. Send SASE for guidelines. Reports in 2 months. Sometimes sends prepublication galleys. Pays 2 copies. Acquires first rights. Staff reviews books and chapbooks of poetry in 500 words. Send books for review consideration.

Also Offers: Website includes editors' address, copy of cover photo, brief description of journal and guidelines.

Advice: The editors say, "Read as much as you can, then do something different."

◐ ONTHEBUS; BOMBSHELTER PRESS, P.O. Box 481266, Bicentennial Station, Los Angeles CA 90048, founded 1975, *ONTHEBUS* editor Jack Grapes, Bombshelter Press poetry editors Jack Grapes and Michael Andrews.

Magazine Needs: *ONTHEBUS* uses "contemporary mainstream poetry—no more than six (ten pgs. total) at a time. No rhymed, 19th Century traditional 'verse.' " They have published poetry by Charles Bukowski, Albert Goldbarth, Ai, Norman Dubie, Kate Braverman, Stephen Dobyns, Allen Ginsberg, David Mura, Richard Jones and Ernesto Cardenal. As a sample Jack Grapes selected "Splitting Hairs" by Joyce Elaine Ross:

> *After I poured my blocks onto the floor and shuffled them,/then made one last attempt to attain some form of poetic/fusion, like William Grant Still's Afro-American Symphony/of classical blues on jazz, I realized that I've never been/able to get others to understand me; that my words always/seem to turn into fishbones and sawdust whenever I tried/to talk about it. And if I could, I would drink my own/ skin, erase the stain of my colors.*

ONTHEBUS is a magazine appearing 2 times/year, 275 pgs., offset printed, flat-spined, with color card cover. Press run is 3,500 for 600 subscribers of which 40 are libraries, 1,200 shelf sales ("500 sold directly at readings"). Subscription: $28/3 issues; Issue #8/9, special double issue: $15. Sample (including guidelines): $12.

How to Submit: Submit 3-6 poems at a time to the above address (send all other correspondence to: 6684 Colgate Ave., Los Angeles CA 90048). Simultaneous submissions and previously published poems OK, "if I am informed where poem has previously appeared and/or where poem is also being submitted. I expect neatly-typed, professional-looking cover letters with list of poems included plus poet's bio. Sloppiness and unprofessional submissions do not equate with great writing." Do not submit mss between November 1 and March 1 or between June 1 and September 1. Submissions sent during those times will be returned unread. Reports in "anywhere from two weeks to two years." Pays 1 copy. Acquires one-time rights. Reviews books of poetry in 400 words (chapbooks in 200 words), single format. Open to unsolicited reviews. Poets may also send books for review consideration.

Book/Chapbook Needs & How to Submit: Bombshelter Press publishes 4-6 flat-spined paperbacks and 5 chapbooks/year. Query first. Primarily interested in Los Angeles poets. "We publish very few unsolicited mss." Reports in 3 months. Pays 50 copies. They also publish the *ONTHEBUS* Poets Anthology Series. Send SASE for details.

Advice: Jack Grapes says, "My goal is to publish a democratic range of American poets and ensure they are read by striving to circulate the magazine as widely as possible. It's hard work and a financial drain. I hope the mag is healthy for poets and writers, and that they support the endeavor by subscribing as well as submitting."

② OPEN HAND PUBLISHING INC., P.O. Box 22048, Seattle WA 98122-0048, phone (206)323-2187, fax (206)323-2188, founded 1981, publisher P. Anna Johnson. Open Hand is a "literary/political book publisher bringing out flat-spined paperbacks as well as cloth cover editions about African-American and multicultural issues." They do not consider unsolicited mss.

Ⓝ Ⓥ OPEN SPACES, 6327 C SW Capitol Hwy., Suite 134, Portland OR 97201-1937, founded 1997, poetry editor Susan Juve-Hu Bucharest.

Magazine Needs: "*Open Spaces* is a quarterly which gives voice to the Northwest on issues that are regional, national and international in scope. Our readership is thoughtful, intelligent, widely read and appreciative of ideas and writing of the highest quality. With that in mind, we seek thoughtful, well-researched articles and insightful fiction, reviews and poetry on a variety of subjects from a number of different viewpoints. Although we take ourselves seriously, we appreciate humor as well." The editor says the magazine is 64 pgs., magazine-sized, sheet-fed printed, cover art and graphics and original art throughout. "We have received many submissions and hope to use 3-4 per issue." Press run is 5,000-10,000. Subscription: $25/year. Sample: $10. Make checks payable to Open Spaces Publications, Inc.

How to Submit: Submit 3-5 poems at a time. Previously published poems and simultaneous submissions OK. Cover letter required. Time between acceptance and publication is 2-3 months. Poems are circulated to an editorial board. Seldom comments on rejections. Reports in 2-3 months. Payment varies. Reviews books and chapbooks of poetry and other magazines in 300 words, single book format. "We solicit reviews."

Advice: The editor says, "In our first 3 issues, we have published the poetry of Vern Rutsala, Pattiann Rogers and William Jolliff. Poetry is presented with care and respect."

Ⓝ Ⓞ OPEN UNIVERSITY OF AMERICA PRESS; OPEN UNIVERSITY OF AMERICA (Specialized: religious, nature, distance learning, English pedagogy), 3916 Commander Dr., Hyattsville MD 20782-1027, phone/fax (301)779-0220, e-mail openuniv@aol.com, website http://www.openuniversityofamerica.com, founded 1965, co-editors Mary Rodgers and Dan Rodgers.

Book/Chapbook Needs: "We buy artistic work outright before copyright or publication by the author. We include these literary pieces always with the author's name in our university publications, catalogues, lists, etc." They publish 4 paperbacks and 4 hardbacks/year. They have "no restrictions on poetry. Shorter is better. One page set up for 6×9 is good. A set of poems (short chapbook) should be uniform." They are interested in receiving work on the topics of "Catholic faith and culture; morality; nature; open learning and English pedagogy (teaching English) K-Ph.D. Pre-published or pre-copyrighted or book-length poems are beyond our capability." They have published poetry by Castina Kennedy, John Tormento, Emebeat Bekele and Raphael Flores. As a sample the editors selected this poem, "Reality," by Rosalee Dansan in *Catholic Teacher Poems, 1945-1995*:

> Yesterday/I had dreams of tomorrow./Somewhere in tomorrowland,/Life with you./But dreams shatter/
> Like glass;/Like mine did when halfway to my mouth,/Before I could taste the sweetness of the wine./
> Today/I do not dream./I have no guarantee of tomorrow/For today I have only today.

Books are usually 100-200 pgs., 6×9, computer/laser printed, perfect-bound (some sewn in library binding), soft cover, includes art.

How to Submit: Submit up to 10 poems at a time. No previously published poems or simultaneous submissions. Cover letter preferred. "We buy poems and small sets of poems outright (price negotiable), so we need pre-copyrighted, pre-published literary work. No whole books. When we publish compilations, we always list the name of the artist/author. Literary work is accepted on its own merit and its usefulness in perpetuity to the Press and to Open University of America. Make sure you want to put your poem for final and irrevocable sale." Reading fee: $1/poem. Time between acceptance and publication is 1-2 years. Poems are circulated to an editorial board. "Two editors plus one consultant select work to be purchased for publication. Note that we purchase all rights for publication, total rights." Seldom comments on rejections. Replies to queries and mss in 2-3 weeks. Order sample books by sending $10 or order off the web.

Advice: The editors say, "Today electronic publishing, overseas sales, and other mass selling mechanisms are running rough-shod over the rights of writers. We buy your verbal art at a fair, negotiated price before copyright and publication. We use your poem/poems always with your name attached to enhance our literary productions. We keep it in perpetuity in our Literary Trust. This is an effective way to get publicity for your name and your work, as well as to earn income."

ORACLE POETRY; ASSOCIATION OF AFRICAN WRITERS; RISING STAR PUBLISHERS (Specialized: ethnic), 2105 Amherst Rd., Hyattsville MD 20783, phone (301)422-2665, fax (301)422-2720, founded 1989, editorial director Obi Harrison Ekwonna.
Magazine Needs: *Oracle Poetry* appears quarterly using works "mainly of African orientation; must be probing and must have meaning—any style or form. Writers must have the language of discourse and good punctuation. No gay, lesbian or erotic poetry." Membership in the Association of African Writers is $20/year. *Oracle Poetry* is 46 pgs., digest-sized, saddle-stapled, print run 500. Subscription: $20/year.
How to Submit: No previously published poems or simultaneous submissions. "Poets may submit materials by fax; however, we prefer submissions by disk in WordPerfect 5.1, or in copies." Reports in 4-6 weeks. Pays 1 copy. Acquires first North American serial rights. Reviews books of poetry.
Also Offers: Sponsors contests. Send SASE for details.
Advice: The editor says, "Read widely, write well and punctuate right."

ORANGE WILLOW REVIEW, P.O. Box 768, Island Lake IL 60042, fax (847)487-6619, e-mail changeling@ameritech.net, founded 1998, editor/publisher Cynthia Warryn Leffner.
Magazine Needs: The *OWR* appears 2-4 times a year and "is a magazine of the arts, literature and psychology which strives to publish work reflecting creativity, originality, craft, intelligence and the ability to take risks with literature. The magazine was founded for humanity about humanity and attempts to show the value of the human experience. We like the surreal, the eclectic, and the deeply psychological. We want to see poetry that utilizes language and vivid, visual imagery to convey an involuntary, inherent response to the world; moments of 'poetic seizure.' The *Orange Willow Review* is a magazine published in memory of Van Gogh and others like him." No pornography or greeting card verse. They have published poetry by Ray Greenblatt and Thomas Catterson. As a sample the editor selected these lines from "China Sequence" by Ray Greenblatt:

> Rain draws maps on windows/tea leaves swim in green cups/crows feet walk/across newspapers./ Wearing caps of mist/rice paddies lie green and silent/by water subdivided,/a person bookmarking/ each field./Buildings with pagoda roofs/and yards of rubbish/crumbling beside high rises/town after town.

The editor says *OWR* is 100-122 pgs., 5½×8½, offset printed and perfect-bound with glossy color text weight cover, includes pen & ink, sketches, computer graphics, oil paint (fine art on cover), ads. Press run is 500. Subscription: $14. Sample: $3. Make checks payable to Cynthia Warryn Leffner.
How to Submit: Submit 6-10 poems at a time. No previously published poems; simultaneous submissions OK. Cover letter with bio and SASE preferred. Disk submissions OK. "We accept poems written in any style, any form, any length. If poems are more than 4 double-spaced pages please only send 3." Time between acceptance and publication is 3 months, "usually sooner. Presently, all work is reviewed by myself and one other assistant. However, we are in the process of adding a review board from members of our writer's groups and workshops." Always comments on rejections. Publishes theme issues occasionally. Send SASE for guidelines and upcoming themes. Reports in 3 months. Sometimes sends prepublication galleys. Pays 2 copies. Acquires first North American serial rights.
Also Offers: Sponsors contests. "We will publish a special issue on 'the artistic experience, mental illness and transcending suffering through art.' We may pay cash awards if funds allow. We are a nonprofit organization. Also, we will expand in the year 2000 to publishing chapbooks."
Advice: The editor says, "We encourage beginners to keep writing and many times comment on rejections. If we especially see promise in a group of poems or a fiction piece, we often ask writers to send us more of his/her best."

ORBIS: AN INTERNATIONAL QUARTERLY OF POETRY AND PROSE; RHYME INTERNATIONAL COMPETITION FOR RHYMING POETRY (Specialized: form), 27 Valley View, Primrose, Jarrow, Tyne-and-Wear NE32 5QT United Kingdom, phone 44 0191-489-7055, fax 44 0191-430-1297, e-mail mikeshields@compuserve.com, founded 1968, editor Mike Shields.
Magazine Needs: *Orbis* considers "all poetry so long as it's genuine in feeling and well executed of its type." They have published poetry by Sir John Betjeman, Ray Bradbury, Seamus Heaney and Naomi Mitchison, as well as US poets Levertov, Piercy, Bell, Geddes, Wilbur, Kumin and many others, "but are just as likely to publish absolute unknowns." The quarterly is 64 pgs. minimum, 6×8½, flat-spined, professionally printed with glossy card cover. They receive "thousands" of submissions a year, use "less than 2%." Press run is 1,000 for 600 subscribers of which 50 are libraries. Single copy: £3.95 ($6); subscription: £15 ($28). Sample: $2 (or £1).
How to Submit: Submit 1 poem/sheet, typed on 1 side only. No bio, no query. No fax or e-mail submissions. Enclose IRCs for reply, not US postage. Reports in 1-2 months. Pays $10 or more/acceptance plus 1 free copy. Each issue carries £50 in prizes paid on basis of reader votes. Editor comments on rejections "occasionally—if we think we can help. *Orbis* is completely independent and receives no grant-aid from anywhere."
Also Offers: They sponsor the Rhyme International Competition for Rhyming Poetry. The competition has 2 categories (open class, any rhyming poem up to 50 lines; strict form class) with prizes averaging £500 in each

class each year (60% of fees received). Entry fee: £2.50/poem, minimum £5 (or $10). They claim to be "the only competition in the world exclusively for rhymed poetry." Write for entry form. Deadline: September 30.

$ ☻ ORCHISES PRESS, P.O. Box 20602, Alexandria VA 22320-1602, e-mail rlathbur@osf1.gmu.edu, website http://www.mason.gmu.edu/~rlathbur, founded 1983, poetry editor Roger Lathbury.

Book/Chapbook Needs: Orchises is a small press publisher of literary and general material in flat-spined paperbacks and in hardcover. "Although we will consider mss submitted, we prefer to seek out the work of poets who interest us." Regarding poetry he states: "No restrictions, really; but it must be technically proficient and deeply felt. I find it increasingly unlikely that I would publish a ms unless a fair proportion of its contents has appeared previously in respected literary journals." He has published *What She Knew* by Peter Filkins and *Believe It or Not* by Jean Monahan. He publishes about 4 flat-spined paperbacks of poetry a year, averaging 96 pgs., and some casebound books. Most paperbacks are $12.95. Hardbacks are $20-21.95 each.

How to Submit: Submit 5-6 poems at a time. No e-mail submissions. Poems must be typed. When submitting, "tell where poems have previously been published." Brief cover letter preferred. Obtain guidelines via website. Reports in 1 month. Pays 36% of money earned once Orchises recoups its initial costs and has a "generous free copy policy."

Also Offers: Website includes submission guidelines, sample poems, book covers and online catalog.

◐ ◉ OSIRIS, AN INTERNATIONAL POETRY JOURNAL/UNE REVUE INTERNATIONALE (Specialized: translations, bilingual), P.O. Box 297, Deerfield MA 01342-0297, phone (413)774-4027, e-mail moorhead@k12s.phast.umass.edu, founded 1972, poetry editor Andrea Moorhead.

Magazine Needs: *Osiris* is a semiannual that publishes contemporary poetry in English, French and Italian without translation and in other languages with translation, including Polish, Danish and German. They want poetry which is "lyrical, non-narrative, multi-temporal, post-modern, well-crafted. Also looking for translations from non-IndoEuropean languages." They have published poetry by Robert Marteau (France), Madeleine Gagnon (Québec), Rezsö Keszthelyi (Hungary), D.G. Jones (Canada), Alexandra Grilikhes (US), and Wally Swist (US). As a sample the editor selected these lines from "Statue" by Alexandra Grilikhes:

> the silence without stars/an ocean of fish at night//the taste of wind in my mouth/I savor, and flowers
> poising/like knives.

Osiris is 40 pgs., 6×9, saddle-stapled with graphics and photos. There are 15-20 pgs. of poetry in English in each issue of this publication. Print run is 500 with 50 subscription copies sent to college and university libraries, including foreign libraries. They receive 200-300 submissions a year, use approximately 12. Single copy: $6; subscription: $12. Sample: $3.

How to Submit: Submit 4-6 poems at a time. "Poems should be sent regular mail." Include short bio and SASE with submission. "Translators should include a letter of permission from the poet or publisher as well as copies of the original text." Reports in 1 month. Sometimes sends prepublication galleys. Pays 5 copies.

Advice: The editor advises, "It is always best to look at a sample copy of a journal before submitting work, and when you do submit work, do it often and do not get discouraged. Try to read poetry and support other writers."

Ⓝ ○ OSRIC PUBLISHING; DISCO GOTHIC ENTERPRISES; THE WHITE CROW (I), P.O. Box 4501, Ann Arbor MI 48106-4501, e-mail chris@osric.com, website http://osric.com, founded 1993, editor Christopher™ Herdt, assistant editor Mrrranda L. Tarrow.

Magazine Needs: *The White Crow* is a quarterly "literate, not literary journal. It contains poetry and fiction that is meaningful and that will appeal to an educated, but not necessarily high-brow audience. Something that even an electrical engineer might enjoy." They want "nothing bigger than a breadbox. No one-pagers that use the word black more than four times and no 'throbbing, beefy torpedo' poems." They have published poetry by Kenneth Pobo, Lyn Lifshin, Mark Senkus and C.D. Chase. The editor says *TWC* is 32 pgs., 5½×8½, sometimes photocopied, sometimes offset printed, saddle-stitched with cardstock, black only cover, includes art and graphics. They receive about 1,000 poems a year, accept approximately 10%. Press run is 500 for 50 subscribers, 250 shelf sales; 100 distributed free to reviewers and associates. Single copy: $2; subscription: $6. Sample (including guidelines): $2. Make checks payable to Osric Publishing.

How to Submit: Submit 5 poems at a time. Previously published poems and simultaneous submissions OK. Cover letter preferred. E-mail and disk submissions OK. Time between acceptance and publication is about 1 month. Poems are circulated to an editorial board. "The editors all get together and drink heavily, eat some food, and rate and berate the submissions." Always comments on rejections. Reports in about 6 months. Pays 1 copy. Acquires first rights. Staff reviews books and chapbooks of poetry and other magazines in 100 words, single book format. Send books for review consideration to Christopher™ Herdt.

USE THE GENERAL INDEX, located at the back of this book, to find the page number of a specific publisher. Also, publishers that were listed in last year's edition but not included in this edition are listed in the General Index with a notation explaining why they were omitted.

Book/Chapbook Needs & How to Submit: Osric Publishing seeks "poetry and short fiction for the literate, not literary." They publish 1 paperback and 1 chapbook/year. Books are usually 32 pgs., 8½×5½, photocopied or offset printed and saddle-stitched with cardstock cover, uses art/graphics. Query first, with a few sample poems and a cover letter with brief bio and publication credits. Replies to queries and mss in 6 months. Pays 5 author's copies (out of a press run of 200). Order sample books by sending $2 to Osric Publishing.
Also Offers: Disco Gothic Enterprises sponsors infrequent contests.
Advice: The editors say, ""No poems about poetry, no poems about writing poetry, no stories about writing stories."

⊠ ⊕ ☻ ◎ OTHER PRESS; ISLINGTON POETRY WORKSHOP (Specialized: nationality, women), 19B Marriott Rd., London N4 3QN England, founded 1992, contact Ms. Frances Presley.
Book/Chapbook Needs: The Other Press publishes primarily experimental poetry by British women, though not exclusively. They publish 1 paperback/year. They do not want traditional poetry by beginners. As a sample the editor chose this poem by Harriet Tarlo:
>   *looking up//cloud circle*
Books are usually paperback, stapled and sometimes include artwork.
How to Submit: No previously published poems; simultaneous submissions OK. Cover letter required. Time between acceptance and publication is 1-2 years. Often comments on rejections. Replies to queries in 1 month. Pays 20 author's copies (out of a press run of 200).

⊠ $ ☻ ◎ THE OTHER SIDE MAGAZINE (Specialized: political, religious, social issues), 300 W. Apsley St., Philadelphia PA 19144, phone (215)849-2178, website http://www.theotherside.org, founded 1965, poetry editor Jeanne Minahan.
Magazine Needs: *The Other Side* is an independent ecumenical magazine that seeks to advance a broad Christian vision that's biblical and compassionate, appreciative of the creative arts, and committed to the intimate intertwining of personal spirituality and social transformation. We weave together first-person essays, insightful analyses, biblical reflection, interviews, fiction, poetry, and an inviting mix of visual art. We strive to nurture, uplift, and challenge readers with personal, provocative writing that reflects the transformative, liberating Spirit of Jesus Christ." The magazine publishes 1-2 poems/issue. "Poetry submissions should include strong imagery, fresh viewpoints, and lively language, while avoiding versifications of religious instruction or syrupy piety. Be warned that only 0.5% of the poems reviewed are accepted." They have published poetry by Kathleen Norris, Paul Ramsey, Carol Hamilton and John Knoepfle. *The Other Side* is magazine-sized, professionally printed on quality pulp stock, 64 pgs., saddle-stapled, with full-color paper cover. Circulation is 13,000 to that many subscriptions. Subscription: $24. Sample: $4.50.
How to Submit: Submit 3 poems at a time. Line length for poetry is 50 maximum. No previously published poems or simultaneous submissions. Editor "almost never" comments on rejections. Send SASE for guidelines. Reports in 1-2 months. Pays $15 plus 2 copies and 2-year subscription.

❧ ✓ $ ◑ OTHER VOICES, Garneau P.O. Box 52059, 8210-109 St., Edmonton, Alberta T6G 2T5 Canada, founded 1988, contact poetry editors.
Magazine Needs: *Other Voices* appears 2 times a year in the Spring and Fall. "We are devoted to the publication of quality literary writing—poetry, fiction, nonfiction; also reviews and artwork. We encourage submissions by new and established writers. Our only desire for poetry is that it is good! We encourage submissions by women and members of minorities, but we will consider everyone's. We never publish popular/sentimental greeting-card-type poetry or anything sexist, racist or homophobic." They have published poetry by Bert Almon, Heidi Greco, Robin S. Chapman, Zoë Landale and Erina Harris. As a sample the editor selected these lines from "One Breast" by Chris Smart:
>   *The word cancer slips/into their house/opens lace curtains, leaves/a trail of mud. A presence/breathes*
>   *at the window/murmurs at the door.//A breast blooms/in the garden.//Once flowers bloomed/on the*
>   *window sills/and the scent flooded/the house.*
The editor says *OV* is 100-120 pgs., 21½×14cm, professionally printed and perfect-bound with color cover, includes art and ads. They receive about 800 poems a year, accept approximately 4%. Press run is 500 for 330 subscribers of which 7 are libraries, 60 shelf sales. Subscription: $18/year in Canada, $23 US, $28 overseas. Sample: $10.
How to Submit: Submit 2-6 poems at a time. Include SAE with IRC. "Please limit your submissions to a maximum of 6 pages of poetry and send only 1 submission every 6 months." No previously published poems or simultaneous submissions. Cover letter preferred. "Please include short bio. Phone numbers, fax numbers and e-mail addresses are helpful." Spring submission deadline: March 15; fall deadline is September 15. "We are currently discussing moving our deadlines up to September 1 and March 1. Poets may want to submit by those dates to be on the safe side." Time between acceptance and publication is 1 month. Poems are circulated to an editorial board. "Poems are read and assessed independently by five poetry editors. After the deadline, we gather and 'haggle' over which poems to accept." Seldom comments on rejections. Publishes theme issues. Send SASE (or SAE with IRCs) for guidelines and upcoming themes or obtain via website. Reports in up to 6 months. Pays small honorarium plus subscription. Acquires first North American serial rights. Reviews books of poetry in

1,000 words, single or double book format. Open to unsolicited reviews. Poets may also send books for review consideration to Editorial Collective.

Also Offers: "We typically hold one contest per year, but the time, fees and theme vary. Check our website for details."

Advice: The editor says, "Please take note of our September and March deadlines. If you just miss a deadline, it could take up to six months for a reply."

⚡ ✓ $ ☺ OUR FAMILY (Specialized: religious, social issues, spirituality/inspirational, themes, family/marriage/parenting), Box 249, Battleford, Saskatchewan S0M 0E0 Canada, phone (306)937-7771, fax (306)937-7644, e-mail ourfamily@marianpress.sk.ca, website http://www.marianpress.sk.ca/ourfamily/, founded 1949, editor Marie-Louise Ternier-Gommers.

Magazine Needs: *Our Family* is a monthly religious magazine for Roman Catholic families. "Any form of poetry is acceptable. In content we look for simplicity and vividness of imagery. The subject matter should center on the human struggle to live out one's relationship with the God of the Bible in the context of our modern world. We do not want to see science fiction poetry, metaphysical speculation poetry, or anything that demeans or belittles the spirit of human beings or degrades the image of God in him/her as it is described in the Bible." They have published poetry by Nadene Murphy and Arthur Stilwell. *Our Family* is 40 pgs., magazine-sized, glossy color paper cover, using drawings, cartoons, two-color ink. Circulation is 10,000 of which 48 are libraries. Single copy: $2; subscription: $17.95 Canada, $23.95 US. Sample: $3.

How to Submit: Will consider poems of 4-30 lines. Simultaneous submissions OK. E-mail and fax submissions OK. "Please include submission in the body of the e-mail. No attachments!" Send SASE or SAE with IRC or personal check for $1.25 (American postage cannot be used in Canada) for writer's guidelines and upcoming themes. Reports within 1 month after receipt. Pays 75¢-$1/line.

Advice: The editor advises, "The essence of poetry is imagery. The form is less important. Really good poets use both effectively."

◖ ☺ OUR JOURNEY (Specialized: recovery issues), 16016 SE Division #327, Portland OR 97236, e-mail wendy@iccom.com or wendy@zzz.com, website http://www.geocities.com/HotSprings/Spa/1416/ourjourney.htm, founded 1994, editor Wendy Apgar.

● *Our Journey* is interested in receiving poetry about hope and moving on which are topics included in every issue.

Magazine Needs: Published by Our Journey, Inc., a 501(c)(3) tax deductable, nonprofit corporation, *Our Journey* is a quarterly newsletter featuring "poetry, articles and occasional book reviews by those and for those involved or interested in the recovery process. This newsletter is a safe way for contributors and readers to address life issues." They want "recovery-based poetry; all inclusive, not limited to recovery of only one (e.g., addictions, incest, pain, abuse, anger, healing, etc.); will consider any length. Each issue has specific topic. No poetry which is not easily understood or which is inappropriately sexually graphic (query editor if unsure about specific poem or essay)." They have published poetry by Ray Hamilton, Karen A. Menard and Kevin Coughlen. As a sample the editor selected this poem, "Fly," by Heidi Sands:

> *Wounds are never too deep/to heal./Letting go of pain is to/accept what I feel./That which I cannot*
> *change,/the past I cannot rearrange./I will fly above the lies./I will soar the open skies./The misfortune*
> *is not/my suffering./It is my parents inability/to repent.*

Our Journey is 14-18 pgs., neatly painted on bond paper and corner stapled, no cover, contains clip art. They receive about 150-200 poems a year, accept approximately 80%. Press run is 200 for 60 subscribers of which 2 are libraries. Single copy: $2.50; subscription: $10/year, $12 Canada, $15 overseas. Sample: $1.50.

How to Submit: Submit any number of poems; 1/page, typed with name and address in upper left corner. "Only mss with SASE will be acknowledged or returned." Previously published poems and simultaneous submissions OK. Cover letter preferred. "Material may also be submitted via e-mail. Two poems per each e-mail, but may send as many e-mail submissions as desire (i.e., 3 e-mails total 6 poems). If accepted for publication a hard copy must then be submitted via snail mail with the completed release form which will be e-mailed upon acceptance." Time between acceptance and publication is within 1 year. If asked, will offer feedback. Publishes theme issues. Upcoming themes: December 1999: Grief, Hope; March 2000: Daily Struggle; June 2000: Masks, Inner Child, Safety & Support; September 2000: Abuse, Moving On. Send SASE for guidelines. Reports in 4-6 weeks, "usually sooner." Pays 2 copies. Acquires one-time rights. Open to unsolicited reviews. Poets may send books for review consideration.

Also Offers: Sponsors 2-4 annual contests for subscribers. Awards: 1st Prize-$20, 2nd Prize-$10, 3rd Prize-$5. Entry fee: $2/poem. Send SASE for details. Website includes writer's guidelines, upcoming issue topics, contest guidelines, non-profit information and links to other recovery-based pages.

◖ ☺ OUTER DARKNESS: WHERE NIGHTMARES ROAM UNLEASHED (Specialized: horror, mystery, science fiction, dark fantasy), 1312 N. Delaware Place, Tulsa OK 74110, phone (918)832-1246, founded 1994, editor Dennis J. Kirk.

Magazine Needs: *Outer Darkness* is a quarterly magazine featuring short stories, poetry and art in the genres of horror, mystery, dark fantasy and science fiction. They want "all styles of poetry, though traditional rhyming verse is preferred. Send verse that is dark and melancholy in nature. Nothing experimental—very little of this

type of verse is published in *Outer Darkness*." They have published poetry by John Grey, Nancy Bennett, John Maclay and Corrine De Winter. *OD* is 40-60 pgs., 8½×5½, photocopied, saddle-stitched, glossy cover, includes cover art, cartoons and illustrations and runs ads for other publications. They receive about 200 poems a year, accept approximately 20%. Press run is 200, 25% to subscribers, 25% to contributors, 25% sample copy sales, 25% to advertisers, free copies, etc. Single copy: $3.95; subscription: $11.95.
How to Submit: Submit up to 3 poems at a time, no longer than 60 lines each. No previously published poems; simultaneous submissions OK. Cover letter preferred. "Poets are encouraged to include cover letters with their submissions, with biographical information, personal interests, past publishing credits, etc. I strongly prefer hardcopy submissions rather than disks." Always comments on rejections. Send SASE for guidelines. Reports in 4-6 weeks. Sends prepublication galleys, when requested. Pays 2 copies with discount on additional copies. Acquires one-time rights.
Advice: The editor says, "I've noticed that interest in traditional metered verse is increasing. This is the type of poetry I feature most frequently in *OD*. Take time and care in writing verse. Maintain a consistent mood and tone; get the most you can out of each line, each word. This obviously takes more time; but, in the end, it will pay off."

OUTERBRIDGE, English A324, The College of Staten Island, 2800 Victory Blvd., Staten Island NY 10314, phone (718)982-3651, founded 1975, editor Charlotte Alexander.
Magazine Needs: *Outerbridge* publishes "the most crafted, professional poetry and short fiction we can find (unsolicited except special features—to date rural, urban and Southern, promoted in standard newsletters such as *Poets & Writers, AWP, Small Press Review*), interested in newer voices. Anti loose, amateurish, uncrafted poems showing little awareness of the long-established fundamentals of verse; also anti blatant PRO-movement writing when it sacrifices craft for protest and message. Poems usually one to four pgs. in length." They have published poetry by Walter McDonald, Thomas Swiss and Naomi Rachel. The digest-sized, flat-spined annual is 100 pgs., about half poetry. Press run is 500-600 for 150 subscribers of which 28 are libraries. They receive about 500-700 submissions a year, use approximately 60. Sample: $6.
How to Submit: Submit 3-5 poems only, anytime except June and July. Include name and address on each page. "We dislike simultaneous submissions and if a poem accepted by us proves to have already been accepted elsewhere, a poet will be blacklisted as there are many good poets waiting in line." Cover letter with brief bio preferred. Publishes theme issues. Send SASE for guidelines and upcoming themes. Reports in 2 months. Pays 2 copies (and offers additional copies at half price). Acquires first rights.
Advice: The editor says, "As a poet/editor I feel magazines like *Outerbridge* provide an invaluable publication outlet for poets (particularly since publishing a book of poetry, respectably, is extremely difficult these days). As in all of the arts, poetry—its traditions, conventions and variations, experiments—should be studied. One current 'trend' I detect is a lot of mutual backscratching which can result in loose, amateurish writing. Discipline!"

OUTPOSTS POETRY QUARTERLY; HIPPOPOTAMUS PRESS, 22 Whitewell Rd., Frome, Somerset BA11 4EL United Kingdom, magazine founded 1944, press founded 1974, editor R. John.
Magazine Needs: *Outposts* is a general poetry magazine. They want "fairly mainstream poetry. No concrete poems or very free verse." They have published poetry by Jared Carter, John Heath-Stubbs, Lotte Kramer and Peter Russell. As a sample we selected these lines from "The Lotus-Eaters" by Ashleigh John:

> Our lives are one long Sunday, when it rained./There were so many things we might have done—/We
> watched the television-set instead,/And the day ended as it had begun./We are the quick who may as
> well be dead:/The nothing-ventured, and the nothing-gained.

Outposts is 60-120 pgs., A5, litho printed and perfect-bound with laminated card cover, includes occasional art and ads. They receive about 54,000 poems a year, accept approximately 1%. Press run is 1,600 for 1,200 subscribers of which 400 are libraries, 400 shelf sales. Single copy: $8; subscription: $26. Sample (including guidelines): $6. Make checks payable to Hippopotamus Press. "We prefer credit cards because of bank charges."
How to Submit: Submit 5 poems at a time. No previously published poems; simultaneous submissions OK. Disk submissions OK. Time between acceptance and publication is 9 months. Seldom comments on rejections, "only if asked." Publishes theme issues occasionally. Send SASE for upcoming themes. Reports in 2 weeks. Sometimes sends prepublication galleys. Pays £8/page plus 1 copy. Buys first rights. Staff reviews books and chapbooks of poetry and other magazines in 400-4,000 words, single and multi-book format. Send books for review consideration to M. Pargitter.
Book/Chapbook Needs & How to Submit: "Hippopotamus Press specializes in first full collections." They publish 6 paperbacks, 6 hardbacks and 6 chapbooks/year. Books are usually 60-300 pgs., A5, litho printed and perfect-bound, cover varies, uses art only for cover. Send full ms. "We only publish those that have already published in the magazines." Pays royalties of 7½-10% plus author's copies. Order sample books by sending for catalogue.
Advice: The editor says, "Read before submitting."

OUTREACH: FOR THE HOUSEBOUND, ELDERLY AND DISABLED (Specialized: senior citizens, disabled, religious), 7 Grayson Close, Stocksbridge, Sheffield S30 5BJ England, phone (0114)288-5346, fax (0114)288-4903, founded 1985, editor J. Kirby.
Magazine Needs & How to Submit: *Outreach* is a quarterly using "semi-religious poetry and short articles;

cowboy, humor, love and romance, mystery, senior citizen and spirituality/inspired poetry. This is a magazine for the housebound, elderly and disabled who need cheering up, not made more depressed or bored!" As a sample, here are lines from "Stairs to God" by Helen S. Rice:

> *Prayers are the stairs/We must climb every day,/If we would reach God/There is no other way.*

Outreach is photocopied from typescript on ordinary paper, folded and saddle-stapled. Faxed submissions OK. Publishes theme issues. Send SAE with IRC for upcoming themes.

☑ ◯ ⬗ ◎ **OUTRIDER PRESS (Specialized: women/feminism, gay/lesbian/bisexual, anthology, humor)**, 937 Patricia Lane, Crete IL 60417-1362, e-mail outriderpr@aol.com, website http://www.outriderpress.com, founded 1988, president Phyllis Nelson.

Book/Chapbook Needs: Outrider publishes 1-3 novels/anthologies/chapbooks annually. They want "poetry dealing with the terrain of the human heart and plotting inner journeys; growth and grace under pressure. No bag ladies, loves-that-never-were, please." They have published poetry by Lyn Lifshin and Maureen Connolly. As a sample we selected these lines from "Marie Writes a Letter to Her Husband (Just Before She Finally Leaves the Womanizing Jerk)" by Pamela Miller, from the anthology *Freedom's Just Another Word*:

> *I wish you a plague of scorpions,/scuttling, brown and sinister as/all my years with you:/scorpions in your coffee,/your hairpiece, your bank account,/nothing but names of scorpion species/in your throbbing/little black book.*

That book is 224 pgs., digest-sized, attractively printed and perfect-bound with glossy card cover, $14.95.

How to Submit: Submit 3-4 poems at a time with SASE. Include name, address and phone/fax number on every poem. Simultaneous submissions OK, if specified. Cover letter preferred. Responds to queries in 3 months, to mss in 6 months. Sometimes sends prepublication galleys. Pays 1 copy.

Also Offers: Outrider publishes a themed anthology annually, with cash prizes for best poetry and short fiction. Submit up to 4 poems, no longer than 1 page in length. Reading fee: $16, $12 for Tallgrass Writers Guild members. Send SASE for guidelines. Deadline: December 31, 1999. Published in July 2000. Our 2000 theme: Earth Beneath, Sky Beyond—The Natural World. The press is affiliated with the Tallgrass Writers Guild, an international organization open to all who support equality of voices in writing. Annual membership fee: $25. Send SASE for information or visit website. Website includes publication titles, prices, ordering information, general guidelines/themes, address for complete guidelines, Tallgrass Writers Guild information and membership.

Advice: The editor says, "We look for visceral truths expressed without compromise, coyness or cliché. Go for the center of the experience. Pull no punches."

$ ◎ **"OVER THE BACK FENCE" MAGAZINE (Specialized: regional)**, P.O. Box 756, Chillicothe OH 45601, phone (740)772-2165, fax (740)773-7626, founded 1994, managing editor Sarah Williamson.

Magazine Needs: A quarterly regional magazine "serving nineteen counties in southern Ohio and 10 counties in Northern Ohio, *'Over The Back Fence'* has a wholesome, neighborly style that is appealing to readers from young adults to seniors." They want rhyming or free verse poetry, 24 lines or less; open to subject matter, "but seasonal works well"; friendly or inspirational work. "Since most of our readers are not poets, we want something simple and likeable by the general public. No profanity or erotic subject matter, please." As a sample the editor selected these lines from "Etchings of the Heart" by Charles Clevenger:

> *I carved a heart upon this tree/With cupid's arrow aimed at thee./'Tho time and space keep us apart,/ This etching holds you in my heart.*

The editor says it is 68 pgs., published on high gloss paper, saddle-stapled with b&w and color illustrations and photos, includes ads. They receive less than 200 poems a year, publish approximately 4-10. Press run is 15,000 for about 2,000 subscribers in Southern Ohio and 5,000 in Northern Ohio, 40% shelf sales. Single copy: $2.95; subscription: $9.97/year. Sample: $4. Make checks payable to Back Fence Publishing, Inc.

How to Submit: Submit up to 4 poems at a time. Previously published poems and simultaneous submissions OK, "if identified as such." Cover letter preferred. "Since we prefer reader-submitted poetry, we would like for the cover letter to include comments about our magazine or contents." Computer disk submissions should be saved in an ASCII text format, Word Perfect or Microsoft Word file. Disk should be labeled with your name, address, daytime phone number, name of format and name of file. Time between acceptance and publication is 6-12 months. Seldom comments on rejections. "We do not publish theme issues, but do feature specific Ohio counties quarterly. Send or call for specific areas." Send SASE for guidelines. Reports in 1-3 months. Pays 10¢/word, $25 minimum. Buys one-time North American print rights.

Advice: The editor says, "While we truly appreciate the professional poet, most of our published poetry comes from beginners or amateurs. We strive for reader response and solicit poetry contributions through the magazine."

☑ ⬗ **OWEN WISTER REVIEW**, Box 3625, University of Wyoming, Laramie WY 82071, phone (307)766-3819, e-mail owr@uwyo.edu, founded 1978.

Magazine Needs: *OWR* is the annual literary and art magazine (appearing in April) of the University of Wyoming. The editor says *OWR* is 100-120 pgs., 6×9, professionally printed and perfect-bound with art on the cover and inside. They receive more than 500 submissions a year, accept 4-6%. Press run is 500. Single copy: $7.95; subscription: $15 for 2 years/2 issues. Sample: $5. Back issues: $5 each.

How to Submit: Submit up to 5 poems. No previously published poems; simultaneous submissions discouraged. Cover letter required. May query by fax; must include mailing address. E-mail submissions OK. "5 poems per e-mail. Spacing between poems." Reads submissions August through November only. Poems are circulated to an editorial board. Send SASE for guidelines. Reports in 2-3 months. Pays 1 copy and 10% discount on additional copies. Acquires first rights.

☑ ✓ ⬤ OXFORD MAGAZINE, 261 Bachelor Hall, Miami University, Oxford OH 45056, phone (513)529-1954, e-mail oxmag@geocities.com, website http://www.geocities.com/Soho/gallery/44100, founded 1984, editor Mike Jones.
 • *Oxford Magazine* has been awarded two Pushcart Prizes.
Magazine Needs: *Oxford Magazine* appears annually, in the spring. "We are open in terms of form, content and subject matter. We have eclectic tastes, ranging from New Formalism to Language poetry to Nuyorican poetry." They have published poetry by Eve Shelnutt, Denise Duhamel and Walter McDonald. *Oxford Magazine* is 220 pgs., 6×9, professionally printed and flat-spined. Press run is 1,000. Sample: $7.
How to Submit: Submit 3-5 poems at a time. No previously published poems. Simultaneous submissions OK. No e-mail submissions. Cover letter preferred. Reads submissions September 1 through January 31. Pays copies only. Buys first North American serial rights.

OXFORD UNIVERSITY PRESS, 198 Madison Ave., New York NY 10016. See listing in Publications of Interest.

Ⓝ ⬤ OYEZ REVIEW, Roosevelt University, 430 S. Michigan Ave., Chicago IL 60605, phone (312)341-3818, founded 1965/66, editor Wilbert Bledsoe.
Magazine Needs: *Oyez Review* is an annual designed "to enlighten the student body of Roosevelt University, to publish the works of the students as well as those of veteran and beginning writers." They want "love poems, spiritual poetry, politically oriented works, urban poetry and performance poetry." They do not want "sexually graphic poetry or racially offensive poetry." They have published poetry by Maria McCray and Marc Smith. As a sample the editor selected these lines from "Last Lovin' Blues" by Reggie Gibson:
> *this night/which is our last my beloved, let us resurrect the embers of dead memory/and recall that*
> *faded dream/this last night*
The editor says *Oyez* is 90 pgs., magazine-sized, includes photos and drawings. They receive about 70 poems a year, accept approximately 30%. Press run is 500. Single copy: $4; subscription: $8/2 issues.
How to Submit: Submit 3 poems at a time. Previously published poems and simultaneous submissions OK. Disk submissions OK. Reads submissions February 24 through July 15 only. Time between acceptance and publication is 7 months. Seldom comments on rejections. Publishes theme issues occasionally. Send SASE for guidelines. Reports in 3 months. Reviews books of poetry in 500 words, single book format. Open to unsolicited reviews. Poets may also send books for review consideration.
Advice: The editor says, "Our major focus is to foster the development of student and beginning authors."

✓ ⬤ OYSTER BOY REVIEW; OFF THE CUFF BOOKS, P.O. Box 83, Chapel Hill NC 27514, e-mail obr@levee67.com, website http://www.levee67.com, founded 1993, poetry editor Jeffery Beam (jeffbeam@email.unc.edu).
Magazine Needs: *Oyster Boy Review* appears 3 times a year. "We're interested in the underrated, the ignored, the misunderstood, and the varietal. We'll make some mistakes. 'All styles are good except the boring kind'— Voltaire." They have published poetry by Jonathan Williams, Cid Corman, Lyn Lifshin and Paul Dilsaver. As a sample the editor selected these lines from "Night" by Thomas Meyer:
> *When it flowers/night fills/with a cruelty/I have done you/whose fruit is sweet*
OBR is 60 pgs., 6½×11, Docutech printed and stapled with paper cover, includes photography and ads. They receive about 1,500 poems a year, accept approximately 2%. Press run is 200 for 30 subscribers, 100 shelf sales; 30 distributed free to editors, authors. Subscription: $12.
How to Submit: Submit up to 5 poems at a time. No previously published poems or simultaneous submissions. Cover letter preferred. E-mail submissions OK. Include poems in body of e-mail message. No attachments. Postal submissions require SASE. Do not submit mss in late December. "Upon acceptance, authors asked to provide electronic version of work and a biographical statement." Time between acceptance and publication is 6 months. Seldom comments on rejections. Obtain guidelines via e-mail or website. Reports in 3 months. Pays 2 copies. Reviews books and chapbooks of poetry in 250-500 words (1st books only), in single or multi-book format. Open to unsolicited reviews. Poets may also send books for review consideration.
Book/Chapbook Needs: *Off the Cuff is not open to submissions or solicitations.* Off the Cuff Books publishes "longer works and special projects of authors published in *Oyster Boy Review.*"
Also Offers: Website includes back issues, submission guidelines, staff, subscription and "where to buy" information.
Advice: The editor says, "*Oyster Boy Review* responds to freshness—to the unschooled enthusiasm that leads to fresh idioms and subjects—without kowtowing to any camps, mainstream or not."

✓ ⬤ P.D.Q. (POETRY DEPTH QUARTERLY), (formerly *The Poet's Guild Quarterly*), 5836 N. Haven Dr., North Highlands CA 95660, phone (916)331-3512, e-mail poetdpth@aol.com, founded 1995, publisher G. Elton Warrick, editor Joyce Odam, web manager Lori Smaltz.

insider report

Poets should make their own way when seeking publication

"Where Do We Get All These Burdens"

Well, you go to the House of Burdens
and you say
I'll take that one, and that one,
and that one, because they all
look good to you;
and then the Burden Salesman says,
Okay . . . they're yours . . .

and you have to put them
all on your shoulders and try
to carry them all in one load
because you were greedy
and they are unreturnable.

Joyce Odam

(originally published in *The Wormwood Review*, Volume 14, Number 3; reprinted by permission of the author)

As editor of *P.D.Q.* (*Poetry Depth Quarterly*) in North Highlands, California, co-editor for a monthly poetry column in *Senior Magazine* and poet with numerous years of writing and submitting experience, Joyce Odam knows more than a little about the processes of crafting and publishing poetry.

Here she shares her knowledge, opinions and experience on writing and publishing poetry, the importance of reading the work of others and the necessity of making your own avenues into the world of poetry publishers.

How did your interest in poetry writing begin? How did you first get published?
I first discovered poetry when I was a child in grammar school, but didn't begin writing poetry until much later. In fact, at the time, I remember becoming bored with my writing because I couldn't break out of a sort of ballad pattern. Even though I was reading, I didn't know how to tap into reading and I was writing all this dull stuff.

Fortunately, I discovered that an adult education class in poetry was being offered here in Sacramento. So I went down, signed up and it was like a burst of confetti. All the information that came at me, things I never knew existed—the forms, the terminology, the metrics. I soaked it all up like a thirsty sponge.

Then, with my teacher's guidance, I began submitting work to local publications that took beginning writers; through those publications I found my own avenues. I received a lot of rejection at first but I learned not to be destroyed by it. Now, my publication credits include such journals and magazines as *Acorn*, *The Bellingham Review*, *Calliope*, *Lactuca*, *Prairie Schooner* and *The Wormwood Review*.

Have publishing opportunities for poets changed since you began submitting your work?

Yes, with the shrinking market and the increasing competition, it's harder and harder to get published. I see little magazines dying because they can no longer financially afford to remain in business. With postage and printing costs, most little magazines are on a starvation diet financially. If publications last more than five years, they've done pretty good.

Do you view Internet journals as a viable option for poets?

I have mixed feelings. The Internet is probably the way to go but I am very uncomfortable with it. I want a book in my hands so I can sit back in my easy chair or sit in bed and read. I don't want to be sitting in front of my computer screen and having to print all this gobbledy-gook with nothing balanced on the page.

However, it is wonderful to have the widening connection and access to all these different voices. But sometimes you can have too much of something, too. Then it swallows you up instead of you tapping into it to suit your tiny appetite. I don't want to feel obligated to get on the playing field. I don't like that kind of direction, nor do I want to be a cow in a cattle run. I want to meander around in my own field.

You mentioned that when you first began in poetry your writing suffered even though you were reading the work of others. How did you eventually learn to tap into the benefits of reading?

Early on I didn't know anything about form or meter or style, or any of the terminology or approaches to writing. I wasn't open to it because I hadn't received it somewhere in me. I was just writing my little emotional pieces and writing songs. I didn't know how to craft my poems. I had to learn some craft.

So you've learned the most from the workshops you've taken?

Well, workshops help but they can also hinder. So you have to learn to approach a workshop from your own state of being. Some people can come in thinking they have to take every comment as gospel. Then some come in so frozen to their work that they won't take any comments from any source. Having a response from other people makes you take a second look at your work, but you also have to stay with your own voice and not be intimidated or persuaded to a voice that is not your own. Workshops *can* be strength-giving if you avail yourself of becoming strong.

On the other hand, I also admire what Mary Oliver said in her book *A Poetry Handbook*: "But, to write well it is entirely necessary to read widely and deeply. Good poems are the best teachers. Perhaps they are the only teachers. I would go so far as to say that, if one must make a choice between reading or taking part in a workshop, one should read."

Reading to me is like having a conversation. You read something and it opens a response. I give a response—an answer or an argument or an agreement. When I read it connects to something in me. Then, when I stop reading, I go with whatever I've connected to and write from that.

As editor of *P.D.Q.* (*Poetry Depth Quarterly*) and a poet with numerous publications to her credit, what have you learned that could help other poets with their own submissions?

Actually, I have learned a lot of humility from being an editor because there is a lot of responsibility connected to it. You are dealing with the work of others and responsible for publishing their work in a final form.

However, one of my pet peeves is poets who submit without a SASE or without sufficient postage. They presume their work is so wonderful that you are going to accept them with open arms and they are going to be the exception to all the rules.

What attracts you to a particular poem?

Choice can be very subjective, based on my own history of preference and recognition. But a basic outline for acceptance that I follow is that the poem works, that all its parts fit and belong. The poem must be careful and self-respectful of how it is put together in all its aspects—from correctness of spelling and punctuation (if used), to appropriateness of language, to its use of line and stanza—all of which are part of the overall consideration. Also, equal care must be given to the poem's visual effect on the page. I am very much in connection with the visual effect, the overall balance of the poem.

I noticed that *P.D.Q.* accepts poetry submissions via e-mail. Has this in anyway affected how you handle submissions?

I don't like e-mail submissions but I read them. I sit back with a deep sigh and say, "Okay let's tackle this." One problem with e-mail submissions is that you will be reading a poem and two lines will go to the next page. As I've said, I like the visual. I like to see how it's going to look on a finished page. But when the poems submitted are rambling one into another and they have all this miscellaneous text and it's small print, it is very disturbing to the eye.

Inevitably, it slows down my approval response because I am annoyed by the presentation. However, I try to be fair to the poetry itself. I have accepted e-mail submissions and I am accepting a little more of them than before. So, maybe the submissions are getting better or maybe the magazine is becoming more known for its requirements.

As an editor, are you often in situations where poets ask advice about submitting their work?

Yes. I think, mostly, people want to know where to send their work. Well, I don't know. I tell them that they need to build their own information. Oh, I may have a recommendation when something is obvious—like if I read something that sounds like the *Lyric* or *Bogg* or *Parting Gifts*. But then poets will follow up on my recommendations and say, "Oh good, now where do I send this next one?" Poets need to learn to do this work themselves. I advise they study the market—read *Poet's Market*, subscribe to a magazine or buy some sample copies.

You have published your own poetry in two "mini-book" collections, *Faces* and *Profiles*. Do you recommend self-publishing to other poets?

I don't mind self-publishing as long as you are careful about the so-called vanity presses. I published my books on my own because I don't have time to knock on the world's door. The world is not going to open up to me and I wanted to get some of my things in book form. So I developed Choice of Words Press. Now, I have these mini-books whenever I give readings; sometimes I give them away and sometimes I sell a few.

I just don't have time to wait for the world to discover me because the world is not going to discover me; there are too many of me out there. I am alone in my own little place here so I have to make my own efforts. If that means getting out there and putting some of my own work in a booklet, I will do that with a clear conscious. Rather than being a small fish in a big pond, poets should try to be a small fish in a small pond and there are a lot of small ponds. There is a lot going on in poetry in a lot of different areas. Poets just have to make the choice to get out and get involved.

—*Chantelle Bentley*

Magazine Needs: *P.D.Q.* wants "original poetry that clearly demonstrates an understanding of craft. All styles accepted." However, they do not want to see "poetry which is overtly religious, erotic, inflammatory or demeans the human spirit." They have published poetry by Jane Blue, Taylor Graham, Simon Perchik and Danyen Powell. As a sample the editor selected these lines from "Dream of Breaking" by Ann Menebroker:

> Do you know the meaning/of this oldness?/The ancient quality/Of time that this/clay pot holds?/Listen to it./The earth is there/The sky is there./Hold it in your hands./Drink from it./Dream about being/Molded dream/Of breaking/and being found.

P.D.Q. is 35-60 pgs., digest-sized, printed on recycled paper and saddle-stapled with a card stock cover with original pen art, interior clip art, and a decorative paper centerfold. They receive 1,800-2,000 poems a year, accept approximately 10%. Press run is 200 of which 5 subscribers are libraries. Single copy: $4; subscription: $16/1 year, $31/2 years, $40/3 years (add $4/year for foreign subscriptions). Make checks payable to G. Elton Warrick.

How to Submit: Submit 3-5 poems of any length, "typewritten and presented exactly as you would like them to appear," maximum 49 characters/line, with name and address on every page. All submissions should include SASE (or SAE with IRC) and cover letter with short 3-10 line bio and publication credits. No simultaneous submissions; previously published poems "occasionally" accepted with publication credits. E-mail submissions OK. Often comments on rejections. Send SASE for guidelines. Reports in 3 months. Pays 1 copy.

Also Offers: Sponsors an annual Open Poetry Contest. 1st Prize: $100; 2nd Prize: $50; and 3rd Prize: $25. Entry fee: $3/poem. Deadline: December 15, 1999. Send SASE for contest guidelines. *P.D.Q.* also submits nominations for the Pushcart Prize.

○ ◎ PABLO LENNIS (Specialized: science fiction/fantasy), 30 N. 19th St., Lafayette IN 47904, founded 1976, editor John Thiel.

Magazine Needs: *Pablo Lennis* appears irregularly, is a "science fiction and fantasy fanzine preferring poems of an expressive cosmic consciousness or full magical approach. I want poetry that rhymes and scans and I like a good rhythmic structure appropriate to the subject. Shorter poems are much preferred. I want them to exalt the mind, imagination, or perception into a consciousness of the subject. Optimism is usually preferred, and English language perfection eminently preferable. Nothing that is not science fiction or fantasy, or which contains morbid sentiments, or is perverse, or does not rhyme or contains slang." They have published poetry by A.J. Dawes, Lloyd Micheal Lohr, Michael Pendragon, Paul Crenshaw and Josh Lareau. As a sample the editor selected these lines from "Jirel of Joiry" by Peter Zenger:

> Now out they go, for the forest without/And the dim high hills are chanting,/And they pass through the
> gates in a mimic rout/For they want to see some necromancing./And the lost horizons are tremulous
> with doubt/And the wayfaring waifs go dancing.

Pablo Lennis is 26 pgs., magazine-sized, photocopied from typescript, side-stapled, using line drawings and hand-lettering. "I get a hundred fifty poems a year and have been using most of them." Press run is "up to 100 copies." Subscription: $20/year, $25 overseas. Sample: $2.

How to Submit: No previously published poems or simultaneous submissions. Send SASE for guidelines. Reports "at once. I generally say something about why the poetry was not used, if it was not. If someone else might like it, I mention an address." Pays 1 copy, 2 if requested. Reviews books of poetry if they are science fiction or fantasy. Open to unsolicited reviews. Poets may also send books for review consideration.

Advice: The editor says, "Poetry is magic. I want spells, incantations, sorceries of a rhythmic and rhyming nature, loftily and optimistically expressed, and I think this is what others want. People buy poetry to have something that will affect them, add new things to their lives. If they want something to think about, they get prose. See how much magic you can make. See how well-liked it is."

$ ◎ PACIFIC COAST JOURNAL; FRENCH BREAD AWARDS; FRENCH BREAD PUBLICA-TIONS, P.O. Box 23868, San Jose CA 95153-3868, e-mail paccoastj@juno.com, website http://www.bjt.net/~stgraham/pcj, founded 1992, editor Stillson Graham.

Magazine Needs: *PCJ* is a quarterly "unprofessional literary magazine that prints first-time authors, emerging authors, established authors, and authors who are so visible that everyone's sick of them." They want "offbeat poetry, visual poetry, poetry that is aware of itself. We don't rule out rhyming poetry, but rarely do we accept it." They have published poetry by Kirby Congdon, Linda Neal and Richard Kostelanetz. As a sample the editor selected these lines by Dayna Severs:

> too many times the door slammed and one hinge came loose/and then/the screen started to rip in a
> couple of places/while the people/ran in and out forgetting to be gentle/and, well,/things slam.

PCJ is 56 pgs., 5½ × 8½, photocopied and saddle-stitched with a card stock cover and b&w photos and artwork. They receive 400-500 poems a year, accept approximately 15%. Press run is 200 for 100 subscribers. Single copy: $3; subscription: $12. Sample: $2.50.

How to Submit: Submit up to 6 poems or 12 pages at a time. No previously published poems; simultaneous submissions OK. Cover letter preferred. Time between acceptance and publication is 6-18 months. Seldom comments on rejections. Send SASE for guidelines or request via e-mail. Reports in 3-4 months. Pays 1 copy. Acquires one-time rights. Reviews novels, short story collections and chapbooks of poetry in 1,500 words, single format. Open to unsolicited reviews (and pays $5 if accepted). Poets may also send books for review consideration.

Book/Chapbook Needs & How to Submit: French Bread Publications also occasionally publishes chapbooks of poetry, short story collections and short novellas. Books are similar to the journal in format. They have published *The Writer's Ancestral Sense of Place* by Errol Miller. Query first with 5-8 sample poems, a cover letter and a list of credits for all the poems in the ms. Replies to queries in 1-2 months, to mss (if invited) in 3-4 months. Pays royalties and 10% of press run.

Also Offers: They also sponsor the French Bread Awards for short fiction/poetry. Entry fee: $6 for a group of up to 4 poems (no longer than 8 pgs. total). 1st Prize: $50. 2nd Prize: $25. Deadline: August 1. Send SASE for details. Website includes guidelines, poetry and contest information.

Advice: The editor says, "Most poetry looks like any other poetry. We want experiments in what poetry is."

[N] ◎ PACIFIC ENTERPRISE MAGAZINE, P.O. Box 1907, Fond du Lac WI 54936-1907, phone (920)922-9218, e-mail rudyled@vbe.com, founded 1998, editor Rudy Ledesma.

Magazine Needs: Appearing 6 times a year, *PEM* is "a literary magazine that combines subjects dealing with entrepreneurial/enterprising ideas. Focus is on poems and personal essays that are autobiographical in nature— that our children's children may know us through our writing and stories." They have no limitations on style or form. "Poems written in a foreign language are welcome as long as the English translation comes with it. No racy themes or content; please, no four-letter words." They have published poetry by Gemino Abad and Jon Pineda. As a sample we selected these lines from "Dear _____," by Eileen Tabios:

> I could be smoking a Cuban lit by a buxom blonde who offered/a pale cleavage with a piece of cedar
> to light my cigar, surrounded/by mahogany walls in a dim bar on Manhattan's Upper East Side. And//
> I could be gliding over pregnant vineyards in Napa Valley/in a hot air balloon, its hide stitched from
> pieces of a rainbow,/a V of birds and a two-seater plane interrupting the horizon. And,//still, I only

would be considering how rarely a smile/sits on your lips, and yet that it sits there with ease/when
you look at me: Thus, you make all my spaces sunlit.

PEM is 36 pgs., magazine-sized, web offset printed and saddle-stitched with 4-color glossy paper cover, includes b&w photos, cartoons and ads. They receive about 300-400 poems a year, accept approximately 20%. Press run is 3,000-10,000 for 500 subscribers of which 10 are libraries; remainder distributed free to potential subscribers. Single copy: $2.95; subscription: $19.95. Sample: $4. Make checks payable to *Pacific Enterprise Institute*.
How to Submit: Submit no more than 5 poems at a time. Previously published poems and simultaneous submissions OK. Cover letter undesired, "but short bio required." E-mail and disk submissions OK. "When submission is by e-mail, include poems in message or attach as text file." Time between acceptance and publication is 1-6 months. Seldom comments on rejections. Send SASE for guidelines. Reports in 2-6 months. Always sends prepublication galleys. Pays 2 copies. Acquires first or one-time rights. Reviews books of poetry. Open to unsolicited reviews. Poets may also send books for review consideration.

✓ ◐ ◎ **PAINTBRUSH: A JOURNAL OF POETRY & TRANSLATION (Specialized: translation, themes, writing); EZRA POUND POETRY AWARD**, Division of Language & Literature, Truman State University, Kirksville MO 63501, phone (660)785-4185, fax (660)785-7486, e-mail pbrush@truman.edu, website http://www.truman.edu/Paintbrush, founded 1974, editor Ben Bennani.
Magazine Needs: *Paintbrush* appears annually in the Fall and is 250-300 pgs., 5½×8½, using quality poetry. Circulation is 500. Sample: $15.
How to Submit: No submissions June, July and August. No e-mail submissions. Send SASE with inquiries and request for samples. Pays 2 copies. Reviews books of poetry.
Also Offers: Sponsors the Ezra Pound Poetry Award. "It's on our website. $2,000 for the best collection of poems." Website includes general information, names of editors, contributors, critical acclaim and competition information.

$ ◐ **PAINTED BRIDE QUARTERLY**, 230 Vine St., Philadelphia PA 19106, website http://www.libertynet. org, editors Kathy Volk Miller and Marion Wrenn, founded 1973.
Magazine Needs: "We have no specifications or restrictions. We'll look at anything." They have published poetry by Robert Bly, Charles Bukowski, S.J. Marks and James Hazen. "*PBQ* aims to be a leader among little magazines published by and for independent poets and writers nationally." The 80-page, digest-sized, perfect-bound magazine uses 40 pgs. of poetry/issue. They receive over 1,000 submissions a year, use approximately 150. Neatly printed, it has a circulation of 1,000 for 850 subscribers, of which 40 are libraries. Subscription: $16. Sample: $6.
How to Submit: Submit up to 6 poems, any length, typed; only original, unpublished work. "Submissions should include a short bio." Seldom comment on rejections. They have a 6- to 9-month backlog. Pays 1-year subscription, 1 half-priced contributor's copy and $5/accepted piece. Publishes reviews of poetry books. "We also occasionally publish critical essays."
Also Offers: Sponsors annual poetry contest and chapbook competition. Entry fee required for both. Send SASE for details.

◐ **PALANQUIN; PALANQUIN POETRY SERIES**, Dept. of English, University of South Carolina-Aiken, 171 University Pkwy., Aiken SC 29801, fax (803)641-3461, e-mail phebed@aiken.sc.edu, founded 1988, editor Phebe Davidson.
Book/Chapbook Needs: The press sponsors annual Fall and Spring chapbooks contests and publishes occasional longer books of poetry. They do not want "sentimental, religious, consciously academic" poetry. They have published poetry by Stuart Bartow, Gay Brewer and Laura Lee Washburn. As a sample the editor selected these lines by Laura Lee Washburn:
    the clouds come down from the sky./They climb monkey-fashion on slick strings./They come leaving
    bruises/against the pale spots of where they have been.
How to Submit: Contest deadlines are April 10 and October 15 annually. Submissions should include 20-25 pages of poetry plus bio and acknowledgements. Include SASE for reply. Reports in 3 months. The $10 reading fee includes a copy of the winning chapbook. Make checks payable to Palanquin Press. The winning ms is published by Palanquin Press and the poet receives $100 and 50 copies of the chapbook. Samples are $5.

✓ ◯ ◐ ◎ **PALO ALTO REVIEW (Specialized: themes)**, 1400 W. Villaret Blvd., San Antonio TX 78224, phone (210)921-5443 or 921-5017, fax (210)921-5115, e-mail eshull@accd.edu, founded 1992, editors Ellen Shull and Bob Richmond.
Magazine Needs: *PAR* is a biannual publication of Palo Alto college. "We invite writing that investigates the

---

THE SUBJECT INDEX, located at the back of this book, can help you select markets for your work. It lists those publishers whose poetry interests are specialized ◎ .

full range of education in its myriad forms. Ideas are what we are after. The *Palo Alto Review* is interested in connecting the college and the community. We would hope that those who attempt these connections will choose startling topics and find interesting angles from which to study the length and breadth of ideas and learning, a lifelong pursuit." The review includes articles, essays, memoirs, interviews, book reviews, fiction and poetry. They want "poetry which has something to say, literary quality poems, with strong images, up to 50 lines. No inspirational verse, haiku or doggerel." They have published poetry by Walt McDonald, Diane Glancy, Virgil Suárez and Wendy Bishop. *PAR* is 60 pgs., 8½×11, professionally printed on recycled paper and saddle-stapled with matte card cover with art; b&w photos, art and graphics inside. They publish about 8 poems in each issue (16 poems/year). Press run is 700 for 400 subscribers of which 10 are libraries, 200 shelf sales. Subscription: $10. Sample: $5.

How to Submit: Submit 3-5 poems at a time. No previously published poems; simultaneous submissions OK. Poems are read by an advisory board and recommended to editors, who sometimes suggest revisions. Always comments on rejections. "Although we frequently announce a theme, the entire issue will not necessarily be dedicated to the theme." Theme for Spring 2000 is "Arts and the Artists" (deadline: December 1, 1999). Send SASE for guidelines and upcoming themes. Reports in 1-3 months. Pays 2 copies. Acquires first North American serial rights. "Please note poems as first published in *Palo Alto Review* in subsequent printings."

Advice: The editors say there are no requirements for submission, "though we recommend the reading (purchase) of a sample copy."

✓ ◯ ◑ **PANDALOON; THE KNEWS REVIEW**, P.O. Box 210973, Milwaukee WI 53221, phone (414)282-7185, fax (414)282-7186, e-mail pandaloon@azml.com, website http://www.azml.com, founded 1997, editor David L. White.

Magazine Needs: *PandaLoon* is a quarterly pocket poetry anthology. "Exactly by its portable pocket size, *PandaLoon* favors the shorter poem. If 'it' cannot be expressed in twenty short lines or less, adding more words will not help. Rhymes are fine. They have to work. Everything has to work. Don't bruise the words shoving them into place. This is not a place for 'concrete' poetry. Editing is 'hands-off.' *PandaLoon* considers that a poem is evidence to the outside world that a poet has grappled with the truth and that intentional obscurity is counterproductive to the poet's overall message." *PandaLoon* is 16 pgs., 4×7, laser printed, saddle-stitched, card cover. Press run is 100. Subscription: $5 for 4 issues. Sample is free with #10 SASE.

How to Submit: Submit up to 3 poems at a time. Previously published poems (with when/where) OK; no simultaneous submissions. Cover letter preferred. E-mail submissions OK. Seldom comments on rejections. Send SASE for guidelines or obtain via e-mail or website. Reports within 3 months. Sometimes sends prepublication galleys. Pays 1 copy. Acquires first North American serial rights.

Also Offers: They also publish *The Knews Review*, "a quarterly newsletter heralding the post-information age that will explore things we already know and bring us home to ourselves." Send SASE for guidelines.

✓ ▣ ◑ **THE PANNUS INDEX; BGB PRESS, INC.**, 14545 N. F.L.W. Blvd. #276, Scottsdale AZ 85260, fax (602)314-7445, e-mail bgbpress@earthlink.net, website http://home.earthlink.net/~bgbpress, founded 1995, poetry editor Leonard Cirino.

Magazine Needs: *The Pannus Index* is an annual online Web-based format, "primarily a genre-thematic journal, past issues (formerly hard copy issues) have delved into satire, decadence, surrealism, Irish and Irish-American writers. Future issues to concentrate on new American Romanticism and important writers of the late 20th century. The Web offers new and exciting directions in producing quality poetry, fiction and nonfiction. By eliminating the need to produce hardcopy, offset printing and a paper trail, we can concentrate on uploading groundbreaking examinations into literary themes previously unexamined. By providing an interactive forum for writers to connect with readers on a personal level, we can close the gap of misinterpretation, close readings, and open up dialogue with our readership. This may prove discouraging to writers not involved in new technological approaches to getting their work out, but we still approach this in the traditional sense of submitting work." They want "real language poetry—Houseman, Williams, Whitman, Pound. Not interested in experimental or modernist bellyaching. No suburban housewife, political or agenda-driven commentary. Absolutely no hack poetry." They have published poetry by Duane Locke, Alan Britt, Paul Roth and Walt Curtis. As a sample they selected these lines from "A Succession of Fine Lives" by Errol Miller:

> The soft spirit of late afternoon/sinks slowly around us in voices exquisitely/vibrant with laughter, with fond attributes/of approaching twilight.

How to Submit: Submit 2-3 poems at a time, length unimportant. Previously published poems OK; no simultaneous submissions. ("If previously published, author must clear first rights from previous publication.") Cover letter preferred. E-mail submissions a priority, "but if you don't have the capabilities, submit via mail with work on disk in a universally understood application (MS Word)." Must include bio and a SASE for manual submissions. Reads submissions in June and September only. Time between acceptance and publication is 2-3 months. Poems are circulated to an editorial board. Seldom comments on rejections. Publishes theme issues. Send SASE for guidelines and upcoming themes or obtain via e-mail or website. Reports in 3-4 weeks. Acquires first North American serial rights. "Must state that poem first appeared in *The Pannus Index* for future re-publishing." Reviews books and chapbooks of poetry and other magazines in 500-1,500 words, multi-book format. Open to unsolicited reviews. Poets may also send books for review consideration to Leonard Cirino, % *The Pannus Index*.

Book/Chapbook Needs & How to Submit: BGB Press, Inc. wants "strong poetry—classic, essential and most importantly, uses language to elevate thought" and publishes 1-2 paperbacks/year. Query—"will talk on individual basis, as interest in project warrants." Replies to queries in 2-3 weeks; to mss in 2 months. Obtain sample books by writing to publisher.

Advice: They say, "Try, try again. Have humility, faith and perserverence. Learn how to write before you write."

PAPERPLATES, 19 Kenwood Ave., Toronto, Ontario M6C 2R8 Canada, phone (416)651-2551, fax (416)651-2910, e-mail paper@perkolator.com, website http://www.perkolator.com, founded 1990, publisher/editor Bernard Kelly.

Magazine Needs & How to Submit: *paperplates* is a quarterly online magazine of general interest featuring short stories, poetry, one-act plays, reviews, travel pieces, essays and interviews. They have no preference for submissions, however they do not want religious poetry. They have published poetry by Richard Ontram and Fraser Sutherland.

How to Submit: Submit 5 poems at a time. Previously published poems and simultaneous submissions OK. Cover letter preferred. E-mail submissions OK with mailing address and phone number. Time between acceptance and publication is up to 1 year. Seldom comments on rejections. Send SASE (or SAE and IRCs) for guidelines. Reports ASAP. Pays 1 hardcopy. Reviews books of poetry. Open to unsolicited reviews. Poets may also send books for review consideration.

PAPIER-MACHE PRESS (Specialized: themes, anthologies, women), 627 Walker St., Watsonville CA 95076, phone (408)763-1420, fax (408)763-1422, founded 1984, acquisitions editor Shirley Coe.

Book/Chapbook Needs: Papier-Mache is a small press publisher of theme anthology books. Their anthologies typically "explore a particular aspect of women's experience, such as aging, parental relationships, work or body image." Their anthologies have included poetry by Sue Saniel Elkind, Lynn Kozma, Patti Tana, Ruth Daigon and Janet Carncross Chandler. As a sample the editor selected these lines from "Drying Apricots" by Maggi Ann Grace, published in *Grow Old Along with Me—The Best Is Yet to Be*:

> They carry their harvest,/now heavy between them,/to sawhorse tables./Their task is familiar/(they
> have been at it for years):/to discard the stone/that alone seems to couple/this fruit. Wife on one side,/
> husband, opposite.

They publish 1-2 anthologies each year. Each anthology contains 20-30 poems, and submissions are accepted only when a particular theme has been announced.

How to Submit: Send SASE for guidelines announcing upcoming themes and submission periods. Pays royalties and several copies. Send SASE for catalog to buy samples; books typically cost $8-14.

Advice: "Papier-Mache's goal is to produce enduring works of beauty, grace and strength that present important social issues. We select well-written, accessible material on theme subjects, develop attractive, high quality book formats, and market them to an audience that might not otherwise buy poetry. We take particular pride in our reputation for dealing with our contributors in a caring, professional manner."

$ PAPYRUS (Specialized: ethnic/nationality), P.O. Box 270797, West Hartford CT 06127-0797, e-mail gwhitaker@imagine.com, website http://www.readersndex.com/papyrus, founded 1994, editor Ginger Whitaker.

Magazine Needs: *Papyrus* is a quarterly "writer's 'craftletter' featuring the Black experience," published by Papyrus Literary Enterprises, Inc. It includes articles on the art of writing; fiction, nonfiction and poetry; marketplace news; and literary notes for the serious beginning writer. They want African-American-centered poetry, but will accept good work by anyone. Shorter works preferred, but nothing against any ethnic group. They have published poetry by Lyn Lifshin, John Grey, Lenard D. Moore and Simon Perchik. As a sample we selected these lines from "I Know the Grandmother One Had Hands" by Jaki Shelton Green:

> I know the grandmother one had hands/but they were always in bowls/folding, pinching, rolling the
> dough/making the bread/I know the grandmother one had hands/but they were always under water/
> sifting rice/bluing clothes/starching lives . . .

Papyrus is 20 pgs., 8½×11, printed in 2 colors and saddle-stitched. They receive about 25 poems a year, publish approximately 50%. Press run is 2,000 for 500 subscribers, 200 shelf sales. Subscription: $8/year. Sample: $2.20.

How to Submit: Submit up to 5 poems at a time. No previously published poems or simultaneous submissions. Work may be submitted on a 3.5 disk, with 2 hard copies. "Macintosh users should submit files in ClarisWorks, Microsoft Word, WordPerfect or MacWrite II. IBM users should submit files saved in ASCII. E-mail submissions OK, but submit work within the body of the e-mail only; no attachments. However, we prefer e-mail queries to blind submissions." Poems are reviewed by 2 senior editors and an independent poetry consultant. Often comments on rejections. Send SASE for guidelines or request via e-mail. Reports in 1 month. Pays $10-25 and 2 copies. Buys first rights.

Also Offers: Sponsors annual contest. Entry fee: $5. Awards $100 for winners in each category of fiction, nonfiction and poetry.

PARADOXISM; XIQUAN PUBLISHING HOUSE; THE PARADOXIST MOVEMENT ASSOCIATION (Specialized: form), University of New Mexico, Gallup NM 87301, e-mail smarand@unm.edu, founded 1990, editor Florentin Smarandache.

Magazine Needs: *Paradoxism*, (formerly *The Paradoxist Literary Movement Journal*), is an annual journal of "avant-garde poetry, experiments, poems without verses, literature beyond the words, anti-language, non-literature and its literature, as well as the sense of the non-sense; revolutionary forms of poetry." They want "avant-garde poetry, one to two pages, any subject, any style (lyrical experiments). No classical, fixed forms." They have published poetry by Paul Georgelin, Titu Popescu, Ion Rotaru, Michéle de LaPlante and Claude LeRoy. *Paradoxism* is 52 pgs., digest-sized, offset printed, soft cover. Press run is 500. "It is distributed to its collaborators, U.S. and Canadian university libraries and the Library of Congress as well as European, Chinese, Indian and Japanese libraries."

How to Submit: No previously published poems or simultaneous submissions. Do not submit mss in the summer. "We do not return published or unpublished poems or notify the author of date of publication." Reports in 3-6 months. Pays 1 copy.

Book/Chapbook Needs & How to Submit: Xiquan Publishing House also publishes 2 paperbacks and 1-2 chapbooks/year, including translations. The poems must be unpublished and must meet the requirements of the Paradoxist Movement Association. Replies to queries in 1-2 months, to mss in 3-6 months. Pays 50 author's copies. Inquire about sample books.

Advice: They say, "We mostly receive traditional or modern verse, but not avant-garde (very different from any previously published verse). We want anti-literature and its literature, style of the non-style, poems without poems, non-words and non-sentence poems, very upset free verse, intelligible unintelligible language, impersonal texts personalized, transformation of the abnormal to the normal. Make literature from everything; make literature from nothing!"

THE PARIS REVIEW; BERNARD F. CONNORS PRIZE, 541 E. 72nd St., New York NY 10021, phone (212)861-0016, fax (212)861-4504, website http://parisreview.com, founded 1953, poetry editor Richard Howard.

● Poetry published in *The Paris Review* was selected for inclusion in the 1992, 1993, 1994, 1995, 1996, 1997 and 1998 volumes of *The Best American Poetry.*

Magazine Needs & How to Submit: This distinguished quarterly (circulation 15,000, digest-sized, 300 pgs.) has published many of the major poets writing in English. Though form, content and length seem open, free verse—some structured, some experimental—tends to dominate recent issues. Because the journal is considered one of the most prestigious in the world, competition is keen and response times can lag. Subscription: $46 (US); $48 (outside US). Sample: $13. Study publication before submitting.

Also Offers: The Bernard F. Connors prize of $1,000 is awarded annually for the best previously unpublished long poem (over 200 lines).

PARIS/ATLANTIC, The American University of Paris, 31 Avenue Bosquet, Paris 75007, France, phone (33 1)01 40 62 05 89, fax (33 1)01 45 89 13, e-mail auplantic@hotmail.com, founded 1982, editor Elise Manley.

Magazine Needs: *Paris/Atlantic* appears biannually and is "a forum for both new and established artists/writers that is based in Paris and is distributed internationally. The contents vary; we publish poetry, prose, paintings, sculpture, sketches, etc." They have published poetry by Ben Wilensky, Joan Payne Kincaid, T. Anders Carson and Joel Brouwer. *Paris/Atlantic* is 80-130 pgs., professionally published with sewn binding and softcover, includes ads. They receive about 400-500 poems a year, accept approximately 40%. Press run is 1,000-1,500; distributed free to bookstores, universities, literary societies, other poets, etc.

How to Submit: Submit any number of poems at a time. "There are no requirements aside from a biography and international postage so we can forward 2 free copies of *Paris/Atlantic* if your work is published." Previously published poems and simultaneous submissions OK. Cover letter including author's name, return address with telephone number, e-mail address or fax number and a short biography required. E-mail and disk submissions OK. "Please cut and paste e-mail submissions. No attachments!" Reads submissions September 1 through November 1 and January 1 through April 1 only. Poems are circulated to an editorial board. "The editorial board reviews work in a roundtable discussion." Send SASE (or SAE and IRC) for guidelines or request via fax or e-mail. Pays 2 copies. Acquires first rights. Rights revert to author upon publication.

Advice: The editor says, "Be heard! The *Paris/Atlantic* Reading Series of Poetry and Prose takes place once a month, for which we invite two poets to perform their work in the Amex Café of The American University of Paris, followed by open mikes. Take advantage to listen and be heard in this international forum, and contact us if you would like to participate."

PARNASSUS LITERARY JOURNAL, P.O. Box 1384, Forest Park GA 30298-1384, phone (404)366-3177, founded 1975, editor Denver Stull.

Magazine Needs: "Our sole purpose is to promote poetry and to offer an outlet where poets may be heard. We welcome well-constructed poetry, but ask that you keep it uplifting, and free of language that might be offensive to one of our readers. We are open to all poets and all forms of poetry, including Oriental, 24-line limit, maximum 3 poems." They have published poetry by Lyn Lifshin, t.k. splake, Mary Ann Henn, Ruth Wildes Schuler and Diana Rubin. As a sample the editor selected this haiku by Matthew Louviere:

> water moccasin/the heron leaps/from its shadow

PLJ, published 3 times/year, is 84 pgs., photocopied from typescript, saddled-stapled, colored card cover, with an occasional drawing. They receive about 1,500 submissions a year, use approximately 350. Currently have about a 1-year backlog. Press run is 300 for 200 subscribers of which 5 are libraries. Circulation includes Japan, England, Greece, India, Korea, Germany and Netherlands. Single copy: $6 US and Canada, $9.50 overseas; subscription: $18 US and Canada, $25 overseas. Sample: $5. Offers 20% discount to schools, libraries and for orders of 5 copies or more. Make checks or money orders payable to Denver Stull.

How to Submit: Submit up to 3 poems, up to 24 lines each, with #10 SASE. Include name and address on each page of ms. "I am dismayed at the haphazard manner in which work is often submitted. I have a number of poems in my file containing no name and/or address. Simply placing your name and address on your envelope is not enough." Previously published poems OK; no simultaneous submissions. Cover letter including something about the writer preferred. "Definitely" comments on rejections. "We do not respond to submissions or queries not accompanied by SASE." Send SASE for guidelines. Reports within 1 week. Pays 1 copy. Acquires all rights. Returns rights to author on publication. Readers vote on best of each issue. Staff reviews books of poetry by subscribers only.

Also Offers: Conducts a contest periodically.

Advice: The editor advises: "Write about what you know. Study what you have written. Does it make sense? A poem should not leave the reader wondering what you are trying to say. Improve your writings by studying the work of others. Be professional."

PARTING GIFTS; MARCH STREET PRESS; FATAL EMBRACE, 3413 Wilshire, Greensboro NC 27408, fax (orders only) (336)282-9754, e-mail rbixby@aol.com, website http://users.aol.com/marchst/, founded 1987, editor Robert Bixby.

Magazine Needs: "I want to see everything. I'm a big fan of Jim Harrison, C.K. Williams, Amy Hempel and Janet Kauffman." He has published poetry by Eric Torgersen, Lyn Lifshin, Elizabeth Kerlikowske and Russell Thorburn. *PG* is 50 pgs., digest-sized, photocopied, with colored matte card cover, appearing twice a year. Press run is 200. Subscription: $12. Sample: $6.

How to Submit: Submit in groups of 3-10 with SASE. No previously published poems, but simultaneous submissions OK. "I like a cover letter because it makes the transaction more human. Best time to submit mss is early in the year." Send SASE for guidelines or obtain via website. Reports in 1-2 weeks. Sometimes sends prepublication galleys. Pays 1 copy.

Book/Chapbook Needs & How to Submit: March Street Press publishes chapbooks. Reading fee: $10.

Also Offers: Website features guidelines, sample issues, book catalog and "fun things" like a name generator and a metaphor generator. They also publish *Fatal Embrace*, an online quarterly, through their website. E-mail submissions OK. "Requirements the same."

PARTISAN REVIEW (Specialized: translations, themes), Dept. PM, 236 Bay State Rd., Boston MA 02215, phone (617)353-4260, founded 1934, editor Edith Kurzweil, editor-in-chief William Phillips.
● Work published in this review has also been selected for inclusion in *The Best American Poetry* (volumes 1995 and 1998).

Magazine Needs: *PR* is a distinguished quarterly literary journal using poetry of high quality. "Our poetry section is very small and highly selective. We are open to fresh, quality translations but submissions must include poem in original language as well as translation. We occasionally have special poetry sections on specified themes." They have published poetry by Charles Wright, Glyn Maxwell, Debora Greger and Wislava Szymbovska. The journal is 160 pgs., 6×9, flat-spined. Circulation is 8,200 for 6,000 subscriptions and shelf sales. Sample: $7.50.

How to Submit: Submit up to 6 poems at a time. No simultaneous submissions. Reports in 2 months. Pays $50 and 50% discount on copies.

PASSAGER: A JOURNAL OF REMEMBRANCE AND DISCOVERY (Specialized: senior citizen, themes), School of Communications Design, University of Baltimore, 1420 N. Charles St., Baltimore MD 21201-5779, e-mail kkopelke@ubmail.ubalt.edu, founded 1989, editors Kendra Kopelke and Mary Azrael.

Magazine Needs: *Passager* is published quarterly and publishes fiction, poetry and interviews that give voice to human experience. "We seek powerful images of remembrance and discovery from writers of all ages. One of our missions is to provide exposure for new older writers." The journal is 32 pgs., 8×8, printed on white linen recycled paper and saddle-stitched. Includes photos of writers. Sample: $4.

How to Submit: Submit 3-5 poems at a time, each 30 lines maximum; fiction, 3,000 words maximum. "We like clean, readable typed copy with name, address and phone number on each page." Simultaneous submissions acceptable if notified. No reprints. "We prefer cover sheets because it makes it personal. We hate pushy cover letters, 'I'm sure you'll find your readers will love my story.'" Does not read mss June through August. Occasionally does special issues. Send SASE for guidelines and upcoming themes. Reports in 3 months. Pays 2 copies.

Also Offers: They sponsor an annual spring poetry contest for new poets over 50 years old, with a $500 1st Prize and honorable mentions; and publication in *Passager*.

PASSAGES NORTH; ELINOR BENEDICT PRIZE, English Dept., 1401 Presque Isle Ave., Northern Michigan University, Marquette MI 49855, phone (906)227-2715, founded 1979, editor-in-chief Kate Myers Hanson

Magazine Needs: *Passages North* is a biannual magazine containing short fiction, poetry, creative nonfiction, essays, interviews and visual art. "The magazine publishes quality work by established and emerging writers." They have published poetry by Jim Daniels, Jack Driscoll, Vivian Shipley and Michael Delp. *PN* is 100 pgs., perfect-bound. Circulation is at 1,000 "and growing." Single copy: $7; subscription: $13/year, $18/2 years, add $10 for international mail. Sample: $2.

How to Submit: Prefers groups of 3-6 poems, typed single-spaced. No simultaneous submissions. "Poems over 100 lines seldom published." Time between acceptance and publication is 6 months. Reads submissions September through May only. Reports in 6-8 weeks. Pays 1 copy.

Also Offers: Sponsors the Elinor Benedict Prize in poetry. Send SASE for details.

$ ☑ ◎ PASSEGGIATA PRESS (Specialized: ethnic, translations), P.O. Box 636, Pueblo CO 81002, phone (719)544-1038, fax (719)576-4689, founded 1973, poetry editor Donald Herdeck.

Book/Chapbook Needs: "Published poets only welcomed and only non-European and non-American poets . . . We publish literature by creative writers from the non-western world (Africa, the Middle East, the Caribbean and Asia/Pacific)—poetry only by non-western writers or good translations of such poetry if original language is Arabic, French, African vernacular, etc." They have published poetry by Derek Walcott, Khalil Hawi, Mahmud Darwish, Julia Fields, Hilary Tham, Houda Naamani and Nizar Kabbani. They also publish anthologies and criticisms focused on relevant themes.

How to Submit: Query with 4-5 samples, bio, publication credits. Replies to queries in 2-4 weeks, to submissions (if invited) in 1-2 weeks. Always sends prepublication galleys. Offers 7.5% royalty contract (5% for translator) with $100-200 advance plus 10 copies. Buys worldwide English rights. Send SASE for catalog to buy samples.

N ◐ ◎ THE PATERSON LITERARY REVIEW; HORIZONTES; ALLEN GINSBERG POETRY AWARDS; THE PATERSON POETRY PRIZE; PASSAIC COUNTY COMMUNITY COLLEGE POETRY CENTER LIBRARY (Specialized: regional, bilingual/foreign language), Poetry Center, Passaic County Community College, Cultural Affairs Dept., 1 College Blvd., Paterson NJ 07505-1179, phone (973)684-6555, e-mail mgellan@pccc.cc.nj.us, website http://www.pccc.cc.nj.us/poetry.

Magazine Needs & How to Submit: A wide range of activities pertaining to poetry are conducted by the Passaic County Community College Poetry Center, including the annual *The Paterson Literary Review* (formerly *Footwork: The Paterson Literary Review*), founded 1979, editor and director Maria Mazziotti Gillan, using poetry of "high quality" under 100 lines; "clear, direct, powerful work." They have published poetry by David Ray, Diane Wakoski, Sonia Sanchez, Laura Boss and Marge Piercy. *TPLR* is 240 pgs., magazine-sized, saddle-stapled, professionally printed with glossy card 2-color cover, using b&w art and photos. Circulation is 1,000 for 100 subscribers of which 50 are libraries. Sample: $10. Send up to 5 poems at a time. Simultaneous submissions OK. Reads submissions September through January only. Reports in 1 year. Pays 1 copy. Acquires first rights.

Magazine Needs & How to Submit: *Horizontes*, founded in 1983, editor José Villalongo, is an annual Spanish language literary magazine using poetry of high quality no longer than 20 lines. Will accept English translations, but Spanish version must be included. They have published poetry by Nelson Calderon, Jose Kozer and Julio Cesar Mosches. *Horizontes* is 120 pgs., magazine-sized, saddle-stapled, professionally printed with full-color matte cover, using b&w graphics and photos. Circulation is 800 for 100 subscribers of which 20 are libraries. Sample: $4. Accepts simultaneous submissions. "On occasion we do consider published works but prefer unpublished works." Reads submissions September through January only. Reports in 3-4 months. Pays 2 copies. Acquires first rights. Staff reviews books of poetry. Send books for review consideration.

Also Offers: The Poetry Center of the college conducts The Allen Ginsberg Poetry Awards Competition each year. Entry fee: $12. Prizes of $300, $150 and $100. Deadline: April 1. Send SASE for rules. They also publish a *New Jersey Poetry Resources* book, the *PCC Poetry Contest Anthology* and the *New Jersey Poetry Calendar*. The Paterson Poetry Prize of $1,000 is awarded each year (split between poet and publisher) to a book of poems published in the previous year. Publishers should write with SASE for application form to be submitted by February 1. Passaic County Community College Poetry Center Library has an extensive collection of contemporary poetry and seeks small press contributions to help keep it abreast. The Distinguished Poetry Series offers readings by poets of international, national and regional reputation. Poetryworks/USA is a series of programs produced for UA Columbia-Cablevision.

◐ ◎ PATH PRESS, INC. (Specialized: ethnic), P.O. Box 2925, Chicago IL 60690, phone (847)424-1620, fax (847)424-1623, e-mail bjjIII@aol.com, founded 1969, president Bennett J. Johnson.

Book/Chapbook Needs & How to Submit: Path Press is a small publisher of books and poetry primarily "by, for and about African-American and Third World people." The press is open to all types of poetic forms; emphasis is on high quality. Submissions should be typewritten in ms format. Writers should send sample poems, credits and bio. The books are "hardback and quality paperbacks."

☑ ◐ ☑ PAVEMENT SAW; PAVEMENT SAW PRESS; PAVEMENT SAW PRESS CHAPBOOK AWARD; TRANSCONTINENTAL POETRY AWARD; BLOODY TWIN PRESS, 7 James St., Scotia NY 12302, e-mail baratiere@megsinet.net, founded 1992, editor David Baratier.

• Please note that Pavement Saw Chapbook Award and Transcontinental Poetry Award are both new additions to this listing.

Magazine Needs: *Pavement Saw*, which appears annually, wants "letters and short fiction, and poetry on any subject, especially work. Length: one or two pages. No poems that tell, no work by a deceased writer and no translations." Dedicates 10-15 pgs. of each issue to a featured writer. They have published poetry by Will Alexander, Sandra Kohler, Naton Leslie, Jendi Reiter, Beth Anderson, Scan Killian and Tracy Philpot. The editor says *PS* is 64 pgs., 6×9, perfect-bound. They receive 7,500-9,000 poems a year, publish less than 1%. Press run is 500 for about 250 subscribers, about 250 shelf sales. Single copy: $4; subscription: $7, $10 for libraries/institutions. Sample: $3.50. Make checks payable to Pavement Saw Press.
How to Submit: Submit 5 poems at a time. "No fancy typefaces." No previously published poems; simultaneous submissions OK, "as long as poet has not published a book with a press run of 1,000 or more." No e-mail submissions. Cover letter required. Seldom comments on rejections. Send SASE for guidelines. Reports in 3-6 months. Sometimes sends prepublication galleys. Pays 2 copies. Acquires first rights.
Book/Chapbook Needs & How to Submit: The press also occasionally publishes books of poetry. "Most are by authors who have been published in the journal."
Also Offers: Sponsors the Pavement Saw Press Chapbook Award. Submit up to 32 pgs. of poetry with a cover letter. Entry fee: $7. Awards publication, $500 and 10% of print run. "Each entrant will receive a copy of the winning chapbook provided a 9×12 SAE with 5 first-class stamps is supplied." Deadline: December 20. Send SASE for guidelines. Also sponsors the Transcontinental Poetry Award. "Each year, Pavement Saw Press will seek to publish at least one book of poetry and/or prose poems from manuscripts received during this competition. Competition is open to anyone who has not previously published a volume of poetry or prose. Writers who have had volumes of poetry and/or prose under 40 pgs. printed or printed in limited editions of no more than 500 copies are eligible. Submissions are accepted during June and July only." Entry fee: $15. Awards publication, $1,000 and a percentage of the press run. Include stamped postcard and SASE for ms receipt acknowledgement and results notification. Send SASE for guidelines. Pavement Saw Press also distributes books for Bloody Twin Press. Send SASE for details.

Ⓝ ⊕ ◯ PEACE & FREEDOM; EASTERN RAINBOW; PEACE & FREEDOM PRESS, 17 Farrow Rd., Whaplode Drove, Spalding, Lincs PE12 OTS England, editor Paul Rance, founded 1985, is a "small press publisher of poetry, music, art, short stories, reviews and general features," and also is a distributor.
Magazine Needs: *Peace & Freedom* is a magazine appearing 2 times a year. "We are looking for poems up to 32 lines particularly from U.S. poets who are new to writing, especially women. The poetry we publish is anti-war, environmental; poems reflecting love; erotic, but not obscene poetry; humorous verse and spiritual, humanitarian poetry. With or without rhyme/metre." They have published poetry by Dorothy Bell-Hall, Doreen King, Bernard Shough, Mona Miller and Andrew Savage. As a sample the editor selected these lines from "No Qualms" by Daphne Richards:

> We humans want our freedom,/and the right to choose our way,/along life's many pathways/as we tread
> them every day.//And yet we ban our animals/from all that we hold dear./We rob them of their dignity,/
> and keep them bound by fear.

Peace & Freedom has a b&w glossy cover, normally 20 A4 pages. Cassette version also available. 50% of submissions accepted. "Poetry is judged on merit, but non-subscribers may have to wait longer for their work to appear than subscribers." Sample: US $5; UK £1.75. "Sample copies can only be purchased from the above address, and various mail-order distributors too numerous to mention. Advisable to buy a sample copy first. Banks charge the equivalent of $5 to cash foreign cheques in the U.K., so advisable to send bills, preferably by registered post." Subscription: US $16, UK £7.50/4 issues.
How to Submit: No simultaneous submissions or previously published poems. Poets are requested to send in bios. Reads submissions all through the year. Publishes theme issues. Send SAE with IRC for upcoming themes. Replies to submissions normally under a month, with IRC/SAE. "Work without correct postage will not be responded to or returned until proper postage is sent." Pays 1 copy. Reviews books of poetry.
Also Offers: Also publishes anthologies. In the Spring 2000, Peace & Freedom Press will publish a paperback anthology entitled *Millennium Memories*—"featuring poetry, prose and art celebrating the past 1,000 years." Send SAE with IRC for guidelines. "*Peace & Freedom* now holds regular contests as does one of our other publications, *Eastern Rainbow*, which is a magazine concerning 20th century popular culture using poetry up to 32 lines. Subscription: US, $13, UK, £6/4 issues. Further details of competitions and publications for SAE and IRC."
Advice: The editor says, "Too many writers have lost the personal touch and editors generally appreciate this. It can make a difference when selecting work of equal merit."

◯ ◑ ◎ PEAKY HIDE (Specialized: form/style), P.O. Box 1591, Upland CA 91785, founded 1996, founding editor Valory Banister.
Magazine Needs: *Peaky Hide* is a quarterly magazine of "almost all poetry. We use some b&w art or photos and occasionally run reviews of chapbooks." They want "experimental, surrealism, post-language, unconventional poetry that is as psychologically unsettling as the magazine's name. The only rule applicable is that tension is evident. We tend to favor short poems with sharp edges. We do not use poems with blatant sentimental or religious imagery. Some visual poetry is used." They have published poetry by Sheila E. Murphy, Errol Miller, Ann Erickson, Scott Keeney, John M. Bennett and Jen Hofer. As a sample the editor selected these lines from her own poem "Tiramisu For A Monday":

An open linoleum floor, unfettered by nothing more than/footprints lazy with haste. Semisweet chocolate
curtains/hung only to make the sun and the cold outside disappear/do not do much against voyeurs
or planning./What would it matter if they were purple? The injuries/are the same and a dessert for a
Monday a decade from/now.

PH is 26-34 pgs., 8½×11, desktop-published and saddle-stapled with light cardstock cover, uses b&w art only.
Accept approximately 40% of poems received a year. Press run is 100 for 12 subscribers; "a number of copies
may be distributed to coffeehouses the editor likes." Subscription: $17 for 4 issues, $8 for 2 issues. Sample: $5.
Make checks payable to Valory Banister.
How to Submit: Submit 3-5 poems at a time. Previously published poems OK; no simultaneous submissions.
Cover letter with brief bio preferred. "I strongly encourage cover letters that include a little about the poet's
individuality and a list of publication credits. I enjoy getting them, and editors are more likely to publish friends
than enemies." Time between acceptance and publication is 4-5 months. "I always try to give comments or
answer specific questions. *PH* publishes many 'new' poets." Publishes theme issues. Send SASE for guidelines
and upcoming themes. Theme for late 1999 is "China, Chartreuse and Candles." Reports in no longer than 4-5
months. Pays 1 copy, additional copies available for $4 each. All rights remain with poets and artists. Reviews
chapbooks of poetry in 250-450 words, multi-book format. Open to unsolicited reviews. Poets may also send
books for review consideration.
Also Offers: "*Peaky Hide* is in the process of publishing chapbooks, but this will be done by *solicitation only*.
We hope to publish 2-3 a year." Titles include *Neurotica* by Nathan Austin and *The Gods of the Salacious
Porcupine* by Damiena S. Carmicheal. Both will cost $2.
Advice: The editor says, "I know not every poet that submits work to me will first examine a sample copy, but
I try to answer requests for sample copies more quickly than I do the submissions I receive so that poets will
have a better idea of the kind of poetry I use. Many poets that review copies of PH or those that are included
within its list of contributors often remark to me that they are propelled within their own artistic visions because
they frequently read PH and magazines like it. These poets come to realize that the work of other poets, the
standards set, are as important as gasoline in an automobile, as fish in an ocean, as French fries in an adolescent's
stomach. . . . there really is something to be said for knowing what's going on and how to get there."

⬤ PEARL; PEARL POETRY PRIZE; PEARL EDITIONS, 3030 E. Second St., Long Beach CA 90803-
5163, phone (562)434-4523 or (714)968-7530, founded 1974, poetry editors Joan Jobe Smith, Marilyn Johnson
and Barbara Hauk.
Magazine Needs: *Pearl* is a literary magazine appearing 2 times/year. "We are interested in accessible, humanistic poetry that communicates and is related to real life. Humor and wit are welcome, along with the ironic and
serious. No taboos stylistically or subject-wise. We don't want to see sentimental, obscure, predictable, abstract
or cliché-ridden poetry. Our purpose is to provide a forum for lively, readable poetry, the direct, outspoken type,
variously known as 'neo-pop' or 'stand-up,' that reflects a wide variety of contemporary voices, viewpoints and
experiences—that speaks to real people about real life in direct, living language, profane or sublime. Our Fall/
Winter issue is devoted exclusively to poetry, with a 12-15 page section featuring the work of a single poet."
They have published poetry by Ron Koertge, Wilma McDaniel, Gerald Locklin, Lisa Glatt, Fred Voss and David
Trinidad. As a sample they selected these lines from "At Terror Street & Reincarnation Way" by Juana Joaquin:
I do not wish to be reincarnated,/Tossed out into this cold world/Naked again. It's taken me all my/
Life to find enough clothes to keep/My skin and soul warm and/I still don't know what to wear.
Pearl is 96-121 pgs., digest-sized, perfect-bound, offset printed, with glossy cover. Press run is 700 for 150
subscribers of which 7 are libraries. Subscription: $18/year includes a copy of the winning book of the Pearl
Poetry Prize. Sample: $7.
How to Submit: Submit 3-5 poems at a time. No previously published poems. "Simultaneous submissions
must be acknowledged as such." Prefer poems no longer than 40 lines, each line no more than 10-12 words to
accommodate page size and format. "Handwritten submissions and unreadable printouts are not acceptable."
No previously published poems; simultaneous submissions OK. "Cover letters appreciated." Reads submissions
September through May only. Time between acceptance and publication is 6-12 months. Send SASE for guidelines. Reports in 6-8 weeks. Sometimes sends prepublication galleys. Pays 2 copies. Acquires first serial rights.
Each issue contains the work of 80-100 different poets and a special 10- to 15-page section that showcases the
work of a single poet.
Book/Chapbook Needs: Pearl Editions "only publishes the winner of the Pearl Poetry Prize. All other books
and chapbooks are *by invitation only*."
Also Offers: "We sponsor the Pearl Poetry Prize, an annual book-length contest, judged by one of our more
well-known contributors. Winner receives publication, $1,000 and 25 copies. Entries accepted during the months
of May, June and July. There is a $20 entry fee, which includes a copy of the winning book." Send SASE for

THE GEOGRAPHICAL INDEX, located at the back of this book, can help you discover
the publishers in your region. Publishers often favor poets (and work) from their own areas.

complete rules and guidelines. Recent books include *Monsters and Other Lovers* by Lisa Glatt, *Dr. Invisible & Mr. Hide* by Charles H. Webb, *Tattooed Woman* by Carolyn E. Campbell and *Bukowski Boulevard* by Joan Jobe Smith.

Advice: The editors add, "Advice for beginning poets? Just write from your own experience, using images that are as concrete and sensory as possible. Keep these images fresh and objective. Always listen to the music."

PECAN GROVE PRESS; CHILI VERDE REVIEW, Box AL 1 Camino Santa Maria, San Antonio TX 78228-8608, phone (210)436-3441, fax (210)436-3782, e-mail palmer@netxpress.com, website http://library.stm arytx.edu/pgpress/index.html, founded 1988, editor H. Palmer Hall, co-editor Cynthia J. Harper (*Chili Verde Review*).

Magazine Needs & How to Submit: Published biannually by Pecan Grove Press and Chili Verde Press, *Chili Verde Review* is "a new magazine that welcomes only original poems by established poets and new voices." They want "poems that are carefully crafted, original, with bright things to say." They have published poetry by John Gilgun, Laurel Speer, Colin Morton, Jenny Browne and Naomi Shihab Nye. The editors say *CVR* is professionally printed and saddle-stitched with cardstock cover featuring a poet walking down a street. Press run is 300 for 97 subscribers. Single copy: $5; subscription: $8/year. "If you want to be our cover poet, send a b&w photo from the back. The editors do like to know a little about you, so do include a cover letter with brief (3-5 line) bio." Sometimes comments on rejections. Reports in 1-6 months. Pays 2 copies and 1-year subscription.

Book/Chapbook Needs: Pecan Grove Press is "interested in fine poetry collections that adhere. A collection should be like an art exhibit—the book is the art space, the pieces work together." They publish 4-6 paperbacks and 2-3 chapbooks/year. They want "poetry with something to say and that says it in fresh, original language. Will rarely publish books of more than 110 pages." They do not want "poetry that lets emotion run over control. We too often see sentiment take precedence over language." They have published poetry by Rick Mulkey, Glen Alyn and Sandra Gail Teichmann. As a sample the editor selected these lines from "This Natural History" by Gwyn McVay:

> Three deer feed in a line at the edge of the wood/And red sky, the spike-buck lifts his head, his weight/
> Suspended on three sinews from the hanging earth,/The does mythical, rounding to white, one/Held
> breath, the space between two trees/And for that reason mostly people can't return/The buck's slight
> black look when he swivels/his head to take in observers, shagbark oak

Books or chapbooks are usually 50-96 pgs., offset, perfect-bound, one-color plus b&w graphic design or photographic cover on index stock.

How to Submit: Submit complete ms. Previously published poems and simultaneous submissions OK. Cover letter required, with some indication of a poet's publication history and some ideas or suggestions for marketing the book. Time between acceptance and publication is 8-12 months. "We do circulate for outside opinion when we know the poet who has submitted a manuscript. We read closely and make decisions as quickly as posisble." Seldom comments on rejections. "We do expect our poets to have a publication history in the little magazines with some acknowledgments." Replies to queries and mss in 1-3 months. After the book has paid for itself, authors receive 50% of subsequent sales and 10 author's copies (out of a press run of 500). "We have no subsidy arrangements, but if author has subvention funds, we do welcome them. Obtain sample books by checking BIP and making purchase. We will send chapbook at random for a fee of $5; book for $10."

Advice: The editor says, "We welcome submissions but feel too many inexperienced poets want to rush into book publication before they are quite ready. Many should try the little magazine route first instead of attempting to begin a new career with book publication."

$ PEER POETRY MAGAZINE; PEER POETRY INTERNATIONAL COMPETITION, 26 (PM) Arlington House, Bath St., Bath, Somerset BA1 1QN United Kingdom, (01225)445298, founded 1995, editor Paul Amphlett.

Magazine Needs: *Peer Poetry Magazine*, published biannually, "is intended to provide poets who have not yet succeeded in 'making their name,' a platform in which they can publish enough of their poetry to allow a number of people in the field to see the quality of their work and at the same time gain for themselves an idea of the informed view of a number of poets with a wide range of views, currently practicing their talent." They want "poetry with natural rhythm, fluent and flowing, having shape and plan; cherishing the sound and beauty of words and ideas. 'Noble sentiments are no substitute for technique and originality.' Highflown language does not make poetry fly high, prose in short lines remains prose; obtrusive rhymes, marching rhythms, produce doggerel!" They have published poetry by Visjna McMaster (Croatia), Jim Norton (Eire), Dick Petter (Saudi Arabia) and Princess Marina Yedi Garoff (UK). As a sample the editor selected these lines from "Cows" by Sue Norris:

> They look at you slowly and calmly./Their tongues would caress you/they come near if you sit with
> them;/lying down in the heat of the day,/eyes looking at you with curiosity,/all together knowingly
> being.

Peer Poetry Magazine is 80 pgs., A4, photocopied, perfect-bound, with b&w card cover. They receive about 750 poems a year, accept approximately 33%. Press run is 300 for 80 subscribers. Single copy: UK £5 plus p&h; subscription: £12 plus p&h.

How to Submit: Submit any number of poems. "We require a sufficient quantity of poems to fill either 1 or preferably a maximum of 2 A4 pages within a double column set-up, using approximately 50-60 lines per single column in 10 or 12 pt. font in clear black type." Previously published poems and simultaneous submissions OK. Cover letter preferred. Time between acceptance and publication is 3-6 months. Poems are circulated to an editorial board. "Selection is based on originality, comprehensibility and quality of imagination." Often comments on rejections. Send SASE (or SAE and IRC) for guidelines. Pays £10/2 published pages of poetry; pays overseas contributors 2 copies.

Also Offers: Sponsors the Peer Poetry International Competition in each issue of the magazine. Readers vote on the winners; analyzed details of voting reactions and editorial comment given in succeeding issue. Send 2 copies of submission with SASE (or SAE and IRC). Include name, address, phone and provide a list of titles on the back of each page.

PEGASUS, 525 Ave. B, Boulder City NV 89005, founded 1986, editor M.E. Hildebrand.
Magazine Needs: *Pegasus* is a poetry quarterly "for serious poets who have something to say and know how to say it using sensory imagery." Avoid "religious, political, pornographic themes." They have published poetry by John Grey, Kerri Brostrom, Nikolas Macioci and Robert K. Johnson. As a sample the editor selected this haiku by Elizabeth Perry:
> When the heart turns cold/it finds warmth in the sparks of/imagination.
Pegasus is 32 pgs., digest-sized, desktop-published, saddle-stapled with colored paper cover. Publishes 10-15% of the work received. Circulation is 200. Subscription: $18. Sample: $5.
How to Submit: Submit 3-5 poems, 3-32 lines. Previously published poems OK, provided poet retains rights; no simultaneous submissions. Send SASE for guidelines. Reports in 2 weeks. Publication is payment. Acquires first or one-time rights.

PELICAN PUBLISHING COMPANY (Specialized: children, regional), Box 3110, Gretna LA 70054-3110, website http://www.pelicanpub.com, founded 1926, editor-in-chief Nina Kooij.
Book/Chapbook Needs: Pelican is a "moderate-sized publisher of cookbooks, travel guides, regional books and inspirational/motivational books," which accepts poetry for "hardcover children's books only, preferably with a regional focus. However, our needs for this are very limited; we do twenty juvenile titles per year, and most of these are prose, not poetry." They have published *Christmas All Over*, by Robert Bernardini. As a sample the editor selected these lines from *A Leprechaun's St. Patrick's Day* by Sarah Kirwan Blazek:
> It is a story that's told/In a magical way/Of leprechaun mischief/On St. Patrick's Day
These are 32-page, large-format (magazine-sized) books with illustrations. Two of their popular series are prose books about Gaston the Green-Nosed Alligator by James Rice and Clovis Crawfish by Mary Alice Fontenot. They have a variety of books based on "The Night Before Christmas" adapted to regional settings such as Cajun, prairie, and Texas. Typically their books sell for $14.95. Write for catalog to buy samples.
How to Submit: They are *currently not accepting unsolicited mss.* Query first with 2 sample poems and cover letter including "work and writing backgrounds and promotional connections." No previously published poems or simultaneous submissions. Reports on queries in 1 month, on mss (if invited) in 3 months. Always sends prepublication galleys. Pays royalties. Buys all rights. Returns rights upon termination of contract.
Also Offers: Website includes writer's guidelines, catalog and company history.
Advice: The editor says, "We try to avoid rhyme altogether, especially predictable rhyme. Monotonous rhythm can also be a problem."

PEMBROKE MAGAZINE, UNCP, Box 1510, Pembroke NC 28372-1510, phone (910)521-6358, fax (910)521-6688, founded 1969 by Norman Macleod, edited by Shelby Stephenson, managing editor Fran Oxendine.
Magazine Needs: *Pembroke* is a heavy (252 pgs., 6×9), flat-spined, quality literary annual which has published poetry by Fred Chappell, Stephen Sandy, A.R. Ammons, Barbara Guest and Betty Adcock. Press run is 500 for 125 subscribers of which 100 are libraries. Sample: $8.
How to Submit: Sometimes comments on rejections. Reports within 3 months. Pays copies.
Advice: Stephenson advises, "Publication will come if you write. Writing is all."

PEMMICAN; PEMMICAN PRESS, P.O. Box 121, Redmond WA 98073-0121, founded 1992, editor Robert Edwards.
Magazine Needs: *Pemmican* is an annual magazine appearing in later winter/early spring designed to publish "the best poetry of imagery, imagination and political commitment we can find. *Pemmican* is not dedicated to advancing any single style, voice or school of poetry. While poets are urged to send their best work, all poets are encouraged to submit poems, women and minorities in particular." They have published poetry by Olga Cabral, Sherman Alexie, John Haines and Maggie Jaffe. *Pemmican* is 80 pgs., 7×8½, saddle-stitched, card stock cover with original art. They receive 1,000-1,200 submissions a year, use less than 10%. Press run is 300-350 for 120 subscribers of which 23 are libraries, 150 shelf sales. Single copy: $5. Sample: $3.50.
How to Submit: Submit 3-10 poems at a time. No previously published poems; simultaneous submissions OK, "but *Pemmican* expects to be notified if a poem has been accepted elsewhere." Cover letter required. "Make sure postage on SASE is adequate for what you want returned." Occasionally comments on rejections. Send SASE for guidelines. Reports in 1-4 week. Pays 1 copy.
Advice: The editor says, "There are no requirements—however, I hope poets realize the importance of small

presses to the survival of American poetry and actively support their favorite magazines. Advice for beginners? Keep writing. Read everything. Don't write to please an editor or to get published. Follow your own voice."

▨ ◐ ◑ PENMANSHIP: A CREATIVE ARTS CALENDAR, P.O. Box 338, Waynesboro VA 22980, website http://www.angelfire.com/me2/, founded 1998, editor Tameka Norris.

Magazine Needs: *Penmanship* is a biannual creative arts calendar. "*Penmanship*'s purpose is to really get us out there! In stores, in everyone's face. Donations are welcomed. Contribute by helping me contribute poetry to a larger audience. I dig avant-garde, concrete, dramatic work with substance. Be sure to intermix passion and control and not one without the other. I want confessional to down right anything. Just make sure it's you writing and not you imagining you're John Clare, Rimbaud or anyone else, but you. No trash talk for the sake of talking trash. There's a difference between erotica and just plain porno." As a sample the editor selected these lines from her poem "Gossiping, Rumors, Lies":

> *There are people out there just waiting/to hate you,/like a hungry stomach growls,/ready to stop the starvation/by cramming any kind of shit in their mouths.*

Penmanship is a 26-page calendar, photocopied and saddle-stapled with b&w cover, uses b&w photos and artwork, ads. Single copy: $5.

How to Submit: Submit 3 poems at a time. Length for poetry is 3 pages maximum. Previously published poems and simultaneous submissions OK. Cover letter preferred. "Some type of letter describing ambitions is greatly desired. Don't forget SASE for response. Fillers are also needed." Reading fee: $5/3 poems. "Additional poems have to be submitted in the accurate batch requirement along with another $5 reading fee. The $5 reading fee serves as purchase of the calendar for those that aren't chosen for publication." Time between acceptance and publication is 1-12 months. Often comments on rejections. Send SASE for guidelines. Reports in 1-4 weeks. Pays $5 refund "or more" and 3 copies. Acquires first or one-time rights or second serial reprint rights. Reviews books and chapbooks of poetry. Open to unsolicited reviews. Poets may also send books for review consideration.

Also Offers: *Penmanship* also publishes an audio cassette series, broadside series and postcard series. Currently no submissions accepted for postcard series. Send SASE for details.

Advice: The editor says, "Forget the ignorant literary scene. If your name is Jacobs, strive to be a Jacobs. Bad poets follow the fads, good poets follow themselves. Ditch that garbage about what trash sells the best. Greedy people will promote anything if it makes them rich. *Penmanship* is closely related to contests when regarding the $5 entry fee, but serves as a regular periodical seeking excellent submissions. If you get published in this zine you should know that the $5 refund is as cheap as we get, and if response is good, the pay you receive in return will be much more than $5 and 3 copies."

⊕ ◑ PENNINE INK, % Mid Pennine Arts, MP The Gallery, Yorke St., Burnley BB11 3JJ Great Britain, founded 1985, editor John Carley.

Magazine Needs: *Pennine Ink* appears annually using poems, short prose items and b&w illustrations. They want "poetry up to 40 lines maximum. Consider all kinds." As a sample the editor selected these lines from "Grace Was Gifted" by Mike Hoy:

> *Had taste, lived quietly/killing weeds, growing roses/- seeds of an elegant life./A wife whose womb didn't bloom/despite green fingers./Adopted royalty, Liz and Maggy,/kept clippings in sagging folders,/ a rag-bag of faded photos.*

The editor says it is 48 pgs., A5, with b&w illustrated cover, small local ads and 3 or 4 b&w graphics. They receive about 400 poems a year, use approximately 40. Press run is 500. "Contributors wishing to purchase a copy of *Pennine Ink* should enclose £2.50 ($6 US) per copy plus postage and packing."

How to Submit: Submit up to 6 poems at a time. Previously published poems and simultaneous submissions OK. Cover letter preferred. Seldom comments on rejections. Reports in 3 months. Reviews small press poetry books in about 200 words.

Advice: The editor adds, "Prose, poetry and illustrations should be accompanied by a suitable stamped, addressed envelope (SASE or SAE with IRCs) for return of work."

⊕ ◑ PENNINE PLATFORM, 7 Cockley Hill Lane, Kirkheaton, Huddersfield HD5 OHW England, phone (0)1484-516804, founded 1973, poetry editor K.E. Smith.

Magazine Needs: *PP* appears 2 times a year. The editor wants any kind of poetry but concrete ("lack of facilities for reproduction"). No specifications of length, but poems of less than 40 lines have a better chance. "All styles—effort is to find things good of their kind. Preference for religious or sociopolitical awareness of an acute, not conventional kind." They have published poetry by Elizabeth Bartlett, Anna Adams, John Ward, Ian Caws, John Latham and Geoffrey Holloway. As a sample the editor selected these lines from "A Vision of Cabez De Vaca" by Cal Clothier:

> *Blanched to a skin manned by bones,/we have blood and our breathing/to prove we are men, and the hungry light/jerking our eyes. We are down to mercy,/gratitude, love, down to humanity.*

The 6×8, 48-page journal is photocopied from typescript, saddle-stapled, with matte card cover with graphics. Circulation is 400 for 300 subscribers of which 16 are libraries. They receive about 300 submissions/year, use about 60, have about a 6-month backlog. Subscription: £8.50 for 2 issues (£12 abroad; £25 if not in sterling). Sample: £4.50.

How to Submit: Submit up to 6 poems, typed. Reports in about 3 months. No pay. Acquires first serial rights.

Editor occasionally comments on rejections. Reviews books of poetry in 500 words, multi-book format. Open to unsolicited reviews. Poets may also send books for review consideration.

N ◐ **PENNSYLVANIA ENGLISH**, Penn State DuBois, DuBois PA 15801-3199, e-mail ajv2@psu.edu, phone (814)375-4814, founded 1988 (first issue in March, 1989), editor Antonio Vallone.
Magazine Needs: *Pennsylvania English*, appearing annually in September, is "a journal sponsored by the Pennsylvania College English Association." They want poetry of "any length, any style." They have published poetry by Liz Rosenberg, Walt MacDonald, Jennifer Richter and Jeff Schiff. The journal is up to 180 pgs., 5½ × 8½, perfect-bound with a full color cover. Press run is 300. Subscription: $11/1 year, $20/2 years.
How to Submit: Submit 3 or more typed poems at a time. Include SASE. They consider simultaneous submissions but not previously published poems. Send SASE for guidelines. Reports in 3 months. Pays 3 copies.

▼ ◯ ◎ PENNY DREADFUL: TALES & POEMS OF FANTASTIC TERROR (Specialized: horror); SONGS OF INNOCENCE; PENDRAGONIAN PUBLICATIONS, 407 W. 50th St. #16, Hell's Kitchen NY 10019, founded 1996, editor and publisher M. Malefica Grendelwolf Pendragon Le Fay.
• "Works appearing in *PD* have received Honorable Mention in *The Year's Best Fantasy and Horror.*"
Magazine Needs: *Penny Dreadful* is a triannual publication (Autumn, Winter, Midsummer). Publishes poetry, short stories, and b&w artwork "which celebrates the darker aspects of Man, the World, and their Creator. We're looking for literary horror in the tradition of Poe, M.R. James, Shelley and LeFanu—dark, disquieting tales designed to challenge the readers' perception of human nature, morality and man's place within the Darkness. Stories and poems should be set prior to 1910 and/or possess a timeless quality: avoid references to 20th century personages/events, graphic sex, strong language, excessive gore and shock elements." *Penny Dreadful* is 48 pags., 5½ × 8½, desktop-published, saddle-stapled with b&w line art. Includes market listings for kindred magazines. Press run is 500 copies, of which 75 are libraries; the rest are mailed to subscribers and other editors. Subscription: $12/1 year (3 issues). Sample: $5. Make checks payable to M. Scarpa.
How to Submit: Submit 3-5 poems with name and address on each page. Poems should not exceed 3 pages (rhymed, metered verse preferred). Previously published poems and simultaneous submissions OK. Cover letter preferred. Reads submissions from June 1 through August of each year only. "Readers are encouraged to submit in April/May." Time between acceptance and publication is up to 1 year. Poems reviewed and chosen by editor. Often comments on rejections. Reports in up to 3 months. Always sends prepublication galleys. Pays 1 copy. Acquires one-time rights.
Magazine Needs & How to Submit: *Songs of Innocence* is a triannual publication (Spring, Midsummer, Fall/Winter). It publishes poetry, short stories, essays and b&w artwork "which celebrate the nobler aspects of mankind and the human experience. We are seeking literary verse in the tradition of Blake, Wordsworth, Emerson, Thoreau, Twain and Whitman. The overall tone of *Songs of Innocence* will most likely be a bit darker than the title leads one to believe: more along the lines of Blake's *Songs of Experience*. Poems and stories must have a modern setting, but those set in the 19th century will have preference. Avoid references to 20th century personages/events, graphic sex, and strong language." The editor says *SOI* is 40 pgs., 8½ × 5½. Press run is 500. Single copy: $5; subscription: $12/year (3 issues). Make checks payable to M. Scarpa. Poems should not exceed 3 pgs.—"rhymed, metered, lyrical verse preferred, but we are open to all styles."

✓ ◐ ◎ PENNY DREADFUL PRESS; THE PENNY DREADFUL REVIEW (Specialized: erotica, form/style), 4210 Park Ave., Nashville TN 37209-3650, phone (615)279-9328, e-mail cramcguirt@aol.com (inquiries only), founded November 1993, "maximum domineditrix" Ms. Penelope Dreadful, assistant subeditrix Ms. Shelley Stoker, assistant editor and factotum C Ra McGuirt.
Magazine Needs: *The Penny Dreadful Review* is a quarterly publication of eclectic tastes. "Our motto: Where Poe Meets Bukowski. We accept poetry, short prose, cartoons and b&w photographs. In *Penny*'s opinion, good poetry is concerned primarily with the dance of words. It avoids intentional obtuseness, moral posturing, emotional caterwauling, and blatant self-aggrandizement. Good poetry doesn't point a finger, or embrace a particular party line, though we do prefer dark humor, erotica, and raw slices of real life in a concrete narrative style." They have published poetry by Brian Daly, Klyd Watkins, Jessica Manke and Julius Air. Chapbook publications by Penny Dreadful Press include *Witness* by Dan Power and *Mute* by James Holder. As a sample the editors selected these lines from "Shoneys 1" by Steve Huff:

> let's go down to shoney's big boy/where all the satanists with teased black hair/sit laughing too loudly
> about their joy in christ . . .

The Penny Dreadful Review is 48 pgs., 5½ × 8½, photocopied and center-stapled. Press run is 500. Subscription: $10/4 issues. Sample: $3. Penny's Dreadful Catalogue, which includes guidelines as well as a complete listing of all chapbooks and back issues of *PDR*, is available for 2 first-class stamps on a SASE.
How to Submit: All submissions should be cleanly and clearly typed or photocopied, with name and address on each page, including SASE. Previously published poems and simultaneous submissions OK. No e-mail submissions. Cover letter preferred. "Tell us a little about yourself; communication is its own reward. We will consider any amount of material, but please include sufficient postage for its return if desired and at the least a SASE for our editorial response." Time between acceptance and publication is up to 1 year. Rarely comments on rejections. Responds in up to 6 months. Pays at least 1 copy. All rights remain with poets.
Advice: "The best way to find out what *PDR* likes to publish is by ordering a sample copy. In our opinion,

'good poetry' is that which is primarily concerned with the dance of words. It avoids intentional obtuseness, moral posturing, emotional caterwauling, and blatant self-aggrandizement. Good poetry doesn't point a self-righteous finger, or embrace a particular party line."

$⬤ PENNYWHISTLE PRESS, P.O. Box 734, Tesuque NM 87574, phone (505)982-0066 or (505)982-2622, fax (505)982-6858 or (505)982-8116, e-mail pnywhistle@aol.com, founded 1986, publisher Victor di Suvero.

Book/Chapbook Needs: Pennywhistle Press "was started as a way to present the work of notable poets to the reading public. Known for its Poetry Chapbook Series, which currently features 24 titles by some of the strongest voices of our time: Francisco X. Alarcón, Dennis Brutus, Joyce Jenkins, Jerome Rothenberg, Suzanne Lummis, Judyth Hill and Sarah Blake, the Press has branched out into the anthology market with the publication of *Saludos! Poemas de Nuevo Mexico*, a bilingual collection of 66 poets presenting their diverse views of this unusual tricultural state, which is also a state of being. Poets in this collection run the spectrum from N. Scott Momaday, Luci Tapahonso and Carolyn Forché to Janet Holmes, Reneé Gregorio and Keith Wilson." The press also has a series entitled Sextet, "an anthology of poetry comprised of six chapbooks by new and established voices." They publish 2 paperbacks and 6 chapbooks a year. They want poetry with "deep, rich imagery; confessional, solid, strong and experimental—generally one page in length." As a sample the editor selected these lines from "A Love Song from the Chimayó Landfill" by Janet Holmes from the anthology, *Saludos! Poemas de Nuevo Mexico*:

> . . . I had merely/two bags of garbage to heave into the heap,/a minor offering beside that of the men/ emptying their truckbeds with shovels. They/were happy, too; yes, everyone was laughing,/as if it were Fiesta, not the dump. I wanted to tell you:/this is how you make me feel, my darling.

Chapbooks are usually 32 pgs., 5¼ × 8⅜, perfect-bound; anthologies are about 200 pgs., 6 × 9, perfect-bound. **How to Submit:** Submit 10 poems at a time. Previously published poems and simultaneous submissions OK. Cover letter preferred. Poems are circulated to an editorial board. "Reviewed by editorial board and then submitted to managing editor and publisher for approval." Replies to queries in 2-4 months, to mss in 1 month. Pays $100 honorarium and 25 author's copies (out of a press run of 1,500).

⬤ ◎ THE PENWOOD REVIEW (Specialized: spirituality), P.O. Box 862, Los Alamitos CA 90720-0862, website: http://www.members.aol.com/bcame39696/penwood.html, founded 1997, editor Lori M. Cameron.

Magazine Needs: *The Penwood Review*, published biannually, "seeks to explore the mystery and meaning of the spiritual and sacred aspects of our existence and our relationship to God." They want "disciplined, high-quality, well-crafted poetry on any subject. Prefer poems be less than two pages. Rhyming poetry must be written in traditional forms (sonnets, tercets, villanelles, sestinas, etc.)" They do not want "light verse, doggerel or greeting card-style poetry. Also, nothing racist, sexist, pornographic or blasphemous." They have published poetry by Carol Kauffman, Jack Niewold, Ellen Hyatt, and Mark Aveyard. As a sample the editor selected these lines from "Afloat at Midnight" by Christopher Salaun:

> This one paddle moves too slowly/for where I want to go. Even/in this darkness, where processions/of trees and muskrats march invisibly by,/I am reaching for the scent of a wild ache,/the groan of all blood and root . . .

The editor says *TPR* has a varying number of pages, 8½ × 11, saddle-stapled with heavy card cover. Press run is 50-100. Single copy: $6; subscription: $12. **How to Submit:** Submit 3-5 poems, 1/page with the author's full name, address and phone number in the upper right hand corner. No previously published poems or simultaneous submissions. Cover letter preferred. Time between acceptance and publication is 6-12 months. "Submissions are circulated among an editorial staff for evaluations." Seldom comments on rejections. Reports in 1-2 months. Pays 1 copy with a discounted subscription. Acquires one-time rights.

■ ○ ◎ PEOPLENET DISABILITY DATENET (Specialized: disabled people, love/romance), P.O. Box 897, Levittown NY 11756-0897, phone (516)579-4043, e-mail mauro@idt.net, website: http://idt.net/~mauro, founded 1987, editor/publisher Robert Mauro.

Magazine Needs: *PDD* is a home page (formerly published as a newsletter) for disabled people focusing on dating, love and relationships. The editor wants "poetry on relationships, love and romance only. The length should remain ten lines or less. We publish beginners, new poets. Prefer free verse, a lot of good imagery—and very little rhyme." *PeopleNet DisAbility DateNet* appears only on the World Wide Web at the above website. **How to Submit:** Submit 3 poems at a time via e-mail only. Poems should be neatly typed with name and e-mail address. No simultaneous submissions. Editor comments on good but rejected mss. Reports "immediately." Acquires first rights.

Also Offers: Website includes writer's guidelines, poems, stories, articles, books, bio and pictures.

Advice: The editor says, "We want to publish poems that express the importance of love, acceptance, inner beauty, the need for love and relationship, and the joy of loving and being loved."

Ⓝ $○⬤ THE PEOPLE'S PRESS, 4810 Norwood Ave., Baltimore MD 21207-6839, phone/fax (410)448-0254, press founded 1997, firm founded 1989, contact submissions editor.

Book/Chapbook Needs: "The goal of the types of material we publish is simply to move people to think and perhaps act to make the world better than when we inherited it." They want "meaningful poetry that is mindful of human rights/dignity." As a sample they selected these lines from "Delusions of Grandeur" by Shirley Richburg:

> They march like soldiers/To and fro./Urgently, they must go/To the porch/To see how many smokes/
> They can choke on

Books are usually 50 pgs., 5½×8, photocopied, perfect-bound and saddle-stitched with soft cover, includes art/graphics.

How to Submit: Query first with 1-5 sample poems and a cover letter with brief bio and publication credits. Previously published poems and simultaneous submissions OK. SASE required for return of work and/or response. Time between acceptance and publication is 6-12 months. Seldom comments on rejections. Replies to queries in 2-6 weeks; to mss in 1-3 months. Pays royalties of 5-20% and 50 author's copies (out of a press run of 500). Order sample books by sending $6.

Also Offers: The People's Press sponsors an annual Poetry Month Contest in April. Entries accepted April 1-15. "Prizes and/or publication possibilities vary from contest to contest." Send SASE for details.

○ ◎ **PEP PUBLISHING; LOVING MORE (Specialized: "ethical multiple relationships")**, P.O. Box 4358, Boulder CO 80306, phone/fax (303)543-7540, e-mail ryam@lovemore.com, website http://www.love more.com, founded 1984, editor Ryam Nearing.

Magazine Needs: *Loving More* is a quarterly that "publishes articles, letters, poems, drawings and reviews related to polyfidelity, group marriage and multiple *intimacy*." They use "relatively short poems, though a quality piece of length would be considered, but topic relevance is essential. Please no swinger or porno pieces. Group marriage should not be equated with group sex." It is 40 pgs., magazine-sized, few ads. Circulation is 2,500. Subscription: $24/year. Sample: $6.

How to Submit: Submit up to 10 poems at a time. Ms should be "readable." Considers simultaneous submissions. Time between acceptance and publication is 2-6 months. Editor comments on rejections "sometimes—if requested." Publishes theme issues. Send SASE for upcoming themes. Guidelines available via e-mail at writers@lovemore.com. Responds "ASAP." Pays 1 copy. Open to unsolicited reviews. Poets may also send books for review consideration.

Advice: The editor says, "We're always looking for good poetry related specifically to our topic. Our readers love it when we find some to include. Writers should read our publication before submitting, and I emphasize no swinger or porno pieces will be published."

◑ **PEQUOD: A JOURNAL OF CONTEMPORARY LITERATURE AND LITERARY CRITICISM**, Dept. of English, New York University, 19 University Place, Room 200, New York NY 10003, phone (212)998-8843, fax (212)995-4019, e-mail pequod.journal@nyu.edu, website http://www.nyu.edu/gsas/dept/eng/journal/pequod, contact poetry editor.

Magazine Needs: *Pequod* is a semiannual literary review publishing quality poetry, fiction, essays and translations. They have published poetry by Sam Hamill, Donald Hall and John Updike. It is 200 pgs., digest-sized, professionally printed, flat-spined with glossy card cover. Subscription: $14. Sample: $10.

How to Submit: Reads submissions September 15 through April 15 only. Always sends prepublication galleys.

☑ ◐ **PEREGRINE: THE JOURNAL OF AMHERST WRITERS & ARTISTS PRESS; THE PERE-GRINE PRIZE; AWA CHAPBOOK SERIES**, P.O. Box 1076, Amherst MA 01004-1076, phone/fax (413)253-7764, e-mail awapress@javanet.com, website http://www.javanet.com/~awapress, founded 1984, managing editor Nancy Rose.

Magazine Needs: *Peregrine*, published annually in October, features poetry, fiction, poems in translation and reviews. Open to all styles, forms and subjects except greeting card verse. They have published poetry by Catherine Strisik, Bill Brown, Fran Harris and Saul Bennett. As a sample the editor selected these lines from "Salvia Leucantha" by Conley Day:

> Never mind they seem still sturdy/against my knife, resisting like firm doubters./Arching as though
> they were slim gray women/full of grace, hair gone from their bodies/but for the purple white tufts on
> their heads. . . .

Peregrine is 104 pgs., digest-sized, professionally printed, perfect-bound with glossy cover. Each issue includes at least one poem in translation and reviews. Press run is 1,000. Single copy: $9; subscription: $20/3 issues; $30/5 issues. Sample: $7. Make checks payable to AWA Press.

How to Submit: Submit 3-5 poems, no more than 76 lines (and spaces) each. No previously published work; simultaneous submissions OK. Include cover letter with bio, 40 word maximum. No e-mail submissions. "No! No! No!" "Each ms is read by several readers. Final decisions are made by the poetry editor." Send #10 SASE or visit website for guidelines. Reads submissions October through April only. Postmark deadline: April 1. Pays 2 copies. Acquires first rights. Reviews books of poetry in 200-500 words. Poets may send books for review consideration. "We will consider review submissions of no more than 750 words (indicate word count), as long as the review is accompanied by the book of poetry reviewed."

Also Offers: The Peregrine Prize, an annual fiction and/or poetry contest. 1st Prize: $500, publication in *Peregrine*, and copies. Entry fee: $10. Submit 1-3 poems, limited to 70 lines (and spaces) per poem. "*Very specific* *contest guidelines!"* Send #10 SASE or visit website for guidelines. After the winners of the Peregrine Prize have been chosen by an outside judge, the editorial staff will select one entry from Western Massachusetts to receive the First Annual "Best of the Nest" Award. The AWA Chapbook Series is *closed* to unsolicited submissions.

⃝ ◗ ◎ **PERMAFROST: A LITERARY JOURNAL; MIDNIGHT SUN POETRY CHAPBOOK CONTEST (Specialized: regional)**, % English Dept., P.O. Box 755720, University of Alaska Fairbanks, Fairbanks AK 99775, fax (907)474-5247, website http://www.uaf.edu/english/index.html, founded 1977, contact poetry editor.

Magazine Needs: An annual published in August, *Permafrost* contains poems, short stories, creative nonfiction and b&w drawings, photographs and prints. "We survive on both new and established writers, and hope and expect to see your best work. We publish any style of poetry provided it is conceived, written and revised with care. While we encourage submissions about Alaska and by Alaskans, we also encourage and welcome poems about anywhere and from anywhere. We have published work by E. Ethelbert Miller, W. Loran Smith, Peter Orlovsky, Jim Wayne Miller, Allen Ginsberg, Jean Genet and Andy Warhol." The journal is about 200 pgs., digest-sized, professionally printed, flat-spined, with b&w graphics and photos. Subscription: $7. Sample: $5.

How to Submit: Submit 3-6 poems, typed, single or double-spaced, and formatted as they should appear. Considers simultaneous submissions. Fax submissions OK. Deadline: March 15. Does not accept submissions between March 15 and September 1. Editors comment only on mss that have made the final round. Send SASE for further guidelines or request via e-mail. Reports in 3 months. Pays 2 copies; reduced contributor rate on additional copies.

Also Offers: *Permafrost* also sponsors the Midnight Sun Poetry Chapbook Contest, as well as an annual fiction contest and a nonfiction contest. Send SASE for guidelines. Contest entry fees: $10, includes a subscription to the journal. Deadline: March 15. Website includes guidelines, contest guidelines, published writers and electronic copy of the journal.

◗ ◎ **PERSPECTIVES (Specialized: religious)**, P.O. Box 470, Ada MI 49301-0470, co-editors Thomas A. Boogart and Evelyn Diephouse, poetry editor Francis Fike (send poetry submissions to Francis Fike at Dept. of English, Hope College, Holland MI 49422-9000), founded 1986.

Magazine Needs: *Perspectives* appears 10 times/year. The journal's purpose is "to express the Reformed faith theologically; to engage issues that Reformed Christians meet in personal, ecclesiastical, and societal life, and thus to contribute to the mission of the church of Jesus Christ." They want "both traditional and free verse of high quality, whether explicitly 'religious' or not. Prefer traditional form. Publish one or two poems every other issue, alternating with a Poetry Page on great traditional poems from the past. No sentimental, trite, or inspirational verse, please." They have published poetry by Len Krisak, Nancy Nicodemus and Frederick Lewis Allen. As a sample the editor selected these lines from "Entering the Kingdom" by Julia Guernsey:

> So she found Dakota Street, a heap/of trash out back, containers grimed with food,/the third floor balcony on which she stood,/remembering Wordsworth's ode to the shrill beep/of a forklift, which came to strip the mound/and struck a nest of rats. Their whiplike tails/slithered, their bodies scratching separate trails/like dice, a chaos over icy ground.

Perspectives is 24 pgs., 8½×11, web offset and saddle-stapled, with paper cover containing b&w illustration. They receive about 50 poems a year, accept 6-10. Press run is 3,300 for 3,000 subscribers of which 200 are libraries. Subscription: $24.95. Sample: $3.50.

How to Submit: No previously published poems or simultaneous submissions. Cover letter preferred. Include SASE. Time between acceptance and publication is 8 months or less. Seldom comments on rejections. Reports in 1-3 months. Pays 5 copies. Acquires first rights.

Ⓝ ◗ **PERUGIA PRESS**, P.O. Box 108, Shutesbury MA 01072, e-mail skan@valinet.com, founded 1997, director Susan Kan.

Book/Chapbook Needs: "Perugia Press publishes first or second books, primarily by women, of poems that express the range of what makes us human." They publish 1 paperback/year. They want "strong, unflinching, lyrical, feminist poetry . . . tend also to publish narrative poems with sensual imagery. No esoteric, 'experimental,' impersonal work." They have published poetry by Gail Thomas. As a sample the director selected these lines from "Ascent" by Almitra David in *Impulse to Fly:*

> Witnesses saw the children plummet,/but she watched them fly, saw each one/soar and ride the wind,/ then tucked her baby under her wings/and took off.

Books are usually 88 pgs., 6×9, offset printed and perfect-bound with 2-color card cover with photo or illustration.

How to Submit: Query first with 7 sample poems and cover letter with brief bio and publication credits. Previously published poems and simultaneous submissions OK. Cover letter preferred. Send SASE for response. Reads submissions in winter only. Time between acceptance and publication is 6 months. Seldom comments on rejections. Replies to queries in 3 weeks; to mss in 6 weeks. Pay is negotiable. Order sample books by sending $6.

🌐 $⦿ **PETERLOO POETS**, 2 Kelly Gardens, Calstock, Cornwall PL18 9SA Great Britain, founded 1977, poetry editor Harry Chambers.
Book/Chapbook Needs: They publish collections of "well-made" poetry (rhyming and free verse) under the Peterloo Poets imprint: flat-spined paperbacks and poetry cassettes. They have published *Undark* by John Glenday and *Safe as Houses* by U.A. Fanthorpe (both Poetry Book Society Recommendations).
How to Submit: Query with 10 sample poems, bio and list of publications. Simultaneous submissions and previously published poems OK if they have not been in book form. Always sends prepublication galleys. Pays 10% royalties, $100 advance (for first volume, $200 for subsequent volumes) and 12 copies. Editor "normally, briefly" comments on rejections.
Also Offers: Sponsors an annual open poetry competition. 1st Prize: £4,000 sterling; 2nd Prize: £1,000 sterling; four other prizes totaling £1,100 sterling. Entry fee: £5 for first poem, £4 for subsequent poems. "Maximum 10 poems—not more than 40 lines per poem." Entries must be previously unpublished. Deadline: March 2. Send IRC for entry form and rules.

⦿ **PHILOMEL; PHILOMATHEAN SOCIETY**, Box H, College Hall, University of Pennsylvania, Philadelphia PA 19104-6303, phone (215)898-8907, founded in 1813, contact editor.
Magazine Needs: *Philomel* is a literary annual using "inventive poetry, no more than 300 words or 3 pgs. per poem." They also use stories, essays and "witty recipes." As a sample they selected these lines from "Tender is the Night" by David Perry Jones:

> Sweep, sweep; the agony settles shoulder-dust deep in the stillness/Of still bolder enmity:/Red-thundered eyes scream shrill shelter in the pelting./Weep, weep; unsated escalation/Clears the wiry field; the carpet rims and folds; two minarets afire/Seethe; black-stones scathe, defile the evening sky . . .

Philomel comes out each spring. It is 80 pgs., 6×9, flat-spined, with glossy card cover. Poems are selected by a committee of the Philomathean Society. Press run is 1,500 for 20 subscribers of which 3 are libraries; 1,400 distributed free to the university community. Sample: $5.
How to Submit: Submit up to 3 poems at a time. Deadline for submissions: February 1, annually. Pays 1 or more copies.

⦿ **PHILOMEL BOOKS**, 345 Hudson St., New York NY 10014, phone (212)414-3610, fax (212)414-3395, an imprint founded in 1980, editorial director Patricia Gauch.
Book/Chapbook Needs: Philomel Books publishes 15-20 hardbacks and 5-7 chapbooks/year. They say, "Since we're a children's book imprint, we are open to individual poem submissions—anything suitable for a picture book. However, publication of poetry collections is usually done on a project basis—we acquire from outside through permissions, etc. Don't usually use unpublished material." They have published poetry by Edna St. Vincent Millay and Walt Whitman.
How to Submit: Query first with 3 sample poems and cover letter including publishing history. Previously published poems and simultaneous submissions OK. Replies to queries in 1 month, to mss in 2. Pay is negotiable.

⦿ **PHOEBE; GREG GRUMMER POETRY AWARD**, George Mason University, 4400 University Dr., Fairfax VA 22030, phone (703)993-2915, website http://www.gmu.edu/pubs/phoebe, founded 1970, poetry editor Mehera Dennison.
Magazine Needs: *Phoebe* is a literary biannual "looking for imagery that will make your thumbs sweat when you touch it." They have published poetry by C.D. Wright, Russell Edson, Burnadette Mayer, Rosemarie Waldrop and Leslie Scalapino. As a sample the editor selected these lines from "Why I Cannot Write At Home" by Jeffrey Schwarz:

> Does the moon yank a black comb/through the sun?/No, Mother does that.// . . .//Then where's the moon all morning?//Knocking and knocking on the outhouse door.

Circulation is 3,000, with 30-35 pgs. of poetry in each issue. *Phoebe* receives 4,000 submissions a year. Single copy: $6; subscription: $12/year.
How to Submit: Submit up to 5 poems at a time; submission should be accompanied by SASE and a short bio. No simultaneous submissions. Reports in 2-3 months. Pays 2 copies.
Also Offers: Sponsors the Greg Grummer Poetry Award. Awards $500 and publication for winner, publication for finalists and a copy of awards issue to all entrants. Submit up to 10 poems, any subject, any form, with name on all pages. No previously published submissions. Entry fee: $10/entry. Deadline: December 15. Contest receives 300-400 submissions. Back copy of awards issue: $6. Send SASE for guidelines.

THE CHAPBOOK INDEX, located at the back of this book, lists those publishers who consider chapbook mss. A chapbook, a small volume of work (usually under 50 pages), is often a good middle step between magazine and book publication.

⬛ ◎ **PHOEBE: JOURNAL OF FEMINIST SCHOLARSHIP THEORY AND AESTHETICS (Specialized: women/feminism)**, Women's Studies Dept., Suny-College at Oneonta, Oneonta NY 13820-4015, phone (607)436-2014, fax (607)436-2656, e-mail omarakk@oneonta.edu, founded 1989, poetry editor Marilyn Wesley, editor Kathleen O'Mara.

Magazine Needs: *Phoebe* is published semiannually. They want "mostly poetry reflecting women's experiences; prefer 3 pages or less." They have published poetry by Barbara Crooker, Graham Duncan and Patty Tana. As a sample we selected these lines from "Rosh Hodesh, In the Room of Mirrors" by Lyn Lifshin:

> eyes over crystal/that a great aunt/might have polished/reflected in a/hall mirror,/candles float/like the moon,/a reflection of a/reflection.

Phoebe is 120 pgs., 7×9, offset printed on coated paper and perfect-bound with glossy card cover, includes b&w art/photos and "publishing swap" ads. They receive about 500 poems a year, accept approximately 8%. Press run is 500 for 120 subscribers of which 52 are libraries. Single copy: $7.50; subscription: $15/year or $25/year institutional. Sample: $5.

How to Submit: No previously published poems. Fax submissions OK. Cover letter preferred. Reads submissions October through January and May through July only. Time between acceptance and publication is 3 months. Seldom comments on rejections. Publishes theme issues occasionally. Send SASE for guidelines. Reports in 12-14 weeks. Sometimes sends prepublication galleys. Pays 2 copies. Staff reviews books and chapbooks of poetry in 500-1,000 words, single book format. Send books for review consideration.

$⬜ **PHOENIX; PHOENIX POETRY CHAPBOOKS; THE PHOENIX ANTHOLOGY OF POETRY COMPETITION; PHOENIX RISING AWARD**, P.O. Box 317, Berkeley CA 94701-0317, founded 1996, editor R.C. Poynter.

Magazine Needs: *Phoenix*, published annually in October, "provides audience for lesser-known poets and publishes work that might be deemed too political or noisy for some magazines." They want "any subject, any style. I believe confessional poets are going to be the lighthouses of the new century; I would like to see form and old school, as well." They do not want "Hallmark-style verse; but I will read every submission sent in the belief that not all great art is dark and angry." They have published poetry by John Vandevoorde, Robert Wooten and Nan Byrne. As a sample the editor included these lines from "Clytemnestra Exposed" by Don Hasso:

> . . . Mad dogs roam your halls/With broken bodies, lamentable loss,/Pitiable and voiceless, faceless and blameless//. . . I saw it all./As did the silent witnesses who marched/Dutifully along, either mute or stupid!

The editor says *Phoenix* is 122 pgs., 8½×11, with glossy cover, authors' photographs and ads. They receive about 300-500 poems/issue, accept approximately 15-20%. Sample: $16.95. Make checks payable Phoenix, Inc.

How to Submit: Submit 6-8 poems at a time with SASE. Previously published poems ("credit must be listed") and simultaneous submissions ("please keep us updated") OK. Cover letter preferred. "We can no longer consider handwritten submissions, sincere apologies. Computer printouts must be dark enough to read! Typewritten submissions can be single-spaced but clean them up please. Don't send your writing with the wrong words ('I love to watch the *sitting* sun') and then tell me in a cover letter that if you've got it wrong, to change it. If you doubt its correctness, fix it before you send it." Time between acceptance and publication is 3 months. Poems are circulated to an editorial board. Send SASE for guidelines. Reports in 1-3 weeks. Sometimes sends prepublication galleys. Pays 4 copies and small honorarium ($5-10/poem). Acquires one-time rights. Reviews chapbooks and books of poetry in a separate insert. Open to unsolicited reviews. "Query." Poets may also send books for review consideration to W. Hall.

Book/Chapbook Needs: Phoenix Poetry Chapbooks publishes 1 paperback and 6 chapbooks/year "of authors we feel would benefit from a larger collection not, rather than one or two poems in a small audience magazine; we publish what we believe is going to be remembered." Chapbooks are usually 24 pgs., 6×9, "copyset," saddle-stitched with cardboard cover and artwork if desired. Pays ⅓ of run.

How to Submit: Query first, with a few sample poems and a cover letter with brief bio and publication credits. Manuscripts for book publication may include poems previously published in magazines. Replies to queries in 1 week, to mss in 1 month. Pays 10-25% royalty and 50 author's copies (out of a press run of 500). "Chapbooks are the only subsidized work at Phoenix; chapbooks are ½ & ½ subsidized, and you receive listed royalties on copies we sell through mail order. (You will probably recoup $100 of an original $250 input—THINK before you agree to this: Can you afford it at this time?) Send $6 for our choice of in-stock chapbooks."

Also Offers: Sponsors the Phoenix Anthology Poetry Competition. Anthology is perfect-bound with glossy cover. $10 entry fee. Awards 4 cash awards. Sponsors theme contests (overcoming addiction, political statements, etc.). Publish special inserts, "Runners" (highlighting one poet), Mini-Run Chaps (50-75 copies of a chapbook without subsidy, "to see whether we can find an audience and perhaps secure a grant to run a full edition run of 250 or more"), and the Phoenix Rising Award with a $1,000 prize for the editor of a small press magazine selected by an outside judge as showing the most promise. Nominations are made by readers, not the editors/publishers themselves. Send SASE for all guidelines.

Advice: The editor says, "We will not reply, in any way, to work that does not include a SASE! Care about your work, and include enough return postage! I will read beginner's writing! We want, we pray for that newcomer's voice that will make all this worthwhile."

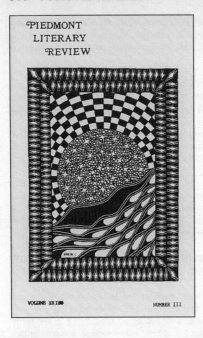

PIEDMONT
LITERARY
REVIEW

VOLUME XXIII

NUMBER III

"For over 22 years, *Piedmont Literary Review* has admitted to a small but finite bias for poetry of form, while judging each work on its own merits," says president William R. Smith. "However, for those who feel that poetry of form is somehow limiting and stodgy, our distinguishing covers—in never-ending variety—provide a visual rebuttal." This cover illustration is part of a series by illustrator Larry Oberc. Says Smith, "The series of drawings, when seen as a whole, provides varying compositions containing repeated and consistent elements—circles, checkered fields, streams of tear-shaped objects, starry fields and masses of out-reaching flame." Published in Lynchburg, Virginia, *Piedmont Literary Review* is digest-sized, saddle-stapled, offset printed from typescript, matte card cover, using black and white graphics, with 40-50 pages of poetry in each issue.

PIEDMONT LITERARY REVIEW; PIEDMONT LITERARY SOCIETY (Specialized: form/style), 1017 Spanish Moss Ln., Breaux Bridge LA 70517, founded 1976, poetry editor Gail White. **Magazine Needs:** If you join the Piedmont Literary Society, $15 a year, you get the quarterly *Review* and a quarterly newsletter containing current market and contest information. Gail White says, "We consider all types of poems—free verse or rhymes—up to 42 lines. Each issue has a special section for oriental forms with an emphasis on haiku." Each also includes short fiction. She wants poems with elegance of style and occasionally accepts humor. Does *not* want pornographic work. "Beginners are welcome, but they compete with mature, competent poets." *PLR* has published poetry by Sharon Kourous, Jeanne Heath Heritage, Carol Hamilton and Georgia Bender. As a sample the editor selected these lines from "Restless Feet" by Elizabeth Howard.

> Fireflies haunt the night;/dogwood blossoms glow in the feverish light;/whippoorwills call, a bobcat
> screams,/a star falls. A ripe time for birthing/the thought gives me gooseflesh/wait, Little one, for a
> proper bed/and a granny to catch you.

PLR is 40 pgs., digest-sized, saddle-stapled, offset printed from typescript, matte card cover, using b&w graphics, with 40-50 pgs. of poetry in each issue. Press run is 300 for 200 subscribers of which 10 are libraries. Sample: $4 (or $3 prepublication) domestic, $6 foreign.
How to Submit: Submit 3-5 poems at a time. (Send haiku submission to Dorothy McLaughlin, 10 Atlantic Rd., Somerset NJ 08872.) Editor often comments on rejections. Send SASE for guidelines. Reports within 3 months. Pays 1 copy. Acquires first rights. Briefly reviews "a few" books of poetry, "mostly contributors' books," in accompanying newsletter.
Also Offers: They also sponsor occasional contests.
Advice: The editor says she is "interested only in poetry which communicates to the thoughtful reader, with special interest in established verse forms and free verse. Not interested in experimental verse."

PIF MAGAZINE; PIF PRIZE FOR POETRY, P.O. Box 538, Dupont WA 98327-0538, phone (615)463-8867, e-mail poetry@pifmagazine.com, website http://www.pifmagazine.com, founded 1995, poetry editor Anne Doolittle, managing editor Richard Luck.
Magazine Needs: *Pif Magazine* appears monthly and is "your home on the Internet for the best poetry, fiction and commentary available. We are fast becoming 'the' litmus test for new authors on the Net." They are open to any form or style. "We want to see poetry that is innovative and takes chances. We're plotting the course for American poetry, not following someone else's example. No stale, staid work that lacks courage or creativity." They have published poetry by Liam Rector, Robert McDowell, David Lehman, Gail Hosking Gilberg and Allison Jenks. *Pif* is 30-36 electronic pgs. They receive about 750 poems a year, accept approximately 15%.
How to Submit: Submit 3-5 poems at a time. No previously published poems; simultaneous submissions OK. Cover letter with short bio preferred. "Tell us a little about the writing of the poem—as well as a brief bio." E-mail and disk submissions only. "No hard-copy submissions will be accepted." For e-mail, include submission in body of message. No attachments." Time between acceptance and publication is 1 month. Seldom comments on rejections. Publishes theme issues. Send SASE or e-mail for guidelines. Reports in 2 months. Sometimes

sends prepublication galleys. Pays $5/poem. Acquires first rights. Reviews books and chapbooks of poetry and other magazines in 250-1,000 words, single book format. Open to unsolicited reviews. Poets may also send books for review consideration to Richard Luck.

Also Offers: Sponsors the Pif Prize for Poetry, an annual award of $150 for the best poem. Honorable mention prizes include subscription to the print magazine, writer's reference books and publication in special "Pif Prize" issue. Submit 2 poems/entry, no more than 100 lines each. Poems must be unpublished but may be on any subject or in any form. Send SASE for guidelines only. Entry fee: $5/entry (2 poems), includes copy of print issue containing winning entries. Deadline: December 1. Competition receives 50-100 entries. Recent contest winners were Leon Shann and Doe Tabor. Judge was Allison Jenks. Winners announced February 1 in online issues of *Pif* (all winners are notified in advance by e-mail or phone).

Advice: The editor says, "Electronic publishing will revolutionize the art of writing as profoundly as did the printing press—and we aim to lead the way. *Pif Magazine* is a premier showcase for new and established poets on the Internet. Many of the poets published in *Pif* have gone on to have collections published by mainstream publishers. Read a couple of issues to get a feel for the type of work we admire. If we love strawberries and you're sending watermelons, well . . .?"

$ 🗹 ◎ PIG IRON; KENNETH PATCHEN COMPETITION (Specialized: themes), P.O. Box 237, Youngstown OH 44501, phone (330)747-6932, fax (330)747-0599, founded 1975, poetry editor Jim Villani.

Magazine Needs: *Pig Iron* is a literary annual devoted to special themes. They want poetry "up to 300 lines; free verse and experimental; write for current themes." They do not want to see "traditional" poetry. They have published poetry by Frank Polite, Larry Smith, Howard McCord, Andrena Zawinski, Juan Kincaid and Coco Gordon. As a sample the editors included these lines from "Cat Call" by Andrenna Zawinski:

> *Curled in the corner of your couch,/like your amber eyed calico cat,/I dove when the earth quaked,/*
> *fell/into the expanse of space stretched/between your arms. You caught me,/held me there,/hair on end,*
> *claws out, screeching./You held me to to your breast, your heart/beat my own rhythm; and I,/star struck*
> *and bewitched,/I purred in your ear.*

Pig Iron is 128 pgs., magazine-sized, flat-spined, typeset on good stock with glossy card cover using b&w graphics and art, no ads. Press run is 1,000 for 200 subscribers of which 50 are libraries. Single copy: $12.95. Subscription: $12.95/year. Sample: $5. (Include $1.75 postage.)

How to Submit: Include SASE with submission. No simultaneous submissions. Fax submissions OK. Send SASE for guidelines. Reports in 3 months. Time between acceptance and publication is 12-18 months. Publishes theme issues. Next theme issue: "Religion in Modernity." Deadline: December 2000. Send SASE for guidelines and upcoming themes. Pays $5/poem plus 2 copies (additional copies at 50% retail). Buys one-time rights.

Also Offers: They sponsor the annual Kenneth Patchen Competition. Send SASE for details.

Advice: The editor says, "Reading the work of others positions one to be creative and organized in his/her own work."

⊕ ◎ PIGASUS PRESS (Specialized: anthologies); THE ZONE; DRAGON'S BREATH; SCAR TISSUE (Specialized: science fiction/fantasy, horror), 13 Hazely Combe, Arreton, Isle of Wight P030 3AJ England, phone (01983)865668, founded 1989, editor Tony Lee.

Magazine Needs: *The Zone*, published biannually, features science fiction stories, interviews, feature articles and poetry. They want "science fiction/fantasy/horror poems. Any length, any style. We are particularly interested in prose poems of 60-70 lines. But please note that genre content is essential." They do not want "non-genre, limericks." They have published poetry by Bruce Boston, Steve Sneyd, Andrew Darlington and John Light. As a sample the editor selected these lines from "Why We Had to Firststrike First" by Steve Sneyd:

> *The creature came right/down nearly to earth dangling/his thousand foot long/penis into town centres/*
> *to catch women's hair/like midnight bat-myths . . .*

The editor says *The Zone* is 68 pgs., A4, "litho printed," saddle-stapled with b&w artwork. Press run varies; "very few" distributed free to review magazines. Single copy: £5.50; subscription: £22. Make checks payable to Tony Lee (those outside UK should pay by international money order in British currency). "We recommend potential contributors buy copies of our magazines to study contents, but it is not compulsory."

How to Submit: Submit 6 poems at a time, one per page with name and address on each. No previously published poems or simultaneous submissions. Cover letter preferred with brief bio. Time between acceptance and publication is 6 months. "The first reading is to get on our short list. The second reading is to select best works before final choice to be published." Often comments on rejections. Publishes theme issues. Send SAE and IRC for guidelines and upcoming themes. Reports "usually" within 6 weeks. Pays 1 copy. Acquires first British rights. "All types of small press books and magazines get brief staff reviews in our *Dragon's Breath* news." Poets may also send books for review consideration to Zine Kat, % Pigasus Press, at the above address.

Book/Chapbook Needs & How to Submit: Pigasus Press, publisher of mini-anthologies, aims "to increase the readership of science fiction poetry." Anthologies are usually 24 pgs., A5, litho printed, saddle-stapled with b&w artwork, including unique graphic poems. Submit up to 5 poems per submission. Introductory letters always welcome. Unpublished poetry is preferred. Replies to mss in a few weeks. Sample books or chapbooks available "by mail order only. Send SAE or IRC for our catalog."

Also Offers: Also publishes *Dragon's Breath* newsletter for international small press review. Published monthly, with information about latest poetry chapbooks and magazines; also market news updates.

Advice: The editor says, "All potential contributors (especially beginners) should read and study our magazines before sending any submissions of work. The sort of poetry we publish is unusual and specialized."

N ⏻ **PIKEVILLE REVIEW**, Humanities Dept., Pikeville College, Pikeville KY 41501, phone (606)432-9612, fax (606)432-9328, e-mail eward@pc.edu, website http://www.pc.edu, founded 1987, editor Elgin M. Ward.

Magazine Needs: "There's no editorial bias though we recognize and appreciate style and control in each piece. No emotional gushing." *PR* appears once yearly in July, accepting about 10% of poetry received. *PR* is 94 pgs., digest-sized, professionally printed and perfect-bound with glossy card cover with b&w illustration. Press run is 500. Sample: $4.

How to Submit: No simultaneous submissions or previously published poems. Editor sometimes comments on rejections. Send SASE for guidelines. Pays 5 copies.

Also Offers: They also sponsor contests. Website includes names of editors, guidelines and most recent editions.

🌐 ⏻ **PINCHGUT PRESS**, 6 Oaks Ave., Cremorne, Sydney, NSW 2090 Australia, phone (02)9908-2402, founded 1948, publishes Australian poetry but is not currently accepting poetry submissions.

N **$** ⏻ ◎ **PINE ISLAND JOURNAL OF NEW ENGLAND POETRY (Specialized: regional)**, P.O. Box 317, West Springfield MA 01090-0317, founded 1998, editor Linda Porter.

Magazine Needs: *Pine Island* appears 3 times a year "to encourage and support New England poets and the continued expression of New England themes." They want poems of "up to thirty lines, haiku and other forms welcome, especially interested in New England subjects or themes. No horror, no erotica. They have published poetry by Larry Kimmel, Roy P. Fairfield and Carol Purington. As a sample the editor selected this poem, "Trinity," by Linda Porter:

> a trinity of apples/grace the handturned bowl/in the parlor.//just in case the pastor should call/or God
> himself stop by

Pine Island is 32 pgs., digest-sized, desktop-published and saddle-stitched, cardstock cover with art. Press run is 100 for 25 subscribers. Subscription: $15. Sample: $5. Make checks payable to Pine Island Journal.

How to Submit: "Writers must be currently residenced in New England." Submit 5 poems at a time. Line length for poetry is 30 maximum. No previously published poems or simultaneous submissions. Cover letter preferred. "Include SASE, prefer first time submissions to include cover letter with brief bio." Time between acceptance and publication is 4 months. Seldom comments on rejections. Send SASE for guidelines. Reports in 2-4 weeks. Pays $1/poem and 1 copy. Buys first rights.

N ⏻ **PINYON POETRY**, Dept. of Languages, Literature & Communications, Mesa State College, Grand Junction CO 81502, phone (970)248-1123, founded 1995, managing editor Michele Gonzales, editor Randy Phillis.

Magazine Needs: *Pinyon Poetry* appears 2 times a year and publishes "the best available contemporary American poetry and b&w artwork." They have "no restrictions other than excellence. We appreciate a strong voice. No inspirational, light verse or sing-song poetry." They have published poetry by Mark Cox, Barry Spacks, Wendy Bishop and Anne Ohman Youngs. As a sample the editor selected these lines from "The Approved Poem" by John McKernan:

> The Approved Poem sits in an oak rocker on the/front porch of a sharecropper's cabin in Logan North/
> Dakota arranging the words alphabetically in a/scrapbook.

The editors say *Pinyon* is about 48 pgs., magazine-sized, offset printed and saddle-stitched, cover varies, includes 8-10 pgs. of b&w art/graphics. They receive about 4,000 poems a year, accept approximately 2%. Press run is 200 for 50 subscribers of which 5 are libraries, 50 shelf sales; 100 distributed free to contributors, friends, etc. Subscription: $8/year. Sample: $4.50. Make checks payable to *Pinyon Poetry*, MSC.

How to Submit: Submit 3-5 poems at a time. No previously published poems or simultaneous submissions. Cover letter preferred. "Name, address and phone number on each page. SASE required." Time between acceptance and publication is 3-12 months. Poems are circulated to an editorial board. "Three groups of assistant editors, led by an associate editor, make recommendations to the editor." Seldom comments on rejections. Send SASE for guidelines. Reports in 1-3 months, "slower in summer." Pays 1 copy/printed page. Acquires one-time rights.

Also Offers: "Each issue contains a 'Featured Poet.' We generally publish 8-15 pages of this one poet's work."

Advice: The editors say, "Send us your best work!"

⏻ ◎ **THE PIPE SMOKER'S EPHEMERIS (Specialized)**, 20-37 120th St., College Point NY 11356-2128, founded 1964, editor/publisher Tom Dunn.

Magazine Needs: "The *Ephemeris* is a limited edition, irregular quarterly for pipe smokers and anyone else who is interested in its varied contents. Publication costs are absorbed by the editor/publisher, assisted by any contributions—financial or otherwise—that readers might wish to make." They want poetry with themes related to pipes and pipe smoking. Issues range from 76-96 pgs., and are 8½ × 11, offset from photoreduced typed copy, saddle-stitched, with colored paper covers and illustrations. The editor has also published collections covering the first and second 15 years of the *Ephemeris*.

How to Submit: Cover letter required with submissions; include any credits. Pays 1-2 copies. Staff reviews books of poetry. Send books for review consideration.

⬜ ◪ ◎ **PIRATE WRITINGS: TALES OF FANTASY, MYSTERY & SCIENCE FICTION; PIRATE WRITINGS PUBLISHING (Specialized: science fiction/fantasy, mystery)**, P.O. Box 329, Brightwaters NY 11718, founded 1992, editor Edward J. McFadden. (Published by DNA Publications. Send all business-related inquiries and subscriptions to DNA Publications, P.O. Box 2988, Radford VA 24143.)
Magazine Needs: *Pirate Writings* is a quarterly magazine "filled with fiction, poetry, art and reviews by top name professionals and tomorrow's rising stars." They want all forms and styles of poetry "within our genres—literary (humorous or straight), fantasy, science fiction, mystery/suspense and adventure. Best chance is 20 lines or less. No crude language or excessive violence. No pornography, horror, western or romance. Poems should be typed with exact capitalization and punctuation suited to your creative needs." They have published poetry by Nancy Springer and John Grey. *Pirate Writings* is 72 pgs., magazine-sized and saddle-stapled with a full-color cover, interior spot color and b&w art throughout. They receive about 150 poetry submissions a year, use approximately 15-25 poems. Subscription: $16/4 issues, $27/8 issues. Sample: $4.95.
How to Submit: Simultaneous submissions OK. Cover letter required; include credits, if applicable. Often comments on rejections. Send SASE for guidelines. Reports in 2-3 months. Pays 1-2 copies. Acquires first North American serial rights. Also "reserves the right to print in anthology."

Ⓝ ⬜ ◪ **PITCHFORK; PITCHFORK PRESS**, 2002 A Guadalupe St. #461, Austin TX 78705, founded 1998, editor Christopher Gibson.
Magazine Needs: *Pitchfork* is a biannual publishing "freaky goodness." They want "erotic, psychotic and surreal poetry. No hack work." They have published poetry by Albert Huffstickler, Thomas Michael McDade and Lyn Lifshin. As a sample the editor selected these lines from "Cupid Pro Creator" by Robert O'Neal:
> *tawdry pink hearts &/blue moons give the feathers to/foreskin, a plump-assed/cherub who splits hairs with his/feckless aim—love or/lust that quickens eggs into/raspberry-shellaced tadpoles?*
Pitchfork is 40-60 pgs., digest-sized, photocopied and saddle-stapled with colored paper cover. Press run varies. Subscription: $6. Sample: $2. Make checks payable to Christopher Gibson.
How to Submit: Submit 3-7 poems at a time. Previously published poems and simultaneous submissions OK. Cover letter preferred. "Include name and address on each page; always include SASE." Time between acceptance and publication is 6 months. Seldom comments on rejections. Send SASE for guidelines. Reporting time varies. Pays 1 copy. Acquires all rights. Returns rights.
Book/Chapbook Needs & How to Submit: Pitchfork Press publishes 2 chapbooks per year. Chapbooks are usually 40-60 pgs., digest-sized, photocopied and side-stapled. Send SASE for details.

☑ ◪ **PITT POETRY SERIES; UNIVERSITY OF PITTSBURGH PRESS; AGNES LYNCH STAR-RETT POETRY PRIZE**, 3347 Forbes Ave., Pittsburgh PA 15261, phone (412)383-2456, fax (412)383-2466, website http://www.pitt.edu/~press, founded 1968, poetry editor Ed Ochester.
Book/Chapbook Needs: Publishes 6 books/year by established poets, and 1 by a new poet—the winner of the Starrett Poetry Prize competition. They want "poetry of the highest quality; otherwise, no restrictions—book mss minimum of 48 pages." Poets who have previously published books should query. Simultaneous submissions OK. Always sends prepublication galleys. They have published books of poetry by Richard Garcia, Larry Levis, Helen Conkling and Alicia Ostriker. Their booklist also features such poets as Peter Meinke, Sharon Olds, Ronald Wallace, David Wojahn and Toi Derricotte.
How to Submit: Unpublished poets or poets "who have published chapbooks or limited editions of less than 750 copies" must submit through the Agnes Lynch Starrett Poetry Prize (see below). For poetry series, submit "entire manuscripts only." No previously published poems or simultaneous submissions. Disk submissions OK with hard copy. Cover letter preferred. Reads submissions from established poets in September and October only. Seldom comments on rejections.
Also Offers: Sponsors the Agnes Lynch Starrett Poetry Prize. "Poets who have not previously published a book should send SASE for rules of the Starrett competition ($15 handling fee), the only vehicle through which we publish first books of poetry." The Starrett Prize consists of cash award of $3,000 and book publication. Reads in March and April only. Competition receives 1,400 entries. Website includes guidelines for poetry series and Agnes Lynch Starrett Poetry Prize, names of editors and descriptions of recently published poetry titles.

◪ **PLAINSONGS**, Dept. of English, Hastings College, Hastings NE 68902-0269, phone (402)463-2402 or 461-7352, founded 1980, editor Dwight C. Marsh.
Magazine Needs: *Plainsongs* is a poetry magazine that "accepts manuscripts from anyone, considering poems on any subject in any style but free verse predominates. Plains region poems encouraged." They have published award poems by Nancy Cherry, Colin Esler, Iris Gribble-Neal, Stephen Herz, Katie Kingston, J. Tarwood and Terry Thomas. As a sample the editor selected these lines from "Groundskeeper" by Rick Alley:
> *Adrift in the trees, the blue jay's noise/is sharp but not unkind. As I learn the ivy is dying//I uncover a woven nest. Seen in the Statue Garden:/a spider asleep on an eyelid, and a hand, snapped//off a marble god, palming the watered grass.*
Plainsongs is 40 pgs., digest-sized, set on laser, printed on thin paper and saddle-stapled with one-color matte

card cover with generic black logo. "Published by the English department of Hastings College, the magazine is partially financed by subscriptions. Although editors respond to as many submissions with personal attention as they have time for, the editor offers specific observations to all contributors who also subscribe." The name suggests not only its location on the Great Plains, but its preference for the living language, whether in free or formal verse. It is committed to poems only, to make space without visual graphics, bio or critical positions. Subscription: $10/3 issues. Sample: $3.

How to Submit: Submit up to 6 poems at a time with name and address on each page. Deadlines are August 15 for fall issue; November 15 for winter; March 15 for spring. Notification is mailed 5-6 weeks after deadlines. Pays 2 copies and 1-year subscription, with 3 award poems in each issue receiving $25. "A short essay in appreciation accompanies each award poem." Acquires first rights.

PLANET: THE WELSH INTERNATIONALIST, P.O. Box 44, Aberystwyth, Ceredigion SY23 3ZZ, Wales, phone 01970-611255, fax 01970-611197, founded 1970, editor John Barnie.

Magazine Needs: *Planet* is a bimonthly cultural magazine, "centered on Wales, but with broader interests in arts, sociology, politics, history and science." They want "good poetry in a wide variety of styles. No limitations as to subject matter; length can be a problem." They have published poetry by J.K. Gill and R.S. Thomas. As a sample the editor selected these lines from "On Home Beaches" by Les Murray:

> *Back, in my fifties, fatter than I was then,/I step on the sand, belch down slight horror to walk/a*
> *wincing pit edge, waiting for the pistol shot/laughter. Long greening waves cash themselves, foam*
> *change/sliding into Ocean's pocket. She turns: ridicule looks down,/strappy, with faces averted, or is*
> *glare and families.*

Planet is 128 pgs., A5 size, professionally printed and perfect-bound with glossy color card cover. They receive about 500 submissions a year, accept approximately 5%. Press run is 1,475 for 1,350 subscribers of which about 10% are libraries, 200 shelf sales. Single copy: £2.75; subscription: £13 (overseas: £14). Sample: £3.56.

How to Submit: No previously published poems or simultaneous submissions. SASE or SAE with IRCs essential for reply. Time between acceptance and publication is 6-10 months. Seldom comments on rejections. Send SASE (or SAE and IRCs if outside UK) for guidelines. Reports within a month or so. Pays £25 minimum. Buys first serial rights only. Reviews books of poetry in 700 words, single or multi-book format.

THE PLASTIC TOWER, P.O. Box 702, Bowie MD 20718, founded 1989, editors Carol Dyer and Roger Kyle-Keith.

Magazine Needs: *The Plastic Tower* is a quarterly using "everything from iambic pentameter to silly limericks, modern free verse, haiku, rhymed couplets—we like it all! Only restriction is length—under 40 lines preferred. So send us poems that are cool or wild, funny or tragic—but especially those closest to your soul." They have published poetry by "more than 400 different poets." It is 38-54 pgs., digest-sized, saddle-stapled; "variety of typefaces and b&w graphics on cheap photocopy paper." Press run is 200. Subscription: $8/year. Copy of current issue: $2.50. "We'll send a back issue free for a large (at least 6×9) SAE with 2 first-class stamps attached."

How to Submit: Submit up to 10 poems at a time. Previously published poems and simultaneous submissions OK. Editors "often" comment on submissions. Send SASE for guidelines. Reports in 3-4 months. Pays 1 copy. Open to unsolicited reviews. Poets may also send books for review consideration.

Advice: Roger Kyle-Keith says, "*PT* is an unpretentious little rag dedicated to enjoying verse and making poetry accessible to the general public as well as fellow poets. We don't claim to be the best, but we try to be the nicest and most personal. Over the past several years, we've noticed a tremendous upswing in submissions. More people than ever are writing poetry and submitting it for publication, and that makes it tougher for individual writers to get published. But plenty of opportunities still exist (there are thousands of little and literary magazines in the U.S. alone), and the most effective tool for any writer right now is not talent or education, but persistence. So keep at it!"

THE PLAZA (Specialized: bilingual), U-Kan, Inc., Yoyogi 2-32-1, Shibuya-ku, Tokyo 151-0053, Japan, phone 81-3-3379-3881, fax 81-3-3379-3882, e-mail plaza@u-kan.co.jp, website http://u-kan.co.jp, founded 1985, poetry editors Leo Nishida and Roger Lakhani.

Magazine Needs: *The Plaza* is a quarterly which "represents a borderless forum for contemporary writers and artists" and includes poetry, fiction and essays published simultaneously in English and Japanese. They want "highly artistic poetry dealing with being human and interculturally related. Nothing stressing political, national, religious or racial differences. *The Plaza* is edited with a global view of mankind." They have published poetry by Al Beck, Antler and Bun'ichirou Chino. As a sample the editors selected these lines from "Rain" by Richard Alan Bunch:

> *We surrendered/through our cravings, embraced/furies in those philosophic limbs./Our days*
> *somersaulted in the wind/bonding with the invisible./There were wrinkling horizons, way back . . .*

The Plaza is 48 pgs., A5, professionally printed and saddle-stapled with card cover. They receive about 2,500 poems a year, accept approximately 4%. Press run is 4,000 for 3,500 subscribers of which 460 are libraries (including 160 overseas), 500 shelf sales. Single copy: 400 yen; subscription: 1,500 yen. Sample available for 5 IRCs (for overseas airmail).

How to Submit: No previously published poems; simultaneous submissions OK. Cover letter required. E-mail and fax submissions OK. "No attachments. Please include telephone and fax numbers with submissions. As *The*

Plaza is a bilingual publication in English and Japanese, it is sometimes necessary, for translation purposes, to contact authors. Japanese translations are prepared by the editorial staff." Seldom comments on rejections. Reports within 1 month. Pays 10 copies plus an additional 10 if self-translated into Japanese. Reviews books of poetry, usually in less than 500 words. Open to unsolicited reviews. Poets may also send books for review consideration.

Also Offers: Website includes contributor's guidelines, publisher's information, introduction of authors, a collection of selected poems, artist's gallery and intercultural events.

Advice: Roger Lakhani says, "*The Plaza* focuses not on human beings but humans being human in the borderless world. It is not international, but intercultural. And it is circulated all over the world—in the American continents, Oceania, Asia, the Middle East, Europe and Africa."

☑ $ ◐ **PLEIADES; PLEIADES/WINTHROP POETRY SERIES; PLEIADES PRESS**, Dept. of English and Philosophy, Central Missouri State University, Warrensburg MO 64093, phone (660)543-4425, e-mail kdp8106@cmsu2.cmsu.edu, website http://www.cmsuvmb.cmsu.edu/englphil/pleiades.html, founded as *Spring Flight* in 1939, reestablished in its present format in 1990, editor R.M. Kinder, co-editor Kevin Prufer.

Magazine Needs: *Pleiades*, a semiannual journal which publishes poetry, fiction, literary criticism, belles lettres (occasionally) and reviews. It is open to all writers. They want "avant-garde, free verse and traditional poetry, and some quality light verse. Nothing pretentious, didactic or overly sentimental." They have published poetry by Alvin Greenberg, Carl Phillips and Eric Pankey. As a sample the editor selected these lines from "How tailors are made" by Graham Foust:

> *Cipher the rate at which things are put/Together. You will discover a love for light//Sleepers who dream they are the only ones/With hands. I'll get lost on the way to your mouth.//If I could have anything I wanted, I would have/Less than I do now. Maybe your blood on a textbook,//Or your breath like some ancient hinge.*

The editor says *Pleiades* is 160 pgs., 5½×8½, perfect-bound with a heavy coated cover and color cover art. They receive about 3,000 poems a year, accept approximately 1-3%. Press run is 1,000, about 200 distributed free to educational institutions and libraries across the country, about 100 shelf sales. Single copy: $6; subscription: $12. Sample: $5. Make checks payable to Pleiades Press.

How to Submit: Submit 3-5 poems at a time. No previously published poems; simultaneous submissions OK with notification. E-mail submissions OK (attach as Microsoft Word files). Cover letter with brief bio preferred. Time between acceptance and publication can be up to 1 year. Each poem published must be accepted by 2 readers and approved by the poetry editor. Seldom comments on rejections. Send SASE for guidelines. Reports in 2-12 weeks. Pays $3/poem and 1 copy or free subscription and 1 copy. Buys first and second serial rights and requests rights for *Wordbeat*, a TV/radio show featuring work published in *Pleiades*. "We are always interested in short reviews of new books of poetry."

Also Offers: Sponsors the Pleiades/Winthrop Poetry Series. "We will select one book of poems in open competition and publish it in our Pleiades Press Series. Louisiana State University Press will distribute the collection." Entry fee: $15. Postmark deadline: March 31. Send SASE for complete guidelines. Website includes new poems and stories, guidelines, masthead, contributors' notes and contents for current issues.

☑ $ ◑ **PLOUGHSHARES**, Emerson College, 100 Beacon St., Boston MA 02116, phone (617)824-8753, founded 1971.

● Work published in *Ploughshares* appears in the 1992, 1993, 1994, 1995, 1996, 1997 and 1998 volumes of *The Best American Poetry*.

Magazine Needs: The magazine is "a journal of new writing guest-edited by prominent poets and writers to reflect different and contrasting points of view." Editors have included Carolyn Forché, Gerald Stern, Rita Dove, Chase Twichell and Marilyn Hacker. They have published poetry by Donald Hall, Li-Young Lee, Robert Pinsky, Brenda Hillman and Thylias Moss. The triquarterly is 250 pgs., 5½×8½. Circulation is 6,000. They receive approximately 2,500 poetry submissions a year. Subscription: $21 domestic; $26 foreign. Sample: $9.95 current issue, $8 sample back issue.

How to Submit: "We suggest you read a few issues before submitting." Simultaneous submissions acceptable. Do not submit mss from April 1 to July 31. Reports in 3-5 months. Always sends prepublication galleys. Pays $50 minimum per poem, $25/printed page per poem, plus 2 copies and a subscription.

☑ $ ◯ ◐ **THE PLOWMAN**, Box 414, Whitby, Ontario L1N 5S4 Canada, phone (905)668-7803, founded 1988, editor Tony Scavetta.

Magazine Needs: *The Plowman* appears semiannually using "didactic, eclectic poetry; all forms. We will also take most religious poetry except satanic and evil. We are interested in work that deals with the important issues

---

🌱 🌐 **SENDING TO A COUNTRY** other than your own? Be sure to send International Reply Coupons (IRCs) instead of stamps for replies or return of your manuscript.

in our society. Social and environment issues are of great importance." *The Plowman* is 20 pgs., 8½×11 (17×11 sheet folded), photocopied, unbound, contains clip art and market listings. They accept 70% of the poetry received. Press run is 15,000 for 1,200 subscribers of which 500 are libraries. Single copy: $5; subscription: $10. Sample free.

How to Submit: Previously published poems and simultaneous submissions OK. Cover letter required. No SASE necessary. Always comments on rejections. Guidelines available free. Reports in 1 week. Always sends prepublication galleys. Pays 1 copy. Reviews books of poetry.

Book/Chapbook Needs & How to Submit: They also publish 125 chapbooks/year. Replies to queries and mss in 1 week. Requires $25 reading fee/book. Pays 20% royalties. They have published *Whispers From the Soul: Volumes I and II* by Ida-May Wagner; *Dark Images* by Irene Kruk; and *Life Is Full of Poetry* by Irene Kruk.

Also Offers: They offer monthly poetry contests. Entry fee: $2/poem. 1st Prize: 50% of the proceeds; 2nd: 25%; 3rd: 10%. The top poems are published. "Balance of the poems will be used for anthologies."

N ⊕ ◯ ◎ **PLUME LITERARY MAGAZINE**, 15 Bolehill Park, Hove Edge, Brighouse, West Yorkshire HD6 2R5 England, phone (01484)7178.8, e-mail plumelit@aol.com, founded 1996, co-editor Jan Bentley.

Magazine Needs: *Plume* is "a biannual magazine committed to a high standard of writing. We accept poetry, fiction, articles and monochrome artwork." They want "well written, original and challenging work, not prescriptive as regards any of the above. No sentimental poetry." They have published poetry by Fiona Curnow, Matthew Barton and Steve Hobson. As a sample the editor selected these lines from "When the Sun Sets in Greece" by Steve Hobson:

> *The night is black skinned, spread tightly over/the olive sea, breathing into breaking/phosphorescence*
> *where the boats are waiting/for the quiet night-talk of fishermen.*

Plume is 40-50 pgs., digest-sized, offset litho printed and saddle-stapled with card cover, b&w illustrations. They receive about 100 poems a year, accept approximately 10%. Press run is 200 for 50 subscribers; 50 distributed free to contributors and other publications. Single copy: £3.50; subscription: £6.50. Sample: £2 (plus .50 p outside EEC).

How to Submit: Submit 2-3 poems at a time with SASE or SAE and IRC. Line length for poetry is 50 maximum. Previously published poems OK; no simultaneous submissions. Cover letter preferred. E-mail submissions OK. Time between acceptance and publication is 6-12 months. Poems are circulated to an editorial board. "Read by editor and poetry editor." Seldom comments on rejections. Send SASE for guidelines. Reports in 2 months. Pays 1 copy. Acquires first rights. Poets may also send books for review consideration.

Also Offers: Sponsors annual poetry and short story competitions. Awards for poetry: £100 1st Prize, £35 2nd Prize, £15 3rd Prize and publication. Entry fee: £2.50/poem. Send SASE (or SAE and IRC) for complete rules.

◎ **POCAHONTAS PRESS, INC.; MANUSCRIPT MEMORIES**, P.O. Drawer F, Blacksburg VA 24063-1020, phone (540)951-0467, fax (540)961-2847, e-mail pocahontas.press@bev.net, founded 1984, president Mary C. Holliman. They are not considering new mss at this time.

◎ **POEM; HUNTSVILLE LITERARY ASSOCIATION**, English Dept., University of Alabama at Huntsville, Huntsville AL 35899, founded 1967, poetry editor Nancy Frey Dillard.

Magazine Needs: *Poem*, appears twice a year, consisting entirely of poetry. "We are open to traditional as well as non-traditional forms, but we favor work with the expected compression and intensity of good lyric poetry and a high degree of verbal and dramatic tension. We equally welcome submissions from established poets as well as from less-known and beginning poets." They have published poetry by Robert Cooperman, Andrew Dillon and Scott Travis Hutchison. *Poem* is a flat-spined, 4⅜×7¼, 90-page journal that contains more than 60 poems (mostly lyric free verse under 50 lines) generally featured 1 to a page on good stock paper with a clean design and a classy matte cover. Circulation is 400 (all subscriptions, including libraries). Sample: $5.

How to Submit: "We do not accept translations, previously published works or simultaneous submissions. We prefer to see a sample of three to five poems at a submission, with SASE. We generally respond within a month. We are a nonprofit organization and can pay only in copy to contributors." Pays 2 copies. Acquires first serial rights.

N ◯ ◎ **POEM DU JOUR**, P.O. Box 416, Somers MT 59932, founded 1999, editor Asta Bowen.

Magazine Needs: *Poem du Jour* is a "weekly one-page broadside circulated in the retail environment." They want "accessible but not simplistic poetry; seasonal work encouraged; humorous, current events, slam favorites; topical work (rural, mountain, outdoors, environmental, Northwest). No erotica, forced rhyme or poems of excessive length." They have published poetry by Tim McNulty. As a sample the editor selected these lines by Jonathan Nelson:

> *. . . I had a cat, and I hated it every way possible./Especially,/Especially,/I hated it when it died.*

Press run is 20-50. Sample: $2. Make checks payable to Asta Bowen—PDJ.

How to Submit: Submit up to 5 poems at a time. Line length for poetry is 50 maximum. Previously published poems and simultaneous submissions OK. Cover letter preferred. "Prefer poems typed with name, address and phone on each page." Time between acceptance and publication varies. Seldom comments on rejections. Send

SASE for guidelines. Reports in 2 months. Sometimes sends prepublication galleys. Pays 1 copy. Acquires one-time rights.
Advice: The editor says, "New/young writers encouraged."

⬤ POEMS & PLAYS; THE TENNESSEE CHAPBOOK PRIZE, English Dept., Middle Tennessee State University, Murfreesboro TN 37132, phone (615)898-2712, founded 1993, editor Gaylord Brewer.
Magazine Needs: *Poems & Plays* is an annual "eclectic publication for poems and short plays," published in April. They have no restrictions on style or content of poetry. They have published poetry by Stephen Dobyns, David Kirby, Vivian Shipley, Charles Bukowski and Ron Koertge. *Poems & Plays* is 88 pgs., 6×9, professionally printed and perfect-bound with coated color card cover and art. "We receive 1,500 poems per issue, typically publish 30-35." Press run is 700. Subscription: $10/2 issues. Sample: $6.
How to Submit: No previously published poems or simultaneous submissions (except for chapbook submissions). Reads submissions October 1 through January 15 only. "Work is circulated among advisory editors for comments and preferences. All accepted material is published in the following issue." Usually comments on rejections. Reports in 1-2 months. Pays 1 copy. Acquires first publication rights only.
Also Offers: "We accept chapbook manuscripts (of poems or short plays) of 24 pages for The Tennessee Chapbook Prize. The winner is printed as an interior chapbook in *Poems & Plays* and receives 50 copies of the issue. SASE and $10 fee (for one copy of the issue) required. Dates for contest entry are the same as for the magazine (October 1 through January 15). Past winners include Maureen Micus Crisick, David Stark, Steven Sater, Angela Kelly and Joe Milosch. The chapbook competition annually receives over 100 manuscripts from the U.S. and around the world."

N $⬤ A POET BORN PRESS, P.O. Box 24238, Knoxville TN 37933, e-mail wm.tell.us@apoetborn.com, website http://www.apoetborn.com, founded 1998, contact Laura Skye.
Book/Chapbook Needs: A Poet Born Press publishes 6-8 paperbacks per year. They want any style or form of poetry, 45 lines or less, including spaces. "Poems should be descriptive of the 20th Century, its people and its issues." No profanity. They have published poetry by Robin Moore, Dwhisperer and Skye. As a sample the editor selected these lines from "One Public Servant" by J. Elsie Madding:
> What was it like—/Going to work each morning,/Calmly ordering the affairs of state,/Striving for wisdom amidst national crises,/Seeking to achieve honorable compromise/Among arguing, bipartitie factions

Books are usually 50-150 pgs., 5½×8½, perfect-bound with 80 lb. cover stock, 1 color or full bleed color covers, includes mostly photographs, some drawings.
How to Submit: Query first with 1-2 sample poems and cover letter with brief bio and publication credits. Line length for poetry is 45 maximum including spaces. Previously published poems and simultaneous submissions OK. E-mail and disk submissions OK. "All poetry must be accompanied by author's name and address, as well as by e-mail address and URL if applicable. Also, author must specify what submission is for: contest, certain publications or call for poems, etc." Time between acceptance and publication is 1-3 months. Poems are circulated to an editorial board. "The editorial staff reviews all submissions for publication and makes their recommendations to the Senior Editor who makes the final selections." Often comments on rejections. "We charge for criticism only on manuscript-length work. Price varies depending on length of manuscript. E-mail for complete details." Replies to queries in 1-2 months. Pays 5-35% royalties "depending on individual contract." 50% of books are author-subsidy published each year. "We have four different subsidy programs. Program is dependent upon work, audience, sales track, and author/press choice. Contracts are specifically tailored to individual authors and their work."
Also Offers: Sponsors three contests per year. 1st Place: $150 plus a brass plaque of poem; 2nd Place: brass plaque of poem; 3rd Place: A Poet Born coffee mug. "All winners receive web publication within 6 weeks of contest and print publication within one year." Entry fee: $5/poem. Website includes complete contest guidelines and submission form, Call for Poems section and permission form, Winners Circle and archive of previous winning poems, Poetry Night listings, poetry news and events, resource links and Teacher's Corner. "Teacher's Corner features lessons in poetry provided by published poets, authors, professors, editors and more. Recent appearances in the Teacher's Corner include: Robert Pinsky, U.S. Poet Laureate; Robin Moore, author of the *French Connection* and *The Green Berets*; Eugene McCarthy, statesman and published poet; and Michael Bugeja, author of *The Art and Craft of Poetry*."

⬤ THE POET HOUSE, P.O. Box 1228, Spring Hill TN 37174-1228, founded 1995, president Michael Salacuse.
Book/Chapbook Needs: Poet House strives "to bring poetry to a wider audience through the CD format." They produce compact disks of recorded poems. They want "short poems no longer than one page. All types of poetry accepted." They do not want vulgar poetry.
How to Submit: Submit 6-10 poems, printed or typed, with name, address and phone on each page. Previously published poems and simultaneous submissions OK. Cover letter required. Poems are circulated to an editorial board. The Poet House board reads each poem and discusses which fits their needs best. Often comments on rejections. Replies to queries in 6 weeks.

✓ ☘ ⃝ **POET LORE; POET LORE NARRATIVE POETRY COMPETITION**, The Writer's Center, 4508 Walsh St., Bethesda MD 20815, phone (301)654-8664, e-mail postmaster@writer.org, website http://www.w riter.org, founded 1889, managing editor Nancy Magill, executive editors Geraldine Connolly and Liz Poliner.
Magazine Needs: *Poet Lore* is a quarterly dedicated "to the best in American and world poetry and objective and timely reviews and commentary. We look for fresh uses of traditional form and devices, but any kind of excellence is welcome. The editors encourage narrative poetry and original translations of works by contemporary world poets." They have published poetry by William Matthews, Denise Duhamel, Susan Terris, R.T. Smith and Cornelius Eady. *Poet Lore* is 6×9, 80 pgs., perfect-bound, professionally printed with glossy card cover. Circulation includes 600 subscriptions of which 200 are libraries. They receive about 3,000 poems a year, use approximately 125. Single copy: $5.50; subscription: $15. Sample: $4.
How to Submit: Submit typed poems, author's name and address on each page, SASE required. Reports in 3 months. Pays 2 copies. Reviews books of poetry. Poets may send books for review consideration.
Also Offers: Sponsors the Poet Lore Narrative Poetry Competition for unpublished poems of 100 lines or more. The annual competition awards $350 and publication in *Poet Lore*. Deadline: November 30. Send SASE for entry form and guidelines. Website includes magazine and contest guidelines, table of contents, current issue and back-issue archives.

🌐 ⃝ **POETIC HOURS; DREAMLANDS POETRY GROUP**, 8 Dale Rd., Carlton, Nottingham NG4 1GT England, founded 1993, editor Nicholas Clark.
Magazine Needs: *Poetic Hours*, published biannually, "is the magazine of the Dreamlands Poetry Group published solely to encourage and publish new poets, i.e., as a forum where good but little known poets can appear in print and to raise money for Third World charities. The magazine features articles and poetry by members of the group and others." They want "any subject, rhyme preferred but not essential; suitable for wide ranging readership, 30 lines maximum." They do not want "gothic, horror, extremist, political, self-interested." As a sample the editor selected these lines from his poem "School Report: Human Race":
> *Does the western world now stand for judgement/Before a clock?/There's a thought!/Whole nations*
> *check two thousand years of progress/Waiting for teachers Millennium Report*
The editor says *Poetic Hours* is 36 pgs., A4, printed, saddle-stapled and illustrated throughout with Victorian woodcuts. They receive about 500 poems a year, accept up to 40%. Press run is 400 of which 12 are for libraries, 300 shelf sales. Subscription: £5, £7 overseas. Sample: £3. Make checks payable to Erran Publishing.
How to Submit: "Poets are encouraged to subscribe or buy a single copy, though not required." Submit up to 5 nonreturnable poems at a time. Previously published poems OK; no simultaneous submissions. Cover letter required. Time between acceptance and publication is 2-3 months. "Poems are read by editors and if found suitable, are used." Always comments on rejections. Publishes theme issues. Upcoming themes listed in magazine. Reports "immediately, whenever possible." Acquires one-time rights. Staff reviews books or chapbooks of poetry. Send books for review consideration.
Also Offers: Dreamlands Poetry Group is non-profit-making and all proceeds go to various national charities, particularly Oxfam and Amnesty International. A page of *Poetic Hours* is set aside each issue for reporting how money is spent.
Advice: The editor says, "We welcome newcomers and invite those just starting out to have the courage to submit work. The art of poetry has moved from the hands of book publishers down the ladder to the new magazines. This is where all the best poetry is found."

Ⓝ ⃝ **POETIC LICENSE POETRY MAGAZINE; BOOKS BY DESIGN**, P.O. Box 311, Kewanee IL 61443-0311, founded 1996, editor Denise Felt, children's editor James Shelton.
Magazine Needs: *PLPM* is a monthly publication with "the purpose of giving new and experienced poets a chance to be published. It includes articles and contests that challenge poets to grow in their craft. We want the best free verse and rhymed poetry by adults and children. No profane, vulgar, pornographic or sloppy work accepted." They have published poetry by Linda Creech, Terri Warden, Elizabeth Fuller and Robert Hentz. As a sample the editor selected these lines from "The Apartment" by Tracy Kreher:
> *My comfortable couch hugs me tenderly./It knows my needs./The book in my hands has caught my*
> *mind/but my ears tend to deceive.*
PLPM is 35-40 pgs., 8½×11, desktop-published, stapled and taped binding with full color cover, includes clip art and ads. They receive about 650 poems a year, accept approximately 95%. Press run is 40 for 30 subscribers. Subscription: $39/year, $68/2 years. Sample: $4.50. Make checks payable to *Poetic License*.
How to Submit: Submit up to 5 poems at a time. Previously published poems and simultaneous submissions OK. Cover letter preferred. "Send double-spaced typed poems with name and address in upper right hand corner. Age required if poet is 14 or younger." Time between acceptance and publication is 1 month. "I judge poems on a 20-point system. Adult submissions with 12 points or less are rejected. Children's submissions with 10 points or less are rejected." Seldom comments on rejections. Publishes theme issues. Send SASE for guidelines and upcoming themes. Reports in 2 weeks. Acquires one-time rights.
Book/Chapbook Needs & How to Submit: They offer chapbook publication services through their press, Books By Design. "We publish quality 8½×11 chapbooks for poets to sell or share with family and friends. We ask poets wishing to publish their chapbook to send for our brochure detailing styles, sizes and cost." They also sponsor an annual chapbook competition through Books By Design. "75% of our publications are subsidized

entirely by the poet. The other 25% are won through our chapbook contest." Send SASE for details on chapbook contest.

Also Offers: Sponsors a quarterly contest anthology on a different theme each February, May, August and November. Anthology chapbooks available at the end of each contest. Send SASE for contest rules. "Magazine and contest anthology winners throughout the year are published in an annual poetry volume called *100 Best Poems*. These are some of the best poems to be found by contemporary poets." Past volumes available.

Advice: The editors say, "The most important thing poets should concern themselves with is excellence. If a poem is rewritten twice or twenty times, it shouldn't matter. The goal is to bring the poem to life. Then it's fit for publication. There is more talent in literate people of all ages than the poets of past centuries could have dreamed. Our goal is to encourage that talent to grow and flourish through exposure to the public."

○ **POETIC REALM; OMNIFIC; THE WRITER'S ADVOCATE**, HC-13, Box 21-AA, Artemas PA 17211-9405, phone (814)458-3102, editor/publisher Kay Weems.

Magazine Needs & How to Submit: *Poetic Realm* is a quarterly of poetry using 36-line, sometimes longer, poems, "anything in good taste" with an Editor's Choice small cash award for each issue. No contributor copies. Subscription: $12/year; $3.50/copy. *Omnific*, a "family-type" quarterly publishes poetry only, 36 lines, sometimes longer; readers vote on favorites, small cash award or copy to favorites. Send SASE for guidelines. No contributor copies. Single copy: $4.50; subscription: $16/year.

Also Offers: She also publishes an annual Christmas anthology. Published/unpublished poetry, 36 lines maximum, Christmas themes. Address to "Christmas Anthology." Deadline: September 30. *The Writer's Advocate*, founded 1988, is a bimonthly newsletter listing over 50 publications and contests for writers, reproducing guidelines of still others. Information is presented in chronological order by deadline date, and then in alphabetical order. Circulation 200-300. Subscription: $24/year; $4/copy. Her other publication, *My Legacy*, is still published but now uses only short stories.

○ **POETIC SPACE: POETRY & FICTION**, P.O. Box 11157, Eugene OR 97440, fax: (541)683-1271, e-mail: poeticspac@aol.com, founded 1983, editor Don Hildenbrand.

Magazine Needs: *Poetic Space*, published annually in the fall, is a nonprofit literary magazine with emphasis on contemporary poetry, fiction, reviews (including film and drama), interviews, market news and translations. Accepts poetry and fiction that is "well-crafted and takes risks. We like poetry with guts. Would like to see some poetry on social and political issues. We would also like to see gay/lesbian poetry and poetry on women's issues. Erotic and experimental OK." Prefers poems under 1,000 words. They have published poetry by Simon Perchik, Paul Weinman, Sherman Alexie, Albert Huffstickler and Lyn Lifshin. The magazine is 30 pgs., 8½×11, saddle-stapled, offset from typescript and sometimes photoreduced. They receive about 200-300 poems a year, accept approximately 25%. Press run is 800 for 50 subscribers of which 12 are libraries. Single copy: $4; subscription: $7/2 issues, $13/4 issues. Send SASE for list of available back issues ($4).

How to Submit: Ms should be typed, double-spaced, clean, name/address on each page. "Submissions without SASE will not be considered." Simultaneous submissions and previously published poems OK. Editor provides some critical comments. Send SASE for guidelines. Reports in 2-4 months. Pays 1 copy, but more can be ordered by sending SASE and postage. Reviews books of poetry in 500-1,000 words. Open to unsolicited reviews. Poets may also send books for review consideration.

Book/Chapbook Needs & How to Submit: Also publishes one chapbook each spring. Their first chapbook was *Truth Rides to Work and Good Girls*, poetry by Crawdad Nelson and fiction by Louise A. Blum ($5 plus $1.50 p&h).

Advice: Don Hildenbrand says, "We like poetry that takes risks—original writing that gives us a new, different perspective."

Ⓝ ○ **POETIC VOICES**, P.O. Box 1684, Durant OK 74702-1684, phone (580)931-0430, e-mail poeticvoices 76@hotmail.com, founded 1998, editor/publisher Brandi Ballew.

Magazine Needs: "*Poetic Voices* is a biannual journal dedicated to giving poets and artists a voice. It includes poetry and artwork by some of today's most talented (though unknown) poets and artists. I want to see poetry full of emotion and imagery. Any style or form accepted. No racist, homophobic or pornographic material." *PV* is 20-30 (possibly more) pgs., 8½×11, neatly printed and saddle-stapled with card cover, includes b&w artwork, ads. They accept approximately 75% of work received. "I try to accept something from each contributor. *Poetic Voices* strives to make the unknown heard." Press run is 125; most distributed free to bookstores and coffeehouses throughout the US. Single copy: $5; subscription: $10/2 issues. Sample (including guidelines): $4.

How to Submit: Submit 3-8 poems at a time with SASE for response. Previously published poems and simultaneous submissions OK. Cover letter required, "containing publication credits, if any." Time between acceptance and publication is 1-6 months. Always comments on rejections. Reports in 1-4 weeks. Pays 1 copy. Poets and artists retain all rights. "Request acknowledgement if work is later printed elsewhere."

Also Offers: Sponsors an annual poetry and art contest. Send SASE for guidelines. Also publishes a newsletter in June.

Advice: The editor says, "Support the local poetry and art scene—not to mention the small press—letters of encouragement and donations are greatly appreciated."

$ POETRY; THE MODERN POETRY ASSOCIATION; BESS HOKIN PRIZE; LEVINSON PRIZE; EUNICE TIETJENS MEMORIAL PRIZE; FREDERICK BOCK PRIZE; GEORGE KENT PRIZE; UNION LEAGUE PRIZE; J. HOWARD AND BARBARA M.J. WOOD PRIZE; RUTH LILLY POETRY PRIZE; RUTH LILLY POETRY FELLOWSHIP, 60 W. Walton St., Chicago IL 60610-3380, e-mail poetry@poetrymagazine.org, website http://www.poetrymagazine.org, founded 1912, editor Joseph Parisi.
   ● Work published in *Poetry* was also selected for inclusion in the 1992, 1993, 1994, 1995, 1996, 1997 and 1998 volumes of *The Best American Poetry*.
Magazine Needs: *Poetry* "is the oldest and most distinguished monthly magazine devoted entirely to verse. Founded in Chicago in 1912, it immediately became the international showcase that it has remained ever since, publishing in its earliest years—and often for the first time—such giants as Ezra Pound, Robert Frost, T.S. Eliot, Marianne Moore and Wallace Stevens. *Poetry* has continued to print the major voices of our time and to discover new talent, establishing an unprecedented record. There is virtually no important contemporary poet in our language who has not at a crucial stage in his career depended on *Poetry* to find a public for him: John Ashbery, Dylan Thomas, Edna St. Vincent Millay, James Merrill, Anne Sexton, Sylvia Plath, James Dickey, Thom Gunn, David Wagoner—only a partial list to suggest how *Poetry* has represented, without affiliation with any movements or schools, what Stephen Spender has described as 'the best, and simply the best' poetry being written." As a sample the editor selected the opening lines of "The Love Song of J. Alfred Prufrock" by T.S. Eliot, which first appeared in *Poetry* in 1915:
   Let us go then, you and I,/When the evening is spread out against the sky/Like a patient etherized upon
   a table;/Let us go, through certain half-deserted streets . . .
Poetry is an elegantly printed, flat-spined, 5½×9 magazine. They receive over 80,000 submissions a year, use approximately 300-350, have up to a 9-month backlog. Press run is 10,000 for 7,000 subscribers of which 53% are libraries. Single copy: $3.50; subscription: $30, $33 for institutions. Sample: $5.
How to Submit: Submit up to 4 poems at a time with SASE. Send SASE for guidelines. Reports in 3-4 months—longer for mss submitted during the summer. Pays $2 a line. Buys all rights. Returns rights "upon written request." Reviews books of poetry in multi-book formats of varying lengths. Open to unsolicited reviews. Poets may also send books to Stephen Young, senior editor, for review consideration.
Also Offers: Seven prizes (named in heading) ranging from $200 to $3,000 are awarded annually to poets whose work has appeared in the magazine that year. Only verse already published in *Poetry* is eligible for consideration and no formal application is necessary. *Poetry* also sponsors the Ruth Lilly Poetry Prize, an annual award of $75,000, and the Ruth Lilly Poetry Fellowship, two annual awards of $15,000 to undergraduate or graduate students to support their further studies in poetry/creative writing. Website includes contents of recent issues, poems by featured poets of the week, writer's guidelines, subscription information, announcement of prize awards and lists of winners, brief history of the magazine and announcements of readings and events.

POETRY & PROSE ANNUAL, P.O. Box 541, Manzanita OR 97130, e-mail info@poetryproseannual.com, website http://www.poetryproseannual.com, founded 1996, editor Sandra Claire Foushee.
Magazine Needs: *Poetry & Prose Annual* "publishes work that focuses on the nature of consciousness and enlightens the human spirit. A general selection of poetry, fiction, nonfiction and photography. We are looking for excellence and undiscovered talent in poems of emotional and intellectual substance. Poems should be original with rhythmic and lyric strength. Innovation and fresh imagery encouraged. Metrical ingenuity recognized. Open to all forms." They have published poetry by Bruce Berger, Anita Endrezze, Tom Crawford and Carlos Reyes. As a sample the editor selected these lines from "All Evening" by Mary Crow:
   Beautiful to be slipping toward a greater/and greater whiteness as if moving/into invisibility or as if
   the whiteness/were a curtain that would open into/some other world, once again green, and new.
PPA is approximately 72 pgs., 7×8½, offset-printed and saddle-stitched with glossy card cover, cover photograph, contains line art and photos inside. Press run is about 1,000. Subscription: $15.
How to Submit: "A $20 submission fee is required. Includes subscription and reader's fee. Any work submitted without submission fee or SASE will not be returned or read. " Submit no more than 200 lines of poetry at a time, typed, with line count, name, address and phone number on first page. Include SASE and brief bio. Previously published poems and simultaneous submissions OK, "but immediate notice requested if accepted elsewhere." E-mail submissions OK. "Submit text from any platform." Cover letter preferred with short bio. Send SASE for guidelines. Reports after deadline. Sometimes sends prepublication galleys. Pays 2 copies. Acquires one-time and reprints rights. Staff reviews books of poetry. Poets may send books for review consideration. Work may also appear in the *Poetry & Prose Annual* website.
Advice: Several new writers will also be chosen from the general selection to be featured in *American Portfolio*—a special selection within the journal showcasing work of several authors in a portfolio.

POETRY BONE, 12 Skylark Lane, Stony Brook NY 11790, website http://www.geocities.com/Athens/Styx/5635, founded 1997, editor Kiel Stuart, editor Reed Coleman.
Magazine Needs: *Poetry Bone* is a biannual journal publishing "general poetry of the highest quality we can find." They want poetry with a maximum length of 29 lines (including title). "Rhyming poetry has to be exceptional." They have published poetry by Simon Perchik. The editors say *PB* is 24 pgs., 5½×8½, laser-printed and saddle-stitched with vellum cover. They receive about 500 poems a year, accept approximately 10%.

Press run is 200 for 100 subscribers of which 20 are libraries, 50 shelf sales. Subscription: $8. Sample: $4.50. Make checks payable to Howard Austerlitz.
How to Submit: Submit 3 poems at a time. No previously published poems or simultaneous submissions. Cover letter undesired. Seldom comments on rejections. Send SASE for guidelines. Reports in about 1 month. Pays 1 copy. Acquires first North American serial rights.
Also Offers: Website includes poetry, notices, editorial, guidelines and mailing address.

○ ◑ **THE POETRY EXPLOSION NEWSLETTER (THE PEN)**, P.O. Box 4725, Pittsburgh PA 15206-0725, phone (412)886-1114, e-mail aford@hillhouse.ckp.edu. website: http://www.incor.com (password: poetry) founded 1984, editor Arthur C. Ford.
Magazine Needs: *The Pen* is a "quarterly newsletter dedicated to the preservation of poetry." Arthur Ford wants "poetry—40 lines maximum, no minimum. All forms and subject matter with the use of good imagery, symbolism and honesty. Rhyme and non-rhyme. No vulgarity." He has published poetry by Veona Thomas and Rose Robaldo. *The Pen* is 12-16 pgs., saddle-stitched, mimeographed on both sides. They receive about 300 poems a year, accept approximately 80. Press run is 850 for 400 subscribers of which 5 are libraries. Subscription: $20. Send $4 for sample copy and more information. Make checks payable to Arthur C. Ford.
How to Submit: Submit up to 5 poems, maximum 40 lines, at a time with $1 reading fee. Also include large SASE if you want work returned. Simultaneous submissions and previously published poems OK. No e-mail submissions. Sometimes publishes theme issues. "We announce future dates when decided. July 15 issue is usually full of romantic poetry." Send SASE or visit website for guidelines and upcoming themes. Editor comments on rejections "sometimes, but not obligated." Pays 2 copies. He will criticize poetry for 15¢ a word. Open to unsolicited reviews. Poets may also send books for review consideration.
Advice: The editor comments: "Even though free verse is more popular today, we try to stay versatile."

○ ◑ ◎ **POETRY FORUM; THE JOURNAL (Specialized: subscription); HEALTHY BODY-HEALTHY MINDS (Specialized: health concerns)**, 5713 Larchmont Dr., Erie PA 16509, phone (814)866-2543 (also fax: 8-10 a.m. or 5-8 p.m.), e-mail 75562.670@compuserve.com, editor Gunvor Skogsholm.
Magazine Needs: *Poetry Forum* appears 3 times/year. "We are open to any style and form. We believe new forms ought to develop from intuition. Length up to 50 lines accepted. Would like to encourage long themes. No porn or blasphemy, but open to all religious persuasions." They have published poetry by Patricia Rourke and Helen Fames. As a sample the editor selected these lines from his poem "Tear":

> *Because the tear down the cheek of a son is the reward of a lifetime of concern, the tear down the*
> *cheek of a brother was what I came for*

The magazine is 7×8½, 38 pgs., saddle-stapled with card cover, photocopied from photoreduced typescript. Sample: $3.
How to Submit: Simultaneous submissions and previously published poems OK. Electronic submissions OK. Submissions via fax and e-mail (ASCII format) OK. Editor comments on poems "if asked, but respects the poetic freedom of the artist." Publishes theme issues. Send SASE for guidelines and upcoming themes or request via fax or e-mail. Sometimes sends prepublication galleys. Gives awards of $25, $15, $10 and 3 honorable mentions for the best poems in each issue. Acquires one-time rights. Reviews books of poetry in 250 words maximum. Open to unsolicited reviews. Poets may also send books for review consideration.
Magazine Needs & How to Submit: *The Journal*, which appears twice a year, accepts experimental poetry of any length from subscribers only. Sample: $3. *Healthy Body-Healthy Minds* is a biannual publication concerned with health issues. They accept essays, poetry, articles and short-shorts on health, fitness, mind and soul. Send SASE for details.
Also Offers: They offer a poetry chapbook contest. Entry fee: $9. Prize is publication and 20 copies. Send SASE for information.
Advice: The editor says, "I believe today's poets should experiment more and not feel stuck in the forms that were in vogue 300 years ago. I would like to see more experimentalism—new forms will prove that poetry is alive and well in the mind and spirit of the people."

☑ $ ○ ◑ ◎ **POETRY HARBOR; NORTH COAST REVIEW (Specialized: regional)**, P.O. Box 103, Duluth MN 55801-0103, phone (218)733-1294, founded 1989, director Patrick McKinnon.
Magazine Needs: Poetry Harbor is a "nonprofit, tax-exempt organization dedicated to fostering literary creativity through public readings, publications, radio and television broadcasts, and other artistic and educational means." Its main publication, *North Coast Review*, is a regional magazine appearing 2 times a year with poetry and prose poems by and about Upper Midwest people, including those from Minnesota, Wisconsin, North Dakota, and the upper peninsula of Michigan. "No form/style/content specifications, though we are inclined toward narrative, imagist poetry. We do not want to see anything from outside our region, not because it isn't good, but because we can't publish it due to geographics." They have published poetry by Mark Vinz, Joe Paddock, Susan Hauser and Jim Northrup. *NCR* is 56 pgs., 7×8½, offset and saddle-stapled, paper cover with various b&w art, ads at back. They receive about 500 submissions a year, use 100-150. Press run is 1,000 for 300 subscribers of which 20 are libraries, 300 shelf sales. Subscription: $21.95/6 issues. Sample: $4.95.
How to Submit: Submit 3-5 pgs. of poetry, typed single-spaced, with name and address on each page. Previously published poems and simultaneous submissions OK, if noted. Cover letter with brief bio ("writer's credits")

required. "We read three times a year, but our deadlines change from time to time. Write to us for current deadlines for our various projects." Send SASE for guidelines. Reports in 1-5 months. Pays $10 plus 2-4 copies. Buys one-time rights.

Book/Chapbook Needs & How to Submit: Poetry Harbor also publishes 1 perfect-bound paperback of poetry and 4-8 chapbooks each biennium. "Chapbooks are selected by our editorial board from the pool of poets we have published in *North Coast Review* or have worked with in our other projects. We suggest you send a submission to *North Coast Review* first. We almost always print chapbooks and anthologies by poets we've previously published or hired for readings." Anthologies include *Poets Who Haven't Moved to St. Paul* and *Days of Obsidian, Days of Grace*, selected poetry and prose by four Native American writers. Complete publications list available upon request.

Also Offers: Poetry Harbor also sponsors a monthly reading series ("poets are paid to perform"), a weekly TV program (4 different cable networks regionally), various radio programming, a prison workshop series and other special events.

Advice: They say, "Poetry Harbor is extremely committed to cultivating a literary community and an appreciation for our region's literature within the Upper Midwest. Poetry Harbor projects are in place to create paying, well-attended venues for our region's fine poets. Poets are now OK to people up here, and literature is thriving. The general public is proving to us that they *do* like poetry if you give them some that is both readable and rooted in the lives of the community."

POETRY IRELAND REVIEW; POETRY IRELAND, Bermingham Tower, Dublin Castle, Dublin 2, Ireland, phone 353.1.6714632, fax 353.1.6714634, e-mail poetry@iol.ie, founded 1979, general manager Niamh Morris.

Magazine Nees: *Poetry Ireland Review*, the magazine of Ireland's national poetry organization, "provides an outlet for Irish poets; submissions from abroad also considered. No specific style or subject matter is prescribed. We strongly dislike sexism and racism." They have published poetry by Seamus Heaney, Michael Longley, Denise Levertov, Medbh McGuckian and Charles Wright. Occasionally publishes special issues. The 6×8 quarterly uses 60 pgs. of poetry in each issue, circulation 1,200, with 800 subscriptions. They receive about 2,000 submissions/year, use 10%, have a 2-month backlog. Single copy: IR£5.99; subscription: IR£24 Ireland and UK; IR£32 overseas (surface). Sample: $10.

How to Submit: Submit up to 6 poems at a time. Include SASE (or SAE with IRC). "Submissions not accompanied by SAEs will not be returned." No previously published poems or simultaneous submissions. Time between acceptance and publication is 1-3 months. Seldom comments on rejections. Send SASE (or SAE with IRCs) for guidelines. Reports in 6-8 weeks. Pays IR£10/poem or 1-year subscription. Reviews books of poetry in 500-1,000 words.

Also Offers: *PIR* is published by Poetry Ireland, an organization established to "promote poets and poetry throughout Ireland." Poetry Ireland offers readings, an information service, library and administrative center, and a bimonthly newsletter giving news, details of readings, competitions, etc. for IR£6/year. They also sponsor an annual poetry competition. Send SASE (or SAE with IRCs) for details.

Advice: The editors advise, "Keep submitting: Good work will get through."

POETRY KANTO, Kanto Gakuin University, Kamariya-cho 3-22-1, Kanazawa-Ku, Yokohama 236-8502, Japan, founded 1984, editor William I. Elliott.

Magazine Needs: *Poetry Kanto* appears annually in August and is published by the Kanto Poetry Center, which also sponsors an annual poetry conference. It publishes well-crafted original poems in English and in Japanese. The magazine publishes "anything except pornography, English haiku and tanka, and tends to publish poems under 30 lines." They have published work by A.D. Hope, Peter Robinson, Naomi Shihab Nye, Nuala Ni Dhomhnaill and Les Murray. The magazine is 60 pgs., digest-sized, nicely printed (the English poems occupy the first half of the issue, the Japanese poems the second), saddle-stapled, matte card cover. Circulation is 700, of which 400 are distributed free to schools, poets and presses; it is also distributed at poetry seminars. The magazine is unpriced. For sample, send SAE with IRCs.

How to Submit: Interested poets should query from October through December with SAE and IRCs before submitting. No previously published poems or simultaneous submissions. Often comments on rejections. Reports on mss in 1-2 weeks. Pays 3-5 copies.

Advice: The editor advises, "Read a lot. Get feedback from poets and/or workshops. Be neat, clean, legible and polite in submissions. SAE with IRCs absolutely necessary when requesting sample copy."

POETRY LIFE (Specialized: subscription), 1 Blue Ball Corner, Water Lane, Winchester, Hampshire SO23 OER England, e-mail adrian.abishop@virgin.net, website http://freespace.virgin.net/poetry. life/, founded 1994, editor Adrian Bishop.

Magazine Needs: *Poetry Life*, published 3 times/year, describes itself as "Britain's sharpest poetry magazine with serious articles about the poetry scene." They want "poets who have passion, wit, style, revelation and loads of imagination." They do not want "poems on pets." They have published articles on James Fenton, Carol Ann Duffy, Les Murray, Benjamin Zephaniah and Simon Armitage. The editor says *Poetry Life* is A4. They accept approximately 1% of the poems they receive. Press run is 1,500. Single copy: £3, £5 overseas.

How to Submit: Previously published poems and simultaneous submissions OK. Cover letter required. "In common with most poetry magazines we now only accept recordings of the poets work on CD. Please do not send manuscripts. If we like what we hear then we will ask for a manuscript." Time between acceptance and publication is 6 months. Poems are circulated to an editorial board. Send SAE with IRCs for guidelines. Reports in 6 months. Reviews books or other magazines. Open to unsolicited reviews. Poets may also send books for review consideration.

Also Offers: Sponsors open poetry competitions. Send SAE with IRCs for guidelines.

THE POETRY MISCELLANY, English Dept., University of Tennessee at Chattanooga, Chattanooga TN 37403, phone (423)755-4629, e-mail suobodni@aol.com or Richard-Jackson@utc.edu, website http://www.utc. edu/~engldept/PM/PMHP.HTML. founded 1971 (in North Adams, MA), poetry editor Richard Jackson.

Magazine Needs: "We publish new and established writers—poems, interviews, essays, translations. We are truly a miscellany: We look at all schools, types, etc." They have published poetry by William Matthews, Marvin Bell, Paula Rankin, Tomaž Šalmun and Donald Justice. As a smaple the editor selected these lines from "Elvis Poem" by Regina Wilkins:

> *But the big things come into your life/only through the little things that give you identity./That's when things like Love beome real./We spent a lot of the fifty dollars in the Snack Bar./We spent a little more at the souvenir shop./The preacher at grandfather's funeral said he could/explain the Bible as plainly as if he had spoken/to Paul himself. I knew when Janis turned down/the Elvis impersonator he'd hit on me. So everything was/back to normal. The world wasn't ending./And we had ten dollars left, which was enough.*

The 16-page tabloid appears annually, professionally printed, with black ink on grey paper. Circulation is 750 for 400 subscribers of which 100 are libraries. They receive about 10,000 submissions a year, use approximately 20, have a 6-12 month backlog. Subscription: $3. Sample: $3.

How to Submit: Submit 3-4 clear copies/submission. Editor "rarely" comments on rejections. Send SASE for guidelines or obtain via e-mail. Reports in 3-4 months. Pays 2 copies.

Also Offers: Publishes chapbooks of translations. Sometimes holds contests "when grants allow."

POETRY MOTEL; POETRY MOTEL WALLPAPER BROADSIDES, P.O. Box 103, Duluth MN 55801, founded 1984, editors Patrick McKinnon, Bud Backen, and Linda Erickson.

Magazine Needs: *Poetry Motel* aims "to keep the rooms clean and available for these poor ragged poems to crash in once they are through driving or committing adultery." They want "poems that took longer than ten minutes to author." No other specifications. They have published poetry by Julie Otten, Willie Smith, Albert Huffstickler, Ron Androla, Linda Wing, Tony Moffeit and Todd Moore. As a sample they selected this poem, "Manitowoc" by Carolyn Ahrens:

> *I did what my father told me to do./I parked the car off/to an angle, shined the brights/and waited. He told me never/to get too close; they can kick you to death/in their dying. And if they come through/the windshield, duck.*

Poetry Motel appears "every 260 days" as a $7 \times 8\frac{1}{2}$ digest, with wallpaper cover, 52 pgs. of poetry, prose, essays, literary memoirs and reviews, with b&w graphics. Press run is 1,000 for 400 subscribers. They receive about 1,500 submissions a year, accept approximately 150, have a 3- to 24-month backlog. Sample: $6.95.

How to Submit: Submit 3-5 pgs. of poetry at a time, with SASE. Simultaneous submissions OK. Informal cover letter with bio credits required. Reports in "1 week to never." Pay varies. Reviews books of poetry. Open to unsolicited reviews. Poets may also send books for review consideration.

Advice: They advise, "Poets should read as much poetry as they can lay their hands on. And they should realize that although poetry is no fraternal club, poets are responsible for its survival, both financially and emotionally. Join us out here—this is where the edge meets the vision. We are very open to work from 'beginners.' "

POETRY NEW YORK: A JOURNAL OF POETRY AND TRANSLATION (Specialized: translations), P.O. Box 3184, Church Street Station, New York NY 10008, e-mail pny33@hotmail.com, founded 1985, editors Burt Kimmelman and Tod Thilleman.

Magazine Needs: *Poetry New York* is an annual. They have published poetry by Wanda Coleman, Jerome Rothenberg, Enid Dame, Amiel Alcalay and Ann Lauterbach, and translations of Mallarme, Hesiod and Makoto Ooka. The editors describe it as 80 pgs., 6×9, perfect-bound. Also publish pamphlet series as supplement. They accept about 20% of "blind submissions." Press run is 700 for 400 shelf sales.

How to Submit: Submit up to 5 poems at a time. Reports in 6 months. Pays 1 copy.

Also Offers: Annual pamphlet contest January 1 to August 15. "E-mail for details."

POETRY NORTHWEST, University of Washington, P.O. Box 354330, Seattle WA 98195, phone (206)685-4750, founded 1959, editor David Wagoner.

THE OPENNESS TO SUBMISSIONS INDEX at the back of this book lists all publishers in this section by how open they are to submissions.

• Poetry published here has also been included in *The Best American Poetry 1996*.

Magazine Needs: *Poetry Northwest* is a quarterly featuring all styles and forms. For instance, lyric and narrative free verse has been included alongside a sonnet sequence, minimalist sonnets and stanza patterns—all accessible and lively. The magazine is 48 pgs., 5½×8½, professionally printed with color card cover. They receive 10,000 poems a year, use approximately 160, have a 3-month backlog. Circulation is 1,500. Subscription: $15. Sample: $4.

How to Submit: Occasionally comments on rejections. Reports in 1 month maximum. Pays 2 copies. Awards prizes of $500, $200 and $200 yearly, judged by the editors.

POETRY NOTTINGHAM INTERNATIONAL; LAKE ASKE MEMORIAL OPEN POETRY COMPETITION; NOTTINGHAM POETRY SOCIETY, 71 Saxton Ave., Heanor, Derbyshire DE75 7PZ England, founded 1946, editor Cathy Grindrod.

Magazine Needs: Nottingham Poetry Society meets monthly for readings, talks, etc., and publishes quarterly its magazine, *Poetry Nottingham International*, which is open to submissions from anyone. "We wish to see poetry that is intelligible to and enjoyable by the intelligent reader." They have published poetry by William Baer, Brian Daldorph and Walter McDonald from the US. As a sample the editor selected these lines from "Pasta" by Kate Scott:

> She hangs the frail strips on chairs, on doors.//As the dampness lifts they start to flutter./She hangs
> them lightly over her arm, padding to the stove.//She boils water, opens wine, puts vegetables in pots./
> Lights click. Smells blossom./Everything feels suddenly invited.

There are at least 44 pgs. of poetry in each issue of the 6×8 magazine, professionally printed with articles, letters, news, reviews, glossy art paper cover. They receive about 1,500 submissions a year, use approximately 120, usually have a 1- to 3-month backlog. Press run is 275 for 200 subscribers of which 20 are libraries. Single copy: £2.25 ($8 US); subscriptions: £15 sterling or $30 US. Sample: $8 or £1.75.

How to Submit: Submit up to 6 poems at any time, or articles up to 500 words on current issues in poetry. No previously published poems. Send SAE and 3 IRCs for stamps. No need to query but requires cover letter. Reports "within 2 months plus mailing time." Pays 1 copy. Staff reviews books of poetry, but space allows only listings or brief review. Send books for review consideration.

Book/Chapbook Needs & How to Submit: Nottingham Poetry Society publishes collections by individual poets who are members of Nottingham Poetry Society.

Also Offers: The Lake Aske Memorial Open Poetry Competition offers cash prizes, annual subscriptions and publication in *Poetry Nottingham*. Open to all.

Advice: The editor says they would like to see "originality, a 'surprise', apt imagery, good sense of rhythm, clear language. Poems most often rejected due to: use of tired language and imagery, use of clichés and inversions, old treatment of an old subject, sentimentality, poor rhythm and scansion, incorrect use of set forms."

POETRY OF THE PEOPLE (Specialized: humor, love, nature, fantasy, themes), P.O. Box 298, Micanopy FL 32667-0298, phone/fax (352)466-3743, e-mail poetryforaquarter@yahoo.com, website http://www.angelfire.com/fl/poetryofthepeople, founded 1986, poetry editor Paul Cohen.

Magazine Needs: *Poetry of the People* is a leaflet that appears 3 times/year. "We take all forms of poetry but we like humorous poetry, love poetry, nature poetry and fantasy. No racist or highly ethnocentric poetry will be accepted. I do not like poetry that lacks images or is too personal or contains rhyme to the point that the poem has been destroyed. All submitted poetry will be considered for posting on website which will be updated every month." They are also accepting poetry written in French and Spanish. They have published poetry by Max Lizard, Prof. Jerry Reminick, Ian Ayers and Noelle Kocot. As a sample the editor selected these lines from "Lunar" by David Vetterlein:

> "I stumble blindly/in coated forests/bound by/howling wolves/I stagger/wandering endless/in that lunar
> maze/called emotion

Poetry of the People varies from 8-32 pgs., 5½×8 to 5½×4⅜, stapled, sometimes on colored paper. Issues are usually theme oriented. It has a circulation between 300 and 2,300. Copies are distributed to Gainesville residents for 25¢ each. Samples: $4 for 11 pamphlets. "Please send donations, the magazine bank account is overdrawn. Suggested donation: $2."

How to Submit: Submit up to 10 poems at a time. Include SASE. Cover letter with biographical information required with submissions. E-mail submissions OK. "I feel autobiographical information is important in understanding the poetry." Poems returned within 6 months. Editor comments on rejections "often." Publish theme issues. Theme for January 2000: "Y2K." Send SASE for upcoming themes. Takes suggestions for theme issues. Sometimes sends prepublication galleys. Pays 10 copies for poetry published in leaflet. Acquires first rights.

Advice: He advises, "Be creative; there is a lot of competition out there."

POETRY REVIEW; NATIONAL POETRY COMPETITION; THE POETRY SOCIETY, 22 Betterton St., London WC2H 9BU United Kingdom, phone (0044)171 420 9880, fax (0044)171 240 4818, e-mail poetrysoc@dial.pipex.com, website http://www.poetrysoc.com, founded 1909, editor Peter Forbes.

Magazine Needs: *Poetry Review*, published quarterly, strives "to be the leading showcase of UK poetry and to represent poetry written in English and in translation." They want "poems with metaphoric resonance." They do not want "inconsequential disconnected jottings." They have published poetry by John Ashbery, Miroslav

Holub, Sharon Olds and Paul Muldoon. As a sample the editor selected these lines from "Addressee Unknown—Retour à L'Expéditeur" by Hans Magnus Enzensberger:

> *Many thanks for the clouds./Many thanks for the* well-tempered *clavier/and, why not, for the warm*
> *winter boots./Many thanks for my strange brain/and for all manner of other hidden organs*

The editor says *Poetry Review* is 96 pgs., 6½×9, paperback, with b&w cartoons and photos. They receive about 30-50,000 poems a year, accept approximately 0.3-0.4%. Press run is 4,750 for 4,000 subscribers of which 400 are libraries, 4 shelf sales; 100 distributed free to contributors and press. Single copy: £5.95; subscription: $56. Sample: $13.

How to Submit: Submit 4 poems at a time. No previously published poems or simultaneous submissions. Time between acceptance and publication is 6 months. Poems are selected by the editor. Seldom comments on rejections. Publishes theme issues. Reports 1-3 months. Sometimes sends prepublication galleys. Pays £40 plus 1 copy. Buys UK first publication rights. Staff reviews chapbooks of poetry or other magazines in single or multi-book format.

Also Offers: Sponsors the annual National Poetry Competition run by the Poetry Society. 1st Prize: £5,000; 2nd Prize: £1,000; 3rd Prize: £500. Entry fee: £5 for first poem, £3/poem thereafter. Deadline: October 31. Send SASE (or SAE and IRC) for guidelines. "The Poetry Society promotes poetry, assists poets and campaigns for poets wherever possible." Offers "Poetry Prescription" reading service: £40 for 100 lines.

POETRY SALZBURG; THE POET'S VOICE; UNIVERSITY OF SALZBURG PRESS, Institut für Anglistik, Universität Salzburg, Akademiestrasse 24, A-5020 Salzburg Austria, phone 0049662 8044 4422, fax 0049 662 80 44 613, founded 1971, editor Dr. Wolfgang Görtschacher, editor James Hogg.

Magazine Needs: *The Poet's Voice* appears twice a year and contains "articles on poetry, mainly contemporary, and 60 percent poetry. Also includes prose and translations. We tend to publish selections by authors who have not been taken up by the big poetry publishers. Nothing of poor quality." They have published poetry by Peter Russell, Desmond O'Grady, James Kirkup, Robert Rehder, Raymond Federman, Rachel Hades, Alice Notley and Rupert Loydell. As a sample we selected this poem, "Afterwards" by Ian Robinson:

> *After the phone call, she put his photograph/face down in the drawer. Then she cooked lunch./That*
> *night, when the television went dead,/she stared at the glistening, empty screen/and could not remember*
> *his face. The cat got up,/stretched and walked to the door. There was wind outside./'I must be getting*
> *old,' she thought/but made no move to go to bed.*

The Poet's Voice is about 140 pgs., A5, professionally printed and perfect-bound with illustrated card cover, sometimes includes art. They receive about 2,000 poems a year, accept approximately 10%. Press run is 400 for 150 subscribers of which 30% are libraries. Single copy: about $11; subscription: $20 (cash only for those sending US funds). Make checks payable to James Hogg. "No requirements, but it's a good idea to subscribe to *Poet's Voice.*"

How to Submit: No previously published poems or simultaneous submissions. Fax submissions OK. Time between acceptance and publication is 6 months. Seldom comments on rejections. Publishes theme issues occasionally. Reports in 2 months. Payment varies. Acquires first rights. Reviews books and chapbooks of poetry and other magazines. Open to unsolicited reviews. Poets may also send books for review consideration.

Book/Chapbook Needs & How to Submit: Poetry Salzburg publishes "collections of at least 100 pages by mainly poets not taken up by big publishers." They publish 2-30 paperbacks/year. Books are usually 100-700 pgs., A5, professionally printed and perfect-bound with card cover, includes art. Query first, with a few sample poems and a cover letter with brief bio and publication credits. Suggests authors publish in *The Poet's Voice* first. Replies to queries in 2 weeks; to mss in about 1 month. Pays 40 author's copies (out of a press run of 300-400).

POETRY USA; NATIONAL POETRY ASSOCIATION, SOMAR, 934 Brannan St., Second Floor, San Francisco CA 94103, phone (415)552-9261, fax (415)552-9271, e-mail poetryusa@nationalpoetry.org, website http://www.nationalpoetry.org, founded 1985, managing editor Adam Shames.

Magazine Needs & How to Submit: *Poetry USA* appears in online format only and "aims to provide a common space for the diversity of voices that make up the American experience. We include poems from all over the country, and often include poetry from young people, people without a home, and people in prison. Poets from the community have been invited to serve as guest editors, choosing different themes for past issues." They publish "shorter poems (under 50 lines, please) accessible to the non-literary general public." Consult website for submission information. Poets retain all rights.

Also Offers: "The National Poetry Association, an all-volunteer organization founded in 1975, is committed to promoting the written, spoken and visual use of language in new and traditional ways." Call or e-mail for more information.

POETRY WALES; SEREN PRESS (Specialized: ethnic), 2 Wyndham St., First Floor, Bridgend, CF31 1EF Wales, founded 1965, editor Robert Minhinnick.

Magazine Needs: *Poetry Wales*, a 72-page, 248×177mm quarterly, circulation 1,000, has a primary interest in Welsh and Anglo-Welsh poets but also considers submissions internationally. Overseas subscription: £18/year. Sample: £4.

How to Submit: Submit 6 poems at a time. No previously published poems. One-page cover letter required; include name, address and previous publications. SASE (or SAE and IRC) must be included for reply. Pays honorarium and 1 copy. Staff reviews books of poetry. Send books for review consideration to Amy L. Wack, reviews editor, Wyndham Street address.

Book/Chapbook Needs & How to Submit: Seren Press publishes books of primarily Welsh and Anglo-Welsh poetry, also biography, critical works and some fiction, distributed by Dufour Editions, Inc., Box 449, Chester Springs PA 19425. They publish 6 poetry paperbacks/year. Books are approximately 64 pgs., 216×138mm, offset printed and perfect-bound, with full color cover. Pays 10% royalties and 6 author's copies. "Authors must have a connection with Wales."

Advice: The editor says, "We would like to see more formal poetry."

POETS AT WORK (Specialized: subscription), VAMC Box 113, 325 New Castle Rd., Box 113, Butler PA 16001, founded 1985, editor/publisher Jessee Poet.

Magazine Needs: All contributors are expected to subscribe. The editor says, "Every poet who writes within the dictates of good taste and within my 20-line limit will be published in each issue. I accept all forms and themes of poetry, including seasonal and holiday, but no porn, no profanity." He has published poetry by Martha Balph, William Middleton, Ann Gasser, Warren Jones and Ralph Hammond. As a sample he selected his poem "An Old Romance":

> I almost loved you . . . did you know?/Sometimes you still disturb my dreams./A summer romance long
> ago/I almost loved you . . . did you know?/We danced to music soft and low/Just yesterday . . . or so
> it seems/I almost loved you . . . did you know?/Sometimes you still disturb my dreams.

Poets at Work, a bimonthly, is generally 36-40 pgs., magazine-sized, saddle-stapled, photocopied from typescript with colored paper cover. Subscription: $20. Sample: $3.50.

How to Submit: If a subscriber, submit 5-10 poems at a time. Line length for poetry is 20 maximum. Simultaneous submissions and previously published poems OK. Reports within 2 weeks. Pays nothing, not even a copy. "Because I publish hundreds of poets, I cannot afford to pay or give free issues. Every subscriber, of course, gets an issue."

Book/Chapbook Needs & How to Submit: Also publishes chapbooks. Send SASE for details.

Also Offers: Subscribers also have many opportunities to regain their subscription money in the numerous contests offered in each issue. Send SASE for flyer for separate monthly and special contests.

Advice: The editor adds, "These days even the best poets tell me that it is difficult to get published. I am here for the novice as well as the experienced poet. I consider *Poets at Work* to be a hotbed for poets where each one can stretch and grow at his or her own pace. Each of us learns from the other, and we do not criticize one another. The door for poets is always open, so please stop by; we probably will like each other immediately."

POETS CORNER; COASTAL PUBLISHING, P.O. Box 456, Glenoma WA 98336-0456, phone (360)498-5341, founded 1997, publisher T.L. Dorn.

Magazine Needs: *Poets Corner* is published 11 times a year "to give new and unknown poets a place to show their art." They want original work. "No copy of old lines such as 'roses are red—I scream' etc." The publisher says *PC* is magazine-sized, desktop-published and photocopied, staple-bound, colored paper cover, includes art/graphics and ads. They receive about 7-900 poems a year, accept approximately 90%. Press run is 1,000 ("growing daily") for 846 subscribers of which 10 are libraries, 30 shelf sales; 90 distributed free to elderly and doctors offices." Subscription: $15/year. Sample: $3. Make checks payable to Coastal Publishing.

How to Submit: Submit 1-3 poems at a time. Length for poetry is 64 lines or 2 pages maximum. Previously published poems and simultaneous submissions OK. Cover letter is "OK." Time between acceptance and publication is 1-3 months. Seldom comments on rejections. Publishes theme issues occasionally. Send SASE for guidelines. Acquires first rights. Poets may also send books for review consideration to T.L. Dorn or Tracy Lynn Davis.

Also Offers: Sponsors annual contest. Cash Prize: $100 or more.

THE POET'S ENERGY (Specialized: metaphysical, New Age, holistic perspective), e-mail poetenergy@aol.com, website http://members.aol.com/poetenergy/page/index.htm, founded 1999, editor Jeffrey Alan Ford.

Magazine Needs: *The Poet's Energy* is a quarterly online publication. "We believe in the oneness that permeates through all living things. We strive to publish only the best holistic poetry that is in circulation. We are looking for insightful, metaphysical poetry from a holistic perspective. We use poems that have either a dark or an uplifting theme. Write from every possible angle of your soul. We do not care to see sickening, fluffy poems that are void of substance. Nor do we perceive nonsensical verse as being art." As a sample the editor selected his poem "Universal Hypocrite":

> Your self-righteousness/Makes you a judgmental fool;/That view makes me you.

How to Submit: Submit 1 poem at a time. Line length for poetry is 40 lines maximum. No previously published poems or simultaneous submissions. Cover letter required. E-mail submissions only. Time between acceptance and publication is 3 months. Seldom comments on rejections. Request guidelines via e-mail or website. Reports in 1-2 months. Pays "nothing. Just the joy of sharing your wisdom with the world."

Advice: The editor says, "Believe in yourself and your art. What may be art to someone, may be trash to another. It simply is what it is."

⬜ 🔘 **POET'S FANTASY (Specialized: fantasy)**, Dept. PM, 227 Hatten Ave., Rice Lake WI 54868-2030, founded 1991, publisher/editor Gloria Stoeckel.

Magazine Needs: *Poet's Fantasy* is a quarterly designed "to help the striving poet see his/her work in print." They want sonnets, haiku and humorous free verse, 4-16 lines. "I accept good, clean poetry. Looking for poems of fantasy, but not exclusively. No profanity or sexual use of words." They have published poetry by earl jay perel and Gary Michael Lawson. *Poet's Fantasy* is 48 pgs., letter-sized, photocopied from typescript and saddle-stapled with colored paper cover, graphics and ads. They receive about 400 poems a year, accept approximately 90%. Press run is 500 for 450 subscribers. Subscription: $20/year; foreign $26/year. Sample: $5.

How to Submit: Submit 3-5 poems at a time. No previously published poems or simultaneous submissions. Often comments on rejections. Send SASE for guidelines. Reports within 2 weeks. Poets must purchase copy their work is in. Acquires first North American serial rights. "I do book reviews if poet sends a complimentary copy of the book and a $3 reading fee. Reviews are approximately 200 to 300 words in length."

Also Offers: Holds contests in each issue and creates greeting cards for poets. "They use verse they wrote and can design their own cover." Send SASE for details. Also publishes a yearly anthology.

🅽 ▣ 🆈 ⬜ **THE POET'S HAVEN**, P.O. Box 1501, Massillon OH 44648, e-mail VertigoXX@PoetsHaven.com, website http://www.PoetsHaven.com, founded 1997, publisher/editor Vertigo Xi'an Xavier.

• *Poet's Haven* has received numerous small website awards including the Nocturnal Society "All-Nighter" Awards.

Magazine Needs: "A completely online publication, *The Poet's Haven* site contains poetry, artwork, stories, book reviews, essays, editorial, quotes and much more. I want to see work that is passionate, emotional, powerful, personal, and/or intimate with either the author or subject, be it fun, sad, light, deep, about love, pain, nature, insanity, or social commentary. No material that is obscene, excessively vulgar, pornographic, racist, or christian." They have published poetry by Barry Brown, Angela Contino Donshes, Terri A. Hateley and Bonnie Langford. As a sample the editor selected this haiku, "Three Card Monte," by Barry Brown:

three card monte fools/me again, love wasn't there/where it should have been.

They receive about 10,000 poems a year, accept approximately 85%.

How to Submit: Previously published poems and simultaneous submissions OK. Cover letter preferred. E-mail and disk submissions OK. "Electronic submissions (e-mail, website, diskette) are preferred, especially for longer works. If you are submitting by carrier mail (snail-mail) and wish to be notified if your work is accepted, include SASE." Time between acceptance and publication is up to 3 months. Seldom comments on rejections. Obtain guidelines via e-mail or website. Reports when published by e-mail or SASE only. Acquires rights to publish on the site permanently and in any future paper publications. Author retains rights to have poems published elsewhere, and have the poem removed from site if desired." Reviews books of poetry in single book format. Poets may also send books for review consideration.

Also Offers: "The site has expanded beyond a simple e-zine into an online community. If a submitter wishes, his/her e-mail address will be included with any of their poems published so that readers can contact them. There are also Message Boards and a Chat Room available for writers and readers to meet and discuss topics of interest to them. The publication is entirely Internet based (at this time), and all pertinent information is available online."

Advice: The editor says, "Multiple submissions (more than one work) are encouraged as they give a wider display of a writer's talents."

▣ 🔘 **POETS ON THE LINE**, P.O. Box 020292, Brooklyn NY 11202-0007, e-mail llerner@mindspring.com, website http://www.echonyc.com/~poets, founded 1995, editor Linda Lerner. Currently not accepting unsolicited work.

🔘 **THE POET'S PAGE**, P.O. Box 372, Wyanet IL 61379, founded 1994, editor/publisher Ione K. Pence.

Magazine Needs: *TPP* is a quarterly "for poets and all who love poetry." They want poetry of "any subject, any length, any style, but we are not interested in shock poetry or vulgarities." *TPP* is approximately 44 pgs., digest-sized and saddle-stapled with colored card stock cover. Subscription: $10. Sample: $3.

How to Submit: No previously published poems; simultaneous submissions OK, "but we must be notified immediately if work is accepted elsewhere. Also, without a SASE or SAE and IRC, submissions go directly into our wastebasket with no response of any kind to the submitter. With submission of manuscript, author grants permission for minimal editing (spelling, grammar, etc.)" Time between acceptance and publication is 9-12 months. Send SASE for guidelines. Reports in 2-3 weeks. Pays 1 copy. All rights retained by authors.

Also Offers: "TPP sponsors an annual poetry contest; but, for your peace of mind and our sanity, please write for full contest rules before submitting contest manuscripts."

⬜ 🔘 **POET'S PARADISE (Specialized: subscription)**, 158-21 78th Ave., Flushing NY 11366-1907, e-mail bonwilly@aol.com, founded 1991, editor/publisher Bunny Williams-Duplessis.

Magazine Needs: *Poet's Paradise*, published 3 times/year features essays, articles, tips on grammar, fiction and nonfiction, with two-thirds devoted to verses. They want "poems that have depth and purpose; nothing trite or forced." They do not want "salacious material." They have published poetry by Kenneth Geisert, Phil Eisenberg and Robert S. Blake. As a sample the editor selected her poem "Metamorphosis":

The canvas of life harbors the scent of greed/Where every stroke caterwauls with rage;/Tinsel thrones

are painted/And purity . . . now tainted . . ./Writhes in the fallout of an age.
Poet's Paradise is 92 pgs., 8½×11, laser-printed, spiral-bound, with inkjet colored cover and interior, with clip art. They receive about 800 poems a year, accept approximately 80%. Press run is 200 for 85 subscribers of which 15 are libraries, 40 shelf sales. Single copy: $5; subscription: $15. Editor sends free tearsheets for anyone interested in sampling the magazine. Make checks payable to Bunny Williams-Duplessis.
How to Submit: Subscription required for consideration. Include SASE with ms. Submit any number of poems with contest fee of $1/poem (of 2-6 lines) or $2/poem (of 7-40 lines). "All poems are entered in a contest whereby subscribers judge the winning poems." Previously published poems and simultaneous submissions OK. E-mail submissions OK. Cover letter preferred. Always comments on rejections. Send SASE for guidelines. Reports in 5-10 days.
Advice: The editor says, "Poets should be open to revision. Read your poem aloud for clarity and continuity. Metaphors are a part of poetry, but obscurity is tedious."

POETS' ROUNDTABLE; POETS' STUDY CLUB OF TERRE HAUTE; POETS' STUDY CLUB INTERNATIONAL CONTEST (Specialized: membership), 826 S. Center St., Terre Haute IN 47807, phone (812)234-0819, founded in 1939, president/editor Esther Alman.
Magazine Needs: Poets' Study Club is one of the oldest associations of amateur poets. It publishes, every other month, *Poets' Roundtable*, a newsletter of market and contest information and news of the publications and activities of its members in a mimeographed, 10-page bulletin (magazine-sized, stapled at the corner), circulation 2,000. They have also published an occasional chapbook-anthology of poetry by members "but do not often do so." Dues: $10/year (includes subscription to *Poets' Roundtable*). Sample free for SASE.
How to Submit: Uses short poems by members only. Simultaneous submissions and previously published poems OK.
Also Offers: They offer an annual Poets' Study Club International Contest, open to all, with no fees and cash prizes—a $25 and $15 award in 3 categories: traditional haiku, serious poetry, light verse. Deadline: February 1. Also contests for members every 2 months.

POETS'PAPER; ANDERIE POETRY PRESS, P.O. Box 85, Easton PA 18044-0085, founded 1998, editor Carole J. Heffley.
Magazine Needs: *Poets'Paper* is a semi-annual newspaper for poets that uses "high-quality poetry in both free verse and form, rhyme and non-rhyme, no line limit." Any theme that is well written, no pornography. They have published poetry by Diana Kwiatkowski Rubin, Tim Scannell and Will Inman. As a sample the editor selected these lines from "Hush" by Frances C. Fabiani:
> . . . it is a silence/a feeling/of no feeling . . .//silence between/raindrops between/expression here/in
> the blink of an eye/gone just stillness/and the void . . .//. . . a pause between breaths/is where you are
Poets'Paper is printed in newspaper format twice yearly, January and August. Uses some photography. Subscription: $9/2 issues. Sample: $5.
How to Submit: "Not accepting submissions until January 2000." No simultaneous submissions. Cover letter with "something about the writer" requested but not required. "SASE must accompany all correspondence." Send SASE for guidelines. Reports in 6-8 weeks. Acquires first rights.

PO'FLYE INTERNATIONAL: A DIGEST OF UNDERCULTURE, P.O. Box 1026, Ashland KY 41105, e-mail poflye@underculture.com, website http://www.poflye.com, publisher Michael Elton Crye.
Magazine Needs: *Poflye Internationale* is a bimonthly publication "founded as a crossroads, a place between trenches, a meeting place where all voices are heard. A gathering of information and inspiration for working artists. We are now catering not only to the ideals involved in the current movements, but also a stronger display of those movements and their talents. Teaching by example if you will. *Po'flye* acts as both a resource and a showcase." They want "the best of the current from otherstream to translation of classics. We've rhymed, we've been sexy, we've been visual, and we've been accused of witchcraft." Regular features include articles/commentary on poetry; book reviews; market, event and contest listings; local resources; and poetry and fiction. "We also do a feature artist, usually dedicating 3-5 pages to a truly great series or longer work." As a sample the editor selected these lines from "Creek Revival" by Thomas Michael McDade:
> City planners embalm/old creeks with brush/and trees that twiddle/off the time fermenting/into a warm
> fertility/that lures the ocean/like a full buck moon./Use skulls, rock, sand,/brick and bones next time/
> whisper loose lips in fear/that eavesdropping/brings the floods/instead of sex/and memory.
The publisher says *Po'flye Internationale* is published in various formats and sizes. Subscription: $10/4 issues. Sample: $3.
How to Submit: Submit any number of poems with SASE. "We also like it when poets send self-published chapbooks, which we can consider as a submission." Previously published poems and simultaneous submissions OK. No e-mail submissions. Include cover letter; "I seek the person and the poetry, they are one and the same and none should hide this from the other." Comments on rejections. Publishes theme issues. Send SASE or e-mail for guidelines. Pays 2 copies. Poet retains all rights. Poets may also send books for review consideration.
Also Offers: Website includes a complete online companion to the print edition of the magazine. "Website is a good place to determine our current moods, current themes, etc."

◎ **POINT JUDITH LIGHT (Specialized: form/style)**, P.O. Box 6145, Springfield MA 01101, founded 1992, editor Patrick Frank.

Magazine Needs: *Point Judith Light* is a biannual publishing individual haiku/senryu, sequences and essays on Eastern philosophy and creativity theory. They want haiku/senryu "which explore the relation of the poet to his/her environment and which focus on life as truly lived; 17 syllables maximum." They have published haiku/senryu by H.F. Noyes, Tom Clausen and Larry Kimmel. As a sample the editor selected this haiku/senryu by Donarella Cardillo-Young:

> *Ringing Liz's school bell/the sound of its chime/floating into space forever*

PJL is desktop-published, 20 pgs. maximum. Press run is 300. Subscription: $10/year.

How to Submit: Previously published poems OK; no simultaneous submissions. Send 20 haiku/senryu maximum. Submissions should be typed. Cover letter with bio required. "I want to have some knowledge of the poet behind the work." Send SASE for guidelines. Reports within 6 months. Acquires first or one-time rights.

Advice: The editor says, "Focus on the aspects of life that are immediately before you. Be yourself. Follow your intuition and be willing to explore and experiment. With James J.Y. Liu, I see poetry as a vehicle to explore external and internal worlds, as well as the language in which it is written. I am particularly interested in promoting the development of haiku/senryu sequencing in English. I am also exploring the connection between haiku, Eastern philosophy and creativity theory. Children's haiku are welcome. Politically relevant haiku are welcome, if they are imagistic and grounded in concrete experience. I also publish sports-related haiku."

◑ **THE POINTED CIRCLE**, 705 N. Killingsworth, Portland OR 97217, founded 1980, advisor Jefferson Ranck.

Magazine Needs: *TPC* is published annually in June. "We are looking for clear, coherent poetry and short fiction with a strong sense of purpose." They have published poetry by Anselm Brocki, Lyn Lifshin, and Mark Dodd. It is about 100 pgs., professionally printed and flat-spined, with card cover and cover art. Press run is 350. Sample: $4.50.

How to Submit: Submit up to 6 poems at a time no longer than 1 page each. "Manuscripts will be returned only if accompanied by SASE with sufficient postage." No simultaneous submissions. Cover letter with bio required. Submit mss from December 1 through February 15 only. "Place name, address, and short bio on cover sheet only, listing titles of submissions. All submissions are read anonymously by student editorial staff; notification about June 1." Send SASE for guidelines. Pays 1 copy. Acquires one-time rights.

🌐 ◯ ◑ ◎ **POLYGON (Specialized: bilingual/foreign language)**, 22 George Square, Edinburgh EH8 9LF Scotland, phone (0131)650 8436, fax (0131)662 0053, e-mail polygon.press@eup.ed.ac.uk, website http://www.eup.ed.ac.uk/polygon/html, founded 1969, contact poetry editor.

Book/Chapbook Needs: Polygon publishes new poets, first-time collections, young voices and Gaelic/English translations. They publish 3 paperbacks and 1 anthology/year. They have published poetry by Ian Hamilton Finlay, Liz Lochhead, Aonghas MacNeacail, Raymond Friel, David Kinloch and Donny O'Rourke. Books are usually 88 pgs., 194×128mm, paperback. Anthologies are 35 pgs., 216×138mm, paperback.

How to Submit: Submit 6 poems at a time. No previously published poems or simultaneous submissions. Cover letter required. Reads submissions April, July, October and December only. Time between acceptance and publication is 6-18 months. Replies to mss in 2-3 months. Query for payment information.

◑ **PORCUPINE LITERARY ARTS MAGAZINE**, P.O. Box 259, Cedarsburg WI 53012, e-mail ppine259@aol.com, website: http://members.aol.com/ppine259, founded 1996, managing editor W.A. Reed.

Magazine Needs: *Porcupine*, published biannually, contains featured artists, poetry, short fiction and visual art work. "There are no restrictions as to theme or style. Poetry should be accessible and highly selective. If a submission is not timely for one issue, it will be considered for another." They have published poetry by Bill Embly, G.K. Wuori, Kenneth Pobo and Andrew Genn-Dorian. As a sample, we selected these lines from "Under the Watchful Eyes of Great Art" by Christine Delea:

> *It's not the eyes following movement,/but red lips, painted pursed or with/a slight smirk, mouths closed tight in custom/or opened in horror or wonder, moving/when I move.*

Porcupine is 100-150 pgs., 8½×5, offset, perfect-bound with full-color glossy cover and b&w photos and art (occasionally use color inside, depending on artwork). They receive about 300 poems a year, accept approximately 10%. Press run is 1,500 for 500 subscribers of which 50 are libraries, 500 shelf sales; 100 distributed free. Single copy: $8.95; subscription: $15.95. Sample: $5.

How to Submit: Submit up to 3 poems, 1/page with name and address on each. Include SASE. "The outside of the envelope should state: 'Poetry.'" No previously published poems or simultaneous submissions. E-mail submissions OK. Time between acceptance and publication is 6 months. "Poems are selected by editors and then submitted to managing editor for final approval." Seldom comments on rejections. Send SASE for guidelines. Reports in 10-12 weeks. Pays 1 copy. Acquires one-time rights.

Also Offers: Website features writer's guidelines, cover art, table of contents and sample poetry.

☑ ◐ **PORTALS PRESS**, 4411 Fontainebleau Dr., New Orleans LA 70125, phone (504)821-7723, e-mail travport@bellsouth.net, founded 1993, publisher/editor John P. Travis.

Book/Chapbook Needs: Portals Press publishes poetry collections, novels and short story collections. They publish 2 paperbacks/year. They want "serious poetry, with depth and some universal extension. No confessional work." They have published poetry by Everette Maddox, Maxine Cassin, Grace Bauer, H.R. Stoneback, Yictove and Kay Murphy. Books are usually 96-128 pgs., 5½×8½, offset printed and perfect-bound with card cover with art.

How to Submit: "Before considering book publication, publish 10 poems in journals or magazines. Previously published poems OK. Cover letter preferred. Poems are circulated to an editorial board. Often comments on rejections. Replies to queries and mss within weeks. Pays 10-20% royalties and 10 author's copies (out of a press run of 500-1,000).

Advice: The publisher says, "As you creatively log the particulars of your specific life experience, strive to capture universals which may resonate with others."

☑ ◎ **PORTLAND REVIEW**, Box 347, Portland State University, Portland OR 97207-0347, phone (503)725-4533, e-mail review@vanguard.vg.pdx.edu, founded 1954, editor Barbara Mann.
Magazine Needs & How to Submit: *Portland Review* is a literary annual published by Portland State University 3 times a year. "Experimental poetry welcomed." The annual is about 128 pgs. They accept about 30 of 300 poems received each year. Press run is 500 for 100 subscribers of which many are libraries. Sample: $6. Simultaneous submissions OK. E-mail submissions OK. Send SASE for guidelines. Pays 1 copy.

N ◎ THE POST-APOLLO PRESS (Specialized: form/style, women), 35 Marie St., Sausalito CA 94965, phone (415)332-1458, fax (415)332-8045, e-mail tpapress@dnai.com, website http://www.dnai.com/~tpa press, founded 1982, publisher Simone Fattal.
Book/Chapbook Needs & How to Submit: The Post-Apollo Press publishes "quality paperbacks by experimental poets/writers, mostly women, many first English translations." They publish 2-3 paperbacks/year. "Please note we are *not* accepting manuscripts at this time due to full publishing schedule."

◎ **POTATO EYES; NIGHTSHADE PRESS; WILLIAM & KINGMAN PAGE POETRY CHAPBOOK COMPETITION**, P.O. Box 76, Troy ME 04987-0076, phone (207)948-3427, fax (207)948-5088, e-mail potatoe yes@uninets.net, website http://www.litline.org/html/potatoeyes.html, founded 1988, editors Roy Zarucchi and Carolyn Page.
Magazine Needs: *Potato Eyes* is a semiannual literary arts journal "with a focus on writers who write about the land and/or quality of life close to the earth. We now accept submissions from throughout the U.S., also from Canada, Australia, England, Ireland and Brazil, although much of our poetry is from Appalachian states." They have published poetry by Daniel Lusk, Howard Nelson, Jack Coulehan, Wendy Bishop and Elizabeth Cohen. *PE* is 100 pgs., 5½×8½, flat-spined, professionally printed, with block cut matte paper cover. Circulation is 800. Subscription: $11 ($14 Canadian). Sample: $6 or $7 Canadian.
How to Submit: The editors say, "those who submit receive a handwritten rejection/acceptance. We are open to any form other than rhymed, in batches of three to five, but we tend to favor poetry with concrete visual imagery, solid intensity and compression. We respect word courage and risk-taking, along with thoughtful lineation. We prefer rebellious to complacent poetry. We prefer a cover letter with brief bio along with SASE." No e-mail submissions, but queries via e-mail are OK. Reports in 1-2 months. Pays 1 copy. Acquires first North American serial rights. Reviews books of poetry. Open to unsolicited reviews. Poets may also send books for review consideration.
Book/Chapbook Needs & How to Submit: Nightshade Press is the imprint under which they publish about 4 books/chapbooks a year, each 24-48 pgs. or longer, "usually with block print or pen-and-ink covers, endsheets and recycled 60 lb. text, 80 lb. covers. Selections come from competitions, mainly, but a few may be from poets who appear first in our magazine." They have published *Mid-Passage* by Wendy Bishop and *Poor People* by Shelby Stephenson. Send SASE for catalog and information and/or send $6 for sample chapbook.
Also Offers: One of the competitions they sponsor is the annual William & Kingman Page Poetry Chapbook Competition. The award is 25 copies of the chapbook and $1,000. Deadline: November 15. Send SASE for guidelines. "We are always open to a sincere offer to guest edit." Website includes guidelines, book listings and competition guidelines.
Advice: They advise, "Beginning poets should devour as much good poetry as possible in order to delineate their own style and voice. Look for a match between substance and sound. We reject fluff but prefer poetry that is multi-layered and pithy. We prefer to receive poetry flat and we do appreciate well done cover letters."

◎ ◎ **POTOMAC REVIEW (Specialized: regional)**, P.O. Box 354, Port Tobacco MD 20677, website http://www.meral.com/potomac, founded 1994, editor Eli Flam.
Magazine Needs: *PR* is published quarterly. They want "poetry with a vivid, individual quality that has vision

---

THE BOOK PUBLISHERS INDEX, located at the back of this book, lists those publishers who consider full-length book collections.

to go with competence, that strives to get at 'the concealed side' of life." They do not want "arch, banal, mannered, surface, flat, self-serving poetry." They have published poetry by Josephine Jacobsen, Roland Flint and Judith McCombs. As a sample the editor selected these lines from "Ignominius" by David Prather:

> I remember the dogs of childhood/comforting my sleep through every phase/of the moon. Like the dog soldiers/who would spear their bright sashes/to the battleground and fight even/the Devil, whose domain is the grass,/always underfoot. . . .

Potomac Review is 128 pgs., 5½×8½, offset printed, perfect-bound, with medium card cover, b&w graphic art, photos and ads. They receive about 1,000 poems a year, accept approximately 5%. Press run is 1,600 for 1,000 subscribers plus about 400 shelf sales. Subscription: $15/year (MD residents add 5%), $28/2 years. Sample: $4.
How to Submit: Submit up to 3 poems, 5 pages at a time with SASE. Simultaneous submissions OK. No previously published poems. Cover letter preferred with brief bio and SASE. Time between acceptance and publication is up to 1 year. Poems are read "in house," then sent to poetry editor for comments and dialogue." Usually comments on rejections. Publishes theme issues. Send SASE for guidelines and upcoming themes. Reports in 1-2 months. Pays 1 copy and offers discount on additional copies. Acquires first North American serial rights. Reviews books or chapbooks of poetry. Send books for review consideration.
Also Offers: Sponsors annual poetry contest, usually open January through March. 1st Prize: $250; winner's poem and some runners-up are published in fall. Entry fee: $15 (provides 1-year subscription). Submit up to 3 poems, any subject, any form. Deadline: March 31, 2000. Competition receives about 170 entries. Send SASE for guidelines.

POTPOURRI; DAVID RAY POETRY AWARD, P.O. Box 8278, Prairie Village KS 66208, phone (913)642-1503, fax (913)642-3128, e-mail Potpourpub@aol.com, website http://www.Potpourri.org, founded 1989, poetry editor Terry Hoyland, haiku editor Jeri Ragan.
Magazine Needs: *Potpourri* is a quarterly magazine "publishing works of writers, including new and unpublished writers. We want strongly voiced original poems in either free verse or traditional. Traditional work must represent the best of the craft. No religious, confessional, racial, political, erotic, abusive or sexual preference materials unless fictional and necessary to plot or characterization. No concrete/visual poetry (because of format)." They have published poetry by X.J. Kennedy, David Ray, Richard Moore, Pattiann Rogers and Tess Gallagher. As a sample the editor selected these lines from "The Last Woman" by Kim Horner:

> When the last woman goes,/Taking faith and myth and the fallow/Earth . . ./. . . who will hold her lambent wake;/Who will watch the dying stars,/Who will staunch the banging of the gate.

It is 76 pgs., 8½×11, professionally printed, saddle-stapled with red & white art on glossy cover, drawings, photos and ads inside. Press run is 1,500 for 850 subscribers. Subscription: $15. Sample: $4.95 with 9×12 envelope; $7.20 overseas.
How to Submit: Submit up to 3 poems at a time, one to a page, length to 75 lines (approximately 30 preferred). Submit seasonal themes 6 months in advance. Address haiku and related forms to Jeri Ragan. No e-mail submissions. Send SASE for guidelines. Reports in 8-10 weeks at most. Pays 1 copy. Acquires first North American serial rights.
Also Offers: The David Ray Poetry Award ($100 or more, depending upon grant monies) is given annually for best of volume. Another annual award is sponsored by the Council on National Literatures and offers $100 and publication in *Potpourri* for selected poem or short story; alternating years (2000 fiction). Send SASE for official guidelines. Deadline: September 1, 2000. Website includes back issues, biographies, submission guidelines, sample writings and literary links.
Advice: The editors advise, "Keep your new poems around long enough to become friends with them before parting. Let them ripen, and, above all, learn to be your own best editor. Read them aloud, boldly, to see how they ripple the air and echo what you mean to say. Unrequited love, children, grandchildren, favorite pets and descriptions that seem to be written for their own sake find little chance here."

POTTERSFIELD PORTFOLIO; POTTERSFIELD PORTFOLIO SHORT POEM COMPETITION, P.O. Box 40, Station A, Sydney, Nova Scotia B1P 6G9 Canada, phone (902)423-8116, e-mail aw486@chebucto.ns.ca, website http://www.chebucto.ns.ca/Culture/WFNS/pottersfield/potters.html, founded 1979, contact poetry editor.
Magazine Needs: Appearing 3 times a year, *Pottersfield Portfolio* is a "literary magazine publishing fiction, poetry, essays and reviews by authors from all around the world. No restrictions on subject matter or style. However, we will likely not use religious, inspirational or children's poetry. No doggerel or song lyrics. And please, no stuff that splashes symbols and images all over the page." They have published poetry by David Zieroth, Don Domanski, Jean McNeil and Alden Nowlan. As a sample the editor selected these lines from "The Coves" by Steve McOrmond:

> You ask the wind/hard questions. Try to see/where the horizon lies, blue seam/between ocean and air,/ between us/and the end of history.

The editor says *Pottersfield* is 96-120 pgs., 6×9, professionally printed and perfect-bound with 2-color cover, includes photos and ads. They receive about 250 poems a year, accept approximately 5%. Press run is 750 for 350 subscribers of which 25 are libraries, 250 shelf sales. Single copy: $8; subscription: $26. Sample: $6. "Subscribers from outside Canada please remit in U.S. dollars."
How to Submit: Submit 6 poems at a time. No previously published poems; simultaneous submissions OK.

Include SAE with IRCs. Cover letter strongly preferred. "Submissions should be on white paper of standard dimensions ($8\frac{1}{2} \times 11$). Only one poem per page." Time between acceptance and publication is 2-3 months. Poems are circulated to an editorial board. "Readers make recommendations to poetry editor." Publishes theme issues occasionally. Send SASE (or SAE with IRC) for guidelines and upcoming themes. "Note: U.S. stamps are no good in Canada." Reports in 3 months. Pays $5/printed page to a maximum of $25 plus 2 copies. Buys first Canadian serial rights. Staff reviews books of poetry in 750 words, single or multi-book format. Send books for review consideration.

Also Offers: Sponsors the *Pottersfield Portfolio* Short Poem Competition. Deadline: February 14 each year. Entry fee: $20 for 3 poems, which must be no more than 20 lines in length. Fee includes subscription. Write for details or consult website.

Advice: The editor says, "Only submit your work in a form you would want to read yourself. Subscribe to some literary journals. Read lots of poetry."

THE PRAGUE REVUE, BOHEMIA'S JOURNAL OF INTERNATIONAL LITERATURE, V Jámě 7, 110 00 Prague 1, Czech Republic, phone (4202)2422-2383, fax (4202)2422-1783, e-mail revue@terminal. cz, website http://www.praguepivo.com, founded 1995, poetry editors William E. Pritts and Todd A. Morimoto, managing editor Clare Wallace.

Magazine Needs: *The Prague Revue*, appearing 2-3 times a year, is a "literary journal with an international focus. We attempt to provide new, talented writers with a forum. Also publish some literary/critical essays on themed topics." They have no preferences as to subject matter, but submissions must be English, Czech or Italian. "Inclusion of English translation will facilitate our decision. *The Prague Revue* reserves the right to generate additional translations for publication." They do not want "epics, tear-jerkers or rhyming verse." They have published poetry by John Kinsella (Australia), Miroslav Holub (Czech Republic), Bohumil Hrabal (Czech Republic) and John Millet. As a sample the editors selected this poem, "Autobus Urbano 45 [madrid]," by Louis Armand:

> in its rainslashed headlights/i am a crouched hyena/who has here awaited the revelations/of hieronymus
> bosch/on the avenida of thousands murdered/forgotten unforgotten/with treacherous claws i give/to
> franco what is franco's/the driver sightless/slips my five coins into their coffins.

PR is 200 pgs., A5, perfect-bound with color cover, includes b&w art and some ads. They receive about 3,000 poems a year, accept approximately 1%. Press run is 2,500 for 1,000 subscribers of which 270 are libraries, 1,200 shelf sales.

How to Submit: Submit no more than 15 pages or 5 poems at a time, typewritten only. Previously published poems (if author holds all rights) and simultaneous submissions OK. However, "strong preference given to previously unpublished works." Cover letter with short bio required. Send SAE with IRC for response and/or return of ms. E-mail, fax and disk (formatted for Microsoft Word) submissions OK. Time between acceptance and publication is 6 months. Poems are circulated to an editorial board. Seldom comments on rejections. Publishes theme issues occasionally. Send SASE for guidelines and upcoming themes or obtain via e-mail or website. Reports in 3-6 months. Pays 2 copies. Acquires first rights.

Also Offers: Website includes *Prague Revue*'s mission, history, submission guidelines, subscription information and latest news on the review.

THE PRAIRIE JOURNAL; PRAIRIE JOURNAL PRESS (Specialized: regional, themes), P.O. Box 61203, Brentwood Post Office, 217-3630 Brentwood Rd. NW, Calgary, Alberta T2L 2K6 Canada, website http://www.geocities.com/Athens/Ithaca/4336/, founded 1983, editor A. Burke.

Magazine Needs: For *The Prairie Journal*, the editor wants to see poetry of "any length, free verse, contemporary themes (feminist, nature, urban, non-political), aesthetic value, a poet's poetry." Does not want to see "most rhymed verse, sentimentality, egotistical ravings. No cowboys or sage brush." They have published poetry by Mick Burrs, Lorna Crozier, Mary Melfi, Art Cuelho and John Hicks. *Prairie Journal* is 40-60 pgs., $7 \times 8\frac{1}{2}$, offset, saddle-stitched with card cover, b&w drawings and ads, appearing twice a year. They receive about 500 poems a year, accept approximately 4%. Press run is 600 for 200 subscribers of which 50% are libraries, the rest are distributed on the newsstand. Subscription: $8 for individuals, $15 for libraries. Sample: $8 ("Use postal money order").

How to Submit: No simultaneous submissions or previously published poems. Guidelines available for postage (but "no U.S. stamps, please"—get IRCs from the Post Office) or on website. "We will not be reading submissions until such time as an issue is in preparation (twice yearly), so be patient and we will acknowledge, accept for publication or return work at that time." Sometimes sends prepublication galleys. Pays $10-50 plus 1 copy. Acquires first North American serial rights. Reviews books of poetry "but must be assigned by editor. Query first."

Book/Chapbook Needs & How to Submit: For chapbook publication, Canadian poets only (preferably from the region) should query with 5 samples, bio, publications. Responds to queries in 2 months, to mss in 6 months. Payment in modest honoraria. They have published *Voices From Earth*, selected poems by Ronald Kurt and Mark McCawley, and *In the Presence of Grace*, by McCandless Callaghan. "We also publish anthologies on themes when material is available."

Advice: A. Burke advises, "Read recent poets! Experiment with line length, images, metaphors. Innovate."

THE PRAIRIE PUBLISHING COMPANY (Specialized: regional), Dept. PM, Box 2997, Winnipeg, Manitoba R3C 4B5 Canada, phone (204)837-7499, founded 1963, publisher Ralph E. Watkins.

Book/Chapbook Needs: The Prairie Publishing Company is a "small press catering to regional market, local history, fantasy, poetry and nonfiction," with flat-spined paperbacks. They want "basically well-crafted poems of reasonable length" and do not want to see "the work of rank amateurs and tentative and time-consuming effort." They have published collections of poetry by Brian Richardson and Brian MacKinnon. Their books are 6×9, handsomely produced, using b&w photos and art along with the poems, glossy card covers. They publish about 1 book a year, 68 pgs. Samples available at a 20% discount—send SASE or SAE and IRC for catalog.

How to Submit: Query with samples. Simultaneous submissions OK. Do not submit mss during summer. Responds to queries in 6 weeks.

Advice: Nancy Watkins notes, "Robert E. Pletta's point that most poets need to do more reading is well taken. We would endorse this suggestion."

PRAIRIE SCHOONER; STROUSSE PRIZE; LARRY LEVIS PRIZE; SLOTE PRIZE; FAULK-NER AWARD; HUGH J. LUKE AWARD; STANLEY AWARD; READERS' CHOICE AWARDS, 201 Andrews, University of Nebraska, Lincoln NE 68588-0334, phone (402)472-0911, fax (402)472-9771, website http://www.unl.edu/schooner/psmain.htm, founded 1927, editor Hilda Raz.

• Poetry published in *PS* has also been selected for inclusion in *The Best American Poetry 1996* and the *Pushcart Prize* anthology.

Magazine Needs: *Prairie Schooner is* "one of the oldest literary quarterlies in continuous publication; publishes poetry, fiction, personal essays, interviews and reviews." They want "poems that fulfill the expectations they set up." No specifications as to form, length, style, subject matter or purpose. They have published poetry by Alicia Ostriker, Marilyn Hacker, Radu Hotinceneasru, Mark Rudman and David Ignatow. As a sample the editor selected these lines from "How to Get in the Best Magazines" by Eleanor Wilner:

> it is time to write/the acceptable poem—/ice and glass, with its splinter/of bone, its pit/of an olive,/the
> dregs/of the cup of abundance,/useless spill of gold/from the thresher, the dust/of it filling the sunlight,
> the chum/broadcast on the black waters/and the fish/—the beautiful, ravenous fish—/refusing to rise.

Prairie Schooner is 200 pgs., 6×9, flat-spined and uses 70-80 pgs. of poetry in each issue. They receive about 4,800 mss (of all types) a year from which they choose 300 pgs. of poetry. Press run is 3,100. Single copy: $7.95; subscription: $22. Sample: $5.

How to Submit: Submit 5-7 poems at a time. No simultaneous submissions. "Clear copy appreciated." Considers mss from September through May only. Publishes theme issues. Send SASE for guidelines. Reports in 3-4 months; "sooner if possible." Always sends prepublication galleys. Pays 3 copies. Acquires all rights. Returns rights upon request without fee. Reviews books of poetry. Open to unsolicited reviews. Poets may also send books for review consideration. Editor Hilda Raz also promotes poets whose work has appeared in her pages by listing their continued accomplishments in a special section (even when their work does not concurrently appear in the magazine).

Also Offers: The $500 Strousse Prize is awarded to the best poetry published in the magazine each year. The Slote Prize for beginning writers ($500), Hugh J. Luke Award ($250), the Stanley Award for Poetry ($500) and six other *PS* prizes are also awarded, as well as the Faulkner Award for Excellence in Writing ($1,000) and the Larry Levis Prize for Poetry ($1,000). Also, each year 5-10 Readers' Choice Awards ($250 each) are given for poetry, fiction and nonfiction. Editors serve as judges. All contests are open only to those writers whose work was published in the magazine the previous year. Website features writer's guidelines, names of editors, subscription info, history, table of contents and current issue.

PRAIRIE WINDS, Box 536, Dakota Wesleyan University, 1200 W. University Ave., Mitchell SD 57301, editor James C. Van Oort.

Magazine Needs: *Prairie Winds* is an annual of poetry, fiction, short essays, photos and art. They are open to all forms, lengths, styles and subjects of poetry except pornographic. They have published poetry by Simon Perchik, Robert Cooperman and Robert Parham. The editor says *PW* is 50-60 pgs., 7½×9¼, offset, bound, gloss litho, no ads. They accept approximately 8% of the poetry received each year. Press run is 700. Sample: $4.

How to Submit: Submit 5-10 poems at a time. No previously published poems; simultaneous submissions OK. Cover letter and SASE required. "We are an annual, published in April. All submissions must arrive by January 4. We do not return submissions." Reads submissions January 4 through 31 only. Send SASE for guidelines. Reports by end of February. Pays 1 copy.

PRAKALPANA LITERATURE; KOBISENA (Specialized: bilingual, form), P-40 Nandana Park, Calcutta 700034, West Bengal, India, phone (91)(033)478-2347, *Kobisena* founded 1972, *Prakalpana Literature* press founded 1974, magazine 1977, editor Vattacharja Chandan.

Magazine Needs: "We are small magazines which publish only Prakalpana (a mixed form of prose and poetry), Sarbangin (whole) poetry, experimental b&w art and photographs, essays on Prakalpana movement and Sarbangin poetry movement, letters, literary news and very few books on Prakalpana and Sarbangin literature. Purpose and form: for advancement of poetry in the super-space age, the poetry must be really experimental and avant-garde using mathematical signs and symbols and visualizing the pictures inherent in the alphabet (within typography) with sonorous effect accessible to people. That is Sarbangin poetry. Length: within 30 lines (up to 4 poems)."

Prakalpana is a mixed form of prose, poetry, essay, novel, story, play with visual effect and it is not at all short story as it is often misunderstood. Better send six IRCs to read *Prakalpana Literature* first and then submit. Length: within 16 pages (up to 2 prakalpanas) at a time. Subject matter: society, nature, cosmos, humanity, love, peace, etc. Style: own. We do not want to see traditional, conventional, academic, religious, mainstream and poetry of prevailing norms and forms." They have published poetry by Dilip Gupta, John M. Bennett and Susan Smith Nash. *Prakalpana Literature*, an annual, is 120 pgs., 7×4½, saddle-stapled, printed on thin stock with matte card cover. *Kobisena*, which also appears once a year, is 16 pgs., digest-sized, a newsletter format with no cover. Both use both English and Bengali. They receive about 400 poems a year, accept approximately 10%. Press run is 1,000 for each, and each has about 450 subscribers of which 50 are libraries. Samples: 15 rupees for *Prakalpana*, 4 rupees for *Kobisena*. *Overseas: 6 IRCs and 3 IRCs respectively or exchange of avant-garde magazines.*
How to Submit: Submit 4 poems at a time. Cover letter with short bio and small photo/sketch of poet/writer/artist required; camera-ready copy (4×6½) preferred. Time between acceptance and publication is within a year. After being published in the magazines, poets may be included in future anthologies with translations into Bengali/English if and when necessary. "Joining with us is welcome but not a pre-condition." Editor comments on rejections "if wanted." Send SAE with IRC for guidelines. No reporting time given. Pays 1 copy. Reviews books of poetry, fiction and art, "but preferably experimental books." Open to unsolicited reviews. Poets, writers and artists may also send books for review consideration.
Advice: He says, "We believe that only through poetry, fiction and art, the deepest feelings of humanity as well as nature and the cosmos can be best expressed and conveyed to the peoples of the ages to come. And only poetry can fill up the gap in the peaceless hearts of dispirited peoples, resulted from the retreat of god and religion with the advancement of hi-tech. So, in an attempt, since the inception of Prakalpana Movement in 1969, to reach that goal in the avant-garde and experimental way we stand for Sarbangin poetry. And to poets and all concerned with poetry we wave the white handkerchief saying (in the words of Vattacharja Chandan), 'We want them who want us.' "

PRAYERWORKS (Specialized: religious), P.O. Box 301363, Portland OR 97294-9363, phone (503)761-2072, fax (503)760-1184, e-mail jay4prayer@aol.com or 76753.3202@compuserve.com, founded 1988, editor V. Ann Mandeville.
Magazine Needs: *Prayer Works* appears weekly "to share prayer concerns with others and to encourage prayer. Contents: 1 devotional and prayer requests, one filler (humorous or catchy)." *PrayerWorks* is 4 pgs., 5½×8, photocopied, desktop-published, folded. They receive about 50 poems a year, accept approximately 25%. Press run is 900 for 900 subscribers. Subscription: free.
How to Submit: Submit 5 poems, 1/page. Previously published poems and simultaneous submissions OK. E-mail submissions OK (Wordperfect or Microsoft Word files). Cover letter preferred. Time between acceptance and publication is 2-6 months. Seldom comments on rejections. Publishes theme issues relating to the holidays. Send SASE for guidelines. Reports in 1-2 months. Pays 5 or more copies.

PREMIERE GENERATION INK, P.O. Box 2056, Madison WI 53701-2056, e-mail poetry@premiere generation.com, website http://www.premieregeneration.com, founded 1998, contact poetry editor.
Magazine Needs: *PGI* appears quarterly and publishes "high quality, honest poetry in a magazine/journal format and also in a multimedia format via website. We are also looking for art, photos, live recordings of poetry (audio or video) to be put on the Web. We also want experimental video poetry which can be mailed by VHS cassette. We would like to see poetry that is less concerned with being perfect than it is with being honest and true. We welcome any length, format, style or subject matter. We do not want to see pretentious and contrived poetry." They have published poetry by Yogesh Chawla, John Ejaife and Sachin Pandya. As a sample they selected these lines from "Starch" (poet unidentified):

> Swollen and oily/on my brittle flesh/you bleed the/trail of words that/cut and disagree as/i wonder
> what broke first-/the condom or my heart

They say *PGI* is 20-30 pgs., 8½×11, photocopied in color and saddle-stapled, cover is color or b&w "depending on issue," includes art/graphics. Single copy: $3; subscription: $10. Sample: $3.
How to Submit: Submit 5 poems at a time. Previously published poems and simultaneous submissions OK. Cover letter preferred. Disk submissions OK. E-mail submissions preferred. "All electronic submissions or disk submissions must be in a readable PC format. Cover letters need not be formal, we prefer casual and personal." Time between acceptance and publication is 4 months. Poems are circulated to an editorial board. "Three editors review all submissions and a collective decision is reached." Often comments on rejections. Send SASE for guidelines or obtain via e-mail or website. Reports in 4-6 weeks. Pays 10 copies. Acquires first or reprint rights.
Also Offers: "We would like to publish books in cooperation with an author. Premiere Generation Ink will chiefly be a means for writers to distribute their art to a larger audience via the Web and the poetry journal. The sales proceeds will go to cover the costs associated with production. Any net profit will be divided equally between the author and the publisher. The main goal of this company is not profit, but rather to distribute quality art to a larger audience. We expect to work closely with the author on the format and layout of the book, and we hope eventually they will become just as much a part of the company as the founders." Order sample books by inquiring via regular mail, e-mail or website. Website includes constant updates of submission criteria and company information.

⬛ **$** ◎ **THE PRESBYTERIAN RECORD (Specialized: inspirational, religious)**, 50 Wynford Dr., North York, Ontario M3C 1J7 Canada, phone (416)441-1111, fax (416)441-2825, e-mail tdickey@presbyterian.ca, founded 1876.

Magazine Needs: *TPR* is "the national magazine that serves the membership of The Presbyterian Church in Canada (and many who are not Canadian Presbyterians). We seek to stimulate, inform, inspire, to provide an 'apologetic' and a critique of our church and the world (not necessarily in that order!)." They want poetry which is "inspirational, Christian, thoughtful, even satiric but not maudlin. No 'sympathy card' type verse a la Edgar Guest or Francis Gay. It would take a very exceptional poem of epic length for us to use it. Shorter poems, 10-30 lines, preferred. Blank verse OK (if it's not just rearranged prose). 'Found' poems. Subject matter should have some Christian import (however subtle)." They have published poetry by Margaret Avison, Andrew Foster, Fredrick Zydek, Kevin Hadduck, T.M. Dickey and Charles Cooper. The magazine comes out 11 times/year. Press run is 55,000. Subscription: $15.

How to Submit: Submit 3-6 poems at a time; seasonal work 6 weeks before month of publication. Simultaneous submissions OK; rarely accepts previously published poems. Poems should be typed, double-spaced. Pays $30-50/poem. Buys one-time rights. Staff reviews books of poetry. Send books for review consideration.

N 🌐 ◎ **PRESENCE (Specialized: form)**, 12 Grovehall Ave., Leeds LS11 7EX United Kingdom, founded 1995, contact Mr. Martin Lucas.

Magazine Needs: *Presence*, published 2-3 times/year, features haiku, senryu, renga, tanka, etc. They want "haiku or haiku-related/haiku-influenced work. Maximum length: 16 lines (including title and spaces)." They do not want "anything longer than 16 lines (except renga), anything tortured, absurd or fantastical, even if in 'haiku form.' " They have published poetry by Richard Goring, Gary Hotham, Jean Jorgensen and Hannah Mitte. As a sample the editor selected this haiku by Martin Lucas:

> a gap in the fence—/next door's cabbage flowers/have come through it

The editor says *Presence* is 44 pgs., A5, photocopied, perfect-bound, with brushdrawn art on card cover and illustrations. They receive about 2,000 poems a year, accept approximately 10%. Press run is 150 for 100 subscribers of which 5 are libraries, 10 shelf sales. Subscription: £5 ($10 US). Sample: £2 ($5 US). Make checks payable in UK funds to Martin Lucas.

How to Submit: Submit 4-12 poems at a time. "Please ensure that separate poems can be identified, and not mistaken for a sequence." No previously published poems or simultaneous submissions. Cover letter preferred. Time between acceptance and publication is 1-6 months. Seldom comments on rejections. Send SASE (or SAE and IRC) for guidelines. Reports within 1 month. Pays 1 copy. Copyright remains with authors. Staff reviews books or chapbooks of poetry or other magazines in 10-500 words, single format. Poets may also send books for review consideration.

Advice: The editor advises beginners, "The more you read the better you'll write. Those who subscribe to read make better poets than those who are motivated solely by seeing their own name in print."

✅ ◎ **THE PRESS OF THE THIRD MIND (Specialized: form)**, 1301 North Dearborn #1007, Chicago IL 60610, phone (312)337-3122, founded 1985, poetry editor "Badly Steamed Lard (anagram of Bradley Last-name)."

Book/Chapbook Needs: Press of the Third Mind is a small press publisher of artist books, poetry and fiction. "We are especially interested in found poems, Dada, surrealism, written table-scraps left on the floors of lunatic asylums by incurable psychotics, etc." They have published poetry by Anthony Stark, Jorn Barger, Michael Kaspar, and Eric Forsburg. As a sample the editor selected the following poem found in a Paul Stuart Department Store "Christmas Wish-List" registry:

> Rob seven banks and escape from the coppers;/Play "hide the salami" with Wendy McWhoppers./Rip out Madonna's cunt by the roots,/Then stomp on her face with my Doc Martens boots

They have a press run of 1,000 with books often going into a second or third printing. Sample for $1.43 postage.

How to Submit: For book publication submit up to 20 sample poems. "No anthologized mss where every poem has already appeared somewhere else." Simultaneous submissions OK, if noted. "Cover letter is good, but we don't need to know everything you published since you were age nine in single-spaced detail." Send SASE for upcoming themes. "Authors are paid as the publication transcends the break-even benchmark." The press has released an 80-page anthology entitled *Empty Calories* and published a deconstructivist novel about the repetition compulsion called *The Squeaky Fromme Gets the Grease*.

N 🖊 **PRESSTHEEDGE**, 3001 Oakridge, Temple TX 76502, e-mail mgreene@sage.net, founded 1996, contact Morrie W. Greene.

Magazine Needs: "*presstheEDGE*, a literary magazine, is a journal-sized semiannual anthology consisting of approximately 100 pages of quality poetry, short stories and art. The only factor affecting acceptance or rejection is quality work. Do not hesitate to submit. Our goal is to provide opportunities for writers so the fine art of writing will flourish as well as provide a quality magazine. We want to see poetry that reaches in deep and grabs the reader. Poetry that is fresh, real contemporary and hits the senses with well-crafted use of metaphor, symbolism, etc. It must be meaningful. Any form or style acceptable. No porn, nothing trite. Traditionalists should submit elsewhere." As a sample the editor selected these lines from his poem "Oracle of Delphi":

> unintelligible yet prophetic sounds in whispers of smoky rust/squeeze out from mystical rocks on the

*sacred ground/like struggling birds flipflopping at our feet/they gasp for air to give life . . . meaning
to the sounds/that are the messages round and red and meaningful/while inside her mouth but hidden
from our alabaster ears*

How to Submit: Submit up to 10 poems at a time. Previously published poems ("please specify") and simultaneous submissions ("notify please") OK. Cover letter preferred. "Format: single spaced, name and address on bottom of each page. E-mail submissions preferred, but snail mail is OK. Include brief bio in cover letter. No handwritten submissions." Deadlines: January 31 for Spring issue, May 31 for Winter issue. Time between acceptance and publication is 1 year. Occasionally comments on rejections. "Send SASE for notification within 4-6 weeks after deadline. If accepted, your realtime address will be required to send author's release form, etc. Hard copy (paper copy) of poems or short stories will not be returned (no need to waste anybody's postage). Author retains all rights, but if the piece is republished, author will credit *presstheEDGE* as the original publisher whenever and wherever else the work may be placed."

Also Offers: Sponsors $50 Editors Choice Award for contributors.

$⃠ PRIDE IMPRINTS, 7419 Ebbert Dr. SE, Port Orchard WA 98367, e-mail pridepblsh@aol.com, website http://www.pride-imprints.com, founded 1989, senior editor Ms. Cris Newport.

Book/Chapbook Needs: Pride Imprints (formerly Pride Publications & Imprints) publishes "thoughtful, quality work; must have some depth." They publish 12 paperbacks/year. They want "a minimum of 100 publishable, quality poems; book length. Any style or subject matter. We will also consider self or vanity published books for distribution." They have published poetry by Jack Rickard, Vacirca Vaughn and Angela Costa.

How to Submit: Query first with SASE. If invited, send entire mss, 100 poems minimum. Previously published poems and simultaneous submissions OK. Cover letter preferred. "A bio with publishing history, a page about the collection's focus, theme, etc., will help in the selection process." Time between acceptance and publication is 1 year. Poems are circulated to an editorial board. "Senior editor reviews all work initially. If appropriate for our press, work given to board for review." Seldom comments on rejections. Replies to queries and to mss in 3 months. Pays 10-15% royalties. Obtain sample books or chapbooks by sending $2 for catalogue.

Also Offers: Website includes writer's guidelines, complete catalog and individual book pages.

N 🌐 ◯ ◎ PRIDE MAGAZINE (Specialized: ethnic), Hamilton House, 55 Battersea Bridge Rd., London SW11 3AX United Kingdom, phone (0171)228-3110, fax (0171)228-3129, e-mail diana@pridemagazine.com, founded 1991, arts editor Diana Evans, editor Dianne St. Hill.

Magazine Needs: *Pride* is a monthly "lifestyle bible for people of colour. It contains arts, features, fashion, beauty and lifestyle sections. They want "short poems on any subject, well-written, imaginative. No clichéd or badly written work." They have published poetry by Dorothea Smart, Aze, Diana Evans and Loren Dixon. As a sample the editor selected these lines from "I Have Known True Beauty" by Robert G. Galbraith:

*The quick glances, continuous questions/And wide-eyed wisdom of the solemn and/Neated haired
young, and the pretty wide-eyed teenage/Girls who dress to display and shock, giggling/The gentle
warm black tenderness that I/Have known and loved*

The editor says *Pride* is 116 pgs., magazine-sized, 4-color, web offset printed, perfect-bound with gloss and metallic print cover, includes photography/illustrations, ads. They receive about 200 poems a year, accept approximately 30%. Press run is 40,000 for 29,000 subscribers, 29,000 shelf sales; 500 distributed free to companies. Single copy: £2.20; subscription: £26. Sample: £3. Make checks payable to Pride Magazine.

How to Submit: Submit 3 poems at a time. Line length for poetry is 10-20 lines maximum. Previously published poems and simultaneous submissions OK. Cover letter preferred. E-mail and disk submissions OK. "Provide SAE with submission." Time between acceptance and publication is 3-6 months. Poems are circulated to an editorial board. "The arts editor and editor read and discuss submissions, then submissions are rejected or filed for publication." Often comments on rejections. Publishes theme issues occasionally. Reports in 3 months. Always sends prepublication galleys. Acquires first or one-time rights. Staff reviews books of poetry in 100 words, single and multi-book format. Send books for review consideration to Diana Evans, arts editor.

⃠ ◎ PRIMAVERA (Specialized: women), P.O. Box #37-7547, Chicago IL 60637, phone (773)324-5920, founded 1975, co-editor Ruth Young.

Magazine Needs: *Primavera* is "an irregularly published but approximately annual magazine of poetry and fiction reflecting the experiences of women. We look for strong, original voice and imagery, generally prefer free verse, fairly short length, related, even tangentially, to women's experience." They have published poetry by Pamela Gemin and Diane Seuss-Brakeman. As a sample the editors selected these lines by Diane Seuss-Brakeman:

*Look around/at where you've/come to./The swamp where/sex and death/intersect./Check it out/
palmettos glazed/with honey,/ants with blood/on the jaws.*

The elegantly printed publication, flat-spined, generously illustrated with photos and graphics, uses 25-30 pgs. of poetry in each issue. They receive over 1,000 submissions of poetry a year, use approximately 25. Circulation is 1,000. Single copy: $10. Sample: $5.

How to Submit: Submit up to 6 poems anytime, no queries. No simultaneous submissions. Editors comment on rejections "when requested or inspired." Send SASE for guidelines. Reports in 1-3 months. Pays 2 copies. Acquires first-time rights.

◎ **PRINCETON UNIVERSITY PRESS; LOCKERT LIBRARY OF POETRY IN TRANSLATION** **(Specialized: translations, bilingual)**, 41 William St., Princeton NJ 08540, phone (609)258-4900, e-mail rebrown@pupress.princeton.edu.

Book/Chapbook Needs: "In the Lockert Library series, we publish simultaneous cloth and paperback (flat-spine) editions for each poet. Clothbound editions are on acid-free paper, and binding materials are chosen for strength and durability. Each book is given individual design treatment rather than stamped into a series mold. We have published a wide range of poets from other cultures, including well-known writers such as Hölderlin and Cavafy, and those who have not yet had their due in English translation, such as Wislawa Szymborska. Manuscripts are judged with several criteria in mind: the ability of the translation to stand on its own as poetry in English; fidelity to the tone and spirit of the original, rather than literal accuracy; and the importance of the translated poet to the literature of his or her time and country." The editor says, "All our books in this series are heavily subsidized to break even. We have internal funds to cover deficits of publishing costs. We do not, however, publish books chosen and subsidized by other agencies, such as AWP."

How to Submit: Simultaneous submissions OK if you tell them. Cover letter required. E-mail submissions OK. Send mss only during respective reading periods stated in guidelines. Send SASE for guidelines to submit. Reports in 2-3 months.

🌱 ✅ $◻ **PRISM INTERNATIONAL**, Creative Writing Program, University of British Columbia, Vancouver, British Columbia V6T 1Z1 Canada, phone (604)822-2514, fax (604)822-3616, e-mail prism@unixg.ubc. ca, website http://www.arts.ubc.ca/prism/, founded 1959, editors Jennica Harper and Kiera Miller, executive editor Laisha Rosnau.

• *Prism International* is known in literary circles as one of the top journals in Canada.

Magazine Needs: "*Prism* is an international quarterly that publishes poetry, drama, short fiction, imaginative nonfiction and translation into English in all genres. We have no thematic or stylistic allegiances: Excellence is our main criterion for acceptance of mss. We want fresh, distinctive poetry that shows an awareness of traditions old and new. We read everything." They have published poetry by Di Brandt, Esta Spalding, Karen Connelly, Derk Wynand and a translation by Seamus Heaney. As a sample the editors selected these lines from "I Like You" by Karen Solie:

> *You name garden pests in order/to better identify the dead./The diazinon has taken care/of the Johnsons, you said,/coming in from the yard,/and made me a salad without/washing your hands.*

Prism is 80 pgs., 6×9, elegantly printed, flat-spined with original color artwork on a glossy card cover. Circulation is for 1,000 subscribers of which 200 are libraries. They receive 1,000 submissions a year, use approximately 80, have a 4- to 6-month backlog. Subscription: $16. Sample: $5.

How to Submit: Submit up to 5 poems at a time, any print so long as it's typed. Include SASE (or SAE with IRCs). No previously published poems or simultaneous submissions. Cover letter with brief introduction and previous publications required. "Translations must be accompanied by a copy of the original. Poets may submit by e-mail, or through our website. Include the poem in the main body of the message." Send Canadian SASE or SAE with IRCs for guidelines. Reports in 2-6 months. Pays $40/printed page plus subscription; plus an additional $10/printed page to selected authors for publication on the World Wide Web. Editors sometimes comment on rejections. Acquires first North American serial rights.

Also Offers: Website includes writer's guidelines, names of editors, samples from past issues and "virtually everything you'd want to know."

Advice: The editors say, "While we don't automatically discount any kind of poetry, we prefer to publish work that challenges the writer as much as it does the reader. We are particularly looking for poetry in translation."

◙ **PROCREATION: A JOURNAL OF TRUTHTELLING IN POETRY & PROSE; SILENT PLANET PUBLICATIONS, LTD.**, 6300-138 Creedmoor Rd., Suite 260, Raleigh NC 27612, phone (919)510-9010, fax (919)510-0210, e-mail editor@procreation.org, website http://www.procreation.org, founded 1996, poetry editor Tanya Register.

Magazine Needs: *ProCreation* appears 3 times/year. "We are a literary journal devoted to the pursuit and expression of truth. In doing so, we echo the Creator's own imaginative, creative activity and so become more fully human. We seek poetry that resonates with artfully encapsulated truth about ultimate reality, including, but not limited to, spiritual truth. All forms are acceptable, provided they do not exceed 100 lines. We do not accept propaganda (however truthful), works of maudlin fiction or sentimental verse, or religious verse not rooted in real-life experience. No erotica." They have published poetry by Luci Shaw, Edward Dougherty and Judith Dupree. As a sample the editor selected these lines from "Christmas Again" by Edward Dougherty:

> *With its ending/already inside us, the story/begins again. This/is the season/of terrible/truths coming/ to live in our flesh. Decisions/will never be measured the same again. The demands/of enerosity-imagine/giving so freely/until even/our selves are gone./Imagine taking such fierce/consequences/ inside, and living/this freedom. No wonder/we put wings/on angels.*

ProCreation is 36-38 pgs., digest-sized, professionally printed on high-quality paper, saddle-stapled, matte card cover, with graphics, photography and line drawings. They receive about 800-1,000 poems a year, accept approximately 10%. Press run is 250 for 100 subscribers, 50 shelf sales; 100 distributed free to media, coffeeshops, independent bookstores and libraries. Subscription: $15/year. Sample: $5. Make checks payable to Silent Planet Publishing.

How to Submit: Submit 5-10 poems at a time with SASE. No previously published poems or simultaneous submissions. No e-mail submissions. Cover letter required. "Previous publications, occupation, interests should be in cover letter, and author should indicate if he desires to be contacted by readers who desire to comment on their work." Time between acceptance and publication is 3-6 months. Poems are circulated to an editorial board. "Each poem is read by each of the editors. We then meet one to three times to select poems to publish. Each poem is thoroughly discussed." Sometimes comments on rejections. Send SASE for guidelines or obtain via e-mail or website. Reports in 1-3 months. Pays 1 copy. Acquires first North American serial rights.
Also Offers: Sponsors a yearly contest with cash awards. Send SASE for guidelines. Website includes writer's guidelines, names of editors, poetry samples, writers' links, profiles of writers and editors' backgrounds.
Advice: The editor says, "One of our goals is to feature the work of relatively new poets who show promise alongside the works of more experienced poets. To this end, submit your best work. Select work with strong imagery and good word choice. Avoid the sentimental, preachy, or abstract. Write out of your experience. Find the extraordinary in the ordinary."

⊘ **PROMETHEUS PRESS**, P.O. Box 1569, Glendale CA 91209-1569, founded 1989. They do not currently accept submissions.

N ◗ **THE PROSE POEM: AN INTERNATIONAL JOURNAL**, English Dept. Providence College, Providence RI 02918, editor Peter Johnson, assistant editors Brian Johnson and Karen Klingon.
Magazine Needs: *The Prose Poem* is published annually. "Please don't send verse poems. Although we don't want to say that we can define 'prose poetry,' we do expect our contributors to at least know the difference between verse and prose poetry, so that they don't waste their time and postage."
How to Submit: Submit 3-5 poems at a time with SASE. No simultaneous submissions. Cover letter with 2-sentence bio required. Reads submissions December through March only. Time between acceptance and publication is 6 months. Subscription: $8/year, $12/2 years. Make checks payable to Providence College. Reports in 3 months. "If we publish an anthology we reserve the right to reprint your published poem in it; we also reserve the right to publish it on our web page." Book reviews are assigned by the editor, "though feel free to query."

◯ ◎ **PROSETRY: NEWSLETTER FOR, BY AND ABOUT WRITERS (Specialized: writing)**, The Write Place, P.O. Box 117727, Burlingame CA 94011, phone/fax (650)347-7613, e-mail prosetry@aol.com, website http://www.prosetry.com, editor P.D. Steele, founded 1986.
Magazine Needs: *Prosetry* is a bimonthly newsletter featuring "new and newly published poets and prose writers. Our purpose is to provide writers with up-to-date information regarding markets, conferences and contests. To help get the juices flowing, to get the writer's work in the hands of an editor, and to offer the writer a forum in which to 'show their wares.' " They want "all forms of poetry. English only (translations OK). No 'off the wall,' profanity, S.M. Gay/lesbian, political OK. We publish very little rhyming poetry. We like different forms: haiku, villanelle, ballade." *Prosetry* is 4 pgs., 8½×11 (17×11 sheet folded), printed on heavy bond paper and 3-hole punched for home binding. Single copy: $2; subscription: $12/year. Sample copy for 2 first-class stamps. Invites new writers.
How to Submit: Submit up to 3 poems, no more than 20 lines, English only (translations OK). Include SASE. Requires 2-line bio. E-mail submissions OK ("we also request SASE for release if we choose to publish"). Include line count, name, mailing address, telephone, fax and e-mail address. Send SASE for guidelines. "All deadlines are first of month." Reports in less than 1 month. Pays 2 copies plus 1-year subscription. Acquires one-time rights; release required. Open to unsolicited reviews. Poets may send chapbooks for review consideration.
Also Offers: Publishes "How-to" *CLIPS©* for writers, $2.50 each. Free list for SASE. "Send articles up to 100 words, of interest to writers in all genres. Previously published OK (give us reprint info). Jokes, minutia, fun gossip about famous writers, quips, famous birthdays." Website includes guidelines, description of newsletter, contact information and additional services, including editing and reviews.
Advice: The editor says, "I'd like to receive less confessional poetry and more humor."

$ ◗ **PROVINCETOWN ARTS; PROVINCETOWN ARTS PRESS**, 650 Commercial St., Provincetown MA 02657-1725, phone (508)487-3167, fax (508)487-8634, founded 1985, editor Christopher Busa.
Magazine Needs: An elegant annual using quality poetry, "*Provincetown Arts* focuses broadly on the artists and writers who inhabit or visit the tip of Cape Cod and seeks to stimulate creative activity and enhance public awareness of the cultural life of the nation's oldest continuous art colony. Drawing upon a century-long tradition rich in visual art, literature and theater, *Provincetown Arts* publishes material with a view towards demonstrating that the artists' colony, functioning outside the urban centers, is a utopian dream with an ongoing vitality." They have published poetry by Bruce Smith, Franz Wright, Sandra McPherson and Cyrus Cassells. *PA* is about 170

MARKETS THAT WERE listed in the 1999 edition of *Poet's Market* but do not appear this year are listed in the General Index with a notation explaining why they were omitted.

pgs., 8¾×11⅞, perfect-bound with full-color glossy cover. Press run is 10,000 for 500 subscribers of which 20 are libraries, 6,000 shelf sales. Sample: $10.

How to Submit: Submit up to 3 typed poems at a time. All queries and submissions should be via regular mail. Reads submissions September 1 through February 1 only. Send SASE for guidelines. Reports in 2-3 months. Usually sends prepublication galleys. Pays $25-100/poem plus 2 copies. Buys first rights. Reviews books of poetry in 500-3,000 words, single or multi-book format. Open to unsolicited reviews. Poets may also send books for review consideration.

Book/Chapbook Needs & How to Submit: The Provincetown Arts Press has published 7 volumes of poetry. The Provincetown Poets Series includes *At the Gate* by Martha Rhodes, *Euphorbia* by Anne-Marie Levine, a finalist in the 1995 Paterson Poetry Prize, and *1990* by Michael Klein, co-winner of the 1993 Lambda Literary Award.

⊕ ◑ ◎ PSYCHOPOETICA (Specialized), Dept. of Psychology, University of Hull, Hull HU6 7RX England, website http://www.fernhse.demon.co.uk/eastword/psycho/, founded 1979, co-editors Dr. Geoff Lowe and Trevor Millum.

Magazine Needs: *Psychopoetica* appears 2 times/year and publishes "short, experimental, rhymed and un-rhymed, light verse, haiku, etc., (and visual poems). We will read and consider any style, any length, providing it's within the arena of 'psychologically-based' poetry. We're not too keen on self-indulgent therapeutic poetry (unless it's good and original), nor sweetly inspirational stuff. We like poetry that has some (or all!) of the following: humor, vivid imagery, powerful feelings, guts and substance, originality, creative style, punch or twist, word-play, good craftsmanship, etc." Published poets include Sheila E. Murphy, Wes Magee, R. Nikolas Macioci, Allen Renfro, Vi Vi Hlavsa and John Brander. It is over 60 pgs., A4, perfect-bound. Single copy: £3.50 ($7); 4-issue subscription: £12 ($24). Make checks payable to G. Lowe. ("American currency payable in dollar notes, please.")

How to Submit: Submit up to 6 poems at a time. Previously published poems ("state where and when") and simultaneous submissions OK. Publishes theme issues. Send SASE (or SAE and IRC) for guidelines and upcoming themes. Editor usually comments on rejections. Pays 1 copy. Authors retain all rights. Occasionally reviews books of poetry in 25 words, single format. Open to unsolicited reviews. Poets may also send books for review consideration.

Advice: They say, "Careful presentation of work is most important. But we continue to be impressed by the rich variety of submissions, especially work that shifts boundaries. Also, we now welcome interesting juxtapositions of words and graphics."

◑ ◎ THE PUCKERBRUSH PRESS; THE PUCKERBRUSH REVIEW (Specialized: regional), 76 Main St., Orono ME 04473-1430, phone (207)866-4868 or 581-3832, press founded 1971, *Review* founded 1978, poetry editor Constance Hunting.

Magazine Needs & How to Submit: *The Puckerbrush Review* is a literary, twice-a-year magazine focused on Maine. The editor looks for freshness and simplicity, but does not want to see "confessional, religious, sentimental, dull, feminist, incompetent, derivative" poetry. As a sample the editor selected these lines from "Canvas for Eyes" by Muska Nagel:

> Our Lady of the Crossroads, stoned by passersby,/mother of all dark lands,/pray for us now:/the
> numbers,/lost, forgotten, scattered, the nameless dead.

For the review, submit 5 poems at a time. Pays 2 copies.

Book/Chapbook Needs & How to Submit: The Puckerbrush Press is a small press publisher of flat-spined paperbacks of literary quality. They have published *Young* by Miriam Colwell and *The Eternal Moment* by Angelica Garnett. For book publication, query with 10 samples. Prefers no simultaneous submissions. Offers criticism for a fee: $100 is usual. Pays 10% royalties plus 10 copies.

◑ ◎ PUDDING HOUSE PUBLICATIONS; PUDDING MAGAZINE: THE INTERNATIONAL JOURNAL OF APPLIED POETRY; PUDDING HOUSE CHAPBOOK COMPETITIONS; PUDDING HOUSE BED & BREAKFAST FOR WRITERS; PUDDING HOUSE WRITERS RESOURCE CENTER (Specialized: political, social issues, popular culture), 60 N. Main St., Johnstown OH 43031, phone (740)967-6060, e-mail pudding@johnstown.net, website http://www.puddinghouse.com, founded 1979, editor Jennifer Bosveld.

Magazine Needs: Pudding House Publications provides "a sociological looking glass through poems that provide 'felt experience' and share intense human situations. Speaks for the difficulties and the solutions. Additionally a forum for poems and articles by people who take poetry arts into the schools and the human services." They publish *Pudding* every several months, also chapbooks, anthologies, broadsides. They "want experimental and contemporary poetry—what hasn't been said before. Speak the unspeakable. Don't want preachments or sentimentality. Don't want obvious traditional forms without fresh approach. Long poems OK as long as they aren't windy. Interested in receiving poetry on popular culture and rich brief narratives, i.e. 'virtual journalism.' (sample sheet $1 plus SASE)." They have published poetry by Knute Skinner, David Chorlton, Mary Winters, Robert Collins and Nita Penfold. *Pudding* is a literary journal with an interest in poetry arts in human service as well. They use about 70 pgs. of poetry in each issue—5½×8½, 70 pgs., offset composed on IBM Microsoft

Works. Press run is 2,000 for 1,400 subscribers of which 40 are libraries. Subscription: $18.95/3 issues. Sample: $6.95.

How to Submit: Submit 3-10 poems at a time with SASE. "Submissions without SASEs will be discarded." No postcards. No simultaneous submissions. Previously published submissions respected but include credits. Likes cover letter. Sometimes publishes theme issues. Send SASE for guidelines. Reports on same day (unless traveling). Pays 1 copy; to featured poet $10 and 4 copies. Returns rights "with *Pudding* permitted to reprint." Staff reviews books of poetry. Send books for review consideration.

Book/Chapbook Needs & How to Submit: Chapbooks considered outside of competitions, no query. $10 reading fee. Send complete ms and cover letter with publication credits and bio. Editor often comments, will critique on request for $4/page of poetry or $75 an hour in person.

Also Offers: Pudding House offers 2 annual chapbook competitions—each requires a $10 reading fee with entry. Deadlines: June 30 and September 30. The competitions award $100, publication and 20 free copies. Pudding House Bed & Breakfast for Writers offers "pretty, comfortable, and clean rooms with desk and all the free paper you can use" as well as free breakfast in large comfortable home ½ block from conveniences. Location of the Pudding House Writers Resource Center and Library on Applied Poetry. Bed & Breakfast is $75 single or double/night, discounts available. Reservations recommended far in advance. Send SASE for details. "Our website is one of the greatest poetry websites in the country—calls, workshops, publication list/history, online essays, games, film assignments, guest pages, Columbus poetry calendar and much more." The website also links to the site for The Unitarian Universalist Poets Cooperative, a national organization. Membership: $10/year.

Advice: Jennifer Bosveld shares, "Editors have pet peeves. I won't respond to postcards or on them. I require SASEs. I don't like cover letters that state the obvious, poems with trite concepts, or meaning dictated by rhyme. Thoroughly review our website; it will give you a good idea about our publication history and editorial tastes."

◢ ◎ PUERTO DEL SOL (Specialized: translations, regional), Box 3E, New Mexico State University, Las Cruces NM 88003-0001, e-mail kwest@nmsu.edu, founded 1972 (in present format), poetry editor Kathleene West.

Magazine Needs: "We publish a literary magazine twice per year. Interested in poems, fiction, essays, photos, originals and translations from the Spanish. Also (generally solicited) reviews and dialogues between writers. We want top quality poetry, any style, from anywhere. We are sympathetic to Southwestern writers, but this is not a theme magazine. Excellent poetry of any kind, any form." They have published poetry by Judith Sornberger, Ana Castillo, Marilyn Hacker, Virgil Suarez and Lois-Ann Yamanaka. As a sample the editor selected these lines from "And Seeing It" by Valerie Martínez:

> Orange, orange. And the hand arching up/to hold it. The woman's hand, the arching./Up. And the
> star exploding, seeing it/where it wasn't, a telescope on the night sky./The thermonuclear flash. The
> explosion.

The 6×9, flat-spined, professionally printed magazine, matte card cover with art. Press run is 1,250 for 300 subscribers of which 25-30 are libraries. Devotes 40-50 pgs. to poetry in each 150-page issue. They use about 50 of the 800 submissions (about 6,000 poems) received each year to fill up the 90 pgs. of poetry the 2 issues encompass. Subscription: $10/2 issues. Sample: $7.

How to Submit: Submit 3-6 poems at a time, 1 poem to a page. Simultaneous submissions OK. Cover letter welcome. Reads mss September 1 to March 1 only. Offers editorial comments on most mss. Reports in 3-6 months. Sometimes sends prepublication galleys. Pays 2 copies.

Advice: The editor says, "We're looking for poems that are risk-taking and honest."

⊕ ◢ PULSAR POETRY MAGAZINE; LIGDEN PUBLISHERS, 34 Lineacre, Grange Park, Swindon, Wiltshire SN5 6DA United Kingdom, phone (01793)875941, e-mail david.pike@virgin.net, website http://www.i-way.co.uk/~swindonlink/, founded 1992, editor David Pike, editorial assistant Jill Meredith.

Magazine Needs: *Pulsar*, published quarterly, "encourages the writing of poetry from all walks of life. Contains poems, reviews and editorial comments." They want "hard-hitting, thought-provoking work; interesting and stimulating poetry." They do not want "racist material. Not keen on religious poetry." They have published poetry by Joanna Ryan, Joy Martin and Gerald England. As a sample the editor selected these lines from "The Watcher" by Lewis Hosegood:

> Somewhere in this tall terraced house, somewhere,/somewhere lives a boy/who surely cannot see me,/
> nor speak my name aloud, yet senses/my interest in origins./He will never go away though I wait here
> and wait. . . .

Pulsar is 28 pgs., A5, professionally printed, saddle-stapled, glossy 2-color cover with photos and ads. Press run is 250 for 100 subscribers of which 40 are libraries; several distributed free to newspapers, etc. Subscription: $30 (£10 UK). Sample: $5. Make checks payable to Ligden Publishers.

How to Submit: Submit 3 poems at a time "preferably typed." No previously published poems or simultaneous submissions. Cover letter preferred; include SAE with IRCs. "Poems can be published in next edition if it is what we are looking for. The editor and assistant read all poems." Time between acceptance and publication is about 1 month. Seldom comments on rejections. Send SASE (or SAE and IRC) for guidelines. Reports within 3 weeks. Pays 1 copy. Acquires first rights. Staff reviews poetry books and poetry audio tapes (mainstream); word count varies. Send books for review consideration.

Advice: The editor says, "Give explanatory notes if poems are open to interpretation. Be patient and enjoy what you are doing. Check grammar, spelling, etc. (should be obvious). Note: we are a non-profit making society."

✔️ 🅞 **PURDUE UNIVERSITY PRESS; VERNA EMERY POETRY PRIZE**, 1207 S. Campus Courts-E, West Lafayette IN 47906, phone (765)494-2038 or (800)933-9637, e-mail libpup@omni.cc.purdue.edu, founded 1960.
Book/Chapbook Needs: They select 1 book/year to publish through the Verna Emery Poetry Prize, which awards $500 on publication plus royalty arrangements. They have published *Murderer's Day* by E.M. Schorb; *No Moon* by Nancy Eimers; *The Body Mutinies* by Lucia Perillo; *Desiring Flight* by Christianne Balk; *Fresh Peaches, Fireworks & Guns* by Donald Platt; *Alcatraz* by Richard Cecil; and poetry by Fleda Brown Jackson, whose book, *Fishing With Blood*, won the GLCA New Writers Award. Final judges for the competition have included Gerald Stern, Andrew Hudgins and Ellen Bryant Voigt.
How to Submit: There is a $15 reading fee. Those interested are urged to send SASE for guidelines, or request via e-mail, as particulars vary from year to year. Deadline: April 15.

🅜 **PYGMY FOREST PRESS; SEMI-DWARF REVIEW**, P.O. Box 7097, Eureka CA 95502, phone (707)268-1274, founded 1987, editor/publisher Leonard Cirino.
Magazine Needs & How to Submit: Pygmy Forest Press publishes *Semi-Dwarf Review* which accepts poetry, translations, memoirs and essays. Send SASE for details. Pays 2 copies.
Book/Chapbook Needs: The press also publishes flat-spined paperbacks. "Forms of any kind/length to 96 pgs., subject matter open; especially ecology, prison, asylum, Third World, anarchist to far right. Prefer Stevens to Williams. I like Berryman, Roethke, William Bronk; dislike most 'Beats.' Open to anything I consider 'good.' Open to traditional rhyme, meter, but must be modern in subject matter. Also open to translations." He has published *Dog* by Michael McIrvin; *Sitting on the Edge of a Cow* by Charles L. Lyndean; *Where the Four Winds Blow* (including epitaphs) by Phillipe Soupault, translated by Pat Nolan; *The Circle & The Line* by Victoria Bouroncle; *Poetry of the Deformed* by Kenn Mitchell; and *Light on The Edge* by Devreaux Baker.
How to Submit: Submit 10-15 poems with bio, acknowledgements, publications. Simultaneous submissions and previously published material OK. Reports on queries in 1-3 weeks, submissions in 2-4 weeks. Usually pays 20% of run ("if author typesets on IBM compatible")—about 25-50 copies. Buys first rights. He comments on "almost every" ms.
Advice: Leonard Cirino says, "I am basically an anarchist. Belong to no 'school.' I fund myself. Receive no grants or private funding. Generally politically left, but no mainline Stalinist or Marxist. Plan to publish one to three books yearly."

🄽 💲🅞 **QED PRESS; CYPRESS HOUSE**, 155 Cypress St., Fort Bragg CA 95437, phone (707)964-9520, fax (707)964-7531, e-mail qedpress@mcn.org, website http://www.cypresshouse.com, founded 1985, senior editor John Fremont.
Book/Chapbook Needs: "QED Press has no determining philosophy. We seek clear, clean, intelligent and moving work." They publish 1-2 paperbacks/year. They want "concrete, personal and spare writing. No florid rhymed verse." They have published poetry by Luke Breit, Paula Tennant (Adams) and Cynthia Frank. As a sample the editor selected this poem, "Ao Lume," by Eugenio de Andrade:

> Nem sempre o homem é um lugar triste./Há noites em que o sorriso/dos anjos/a torna habitável e leve:/com a cabeça no teu regaço/é um cão ao lume a correr às lebres.

Translated from Portuguese by Alexis Levitin:

> Man is not always a place of sorrow./There are nights in which the smile/of angels/makes him habitable and light:/with his head in your lap/he's a dog by the fire chasing after hares.

Books are usually around 100 pgs., 5½×8½, offset printed, perfect-bound, full-color CS1 10 pt. cover.
How to Submit: "We prefer to see all the poems (about 100 pages worth or 75-80 poems) to be bound in a book." Previously published poems and simultaneous submissions OK. Cover letter required. "Poets must have prior credits in recognized journals, and a minimum of 50% new material." Time between acceptance and publication is 3-6 months. Poems are circulated to an editorial board. "We publish only 1-2 poetry books each year—by consensus." Seldom comments on rejections. Replies to queries and mss in 3 months. Pays royalties of 7½-12% and 25 author's copies (out of a press run of 500-1,000). Order sample books by sending SASE for catalog.
Also Offers: Through the imprint Cypress House, they offer subsidy arrangements "by bid with author retaining all rights and inventory. We are not a vanity press." 50% of books are author-subsidy published each year.

✔️ 🅞 **QOPH; PLEROMA PRESS**, P.O. Box 1009, Paia HI 96779, e-mail qoph@hotmail.com, founded 1998, editor Andrew Rawnsley.
Magazine Needs: *Qoph* is a journal of "writing and ideas which penetrate reality, that pierces the veils of illusion; prose and poetry, criticism and creative; to establish a focused place for intuitive creativity and truly fresh 21st century ideas; blending art, science and spirit in a meaningful way; synthesis; esoteric yet grounded." They want "evocative, innovative, imaginative poetry and prose that connects word, sound and image in a musical way; powerful shamanic process; no restrictions on form or style; poetry with a vision. We are looking especially for conceptual and abstract writing that is spiritually potent." They have published poetry by Tobey

Hiller. The editor says *Qoph* is 32-40 pgs., digest-sized, laser-printed and saddle-stapled, heavy card stock cover, includes cover and inside art and photography. Press run is 200. Single copy: $4; subscription: $12/4 issues. Sample: $3. "Please use money orders made payable to Andrew Rawnsley. We would prefer contributors read the journal (and hopefully subscribe) so that they know our 'vibe'. Many people submitted material without doing this, and have sent unsuitable work."

How to Submit: Submit up to 6 poems at a time. Previously published poems OK; no simultaneous submissions. Cover letter required including "why you are submitting, what your poetry is seeking to do, who you are . . ." E-mail submissions OK. Send both as text in the body of the e-mail and as attachments (MS Word or simple text files.). Disk (Macintosh/MS Word) OK "as long as hard copies come later." Time between acceptance and publication is up to 1 year. Sometimes comments on rejections, "depending on quality of work and time available." Send SASE for guidelines (preferred) or obtain via e-mail. Reports in 3-12 weeks. Pays subscription and 2 copies. Acquires first or one-time rights. Reviews books and chapbooks of poetry and other magazines in 200-300 words, single or multi-book format. Open to unsolicited reviews. Poets may also send books for review consideration.

Book/Chapbook Needs & How to Submit: Pleroma Press publishes occasional chapbooks *by invitation only.* "Limited press, high quality paper, cover stock and artwork. Specialized, esoteric themes."

Advice: The editor says, "Poetry and art should make you open-minded, don't become elitist and exclusionary—the epitome of close-mindedness. Scenes are superficial—be yourself. Send us work that is powerful, makes a difference, balancing light with dark, movement with stasis, wisdom with enthusiasm. Say it with confidence."

N ⊕ $□ ② QUADRANT MAGAZINE, P.O. Box 1495, Collingwood, Victoria 3066 Australia, phone (03)9417 6855, fax (03)9416 2980, e-mail quadrnt@o2email.com.au, founded 1956, editor P.P. McGuinnes, literary editor Les Murray.

Magazine Needs: *Quadrant*, published 10 times/year, is a "magazine of literature and ideas; about 10% of pages devoted to poetry." They have published poetry by John Ridland, Geoff Page and Kathleen Stewart. *Quadrant* is 88 pgs., 7⅛ × 10¾, professionally printed on newsprint, saddle-stapled, CS2 cover stock with some art and ads. They receive several thousand poems a year, accept approximately 5%. Press run is 8,000 for 3,000 subscribers of which 500 are libraries, 2,500 shelf sales; 130 distributed free. Subscription: $54 (in Australia). Sample: $5.50.

How to Submit: No previously published poems or simultaneous submissions. Cover letter preferred. Time between acceptance and publication is 6 months. "Assessment made by literary editor." Seldom comments on rejections. Send SASE (or SAE and IRCs) for guidelines. Pays $30/poem plus 1 copy. Buys first Australian serial rights. Reviews books of poetry. Open to unsolicited reviews.

N ⊕ $□ ② QUANTUM LEAP; Q.Q. PRESS, 81 Breval Crescent, Hardgate, Clydebank G81 6LS Scotland, United Kingdom, phone (01389)874953, founded 1997, editor Alan Carter.

Magazine Needs: *Quantum Leap* is a quarterly poetry magazine. They want "all kinds of poetry—free verse, rhyming, whatever—as long as it's well written and preferably well punctuated, too. We rarely use haiku." They have published poetry by Dr. Stella Browning, Roger Harvey, Fiona Curnow and Dylan Thomas. As a sample the editor selected these lines from "Tumulus, Coniston" by John H. Hope:

> *Sleep cold tonight./They'll build a mortuary house of wood,/Wattle-woven, leaf-bright thatch,/Dark resting-place when they despatch/My spirit to the womb of motherhood/Beyond the light*

QL is 40 pgs., digest-sized, desktop-published and saddle-stapled with card cover, includes clip art and ads for other magazines. They receive about 2,000 poems a year, accept approximately 10%. Press run is 180 for 160 subscribers. Single copy: $9; subscription: $32. Sample: $6. Make checks payable to Alan Carter. "All things being equal in terms of a poem's quality, I will often favor that of a subscriber (or someone who has at least bought an issue) over a nonsubscriber, as it is they who keep us solvent."

How to Submit: Submit 6 poems at a time. Line length for poetry is 36 ("normally"). Previously published poems and simultaneous submissions OK. Cover letter required. "Within the UK, send a SASE, outside it, send IRCs to the value of what has been submitted." Time between acceptance and publication is usually 3 months. Seldom comments on rejections. Send SASE (or SAE and IRC) for guidelines. Reports in 3 weeks. Pays £2 sterling. Acquires first or second British serial rights.

Book/Chapbook Needs: Under the imprint "Collections," Q.Q. Press offers subsidy arrangements "to provide a cheap alternative to the 'vanity presses'—poetry only." They charge £100 sterling for 50 32-page books (A4), US $250 plus postage. Please write for details. Order sample books by sending $12 (postage included).

Also Offers: Sponsors open poetry competitions and competitions for subscribers only. Send SAE and IRC for details.

Advice: The editor says, "Submit well-thought-out, well-presented poetry, preferably well punctuated, too. If rhyming poetry, make it flow and don't strain to rhyme. I don't bite, and I appreciate a short cover letter, but not a long, long list of where you've been published before!"

☑ ◐ ◎ QUARTER AFTER EIGHT; PROSE WRITING CONTEST (Specialized: form/style), Ellis Hall, Ohio University, Athens OH 45701, fax (740)593-2818, website http://www.-as.phy.ohiou.edu/Depart ments/English/Litjournals.html, founded 1993, editors Tom Noyes, Bonnie Proudfoot, Imad Rahman and Andy Touhy.

Magazine Needs: *Quarter After Eight* is "an annual journal of prose and commentary devoted to the exploration of prose in all its permutations. We are interested in reading fiction, sudden fiction, prose poetry, creative and critical non-fiction, interviews, reviews, letters, memoirs, translations and drama. We do not publish traditional poetry, but we do welcome work that provocatively explores—even challenges—the prose/poetry distinction. Our primary criteria in evaluating submissions are freshness of approach and an address to the prose form." They have published poetry by Rosmarie Waldrop, Nathaniel Tarn and Diane Glancy. As a sample the editor selected these lines from "Whining Prairie" by Maureen Seaton:

> *I don't want to die in this wild onion smelly belly mire of the midwest stinking marsh this drenchy swaly swamp but I might and who would note the fragrant corruption of my poor elan this moorish bog this poachy few who come from sea with salt and myrrh to burn my rotting flesh?*

QAE is 310 pgs., 6×9, professionally printed and perfect-bound with glossy card cover, includes b&w photos and ads. They receive about 1,000 poems a year, accept approximately 3%. Press run is 1,000 for 200 subscribers of which 50 are libraries, 500 shelf sales. Sample: $10.
How to Submit: Submit 4-6 poems at a time. No previously published poems; simultaneous submissions OK. Disk submissions with hard copy OK. "Include publishing history. We encourage readers/submitters to obtain a copy of the magazine." Reads submissions September 15 through March 15 only. Time between acceptance and notification is 6-8 weeks. Poems are circulated to an editorial board. "Editorial board makes final decisions; a pool of readers handles first reads and commentary/input on editorial decisions." Often comments on rejections. Send SASE for guidelines. Reports in 6-8 weeks. Pays 2 copies. Acquires first North American serial rights. Reviews books of poetry in 800-1,200 words, single or multi-book format. Send books for review consideration to Book Review Editor.
Also Offers: Sponsors an annual Prose Writing Contest with $500 cash award. Reading fee: $10. Winner is published in subsequent issue. Maximum length 10,000 words—can be a sequence of poems.
Advice: The editor says, "*QAE* is a somewhat specialized niche. Check out the magazine and explore the boundaries of genre."

▨ ◎ QUARTERLY REVIEW OF LITERATURE POETRY BOOK SERIES; QRL PRIZE AWARDS (Specialized: subscription, translation), 26 Haslet Ave., Princeton NJ 08540, website www.princeton.edu/~qrl, founded 1943, poetry editors T. Weiss and R. Weiss.
Book/Chapbook Needs & How to Submit: After more than 35 years as one of the most distinguished literary journals in the country, *QRL* now appears as the *QRL Poetry Book Series*, in which 4-6 poetry books, a poetic play of a book of a poet in translation are chosen in open competition. The selected poetry books are combined in one annual volume with each of the 4-6 poets receiving $1,000 and 100 copies. The resulting 300- to 400-page volumes are printed in editions of 3,000-5,000, selling in paperback for $12, in hardback for $20. Subscription—2 paperback volumes containing 10 books: $20. Send SASE for details.

✔ ☟ $ ▨ QUARTERLY WEST, 200 S. Central Campus Dr., Room 317, University of Utah, Salt Lake City UT 84112-9109, phone (801)581-3938, website http://www.chronicle.edu/QW/Qw.html, founded 1976, editor Margot Schilpp, poetry editors Melanie Figg and Heidi Czerwiec Blitch.
   ● Poetry published in *Quarterly West* has appeared in *The Best American Poetry 1997* and won the 1998 Pushcart Prize.
Magazine Needs: *Quarterly West* is a semiannual literary magazine that seeks "original and accomplished literary verse—free or formal. No greeting card or sentimental poetry." Also publishes translations. They have published poetry by Robert Pinsky, Eavan Boland, Albert Goldbarth, William Matthews, Agha Shahid Ali and Heather McHugh. *QW* is 220 pgs., 6×9, offset printed with 4-color cover art. They receive 1,500 submissions a year, accept less than 1%. Press run is 1,900 for 500 subscribers of which 300-400 are libraries. Subscription: $12/year, $21/2 years. Sample: $7.50.
How to Submit: Submit 3-5 poems at a time; if translations, include original. No previously published poems; simultaneous submissions OK, with notification. Seldom comments on rejections. Send SASE for guidelines. Reports in 1-6 months. Pays $15-100 plus 2 copies. Buys all rights. Returns rights with acknowledgement and right to reprint. Reviews books of poetry in 1,000-3,000 words. Open to unsolicited reviews. Poets may also send books for review consideration.
Also Offers: Website includes guidelines, staff, examples of recently published poems, graphic of cover and a list of contributors.

◎ QUEEN OF ALL HEARTS (Specialized: religious), 26 S. Saxon Ave., Bay Shore NY 11706, phone (516)665-0726, fax (516)665-4349, e-mail pretre@worldnet.att.net, founded 1950, poetry editor Joseph Tusiani.
Magazine Needs: *QOAH* is a magazine-sized bimonthly that uses poetry "dealing with Mary, the Mother of Jesus—inspirational poetry. Not too long." They have published poetry by Fernando Sembiante and Alberta Schumacher. The professionally printed magazine is 48 pgs., heavy stock, various colors of ink and paper, liberal use of graphics and photos, has approximately 3,000 subscriptions at $20/year. Single copy: $2.50. Sample: $3. They receive 40-50 submissions a year, use approximately 2/issue.
How to Submit: Submit double-spaced mss. Reports within 3-4 weeks. Pays 6 copies (sometimes more) and complimentary subscription. Editor sometimes comments on rejections.
Advice: His advice: "Try and try again! Inspiration is not automatic!"

☑ $ ◎ **ELLERY QUEEN'S MYSTERY MAGAZINE (Specialized: mystery)**, 475 Park Ave. S, 11th Floor, New York NY 10016, founded 1941.

Magazine Needs: *EQMM*, appears 11 times/year, primarily using short stories of mystery, crime or suspense. "We also publish short limericks and verse pertaining to the mystery field." As a sample the editor selected these lines from "Coffee Olé" by Marie E. Truitt:

> *But once he married, breakfasts were the nastiest of scenes;/On making coffee, Wifie didn't know a*
> *hill of beans./The bitter taste! . . . the inch-deep dregs! . . . he couldn't take much more!/It went from*
> *bad to mega-bad, till Fred let out a roar:/"I've had enough! It's Splitsville! There's just no other*
> *course!/And I hold within this cup, my Dear, the grounds for our divorce!"*

EQMM is 144 pgs., 5¼ × 8⁵⁄₁₆, professionally printed on newsprint, flat-spined with glossy paper cover. Subscription: $33.97. Sample: $2.95 (available on newsstands).

How to Submit: No previously published poems; simultaneous submissions OK. Include SASE with submissions. Reports in 3 months. Pays $5-50 plus 3 copies.

◩ $ ◿ ◎ **QUEEN'S QUARTERLY: A CANADIAN REVIEW (Specialized: regional)**, Queen's University, 184 Union St., Kingston, Ontario K7L 3N6 Canada, phone (613)545-2667, e-mail qquartly@post.quee nsu.ca, website http://www.info.queensu.ca/quarterly, founded 1893, editor Boris Castel.

Magazine Needs: *Queen's Quarterly* is "a general interest intellectual review featuring articles on science, politics, humanities, arts and letters, extensive book reviews, some poetry and fiction. We are especially interested in poetry by Canadian writers. Shorter poems preferred." They have published poetry by Evelyn Lau, Sue Nevill and Raymond Souster. There are about 12 pgs. of poetry in each issue, 6 × 9, 224 pgs. Circulation is 3,500. They receive about 400 submissions of poetry a year, use approximately 40. Subscription: $20 Canadian, $25 US for US and foreign subscribers. Sample: $6.50 US.

How to Submit: Submit up to 6 poems at a time. No simultaneous submissions. E-mail submissions OK. Reports in 1 month. Pays usually $50 (Canadian)/poem, "but it varies," plus 2 copies.

$ ▢ ◎ **RADIANCE: THE MAGAZINE FOR LARGE WOMEN (Specialized: women)**, P.O. Box 30246, Oakland CA 94604, phone/fax (510)482-0680, e-mail radmag2@aol.com, website http://www.radiancema gazine.com, founded 1984, publisher/editor Alice Ansfield.

Magazine Needs: *Radiance* appears quarterly. "Now fourteen years in print, *Radiance* offers support, information, and inspiration for women *all* sizes of large. *Radiance* has grown to become one of the leading resources in the worldwide size acceptance movement. Each issue features dynamic large women from all walks of life, along with articles and essays on health, media, fashion, and politics. Our focus is on celebrating body acceptance. We now have a 'young activists' column—devoted to helping plus-size children feel seen, love, and vauled for who they are, whatever their size. Keeping in mind that our magazine is geared toward large women, we look for poetry from women of any size and men who don't accept society's stereotypical standards of beauty and weight—but who celebrate women's bodies, sexuality, search for self-esteem and personal growth." As a sample she quotes "Homage to My Hips" by Lucille Clifton:

> *these hips are big hips/they need space to/move around in./they don't fit into little/petty places. these*
> *hips/are free hips./they don't like to be held back./these hips have never been enslaved,/they go where*
> *they want to go/they do what they want to do./these hips are mighty hips./these hips are magic hips./*
> *i have known them/to put a spell on a man and/spin him like a top!*

Radiance is 60 pgs., magazine-sized, professionally printed on glossy stock with full-color paper cover, saddle-stapled, 4-color graphics, photos and ads. Circulation is 14,000 "and growing" for 5,000 subscriptions, 8,000 selling on newsstands or in bookstores; 2,000 distributed free to media and clothing stores for large women. Subscription: $20/year. Sample: $3.50.

How to Submit: Submit typed ms. Assistant Editor usually comments on rejections. Send SASE for guidelines. Reports in 4-6 months. Pays $10-15 plus contributor's copy. Buys one-time rights. Reviews related books of poetry in 500-800 words.

☑ ◿ **RAG MAG; BLACK HAT PRESS**, P.O. Box 12, Goodhue MN 55027, phone (651)923-4590, founded 1982, poetry editor and publisher Beverly Voldseth.

Magazine Needs: *Rag Mag* accepts poetry of "any length or style. No pornographic SM violent crap." They have published poetry by Robert Bly, Ann Niedringhouse and Kerri Brostrom. As a sample the editor selected these lines from "What the Plants Say" by Tom Hennen:

> *Weed, it is you with your bad reputation that I/love the most. Teach me not to care what anyone/has*
> *to say about me. Help me to be in the world/for no purpose at all except for the joy of sunlight/and*
> *rain. Keep me close to the edge where every-/thing wild begins.*

Rag Mag, appearing twice a year (usually in April and October), is 80-112 pgs., perfect-bound, 6 × 9, professionally printed in dark type with ads for books, matte card cover. The editor says she accepts about 10% of poetry received. Press run is 250 for 80 subscribers of which 8 are libraries. Subscription: $10. Sample: $6.

How to Submit: "Send up to eight pages of your best work with brief bio. Something that tells a story, creates images, speaks to the heart. Please proofread carefully before submitting. Poetry will be published as is." *Name and address on each page. SASE required for return of work or response.* Previously published poems and simultaneous submissions OK, "but please acknowledge both." Send SASE for guidelines. Pays 1 copy. Acquires first or one-time rights. Reviews books of poetry. Open to unsolicited reviews but has room for only 1 or 2/issue. Poets may also send books for review consideration.

Book/Chapbook Needs & How to Submit: Black Hat Press is *not* considering chapbooks or book-length mss of any kind until further notice. They have published *Boom Town* by Diane Glancy and *Crawling Out the Window* (a book of prose poems) by Tom Hennen. Black Hat Press also publishes a yearly poetry calendar open to submissions from poets residing in MN. Send SASE for details to Poetry Calendar, P.O. Box 130121, Roseville, MN 55113.

THE RAINTOWN REVIEW; THE RAINTOWN REVIEW: A FORUM FOR THE ES-SAYIST'S ART; HARMONA PRESS (Specialized: form/style), P.O. Box 370, Pittsboro IN 46167, founded 1996, editor Harvey Stanbrough.

Magazine Needs: *The Raintown Review* is published quarterly, in March, June, September and October, contains only poetry. They want well-crafted poems—metered, syllabic, or free-verse. They have published poetry by Janice L. Braud, William J. Middleton, Sally-Ann Hard and Jane B. Roth. As a sample the editor selected these lines from "Ode to Legs" by Dara McLaughlin:

> *Was it nature's reckless throw of indiscriminate die/Part of a grand, irreversible plan/Or did I share*
> *a night or two/hunkered down with the devil?*

TRR is about 60 pgs., chapbook-sized, desktop-published and saddle-stapled with card cover. They receive about 900 poems a year, accept approximately 10-15%. Press run is about 200 with most going to subscribers and contributors. Subscription: $15/year. Sample: $4.50.

How to Submit: Submit up to 6 poems at a time. Previously published poems and simultaneous submissions OK. Cover letter preferred. Disk submissions OK. "We prefer contributors write for guidelines before submitting work." Often comments on rejections. Send SASE for detailed guidelines. Reports in 2-3 weeks. Pays 1 copy. Acquires first or one-time rights.

Book/Chapbook Needs: HarMona Press publishes chapbooks through subsidy arrangements only.

Also Offers: Sponsors contests. Write for details.

Advice: The editor says, "If you want glowing reviews, send your manuscript to your mother. For valid critique, send it to an editor."

RALPH'S REVIEW; RC'S STAMP HOT LINE, 129A Wellington Ave., Albany NY 12203, e-mail rcpub@juno.com, founded 1988, editor R. Cornell.

Magazine Needs: *Ralph's Review*, published quarterly, contains "mostly new writers, short stories and poems." They want "horror/fantasy, environmental. No more than 30 lines." They do not want "rape, racial, political poems." They have published poetry by Kim Laico and John Grey. The editor says *Ralph's Review* is 20-35 pgs., 8½×11, photocopied, sometimes with soft cover, with art, cartoons and graphics. They receive about 80-100 poems a year, accept approximately 40%. Press run is 75-100 for 35 subscribers of which 3 are libraries; 30-40 distributed free to bookstores, toy stores, antique and coffee shops. Single copy: $2; subscription: $15. Make checks payable to R. Cornell.

How to Submit: Submit up to 5 poems, with a $3 reading fee and SASE. Previously published poems and simultaneous submissions OK. Cover letter required. Time between acceptance and publication is 2-4 months. Seldom comments on rejections. Publish theme issues. Send SASE or e-mail for guidelines and upcoming themes. Reports in 2-3 weeks. Pays 1 copy. Acquires all rights. Returns rights 1 year after acceptance. Reviews books in up to 5,000 words in single-book format. Open to unsolicited reviews. Poets may also send books for review consideration.

Advice: The editor says, "Books are selling like crazy; keep writing, check out current trends, submit to as many publications as you can afford."

RAMBUNCTIOUS PRESS; RAMBUNCTIOUS REVIEW, 1221 W. Pratt, Chicago IL 60626, founded 1982, poetry editors Richard Goldman, Beth Hausler and Nancy Lennon.

Magazine Needs: *Rambunctious Review* appears once yearly. They want "spirited, quality poetry, fiction, photos and graphics. Some focus on local work, but all work is considered." As a sample the editors selected these lines from "I Grew Up in Arles" by Anne Valdez:

> *I grew up in Arles, South Chicago,/The town where Vincent lived/I never knew the tavern/cafe/bars/*
> *But I knew the trees and houses/And people with spider-jointed fingers.*

RR is 48 pgs., 7×10, handsomely printed and saddle-stapled. They receive about 700-800 submissions a year, accept approximately 50-60. Circulation is about 500 for 200 subscribers. Sample: $4.

How to Submit: Will consider simultaneous submissions. No submissions accepted June 1 through August 31. No queries. Occasionally comments on mss. Publishes theme issues. Reports in 9 months. Pays 2 copies.

VISIT THE WRITER'S DIGEST WEBSITE at www.writersdigest.com for hot new markets, daily market updates, writers' guidelines and much more.

insider report

Adversity leads poet to her life's work

Stellasue Lee

Twelve years ago, poet and editor Stellasue Lee had little time or interest for poetry. Having been diagnosed with a terminal illness, Lee was spending 20 hours a day confined to bed. She says, "During that time, I developed this perfectly natural need to leave something of myself, so I began to write a novel. I had also heard about a writers' conference in Port Townsend, Washington. I didn't know how I was going to get the wherewithal to attend a ten-day conference, but I was determined to go and did go. Then one night during the conference, I was sitting out in the bluff of Puget Sound looking over the straits and I had an epiphany—I wanted to live. I really wanted to live, and I wanted to learn how to write." After the conference, Lee returned home to Los Angeles determined to find a way to achieve her goals.

Lee's first step was to consult another physician about her diagnosis—hemolytic anemia. That physician determined the anemia was the result of another medical problem. Lee underwent major surgery within one week of the consultation and had a large tumor removed. "I looked better two days after the surgery than I had looked for the preceding four years." With one goal achieved, Lee went on a quest to find a mentor to help her learn to write. "I attended every single writing event in Los Angeles. One Saturday morning I was sitting in Women's Writers West and Jack Grapes came in to do the feature. I thought, 'My God, I could really learn from him.'" Again turning a wish into reality, Lee began working with Grapes, the editor of *ONTHEBUS Magazine* and a popular writing instructor in the Los Angeles area. Lee says, "Jack teaches his students how to write by using good writing as an example. It took me a while, but I learned how to write."

Through the readings she did while studying with Grapes, Lee learned appreciation for another writing form besides the novel—poetry. "I just fell in love with poetry. I had never read much poetry, had never really thought much about poetry, but I just flat fell in love with it. The last ten years I have spent totally immersed in poetry." To date, Lee's poems have been published in over 60 journals. They also have been included in three collections published by

STELLASUE LEE

Poet and Poetry Editor
Publication: Rattle

Bombshelter Press, *After I Fall*, *Over to You* and *13 Los Angeles Poets*.

While immersed in poetry, Lee also inadvertently guided herself toward a new career. Because of her prolonged illness, she had left her job as a real estate broker—a position she occupied for more than 20 years—and was working 3 part-time jobs to sustain herself. But a pivotal event during a poetry party she was attending changed all that: Lee says, "I was talking to fellow poet Fred Fox about his work when he asked about the black eye I had obtained that very same day. I told him one of my bosses had thrown a paperweight that accidentally hit me. Fred said it was an unforgivable act and that it couldn't go on another minute. He gave me an address and said, 'You show up here on Tuesday for a job interview.'"

"After Watching Too Many Spy Movies"

She mistook me for a German friend she had
met while traveling and she was surprised
to find me in the states with such improved English.
I told her I have always been American,
but while in Germany, I fake my accent.
She slapped me and asked me if that was all I faked.
By then, I figured it was time to tell her the facts,
that I was a secret agent and caring for any woman
was against the rules—I told her that was why
I had to leave so soon: I feared loving her too much.
Her eyes camped in bewilderment.
She asked me why then I pretended to be gay in Germany
and why I chose to lead her brother on so strongly.
I had stepped deeply into a failing script, so I insisted
that her brother was, in fact, not really her brother.
Then I turned and ran sideways across the street,
disappearing like coincidence behind a rolling bus.

(by Sam Pierstorff, originally published in *Rattle*, Issue number 10, Volume 4, Number 2, Winter 1998; reprinted by permission of the author)

The address was for a real estate management company run by Fox's son, Alan. Alan Fox hired Lee to manage the staff of a 250-unit apartment building. Six months later the apartment building was sold. Alan Fox, who, coincidentally, was also a student of Grapes, then offered Lee the editorship of his publication *Rattle*. Lee says, "*Rattle* had begun as a class project but Alan had a bigger vision for the publication. He said, 'Stellasue, take it any place you want.' At the time, I had been on the staff of *ONTHEBUS* but I wasn't familiar with all the ins and outs of editing or marketing a literary journal." Despite her lack of editorial experience, Lee has been very successful with *Rattle*, taking it from a chapbook with a print run of 300 copies to a nearly 200-page, perfect-bound, professionally printed journal with a print run of 4,000 copies and carried by such major distributors as Ingram.

Through her position as poetry editor of *Rattle*, Lee receives in excess of 5,000 submissions a year with each submission containing anywhere from 3 to 10 poems. With all those submissions, Lee has a method to prevent burnout. "Every envelope I open, every group of poems I unfold, I do it deliberately with the idea that this is going to be the best piece I have ever read. Ninety-nine percent of the time, I can tell within the first three lines if this is someone who knows how to write. However, in spite of that, I have made a pledge to myself to honor the writer by reading the entire submission from beginning to end. I will make comments from time to time. Although I've found that even though authors say they want comments, few accept them gracefully."

Lee feels that quite a few of the submissions she receives are from people who are what she calls "loving hands at home." She adds, "Sometime back in school, these people may have read a poem by Robert Frost that they liked and thought, 'Well, I can do that.' So they sit down and write rhyming poetry about birds and bees and trees and flowers. They think they create a nice image that is poetry. But poetry goes much deeper. Poetry is voice and the voice is a musical instrument that should be able to cover every octave.

"You should be able to write like you talk or write from a deep voice with deep rich imaging. You should be able to know something of the speech-making voice of the Bible or the big speech-making voice of Martin Luther King. That is all a part of the musical instrument of the voice. And you don't get that without really opening yourself up to training, and training is reading."

By reading the classics as well as the work of up-and-coming poets, Lee says beginning poets can better determine the quality of their own work. "You have to know what other poets are doing to be able to determine what's good and what isn't, what works and what doesn't in your own poetry. I think it is so natural for writers, because of the loneliness of writing and the lack of feedback, to not really know if what they have written is good. Even for those who've been published a lot that issue continues to crop up. Evaluating your own writing is a constant soul-searching process."

Also committed to supporting writers, Lee often lectures at universities about the passion and commitment of writing and what it takes to be a writer. "No one should be fooled into thinking the time and effort they devote to improving their writing won't take away from their families or from other activities. But if you have a passion for something, you should be willing to put in the required effort. However, if it is too much effort, then maybe you should have a passion for something else. When I accept a submission, I consider that as validation for the time and effort the author has put into the piece, that what they are doing is important and people appreciate it."

—*Chantelle Bentley*

Also Offers: They run annual contests in poetry, fiction and short drama. Send SASE for information.

📷 🖉 **RARACH PRESS (Specialized: bilingual/foreign language)**, 1005 Oakland Dr., Kalamazoo MI 49008, phone (616)388-5631, founded 1981, owner Ladislav Hanka. Not open to unsolicited mss.

N $🖉 RATTAPALLAX; REPOSSESSED HEAD PUBLISHING HOUSE, 532 La Guardia Place, Suite 353, New York NY 10012, phone (212)560-7459, e-mail rattapallax@hotmail.com, website http://www.ratta pallax.com, founded 1998, editor-in-chief George Dickerson, senior editor Judith Werner.
Magazine Needs: "A biannual journal of contemporary literature, *Rattapallax* is Wallace Steven's word for the sound of thunder." They want "extraordinary work in poetry and short fiction—words that are well-crafted and sing, words that recapture the music of the language, words that bump into each other in extraordinary ways and leave the reader touched and haunted by the experience. We do not want ordinary words about ordinary things." They have published poetry by Lamont B. Steptoe, Kate Light, Karen Swenson and Rick Pernod. As a sample the editors selected these lines from "This kindled by *Guade Virgo Salutata*, a motet by John Dunstable, c. 1400" by Mark Nichols:

> *Slow-spreading English music, as though/we watched a pale drawing-off of the night/from delicate fields, and heard a haunt/of griffins in a fog close by the house./How one of the griffins, without fire, has wrought,/by a concentration of time, a face in gnarled elmwood. . . .*

The editors say *Rattapallax* is 128 pgs., magazine-sized, offset printed and perfect-bound, with 12 pt. C1S cover, includes photos, drawings, and CD with poets. They receive about 5,000 poems a year, accept approximately 2%. Press run is 2,000 for 100 subscribers of which 50 are libraries, 1,200 shelf sales; 200 distributed free to contributors, reviews and promos. Single copy: $7.95; subscription: $14/1 year. Sample (including guidelines): $7.95. Make checks payable to Repossessed Head.
How to Submit: Submit 3-5 poems at a time. No previously published poems; simultaneous submissions OK. Cover letter preferred. E-mail submissions OK. "SASE is required and e-mailed submissions should be sent as simple text." Reads submissions all year; issue deadlines are May 1 and November 1. Time between acceptance and publication is 2-6 months. Poems are circulated to an editorial board. "The editor-in-chief, senior editor and associate editor review all the submissions then decide on which to accept every week. Near publication time, all accepted work is narrowed and unused work is kept for the next issue." Often comments on rejections. Obtain guidelines via e-mail or website. Reports in 2 months. Always sends prepublication galleys. Acquires first rights.
Book/Chapbook Needs & How to Submit: Repossessed Head Publishing House publishes "contemporary poets and writers with unique powerful voices." They publish 5 paperbacks and 3 chapbooks/year. Books are usually 64 pgs., 6×9, offset printed and perfect-bound with 12 pt. C1S cover, include drawings and photos. Query first with a few sample poems and cover letter with brief bio and publication credits and SASE. Requires authors to first be published in *Rattapallax*. Replies to queries in 1 month; to mss in 2 months. Pays royalties of 10-25%. Order sample books by sending SASE and $7.
Also Offers: Website includes information about the journal, submission guidelines, upcoming readings, names of editors, sample poems and links.

🖉 **RATTLE**, 13440 Ventura Blvd. #200, Sherman Oaks CA 91423, phone (818)788-3232 or (818)999-5080, fax (818)788-2831, e-mail stellasuel@aol.com, website http://www.rattle.com, founded 1994, editor Alan Fox, poetry editor Stellasue Lee.
Magazine Needs: *Rattle* is a biannual poetry publication which also includes interviews with poets, essays and reviews. They want "high quality poetry of any form, three pages maximum. Nothing unintelligible." They have published poetry by Charles Bukowski, Philip Levine, Yusef Komunyakaa, Colette Inez, Dorianne Laux, Virginia Hamilton Adair and Sam Hamill. As a sample the editor selected these lines from "Other Than Where You Were" by Willie James King:

> *You look long into/the black blue nostrils/of a mule, half-a-dollar-sized/holes, laced by the liquid of/ its breathing, as fog, white as/fire, oozes out of the openings/to stab winter's air, before it/disappears, as ghosts are said/to do; and, you watch, while/it lips brown blades of sage/left in the late fall field, where/it grazes; its eyes, like new/marbles, glued to you and/all that you do,*

Rattle is 176 pgs., 5½×8½, neatly printed and perfect-bound with 4-color coated card cover. They receive about 5,000 poems a year, accept approximately 200. Press run is 4,000. Subscription: $28/2 years. Sample: $8. Make checks payable to Alan Fox.
How to Submit: Submit up to 5 poems at a time. Includes SASE. No previously published poems or simultaneous submissions. Cover letter, address, telephone number and e-mail address if possible is required as well as a bio. E-mail and fax submissions OK. Reads submissions all year. Seldom comments on rejections. Reports in 6-8 weeks. Pays 2 copies. Rights revert to authors upon publication. Welcomes essays up to 2,000 words on the writing process and book reviews on poetry up to 250 words. Send books for review consideration.

🖉 📷 **RAW DOG PRESS; POST POEMS (Specialized: humor)**, 151 S. West St., Doylestown PA 18901-4134, phone (215)345-6838, website http://www.freeyellow.com/members/rawdog, founded 1977, poetry editor R. Gerry Fabian.
Magazine Needs: "Publishes Post Poems annual—a postcard series. We want short poetry (three to seven lines) on any subject. The positive poem or the poem of understated humor always has an inside track. No taboos,

however. All styles considered. Anything with rhyme had better be immortal." They have published poetry by Don Ryan, Lyn Lifshin, John Grey, Wes Patterson and the editor, R. Gerry Fabian, who selected his poem, "Arc Welder," as a sample:

> After years of burning/he pressed his lips against hers/and sealed out any doubt.

How to Submit: Submit 3-5 poems at a time. Send SASE for catalog to buy samples. The editor "always" comments on rejections. Pays copies. Acquires all rights. Returns rights on mention of first publication. Sometimes reviews books of poetry.

Book/Chapbook Needs & How to Submit: Raw Dog Press welcomes new poets and detests second-rate poems from 'name' poets. We exist because we are dumb like a fox, but even a fox takes care of its own."

Also Offers: He says he will offer criticism for a fee; "if someone is desperate to publish and is willing to pay, we will use our vast knowledge to help steer the ms in the right direction. We will advise against it, but as P.T. Barnum said. . . ." Website includes basic Raw Dog Press information, general poets' Q and A and general writer's guidelines.

Advice: The editor also says, "I get more poems that do not fit my needs. At least one quarter of all poets waste their postage because they do not read the requirements."

☑ ◑ **THE RAW SEED REVIEW**, 780 Merion Greene, Charlottesville VA 22901, founded 1998, editor Sam Taylor.

Magazine Needs: The Raw Seed Review appears biannually and intends "to be a mecca of imagination, intensity and innovation. We encourage a more expansive and fluid 'realism' than the one that has dominated contemporary poetry, a realism rooted in an awareness that all language is myth and that the world itself is utterly mysterious." They want "poetry motivated by inner urgency and inspired by an original vision. Work that explores and creates reality, foraging in new directions, and opening into the unknown. No unnecesary, sentimental, dogmatic or superficial work." They have published poetry by James Grabill, Alexandra Grilikhes, Martin Nakell, Duane Locke and Leonard Cirino. TRSR is 80 pgs., 6×9, professionally printed, perfect-bound with color cover, includes art and photography. Accept approximately 5% of poems received. Press run is 500. Subscription: $12 for 2 issues. Sample: $7.

How to Submit: Submit 2-6 poems at a time. Previously published poems (only if exceptional) and simultaneous submissions OK. Cover letter preferred with "brief, sincere comments on the author's artistic perspective, plus short bio and credits." Time between acceptance and publication is 1-6 months. "Editor makes final decision after consultation with assistant editor." Sometimes comments on rejections; always for subscribers. "Usually reports within six weeks—sometimes work under serious consideration is held up to four months." Reports in 1-12 weeks. Pays 1-3 copies. Acquires first rights. Staff reviews books and chapbooks of poetry and other magazines. Send books for review consideration.

Advice: The editor says, "We are particularly interested in how the unknown is encountered within our world and in the interaction between the timeless soul and the modern face of the earth. We highly recommend sampling an issue before submitting. Advice for beginners: Plunge deep within yourself, beneath identity, language and reason; then reemerge into language. Follow the intuitive imagery and instincts in the body and subconscious."

◑ **RB'S POETS' VIEWPOINT**, P.O. Box 940, Eunice NM 88231, phone (505)394-2611, founded 1989, editor Robert Bennett.

Magazine Needs: RB's published bimonthly, features poetry and cartoons. They want "general and religious poetry, sonnets and sijo with a 21-line limit." They do not want "vulgar language." They have published poetry by Marion Ford Park, Ruth Ditmer Ream, Ruth Halbrooks and Delphine Ledoux. As a sample the editor selected these lines from "Star Fantasy" by Mary Strand:

> On the hill where Will-O-Wisps camp/I danced to the chirpings of crickets/by the glow of the lightning-bug's lamp./When the stars in their celestial thickets/beckoned me with come-hither winks/I climbed a dangling moonbeam/& skipped on heavenly rinks.

RB's is 34 pgs., digest-sized, photocopied, saddle-stapled with drawings and cartoons. They receive about 400 poems a year, accept approximately 90%. Press run is 60. Subscription: $8. Sample: $2. Make checks payable to Robert Bennett.

How to Submit: Submit 3 poems typed single space with a $1.50 per poem reading fee. Previously published poems and simultaneous submissions OK. Reads submissions February, April, June, August, October and December only. Time between acceptance and publication is 1 month. "Poems are selected by one editor." Often comments on rejections. Send SASE for guidelines. Reports in 1 month. Pays 1 copy. Acquires one-time rights.

Also Offers: Sponsors contests for general poetry, religious poetry, sonnets and sijo with 1st Prizes of $20, $6 and $5, respectively, plus publication in RB's. There is a $1.50 per poem entry fee, except the sijo category, which has a 50¢ per poem fee. Send SASE for guidelines.

☑ ◑ **RE:AL—THE JOURNAL OF LIBERAL ARTS**, Dept. PM, Box 13007, Stephen F. Austin State University, Nacogdoches TX 75962, phone (409)468-2059, e-mail f_real@titan.sfasu.edu, website http://www.titan.sfasu.edu, founded 1968, editor W. Dale Hearell.

Magazine Needs: RE:AL is a "Liberal Arts Forum" using short fiction, drama, reviews and interviews; contains editorial notes and personalized "Contributors' Notes"; printed in the fall and spring. They "hope to use from 90 to 110 pages of poetry per issue, typeset in editor's office. RE:AL welcomes all styles and forms that display craft, insight and accessibility." They receive between 60-100 poems/week. "We need a better balance between open and generic forms. We're also interested in critical writings on poems or writing poetry and translations with a bilingual format (permissions from original author)." It is handsomely printed, "reserved format," perfect-bound with line drawings and photos. Circulation approximately 400, "more than half of which are major college libraries." Subscriptions also in Great Britain, Ireland, Italy, Holland, Puerto Rico, Brazil, Croatia, and Canada. Subscription: $20-$30 for institutions. Sample: $10.

How to Submit: Submit original and copy. "Editors prefer a statement that ms is not being simultaneously submitted; however, this fact is taken for granted when we receive a ms." Writer's guidelines for SASE. They acknowledge receipt of submissions and strive for a 1-month decision. Submissions during summer semesters may take longer. Pays 2 copies. Reviews are assigned, but queries about doing reviews are welcome.

⊕ ∅ REALITY STREET EDITIONS, 4 Howard Court, Peckham Rye, London SE15 3PH United Kingdom, phone (0171)639-7297, e-mail 100344.2546@compuserve.com, editor Ken Edwards. They currently do not accept unsolicited mss.

▨ ⊕ ∅ THE REATER; WRECKING BALL PRESS, 18 Church St., North Cave, Brough, East Yorkshire HU15 2LW United Kingdom, phone (01430)424346, founded 1997, editor Shane Rhodes.
Magazine Needs: *The Reater* appears 2 times a year and "accepts good hammered home poetry—also accepts b&w photographs and illustrations." They want "any form, any length; any subject matter can be made interesting if you're worth your salt. As for purpose, you do it because you can't help doing it. Strictly no flowers, just blunt chiselled poetry. No religious verse." They have published poetry by Charles Bukowski, Gerald Locklin and Labi Siffre. As a sample the editor selected these lines from "Even in the Dust We Brush From Our Shelves" by Fred Voss:

> There is something that has never died/in each cat/on a balcony/as we spend our lives chiselling our
> names into the headstones/of our graves,/there is something that has never died . . .

The Reater is approximately 200 pgs., 6×9, professionally printed and perfect-bound with color texturized card cover, includes b&w photos. Press run is 900 for 400 subscribers of which 150 are libraries, 400 shelf sales; 100 distributed free to contributors.Subscription: £18/year (UK), $36/2 issues (US). Sample: £9.50 (UK), $20 (US). Make checks payable to Wrecking Ball Press.
How to Submit: Submit 4-10 poems at a time. No previously published poems. Cover letter preferred. "Handwritten manuscripts will not be looked at." Seldom comments on rejections. Send SASE (or SAE and IRC) for guidelines. Reports in 3-4 months. Pays 1 copy. Reviews books and chapbooks of poetry. Poets may also send books for review consideration.

⊕ ∅ THE RED CANDLE PRESS; CANDELABRUM, 9 Milner Rd., Wisbech, Cambs PE13 2LR England, founded 1970, editor M.L. McCarthy, M.A., administrative editor Helen Gordon, B.A.
Magazine Needs: Red Candle Press was "founded to encourage poets working in traditional-type verse, metrical unrhymed or metrical rhymed. We're more interested in poems than poets: that is, we're interested in what sort of poems an author produces, not in his or her personality." They publish the magazine, *Candelabrum*, twice yearly (April and October). They want "good-quality metrical verse, with rhymed verse specially wanted. Elegantly cadenced free verse is acceptable. No weak stuff (moons and Junes, loves and doves, etc.) No chopped-up prose pretending to be free verse. Any length up to about 40 lines for *Candelabrum*, any subject, including eroticism (but not porn)—satire, love poems, nature lyrics, philosophical—any subject, but nothing racist or sexist." They have published poetry by Peter Russell, Ann Keith, Michael Newman and Andrea Abraham. The editors offer these lines by Michael Fantina as a sample:

> Spoons of hammered silver sit and merge/With pewter plates and well-honed disks of steel/Strewn like
> fallen dolmens. Like some black eel,/Familiar of a mage or demiurge,/The adder coils around the
> cranium,/Dark skull, once blended in delirium.

The digest-sized magazine, staple-spined, small type, exemplifies their intent to "pack in as much as possible, wasting no space, and try to keep a neat appearance with the minimum expense." They get in about 40 pgs. (some 70 poems) in each issue. They receive about 2,000 submissions a year, use approximately 5% of those, sometimes holding over poems for the next year. Press run is 900 for 700 subscribers of which 22 are libraries. Sample: $4 in bills only; checks not accepted.
How to Submit: "Submit anytime. IRCs essential for reply and please check the weight if you wish your ms returned. Each poem on a separate sheet please, neat typescripts or neat legible manuscripts. Please no dark, oily photostats, no colored ink (only black or blue). Author's name and address on each sheet, please." No simultaneous submissions. Reports in about 2 months. Pays 1 copy.
Advice: The editor comments, "Traditional-type poetry is much more popular here in Britain, and we think also in the United States, now than it was in 1970, when we founded *Candelabrum*. We always welcome new poets, especially traditionalists, and we like to hear from the U.S.A. as well as from here at home. General tip: Study the various outlets at the library, or buy a copy of *Candelabrum*, or borrow a copy from a subscriber, before you go to the expense of submitting your work. The Red Candle Press regrets that, because of bank charges, it is unable to accept dollar cheques. However, it is always happy to accept U.S. dollar bills."

⦿ **RED CEDAR REVIEW**, 17C Morrill Hall, Dept. of English, Michigan State University, East Lansing MI 48824, e-mail rcreview@pilot.msu.edu, website http://www.msu.edu/~rcreview, founded 1963, poetry editor Carrie Preston.

Magazine Needs: *Red Cedar* is a literary biannual which uses poetry—"any subject, form, length; the only requirement is originality and vision." The editor encourages work "that shows careful thought and unification of imagery." They have published poetry by Margaret Atwood, Diane Wakoski, Jim Harrison and Stuart Dybek. As a sample the editor selected these lines from "Last Words" by Gary Duehr:

> *Do flowers, flowering, go through/Excruciating amounts of pain to put out/Buds, petals?—the opposite/*
> *Of pre-amputees, cut to cut off their/Naked suffering;/Waiting, drugless, they beg for anything/But the*
> *next breath in.*

The review is 120 pgs., digest-sized. They receive about 500 submissions a year, use approximately 20. Press run is 400 for 200 subscribers of which 100 are libraries. Single copy: $5; subscription: $10. Sample: $3.50.

How to Submit: Submit up to 5 poems at a time with SASE. No previously published poems. Simultaneous submissions are discouraged. Reports in 1-4 months. Pays 2 copies. Sometimes comments on rejections. Send SASE for submission guidelines.

Also Offers: Website includes guidelines, subscription information, order forms for sample copies, and biographical information about our staff.

⦿ **RED DANCEFLOOR PRESS; RED DANCEFLOOR**, P.O. Box 4974, Lancaster CA 93539-4974, fax (805)946-8082, e-mail dubpoet@as.net, website http://www.web.as.net/~dubpoet, founded 1989, editor David Goldschlag.

Magazine Needs & How to Submit: The press publishes the magazine, *Red Dancefloor*. However, the magazine has suspended publication until further notice.

Book Needs: Red Dancefloor Press also publishes full-length books and poetry audiotapes. No restrictions on form, length or subject matter. They have published poetry by Sean T. Dougherty, Gerry Lafemina, Laurel Ann Bogen and Michael Stephans. As a sample the editor selected the first stanza from "The Novena of Payphones" in *Nicotine Jukebox* by Marc C Jacksina:

> *The coins are rolling between/my fingers like rosary beads.//This prayer to hear your voice/is a long-*
> *shot scratched on a/cocktail napkin, the whisper/trapped in the space/between hello and click/stained*
> *by liquor, as clear as the air/I breathe on the way to the car//out of cigarettes,/and drunk.*

He says, the author may want to get a copy of a book, chapbook or tape before submitting. (Send 5½×8½ SASE with first-class stamp for catalog.)

How to Submit: "We openly accept submissions for books and tapes, but *please* query first with ten samples and a cover letter explaining which area of our press you are interested in. Listing credits in a cover letter is fine, but don't go crazy." E-mail and fax submission OK. "E-mail submissions may be embedded in the message itself or attached as ASCII, MS Word or Wordperfect files." Queries and submissions via e-mail "strongly encouraged."

🅝 ⬇ $⦿ **RED DEER PRESS**, Box 5005, 56 Ave. & 32 St., Red Deer, Alberta T4N 5H5 Canada, phone (403)342-3321, fax (403)357-3639, e-mail kgough@rdc.ab.ca, founded 1975, poetry editor Nicole Marcotic.

Book/Chapbook Needs & How to Submit: Red Deer Press publishes 1 poetry paperback per year under the imprint Writing West. They have published poetry by Monty Reid, Stephen Scobie and Nicole Marcotic. Books are usually 80-100 pgs. Submit 8-10 poems at a time. Simultaneous submissions OK. Cover letter required. "Must include SASE. Canadian poets are preferred." Time between acceptance and publication is 4-6 months. Replies to queries in 4-6 months. Pays royalties.

⦿ **RED DRAGON PRESS**, P.O. Box 19425, Alexandria VA 22320-0425, founded 1993, editor/publisher Laura Qa.

Book/Chapbook Needs: Red Dragon Press publishes 3-4 chapbooks/year. They want "innovative, progressive and experimental poetry and prose using literary symbolism, and aspiring to the creation of meaningful new ideas, forms and methods. We are proponents of works that represent the nature of man as androgynous, as in the fusing of male and female symbolism, and we support works that deal with psychological and parapsychological topics." They have published poetry by Suzette Bishhop, Patrick Russell Gibbons, Laura Qa and Dee Snyder. As a sample the editor selected these lines from "In the Beauty Parlor" by Grace Cavalieri:

> *Language was not built for her so/she murmured a thank you that/came out like a growl/which meant*
> *she was grateful/for something she/wanted/instead of something she didn't.*

Chapbooks are usually 64 pgs., 8½×5⅜, offset printed, perfect-bound on trade paper with 1-10 illustrations.

How to Submit: Submit up to 5 poems at a time with SASE. Previously published poems and simultaneous submissions OK. Cover letter preferred with brief bio. Reading fee: $5 for poetry and short fiction, $10 for novels; check or money order payable to Red Dragon Press. Time between acceptance and publication is 8 months. Poems are circulated to an editorial board. "Poems are selected for consideration by the publisher, then circulated to senior editor and/or poets previously published for comment. Poems are returned to the publisher for further action; i.e., rejection or acceptance for publication in an anthology or book by a single author. Frequently submission of additional works is required before final offer is made, especially in the process for a book by a single author." Often comments on rejections. Charges criticism fee of $10 per page on request.

Reports on queries in 6-10 weeks, to mss in 6-12 months. For sample books, purchase at book stores, or mail order direct from Red Dragon Press at the above address.

$ ⊘ RED HEN PRESS; RED HEN POETRY CONTEST, P.O. Box 902582, Palmdale CA 93590-2582, fax (818)831-0649, e-mail redhen@vpg.net, website http://www.vpg.net/redhen, founded 1993, publisher Mark E. Cull, editor Kate Gale.

Book/Chapbook Needs: Red Hen Press wants "good literary fiction and poetry" and publishes 4 paperbacks, one selected through a competition. "Translations are fine. No rhyming poetry." They have published poetry by Dr. Benjamin Saltman, Dr. Angela Ball, Ricardo Means Ybarra and Marlene Pearson. Books are usually 64-96 pgs., 5×7 or 6×9, professionally printed and perfect-bound with trade paper cover, includes paintings and photos.

How to Submit: Submit 5 poems at a time. Previously published poems and simultaneous submissions OK. Cover letter preferred. E-mail submissions OK. Time between acceptance and publication is 1 year. Poems are circulated to an editorial board. "One main poetry editor plus three to four contributing editors review the work." Seldom comments on rejections. Replies to queries in 1 month. Pays 10% royalties and 50 author's copies. To obtain sample books "write to our address for a catalog."

Also Offers: Sponsors the Red Hen Poetry Contest for a full-length collection (46-68 pgs.). Deadline is in June.

Advice: The editor says, "Be willing to help promote your own book and be helpful to the press. Writers need to help small presses survive."

⊕ ✓ ⊘ ⊘ RED HERRING; NORTHERN POETRY LIBRARY, MidNAG, East View, Stakeford, Choppinghm, Northumberland NEG2 5TR England, contact Pat Hallam.

Magazine Needs: *Red Herring* appears 2-3 times a year and "welcomes new original poetry of all kinds." They have published poetry by W.N. Herbert, Sean O'Brien and Matthew Sweeney. As a sample they selected these lines from "Sometimes" by Tom Kelly:

> He's making his point,/stabbing his fingers/at the air, his kids, I presume,/stand near the mother,/as he
> seethes/intoning his hate, his troubles/to those he loves/sometimes.

RH is 1 A3 sheet folded. They receive about 350 poems a year, accept approximately 15%. Press run is 3,000. "Most available free in Northumberland libraries." Single copy: £1. Make checks payable to Northumberland County Council.

How to Submit: No previously published poems; simultaneous submissions OK. "Copies preferred, as submissions cannot be returned." Time between acceptance and publication is 4 months. Poems are circulated to an editorial board. Seldom comments on rejections. Reports in 4 months. Pays 5 copies.

Also Offers: "The Northern Poetry Library was created in 1968 and aims to acquire all books of poetry in English by living writers published in the United Kingdom. Anyone who lives in the region covered by Cleveland, Cumbria, Durham, Northumberland and Tyne and Wear can be a member. (If you live outside this region you can become an associate member.) Membership is free and you can borrow books by post as well as by visiting the library, which is housed in Morpeth Library, Northumberland. The library also provides magazines, information on poets and poetry, and access to English Poetry, the database. The Northern Poetry Library is the most comprehensive collection of contemporary poetry in England outside London—a resource full of the pleasure of words and creativity."

$ ☯ ◎ RED MOON PRESS; THE RED MOON ANTHOLOGY; AMERICAN HAIBUN & HAIGA (Specialized: form/style), P.O. Box 2461, Winchester VA 22604-1661, phone (540)722-2156, e-mail redmoon @shentel.net, founded 1994, *American Haibun & Haiga* founded 1999, editor/publisher Jim Kacian.

Magazine Needs: *American Haibun & Haiga*, published annually in September, is the first western journal dedicated to these forms. *AH&H* is 120 pages, digest-sized, offset printed on quality paper with heavy stock four-color cover. They anticipate receiving several hundred submissions per year, and accepting about 10%. Expected print run will be 300 for subscribers and commercial distribution. Subscription: $15. A brief sample of the form will be available for SASE.

How to Submit: Submit up to 3 haibun or haiga at a time with SASE. No previously published work or simultaneous submissions. E-mail submissions OK. Submissions will be read by at least two editors. Time between acceptance and publication varies according to time of submission. Pays contributor's copies. Acquires first North American serial rights. "Only haibun and haiga will be considered. If the submitter is unfamiliar with the form, consult *Journey to the Interior*, edited by Bruce Ross, for samples and some discussion."

Book/Chapbook Needs: Red Moon Press "is the largest and most prestigious publisher of English-language haiku and related work in the world." They publish *The Red Moon Anthology,* an annual volume, the finest English-language haiku and related work published anywhere in the world in the previous 12 months. The anthology is 60 pgs., digest-sized, offset printed, perfect-bound, glossy 4-color heavy-stock cover. Inclusion is by nomination of the editorial board only. The press also publishes 6-8 volumes per year, usually 3-5 individual collections of English-language haiku, as well as 1-3 books of essays or criticism of haiku. Under other imprints the press also publishes chapbooks of various sizes and formats.

How to Submit: Query with book theme and information, and 30-40 poems, or draft of first chapter. Replies to queries in 2 weeks, to mss (if invited) in 2-3 months. "Each contract separately negotiated."

Advice: The editor says, "Haiku is a burgeoning and truly international form. It is nothing like what your fourth-grade teacher taught you years ago, and so it is best if you familiarize yourself with what is happening in the form (and its close relatives) today before submitting. We strive to give each poem, and every other work, plenty of space in which to resonate, and to provide a forum where the best of today's practitioners can be published with dignity and prestige."

◯ ⊘ **RED OWL MAGAZINE**, 35 Hampshire Rd., Portsmouth NH 03801-4815, phone (603)431-2691, e-mail redowlmag@aol.com, founded 1995, editor Edward O. Knowlton.
Magazine Needs: *Red Owl* is a biannual magazine of poetry and b&w art. "Ideally, poetry here might stress a harmony between nature and industry; add a pinch of humor for spice. Nothing introspective or downtrodden. Sometimes long poems are OK, yet poems which are 10 to 20 lines seem to fit best." They are also open to poems on the subjects of animals, gay/lesbian issues, horror, psychic/occult, science fiction/fantasy and women/feminism. They have published poetry by John Binns, John Grey, Albert Huffstickler, Nancy McGovern and Dawn Zapletal. As a sample the editor selected these lines from "Night Eye" by Nancy McGovern:

> colors shifting to mute tones/as though the skull of earth/held a candle within whose/wax draws sun-
> fire to/illuminate the center/and glow in the moon.

Red Owl is about 70 pgs., 8½×11, neatly photocopied in a variety of type styles and spiral-bound with a heavy stock cover and b&w art inside. "Out of a few hundred poems received, roughly one third are considered." Press run is 100 for 65 subscribers, 10 shelf sales. Single copy: $10; subscription: $20. Sample (including brief guidelines): $10. Makes checks payable to Edward O. Knowlton.
How to Submit: Submit 4 poems at a time. No previously published poems or simultaneous submissions. E-mail submissions OK "Relay cover letter and each poem separately." Cover letter preferred. "I only use the 'Net to answer questions; I'd prefer to receive the submissions I get via the U.S.P.S. since I feel it's more formal—and I'm not in that big of a hurry, nor do I feel that the world is coming to an end. . . ." Seldom comments on rejections. Reports in 3 weeks to 3 months. Pays 1 copy.
Advice: The editor says, "Try and be bright; hold your head up. Yes, there are hard times in the land of plenty, yet we might try to overshadow them. . . ."

⊘ **RED RAMPAN' PRESS; RED RAMPAN' REVIEW; RED RAMPAN' BROADSIDE SERIES**, Bishop House, 518 East Court St., Dyersburg TN 38024-4714, founded 1981, poetry editor Larry D. Griffin. Presently not accepting poetry.

🅽 ◯ ⊘ **RED ROCK REVIEW; RED ROCK POETRY AWARD**, English Dept. J2A, Community College of Southern Nevada, 3200 E. Cheyenne Ave., North Las Vegas NV 89030, phone (702)651-4094, e-mail rich_logsdon@ccsn.nevada.edu, website http://www.ccsn.nevada.edu/academics/departments/English/redrock.h tm, founded 1994, editor-in-chief Dr. Rich Logsdon, associate editor Todd Moffett.
Magazine Needs: *RRR* appears biannually and publishes "the best poetry available." They have published poetry by Stephen Liu, Alberto Rios, Naomi Shahib Nye and Katharine Coles. As a sample the editors selected these lines (poet unidentified):

> Oil paint, I've read/never completely dries./The breasts of Venus droop./Mona Lisa finally drops the
> smile./Glass, I've heard, is a liquid./Windows silently slide at night,/a slow motion sink, always/toward
> the floor, Christ ascending

They say *RRR* is about 130 pgs., magazine-sized, professionally printed and perfect-bound with 10 pt. cornwall, C1S cover. Accept approximately 15% of poems received a year. Press run is 1,000. Sample: $5.50.
How to Submit: Submit 2-3 poems at a time. No previously published poems; simultaneous submissions OK. Cover letter required. E-mail and disk submissions OK. Reads submissions September 1 through August 31 only. Time between acceptance and publication is 3 months. Poems are circulated to an editorial board. "Poems go to poetry editor, who then distributes them to three readers." Seldom comments on rejections. Send SASE for guidelines. Reports in 2 months. Pays 1 copy. Acquires first North American serial rights. Reviews books and chapbooks of poetry in 500-1,000 words, multi-book format. Open to unsolicited reviews. Poets may also send books for review consideration.
Also Offers: Sponsors the annual Red Rock Poetry Award. Winner receives $500 plus publication in the *Red Rock Review*. Submit up to 3 poems of not more than 20 lines each, typed on 8½×11 white paper. Reading fee: $6/entry (3 poems). Deadline: October 31. Send SASE for complete rules. Website includes sample poetry, names and pictures of staff and guidelines.

🅽 ◎ **REFLECT (Specialized: form/style)**, 1317-D Eagles Trace Path, Chesapeake VA 23320, founded 1979, poetry editor W.S. Kennedy, assistant editor Clara Holton.
Magazine Needs: They use "spiral poetry: featuring an inner-directed concern with sound (euphony), mystical references or overtones, and objectivity—rather than personal and emotional poems. No love poems, pornography, far left propaganda; nothing overly sentimental." They have published poetry by Marikay Brown, H.F. Noyes, Joe Malone, Ruth Wildes Schuler and Stan Proper. As a sample the editor selected these lines from "April Sashays in Lime Heels" by Edward C. Lynskey:

> April sashays across ashy mews,/in lime heels and lilac breath,/swells sappy stalks, and shoos/winter
> north, the killing guest.//Hyacinths blush and daffodils/blink as a wisp of apple smoke/curlicues through
> screens until/kale yards wakes in a rainy soak.

The quarterly is 48 pgs., digest-sized, saddle-stapled, typescript. Subscription: $8. Sample: $2.
How to Submit: Submit 4 or 5 poems at a time. All submissions should be single-spaced and should fit on one typed page. No previously published poems or simultaneous submissions. Sometimes comments on rejections. Send SASE for guidelines. Reports within a month. Pays 1 copy to nonsubscribers, 2 copies to subscribing contributors. Acquires first rights. Occasionally reviews books of poetry in 50 words or more.

○ **REFLECTIONS OF YOU® JOURNAL**, P.O. Box 523018, Springfield VA 22152-5018, phone (703)913-0726, fax (703)913-0125, e-mail rflection@aol.com, founded 1996, editor-in-chief Shar'Ron "Maxx" Mahaffey.
Magazine Needs: *ROYJ*, published 4 times/year, is "a magazine of insight and perspective for people actively working on their emotional, mental and spiritual well-being. *ROYJ* stimulates the mind, uplifts the spirit, and nourishes the soul. Included are informative and thought-provoking articles, inspiring essays, uplifting poetry, profiles, laughter, and much more." They want "10-30 lines, free verse, traditional, conversational. Subject matters: spirituality, relationships, friendship, marriage, parenting, ethnic, moral and social issues, family, love." They do not want material that is religious or preachy. They have published poetry by Carrie Crippen Fisher and Shirley Leighton. As a sample the editor selected these lines from her poem "Reflections of You":

> . . . . *My experiences, someone has lived them/My hopes, someone has rejoiced in them/My tears, someone has cried them/My understanding, someone understood it first/Therefore, my soul is the reflection/Of someone whom I may or may not know/Reflections of you . . .*

ROYJ is 38 pgs., 8½×11, offset printed on uncoated stock, saddle-stapled, with semi glossy cover, b&w drawings, art, clip art and photos. They receive about 350 poems a year, accept approximately 80%. Press run is 2,500 for 1,000 subscribers of which 2 are libraries; 300 distributed free to mailing lists. Single copy: $6; subscription: $22. Sample (including guidelines): $6.25. Make checks payable to A&M Publishing Company.
How to Submit: Submit 3 poems at a time. No previously published poems or simultaneous submissions. Time between acceptance and publication is within a year. Usually comments on rejections. Publishes theme issues. Send SASE for upcoming themes. Reports in 4-6 weeks. Usually sends prepublication galleys. Pays 2 copies. Acquires first serial rights. Reviews books or chapbooks of poetry or other magazines. Open to unsolicited reviews. Poets may also send books for review consideration to Poetry Editor, at the above address.
Advice: The editor advises, "Listen to the rhythm of your heart and let inspiration flow effortless. Speak to the heart of the reader from your heart."

Ⓝ $⃠ THE REJECTED QUARTERLY; BLACK PLANKTON PRESS, P.O. Box 1351, Cobb CA 95426, phone (707)928-5511, e-mail bplankton@juno.com, press founded 1983, magazine founded 1998, editor Daniel Weiss, associate editor Jeff Ludecke.
Magazine Needs: *The Rejected Quarterly* is published "to provide an outlet for literature that doesn't fit anywhere else." They want "original, unassuming, out-of-state poetry." They have published poetry by Brian C. Felder and Julie Babcock. As a sample the editor selected these lines from "To the Erstwhile Contributor" by Ken Waldman:

> *Dear Poetry, he writes,/forgetting Editor, and signs/A new Poet, Billy Rochester. Typical/of the submission, which, full/of typos, does charm enough/to almost win me, I respond:*

The editor says *TRQ* is 40-48 pgs., magazine-sized, saddle-stitched, with glossy 80 lb. coated cover, ads. They receive about 150 poems a year, accept approximately 5%. Press run is 150 for 75 subscribers, 25 shelf sales; 30 distributed free to editors, book companies, etc. Sample: $5.50. Make checks payable to Black Plankton Press.
How to Submit: Submit up to 3 poems at a time. No previously published poems or simultaneous submissions. Cover letter preferred. "We prefer five rejection slips to accompany poems." Time between acceptance and publication is 3 weeks to 6 months. "Poems are circulated to both editors." Often comments on rejections. Send SASE for guidelines. Reports in 2 months. Pays $5 and/or 1 copy. Acquires first rights.
Advice: The editors say, "We like things that are different—but not for the sake of being different."

Ⓝ ▣ ○ RENAISSANCE ONLINE MAGAZINE, 168 Orient Ave., Pawtucket RI 02861, e-mail submit@renaissancemag.com or kridolfi@renaissancemag.com, website http://www.renaissancemag.com, founded 1996, editor Kevin Ridolfi.
Magazine Needs: "Updated monthly, *Renaissance Online* strives to bring diversity and thought-provoking writing to an audience that usually settles for so much less. Poetry should reveal a strong emotion and be able to elicit a response from the reader. No nursery rhymes or profane works." As a sample the editor selected these lines from "Dasein" by David Hunter Sutherland:

> *What can't be held send/into sleep, into turn by gentle turn/if ring worn age, covetable grace/beauty,*

sadness and you spread/over this air-woven awning of clouds/to defy life's strange author
They receive about 40 poems a year, accept approximately 50%.
How to Submit: Submit 3 poems at a time. Previously published poems and simultaneous submissions OK. Cover letter preferred. E-mail submissions OK. "We prefer e-mail submissions. *Renaissance Online Magazine* is only published online and likes to see potential writers read previous works before submitting." Time between acceptance and publication is 3 months. Poems are circulated to an editorial board. "Poems are read by the editor, when difficult acceptance decisions need to be reached, the editorial staff is asked for comments." Often comments on rejections. Publishes theme issues occasionally. Send SASE for guidelines or obtain via website. Reports in 1 month. Acquires all online publishing rights. Reviews books of poetry. Open to unsolicited reviews, "but inquire first."
Also Offers: Website includes the entire magazine, including content, archives, guidelines and contact information.

🌐 $ 🔘 **RENDITIONS: A CHINESE-ENGLISH TRANSLATION MAGAZINE (Specialized: translations)**, Research Center for Translation, CUHK, Shatin, NT, Hong Kong, phone 852-2609-7399, fax 852-2603-5110, e-mail renditions@cuhk.edu.hk, website http://www.cuhk.edu.hk/renditions, editor Dr. Eva Hung.
Magazine Needs: *Renditions* appears twice a year. "Contents exclusively translations from Chinese, ancient and modern." They also publish a paperback series of Chinese literature in English translation. They have published translations of the poetry of Gu Cheng, Shu Ting, Mang Ke and Bei Dao. *Renditions* is about 150 pgs., magazine-sized, elegantly printed, perfect-bound, all poetry with side-by-side Chinese and English texts, using some b&w and color drawings and photos, with glossy 4-color card cover. Annual subscription: $17/1 year; $25/2 years: $42/3 years. Sample: $15.
How to Submit: E-mail and fax submissions OK. "Chinese originals should be sent by regular mail because of formatting problems." Publishes theme issues. Reports in 2 months. Pays "honorarium" plus 2 copies. Use British spelling. They "will consider" book mss, for which they would like a query with sample translations. Submissions should be accompanied by Chinese originals. Books pay 10% royalties plus 10 copies. Mss usually not returned. Editor sometimes comments on rejections.
Also Offers: Website includes information on *Renditions* magazine; Research Centre for Translation; ordering information for paperback books and forthcoming issues of *Renditions* and links to related sites.

$ 🔘 **REVIEW: LATIN AMERICAN LITERATURE AND ARTS (Specialized: ethnic, regional, translations)**, 680 Park Ave., New York NY 10021, phone (212)249-8950 ext. 366, fax (212)249-5868, founded 1968, managing editor Daniel Shapiro.
Magazine Needs: *Review* is a biannual magazine which serves as a "major forum for Latin American literature in English translation and articles on Latin American visual and performing arts." They want contemporary Latin American poetry and fiction. They have published poetry by Alberto Blanco, Octavio Paz and Blanca Varela. It is 100 pgs., 8½×11, with b&w photos of Latin American art. They receive 50-100 submissions, accept the work of 1-2 poets. Press run is 10,000 for 6,000 subscribers of which 500 are libraries. Subscription: $19.95 for individuals, $29.95 for institutions, $31 for international. Two-year subscription: $32 for individuals, $52 for institutions, $54 for international. Sample: $9.
How to Submit: Query before submitting work. Previously unpublished poetry and fiction only. Cover letter required. Reports in 2-3 months. Pays $100-300. Reviews books of poetry by Latin Americans. *Review* is published by the Americas Society, a not-for-profit organization.

🔘 **REVISTA/REVIEW INTERAMERICANA (Specialized: ethnic, regional)**, Inter-American University of Puerto Rico, Box 5100, San Germán, Puerto Rico 00683, phone (787)264-1912 ext. 7229 or 7230, fax (787)892-6350, e-mail reinter@sg.inter.edu, editor Anibal José Aponte.
Magazine Needs: The *Revista/Review* is a bilingual scholarly journal oriented to Puerto Rican, Caribbean and Hispanic American and inter-American subjects, poetry, short stories and reviews. Press run is 400.
How to Submit: Submit at least 5 poems in Spanish or English, blank verse, free verse, experimental, traditional and avant-garde, typed exactly as you want them to appear in publication. No simultaneous submissions. Cover letter with brief personal data required. Publishes theme issues. Send SASE for guidelines and upcoming themes. Pays 2 copies. Open to unsolicited reviews.
Advice: The editor says, "It is very difficult to really get the feel of a poet's merit when only one or two poems are submitted."

🔘 **RFD: A COUNTRY JOURNAL FOR GAY MEN EVERYWHERE (Specialized: gay)**, P.O. Box 68, Liberty TN 37095, phone (615)536-5176, website http://www.rfdmag.org, founded 1974, poetry editor Tom Seidner.
Magazine Needs: *RFD* "is a quarterly for gay men with emphasis on lifestyles outside of the gay mainstream—poetry, politics, profiles, letters." They want poetry that "illuminates the uniqueness of the gay experience. Themes that will be given special consideration are those that explore the rural gay experience, the gay perspective on social and political change, and explorations of the surprises and mysteries of relationships." They have published poetry by Antler, James Broughton, Gregory Woods and Winthrop Smith. *RFD* has a circulation of 3,800 for 1,300 subscribers. Single copy: $6.50; subscription: $32 first class, $20 second class. Sample: $6.50.

How to Submit: Submit up to 5 poems at a time. Simultaneous submissions OK. Send SASE for guidelines. Editor sometimes comments on rejections. Reports in 6-9 months. Pays 1 copy. Open to unsolicited reviews.
Advice: The editor says, *"RFD* looks for interesting thoughts, succinct use of language and imagery evocative of nature and gay men and love in natural settings."

RHINO, P.O. Box 554, Winnetka IL 60093, website http://www.artic.edu/~ageorge/RHINO, founded 1976, editors Deborah Rosen and Alice George.
Magazine Needs: *Rhino* "is an annually published poetry journal. We seek poetry, short shorts, translations, and occasional essays on poetry which manifest the author's passion, originality and artistic conviction. Wisdom, wit and a love affair with language are most welcome. Prefer poems under 100 lines." They have published poetry by Susan Terris, Colette Inez, David Starkey, James Armstrong and Maureen Seaton. *Rhino* is a 96-page journal, digest-sized, matte card cover with art, on high-quality paper. They receive 1,000 submissions a year, use approximately 60-80. Press run is 1,000. Sample: $5.
How to Submit: Submit 3-5 poems with SASE. No previously published submissions; simultaneous submissions OK with notification. Submissions are accepted April through November 30. Send SASE for guidelines. Reports in 2-3 months. Pays 2 copies. Acquires first rights only.
Also Offers: Website includes writer's guidelines, ordering info, table of contents and excerpts from current issue, literary challenges and a schedule of Chicago-area workshops, events and literary links.

RICHMOND COMMUNICATIONS LLC, P.O. Box 1539, New York NY 10021, e-mail puppyh se@aol.com, founded 1998, president Richard Hurowitz.
Book/Chapbook Needs: Richmond Communications LLC publishes poetry of all kinds. "We obtain electronic publishing rights and distribute for download directly over the Internet. We only do electronic publishing from our website. We are able to accept a great deal of poetry. We are looking for interesting and exceptional poetry."
How to Submit: Submissions should be on disk in Microsoft Word saved as one file. Previously published poems and simultaneous submissions OK. Cover letter required. Charges a $50 posting fee. Time between acceptance and publication is several weeks. Seldom comments on rejections. Replies to queries and mss in 1 month. Generally pays 20% royalties, no advances.
Advice: The president says, "Our publishing house only does books electronically. We are especially interested in giving voice to talented poets and are anxious to publish good works of all kinds."

RIO: A JOURNAL OF THE ARTS, % Cynthia Davidson, 104 Hoyt Lane, Port Jefferson NY 11777, phone (516)474-8265, e-mail cdavidson@ccmail-sunysb-edu, website http://www.engl.vic.edu/rio/rio.ht ml, founded 1997, editor/publisher Cynthia Davidson, associate editor Orlando Menes, associate editor Gail Lukasik.
Magazine Needs: *Rio* is a biannual online journal containing "poetry, short fiction, creative nonfiction, scannable artwork/photography and book reviews. Query for anything else." They want poetry of any length or form. "Experiments encouraged with voice, image or language. No greeting card verse or sentimentality; no purely therapeutic rants against mom, dad, boss, a gender." They have published poetry by Michael Anania, Liviu Ioah Stoiciu, Eleni Fourtourni, Michael Waters, Terry Wright, Ralph Mills, Jr., David Shevin and Briar Wood. As a sample the editor selected these lines from "XI. The Sun Has Wings" by Roberta Gould:

> Each worm in the cabbage/is joyous/Each saw-toothed form/smiles freely/Even the question mark
> shimmers/flexed to new functions

Accept approximately 20% of poems received a year. Back issues are available on the website, or printout for $8. Make checks payable to Cynthia Davidson.
How to Submit: Submit 5-8 poems at a time. Previously published poems and simultaneous submissions OK. Cover letter preferred. E-mail and disk submissions OK. "For electronic submissions, use text (ASCII) or Macintosh attachments, or e-mail submissions in body of e-mail message." Time between acceptance and publication is 4-6 months. Seldom comments on rejections. Send SASE for guidelines or obtain via website. Reports in 2-6 months. Acquires all rights. Rights revert to authors immediately upon publication. Reviews books and chapbooks of poetry in 500-1,200 words, single book format. Open to unsolicited reviews. Send books for review consideration.
Advice: The editors say, "We're looking for writers who do not fall into an easy category or niche."

RIO GRANDE PRESS; SE LA VIE WRITER'S JOURNAL, 4320 Canyon, Suite A12, Amarillo TX 79109, founded 1987, editor/publisher Rosalie Avara.
Magazine Needs: *Se La Vie Writer's Journal* is a quarterly journal with book reviews and cartoons about poetry and writing, and monthly and quarterly contests in poetry, essays and short stories. Publishes 70% of mss received/ quarter, "dedicated to encouraging novice writers, poets and artists; we are interested in original, unpublished mss that reflect the 'life' theme (La Vie). Poems are judged on originality, clarity of thought and ability to evoke emotional response." They have published poetry by Alan Frame, Angie Monnens and Lyn Lifshin. *SLVWJ* is 64 pgs., digest-sized, photocopied from typescript, saddle-stapled. Sample: $2. Make checks payable to Rosalie Avara.
How to Submit: Submit poems of up to 20 lines, 40 characters/line (pica) with SASE. Entry fee: $2/poem or 3 for $5. Prizes: $15, $10, $5 and Honorable Mention. Publishes some theme issues. Send SASE for guidelines

and upcoming themes. Staff reviews books of poetry. Send books for review consideration before 15th of January, April, July or October.

Also Offers: Also offers a quarterly contest. Submit poems up to 30 lines, 40 characters/line (pica) with SASE. Any subject, any style ("in good taste"). Entry fees: $3/poem or 2 for $5. Prizes: $25, $15, $10, $5 or Honorable Mention. Also publishes several poetry/short story anthologies annually. "No fee or purchase necessary." Cash prizes. Send SASE for guidelines.

RIO GRANDE REVIEW, 105 East Union, El Paso TX 79968-0622, contact poetry editor.

Magazine Needs: *Rio Grande Review*, a biannual student publication from the University of Texas at El Paso, contains poetry; flash, short, and nonfiction; short drama; photography and line art. They have published poetry by B.Z. Niditch, Lyn Lifshin, Lawrence Welsh and Naomi Shihab Nye. *RGR* is 95 pgs., 6×9, professionally printed and perfect-bound with card cover with line art, line art inside. Subscription: $10/year, $20/2 years.

How to Submit: Include bio information with submission. "Submissions are recycled regardless of acceptance or rejection." SASE for reply only. Send SASE for guidelines. Pays copies. "Permission to reprint material remains the decision of the author. However, *RGR* does request it be given mention."

$ RIVELIN GRAPHEME PRESS, 4 Merlin House, Church St., Hungerford, Berkshire RG17OJG England, founded 1984, poetry editor Snowdon Barnett.

Book/Chapbook Needs & How to Submit: Rivelin Grapheme Press publishes only poetry. Query first with biographical information, previous publications and a photo, if possible. If invited, send book-length manuscript, typed, double-spaced, photocopy OK. Payment is 20 copies of first printing up to 2,000, then 5% royalties on subsequent printings.

RIVER CITY, English Dept., University of Memphis, Memphis TN 38152, phone (901)678-4591, fax (901)678-2226, founded 1980, editor Dr. Thomas Russell.

● Poetry published here has also been included in *The Best American Poetry 1996*.

Magazine Needs: *River City* publishes fiction, poetry, interviews and essays. Contributors have included John Updike, Marvin Bell, Philip Levine, Maxine Kumin, Robert Penn Warren, W.D. Snodgrass, Mary Oliver, Fred Busch, Beth Bentley, Mona Van Duyn and Peter Porter. The biannual is 160 pgs., 7×10, perfect-bound, professionally printed with 4-color glossy cover. Publishes 40-50 pgs. of poetry in each issue. Circulation is 2,000. Subscription: $12. Sample: $7.

How to Submit: Submit no more than 5 poems at a time. Include SASE. Does not read mss June through August. Reports in 2-12 weeks. Pays 2 copies (and cash when grant funds available).

RIVER KING POETRY SUPPLEMENT, P.O. Box 122, Freeburg IL 62243, phone (618)234-5082, fax (618)355-9298, e-mail riverkng@icss.net, founded 1995, editor Wayne Lanter.

Magazine Needs: *RKPS*, published 3 times/year (April, August, December), features "all poetry with commentary about poetry." They want "serious poetry." They do not want "light verse." They have published poetry by Alan Catlin, R.G. Bishop, John Dickson, Allison Joseph and Martha Vertreace. The editor says *River King* is 8 pgs., 17×11 with newsprint. They receive about 2,000 poems a year, accept approximately 8%. Press run is 4,500 of which 600 are for libraries.

How to Submit: Submit 5 poems at a time. No previously published poems; simultaneous submissions OK. E-mail submissions OK. Cover letter preferred. Time between acceptance and publication is 2 months. Often comments on rejections. Reports in 1 month. Pays 10 copies.

$ RIVER OAK REVIEW, P.O. Box 3127, Oak Park IL 60303, phone (708)524-8725, founded 1993.

Magazine Needs: *River Oak Review* is a biannual literary magazine publishing high quality short fiction, creative nonfiction and poetry. Regarding work, they say, "quality is primary, but we probably wouldn't publish poems longer than 100 lines or so." They have published poetry by Billy Collins, Kathleen Norris, Steve Lautermillk and Maureen Seaton. *ROR* is 128 pgs., 6×9, neatly printed and perfect-bound with glossy 4-color card cover with art. They receive about 1,500-2,500 poems a year, publish approximately 1-2%. Press run is 1,300 for 750 subscribers, 200 shelf sales. Single copy: $6; subscription: $12. Sample: $5. Make checks payable to River Oak Arts.

How to Submit: Submit 4-6 poems at a time. No previously published poems; simultaneous submissions OK if notified. Cover letter preferred. Poems are circulated to readers, then an editorial board, then the editor. Seldom comments on rejections. Send SASE for guidelines. Reports in 3 months. Always sends prepublication galleys. Pays $10-50 and 2 copies. Buys first North American serial rights.

Also Offers: They also sponsor a poetry contest in December with an award of $500 and publication in the spring issue of *River Oak Review*. Submit up to 4 poems at a time (maximum 500 lines only); typed, double spaced; with name, address, phone on cover letter only. Entries are not returned. Send postcard for notification of receipt and SASE for winners. Winners will be announced in spring. Send SASE for guidelines.

Advice: The editor says, "Read literary magazines; read new poetry books; only submit if it's excellent."

☑ ☯ $◪ **RIVER STYX MAGAZINE; BIG RIVER ASSOCIATION**, 634 N. Grand Ave., 12th Floor, St. Louis MO 63103, website http://www.riverstyx.org, founded 1975, editor Richard Newman, senior editors Michael Castro and Quincy Troupe, managing editor Carrie Robb.

● Poetry published in *River Styx* has been selected for inclusion in the 1994, 1996 and 1998 volumes of *The Best American Poetry* and *Pushcart Prize* anthologies.

Magazine Needs: *River Styx*, published 3 times/year, is "an international, multicultural journal publishing both award-winning and previously undiscovered writers. We feature poetry, short fiction, essays, interviews, fine art and photography." They want "excellent poetry—original, energetic, musical and accessible. Please don't send us chopped prose or opaque poetry that isn't about anything." They have published work by Jared Carter, R.S. Gwynn, Marilyn Hacker, Timothy Liv and Martha Zweig. As a sample the editor selected these lines from "The Dismal Science" by Donald Finkel:

> He could pick up an epic this morning/from the take-away rack at the local supermarket./All over the city young men are scribbling, scribbling,/and old women, and schoolchildren, and several chimpanzees.//The young man persists in his kitchen, parboiling a dithyramb/while the sows go farrowing on in Iowa./Welcome to the eleventh plague: plenty.

River Styx is 100 pgs., 6×9, professionally printed on coated stock, perfect-bound with color cover and b&w art, photographs and ads. They receive about 8,000 poems/year, publish 60-75. Press run is 2,500 for 1,000 subscribers of which 80 are libraries. Sample: $7.

How to Submit: Submit 3-5 poems at a time, "legible copies with name and address on each page." Time between acceptance and publication is within 1 year. Reads submissions May 1 through November 30 only. Guidelines available for SASE. Editor sometimes comments on rejections. Reports in 3-5 months. Pays 2 copies plus 1-year subscription plus $8/page if funds available. Buys one-time rights.

Also Offers: Sponsors annual poetry contest. Past judges include Marilyn Hacker, Philip Levine and Molly Peacock. Deadline: May 31. Send SASE for guidelines.

◖ **RIVERRUN**, Glen Oaks Community College, 62249 Shimmel Rd., Centreville MI 49032-9719, founded 1974, contact poetry editor.

Magazine Needs: *Riverrun* is a literary biannual, using 30-40 magazine-sized pages of poetry in each issue. "We are a true miscellany. We publish a variety of styles, but we do give preference to more formal verse, that is less marketable in these times. Send rhyme, send structure; send sonnets, sestinas, villanelles, and ballads. Greeting card verse, of course, has other markets. However, feel free to send all poetry. There is structured verse we hate and free verse we love. We usually avoid anything over two manuscripts pages in length." They receive 200 poems/month, use up to 200/year. Press run is 675. Sample: $5.

How to Submit: Submit 3-7 poems at a time with SASE for response. No previously published poems; simultaneous submissions OK. Send SASE for guidelines. Reports in 1-6 months. Pays 1 copy.

Advice: The editor says, "We proudly publish an extremely broad range of individuals well-known to small press circles and beyond, but we also pride ourselves on devoting occasional space to local poets and as-yet-unpublished poets."

◖ **RIVERSTONE, A PRESS FOR POETRY; RIVERSTONE POETRY CHAPBOOK AWARD**, 1184A MacPherson Dr., West Chester PA 19380-3814, founded 1992.

Book/Chapbook Needs: Riverstone publishes 1 perfect-bound chapbook a year through an annual contest. They have published chapbooks by Gia Hansbury, Jefferson Carter, Marcia Hurlow, Margo Stever, Cathleen Calbert and Gary Myers. As a sample the editor selected these lines by Anita Barrows:

> You have survived yourself, now empty yourself./What were you looking for, there in all the old places?/ Grief & rage are the tasks of the day. Now, awake/in the darkness, an uneasy peace settles/in you, a drifting in the limbs.

That's from the chapbook *A Record*, which won the 1998 Riverstone Poetry Chapbook Award. It is 44 pgs., digest-sized, attractively printed on 80 lb. paper and perfect-bound with spruce green endleaves and a stippled beige card stock cover with matching spruce green ink.

How to Submit: To be considered for the contest, submit $8 reading fee and chapbook ms of 24-36 pgs., "including poems in their proposed arrangement, title page, contents and acknowledgments. All styles welcome." Previously published poems OK, multiple entries and simultaneous submissions. Include 6×9 SASE or larger for notification and copy of last year's chapbook. No further guidelines. Contest deadline: June 1 postmark. Winner receives publication, 50 author's copies and a cash prize of $100. Sample: $5.

◖ **ROCKET PRESS**, P.O. Box 730, Greenport NY 11944-0730, e-mail RocketUSA@delphi.com, website http://people.delphi.com/ROCKETUSA, founded 1993, editor Darren Johnson.

Magazine Needs: *Rocket Press* features "styles and forms definitely for the 21st century." The editor wants "experimental and eccentric poetry that's tight and streamlined. No rhyme. Don't use the words 'poem,' 'love' or 'ode.'" They have published poetry by Ben Ohmart, Albert Huffstickler and Cheryl Townsend. As a sample the editor selected these lines from "The Bovine Photograph" by Brandon Freels:

> At the art museum/we both stood in front of the/bovine photograph.//"It's sexy," Kris said./"I think it's just a sexy photo!"//"Look at those thighs!"/Someone in the background/mumbled.//"You know,"/ I said. "It is kind of sexy."

Rocket Press is a newspaper tabloid, 20 pgs., professionally printed, with a circulation over 2,000. They receive about 1,000 poems a year, accept approximately 1-2%. Press run is 2,000 for 200 subscribers of which 2 are libraries, 400 shelf sales. Sample: $1.50.

How to Submit: Submit 3 poems at a time. E-mail submissions OK. No previously published poems; simultaneous submissions OK. Time between acceptance and publication is 6-12 months. Often comments on rejections. "Subscribers get fuller critiques." Reports in less than 3 months. Pays 1 copy. Acquires one-time rights. Editor includes his own blurb reviews "of anything cool."

Advice: The editor says, "In our sixth year of publication, we've just about seen it all—please change that. Let's break all the rules in the new millennium."

THE ROCKFORD REVIEW; ROCKFORD WRITERS' GUILD, P.O. Box 858, Rockford IL 61105, founded 1971, editor David Ross.

Magazine Needs: *TRR* is a publication of the Rockford Writers' Guild which appears 3 times/year, publishing their poetry and prose, that of other writers throughout the country and contributors from other countries. *TRR* seeks experimental or traditional poetry of up to 50 lines. "We look for the magical power of the words themselves, a playfulness with language in the creation of images and fresh insights on old themes, whether it be poetry, satire or fiction." They have published poetry by Cindy Guentherman, Richard Vargas and Christine Swanberg. *TRR* is about 50 pgs., digest-sized, meatly printed and saddle-stapled with card cover with b&w illustration. Circulation is 750. Single copy: $5; subscription: $18 (3 issues plus the Guild's monthly newsletter, *Write Away*).

How to Submit: Submit up to 3 poems at a time with SASE. No previously published poems; simultaneous submissions OK. Reports in 6-8 weeks. Pays 1 copy and "you will receive an invitation to be a guest of honor at a Contributors' Reading & Reception in the spring." Acquires first North American serial rights.

Also Offers: They offer Editor's Choice Prizes of $25 for prose, $25 for poetry each issue. The Rockford Writers' Guild is a nonprofit, tax-exempt corporation established "to encourage, develop and nurture writers and good writing of all kinds and to promote the art of writing in the Rockford area." They offer lectures by Midwest authors, editors and publishers, and workshops. Membership: $25/year. Write for further information.

RONSDALE PRESS (Specialized: regional), 3350 W. 21st Ave., Vancouver, British Columbia V6S 1G7 Canada, e-mail ronhatch@pinc.com, website http://www.ronsdalepress.com, founded 1988, director Ronald B. Hatch.

Book Needs: Publishes 3 flat-spined paperbacks of poetry/year—by Canadian poets only—classical to experimental. "Ronsdale looks for poetry manuscripts which show that the writer reads and is familiar with the work of some of the major contemporary poets. It is also essential that you have published some poems in literary magazines. We have never published a book of poetry when the author has not already published a goodly number in magazines." They have published *Taking the Breath Away* by Harold Rhenisch, *Two Shores/Deux rives* by Thuong Vuong-Riddick, and *Burning Stone* by Zoë Landale. As a sample the director selected these lines from "The Process" in *The Edge of Time* by Robin Skelton:

> *Begin with listening—the voice/elsewhere and here, a gleam of brown,/its movements fluent and its*
> *flying leaps/the sudden judgement of a heart in shock/at precipices we'd not thought to find.*

How to Submit: Query first, with sample poems and cover letter with brief bio and publication credits. Previously published poems and simultaneous submissions OK. Often comments on rejections. Replies to queries in 2 weeks, to mss in 2 months. Pays 10% royalties and 10 author's copies. Write for catalog to purchase sample books.

Also Offers: Website includes catalogs, list of upcoming events, and writer's guidelines.

Advice: The director adds, "Ronsdale looks for poetry with echoes from previous poets. To our mind, the contemporary poet must be well-read."

ROOM OF ONE'S OWN (Specialized: women), P.O. Box 46160 Station D, Vancouver, British Columbia V6J 5G5 Canada, website http://www.islandnet.com/Room/enter, founded 1975.

Magazine Needs: *Room of One's Own* is a quarterly using "poetry by and about women, written from a feminist perspective. Nothing simplistic, clichéd. Short fiction also accepted." It is 96 pgs., 9×6. Press run is 1,000 for 420 subscribers of which 50-100 are libraries; 350 shelf sales. Subscription: $22 ($32 US or foreign). Sample: $8 plus IRCs.

How to Submit: "We prefer to receive 5-6 poems at a time, so we can select a pair or group." Include bio note. No simultaneous submissions. The mss are circulated to a collective, which "takes time." Publishes theme issues. Send SAE with 1 IRC for guidelines and upcoming themes. Reports in 6 months. Pays honorarium plus 2 copies. Buys first North American serial rights. "We solicit reviews." Send books for review consideration, attn. book review editor.

ROSE ALLEY PRESS, 4203 Brooklyn Ave. NE #103A, Seattle WA 98105, phone (206)633-2725, e-mail rosealleypress@juno.com, founded 1995, publisher/editor David D. Horowitz. "We presently do not read unsolicited manuscripts."

✓ $☑ ◎ **ROSEBUD (Specialized: themes)**, P.O. Box 459, Cambridge WI 53523, phone (907)822-5146 or (800)786-5669, website http://www.hyperionstudio.com/rosebud, founded 1993, editor Rod Clark, poetry editor John E. Smelcer.

Magazine Needs: *Rosebud* is an attractive quarterly "for people who enjoy good writing." The editor says it is "a reader's feast for the eye, ear and heart" which has rotating themes/departments. They want contemporary poetry with "strong images, real emotion, authentic voice; well crafted, literary quality. No inspirational verse." *Rosebud* is 136 pgs., 7×10, offset printed and perfect-bound with full-color coated card cover, art, graphics and ads. They receive about 700 poems a year, accept approximately 10%. Press run is 10,000 for 2,000 subscribers, 8,000 shelf sales. Subscription: $22. Sample: $5.95.

How to Submit: Submit 3-5 poems at a time. Previously published poems and simultaneous submissions OK. Often comments on rejections. Send SASE for guidelines and explanation of themes/departments. Reports in 3 months. Pays $45/piece and 3 copies. Buys one-time rights.

Also Offers: Each year they award 3 prizes of $150 for work published in the magazine.

Advice: The editor says, "We are seeking stories, articles, profiles and poems of love, alienation, travel, humor, nostalgia and unexpected revelation. And something has to 'happen' in the pieces we choose."

◖ ◎ **RUAH; POWER OF POETRY (Specialized: spirituality)**, Dominican School of Philosophy/Theology, 2401 Ridge Rd., Berkeley CA 94709, phone (510)849-2030, fax (510)849-1372, e-mail cjrenz@usa.net, founded 1990, general editor C.J. Renz, O.P., editor Gregory Thielen.

Magazine Needs: *Ruah*, an annual journal published in May, "provides a 'non-combative forum' for poets who have had few or no opportunities to publish their work. Theme: spiritual poetry. The journal has three sections: general poems, featured poet, and chapbook contest winners." They want "poetry which is of a 'spiritual nature,' i.e., describes an experience of the transcendent. No religious affiliation preferences; no style/format limitations. No 'satanic verse'; no individual poems longer than four typed pages." They have published poetry by Benjamin Alire Saens, Jean Valentine, Alberto Rios and Naomi Shihab Nye. *Ruah* is 60-80 pgs., 5½×8½, photocopied and saddle-stapled or perfect-bound, glossy card stock cover, b&w photo, includes occasional b&w sketches of original artwork. They receive about 250 poems a year, accept approximately 10-20%. Press run is 250 for about 100 subscribers of which 7 are libraries, 10 shelf sales; 50 distributed free to authors, reviewers and inquiries. Subscription: $10. Sample: $5. Make checks payable to Power of Poetry/DSPT.

How to Submit: Submit 3-5 poems at a time. No previously published poems; simultaneous submissions OK. E-mail submissions OK. "Do not mail submissions to publisher's address. Contact general editor via e-mail for current address or send written inquiries to Dominican School." Reads submissions December through March only. Time between acceptance and publication is 3-6 months. Poems are circulated to an editorial board. "Poems reviewed by writers and/or scholars in field of creative writing/literature." Send SASE for guidelines. Reports in 3-6 months. Pays 1 copy/poem. Acquires first rights.

Book/Chapbook Needs & How to Submit: Power of Poetry publishes 1 chapbook of spiritual poetry through their annual competition. Chapbooks are usually 24 pgs., and are included as part of *Ruah*. "Poets should e-mail editor for contest guidelines and submission address or write to Dominican School." Reading fee: $10. Deadline: December 15. Replies to queries in 3-6 weeks; to mss in 3-6 months. Winner receives publication in a volume of *Ruah* and 25 author's copies (out of a press run of 250).

Advice: The editors say, "*Ruah* is a gathering place in which new poets can come to let their voice be heard alongside of and in the context of 'more established' poets. The journal hopes to provide some breakthrough experiences of the Divine at work in our world."

$◖ ◎ **RURAL HERITAGE (Specialized: rural, humor)**, 281 Dean Ridge Lane, Gainesboro TN 38562-5039, phone (931)268-0655, e-mail editor@ruralheritage.com, website http://www.ruralheritage.com, founded 1976, editor Gail Damerow.

Magazine Needs: *Rural Heritage* uses poetry related to draft animal power, livestock, rural living. "Traditional meter and rhyme only. Poems must have touch of humor or other twist. Please, no comparisons between country and city life and no religious, political or issues-oriented material." As a sample the editor selected this poem, "Easy Choice" by John M. Floyd:

> *"You get rid of that/Plow horse right now,"/Said Jim's wife,/"Or I want a divorce."/So he put the old*
> *nag/On a boat to Mau Mau,/And then plowed a few rows/With his horse.*

RH is magazine-sized, bimonthly, using b&w photos, graphics and ads, 4-6 poems/issue. Circulation is 3,500. Subscription: $22. Sample: $6.

How to Submit: Submit up to 3 poems at a time, one/page. "Previously published poems are OK if we are told where and when. Simultaneous submissions must be withdrawn before we publish. We welcome submissions via e-mail—one verse per message please. Don't forget your snail mail address so we'll know where to send the check if your verse is accepted." Time between acceptance and publication is 4-6 months. "We often group poems by theme, for example plowing, threshing and so forth according to season. Verse may also be coupled with an article of similar theme such as maple sugaring, mule teams, etc." Send SASE for guidelines. Reports ASAP. Pays on publication, $5 and up (depending on length) and 2 copies.

Advice: The editor says, "We receive too much modern poetry (free verse), not enough traditional (true meter & rhyme), not enough humor. We get too much image poetry (we prefer action) and most poems are too long—we prefer 12 lines or less."

insider report

Red Dragon Press: things are different here

Laura Qa didn't expect to own a press, nor did she anticipate she'd be a poet. While in school she pursued mathematics and almost shunned the liberal arts, and her first
piece of published writing was not a limerick, sonnet or
sestina—it was a computer manual. Now, however, she's
authored two poetry books (*Tribute to the Hound, The Voice
of the Image*), co-authored a third (*Personal Values: Writings
by Uncommon Women*, with Elizabeth Croyden and Dee
Snyder), and owns Red Dragon Press, which had its inception in 1993 and has published 12 books since.

©Bachrach

Laura Qa

If the name Qa sounds a little different, that's because
it is. She says, "It's the Egyptian word for the soul. I felt
like I needed to choose my own name, something that was
separate from anything I'd known, a name that didn't connect with my family, my past,
or someone else's family. I just wanted a name that represented the poetry itself. The
poetry I write and the poets I publish all have the same experience of poetry coming
through us to the reader or listener. And for me poetry is a matter of the soul."

When asked what she means by "poetry is a matter of the soul," Qa says, "By soul
I mean depth of the human spirit. It's hard to describe without using these two words,
soul and spirit. Holistic-type thinking appeals to me."

Red Dragon Press looks for poetry that is authentic to one's experience, poetry
that doesn't try to manipulate or persuade. Says Qa, "Most language we hear and
read today is very restrictive and tries to channel the way we think. It is used to sell,
exploit or persuade—not to relate honestly. Poetry is a way to think beyond what
you've heard and what you've been told. It should be honest and strive for truth."

No wonder Qa looks for one thing in all poems she writes and publishes: depth.
"Communicating depth and helping people to strive for depth in their own lives and
perceptions of self and what they're looking for in life is what I'm trying to do," she says.

LAURA QA

Company: Red Dragon Press
Title: Editor/Publisher
Founded: 1993

"It's actually not just depth but a movement toward
depth—it's a constant motion, a striving for, and that
movement is conveyed by words and sound."

That Qa emphasizes "sound" is significant: Red
Dragon Press takes a strong interest in performance
poets. "Performing helps to perfect the work," says

Qa, who thinks performance poetry helps create a bond between the poet and the person receiving the poetry. "You get an immediate response when you're presenting the poetry in performance. A lot depends upon the skill of the listener, and the listener's mood at that moment—the poet can convey more or less complicated thoughts or images through performance. The poet as a performer has to be sensitive to the audience. Also, some people understand better when something is verbalized. They get more from hearing and seeing poetry than reading it. Performance adds a new dynamic, and I'm interested in that."

"Vox Angelica"

Pages ravaged by painful eyes
within a cover of chalky print,
transformed by envisaged holiness,
are held in habitual placement
within the sanctuary of hope
exalting immortality.

The words cannot detach the cord
sustaining proclivities to order—
they resign to external obedience
colored as educated values
reasoning common expectations
as "God's will on earth be done."

But having read and truly tried
the meaning of silent images,
wisdom chooses a memory beneath
green earth martyred for paper and ink—
and fantasies claim all the universe
for the soul is a solitary church.

(from *Tribute to the Hound*, published by Red Dragon Press, 1995; reprinted by permission of the author)

But, by performing their work, it's possible that some poets might be tempted to exaggerate a bit to get a point across. There's a possibility the performance could undermine the poetry. "No," says Qa. "That's drama, that's theater, that's not performance poetry. What I consider good performance poetry is having the message conveyed in an honest way. In performance the receiver gets something beyond the poem—a gesture, inflection, props, singing, music, whatever. These are new and honest dimensions that can be added by performing a poem."

Qa says the mission of Red Dragon Press is to publish poets who write about subjects and ideas that are "different." What other editors might write off, Qa welcomes. "Red Dragon is an androgynous press. If you write a fabulous poem but it's too one-sexed, you probably will not be published by us. We want work from a person who helps the reader feel the qualities of both sexes."

What precisely does she mean by "Red Dragon is an androgynous press?" For Qa, it's quite simple. "I think we can all agree that most of literature has been written from the male perspective. Well, people should not have to follow traditional roles or traditional behaviors." For example, if the poem is written by a man, a woman should be able to feel what is going on with him. Likewise, if the poem is written by a woman, a man should be able to feel what she's feeling. Qa adds, "There is no reason a man should not feel free to write about what it's like to be nurturing and soft, even though that is deemed a 'female' attribute. And a woman should be free to write about, say, feeling sexual pleasure or anger, things usually associated with men. For me, poetry should inspire both the writer and the reader to creativity and expanded ways of thinking—androgynous writing does that."

Now don't think that Red Dragon is a feminist press, because it's not, and Qa adamantly refutes such a suggestion. "Androgynous is not feminist. We aren't and don't want to be labeled a feminist press. We've published a number of male poets and will continue to do so in the future."

Another subject Qa embraces that most other poetry publishers might steer clear of are poems that deal with the parapsychological. If you write about any experiences of ESP, psycho-kinesis, mental telepathy, dream telepathy, out of body experiences and the like, Qa is interested. "I love to see how someone feels and communicates such experiences in a poem. I'm particularly interested in the visual images and impressions someone gets when they experience these things. Waking impressions from a dream or semiconscious state really appeal to me. Sometimes poems about these extraordinary experiences are more real than poems about normal things."

Red Dragon's interests do not end there. Qa is also looking for poetry that deals with new and evolving symbols and myths, such as cars, computers, cyberspace, microwaves, space ships, virtual reality—concepts and images that those before us didn't have the opportunity to write about. Says Qa, "A hundred years ago a poet couldn't have used the automobile as an image because it hadn't been invented, but today it's a very prominent symbol, almost a modern myth. Instead of a stairway to heaven now we have the highway to heaven. I want to see what poets have to say about other things in our modern lives that might be new myths or symbols."

Is there anything else that sets Red Dragon Press apart from other poetry publishers? "We certainly don't have an academic approach to poetry," says Qa. "I look for poetry that's more intuitive. And we do lean toward poets who are actively involved in the support of poetry as well as currently pursuing the artist's nature as writer and performer. A poet doesn't need to be a performance artist to be published by Red Dragon Press, but I always encourage poets to present their work or work-in-progress in a performance atmosphere. I believe performance is an important mechanism in the creation of the type of work we publish. I suppose this is because we believe the sound of a poem should reflect the meaning and intent of its words."

—Don Prues

✓ 🌐 ○ ◑ **RUSTIC RUB; WOODMAN'S PRESS**, 7 Copse End, Fleet, Hampshire GU13 8EQ England, phone (01252)812742, or for magazine sales in the US, Randy Lusk, 903 Ridgewood Rd., Austin TX 78746, founded 1993, editor/publisher Jay Woodman.

Magazine Needs: *Rustic Rub*, published biannually, "concentrates on exciting poetry. Also publishes interviews and information for performers, etc." They want "originality and vitality, not pretenders. Open to wide variety of styles/forms of any length." They do not want "uninspired formulaic poetry typically engendered by competitions." They have published poetry by Ian Robinson, Albert Huffstickler, Norman Jope and an interview with Tess Gallagher. As a sample the editor selected these lines from "Twilight on Trinity" by Albert Huffstickler:
> . . . *watching the rain,/thinking about/the letter I'd write/if I were going/to write while down/below on this borderland street/the named and the nameless/walk side by side in the slow fall.*

Rustic Rub is 92 pgs., A5, perfect-bound, desktop-published, medium card cover with b&w artwork and ads. They receive about 700 poems a year, accept approximately 10%. Press run is 350 for 150 subscribers of which 5 are libraries; 100 distributed free to contributors. Single copy: $8/£4; subscription: $15/£7.50. Sample: $8. Make checks payable to R. Lusk for USA or J. Woodman for UK.

How to Submit: Submit 6 poems at a time. No previously published poems or simultaneous submissions. Cover letter preferred. Time between acceptance and publication "can be immediate, up to three months." The editor says, "My decisions are mostly personal." Often comments on rejections. Reports "usually straightaway." Pays 1 copy. Acquires first British serial rights.

Book/Chapbook Needs & How to Submit: Woodman's Press is a subsidy publisher, *currently closed to unsolicited mss.* Chapbooks vary, usually perfect-bound. "I expect poets to cover their costs and market their own books. I merely facilitate self-publishing."

Advice: The editor advises, "always look at a copy of a magazine before submitting, as that is the best way to guage their needs. Also, please address all mail with the editor's name first."

$ ◑ 📀 **SACHEM PRESS (Specialized: translations, bilingual)**, P.O. Box 9, Old Chatham NY 12136-0009, founded 1980, editor Louis Hammer.

Book/Chapbook Needs: Sachem, a small press publisher of poetry and fiction, both hardcover and flat-spined paperbacks. The editor wants to see "strong, compelling, even visionary work, English-language or translations." He has published poetry by Cesar Vallejo, Yannis Ritsos, 24 leading poets of Spain (in an anthology), Miltos Sahtouris and himself. The paperbacks average 120 pgs. and the anthology of Spanish poetry contains 340 pgs. Each poem is printed in both Spanish and English, and there are biographical notes about the authors. The small books cost $6.95 and the anthology $11.95.

How to Submit: No new submissions, only statements of projects, until January 2000. Submit mss January through April only. Royalties are 10% maximum, after expenses are recovered, plus 50 author's copies. Rights are negotiable. Book catalog is free "when available," and poets can purchase books from Sachem "by writing to us, 33⅓% discount."

📀 **SACRED JOURNEY: THE JOURNAL OF FELLOWSHIP IN PRAYER (Specialized: religious)**, 291 Witherspoon St., Princeton NJ 08542, phone (609)924-6863, fax (609)924-6910, founded 1950, contact Editor.

Magazine Needs: *SJ* is an interfaith bimonthly "concerned with prayer, meditation and spiritual life" using short poetry "with deep religious (or spiritual) feeling." It is 48 pgs., digest-sized, professionally printed, saddle-stapled with glossy card cover. They accept about 2% of submissions received. Press run is 10,000. Subscription: $16. Sample free.

How to Submit: Submit 5 poems at a time, double-spaced. Simultaneous submissions and "sometimes" previously published poems OK. Cover letter preferred. Reports in 2 months. Pays 5 copies.

$ 📀 **ST. ANTHONY MESSENGER (Specialized: religious)**, 1615 Republic St., Cincinnati OH 45210-1298, website http://www.americancatholic.org, poetry editor Susan Hines-Brigger.

Magazine Needs: *St. Anthony Messenger* is a monthly 56-page magazine, circulation 359,000, for Catholic families, mostly with children in grade school, high school or college. In some issues, they have a poetry page that uses poems appropriate for their readership. Their poetry needs are limited but poetry submissions are always welcomed. As a sample here is "A Valentine for Darby" by Jean M. Syed:
> *Why do I love you, my potbellied love?/Not for your pregnant form or shiny pate./Were these on tender those decades ago,/would I have been so indiscriminate/as to let you win my heart? No princess/from passion ever took a frog to mate.*

How to Submit: "Submit seasonal poetry (Christmas/Easter/nature poems) several months in advance. Submit a few poems at a time; do not send us your entire collection of poetry. We seek to publish accessible poetry of high quality." Send regular SASE for guidelines and 9×12 SASE for free sample. Pays $2/line on acceptance. Buys first worldwide serial rights. *St. Anthony Messenger* poetry occasionally receives awards from the Catholic Press Association Annual Competition.

✓ $ ○ 📀 **ST. JOSEPH MESSENGER AND ADVOCATE OF THE BLIND (Specialized: religious)**, 537 Pavonia Ave., P.O. Box 288, Jersey City NJ 07303, founded 1898, poetry editor Sister Mary Kuiken,-C.S.J.P.

Magazine Needs: *St. Joseph Messenger* is semiannual, (16 pgs., 8 × 11). They want "brief but thought-filled poetry; do not want lengthy and issue-filled." Most of the poets they have used are previously unpublished. They receive 400-500 submissions a year, use approximately 50. There are about 2 pgs. of poetry in each issue. Circulation 15,000. Subscription: $5.

How to Submit: Sometimes comments on rejections. Publishes theme issues. Send SASE for guidelines, free sample and upcoming themes. Reports within 2 weeks. Pays $10-25/poem and 2 copies.

$ ◐ SALMON RUN PRESS; NATIONAL POETRY BOOK AWARD, P.O. Box 672130, Chugiak AK 99567-2130, founded 1991, editor/publisher John E. Smelcer.

Book/Chapbook Needs: Salmon Run publishes 2-3 books/year. They want "quality poetry by established poets, any subject, any style. No poetry that is not representative of the highest achievement in the art." They have published Galway Kinnell, Ursula K. Le Guin, X.J. Kennedy, Molly Peacock, Denise Levertov, Denise Duhamel, Philip Levine and Luis Omar Salinas. As a sample the editor selected these lines from Philip Levine's "Peter's Gift":

> My friend Peter found a strange newcomer/in the walnut tree. Late June,/near dusk, the soft light
> hanging on,/he stills us, and at first I catch nothing,/and then the soft voice, the bubbling.

Their books are flat-spined and professionally printed on heavy, natural-colored paper with glossy color covers.

How to Submit: Query first with sample poems and cover letter with brief bio. Previously published poems and simultaneous submissions OK. Usually comments on rejections. Replies to queries within 1-3 weeks, to mss in 1-2 months. Pays 10% royalties, sometimes advances and a negotiable number of author's copies.

Also Offers: They also sponsor a pamphlet series ("by invitation only") and the National Poetry Book Award for book-length mss of 48-96 pgs. $10 reading fee and SASE required. Entries must be postmarked by December 30. The winning ms will be published in book form, nationally distributed and receive $1,000 prize.

◖ ◑ SALT HILL; SALT HILL POETRY PRIZE; SALT HILL HYPERTEXT PRIZE, English Dept., Syracuse University, Syracuse NY 13244, website http://www-hl.syr.edu/cwp, founded 1994, editor James Wagner.

• Poetry published in *Salt Hill* has also been included in *The Best American Poetry 1998*.

Magazine Needs: *Salt Hill*, published biannually, features "high-quality contemporary writing including poetry, fiction, essays, book reviews and artwork." They want "all kinds of high quality original work, from four lines to four pages, to free verse and prose poems. We are interested in poetry that does more than simply deliver a tight, well-defined anecdote. We like to see the kind of intellectual and emotional engagement we feel is representative of a mature poetic imagination." They do not want "badly written sentimental work without soul. Experimental work welcome." They have published poetry by Bei Dao, Daniela Crăsnaru, Bill Knott and Eléna Rivera. As a sample the editor selected these lines from "2 Bachelard" by Michael Burkard:

> Days go by. 2 Bachelard begins to feel like a street. I/stare at this weak brown slip called a receipt
> with its clear/but incomplete scrawl and an entire world of passion and/rain and the inner and outer
> city returns to me. Yes, a/street. A sign. A smell. A love, a life, a love of life when/you could not let go
> of either.

The editor says *Salt Hill* is 120-150 pgs., 5½ × 8½, perfect-bound, with art, photography and ads. They receive about 3,000 poems a year, accept approximately 2%. Press run is 1,000. Subscription: $15. Sample: $8.

How to Submit: Submit 5 poems at a time. No previously published poems; simultaneous submissions OK. Cover letter preferred with a brief bio. Time between acceptance and publication is 2-8 months. Seldom comments on rejections. Send SASE for guidelines. Reports in 2-6 months. Pays when funds available and 2 copies. Buys one-time rights. Reviews books or chapbooks of poetry or other magazines in 900-3,000 words and/or essay reviews of single/multi book format. Open to unsolicited reviews. Poets may also send books for review consideration to Book Review Editor, at the above address.

Also Offers: Sponsors annual *Salt Hill* Poetry Prize, awarding $500 1st Prize and publication, $100 2nd Prize and publication and $50 3rd Prize and publication. Submit unpublished poems with name, address and phone on each. Reading fee is $5 for up to 150 lines (1-3 poems); $3 extra for every additional 100 lines. Include SASE. Postmark deadline May 1. Also sponsors Salt Hill Hypertext Prize, awarding $500 1st Prize and web publication, $100 2nd Prize and web publication, 3rd Prize web publication. See website for details. Reading fee: $10. Address envelope to Web Contest. Send url address, or work as an attachment to jsparker@mailbox.syr.edu, or address envelope with floppy disks to Web Editor (disks will not be returned). Deadline: January 31.

MARKET CONDITIONS are constantly changing! If you're still using this book and it is 2001 or later, buy the newest edition of *Poet's Market* at your favorite bookstore or order directly from Writer's Digest Books (800)289-0963.

⊘ **SANDPIPER PRESS**, P.O. Box 286, Brookings OR 97415-0028, phone (541)469-5588, founded 1979. They currently do not accept unsolicited poetry.

Ⓝ ◖ **SANTA BARBARA REVIEW**, P.O. Box 808, Summerland CA 93067, founded 1993, editor Patricia Stockton Leddy.
Magazine Needs & How to Submit: Santa Barbara Review is an annual literary arts journal appearing in February publishing poetry, fiction and essays, including essays on poetry. The editor says *SBR* is 196-240 pgs., 6×9, professionally printed and perfect-bound with b&w and color coated card cover and b&w illustrations inside. They use 12-18 poems each issue. Single copy: $10; subscription: $10. Pays 2 copies.
Advice: The editor says, "As far as length is concerned, make every image, word or trope count."

$⊘ **SARABANDE BOOKS, INC.; THE KATHRYN A. MORTON PRIZE IN POETRY**, 2234 Dundee Rd., Suite 200, Louisville KY 40205, phone (502)458-4028, fax (502)458-4065, e-mail sarabandeb@aol.com, website http://www.SarabandeBooks.org, founded 1995, editor-in-chief Sarah Gorham.
Book/Chapbook Needs: Sarabande Books publishes books of poetry and short fiction. They want "poetry of superior artistic quality. Otherwise no restraints or specifications." They have published poetry by Michael Burkard, Belle Waring, Baron Wormser and Kathleen Halme.
How to Submit: Query with 10 sample poems during the month of September only. No fax or e-mail submissions. SASE must always be enclosed. Previously published poems OK if acknowledged as such. Simultaneous submissions OK "if notified immediately of acceptance elsewhere." Seldom comments on rejections. Replies to queries in 3 months, to mss (if invited) in 6 months. Send SASE or visit website for guidelines. Pays 10% royalties and author's copies.
Also Offers: The Kathryn A. Morton Prize in Poetry is awarded to a book-length ms (at least 48 pgs.) submitted between January 1 and February 15. $15 handling fee and entry form required. Send SASE for guidelines beginning in November. Winner receives a $2,000 cash award, publication and a standard royalty contract. All finalists are considered for publication. "At least half of our list is drawn from contest submissions." Entry fee: $15. Reads entries January 1 through February 15 only. Competition receives 1,200 entries. Website includes guidelines and application form for contest, interviews with authors, ordering information and general information on press.

■ ◎ **SATIRE (Specialized: humor)**, P.O. Box 340, Hancock MD 21750-0340, e-mail satire@intrepid.net, website http://www.satire.org, founded 1994, editor Larry Logan.
Magazine Needs: Now exclusively published as an e-zine, *Satire* is "the literary journal of the satiric." They want "humor/satire." They publish "original poetry, short stories, articles, essays and cartoons. While we do enjoy the classic satiric form, we are flexible with other related genres of humor: parody, wit, lampoonery, farce, caricature, burlesque, etc. If the work can make the reader laugh, and then make the reader think, it is what we value." They receive about 100-150 poems a year, use approximately 15-20.
How to Submit: Submit up to 5 poems at a time. "Keep poetry under 1,000 words." Accepts previously published poems (but prefer unpublished works); simultaneous submissions OK. Cover letter preferred. E-mail submissions OK, "but may limit unique typographic aspects of the work (italics, symbols, etc.). Always include SASE or e-mail address for reply." Time between acceptance and publication is 3-6 months. Editor makes final selections. Seldom comments on rejections. Send SASE for guidelines or obtain via website. Reports in 3 months. Acquires one-time rights.

⊘ **SATURDAY PRESS, INC.**, Box 43548, Upper Montclair NJ 07043, phone (973)256-5053, fax (973)256-4987, e-mail saturdaypr@aol.com, founded 1975, editor S. Ladov. "We do not plan to read manuscripts in the foreseeable future."

$◎ **SCAVENGER'S NEWSLETTER; KILLER FROG CONTEST (Specialized: science fiction/ fantasy, horror, mystery, writing)**, 519 Ellinwood, Osage City KS 66523-1329, phone (785)528-3538, e-mail foxscav1@jc.net, website http://www.cza.com/scav/index/html, editor Janet Fox.
Magazine Needs: *Scavenger's Newsletter* may seem an odd place to publish poems, but its editor, Janet Fox, uses 1-2 every month. The *Newsletter* is a booklet packed with news about science fiction and horror publications. Ms. Fox prefers science fiction/fantasy, horror and mystery poetry and will read anything that is offbeat or bizarre. Writing-oriented poetry is occasionally accepted but "poems on writing must present fresh ideas and viewpoints. Poetry is used as filler so it must be ten lines or under. I like poems with sharp images and careful craftsmanship." They have published poetry by K.S. Hardy, James A. Lee, Brian Rosenberger and Ann K. Schwader. As a sample she selected this poem, "Pac Woman" by Francis W. Alexander:

> *Venus/putting a fierce bite/on the moon's backside*

Scavenger's Newsletter is 22-28 pgs., printed at a quick printing shop for 800 subscribers. Subscription: $18/ year; $9/6 months. Sample (including guidelines): $2.50.
How to Submit: Submit 3-6 poems at a time. Previously published poems, submissions by e-mail (no attachments) and simultaneous submissions OK (if informed)—reprints if credit is given. Send SASE for guidelines or request via e-mail. At last report was "accepting about 1 out of 20 poems submitted. I am currently reading selectively. "I have made the notice 'reading selectively due to backlog' a permanent part of the guidelines, since

I do usually have quite a bit of material on hand yet do not want to close to the exceptional piece." Reports in 1 month or less. Pays $2 on acceptance plus one copy. E-mail submissions may choose cash or subscription. Buys one-time rights. Staff reviews science fiction/fantasy/horror and mystery chapbooks, books and magazines only. Send materials for review to either: Jim Lee, 801 - 26th St., Windber PA 15963 or Steve Sawicki, 186 Woodruff Ave., Watertown CT 06795.

Also Offers: "I hold an annual 'Killer Frog Contest' for horror so bad or outrageous it becomes funny. There is a category for horror poetry. Has been opening April 1, closing July 1 of each year. Prizes are $25 each in four categories: poetry, art, short stories and short short stories, plus the 'coveted' Froggie statuette." The last contest had no entry fee but entrants wanting the anthology pay $4.50. Winners list available for SASE. Website features guidelines, information about *Scavenger's Newsletter*, Killer Frog Contest information and other projects.

N **↻** **⊘** **SCHOLASTIC CANADA LTD.; NORTH WINDS PRESS**, 175 Hillmount Rd., Markham, Ontario L6C 1Z7 Canada, website http://www.scholastic.com, founded 1971.

Book/Chapbook Needs: Publishes entertaining, high-quality novels and picture books for children. "A good story is prerequisite; very little poetry published. We publish 2 picture books per year that feature poetry."

How to Submit: "However, we are not currently accepting unsolicited mss. Accepting query letters only."

N **$** **◎** **SCIENCE FICTION POETRY ASSOCIATION; STAR*LINE (Specialized: science fiction, horror); THE RHYSLING ANTHOLOGY**, 1300 Kicker Rd., Tuscaloosa AL 35404, phone (205)553-2284, e-mail dragontea@earthlink.net, website http://dm.net/~bejay/sfpa.htm, founded 1978, editor David Kopaska-Merkel.

Magazine Needs: The Association publishes *Star*Line*, a bimonthly newsletter and poetry magazine. They are "open to all forms—free verse, traditional forms, light verse—so long as your poetry shows skilled use of the language and makes a good use of science fiction, science, fantasy, horror or speculative motifs." The Association also publishes *The Rhysling Anthology*, a yearly collection of nominations from the membership "for the best science fiction/fantasy long and short poetry of the preceding year." The magazine has published poetry by Lawrence Schimel, Kendall Evans, Charlie Jacob, Terry A. Garey and Timons Esaias. The digest-sized magazine and anthology are saddle-stapled, photocopied, with numerous illustrations and decorations. They have 250 subscribers of which 1 is a library. Subscription: $13/6 issues. Sample: $2. Send requests for copies/membership information to John Nichols, Secretary-Treasurer, 6075 Bellevue Dr., North Olmstead OH 44070. Submissions to *Star*Line* only. They receive about 300-400 submissions a year, use approximately 80—mostly short (under 50 lines).

How to Submit: Send 3-5 poems/submission, typed. No simultaneous submissions, no queries. E-mail submissions OK "as part of the e-mail message, no attachments." Include brief cover letter. Reports in a month. Pays 5¢/line plus 1¢/word and a copy. Buys first North American serial rights. Reviews books of poetry "within the science fiction/fantasy field" in 50-500 words. Open to unsolicited reviews. Poets may also send books for review consideration to Todd Earl Rhodes, 735 Queensbury Loop, Winter Garden FL 34787-5808. A copy of *The Rhysling Anthology* is $3.

Also Offers: Website includes guidelines, editor's address, ordering and subscription address and links to *Rhysling Anthology* winners list.

$ **◎** **SCIENCE OF MIND (Specialized: spirituality/inspirational)**, 3251 W. Sixth St., P.O. Box 75127, Los Angeles CA 90020-5096, phone (213)388-2181, fax (213)388-1926, e-mail edit@scienceofmind.com, website http://www.scienceofmind.com, founded 1927, publisher/editor Elaine Sonne. Send all poetry mss to editorial associate Sylvia Delgado, sdelgado@scienceofmind.com.

Magazine Needs: *Science of Mind*, published monthly, "is a correlation of laws of science, opinions of philosophy, and revelations of religion applied to the needs and aspirations of humankind. A practical teaching, it helps thousands of people experience health, happiness, peace and love." They want "poems inspirational in theme and characterized by an appreciation of *Science of Mind* principles. Average length is 8-12 lines. Maximum length is 25-30 lines." They do not want "religious poetry, stuff about Christ and redemption." They have published poetry by Terri Glass and Eva Poole-Gilson. As a sample the editor selected these lines from "Such Beauty" by John D. Engle, Jr.:

> There is such beauty in the world today,/Flowing through me and around me like a current/Till I am
> charged and tingling from its force!/It lives in all I see or hear or touch./It glows and sings and dances
> in its fervor./Such beauty! Such forceful beauty in the world, . . .

The editor says *Science of Mind* is 112 pgs., digest-sized, web offset printed, perfect-bound with 4-color cover and color ads. They receive about 200 poems a year, accept approximately 6-8. Press run is 78,000 for 55,000 subscribers, 15,000 shelf sales. Single copy: $2.50; subscription: $19.95. Sample: $5.

How to Submit: Submit maximum of 3 poems at a time. No previously published poems; simultaneous submissions OK. No e-mail or fax submissions. Cover letter preferred. "Must include SASE for response." Time between acceptance and publication is 1 year ("each issue has a theme, so we may keep a poem until the right theme comes along"). Poems are read by the assistant editor, and if approved, sent to the editor for final decision. Publishes theme issues. Reports "not soon at all—most are rejected right away, but acceptances may take months." Pays $25 and 10 copies. Buys first North American serial rights.

◐ ◎ **SCORE MAGAZINE; SCORE CHAPBOOKS AND BOOKLETS (Specialized: form)**, 1015 NW Clifford St., Pullman WA 99163, phone (509)332-1120, e-mail orion@pullman.com, poetry editors Crag Hill and Spencer Selby.

Magazine Needs: Score Chapbooks and Booklets is a small press publisher of visual poetry in the annual magazine *Score*, booklets, postcards and broadsides. They want "poetry which melds language and the visual arts such as concrete poetry; experimental use of language, words and letters—forms. The appearance of the poem should have as much to say as the text. Poems on any subject; conceptual poetry; poems which use experimental, non-traditional methods to communicate their meanings." They don't want "traditional verse of any kind—be it free verse or rhymed." They have published poetry by Karl Kempton, A.L. Nielsen, Bruce Andrews, Larry Eigner and Jacques Debrot. They say that it is impossible to quote a sample because "some of our poems consist of only a single word—or in some cases no recognizable words." *Score* is 48-72 pgs., magazine-sized, offset printed, saddle-stapled, using b&w graphics, 2-color matte card cover. Press run is 200 for 25 subscribers, of which 6 are libraries, about 40 shelf sales. Sample: $10.

How to Submit: We strongly advise looking at a sample copy before submitting if you are not familiar with visual poetry. Previously published poems OK "if noted." No simultaneous submissions. Send SASE for guidelines. Pays 2 copies. Open to unsolicited reviews. Poets may also send books for review consideration.

Book/Chapbook Needs & How to Submit: For chapbook consideration send entire ms. No simultaneous submissions. Almost always comments on rejections. Pays 25% of the press run. They subsidy publish "if author requests it."

N ◯ **THE SCREAMING RAY REVIEW; THE SCREAMING RAY PAMPHLET SERIES**, P.O. Box 1511, Willoughby OH 44096-1511, founded 1997, co-editors Charlotte Richey and D.T. Holt.

Magazine Needs & How to Submit: *The Screaming Ray Review* is a poetry magazine published at least 2 times a year. "We have no restrictions on style, however we do ask that your work be no longer than two pages. Please include a SASE with your work." As a sample we selected these lines from "There's a Radio Playing My Song" by Mark Weber:

> *i've been on the pancakes lately//which, is not a whole lot different/than being on the wine//but i don't drink wine anymore//i do pancakes//drop an egg in there/along with the flour/dice up an apple, a red delicious/melt liberal amount of butter/into the iron skillet//and start flapping them babies*

TSRR is 12-24 pgs., digest-sized, desktop-published and saddle-stapled with b&w paper cover, uses b&w art and photos. Subscription: $2/1 issue, $3/2 issues, $6/4 issues. Sample: $2. Make checks payable to Charlotte Richey. Pays 2 copies.

Also Offers: "The Screaming Ray Pamphlet Series features a longer poem or a few short poems by one poet. We plan to publish them whenever we can. *Submission is by invitation only.*" The price is $1/pamphlet or 3 for $2.

❀ ◐ **SCRIVENER**, 853 Sherbrooke St. W., Montreal, Quebec H3A 2T6 Canada, phone (514)398-6588, fax (514)398-8146, founded 1980.

Magazine Needs: *Scrivener* is an annual review of contemporary literature and art published in March by students at McGill University. With a circulation throughout North America, *Scrivener* publishes the best of new Canadian and American poetry, short fiction, criticism, essays, reviews and interviews. "*Scrivener* is committed to publishing the work of new and unpublished writers." They have published poetry by Lyn Lifshin, B.Z. Niditch, Jon Durbin, Kathleen Frederickson and Catherine T. Black. As a sample they selected these lines from "Orals" by Lyn Lifshin:

> *half of them cough. The one with a limp/wittily grunts toward me, "you remind me of Theda Bara."/ A distant relative I blush, because it's true./Already his eyes are full of no. Smoke boils up from the table./The scraped faces freeze on me until I wish I hadn't come . . .*

Scrivener is a book-sized review, 100 pgs., printed on natural recycled paper and bound with a flat spine and one color matte card cover; all graphics and ads are black and white. They receive about 500 submissions a year, accept approximately 50. Subscription: $4 Canadian plus $1 for postage. Sample: $5.

How to Submit: January 15 deadline for submissions; contributors encouraged to submit in early fall. Send 5-10 poems, one poem/page; be sure that each poem be identified separately, with titles, numbers, etc. Do not send originals of work as submissions are not returned. "Poets may contact our editorial staff regarding submission guidelines, deadlines, etc. We operate at full capacity only during the academic year; our editors may be difficult to reach in the summer." Reports in 6 months. Pays 1 copy (multiple copies available upon request).

Also Offers: The Scrivener Poetry Supplement "publishes a large body of work of three or four poets, and includes introductions to each of the poets' works."

☑ **$**◯ **SCROLL PUBLICATIONS; SCROLL BI-MONTHLY MAGAZINE**, 88 County Rd. 232, Durango CO 81301, phone (970)247-2054, website http://www.scroll.com, founded 1990, editor Cherylann Gray.

Magazine Needs: *Scroll Bi-Monthly Magazine* contains "humor, comics, slogans, music, short stories, fiction/nonfiction, artwork, recipes and poetry. We are strictly devoted to preserving the works and dreams of the original artist." They want poetry of any form or style, on any subject; length, no more than 30 lines. Nothing profane or vulgar. They have published poetry by Daniel Gray and Jenny Jacobs. As a sample the editor selected these lines from "Grandmothers" by Eve Mackintosh:

Grandmothers are rocks thrown into deep wells/Each brick fitted painstakingly to form/Solid foundations for dream castles created/by her children and offspring.

The editor says *Scroll* is 75-80 pgs., 8½×11½, soft paperback, includes art, ads. They receive about 500 poems a year, accept approximately 65%. Press run is 150. Single copy: $6; subscription: $20. Sample: $4. Make checks payable to Cherylann Gray.

How to Submit: Submit up to 5 poems at a time. Reading fee: $4/5 poems. Previously published poems and simultaneous submissions OK. Cover letter preferred. E-mail and disk submissions OK. Time between acceptance and publication is 3-6 months. Poems are circulated to an editorial board. Often comments on rejections. Publishes theme issues occasionally. Send large SASE for guidelines and upcoming themes. Reports in 2 months. Always sends prepublication galleys. Pays 2 copies. Acquires first or one-time rights. Reviews chapbooks of poetry. Open to unsolicited reviews. Poets may also send books for review consideration.

Book/Chapbook Needs & How to Submit: Scroll Publications publishes 3 chapbooks and 3 anthologies/year. Query first, with 3-4 sample poems and a cover letter with brief bio and publication credits. Replies to queries in 2 months; to mss in 3 months. Pays 40-50% royalties and 50 author's copies (out of a press run of 200).

Also Offers: Sponsors biannual contest. Awards prizes of $250, $100 and $50 plus publication. Submit up to 7 poems, 30 lines maximum, with large SASE.

Advice: The editor says, "We want poetry that's strong in nature, life and real experiences, thoughts and dreams."

N ○ ◎ SEA OATS (Specialized: form), 6815 41 Dr. N., Riviera Beach FL 33404, phone (561)882-1428, founded 1993, editor Robert Henry Poulin.

Magazine Needs: *Sea Oats* appears biannually and is published by the Haiku Poets of South Florida. They want haiku, tanka and senryu. We prefer poetry of explosive moments as seen in nature or felt from the heart with brevity and juxtaposed as a happening event with images expressed in common language." They have published poetry by Robert Spiess, "Mimi" Davis, John Stevenson, Robert Major and Geraldine C. Little. As a sample the editor selected this haiku by H.F. Noyes:

Among spring snowflakes/falling blossoms/lose the way

Sea Oats is 8 pgs., 8½×11, corner-stapled. "We accept at least one from every person who submits." Press run is 300 for 150 subscribers of which 5 are libraries. Subscription: $5, includes 2 issues, membership. Make checks payable to Robert Henry Poulin.

How to Submit: Submit any number of poems. No previously published poems or simultaneous submissions. Cover letter preferred "of new poets, bio desired with birthday." Send SASE for guidelines. Reports "ASAP."

$ ○ SEASONS OF THE MUSE; CALLIOPE PRESS, 2 Jasmine Court, Millbrae CA 94030, founded 1996, editor/publisher Dawn Zapletal.

Magazine Needs: *SOTM* appears quarterly "with the seasons, to give new and established poets a showcase for their work." They want poetry of all types; "free verse, haiku, rhyme. No religious, political or pornographic work." As a sample the editor selected these lines from "Send For Rod" by Rachael Trayar:

Time to call in a man with mud on his shoes,/and dirt under his fingernails./A man with tomatoes and cucumbers/and melons to give away,/and sweet roses for the soul to feed on.

The editor says *SOTM* is 4-6 pgs., 8½×11, corner stapled, with cover graphics. "No samples or subscriptions available. Only published poets receive copies."

How to Submit: Submit 4 poems at a time with $1 reading fee, "stamps or cash only. No checks, please." Line length for poetry is 24 maximum. Previously published poems and simultaneous submissions OK. Send SASE for reply. Does not return material. Poems are circulated to a 3-member editorial board. Decisions must be unanimous for acceptance. Always comments on rejections. Reports in 1 week to 1 month. Pays $1 plus 1 copy.

Also Offers: Sponsors an Editor's Choice Award in each issue. The best poem from each issue receives $5.

Advice: The editor says, "No vague inaccessible poetry."

N $ ○ SEATTLE REVIEW, Padelford Hall, Box 354330, University of Washington, Seattle WA 98195, phone (206)543-7884, e-mail seaview@english.washington.edu, founded 1978, poetry editor Colleen McElroy.

Magazine Needs: *Seattle Review* appears in the fall and spring using "contemporary and traditional" poetry. They have published poetry by William Stafford, Tess Gallagher, Marvin Bell and Walter McDonald. The review is 110 pgs., professionally printed, flat-spined, with glossy card cover. Press run is 800 for 250 subscribers of

**FOR EXPLANATIONS OF THESE SYMBOLS,
SEE THE INSIDE FRONT AND BACK COVERS OF THIS BOOK.**

which 50 are libraries, 400 shelf sales. Single copy: $6; subscription: $10. Sample: $3.
How to Submit: Reads submissions October 1 through May 31 only. Publishes theme issues. Send SASE for guidelines and upcoming themes. Reports in 2-6 months. Pay "varies, but we do pay" plus 2 copies.
Advice: The editors offer these "practical suggestions: Cover letters with submissions do help. A cover letter provides something about the author and tells where and for what s/he is submitting. And don't let those rejection letters be cause for discouragement. Rejections can often be a matter of timing. The journal in question may be publishing a special issue with a certain theme (we've done a number of themes—'all-fiction,' 'all-poetry,' 'Asian-American,' 'environmental hazards,' 'Beauty and the Beasts,' etc.). Also, editorial boards do change, and new editors bring their individual opinions and tastes in writing. Good poetry will eventually be published if it is circulated."

SECOND AEON PUBLICATIONS, 19 Southminster Rd., Roath, Cardiff CF2 S4T Wales, phone/fax 01222-493093, e-mail peter.finch@dial.pipex.com, founded 1966, poetry editor Peter Finch. Does not accept unsolicited mss.

SEEDHOUSE, P.O. Box 883009, Steamboat Springs CO 80477, phone (970)879-6978, e-mail seedhouse98@yahoo.com, founded 1998, editor-in-chief Barbara Block.
Magazine Needs: *Seedhouse* is "a bimonthly literary magazine for modern writers and poets. Accepts poetry, essays, short stories, nonfiction and b&w artwork." They want "any good poetry. No juvenile work." They have published poetry by Michael White, Colorado Award Winner, and Mary Crow, Poet Laureate of Colorado. As a sample the editor selected these lines from "Cliff Dwellers" by Ron Chappell:

> still they roam the hidden reaches/ . . . archaic margins of my mind/and they call me, seek to know
> me/from an age beyond some border/where the eons gather stardust/from a people lost in time.

The editor says *Seedhouse* is 16 pgs., magazine-sized, includes b&w art/graphics. Press run is 1,000 for 500 subscribers. Single copy: $2.75; subscription: $15. Sample: $3.30. Make checks payable to *Seedhouse Magazine*.
How to Submit: Submit 3 poems at a time. Line length for poetry is 80 maximum. Previously published poems and simultaneous submissions OK. E-mail and disk submissions in Word Perfect or MS Word OK. Cover letter preferred. "We prefer typed submissions, double-spaced, in an easy to read font. Include name, address, phone, and three-sentence bio." Often comments on rejections. Publishes theme issues occasionally. Send SASE for guidelines and upcoming themes. Reports in 3 months. Pays 2 copies. Acquires one-time rights.
Also Offers: Sponsors an annual summer writing contest for short stories and poetry. 1st Place winners: $50 plus 1-year subscription; 2nd Place winners: $30; 3rd Place: $20.
Advice: The editor says, "Proofread your work carefully. Be sure to retain original."

SEEDS POETRY MAGAZINE; HIDDEN BROOK PRESS; SEEDS POETRY CONTEST, 412-701 King St. W., Toronto, Ontario M5V 2W7 Canada, e-mail writers@pathcom.com, website http://www.pathcom.com/~writers, founded 1994, publisher/editor Richard M. Grove.
Magazine Needs: *SEEDS* is published in a paper-based form and on the web approximately 2 times a year. "*SEEDS* is dedicated to being an accessible venue for writers, no matter what their status is in the publishing world. It doesn't matter whether you've ever been published or not. We publish well-crafted poetry from around the world, so send us any style of poetry you love to write. Send us your newly written or previously published work but be sure it is your absolute top shelf, best stuff. Don't save it for the bottom drawer or the future. We do not appreciate obscure, self-indulgent word games. We are not very interested in reading rhymed verse though we do on occasion publish such poetry if it suits us personally. We are not at all interested in reading about one-night stands, love-lorn angst or the teen heart throb. Save this for your bottom drawer. Religious dogma and spiritually sappy work are usually not our cup of tea but we have published some interesting references to God, the universe and spiritual epiphanies. Our goal is to publish well-written, memorable work whether it is humorous, traumatic, nature poems, cityscapes or just the insight or outlook about life. Push your poetry to the edge but not too far over the edge for us. Oh and keep the four letter words to a minimum. We have published very few of them." The editor says *SEEDS* is 32 pgs., magazine-sized, offset printed and saddle-stitched with b&w cover, includes ads. They receive about 200 poems a year, accept approximately 25%. Press run is 500 for 250 subscribers. Subscription: $15. Sample: $5. Make checks payable to Hidden Brook Press.
How to Submit: Submit 3 hard copy poems at a time, "any number of poems on 3.5 disk or e-mail." Line length for poetry is 3-200 maximum. Previously published poems and simultaneous submissions OK. E-mail and disk submissions OK. "If submitting by surface mail, please include SASE and short bio. Send mail submissions in the body of the message only, no attachments. Work, if accepted, is filed to fit with future themes, styles and formats of other works. Authors will be notified as to whether or not the editor is interested in keeping work on file." Obtain guidelines via website. Reports "as soon as possible." Pays 1 copy for work published in paper-based *SEEDS*. Staff reviews chapbooks of poetry in 300 words. Send books for review consideration.
Book/Chapbook Needs & How to Submit: Hidden Brook Press publishes 2 annual anthologies, *The Open Window* and *No Love Lost*. Send SASE (or SAE and IRC) for theme and submission information.
Also Offers: Sponsors the *SEEDS* Poetry Contest, awards $100, $50 and $25 plus publication. Entry fee: $12 for 3 poems. Deadlines: April 30 and October 30 annually. Send SASE (with IRCs) for details or request via e-mail. Also publishes an annual anthology. Send SASE (or SAE with IRCs) for submission guidelines.
Advice: The publisher says, "The paper-based *SEEDS* and the website *SEEDS* are two different poetry publica-

tions containing a different selection of poems and published at different times of the year."

○ SEEMS, P.O. Box 359, Lakeland College, Sheboygan WI 53082-0359, phone (920)565-1276, fax (920)565-1206, founded 1971.

Magazine Needs: *Seems* is published irregularly (33 issues in 28 years). This is a handsomely printed, nearly square (7×8¼) magazine, saddle-stapled, generous with white space on heavy paper. Two of the issues are considered chapbooks, and the editor, Karl Elder, suggests that a way to get acquainted would be to order *Seems #14, What Is The Future Of Poetry?* for $5, consisting of essays by 22 contemporary poets, and "If you don't like it, return it and we'll return your $5." *Explain That You Live: Mark Strand with Karl Elder* (#29) is available for $3. There are usually about 20 pgs. of poetry/issue. Elder has published poetry by Kim Bridgford, William Greenway, Joanne Lowery, Dave Oliphant and Kelly Shuford. He said it was "impossible" to select 6 illustrative lines. Print run is 350 for 200 subscribers of which 20 are libraries. Single copy: $4; subscription: $16/4 issues.

How to Submit: There is a 1- to 2-year backlog. "People may call or fax with virtually any question, understanding that the editor may have no answer." Reports in 1-3 months. Pays 1 copy. Acquires first North American serial rights. Returns rights upon publication.

Advice: The editor says, "We'd like to consider more prose poems."

▣ ◉ SEMIQUASI PRESS; RED DOT (Specialized: form/style), P.O. Box 55892, Fondren Station, Jackson MS 39296-5892, phone (601)969-9324, e-mail mempath@hotmail.com, founded 1989, publisher/editor A. di Michele, editor (chapbooks) Alef M. Baba.

• Semiquasi Press has been featured in Boise State University's SZ2 (Some Zines Two) exhibition (1996) and in the annual Poets House Poetry Publication Showcase (1995, 1996, 1997).

Magazine Needs: *Red Dot*, published in association with La College de Phénomenographie, is an annual "barrage of disjointedly, articulated poems and poetic discourse." They want "experimental work—meaning: concrete, cut-up, automatic, post-syntactic, collaborative, phenomenological, chance; poetry that combines or fuses the style/direction of, say, *Finnegan's Wake* with haiku . . . epic instances." They do not want "witty, sentimental work, or rhyming poems (unless unintentional)." They have published poetry by Guy R. Beining, Joel Dailey and John Lowther. As a sample the editor selected these lines from "Untitled" by Frank O'Royler:

> *Apropos, reverse vulnerable, a gem/abrigate could even structure an ear of worry/to be helium of ol'*
> *you soulmates. Her's is/quorum diabetes, (to menthol)*

The editor says *Red Dot* is 20-60 pgs., 8½×7, offset or letterpress printed, saddle-stapled or hand-bound with cardstock cover, includes collage art. They receive about 500 poems a year, accept approximately 10%. Press run is 200-400 for 100 subscribers of which 10 are libraries, 100 shelf sales; 50 distributed free (traded) to like publishers.

How to Submit: Submit 5-10 poems at a time. Previously published poems and simultaneous submission OK. Cover letter preferred. Reads submissions February 14 through November 2 only. "However, we accept submissions year-round." Often comments on rejections. Reports in 2 months. Sometimes sends prepublication galleys. Pays 1 copies. Reviews books and chapbooks of poetry. Poets may send books for review consideration.

Book/Chapbook Needs & How to Submit: Semiquasi Press is interested in "post-experimental, post-colonial, post-leftist work" and publishes 3-6 chapbooks/year under the imprint Semiquasi Editions. Chapbooks are usually 8-24 pgs., size varies, offset or letterpress printed or photocopied, saddle-stapled or hand-bound with cardstock cover. Query first with 5-10 sample poems and cover letter with brief bio and publication credits. Replies to queries in 2 weeks, to mss in 2 months. Pays up to 25 author's copies (out of a press run of 200). Obtain sample chapbooks by sending $10.

Advice: The editor says, "Experimentation is more than creating meaninglessness . . . it is the allowing of meaning to issue forth from deeper founts and in stranger garb."

▣ ○ ◉ SENECA REVIEW (Specialized: translations), Hobart and William Smith Colleges, Geneva NY 14456-3397, phone (315)781-3392, fax (315)781-3348, website http://www.hws.edu/~senecareview/, founded 1970, editor Deborah Tall, associate editor John D'Agata.

• Poetry published in *Seneca Review* has also been included in the 1994 and 1997 volumes of *The Best American Poetry* and in the 1998 Pushcart Anthology.

Magazine Needs: *Seneca Review* is a biannual. They want "serious poetry of any form, including translations. No light verse. Also essays on contemporary poetry and lyrical nonfiction." They have published poetry by Seamus Heaney, Rita Dove, Denise Levertov, Stephen Dunn and Hayden Carruth. *Seneca Review* is 100 pgs., 6×9, professionally printed on quality stock and perfect-bound with matte card cover. You'll find plenty of free verse here—some accessible and some leaning toward experimental—with the emphasis on voice, image and diction. All in all, poems and translations complement each other and create a distinct editorial mood each issue. They receive 3,000-4,000 poems a year, accept approximately 100. Press run is 1,000 for 500 subscribers of which half are libraries, about 250 shelf sales. Subscription: $8/year, $15/2 years. Sample: $5.

How to Submit: Submit 3-5 poems at a time. No simultaneous submissions or previously published poems. Reads submissions September 1 through May 1 only. Reports in 6-12 weeks. Pays 2 copies and a 2-year subscription.

Also Offers: Website includes guidelines, excerpts from current issue, profile of editors, available back issues, subscription info, info for advertisers and book stores.

⚐ $⃠ ◎ **SENSATIONS MAGAZINE (Specialized: membership/subscription, themes)**, 2 Radio Ave., A5, Secaucus NJ 07094, founded 1987, publisher/executive editor David Messineo.

● "*Sensations Magazine* is a three-time winner in the American Literary Magazine Awards, including First Place for our tabloid-sized issue on 'The 100th Anniversary of Coney Island's Amusement Parks,' which contained over 100 5×7 photos with the poetry and fiction."

Magazine Needs: *Sensations Magazine* is "an unusual mix of contemporary poetry, contemporary fiction and historical research." *Sensations Magazine* releases 1 issue/year, and alternates between theme and non-theme issues. It will release Issue 20 in 2000. "Theme is 'Scenic New Jersey.' Also in that issue will be 'Secaucus in Poetry,' a collection of verse inspired by Secaucus, NJ, which is celebrating its 100th anniversary." As a sample the publisher selected these lines from "Tituba's Defiance" by Jacqueline de Weever, which appeared in Issue 18, "The 350th Anniversary of American Witchhunts, 1648-1998":

> Zig-zag sharpens/life's bulk rations/Salem's a run down place/wooden minds encaged in bark./I travel in silk/not spun by worms.//Salem/can't/tie me./Witch. Sorcerer. Life./Fire doesn't frighten me.

Sensations Magazine averages over 100 pgs., 8½×11, desktop-published on coated stock, velo-bound, and often includes full color on the cover and color photos inside. Check (or international money order) must be made payable to David Messineo.

How to Submit: "Writers must first send a SASE for current submission guidelines. Do not send poetry before receiving submission requirements; such 'poetry dumps' will be tossed, unread." No previously published poems; simultaneous submissions OK. Responds 1 month after postmark deadline. Pays on acceptance. "*Sensations Magazine* has previously paid $3.25/line for the top 2 poems per issue: the highest 'per line' rate in America. To pay writers significantly and to maintain excellent production standards, we typically require writers to make an up-front payment with their submissions, to fund all we do for you."

Advice: Mr. Messineo says, "If you merely want a publication credit to add to a 'comma-list' in your bio, or don't care how your work is presented in publication, we're not for you. If you would appreciate having your poetry critiqued on up to 20 different categories, or would just like to be treated with personal courtesy and decency instead of as 'one among thousands' for a change, it's definitely worth your time to send an SASE to our address for the current submission requirements. Purchase of a back issue, as always, is recommended; rates and availability will be included with all inquiries we receive. Good luck!"

⊘ **SERPENT & EAGLE PRESS**, 10 Main St., Laurens NY 13796, phone (607)432-2990, founded 1981, poetry editor Jo Mish. They are currently not accepting poetry submissions.

◎ **SEVEN BUFFALOES PRESS; AZOREAN EXPRESS; BLACK JACK; VALLEY GRAPEVINE; HILL AND HOLLER ANTHOLOGY SERIES (Specialized: rural, regional, anthologies)**, Box 249, Big Timber MT 59011, founded 1973, editor Art Coelho.

Magazine Needs & How to Submit: The editor says, "I've always thought that rural and working class writers, poets and artists deserve the same tribute given to country singers." These publications all express that interest. For all of them Art Coelho wants poetry oriented toward rural and working people, "a poem that tells a story, preferably free verse, not longer than 50-100 lines, poems with strong lyric and metaphor, not romantical, poetry of the heart as much as the head, not poems written like grocery lists or the first thing that comes from a poet's mind, no ivory tower, and half my contributors are women." He has published poetry by R.T. Smith, James Goode, Leo Connellan and Wendell Berry. *The Azorean Express* is 35 pgs., 5½×8½, side-stapled. It appears twice a year. Circulation 200. Sample: $6.75. Submit 4-8 poems at a time. No simultaneous submissions. Reports in 1 month. Pays 1 copy. *Black Jack* is an anthology series on Rural America that uses rural material from anywhere, especially the American West; *Valley Grapevine* is an anthology on central California, circulation 750, that uses rural material from central California; *Hill and Holler*, Southern Appalachian Mountain series, takes in rural mountain lifestyle and folkways. Sample of any postpaid: $6.75.

Book/Chapbook Needs & How to Submit: Seven Buffaloes Press does not accept unsolicited mss but publishes books solicited from writers who have appeared in the above magazines.

Advice: Art Coelho advises, "Don't tell the editor how great you are. This one happens to be a poet and novelist who has been writing for 30 years. Your writing should not only be fused with what you know from the head, but also from what you know within your heart. Most of what we call life may be some kind of gift of an unknown river within us. The secret to be learned is to live with ease in the darkness, because there are too many things of the night in this world. But the important clue to remember is that there are many worlds within us."

$⃠ ⚐ **THE SEWANEE REVIEW**, University of the South, Sewanee TN 37383-1000, phone (931)598-1246, e-mail rjones@sewanee.edu, website http://www.sewanee.edu/sreview/home.html, founded 1892, thus being our nation's oldest continuously published literary quarterly, editor George Core.

Magazine Needs: Fiction, criticism and poetry are invariably of the highest establishment standards. Many of our major poets appear here from time to time. *SR* has published poetry by Catharine S. Brosman, Wendell Berry, Donald Hall, Anthony Hecht and Howard Nemerov. Each issue is a hefty paperback of nearly 200 pgs., conservatively bound in matte paper, always of the same typography. Truly a magazine open to all styles and forms, issues we critiqued featured formal sequences, metered verse, structured free verse, sonnets, and lyric and narrative forms—all accessible and intelligent. Circulation: 3,200. Sample: $6.25.

How to Submit: Reports in 3-6 weeks. No simultaneous submissions. No fax or e-mail submissions. "Unsolicited works should not be submitted between June 1 and August 31. A response to any submission received during that period will be greatly delayed." Pays 70¢/line, plus 2 copies (and reduced price of $4 for additional copies). Also includes brief, standard and essay-reviews.

Also Offers: Website includes submission guidelines, subscription costs, selections from the magazine and links to useful references, publishers, etc.

[N] [◯] SHADES OF DECEMBER, P.O. Box 244, Selden NY 11784, e-mail eilonwy@innocent.com, website http://www2.crosswinds.net/new-york/~shadesof12/, founded 1998, editor-in-chief Alexander C.P. Danner and Brandy L. Straus.

Magazine Needs: Published quarterly, *Shades of December* "provides a forum that is open to all forms of writing (poetry, prose, drama, etc.). Topics and tones range from the academic to the whimsical. We are open to any genre and style. No trite greeting-card verse." They have published poetry by Joe Lucia, Anne O'Malley, Jonathan Russell and Emily Rivard. As a sample the editor selected this poem, "From: Poetry To: Entropy" by Carl Marcum:

> Even asleep in your bed you're spinning/at hundreds of miles an hour./Only your covers and a
> misplaced faith in gravity/keep you from waking light years/away from yourself.

SOD is 52 pgs., digest-sized, neatly printed and saddle-stapled with colored cardstock cover, uses b&w graphics. Single copy: $2.75; subscription: $12. Sample: $3. Make checks payable to Alexander C.P. Danner.

How to Submit: Submit 2-6 poems at a time. No previously published poems; simultaneous submissions OK. Cover letter preferred. E-mail submissions OK. "Cover letter should include brief 50-word bio listing previous publications/noteworthy facts. Include SASE. All electronic submissions should be in an IBM-recognizable format (any version MS Word, Corel Word Perfect)." Time between acceptance and publication is 1-4 months. Seldom comments on rejections. Publishes theme issues occasionally. Send SASE for guidelines or obtain via e-mail or website. Reports in 4-6 weeks. Sometimes sends prepublication galleys. Pays 2 copies. Acquires one-time rights.

Also Offers: Website includes guidelines, subscription/ordering information, upcoming themes and sample pieces.

$ [◯] SHAMAL BOOKS (Specialized: ethnic, anthologies), Dept. PM, GPO Box 16, New York NY 10116, phone (718)622-4426, founded 1976, editor Louis Reyes Rivera.

Book/Chapbook Needs: Shamal Books is a small press whose purpose is "to promote the literary efforts of African-American and Caribbean writers, particularly those who would not otherwise be able to establish their literary credentials as their concerns as artists are with the people." The press publishes individual and "anthological" books and chapbooks, mostly flat-spined paper texts. They have published poetry by Sandra Maria Esteves and Rashidah Ismaili. The editor wants to see "poetry that clearly demonstrates an understanding of craft, content and intent as the scriptural source of the word guiding and encouraging the intellect of the people."

How to Submit: The editor does not consider unsolicited submissions of individual mss, but will look at work only while anthologies are open. Submit 2 sample poems. Mss should be "neat and single-spaced." Cover letter "leaning toward personal goals and poetic principles" required. Replies to queries within 2 months. Royalties for book authors are 15%. The editor says that he will subsidy publish "delicately—depends on resources and interest in work." His projects include "an international anthology; drama; books on language as a weapon; a collectivized publisher's catalog of Third World presses working out of NYC."

Advice: His advice to poets: "Certainly to study the craft more and to research more into the historical role that has been the hallmark of poetry across class and caste conscious lines that limit younger perspectives. Not to be as quick to publish as to be in serious study, then while looking to publish, looking as well into collective ventures with other poets for publication and distribution. Above all, read!"

[◯] SHARING MAGAZINE (Specialized: religious, Christian healing), 6807 Forest Haven, San Antonio TX 78240, phone/fax (210)681-5146, founded 1932, editor Marjorie George.

Magazine Needs: *Sharing* is published monthly by the Order of St. Luke, a Christian healing ministry. They want poetry "on the subject of Christian healing only." The editor says *Sharing* is 32 pgs., 5½×8½, offset printed. They receive about 50 poems a year, accept approximately 25%. Press run is 9,000. Single copy: $1.75; subscription: $12/year.

How to Submit: Submit up to 4 poems at a time. Previously published poems and simultaneous submissions OK. Cover letter preferred. E-mail and disk submissions OK. Send SASE for guidelines. Reports in 2-4 weeks. Pays 5 copies. Acquires first or one-time rights.

Advice: The editor says, "We are a very limited market and specific to poems on the topic of Christian healing."

[◯] SHATTERED WIG REVIEW, 425 E. 31st, Baltimore MD 21218, phone (410)243-6888, website http://www.normals.com/~normals/, founded 1988, contact Sonny Bodkin.

Magazine Needs: *SWR* is a semiannual using "everything in particular. Prefer sleaking nurse stories, absurdist trickles and blasts of Rimbaud. Exploring the thin line between reality and societal hallucination." They have published poetry by Gary Blankenburg, Cynthia Hendershot and Dan Raphael. As a sample the editor selected these lines from "Answering" by John M. Bennett:

> Seems like falling over chair, rings I skull-clapped/that stoney wall he dandruffs in, dithering before's/

When asked about the cover illustration for Issue 17 of *Shattered Wig Review* and its relationship to the overall theme of the publication, co-editor Rupert Wondolowski summed it up this way: "Human life has been reduced to facsimiles—some of them eerily floating heads, others are heads stuck on Pez stands." The cover illustration is by T. Duggan, "a sailor/travel writer, computer graphic designer, visual artist and technical support for the Baltimore avant-garde musical group Your Father's Moustache." *Shattered Wig Review* appears semiannually and publishes "liquid, messy poetry, oozing the stuff of life. We consider poetry in its broadest form—any moments of clarity." The magazine is about 70 pages, 8½ × 8½, photocopied and side-stapled with card stock covers with original artwork.

> *slump in the socket, an (eye slucked back in)/what I doubled seeing, like "crawling over air, sinks/I"*
> *dreaming my lid-blink closed . . . (so the far down/dull flat seems, like's phoney) all night looking*

SWR is approximately 70 pgs., 8½ × 8½, photocopied, side-stapled with card stock covers with original artwork, art and graphics also inside. They receive about 10 submissions a week, accept about 20%. Press run is 300 for 100 subscribers of which 10 are libraries, 100 shelf sales. Subscription: $9 (2 issues). Sample: $4.
How to Submit: Previously published poems and simultaneous submissions OK. Seldom comments on rejections. Reports within a month. Pays 1 copy. Acquires one-time rights. Occasionally reviews books of poetry in 100 words. Open to unsolicited reviews. Poets may also send books for review consideration. The editor says there are no requirements for contributors except "that the contributor include us in their nightly prayers."

SHEILA-NA-GIG, 23106 Kent Ave., Torrance CA 90505, e-mail grimmgirl@aol.com, founded 1990, editor Ms. Hayley R. Mitchell.
Magazine Needs: *Sheila-Na-Gig* appears once a year in January as a large general issue. The editor says she is partial to free verse but accepts many styles and subject matter. She generally does not publish poems over 3 pages, religious poetry or rhyming verse. They have published work by Lyn Lifshin, Gerald Locklin, Michael McNeilley, Denise Duhamel, Joan Jobe Smith and Charles Webb. *Sheila-Na-Gig* is 100-150 pgs., digest-sized, flat-spined, photocopied from laser prints with matte card cover. Subscription: $7/year, $12/2 years. Sample: $7 for current issue ($6 for back issues). Please make checks payable to *Sheila-Na-Gig.*
How to Submit: Submit up to 5 poems with cover letter, short bio and SASE. No e-mail submissions. Reads submissions January through May 31 only. Reports in 6-8 weeks. Pays 1 copy. Acquires first rights.
Also Offers: Sponsors the Featured Poet contest. Submit 5-10 previously unpublished poems with SASE. Deadline: June 30, 2000. Entry fee: $10. "Include a cover letter with name, address, 50-word bio, e-mail address, poem titles and check number. Please do not include your name on poems." 1st place: $500 plus publication; 2nd and 3rd place: publication and 5 copies. "All entrants receive a copy of *Sheila-Na-Gig,* and all poems are considered for publication."

$ SHENANDOAH; THE JAMES BOATWRIGHT III PRIZE FOR POETRY, Troubadour Theater, 2nd Floor, Washington and Lee University, Lexington VA 24450-0303, phone (540)463-8765, fax (540)463-8461, e-mail lleech@wlu.edu, website http://www.wlu.edu/~shenando, founded 1950, editor R.T. Smith, managing editor Lynn L. Leech.
● Poetry published in *Shenandoah* has been included in the 1993 and 1997 volumes of *The Best American Poetry.*
Magazine Needs: Published at Washington and Lee University, it is a quarterly literary magazine. They have published poetry by Mary Oliver, Margaret Gibson, W.S. Merwin and Brendan Galvin. As a sample the editor selected "The Ghost Orchid" by Michael Longley:
> Added to its few remaining sites will be the stanza/I compose about leaves like flakes of skin, a colour/
> Dithering between pink and yellow, and then the root/That grows like coral among shadows and leaf-
> litter./Just touching the petals bruises them into darkness.
The magazine is 120 pgs., 6 × 9, perfect-bound, professionally printed with full-color cover. Generally, it is open to all styles and forms. Circulation is 1,900. Subscription: $15/year; $28/2 years; $40/3 years. Sample: $5.
How to Submit: All submissions should be typed on one side of the paper only. Your name and address must be clearly written on the upper right corner of the ms. Include SASE. Reads submissions September 1 through May 30 only. Reports in 3 months. Payment includes a check, 1-year subscription and 1 copy. Buys first publication rights. Staff reviews books of poetry in 7-10 pages, multi-book format. Send books for review consideration. Most reviews are solicited.
Also Offers: Sponsors The James Boatwright III Prize For Poetry. A $1,000 prize awarded annually to the

author of the best poem published in *Shenandoah* during a volume year.

N ☉ SHIRIM, A JEWISH POETRY JOURNAL (Specialized: ethnic), 4611 Vesper Ave., Sherman Oaks CA 91403, phone (310)476-2861, founded 1982, editor Marc Dworkin.
Magazine Needs: *Shirim* appears biannually and publishes "poetry that reflects Jewish living without limiting to specific symbols, images or contents." They have published poetry by Robert Mezcy, Karl Shapiro and Grace Schulmon. The editor says *Shirim* is 40 pgs., 4×5, desktop-published and saddle-stapled with card stock cover. Press run is 200. Subscription: $7. Sample: $4.
How to Submit: Submit 4 poems at a time. No previously published poems or simultaneous submissions. Cover letter preferred. Seldom comments on rejections. Publishes theme issues regularly. Reports in 3 months. Acquires first rights.

$ ☉ SHOFAR (Specialized: children, ethnic, religious), 43 Northcote Dr., Melville NY 11747-3924, phone/fax (516)643-4598, founded 1984, publisher/editor Gerald H. Grayson.
Magazine Needs: *Shofar* is a magazine for Jewish children 9-13, appearing monthly October through May (double issues December/January and April/May). It is 32 pgs., magazine-sized, professionally printed, with color paper cover. Press run is 17,000 for 16,000 subscribers of which 1,000 are libraries. Subscription: $14.95. Sample: $1.01 postage and 9×12 SAE.
How to Submit: They will consider simultaneous submissions and "maybe" previously published poems. Send SASE for guidelines. Submit holiday theme poems at least 4 months in advance. Reports in 6-8 weeks. Pays 10¢/word plus 5 copies. Buys first North American serial rights.

□ ◒ SIDEWALKS, P.O. Box 321, Champlin MN 55316, founded 1991, editor Tom Heie.
Magazine Needs: *Sidewalks* is a semiannual anthology of poetry, short prose and art, published to promote the work of emerging and published writers and artists. They want "poetry that uses strong, original images and language, showing attention to craftsmanship, but not self-conscious; poetry that shows insight. No porno, kinky sex or rhyming verse." They have published poetry by Mark Vinz, Jay Meek, Michael Dennis Browne and Kenneth Pobo. As a sample the editor selected the last stanza of "The Winter Heart" by Mary Kay Rummel:

> *She searches for the bear, remembering/how she'd watched her roll down the road/on round haunches.*
> *She knows they both/will wake with lust some morning/will walk on the ice in shoes of fire.*

Sidewalks is 76-80 pgs., 5½×8½, professionally printed and perfect-bound with matte card cover and b&w art. They receive 600-800 poems a year, accept approximately 10%. Press run is 300 for 100 subscribers, 50 shelf sales. Single copy: $6; subscription: $9. Sample: $5.
How to Submit: Submit 3-6 poems at a time, name and address on each. No previously published poems or simultaneous submissions. Cover letter preferred. Deadlines: May 31 and December 31. Three readers read and vote on submissions; then a group meets to select the best work. Seldom comments on rejections. Send SASE for guidelines. Reports 1 month after deadline. Pays 1 copy. Acquires first rights.
Advice: The editor says, "Sidewalks [are] those places where a child first meets the world, [a] place of discovery, of myth, power, incantation . . . a world in itself, places we continue to meet people, ignoring some, smiling at others, preoccupied, on our way somewhere, . . . [places] where we pass with just a glance or smile or protectively turn up our collar on a windy day, . . . paths to and from neighbors, to the corner grocery . . . paths that bring us home."

□ ◒ SIERRA NEVADA COLLEGE REVIEW, P.O. Box 4269, Incline Village NV 89450, founded 1990, editor June Sylvester.
Magazine Needs: *SNCR* is an annual literary magazine featuring poetry and short fiction by new writers. They want "high quality, image-oriented poems that suggest or surprise; no limit on length, style, etc. No light verse, sloppy sentiment, purposeful obscurity, clichés or cuteness." They have published poetry by Marisella Veiga, Ivanov Y. Reyez, Colleen O'Brien and B.Z. Niditch. As a sample the editor selected these lines from "The Book of Ruth" by Margaret Almon:

> *I must not dream of anger./Placing a kernel/in the bend of his knee,/willing it to sprout into tangles/*
> *around his throat—/tangles like the ones in my hair/that break the comb./Placing a sheaf beneath his*
> *bed,/his body becoming a field of bruises.*

The editor says *SNCR* is approximately 75 pgs., with cover art only. "We receive approximately 500 poems a year and accept approximately 50." Press run is 500. Subscription: $5/year. Sample: $2.50.
How to Submit: Submit 5 poems at a time. No previously published poems; simultaneous submissions OK. Include brief bio. Reads submissions September 1 through April 1 only. Often comments on rejections. Reports in 3 weeks to 3 months. Pays 2 copies.
Advice: The editor says, "We delight in publishing the unpublished or underpublished writer. We look specifically for subtlety and skill."

$ □ ☉ THE SILVER WEB: A MAGAZINE OF THE SURREAL (Specialized: science fiction, horror), P.O. Box 38190, Tallahassee FL 32315, e-mail annk19@mail.idt.net, founded 1989, editor Ann Kennedy.
Magazine Needs: *The Silver Web* is a semiannual publication featuring fiction, poetry, art and thought-provoking

articles. They want "works ranging from speculative fiction to dark tales and all weirdness in between; specifically works of the surreal. We are looking for well-written work that is unusual and original. No genre clichés, that is, no vampires, werewolves, zombies, witches, fairies, elves, dragons, etc. Also no fantasy, sword and sorcery. Poems must use standard poetic conventions whether free verse or rhyming." They have published poetry by Glenna Holloway, Simon Perchik, Tippi N. Blevins and Jacie Ragan. As a sample we selected these lines from "Empty House" by Fabian Peake:

> *You walk the pavement/of my street in your/scuffed black shoes,/dragging behind you/(on lengths of*
> *string/tied to your belt),/a hundred paintbrushes/dancing like drumsticks . . .*

The Silver Web is 90 pgs., 8½×11, offset printed, perfect-bound with full-color cover and b&w photos, art and ads. They receive 10-20 poems a week, accept 10-20 a year. Press run is 2,000 for more than 300 subscribers. Subscription: $12. Sample: $7.20, $7.95 Canada and overseas.

How to Submit: Submit up to 5 poems at a time. Previously published poems OK, but note previous credit. Simultaneous submissions also OK. E-mail for queries and information only. "Cover letters are enjoyed but not essential. Provide an SASE with proper postage to ensure a response." Reads submissions January 1 through September 30 only. "You may receive a form rejection, but I will do my best to give personal comments as time allows." Send SASE for guidelines or request via e-mail. Reports in 6-8 weeks. Always sends prepublication galleys. Pays $10-50, 2 copies and discount on additional copies. Buys first or one-time rights.

◎ **SILVER WINGS/MAYFLOWER PULPIT (Specialized: religious, spirituality/inspirational); POETRY ON WINGS, INC.**, P.O. Box 1000, Pearblossom CA 93553-1000, phone (805)264-3726, e-mail poetwing@yahoo.com, founded 1983, published by Poetry on Wings, Inc., poetry editor Jackson Wilcox.

Magazine Needs: "As a committed Christian service we produce and publish *Silver Wings/Mayflower Pulpit*, a bimonthly poetry magazine. We want poems with a Christian perspective, reflecting a vital personal faith and a love for God and man. Will consider poems from 3-20 lines. Short poems are preferred. Poems over 20 lines will not even be read by the editor. Quite open in regard to meter and rhyme." They have published poetry by Elva McAllaster, Mary Ann Henn, Fred Forster and C. David Hay. As a sample the editor selected these lines from "The First Step is the Hardest" by Deborah Esling:

> *Eaglets never learn to fly/While clinging to the limb.//A lesson gleaned from nature—/When faith*
> *outweighs the fear,/First steps can be taken/And miracles appear.*

Silver Wings/Mayflower Pulpit is 16 pgs., digest-sized, offset with cartoon-like art. Each issue contains a short inspirational article or sermon plus 15-20 poems. They receive about 1,500 submissions a year, use approximately 260. Circulation is 300 with 250 subscribers, 50 shelf sales. Subscription: $10. Sample: $2.

How to Submit: Submit typed ms, double-spaced. Include SASE. No previously published poems; simultaneous submissions OK. Time between acceptance and publication can be up to 2 years. Send SASE for guidelines and upcoming themes. Reports in 3 weeks, providing SASE is supplied. Pays 1 copy. "We occasionally offer an award to a poem we consider outstanding and most closely in the spirit of what *Silver Wings* seeks to accomplish." Acquires first rights.

Advice: The editor says, "We have felt that the state of secular poetry today is thrashing in a stagnant pond out of which it cannot extract itself. We want to lift our poetry to a high road where God's sunlight is shining. We even encourage poets with little ability but having an upward mobile commitment."

☑ ◑ ⊘ **SILVERFISH REVIEW; SILVERFISH REVIEW PRESS; GERALD CABLE POETRY CONTEST**, P.O. Box 3541, Eugene OR 97403, phone (541)344-5060, e-mail sfrpress@aol.com, website http://www.qhome.com/silverfish, founded 1979, poetry editor Rodger Moody.

Magazine Needs: *Silverfish* is a biannual (June and December) literary magazine. "The only criterion for selection of poetry is quality. In future issues, *Silverfish Review* will also showcase the short short story." They have published poetry by Chelsey Minnis, Denise Duhamel, Dick Allen, Ivan Arguelles, Gary Young, Robert Gregory, Kevin Bowen, Richard Jones, Floyd Skloot and Judith Skillman. The magazine is 48 pgs., digest-sized, professionally printed in dark type on quality stock, matte card cover with art. There are 30-34 pgs. of poetry in each issue. They receive about 1,000 submissions of poetry a year, use approximately 20, have a 6- to 12-month backlog. Circulation is 500. Subscription for institutions: $12; for individuals: $8. Sample: $4, single copy orders should include $1.50 for p&h.

How to Submit: *SR* is suspended until the summer of 2000 and *not open to submissions*. It will open to submissions in the year 2000. When open, submit at least 5 poems to editor. No simultaneous submissions. Reports in about 2-3 months. Pays 2 copies and 1-year subscription, plus small honorarium when grant support permits. Reviews books of poetry. Open to unsolicited reviews. Poets may also send books for review consideration.

Also Offers: Silverfish Review Press sponsors the Gerald Cable Poetry Contest. A $1,000 cash award and publication by SRP is awarded annually to the best book-length ms or original poetry by an author who has not yet published a full-length collection. No restrictions on the kind of poetry or subject matter; translations not acceptable. A $20 reading fee must accompany the ms; make checks payable to Silverfish Review Press. Send SASE for rules.

Also Offers: Website includes contest information and information on back of books published by SRP.

○ ◙ **SIMPLE VOWS; IMPRIMATUR PRESS**, P.O. Box 681597, San Antonio TX 78268, founded 1997, first issue appeared July 1998, co-editor Kemp Gregory, co-editor Charles Fuhrken, production editor Jon Gordon.
Magazine Needs: *Simple Vows* is published biannually "to provide a high-quality venue for writers in general (short story writers, playwrights, diarists, etc.) and for poets in particular." They want "lean, uncluttered, luminous, rhythmical work about experiences that matter. No artless simplistic expression, on the one hand, and overornate, rarefied (and usually obtuse) academic experiments, on the other." They have published poetry by Gerald Locklin, Susanne Bowers and Albert Huffstickler. As a sample Kemp Gregory selected these lines from his poem "Jonah's Fifth Avenue Prayer":
  Sunday morning./The bells are ringing/for me and my God,/Dearly beloved/We are separated/for good.
The editors say *SV* is 80 pgs., 5×8, saddle-stitched with card stock cover, includes b&w line art. They receive about 500 poems a year, accept approximately 5-10%. Press run is 200. Single copy: $6; subscription: $10. Sample: $6. Make checks payable to Kemp Gregory.
How to Submit: Submit 3-6 poems at a time. Previously published poems and simultaneous submissions OK. Cover letter required. "Keep cover letter to a page, please. List most recent credits (a few). Tell us a little about you (job, reasons for writing, etc.)." Time between acceptance and publication is 4-6 months. Often comments on rejections. Send SASE for guidelines. Reports in 2-3 months. Pays 1 copy. Acquires first or one-time rights. Staff reviews other magazines in 500 words, single book format.
Advice: The editors say, "Everyone is saying this, but too many poets still aren't listening: if you want to be a good poet, you must read poetry of all kinds. Know the rules of the game and the greats who have played it."

[N:] ○ **SIMPLY WORDS MAGAZINE**, 605 Collins Ave. #23, Centerville GA 31028, phone/fax (912)953-9482, e-mail simplywords@hotmail.com, website http://welcome.to/simplywords, founded 1991, editor Ruth Niehaus.
Magazine Needs: *Simply Words* is a quarterly magazine publish "to keep poetry alive." They are open to all type, forms and subjects. "No foul language or overtly sexual works." They have published poetry by Marian Ford Parks, Najwa Salam Brax, Sarah Jensen and James Cannon. As a sample the editor selected these lines (poet unidentified):
  Through the window/A star among the branches/In the winter light
The editor says *SWM* is 20-24 pgs., magazine-sized, deskjet printed and spiral-bound, uses clip art. They receive about 500 poems a year, accept approximately 90%. Press run is "limited to subscriptions and orders in house before we print." Subscription: $18.50/year. Sample: $5.
How to Submit: Line length for poetry is 24 maximum. Previously published poems OK; no simultaneous submissions. Cover letter preferred. SASE required. Reading fees: $1/poem, $3 for 3 or more poems. Time between acceptance and publication is "anytime within a year." Seldom comments on rejections. Publishes theme issues occasionally. Send SASE for guidelines and upcoming themes or obtain via e-mail. Reports in 4-6 weeks. Acquires one-time rights.
Also Offers: "We also accept short stories and articles about the 'writing' life and how to be a better poet/writer. Reading fees apply." Website includes some guidelines and general information.
Advice: The editor says, "Learn the ropes—research your craft and always, always get guidelines."

$ ◙ **SING HEAVENLY MUSE! (Specialized: feminist)**, Box 13320, Minneapolis MN 55414, founded 1977, contact editorial circle.
Magazine Needs: Fosters "the work of women poets, fiction writers and artists. The magazine is feminist in an open, generous sense: We encourage women to range freely, honestly and imaginatively over all subjects, philosophies and styles. We do not wish to confine women to women's subjects, whether these are defined traditionally, in terms of femininity and domesticity, or modernly, from a sometimes narrow polemical perspective. We look for explorations, questions that do not come with ready-made answers, emotionally or intellectually." For poetry they have "no limitations except women's writing or men's writing that reflects awareness of women's consciousness." They have published poetry by Alexis Rotella, Jill Breckenridge and Amirh Bahati. The magazine appears once a year in a 6×9, flat-spined, 125-page format, offset from typescript on heavy stock, b&w art, glossy card color cover. They receive about 1,500 submissions a year, use approximately 50-60. Press run is 1,000 for 275 subscribers of which 50 are libraries. Single copy: $8 plus $2 p&h; subscription: $15/2 issues, $20/3 issues ($16 low income), $38/6 issues. Sample: $4. "Copies are also available in bookstores nationwide that carry small press women's literature."
How to Submit: Submit up to 6 poems at a time, name and address on each page. No simultaneous submissions. Editors sometimes comment on rejections. Send SASE for guidelines, information about upcoming reading periods and themes. Reports in 4-5 months. Pays "usually $25 plus two copies."

FOR AN EXPLANATION of symbols used in this book, see the Key to Symbols on the front and back inside covers.

$ ⬛ ◎ SISTERS TODAY (Specialized: spirituality/inspirational), The Liturgical Press, Collegeville MN 56321, phone (320)363-7065, e-mail mwagner@csbsju.edu, send submissions to: poetry editor Sister Mary Virginia Micka, C.S.J., 1884 Randolph, St. Paul MN 55105.
Magazine Needs: *Sisters Today* has been published for about 60 years. Though it is a Roman Catholic magazine, poetry may be on any topic, but "should clearly be *poems*, not simply *statements* or *prayers*." They want "short poems (not over 25 lines) using clean, fresh images that appeal to the reader's feelings in a compelling way." They do not want poetry that depends "heavily on rhyme, verbal 'tricks' or excessive capitalization, manipulation of spacing, etc." *ST*, appearing 6 times/year, is 80 pgs., 6×9, saddle-stapled, professionally printed with matte card cover. They receive about 50 poems a month, accept 3-4.
How to Submit: Submit up to 5 poems at a time. No simultaneous submissions. Original poems much preferred. They require "each poem typed on a separate standard-size typing sheet, and each page must carry complete legal name, address and social security number typed in the upper right corner. Manuscripts without SASE will not be returned." Time between acceptance and publication is 6-12 months. Send SASE to St. Paul, MN address (above) for guidelines. Reports within 1-2 months. Pays $10/poem and 2 copies. Buys first rights.

⬛ SITUATION, 10402 Ewell Ave., Kensington MD 20895, founded 1991, contact Mark Wallace and Joanne Molina.
Magazine Needs: *Situation* appears several times/year and is interested in "innovative work that explores how writing creates, dismantles, or restructures the possibility of identity. A poetry of situation. Works involving questions of race, class, gender or sexual preference are all encouraged." They want experimental or avant-garde poetry; "less likely to accept poetry in traditional forms." They have published poetry by Charles Bernstein, Sterling Plumpp, Joan Retallack and Stephen-Paul Martin. As a sample we selected these lines from "Arlem" by Renee Gladman:
> having decided on neither extreme because she is always/already in the middle I sat through intermission tapping my/foot to its duration. You ask me why I mourn the leaving/before you have left as if any answer would bring us closer/to the problem of poetry.
Situation is 24 pgs., 7×8½, neatly printed on bond paper, saddle-stapled, no cover. They receive about 200 submissions a year, accept approximately 15%. Press run is 200 for 100 subscribers of which 5 are libraries. Subscription: $10. Sample: $3. Make checks payable to Mark Wallace.
How to Submit: Submit 7 poems at a time. No previously published poems. Cover letter required. "All submissions must be accompanied by SASE." Time between acceptance and publication is usually 6 months. Seldom comments on rejections. Send SASE for guidelines or request via e-mail. Reports in 3 months. Sometimes sends prepublication galleys. Pays 2 copies. Acquires first rights.

✓ $⬛ SIXTH CHAMBER; SIXTH CHAMBER USED BOOKS; SIXTH CHAMBER PRESS, 1332 Grand Ave., St. Paul MN 55105, phone (651)690-9463, website http://www.sixthchamber.com, founded 1995, editor James Williams.
Magazine Needs: *Sixth Chamber* is an annual publication with "no agenda. We focus on individual pieces of good quality poetry and prose." They want poetry of no more than 100 lines; prose no more than 1,500 words. "No poems that feature wicked mothers or fathers." They have published poetry by Darin Smith, Jeffry Little, Chaunce Stanton and Chris Hubbuch. As a sample the editor selected this poem (poet unidentified):
> My ancestors distrusted people with arched/feet long fingernails, dark skin, people/who worshipped outside their homes/and people who used hand gestures./At times they killed such people. Other times/ they simply refrained from marrying them.
SC is 35 pgs., 4¼×5½, desktop-published and inhouse printed, saddle-stapled with card stock cover, includes art. They receive about 300 poems a year, accept approximately 10%. Press run is 300. Single copy: $2.50. Sample: $4. Make checks payable to Sixth Chamber Used Books.
How to Submit: Submit 5 poems at a time. No previously published poems or simultaneous submissions. Cover letter preferred. Time between acceptance and publication is 3 months. Send SASE for guidelines. Reports in 1 month. Always sends prepublication galleys. Pays 1 copy. Acquires first rights. Reviews chapbooks of poetry. Send books for review consideration.
Book/Chapbook Needs & How to Submit: Sixth Chamber Press "focuses on quality of pieces not styles or philosophies" and publishes 5 chapbooks/year. Format for chapbooks is similar to that of the journal. Replies to queries in 1 month. Pays 30% royalties and 1 author's copy. Obtain sample chapbooks by sending SASE for information.

🌐 ◯ SKALD, 2 Greenfield Terrace, Menai Bridge, Anglesey LL59 5AY Wales, United Kingdom, phone 1248-716343, founded 1994, contact Ms. Zoë Skoulding.
Magazine Needs: *Skald* appears approximately 3 times a year and contains "poetry and prose in Welsh or English. We focus on writers in Wales though submissions from elsewhere are welcome." They want "interesting and varied poetry in Welsh and English. Nothing didactic, sentimental or nostalgic." As a sample Ms. Skoulding selected these lines from "Life Story" by Malcolm Bradley:
> Unexplored eccentric swelling/fills my lunar skull./An atrocity of emptiness/leaves each glib cell/to the slow abstract/click of extinction.
Skald is 30-40 pgs., A5, professionally printed and saddle-stapled with textured card cover, contains b&w artwork.

They receive about 300 poems a year, accept approximately 25%. Press run is 300 for 20 subscribers, 250 shelf sales; 20 distributed free to other magazines, art boards. Single copy: £3; subscription: £8/year (payments in sterling only).
How to Submit: Submit 2 poems at a time. No previously published poems or simultaneous submissions. Cover letter preferred. Time between acceptance and publication is 4 months. Often comments on rejections. Reports in 1 month. Pays 1 copy.

⬜◐◎ **SKIPPING STONES: A MULTICULTURAL CHILDREN'S MAGAZINE; ANNUAL YOUTH HONOR AWARDS (Specialized: bilingual, children/teen, ethnic/nationality, nature/ecology, social issues)**, P.O. Box 3939, Eugene OR 97403, phone (541)342-4956, e-mail skipping@efn.org, website http://www.nonviolence.org/skipping/, founded 1988, editor Arun Toké.
Magazine Needs: *Skipping Stones* is a "nonprofit magazine published bimonthly during the school year (5 issues) that encourages cooperation, creativity and celebration of cultural and environmental richness." They want poetry by youth under 18; 30 lines maximum on "nature, multicultural and social issues, family, freedom . . . uplifting." No work by adults. As a sample we selected these lines from "The Sound and Rhythm of the Drum" by Alexander Harvey, age 10, from Washington, DC:

> The rhythm is as natural as laying eggs is to a chicken/My great ancestors of the past, all heard the
> rhythm of the drum./It's sounds are as beautiful/As a pack of wild horses running on the great plains.//
> Our ancestors have struggled to grow./When our ancestors spirits are low and bum/It lifts us up far
> into the sun./That's the rhythm and sound, of the drum.

SS is 8½×11, saddle-stitched, printed on recycled paper. They receive about 500-1,000 poems a year, accept approximately 10%. Press run is 3,000 for 1,700 subscribers. Subscription: $25. Sample: $5.
How to Submit: Submit up to 3 poems at a time. No previously published poems; simultaneous submissions OK. Cover letter preferred. "Include your cultural background, experiences and what was the inspiration behind your creation." Time between acceptance and publication is 3-9 months. Poems are circulated to a 3-member editorial board. "Generally a piece is chosen for publication when all the editorial staff feel good about it." Seldom comments on rejections. Publishes theme issues. Send SASE for guidelines and upcoming themes. Reports in 2-4 months. Pays 1 copy, offers 25% discount for more. Acquires all rights. Returns rights after publication, but "we keep reprint rights."
Also Offers: Sponsors Annual Youth Honor Awards for 7-17 year olds. Theme for Annual Youth Honor Awards is "Multicultural and Nature Awareness." Deadline: June 20. Entry fee: $3, includes free issue containing the winners. Send SASE for details.

◐◎ **THE SKY; NUDE POETRY PRESS (Specialized: form/style)**, 3595 3A Gorsuch Rd., Nashport OH 43830, phone (740)450-2432, founded 1997, editor A. Scott Britton, editor Amanda Grimm.
Magazine Needs: *The Sky* appears monthly to "give the world the opportunity to experience good poetry and know the current movements and theories thereof. We want poetry that is experimental in both content and form—Beat, post-Beat independent, Dada, surreal, concrete, visual, and, of course, new movements. We do not want poetry written by poets who let rules limit their purpose and thought." They have published poetry by Dave Church, Ed Galing, Nelson Heise and Scott Rinehart. As a sample the editor selected these lines from "E7, A7, B7" by Mark Sonnenfeld:

> KEEP/to the surface phenomenon on private farm, a car/it is black. Oh come now it is written/on all
> the aspirin boxes, Dr. symptoms, coffins committed a patch/a porch light is on over a ways, a pitch, a
> sound, a frequency everyday bombed.

The Sky is 6-28 pgs., 8½×11, photocopied and saddle-stapled with color paper cover, includes art ("sometimes color, always b&w"). They receive about 600 poems a year, accept approximately 40%. Press run is 300 for 25 subscribers; 50 distributed free to other publishers. Subscription: $20. Sample: $3. Make checks payable to A. Scott Britton.
How to Submit: Submit 5-6 poems at a time. No previously published poems or simultaneous submissions. Cover letter preferred. Time between acceptance and publication is 3-4 months. Always comments on rejections. Send SASE for guidelines. Reports in 1-2 months. Sometimes sends prepublication galleys. Pays 1 copy. Rights remain with poet.
Book/Chapbook Needs & How to Submit: Nude Poetry Press "publishes material that takes risks." Through the Nude Poetry Chapbook Series, they publish 3 chapbooks/year. Chapbooks are usually 20-40 pgs., 4¼×5½, photocopied and saddle-stapled with color card stock cover. Query first, with a few sample poems and a cover letter with brief bio and publication credits. Replies to queries and mss in 1-4 weeks. Pays honorarium or 30 author's copies (out of a press run of 200).
Also Offers: "We publish a monthly broadside collection, as well as a monthly pamphlet collection. Each broadside and pamphlet is printed in increments of 200 copies, usually featuring a single poet each month."

✓⬜◐◎ **SKYLARK (Specialized: themes)**, Purdue University Calumet, 2200 169th St., Hammond IN 46323, phone (219)989-2262, fax (219)989-2160, founded 1972, editor-in-chief Pamela Hunter, poetry editor Cathy Michniewicz.
Magazine Needs: *Skylark* is "a fine arts annual, one section (about 25 pages) of which is devoted to a special theme." They are looking for "fresh voices, original images, concise presentation and honesty; poems up to 30

lines; narrative poems to 75 lines. No horror, nothing extremely religious, no pornography." They are also interested in receiving more prose poems and more well-crafted surrealistic poems. They have published poetry by Charles Eaton, Sandra Fowler, John Grey, Ward Kelley and Philip Lister. As a sample the editor selected these lines from "My Father's Cedar" by Joanne Kennedy:

> *My house is holy with cedar-scent/each Christmas now,/a fragrance faint and fresh/that moves through rooms like memories—/blessed, hurtful, precious—of my father.*

Published in December, *Skylark* is 100 pgs., magazine-sized, professionally printed, perfect-bound, with four-color cover and three four-color section-opening pages inside the magazine. Press run is 900-1,000 for 50 subscribers of which 12 are libraries. Single copy: $8. Sample (back issues): $6.

How to Submit: Submit up to 6 poems at a time. "Cover letter encouraged. No previously published poems or simultaneous submissions. Inquire (with SASE) as to annual theme for special section." Fax submissions OK followed by SASE within 2 weeks. The theme for 2000 is "The American Worker." Send SASE for themes and guidelines. Mss are read between November 1 and April 30. Reports in 4 months. Pays 1 copy/published poem. Acquires first rights. Editor may encourage rejected but promising writers.

Advice: She says she would like to receive "poems with greater coordination of form and content, sharper, more original imagery and a carefully-edited text."

◪ SLANT: A JOURNAL OF POETRY, Box 5063, University of Central Arkansas, 201 Donaghey Ave., Conway AR 72035-5000, phone (501)450-5107, website http://www2.uca.edu/english/Slant/HOMPAGE.html, founded 1987, editor James Fowler.

Magazine Needs: *Slant* is an annual using *only* poetry. They use "traditional and 'modern' poetry, even experimental, moderate length, any subject on approval of Board of Readers; purpose is to publish a journal of fine poetry from all regions of the United States and beyond. No haiku, no translations." They have published poetry by William Doreski and Carolyn Gregory. As a sample the editor selected these lines from "Celestial Couches" by John O'Dell:

> *And who shared the impatient flash point/of your peculiar dreams, your explosive/visions of incandescent worlds which lay/shimmering just beyond your grasp?/Or were you then but a solitary meteor/of prophecy ablaze across your village/sky a brief moment, then fast forgotten?*

Slant is 125 pgs., professionally printed on quality stock, flat-spined, with matte card cover. They receive about 1,500 poems a year, accept approximately 70-80. Press run is 200 for 70-100 subscribers. Sample: $10.

How to Submit: Submit up to 5 poems of moderate length with SASE between September and mid-November. "Put name, address and phone on the top of each page." No simultaneous submissions or previously published poems. Editor comments on rejections "on occasion." Allow 3-4 months from November 15 deadline for response. Pays 1 copy.

Also Offers: Website includes guidelines, editor/board of readers, table of contents from 1998 volume and index 1987-1996.

Advice: The editor says, "I would like to see more formal verse."

◎ SLATE & STYLE (Specialized: blind writers), Dept. PM, 2704 Beach Dr., Merrick NY 11566, phone (516)868-8718, fax (516)868-9076, e-mail LoriStay@aol.com, editor Loraine Stayer.

Magazine Needs: *Slate & Style* is a quarterly for blind writers available on cassette, in large print, Braille and e-mail, "including articles of interest to blind writers, resources for blind writers. Membership/subscription is $10 per year, all formats. Division of the National Federation of the Blind." Poems may be "5-36 lines. Prefer contributors to be blind writers, or at least writers by profession or inclination, but prefer poems not about blindness. No obscenities. Will consider all forms of poetry including haiku. Interested in new talent." They have published poetry by Stephanie Pieck, Louise Hope Bristow, Janet Wolff and Ken Volonte. As a sample the editor selected these lines from "To Matthew" by M.J. Lord:

> *I feel your hand reach out to me./A velvety soft palm and tiny fingers/reach through my skin,/grab my hand with an amazing strength./Your father lies beside me,/as he dreams of your premature birth.*

The print version is 28-32 pgs., magazine-sized, stapled, with a fiction and poetry section. Press run is 200 for 160 subscribers of which 4-5 are libraries. Subscription: $10/year. Sample: $2.50.

How to Submit: Submit 3 poems once or twice a year. No simultaneous submissions or previously published poems. Cover letter preferred. "On occasion we receive poems in Braille. I prefer print, since Braille slows me down. Typed is best." Fax submissions OK. Do not submit mss in July. Editor comments on rejections "if requested." Send SASE for guidelines. Reports in "two weeks if I like it." Pays 1 copy. Reviews books of poetry. Open to unsolicited reviews. Poets may also send books for review consideration.

Also Offers: They offer an annual poetry contest. Entry fee: $5/poem. Deadline: May 1. Write for details.

Advice: Loraine Stayer says, "Poetry is one of the toughest ways to express oneself, yet ought to be the easiest to read. Anything that looks simple is the result of much work."

◪ ◎ SLIPSTREAM (Specialized: themes), Box 2071, New Market Station, Niagara Falls NY 14301-0071, phone (716)282-2616 (after 5PM, EST), website http://www.wings.buffalo.edu/libraries/units/pl/slipstream, founded 1980, poetry editors Dan Sicoli, Robert Borgatti and Livio Farallo.

Magazine Needs: *Slipstream* is a "small press literary mag that is about 90% poetry and 10% fiction/prose, some artwork. The editors like new work with contemporary urban flavor. Writing must have a cutting edge to get our attention. We like to keep an open forum, any length, subject, style. Best to see a sample to get a feel. Like city stuff as opposed to country. Like poetry that springs from the gut, screams from dark alleys, inspired by experience." No "pastoral, religious, traditional, rhyming" poetry. They have published poetry by M. Scott Douglass, Lyn Lifshin, Gerald Locklin, Duane Sprow, Belinda Subraman, A.D. Winans, Gailmarie Pahmeier and Dancing Bear. As a sample the editors selected these lines from "Confirmation" by Jennifer Lagier:

> *Ironically, it's a nun who/orders my mother to purchase/my first pair of high heels,/nylons, the superfluous bra,/rubber straight-jacket girdle.*

Slipstream appears 1-2 times a year in a 7 × 8½ format, 80-100 pgs., professionally printed, perfect-bound, using b&w photos and graphics. It contains mostly free verse, some stanza patterns. They receive over 2,500 submissions of poetry a year, use less than 10%. Press run is 500 for 400 subscribers of which 10 are libraries. Subscription: $15/2 issues and 2 chapbooks. Sample: $6.

How to Submit: Editor sometimes comments on rejections. Publishes theme issues. Send SASE for guidelines and upcoming themes. "Reading for a general issue through 1998." Reports in 2-8 weeks, "if SASE included." Pays 1 copy.

Also Offers: Annual chapbook contest has December 1 deadline. Reading fee: $10. Submit up to 40 pgs. of poetry, any style, previously published work OK with acknowledgments. Winner receives $1,000 and 50 copies. All entrants receive copy of winning chapbook and an issue of the magazine. Past winners have included Richard Amidon, Sherman Alexie, Katharine Harer, Matt Buys, Leslie Anne Meilroy, and most recently, Rene Christopher for "Longing Fervently for Revolution." Website includes guidelines, announcements, samples of poetry, annual poetry chapbook winner, back issues and order form.

Advice: Dan Sicoli advises, "Do not waste time submitting your work 'blindly.' Sample issues from the small press first to determine which ones would be most receptive to your work."

☐ SLUGFEST, LTD., P.O. Box 1238, Simpsonville SC 29681, founded 1991, contact M.T. Nowak.
Book/Chapbook Needs: Publishes 2 chapbooks/year. They want "any type of poetry, less than 3 pages or 300 lines. No pornographic or bad work." They have published poetry by Conti, Semenovich, Nowak and Arnold. Chapbooks are usually about 60 pgs., 5½ × 8½.
How to Submit: Submit 3-5 poems at a time. Previously published poems and simultaneous submissions OK. Time between acceptance and publication is 3-6 months. Poems are circulated to an editorial board. Reports in 1-4 weeks. Always comments on rejections. Pays 1 copy. Send SASE for more details.

☑ SMALL POND MAGAZINE OF LITERATURE, P.O. Box 664, Stratford CT 06497, phone (203)378-4066, founded 1964, editor Napoleon St. Cyr.
Magazine Needs: *SPML* is a literary triquarterly that features poetry . . . "and anything else the editor feels is interesting, original, important." Poetry can be "any style, form, topic, except haiku, so long as it is deemed good, but limit of about 100 lines." Napoleon St. Cyr wants "nothing about cats, pets, flowers, butterflies, etc. Generally nothing under eight lines." The magazine is 40 pgs., digest-sized, offset from typescript on off-white paper, with colored matte card cover, saddle-stapled, artwork both on cover and inside. Circulation is 300, of which about a third go to libraries. Subscription: $10/3 issues. Sample (including guidelines): $3 for a random selection, $4 current.
How to Submit: The editor says he doesn't want 60 pages of anything; "dozen pages of poems max." Name and address on each page. No previously published poems or simultaneous submissions. Brief cover letter preferred. Time between acceptance and publication is within 3-15 months. Reports in 10-30 days (longer in summer). Pays 2 copies. Acquires all rights. Returns rights with written request including stated use. "One-time use per request." All styles and forms are welcome here. The editor usually responds quickly, often with comments to guide poets whose work interests him.
Advice: He says, "I would like to receive more good surreal verse."

☐ ◎ SMILE; SMILE SUBSCRIBERS QUARTERLY POETRY CONTEST (Specialized: spirituality/inspirational, humor), P.O. Box 5090, Brookfield CT 06804-5090, founded 1994, editor/publisher Joyce M. Johnson.
Magazine Needs: *SMILE* is published quarterly "to provide uplifting cheerful poetry for shut-ins and to be a resource for poets who write spiritual poems. *SMILE* is an ecumenical Christian journal open to all people of good will. (Not a 'religious' publication)." They want "inspirational poetry and light-hearted verse with upbeat humor, any style, 24 lines maximum, no lines wider than 40 characters. No profane, morbid work; suggestive sex or negative complaints." They have published poetry by Tim Scannell, Kae Carter Jaworski and Sr. Jo-Ann Iannotti. As a sample the editor selected these lines from "Some Quiet Moment" by Raymond John Flory:

> *Look to this day/for out of it/will arise/in some quiet moment/something beautiful/from God.*

SMILE is 32 pgs., 8½ × 11, photocopied and corner-stapled, includes b&w art from readers and clip art, exchange ads only. They receive about 900 poems a year, accept approximately 50%. Press run is 300 for 95 subscribers; 100 distributed free to shut-ins, senior congregate facilities. Subscription: $12. Sample: $3. "It is not necessary to subscribe but subscribers receive first limited space and also may enter quarterly contest. Each subscriber may choose a shut-in to receive a free subscription or editor will choose one."
How to Submit: Submit no more than 3 poems at a time. Previously published poems OK; no simultaneous submissions. Cover letter preferred. Time between acceptance and publication is 2-3 months. Always comments

on rejections. Send SASE for guidelines. Reports in 3-4 weeks. Pays 1 copy. Acquires first or one-time rights. Open to unsolicited reviews. Poets may also send books for review consideration if a subscriber.

Also Offers: Sponsors the *SMILE* Subscribers Quarterly Poetry Contest. Awards 1st Prize: $25; 2nd Prize: $15; and 3rd Prize: $10 plus at least one Honorable Mention award. "The only requirement to participate in this contest is the contribution of three first-class postage stamps. These stamps will be used to offset the postage expense for mailing free issues of *SMILE* to seniors and/or shut-in readers. Contestant must be a subscriber, poem should be no more than 24 lines, and each line should be no more than 40 characters across. There is a limit of one poem for each quarterly issue."

Advice: The editor says, "I urge older people to have confidence in their poetic ability. I have become aware of the great amount of creative talent there is among seniors. 'If you don't try, you'll never know.' "

$ ◐ THE SMITH; THE GENERALIST ASSOCIATION, 69 Joralemon St., Brooklyn NY 11201-4003, founded 1964, editor Harry Smith, associate editor Michael McGrinder.

Book/Chapbook Needs: The Smith publishes 3 to 5 books yearly. They have published *Poems New & Selected 1962-1992* by Lloyd Van Brunt and *Your Heart Will Fly Away* by David Rigsbee. As a sample the editor selected these lines from "For the Women" from Glenna Luschei's *Matriarch*:

> All the people who gave me blood are/in my veins. It was a flood of love./If I had known my daughter had chosen/my womb to learn from me/I would have treated her in a different/way. Last night the raccoons got our/mother duck. She never left the nest./The message is not to get upset/with nature, to let it have its way.

How to Submit: "Send three to six poem sampling with query. Include SASE for reply and/or return of poems. Do not send complete manuscript. Unable to accept registered or certified mail. No jingles, no standard academic verse. The decision process is relatively slow—about three months—as many mss are offered. Readers' reports are often passed along and the editor often comments." Always sends prepublication galleys. Pays 15% royalties, $500 advance, 10 copies. Send SASE for catalog or send $3 for a "slightly irregular" book ("with bumped corners or a little dust").

Advice: The editor advises, "Revert to earlier models. *Avoid* university wordshops where there are standard recent models leading to standard mod verse. A close reading of *The Pearl Poet* will be more nourishing than all the asparagus of John Ashbery or Robert Bly."

◐ GIBBS SMITH, PUBLISHER; PEREGRINE SMITH POETRY COMPETITION, P.O. Box 667, Layton UT 84041-0667, founded 1971, poetry series established 1988, poetry editor Gail Yngve.

Book/Chapbook Needs: They want "serious, contemporary poetry of merit." They have published *Perfect Hell* by H.L. Hix and *1-800-HOT-RIBS* and *Rock Farm* by Catherine Bowman. Books are selected for publication through competition for the Peregrine Smith Poetry Prize of $500 plus publication.

How to Submit: Entries are received in April only and require a $15 reading fee and SASE. Mss should be 48-64 typewritten pgs. "We publish only one unsolicited poetry ms per year—the winner of our annual Peregrine Smith Poetry Contest. For guidelines to the contest, interested poets should send a request with SASE through the mail." The winner of the 1998 contest was Gary Young's *Braver Deeds*. The judge for the series is Christopher Merrill.

⊕ $ ◐ ◑ SMITHS KNOLL, 49 Church Rd., Little Glemham, Woodbridge, Suffolk IP13 0BJ England, phone (01728)747951, founded 1991, co-editors Roy Blackman and Michael Laskey.

Magazine Needs: *Smiths Knoll* is a magazine appearing 3 times/year. They look for poetry with honesty, depth of feeling, lucidity and craft. As a sample the editors selected these lines from "Cut Lip" by John Lynch:

> The way she held out her hand/As if to say Daddy, what's this?//I hushed her, wiped her tears,/It's only blood I said//Later, on the motorway,/streams of tail-lights pouring red.

Smiths Knoll is 60 pgs., A5, offset-litho, perfect-bound, with 2-color card cover. They receive 6,000-8,000 poems a year, "accept about one in forty." Press run is 500 for 350 subscribers. Single copy: £4.50; subscription: £12/3 issues (outside UK).

How to Submit: Submit up to 5 poems at a time to the co-editors. "We would consider poems previously published in magazines outside the U.K." No simultaneous submissions. Poems only. Doesn't commission work. "Cover letters should be brief: name, address, date, number of poems sent (or titles). We don't want life histories or complete publishing successes or what the poems are about. We do want sufficient IRCs for return of work. Constructive criticism of rejections where possible." Tries to report within 1 month (outside UK). Pays £5 plus 1 copy/poem.

⊕ $ ◐ SMOKE; SPIKE, First Floor, Liver House, 96 Bold St., Liverpool L1 4HY England, phone (0151)709-3688, founded 1974, editor Dave Ward.

Magazine Needs: *Smoke* is a biannual publication of poetry and graphics. They want "short, contemporary poetry, expressing new ideas through new forms." They have published poetry by Carol Ann Duffy, Roger McGough, Jackie Kay and Henry Normal. The editor says *Smoke* is 24 pgs., A5, offset litho printed and stapled with paper cover, includes art. They receive about 3,000 poems a year, accept approximately 40 poems. Press run is 500 for 250 subscribers of which 18 are libraries, 100 shelf sales; 50 distributed free to contributors/other

insider report

Improve your poetry, as well as the poetry community, by getting involved

"Rural Route #1
Covington, Ohio"

*A straw matted living room
textured our unraveling lives:*

*Six unpainted two-by-four kids
A slant-roofed grandmother.
A set of green-shuttered parents
battened down for the next disaster.*

(from *Rings of Saturn, Selected and New Poems*, published by West Anglia Publications, 1999;
reprinted by permission of the author)

Kathleen Iddings

Unlike many artists who struggle day in and day out to get their work published, Kathleen Iddings became a poet, editor and publisher within the same year. This feat followed several others, including 13 years as an elementary school teacher, a career in photojournalism (her photos appeared in *Newsweek* and several newspapers), and a stint as a PR manager for a memory expert. Iddings credits these early experiences for her ability to make the transition from poet to editor.

In 1981, during a weekly workshop, Iddings's talent garnered the attention of fellow workshop members Ric Solano, Tom Gayton and Ron Salisbury, who wanted to begin publishing national anthologies. Having been published widely through her photojournalism and PR work, Iddings was offered a position on the editorial staff, and thus became a founding member of San Diego Poet's Press. Also wanting to publish individual's poetry books, Iddings consequently established La Jolla Poet's Press. To date, the presses have published 5 anthologies and 35 individual collections, and sponsor the annual National Poetry Book Series Awards, and American Book Series Awards.

Iddings's list of successes include five volumes of poetry (all published with West Anglia Publications): *The Way of Things* (1984); *Invincible Summer* (1985); *Promises to Keep* (1987); *Selected and New Poems, 1980-1990* (1991); and *Rings of Saturn* (1998). Her individual poems have appeared in textbooks, anthologies and journals such as *Yearbook of American Poetry* (Monitor Book Co.); *A New Geography of Poets* (Arkansas Press); and *The Connecticut Review*. She has received numerous awards including a

NEA Fellowship, Carnegie Author's Grants and PEN Writer's Grants. She judges numerous poetry contests and has given over 75 readings. Clearly, Iddings has dedicated a great portion of her life to poetry, and here she discusses that dedication and the role of poetry in the world today.

Describe your experiences as a beginning poet. How did you get published?
While working with a memory expert, I attended a poetry reading by local poet Linda Brown. Her work was so open, honest and moving that I wanted to learn to express myself through poetry. Her class was the next evening and I was in attendance.

With the help of *Poet's Market*, I began submitting my poetry for publication after several months of writing. By checking the poetry samples that accompany each listing, I determined if they published my style of work. For my stronger poems, I selected markets that published fewer poems per year and were considered more competitive markets. If rejected by these, I would lower my expectations to a market that published more poems per year.

Twenty poems were accepted my first year writing poetry—some in the more difficult markets—and three were deemed finalists in a national contest. I received numerous rejections as well. My early poems, which focused on my childhood in rural Ohio as well as political, philosophical, pastoral and erotic themes, appeared in my first book, *The Way of Things*.

What did you learn early on that you were able to apply as your career progressed?
As an educator, I knew the value of studying with the best poets/teachers possible, and did so locally with Linda Brown and Steve Kowit, who are both excellent. From them, and the many poets with whom I studied during summer conferences (Galway Kinnell, Sharon Olds, Tess Gallagher, Robert Pinsky, Carolyn Forche, Louise Gluck, to name a few), I learned the necessity of revising, the value of reading the finest works of poetry, and the wisdom of using feedback from fine poets in good workshops or classes to improve. These poets generously gave their time, expertise and friendship, and for this I owe them forever.

You have seen the industry as a poet, an editor and a publisher. Has your view of poetry or publishing changed because of this?
As an editor screening 400 to 500 manuscripts per contest, I find a number of extraordinary poets. They are published widely in the finest places and winning national contests for individual poems but cannot get a publisher. Without a nationally recognizable name, larger presses know the books won't move, and many don't risk publishing these books no matter how excellent the poetry. Small presses serve to bring these poets to the fore.

And that was your goal in establishing San Diego Poet's Press and La Jolla Poet's Press. What do you look for when considering manuscripts?

Excellence is my criterion in considering manuscripts. For me, an excellent poem is unique, well-crafted, interesting, moving and unforgettable. I think a poet reaches this level of writing by studying how to craft poetry from fine teachers. Poets need to revise until the poem is the best it can be. Objective feedback from mentors is important in learning to revise.

What are some common mistakes beginning poets make?

From the submissions I receive, it's obvious some poets do not realize they need a serious study of the craft of poetry to write well, and that revising until the poem is a work of art is a requirement for good poetry. Beginners need strong teachers and/or good workshops to improve.

Do you see any drawbacks to the workshop atmosphere?

In my 20 years of writing poetry, I have been almost constantly involved in various poetry workshops or classes. I know they have taught me to craft better poetry. I have seen other poets' works improve, some dramatically, in one semester. If the leader of the workshop is a good poetry teacher, I see few drawbacks, especially if a poet attends a variety of workshops with different teachers and poets in attendance.

You've mentioned revision several times as integral to a poet's success. How should poets go about revising their work?

Revising endlessly is typical of most good poets. I've heard many poets say their poems are never done, they finally abandon them and submit them for publication. Hard and dedicated work pays off. I revise poems, even after they are published or win awards.

Putting a poem aside for a few days, weeks or months before considering it a finished poem is helpful. One can be more objective later, after the creative fires have cooled. It is then a poet can check the crafting closely.

If a poet does not know how to revise, I would urge them to find a good mentor. Without the ability to revise, writing good poetry is not likely to happen.

What other resources or experiences would you recommend to poets?

Besides using *Poet's Market*—I consider it the "poet's Bible"—I feel strongly that poets become involved in poetry-related projects in their communities. Poetry, like any of the arts, needs backing, whether through volunteer work or providing financial help for valuable projects. Get involved in starting a writing center, or a writer's magazine for the community. Attend poetry readings. Start a small press and make chapbooks for fine poets. Start a workshop with a good poet/teacher to lead it. Teach poetry in prisons or to the elderly in nursing homes. In order to improve, surround yourself with other enthusiastic poets.

You have been commended by Helynn Hoffa (editor of West Anglia Publications) for "doing much to keep poetry alive" through your own projects which include teaching poetry, and sending poetry abroad and to numerous prison libraries. What is the role of poetry in the world today?

I think we have only scratched the surface of the value poetry can be in our lives today. During my 20 years as poet, editor and publisher, my involvement in poetry-related projects has made me draw this conclusion. When I included a poem about a childhood friend's abuse in a classroom, a third grader took me aside when I had finished. He cupped his hands around a quickly scrawled poem, so no one else could see it. It revealed that his stepfather was beating him and his mother every day. The last line was, " . . . and I hate the son of a bitch." I told him it was a wonderful, expressive poem and that I was very sorry this was happening. Intervention followed.

Months later, a teen asked me to read her poem after everyone was gone. It was about the incest she was suffering by her father and her clear intent to commit suicide. A counselor was talking to her within 15 minutes. Other poets who read to students and include an abuse poem in their readings have had similar experiences. Because abuse is the big secret kids don't usually tell, I include this abuse poem when reading to young people. Saving children's lives and uncovering abuse is a worthy use for this art.

A different kind of need came my way when I received a letter from a professor in Estonia when they were still under the thumb of the USSR. The only American poetry books in his country were of Emily Dickinson and Walt Whitman, and he wanted contemporary American poets' work to translate for Estonians. He indicated the political aspects of their country's situation and the resulting food shortage. He and his wife went to the market many times daily in hopes that some food had come in and to be there before it would all be sold. In spite of this extremely serious situation, all he was asking for was *poetry*. After sending books from my own stock, I sent his appeal to many fine poets, editors, anthologers and publishers throughout the country. The response was great.

I believe through poetry, more than any other art form, people may come to better appreciate and understand each other. Exposure to poetry could ensure less depression by the elderly in nursing homes and could make a positive difference for those in prisons and those who emerge from them. We would learn a lot from these people's poetry. Poets and writers I think would agree that when writing, we are less lonely. Through writing we rise above our surroundings and can be anywhere we wish to be. What a gift to give to those confined!

—*Amanda Heele*

mags. Subscription: $5 (cash). Sample: $1. Make checks payable to Windows Project (cash preferred/exchanges rate on cheques not viable).

How to Submit: Submit 6 poems at a time. Previously published poems and simultaneous submissions OK. Cover letter preferred. Time between acceptance and publication is 6 months. Seldom comments on rejections. Reports in 2 weeks. Pays 1 copy.

Book/Chapbook Needs & How to Submit: Spike publishes "challenging and 'non-literary' work—mainly Merseyside." They publish 2 paperbacks and 3 chapbooks/year. Books are usually 64 pgs., A5, offset litho printed and perfect-bound with laminated board cover, cover art only. Query first, with a few sample poems and a cover letter with brief bio and publication credits. Replies to queries and mss in 2 months. Pays 10% royalties and 160 author's copies (out of a press run of 1,000).

$ **SNOWAPPLE PRESS**, P.O. Box 66024, Heritage Postal Outlet, Edmonton, Alberta T6J 6T4 Canada, founded 1991, editor Vanna Tessier.

Book/Chapbook Needs: Snowapple Press is an "independent publisher dedicated to writers who wish to contribute to literature." They publish 4-5 paperbacks/year. They want "contemporary, expansive, experimental and literary poetry." They have published poetry by Gilberto Finzi, Peter Prest, Vanna Tessier, Bob Stallworthy and Paolo Valesio. Books are usually 120-160 pgs., offset printed with #10 colored card cover with "art/graphics suitable to theme."

How to Submit: Submit 5 poems at a time, 14-75 lines each. Previously published poems and simultaneous submissions OK. Cover letter preferred. Reads submissions September through March 31 only. Time between acceptance and publication is 12-18 months. Poems are circulated to an editorial board. Replies in 3-4 weeks. Pays 10% royalty, $100 honorarium and 25 author's copies (out of a press run of 500).

Also Offers: Sponsors an occasional anthology contest. Send SASE (or SAE and IRC) with all correspondence.

$ **SNOWY EGRET (Specialized: nature)**, P.O. Box 9, Bowling Green IN 47833, founded 1922 by Humphrey A. Olsen, editor Philip Repp.

Magazine Needs: They want poetry that is "nature-oriented: poetry that celebrates the abundance and beauty of nature or explores the interconnections between nature and the human psyche." As a sample they selected the opening lines of "In a Climax Forest" by Conrad Hilberry:

> The wooden past grows larger, I grow less/and less convincing in this sullen air/that wants a wind to stir its emptiness.

Snowy Egret appears twice a year in a 60-page, magazine-sized format, offset, saddle-stapled, with original graphics. They receive about 500 poems a year, accept approximately 20. Press run is 800 for 500 subscribers of which 50 are libraries. Sample: $8.

How to Submit: Send #10 SASE for writer's guidelines. Reports in 1 month. Always sends prepublication galleys. Pays $4/poem or $4/page plus 2 copies. Buys first North American or reprint rights. Open to unsolicited reviews. Poets may also send books for review consideration.

SO TO SPEAK: A FEMINIST JOURNAL OF LANGUAGE AND ART (Specialized: women/feminism), Sub 1, Room 254A, George Mason University, 4400 University Dr., Fairfax VA 22030-4444, phone (703)993-3625, e-mail sts@gmu.edu, founded 1991, poetry editor Hope Smith.

Magazine Needs: *So To Speak* is published 2 times a year. "We publish high-quality work about women's lives—fiction, nonfiction (including book reviews and interviews), b&w photography and artwork along with poetry. We look for poetry that deals with women's lives, but also lives up to a high standard of language, form and meaning. We are most interested in more experimental, high-quality work by new poets. There are no formal specifications. We like work that takes risks successfully. No unfinished/unpolished work without strength or depth. We get tired of poetry that uses what we consider 'stale' feminist issues or topics." They have published poetry by Heather Fuller, Carolyn Forché, Allison Joseph, Sharon Dolin and Lynne Hugo. *So To Speak* is 150 pgs., digest-sized, photo-offset printed and perfect-bound, with glossy cover, includes b&w photos and art, ads. They receive about 300 poems a year, accept approximately 10%. Press run is 1,000 for 350 subscribers, 50 shelf sales; 500 distributed free to students/submitters. Subscription: $10. Sample: $5.

How to Submit: Submit 1-3 poems at a time. No previously published poems; simultaneous submissions OK. Cover letter preferred. Disk submissions OK. "Please submit poems as you wish to see them in print. We do have an e-mail address but do not accept e-mail submissions. Be sure to include a cover letter with contact info, publications credits, and awards received." Reads submissions all year, "but August 15 through November 1 and December 31 through April 15 are best." Time between acceptance and publication is 6-8 months. Seldom comments on rejections. Publishes theme issues occasionally. Send SASE for guidelines and upcoming themes. Reports in 6-8 months. Pays 2 copies. Acquires one-time rights. Reviews books and chapbooks of poetry and other magazines in 750 words, single book format. Open to unsolicited reviews. Poets may also send books for review consideration.

Also Offers: *So To Speak* runs an annual poetry contest. "We advertise it well. Our Autumn 1998 judge was Beth Joselow, DC poet and playwright."

Advice: The editor says, "Language can be manipulated and made into beautiful phrases, but to be in *So To Speak* a poem must add up to something."

☐ **SO YOUNG!; ANTI-AGING PRESS, INC.**, P.O. Box 141489, Coral Gables FL 33114, phone (305)662-3928, fax (305)661-4123, e-mail julia@icanect.net, founded 1992 press, 1996 newsletter, editor Julia Busch.
Magazine Needs: *So Young!* is a bimonthly newsletter publishing "anti-aging/holistic health/humorous/philosophical topics geared to a youthful body, attitude and spirit." They want "short, upbeat, fresh, positive poetry. The newsletter is dedicated to a youthful body, face, mind and spirit. Work can be humorous, philosophical fillers. No off color, suggestive poems or anything relative to first night, or unrequited love affairs." *So Young!* is 12 pgs., 8½×11 (11×17 sheets folded), unbound. They receive several hundred poems a year, use approximately 6-12. Press run is 700 for 500 subscribers. Subscription: $35. Sample: $6.
How to Submit: Submit up to 10 poems at a time. Previously published poems and simultaneous submissions OK. Cover letter preferred. Time between acceptance and publication "depends on poem subject matter—usually 6-8 months." Send SASE for guidelines. Reports in 2 months. Pays 10 copies. Acquires one-time rights.

☑ $☐ ◐ ◎ **THE SOCIETY OF AMERICAN POETS (SOAP); IN HIS STEPS PUBLISHING COMPANY; THE POET'S PEN; PRESIDENT'S AWARD FOR SUPERIOR CHOICE (Specialized: religious)**, P.O. Box 3563, Macon GA 31205-3563, phone (912)788-1848, fax (912)788-0925, e-mail DrRev@msn.com, website http://www.geocites.com/Athens/7283, founded 1984, editor Dr. Charles E. Cravey.
Magazine Needs: *The Poet's Pen* is a literary quarterly of poetry and short stories. "Open to all styles of poetry and prose—both religious and secular. No gross or 'X-rated' poetry without taste or character." They have published poetry by Henry Gurley, Pat Stephenson and Robert Dixon. As a sample the editor selected these lines from "Resignation" by Vivian Bolland Schroeder:

> Reminiscent of dry antiquated leaves/scuttling crisp and russet/Before windswept autumn,/Her every
> moment seems to rustle."

The Poet's Pen uses poetry primarily by members and subscribers, but outside submissions are also welcomed. (Membership: $25/year.)
How to Submit: Submit 3 poems at a time, include name and address on each page. "Submissions or inquiries will not be responded to without a SASE. We do stress originality and have each new poet and/or subscriber sign a waiver form verifying originality." Simultaneous submissions OK; previously published poems OK, if permission from previous publisher is included. E-mail and fax submissions OK. Publishes seasonal/theme issues. Send SASE for upcoming themes or obtain via e-mail or website. Sometimes sends prepublication galleys. Editor "most certainly" comments on rejections.
Book/Chapbook Needs & How to Submit: In His Steps publishes religious and other books and publishes music for the commercial record market. Query for book publication. 60/40 split of pay.
Also Offers: Sponsors several contests each quarter which total $250-500 in cash awards. Editor's Choice Awards each quarter, prizes $50, $25 and $15. President's Award for Superior Choice has a prize of $50; deadline is November 1. They also publish a quarterly anthology that has poetry competitions in several categories with prizes of $25-100.
Advice: The editor says, "We're looking for poets who wish to unite in fellowship with our growing family of poets nationwide. We currently have over 850 poets and are one of the nation's largest societies, yet small enough and family operated to give each of our poets individual attention and pointers."

Ⓝ $◖ **SOFT SKULL PRESS, INC.**, 98 Suffolk #3A, New York NY 10002, e-mail sander@softskull.com, website http://www.softskull.com, founded 1992, editor Sander Hicks.
Book/Chapbook Needs: Soft Skull Press, Inc. "likes books that reinvent genre, like the poetic/political memoir of socialist poet Sparrow's 'Republican Like Me: A Diary of My Presidential Campaign.'" They publish 10 paperbacks and 2 hardbacks/year. They want poetry that is "angry, politically sharpened by struggle, honest, hard-working, post punk/hip hop-influenced beauty. No post-modern, ultra-subjective, bourgeois work." They have published poetry by Cynthia Nelson, John S. Hall, Tracie Morris and Sparrow. As a sample the editor selected these lines from a poem by Todd Colby:

> Ask the children/which member of their family/they would be willing to sacrifice for hot pig.

Books are usually 120 pgs., offset printed and perfect-bound, uses art.
How to Submit: Query first with 10-20 sample poems, cover letter, brief bio, publication credits and SASE. Previously published poems and simultaneous submissions OK. Time between acceptance and publication is 1 year. Poems are circulated to an editorial board. "Interns, volunteers, shareholders and comrades of press are on Editorial Board." Seldom comments on rejections. "If we like it but can't publish it, we'll say so." Replies to queries in 1 month; to mss in 6 months. Pays royalties of 6-8% plus advance of $10-100 and 25 author's copies (out of a press run of 1,500). Additional copies sold to author at 55% discount. Order sample books by sending $8 each.

Ⓨ $◎ **SOJOURNERS (Specialized: religious, political)**, 2401 15th St. NW, Washington DC 20009, phone (202)328-8842, fax (202)328-8757, website http://www.sojourners.com, founded 1975, poetry editor Rose Berger.
• The poetry section of *Sojourners* has received awards from the Associated Church Press and Evangelical Press Association.
Magazine Needs: *Sojourners* appears 6 times/year, "with approximately 40,000 subscribers. We focus on faith, politics and culture from a radical Christian perspective. We publish one or two poems/month depending on

length. All poems must be original and unpublished. We look for seasoned, well-crafted poetry that reflects the issues and perspectives covered in our magazine. We highly discourage simplistic, rhyming poetry. Poetry using non-inclusive language (any racist, sexist, homophobic poetry) will not be accepted." *Sojourners* is about 70 pgs., magazine-sized, offset printed and saddle-stapled with 4-color paper cover, includes photos and illustrations throughout. They receive about 400 poems a year, accept approximately 6-8. Press run is 50,000 for 40,000 subscribers of which 500 are libraries, 2,000 shelf sales. Single copy: $4; subscription: $30. Sample: free.

How to Submit: Submit up to 3 poems at a time. Line length for poetry is 50 maximum. Cover letter with brief (3 sentences) bio required. Editor occasionally comments on submissions. Publishes theme issues. Send SASE for guidelines. Reports in 4-6 weeks. Pays $25/poem plus 5 copies. "We assume permission to grant reprints unless the author requests otherwise."

N ⬭ ⬭ **SOMNILOQUY; SOMNILOQUY . . . ONLINE**, P.O. Box 720862, Orlando FL 32872-0862, phone (407)273-4942, e-mail editor@somniloquy.com, website http://www.somniloquy.com, founded 1996, managing editor Tracey Hessler.

Magazine Needs: *Somniloquy* is a "quarterly multi-genre journal which strives to published the best in prose and poetry." They want any style or format of poetry, 2 pages/poem maximum. No pornography or sexually explicit language. They have published poetry by Dave Taub, Kt. Frankovich and Liz Larraby. As a sample the editor selected these lines from "Child at a Grave" by Dave Taub:

> *Knees bent to grasses and dust (to dust)/These solemn hours . . ./Deep to the eyes of youth./Searching*
> *for still younger days/shared from the womb/The breeze passing through the oaks and ashes (to ashes)/*
> *Here lies memories of a child's mind:/Yellow frock, fading sun/and crocuses around a small wooden*
> *cross/Naive enough to know only heaven.*

Somniloquy is 52 pgs., 7×8½, desktop-published and side-stapled and taped with coated paper cover, uses computer-generated graphics. They receive about 500 poems a year, accept approximately 25%. Press run is 150 for 78 subscribers, 18 shelf sales. Single copy: $5; subscription: $16.97/year (4 issues). Sample (including guidelines): $6.26 (US). Make checks payable to T. Hessler RTWG.

How to Submit: Submit up to 3 poems at a time. Line length for poetry is 100 maximum. Previously published poems and simultaneous submissions OK. Cover letter preferred. E-mail and disk submissions OK. Reads submissions year-round; seasonal, 6 months in advance. Time between acceptance and publication is 3½ months. Poems are circulated to an editorial board. "Each of four editors reads and critiques each submission." Often comments on rejections. Send SASE for guidelines or obtain via e-mail or website. Reports in 2 months. Pays 1 copy. Acquires first North American serial rights. Reviews books of poetry in 500 words, single book format. Open to unsolicited reviews.

Also Offers: Website includes guidelines, editors' names, submission form, content from past issues, writers' links and message board.

Advice: The editor says, "Send only finished, polished work which you consider your best."

🌑 ✓ **$** ⬭ **SONO NIS PRESS**, P.O. Box 5550, Station B, Victoria, British Columbia V8R 6S4 Canada, phone (250)598-7807, fax (250)598-7866, e-mail sononis@islandnet.com, website http://www.islandnet.com/~sononis/, founded 1968, contact the editor.

Book/Chapbook Needs: Publishes 2 paperbacks/year. "We publish contemporary poetry, usually 2 mss a year, and 6-8 nonfiction titles (predominantly history)." They want "75 pages minimum; literature not limerick; connected or isolated poems acceptable. No rhyming ballads; haiku or religious verse." They have published poetry by Brian Brett, Linda Rogers and Sandy Shreve. As a sample the editor selected these lines from "Heaven Cake" in *Heaven Cake* by Liliane Welch:

> *She is breaking her first/egg on the side of the metal bowl./It sounds like bedpans and nurses,/the girl*
> *who sat with Grandpa last night/holding his bruised hand in her own/until his old heart/stopped*
> *singing in hers.*

Books are usually 80-120 pgs., 6×9 with laminated color cover.

How to Submit: Previously published poems OK, "if magazine publication only"; simultaneous submissions OK. Cover letter preferred. "Hard copy traditional submission only. No fax or e-mail submissions. Brief bio information and publication history helpful." Time between acceptance and publication is 14 months. Replies to queries in 2 months; to mss in 3 months. Pays "10% of suggested list for all books sold at normal discounts, 10% of net if deep discount," plus 10 author's copies (out of a press run of 600). For sample books, order direct or check local library.

Advice: The editor says, "We are publishing only two poetry books a year—usually one established poet and

---

ALWAYS include a self-addressed, stamped envelope (SASE) when sending a ms or query to a publisher within your own country. When sending material to other countries, include a self-addressed envelope and International Reply Coupons (IRCs), available at many post offices.

one new poet. We never publish non-Canadians as the marketing is difficult. We are finding it harder and harder to publish limited market books. Promotion oriented authors are a bonus."

☑ ◯ ◉ **SOUL FOUNTAIN**, 90-21 Springfield Blvd., Queens Village NY 11428, phone/fax (718)479-2594, e-mail davault@aol.com, website http://www.TheVault.org, founded 1997, editor Tone Bellizzi.

Magazine Needs: *Soul Fountain* appears 4 times a year and publishes poetry, art, photography, short fiction and essays. They are "open to all. Our motto is 'Fear no Art.' We publish all quality submitted work, and specialize in emerging voices. We are particularly interested in visionary, challenging and consciousness-expanding material." They have published poetry by Robert Dunn, Thomas Catterson, Jay Chollick and Paula Curci. *Soul Fountain* is 24 pgs., 8½×11, offset printed and saddle-stapled. Subscription: $10. Sample: $3.50. Make checks payable to Hope for the Children Foundation.

How to Submit: Submit 2-3 "camera-ready" poems at a time. Previously published poems and simultaneous submissions OK. E-mail submissions OK. Time between acceptance and publication is 6 months. Publishes theme issues occasionally. Send SASE for upcoming themes. Pays 1 copy. "For each issue there is a release/party/performance, 'Poetry & Poultry in Motion,' attended by all poets, writers, artists, etc., appearing in the issue."

Also Offers: *Soul Fountain* is published by The Vault, "a not-for-profit arts project of the Hope for the Children Foundation; a growing, supportive community committed to empowering young and emerging artists of all disciplines at all levels to develop and share their talents through performance, collaboration and networking."

N ◉ SOUNDS OF A GREY METAL DAY; CREATIVE EXPRESSIONS PROJECT (Specialized: prisoners), % Jacqueline Helfgott, Dept. of Criminal Justice, Seattle University, 900 Broadway, Seattle WA 98122, phone (206)296-5477, fax (206)296-5997, e-mail jhelfgot@seattleu.edu, founded 1993, outside program coordinator/assistant professor of criminal justice Jacqueline Helfgott, inside coordinator Patrick Bolt.

Magazine Needs: *Sounds of a Grey Metal Day* appears annually in November/December and publishes writing and art by prisoners and volunteers participating in the Creative Expressions Project. "We've never accepted poems from people not in the program, but are willing to review prisoner submissions in the future." They want "poetry by prisoners about anything or poetry about prisons/imprisonment." *SGMD* is 75-85 pgs., magazine-sized, printed in "prison print shop" and saddle-stapled, textureed card stock cover, includes b&w drawings. Press run is 500. Single copy: $5. Make checks payable to Jackie Helfgott, money orders to CIPC.

How to Submit: Submit up to 3 poems at a time. No previously published poems or simultaneous submissions. Cover letter preferred. Disk submissions OK. Time between acceptance and publication varies. Poems are circulated to an editorial board. "Poems are circulated among committee of prisoners, volunteers, coordinators and selected by vote based on available space for outside submissions." Reports in 2 months. Pays 2 copies.

◯ ◐ ◉ **THE SOUNDS OF POETRY; THE LATINO POETS' ASSOCIATION (Specialized: bilingual/foreign language)**, 2076 Vinewood, Detroit MI 48216-5506, phone (313)843-2352, founded 1983, publisher/editor Jacqueline Rae Sanchez.

Magazine Needs: *The Sounds of Poetry* is published 3 times/year to "promote throughout the world an awareness (through poetry) that we are quite diverse, yet the same. We all love, hurt, laugh and suffer. We are open to all types of poetry with substance, grit, feeling; prefer one column and/or shorter poetry. Always in need of fillers. Do not want to see fluff, insincere gibberish, foul language, nor porn, although light erotica is acceptable." They have published poetry by Ann Holdreith, Gil Saenz, Jessica Sanchez and Lladoow S. Shevshenko. The publisher says *SOP* is 24-32 pgs., digest-sized, saddle-stitched. "We use approximately 50-98 poems per issue representing at least 18 different states plus three or more other countries as well." Press run is 200. Subscription: $10. Sample: $4.50.

How to Submit: Submit 5 poems at a time. Previously published poems OK ("only if credit is listed on poem sheet submitted"); prefer no simultaneous submissions. Cover letter with titles of poems and bio preferred. "Type poems on an 8½×11 sheet of white paper, one poem per page unless submitting brief fillers (four titled fillers per sheet is OK), handwritten poems will be returned. Name, address and phone number should appear on each sheet submitted." Reads submissions January through October only. Time between acceptance and publication can be from several months to a couple years. Seldom comments on rejections. Publishes theme issues. Send SASE for guidelines. Reports in 1-6 months. Pays 1 copy to contributor, 2 to subscriber. Poets may also send books for review consideration; "mark 'Review Copy' and enclose cover letter. We do not review excerpts of books/chapbooks."

Also Offers: "The Latino Poets' Association is a multicultural, multilingual, non-profit association whose 'purpose is to promote within the community and throughout the USA an appreciation and education of the writing/recitals of poetry by Latinos and those people who support the work of Latinos.' A person does not have to be Latino in order to join the L.P.A. Some L.P.A. poets write and recite only in Spanish, others write/recite in English, Spanish and French." Yearly membership: $25. Members have the opportunity to read at scheduled events. The L.P.A. meets monthly at The Olde Coffee Shoppe, 5423 W. Vernor, Detroit MI, George Atan, proprietor, (313)842-5911; and The Bowen Branch Library-DPL, 3648 W. Vernor, Detroit MI, Ellen Simmons is library manager (313)297-9381. Send SASE for a schedule of L.P.A. events.

Advice: The editor says, "Write poetry using the knowledge you have, research and expand, add your own feelings, emotions then take that same poetry to your ultimate heights. Write and rewrite until you are comfortable with your work. Attend poetry readings, listen closely to other poets as they read their material. Participate in open-mike readings, get feedback from other poets but ultimately use your own gut instincts."

☑ ▣ ◎ SOUR GRAPES: ONLINE VINE FOR REJECTED WRITERS AND OTHER TOR-MENTED SOULS (Specialized), 26 Sheridan St., Woburn MA 01801-3542, e-mail sandyberns@netscape.net, website http://Members.xoom.com/Sandyberns/sourgrapes.htm, hardcopy founded 1995, discontinued 1998, website founded 1997.
Needs: *Sour Grapes* website, published "haphazardly," is "dedicated to the discouraged, disgruntled, disillusioned and dejected writers of the universe." They want "insightful verse that is thought-provoking, creates an image or stirs a feeling. Poems don't have to be gripe-related, but should be of normal length—no epics, please. Almost any form style or subject is acceptable." They don't want " 'Experimental Poems' such as lines printed horizontally and vertically. If it looks like a crossword puzzle—don't send it here. No 'Gratuitous Profanity,' show us poetic language—not street talk."
How to Submit: Submit no more than 5 poems at one time. If submitting all haiku or very short poems, the limit is 5. Prefer e-mail submissions ("text in the body of the e-mail is preferred"). Please include cover letter with short bio and credits. Regular mail submissions should include SASE for return of mss. Often comments on rejections. Response time "may vary but will not be unreasonable." Guidelines available on the website. "Payment, none. We're too cheap. Our site is free and open to everyone."
Advice: The editor says, "Only submissions that follow our guidelines will be considered."

Ⓝ ⊕ ◗ SOUTH–A POETRY MAGAZINE FOR THE SOUTHERN COUNTIES; WANDA PUB-LICATIONS, 61 West Borough, Wimborne, Dorset BH21 1LX England, phone (01202)889669, fax (01202)881061, e-mail wanda@wanda.demon.co.uk, founded 1972, administrator Mick Fealty.
Magazine Needs: *South* is published biannually "to give voice to poets writing in the South of England. As the magazine passes through the hands of seven editorial groups, our policy is open." They have published poetry by Ian Caws, Peter Abbs, Colin Nixon and Jeremy Hooker. *South* is 68 pgs., 6×9, litho-printed and saddle-stapled with gloss laminated, duotone cover, includes photographs. They receive about 1,000 poems a year, accept approximately 10%. Press run is 400 for 200 subscribers of which 15 are libraries, 170 shelf sales; 15 distributed free to other magazines and reviewers. Single copy: £3.50; subscription: £6/2 issues, £11/4 issues. Make checks payable to Wanda Publications.
How to Submit: Submit 6 poems at a time. Previously published poems OK; no simultaneous submissions. Cover letter preferred. E-mail and disk submissions OK. Time between acceptance and publication is 5 months. Poems are circulated to an editorial board. "Each issue is selected by a different editorial group." Reports in 5 months. Pays 1 copy. Staff reviews books of poetry and other magazines in 400 words, multi-book format. Send books for review consideration.

Ⓝ ◗ SOUTH CAROLINA REVIEW, English Dept., 801 Strode Tower, Clemson University, Box 341503, Clemson SC 29634-1503, phone (803)656-5404 or 656-3457, fax (803)656-1345, founded 1968, managing editor Wayne Chapman.
Magazine Needs: *South Carolina Review* is a biannual literary magazine "recognized by the *New York Quarterly* as one of the top 20 of this type." They will consider "any kind of poetry as long as it's good. No stale metaphors, uncertain rhythms or lack of line integrity. Interested in seeing more traditional forms. Format should be according to new MLA Stylesheet." They have published poetry by Pattiann Rogers, J.W. Rivers and Claire Bateman. It is 200 pgs., 6×9, professionally printed, flat-spined and uses about 8-10 pgs. of poetry in each issue. Reviews of recent issues back up editorial claims that all styles and forms are welcome; moreover, poems were accessible and well-executed. Circulation is 600, for 400 subscribers of which 250 are libraries. They receive about 1,000 submissions of poetry a year, use approximately 10, have a 2-year backlog. Sample: $10.
How to Submit: Submit 3-10 poems at a time in an "8×10 manila envelope so poems aren't creased." No previously published poems or simultaneous submissions. "Editor prefers a chatty, personal cover letter plus a list of publishing credits." Do not submit during June, July, August or December. Publishes theme issues. Reports in 2-3 months. Pays copies. Staff reviews books of poetry.

Ⓝ ◎ THE SOUTH 666 BITCH (Specialized: form/style, gay, horror, erotica, psychic/occult, social issues); MANDRAKE, 902 Poplar St., Erie PA 16502-1252, founded 1997, editor "That Bitch".
Magazine Needs: *The South 666 Bitch* appears 2-4 times a year and is "eager to offend those (what be) easily offended! 'That Bitch' prefers pro-anti, pro-beat, pro-morbid, pro-street poetry; 3-40 lines." Does not want to see "anything pretentious." They have published poetry by R.L. Nichols, Alice Olds-Ellingson, Joe R and Paul Weinman. The editor says *Bitch* is 6-8 pgs., 8½×11, photocopied and side-stapled with plenty of art and lots of ads. Accept approximately 2-10% of poems received. Press run is 36 for 2 subscribers. Sample: $1.
How to Submit: Submit 3 poems at a time. Previously published poems and simultaneous submissions OK. "Check your work for typos and uncorrect grammar (if unintentional)." Reads submissions January 2 through October 27 only. Time between acceptance and publication is 6 months. Seldom comments on rejections. Publishes theme issues occasionally. Reports in 6 months. Pays 1-2 copies.
Advice: " 'That Bitch' publishes only six poets per issue. Also: read Joe R and share da vibe!"

🕐 ◎ **THE SOUTHERN CALIFORNIA ANTHOLOGY** (Specialized: anthology); **ANN STAN-FORD POETRY PRIZES**, c/o Master of Professional Writing Program, WPH 404, University of Southern California, Los Angeles CA 90089-4034, phone (213)740-3252, founded 1983.

Magazine Needs: *TSCA* is an "annual literary review of serious contemporary poetry and fiction. Very open to all subject matters except pornography. Any form, style OK." They have published poetry by Robert Bly, Donald Hall, Allen Ginsberg, Lisel Mueller, James Ragan and Amiri Baraka. The anthology is 144 pgs., digest-sized, perfect-bound, with a semi-glossy color cover featuring one art piece. A fine selection of poems distinguish this journal, and it has an excellent reputation, well-deserved. The downside, if it has one, concerns limited space for newcomers. Circulation is 1,500, 50% going to subscribers of which 50% are libraries, 30% are for shelf sales. Sample: $5.95.

How to Submit: Submit 3-5 poems between September 1 and January 1 only. No simultaneous submissions or previously published poems. All decisions made by mid-February. Send SASE for guidelines. Reports in 4 months. Pays 2 copies. Acquires all rights.

Also Offers: The Ann Stanford Poetry Prizes ($1,000, $200 and $100) have an April 15 deadline, $10 fee (5 poem limit), for unpublished poems. Include cover sheet with name, address and titles and SASE for contest results. All entries are considered for publication, and all entrants receive a copy of *SCA*.

◖ **SOUTHERN HUMANITIES REVIEW; THEODORE CHRISTIAN HOEPFNER AWARD**, 9088 Haley Center, Auburn University, Auburn AL 36849-5202, e-mail shrengl@mail.auburn.edu, founded 1967, co-editors Dan Latimer and Virginia M. Kouidis.

Magazine Needs: *Southern Humanities Review* is a literary quarterly "interested in poems of any length, subject, genre. Space is limited, and brief poems are more likely to be accepted. Translations welcome, but also send written permission from the copyright holder." They have published poetry by Eamon Grennan, Donald Hall, Brendan Galvin, Susan Ludvigson, Andrew Hudgins, Bin Ramke and Fred Chappell. *SHR* is 100 pgs., 6×9, circulation 700. Subscription: $15/year. Sample: $5.

How to Submit: "Send 3-5 poems in a business-sized envelope. Avoid sending faint computer printout." No previously published poems or simultaneous submissions. No e-mail submissions. Reports in 1-2 months, possibly longer in summer. Always sends prepublication galleys. Pays 2 copies. Copyright reverts to author upon publication. Reviews books of poetry in approximately 750-1,000 words. Send books for review consideration.

Also Offers: Sponsors the Theodore Christian Hoepfner Award, a $50 award for the best poem published in a given volume of *SHR*.

Advice: The editors advise, "For beginners we'd recommend study and wide reading in English and classical literature, and, of course, American literature—the old works, not just the new. We also recommend study of or exposure to a foreign language and a foreign culture. Poets need the reactions of others to their work: criticism, suggestions, discussion. A good creative writing teacher would be desirable here, and perhaps some course work too. And then submission of work, attendance at workshops. And again, the reading: history, biography, verse, essays—all of it. We want to see poems that have gone beyond the language of slippage and easy attitudes."

ℕ ◯ ◎ **SOUTHERN INDIANA REVIEW** (Specialized: regional), Liberal Arts, University of Southern Indiana, 8600 University Blvd., Evansville IN 47712, phone (812)465-1630, fax (812)465-7512, e-mail twilhelm@usi.edu, website http://www.usi.edu/libarts/english/review.htm, founded 1993, fiction editor Thomas A. Wilhelmus, managing editor Teresa J. Kramer.

Magazine Needs: Published biannually, *Southern Indiana Review* "celebrates the American heartland through poetry, fiction, nonfiction and artwork." They want poetry from Midwestern writers or on Midwestern themes. They have published poetry by Liam Rector, Ellen Bryant Voigt, Heather McHugh and Allison Joseph. *SIR* is 180 pgs., 6×9, professionally printed and perfect-bound with 4-color glossy cover, includes b&w photos and art. They receive about 1,500 poems a year, accept approximately 10%. Press run is 375. Subscription: $10. Sample: $6.

How to Submit: No previously published poems; simultaneous submissions OK. Cover letter preferred. E-mail and disk submissions OK. Reads submissions September through December. Time between acceptance and publication is 6 months. Seldom comments on rejections. Send SASE for guidelines or obtain via website. Reports in 3 months. Sometimes sends prepublication galleys. Pays 1 copy. Open to unsolicited reviews.

◖ **SOUTHERN POETRY REVIEW; GUY OWEN POETRY PRIZE**, Advancement Studies, Central Piedmont Community College, Charlotte NC 28235, phone (704)330-6002, fax (704)330-6455, editor Ken McLaurin, founded 1958.

Magazine Needs: *SPR* a semiannual literary magazine "with emphasis on effective poetry. There are no restrictions on form, style or content of poetry; length subject to limitations of space." They have published work by R.T. Smith, Colette Inez, Dabney Stuart, Peter Cooley and Susan Ludvigson. *Southern Poetry Review* is 80 pgs., 6×9, handsomely printed on buff stock, flat-spined with textured, one-color matte card cover. Circulation is 1,000. Subscription: $8/year. Sample: $3.

How to Submit: Queries answered with SASE. Submit up to 3-5 poems at a time. Reads submissions September 1 through May 31 only. Pays 1 copy. Acquires first-time rights. Staff reviews books of poetry. Send books for review consideration.

Also Offers: Also sponsors the annual Guy Owen Poetry Prize of $500. Entry fee is an $8 subscription;

submission must be postmarked in April. Submit 3-5 poems with SASE.

Advice: This is the type of literary magazine to settle back with in a chair and read, particularly during dry creative spells, to inspire one's muse. It is recommended as a market for that reason. It's a tough sell, though. Work is read closely and the magazine reports in a timely manner.

▼ $◐ THE SOUTHERN REVIEW, 43 Allen Hall, Louisiana State University, Baton Rouge LA 70803, phone (225)388-5108, fax (225)388-5098, e-mail bmacon@lsu.edu, website http://www.lsu.edu/guests/wwwtsm, founded 1935 (original series), 1965 (new series), poetry editors James Olney and Dave Smith.
- Work published in this review has been included in the 1995, 1996 and 1998 volumes of *The Best American Poetry*.

Magazine Needs: *The Southern Review* "is a literary quarterly that publishes fiction, poetry, critical essays and book reviews, with emphasis on contemporary literature in the U.S. and abroad, and with special interest in southern culture and history. Selections are made with careful attention to craftsmanship and technique and to the seriousness of the subject matter. We are interested in any variety of poetry that is well crafted, though we cannot normally accommodate excessively long poems (say 10 pgs. and over)." They have published poetry by Norman Dubie, Margaret Gibson, Seamus Heaney, Yusef Komunyakaa, Susan Ludvigson and Robert Penn Warren. The beautifully printed quarterly is massive: 6¾×10, 240 pgs., flat-spined, matte card cover. They receive about 6,000 submissions of poetry a year. All styles and forms seem welcome, although accessible lyric and narrative free verse appear most often in recent issues. Press run is 3,100 for 2,100 subscribers of which 70% are libraries. Subscription: $25. Sample: $8.

How to Submit: "We do not require a cover letter but we prefer one giving information about the author and previous publications." Prefers submissions of up to 4 pgs. Send SASE for guidelines. Reports in 2 months. Pays $20/printed page plus 2 copies. Buys first North American serial rights. Staff reviews books of poetry in 3,000 words, multi-book format. Send books for review consideration.

Also Offers: Website includes guidelines, subscription information, current table of contents, relevant addresses, names, etc.

Ⓝ ⊕ ◐ ◎ SOUTHFIELDS; SOUTHFIELDS PRESS; VENNEL PRESS; AU QUAI (Specialized: ethnic/nationality), 8 Richmond Rd., Staines, Middlesex TW18 2AB England, founded 1994, co-editors Richard Price, David Kinloch and Raymond Friel.

Magazine Needs: *Southfields* is a biannual journal that publishes "Scottish poetry of a wide range of styles and commitments, articles on key Scottish writing of any period, independent poetry from other countries, translations into the languages of Scotland, occasional art criticism, memoir and cross-genre prose. They want "Scottish poetry of a wide range of styles and commitments, but independent poetry from other countries, too. We do not want to see poetry which suggests the poet has not read an issue of the magazine before." They have published poetry by Gael Turnbull, Haryette Mullen, Fiona Templeton and Angela McSeveney. As a sample the editor selected these lines from "Compressor" by Richard Price:

> A mash of half-bricks, off-cuts of board, glaur. The first foam of alyssum./Bungalows crating up the
> fields. Skelfy yellow rafters dreeping girls. Finished halls./A gripped man-hole lid, a lazy boy. A bath
> of petrol, a cigarette's disfigurement, teenage inferno./Twenty years later: a carpenter, a father, a face
> saved.

The editor says *Southfields* is 72-84 pgs., magazine-sized, offset litho printed and perfect-bound, cover varies, occasional ads. They receive about 300 poems a year, accept approximately 15%. Press run is 200. Single copy: $10 (US); subscription: $20 (US). Sample: $8 (US). Make checks payable to Southfields Press.

How to Submit: Submit 3-6 poems at a time. No previously published poems or simultaneous submissions. Cover letter preferred. Time between acceptance and publication is 2 months. Poems are circulated to an editorial board. "If the first editor likes a poem enough it is sent to the second editor, etc." Seldom comments on rejections. Reports in 2 months. Sometimes sends prepublication galleys. Pays 1 copy. Acquires first rights. Reviews books and chapbooks of poetry and other magazines in up to 1,500 words, single or multi-book format. Open to unsolicited reviews. Poets may also send books for review consideration to Richard Price.

Book/Chapbook Needs & How to Submit: Under Vennel Press, they publish Scottish and independent poetry from other countries; under the Au Quai imprint, translations. They publish 0-1 paperbacks and 1-5 chapbooks/year. Query first with a few sample poems and cover letter with brief bio and publication credits. Replies to queries in 2 weeks; to mss in 2 months. Pays 10% author's copies. Order sample books/chapbooks by sending $20 payable to Vennel Press.

▼ $◐ SOUTHWEST REVIEW; ELIZABETH MATCHETT STOVER MEMORIAL AWARD, 307 Fondren Library West, P.O. Box 750374, Southern Methodist University, Dallas TX 75275-0374, phone (214)768-1037, founded 1915, editor Willard Spiegelman.
- Poetry published in *Southwest Review* has been included in the 1993, 1994, 1995 and 1998 volumes of *The Best American Poetry*.

Magazine Needs: *Southwest Review* is a literary quarterly that publishes fiction, essays, poetry and interviews. "It is hard to describe our preference for poetry in a few words. We always suggest that potential contributors read several issues of the magazine to see for themselves what we like. But some things may be said: We demand very high quality in our poems; we accept both traditional and experimental writing, but avoid unnecessary obscurity and private symbolism; we place no arbitrary limits on length but find shorter poems easier to fit into our format than longer ones. We have no specific limitations as to theme." They have published poetry by Adrienne Rich, Amy Clampitt, Albert Goldbarth, Leonard Nathan, Molly Peacock and Charles Wright. The journal is 6×9, 144 pgs., perfect-bound, professionally printed, with matte text stock cover. They receive about 1,000 submissions of poetry a year, use approximately 32. Poems tend to be lyric and narrative free verse combining a strong voice with powerful topics or situations. Diction is accessible and content often conveys a strong sense of place. Circulation is 1,500 for 1,000 subscribers of which 600 are libraries. Subscription: $24. Sample: $6.

How to Submit: No simultaneous submissions or previously published work. Send SASE for guidelines. Reports within a month. Always sends prepublication galleys. Pays cash plus copies.

Also Offers: The $150 Elizabeth Matchett Stover Memorial Award is awarded annually for the best poem, chosen by editors, published in the preceding year.

SOUTHWESTERN AMERICAN LITERATURE (Specialized: regional), Center for the Study of the Southwest, Southwest Texas State University, San Marcos TX 78666, phone (512)245-2232, fax (512)245-7462, e-mail mb13@swt.edu, website http://www.english.swt.edu/css/cssindex.htm, founded 1971, editor Dr. Mark Busby, editor Dr. Dick Heaberlin.

Magazine Needs: *Southwestern American Literature* is "a biannual scholarly journal that includes literary criticism, fiction, poetry and book reviews concerning the Greater Southwest. While we are a regional journal, we enjoy seeing poetry of all subject matters, not just about tumbleweeds, longhorns and urban cowboys." They have published poetry by Naomi Shihab Nye, Alberto Rios, Alison Deming and Simon J. Ortiz. As a sample the editor selected these lines from "Light" by Simon J. Ortiz:

> Out to mail a letter at the corner mailbox,/morning moment, the sunlight caught/me striding loosely uphill. I cannot mistake/this morning for what it is: sunshine/air quick and rich in spirit, alert in my eye.

The editors say *SAL* is 100-125 pgs., 6×9, professionally printed and perfect-bound with 80 lb. embossed bond cover. They receive about 200 poems a year, accept approximately 10%. Press run is 300 for 225 subscribers of which 80 are libraries. Subscription: $14/year. Sample: $7.

How to Submit: Submit 3 poems at a time. No previously published poems; simultaneous submissions OK. Cover letter preferred. "Two copies of manuscript should be submitted along with SASE." No e-mail submissions. Time between acceptance and publication is 2-6 months. Poems are circulated to an editorial board. "Each poem that is accepted has been recommended by at least two members of our editorial board." Seldom comments on rejections. Publishes theme issues occasionally. Obtain guidelines via e-mail. Reports in 6 weeks. Pays 1 copy. Acquires all rights. Returns rights upon publication. Staff reviews books of poetry in 500-1,000 words, single or multi-book format. Send books for review consideration.

SOU'WESTER, Box 1438, Southern Illinois University, Edwardsville IL 62026, phone (618)650-3190, founded 1960, managing editor Fred W. Robbins, associate editor Nancy Avdoian.

Magazine Needs: *Sou'wester* appears twice a year. "We lean toward poetry with strong imagery, successful association of images, and skillful use of figurative language." They have published poetry by R.T. Smith, Susan Swartwout and William Jolliff. There are 30-40 pgs. of poetry in each 6×9, 100-page issue. The magazine is professionally printed, flat-spined, with textured matte card cover, circulation is 300 for 500 subscribers of which 50 are libraries. They receive 3,000 poems (from 600 poets) each year, use approximately 36-40, have a 4-month backlog. Subscription: $10/2 issues. Sample: $5.

How to Submit: Simultaneous submissions OK. Does not read during August. Rejections usually within 4 months. Pays 2 copies. Acquires all rights. Returns rights. Editor comments on rejections "usually, in the case of those that we almost accept."

Advice: He says, "Read poetry past and present. Have something to say and say it in your own voice. Poetry is a very personal thing for many editors. When all else fails, we may rely on gut reactions, so take whatever hints you're given to improve your poetry, and keep submitting."

THE SOW'S EAR POETRY REVIEW, 19535 Pleasant View Dr., Abingdon VA 24211-6827, phone (540)628-2651, e-mail richman@preferred.com, founded 1988, managing editor Larry Richman, graphics editor Mary Calhoun.

Magazine Needs: *The Sow's Ear* is a quarterly. "We are open to many forms and styles, and have no limitations on length. We try to be interesting visually, and we use graphics to complement the poems. Though we publish some work from our local community of poets, we are interested in poems from all over. We publish a few by previously unpublished poets." They have published poetry by Allen C. Fischer, Penelope Scambly Schott, Susan Terris and Madeline Tiger. *TSE* is 32 pgs., 8½×11, saddle-stapled, with matte card cover, professionally printed. They receive about 2,000 poems a year, accept approximately 100. Press run is 600 for 500 subscribers of which 15 are libraries, 20-40 shelf sales. Subscription: $10. Sample: $5.

How to Submit: Submit up to 5 poems at a time with SASE. No previously published poems; simultaneous submissions OK if you tell them promptly when work is accepted elsewhere. Enclose brief bio. No e-mail submissions. Send SASE or e-mail for guidelines. Reports in 3-6 months. Pays 2 copies. Buys first publication rights. Most prose (reviews, interviews, features) is commissioned.

Also Offers: They offer an annual contest for unpublished poems, with fee of $2/poem, prizes of $1,000, $250 and $100, and publication for 15-20 finalists. For contest, submit poems in September/October, with name and address on a separate sheet. Submissions of 5 poems/$10 receive a subscription. Include SASE for notification. 1998 Judge: Maggie Anderson. They also sponsor a chapbook contest in March/April with $10 fee, $500 1st Prize, publication, 25 copies and distribution to subscribers; 2nd Prize $200 and 3rd Prize $100. Send SASE or e-mail for chapbook contest guidelines.

Advice: The editor says, "Four criteria help us to judge the quality of submissions: Does the poem make the strange familiar or the familiar strange or both? Is the form of the poem vital to its meaning? Do the sounds of the poem make sense in relation to the theme? Does the little story of the poem open a window on the Big Story of the human situation?"

$ ⓘ SPARROW: THE YEARBOOK OF THE SONNET (Specialized: form), 103 Waldron St., West Lafayette IN 47906, founded 1954, editor/publisher Felix and Selma Stefanile.

Magazine Needs: *Sparrow* appears every October. "We are noted for our devotion to the publication of formal, contemporary sonnets. We occasionally publish other types of structured verse, but only rarely, and only when the poem seems to compel us to take it. No subject restrictions. We don't publish poems in poor taste." They have published poetry by Michael J. Bugeja, Annie Finch, Timothy Murphy and Katherine McAlpine. As a sample the editor selected these lines from "The Trumpet Shall Sound" by Dessa Crawford:

> *The balance is perfection, the clear tone/of trumpet banked a sixth above the bass./Neither voice could*
> *say as much alone:/they're yoked in opposition, pace by pace.*

Sparrow is about 100 pgs., 8½ × 11, attractively printed, perfect-bound with light card cover, using occasional graphics only by invitation. They receive about 2,000 mss a year, use less than 1%. Press run is 650 for about 400 subscribers of which about 50 are libraries, 200 shelf sales. Single copy: $6. Sample back issue: $5.

How to Submit: Submit 4-5 poems at a time, typed on 8½ × 11 bond paper. One poem to a page with name and address on each. No simultaneous submissions. No material returned without SASE. "We have a very cynical attitude toward long cover letters." Reads submissions January through September only. Seldom comments on rejections. "We are not in the business of offering criticism or advice." Send SASE with all queries. Reports in 6 weeks. Sends prepublication galleys. Pays $3 a sonnet plus 1 copy. Buys first and non-exclusive reprint rights. "We also offer a $25 prize for the best sonnet each issue." Reviews books of poetry only rarely.

Advice: The editor says, "We are now essentially a 'new' magazine with a fine, old name. We pride ourselves on our liveliness and our currency. We also publish scores of musical settings for sonnets, by special arrangement with the composer. We are really not a market for beginners and the MFA degree does not elicit special consideration from us."

◑ ⓓ SPELUNKER FLOPHOUSE, P.O. Box 617742, Chicago IL 60661, phone (773)561-6642, fax (773)561-6918, e-mail spelunkerf@aol.com, website http://members.aol.com/spelunkerf/, founded 1995, editors Chris Kubica and Wendy Morgan.

Magazine Needs: *spelunker flophouse* is an annual literary magazine, published in January, offering "high quality poetry, fiction and artwork for an intelligent, imaginative readership. We are extremely interested in poetry that shows a high consciousness of language, rhythm, and structure and attempts to deal with the minute, seemingly insignificant aspects/details of daily life. To quote the cliché, less is definitely more. However, we have little interest in poetry that deals directly with the larger aspects/summaries/absolutes of life, for instance obvious religious, political, or social commentary. Discussing emotions (telling without showing) without illustrations of specific/vivid/tangible scenes, objects, situations, language, or people is not looked upon favorably by the editors." As a sample the editors selected this poem, "if," by David Ignatow:

> *I must accept aches and pains of the body/that is my presence, if I am to accept/my presence in the*
> *empty room,/with no motive for being/in an empty room, and so/no motive for being, If/I can accept*
> *aches and pains,/I exist.*

spelunker flophouse is 96 pgs., 8½ × 7 (half legal), offset printed and perfect-bound with 4-color glossy card cover. "We publish fiction, poetry, b&w artwork, creative nonfiction, and ads." They receive about 4,000 poems a year, accept approximately 40. Press run is 1,500. Subscription: $9.95/year, $17.95/2 years. Sample: $9.95.

How to Submit: "Submit 3-5 poems at a time so that we may get a round survey of your work. Print name/address/phone on every first page, full name on subsequent pages. One poem per page, please. Submit on clean, white letter-sized paper. Electronic submissions are not accepted. However, electronic requests for guidelines and queries about submissions are accepted if brief. Please make every effort to include cover letters—tell us about the colorful, intense, perhaps quixotic hollow in which you live (include publication credits and a brief bio if you can). We favor submitters who clearly illustrate the fact that they've read our magazine." No previously published poems; simultaneous submissions OK if notified. Often comments on rejections. Send SASE for guidelines or request via e-mail. Reports in approximately 2 months. Always sends prepublication galleys. Pays "copies and occasional small sums." Acquires first North American serial rights. "Cite us if published again elsewhere, we retain rights to anthologize work(s) with proper credit and notification given."

Also Offers: Sponsors an annual contest awarding $500 and publication in the magazine for a piece of previously unpublished fiction, nonfiction, poetry and artwork. Entry fee: $10/5 poems. Deadline (postmarked): September 1. All entrants may order a copy of winning issue for an additional $4.95. Send SASE for complete entry requirements. Website includes guidelines, sample work, links, table on contents, the magazine's heritage and contest for a free subscription.

Advice: The editors say, "We offer the best poetry, fiction, creative nonfiction and artwork we can in an inventive, original format. We cooperate regularly with other literary magazines. Support this necessary forum for the arts by purchasing copies of literary magazines, reading them, and increasing local awareness of magazines/forums such as ours whenever possible. Study the market; then submit. And keep in touch! We love to hear from members/supporters of the literary community."

SPILLWAY, 20592 Minerva Lane, Huntington Beach CA 92646, phone (714)968-0905, founded 1991, editors Mifanwy Kaiser and Mark Bergendahl.

Magazine Needs: *Spillway* is a biannual journal, published in March and September, "celebrating writing's diversity and power to affect our lives. Open to all voices, schools and tendencies. We usually do not use writing which tells instead of shows, or writing which contains general, abstract lines not anchored in images. We publish poetry, translations, reviews, essays and b&w photography." They have published poetry by John Balahan, Sam Hamill, Richard Jones and Susan Terris. *Spillway* is about 160 pgs., digest-sized, attractively printed, perfect-bound, with 2-color or 4-color card cover. Press run is 1,000. Subscription: $14/2 issues, $24/4 issues. Sample (including guidelines): $10. Make checks payable to Spillway, Mifanwy Kaiser.

How to Submit: Submit 3-6 poems at a time, 10 pages total. Previously published work ("say when and where") and simultaneous submissions ("say where also submitted") OK. Cover letter including brief bio and SASE required. "No cute bios—we need professional ones." Reports in 2 weeks to 6 months. Pays 1 copy. Acquires one-time rights. Reviews books of poetry in 500-2,500 words maximum. Open to unsolicited reviews and essays, 10 pages words maximum. Poets may also send books for review consideration.

Advice: The editors say, "We have no problem with simultaneous or previously published submissions. Poems are murky creatures—they shift and change in time and context. It's exciting to pick up a volume, read a poem in the context of all the other pieces and then find the same poem in another time and place. And, we don't think a poet should have to wait until death to see work in more than one volume. What joy to find out that more than one editor values one's work. Our responsibility as editors, collectively, is to promote the work of poets as much as possible—how can we do this if we say to a writer you may only have a piece published in one volume and only one time?"

SPIN; POETRY ORBITAL WORKSHOPS, % Postal Agency, Ngakawau, Buller, New Zealand, phone 03 7828608, founded 1986, contact Leicester Kyle.

Magazine Needs: *SPIN* appears 3 times/year, March, July, November, and publishes poetry. "We have no hard and fast rules but appreciate poetry that excels in its form and content. No stereotyped, imitative or boring work." They have published poetry by George Gott, Catherine Maur, John O'Connor and Joanna Weston. As a sample the editor selected these lines from "Like Florida" by David Gregory:

> *No new ways of telling time,/winking heart monitor digitals,/cruel and precise./Autumn is made*
> *apocryphal;/she extends herself south,/ahead of the shadows.*

SPIN is 72 pgs., A5, photocopied and saddle-stitched with light card cover. They receive about 600 poems a year, accept approximately 25%. Press run is 150 for 110 subscribers of which 6 are libraries. Single copy: NZ 6.50; subscription: NZ 18. Sample: NZ 4.50.

How to Submit: "We expect contributors to subscribe/purchase. We are unable to supply contributors copies." Submit approximately 6 poems at a time. No previously published poems or simultaneous submissions. Cover letter preferred. "All submissions returned at each publication." Time between acceptance and publication is 1 month. Sometimes comments on rejections. Publishes theme issues. Reports within 3 months. Reviews books of poetry in 1-page (or more), or in multi 3-4 line notices. Open to unsolicited reviews. Poets may also send books for review consideration.

Also Offers: Subscription covers (optional) membership in poetry orbital workshops. "Each workshop or 'orbit' comprises four or five poets who by post submit poems to each other for reading and comment." Send SASE (or SAE and IRC) for details.

SPINDRIFT, Shoreline Community College, 16101 Greenwood Ave. N., Seattle WA 98133, phone (206)546-5864, founded 1962, faculty advisor varies each year, currently Carol Orlock.

Magazine Needs: *Spindrift* is open to all varieties of poetry except greeting card style. They have published poetry by Lyn Lifshin, Mary Lou Sanelli, James Bertolino, Edward Harkness and Richard West. *Spindrift*, an annual, is 125 pgs., handsomely printed in an 8″ square, flat-spined. Circulation is 500. Single copy: $6.50. Sample: $5.

How to Submit: "Submit two copies of each poem, six lines maximum. Include SASE and cover letter with

OPENNESS TO SUBMISSIONS: ○ beginners; ◐ beginners and experienced; ◑ mostly experienced, few beginners; ◎ specialized; ⊘ closed to unsolicited mss.

2-3 lines of biographical information including name, address, phone number, e-mail address and a list of all materials sent. We accept submissions until February 1; editorial responses are mailed by March 15." Send SASE for guidelines. Pays 2 copies. All rights revert to author upon publication.

Advice: The editors advise, "Read what the major contemporary poets are writing. Read what local poets are writing. Be distinctive, love the language, avoid sentiment."

✓ ◐ ◑ **SPINNING JENNY**, Black Dress Press, P.O. Box 213, New York NY 10014, website http://www.blackdresspress.com, founded 1994, first issue Fall 1995, editor C.E. Harrison.

Magazine Needs: *Spinning Jenny* appears once a year. They have published poetry by Denise Duhamel, Matthew Lippman, Michael Loncar, Sarah Messer and a play by Jeff Hoffman. As a sample the editor selected these lines from "Infidelity" by Michael Morse:

> *The stranger takes off his shirt,/and in your own good mind it's the kiss.//When you lean forward and close the eyes,/the stars and their just torments/wheel off to the somewhere-else.*

SJ is 96 pgs., 5¼×9¼, perfect-bound with heavy card cover. "We accept less than 5% of unsolicited submissions." Press run is 1,500. Single copy: $6; subscription: $12/2 issues. Sample: $6.

How to Submit: No previously published poems; simultaneous submissions not encouraged. E-mail submissions OK. Seldom comments on rejections. Send SASE for guidelines. Reports within 2 months. Pays contributor copies. Authors retain rights.

Also Offers: Website includes guidelines, address/contact information, subscription info, sample work and links.

◐ **THE SPIRIT THAT MOVES US; THE SPIRIT THAT MOVES US PRESS**, P.O. Box 720820-PM, Jackson Heights, Queens NY 11372-0820, phone (718)426-8788, founded 1974, poetry editor Morty Sklar.

Magazine Needs & How to Submit: *"The Spirit That Moves Us* will be continuing its *Editor's Choice* series and publishing regular issues only occasionally. *Editor's Choice* consists of selections from other literary magazines and small presses, where we choose from nominations by the editors of those magazines and presses." They have published poetry by Rhina Espaillat, Darryl Holmes, Barbara Unger and Susan Montez. As a sample the editor selected these lines from "Jamaica, Queens, 1963" by Julia Alvarez:

> *Everyone seemed more American/than we, newly arrived,/foreign dirt still on our soles./Watched at first, by year's end/we were melted into the block,/owned our own mock Tudor house.*

That poem appeared in *Patchwork of Dreams: Voices from the Heart of the New America*, an anthology, which they offer as a sample for $8 plus $1 postage (regularly $12 plus $1.50 postage) or their *15th Anniversary Collection* for $6 and free shipping. Publishes theme issues. Send SASE for upcoming themes and time frames.

Advice: The editor's advice: "Write what you would like to write, in a style (or styles) which is/are best for your own expression. Don't worry about acceptance, though you may be concerned about it. Don't just send work which you think editors would like to see, though take that into consideration. Think of the relationship between poem, poet and editor as personal. You may send good poems to editors who simply do not like them, whereas other editors might."

◎ **SPITBALL: THE LITERARY BASEBALL MAGAZINE; CASEY AWARD (Specialized: sports/recreation)**, 5560 Fox Rd., Cincinnati OH 45239, phone (513)385-2268, founded 1981, poetry editor William J. McGill.

Magazine Needs: *Spitball* is "a unique literary magazine devoted to poetry, fiction and book reviews exclusively about baseball. Newcomers are very welcome, but remember that you have to know the subject. We do and our readers do. Perhaps a good place to start for beginners is one's personal reactions to the game, a game, a player, etc. and take it from there." The 96-page, digest-sized biannual is computer typeset and perfect-bound. They receive about 1,000 submissions a year, use approximately 40. "Many times we are able to publish accepted work almost immediately." Circulation is 1,000 for 750 subscribers of which 25 are libraries. Subscription: $12. Sample: $6. "We now require all first-time submitters to purchase a sample copy for $6. This is a one-time only fee, which we regret but economic reality dictates that we insist those who wish to be published in *SB* help support it, at least at this minimum level."

How to Submit: "We are not very concerned with the technical details of submitting, but we do prefer a cover letter with some bio info. We also like batches of poems and prefer to use several of same poet in an issue rather than a single poem." Pays 2 copies.

Also Offers: "We sponsor the Casey Award (for best baseball book of the year) and hold the Casey Awards Banquet every January. Any chapbook of baseball poetry should be sent to us for consideration for the 'Casey' plaque that we award to the winner each year."

Advice: The editor says, "We encourage anyone interested to submit to *Spitball*. We are always looking for fresh talent. Those who have never written 'baseball poetry' before should read some first probably before submitting. Not necessarily ours."

N ⊕ ◯ **SPLIZZ**, 4 St. Marys Rise, Burry Port, Carms SA16 OSH Wales, founded 1993, editor Amanda Morgan.

Magazine Needs: *Splizz*, published quarterly, features poetry, prose, reviews of contemporary music, background to poets and art. They want "any kind of poetry. We have no restrictions regarding style, length, subjects." They do not want "anything racist or homophobic." They have published poetry by writers from throughout the world. The editor says *Splizz* is 40-44 pgs., A5, saddle-stapled with art and ads. They receive about 100-200 poems a year, accept approximately 90%. Press run is 100 for 25 subscribers. Single copy: £1.30, 5 IRCs elsewhere; subscription: £5 UK, £10 elsewhere. Sample: £1.30 UK, 5 IRCs elsewhere. Make checks payable to Amanda Morgan (British checks only).

How to Submit: Submit 5 poems, typed submissions preferred. Include SAE with IRCs. Previously published poems and simultaneous submissions OK. Cover letter required with short bio. Time between acceptance and publication is 2-4 months. Often comments on rejections. Charges criticism fee: "Just enclose SAE/IRC for response, and allow one to two months for delivery." Send SASE (or SAE and IRC) for guidelines. Reports in 1-2 months. Sometimes sends prepublication galleys. Reviews books or chapbooks of poetry or other magazines in 50-300 words. Open to unsolicited reviews. Poets may also send books for review consideration.

Advice: The editor says, "Beginners seeking to have their work published, send your work to *Splizz*, as we specialize in giving new poets a chance."

THE SPOON RIVER POETRY REVIEW (Specialized: regional, translations); EDITORS' PRIZE CONTEST, 4240/English Dept., Illinois State University, Normal IL 61790-4240, website http://www.lit line.org/spoon, founded 1976, editor Lucia Getsi.

Magazine Needs: *SRPR* is a "poetry magazine that features newer and well-known poets from around the country and world." Also features 1 Illinois poet/issue at length for the magazine's Illinois Poet Series. "We want interesting and compelling poetry that operates beyond the ho-hum, so-what level, in any form or style about anything; language that is fresh, energetic, committed, filled with a strong voice that grabs the reader in the first line and never lets go." They also use translations of poetry. They have published poetry by Stuart Dybek, Leslie Andrienne Miller, Allison Joseph, Sheryl St. Germain and Dave Smith. As a sample the editors included these lines from "Contract" by Karen Themstrup·

> A face unravels like a sweater snagged on a nail—first/the eyes get wobbly, then the cheeks shiver,
> the/mouth shakes, everything slips apart/as if it was never there—

SRPR appears biannually, 128 pgs., digest-sized, laser set with card cover using photos, ads. They receive about 3,000 poems a month, accept approximately 1%. Press run is 1,500 for 700 subscribers, of which 100 are libraries and shelf sales. Subscription: $14. Sample (including guidelines): $9.

How to Submit: "No simultaneous submissions unless we are notified immediately if a submission is accepted elsewhere. Include name and address on every poem." Do not submit mss May 1 through September 1. Editor comments on rejections "many times, if a poet is promising." Reports in 2 months. Pays a year's subscription. Acquires first North American serial rights. Staff reviews books of poetry. Send books for review consideration.

Also Offers: Sponsors the Editor's Prize Contest for previously unpublished work. One poem will be awarded $500 and published in the fall issue of *SRPR*, and two runners-up will receive $100 each and publication in the fall issue. Entries must be previously unpublished. Entry fee: $15, including 1-year subscription. Deadline: April 15. Write for details. Recent winners were Judith Westley and Aleida Rodríguez. Website includes guidelines, cover pictures, contest guidelines, subscription information and poems.

SPOONFED, P.O. Box 21036, Washington DC 20009-1036, phone (202)667-5248, e-mail spoonfe d99@aol.com, website http://members.aol.com/spoonfed99/spoonfedl.html, founded 1995, managing editor Thomas Drymon.

Magazine Needs: *SpoonFed* is a quarterly publication "for queer writers and artists who critically examine issues about family, religion, politics, sex, identity, orientation, culture, relationships, race and class. The publication serves as a venue for emerging, under-recognized, and previously unpublished queer artists." Any style of poetry is acceptable. They have published poetry by Leslea Newman and Hiram Laren. As a sample we selected these lines from "Underneath the Real Inside" by Gigi Ross-Fowler:

> Sometimes, alone, I sit atop a cliff,/city ruins crumble, behind, below./Your face appears in silence
> before me./Sometimes, troubled, I slump in my chair, neck//muscles tensed against the pressure, her
> touch./Your hum overcomes that heat in my head./But when I sketch your contours with words, then/
> no shimmer of breath disturbs the air.

SpoonFed is 16-24 pgs., 7 × 6¾, offset printed and saddle-stitched with paper self-cover, includes photography, illustration, comics. They receive about 120 poems a year, accept approximately 8%. Press run is 2,500; all distributed free to bookstores, coffeehouses, record stores in DC. Sample: $2 (metro area).

How to Submit: Submit 5-8 poems at a time. Line length for poetry is 40 maximum. Previously published poems and simultaneous submissions OK. Cover letter preferred. E-mail and disk submissions OK. Time between acceptance and publication is 3-6 months. Poems are circulated to an editorial board. "Board compromised of four writers review selections for quality and appropriateness and theme." Seldom comments on rejections. Publishes theme issues. Send SASE for guidelines and upcoming themes. Reports in 3-6 months. Pays 3-5 copies. Acquires one-time rights. Reviews books and chapbooks of poetry in less than 1,200 words, single book format. Open to unsolicited reviews. Poets may also send books for review consideration.

Also Offers: Website includes addresses, submission guidelines, mission statement, themes, past issues/content.

Advice: The editor says, "*SpoonFed* provides an outlet for expression for queer people involved in various artistic disciplines including writing (short fiction, poetry, journalism), photography, graphic arts, comics, painting, sculpture, collage, etc. It encourages collaboration between artists of different disciplines and expansion of individual artists' means of expression. It hopes to strengthen and build upon the existing queer art community in the metropolitan DC area, creating a network of artists working with artists and other arts organizations."

SPOUT MAGAZINE, 28 W. Robie, St. Paul MN 55107, founded 1989, editors John Colburn and Michelle Filkins.

Magazine Needs: *Spout* appears approximately 3 times/year providing "a paper community of unique expression." They want "poetry of the imagination, poetry that surprises. We enjoy the surreal, the forceful, the political, the expression of confusion." No light verse, archaic forms or language. They have published poetry by Simon Perchik, Sheila E. Murphy, Lyn Lifshin and Jeffrey Little. As a sample the editor selected these lines from "English Lesson" by Mary Hale Jackson:

> He says, I see my wife,/my children and the/soldiers under me.//I say, You had a dream.//Yes. Dream. How do you/spell it?

The editor says *Spout* is 40-60 pgs., saddle-stapled, card stock or glossy cover is a different color each issue. They receive about 400-450 poems a year, accept approximately 10%. Press run is 200-250 for 35-40 subscribers, 100-150 shelf sales. Single copy price: $4; subscription: $12. Sample: $4.

How to Submit: Submit up to 6 poems at a time. Previously published poems and simultaneous submissions OK. Cover letter preferred. Time between acceptance and publication is 2-3 months. Poems are circulated to an editorial board. "Poems are reviewed by two of three editors, those selected for final review are read again by all three." Seldom comments on rejections. Send SASE for guidelines. Reports in 3-4 months. Pays 1 copy.

SPRING: THE JOURNAL OF THE E.E. CUMMINGS SOCIETY (Specialized), 33-54 164th St., Flushing NY 11358-1442, phone (718)353-3631 or (718)461-9022, fax (718)353-4778, editor Norman Friedman.

Magazine Needs: *Spring* is an annual publication designed "to maintain and broaden the audience for Cummings and to explore various facets of his life and art." They want poems in the spirit of Cummings, primarily poems of one page or less. Nothing "amateurish." They have published poetry by John Tagliabue, Ruth Whitman, M.L. Rosenthal, William Jay Smith and Theodore Weiss. *Spring* is about 180 pgs., 5½×8½, offset and perfect-bound with light card stock cover. Press run is 700 for 200 subscribers of which 15 are libraries, 450 shelf sales. Subscription or sample: $17.50.

How to Submit: No previously published poems or simultaneous submissions. Fax submissions OK. Cover letter required. Reads submissions January through March only. Seldom comments on rejections. Reports in 6 months. Pays 1 copy.

Advice: "Contributors are encouraged to subscribe."

SPRING TIDES (Specialized: children), Savannah Country Day School, 824 Stillwood Dr., Savannah GA 31419-2643, founded 1989.

Magazine Needs: *Spring Tides* is an annual literary magazine by children 5-12 years of age. "Children from ages five through twelve may submit material. Please limit stories to 1,200 words and poems to 20 lines. All material must be original and created by the person submitting it. A statement signed by the child's parent or teacher attesting to the originality must accompany all work." *ST* is 28 pgs., digest-sized, attractively printed and saddle-stapled with glossy card cover, includes b&w and 4-color art. Press run is 500; given to student at SCDS and sold to others. Single copy: $5.

How to Submit: Simultaneous submissions OK. SASE required. "Poems with or without illustrations may be submitted." Reads submissions January through August only. Poems are circulated to an editorial board. Always comments on rejections. Send SASE for guidelines. Reports in 4 months. Pays 1 copy.

SPUNK, Box 55336, Hayward CA 94545, phone (415)397-2596, founded 1996, editor Violet Jones.

Magazine Needs: Appearing 2 times a year, *Spunk: The Journal of Spontaneous Creativity* contains "short fiction, poetry and b&w artwork (comics OK). We are an outlet for the muses who drive us to write when we are in the middle of doing something else. No restrictions (on form, that is). We want only explosive, spontaneous creativity. No smugness, no needlepoint, no half-stepping." They have published poetry by Catfish McDaris, Tim Scannell and John Sweet. *Spunk* is 30-50 pgs., 5½×8½, photocopied and side-stapled with light card cover, b&w art only, ads. They receive about 800-1,000 poems a year, accept approximately 10%. Press run is 500; all distributed free to anyone who really, really wants them. Sample: $2. No checks.

How to Submit: Submit any number of poems at a time. No previously published poems or simultaneous submissions. Cover letter preferred. "Just make us happy we opened the envelope—how you do this is up to you." Time between acceptance and publication is 6-12 months. Poems are circulated to an editorial board. "Our extremely small staff gets together now and then, we drink large amounts of coffee/tea and work through the 'in' pile until we have a zine." Often comments on rejections. Publishes theme issues occasionally. Send SASE for guidelines and upcoming themes. Reports in 6-12 months. Pays 1 copy. Acquires first North American serial rights. Staff occasionally reviews books and chapbooks of poetry and other magazines in 100-500 words, single book format. Send books for review consideration.

Advice: The editor says, "*SPUNK* is 30 pages of pure vim. Send us a shot in the dark if you like, but *SPUNK* is always worth the postage (to see it in the flesh), and then you can see what we publish. Keep doin' what you doin' . . ."

N ◨ **SPUYTEN DUYVIL**, 1852 Cathedral Station, New York NY 10025, fax (212)727-8228, e-mail spuyte nduyvil@mailcity.com, founded 1982.
Book/Chapbook Needs: Publishes works of "quality content and form of perennial interest." Publishes 2 paperbacks, 2 hardbacks and 2 chapbooks/year. "Open to any formats of course, restrictions would be that to which not enough editing and testing of the waters has surfaced." They have published poetry by Michael Stephens, Mark Rudman, Richard Pevear, Robert Creeley and Leonard Schwartz. Books or chapbooks are usually 60-100 pgs., 6×9, perfect-bound with color art covers.
How to Submit: "Only published poets need apply." Previously published poems OK; no simultaneous submissions. Cover letter required. "Send ms ideas, or e-mail ideas and/or the actual mogombo. We'll get to you as soon as possible with a yeh or nay." Prefers not to read submissions during the summer. Poems are circulated to an editorial board and must be approved by all four editors.
Also Offers: Sponsors the annual Poetry Book Contest from May 1 to December 31. Send e-mail with address for guidelines.

N $ ◯ ◨ **STAR RISING**, P.O. Box 1139, Sedona AZ 86339-1139, founded 1997, editor/publisher Leondra May.
Magazine Needs: *Star Rising* appears quarterly and publishes "poetry on life experiences to bring a greater understanding of life to the reader through the art of words." They want "poetry on life matters from the heart and experience. Poetry that takes you to the experiences and makes you think and feel. All subject matters; any length or style. No porn or graphic horror." They have published poetry by Robin May and Kristen Odenthal. As a sample the editor selected these lines from "Til' Morrow" by Robin May:

> Lies told, dreams stolen, thoughts provoked/To the times of weathered vanes and scattered yoke/Hold
> my hand and see the pain/Gazing out the window into the rain/A chance to be forever in sorrow/This
> time of now til' morrow.

The editor says *SR* is 20 pgs., 6×9, offset printed and stapled with 12 pt. cover, includes line drawings. They receive about 100 poems a year, accept approximately 20%. Press run is 200 for 50 subscribers; 100 distributed free. Subscription: $28. Sample: $7. Make checks payable to *Star Rising*.
How to Submit: Submit 5 poems at a time. Previously published poems and simultaneous submissions OK. Cover letter preferred. Time between acceptance and publication is 2 months. Poems are circulated to an editorial board. Poems are selected by two editors. Often comments on rejections. Publishes theme issues occasionally. Send SASE for guidelines and upcoming themes. Reports in 2 weeks. Pays 2 copies. Acquires first or one-time rights. Staff reviews books and chapbooks of poetry in single book format.
Book/Chapbook Needs & How to Submit: *Star Rising* also publishes books of poems "to bring thought and feeling back into poetry. We would like to see more old-style poetry such as that of Poe, Byron and Dickinson." They publish 2 paperbacks and 2 chapbooks/year. Books are usually 60-200 pgs., 6×9, offset printed and perfect-bound or stapled with 12 pt. glossy cover, include line drawings. Query first with a few sample poems and cover letter with brief bio and publication credits. Replies to queries in 2 weeks; to mss in 1 month. Pays royalties of 40% plus author's copies (out of a press run of 500). Order sample books by sending for list of books.
Advice: The editor says, "Write, write, write. Keep your creativity flowing and send the poems often even the ones you consider not so good. We would like to see more work done as an art form with thought and feelings to bring the words alive."

◯ ◨ **STATE STREET REVIEW**, FCCJ North, 4501 Capper Rd., Jacksonville FL 32218, phone (904)766-6697, fax (904)766-6654, e-mail hdenson@fccj.cc.fl.us, website http://astro.fccj.cc.fl.us/WritersFestival/, founded 1990, poetry and fiction editor Howard Denson.
Magazine Needs: A biannual that "sometimes has to settle for being an annual," *State Street Review* strives "to publish the best prose and poetry that we can get our hands on." They want "good, sharp poems. Generally no longer than 30 lines. No restrictions other than quality." They don't want "stuff that's been done before." They have published poetry by Peter Meinke, Enid Shomer, Scott Ward and Jane Ellen Glasser. As a sample the editor selected these lines from "Piet Mondrian" by Louis Phillips:

> Mondrian. Piet/Did not sculpt the Piet/Instead he settled on subjects less theatrical,/But slightly more
> geometrical.

The editor says *State Street Review* is 70-90 pgs., 5×8, offset printed, true binding with b&w photos and line art. They receive about 300-500 poems a year, accept approximately 40-60. Press run is 300-500 for 20 subscribers, 200-400 shelf sales, with 100 distributed free to libraries. Single copy: $5. Sample: $3.
How to Submit: Submit 5 poems at a time. No previously published poems, simultaneous submissions OK. "It won't hurt our feelings if a piece has been accepted elsewhere while we scraped together the money for our next issue." No fax or e-mail submissions. Cover letter preferred with information for contributors' page. "For longer poems, we appreciate diskettes in WordPerfect, ASCII or RTF format." Time between acceptance and publication is 1-6 months. Poems are circulated to an editorial board. Always comments on rejections. Send SASE for guidelines or obtain via e-mail. Reports in 1-6 months. Always sends prepublication galleys. Pays 2 copies. Acquires first North American serial rights. May review books or chapbooks of poetry in the future. Open to unsolicited reviews. Poets may also send books for review consideration.

☑ ◖◗ ◎ **THE WALLACE STEVENS JOURNAL (Specialized)**, Liberal Arts, Clarkson University, Box 5750, Potsdam NY 13699-5750, phone (315)268-3967, fax (315)268-3983, e-mail duemer@clarkson.edu, founded 1977, poetry editor Prof. Joseph Duemer.

Magazine Needs: *The Wallace Stevens Journal* appears biannually using "poems about or in the spirit of Wallace Stevens or having some relation to his work. No bad parodies of Stevens' anthology pieces." They have published poetry by David Athey, Jacqueline Marcus, Charles Wright, X.J. Kennedy, A.M. Juster and Robert Creeley. As a sample the editor selected these lines from "A Holograph Draft" by Richard Epstein:

> Dear Sir:/I have received your letter of/the 26th. The offer it contains,/that in exchange for ~~mermaids~~
> a warranty deed/to 1464 we drop our claim/for 16,000 ~~blackbirds~~ dollars, will not do./Our client has
> decided to obtain/~~a pair of scarlet boots~~ a writ of execution to be served/at his discretion. I remain,
> most truly,/~~the Rajah of Molucca blithely yours~~/your obedient servant, Wallace Stevens

The editor describes it as 80-120 pgs., 6×9, typeset, flat-spined, with cover art on glossy stock. They receive 200-300 poems a year, accept approximately 15-20. Press run is 900 for 600 subscribers of which 200 are libraries. Subscription: $15. Sample: $4.

How to Submit: Submit 3-5 poems at a time. "We like to receive clean, readable copy. We generally do not publish previously published material, though we have made a few exceptions to this rule. No fax or e-mail submissions, though requests for information are fine." Reports in 4-10 weeks. Always sends prepublication galleys. Pays 2 copies. Acquires all rights. Returns rights with permission and acknowledgment. Staff reviews books of poetry. Send books for review consideration "only if there is some clear connection to Stevens." *The Wallace Stevens Journal* is published by the Wallace Stevens Society.

Advice: The editor says, "Brief cover letters are fine, even encouraged. Please don't submit to *WSJ* if you have not read Stevens. We like parodies, but they must add a new angle of perception. Most of the poems we publish are not parodies but meditations on themes related to Wallace Stevens and those poets he has influenced. Those wishing to contribute might wish especially to examine the Fall 1996 issue which has a large and rich selection of poetry."

◖◗ ◎ **STICKS; STICKS ANTHOLOGY (Specialized: form)**, P.O. Box 399, Maplesville AL 36750-0399, press founded 1989, mini-anthology 1991, editor/publisher Mary Veazey.

Magazine Needs: *Sticks*, appearing irregularly, is "a mini-anthology of mostly short poems. All styles, subjects." The editor has published poetry by X.J. Kennedy and Richard Kostelanetz. As a sample she selected this poem, "After a Night on the Town" by Bob Grumman:

> Poem lay in the ditch/between the blonde and her voice,/morose and unhovered,/but filigreeing.

Sticks is a 4¼×5½, saddle-stapled or saddle-sewn booklet, professionally printed on Mohawk Superfine paper, 32 pgs. Press run is about 200. *Sticks* I through IV available for $3 each; sewn binding by request.

How to Submit: Submit up to 3 poems at a time. "As with any anthology, previously published material is encouraged and welcomed. While many poems are first-time publications, others are selected from chapbooks; a few are 'recycled; from the past. No guidelines." Does not usually comment on rejections. Reports in 1 month or so. Pays 10 copies. Featured poets may receive 15-50 copies.

Advice: The editor says, "Please devise a Renaissance persona to submit to this anthology: ladies and gentlemen who view poetry as a part of the refined lifestyle, as almost a handwritten manuscript passed from friend to friend. Like Ben Jonson, be interested not only in the careful craftsmanship of writing but also in good criticism and the distribution and preservation of writing of lasting value. If you're in a rush, get yet to the shimmering internet and leave us bookworms to our fine paper and dip pens! 'Read not the Times, Read the Eternities,' said Thoreau. Written any good Eternities lately? Send 'em on!"

◖◗ ◎ **STILL WATERS PRESS (Specialized: women)**, 459 S. Willow Ave., Galloway NJ 08201-4633, website http://www.netcom.com/~salake/StillWatersPoetry.html, founded 1989, editor Shirley Lake.

Book/Chapbook Needs: Still Waters is a "small press publisher of poetry chapbooks and poet's handbooks (contemporary craft). Especially interested in works by, for and about women. We prefer poetry firmly planted in the real world, but equally mindful of poetry as art. The transformation from pain to perseverance, from ordinary to extraordinary, from defeat to triumph, pleases us. But we reject Pollyanna poetry immediately. Nothing sexist, in either direction, nothing sexually erotic. No rhymed poetry unless you're a master of form who can meticulously avoid strange manipulations of syntax simply to achieve end-rhyme. No patriarchal religious verse. Preferred length: four lines to two pages per poem. Form: no restrictions—we expect content to dictate the form." They have published poetry by Linda Milstein and Susan Cavanaugh. The press publishes 4-8 chapbooks/year, averaging 28 pgs. Sample chapbooks: $5; writer's guide booklets: $3.

How to Submit: Send SASE for guidelines, then query. Simultaneous submissions and previously published poems OK. Always sends prepublication galleys. Pays 10% of the press run. Royalties on second and subsequent press runs. Acquires first or reprint rights.

Also Offers: They hold 2 annual contests, each with $10 reading fee. Send SASE for detailed guidelines.

Advice: The editor says, "Read other poets, contemporary and traditional. Attend workshops, establish rapport with local peers, attend readings. Keep your best work in circulation. Someone out there is looking for you."

◖◗ $ ◎ **STONE SOUP, THE MAGAZINE BY YOUNG WRITERS AND ARTISTS; THE CHILDREN'S ART FOUNDATION (Specialized: children)**, P.O. Box 83, Santa Cruz CA 95063, phone

(408)426-5557, fax (408)426-1161, e-mail editor@stonesoup.com, website http://www.stonesoup.com, founded 1973, editor Ms. Gerry Mandel.
• *Stone Soup* has received both Parents' Choice and Edpress Golden Lamp Honor Awards.
Magazine Needs: *Stone Soup* publishes writing and art by children through age 13; they want to see free verse poetry but no rhyming poetry, haiku or cinquain. *Stone Soup*, published 6 times/year, is a handsome 7×10 magazine, professionally printed on heavy stock with 4-6 full-color art reproductions inside and a full-color illustration on the coated cover, saddle-stapled. A membership in the Children's Art Foundation at $32/year includes a subscription to the magazine. The editor receives 5,000 poetry submissions a year, uses approximately 20. There are 2-4 pgs. of poetry in each issue. Circulation is 20,000 for 13,000 subscribers, 5,000 to bookstores, 2,000 other. Sample: $5.
How to Submit: Submissions can be any number of pages, any format. Include SASE. No simultaneous submissions. E-mail submissions OK. Criticism will be given when requested. "We prefer submissions by mail because we need an SASE in order to respond. Submissions that arrive via fax or e-mail will receive a response only if they are accepted." Send SASE for guidelines or obtain via e-mail or website. Reports in 1 month. Pays $25 and 2 copies plus discounts. Buys all rights. Returns rights upon request. Open to reviews by children. Children through age 13 may also send books for review consideration.
Also Offers: Website features writer's guidelines, sample issue, philosophy, and related materials featuring children's writing and art.

STONE SOUP MAGAZINE, 37 Chesterfield Rd., London W4 3HQ Great Britain, phone/fax 181 742 7554, founded 1995, editor Mr. Igor Klikovac.
Magazine Needs: Appearing quarterly, *Stone Soup* is "an international magazine for new writing—mainly poetry and theory, combined with some fiction and criticism. Edited by English poet Ken Smith and Bosnian poet Igor Klikovac, the magazine is printed bilingually, in English and the languages of former Yugoslavia, but it also attracts a broad audience across Europe. It tends to regularly bring the most interesting work from Eastern Europe and combines it with well-established authors from the West." They have "no limitations at all" on poetry. They have published poetry by Adam Zagajewski (Poland), Alain Bosquet (France) and Janos Pilinszky (Hungary). As a sample the editor selected these lines from "The Forms Of Love, VII" by Ales Debeljak:

> Nothing is attainable. No voice is ever doubled./As if it had never happened. Things move on, orderly./
> In the morning the sun will rise again. Blood runs through the veins./You are nothing. For everybody
> else but one woman, you are/a deep darkness on the river bottom

SS is 66 pgs., magazine-sized, professionally printed and perfect-bound with 4-color card cover, includes b&w photos. They receive about 5,000 poems a year, accept approximately 5%. Press run is 5,000 for 1,200 subscribers of which 280 are libraries, 3,400 shelf sales; 300 distributed free to the press/complimentary. Subscription: individial £16 inland, £18 Europe, £21 rest of world; institutional £19.50 Inland, £21.50 Europe, £23.50 rest of world.
How to Submit: Submit 6-10 poems at a time. No previously published poems or simultaneous submissions. Cover letter preferred. Disk submissions OK. "Short bio-bibliographical note is desirable." Time between acceptance and publication is 2 months. Poems are circulated to an editorial board. "All submissions are read by three of our editors; if liked, a contribution is discussed by the editorial board and, then, accepted or refused." Always comments on rejections. Send SASE for guidelines. Reports in 2-3 months. Pays 2 copies. Acquires first rights. Reviews books of poetry in 2,000 words, single or multi-book format. Open to unsolicited reviews. Poets may also send books for review consideration.

STONEFLOWER PRESS; ENTRE NOUS; STONEFLOWER LITERARY JOURNAL, P.O. Box 90507, San Antonio TX 78209, e-mail stonflower@aol.com, founded 1995 (*Stoneflower*), 1997 (*Entre Nous*), editor Brenda Davidson-Shaddox.
Magazine Needs: *Entre Nous*, very open to new writers, published quarterly, strives to offer a forum for creative people who have daring for the new and respect for the traditional. *Entre Nous* wants any subject, style or form up to 40 lines long; does not want pornographic, didactic or religious work. *Stoneflower Literary Journal* no longer accepts unsolicited mss. The editor says *Entre Nous* is 40-50 pgs., 4¼×5½, 50 lb. paper, saddle-stapled with medium card cover, pen and ink drawings and b&w photos. They receive about 250 poems, accept approximately 20%. Press run for *Entre Nous* is 300. Single copy: $5 plus 6×9 envelope with $1.24 postage; subscription: $20. Sample: $2.50 plus 6×9 envelope and $1.24 postage. Make checks payable to Stoneflower Press.
How to Submit: Submit up to 6 poems at a time. "Poems should appear on page as poet wants it printed with clean, clear type suitable for scanning. Include a short bio. E-mail submissions OK, "but do not send as an attachment." Previously published poems and simultaneous submissions OK. Time between acceptance and publication is up to 1 year. Poems are circulated to an editorial board. Reading staff does first reading for general acceptability. Poetry editor makes final selections. Seldom comments on rejections. Publishes theme issues. Send SASE for guidelines and upcoming themes. Reports within 3 months. Acquires one-time rights.
Also Offers: *Stoneflower* sponsors annual literary contest with $50 1st Prize, $10 2nd Prize and copies to honorable mentions. Submit poems May through March only, with title, name, address and phone on cover sheet and number of lines in upper right of first page. Send SASE for more information.
Advice: The editor says, "Read our journal and others; go to readings. Follow guidelines exactly, otherwise the

ms will not be read. A submission letter to an editor does nothing to improve your chances for publication. Your work will speak for itself."

☑ ☗ ◐ **STORY LINE PRESS; NICHOLAS ROERICH POETRY PRIZE**, Three Oaks Farm, P.O. Box 1240, Ashland OR 97520-0055, phone (541)512-8792, fax (541)512-8793, e-mail mail@storylinepress.com, website http://www.storylinepress.com, Story Line Press founded 1985, executive director Robert McDowell.
  • Books published by Story Line Press have recently received such prestigious awards as The Lenore Marshall Prize, The Whiting Award and The Harold Morton Landon Prize.
Book/Chapbook Needs: Story Line Press publishes each year the winner of the Nicholas Roerich Poetry Prize ($1,000 plus publication and a paid reading at the Roerich Museum in New York; a runner-up receives a full Story Line Press Scholarship to the Wesleyan Writers Conference in Middletown, CT [see listing in Conferences and Workshops section]; $20 entry and handling fee). The press also publishes books about poetry and has published collections by such poets as Alfred Corn, Annie Finch, Donald Justice, Mark Jarman and David Mason.
How to Submit: Deadline for Nicholas Roerich Poetry Prize competition is October 31st. Send SASE for complete guidelines.
Also Offers: Story Line Press annually publishes 10-15 books of poetry, literary criticism, memoir, fiction and books in translation. Query first. Website includes catalog, guidelines and e-mail links.

🅝 ◎ **STORYBOARD; UNIVERSITY OF GUAM PRESS (Specialized: regional)**, Division of English, University of Guam, Mangilau Guam 96921, phone (671)735-2749, e-mail jtalley@uoga.uog.edu, founded 1991, general editor Jeannine E. Talley.
Magazine Needs: *Storyboard* appears annually and "exists primarily to encourage indigenous Pacific writers and poets to write publishable materials and to encourage writings about the Pacific region." They want work by indigenous Pacific writers or work about the Pacific Region. They have published poetry by Eileen Tabios and K.K. Todorovich. As a sample the editor selected this poem (poet unidentified):
> Your face is/marble-cold/your countenances/a slab of stone./Yet your eyes are/soft fires/amd their glance/a feather's fall.
The editor says *Storyboard* is 104 pgs., magazine-sized, offset printed and perfect-bound with linen cover, uses photos and b&w art. They receive about 150 poems a year, accept approximately 10%. Press run is 500 for 100 subscribers of which 25 are libraries, 200 shelf sales; remainder distributed free to schools in the region. Subscription: $7.50. Sample: $6.
How to Submit: Submit 5 poems at a time. Line length for poetry is 8 minimum, 70 maximum. No previously published poems; simultaneous submissions OK. Cover letter with short bio and SASE preferred. Reads submissions September through May. Time between acceptance and publication is 6-8 months. Poems are circulated to an editorial board. "The board outright rejects poems that do not meet our criteria as to focus on Pacific region and writers. Selections made on artist aesthetic merit." Seldom comments on rejections. Publishes theme issues occasionally. Send SASE for guidelines. Reports in 6 months "if considered for publication." Pays 2 copies. Acquires first North American serial rights.
Also Offers: Website includes samples of writings, cover and guidelines.

◐ **THE STORYTELLER**, 2441 Washington Rd., Maynard AR 72444, phone (870)647-2137, website http://www.angelfire.com/ar/coolwriters, founded 1996, editor Regina Williams.
Magazine Needs: *The Storyteller*, a quarterly magazine, "is geared to, but not limited to new writers and poets." They want "any form up to 40 lines, any matter, any style, but must have a meaning. Do not throw words together and call it a poem. Nothing in way of explicit sex, violence, horror or explicit language. I would like it to be understood that I have young readers, ages 9-18." As a sample the editor selected this poem by Bryan Byrd:
> This is the land of my memories:/Where forgotten river towns leak slowly into the Mississippi;/Crumbling and ivy covered,/They jealously watch the trains and barges go by.
Storyteller is 64 pgs., 8½×11, desktop-published and saddle-stapled with colored light card cover, original pen & ink drawings on cover, ads. They receive about 300 poems a year, accept approximately 40%. Press run is 600 for over 500 subscribers. Subscription: $20. Sample: $6 (if available).
How to Submit: Submit 2 poems at a time, typed and double-spaced. Previously published poems and simultaneous submissions OK, "but must state where and when poetry first appeared." Cover letter preferred. Reading fee: $1/poem. Time between acceptance and publication is 9 months. Poems are circulated to an editorial board. "Poems are read and discussed by staff." Often comments on rejections. Offers criticism service for $5/poem. Publishes theme issues occasionally. Send SASE for guidelines and upcoming themes. Reports in 4-5 weeks. Acquires first or one-time rights. Reviews books and chapbooks of poetry. Open to unsolicited reviews. Poets may also send books for review consideration to associate editor Ruthan Riney.
Also Offers: Sponsors a quarterly contest. "Readers vote on their favorite poems. Winners receive copy of magazine and certificate suitable for framing." Website includes guidelines, editors' names and sample poetry.
Advice: The editor says, "I want to read what comes from your heart, whether good or bad. This is probably the easiest place to get your work in print—if it is well written. Thrown together words will not find a place in *The Storyteller*."

☑ ⬙ **STOVEPIPE, A JOURNAL OF LITTLE LITERARY VALUE; SWEET LADY MOON PRESS; SOCIETY OF UNDERGROUND POETS**, P.O. Box 1076, Georgetown KY 40324, e-mail troyteegarden@w orldradio.org, founded 1995, editor Troy Teegarden, reader of poetry Kate Teegarden.

Magazine Needs: *STOVEPIPE* is a quarterly journal of poetry, short fiction and b&w art. They are "open to most anything, but the best idea is to order a copy of *STOVEPIPE* first. We extremely dislike forced rhyme poetry, cheesy Hallmark-esque lines and religious poetry." They have published poetry by Bob Holman, t. kilgore splake and Michael Crossley. As a sample we selected these lines from "Just Before It Rains" by Maura Gage:

> He lights her cigarette,/pours her martini,/watches her long/muscular legs as/she pulls away/and then
> steps lightly/towards him./She undresses/slowly, piece by piece,/until she's naked/by the window,/the
> neighbors/just outside/the bluing sky—/clouds beyond the building/over the bridge like/intricate lace.

STOVEPIPE is 24-60 pgs., 5½×8½, offset-printed and saddle-stapled with card stock cover, includes b&w art and photos. Accept approximately 15% of poems received. Press run is 250 for 25 subscribers of which 5 are libraries, 50 shelf sales. Subscription: $10, "includes extra stuff." Sample: $2 US; $2.50 Can/Mex; $3.50 world. Make checks payable to Troy Teegarden.

How to Submit: Submit 3-5 poems at a time. Previously published poems and simultaneous submissions OK. Cover letter preferred. "Must be informed on where previously published, what poems were published and when. Also must be informed of simultaneous submissions. Time between acceptance and publication is usually 1-3 months. Often comments on rejections. Reports in 1 month. Pays 1-3 copies.

Book/Chapbook Needs & How to Submit: Sweet Lady Moon Press publishes 2-4 chapbooks/year—"if we like it, we publish it." Chapbooks are usually 60 pgs., 5½×8½, offset printed and saddle-stapled with heavy card stock cover, includes b&w art and photos. "We usually solicit the poets we'd like to publish, but are open to a sample of five poems and cover letter with bio." Replies to queries in 1 month. Payment varies. Obtain sample chapbooks by writing for catalog.

Also Offers: Sponsors The Society of Underground Poets (SoUP), a weekly one-hour radio show broadcast on WRVG from Georgetown, KY. "We are interested in poetry along with music, spoken word performances, taped recordings of poets and writers reading their works and lots of other stuff. We regularly interview national award-winning poets along with writers and editors from the smallest of presses. We also receive large amounts of books from established publishers and review them on the show right beside the latest issue of your zine or chapbook. Also featured each week is a regular section called News from the Writing World, put together by Heather Blakeslee at *Poets & Writers*, where we keep you updated on the latest news from around the globe. Send us your best stuff and we'll get it on the air." Send SASE for more information.

Advice: The editors say, "Send us your best stuff. We enjoy reading poetry and short prose all year round."

$ ⬙ **STRAIGHT; STANDARD PUBLISHING CO. (Specialized: religious, teens)**, 8121 Hamilton Ave., Cincinnati OH 45231, phone (513)931-4050, editor Heather E. Wallace. Standard is a large religious publishing company.

Magazine Needs: *Straight* is a weekly take-home publication (digest-sized, 12 pgs., color newsprint) for teens. Poetry is by teenagers, any style, religious or inspirational in nature. No adult-written poetry. As a sample the editor selected "Why Grace to Me" by Janice Dru:

> This beat-up soul has/Not much to give,/Not much to say . . ./Not much at all./Yet through it all,/It is
> showered with Your grace.

Teen author must include birthdate and social security number.

How to Submit: Submit 1-5 poems at a time. Simultaneous submissions OK. Time between acceptance and publication is 9-12 months. Publishes theme issues. Guidelines and upcoming themes available for SASE. Reports in 4-6 weeks. Pays $10/poem plus 5 copies. Buys first or reprint rights.

Advice: The editor says, "Many teenagers write poetry in their English classes at school. If you've written a poem on an inspirational topic, and your teacher's given you an 'A' on it, you've got a very good chance of having it published in *Straight*."

$ ⬙ **THE STRAIN**, 1307 Diablo Dr., Crosby TX 77532-3004, poetry editor Michael Bond.

Magazine Needs: *The Strain* is a monthly magazine using "experimental or traditional poetry of very high quality." They do not include sample lines of poetry here as they "prefer not to limit style of submissions."

How to Submit: Simultaneous submissions and previously published poems OK. Guidelines issue: $5 and 8 first-class stamps. Pays "no less than $5. We would prefer you submit before obtaining the guidelines issue which mostly explains upcoming collections and collaborations." Send books for review consideration.

USE THE GENERAL INDEX, located at the back of this book, to find the page number of a specific publisher. Also, publishers that were listed in last year's edition but not included in this edition are listed in the General Index with a notation explaining why they were omitted.

insider report

Turning life into compelling poetry

Many poets write about family life. Colette Inez has made her family life her poet's life as well.

Colette Inez

Born under unusual circumstances, Inez was the illegitimate child of an American priest and a French scholar. Raised during her early years in a Belgian orphanage, she came to the United States at the age of eight. Inez's upbringing has figured heavily in her six major collections of poems, most prominently in *Family Life* (Story Line Press, 1988); as a recurring theme in *Getting Under Way: New & Selected Poems* (Story Line Press, 1993); and in her most recent book, *Clemency* (Carnegie Mellon University Press, 1998).

In *Family Life*, Inez traces, in more or less linear fashion, her autobiography from childhood to the mid-1980s. *Clemency*, published a decade later, returns to delve more deeply into the circumstances of her birth. Inez says the subject kept coming back to her, in part, because of increased encounters with her birth family after her mother's death. Inez's father, ordained a monsignor the year she was born, died when she was a child.

Some readers might wonder why a writer would return again and again to the same subject. Wouldn't it be more interesting to write about new things? Inez admits that this question has occurred to her. "You have the feeling you're overstaying your subject." However, she adds, her most recent poems about her parents are different than her earlier ones—a fundamental letting go of the past. Writing about her past has allowed Inez to put her life into greater perspective, which allows the "clemency" of the book's title to come from her toward the parents she has written about so much. As she says in one poem, "I will have my say."

This process of forgiveness is illustrated fully in these stanzas from "Lady in the Stacks," one of the strongest poems in *Clemency*:

COLETTE INEZ

Poet
Recent Title: Clemency
(Carnegie Mellon University Press)

You, in the dust of the Biblioteque
Nationale indexing the Popes, Leo Xs
in their capelets of fur, high-minded
Lady Em in your cloche, clodhoppers
and woolen hose cutting a figure
in the archives of lost saints.

My tracer of missing flagellants,
you fingered codicils in the Vatican.
Ladder rungs were scuffed with your climb
to beatitudes shelved in the dust
of Lourdes. You sought an account
from Bernadette who scrubbed

for Christ, our Lord, faith
in the perfect floor. Lady Em, you
to whom I was more than a footnote
on the page of a crosschecked gloss,
I hold the fading words of this worn
chronicle, my scholar, my lost mother.

In this poem, Inez recalls her mother as a young scholar researching classical literature in libraries, and traces her own attempts to understand her mother and her
birth: "I told my story again and again/trying to get it clear." The tone, though, is not
one of anger but forgiveness: "I, your daughter, upholder of words,/reconciled to your
diffidence."

The compassion evident in this poem is in sharp contrast to a poem from Inez's
first book, in which she imagines her conception. In that poem, "A Collar Rounds My
Thoughts," Inez imagines herself as "I, your bastard child." She addresses her priest
father, "burning to know your life." The tone is one of anger, not forgiveness. It is a
tone that marked much of Inez's earlier poetry about her family, but has perceptibly
softened and shifted in *Clemency*.

What is distinctive about Inez's work, apart from its subject, is its style. Inez does
not write in traditional form, but her work has a strong, musical intensity that gives
her scenes and stories a rich memorability. Her poetry combines lyric and narrative,
or song and story, in interesting ways; the stories are given intensity by her lyricism,
while her lyrics are made more intriguing by the stories they tell. The combination in
her work has led critics to praise both her lyricism and her narrative skills. For her
part, though, Inez is not overly concerned about the labels that critics apply to her
work. "I'm not really concerned about these types of definitions," she says.

What may be more important than critical labels is the example Inez's work offers
to other writers. For instance, developing poets can take instruction from the way
Inez takes autobiographical material and turns it into verse that is charged with energy
and is compelling as story. This is not a simple task for any writer. "My subject matter
is always bordering on pathos," she says. "I have to struggle to give it distance."

Inez has offered examples to developing writers in other ways as well. Earlier in
her career, she taught developing readers and writers in anti-poverty outreach programs. Her own upbringing allowed her "a lot of identification with outsiders," and
she was committed to teaching. But the demands of the classroom were so great that
"I became a person who writes on weekends," to the detriment of her poetry. Inez

chose to concentrate more on her writing, and in recent years has settled on a part-time schedule that gives her sufficient time to write. She currently teaches in the writing program at Columbia University, and periodically teaches as a visiting professor at other universities, including Bucknell, Ohio and Cornell.

As a teacher, Inez likes to give her students varied assignments to stimulate their creativity. And working with students has a positive effect on her own writing, because sometimes it leads her in new directions. Many students from other countries enroll in Columbia's writing program, and they introduce her to new styles of poetry from other cultures. For instance, after asking her students to work on a ghazal—a Persian style comprised of couplets—she decided to try the form herself. "I don't need to bellyache now," she says. "I'm actually getting inspiration. It's the opposite of being depleted. I'm being replenished."

While Inez's life as a poet is set in large part in the classroom, she is encouraged that the readership for poetry in the United States seems to be healthy, diverse, and growing. After all, poetry is not limited to the classroom. "There's an awful lot of people who want to read their poetry aloud who aren't interested in reading poetry on the page. I think that stuff is growing in the U.S.," Inez says. "I think the more variety we have, the better; I'm interested in the beauty of language." As most readers of Inez would agree, her poetry demonstrates this interest.

—*Kevin Walzer*

STRIDE PUBLICATIONS, 11 Sylvan Rd., Exeter, Devon EX4 6EW England, e-mail stride@madbear .demon.co.uk, website http://www.madbear.demon.co.uk/stride/, founded 1982, managing editor R.M. Loydell.
Book/Chapbook Needs: Stride Publications publishes poetry, poetry sequences, prose and experimental novels, and an occasional arts magazine. The editor wants to see any poetry that is "new, inventive, nothing self-oriented, emotional, no narrative or fantasy, rhyming doggerel, light verse or the merely-confessional." He has published work by Peter Redgrove, William Everson, Sheila E. Murphy, Peter Finch and Charles Wright. Stride Publications publishes paperbacks 60-100 pgs. of poetry, plus a few novels and anthologies.
How to Submit: Unsolicited submissions for book publication are accepted. "All submissions must be typewritten/word-processed and have an SAE included" with IRCs. Authors should obtain submission guidelines first via e-mail or by sending SASE with return postage or IRCs. Cover letter required with bio, summary and review quotes. Queries will be answered in 6 weeks and mss reported on in 3 months or more. Pays 30 author's copies. Magazine reviews books and tapes of poetry in 100-200 words, multi-book format. Send books etc. for review consideration.

STRUGGLE: A MAGAZINE OF PROLETARIAN REVOLUTIONARY LITERATURE (Specialized: political, science fiction/fantasy, workers' social issues, women/feminism, anti-racism), P.O. Box 13261, Detroit MI 48213-0261, phone (313)273-9039, founded 1985, editor Tim Hall.
Magazine Needs: *Struggle* is a "literary quarterly, content: the struggle of the working people and all oppressed against the rich. Issues such as: racism, poverty, women's rights, aggressive wars, workers' struggle for jobs and job security, the overall struggle for a non-exploitative society, a genuine socialism." The poetry and songs they use are "generally short, any style, subject matter must criticize or fight—explicitly or implicitly—against the rule of the billionaires. We welcome experimentation devoted to furthering such content." They have published poetry by Jamie Cavanagh, Rowena Silver, Evan Gwyn Williams, Paul Grams and Gregory Gilbert Gumbs. As a sample the editor selected these lines from "These Are" by Luis Cuauhtemoc Berriozabal:

> These are the scars like leaves behind/A disemboweled cat on the highway/A malnourished child in
> Rwanda/A "slave-wage-made" Barbie doll amongst/The debris of the latest plane crash

Struggle is 36 pgs., digest-sized, photocopied with occasional photos of artwork, short stories and short plays as well as poetry and songs. Subscription: $10 for 4 issues. Sample: $2.50. Make checks payable to "Tim Hall—Special Account."
How to Submit: Submit up to 8 poems at a time. Accepted work usually appears in the next issue. Editor tries to provide criticism "with every submission." Tries to report in 3-4 months. Pays 2 copies.

Advice: Tim Hall says, "Show passion and fire. Humor also welcome. Prefer powerful, colloquial language over academic timidity. Look to Neruda, Lorca, Bly, Whitman, Braithwaite, Pietri, Aretha Franklin, the rappers, Aime Cesaire. Formal experiments, traditional forms both welcome. Especially favor: works reflecting rebellion by the working people against the rich; works against racism, sexism, militarism, imperialism; works critical of our exploitative culture; works showing a desire for—or fantasy of—a non-exploitative society; works attacking the Republican New Stone Age and the Democrats' surrender to it."

$ ◎ STUDENT LEADERSHIP JOURNAL (Specialized: students, religious), Dept. PM, P.O. Box 7895, Madison WI 53707-7895, phone (608)274-4823 ext. 425 or 413, editor Jeff Yourison.
Magazine Needs: *Student Leadership* appears 3 times/year and is a "magazine for Christian student leaders on secular campuses. We want poetry with solid Biblical imagery, not preachy or trite. Also, we accept little rhymed poetry; it must be very, very good." *Student Leadership* is 32 pgs., magazine-sized, full color, with no advertising, 70% editorial, 30% graphics/art. Press run is 8,000 going to college students in the US and Canada. Subscription: $12. Sample: $4.
How to Submit: No simultaneous submissions. Previously published poems OK. "Would-be contributors should read us to be familiar with what we publish." Best time to submit mss is March through July ("We set our year's editorial plan"). Editor "occasionally" comments on rejections. Send SASE for guidelines. Reports in 2-3 months. Time between acceptance and publication is 1-24 months. Pays $25-50/poem plus 2 copies. Buys first or reprint rights.
Advice: He says, "Try to express feelings through images and metaphor. Religious poetry should not be overly didactic, and it should never moralize!"

⊕ ◐ ◎ STUDIO, A JOURNAL OF CHRISTIANS WRITING (Specialized: religious, spirituality), 727 Peel St., Albury, New South Wales 2640 Australia, phone/fax 61 2 6021 1135, founded 1980, publisher Paul Grover.
Magazine Needs: *Studio* is a quarterly journal publishing "poetry and prose of literary merit, offering a venue for previously published, new and aspiring writers, and seeking to create a sense of community among Christians writing." The journal also publishes occasional articles as well as news and reviews of writing, writers and events of interest to members. In poetry, the editors want "shorter pieces but with no specification as to form or length (necessarily less than 200 lines), subject matter, style or purpose. People who send material should be comfortable being published under this banner: *Studio, A Journal of Christians Writing*." They have published poetry by John Foulcher and other Australian poets. *Studio* is 36 pgs., digest-sized, professionally printed on high-quality recycled paper, saddle-stapled, matte card cover, with graphics and line drawings. Circulation is 300, all subscriptions. Subscription: $40 (Aud) for overseas members. Sample available (airmail to US) for $8 (Aud).
How to Submit: Submissions must be typed and double-spaced on one side of A4 white paper. Simultaneous submissions OK. Name and address must appear on the reverse side of each page submitted. Cover letter required; include brief details of previous publishing history, if any. SASE (or SAE with IRC) required. Reporting time is 2 months and time to publication is 9 months. Pays 1 copy. Acquires first Australian rights. Reviews books of poetry in 250 words, single format. Open to unsolicited reviews. Poets may also send books for review consideration.
Also Offers: The magazine conducts a biannual poetry and short story contest.
Advice: The editor says, "The trend in Australia is for imagist poetry and poetry exploring the land and the self. Reading the magazine gives the best indication of style and standard, so send a few dollars for a sample copy before sending your poetry. Keep writing, and we look forward to hearing from you."

✿ ◐ SUB-TERRAIN; ANVIL PRESS; LAST POEMS POETRY CONTEST, P.O. Box 1575, Bentall Centre, Vancouver, British Columbia V6C 2P7 Canada, phone (604)876-8710, fax (604)899-2667, e-mail subter@pinc.com, website http://www.anvilpress.com, founded 1988, poetry editor Paul Pitre.
Magazine Needs: Anvil Press is an "alternate small press publishing *sub-TERRAIN*—a socially conscious literary quarterly whose aim is to produce a reading source that will stand in contrast to the trite and pandered—as well as broadsheets, chapbooks and the occasional monograph." They want "work that has a point-of-view; work that has some passion behind it and is exploring issues that are of pressing importance (particularly that with an urban slant); work that challenges conventional notions of what poetry is or should be; work with a social conscience. No bland, flowery, uninventive poetry that says nothing in style or content." As a sample the editor selected these lines from "Eidetic" by Quentin Tarantino:

> In fluid and electrics the alligator brain holds it all/rigid, refined and encyclopedic, the chemical well/
> contains a green bathing suit, improbable sex acts,/inclusive results from the elector of nineteen eighty-
> six/a bowl of stinging Thai soup and the origin of scars/all held static and wet in the ancient clock,
> the first mind.

Sub-TERRAIN is 40 pgs., 7½ × 10½, offset printed, with a press run of 3,000. Subscription: $18. Sample: $5.
How to Submit: Submit 4-6 poems at a time. Simultaneous submissions OK; no previously published poems. No fax or e-mail submissions. Reports in 4-6 months. Pays money only for solicited work; for other work, 4-issue subscription. Acquires one-time rights for magazine. "If chapbook contract, we retain right to publish subsequent printings unless we let a title lapse out-of-print for more than one year." Staff occasionally reviews small press poetry chapbooks.

Book/Chapbook Needs & How to Submit: For chapbook or book publication submit 4 sample poems and bio, no simultaneous submissions. No fax or e-mail submissions. "Only those manuscripts accompanied by a self-addressed stamped envelope (SASE) will be considered. But I must stress that we are a co-op, depending on support from an interested audience. New titles will be undertaken with caution. We are not subsidized at this point and do not want to give authors false hopes—but if something is important and should be in print, we will do our best. Response time can, at times, be lengthy; if you want to be assured that your manuscript has been received, include a self-addressed stamped postcard for notification." Editor provides brief comment and more extensive comments for fees.

Also Offers: Sponsors Last Poems Poetry Contest for "poetry that encapsulates North American experience at the close of the 20th Century." Submit up to 4 poems. Entry fee: $15. Deadline: January 31. Winner announced March 1. Prize: $250, plus publication in Spring issue. Entrants receive a 4-issue subscription. Send SASE (or SAE and IRC) for more information.

Advice: He says, "It is important that writers intending to submit work have an idea of what work we publish. Read a sample copy before submitting."

◐ SULPHUR RIVER LITERARY REVIEW, P.O. Box 19228, Austin TX 78760-9228, founded 1978, reestablished 1987, editor/publisher James Michael Robbins.

Magazine Needs: *Sulphur River* is a semiannual of poetry, prose and artwork. They have "no restrictions except quality." They do not want poetry that is "trite or religious or verse that does not incite thought." They have published poetry by William Aarnes, Patricia Dubrava, Robert Jergent, Walter McDonald, James Scofield, Barbara F. Lefcowitz and Jamie Simpson. *SRLR* is digest-sized, perfect-bound, with glossy cover. They receive about 2,000 poems a year, accept approximately 4%. Press run is 400 for 200 subscribers, 100 shelf sales. Subscription: $12. Sample: $7.

How to Submit: No previously published poems or simultaneous submissions. Often comments on rejections, although a dramatic increase in submissions has made this increasingly difficult. Reports in 1 month. Sometimes sends prepublication galleys. Pays 2 copies.

Advice: The editor says, "Poetry is, for me, the essential art, the ultimate art, and any effort to reach the effect of the successful poem deserves some comment other than 'sorry.' This is why I try to comment as much as possible on submissions, though by doing so I risk my own special absurdity. So be it. However, there can be no compromise of quality if the poem is to be successful or essential art."

$◐ SUMMER STREAM PRESS, P.O. Box 6056, Santa Barbara CA 93160-6056, phone (805)962-6540, founded 1978, poetry editor David D. Frost.

Book/Chapbook Needs: Publishes a series of books (Box Cars) in hardcover and softcover, each presenting 6 poets, averaging 70 text pgs. for each poet. "The mix of poets represents many parts of the country and many approaches to poetry. The poets previously selected have been published, but that is no requirement. We welcome traditional poets in the mix and thus offer them a chance for publication in this world of free-versers. The six poets share a 15% royalty. We require rights for our editions worldwide and share 50-50 with authors for translation rights and for republication of our editions by another publisher. Otherwise all rights remain with the authors." They have published poetry by Virginia E. Smith, Sandra Russell, Jennifer MacPherson, Nancy Berg, Lois Shapley Bassen and Nancy J. Wallace.

How to Submit: To be considered for future volumes in this series, query with about 12 sample poems, no cover letter. Replies to query in 6 months, to submission (if invited) in 1 year. Previously published poetry and simultaneous submissions OK. Editor usually comments on rejections. Always sends prepublication galleys. Pays 6 copies plus royalties.

Advice: He says, "We welcome both traditional poetry and free verse. However, we find we must reject almost all the traditional poetry received simply because the poets exhibit little or no knowledge of the structure and rules of traditional forms. Much of it is rhymed free verse."

☑ ◐ A SUMMER'S READING, 409 Lakeview Dr., Sherman IL 62684, phone (217)496-3012, founded 1996, contact Ted Morrissey and Barbara Hess.

Magazine Needs: *A Summer's Reading*, published annually in June, strives "to provide one more well edited, attractive outlet for new and emerging writers, poets and artists. Willing to look at all kinds of poetry, prefer free verse or blank verse with clear images and ideas." They do not want "sappy 'greeting card' stuff." They have published poetry by Kathy Kennedy Tapp, Fernard Roqueplan and Elsie Pankowski. As a sample the editor selected these lines from "Sabbatical" by Zarina Mullan Plath:

> In India I once listened to geckos/falling from the ceiling, stretching/my hands toward the spun threads/
> of mosquito netting, a fairy-cloth/holding me safe, I believed, from tigers/and cobras.

The editor says *A Summer's Reading* is approximately 80 pgs., offset printed, with color cover, b&w artwork. Press run is 200 for 50 subscribers. Subscription: $6. Sample: $6.

How to Submit: Submit up to 10 poems with name, address, phone and line count on each. Simultaneous submissions OK if so noted. Cover letter preferred with brief bio and publishing history. Time between acceptance and publication is 3-12 months. "Both editors read all submissions—may ask others for their opinions if needed." Sometimes comments on rejections. Send SASE for guidelines. Reports in 3-12 weeks. Always sends prepublication galleys. Pays 2 copies. Acquires one-time rights plus request for acknowledgement if reprinted. May include

staff-written reviews of poetry books in the future. Poets may also send books for review consideration.
Advice: The editor says, "Don't hesitate to submit—we will be respectful and fair to your work. We strive to publish newcomers with emerging and established artists. We would like to see more translations (include original text)."

$⦿ THE SUN, 107 N. Roberson St., Chapel Hill NC 27516, phone (919)942-5282, founded 1974, editor Sy Safransky.
Magazine Needs: *The Sun* is "noted for honest, personal work that's not too obscure or academic." We avoid traditional, rhyming poetry, as well as limericks, haiku and religious poetry. We're open to almost anything else: free verse, prose poems, short and long poems." They have published poetry by Alison Seevak, Kip Knott, Red Hawk, Sybil Smith and Lou Lipsitz. As a sample the editor selected these lines from "Nudging a Poem" by Robert Bly:

> To nudge a poem along toward its beauty./Is that selfishness? Is it something silly?/Do others love
> poems as I do? Longing/To find you in a phrase, and be close/There, kissing the walls and the door
> frame./Happy in the change of a single word.

The Sun is 48 pgs., magazine-sized, printed on 50 lb. offset, saddle-stapled, with b&w photos and graphics. Circulation is 36,000 for 34,000 subscriptions of which 500 are libraries. They receive 3,000 submissions of poetry a year, use approximately 36, have a 1- to 3-month backlog. Subscription: $34. Sample: $5.
How to Submit: Submit up to 6 poems at a time. Poems should be typed and accompanied by a cover letter. Previously published poems OK, but simultaneous submissions are discouraged. Send SASE for guidelines. Reports within 3 months. Pays $50-200 on publication plus copies and subscription. Buys first serial or one-time rights.

N ◯ ⦿ SUN POETIC TIMES, 10362 Sahara Dr. #2203, San Antonio TX 78216, phone (210)530-9849, e-mail sunpoets@hotmail.com, founded 1994, editor Rod C. Stryker, assistant editor Tanya R. Keyser.
Magazine Needs: *Sun Poetic Times, a literary & artistic magazine*, appears quarterly to "publish all types of literary and visual art from all walks of life. We take all types. Our only specification is length—1 page in length if typed, 2 pages if handwritten (legibly)." They have published poetry by Naomi Shihab Nye, Chris Crabtree, Trinidad Sanchez, Jr. and Garland Lee Thompson, Jr. As a sample the editors selected these lines from "Measurements" by Tom Cox:

> We talk among ourselves in mysterious tongues/telling each other lies with stiff lips/in the place where
> the mountain meets the moon/amplified guitars screaming in the night/bonfires illuminating the paths
> converging on what we have/called sacred ground

SPT is 24-28 pgs., 7×8½, attractively printed and saddle-stapled with glossy card stock cover, uses b&w line drawings/halftones. They receive about 200 poems a year, accept approximately 50%. Press run is 100, 65-70 shelf sales. Subscription: $6 for 2 issues, $12/1 year (4 issues). Sample: $3 and SASE. Make checks payable to Sun Poetic Times.
How to Submit: Submit 3-5 poems at a time. No previously published poems; simultaneous submissions OK. Cover letter preferred. E-mail submissions OK. "In cover letters, we like to hear about your publishing credits, reasons you've taken up the pen and general BS like that (biographical info.)." Time between acceptance and publication is 4-8 months. Seldom comments on rejections. Publishes theme issues occasionally. Send SASE for guidelines and upcoming themes. E-mail queries welcome. Reports in 2-3 months. Pays 1 copy. Rights revert back to author upon publication.

⦿ SUNSTONE, 343 N. 300 W., Salt Lake City UT 84103-1215, founded 1974, poetry editor Dixie Partridge.
Magazine Needs: Appearing 6-8 times a year, *Sunstone* publishes "scholarly articles of interest to an open, Mormon audience; personal essays; fiction; and poetry." They want "both lyric and narrative poetry that engages the reader with fresh, strong images, skillful use of language and a strong sense of voice and/or place. No didactic poetry, sing-song rhymes or in-process work." They have published poetry by R.A. Christmas, Susan Howe, Anita Tanner, Robert Cooperman, Sean Brendan Brown and Niranjan Mohanty. As a sample the editor selected these lines from "Sonora" by Georganne O'Connor:

> . . . the wind's hot breath steals the air from your chest/and every bead of sweat from your skin./From
> the canyon floor, I see hills/robbed of rain, studded with giant saguaro,/the sentinels. They have seen
> us coming./In the accordian folds of their flesh,/elf owl rests, insulated from heat. . . .

Sunstone is 96 pgs., 8½×11, professionally printed and saddle-stapled with a semi-glossy paper cover. They receive over 500 poems a year, accept 40-50. Press run is 10,000 for 8,000 subscribers of which 300 are libraries, 700 shelf sales. Subscription: $36/8 issues. Sample: $4.95.
How to Submit: Submit up to 5 poems with name and address on each poem. "We rarely use poems over 40 lines." No previously published poems or simultaneous submissions. Time between acceptance and publication is 18 months or less. Seldom comments on rejections. Send SASE for guidelines. Reports in 3 months. Pays 3 copies. Acquires first North American serial rights. Reviews books of poetry. Open to unsolicited reviews. Poets may also send books for review consideration. Address to book review editor–poetry.
Advice: The editor says, "Poems should not sound like a rewording of something heard before. Be original; pay attention to language, sharp imagery. Contents should deepen as the poem progresses. We've published

poems rooted strongly in place, narratives seeing life from another time or culture, poems on religious belief or doubt—a wide range of subject matter."

⬤ ◢ ◎ **SUPERIOR POETRY NEWS (Specialized: translations, regional, humor); JOSS (Specialized: spirituality/inspirational/psychic/occult); SUPERIOR POETRY PRESS**, P.O. Box 424, Superior MT 59872, founded 1995, editors Ed and Guna Chaberek.

Magazine Needs: *Superior Poetry News* appears 4 times a year and "publishes the best and most interesting of new poets, as well as established poets, we can find. Also, we encourage lively translation into English from any language." They want "general, rural, Western or humorous poetry; translations; 40 lines or under. Nothing graphically sexual; containing profanity." They have published poetry by Makyo, Roberts Mūks, Cae Pitharoulis and Charles L. Wright. As a sample the editor selected these lines from "Amrita" by Roberts Mūks, translated from Latvian:

> Birds and other flying things die quietly/making no noise about life/and death, no last words/leaving
> no trace

SPN is 12-20 pgs., 8½×5, photocopied and saddle-stapled with handcrafted cover, "relevant artwork accepted, ads open to subscribers (1 free per issue)." They receive about 500 poems a year, accept approximately 25%. Press run is 75 for 50 subscribers; 3-5 distributed free to libraries. Single copy: $1.50; subscription: $4. Sample: $2.

How to Submit: Submit 3-5 poems at a time. Previously published poems and simultaneous submissions OK (if stated). Cover letter with short bio preferred. Time between acceptance and publication is 1-3 months. Seldom comments on rejections, "but will if requested." Send SASE for guidelines. Reports in 1 week. Pays 1 copy. Acquires first rights. Staff reviews books and chapbooks of poetry and other magazines in 50-100 words, single book format. Send books for review consideration with return postage (overseas contributors please include two IRCs).

Magazine Needs & How to Submit: Superior Poetry Press also publishes *JOSS: A journal for the 21st century.* Published quarterly, *JOSS* features "all material which serves to project and uplift the human spirit for the great adventure of the next one hundred years. Writers of New Age, holistic, occult, prophetic material as well as visionary writers and poets in mainstream religious, philosophical, scientific and social disciplines are encouraged to submit." Subscription: $12/yr. Sample: $3.50. Submit poems of up to 40 lines in length. Pays 1 copy.

⬤ ◎ **SUZERAIN ENTERPRISES; LOVE'S CHANCE MAGAZINE; FIGHTING CHANCE MAGAZINE (Specialized: romance, horror, science fiction)**, P.O. Box 60336, Worcester MA 01606, founded 1994, editor/publisher Milton Kerr.

Magazine Needs: *Love's Chance Magazine* and *Fighting Chance Magazine* are each published 3 times/year to "give unpublished writers a chance to be published and to be paid for their efforts." *Love's Chance* deals with romance; *Fighting Chance* deals with dark fiction, horror and science fiction. "No porn, ageism, sexism, racism, children in sexual situations." As a sample the editor selected these lines by Jacqui Burnett:

> Clashing./His personalized savior versus/her enhanced Cinderella attitude./Both of them lugging their
> old baggage./Minus the shouting, pouting,/or even dissing each other./They tried defining love and
> lust/without giving up their real intentions./Each hoping not to lose the other/or themselves.

Both magazines are 15-30 pgs., 8½×11, photocopied and side-stapled, computer-designed paper cover. Both receive about 500 poems a year, accept approximately 10%. Press runs are 100 for 70-80 subscribers. Subscription: $12/year for each. Samples: $4 each. Make checks payable to Suzerain Enterprises.

How to Submit: For both magazines, submit 3 poems at a time. Line length for poetry is 20 maximum. Previously published poems and simultaneous submissions OK. Cover letter preferred. "Proofread for spelling errors, neatness; must be typewritten in standard manuscript form. No handwritten manuscripts." Time between acceptance and publication is 6-12 weeks. Often comments on rejections. Send SASE for guidelines. Reports in 6 weeks. Acquires first or one-time rights.

Advice: The editor says, "Proofread and edit carefully. Read and write, then read and write some more. Keep submitting and don't give up."

⬤ ◢ **SWEET ANNIE & SWEET PEA REVIEW**, 7750 Highway F-24 W, Baxter IA 50028, phone (515)792-3578, fax (515)792-1310, e-mail anniespl@netins.net, founded 1995, contact Beverly A. Clark.

Magazine Needs: *SA&SPR*, published quarterly, features short stories and poetry. They want "poems of outdoors, plants, land, heritage, women, relationships, olden times—simpler times." They do not want "obscene, violent, explicit sexual material, obscure, long-winded materials, no overly religious materials." They have published poetry by Anne Carol Betterton, Mary Ann Wehler, Susan Clayton-Goldner and Brenda Serotte. As a sample the editor selected these lines from "Brooding the Heartlands" by M.L. Liebler:

> There were those days/Lonesome out on/The Dakota Plains. Lonesome/In my prairie rose daydreams—/
> memories brooding across the heartland.

SA&SPR is 56 pgs., 5¼×8½, offset printed, saddle-stapled, bond paper with onion skin page before title page, medium card cover, and cover art. They receive about 200 poems a year, accept approximately 25-33%. Press run is 100 for 30 subscribers, 20 shelf sales; 25-35 distributed free to contributors. Subscription: $24. Sample: $7. Make checks payable to Sweet Annie Press.

How to Submit: Submit 6-12 poems at a time. No previously published poems; simultaneous submissions OK. No e-mail submissions. Cover letter preferred with personal comments about yourself and phone number. Time between acceptance and publication is 6-9 months. "We select for theme first, select for content second; narrow selections through editors." Often comments on rejections. Publishes theme issues. Themes for 1999-2000 are Eclectic Woman, Eclectic Man, About Him!, Olden Times and Celebrating Gaia. Send SASE for guidelines and upcoming themes. Reports in 6 months or sooner. Pays 1 copy. Acquires all rights. Returns rights with acknowledgment in future publications. Will review chapbooks of poetry or other magazines of short length, reviews 500 words or less. Open to unsolicited reviews. Poets may also send books for review consideration.

☑ ◑ SYCAMORE REVIEW, Dept. of English, Purdue University, West Lafayette IN 47907, phone (765)494-3783, fax (765)494-3780, e-mail sycamore@expert.cc.purdue.edu, website http://www.sla.purdue.edu/academic/engl/sycamore/, founded 1988 (first issue May, 1989), editor-in-chief Numsiri C. Kunakemakorn, poetry editor changes each year; submit to Poetry Editor.
Magazine Needs: "We accept personal essays, short fiction, drama, translations and quality poetry in any form. We aim to publish many diverse styles of poetry from formalist to prose poems, narrative and lyric." They have published poetry by Mark Halliday, Joshua Clover, Bill Knott, Charles H. Webb, Kathleen Pierce and Catherine Bowman. The magazine is semiannual in a digest-sized format, 160 pgs., flat-spined, professionally printed, with matte, color cover. Press run is 1,000 for 500 subscribers of which 50 are libraries. Subscription: $12; $14 outside US. Sample: $7. Make checks payable to Purdue University (Indiana residents add 5% sales tax.)
How to Submit: Submit 3-6 poems at a time. Name and address on each page. No previously published poems except translations; simultaneous submissions OK, if notified immediately of acceptance elsewhere. No submissions accepted via fax or e-mail. Cover letters not required but invited; include phone number, short bio and previous publications, if any. "We read September 1 through March 31 only." Guidelines available for SASE. Reports in 4 months. Pays 2 copies. Acquires first North American rights. After publication, all rights revert to author. Staff reviews books of poetry. Send books to editor-in-chief for review consideration.
Also Offers: Website includes current issue information, writer's guidelines, online versions of out-of-print editions, back issue information and subscription information.
Advice: The editor says, "Poets who do not include SASE do not receive a response."

◑ SYMBIOTIC OATMEAL; SYMBIOTIC PRESS, SYMBIOSIS PRESS, SLAP-DASH-UGLY CHAP-BOOK SERIES, P.O. Box 14938, Philadelphia PA 19149, founded 1997, editor Ms. Juan Xu.
Magazine Needs: *Symbiotic Oatmeal* is published 2 times a year and contains poetry, art and fun." They want poetry of "any style under three pages, would like to see more work from Asian Americans. No poor taste, poorly written work." They have published poetry by Giovanni Malitan, Yen Li, John Sweet and Michael Hafer. As a sample the editor selected these lines from "Zodiac" by Joseph Farley:
> *There is a morning out there,/beyond the horizon,/waiting for prayers/to call it out of darkness/and light the world*

SO is about 6 pgs., magazine-sized, photocopied and side-stapled. They receive about 50 poems a year, accept approximately 25%. Press run is 100. Single copy: $2 cash or 6 first-class stamps.
How to Submit: Submit 5 poems at a time. Previously published poems and simultaneous submissions OK. Cover letter required. Disk submissions OK. "Disk submissions must be on a diskette formatted in DOS and in WordPerfect format." Time between acceptance and publication is 1-5 months. Seldom comments on rejections. Offers criticism service. "I have a M.A. in English. If someone wants me to read a book manuscript, proof and give feedback I will need compensation of $25 or more, depending on length." Reports in 3 months. Pays 1 copies.
Book/Chapbook Needs & How to Submit: Symbiotic Press/Symbiosis Press publishes chapbooks. However, "Don't query about chapbooks. Projects are lined up until 2000."

⬚ $◑ SYNAESTHESIA PRESS; SYNAESTHESIA PRESS CHAPBOOK SERIES, P.O. Box 1763, Tempe AZ 85280-1763, phone (602)280-9092, e-mail synaepress@aol.com, website http://synaesthesiapress.com, founded 1995, editor Jim Camp.
Book/Chapbook Needs: Synaesthesia Press wants to publish "work seldom seen elsewhere." Under the Synaesthesia Press Chapbook Series, they publish 4 chapbooks/year. The editor has "no real specifications to form/style; I want to read fresh poetry that stimulates the reader." He does not want to see "the same garbage most little mags publish." They have published poetry by Jack Micheline, Tszurah Litzky, Roxie Powell and Steve Fisher. Chapbooks are usually 16 pgs., digest-sized, offset/hand press printed, sewn-wrap binding, 80 lb. cardstock cover.
How to Submit: Submit 16 poems at a time. Previously published poems and simultaneous submissions OK.

THE SUBJECT INDEX, located at the back of this book, can help you select markets for your work. It lists those publishers whose poetry interests are specialized ◎ .

Cover letter preferred. Time between acceptance and publication is 6 months. Replies to queries in 1 month. Pays honorarium of $200 and 6 author's copies (out of a press run of about 250). Order sample chapbooks by sending $5.

Advice: The editor says, "Don't quit—submit!"

SYNCOPATED CITY, P.O. Box 2382, Providence RI 02906, e-mail samuelgray@bigfoot.com, founded 1995, editor Liti Kitiyakara, poetry editors Margaret Balch-Gonzalez, Jerry Fogel and Milton Mannix. **Magazine Needs:** *Syncopated City*, published quarterly, strives "to provide an outlet for the expression of creativity." They want "poetry of any subject and style; generally 50 lines or less, but will consider longer poems if truly outstanding." They do not want greeting card verse or untitled work. They have published poetry by John Grey, Hugh Fox, Lorette Thiessen and Ryan G. Van Cleave. As a sample the editor selected these lines from "Maybe Birds Would Carry It Away" by Christopher Woods:

> But she won't open the locket./She can't./Maybe it's been too long./The hair might dissolve in the air./
> Maybe birds would carry it away.

Syncopated City is 60 pgs., 5½×8½, photocopied, saddle-stapled with cardstock cover, original b&w artwork and ads. They receive about 800 poems a year, accept approximately 20%. Press run is 150-200, mostly shelf sales, about 10% subscriptions including the Rockefeller Library at Brown University; 20-25 distributed free to reviewers and contributors. Subscription: $15. Sample: $4. Make checks payable to Gerald Fogel. **How to Submit:** Submit up to 5 poems at a time, preferably under 50 lines, with full name on every page. Previously published poems and simultaneous submissions OK "if notified and poet retains rights." E-mail submissions OK ("attach file"). Cover letter preferred. Time between acceptance and publication is 3-12 months. Often comments on rejections. Send SASE for guidelines. Reports in 1-6 months. Pays 1 copy, additional copies half price. Acquires one-time rights. **Advice:** The editor says, "Quality is important, but it is equally important to make us think, make us feel. Don't feel it's necessary to conform—originality is important. We lean toward poetry that is more art than craft. Don't be afraid to be original, evoke thoughts and feelings."

TAK TAK TAK, BCM Tak, London WC1N 3XX England, founded 1986, editors Andrew and Tim Brown. *Tak Tak Tak* appears occasionally in print and on cassettes. "However, we are currently not accepting submissions."

TAKAHE, P.O. Box 13335, Christchurch 8001 New Zealand, phone (03)359-8133, founded 1990, poetry editor Bernadette Hall. **Magazine Needs:** "*Takahe* appears three to four times a year, and publishes short stories and poetry by both established and emerging writers. The publisher is the Takahe Collective Trust, a nonprofit organization formed to help new writers and get them into print. While insisting on correct British spelling (or recognized spellings in foreign languages), smart quotes, and at least internally consistent punctuation, we, nonetheless, try to allow some latitude in presentation. Any use of foreign languages must be accompanied by an English translation." No style, subject or form restrictions. Length: "A poem can take up to two pages, but we have published longer." They have published poetry by John Allison, Sarah Quigley, Mark Pirie and Kapka Kassabova. The editor says *Takahe* is 60 pgs., A4. They receive about 250 poems a year, accept approximately 30%. Press run is 320 for 200 subscribers of which 30 are libraries, 40 shelf sales. Single copy: $NZ6; subscription: $NZ24 within New Zealand, $NZ32 elsewhere. **How to Submit:** Previously published poems OK; no simultaneous submissions. Cover letter required. IBM compatible disk submissions OK. Time between acceptance and publication is 4 months. Often comments on rejections. Send SASE for guidelines. Reports in 4 months. "Payment varies but currently NZ$30 total for any and all inclusions in an issue plus 2 copies." Acquires first or one-time rights.

TALE SPINNERS; MIDNIGHT STAR PUBLICATIONS (Specialized: rural/pastoral), R.R. #1, Ponoka, Alberta T4J 1R1 Canada, phone (403)783-2521, founded 1996, editor/publisher Nellie Gritchen Scott. **Magazine Needs:** *Tale Spinners* is a quarterly " 'little literary magazine with a country flavour,' for writers who love country and all it stands for." The editor wants poetry, fiction, anecdotes, personal experiences, etc. pertaining to country life. Children's poetry welcome." No scatological, prurient or sexually explicit or political content." She has published poetry by June Hudy, John M. Floyd and Ray Ens. As a sample the editor selected these lines from "Queen"by Eileen Burnett:

> the greatest insult offered me/before I married down/was young swain stuttering 'you are . . . l . . .
> like a .like a Jersey cow/having encountered many a cow/I would know I was Blue Ribbon Class if/
> called a Jersey now.

TS is 48 pgs., 5½×8, photocopied and saddle-stapled with light cardstock cover, uses clip art or freehand graphics. They receive about 80 poems a year, accept approximately 80%. Press run is 75 for 50 subscribers. Subscription: $18. Sample: $4. **How to Submit:** Submit up to 6 poems at a time. Previously published poems OK. Cover letter ensured a reply. "Short poems preferred, but will use narrative poems on occasion." Time between acceptance and publication is 3 months. Often comments on rejections. Reports in 2 weeks. Pays 1 copy.

Book/Chapbook Needs & How to Submit: Midnight Star Publications publishes chapbooks and soft cover novels as well as collections of poetry and fiction. Query first, with a few sample poems and a cover letter with brief bio and publication credits.

◗ **TALKING RIVER REVIEW**, Lewis-Clark State College, 500 Eighth Ave., Lewiston ID 83501, phone (208)799-2307, founded 1994, contact poetry editor.
Magazine Needs: *Talking River Review*, published biannually, considers itself a "high-quality literary magazine." They want "any length, any style, any subject. We print one long poem each issue (up to 15 pages). Send your best work." They do not want "sexist, racist or simple-minded poetry." They have published poetry by Stephen Dunn, Robert Wrigley and Dorianne Laux. As a sample the editor selected these lines from "Poverty" by Pattiann Rogers:

> *The lament wasn't in the stiff/whips of willow or the ice-captures/on pondweed and underwater tubers,/ as we expected. No moan rose/from the frost-blackened spikelets/of bluejoint or twisted cattail.*

The editor says *Talking River Review* is 150 pgs., perfect-bound with color cover and some color art. They receive about 3,000 poems a year, accept less than 5%. Press run is 600 for 350 subscribers of which 50 are libraries, 100 shelf sales; 150 distributed free to students/contributors. Single copy: $6; subscription: $12. Sample: $5.
How to Submit: Submit up to 5 poems at a time. No previously published poems; simultaneous submissions OK. Cover letter preferred. Reads submissions September 1 through March 1 only. Time between acceptance and publication is 4 months. "Faculty advisor picks poems for board to consider; majority rules." Often comments on rejections. Send SASE for guidelines. Reports in 1-3 months. Sometimes sends prepublication galleys. Pays 1-year subscription and 2 copies. Acquires first rights.

$◙ **TAMPA REVIEW**, Dept. PM, University of Tampa, 401 W. Kennedy Blvd., Tampa FL 33606-1490, founded 1964 as *UT Poetry Review*, became *Tampa Review* in 1988, editor Richard Mathews, poetry editors Kathryn Van Spanckeren and Donald Morrill. Send poems to Poetry Editor, *Tampa Review*, Box 19F, The University of Tampa, Tampa FL 33606-1409.
Magazine Needs: *Tampa Review* is an elegant semiannual of fiction, nonfiction, poetry and art (not limited to US authors) wanting "original and well-crafted poetry written with intelligence and spirit. We do accept translations, but no greeting card or inspirational verse." They have published poetry by Richard Chess, Naomi Shihab Nye, Jim Daniels and Stephen Dunn. As a sample the editors selected these lines from "Stranger" by Pattiann Rogers:

> *The corridors and implications/Of my place, shaped by cat present/And gone, shapes cat lost and recovered./Strange reordering strangeness—come/Next time, wolf, butterfly, sloth, slug, wraith, wind.*

TR is 78-96 pgs., 7½×10½ flat-spined, with a matte card color cover. They receive about 2,000 poems a year, accept approximately 50-60. Press run is 750 for 175 subscribers of which 20 are libraries. Sample: $5.
How to Submit: Submit 3-6 poems at a time, typed, single-spaced. No previously published poems or simultaneous submissions. Unsolicited mss are read between September and December only. Send SASE for guidelines. Reports by mid-February. Sometimes sends prepublication galleys. Pays $10/printed page plus 1 copy and 40% discount on additional copies. Buys first North American serial rights.

◖ ◗ **TAPROOT LITERARY REVIEW; TAPROOT WRITER'S WORKSHOP ANNUAL WRITING CONTEST**, P.O. Box 204, Ambridge PA 15003, phone (724)266-8476, e-mail taproot10@aol.com, founded 1986, editor Tikvah Feinstein.
Magazine Needs: *Taproot* is an annual publication, open to beginners. "We publish some of the best poets in the U.S. *Taproot* is a very respected anthology with increasing distribution. We enjoy all types and styles of poetry from emerging writers to established writers to those who have become valuable and old friends who share their new works with us." Writers published include Rochelle Mass, T. Anders Carson, Rachel Oliver, Marlene Meehl and Elizabeth Howkins. As a sample the editor selected these lines from "The Vantage Point of Paralysis" by Wendy Smyer Yu:

> *I will watch death crawl slowly toward the hollow of my throat./He will devour my vision and my voice,/leaving only a card pace of nightmares/strung up against a blue-eyed sky.*

The review is approximately 95 pgs., offset printed on white stock with one-color glossy cover, art and no ads. Circulation is 500, sold at bookstores, readings and through the mail. Single copy: $6.95; subscriptions $7.50. Sample: $5.
How to Submit: Submit up to 5 poems, "no longer than 30 lines each." Nothing previously published or pending publication will be accepted. Cover letter with general information required. E-mail submissions OK. "We would rather have a hard copy. Also, we cannot answer without a SASE." Submissions accepted between September 1 and December 31 only. Send SASE for guidelines. Sometimes sends prepublication galleys. Pays 2 copies. Send books for review consideration.
Also Offers: Sponsors the annual Taproot Writer's Workshop Annual Writing Contest. 1st Prize: $25 and publication in *Taproot Literary Review*; 2nd Prize: publication; and 3rd Prize: publication. Submit 5 poems of literary quality, any form and subject except porn. Entry fee: $10/5 poems, provides copy of review. Deadline: December 31. Winners announced the following March.
Advice: The editor says, "We publish the best poetry we can in a variety of styles and subjects, so long as it's literary quality and speaks to us."

☑ ◎ **TAR RIVER POETRY**, English Dept., East Carolina University, Greenville NC 27858-4353, phone (252)328-6046, fax (252)328-4889, founded 1960, editor Peter Makuck, associate editor Luke Whisnant.
Magazine Needs: "We are not interested in sentimental, flat-statement poetry. What we would like to see is skillful use of figurative language." *Tar River* is an "all-poetry" magazine that accepts dozens of poems in each issue, providing the talented beginner and experienced writer with an excellent forum that features all styles and forms of verse. They have published poetry by Betty Adcock, Michelle Boisseau, Richard Jackson, Janet Holmes, Lance Larsen and Gray Jacobik. As a sample the editors selected these lines from "Notes For The Program" by William Stafford:

> Just the ordinary days, please.//I wouldn't want them any better.//About the pace of life, it seems best to have/slow, if-I-can-stand-them revelations.//And take this message about the inevitable://I've decided it's all right if it comes.

Tar River appears twice yearly and is 60 pgs., digest-sized, professionally printed on salmon stock, some decorative line drawings, matte card cover with photo. They receive 6,000-8,000 submissions a year, use approximately 150-200. Press run is 900 for 500 subscribers of which 125 are libraries. Subscription: $10. Sample: $5.50.
How to Submit: Submit 3-6 poems at a time. "We do not consider previously published poems or simultaneous submissions. Double or single-spaced OK. Name and address on each page. We do not consider mss during summer months." Reads submissions September 1 through April 15 only. Editors will comment "if slight revision will do the trick." Send SASE for guidelines. Reports in 4-6 weeks. Pays 2 copies. Acquires first rights. Reviews books of poetry in 4,000 words maximum, single or multi-book format. Poets may send books for review consideration.
Advice: The editors advise, "Read, read, read. Saul Bellow says the writer is primarily a reader moved to emulation. Read the poetry column in *Writer's Digest*. Read the books recommended therein. Do your homework."

Ⓝ ◎ **TEA PARTY**, P.O. Box 1492, Lafayette CA 94549, phone (510)638-4320, e-mail tpartymag@aol.com, founded 1995, editor David Pang.
Magazine Needs: Appearing 2 times a year, *Tea Party* "is a journal for the merry bohemian. It incorporates scenes, people, feelings, unbridled and uncensored eruptions of ideas and thought provoking interviews and reviews—and always literary." They want "vigorous ideas from the unconventional perspective: whether it be a house-wrecking emotion of hurricane darkness . . . on a nice Easter morning in Whitefish, Montana; to the ethereal musings drifting languidly upon a snowflake in a quiet morning . . . at a slam-dance rave in Alaska. Tell us something new. No poetry from people who don't get out of their hometown rut, who compose poetry at Starbucks or Borders, and no poets who aspire to be published by Hallmark or in *The New Yorker*." They have published poetry by Janice Decker, Robert Klein Engler, Buzzsaw and Maya Archer. *Tea Party* is 50-60 pgs., 8½×11, offset printed and saddle-stapled with 4-color coated paper cover, includes b&w artwork, illustrations and photography, ads. They receive about 100 poems a year, accept approximately 10%. Press run is 1,500 for 350 subscribers of which 50 are libraries, 200 shelf sales; 300 distributed free to "the economically disadvantaged." Subscription: $12/4 issues. Sample: $4. Make checks payable to Tea Party Productions.
How to Submit: Submit 3-5 poems at a time. No previously published poems; simultaneous submissions OK. E-mail submissions OK. Cover letter required. "Please include a brief biography and photograph (optional) to be included in the magazine." Reads submissions January 15 through February 15 and July 15 through August 15. Time between acceptance and publication is 3 months. Poems are circulated to an editorial board of 3 people. "Each person scores the poetry from a scale of one to five." Seldom comments on rejections. Publishes theme issues occasionally. Send SASE for upcoming themes. Reports in 1 month. Sometimes sends prepublication galleys. Pays 2 copies. Acquires first North American serial rights. Reviews other magazines in 100 words, single book format. Open to unsolicited reviews. Poets may also send books for review consideration to Chuck Lee at the above address.
Also Offers: "*Tea Party* likes to see illustration or artwork combined with poetry. *Tea Party* also publishes avant-garde photo greeting cards with poetry to compliment."

Ⓝ ◎ **TEACUP**, 8665 Hellgate Station, Missoula MT 59807, founded 1995, co-editors Sally Cobau and Rhian Ellis.
Magazine Needs: *TEACUP* appears 3 times a year and publishes "high quality, exciting, engaging poetry and prose with photographs and artwork." They want "high quality poetry, but not limited to a particular style." They have published poetry by Heather McHugh, Sarah Davis and Henrietta Goodman. As a sample the editor selected these lines from "On the Corner" by Charles Simic:

> The elegant lone woman/Stood waiting so long,/The evening shadow took pity/And came to keep her company

TEACUP is about 45 pgs., digest-sized, professionally printed and saddle-stapled with light card cover, includes local Missoula ads. They receive about 500 poems a year, accept approximately 10%. Press run is 300. Sample: $3.
How to Submit: Submit 5 poems at a time. No previously published poems; simultaneous submissions OK. Cover letter preferred. SASE required for response. Time between acceptance and publication is 6 months. Poems are circulated to an editorial board. "Currently we have three people who decide on the poems we publish."

Often comments on rejections. Publishes theme issues occasionally. Send SASE for guidelines and upcoming themes. Reports in 1-3 months. Pays 2 copies. Acquires first rights.

Advice: "We love 'discovering' new writers."

"TEAK" ROUNDUP (Specialized: subscribers); WEST COAST PARADISE PUBLISHING, #5-9060 Tronson Rd., Vernon, British Columbia V1H 1E7 Canada, phone (250)545-4186, fax (250)545-4194, editors Yvonne and Robert G. Anstey.

Magazine Needs: *"Teak" Roundup* is an international quarterly open to the work of subscribers only. They publish work from authors and poets across North America and beyond. As a sample the editors selected these lines from "A Joyous Moment" by Martin Goorhigian:

> Let the rivers flow/Through verdant lands/Where flocks browse/Carelessly beneath/The endless sun/
> And flowers bloom for eternity.

TR is 52 pgs., A5, offset printed, saddle-stapled, medium card cover with clip art, photos and ads. Subscription: $17 Canadian, $13 US, $24 overseas. Sample: $5 Canadian, $3 US, $8 overseas.

How to Submit: Accepts work from subscribers only. Submit 3-5 poems at a time. Line length for poetry is 40 maximum, but "good work makes room for exceptions." Fax submissions OK. SASE (or SAE with IRC) required for response. Publishes theme issues. Send SASE for guidelines and upcoming themes. No payment. "It is our goal to become a paying market when circulation makes it feasible." Reports in 1 week.

Also Offers: West Coast Paradise Publishing also publishes books and chapbooks. Send SASE for catalog.

TEARS IN THE FENCE, 38 Hodview, Stourpaine, Nr. Blandford Forum, Dorset DT11 8TN England, phone 0044 1258-456803, e-mail poets@in2it.co.uk, founded 1984, general editor David Caddy, poetry editor Sarah Hopkins.

Magazine Needs: *Tears in the Fence* is a "small press magazine of poetry, fiction, interviews, articles, reviews and graphics. We are open to a wide variety of poetic styles. Work that is unusual, perceptive, risk-taking as well as imagistic, lived and visionary will be close to our purpose. However, we like to publish a variety of work." They have published poetry by Edward Field, K.V. Skene, John Freeman, Donna Hilbert and Lee Harwood. As a sample they selected these lines from "I Looked Down On A Child Today" by Barry MacSweeney:

> I looked down on a child today, not because he or she was smaller than me/or because I was being
> in my middle-aged way bairnbarren and condescending/but because he or she was dying or dead
> between the kerbstone and the wheel

Tears in the Fence appears 2 times/year. It is 96 pgs., A5, docutech printed on 110 gms. paper and perfect-bound with matte card cover and b&w art and graphics. It has a press run of 700, of which 356 go to subscribers. Subscription: $15/3 issues. Sample: $5.

How to Submit: Submit 6 typed poems with IRCs. Cover letter with brief bio required. Publishes theme issues. Send SASE (or SAE and IRC) for upcoming themes. Reports in 3 months. Time between acceptance and publication is 8-10 months "but can be much less." Pays 1 copy. Reviews books of poetry in 2,000-3,000 words, single or multi-book format. Open to unsolicited reviews. Send books for review consideration.

Also Offers: The magazine is informally connected with the East Street Poets literary promotions, workshops and publications. They also sponsor an annual pamphlet competition open to poets from around the world. Also publishes books. Books published include *Hanging Windchimes In A Vacuum*, by Gregory Warren Wilson, *Heart Thread* by Joan Jobe Smith and *The Hong Kong/Macao Trip* by Gerald Locklin.

Advice: The editor says, "I think it helps to subscribe to several magazines in order to study the market and develop an understanding of what type of poetry is published. Use the review sections and send off to magazines that are new to you."

TEBOT BACH, 20592 Minerva Lane, Huntington Beach CA 92646, phone (714)968-0905, editors/publishers Mifanwy Kaiser and Mark Bergendahl.

Book/Chapbook Needs & How to Submit: Tebot Bach (Welsh for "little teapot") publishes books of poetry. Titles include *48 Questions* by Richard Jones and *The Way In* by Robin Chapman. Query first with sample poems and cover letter with brief bio and publication credits. Include SASE. Replies to queries and mss, if invited, in 1 month. Time between acceptance and publication is 1-2 years. Write to order sample books.

$ TEMPORARY VANDALISM RECORDINGS; FREEDOM ISN'T FREE; ESTHER—A DRIVING LITERARY MAGAZINE, P.O. Box 6184, Orange CA 92863-6184, e-mail tvrec@yahoo.com, founded 1991 (Temporary Vandalism Recordings), 1994 (*Freedom Isn't Free*), 1995 (*Esther*), editors Robert Roden and Barton M. Saunders.

Magazine Needs: *Freedom Isn't Free*, is published biannually. "Form, length, style and subject matter can vary. It's difficult to say what will appeal to our eclectic tastes." They do not want "strictly rants, overly didactic poetry." They have published poetry by M. Jaime-Becerra, Daniel McGinn, Jerry Gordon, Margaret Garcia and S.A. Griffin. As a sample the editor selected these lines from "Train/Station" by Michael Salovaara:

> Train/Boys laugh/Against the silence/Of those who laughed/Yesterday//Station/My Stop?/A collective
> wonder/Nobody moves/Guess not

FIF is 32 pgs., 4¼×5½, saddle-stapled, photocopied with colored card cover and some ads. They accept less than 15% of poems received. Press run is 300. Single copy free. Sample: $1. Make checks payable to Robert Roden.

How to Submit: Submit 5 neatly typed poems at a time. Previously published poems and simultaneous submissions OK. E-mail submissions OK. Cover letter preferred. Time between acceptance and publication is 3 months. "Two editors' votes required for inclusion." Seldom comments on rejections. Reports 3-6 months. Pays 2 copies. Acquires one-time rights.

Book/Chapbook Needs & How to Submit: Temporary Vandalism Recordings strives "to make the world safe for poetry (just kidding)." They publish 3 chapbooks/year. Chapbooks are usually 40 pgs., photocopied, saddle-stapled, press run of 100 intially, with reprint option if needed. Submit 10 sample poems, with SASE for response. "Publication in some magazines is important, but extensive publishing is not required." Replies in 3 months. Pays 50% royalty (after costs recouped) and 5 author's copies (out of a press run of 100). For sample chapbooks send $5 to the above address.

Advice: Mr. Roden says, "The magazine *Esther* is not sold or printed, it consists of poems displayed in the windows of my car and is a quarterly publication in that format. Hope to someday release a 'best of' anthology."

10TH MUSE, 33 Hartington Rd., Newtown, Southampton, Hants SO14 0EW England, founded 1990, editor Andrew Jordan.

Magazine Needs: *10th Muse* "used to be dull—like a typical small press 'literary' magazine—then it became challenging and entertaining. I include poetry and reviews, as well as short prose (usually no more than 2,000 words) and some graphics. The reviews can be deadly serious or spoofs; they often contain 'satire.' " The editor wants "poetry that I have to work at liking and/or with a strong 'lyric' aspect. I'm interested in 'experimentation' but I do not hold prejudices against 'closure.' I enjoy 'experimental' work that corresponds with the 'tradition.' I like humour, but in terms of 'ideas' rather than 'tone.' " They have published poetry by Peter Redgrove, Sheila E. Murphy, Peter Riley, Courtesy Ordus and Belinda Subraman. As a sample the editor selected these lines from "Photograph of Wittey Court, Worcestershire" by Melaine Byfield:

> Know the price/And the doing/And the ruin/I stood on the brink of the ha-ha/and laughed

10th Muse is 48-72 pgs., A5, photocopied, saddle-stapled, with card cover, no ads. Press run is 200. "U.S. subscribers—send $10 in bills for 2 issues, $5 for single copy."

How to Submit: Submit up to 6 poems. Include SASE (or SAE with IRCs). Often comments on rejections. Reports in 2-3 months. Pays 1 copy. Staff reviews books of poetry. Send books for review consideration.

Advice: The editor says, "Poets should read a copy of the magazine first."

TERRIBLE WORK; SPINELESS PRESS, 21 Overton Gardens, Mannamead, Plymouth, Devon PL3 5BX United Kingdom, founded 1993, contact Tim Allen.

Magazine Needs: *Terrible Work*, published triannually, features "poetry/art/reviews illustrating the variety of non-mainstream work; new writers especially." They want "post-modern, experimental, language, interesting, naive, warm, cold, speculative, minimal, expansionist, high-quality, computer, etc." They do not want "traditional formal, realist, well-crafted anecdotes, message/preaching, mystical, right-wing, bad poetry." They have published poetry by Peter Redgrove, Bruce Andrews, Rosmarie Waldrop and Sheila E. Murphy. As a sample the editor selected these lines from "Investigations" by Steve Carll:

> The arms encircle nothing;/The eyes' radiance opens/Only elsewhere, flickering/Indifferent when I'm outside/the glass//Simple and regressive,/I fall back on you,/Each time breaking/New little bones in/ Each of us.

The editor says *Terrible Work* is 92 pgs., A5, perfect-bound, spined, laminated cover and graphics. They receive about 1,000 poems a year, accept approximately 10%. Press run is 300 for 200 subscribers of which 7 are libraries, 30 shelf sales; some distributed free as review copies. Single copy: $7.50 (£3.50 UK); subscription: $20 (£9 UK). Sample: $4. Make checks payable to *Terrible Work*.

How to Submit: Submit 5 poems at a time. No previously published poems or simultaneous submissions. Cover letter required with "a brief history of publications, etc." Time between acceptance and publication is up to 4 months. Often comments on rejections. Send SASE (or SAE and IRC) for guidelines. Reports in up to 4 months. Pays 1 copy. Staff reviews books of poetry or other magazines "of critical and partisan reviewing." Poets may also send books for review consideration.

Book/Chapbook Needs & How to Submit: Spineless Press publishes 5 chapbooks/year of "experimental and more interesting quality poets—particularly those not well known." Chapbooks are usually under 60 pgs., A5, stapled, but good quality production and design. *"No submissions. By invitation only."*

Advice: The editor says, "For submissions from USA/Canada for the magazine we are more interested in high-quality experimental work. We will trade copies of *TW* for interesting USA magazines/chapbooks."

TEXAS REVIEW; TEXAS REVIEW PRESS; X.J. KENNEDY POETRY COMPETITION, Sam Houston State University, Dept. of English and Foreign Languages, Huntsville TX 77341-2146, website http://www.shsu.edu/~eng_www/trp.html, founded 1976, contact Paul Ruffin.

Magazine Needs: *The Texas Review*, published biannually, is a "scholarly journal publishing poetry, short fiction, essays and book reviews." They have published poetry by Donald Hall, X.J. Kennedy and Richard Eberhart. *The Texas Review* is 152 pgs., digest-sized, offset printed, perfect-bound, bond paper with 4-color cover and ads. Press run is 1,000 for 500 subscribers of which 250 are libraries. Single copy: $12; subscription: $24. Sample: $5. Make checks payable to Friends of *Texas Review*.

How to Submit: No previously published poems or simultaneous submissions. Include SASE. Reads submissions September 1 through June 1 only. Time between acceptance and publication is 6 months. Poems are circulated to an editorial board. Seldom comments on rejections. Publishes theme issues. Send SASE for guidelines. Reports in a few months. Pays 1 year subscription and 1 copy (may request more). Acquires all rights. Returns rights "for publication in anthology." Open to unsolicited reviews.

Also Offers: Sponsors the X.J. Kennedy Poetry Competition. Winning mss will be published. For contest guidelines send SASE specifying "for poetry/fiction contest guidelines." Website includes catalog, contest guidelines and editors.

◎ ⊘ **TEXAS TECH UNIVERSITY PRESS (Specialized: series)**, P.O. Box 41037, Lubbock TX 79409-1037, phone (806)742-2982, fax (806)742-2979, e-mail ttup@ttu.edu, website http://www.ttup.ttu.edu, founded 1971, editor Judith Keeling. Does not read unsolicited manuscripts.

◻ ◎ **TEXAS YOUNG WRITERS' NEWSLETTER (Specialized: teen/young adult)**, P.O. Box 942, Adkins TX 78101, e-mail scurrie@trinity.edu, founded 1994, editor Susan Curne.

Magazine Needs: *TYWN*, published 9 times/year, is a "newsletter publishing information on the art and business of writing for young writers, as well as poetry and short stories by young people ages 12-19." They want "positive poetry, upbeat, no more than 30 lines—rhymed or unrhymed." They do not want "depressing poetry, boring poetry, unoriginal poetry, 'roses-are-red-violets-are-blue' poetry." *TYWN* is 6-8 pgs., 8½×11, photocopied and stapled, desktop-published with clip art. They receive about 100 poems a year, accept approximately 25%. Press run is 150. Subscription: $10. Sample: $1. Make checks payable to Susan Currie, *TYWN*.

How to Submit: Contributors must be 12-19 years old. Submit 3-5 poems at a time. No previously published poems or simultaneous submissions. Cover letter preferred with author's age and bio. Submissions on disk OK in .wri or .txt formats. Time between acceptance and publication is 8 months. Always comments on rejections. Send SASE for guidelines or request via e-mail. Reports in 1 month. Sometimes sends prepublication galleys. Pays 5 copies. Acquires first rights.

Advice: The editor says, "We look for good writing. But we also look for potential in our submitters, and even if their work is returned, we work with them to improve. We're more than willing to help."

❖ ◻ **TEXTSHOP**, First Year Services, University of Regina, Regina, Saskatchewan S4S 0A2 Canada, fax (306)585-4827, e-mail andrew.stubbs@uregina.ca, founded 1993, editors Andrew Stubbs, Judy Chapman and Richelle Leonard.

Magazine Needs: *Textshop* is an annual "collaborative writing journal" appearing in November that seeks "experimental, postmodern poetry; one page in length, or sequences up to five pages. No thematic poetry." They have published poetry by Bruce Bond and Judith Miller. As a sample the editor selected these lines from "Connections" by Rienzi Crusz:

> Come summer/and the family is back/to its sun beginnings;/suck the sweet rambuttan,/let the mango
> juice run down your shirt

Textshop is over 80 pgs., 7½×10, flat-spined with coated card cover with color graphics and images. They receive 400-500 poems a year, accept approximately 20%. Press run is 350 for 25 subscribers of which 15 are libraries, 200 shelf sales. Single copy: $10 Canadian, $8.50 US.

How to Submit: Submit 5 poems at a time. "New material only." No simultaneous submissions. E-mail and fax submissions OK. Cover letter with capsule bio required. Reads submissions January through April. Poems are circulated to an editorial board. Always comments on rejections. Reports in 2-3 months. Publishes theme issues. Send SASE for guidelines. Pays 2 copies "plus 1 on request." At the end of each issue, in sections titled "Reactions," the editors also include written commentary regarding the work published in the issue.

❖ ◻ ◎ **THALIA: STUDIES IN LITERARY HUMOR (Specialized: subscribers, humor)**, Dept. of English, University of Ottawa, Ottawa, Ontario K1N 6N5 Canada, phone (613)230-9505, fax (613)565-5786, e-mail jtaverni@aixl.uottawa.ca, editor Dr. J. Tavernier-Courbin.

Magazine Needs: *Thalia* appears twice a year using "humor (literary, mostly). Poems submitted must actually be literary parodies." The editor describes it as 7×8½, flat-spined, "with illustrated cover." Press run is 500 for 475 subscribers. Subscription: $25 (US funds) for individuals, $27 (US funds) for libraries. Sample: $8 up to volume 11, $15 and $20 for volume 12-15 respectively (double issues).

How to Submit: Contributors must subscribe. Simultaneous submissions OK but *Thalia* must have copyright. Will authorize reprints. Publishes occasional theme issues. Query for guidelines and upcoming themes. "Queries via phone, fax or e-mail OK. However, submissions must be in hard copy." Editor comments on submissions. Reports in 3-4 months. Reviews books of poetry. "Send queries to the editor concerning specific books."

✔ $ ⊘ ◎ **THEMA (Specialized: themes)**, Thema Literary Society, P.O. Box 8747, Metairie LA 70011-8747, e-mail bothomos@juno.com, website http://www.litline.org, founded 1988, editor Virginia Howard, poetry editor Gail Howard. Address poetry submissions to: Gail Howard, poetry editor, Box 117, 1959 N. Peacehaven Rd., Winston-Salem NC 27106.

Magazine Needs: *Thema* is a triannual literary magazine using poetry related to specific themes. "Each issue is based on an unusual premise. Please, please send SASE for guidelines before submitting poetry to find out the upcoming themes. Upcoming themes (and submission deadlines) include: 'Toby came today' (11-1-99), 'Addie hasn't been the same' (3-1-00), 'Scraps' (7-1-00). No scatologic language, alternate life-style, explicit love poetry." They have published poetry by James Penha, Mary Winters, Joyce K. Gordon and Richard Downing. As a sample the editor selected these lines from "A Celebration of Midges" by L.G. Mason:

> dancers maypole the lamps,/marry the walls and ceiling/as well as the sky

Thema is 200 pgs., digest-sized, professionally printed, with matte card cover. They receive about 400 poems a year, accept approximately 8%. Press run is 500 for 270 subscribers of which 30 are libraries. Subscription: $16. Sample: $8.

How to Submit: Submit up to 3 poems at a time with SASE. All submissions should be typewritten and on standard 8½×11 paper. Submissions are accepted all year, but evaluated after specified deadlines. Send SASE for guidelines and upcoming themes. Editor comments on submissions. Pays $10/poem plus 1 copy. Buys one-time rights.

Also Offers: Website includes writer's guidelines, table of contents of current issue, subscription information and a list of back issues.

THIN COYOTE; LOST PROPHET PRESS, 3300 3rd Ave. South, Minneapolis MN 55408, phone (612)823-1047, founded 1992, publisher/editor Christopher Jones, co-editor Maggie McKnight.

Magazine Needs: *Thin Coyote* is a quarterly magazine "churning up whirlwinds of creative endeavor by the planet's scofflaws, mule skinners, seers, witchdoctors, maniacs, alchemists and giant-slayers. Get in touch with your inner shapeshifter and transcribe his howls, growls and wails. No singsong rhyming crap; no greeting card devotional stuff or I'll come over to your house and put a terrible hurtin' on you." They have published poetry by Jonis Agee, John Millett, Pat McKinnon and Paul Weinman. As a sample the editor selected these lines from "invading dusk" by Laura Joy Lustig:

> jaded/with no snooze/because someone/is beside me/making me look/at myself/making shy nipples/
> pink gumballs/(because love/don't make me come)

TC is 40-60 pgs., 8½×11, docutech printed and perfect-bound with b&w cardstock cover, includes b&w photos and ads. They receive about 1,200 poems a year, accept approximately 5-10%. Press run is 300 for 30 subscribers of which 20 are libraries, 270 shelf sales. Single copy: $5; subscription: $15. Sample: $5. Make checks payable to Christopher Jones/*Thin Coyote*.

How to Submit: Submit 5 poems at a time. Previously published poems and simultaneous submissions OK. Cover letter preferred. Time between acceptance and publication is 2-4 months. Often comments on rejections. Send SASE for guidelines. Reports in 1-2 months. Pays 1 copy. Acquires first or one-time rights. Reviews books and chapbooks of poetry and other magazines. Open to unsolicited reviews. Poets may also send books for review consideration to Christopher Jones.

Book/Chapbook Needs & How to Submit: Lost Prophet Press publishes "primarily poetry, some short stories." They publish 2-3 chapbooks/year. Chapbooks are usually 30-40 pgs., 5½×8, offset printed and saddle-stapled with cardstock cover, includes art. Query first, with a few sample poems and a cover letter with brief bio and publication credits. Replies to queries in 1 month; to mss in 2 weeks. Pays advance or 25% of run.

THIRD COAST, Dept. of English, Western Michigan University, Kalamazoo MI 49008-5092, phone (616)387-2675, fax (616)387-2562, website http://www.wmich.edu/thirdcoast, founded 1995, contact poetry editors.

Magazine Needs: *Third Coast* is a biannual national literary magazine of poetry, prose, creative nonfiction and translation. They want "excellence of craft and originality of thought. Nothing trite." They have published poetry by Chase Twichell, Robin Behn, Richard Lyons, Lisa Sewell, Nance Van Winckel, Philip Levine and Tomaž Šalamun. As a sample they selected these lines from "Where Nothing Happens" by Richard Lyons:

> I/A monk's cell cools a cracked tan bowl & a missal.//Overhead, the sun boils its egg,/guilty for
> everyone it's encouraged, pulling them like scavengers//into a world that won't satisfy. Why stand
> beneath/the rose chapel-window where everything escapes?//An olive tree ghosts its rosary along the
> top of the wall./Only now does the light yield what no one wants, what exactly it is.//A red trumpet
> blossom climbs the gatepost.

Third Coast is 140 pgs., 6×9, professionally printed and perfect-bound with a 4-color cover with art. They receive about 2,000 poems a year, accept 3-5%. Press run is 1,000 for 100 subscribers of which 20 are libraries, 350 shelf sales. Single copy: $6; subscription: $11/year, $20/2 years, $29/3 years.

How to Submit: Submit up to 5 poems at a time. Poems should be typed and single-spaced, with the author's name on each page. Stanza breaks should be double-spaced. No previously published poems or simultaneous

THE GEOGRAPHICAL INDEX, located at the back of this book, can help you discover the publishers in your region. Publishers often favor poets (and work) from their own areas.

submissions. No electronic submissions. Cover letter preferred. Poems are circulated to assistant poetry editors and poetry editors; poetry editors make final decisions. Seldom comments on rejections. Send SASE for guidelines. Reports in 3-4 months. Pays 2 copies and 1-year subscription. Acquires first rights.
Also Offers: Website includes table of contents from past issues, poetry samples and writer's guidelines.

🌐 ◯ ◑ **THE THIRD HALF LITERARY MAGAZINE; K.T. PUBLICATIONS**, 16, Fane Close, Stamford, Lincolnshire PE9 1HG England, phone (01780)754193, founded 1987, editor Mr. Kevin Troop.
Magazine Needs: *TTH* appears "as often as possible each year." The editor wants "meaningful, human and humane, funny poems up to 40 lines. Work which actually says something without being obscene." They have published poetry by Lee Bridges (Holland), Ann Keith (Amsterdam), Toby Litt (Prague) and Edmund Harwood, Michael Newman, Louise Rogers and Steve Sneyd (Britain). *TTH* is up to 100 pgs., A5, perfect-bound, illustrated, printed on white paper with glossy cover. Press run is over 200.
How to Submit: Submit 6 poems at a time. No simultaneous submissions. Cover letter and suitable SAE required. Publishes theme issues. Send SAE with IRCs for guidelines and upcoming themes. Reports ASAP. Pays 1 copy. *The Third Half* is priced at £4.95 each, £5.50 by post in UK, £8 overseas.
Book/Chapbook Needs & How to Submit: K.T. Publications also publishes other books in a Minibooks Series, for use in the classroom. Individual booklets vary in length and are perfect-bound with glossy covers. "Procedure for the publication of books is explained to each author; each case is different."

$ ◑ **THIRST MAGAZINE; CARPE DIEM PUBLISHING**, 1705 E. 17th St., Suite #400, The Dalles OR 97058, phone (541)296-1552, e-mail waconner@aol.com or THIRST@netcnct.net, founded 1994, editor Jessica E. Griffin.
Magazine Needs: *THIRST* is a bimonthly independent variety magazine which focuses on music, literature and film important and noteworthy in the cyberpunk methodology. Poetry submitted to *THIRST* must be cyberpunk in style, mood, or tone. Topics should be about computer lifestyle, drugs, sex, etc. No dreary poetry drudged from high school assignments." The editor says *THIRST* is 40-90 pgs., 8½×7, saddle-stitched, full color cover of an original art, b&w graphics included inside. They receive about 100-300 poems a year, accept approximately 10-12%. Press run is 400 for 100 subscribers. Single copy: $3.25; subscription: $25. Sample: $4.20. Make checks payable to Carpe Diem Publishing.
How to Submit: Submit 3 poems at a time. Previously published poems and simultaneous submissions OK. Cover letter required. "Poems can take any format and should. Poets should keep in mind the visual arrangement of their work as to make the best representation of the content of the poem." E-mail submissions OK, "but name, address, phone number and correct e-mail for response must be included." Time between acceptance and publication is 3-12 months. Publishes theme issues. Send SASE for guidelines and upcoming themes. Reports in 3-12 months. Pays 4¢/word, minimum of $4.50, and 1 copy. Acquires first North American serial or one-time rights. "Our staff reviews all literature (fiction/nonfiction) and poetry that might be of interest to cyberpunks." Open to unsolicited reviews. Poets may also send books for review consideration to Attention: William A. Conner, editor.

◑ 🔲 **13TH MOON (Specialized: women)**, English Dept., University at Albany, State University of New York, Albany NY 12222, phone (518)442-4181, e-mail moon13@csc.albany.edu, website http://www.albany.edu/english/Moon, founded 1973, editor Judith Emlyn Johnson.
Magazine Needs: *13th Moon* is a feminist literary magazine appearing yearly (one double issue). Beyond a doubt, a real selection of forms and styles is featured here. For instance, free verse has appeared with formal work, concrete poems, long poems, stanza patterns, prose poems, a crown of sonnets and more. *13th Moon* is a 6×9, flat-spined, handsomely printed format with glossy card cover, using photographs and line art. Press run is 2,000 for 690 subscribers of which 61 are libraries, 700 shelf sales. Subscription: $10. Sample: $10.
How to Submit: Submit 3-5 poems at a time. No previously published poems or simultaneous submissions. Reads submissions September 1 through May 30 only. Publishes theme issues. Send SASE for guidelines and upcoming themes. Themes include "special issues on women's poetics, one focusing on poetry, one on narrative forms." Pays 2 copies. Acquires first North American serial rights.
Also Offers: Website includes writer's guidelines, names of editors, poetry and a price list for back issues.

$ ◯ ◑ **32 PAGES; RAIN CROW PUBLISHING**, 2127 W. Pierce Ave., Apt. 2B, Chicago IL 60622-1824, e-mail 32pp@rain-crow-publishing.com, website http://rain-crow-publishing.com/32pp/, founded 1997, editor-in-chief Michael S. Manley.
Magazine Needs: Appearing 4-6 times per year, *32 Pages* is a magazine of poetry, short fiction, drama, essays, creative nonfiction, and graphical storytelling in English or translation." They want "narrative, lyric or formal poetry. No length or subject restrictions. No light verse, 'language' poetry, visual poetry or 'concrete' poetry." They have published poetry by Neil Myers, David Kirby and Mary Winters. As a sample the editor selected these lines from "Homopoeticus" by Fred Santiago Arroyo:

> Mine swirled baby roses on the blades of machetes/over the labels of rum bottles/his red fingers
> pressing petals along their stems/little necklaces of blood around their necks/On walls outside Anasco,
> Lares, along the sea-walls of Arecibo/he soothed graffiti tortured walls with yellow tulips.

32 Pages is 32 pgs., 8½×11, offset printed with "paste and fold binding", glossy paper cover, includes b&w

line drawings, ads. They receive about 25 poems/month. Press run is 1,000 for subscribers and shelf sales; also distributed free to writing centers. Subscription: $10 for 6 issues. Sample: $2.50. Make checks payable to Rain Crow Publishing.

How to Submit: Submit up to 5 poems at a time—typed, 1 poem/page. Previously published poems and simultaneous submissions OK. Cover letter preferred. E-mail submissions OK, plain text or MS Word. "Cover letters should just give a brief introduction and list of publications. Don't go overboard, don't explain your poems or your theories of poetry." Time between acceptance and publication is 3 months. Seldom comments on rejections. Publishes theme issues occasionally. Send SASE for guidelines. "Themes are announced on website and in preceding issues." Reports in 4 months. Always sends prepublication galleys. Pays $5/page plus 2 copies and subscription. Acquires first or one-time rights.

Advice: The editor says, "We look for poetry that crystalizes and conveys experience, using language as the means, not the goal itself. Be persistent, read the magazine you submit to (and those you don't!)."

THISTLEDOWN PRESS LTD. (Specialized: regional), 633 Main St., Saskatoon, Saskatchewan S7H 0J8 Canada, phone (306)244-1722, fax (306)244-1762, e-mail thistle@sk.sympatico.ca, website http://www.thistledown.sk.ca, founded 1975, editor-in-chief Patrick O'Rourke.

Book/Chapbook Needs: Thistledown is "a literary press that specializes in quality books of contemporary poetry by Canadian authors. Only the best of contemporary poetry that amply demonstrates an understanding of craft with a distinctive use of voice and language. Only interested in full-length poetry mss with 53-71 pgs. minimum." They published *Wormwood Vermouth*, *Warphistory* by Charles Noble and *Zhivago's Fire* by Andrew Wreggitt.

How to Submit: Do not submit unsolicited mss. Canadian poets must query first with letter, bio and publication credits. No e-mail or fax queries or submissions. Submission guidelines available upon request. Replies to queries in 2-3 weeks, to submissions (if invited) in 3 months. No authors outside Canada. No simultaneous submissions. "Please submit quality laser-printed or photocopied material." Always sends prepublication galleys. Contract is for 10% royalty plus 10 copies.

Advice: They comment, "Poets submitting mss to Thistledown Press for possible publication should think in 'book' terms in every facet of the organization and presentation of the mss: Poets presenting mss that read like good books of poetry will have greatly enhanced their possibilities of being published. We strongly suggest that poets familiarize themselves with some of our poetry books before submitting a query letter."

THORNY LOCUST, P.O. Box 32631, Kansas City MO 64171-5631, founded 1993, editor Silvia Kofler, associate editor Celeste Kuechler.

Magazine Needs: Thorny Locust, published quarterly, is a "literary magazine that wants to be thought-provoking, witty and well-written." They want "poetry with some 'bite' e.g., satire, epigrams, black humor and bleeding-heart cynicism." They do not want "polemics, gratuitous grotesques, sombre surrealism, weeping melancholy or hate-mongering." They have published poetry by Victoria Garton, Don Mager, Simon Perchik and Brian Daldorph. As a sample the editor selected these lines from "It's Broken" by Philip Miller:

> The Chinese teacup/with its delicate cypresses. . . . /A hairline crack began years ago, but we could
> not resist using it from time to time. . . /Today when I poured the boiling water/ . . . I heard the crack
> open . . ./the cup shattering . . ./where we had walked together. . . .

Thorny Locust is 28-32 pgs., 7×8½, desktop-published, saddle-stapled with medium cover stock, drawings and b&w photos. They receive about 350-400 poems a year, accept approximately 35%. Press run is 150-200 for 30 subscribers of which 6 are libraries; 60 distributed free to contributors and small presses. Single copy: $4; subscription: $15. Sample: $3. Make checks payable to Silvia Kofler.

How to Submit: Submit 3 poems at a time. "If you do not include a SASE with sufficient postage, your submission will be pitched!" No previously published poems; simultaneous submissions OK. Cover letter preferred. "When possible, we prefer material on a mini-disk in Word Perfect 5.1 or Microsoft Word (Mac or IBM) with a hard copy. Otherwise, poetry and fiction must be typed, laser-printed or in a clear dot-matrix." Time between acceptance and publication is 1-2 months. Seldom comments on rejections. Send SASE for guidelines. Reports in 2-3 months. Pays 1 copy. Acquires one-time rights.

Advice: The editor says, "Never perceive a rejection as a personal insult, keep on trying. Take advice."

THOUGHTS FOR ALL SEASONS: THE MAGAZINE OF EPIGRAMS (Specialized: form, humor), % editor Prof. Em. Michel Paul Richard, 478 NE 56th St., Miami FL 33137-2621, founded 1976.

Magazine Needs: TFAS "is an irregular serial: designed to preserve the epigram as a literary form; satirical. All issues are commemorative." Rhyming poetry and nonsense verse with good imagery will be considered although most modern epigrams are prose. As a sample the editor selected this poem by Neil Megaw:

> Leonardo never had to be fretful/Landing great ideas by the netful./If I hook one a week/It's a poor
> little freak/With a look in its eyes most regretful.

TFAS is 84 pgs., offset from typescript and saddle-stapled with full-page illustrations, card cover. The editor accepts about 20% of material submitted. Press run is 500-1,000. There are several library subscriptions but most distribution is through direct mail or local bookstores and newsstand sales. Single copy: $4.75 plus $1.50 postage.

How to Submit: Submit at least 1 full page of poems at a time, with SASE. Simultaneous submissions OK, but not previously published epigrams "unless a thought is appended which alters it." Editor comments on rejections. Publishes 1 section devoted to a theme. Theme for September 2000: "The Third Millenium." Send SASE for guidelines. Reports in 1 month. Pays 1 copy.

☑ 🖉 **360 DEGREES**, 588 Sutter St. #414, San Francisco CA 94102, founded 1993, managing editor Karen Kinnison.

Magazine Needs: *360 Degrees* is a biannual review, containing literature and artwork. "We are dedicated to keeping the art of poetic expression alive in America." They say they have "no real limits" on poetry, "only the limits of the submitter's imagination." However, they do not want to see "greeting card verse, simplified emotions or religious verse." They have published poetry by Sean Brendan-Brown, David Fedo and Lyn Lifshin. As a sample the editor selected these lines from "Where Heroes Gather" by David Demarest:

> *"It is the encounter of a lifetime,/the endless strudggle, like Sisyphus and his rock,/where the sun*
> *confronts the moon's sad and silent side/and rises again the better for it,/free, perhaps, yet forever*
> *locked within dark gates."*

360 Degrees is 40 pgs., digest-sized, neatly printed and saddle-stapled. They receive about 1,000 poems a year, accept approximately 80. Press run is 500 for 100 subscribers. Subscription: $15. Sample: $5.

How to Submit: Submit 3-6 poems at a time. Include SASE. No previously published poems; simultaneous submissions OK. "Just let us know if a particular piece you have submitted to us has been accepted elsewhere." Cover letter preferred. Seldom comments on rejections. Send SASE for guidelines. Reports within 3 months. Pays 1 copy.

Advice: The editor says, "We are a small, but excellent review. Most of the poems we accept not only show mastery of words, but present interesting intelligent ideas. The mastery of language is something we expect from freelancers, but the content of the idea being expressed is the selling point."

☒ $🖉 **THE THREEPENNY REVIEW**, P.O. Box 9131, Berkeley CA 94709, phone (510)849-4545, founded 1980, poetry editor Wendy Lesser.

● Work published in this review has also been included in the 1993, 1994, 1995 and 1998 volumes of *The Best American Poetry*.

Magazine Needs: *Threepenny Review* "is a quarterly review of literature, performing and visual arts, and social articles aimed at the intelligent, well-read, but not necessarily academic reader. Nationwide circulation. Want: formal, narrative, short poems (and others). Prefer under 100 lines. No bias against formal poetry, in fact a slight bias in favor of it." They have published poetry by Thom Gunn, Frank Bidart, Seamus Heaney, Czeslaw Milosz and Louise Glück. There are about 9-10 poems in each 36-page tabloid issue. They receive about 4,500 submissions of poetry a year, use approximately 12. Press run is 10,000 for 8,000 subscribers of which 150 are libraries. Subscription: $20. Sample: $7.

How to Submit: Submit up to 5 poems at a time. Do not submit mss June through August. Send SASE for guidelines. Reports in 3-8 weeks. Pays $100/poem plus year's subscription. Buys first serial rights. Open to unsolicited reviews. "Send for review guidelines (SASE required)."

🔃 ◯ **THE THRESHOLD; CROSSOVER PRESS**, P.O. Box 101362, Pittsburgh PA 15237, phone (412)559-2269, fax (412)364-3273, e-mail lazarro@aol.com, website http://members.aol.com/lazarro/threshold/home.htm, founded 1996, editor D.H. Laird, poetry editor Monique Wetli.

Magazine Needs: "*The Threshold* is a quarterly magazine for writers by writers. Bottom line, if we like it, we print it. We're not interested in trends or what is marketable. We want imaginative, thoughtful poetry. Open to all styles and subject matter." They have published poetry by Frank Anthony and Elena Geil. As a sample the editor selected these lines from "The Cellest" by Ace Boggess:

> *As if a potent aphrodisiac, an inducement to tranquil euphoria, I hear one of them sigh./Careful,*
> *meandering streams of thought echo from the subconscious, the id, demanding relegation./My thoughts,*
> *no doubt, are theirs.*

The Threshold is 48 pgs., magazine-sized, attractively printed and saddle-stitched with cardstock cover with b&w illustration, includes b&w illustrations and ads. They receive about 100 poems a year, accept approximately 10%. They publish approximately 4-6 poems/issue. Press run is 500 for 100 subscribers, 300 shelf sales. Single copy: $5.95; subscription: $22. Sample: $6. Make checks payable to Crossover Press.

How to Submit: Submit up to 4 poems at a time. No previously published poems; simultaneous submissions OK. Cover letter preferred. Disk submissions OK. "Poets should provide a brief biography." Time between acceptance and publication is 4 months. Often comments on rejections. Publishes theme issues occasionally. Send SASE for guidelines. Reports in 4-6 months. Pays 1 copy. Acquires one-time rights.

Also Offers: Website includes guidelines, editor's name, excerpts from poetry and short story collections.

Advice: The editors say, "Good writers are a dime a dozen. Good story tellers are priceless!"

◯ **THUMBPRINTS**, Thumb Area Writer's Club, P.O. Box 27, Sandusky MI 48471, founded mid-1980s, co-editor/president S.R. Elwood, co-editor Ron Curell.

Magazine Needs: *Thumbprints* appears monthly "to give writers a chance to be published." They want "any style of poetry, 40 lines maximum." No "vulgar language or sex of any kind. No satanic or witchcraft poetry." They have published poetry by Janet Murphy. The editor says *Thumbprints* is 8-10 pgs., 8½×11, photocopied and corner stapled with original art on cover. They receive about 300 poems a year, accept approximately 98%.

Press run is 30-60 copies depending on submissions. Subscription: $10. Sample: $1. Make checks payable to Thumb Area Writer's Club.

How to Submit: Submit up to 5 poems at a time. Include SASE with all submissions. Line length for poetry is 40 maximum. Previously published poems and simultaneous submission OK. Cover letter preferred. Time between acceptance and publication is 1-2 months. Often comments on rejections. Publishes theme issues occasionally. Send SASE for guidelines and upcoming themes. Pays 1 copy. Author retains all rights.

N ⊕ 🄯 **THUMBSCREW**, P.O. Box 657, Oxford OX2 6PH United Kingdom, e-mail tim.kendall@bristol.ac.uk (no poems by e-mail), website http://www.bris.ac.uk/Depts/English/jl_thumb.html, founded 1994, editor Tim Kendall.

Magazine Needs: "Appearing 3 times a year, *Thumbscrew* is an international poetry magazine featuring poetry and criticism from well-known and new writers." They have published poetry by Paul Muldoon, Anne Stevenson, Michael Longley and Seamus Heaney. The editor says *Thumbscrew* is 100 pgs., magazine-sized, perfect-bound with laminated board cover. They receive about 6,000 poems a year, accept approximately 1%. Press run is 600 for 400 subscribers of which 50 are libraries, 200 shelf sales. Subscription: $27.50. Sample: $9.50.

How to Submit: Submit 2-5 poems at a time. No previously published poems or simultaneous submissions. Cover letter preferred. "Send clear typed copies, with each page including name and address of author." Time between acceptance and publication is 3 months. Seldom comments on rejections. Publishes theme issues occasionally. Reports in 2-3 months. Pays 1-2 copies. Acquires all rights. Copyright returned to author after publication. Reviews books and chapbooks of poetry in 1,000 words, single book format. Open to unsolicited reviews. Poets may also send books for review consideration.

✔ ▣ 🄯 **THUNDER RAIN PUBLISHING; CORP.; L'INTRIGUE WEB MAGAZINE; THUNDER RAIN WRITER AWARD; LOUISIANA POETRY BOOK CONTEST**, 34326 W.N. Sibley Rd., Walker LA 70785, phone (225)686-2002, fax (225)686-2285, e-mail rhi@thunder-rain.com, website http://www.thunder-rain.com, founded 1996, president/editor Katherine Christoffel, associate editor Phyllis Jean Green, poetry editor David Ritchie, webmaster Mike Blezien.

Magazine Needs: *L'Intrigue* is an annual arts web magazine with periodical updates. Accepts submissions of poetry, fiction, feature stories, and reviews on all literary material. Welcomes information on literary events. "*L'Intrigue* celebrates the work of new and up-and-coming writers." They have published poetry by Peter Tomassi, Raymond HV Galluci, Dennis Collins Johnson and Miral Brisca. As a sample they selected these lines from "I, Emmanuel" (a poem dedicated to the homeless) by poetry editor David Ritchie:

> I, Emmanuel, was born where/the winds never still;/where swallows dive and loop;/return, and return
> again/My life was an open flower/arrayed in beauty, aligned/with the sun./I had time to rest,/to listen
> to the sound of easy winds/sweep across the lake, and/see the blue turn to rosewater/as the sun set.

They receive about 200 poems a year, accept approximately 75%.

How to Submit: Simultaneous submissions OK. Short bio preferred. E-mail submissions OK. Send SASE for guidelines or visit website. Acquires first North American serial rights.

Also Offers: Sponsors the annual Thunder Rain Writer Award of $100 for poetry, essays, fiction and feature stories. Also sponsors *The Louisiana Poetry Book* Contest. "May enter 3 poems for submission fee of $5, contact is made if poetry is accepted for book/contest. Poetry must be original work, not previously published, reflect the state of Louisiana. Copyright remains with writer. $100 award given to one poet, and most reflected poetry published in *The Louisiana Poetry Book*."

🄯 **TIA CHUCHA PRESS**, P.O. Box 476969, Chicago IL 60647-2304, phone (773)377-2496, fax (773)296-0968, e-mail guild@charlie.cns.iit.edu, website http://www.nupress.nwu.edu/guild, founded 1989, director Luis J. Rodriguez.

Magazine Needs: They publish 2-4 paperbacks a year, "multicultural, lyrical, engaging, passionate works informed by social, racial, class experience. Evocative. Poets should be knowledgeable of contemporary and traditional poetry, even if experimenting. Ours is a culturally diverse, performance-oriented publishing house of emerging socially-engaged poetry. There are no restrictions as to style or content—poetry that 'knocks us off our feet' is what we are looking for." They have published *Talisman* by Afaa Michael Weaver and *You Come Singing* by Virgil Suarez. As a sample the editor selected these lines from "Eating in Anger" in *Fallout* by Kyoko Mori:

> My friend lived with a man who ate/peanut butter when they fought. She/found the spoons in his
> pockets, sticky/inverted mirrors in which her angry/words blurred backwards. . . .

How to Submit: Submit complete ms of 50 pages or more with SASE ("preferably 60-100 pages"). "We publish only in English, but will look at bilingual editions if they are presented in both languages." Simultaneous submissions OK, if notified. Only original, unpublished work in book form. "Although, we like to have poems that have been published in magazines and/or chapbooks." Deadline: June 30. Do not submit via fax. Reads submissions during the summer months. Pays 5 copies.

Advice: They say, "We are known for publishing the best of what is usually spoken word or oral presentations of poetry. However, we like to publish poems that best work on the page. Yet, we are not limited to that. Our authors come from a diversity of ethnic, racial and gender backgrounds. Our main thrust is openness, in forms as well as content. We are cross-cultural, but we don't see this as a prison. The openness and inclusiveness is a foundation to include a broader democratic notion of what poetry should be in this country."

$○◐◎ TICKLED BY THUNDER, HELPING WRITERS GET PUBLISHED SINCE 1990 (Specialized: subscribers), 7385 129th St., Surrey, British Columbia V3W 7B8 Canada, e-mail thunder@istar. ca, website http://www.home.istar.ca/~thunder, founded 1990, publisher/editor Larry Lindner.
Magazine Needs: *Tickled by Thunder*, appears 4 times/year, using poems about "fantasy particularly, about writing or whatever. Require original images and thoughts. Keep them short (up to 40 lines)—not interested in long, long poems. Nothing pornographic, childish, unimaginative. Welcome humor and inspirational verse." They have published poetry by Laleh Dadpour Jackson and Helen Michiko Singh. It is 24 pgs., digest-sized, published on Macintosh. 1,000 readers/subscribers. Subscription: $12/4 issues. Sample: $2.50. Send SASE (or SAE and IRC) for guidelines.
How to Submit: Include 3-5 samples of writing with queries. No e-mail submissions. Cover letter required with submissions; include "a few facts about yourself and brief list of publishing credits." Reports in 3-6 months. Pays 2¢/line to $2 maximum. Buys first rights. Editor comments on rejections "80% of the time." Reviews books of poetry in up to 300 words. Open to unsolicited reviews. Poets may also send books for review consideration.
Also Offers: They offer a poetry contest 4 times/year. Deadlines: the 15th of February, May, August and October. Entry fee: $5 for 1 poem; free for subscribers. Prize: cash, publication and subscription. We publish chapbooks. "We are interested in student poetry and publish it in our center spread: *Expressions*." Send SASE (or SAE and IRC) for details. Website includes writer's guidelines and names of editors.

◐ TIGHTROPE; SWAMP PRESS, 323 Pelham Rd., Amherst MA 01002-1654, founded 1977, chief editor Ed Rayher.
Magazine Needs: *Tightrope*, appearing 1-2 times a year, is a literary magazine of varying format. Circulation is 300 for 150 subscribers of which 25 are libraries. Subscription: $10/2 issues. Sample: $6.
How to Submit: Submit 3-6 poems at a time. No simultaneous submissions. Time between acceptance and publication is 6-12 months. Sometimes comments on rejections. SASE required. Reports in 2 months. Pays "sometimes" and provides 2 copies. Acquires first rights.
Book/Chapbook Needs & How to Submit: *The editor is not presently accepting unsolicited submissions for chapbook publication.* Swamp Press is a small press publisher of poetry and graphic art in limited edition, letterpress chapbooks. Swamp Press has published books by Edward Kaplan, editor Ed Rayher, Alexis Rotella (miniature, 3×3, containing 6 haiku), Sandra Dutton (a 4 foot long poem), Frannie Lindsay (a 10×13 format containing 3 poems), Andrew Glaze, Tom Haxo, Carole Stone and Steven Ruhl. Pays 5-10% of press run and, if there is grant money available, an honorarium (about $50). Send SASE for catalog.

◖ TIMBER CREEK REVIEW, 3283 UNCG Station, Greensboro NC 27413, phone (336)334-6970, e-mail Timber_Creek_Review@hoopsmail.com, *TCR* founded 1994, editor J.M. Freiermuth, associate editor Celestine Woo.
Magazine Needs: Magazine appears quarterly using "primarily short stories and ten to twenty poems. We read all forms of poetry, but shorter poems stand a better chance of being selected. I like to have five or six poems to thirty lines that can fill a page. Occasionally include poems from two to four pages. There was one issue that had about twenty-five sonnets." They have published poetry by Anselm Brocki, Randy W. Oakes, David Fedo, Taylor Graham and Hugh Fox. The editors say *TCR* is 76-84 pgs., 5½×8½, computer generated on copy paper, saddle-stapled with 85 lb. colored paper cover, occasionally uses graphics. They publish about 60 of 600-800 submitted poems per year. Subscription: $15 domestic, $16 Canada, $24 international. Sample: $4.25. Make checks payable in US dollars to J.M. Freiermuth.
How to Submit: No previously published poems; simultaneous submissions OK. Cover letter required. "There are no automatons here, so don't treat us like machines. We recognize the names of a couple hundred poets on sight, but if you are not a dead white guy, we may not recognize your name at the bottom of the poem. Include a few lines about you to break the ice; the names of three or four magazines that have published you in the last year would show your reality; and a bio blurb of 37 words including the names of two or three of the magazines (where you aspire to be?) you send the occasional subscription check could help. If you are not sending a check to some little magazine that is supported by subscriptions and the blood sweat and tears of the editors, why would you send your poetry to any of them and expect to receive a warm welcome?" Seldom comments on rejections. Reports in up to 6 months. Pays 1 copy. Acquires one-time rights.
Advice: The editors say, "Stop watching TV and read that book of poetry your last poem appeared in. If you are not reading other people's poetry, they are probably not reading yours either. Was it worth wasting the tree?"

$◎ TIMBERLINE PRESS, 6281 Red Bud, Fulton MO 65251, phone (573)642-5035, founded 1975, poetry editor Clarence Wolfshohl.
Book/Chapbook Needs: "We do limited letterpress editions with the goal of blending strong poetry with well-crafted and designed printing. We lean toward natural history or strongly imagistic nature poetry but will look at any good work. Also, good humorous poetry." They have published the book *Of Belly and Bone* by Peter D. Zivkovic. Sample copies may be obtained by sending $5, requesting sample copy, and noting you saw the listing in *Poet's Market*. Reports in under 1 month. Pays "50-50 split with author after Timberline Press has recovered its expenses."
How to Submit: Query before submitting full ms.

N □ ○ ◎ **TIMBOOKTU (Specialized: ethnic/nationality)**, P.O. Box 933, Mobile AL 36601-0933, e-mail editor@timbooktu.com, website http://www.timbooktu.com, founded 1996, editor Memphis Vaughan, Jr.
Magazine Needs: *TimBookTu* is a biweekly online journal. They want "positive, creative and thought-provoking poetry that speaks to the diverse African-American culture and the African diaspora." They have published poetry by Zamoundie Allie, Jamal Sharif, John Riddick, Rodney Coates, Michael Rodriguez and Richard "Goldie" Parks. They receive about 500 poems a year, accept approximately 98%.
How to Submit: Submit 3 poems at a time. Previously published poems and simultaneous submissions OK. E-mail and disk submissions OK. Cover letter preferred. Time between acceptance and publication is 2 weeks. Always comments on rejections. Send SASE for guidelines. Reports in 2 weeks. Poets may send books for review consideration.

♣ ○ ◎ **TIME FOR RHYME (Specialized: form/style)**, P.O. Box 1055, Battleford, Saskatchewan S0M 0E0 Canada, phone (306)445-5172, founded 1995, editor Richard W. Unger.
Magazine Needs: *Time for Rhyme*, published quarterly, aims to "promote traditional rhyming poetry. Other than short editorial, contents page, review page, PoeMarkets (other markets taking rhyme), this magazine is all rhyming poetry." They want "any rhyming poetry in any form up to about 32 lines on nearly any subject." They do not want "obscene (4-letter words), pornographic, profane, racist or sexist. No e.e. cummings' style either." They have published poetry by Elizabeth Symon, Sharron R. McMillan, Anthony Chalk and J. Alvin Speers. *Time for Rhyme* is 32 pgs., 4 × 5½, photocopied, hand-bound with thread, hand press printed cover, with clip art, handmade rubber stamps, letterpress art and ads. They receive several hundred poems a year, accept approximately 25%. Subscription: $12. Sample: $3.25.
How to Submit: "Preference given to subscribers, however, no requirements." Previously published poems OK ("But must ensure poet retained rights on it. Prefer unpublished"). No simultaneous submissions. Cover letter preferred, list titles submitted and if first submission here give brief list of publications poet has been published in. No poems published yet? Send some general information." Often comments on rejections. Send SASE (or SAE and IRC) for guidelines. "Americans submitting can save money by sending SAE and $1 US bill (cheaper than IRC). Please no SASE with U.S. stamps." Reports ASAP. Pays 1 copy. Acquires first North American serial rights—will consider second serial rights. Staff reviews books/magazines containing mostly or all rhyming poetry. Reviews vary in length but up to about 100 words. Send books for review consideration.
Advice: The editor says, "though non-rhyming poetry can be excellent, *Time for Rhyme* was created to be a platform for poets who prefer rhyme and as a source for those who prefer to read it. Old-fashioned values popular here too. Might be best to read a back issue before submitting."

○ ◐ ◎ **TIME OF SINGING, A MAGAZINE OF CHRISTIAN POETRY (Specialized: religious, themes)**, P.O. Box 149, Conneaut Lake PA 16316, fax (814)382-7149, e-mail timesing@toolcity.net, founded 1958-1965, revived 1980, editor Lora H. Zill.
Magazine Needs: *Time of Singing* appears 4 times a year. "We tend to be traditional. We like poems that are aware of grammar. Collections of uneven lines, series of phrases, preachy statements, unstructured 'prayers,' and trite sing-song rhymes usually get returned. We look for poems that 'show' rather than 'tell.' The viewpoint is unblushingly Christian—but in its widest and most inclusive meaning. Moreover, it is believed that the vital message of Christian poems, as well as inspiring the general reader, will give pastors, teachers, and devotional leaders rich current sources of inspiring material to aid them in their ministries. Would like to see more forms. They have published poetry by Tony Cosier, John Grey, Luci Shaw, Bob Hostetler, Mary Herbert, Frances P. Reid and Charles Waugaman. As a sample the editor selected these lines from "Stone Pillars" by Elizabeth Howard:

> Manoah brought his broken/body home. We grieved/two wheat straws leaning/into each other for
> succor,/but one pale day, joy/crept onto the hearth,/legs as spindly/as a grasshopper nymph's/on a
> frosty morning.

Time of Singing is 40 pgs., digest-sized, offset from typescript with decorative line drawings scattered throughout. The bonus issues are not theme based. They receive over 800 submissions a year, use about 175. Circulation is 350 for 150 subscribers. Single copy: $6; subscription: $15 US, $18 Canada, $27 overseas. Sample: $4.
How to Submit: Submit up to 5 poems at a time, single-spaced. "We prefer poems under 40 lines, but will publish up to 60 lines if exceptional." Simultaneous submissions and previously published poems OK. Time between acceptance and publication is 6-12 months. Editor comments with suggestions for improvement if close to publication. Publishes theme issues "quite often." Send SASE for guidelines and upcoming themes. Reports in 1-2 months. Pays 1 copy.
Also Offers: Sponsors several theme contests for specific issues. Send SASE for guidelines and upcoming themes.

✓ ◐ **THE TMP IRREGULAR; TAMAFYHR MOUNTAIN PRESS**, (formerly *Hodge Podge Poetry* and Hodge Podge Press), P.O. Box 2996, Taos NM 87571, e-mail kpg@newmex.com, founded 1995, editor Kenneth P. Gurney.
Magazine Needs: *The TMP Irregular* publishes 3-4 issues a year on an irregular basis "as it happens, in deference to time, money, acts of God and the input of poetry worthy of these pages, for the love of poetry and the joy of producing a publication that helps us poets achieve a small part of our fame and glory." They want

"typed, original, unpublished work and select poems that the editor finds moving or compelling." They don't want "poems of excessive prejudice or swearing." They have published poetry by Antler, Eileen Tabios, Ann Boger and Jo Speer. *The TMP Irregular* is 44 pgs., 5½×8½, desktop published, saddle-stapled with medium card cover with art, no ads. They receive about 2,400 poems a year, accept approximately 160. Press run is 200 for 35 subscribers of which 4 are libraries, 30 distributed free. Subscription: $20/4 issues. Sample: $5. Make checks payable to Tamafyhr Mountain Press.
How to Submit: Submit up to 5 poems at a time, one poem per page, typed, name and address on each page. Include SASE. "Send copies. Work will not be returned." Simultaneous submissions OK. No electronic submissions. "Cover letters are generally ignored, unless you tell me something interesting about you that is not related to poetry." Reports in 1 month, "sometimes less." Pays 1 copy.

TO TOPIO: AN ANNUAL ANTHOLOGY OF POETRY FOR THE INTERNATIONALLY MINDED (Specialized: anthology), 712 NW 13th St., Corvallis OR 97330, phone (541)753-9955, e-mail weaverr@ucs.orst.edu, founded 1996, submissions editor Joseph Ohmann-Krause, founder Roger Weaver.
Magazine Needs: *To Topio* is published annually (Summer/Fall). "The landscape, site or locality that *To Topio* refers to is global, so we welcome quality poetry from all over the world and in any language, so long as it is accompanied by an English translation approved by the author and so indicated with the author's legible signature." The editors say *To Topio* is 50-100 pgs., digest-sized, perfect-bound with card cover. Subscription: $5.25.
How to Submit: Submit up to 6 poems or pages with name and address on each page. No previously published poems; simultaneous submissions OK. Cover letter preferred. Reads submissions September 1 through March 15 only. Poems are circulated to an editorial board with two editors agreeing on the acceptances. Seldom comments on rejections. Publishes theme issues. Theme for issue #3 is Poetry In Other Languages. Deadline: March 15, 2000. Send SASE for guidelines and upcoming themes. Pays 1 copy. Acquires one-time rights.
Also Offers: "Poetry Enterprises provides copyrighted but free materials for poets and artists, students and teachers. Send a SASE and request for information on traditional poetry, free verse or prose poetry."

$ TOUCH (Specialized: religious, teens, themes), P.O. Box 7259, Grand Rapids MI 49510, phone (616)241-5616, founded 1970, poetry editor Carol Smith.
Magazine Needs: *Touch* is a 24-page edition "written for girls 9-14 to show them how God is at work in their lives and in the world around them. *Touch* is theme-oriented. We like our poetry to fit the theme of each issue. We send out a theme update biannually to all our listed freelancers. We prefer short poems with a Christian emphasis that can show girls how God works in their lives." They have published poetry by Janet Shafer Boyanton and Iris Alderson. As a sample the editor selected this poem, "Thanks for Funny Things," by Lois Walfrid Johnson:
> Thank You for funny things,/for the bubbling feeling of/giggles that fill my insides,/push up,/and spill over/in a shout of joy!/Thank You, Lord./Thank You!

Touch is published 10 times a year, magazine-sized. They receive 150-200 submissions of poetry/year, use 1 poem in each issue, have a 6-month backlog. Circulation is 15,500 subscribers. Subscription: $12.50 US, $15 Canada, $20 foreign. Sample and guidelines: $1 with 8×10 SASE.
How to Submit: Poems must not be longer than 20 lines—prefer much shorter. Simultaneous submissions OK. Query with SASE for theme update. Reports in 2 months. Pays $10-15 and copies.

TOUCHSTONE, Viterbo College, La Crosse WI 54601-4797, phone (608)796-3484, fax (608)796-3050, e-mail rjuppel@mail.viterbo.edu, founded 1950, moderator Richard Ruppel.
Magazine Needs: Published annually in April, *Touchstone* is a literary journal containing poetry, short stories and artwork. As a sample the moderator selected these lines from "The Choice" by Kerri Brostrom:
> Why did you come to me/like a streak of scarlet,/a swift red explosion/landing in my passion?

The magazine is 110 pgs., digest-sized, perfect-bound, with semi-glossy card cover. Press run is 1,200 for 100 subscribers of which 25 are libraries. Subscription: $15. Sample: $15.
How to Submit: Cover letter required; include "a note of origination" (i.e., that the work is original). "Poets may submit via fax, e-mail or snail-mail." Reads submissions August 1 through March 1 only. Send SASE for guidelines. Reports in 2 months. Pays 1 copy.

TOUCHSTONE LITERARY JOURNAL; TOUCHSTONE PRESS (Specialized: translations), P.O. Box 8308, Spring TX 77387-8308, e-mail guidamj@flex.net, founded 1975, poetry editor William Laufer, managing editor Guida Jackson.
Magazine Needs: *Touchstone Literary Journal* is an annual appearing in December that publishes "experimental or well-crafted traditional form, including sonnets, and translations. No light verse or doggerel." They have published poetry by Walter Griffin, Walter McDonald, Paul Ramsey and Janice Whittington. *Touchstone* is 100 pgs., digest-sized, flat-spined, professionally printed in small, dark type with glossy card cover. Subscription: $7.50. Sample: $4.
How to Submit: Submit 5 poems at a time. "Cover letter telling something about the poet piques our interest and makes the submission seem less like a mass mailing." Sometimes sends prepublication galleys. Pays 2 copies. Reviews books of poetry. Open to unsolicited reviews. Poets may also send books for review consideration to Review Editor.

Book/Chapbook Needs & How to Submit: Touchstone Press also publishes an occasional chapbook. Send SASE for chapbook submission guidelines. "We previously published a book-length epic, *Kingdom of the Leopard: An Epic of Old Benin* by Nigerian poet chi chi layor. We are open to new projects. Query first, with SASE. Absolutely no mail is answered without SASE."

N̄ $□ TRADITION MAGAZINE, P.O. Box 492, Anita IA 50020, phone (712)762-4363, founded 1976, editor Bob Everhart.

Magazine Needs: *Tradition* is a bimonthly "house magazine for our non-profit association devoted to presevation of pioneer music. Poetry needs to be related to pioneer music." The editor says *Tradition* is 56 pgs., magazine-sized, staple bound. They receive about 5 poems a year, accept approximately 50%. Press run is 2,500 for 2,000 subscribers. Subscription: $20. Sample: $3.75. Make checks payable to NTCMA.

How to Submit: Submit 2 poems at a time. Previously published poems and simultaneous submissions OK. Cover letter preferred. Time between acceptance and publication is 3 months. Publishes theme issues. Reports in 3 months. Pays $1/poem and 5 copies. Buys one-time rights. Reviews books of poetry and other magazines in multi-book format. Open to unsolicited reviews. Poets may also send books for review consideration to.

□ ◎ TRANSCENDENT VISIONS (Specialized: psychiatric survivors, ex-mental patients), 251 S. Olds Blvd. 84-E, Fairless Hills PA 19030-3426, phone (215)547-7159, founded 1992, editor David Kime.

Magazine Needs: *Transcendent Visions* appears 3 times a year "to provide a creative outlet for psychiatric survivors/ex-mental patients." They want "experimental, confessional poems; strong poems dealing with issues we face. Any length or subject matter is OK but shorter poems are more likely to be published. No rhyming poetry." They have published poetry by Lyn Lifshin, Chriss-Spike Quatrone and Paul Weinman. As a sample the editor selected these lines from "It (Fear)" by Gloria del Vecchio:

> *What has happened to the rat?/Is it on some remote street with its/mouth and anus ruining space?/*
> *Suddenly, out of the chimney/the rat leaps into the room and/climbs up the paintings of large women.*

TV is 24 pgs., 8½×11, photocopied and corner-stapled with paper cover, b&w line drawings. They receive about 100 poems a year, accept approximately 40%. Press run is 200 for 50 subscribers. Subscription: $6. Sample: $2. Make checks payable to David Kime.

How to Submit: Submit 5 poems at a time. Previously published poems and simultaneous submissions OK. Cover letter preferred. "Please tell me something unique about you, but I do not care about all the places you have been published." Time between acceptance and publication is 3 months. Reports in 3 weeks. Pays 1 copy of issue in which poet was published. Acquires first or one-time rights. Staff reviews books and chapbooks of poetry and other magazines in 20 words. Send books for review consideration.

Also Offers: "I also publish a political zine called *Crazed Nation*, featuring essays concerning mental illness."

◐ ◎ TRESTLE CREEK REVIEW (Specialized: regional), English Dept. North Idaho College, 1000 W. Garden, Coeur d'Alene ID 83814, phone (208)769-3384, fax (208)769-3431, founded 1982-83, poetry editor Chad Klinger et al.

Magazine Needs: *Trestle Creek* is a "2-year college creative writing program production. Purposes: (1) expand the range of publishing/editing experience for our small band of writers; (2) expose them to editing experience; (3) create another outlet for serious, beginning writers. We're fairly eclectic but prefer poetry on the Northwest region, particularly the innermountain West (Idaho, Montana, etc.). We favor poetry strong on image and sound, and country vs. city; spare us the romantic, rhymed clichés. We can't publish much if it's long (more than two pgs.)." This publication features both free and formal verse by relative newcomers. They have published poetry by Jesse Bier, Walter Griffin, Lance Olsen and Mary Winters. As a sample Chad Klinger selected these lines from "Trying to Pen What You Wish You Hadn't Said" by Daniel Mills:

> *What you said won't return to be fenced,/a stallion of wild syllables your tongue tries roping back—/*
> *but the words stumble, go lame,/beg for you to shoot them.*

TCR is a 57-page annual, digest-sized, professionally printed on heavy buff stock, perfect-bound, matte cover with art. Press run is 500 for 6 subscribers of which 4 are libraries. The editors receive 100 submissions a year, use approximately 30. Sample: $5.

How to Submit: Submit before March 1 (for May publication), no more than 5 pgs. No previously published poems or simultaneous submissions. Reports by March 30. Pays 2 copies.

Advice: The editor advises, "Be neat; be precise; don't romanticize or cry in your beer; strike the surprising, universal note. Know the names of things."

THE CHAPBOOK INDEX, located at the back of this book, lists those publishers who consider chapbook mss. A chapbook, a small volume of work (usually under 50 pages), is often a good middle step between magazine and book publication.

N ◐ ◎ TRI LINGUA (Specialized: ethnic/nationality), P.O. Box 24927, New Orleans LA 70184-4927, e-mail trilingua@aol.com, website http://members.aol.com/TriLingua, founded 1999, editor Anne Marie Giovingo.

Magazine Needs: Published biannually, *Tri Lingua* is "a place for American, French and Italian poets and writers to present their work in side-by-side translation. *Tri Lingua* also publishes poems without translation and invites readers to submit translations." They want "poems of any length or form, also short stories and essays which reflect the individual and respect and explore the language. Translations of published and unpublished works of other poets are also welcomed. No poems in their first stages of revision." The editor says *Tri Lingua* is about 62 pgs., magazine-sized, "uniquely handmade" and perfect-bound with 4-color soft cover. Subscription: $20 US, $28 outside US. Sample: $10 US, $14 outside US. Make checks payable to Anna Publishing.

How to Submit: Submit 3-6 typed poems at a time. Previously published poems and simultaneous submissions OK, "if clearly stated in the cover letter." E-mail submissions OK, "if queried first." Cover letter with brief bio required. Include SASE or IRCs for returns. Time between acceptance and publication is 1-6 months. Poems are circulated to an editorial board. Seldom comments on rejections. Send SASE (or SAE and IRC) for guidelines or obtain via e-mail or website. Reports in 2-4 months. Sometimes sends prepublication galleys. Pays 1 copy. Acquires first and reprint rights. Staff reviews books of single and multi-book format. Send books for review consideration.

Also Offers: Website includes submission guidelines.

⊻ ◐ TRIQUARTERLY MAGAZINE; TRIQUARTERLY BOOKS/NORTHWESTERN UNIVERSITY PRESS, 2020 Ridge Ave., Evanston IL 60208-4302, phone (847)491-7614, fax (847)467-2096, website http://www.triquarterly.nwu.edu, editor Susan Hahn.

• Work appearing in *TriQuarterly* has been included in *The Best American Poetry* (1993, 1994, 1995, 1996 and 1997) and the *Pushcart Prize* anthology.

Magazine Needs: *TriQuarterly* magazine "accepts a wide range of verse forms and styles of verse (long poems, sequences, etc.) with the emphasis solely on excellence, and some issues are published as books on specific themes." They have published poetry by Tom Sleigh, Linda McCarriston, Alice Fulton, Campbell McGrath, Susan Stewart and Theodore Weiss. *TriQuarterly*'s three issues per year are 200 pgs., 6×9, professionally printed and flat-spined with b&w photography, graphics, glossy card cover. There are about 40 or more pgs. of poetry in each issue. They receive about 3,000 poems a year, use approximately 60, 1 year backlog. Press run is 5,000 for 2,000 subscribers of which 35% are libraries. Single copy: $11.95; subscription: $24. Sample: $5.

How to Submit: No simultaneous submissions. No fax or e-mail submissions. Reads submissions October 1 through March 31 only. Sometimes works with poets, inviting rewrites of interesting work. Reports in 3 months. Always sends prepublication galleys. Pays 2 copies, additional copies available at a 40% discount. Acquires first North American serial rights. "We suggest prospective contributors examine sample copy before submitting." Reviews books of poetry "at times."

Book/Chapbook Needs & How to Submit: TriQuarterly Books (an imprint of Northwestern University Press) publishes 8-10 books/year of fiction, literary essays and poetry. They have published poetry by Bruce Weigl, Adrian C. Louis and Muriel Rukeyser. Query with up to 10 sample pages of poetry with SASE, "but we cannot consider unsolicited manuscripts without a prior query." Send SASE for additional information.

◐ ◎ TROUBADOUR; TOWERS AND RUSHING, LTD. (Specialized: style), P.O. Box 691745, San Antonio TX 78269-1745, phone/fax (210)696-1363, e-mail rgribel@express-news.net, website http://www.bcity.com/trouba, *Troubadour* founded 1997, Towers and Rushing Ltd. founded 1986, publisher/editor Dr. Ron Ribble.

Magazine Needs: *Troubadour*, published biannually (March and October), intends "to bridge the gap between the general reader and the contemporary world of poetry." They want "excellently crafted, accessible poetry written in formal styles, but will accept any style that has the flavor of tradition and formality. Preference for formal poetry [we estimate that 80% of the poetry published will be lyric poetry] but we will consider and publish any style that has the right spirit and impact." They do not want "forced rhyme or inversion, no epics, no self-pitying or self-indulgent verse, no useless profanity, mush or schlock." They have published poetry by Richard Wakefield, Richard Moore, Ed Wier, Ed Meek, Emily Long, Brooke Wiese and Gale White. As a sample the editor selected these lines from "Palisades Park" by Jeanne Heath Heritage:

> Palm trees rustle, dry fronds fall./White winged, a gull soars to the sky./A small boy throws a bright
> red ball./I toss it back and then I cry.

Troubadour is 48 pgs., 8½×5½, perfect-bound, with semi-gloss cover. The most recent issue we received contained 35 pgs. of poetry, a 1-page tribute to Poet Laureate Robert Pinsky, an exchange of ideas with JD McClatchy and an interview with Robert Goulet. Single copy: $6.50; subscription: $10.

How to Submit: Submit up to 3 poems at a time. Line length for poetry is 32 maximum. No previously published poems or simultaneous submissions. Cover letter preferred with "whether poet has been published before or not and a little bit about who the poet is—not how wonderful he or she may be. SASE required or no response." No electronic submissions. Does not read submissions during December and August. Time between acceptance and publication is 2-5 months. "Editor/publisher will make selections with selected input from advisory editor." Seldom comments on rejections. Send SASE for guidelines. Reports in 2 months. Pays honoraria to invitees and 2 copies to subscribers, 1 to non-subscribers. Acquires one-time rights.

Advice: The editors says, "we have interviewed folks like Rita Dove, Richard Moore, Robert Pinsky, Robert

Hass, Gerald Stern, X.J. Kennedy and J.D. McClatchy. All assert that being a good reader is a necessary but not sufficient prerequisite for being a good poet. Before submitting be certain you understand what 'good' poetry is. Sampling the journal you intend to submit to is probably the best way to know whether or not you create what they hunger for."

N $ ⬛ ◎ **TRUE ROMANCE (Specialized: women); STERLING MACFADDEN**, 233 Park Ave. S., New York NY 10003, editor Pat Vitucci.

Magazine Needs: *True Romance* is a monthly magazine publishing "subjects of interest to women—family, careers, romance, tragedy, personal crises." They want "poems that express a unique point of view. Poems that address topics. No Hallmark greeting cards." The editor says *TR* is 76 pgs., magazine-sized.

How to Submit: Submit 3 poems at a time. Line length for poetry is 8 minimum, 24 maximum. No previously published poems or simultaneous submissions. Send SASE for guidelines before submitting. Reports in 3 months. Pays $10-40. Buys all rights.

⬛ ◎ **TSUNAMI INC.; THE TEMPLE, GU SI, EL TEMPLO (Specialized: foreign language)**, P.O. Box 100, Walla Walla WA 99362-0033, phone (509)529-0813, e-mail tsunami@wwics.com, website http://www.wwics.com/~tsunami, founded 1995, editor Charles Potts.

Magazine Needs: *The Temple, Gu Si, El Templo* is a quarterly tri-lingual poetry magazine. It contains poems in Chinese, Spanish and English; also news, reviews and events. They want "signature poems exhibiting artistic control, intellectual rigor, emotional commitment and a command of subject matter. No rhymes, haiku; formalist, overly clever or academic work." They have published poetry by Teri Zipf, John Oliver Simon and Sharon Doubiago. As a sample the editor selected these lines from "The Wheel" by Stephen Thomas:

> My daddy made me reinvent the wheel . . ./on the lathe which I'd invented more than once/and would again. The spoke wire/trembled like a martyr,/as I drew it out from the/extruder in the hissing workshop air.

The Temple is 80 pgs., 7×10, web press printed on newsprint and saddle-stapled, includes ads for books and other magazines. They receive about 5,000 poems a year, accept approximately 1%. Press run is 5,000 for 300 subscribers of which 10 are libraries; 600 distributed free to poets at festivals. Subscription: $20. Sample: $5. Make checks payable to Tsunami Inc. "Familiarity is critical, poets must buy and read a sample first or be a subscriber."

How to Submit: Submit 3-5 poems at a time. Previously published poems OK; no simultaneous submissions. Cover letter preferred. "Send poems in 9×12 envelopes." Send Spanish mss to John Oliver Simon, 2209 California St., Berkeley CA 94705. Send Chinese mss to Denis Mair, 9200 Glendon Way, Rosemead CA 91770. Time between acceptance and publication is 1-3 months. Seldom comments on rejections. Send SASE for guidelines. Reports in 2-8 weeks. Pays 10 copies. Acquires first North American serial or one-time rights. Reviews books and chapbooks of poetry and other magazines in single or multi-book format. Open to unsolicited reviews. Poets may also send books for review consideration.

Book/Chapbook Needs: Tsunami Inc. publishes 3 paperbacks/year. Books are published by invitation only.

Advice: The editor says, "Beginners send one to three poems, large envelope, SASE for reply. Know the contents of the magazine to date: we publish original poetry in Spanish and Chinese with English translations."

⬛ ◎ **TUCUMCARI LITERARY REVIEW (Specialized: form/style)**, 3108 W. Bellevue Ave., Los Angeles CA 90026, founded 1988, editor Troxey Kemper.

Magazine Needs: *Tucumcari* appears every other month. "Prefer rhyming and established forms, including sonnet, rondeau, triolet, kyrielle, villanelle, terza rima, limerick, sestina, pantoum and others, 2-100 lines, but the primary goal is to publish good work. No talking animals. No haiku. No disjointed, fragmentary, rambling words or phrases typed in odd-shaped staggered lines trying to look like poetry. The quest here is for poetry that will be just as welcome many years later as it is now." They have published poetry by Elizabeth Dabbs, Fontaine Falkoff, Andy Peterson, Jim Dunlap and Dawn Zapletal. As a sample the editor selected these lines from "Mistaken Identity" by Leon H. Nunn:

> The well arranged lady and the disquieted man/sat sipping wine at a table/in a darkened corner near the exit/of a restaurant "Bar and Band."/The attentive waiter watched the couple for the next order/ and saw the man slump to the floor./He dashed to the table and said to the lady/"Your husband just fell to the floor."/"Not so," said the lady,/"my husband just entered the front door."

The magazine is 48 pgs., digest-sized, saddle-stapled, photocopied from typescript, with card cover. Press run is 150-200. Subscription: $12, $20 for overseas. Sample: $2, $4 for overseas.

How to Submit: Submit up to 4 poems at a time. Simultaneous submissions and previously published poems OK. Sometimes comments on rejections. Send SASE for guidelines. Reports within 1 month. Pays 1 copy. Acquires one-time rights.

Advice: The editor says, "Writing is welcomed from amateurs, in-betweens and professors/scholars. Many college professors and writing teachers submit rhyming poems here. They say they're sick of non-rhyme junk. Oddly, some of the work by amateurs is more interesting than erudite, obscure allusions to Greek/Roman mythology personages and events—more honest, earnest and heart-felt. The main measure of acceptability is: Is it interesting? Is it good? What counts is what it says not whether the work is handwritten on lined notebook paper or presented on expensive computer-generated equipment/paper which often is very difficult to read."

⊘ **TURKEY PRESS**, 6746 Sueno Rd., Isla Vista CA 93117-4904, founded 1974, poetry editors Harry Reese and Sandra Reese. "We do not encourage solicitations of any kind to the press. We seek out and develop projects on our own."

🅽 ♣ ⅄ $ ◎ **TURNSTONE PRESS LIMITED (Specialized: regional)**, 607-100 Arthur St., Winnipeg, Manitoba R3B 1H3 Canada, phone (204)947-1555, fax (204)942-1555, e-mail editor@turnstonepress.mb.ca, website http://www.TurnstonePress.com, founded 1976, contact acquisitions editor-poetry.

• Books published by Turnstone Press have won numerous awards, including the McNally Robinson Book of the Year Award, the Canadian Author's Association Literary Award for Poetry and the Lampert Memorial Awards.

Book/Chapbook Needs: "Turnstone Press publishes Canadian authors with special priority to prairie interests/themes." They publish 2 paperbacks/year. They have published poetry by Di Brandt, Catherine Hunter, Patrick Friesen and Dennis Cooley. Books are usually 5½×8½, offset printed and perfect-bound with quality paperback cover.

How to Submit: Query first with 10 sample poems and cover letter with brief bio and publication credits. Previously published poems and simultaneous submissions OK. Cover letter preferred. "Please enclose SASE (or SAE with IRC) and if you want the submission back, make sure your envelope and postage cover it." Time between acceptance and publication is 6 months. Poems are circulated to an editorial board. "The submissions that are approved by our readers go to the editorial board for discussion." They receive more than 1,000 unsolicited mss a year, about 10% are passed to the editorial board. Replies to queries in 2 months; to mss in 3 months. Pays royalties of 10% plus advance of $200 and 10 author's copies (out of a press run of 500).

Advice: They say, "Competition is extremely fierce in poetry. Most work published is by poets working on their craft for many years."

⊘ **24.7; RE-PRESST**, 30 Forest St., Providence RI 02906, founded 1994, poetry editor David Church. Currently not accepting submissions.

⊘ **TWILIGHT ENDING**, 21 Ludlow Dr., Milford CT 06460-6822, phone (203)877-3473, founded 1995, editor/publisher Emma J. Blanch.

Magazine Needs: *Twilight Ending* appears 3 times/year publishing "poetry and short fiction of the highest caliber in English." They have featured the work of poets from the US, Canada, Europe, Japan, New Zealand and India. They want "poems with originality in thought and in style, reflecting the latest trend in writing, moving from the usual set-up to a vertical approach. We prefer unrhymed poetry, however we accept rhymed verse if rhymes are perfect. We look for the unusual approach in content and style with clarity. No haiku. No poems forming a design. No foul words. No translations. No bio. No porn." The editor says *TE* is 5½×8½, "elegantly printed on white linen with one poem with title per page (12-30 lines)." They receive about 1,500 poems a year, accept approximately 10%. Press run is 100 for 50 subscribers of which 25 are libraries. Sample: $5 US, $6 Canada, $6.50 Europe, $7.50 India, Japan and New Zealand. Make checks payable to Emma J. Blanch.

How to Submit: Submit 3-4 poems at a time, typed, single spaced. No previously published poems or simultaneous submissions nor poems submitted to contests while in consideration for *Twilight Ending*. Include SASE for reply (overseas contributors should include 2 IRCs). No fax or e-mail submissions. "When accepted, poems and fiction will not be returned so keep copies." Submission deadlines: mid-December for Winter issue, mid-April for Spring/Summer issue, mid-September for Fall issue. No backlog, "all poems are destroyed after publication." Often comments on rejections. Send SASE for guidelines. Reports in 1 week. Pays nothing—not even a copy. Acquires first rights.

Advice: The editor says, "If editing is needed, suggestions will be made for the writer to rework and resubmit a corrected version. The author always decides; remember that you deal with experts."

🅽 ⊘ **TWO GIRLS REVIEW**, 3331 NE 39th Ave., Portland OR 97212, phone (503)284-4724, e-mail lilnub @aol.com, founded 1995, managing editor Lidia Yukman, poetry editor Brigid Yukman.

Magazine Needs: *two girls review* is published biannually and "committed to printing under-represented experimental writing." Their poetry needs are open. "We respond to literary, experimental, mixed-genre." The editors say *tgr* is 100 pgs., 9×12, perfect-bound. They receive about 250 poems a year, accept approximately 15-25%. Press run is 2,000 for 100 subscribers of which 10 are libraries, 1,500 shelf sales; 200 distributed free to writers/literary agencies. Single copy: $6.95; subscription: $12/year, $24/2 years. Sample: $4.

How to Submit: Simultaneous submissions OK; may take previously published poems. Time between acceptance and publication is 6-12 months. Poems are circulated to an editorial board. Seldom comments on rejections. Publishes theme issues. Send SASE for upcoming themes. Reports in 2-6 months. Sometimes sends prepublication galleys on request. Pays 2 copies. All rights revert to author. Reviews books of poetry, single book format. Open to unsolicited reviews. Poets may also send books for review consideration.

Also Offers: Sponsors yearly contests for fiction, poetry and mixed-genre or experimental works. Themes vary. Send SASE for details.

Advice: The editors say, "Be relentless. Torque the lines."

U.S. 1 WORKSHEETS

U.S. 1 Poets' Cooperative
Princeton, New Jersey

VOLUME 38/39

The cover artwork for Volume 38/39 of *U.S. 1 Worksheets* is a full-color reproduction of "Chinese Opera Singer," an enamel by Vida Chu, an artist and writer based in Princeton, New Jersey. The cover was designed by artist and graphic designer Mary Szilaggi Durkee. "The artwork was chosen for its striking beauty, solidity and depth," says editor Winifred Hughes. "We wanted a cover with a strong visual image that reflects the poetic vision of the magazine. *U.S. 1 Worksheets* primarily publishes poetry, and our new format highlights each individual poem and its author. Poetry is our mainstay." Published by U.S. 1 Poets' Cooperative since 1973, *U.S. 1 Worksheets* is 72 pages, 5½ × 8½, saddle-stapled, with color cover art.

TWO RIVERS REVIEW; ANDERIE POETRY PRESS, 215 McCartney St., Easton PA 18042, e-mail tworiversreview@juno.com (guidelines/inquiries only), founded 1998, submissions editor Philip Memmer.
Magazine Needs: *Two Rivers Review* appears biannually and "seeks to print the best of contemporary poetry. All styles of work are welcome, so long as submitted poems display excellence." They have published poetry by Billy Collins, Mark Jarman, Naomi Shihab Nye, Michael McFee and Lee Upton. As a sample the editor selected these lines from "This Animal" by Julie Suk:

> What I thought was a chipmunk/unfolds to a wren,/its distrustful eyes locked on me./My poor sight
> lifted too late/to see the truth fly away.

The editor says *TRR* is 48-60 pgs., digest-sized, professionally printed on cream-colored paper, with card cover. Subscription: $15. Sample: $7.50.
How to Submit: Submit no more than 4 poems at a time with cover letter and SASE. No previously published poems; simultaneous submissions OK, "but please inform the editor in the cover letter." No electronic submissions. Reports within 6 weeks. Acquires first rights.

TYRO PUBLISHING, 194 Carlbert St., Sault Ste. Marie, Ontario P6A 5E1 Canada, phone (705)253-6402, fax (705)942-3625, e-mail tyro@sympatico.ca, founded 1984, editor Stan Gordon.
Book/Chapbook Needs: They only consider full-length mss for book publication. They have published *The Lonliness Machine* by Denis Robillard; *Doc's Log* by A.B. Normalle; and *Read Me A Poem* by Lisa Marie Brennan.
How to Submit: Query first with at least 6 sample poems. Mss should be in standard format. E-mail submissions OK. "Send samples as attached file. State word processor used. E-mail submissions will be given priority." Send e-mail for guidelines and further information. Always sends prepublication galleys.

U.S. 1 WORKSHEETS; U.S. 1 POETS' COOPERATIVE, P.O. Box 127, Kingston NJ 08528-0127, founded 1973.
Magazine Needs: *U.S. 1 Worksheets* is a literary annual, circulation 500, which uses high-quality poetry and fiction. "We use a rotating board of editors; it's wisest to query when we're next reading before submitting. A self-addressed, stamped postcard will get our next reading period dates." They have published poetry by Alicia Ostriker, Elizabeth Anne Socolow, Jean Hollander, Frederick Tibbetts, Lois Marie Harrod, James Haba, Charlotte Mandel and David Keller. *U.S. 1 Worksheets* is 72 pgs., 5½ × 8½, saddle-stapled, with color cover art. "We read a lot but take very few. Prefer complex, well-written work." Subscription: $7.
How to Submit: Submit 5 poems at a time. Include name, address and phone number in upper right-hand corner. No simultaneous submissions; rarely accepts previously published poems. Requests for sample copies, subscriptions, queries, back issues, and all mss should be addressed to the editor (address at beginning of listing). Pays 1 copy.

⭕ ◎ **THE ULTIMATE UNKNOWN (Specialized: science fiction, horror)**, P.O. Box 219, Stream-wood IL 60107-0219, e-mail ralitsa@sprynet.com, website http://www.wimall.com/cassini, founded 1995, editor David D. Combs.

Magazine Needs: *The Ultimate Unknown*, published quarterly, is a "literary magazine of science fiction, horror and the future." They want "science fiction, horror, future and politics of 20-30 lines, any style or meter." They do not want "profanity of any kind or excessive violence." They have published poetry by John Grey. *The Ultimate Unknown* is 100 pgs., photocopied, saddle-stitched with color cover, art and ads. They receive about 50 poems a year, accept approximately 75%. Press run is 250 for 100 subscribers, 10 shelf sales; 50 distributed free to authors, advertisers and reviewers. Subscription: $14. Sample: $4. Make checks payable to Combs Press.

How to Submit: "I encourage the author to subscribe, but this is not required, and only done after the accep-tance." Submit any number of poems, each on a separate piece of paper with name and address. Previously published poems and simultaneous submissions OK. Cover letter preferred. Time between acceptance and publi-cation is 3-6 months. "All poems are judged on an individual basis and accepted for their own merits." Always comments on rejections. Publishes theme issues. Send SASE for guidelines and upcoming themes. Reports in 2-3 months. Pays 1 copy. Acquires first North American serial or one-time rights. Staff reviews books or chapbooks of poetry or other magazines in 1-3 paragraphs. Send books for review consideration.

Advice: The editor says, "We are very open to new poets. We give full credit to all poets."

💲◪ **ULTRAMARINE PUBLISHING CO., INC.**, P.O. Box 303, Hastings-on-Hudson NY 10706-1817, phone (914)478-1339, fax (914)478-1365, e-mail washbook@sprynet.com, founded 1974, editor C.P. Stephens.

Book/Chapbook Needs: "We mostly distribute books for authors who had a title dropped by a major pub-lisher—the author is usually able to purchase copies very cheaply. We use existing copies purchased by the author from the publisher when the title is being dropped." Ultramarine's list includes 250 titles, 90% of them cloth bound, one-third of them science fiction and 10% poetry.

How to Submit: Authors should query before making submissions; queries will be answered in 1 week. No queries/submissions via fax. Simultaneous submissions OK, but no disks. The press pays 10% royalties. "Distrib-utor terms are on a book-by-book basis, but is a rough split."

🌐 ✅ ⭕ ◪ **UNDERSTANDING MAGAZINE; DIONYSIA PRESS LTD.**, 20 A Montgomery St., Edinburgh, Lothion EH7 5JS Great Britain, phone (0131)4782572, fax (0131)4782572, e-mail denise.smith@cabl einet.co.uk, founded 1989, contact Denise Smith.

Magazine Needs: *Understanding Magazine*, published 1-2 times/year, features "poetry, short stories, parts of plays, reviews and articles." They want "original poetry." They have published poetry by Susanne Roxman and Ron Butlin. As a sample we selected these lines from "Private Axis" by Thom Nairn:

> *The circles grow relentlessly,/His passage, inscrutably centrifugal/On this terminal cycle to silence.*

The editor says *Understanding* is A5 and perfect-bound. They receive 2,000 poems a year. Press run is 1,000 for 500 subscribers. Single copy: £4.50; subscription: £9. Sample: £3. Make checks payable to Dionysia Press.

How to Submit: Submit 5 poems at a time. No previously published poems; simultaneous submissions OK. E-mail and fax submissions OK. Time between acceptance and publication is 6-10 months. Poems are circulated to an editorial board. Often comments on rejections. Reports in 2-6 months. Always sends prepublication galleys. Pays 1 copy. Acquires all rights. Returns rights after publication. Staff reviews books or chapbooks of poetry or other magazines. Send books for review consideration.

Book/Chapbook Needs & How to Submit: Dionysia Press Ltd., publishes 2-7 paperbacks and chapbooks of poetry/year. "Sometimes we select from submissions or competitions." They have published *The Louisiana Molegrip* by Keith Bennett, *Broken Angels* by Susanna Roxman and *And Here's What You Could Have Won* by Paul Hullah. Books are usually A5, perfect-bound, hard cover with art. Query first, with a few sample poems and cover letter with brief bio and publication credits. Replies to queries in 2-6 months. Pays author's copies. "We usually get arts council grants or poets get grants for themselves." For sample books or chapbooks, write to the above address.

Also Offers: Sponsors poetry competitions with cash prizes. Send SASE for guidelines.

🅈 ◎ **UNIVERSITY OF ARIZONA PRESS (Specialized: ethnic/nationality)**, 1230 N. Park Ave., Suite 102, Tucson AZ 85719, phone (520)621-1441, fax (520)621-8899, website http://www.uapress.arizona.edu, founded 1959, editor-in-chief Christine Szuter, acquiring editor Patti Hartmann.

• In 1998, their book *Blue Horses Rush By*, by Luci Tapahonso, received the Mountains & Plains Booksell-ers Association Poetry Award.

Book/Chapbook Needs: The University of Arizona Press publishes work by Native American poets (Sun Track series) and Chicano poets only (Camino Del Sol series). They publish 2 paperbacks/year. They have published poetry by Demetria Martinez, Juan Felipe Herrera, Luci Tapahonso, Ofelia Zepeda, Simon Ortiz and Carter Revard. As a sample the editor selected this poem from *Blue Horses Rush In*:

> *Before the birth, she moved and pushed inside her mother./Her heart pounded quickly and we recognized/the sound of horses running:/the thundering of hooves on the desert floor.*

Books are 80-140 pgs., offset-printed and perfect-bound with 4-color laminated cover, include art.

How to Submit: Query first, with a few sample poems and a cover letter with brief bio, publication credits and résumé. Previously published poems and simultaneous submissions OK. Time between acceptance and publication is approximately 2 years. "All manuscripts are sent to two independent reviewers and require two approvals prior to publication." Seldom comments on rejections. Replies to queries in 1 month; to mss in 3 months. Payment varies. Obtain sample books by visiting website.

UNIVERSITY OF CENTRAL FLORIDA CONTEMPORARY POETRY SERIES, % English Dept., University of Central Florida, Orlando FL 32816-1346, phone (407)823-2212, founded 1968, poetry editor Judith Hemschemeyer.
Book/Chapbook Needs: Publishes two 50- to 80-page hardback or paperback collections each year. "Strong poetry on any theme in the lyric-narrative tradition." They have published poetry by Robert Cooperman, Katherine Soniat and John Woods.
How to Submit: Submit complete paginated ms with table of contents and acknowledgement of previously published poems. Simultaneous submissions OK. "Please send a reading fee of $7, a SASE for return of ms, and a self-addressed postcard for acknowledgment of receipt of ms." Reads submissions September through April only. Reports in 3 months. Time between acceptance and publication is 1 year.

THE UNIVERSITY OF CHICAGO PRESS; PHOENIX POETS SERIES, 5801 Ellis Ave., Chicago IL 60637, phone (773)702-7700, fax (773)702-9756, website http://www.press.uchicago.edu, founded 1891, poetry editor Randolph Petilos.
Book/Chapbook Needs: The University of Chicago Press publishes scholarly books and journals. "We may only publish four books in Phoenix Poets per year, and perhaps two or three books of poetry in translation per year. We occasionally publish a book of poems outside Phoenix Poets, or as a reprint from other houses." They have published poetry by Michael Chitwood, Greg Miller, Jason Sommer, Peter Sacks and Susan Hahn.
How to Submit: By invitation only. No unsolicited mss.

UNIVERSITY OF GEORGIA PRESS; CONTEMPORARY POETRY SERIES, 330 Research Dr., Suite B100, University of Georgia, Athens GA 30602-4901, phone (706)369-6135, e-mail mnunnell@ugapress.uga.edu, press founded 1938, series founded 1980, series editor Bin Ramke, poetry competition coordinator Margaret Nunnelley.
Book/Chapbook Needs: Through its annual competition, the press publishes 4 collections of poetry/year, 2 of which are by poets who have not had a book published, in paperback editions. They have published poetry by Marjorie Welish, Arthur Vogelsang, C.D. Wright, Martha Ronk and Paul Hoover.
How to Submit: "Writers should query first for guidelines and submission periods. Please enclose SASE." There are no restrictions on the type of poetry submitted, but "familiarity with our previously published books in the series may be helpful." No fax or e-mail submissions. $15 submission fee required. Make checks payable to University of Georgia Press. Manuscripts are *not* returned after the judging is completed. Always sends prepublication galleys.

UNIVERSITY OF IOWA PRESS; THE IOWA POETRY PRIZES, 119 West Park Rd., 100 Kuhl House, Iowa City IA 52242-1000.
Book/Chapbook Needs: The University of Iowa Press offers annually The Iowa Poetry Prizes for book-length mss (50-150 pgs.) by poets who have already published at least one full-length book in an edition of at least 500 copies. Winners will be published by the Press under a standard royalty contract. (This competition is the only way in which this press accepts poetry.)
How to Submit: Mss are received annually in May only. All writers of English are eligible, whether citizens of the US or not. Poems from previously published books may be included only in mss of selected or collected poems, submissions of which are encouraged. Simultaneous submissions OK if press is immediately notified if the book is accepted by another publisher. No reading fee is charged, but stamped, self-addressed packaging is required or mss will not be returned. Include name on the title page only.
Advice: "These awards have been initiated to encourage poets who are beyond the first-book stage to submit their very best work."

THE UNIVERSITY OF MASSACHUSETTS PRESS; THE JUNIPER PRIZE, P.O. Box 429, Amherst MA 01004-0429, phone (413)545-1227, fax (413)545-1226, website http://www.umass.edu/umpress, founded 1964.
Book/Chapbook Needs: The press offers an annual competition for the Juniper Prize, in alternate years to first and subsequent books. In even-numbered years (2000, 2002, etc.) only subsequent books will be considered: mss whose authors have had at least one full-length book or chapbook of poetry published or accepted for publication. Such chapbooks must be at least 30 pages, and self-published work is not considered to lie within this "books and chapbooks" category. In odd-numbered years (1999, 2001, etc.) only "first books" will be considered: mss by writers whose poems may have appeared in literary journals and/or anthologies but have not been published, or been accepted for publication, in book form. They have published *The Double Task* by Gray Jacobik; *El Coro: A Chorus of Latino and Latina Poetry* edited by Martín Espada; and *Fugitive Red* by Karen Donovan. "Poetry books are approximately $14 for paperback editions and $24 for cloth."
How to Submit: Submissions must not exceed 60 pgs. in typescript (generally 50-55 poems). Include paginated contents page; provide the title, publisher and year of publication for previously published volumes. A list of

poems published or slated for publication in literary journals and/or anthologies must also accompany the ms. Such poems may be included in the ms and must be identified. "Mss by more than one author, entries of more than one ms simultaneously or within the same year, and translations are not eligible." Entry fee: $10 plus SASE for return of ms or notification. Entries must be postmarked not later than September 30. The award is announced in April/May and publication is scheduled for the following spring. The amount of the prize is $1,000 and is in lieu of royalties on the first print run. Poet also receives 12 copies in one edition or 6 copies each if published in both hardcover and paperbound editions. Fax, call or send SASE for guidelines and/or further information to the above address. Entries are to be mailed to Juniper Prize, University of Massachusetts, Amherst MA 01004.
Also Offers: Website includes historical information about the press, staff listing, our books-in-print and seasonal catalogs, and excerpts from recently published books.

Ⓞ UNIVERSITY OF TEXAS PRESS, P.O. Box 7819, Austin TX 78713-7819, website http://www.utexas. edu/utpress, founded 1950. They are not accepting unsolicted manuscripts.

N Ⓞ Ⓞ UNLIKELY STORIES: A COLLECTION OF LITERARY ART, 209 West Dixie Ave., Marietta GA 30060, e-mail unlikely@flash.net, website http://www.flash.net/~unlikely, founded 1998, editor Jonathan Penton.
Magazine Needs: "*Unlikely Stories* is a monthly online publication containing poetry, fiction and nonfiction which falls under my own highly subjective definition of 'literary art.' I especially like work that has trouble finding publication due to adult, offensive or weird content." They want "any subject matter, including those normally considered taboo. I like informal poetry, but am open to formal poetry that demonstrates an understanding of good meter. No emotionless poetry, lies. 'I'll love you forever' is a lie; spare me." They have published poetry by Michael McNeilley, Elisha Porat, Ben Ohmart and B.M. Bradley. They receive about 500 poems a year, accept approximately 30%.
How to Submit: Submit 3 or more poems at a time. Previously published poems and simultaneous submissions OK. Cover letter preferred. E-mail and disk submissions OK. "*Unlikely Stories* is designed to promote acquaintanceship between readers and authors therefore, only multiple submissions will be accepted. I greatly prefer to see a bio; there is no maximum length." Time between acceptance and publication is 1 month. Often comments on rejections, if requested. Send SASE for guidelines or obtain via e-mail or website. Reports in 2-4 weeks. Acquires one-time rights.
Also Offers: "If a contributor asks me a question, or for editorial or business advise. I'll answer. I have edited full manuscripts for a fee." Website includes guidelines, contact information, complete content and interviews with select artists.
Advice: The editor says, "Write from the heart, if you must, but write from that part of you which is unique."

Ⓞ Ⓞ UPRISING; THE JEREMIAH REEVES POETRY PRIZE FOR JUSTICE (Specialized: political, ethnic/nationality), 241 Noble Ave., Montgomery AL 36104, phone (334)265-7613, e-mail Geri34825@aol.com, founded 1997, editor Geri Moss.
Magazine Needs: *Uprising* is a quarterly poetry journal especially interested in political poems and work on Native Americans. They want "free verse, well written work, very little if any rhyme. I want fire, thought and feeling; make the reader feel what you feel. Poems should be 32 lines or under, more if poem is exceptional. No religious, haiku or pornography." They have published poetry by Catfish McDaris, Mark Swan and Willie J. King. As a sample the editor selected these lines from "Recovering" by Fernand Roquepan:

> You are storyteller, a savage-plucked/creativity salvaged from left-hand columns/of charred books
> and torn broadsides,/(your imagined) conviviality sequestered/from vanquished mobs whose sanguine
> lyrics/toss bricks and leach needed lexicons.

Uprising is 15-20 pgs., 8½×11, desktop-published and glued into paper cover. They receive about 300 poems a year, accept approximately 25%. Press run is 150. Subscription: $16/year. Sample: $4. Make checks payable to Geri Moss.
How to Submit: Submit 3 poems at a time. No previously published poems; simultaneous submissions OK. Cover letter preferred. E-mail submissions OK, "no more than 30 lines." Time between acceptance and publication is 1-3 months. Seldom comments on rejections. Publishes theme issues occasionally. Send SASE for guidelines and upcoming themes. Reports in 1-3 months. Pays 1 copy. Acquires first rights. Open to unsolicited reviews. Send books for review consideration.
Also Offers: Sponsors The Jeremiah Reeves Poetry Prize for Justice. 1st Prize: $500, publication in contest issue and free copy; 2nd Prize: $150; 3rd Prize: $75; 4th Prize: $25. Poems can be up to 2 pgs. long. Reading fee: $5/3 poems. Proceeds from contest will go to support the E.J.I. & the Southern Poverty Law Center of Alabama to help fight injustice. Contest announced March each year. Deadline: January 15, but submissions accepted all year.
Advice: The editor says, "Poets write what you feel, don't be afraid to submit your work with the best out there. Read. Join a book swapping club and remember editors are poets who were not great poets."

Ⓞ Ⓞ UPSOUTH (Specialized: regional, religious), P.O. Box 20133, Bowling Green KY 42101-6133, phone (502)843-8018, e-mail galen.smith@bgamug.org, founded 1993, editor Galen Smith.
Magazine Needs: "*Upsouth* is a quarterly international newsletter for Southern and Catholic writers. We ask

for tasteful poems, columns, essays, etc. No works of non-Christian views will be accepted. But the works do not necessarily have to be religious or spiritual to be accepted. Our intention is to be a creative outlet for spiritual or inspirational works, but *Upsouth* also has an interest in Southern culture and its literary figures and their writings, too. We do accept works from writers and poets from other regions of the U.S. and other parts of the world. We also accept works from non-Catholic writers and writers with other religious beliefs." They have published poetry by Rory Morse, Joyce Bradshaw and Leah Maines. As a sample the editor selected these lines from "Dear Heavenly Father" by Raymond Flory:

> This day,/in this place/hold me once again./May I feel the touch

Upsouth is 12-16 pgs., 8½ × 11, photocopied and corner-stapled, includes clip art. They receive about 100 poems a year, accept approximately 10%. Press run is 75 for 50 subscribers of which 10 are libraries, 10 shelf sales. Subscription: $8. Sample: $2. "We are more likely to publish your poem if you subscribe."

How to Submit: Submit 3 poems at a time. Line length for poetry is 21 maximum. Include SASE. Previously published poems and simultaneous submissions OK. Cover letter preferred. Seldom comments on rejections. Publishes theme issues occasionally (related to the seasons). Send SASE for guidelines. Reports in 2-8 weeks. Pays 1 copy. Author retains all rights. Reviews books and chapbooks of poetry and other magazines in 250 words. Open to unsolicited reviews. Poets may also send books for review consideration.

Advice: The editor says, "We like for you to subscribe to *Upsouth*. We consider you as a friend and write you personal and encouraging letters. Our motto is 'your writing can change the world!'"

N ⚑ ◯ URBAN GRAFFITI, P.O. Box 41164, Edmonton, Alberta T6J 6M7 Canada, founded 1993, editor Mark McCawley.

Magazine Needs: Appearing 2 times a year, *Urban Graffiti* is "a litzine of transgressive, discursive, post-realist writing concerned with hard-edged urban living, alternative lifestyles, deviance—presented in their most raw and unpretentious form." They want "free verse, prose poetry; urban themes and subject matter; transgressive, discursive, post-realist and confessional work. No metaphysical, religious or Hallmark verse." They have published poetry by Lyn Lifshin, Carolyn Zonailo, Beth Jankola, Daniel Jones and Allan Demeule. As a sample the editor selected these lines from "Extremities" by Martin O'Rourke:

> still, watching you sleep, I wonder./What other deep cuts are you hiding?/If only I could slip inside
> your skin/as easily as your breath and remove them./If only I had healer's touch,/I could wipe them
> clean away.

The editor says *Urban Graffiti* is 28 pgs., magazine-sized, photocopied and saddle-stapled with paper cover, includes art/graphics. They receive about 100 poems a year, accept 10-15%. Press run is 250. Single copy: $5; subscription: $10/3 issues. Make checks payable to Mark McCawley.

How to Submit: Submit 5-8 poems at a time. No previously published poems or simultaneous submissions. E-mail submissions OK. Cover letter "with creative bio" required. Time between acceptance and publication is 6-12 months. Seldom comments on rejections. Send SASE for guidelines. Reports in 2-6 months. Pays 5 copies. Acquires first North American serial and first anthology rights. Reviews books and chapbooks of poetry and other magazines in 500-1,000 words, multi-book format. Poets may also send books for review consideration.

Advice: The editor says, "If it's raunchy, realistic, angry, sarcastic, caustic, funny, frightening, brutally honest . . . then that's what we're looking for at *UG*."

N ◯ URBAN SPAGHETTI: LITERARY ARTS JOURNAL, P.O. Box 5186, Mansfield OH 44901-5186, e-mail editor@urban-spaghetti.com, website http://www.urban-spaghetti.com, founded 1998, co-editors Cheryl Dodds and Philip Richardson.

Magazine Needs: "*Urban Spaghetti* is a biannual literary arts journal located in mid-Ohio featuring poetry, short stories and artwork from around the world. Our focus extends a hand to new poets who share a sense of social responsibility in their writing, and offer a fresh presentation and language which challenges us." They want "quality verse. All styles are accepted, but please send your best. Rhymed verse has its place. However, that place is not *Urban Spaghetti*." They have published poetry by David Citino, Lyn Lifshin, Marge Piercy and Andrea Potos. As a sample we selected these lines from "Slogans" by Philip Avery:

> He's folding into madness/The way his mother used to be/Asking questions of his feet/Does the ocean
> rush ashore/Or push the land away/Does the sky turn black/When there's nothing left to see/And what
> time is dinner served/When there's nothing left to eat

US is 60-100 pgs., digest-sized, offset litho printed and perfect-bound with slick 90 lb. paper cover, includes b&w photos and drawings. They receive about 1,200 poems a year, accept approximately 10%. Press run is 500. Single copy: $7.

How to Submit: Submit 7 poems at a time with $7 reading fee. Line length for poetry is 100 maximum. Previously published poems (with appropriate permissions) and simultaneous submissions (with notification) OK. Cover letter preferred. "All poetry submitted to *Urban Spaghetti* will be considered for publication and must be accompanied by $7 reading fee and SASE. Non-accepted submissions will be returned if proper postage and envelope are provided. Sorry, we cannot accept e-mail submissions." Reads submissions February through May for the Summer issue and August through November for the Winter issue. However, *US* accepts submissions throughout the year. Seldom comments on rejections. Publishes theme issues occasionally. Send SASE for guidelines. Reports in 6-8 weeks. "Sooner if e-mail address is provided." Pays 2 copies. Copyright reverts to author upon publication.

$ ▣ ◎ THE URBANITE; URBAN LEGEND PRESS (Specialized: horror, fantasy, themes), P.O. Box 4737, Davenport IA 52808-4737, founded 1991, editor Mark McLaughlin.
Magazine Needs: *The Urbanite* appears 3 times a year "to promote literate, character-oriented and entertaining fiction and poetry in the genre of surrealism." Each issue is based on a particular theme. Send SASE for details. They want contemporary fantasy/surrealism (maximum 2 pages/poem). No "slice-of-life, sentimental, gore, porn, Western, haiku or rambling rants against society." They have published poetry by John Benson, Tina Reigel and Wayne Edwards. As a sample the editor selected these lines from "Tree" by Pamela Briggs:
>　Another cold spring/Is that a train a siren a wolf howling/or just a chainsaw cutting into something
>　living/because it doesn't fit everyone's idea/of what a tree should be?
The Urbanite is 64-92 pgs., 8½×11, saddle-stitched or perfect-bound with 2-color glossy cover. They receive 500 poems a year, accept less than 10%. Press run is 500-1,000. Subscription: $13.50/3 issues. Sample: $5. Make checks payable to Urban Legend Press.
How to Submit: Submit up to 3 poems at a time. No simultaneous submissions. "Query first regarding previously published work." Cover letter required. Sends checklist reply form, but sometimes comments on rejections. Publishes theme issues. Send SASE for guidelines and upcoming themes. Reports within 1 month, sometimes longer. Pays $10/poem and 2 copies. Buys first North American serial rights and nonexclusive rights for public readings. ("We hold readings of the magazine at libraries, literary conventions and other venues.") Rights revert to the writer after publication.
Book/Chapbook Needs & How to Submit: In addition to the magazine, Urban Legend Press publishes 1 or more chapbooks a year. Interested poets should "submit to the magazine first, to establish a relationship with our readers." More poetry chapbooks are planned for the future.

🌐 ✔ ▣ ◎ URTHONA MAGAZINE (Specialized: religious, Buddhism), 3 Coral Park, Henley Rd., Cambridge CB1 3EA United Kingdom, phone 01223 566567, fax 01223 566568, e-mail windhorset@aol.com, website http://www.ziplink.net/~vajramat/urthona.html, founded 1992, poetry editor Ian Tromp.
Magazine Needs: *Urthona*, published biannually, explores the arts and western culture from a Buddhist perspective. They want "poetry rousing the imagination." They do not want "undigested autobiography, political, or New-Agey poems." They have published poetry by Peter Abbs, Robert Bly and Peter Redgrove. As a sample the editor selected these lines from "The Shower" by Ananda:
>　And somewhere there is gold,/and a song almost getting started/in the street we're leaving by://
>　something like tenderness, how/the spring light races and dies/over the washed squares
Urthona is 60 pgs., A4, offset printed, saddle-stapled with 4-color glossy cover, b&w photos, art and ads inside. They receive about 300 poems a year, accept approximately 40. Press run is 900 for 50 subscribers of which 4 are libraries, 500 shelf sales; 50 distributed free to Buddhist groups. Subscription: £8.50 (surface), £11.50 (airmail)/2 issues; £15 (surface), £22 (airmail)/4 issues. Sample (including guidelines): £3.50.
How to Submit: Submit 6 poems at a time. No previously published poems or simultaneous submissions. Cover letter preferred. Fax submissions OK. Reads submissions January through July only. Time between acceptance and publication is 6-8 months. Poems are circulated to an editorial board and read and selected by poetry editor. Other editors have right of veto. Reports in 1-2 months. Pays 1 copy. Acquires one-time rights. Reviews books or chapbooks of poetry or other magazines in 600 words. Open to unsolicited reviews. Poets may also send books for review consideration.
Also Offers: Sponsors annual contest with £150 1st Prize, £80 2nd Prize and five 3rd Prizes of a 2-year subscription. Submit any number of poems with a £1.50/poem entry fee. Poems must be no longer than 40 lines; 1 poem/page. Put name, address and phone on separate sheet only. Entries not returned. Deadline: January 15.

✔ $ ▢ URTHONA PRESS; BLACK SWAN PUBLICATIONS; WILLIAM BLAKE PRIZE COMPETITION, 166 W. Haywood St., #3, Asheville NC 28801, fax (828)251-6411, e-mail davehopes@earthlink.com, website http://www.urthona.org, founded 1995, editors David Hopes and Butch Lily.
Book/Chapbook Needs: Urthona Press strives to "bring the best of poetry to an expanded audience." They publish 3 paperbacks/year. One book a year is selected through the William Blake Prize Competition. The winner also receives half of the profits after expenses. Entry fee: $10. Deadline: October 31. Write for more information. They want "the best of the modern mode—like the mystical or explanatory." They do not want "workshop poems or APR clones." They have published poetry by Ann Dunn and David Hopes. Books are usually 50-100 pgs., perfect-bound, "we are noted for our beautifully designed books."
How to Submit: Submit complete ms. Previously published poems and simultaneous submissions OK. E-mail submissions OK. Cover letter preferred. Time between acceptance and publication is 1 year. Poems are circulated to an editorial board. Often comments on rejections. Replies to queries "immediately," to mss in 6 months. Pays 50% of profits after expenses and 10 author's copies (out of a press run of 1,000). "We accept but do not require subsidation." For sample books, call the above number.

◎ UTAH STATE UNIVERSITY PRESS; MAY SWENSON POETRY AWARD, Logan UT 84322-7800, phone (435)797-1362, fax (435)797-0313, e-mail mspooner@press.usu.edu, website http://www.usu.edu/~usupress, founded 1972, poetry editor Michael Spooner, publishes poetry only through the May Swenson Poetry Award competition annually. They have published *May Out West* by May Swenson; *Plato's Breath* by Randall Freisinger; *The Hammered Dulcimer* by Lisa Williams. See website for details.

insider report

Poet uses language to connect with the community of his youth

Michael Chitwood's fascination with language initially grew out of what he calls his "childhood infection" with evangelical Christianity in a small rural town in the foothills of the Blue Ridge Mountains. "I guess the poetry that first affected me was the poetry of the King James Bible. I grew up in a very religious family and, basically, that was the only reading I saw performed in the community, those wonderful cadences from the King James."

Photo by John Rosenthal

Michael Chitwood

Chitwood also cites the day-to-day vocal cadences and rhythms of his childhood community as a driving force behind his decision to become a writer. "I grew up in a place that was not bookish at all. It's predominantly a farming and factory community. There were no readers in my family, but there were storytellers, and the accent of the place is really what I think made me want to write and try to capture that accent. And I mean the deep accent that carries the emotion of a place."

After graduating from high school, Chitwood left the area to pursue a degree in English at Emory and Henry College in southwest Virginia, and later an M.F.A. from the University of Virginia. Over the next 20 years, he pursued parallel careers as both a poet and a well-published journalist. He has published several books and chapbooks of poetry, including *Salt Works* (Ohio Review Books, 1992), *Whet* (Ohio Review Books, 1995) and, most recently, *The Weave Room* (University of Chicago Press, 1998).

The Weave Room explores the community where Chitwood grew up and is a meditation on the range of social and personal tensions centered around the local textile mill where many from the community made their living. "Community becomes very important in *The Weave Room*, because it's a community under stress because of unionization," says Chitwood. "It's a community whose very strong bonds are being tested because there's division in opinion of people who want the union and those who don't. The irony is the union that is supposed to bring the community together is, in this place at this particular time, what drives people apart. And that seemed to me like a rich vein for poetry."

MICHAEL CHITWOOD

Poet
Recent Title: The Weave Room
   (University of Chicago Press)

Chitwood recalls the initial moment of inspiration as a sudden surge of feelings and images triggered by a visit to the textile mill with his father, a retired personnel manager from the mill. "*The Weave Room* happened to me as a kind of fever. There is a particular gesture that you have to do when you're in the weave room, because of the noise. It's so loud, and you're wearing ear protection. People put one hand on a shoulder and get right up in the person's ear. You say what you have to say, and then the other person has to do that back. It seemed like such a determined act of communication in the noise of this place. And from watching my father do that, all of these memories and all of these images started to rush back at me. It had been about 20 years since I worked there, but I guess I had been storing these images, and I wrote the bulk of the book in about 6 months."

"Entering the Weave Room"

> At the start bell,
> they pull the stained handle,
> and the great doors
> swing open. The blast
> is warm, a roaring hush.
> They step into this lush wind,
> like the back draft
> from a huge, unearthly flock.
>
> The strings jump in the harnesses
> of these clattering, greasy harps,
> the music here is
> how you make it.

(from *The Weave Room*, 1998, The University of Chicago Press; reprinted by permission of the author)

The clatter and racket of the textile looms permeate the fabric of the poems. In this noise, words take on special significance and seem to be the source of many strange powers and events. In one poem, an old man mutters incantations over the burned arm of another worker and by this seems to aid the healing of the injury. In another, a woman is said to remove warts by speaking to them. One worker makes dogs cringe and whine with the power of his inaudible voice. Chitwood believes these elements in the poems are an expression of his fascination with the intention and effort required when using words to communicate in the noisy environment of the textile mill. "In the weave room, basically, you're deaf. You get pieces of words. You have to speak in clipped phrases because you can't hear. Words take on a power they don't have outside of the weave room, or that they don't have unless you're a writer because words are your tools. I was fascinated with how people who might not be as attentive to language became that way because of where they worked and because of both the sound and lack of sound of their environment."

Chitwood also feels these poems represent the first time the two different sides of his personality as a journalist and poet came together and formed a whole. "Before

The Weave Room, I didn't see a whole lot of connection between my work as a journalist and my work with poetry. With *The Weave Room*, though, I did attempt to do much more documenting of a way of life, a people and a place. And so, my work as a journalist, as a note-taker, as a person who tries to fill in the blanks in a story, really came into play."

In spite of the speed with which he initially wrote the poems, Chitwood is quick to emphasize the amount of time he later takes to hone and shape his poems. "For me, poems happen in revision. The meat of them happened maybe with the first draft, but what finally fashioned them into poems worth keeping is the revision process. It's very rare for me to go back to it in a week and say there's nothing I want to change, or that nothing could benefit from better arrangement, more work."

Attention to the different levels of structure within each poem is an important component of Chitwood's craft. "Free verse has been my chosen form, although every poem brings its own formality, whether it is in pentameter or not. For me, it's often a set of images that have cohesion to them."

When it comes to the craft of seeking publication, Chitwood believes poets can benefit from sustained relationships with editors. "It's hard to get a book of poems published. So if you establish yourself with an editor, either at a magazine or a press, it's extremely beneficial. If they liked your work enough to publish it one time, I think they feel somewhat invested with you and so you are much more likely to receive a favorable reaction to the second book or the third book."

While acknowledging the importance of publication to a poet's development, Chitwood emphasizes the need for poets to return to their basic love of words and to refill their wells by reading extensively and recognizing their debt to the larger cultural stream of poetry. "The primary advice I would offer is read, read, read. Read what's going on now. Read the literary magazines. You should never be submitting to a literary magazine you haven't read. If you're serious about writing poetry, you should be subscribing to several literary magazines and picking up others at the library. You should be buying books of poetry. I think all writers are readers, and if they're not, they don't stay writers for long. So, reading is essential to me. I read poetry every day, so I'm always looking for new poets to like as well as returning to my favorites."

As a teacher of creative writing at the University of Chicago and as a visiting lecturer at other university writing programs, Chitwood's advice to aspiring poets is to focus on the particularity of words and images. "The thing I emphasize most with my students is the use of concrete images and the avoidance of abstract. We all want to write about the big ideas, and that's what we do write about, but it only works if you write about it in the particular and in the concrete. I think when students first start to write, they want to write about words with capital letters like 'Love,' 'Anger,' 'Hate' and 'Injustice.' You can practically see the words. But what you discover the longer you write is the only way to write about those issues, those very important issues, is to write about them in the particular, in the individual and in the touchable things of our lives."

—*Ian Bessler*

◎ **VEGETARIAN JOURNAL; THE VEGETARIAN RESOURCE GROUP (Specialized: children/ teens, vegetarianism)**, P.O. Box 1463, Baltimore MD 21203, website http://www.vrg.org, founded 1982.
Magazine Needs: The Vegetarian Resource Group is a publisher of nonfiction. *VJ* is a bimonthly, 36 pgs., 8½×11, saddle-stapled and professionally printed with glossy card cover. Circulation is 20,000. Sample: $3.
How to Submit: "Please no submissions of poetry from adults; 18 and under only."
Also Offers: The Vegetarian Resource Group offers an annual contest for ages 18 and under, $50 savings bond in 3 age categories for the best contribution on any aspect of vegetarianism. "Most entries are essay, but we would accept poetry with enthusiasm." Postmark deadline: May 1. Send SASE for details.

⚘ ◖ ◎ **VEHICULE PRESS; SIGNAL EDITIONS (Specialized: regional)**, P.O. Box 125 Station Place du Parc, Montreal, Quebec H2W 2M9 Canada, phone (514)844-6073, fax (514)844-7543, poetry editor Michael Harris, publisher Simon Dardick.
Book/Chapbook Needs: Vehicle Press is a "literary press with a poetry series, Signal Editions, publishing the work of Canadian poets only." They publish flat-spined paperbacks and hardbacks. They have published *White Stone: The Alice Poems* by Stephanie Bolster (winner of the 1998 Governor-General's Award for Poetry); *Facts* by Bruce Taylor and *Keep It All* by Yves Boisurt, translated by J. Cowan. As a sample they selected these lines by Carla Hartsfield:
> *Isn't it possible men/are jealous of women?/How we root ourselves/in autonomy. Like trees/women can be both things:/wound and tourniquet.*

They publish Canadian poetry which is "first-rate, original, content-conscious."
How to Submit: Query before submitting.

✓ ⚘ ◖ **VERSE**, Plymouth State College, Plymouth NH 03264, fax (603)535-2584, founded 1984, editors Brian Henry and Andrew Zawacki.
 • Poetry published in this journal also appeared in the 1997 volume of *The Best American Poetry*.
Magazine Needs: *Verse* appears 3 times/year and is "an international poetry journal which also publishes interviews with poets, essays on poetry and book reviews." They want "no specific kind; we look for high-quality poetry. Our focus is not only on American poetry, but on all poetry written in English, as well as translations." They have published poetry by August Kleinzahler, Charles Wright, Heather McHugh, John Ashbery, James Tate, Gary Soto, Tomaz Salamun, Karen Volkman, Medbh McGuckian and Simon Armitage. As a sample the editor included these lines from "The Definition of Swan" by Geoffrey Nutter:
> *One that resembles or emulates a swan/may be rightly called a "Swan," or more precisely,/"one who emulates a swan." We may say that he is swan-like./If he is long-necked and beautiful, or if he flies strongly/when once started, or sleeps in mim,/we may put him to sleep in a swannery./To "swan" is to wander aimlessly.*

Verse is 128-256 pgs., digest-sized, professionally printed and perfect-bound with card cover. They receive about 5,000 poems a year, accept approximately 100. Press run is 1,000 for 600 subscribers of which 200 are libraries, 200 shelf sales. Subscription: $15 for individuals, $27 for institutions. Current issue $6. Sample: $5.
How to Submit: Submit up to 5 poems at a time. No previously published poems; simultaneous submissions OK. Cover letter required. Time between acceptance and publication is 3-9 months. Reports in 2 months. Often comments on rejections. "The magazine often publishes special features—recent features include Scottish poetry, Latino poets, prose poetry, women Irish poets, and Australian poetry." Always sends prepublication galleys. Pays 2 copies plus a one-year subscription. Open to unsolicited reviews. Poets may also send books for review consideration.

⊕ ◖ **VIGIL; VIGIL PUBLICATIONS**, 12 Priory Mead, Bruton, Somerset BA10 0DZ England, founded 1979, poetry editor John Howard Greaves.
Magazine Needs: *Vigil* appears 2 times/year. They want "poetry with a high level of emotional force or intensity of observation. Poems should normally be no longer than 40 lines. Color, imagery and appeal to the senses should be important features. No whining self-indulgent, neurotic soul-baring poetry. Form may be traditional or experimental." They have published poetry by Michael Newman, Claudette Bass, David Flynn, Sheila Murphy and Karen Rosenberg. As a sample we selected these lines from "A Language We Shared" by Mel C. Thompson:
> *It feels lonely in our Orthodox Church/where we proclaim our lack of racism/in rooms full of colorless faces.//"Gringo," a Guatemalan poet told me,/"You could not even buy/yourself a soul."*

The digest-sized magazine is 40 pgs., saddle-stapled, professionally printed with colored matte card cover. They receive about 400 poems a year, accept approximately 60. Press run is 250 for 85 subscribers of which 6 are libraries. Subscription: £8. Sample: £3.
How to Submit: Submit up to 6 poems at a time in typed form. No previously published poems. Send SASE (or SAE and IRC) for guidelines. Sometimes sends prepublication galleys. Pays 1 copy. Editor sometimes comments on rejections.
Book/Chapbook Needs & How to Submit: Query regarding book publication by Vigil Publications. The editor offers "appraisal" for £10 for a sample of a maximum of 6 poems.

✓ ◐ **VIRGINIA LITERARY REVIEW**, 413 Newcomb Hall Station #2, Charlottesville VA 22904, e-mail tmw5G@virginia.edu, founded 1979, editor-in-chief Travis Wheeler.
Magazine Needs: *Virginia Literary Review* is published biannually "to bring together a variety of work having edge. Preferred from submissions is the fresh rendering of the traditional or experimentation. Only content in which the writer has invested, though sentimental verse and prose will not be used. All artistic media (i.e. photography and other b&w artwork)." They have published poetry by Simon Perchik, Madison Morrison and Virgil Suarez. As a sample the editor selected these lines from "Beyond the Blue Arcades of Earth" by Errol Miller:

> Eating the earth, stuffing/our mouths, our faces, our lives, until/there's blue silk/underneath, a great ghastly/projectile of a train carrying us off to somewhere/like Lincoln's farewell mourning, you watch/ the sun go down, the moon come up, you . . .

VLR is 35-40 pgs., 6½×10½, offset printed, saddle-stitched with full color process on 80 lb. cover stock with b&w inside, color front and back, ads. They receive about 400 poems a year, accept 5-10%. Press run is 2,000 for a few subscribers; most distributed free to UVA grounds, community of Charlottesville and sometimes Washington, DC. Subscription: $8/2 issues. Sample: $5.
How to Submit: Submit 3-5 poems at a time. Previously published poems OK. Cover letter with brief bio preferred. E-mail submissions OK. Reads submissions September 1 through November 1 and January 1 through March 1 only. Time between acceptance and publication is 1 month. Poems are circulated on an editorial board. "They are read and discussed by staff and editors, selections made six weeks prior to publication with final decisions handled by the editorial board." Reports in 2-3 months. Pays 2 copies. Acquires first North American serial or one-time rights.

$ ☑ **THE VIRGINIA QUARTERLY REVIEW; EMILY CLARK BALCH PRIZE**, 1 West Range, Charlottesville VA 22903, phone (804)924-3124, fax (804)924-1397, founded 1925.
Magazine Needs: *The Virginia Quarterly Review* uses about 15 pgs. of poetry in each issue, no length or subject restrictions. Issues have largely included lyric and narrative free verse, most of which features a strong message or powerful voice. The review is 220 pgs., digest-sized, flat-spined, circulation 4,000.
How to Submit: Submit up to 5 poems and include SASE. "You will *not* be notified otherwise." No simultaneous submissions. Reports in 3 months or longer "due to the large number of poems we receive." Send SASE for submission details; do not request via fax. Pays $1/line.
Also Offers: They also sponsor the Emily Clark Balch Prize, an annual prize of $500 given to the best poem published in the review during the year.

✓ $ ◎ **VISTA PUBLISHING, INC. (Specialized: nurses)**, 473 Broadway, Long Branch NJ 07740, phone (732)229-6500, fax (732)229-9647, e-mail info@vistapubl.com, website http://www.vistapubl.com, founded 1991, contact Carolyn S. Zagury.
Book/Chapbook Needs: Provides "a forum for the creative and artistic side of our nursing colleagues." Publishes 10 paperback/year. They want "poetry written by nurses, relating to nursing or healthcare." They have published poetry by Craig Betson, Susan Farese, Sarah Kimberly Eiland and Judy Schaefer. Books are usually 100 pgs., 6×9, trade paper, perfect-bound with illustrations if appropriate and 4-color cover.
How to Submit: Submit complete ms. No previously published poems; simultaneous submissions OK. E-mail submissions OK. Cover letter preferred. Has backlog to Fall 2000. Time between acceptance and publication is 2 years. Often comments on rejections. Replies in 3 months. Pays "percentage of profits."
Also Offers: Website includes contact information and a list of all current titles with prices and ordering information.

◎ **VOICES FROM THE WELL (Specialized: open mic/spoken word performers in the Twin Cities area)**, 402 S. Cedar Lake Rd., Minneapolis MN 55405, founded 1997, editor/publisher Laura Winton.
Magazine Needs: *Voices From the Well* appears 2 times a year "to showcase open mic/spoken word poets." They want "good poetry—any length or style. I prefer post-modern styles, but am open. No prosey storytelling poems; rhyming, sentimental poems; anything you'd be afraid to read to a bar full of other poets. We also take fiction up to 2,500 words and scenes/excerpts from plays/performance art pieces." They have published poetry by Leigh Herrick, Terrence J. Folz, Esther Perry and Lyle Daggett. As a sample the editor selected these lines from "Parthenogenesis" by Dave Okar:

> We are heralds at the gate/of civilization and wear the City like a runway/dressed with late fashion lines. Adam/& Eve return to sort differences with the snake/and take his submissive fangs into the temple.

The editor says *VFTW* is 20 pgs., 8½×11, newsprint and saddle-stitched cover, art on both covers, some inside art (all original), ads. Accept approximately 50-60% of poems received. Press run is 1,000 for 10 subscribers, 30 shelf sales; 40 distributed free to contributors, reviewers. Single copy: $3; subscription: $10/4 issues. Sample: $3-5. Make checks payable to Laura Winton. "To be considered poets must read at an open mic in their community. I prefer people be an ongoing part of their spoken word scene."
How to Submit: Submit 5-6 poems at a time. Previously published poems and simultaneous submissions OK. Disk submissions OK with hard copy. Time between acceptance and publication is 2-6 months. Seldom comments on rejections. Publishes theme issues occasionally. Reports in 2-6 months. Pays 3 copies plus half price discount

on additional copies. Acquires first or one-time rights. Reviews books of poetry and other magazines in 500 words, single or multi-book format.

Advice: The editor says, "Make your own scene! Don't wait for someone else to 'find' you. You can be a 'working poet,' with a little ingenuity and ambition. Poets should use every avenue available—lit mags, readings, self-publishing, cable access, etc., to make themselves visible."

⊕ ✓ ⊙ ◎ **VOICES ISRAEL (Specialized: anthology); REUBEN ROSE POETRY COMPETITION; MONTHLY POET'S VOICE (Specialized: members)**, P.O. Box 661, Metar Israel 85025, phone 972-7-6519118, fax 972-7-6519119, e-mail aschatz@bgumail.bgu.ac.il, website http://members.tripod.com/~VoicesIsrael, founded 1972, editor-in-chief Amiel Schotz, with an editorial board of 7.

Magazine Needs: *"Voices Israel* is an annual anthology of poetry in English coming from all over the world. You have to buy a copy to see your work in print. Submit all kinds of poetry (up to 4 poems), each no longer than 40 lines, in seven copies." They have published poetry by Yehuda Amichai, Eugene Dubnov, Alan Sillitoe and Gad Yaacobi. As a sample the editor selected these lines from "Tapestry" by Helen L. Schoenberg:

> It breaks the white on the wall/with its appalling knitted self/full of ugly flowers and/orange and yellow
> lines/On the floor it might look worse

Voices Israel is approximately 121 pgs., 6½×9⅜, offset from laser output on ordinary paper, flat-spined with varying cover. Circulation is 350. Subscription: $15. Sample back copy: $10. Contributor's copy: $15 airmail.

How to Submit: Previously published poems OK, "but please include details and assurance that copyright problems do not exist." No simultaneous submissions. Cover letter with brief biographical details required with submissions. Deadline: end of February each year. Reports in fall.

Also Offers: Sponsors the annual Reuben Rose Poetry Competition. Send poems of up to 40 lines each, plus $5/poem to P.O. Box 236, Kiriat Ata, Israel. Poet's name and address should be on a separate sheet with titles of poems. *The Monthly Poet's Voice*, a broadside edited by Ezra Ben-Meir, is sent only to members of the Voices Group of Poets in English.

Advice: The editor advises, "We would like to see more humorous but well constructed poetry. We like to be surprised."

Ⓝ ⊟ ◯ **VOIDING THE VOID**, % E. Lippincott, 8 Henderson Place, New York NY 10028, phone (212)628-2799, e-mail eelipp@aol.com, website http://www.vvoid.com, founded 1997, editor-in-chief Erin E. Lippincott.

Magazine Needs: *Voiding The Void* is "a monthly existential-esque reader for those for whom things sometimes/often seem (though another perceivable 'seeming' is never ruled out, of course) to suck." Their poetry needs are "very open, if author feels the work is in keeping with *Voiding The Void*'s theme of 'tangibility.' " They have published poetry by Barbara Lopez, Wynne Lippincott and Andrew Tiffen. As a sample the editor selected these lines (poet unidentified):

> She is caught in the inevitable fury/which results from finding the secret/everyone searches, but few
> unearth/its crusty pages. With those pages clenched/in her white-knocked fists, she runs.

VTV appears both on hard copy (one 8½×11 sheet printed on two sides) and one the web. They receive about 200 poems a year, accept approximately 95%. Press run is about 150 for approximately 100 subscribers. Single copy: 1 first-class stamp; subscription: $3.96/year. Make checks payable to E. Lippincott ("or simply send postage").

How to Submit: Submit up to 5 poems at a time. Line length for poetry is 50 "or so" maximum. Simultaneous submissions OK. Cover letter preferred. E-mail and disk submissions OK. Time between acceptance and publication is 1-3 months. Always comments on rejections. Publishes theme issues occasionally. Obtain guidelines and upcoming themes via e-mail or website. Reports in 1-2 months. Pays 5 copies. Acquires one-time rights. Reviews books of poetry in up to 2,000 words, single book format. Open to unsolicited reviews. Poets may also send books for review consideration.

Also Offers: Website includes writer's guidelines, correspondence information, e-mail access to editor, all back issues as well as the main display of the current issue of the hard copy.

◑ ◎ **VOL. NO. MAGAZINE (Specialized: themes)**, 24721 Newhall Ave., Newhall CA 91321, phone (805)254-0851, founded 1983, poetry editors Richard Weekley, Jerry Danielsen and Don McLeod.

Magazine Needs: *Vol. No.* appears annually and "publishes lively, concise, unafraid works. Vivid connections. No trivial, clichéd or unthoughtout work. Work that penetrates the shadow within. One-page poems have the best chance." They have published poetry by Octavio Paz, Anne Marple, Jane Hirshfield and Julian Pulley. *Vol. No.* is 32 pgs., digest-sized, saddle-stapled, circulation 300. They receive about 600 poems a year, use approximately 60, have a 6-month backlog. Subscription: $10/2 issues. Sample: $5.

🍁 ⊕ **SENDING TO A COUNTRY** other than your own? Be sure to send International Reply Coupons (IRCs) instead of stamps for replies or return of your manuscript.

How to Submit: Submit up to 6 poems at a time. Simultaneous submissions OK. Publishes theme issues. Send SASE for guidelines and upcoming themes. Reports in 1-5 months. Pays 2 copies.

$ ◎ WAKE FOREST UNIVERSITY PRESS (Specialized: bilingual/foreign language, ethnic/nationality), P.O. Box 7333, Winston-Salem NC 27109, phone (336)758-5448, fax (336)758-4691, e-mail wfupress @wfu.edu, founded 1976, director and poetry editor Dillon Johnston.
Book/Chapbook Needs: "We publish only poetry from Ireland and bilingual editions of French poetry in translation. I am able to consider only poetry written by Irish poets. I must return, unread, poetry from American poets." They have published *Collected Poems* by John Montague; *Ghost Orchid* by Michael Longley; *Selected Poems* by Medbh McGuckian; and *Opera Et Cetera* by Ciaran Carson. As a sample the editor selected the poem "Nights Thoughts" from *The Yellow Book* by Derek Mahon:
> windows flung wide on briny balconies/above an ocean of roofs and lighthouse beams;/like a storm
> lantern the wintry planet swings.

How to Submit: Query with 4-5 samples and cover letter. No simultaneous submissions. Replies to queries in 1-2 weeks, to submissions (if invited) in 2-3 months. Sometimes sends prepublication galleys. Publishes on 10% royalty contract with $500 advance, 6-8 author's copies. Buys North American or US rights.
Advice: They say, "Because our press is so circumscribed, we get few direct submissions from Ireland. Our main problem, however, is receiving submissions from American poets, whom we do not publish because of our very limited focus here. I would advise American poets to read listings carefully so they do not misdirect to presses such as ours, work that they, and I, value."

$ ◑ ◎ THE WAR CRY (Specialized: religious), 615 Slaters Lane, P.O. Box 269, Alexandria VA 22313, phone (703)684-5500, fax (703)684-5539, e-mail warcry@usn.salvationarmy.org, website http://publications.salv ationarmyusa.org, founded 1880, editor-in-chief Lt. Colonel Marlene Chase.
Magazine Needs: *The War Cry*, appearing biweekly, publishes "reports, commentary and testimonies that proclaim the gospel of Jesus Christ and His power to change lives today." They want "Christian poetry, any style, 16 lines maximum." As a sample the editor selected these lines from "Merciful Heavens!" by Ruth Glover:
> Today my skies are clear;/The night is gone,/And all my midnight sighs/And foolish fears/Have faded
> with the dawn;

The editor says *The War Cry* is 24 pgs., with photos and graphics. Press run is 300,000. Sample available for SASE.
How to Submit: Submit any number of poems at a time. Previously published poems and simultaneous submissions OK. Fax and e-mail submissions accepted. Cover letter preferred. Time between acceptance and publication varies. "Poems are screened by an editor who acts as a 'first reader,' then good ones are passed on to the editor-in-chief." Seldom comments on rejections. Publishes theme issues. Send SASE for guidelines and upcoming themes. Reports in up to 1 month. Pays 15-20¢/word and 2 copies. Buys one-time and reprint rights.
Also Offers: Website features writer's guidelines, interviews and forums.

✓ ◑ WARTHOG PRESS, 29 South Valley Rd., West Orange NJ 07052, phone (973)731-9269, founded 1979, poetry editor Patricia Fillingham.
Book/Chapbook Needs: Warthog Press publishes books of poetry "that are understandable, poetic." They have published *From the Other Side of Death* by Joe Lackey; *Wishing for the Worst* by Linda Portnay; and *Hanging On* by Joe Benevento.
How to Submit: Query with 5 samples, cover letter and SASE. "A lot of the submissions I get seem to be for a magazine. I don't publish anything but books." Simultaneous submissions OK. Ms should be "readable." Comments on rejections, "if asked for. People really don't want criticism." Pays copies, but "I would like to get my costs back."
Advice: Patricia Fillingham feels, "The best way to sell poetry still seems to be from poet to listener."

Ⓝ ⊕ ◑ ◎ WASAFIRI (Specialized: ethnic/nationality), Dept. of English, Queen Mary and Westfield College, University of London, Mile End Rd., London E1 4NS United Kingdom, phone +44(0171)775 3120, fax +44(0181)980 6200, e-mail wasafiri@qmw.ac.uk, website http://www.qmw.ac.uk/~english/publications/was afiri.html, founded 1984, editor Susheila Nasta, managing editor Richard Dyer.
Magazine Needs: *Wasafiri*, published biannually, "promotes new writing and debate on African, Asian, Caribbean and associated literatures." They want "African, Asian, Caribbean, diaspora, post-colonial, innovative, high-quality poetry." They have published poetry by Vikram Seth, Fred D'Aguiar, Marlene Nourbese Philip and Kamau Brathwaite. *Wasafiri* is 80 pgs., A4, professionally printed on coated stock, perfect-bound, with full color glossy cover, graphics, photos and ads. They receive about 350 poems a year, accept approximately 30%. Press run is 1,200 for 1,000 subscribers of which 450 are libraries, 300 shelf sales; 50 distributed free to arts council literature panel and education board. Single copy: $7.50; subscription: £18 individuals; £30 institutions/overseas. Sample: £5, £6 overseas.
How to Submit: Submit 3 poems at a time. No simultaneous submissions. Cover letter required. Disk submissions (Word or WordPerfect) OK. Time between acceptance and publication is 6-12 months. Poems are circulated to an editorial board. "Poems are considered by the editor and managing editor. Where guest editors are involved, poetry is considered by them also. Associate editors with expertise are asked to participate also." Often comments

on rejections. Publishes theme issues. Send SASE (or SAE and IRC) for guidelines and upcoming themes or obtain via e-mail or website. Special theme issues include "Mauritian Literature" (Autumn 1999); "Migrant Writing in Europe" (Spring 2000); and "Creative Writing" (Autumn 2000). Reports in 6-12 months. Sometimes sends prepublication galleys. Pays 1 copy. Acquires all rights. Returns rights with editor's permission. Reviews books or chapbooks of poetry or other magazines. Open to unsolicited reviews. Poets may also send books for review consideration.

WASCANA REVIEW, Dept. of English, University of Regina, Regina, Saskatchewan S4S 0A2 Canada, phone (306)585-4302, fax (306)585-4827, e-mail kathleen.wall@uregina.ca, founded 1966, editor Kathleen Wall.

Magazine Needs: *Wascana Review* appears twice a year publishing contemporary poetry and short fiction along with critical articles on modern and post-modern literature. "We look for high-quality literary poetry of all forms. No haiku or doggerel. No long poems. No concrete poetry." They have published poetry by Beth Goobie, Robert Cooperman, Lea Littlewolfe and Susanna Roxman. The editor says *WR* is a trade-sized paperback, 75-100 pgs., no art/graphics, no ads. They receive about 200-300 submissions a year, accept under 10%. Press run is 400 for 192 subscribers of which 134 are libraries, 100 shelf sales. Subscription: $10/year, $12 outside Canada. Sample: $5.

How to Submit: No previously published poems or simultaneous submissions. Cover letter required. SASE (or SAE and IRCs) necessary for return of mss. "Poems are read by at least two individuals who make comments and/or recommendations. Poetry editor chooses poems based on these comments. Poets may request information via e-mail. But no faxed or e-mailed submissions, please." Poets may also send SASE for guidelines and upcoming themes. Often comments on rejections. Reports within 6 months. Pays $10/page plus contributor's copy and 1-year subscription. Buys first North American serial rights. Reviews books of poetry in both single and multi-book format.

Advice: The editor says, "*WR* will be featuring special issues from time to time. Poets should watch for news of these in upcoming editions."

WASHINGTON SQUARE, A JOURNAL OF THE ARTS, 19 University Place, Third Floor, New York University Graduate Creative Writing Program, New York NY 10003, founded 1994 as *Washington Square* (originally founded in 1979 as *Ark/Angel*), editor Jennifer Keller.

Magazine Needs: Published semiannually, *Washington Square* is "a non-profit literary journal publishing fiction, poetry and essays by new and established writers. It's edited and produced by the students of the NYU Creative Writing Program." They want "all poetry of serious literary intent. No lazy poetry." They have published poetry by Marilyn Chin, Paul Muldoon, Pattiann Rogers, Sharon Olds and Philip Levine. The editor says *WS* is 128 pgs. Press run is 1,000. Subscription: $12. Sample: $6.

How to Submit: Submit up to 6 poems at a time. No previously published poems; simultaneous submissions OK if noted. Time between acceptance and publication is 1-6 months. Poems are circulated to an editorial board. "The poetry editors and editorial staff read all submissions, discuss and decide which poems to include in the journal." Sometimes comments on rejections. Send SASE for guidelines or obtain via website. Reports in 4-6 weeks. Acquires first North American serial rights. Sometimes reviews books and chapbooks of poetry and other magazines in 300 words. Open to unsolicited reviews. Poets may also send books for review consideration.

Also Offers: Sponsors the *Washington Square* Literary Contest, an annual award of $250 and publication in *Washington Square*. Submissions must be previously unpublished and must include the author's name on the back of each page. Send SASE for entry form and guidelines. Entry fee: $10 (includes subscription).

WATER MARK PRESS, 138 Duane St., New York NY 10013, founded 1978, editor Coco Gordon. Currently they do not accept any unsolicited poetry.
- Note: Please do not confuse Water Mark Press with the imprint Watermark Press, used by other businesses.

WATERWAYS: POETRY IN THE MAINSTREAM (Specialized: themes); TEN PENNY PLAYERS (Specialized: children/teen/young adult); BARD PRESS, 393 St. Paul's Ave., Staten Island NY 10304-2127, phone (718)442-7429, fax (718)442-4978, e-mail 72713.3625@compuserve.com, website http://www.tenpennyplayers.org, founded 1977, poetry editors Barbara Fisher and Richard Spiegel.

Magazine Needs: Bard Press "publishes poetry by adult poets in a magazine [*Waterways*] that is published 11 times/year. We do theme issues and are trying to increase an audience for poetry and the printed and performed word. The project produces performance readings in public spaces and is in residence year round at the New York public library with workshops and readings. We publish the magazine *Waterways*, anthologies and chapbooks. We are not fond of haiku or rhyming poetry; never use material of an explicit sexual nature. We are open to reading material from people we have never published, writing in traditional and experimental poetry forms. While we do 'themes,' sometimes an idea for a future magazine is inspired by a submission so we try to remain open to poets' inspirations. Poets should be guided however by the fact that we are children's and animal rights advocates and are a NYC press." They have published poetry by Ida Fasel, Kit Knight, Terry Thomas and Will Inman. *Waterways* is 40 pgs., 4¼×7, photocopied from various type styles, saddle-stapled, using b&w drawings, matte card cover. They use 60% of poems submitted. Press run is 150 for 58 subscribers of which 12 are libraries. Subscription: $20. Sample: $2.60.

How to Submit: Submit less than 10 poems for first submission. Simultaneous submissions OK. Send SASE for guidelines for approaching themes. "Since we've taken the time to be very specific in our response, writers should take seriously our comments and not waste their emotional energy and our time sending material that isn't within our area of interest. Sending for our theme sheet and for a sample issue and then objectively thinking about the writer's own work is practical and wise. Manuscripts that arrive without a return envelope are not sent back." Editors sometimes comment on rejections. Reports in less than a month. Pays 1 copy. Acquires one-time publication rights.

Book/Chapbook Needs & How to Submit: Chapbooks published by Ten Penny Players are "by children and young adults only—*not by submission*; they come through our workshops in the library and schools. Adult poets are published through our Bard Press imprint, *by invitation only*. Books evolve from the relationship we develop with writers we publish in *Waterways* and whom we would like to give more exposure."

Also Offers: They hold contests for children only.

Advice: The editors advise, "We suggest that poets attend book fairs. It's a fast way to find out what we are publishing. Without meaning to sound 'precious' or unfriendly, the writer should understand that small press publishers doing limited editions and all production work inhouse are working from their personal artistic vision and know exactly what notes will harmonize, effectively counterpoint and meld. Many excellent poems are sent back to the writers by *Waterways* because they don't relate to what we are trying to create in a given month."

WAY STATION MAGAZINE, 1319 S. Logan-MLK, Lansing MI 48910-1340, founded 1989, managing editor Randy Glumm.

Magazine Needs: *Way Station*, published occasionally, strives "to provide access and encourage beginning writers, while courting the established." They want "emerging cultures, world view, humanity direction, relationships—try all. No rhyme unless truly terrific." They do not want "religious or openly militant gay or lesbian poetry. Use common sense and discretion." They have published poetry by Charles Bukowski, Diane Wakoski, Stuart Dybek, Ethridge Knight and Terri Jewell. *Way Station* is 52 pgs., 8½×11, offset printed, saddle-stitched with heavy card cover, b&w art, photos and ads. They receive about 300 poems a year, accept approximately 20-30%. Press run is 1,000 for 35 subscribers of which 2 are libraries, 200 shelf sales; 500 distributed free to potential advertisers, readers, libraries and universities. Subscription: $18. Sample: $6.

How to Submit: Submit 5 poems with name and address on each page and $5 processing fee (returned if work is rejected). Previously published poems and simultaneous submissions OK. Cover letter preferred. Time between acceptance and publication is 1-2 months, sometimes longer. "If not struck immediately, I then put it aside and re-read later 3-4 times. I might also circulate if through a panel of volunteer readers." Often comments on rejections. Send SASE for guidelines. Reports in 1-2 months. Pays 2 copies. Acquires one-time or first North American serial rights. Reviews books or chapbooks of poetry or other magazines "if I have time." Open to unsolicited reviews. Poets may also send books for review consideration.

Advice: The editor says, "It's best to check out your own work. Get advice from coaches, instructors prior to submitting. Also get sample copies of magazines you intend to submit to—this can only help you."

WELCOME HOME; MOTHERS AT HOME, INC. (Specialized: mothers, parenting, families, children), 8310A Old Courthouse Rd., Vienna VA 22182, e-mail mah@mah.org, website http://www.mah.org, founded 1984, manuscript coordinator Kate Murphy.

Magazine Needs: *Welcome Home* is a monthly publication of "support and encouragement for at-home mothers." They want "poetry about the experience of parenting. Nothing long or obscure." *WH* is 32 pgs., digest-sized, professionally printed and saddle-stapled with paper cover, includes original art and photos. They receive about 240 poems a year, accept approximately 8%. Press run is 16,000 for 14,000 subscribers of which 200 are libraries. Subscription: $18. Sample: $2. Make checks payable to *Welcome Home*.

How to Submit: Previously published poems and simultaneous submissions OK. Cover letter preferred. Disk submissions OK. "We prefer paper mailed to the office." Time between acceptance and publication is 6 months. Poems are circulated to an editorial board. Seldom comments on rejections. Publishes theme issues occasionally. Send SASE for guidelines. Reports in 1 month. Pays $10 and 5 copies. Acquires one-time rights.

Also Offers: Website includes writer's guidelines.

WELLSPRING, % James Sprunt Community College, P.O. Box 398, Kenansville NC 28349-0398, phone (910)296-2481, fax (910)296-1636, e-mail dlrobert@duplinnet.com, founded 1991, co-editors Dave Roberts and Becke Roughton.

Magazine Needs: *Wellspring* appears annually in September "to publish high quality poetry, fiction, nonfiction, drawings, and photographs by artists and writers ranging from students to professionals." They want "any kind of poetry as long as it is well written. No poetry that is overly sentimental or contains major profanity." They have published poetry by Anthony Abbott, Maureen Ryan Griffin, Al Maginnes and R.T. Smith. As a sample the editor selected these lines from "Pete Knows" by Mary Wilmer:

> My black cat, Pete, lies/in the sun on the blue oriental/bathing himself with his bright/pink tongue,
> hind leg poised/in the air, attention focused,/like a ballet dancer in arabesque.

Wellspring is about 84 pgs., 6×9, offset printed and perfect-bound with 80 lb. cover stock cover, includes b&w

drawings and photos. They receive about 200 poems a year, accept approximately 10%. Press run is 500 for 50 subscribers, 300 shelf sales. Single copy: $5. Sample back issue: $3. Make checks payable to JSCC-Wellspring. **How to Submit:** Submit up to 5 poems at a time. No previously published poems; simultaneous submissions OK (please indicate in cover letter). Cover letter preferred. "Include brief bio in cover letter or separately. Submit letter-quality copies suitable for scanning." Reads submissions year round, "but those mailed after December 31 may be considered for a later issue." Time between acceptance and publication is 6-12 months. Poems are circulated to an editorial board. "Students and faculty members at James Sprunt Community College provide preliminary evaluations; co-editors make final selections." Seldom comments on rejections. Send SASE for guidelines. Reports in 2 months. Pays 1 copy. Acquires first North American serial rights.

$ ◓ WESLEYAN UNIVERSITY PRESS, 110 Mt. Vernon, Middletown CT 06459, phone (860)685-2420, founded 1957, editor-in-chief Suzanna Tamminen.
Book/Chapbook Needs: Wesleyan University Press is one of the major publishers of poetry in the nation. They publish 4-6 titles/year. They have published poetry by James Dickey, Joy Harjo, James Tate and Yusef Komunyakaa.
How to Submit: Send query and SASE. Considers simultaneous submissions. Send SASE for guidelines. Responds to queries in 6-8 weeks, to mss in 2-4 months. Pays royalties plus 10 copies. Poetry publications from Wesleyan tend to get widely (and respectfully) reviewed.

◓ WEST ANGLIA PUBLICATIONS, P.O. Box 2683, La Jolla CA 92038, editor Helynn Hoffa, publisher Wilma Lusk.
Book Needs: West Anglia Publications wants only the best poetry and short stories and publishes 1 paperback/year. They want "contemporary poems, well wrought by poets whose work has already been accepted in various fine poetry publications. No poets who have not published in various poetry publications, nor studied the craft/art of poetry." They have published poetry by Gary Morgan, Robert Wintringer and John Theobald. As a sample the editor selected these lines from "Alone" in *Rings of Saturn, Selected and New Poems, 1990* by Kathleen Iddings:

> Tonight a hot wind/stirs the eucalyptus./Umbrella oaks temple the silence./How many wickless days/
> have I clung/to this forked bough?/In the brittle crackle of leaves/Earth's low notes curl silver./Moon's
> match strikes igniting stars./Below me the yoked road,/lost in its wandering/enters the long tunnel of
> night./Where are the wild flowers/to soften the armored mountain?

Books are usually approximately 75-100 pgs., 5½ × 8½, perfect-bound. Sample book: $10.
How to Submit: Query with 6 poems, cover letter, professional bio and SASE.

◒ WEST BRANCH, Bucknell Hall, Bucknell University, Lewisburg PA 17837, founded 1977.
Magazine Needs: *West Branch* is a literary biannual, using quality poetry. Free verse is the dominant form—lyric, narrative and dramatic—occasionally longer than one page, with the emphasis on voice and/or powerful content. They have published poetry by D. Nurkse, Deborah Burnham, Jim Daniels, Anneliese Wagner, Betsy Sholl, David Citino, Barbara Crooker and David Brooks. It is 100-120 pgs., digest-sized, circulation 500. Subscription: $7, $11/4 issues. Sample: $3.
How to Submit: Submit 3-6 poems. Line length for poetry is 20 minimum, 40 maximum. No simultaneous submissions. "Each poem is judged on its own merits, regardless of subject or form. We strive to publish the best work being written today." Reports in 6-8 weeks. Pays copies and subscription. Acquires first rights. Reviews books and chapbooks of poetry but only those by writers who have been published in *West Branch*.

⚇ $ ◒ ◎ WEST COAST LINE (Specialized: regional), 2027 EAA, Simon Fraser University, Burnaby, British Columbia V5A 1S6 Canada, phone (604)291-4287, founded 1990, editor Roy Miki.
Magazine Needs: *West Coast Line* is published 3 times/year and "favors work by both new and established Canadian writers, but it observes no borders in encouraging original creativity. Our focus is on contemporary poetry, short fiction, criticism and reviews of books." They have published poetry by Rodrigo Toscano, Nicole Brossard, Hiromi Goto and Pasquale Verdicchio. The magazine is 144 pgs., 6 × 9, handsomely printed on glossy paper and flat-spined. They receive about 500-600 poems a year, accept approximately 20. Approximately 40 pages of poetry/issue. Press run is 800 for 500 subscribers of which 350 are libraries, 150 shelf sales. Single copy: $10; subscription: $25.
How to Submit: Submit poetry ". . . in extended forms; excerpts from works in progress; experimental and innovative poems; to 400 lines." No previously published poetry or simultaneous submissions. Time between acceptance and publication is 2-8 months. Publishes theme issues. Send SASE for guidelines or request via e-mail. Reports in 3-4 months. Pays $8 (Canadian)/printed page plus a 1-year subscription and 2 copies. Mss returned only if accompanied by sufficient Canadian postage or IRC.

THE OPENNESS TO SUBMISSIONS INDEX at the back of this book lists all publishers in this section by how open they are to submissions.

Advice: The editor says, "We have a special concern for contemporary writers who are experimenting with, or expanding the boundaries of, conventional forms of poetry, fiction and criticism. That is, poetry should be formally innovative. We recommend that potential contributors send a letter of inquiry before submitting a manuscript."

WEST WIND REVIEW (Specialized: anthology), 1250 Siskiyou Blvd., Ashland OR 97520, phone (541)552-6581, e-mail westwind@tao.sou.edu, website http://www.sou.edu/stu_affa/westwind/index.htm, founded 1980.

Magazine Needs: *West Wind Review* publishes an annual anthology each spring in May, editor of anthology changes yearly. They are "looking for sensitive but strong verse that celebrates all aspects of men's and women's experiences, both exalted and tragic. We are looking to print material that reflects ethnic and social diversity." They have published poetry by Simon J. Ortiz and Lawson F. Inada. As a sample the editor selected these lines from "after the burnin moon" by Clarissa Armstrong:

> given to daydreams that make her go weak in the knees; of her/limbs wrapped 'round Rooney's back
> like writhing white snakes,/of pushing a carriage full of sky-eyed babies; and her/own secret garden
> of bushes budding paper money in Spring. Of/babies bawling soft as lambs in the wake of wet-woolen
> sleep

The anthology is usually 224 pgs., digest-sized, handsomely printed and flat-spined. They receive about 1,200 submissions a year, publish 50-60 poems, 10 short stories and 16 pgs. of art. Press run is 600. Sample: "at current year's price."

How to Submit: Submit up to 5 poems not exceeding 50 lines each. Manuscripts should have poet's name and address on first page." Include SASE. No previously published poems; simultaneous submissions OK. Cover letter required with name, address, phone number and a brief bio. No e-mail submissions. Deadline: November 15 for publication in late May. Send SASE for guidelines. Reports in March. Pays 1 copy.

Also Offers: Offers $25 award for best poem. Website includes "general 'who are we' e-mail address, cool links to other poetry sites."

WESTERLY; PATRICIA HACKETT PRIZE, Centre for Studies in Australian Literature, University of Western Australia, Nedlands 6907, Australia, phone (08)9380-2101, fax (08) 9380-1030, e-mail westerly@uniwa.uwa.edu.au, website http://www.arts.uwa.edu.au/westerly, founded 1956, editors Dennis Haskell and Delys Bird.

Magazine Needs: *Westerly* is a literary and cultural quarterly publishing quality short fiction, poetry, literary critical, socio-historical articles and book reviews with special attention given to Australia and the Indian Ocean region. "No restrictions on creative material. Our only criterion [for poetry] is literary quality. We don't dictate to writers on rhyme, style, experimentation, or anything else. We are willing to publish short or long poems. We do assume a reasonably well-read, intelligent audience. Past issues of *Westerly* provide the best guides. Not consciously an academic magazine." The quarterly magazine is 144 pgs., 5½×8½, "electronically printed," with some photos and graphics. Press run is 1,200. Single copy: $8 (Aus.) plus overseas postage via surface mail; subscription: $38 (Aus.)/year or $10 by e-mail. Sample: $8 (Aus.) surface mail, $12 (Aus.) airmail.

How to Submit: Submit up to 6 poems at a time. Fax and e-mail submissions OK ("but replies may only be made for acceptances.") "Please do not send simultaneous submissions. Covering letters should be brief and nonconfessional." Time between acceptance and publication is 3 months. Publishes occasional theme issues. Reports in 2-3 months. Pays minimum of $30 plus 1 copy. Buys first publication rights; requests acknowledgment on reprints. Reviews books of poetry in 500-1,000 words. Open to unsolicited reviews. Poets may also send books to Reviews Editor for review consideration.

Also Offers: The Patricia Hackett Prize (value approx. $500) is awarded in March for the best contribution published in *Westerly* during the previous calendar year. Website includes details of past issues, subscription form and current issue.

Advice: The advice of the editors is: "Be sensible. Write what matters for you but think about the reader. Don't spell out the meanings of the poems and the attitudes to be taken to the subject matter—i.e., trust the reader. Don't be swayed by literary fashion. Read the magazine if possible before sending submissions."

WESTERN ARCHIPELAGO REVIEW (Specialized: regional), P.O. Box 803282, Santa Clarita CA 91380, phone (213)383-3447, e-mail adorxyz@aol.com, founded 1999, editor Jovita Ador Lee.

Magazine Needs: *WAR* "publishes verse with a focus on the civilizations of Asia and the Pacific. All types of verse considered." As a sample the editor selected these lines (poet unidentified):

> Angel of death, the High Priestess dances,/Turning her silk;/Servant of the temple, covered in black
> robes,/Black cloth of Bali.

The editor says *WAR* is 12 pgs., 5½×8½, with glossy cover. Press run is 100. Subscription: $9. Sample: $3. Make checks payable to GoodSAMARitan Press

How to Submit: Submit 3 poems at a time. Previously published poems and simultaneous submissions OK. E-mail, fax and disk submissions OK. Cover letter with SASE required. Reads submissions September to June. Time between acceptance and publication is 6 weeks. Poems are circulated to an editorial board. Send SASE for guidelines. Reports in 6 weeks. Acquires all rights. Does not return rights. Reviews books and chapbooks of poetry and other magazines in 100 words. Poets may send books for review consideration.

$ **WESTERN DIGEST (Specialized: cowboy poetry)**, 400 Whiteland Dr. NE, Calgary, Alberta T1Y 3M7 Canada, phone (403)280-3424, e-mail crossbow@cadvision.com, website http://www.smithy.net/cross bow/index.html, founded 1995, publisher Douglas Sharp.

Magazine Needs: *Western Digest* is a bimonthly magazine of western fiction and cowboy poetry. They want "cowboy poetry of 16-48 lines, rhyming with equal length stanzas. Prefer humorous poems." The publisher says *WD* is 20 pgs., 8½×11. They receive about 20 poems a year, accept approximately 70%. Press run is 300 for 200 subscribers. Subscription: $18. Sample: $4.

How to Submit: Previously published poems and simultaneous submissions OK. Cover letter required. E-mail submissions OK. Often comments on rejections. Reports in 3 weeks. Pays $1/line (Canadian) and 1 copy.

$ **WESTERN HUMANITIES REVIEW**, Dept. of English, 3500 LNCO, University of Utah, Salt Lake City UT 84112, phone (801)581-6070, fax (801)585-5167, e-mail whr@lists.utah.edu, founded 1947, managing editor Jenny Mueller.

● Poetry published in this review has been selected for inclusion in the 1992, 1993, 1995 and 1998 volumes of *The Best American Poetry*.

Magazine Needs: *WHR* is a quarterly of poetry, fiction and a small selection of nonfiction. They want "quality poetry of any form, including translations." They have published poetry by Philip Levine, Bin Ramke, Lucie Brock-Broido, Timothy Liu and Pattiann Rogers. *WHR* is 96-125 pgs., 6×9, professionally printed on quality stock and perfect-bound with coated card cover. They receive about 900 submissions a year, accept less than 10%, publish approximately 60 poets. Press run is 1,100 for 1,000 subscribers of which 900 are libraries. Subscription: $20 to individuals in the US. Sample: $6.

How to Submit: "We do not publish writer's guidelines because we think the magazine itself conveys an accurate picture of our requirements." No previously published poems; simultaneous submissions OK. No fax or mail submissions. Reads submissions October 1 through May 31 only. Time between acceptance and publication is 3-6 issues. Managing editor Jenny Mueller makes an initial cut then the poetry editor makes the final selections. Seldom comments on rejections. Occasionally publishes special issues. Reports in 1-6 months. Pays $35/poem and 2 copies. Acquires first serial rights.

Also Offers: They also offer an annual spring contest for Utah poets. Prize is $250.

$ **WESTERN PRODUCER PUBLICATIONS; WESTERN PEOPLE (Specialized: regional)**, P.O. Box 2500, Saskatoon, Saskatchewan S7K 2C4 Canada, phone (306)665-3500, fax (306)934-2401, e-mail people@producer.com, founded 1923, managing editor Michael Gillgannon.

Magazine Needs: *Western People* is a magazine supplement to *The Western Producer*, a weekly newspaper, circulation 100,000, which uses "poetry about the people, interests and environment of rural Western Canada." The magazine-sized supplement is 16 pgs., newsprint, with color and b&w photography and graphics. They receive about 500 submissions of poetry a year, use 60-70. Sample free for postage (2 oz.)—and ask for guidelines.

How to Submit: Submit up to 3 poems at a time, 1 per page. Name, address and telephone number in upper-left corner of each page. Reports within 2 weeks. Pays $15-50/poem.

Advice: The editor comments, "It is difficult for someone from outside Western Canada to catch the flavor of this region; almost all the poems we purchase are written by Western Canadians."

WESTVIEW: A JOURNAL OF WESTERN OKLAHOMA, 100 Campus Dr., SWOSU, Weatherford OK 73096, phone (580)774-3168, founded 1981, editor Fred Alsberg.

Magazine Needs: *Westview* is a biannual publication that is "particularly interested in writers from the Southwest; however, we are open to work of quality by poets from elsewhere. We publish free verse, prose poems and formal poetry." They have published poetry by Walter McDonald, Robert Cooperman, Alicia Ostriker and James Whitehead. *Westview* is 44 pgs., magazine-sized, saddle-stapled, with glossy card cover in full-color. They receive about 500 poems a year, accept approximately 5%. Press run is 700 for 300 subscribers of which about 25 are libraries. Subscription: $10/2 years. Sample: $4.

How to Submit: Submit 5 poems at a time. Cover letter including biographical data for contributor's note required with submissions. "Poems on 3.5 computer disk are welcome so long as they are accompanied by the hard copy and the SASE has the appropriate postage." Editor comments on submissions "when close. Mss are circulated to an editorial board; we usually respond within two to three months." Pays 1 copy.

WEYFARERS; GUILDFORD POETS PRESS, 1 Mountside, Guildford, Surrey GU2 5JD United Kingdom (for submissions), 9, White Rose Lane, Woking, GU22 7JA United Kingdom (for subscriptions), phone (01483)504566, founded 1972, administrative editor Martin Jones, poetry editors Stella Stocker, Martin Jones and Jeffery Wheatley.

Magazine Needs: They say, "We publish *Weyfarers* magazine three times a year. All our editors are themselves poets and give their spare time free to help other poets." They describe their needs as "all types of poetry, serious and humorous, free verse and rhymed/metered, but mostly 'mainstream' modern. Excellence is the main consideration. No hard porn, graphics, way-out experimental. Any subject publishable, from religious to satire. Not more than 40 lines." They have published poetry by Kenneth Pobo and Richard Ball (US), Michael Henry and Susan Skinner. As a sample the editors selected these lines from "The Lonely Places" by R.L. Cook:

> . . . *Set in the rim of the globe, spots on the atlas,/Stern, hard & desolate,/Far from the bedlam towns,*

> these lonely places,/Have waited & will wait,//Till they are left, one day, to the cold-eyed seabirds,/
> Gannet, guillemot, gull,/And the last croft, crumbling covered by the bracken,/And the wild sheep's
> skull . . .

The digest-sized, saddle-stapled format contains about 28 pgs. of poetry (of a total of 32 pgs.). They receive about 1,200-1,500 poems a year, accept approximately 125. The magazine has a circulation of "about 300," including about 200 subscribers of which 5 are libraries. Sample (current issue): $5 in cash US or £2 UK.

How to Submit: Submit up to 6 poems, one poem/sheet. No previously published poems or simultaneous submissions. Closing dates for submissions are end of January, May and September. Usually comments briefly on rejections. Pays 1 copy.

Also Offers: "We are associated with Surrey Poetry Center, which has an annual Open Poetry Competition. The prize-winners are published in *Weyfarers*."

Advice: Their advice to poets is, "Always read a magazine before submitting. And read plenty of modern poetry."

WHELKS WALK REVIEW; WHELKS WALK PRESS, 37 Harvest Lane, Southampton NY 11968, phone (516)283-5122, fax (516)283-1902, e-mail whelkswalk@aol.com, website http://members.aol.com/Whelks Walk/Whelk.html, press founded 1995, magazine founded 1998, publisher Marianne Mitchell, editor-in-chief Joan Peternel.

Magazine Needs: *Whelks Walk Review* is "a biannual magazine of the arts—verbal, visual and performing. For a general audience. Includes poems, fiction, essays, reviews, interviews." They want "all forms except non-verbal and prose poems. No pornography; no vulgar slang; no obscenities." They have published poetry by Michael Bugeja, Emma Crebolder, Aleš Debeljak and Harvey Shapiro. As a sample the editor selected these lines from "Houses Remember Me" by Diana Chang:

> After I left . . . a corner of that first place/and an early moment there still search for me,/I like to think.

The editor says *WWR* is 105-120 pgs., 5×7, typeset and perfect-bound, 2-color cover, includes photos, drawings. Subscription: $15/year (for 2 issues). Single copy: $8. Sample or back copy: $5. Make checks payable to Whelks Walk Press.

How to Submit: Submit up to 4 poems at a time. Previously published poems OK (occasionally); no simultaneous submissions. Cover letter preferred but not necessary. Deadlines: June 15 and December 15. Time between acceptance and publication is several days to several months. Send SASE for guidelines. Reports in several days to several months. Pays 1 copy. Acquires first or one-time rights.

Book/Chapbook Needs & How to Submit: Query. "Under Whelks Walk Press, we have published one chapbook (1995) which includes several genres (poems, fiction, essays, interview, review). We have also published one full-length paperback book of poems (1997), 103 pgs. We are currently busy bringing out our magazine, *Whelks Walk Review*. We may publish a full-length book, poems or fiction, in 2000." Send SASE for details.

$ WHETSTONE; WHETSTONE PRIZE, P.O. Box 1266, Barrington IL 60011-1266, phone (847)382-5626, fax (847)382-3685, editors Sandra Berris, Marsha Portnoy and Jean Tolle.

Magazine Needs: *Whetstone* appears annually in late November and publishes poetry, short fiction, novel excerpts and creative nonfiction. "We favor the concrete over the abstract, the accessible over the obscure. We like poets who use words in ways that transform them and us, whose images add a new dimension, whose meaning goes beyond first impression." They have published poetry by Michael Atkinson, Helen Reed and Susan Terris. As a sample an editor selected these lines from "November" by Ted May:

> Thanksgiving! set the feast/for the flowers are starving/and will burn ferociously

It is 96 pgs., digest-sized, professionally printed, perfect-bound with semi-gloss card cover. Press run is 850 for 200 subscribers of which 5 are libraries, 600 shelf sales. Subscription: $8.50; back issues $5. Sample (including guidelines): $5. Make checks payable to BAAC.

How to Submit: Submit up to 7 poems at a time. Reports in 3-4 months. Always sends prepublication galleys. Pays 2 copies plus a monetary amount that varies. Buys first North American serial rights.

Also Offers: Awards the Whetstone Prize of $500 for the best poetry or fiction in each issue, and additional prizes as well.

WHISKEY ISLAND MAGAZINE, English Dept., Cleveland State University, Cleveland OH 44115, phone (216)687-2056, fax (216)687-6943, e-mail whiskeyisland@popmail.csuohio.edu, website http://www.csuo hio.edu/whiskey_island, founded 1968, student editors change yearly, contact poetry editor.

Magazine Needs: *Whiskey Island* appears biannually in January and July and publishes poetry, fiction, nonfiction and an interview each issue. They want "advanced writing. We want a range of poetry from standard to experimental and concrete poetry. Thought provoking." They have published poetry by Vivian Shipley, Kathleene West, Claudia Rankine, Patricia Smith and Dennis Saleh. As a sample the editor selected these lines from "Pigeon Bones & a Pair of Pants" by Ben Gulyas:

> he is . . . in his dreams/a man, mad with the deep blue of wooden corners/under a high eclipse where
> moon & sun/make dark luminous love/he is a man mad with something that breaks him open/and
> makes him sing—

Whiskey Island Magazine is 86-120 pgs., 6×9, professionally printed and perfect-bound with glossy stock cover and b&w art. They receive 1,000-1,500 poetry mss a year, accept approximately 6%. Press run is 1,200 for 200 subscribers of which 20 are libraries, about 200 shelf sales. Subscription: $12, $20 overseas. Sample: $5. Make checks payable to *Whiskey Island Magazine*.

How to Submit: Submit up to 10 pgs. of poetry at a time. Include SASE for reply/ms return. Include name, address, e-mail, fax and phone number on each page. No previously published poems or simultaneous submissions. Include cover letter with brief bio. Fax submissions OK. E-mail submissions OK for mss outside of US. Send as MSWord, WordPerfect or ASCII files. Reads submissions September through May only. "Poets may fax inquiries and work that runs a few pages (longer submissions should be mailed). They may e-mail requests for submission and contest information." Poems are circulated to an editorial committee. Send SASE for guidelines or obtain via website. Reports within 4 months. Pays 2 copies, and 1 year subscription.

Also Offers: Sponsors an annual poetry contest. 1st Prize: $300; 2nd Prize: $200; 3rd Prize: $100. Entry fee: $10. Entries accepted October 1 through January 31. Query regarding contest for 2000. "Our website provides writer's guidelines, contest information, a history of the publication, and will, in the future, include poetry and fiction."

Advice: The editor says, "Send a full ten pages of poetry. We like to see a broad sample of your work. Include SASEs and your name, address and phone for reply."

WHITE EAGLE COFFEE STORE PRESS; FRESH GROUND (Specialized: anthology), P.O. Box 383, Fox River Grove IL 60021-0383, phone (847)639-9200, e-mail wecspress@aol.com, website http://members.aol.com/wecspress, founded 1992.

Magazine Needs & How to Submit: *Fresh Ground* is an annual anthology, appearing in November, that features "some of the best work of emerging poets. We're looking for edgy, crafted poetry. Poems for this annual are accepted during May and June only."

Book/Chapbook Needs: White Eagle is a small press publishing 5-6 chapbooks/year. "Alternate chapbooks are published by invitation and by competition. Author published by invitation becomes judge for next competition." They are "open to any kind of poetry. No censorship at this press. Literary values are the only standard. Generally not interested in sentimental or didactic writing." They have published poetry by Timothy Russell, Peter Blair, David Craig, Leilani Wright and Jill Peláez Baumgaertner. As a sample the editors included these lines from "Volunteer" in *The Wide View* by Linda Lee Harper:

> Her Head-Start students love her bosom plush as a divan./They celebrate and grieve there, noodle/
> their faces deeper, deeper, dangerous comfort./But she holds their fears close as if to absorb them/into
> her girth like calories from so much pasta,/each little rigatoni head, a child's dread allayed.

Sample: $5.95.

How to Submit: Submit complete chapbook ms (20-24 pgs.) with a brief bio, 125-word statement that introduces your writing and $10 reading fee. Previously published poems and simultaneous submissions OK, with notice. No electronic submissions. Competition deadlines: March 30 for spring contest; September 30 for fall contest. Send SASE for guidelines. "Each competition is judged by either the author of the most recent chapbook published by invitation or by previous competition winners." Seldom comments on rejections. Reports 3 months after deadline. All entrants will receive a copy of the winning chapbook. Winner receives $200 and 25 copies.

Advice: They say, "Poetry is about a passion for language. That's what we're about. We'd like to provide an opportunity for poets of any age who are fairly early in their careers to publish something substantial. We're excited by the enthusiasm shown for this press and by the extraordinary quality of the writing we've received."

WHITE PINE PRESS; THE WHITE PINE PRESS POETRY PRIZE, P.O. Box 236, Buffalo NY 14201, e-mail wpine@whitepine.org, website http://www.whitepine.org, founded 1973, editor Dennis Maloney, managing director Elaine LaMattina.

Book/Chapbook Needs & How to Submit: White Pine Press publishes poetry, fiction, literature in translation, essays—perfect-bound paperbacks. "*At present we are accepting unsolicited mss only for our annual competition, The White Pine Poetry Prize*. This competition awards $500 plus publication to a book-length collection of poems by a US author. Entry fee: $15. Deadline: October 31. Send SASE for details." No e-mail submissions. They have published *The Four Questions of Melancholy* by Tomaž Šalamun; *Pretty Happy!* by Peter Johnson; and *Bodily Course* (winner of the Poetry Prize) and *Treehouse* by William Kloefkorn. Send for free catalog.

Also Offers: Website includes writer's guidelines, poetry contest guidelines, list of current and backlist titles.

WHITE WALL REVIEW, 63 Gould St., Toronto, Ontario M5B 1E9 Canada, phone (416)977-9924, e-mail whitewal@acs.ryerson.ca, founded 1976, editors change every year.

Magazine Needs: *White Wall Review* is an annual, appearing in May, "focused on publishing clearly expressed, innovative poetry. No style is unacceptable." They have published poetry by Kenneth Bullock Jr. and J.P. Lamarche. As a sample the editors selected these lines from an untitled poem by Scott Carlson:

THE BOOK PUBLISHERS INDEX, located at the back of this book, lists those publishers who consider full-length book collections.

> *you made me watch you/while your fingers fancied/the best part of being your lover/is when the candles*
> *make the jasper/foreshadow your cervix with the travesty/spectrum of a prism.*

WWR is between 90-144 pgs., digest-sized, professionally printed and perfect-bound with glossy card cover, using b&w photos and illustrations. Press run is 250. Subscription: $9 in Canada, $9.50 in US and elsewhere. Sample: $5.

How to Submit: Submit up to 5 poems at a time. A critique composed of 5 editors' comments is available for $5. "Please do not submit between January and August of a given year." Cover letter required; include short bio. Reports "as soon as we can (usually in April or May). Pays 1 copy. They say, "Poets should send what they consider their best work, not everything they've got."

N ◯ ◎ TAHANA WHITECROW FOUNDATION; CIRCLE OF REFLECTIONS (Specialized: ethnic), 2350 Wallace Rd. NW, Salem OR 97304, phone (503)585-0564, e-mail tahana@open.org, website http://www.open.org/tahana, founded 1987, executive director Melanie Smith.

Magazine Needs & How to Submit: The Whitecrow Foundation conducts one spring/summer poetry contest on Native American themes in poems up to 30 lines in length. Deadline for submissions: May 31. No haiku, Seiku, erotic or porno poems. Fees are $2.75 for a single poem, $10 for 4. Winners, honorable mentions and selected other entries are published in a periodic anthology, *Circle of Reflections*. Winners receive free copies and are encouraged to purchase others for $4.95 plus $1 handling in order to "help ensure the continuity of our contests." As a sample Melanie Smith selected these lines by David E. Sees:

> *Alas . . ./I see/I hear . . ./my grandchild/move and speak . . ./the only thing native/is the complexion/*
> *of his skin . . . his eyes and hair . . ./alas . . . forgive/this lonely tear*

Obtain guidelines via e-mail. Reviews books of poetry for $10 reading fee (average 32 pages).

Advice: Melanie Smith adds, "We seek unpublished Native American writers. Poetic expressions of full-bloods, mixed bloods and empathetic non-Indians need to be heard. Future goals include chapbooks and native theme art. Advice to new writers. Keep writing, honing and sharpening your material; don't give up—keep submitting."

◯ ◖ ◎ WHOLE NOTES; WHOLE NOTES PRESS (Specialized: children, translations), P.O. Box 1374, Las Cruces NM 88004-1374, *WN* founded 1984, Whole Notes Press founded 1988, editor Nancy Peters Hastings.

Magazine Needs: *WN* appears twice a year and tends toward close observation of the natural world, the beauty of nature and a poetry which affirms the human spirit. "All forms will be considered." As a sample the editor selected these lines from "Over Dangerous Wet Rocks" by Joyce Odam:

> *Once you led me over dangerous wet rocks/into the sea-edge of a dwindling summer.//We were not*
> *there/to honor time or its commitments;//we were there for something/or our loss and of our finding.//*

WN is 32 pgs., digest-sized, "nicely printed," staple bound, with a "linen 'fine arts' cover." They receive about 800 poems a year, accept approximately 10%. Press run is 400 for 200 subscriptions of which 10 are libraries. Subscription: $6. Sample: $3.

How to Submit: Submit 3-5 poems at a time. Some previously published poems used; no simultaneous submissions. Reports in 2 months. Pays 1 copy.

Book/Chapbook Needs & How to Submit: Whole Notes Press publishes 1 chapbook/year by a single poet. They have published chapbooks by Dan Stryk (*A Sea Change*), Robert Dorsett (*Threshold*) and Roy Scheele (*To See How it Tallies*). For 20-page chapbook consideration, submit 3-5 samples with bio and list of other publications. Pays 25 copies of chapbook. Editor sometimes comments on rejections.

Advice: The editor says, "In the fall of each even-numbered year I edit a special issue of *WN* that features writing by young people (under 21). Overall, we'd like to see more translations and more poems about rural experiences."

◯ WILD WORD; WILDER WORD, P.O. Box 2132, Idyllwild CA 92549, phone (909)659-2265, fax (909)659-4533, e-mail poemslady@aol.com, founded 1996, publisher Lorraine Lawhorne.

Magazine Needs: *Wild Word* appears monthly "to give unknown poets a forum in which to be published and read." And, *Wilder Word* appears annually "to provide the more erotic/shocking the same chance." They want all styles and formats of poetry; short stories and artwork are also considered. They have published poetry by Robert Kensington and "Poet Wings." As a sample the editor selected this poem, "Love's Haiku," by Lori Jo Dickinson:

> *we fly in formation, wing tip to wing tip/In perfect tandem/together forever. mated.*

Wild Word is about 48 pgs., digest-sized, laser-printed and saddle-staple with 80 lb. cardstock cover with b&w illustration, b&w photos and illustrations inside, "ads are kept to the front page and in the rear pages so as not to interrupt the flow." Press run is 500 for 50 subscribers, about 400 shelf sales. Subscription: $35/year. Sample: $3.99.

How to Submit: Submit 3-5 pages of poetry at a time. No previously published poems; simultaneous submissions OK. Cover letter preferred. E-mail submissions OK. Time between acceptance and publication is 2-4 months. Seldom comments on rejections. Publishes theme issues. Send SASE for guidelines and upcoming themes. Reports in 2-4 months. Pays 1 copy.

Advice: The publisher says, "Poetry should have life, passion and a soul. The reader should be drawn in so when they come to the end they have goose bumps and are only able to mutter 'Wow.' Rhyming? Don't stretch it!"

⟨⟩ **THE WILLIAM AND MARY REVIEW**, Campus Center, College of William and Mary, P.O. Box 8795, Williamsburg VA 23187-8795, phone (757)221-3290, founded 1962.

Magazine Needs: The *Review* is a 120-page annual, appearing in April, "dedicated to publishing new work by established poets as well as work by new and vital voices." They have published poetry by Dana Gioia, Robert Morgan, Cornelius Eady, Amy Clampitt, Elizabeth Alexander, Robert Hershon, Diane Ackerman, Agha Shahid Ali, Bruce Weigl, Robert Bly and Phyllis Janowitz. As a sample the editor selected these lines from "The Broken-footed Angel" by Andrew Zawacki:

> She crossed her legs, and the leaves outside/Were composed. In between two movements, I asked her/
> Which words really mattered anymore. "Poetry," she said,/"is an arrangement of the space between
> us."/I wasn't quite sure how to take this . . .

The *Review* is about 100 pgs., 6×9, professionally printed on coated paper and perfect-bound with 4-color card cover, includes 4-color artwork and photos. They receive about 5,000 poems a year, accept approximately 15-20. Press run is 3,500. They have 250 library subscriptions, about 500 shelf sales. Sample: $5.50.

How to Submit: Submit 1 poem/page, batches of up to 6 poems addressed to Poetry Editors. Cover letter required; include address, phone number, past publishing history and brief bio note. Reads submissions September 15 through February 15 only. Reports in approximately 4 months. Pays 5 copies.

⟨⟩ **WILLOW REVIEW; COLLEGE OF LAKE COUNTY READING SERIES**, College of Lake County, 19351 W. Washington St., Grayslake IL 60030-1198, phone (847)223-6601, ext. 2956, fax (847)548-3383, founded 1969, editor Paulette Roeske.

Magazine Needs: "We are interested in poetry and fiction of high quality with no preferences as to form, style or subject." They have published poetry by Lisel Mueller, Lucien Stryk, David Ray, Louis Rodriguez, John Dickson and Garrett Hongo and interviews with Gregory Orr, Diane Ackerman and Li-Young Lee. As a sample the editor selected this poem, "Daddy Long Legs" by Elaine Fowler Palencia:

> His mind trapped forever/In a dream of shadows/My son hunts bugs./All the day long/Along the house
> foundations/Mewling gently/He pulls up grass/Lets daylight under bricks/To watch the bugs scurry./
> One day while I'm sunning/He opens his palm to me/And smiles./There sit five grey buttons/Pulsing
> with surprise/At the loss of their legs//How like a god he is,/My thoughtless child.

The editor says she selected this particular sample because "Palencia's powerful poem represents the simultaneous simplicity of language and complexity of idea I admire, along with a relentless credibility." The review is an 88- to 96-page, flat-spined annual, 6×9, professionally printed with a 4-color cover featuring work by an Illinois artist. Editors are open to all styles, free verse to form, as long as each poem stands on its own as art and communicates ideas. Circulation is 1,000, with distribution to bookstores nationwide. Subscription: $13 for 3 issues, $20 for 5 issues. Sample back issue: $4.

How to Submit: Submit up to 5 poems or short fiction/creative nonfiction up to 4,000 words. "We read year round but response is slower in the summer months." Sometimes sends prepublication galleys. Pays 2 copies. Acquires first North American serial rights. Prizes totaling $400 are awarded to the best poetry and short fiction/creative nonfiction in each issue.

Also Offers: The reading series, 4-7 readings/academic year, has included Angela Jackson, Thomas Lux, Charles Simic, Isabel Allende, Donald Justice, Gloria Naylor, David Mura, Galway Kinnell, Lisel Mueller, Amiri Baraka, Stephen Dobyns, Heather McHugh, Linda Pastan, Tobias Wolff, William Stafford and others. One reading is for contributors to *Willow Review*. Readings are usually held on Thursday evenings, for audiences of about 150 students and faculty of the College of Lake County and other area colleges and residents of local communities. They are widely publicized in Chicago and suburban newspapers.

✓ ⟨⟩ ◎ **WILLOW SPRINGS (Specialized: translations)**, 705 W. First Ave., MS-1, Eastern Washington University, Spokane WA 99201, phone (509)623-4349, fax (509)623-4238, founded 1977.

Magazine Needs: "We publish quality poetry and fiction that is imaginative, intelligent, and has a concern and care for language. We are especially interested in translations from any language or period." They have published poetry by James Grabill, Michael Heffernan, Robert Gregory and Paul Zimmer. *Willow Springs*, a semiannual, is one of the most visually appealing journals being published. It is 128 pgs., 6×9, professionally printed, flat-spined, with glossy 4-color card cover with art. They receive about 4,000 poems a year, accept approximately 1-2%. Editors seem to prefer free verse with varying degrees of accessibility (although an occasional formal poem does appear). Press run is 1,500 for 700 subscribers of which 30% are libraries. Subscription: $10.50/year, $20/2 years. Sample: $5.50.

How to Submit: Submit September 15 through May 15 only. "We do not read in the summer months." Include name on every page, address on first page of each poem. Brief cover letter saying how many poems on how many pages preferred. No simultaneous submissions. Send SASE for guidelines. Reports in 1-3 months. Pays 2 copies plus a copy of the succeeding issue, others at half price, and cash when funds available. Acquires all rights. Returns rights on release. Reviews books of poetry and short fiction in 200-500 words. Open to unsolicited reviews. Poets may also send books for review consideration.

Also Offers: They have annual poetry and fiction awards ($100 and $250 respectively) for work published in

the journal.
Advice: The editor says, "We like poetry that is fresh, moving, intelligent and has no spare parts."

WIND PUBLICATIONS; WIND MAGAZINE, P.O. Box 24548, Lexington KY 40524, phone (606)885-5342, e-mail wind@lit-arts.com, website http://www.lit-arts.com/wind, *Wind Magazine* founded in 1971, editor/publisher Charlie G. Hughes, poetry editor Leatha Kendrick.
Magazine Needs: "Although we publish poets of national repute, we are friendly toward beginners who have something to say and do so effectively and interestingly. No taboos, no preferred school, form, style, etc. Our interests are inclusive. Competition is keen; send only your best." *Wind* appears twice a year (spring and fall) and is about 100 pgs., digest-sized, perfect-bound, containing approximately 40% poetry, also short fiction, essays and reviews ("Editor's Choice"). "We accept about 1% of submissions." Subscription: $10/year. Sample: $4.50.
How to Submit: Submit 3-5 poems at a time. No simultaneous submissions. "Cover letter optional; short bio desirable." Editor comments on submissions which are near misses. Reports in 6-8 weeks. Time between acceptance and publication is within 1 year. Sometimes sends prepublication galleys. Pays 1 copy plus discount on extras. "Your submission is understood to guarantee Wind Publications first North American serial rights and anthology reprint rights only."
Book/Chapbook Needs & How to Submit: Wind Publications sponsors a yearly poetry chapbook competition. Reading fee: $10. Send SASE for contest guidelines or obtain via website. Also sponsor poetry and fiction competitions. Send SASE for more information.

WINDHOVER: A JOURNAL OF CHRISTIAN LITERATURE; NEW TEXAS '98 (Specialized: religious), 900 College St., Box 8008, University of Mary Hardin-Baylor, Belton TX 76513, phone (254)295-4564, e-mail dwnixon@umhb.edu, founded 1996, editor Donne Walker-Nixon.
Magazine Needs: "*Windhover* annually publishes poetry and fiction by writers of faith. We're open to all types of poetry. Nothing trite or didactic." They have published poetry by Walt McDonald, Marjorie Maddox, David Brendan Hopes and Kelly Cherry. The editor says *Windhover* is 160 pgs., magazine-sized, perfect-bound. They receive about 150 poems a year, accept approximately 10%. Press run is 500 for 50 subscribers. Subscription: $8/year. Sample: $6. Make checks payable to *Windhover*.
How to Submit: Submit 4 poems at a time. No previously published poems; simultaneous submissions OK. E-mail and disk submissions OK. "We work best with e-mail submissions." Time between acceptance and publication is 4 months. Poems are circulated to an editorial board. "We send poems to members of the editorial board for advisement. If poems are sent via e-mail, response time is shorter." Often comments on rejections. Send SASE for guidelines or obtain via e-mail. Reports in 3 months. Sometimes sends prepublication galleys. Pays 2 copies. Acquires one-time rights. Reviews books and chapbooks of poetry in 300 words, single book format. Open to unsolicited reviews. Poets may also send books for review consideration.

WINDSOR REVIEW, English Dept., University of Windsor, Windsor, Ontario N9B 3P4 Canada, phone (519)253-3000 ext. 2332, fax (519)973-7050, e-mail uwrevu@uwindsor.ca, founded 1965, poetry editor John Ditsky.
Magazine Needs: *Windsor Review* appears twice a year and features poetry, short fiction and art. "Open to all poetry but no epics." They have published poetry by Ben Bennani, Walter McDonald, Larry Rubin and Lyn Lifshin. It is professionally printed, 100 pgs., digest-sized. They receive about 500 poems a year, accept approximately 15%. Press run is 400. Subscription: $19.95 (+7% GST) individuals, $29.95 (+7% GST) institutions (Canadian); $19.95 individuals, $29.95 institutions (US). Sample: $7.
How to Submit: Submit 5-10 poems at a time, typed. No simultaneous submissions. Queries via e-mail, poetry submissions via fax OK. No e-mail submissions. Reports in 6 weeks. Pays 1 copy.

WINGS MAGAZINE, INC., e-mail tomjones1965@juno.com, website http://members.aol.com/wing smag/, founded 1991, publisher/editor Thomas Jones, poetry editor Michael Del Mastro.
Magazine Needs: *Wings* is an exclusively online publication. "We want to publish the work of poets who are not as widely known as those published in larger journals but who nevertheless produce exceptional, professional material. We also publish personal essays, fiction and plays." They want "poetry with depth of feeling. No jingly, rhyming poetry. If it rhymes, it should be new and not clichéd. Poetry on any theme, 80 lines or less, any style." They receive about 200 poems a year. "No requirements but we encourage poets to check out our website and get an idea of the kind of material we publish."
How to Submit: Submit up to 5 poems at a time. "Send e-mail to the above juno address asking for the *Wings* mailing address." Previously published poems and simultaneous submissions OK. Cover letter preferred with 5-line bio, "so if accepted, it can be included with publication. We want submissions sent to us on paper and will only ask for disk or e-mail if submission is accepted." Requires SASE for mailed submissions. ASCII text format for e-mail and disk submisisons (IBM PC compatible only—no Mac). Sometimes comments on rejections. Reports in 2-8 weeks. Staff reviews books and chapbooks of poetry and other magazines in single book format.
Also Offers: Sponsors at least 1 online contest each year. See *Poets & Writers* or *AWP Chronicle* for advertisements.
Advice: The publisher says, "We don't want doggerel. We want sincere, well-crafted work. Poetry has been

reduced to second class status by commercial publishing; and we want to restore it to the level of fiction (novels) or plays, in a heroic (that is, human) sense."

WISCONSIN ACADEMY REVIEW (Specialized: regional), 1922 University Ave., Madison WI 53705, phone (920)263-1692, fax (608)265-3039, founded 1954, poetry editor Faith B. Miracle.
Magazine Needs: The *Wisconsin Academy Review* "distributes information on scientific and cultural life of Wisconsin and provides a forum for Wisconsin (or Wisconsin background) artists and authors." They want "good lyric poetry; traditional meters acceptable if content is fresh. No poem over 65 lines." They have published poetry by Credo Enriquez, Jean Feraca, Felix Pollak, Ron Wallace, Sara Rath and Lorine Niedecker. The *Review* is a 52-page quarterly, magazine-sized, professionally printed on glossy stock, glossy card color cover. Press run is 1,800 for 1,500 subscribers of which 100 are libraries. They use 3-6 pgs. of poetry/issue. They receive about 150 submissions a year, accept approximately 24. They have a 6- to 12-month backlog. Sample: $3.
How to Submit: Submit 5 pages maximum, double-spaced, with SASE. Must include Wisconsin connection if not Wisconsin return address. Sometimes comments on rejections. Reports in 10-12 weeks. Always sends prepublication printouts. Pays 3 copies. Staff reviews books of poetry with Wisconsin connection only. Send related books for review consideration.
Advice: The editor says, "We would like to receive good traditional forms—not sentimental rhymes."

WISCONSIN REVIEW; WISCONSIN REVIEW PRESS, Box 158, Radford Hall, University of Wisconsin-Oshkosh, Oshkosh WI 54901, phone (920)424-2267, founded 1966, contact poetry editor.
Magazine Needs: *Wisconsin Review* is published 3 times/year. "The poetry we publish is mostly free verse with strong images and fresh approaches. We want new turns of phrase." They have published poetry by Stephen Perry, Lyn Lifshin, Karla Huston, Herman Asarnow, Bill Garten and John McKernan. As a sample the editor selected these lines from "False Candles" by Fernand Roqueplan:

> Here's our town, rundown/without smiths or merlot. Rust blighted with apples/and our local vintner Ingo Rosado salted his vines/instead of surrendering to Gallo./Love begs real candlelight. Zoned/ seaside cottages as sensual as high-rises/where lovers share through sheetrock walls/kinship to the thousand others/booming back in symphony.

The *Review* is 80-100 pgs., 6×9, elegantly printed on quality white stock, glossy card cover with color art, b&w art inside. They receive about 1,500 poetry submissions a year, use approximately 75; 40-50 pgs. of poetry in each issue. Press run is 1,600 for 40 subscribers of which 20 are libraries. Single copy: $4; subscription: $10.
How to Submit: Submit mss September 15 through May 15. Offices checked bimonthly during summer. Submit up to 4 poems at a time, one poem/page, single-spaced with name and address of writer on each page. Simultaneous submissions OK, but previously unsubmitted works preferable. Cover letter also preferred; include brief bio. Mss are not read during the summer months. Send SASE for guidelines. Reports within 2-6 months. Pays 2 copies.

$ A WISE WOMAN'S GARDEN (Specialized: women, psychic, humor, nature, animals, love/ romance/erotica, health concerns, mystery, fantasy, senior citizen, social issues, spirituality), P.O. Box 403, Racine WI 53401-0403, phone (414)632-2373, founded 1994, editor Katus Hortus (a.k.a. Katarzyna Rygasiewicz).
Magazine Needs: *A Wise Woman's Garden* appears 10-12 times a year "to connect readers with nature, landscape, metaphor magicks, the four elements (earth, water, air, fire) witnessed to in heart and mind." She wants "medicine-shield balanced poetry. No first drafts, typos, grammar impossibles, bleep-bleep-expletives." She has published poetry by Jane Farrell, Harvey Taylor, DyAnne Korda, Catherine Cofell and Elaine Cavanaugh. As a sample the editor selected these lines from "Prayers for Morning" by Jessica Jordan Nudels:

> May my writing flow like rivers/May I be a river bed/May the waters pass through me clear and cool/ May the fish pass over me/May the rocks lie in me/May I write rivers

AWWG is 12-16 pgs., 4¼×11, photocopied on colored paper, bound by hand, "corded 2-color classic 'J' book binder stitch," occasional sketches and cartoons. Press run is 450 for 70 subscribers; most distributed free through Racine and Kenosha WI coffeehouses, libraries and galleries. Subscription: $22 regular; $17 libraries; $11 for poets accepted for printing. Sample (including guidelines): $2. "Issues are linked to sun-sign astrological imagery at month's beginning (example: March-Pisces). Please supply birthdate for appropriate astrological linkage."
How to Submit: Submit 3-7 poems at a time. Previously published poems and simultaneous submissions OK. Cover letter preferred, with bio or "fantastickal anecdotes." Reads submissions February 2 through October 31 only. Time between acceptance and publication is 1-18 months. Often comments on rejections. Reports in 1-12 months. Sometimes sends prepublication galleys. Pays $5/poem plus 10 copies. Acquires first or one-time rights.
Advice: The editor says, "Earth is capitalized (sacral respect). Poems automatically rejected for using the word 'dirt.' 'Soil' is a living organism. Find the magicks in your regional landscape and sculpt-sing them with all your knack. Wisconsin readers are ever friendly and grateful."

THE WISHING WELL (Specialized: membership, women/feminism, lesbian/bisexual), P.O. Box 178440, San Diego CA 92177-8440, phone (619)270-2779, e-mail laddiewww@aol.com, website http://www.sdc w.org/members/wishingwell, founded 1974, editor/publisher Laddie Hosler.
Magazine Needs: *The Wishing Well* is a "contact magazine for women who love women the world over;

members' descriptions, photos, letters and poetry published with their permission only; resources, etc., listed. I publish writings only for and by members so membership is required." 1-2 pgs. in each issue are devoted to poetry, "which can be up to 8" long—depending upon acceptance by editor, 3" width column." It is 7×8½, offset printed from typescript, with soft matte card cover. It appears bimonthly and goes to 100 members, 200 nonmembers. A sample is available for $5. Membership in *Wishing Well* is $35 for 3-5 months, $60 for 5-7 months, $120 for 15 months.

How to Submit: Membership includes the right to publish poetry, a self description (exactly as you write it), to have responses forwarded to you, and other privileges. Personal classifieds section, 50¢/word for members and $1/word for nonmembers.

Also Offers: Website includes membership application and introductory letter describing membership with *The Wishing Well*.

☑ ▣ ◯ **WOLF HEAD QUARTERLY**, P.O. Box 30057, Kansas City MO 64112, e-mail TheWHQ@aol.com, website http://members.aol/thewhq, founded 1994, managing editor W.H. Mitchell.

Magazine Needs: *Wolf Head Quarterly* "endeavors to cultivate the senses of each reader by publishing quality prose and poetry by writers from across the country." They want "a wide range of styles and subjects, no more than five pages." They do not want "overly political poems and foul language." They have published poetry by Joan Joffe Hall, Gayle Elen Harvey, Peter Orner and Lynn Veach Sadler. *Wolf Head Quarterly* is published exclusively on the World Wide Web. They receive about 400-800 poems a year, accept approximately 4-5%. "There is no no cover price or subscriptions; the website is free for those with Internet access."

How to Submit: Submit 5 poems at a time with SASE. E-mail submissions OK "with an attached PC compatible document, or include the work in the e-mail itself." No previously published poems or simultaneous submissions. Cover letter preferred. Time between acceptance and publication is 1-3 months. "Poems are circulated to our three editors who read all submissions and decide as a group." Send SASE for guidelines. Reports in 1-3 months. Always sends prepublication galleys. Acquires first North American serial rights.

Also Offers: Website includes the current issue, back issues, guidelines and author bios.

Advice: The editor says, "Beginners should not feel discouraged. Magazines not only pick the best of the lot, but rather pick the best of the best they receive."

◓ **WOLFSONG PUBLICATIONS**, 3123 S. Kennedy Dr., Sturtevant WI 53177, e-mail wolfsong@wi.net, founded 1974, editor/publisher Gary C. Busha.

Book/Chapbook Needs: Wolfsong is "a small press with a well known, respected reputation for publishing talented, serious poets." They publish 1-3 chapbooks/year. They are open to all types of poetry, but have a bias toward nature/fishing and Wisconsin/Midwest Writers. They have published poetry by Chris Halla, Dave Etter, Russell King, Robert Schuler and Doug Flaherty. As a sample the editor selected these lines from "April 10" in *Grace: A Book of Days* by Robert Schuler:

> Crocuses blossom/lavendar out of snow and mud/Canada geese honking/circling the house/in the soft
> evening rain.

Chapbooks are usually 30-36 pgs., 5½×8½, offset printed or photocopied, saddle-stitched with line art on cover. Sample: $3.50.

How to Submit: Query first. "Serious poets should send SASE for guidelines. Poets should have 5-10 publishing credits in respectable magazines and journals." No previously published poems or simultaneous submissions. Seldom comments on rejections. Replies to queries in up to 2 weeks. Pays 5 author's copies (out of a press run of 200-300).

Advice: The editor says, "Read extensively. Read literature, including all the classics. Read poetry and learn what poetry is, how it's written and apply those standards to your own work. You need to develop a critical eye and apply that eye to your own work. You need to know the elements of good writing and understand why something that is good stands the test of time, while the 95% of everything else is—thankfully—soon forgotten."

☑ $ ◓ **WOMEN'S REVIEW OF BOOKS**, Wellesley College, Wellesley MA 02481, website http://www.wellesley.edu/WCW/CRW/WROB/welcome.html, founded 1983, contact Robin Becker.

Magazine Needs: *WROB* is a monthly review of works by and about women, in all fields, including some poetry reviews. They want "good stuff. No junk." They have published poetry by Alicia Ostriker, Maxine Kumin and Celia Gilbert. The editor says *WROB* is 32 pgs., tabloid-sized (10×15), published on newsprint. They receive about 200 poems a year, accept approximately 5%. Press run is 14,000 for 10,000 subscribers of which 1,000 are libraries, 3,000 shelf sales. Single copy: $3; subscription: $23. Sample copy is free.

How to Submit: Submit 2 poems at a time. No previously published poems or simultaneous submissions. Cover letter required. Reads submissions in March and April only. Time between acceptance and publication is up to 18 months. Seldom comments on rejections. Reports in 2-3 months. Pays $75 plus unlimited copies. Buys first North American serial rights. Staff reviews books or chapbooks of poetry in 500-2,000 words. Send books for review consideration.

☑ ◓ ◉ **WOMENWISE (Specialized: women/feminism, health concerns)**, %BWHBC, P.O. Box 192, West Somerville MA 02144, founded 1978, run by an editorial committee, contact editor Luita D. Spangler.

Magazine Needs: *WomenWise* is "a quarterly newspaper that deals specifically with issues relating to women's health—research, education, and politics." They want "poetry reflecting status of women in society, relating specifically to women's health issues." They do not want "poetry that doesn't include women or is written by men; poetry that degrades women or is anti-choice." *WomenWise* is a tabloid newspaper, 12 pgs., printed on quality stock with b&w art and graphics. Press run is 3,000. Single copy: $3.50. Subscription: $15/year.

How to Submit: Submissions should be typed, double-spaced. Reads submissions March, June, September and December only. Publishes theme issues. Send SASE for upcoming themes. Reporting time and time to publication varies. Pays 5 copies. Acquires first North American serial rights. Staff reviews books of poetry in "any word count," single format.

Advice: They say they often receive mss with no SASE. "We throw them away. Please remember that we are a nonprofit organization with limited resources." The editor adds, "We receive a great deal of badly written free verse. We would appreciate receiving more poetry in traditional form, as well as more poetry in free verse written with skill and care."

✓ ◎ **WOODLEY MEMORIAL PRESS (Specialized: regional)**, English Dept., Washburn University, Topeka KS 66621, phone (785)234-1032, e-mail zzlaws@washburn.edu, website http://www.wuacc.edu/refere nce/woodley-press/index.html, founded 1980, editor Robert Lawson.

Book/Chapbook Needs: Woodley Memorial Press publishes 1-2 flat-spined paperbacks a year, about half being collections of poets from Kansas or with Kansas connections, "terms individually arranged with author on acceptance of ms." They have published *Looking for the Pale Eagle* by Stephen Meats, *Killing Seasons* by Christopher Cokinos, and *Gathering Reunion* by David Tangeman. As a sample the editor selected these lines from "The Drowning" in *The Gospel of Mary* by Michael Page:

> I hear/there's a gospel of Mary./It is a fragment/and she is naturally saddened.

Samples may be individually ordered from the press for $5.

How to Submit: Replies to queries in 2 weeks, to mss in 2 months. Time between acceptance and publication is 1 year.

Also Offers: Website features descriptions of books, board members' short bios and writers' guidelines.

◐ ◎ **WORCESTER REVIEW; WORCESTER COUNTY POETRY ASSOCIATION, INC. (Specialized: regional)**, 6 Chatham St., Worcester MA 01609, phone (508)797-4770, website http://www.geocities.com/paris/leftbank6433, founded 1973, managing editor Rodger Martin.

Magazine Needs: *WR* appears annually "with emphasis on poetry. New England writers are encouraged to submit, though work by other poets is used also." They want "work that is crafted, intuitively honest and empathetic, not work that shows the poet little respects his work or his readers." They have published poetry by Kathleen Spivack, Bruce Weigl and Walter McDonald. *WR* is 160 pgs., 6×9, flat-spined, professionally printed in dark type on quality stock with glossy card cover. Press run is 1,000 for 300 subscribers of which 50 are libraries, 300 shelf sales. Subscription: $20 (includes membership in WCPA). Sample: $5.

How to Submit: Submit up to 5 poems at a time. "I recommend three or less for most favorable readings." Simultaneous submissions OK "if indicated." Previously published poems "only on special occasions." Editor comments on rejections "if ms warrants a response." Publishes theme issues. Send SASE for guidelines and upcoming themes. Reports in 4-6 months. Pays 2 copies. Buys first rights.

Also Offers: They have an annual contest for poets who live, work, or in some way (past/present) have a Worcester County connection or are a WCPA member.

Advice: The editor advises, "Read some. Listen a lot."

◑ **WORD PROCESS**, 623 N. Monterey St. #1, Alhambra CA 91801-1505, founded 1996, editor Don Craig Campbell.

Magazine Needs: *Word Process* is a monthly that publishes 3 poems on a folded 8½×11 cardstock. "Our motto is 'cool poetry . . . for your refrigerator!'" They want "quality poetry—35 lines maximum (including line breaks)." They do not want "poetry without images." They have published poetry by Charles Ardinger, David Minjares and Laura Joy Lustig. As a sample the editor selected these lines from "Tulips And Rainbows" by Rosalee:

> My grandmother believes in Springtime/so she plants seeds in November/her leafy hands patting the soil/the way she touches the top of my head

They receive about 400 poems a year, accept approximately 36. Press run is 500 for 175 subscribers; 325 distributed free at poetry readings and workshops. Subscription: $10/year. Sample: $1. Make checks payable to Don Craig Campbell.

How to Submit: Submit 3-5 poems at a time. Previously published poems and simultaneous submissions OK. "Please send brief biographical information (i.e., recent publications, reading notice, chapbook available,

---

MARKETS THAT WERE listed in the 1999 edition of *Poet's Market* but do not appear this year are listed in the General Index with a notation explaining why they were omitted.

geographical, etc.).'' Time between acceptance and publication is 4-6 months. Seldom comments on rejections. Reports in 3-6 months. Pays 6-month subscription.

Also Offers: Sponsors annual contest with $100 first prize, $50 second and $25 third. Write for more information.

✔ ▣ ◎ **WORD SALAD; WORD SALAD POETRY CONTEST**, 3224 N. College Rd., Suite C, B-107, Wilmington NC 28405, e-mail whealton@wordsalad.net, website http://wordsalad.net, founded 1995, publisher Bruce Whealton, editor Lynn Krupey.

Magazine Needs: Published quarterly on the Web, *Word Salad* ''continuously accepts original poetry. Although we do not restrict ourselves to one subject area or style, the Web allows us to receive a large number of poems and select the highest quality and we offer a world wide exposure. We are open to any form, style or subject matter; length should be no more than two typed pages. We especially like poetry dealing with oppressed/vulnerable populations, i.e., persons with mental illness, the poor/homeless. No greeting card verse or forced rhyme; most love poems unless you have something original to say. We invite gay/lesbian/bisexual poetry.'' They have published poetry by Scott Urban and Jean Jones. As a sample we selected these lines from ''Denial'' by Paula Martin:

> Her every thought, word, and action/Consumed by the/Food That she will not face—/Unknowingly digesting/Her very soul/As the meal/Remains untouched/and we all stand by,/Silverware in hands,/ Ready to help her/Eat,/If only she would take/The first bite

They receive about 1,200 poems a year, accept approximately 10%.

How to Submit: Submit 2 poems at a time. No previously published poems or simultaneous submissions. Cover letter preferred. E-mail and disk submissions OK. ''We receive 200-300 poems per quarter and publish 20-30. Most of the submissions are received via e-mail. We ask that poets read the submission guidelines on the Web.'' Time between acceptance and publication is about 3 months. Seldom comments on rejections. Publishes theme issues occasionally. Obtain guidelines and upcoming themes via website. Reports in about 3 months. Sometimes sends prepublication galleys. Open to unsolicited reviews.

Also Offers: Sponsors annual poetry contest. See website for announcements. Winners are announced May 31. ''*Word Salad* is linked to a directory of online resources related to writing and creativity. Additionally, we have a web-based chat program that allows live chat discussions.''

◎ **THE WORD WORKS; THE WASHINGTON PRIZE**, P.O. Box 42164, Washington DC 20015, phone (703)527-9384, e-mail wordworks@shirenet.com, website http://www.writer.org/wordwork/wordwrk1.htm, founded 1974, editor-in-chief Hilary Tham, poetry editors Karren Alenier, J.H. Beall, Robert Sargent and Miles David Moore.

Book/Chapbook Needs: Word Works ''is a nonprofit literary organization publishing contemporary poetry in single author editions usually in collaboration with a visual artist. We sponsor an ongoing poetry reading series, educational programs, the Capital Collection—publishing metropolitan Washington D.C. poets, and the Washington Prize—an award of $1,000 for a book-length manuscript by a living American poet.'' Previous winners include *Tipping Point* by Fred Marchant; *Stalking the Florida Panther* by Enid Shomer; *Farewell to the Body* by Barbara Moore; *The CutOff* by Jay Rogoff; and *Spinoza's Mouse* by George Young. Submission open to any American writer except those connected with Word Works. Send SASE for rules. Entries accepted between February 1 and March 1. Postmark deadline is March 1. Winners are announced at the end of June. They publish perfect-bound paperbacks and occasional anthologies and want ''well-crafted poetry, open to most forms and styles (though not political themes particularly). Experimentation welcomed.'' As a sample the editors selected these lines from ''Cheek to Cheek'' in *Following Fred Astaire* by Nathalie Anderson:

> Anyone can wear the fresh face, bat the lashes,/make the goo-goo eyes, playing at first love, calf love,/ true love. What's tricky is to get the deep sunk tug,/the wrench infinitesimal, that makes it right,/that makes it clear it's meant, and meant to last, to be./Then you can walk on air, dance on ceilings, swing your/many partners: then it's love, again. Any school girl/knows that in the right arms the kitchen maid turns queen . . .

''We want more than a collection of poetry. We care about the individual poems—the craft, the emotional content and the risks taken—but we want manuscripts where one poem leads to the next. We strongly recommend you read the books that have already won the Washington Prize. Buy them, if you can, or ask for your libraries to purchase them. (Not a prerequisite.) Most books are $10.

How to Submit: ''Currently we are only reading unsolicited manuscripts for the Washington Prize.'' Simultaneous submissions OK, if so stated. Always sends prepublication galleys. Payment is 15% of run (usually of 500). Send SASE for catalog to buy samples. Occasionally comments on rejections.

Also Offers: Website includes a history of the Word Works; guidelines for the Washington Prize; list and description of books; ordering instructions; book descriptions; how to apply for the Miller Cabin Poetry Series and Young Poets Competition; trip for writers to Tuscany, Italy; membership info; how to volunteer; and list of staff members.

Advice: The editors advise, ''Get community support for your work, know your audience and support contemporary literature by buying and reading the small press.''

⬛ ◎ **WORDS OF WISDOM (Specialized: humor, light verse)**, 3283 UNCG Station, Greensboro NC 27413, phone (336)334-6970, e-mail wowmail@hoopsmail.com, founded 1981, editor Mikhammad Abdel-Ishara, associate editor Celestine Woo, publisher J.M. Freiermuth.

Magazine Needs: *WoW* appears quarterly using primarily short stories and 10-15 poems. "We read all forms of poetry, but shorter poems stand a better chance of being selected. I like to have 2 or 3 poems to 30 lines that can fill a page. Occasionally, we include a page of haiku, limericks or other short light forms." They have published poetry by Lois Greene Stone, Joseph S. Salemi, Rod Farmer, Paul Shore, Daniel Green and Phyllis Jean Green. The editors say *WoW* is 76-88 pgs., 5½×8½, computer-generated on copy paper, saddle-stapled with 40 lb. colored paper cover, occasionally uses graphics. They receive 500-600 poems a year, accept approximately 65. Subscription: $15 domestic, $16 Canada, $24 international. Sample: $4. Make checks payable in US dollars to J.M. Freiermuth.

How to Submit: No previously published poems; simultaneous submissions OK. Cover letter required. "There are no automatons here, so don't treat us like machines. We may not recognize your name at the bottom of the poem. Include a few lines about yourself to break the ice, the names of 3 or 4 magazines that have published you in the last year would show your reality, and a bio blurb of about 37 words including the names of 2 or 3 of the magazines (where you aspire to be?) you send the occasional subscription check could help. If you are not sending a check to some little magazine that is supported by subscriptions and the blood, sweat and tears of the editors, why would you send your poetry to any of them and expect to receive a warm welcome?" Reports in 1-6 months. Seldom comments on rejections. Pays 1 copy, extra copies available at $3.75. Acquires one-time rights.

Advice: The editors say, "Stop watching TV and read a book of poetry."

✅ ♟ **$** ◎ **WORDSONG; BOYDS MILLS PRESS (Specialized: children/teen/young adult)**, 815 Church St., Honesdale PA 18431, phone (800)490-5111, fax (570)253-0179, founded 1990, manuscript coordinator Beth Troop, editor-in-chief Dr. Bernice E. Cullinan.

- Wordsong's *Been to Yesterdays* received the Christopher Award and was named a Golden Kite Honor Book.

Book/Chapbook Needs: Wordsong is the imprint under which Boyds Mills Press (a *Highlights for Children* company) publishes books of poetry for children of all ages. They want quality poetry which reflects childhood fun, moral standards and multiculturalism. We are not interested in poetry for adults or that which includes violence or sexuality or promotes hatred." They have published *The Purchase of Small Secrets* by David L. Harrison and *Tea Party Today* by Eileen Spinelli. As a sample the editor selected these lines from "Teatime" in *Tea Party Today*:

> Teatime, teatime/Here's the tray/Cups and saucers/Pink and gray/Linen napkins/Copper pot—/Come and get it/While it's hot.

How to Submit: "Wordsong prefers original work but will consider anthologies and previously published collections. We ask poets to send collections of 25-45 poems with a common theme; please send complete book manuscripts, not single poems. We buy all rights to collections and publish on an advance-and-royalty basis. Wordsong guarantees a response from editors within one month of our receiving submissions or the poet may call us toll free to inquire. Please direct submissions to Beth Troop, manuscript coordinator." No fax or e-mail submissions. Always sends prepublication galleys.

Advice: Dr. Cullinan says, "Poetry lies at the heart of the elementary school literature and reading program. In fact, poetry lies right at the heart of children's language learning. Poetry speaks to the heart of a child. We are anxious to find poetry that deals with imagination, wonder, seeing the world in a new way, family relationships, friends, school, nature and growing up."

$ ◎ **WORDWRIGHTS! A MAGAZINE FOR PEOPLE WHO LOVE THE WRITTEN WORD; ARGONNE HOTEL PRESS**, The Argonne Hotel, 1620 Argonne Place NW, Washington DC 20009, phone (202)328-9769, e-mail poet430@yahoo.com, website http://www.wordwrights.com, founded 1993, publisher/editor-in-chief R.D. Baker.

Magazine Needs: *WordWrights!* appears 3 times a year and contains "interesting and entertaining poetry and prose by both new and established writers." They want "anything that is interesting and poetic. No bad poetry or handwritten manuscripts." They have published poetry by Henry Taylor, Grace Cavalieri, Rose Solari and David Franks. *WW* is 64 pgs., 8½×11, offset printed and saddle-stitched with glossy, full color cover, includes color and b&w author photos. They receive about 1,000 poems a year, accept approximately 10%. Press run is 5,000. Single copy: $5.95; subscription: $15/year, $25/2 years. Sample: $5.

How to Submit: Mss not to exceed 12 pgs. No previously published poems; simultaneous submissions OK. Reading fees: $5 (waived for subscribers). Time between acceptance and publication is 6 months. Seldom comments on rejections. Send SASE for guidelines. Reports in 3 months. Always sends prepublication galleys. Pays $50/ms. Rights revert to author upon publication. Staff reviews books and chapbooks of poetry and other magazines. Send books for review consideration.

Book/Chapbook Needs & How to Submit: Argonne Hotel Press publishes 4 poetry chapbooks/year. Chapbooks are usually 40 pgs., digest-sized, stapled with glossy b&w cover, includes author photos. Query first, with a few sample poems and a cover letter with brief bio and publication credits. "We only publish poets who have

appeared in *WordWrights*!"Replies to queries in 3 months. Pays $25 and 25 author's copies (out of a press run of 500). Obtain sample chapbooks by sending $5.
Also Offers: In each issue of *WordWrights*, three published mss are awarded "Best of Issue" awards of $100, $200 or $300.

WORKS MAGAZINE (Specialized: science fiction), 12 Blakestones Rd., Slaithwaite, Huddersfield, Yorks HD7 5UQ United Kingdom, phone/fax 01484 842324, e-mail dwworks@aol.com, founded 1989, editor Dave W. Hughes.
Magazine Needs: *Works* is a biannual using "speculative and imaginative fiction and poetry favoring science fiction." They want "surreal/science fiction poetry. Nothing more than 50 lines. No romance or general work." They have published poetry by Andy Darlington, Steve Sneyd, Paul Weinman and Brian Aldiss. *Works* is 40 pgs., A4, offset printed, on colored paper, saddle-stapled with b&w glossy cover and interior b&w art. They receive about 150 poems a year, use approximately 36. Press run is 400 for 200 subscribers of which 4 are libraries, 50 shelf sales. Single copy: £2 (£4.50 for US); subscription: £7.50/4 issues (£14 US).
How to Submit: No simultaneous submissions. Cover letter required. Disk submissions acceptable: IBM (3.5 inch) ASCII files only. Often comments on rejections. Send SASE (or SAE and IRC) for guidelines. Reports within a month. Pays 1 copy.
Advice: The editor says, "Study the market."

WORLD LETTER, 729 Kimball Rd., Iowa City IA 52245, phone (319)337-6022, founded 1990, editor Jon Cone.
Magazine Needs: *World Letter* is an irregularly published international literary review of poetry, prose and art. They have no specific poetry needs, but do not want to see "poetry lacking in music and mystery. However, almost all material is solicited by the editor." They have published poetry by Charles Bukowski, Amiri Baraka, James Laughlin and Cid Corman. *World Letter* is 30-40 pgs., size varies, offset printed or photocopied, saddle-stitched with paper cover, includes b&w illustrations. Press run is 200-300 for 100 subscribers of which 20 are libraries; 20 distributed free to editors, reviewers. Sample: $6. Make checks payable to Jon Cone.
How to Submit: Submit 5 poems at a time. No previously published poems or simultaneous submissions. Cover letter preferred. Time between acceptance and publication is 1 year. Often comments on rejections. Reports in 2 weeks. Pays 2 copies. Acquires first rights.
Also Offers: "I will consider giving detailed critiques of poetry manuscripts. Interested poets should contact me before sending anything, so that an equitable fee can be decided."
Advice: The editor says, "Read widely and constantly. Never be discouraged by rejection. Let your writing be its own reward. Consider publishing your own work, but avoid vanity presses as they are expensive and exploitive!"

WORM FEAST!; TAPE WORM; VIDEO WORM; FREAKIN' EINSTEN, WORKIN' CLASS ZERO; KNIGHTMAYOR PRODUCTIONS, P.O. Box 7030, Fallschurch VA 22046, e-mail llori@knightmayor.com, website http://knightmayor.com, founded 1981, editor Llori Steinberg.
● Knightmayor's paper-based zines are going electronic. Check out their website for the specific changes.
Magazine Needs: *WoRM fEASt!* is an underground monthly. *Tape WoRM* is an audio magazine with music, poetry, comedy and more. *Video WoRM* is a video endeavor with movies, visual art, animation, music videos, news events and more. Send SASE for details. *Freakin' Einstein, Workin' Class Zero* features "essays, 'you work for nothing get paid nothing rants.'" For *Wf* they want "as strange as humanoids can get; no traditional verse, no rhyme (unless it's way off the keister), no haiku, no love poems unless one-sided and morbid/dark and unusually sickening; and no Christian poetry." They have published poetry by Gregory K.H. Bryant, Robert Howington, C.F. Roberts, Bill Shields and Vinnie Van Leer.
How to Submit: Send 1 poem at a time. Previously published poems OK. Cover letter with SASE required; "don't have to be professional, just state the facts and why you're interested in submitting. We report as quickly as we can." E-mail submissions OK. Sometimes sends prepublication galleys. Send SASE or visit website for submission guidelines. Reviews books of poetry. Open to unsolicited reviews. Poets may also send books for review consideration.
Book/Chapbook Needs & How to Submit: "We publish chapbooks for poets' personal use. They buy and they sell." Cost is $100 for 100 chapbooks of under 15 pgs. each.
Also Offers: Sponsors contests. Send SASE for details.
Advice: The editor says, "We want everything from serious to sick, profound to profane, from sane to insane, from graceful to gory—get it?"

THE WRITER; POET TO POET, 120 Boylston St., Boston MA 02116-4615, website http://www.channel1.com/the writer, founded 1887.
Magazine Needs: This monthly magazine for writers has a quarterly instructional column, "Poet to Poet," to which poets may submit previously unpublished work for possible publication and comment. Single copy: $3.50 back issues; $2.75 newsstand; subscription: $29 (introductory offer: 5 issues for $12).
How to Submit: Submit up to 3 poems, no longer than 30 lines each, name and address on each page, 1 poem

to a page. Send SASE for guidelines only; do not send SASE with submission. There is no pay and mss are not acknowledged or returned. Acquires first North American serial rights.

■ Ø **THE WRITER'S BLOCK**, P.O. Box 538, Whitewater WI 53190, fax (414)472-9412, e-mail editor-twb@cni-usa.com, founded 1996, editor Kellie Eggert.
• *"The Writer's Block* was out of circulation for much of 1998 but is now back in print."
Magazine Needs: *The Writer's Block* is a monthly literary magazine "providing a comfortable neighborhood atmosphere for writers of all ages and experience levels. We focus on poems and short stories, but also interview writers, discuss literary 'hot topics' and provide many opportunities for readers to get involved with us and with each other. We also have a kids' section, 'Building Blocks,' and a section on handling writer's block in each issue." Some people write for the sheer beauty of the sound of the words or of the images used; some write to evoke truth, to show something about our lives. We feel that the best poetry encompasses both of these—that it is both a sensual and an intellectual experience. However, we recognize that our neighborhood is made up of people with varying tastes and we will look at any poetry which the poet feels is good enough to be reviewed. No overly didactic, blatantly political, occult or pornographic poetry." They have published poetry by Laurel Yourke, Peg Sherry, Matt Welter, Richard Roe and Roberta Fabiani. As a sample the editor selected this poem by Lynn Renor:
> Scarlet fire backlights a single silhouette/as the form strides into the flickering distance/away, into the curve of time . . .

TWB is 50 pgs., digest-sized, professionally printed and perfect-bound, card stock cover, contains graphics, photos and contributor's artwork. They receive between 1,200-1,500 poems a year and use 20-25%. Press run is 125 for 75 subscribers, 50 shelf sales. Subscription: $15.50/6 months, $28.50/year. Sample: $2.95.
How to Submit: Submit 5 poems at a time with a #10 or larger SASE. Previously published poems OK; no simultaneous submissions. Fax submissions OK "provided the author includes a signed cover sheet noting the names of the pieces, an e-mail address and a recognition that faxed material will not be returned." No e-mail submissions. Cover letter required. "Cover letter should list the poems being submitted and should discuss (briefly) either the works themselves or writing in general (there is more detail in the guidelines). Cover letter must be signed by the author. All SASEs should be legal-sized." Time between acceptance and publication is 2-3 months. "I read each work then discuss it with my editorial assistant in depth before making a determination. We read each piece a minimum of two times, usually three to four. If we have questions, I contact the author. Whether the poem is accepted or rejected, I write back a personal letter offering a 'sickeningly large' amount of comments. I work individually with each poet to the extent of his/her interest and our mutual schedules." Publishes theme issues. Send SASE for guidelines and upcoming themes or request via e-mail. Reports in 1-2 months. Acquires first or one-time rights.
Advice: The editor says, "For beginners, remember that there are as many kinds of editors as there are poets. Learn from their comments, but don't be discouraged by them. Remember that your poems are that—yours. You are the artist; you have the vision. Think of looking for publications as similar to picking out a frame for a painting: one frame may not work, but that does not mean that either the frame or the painting is flawed, simply badly matched. Keep on looking—the right frame is out there! If I can help, let me know."

■ $☐ **WRITER'S BLOCK MAGAZINE; WRITER'S BLOCK CONTEST**, P.O. Box 32, 9944-33 Ave., Edmonton, Alberta T6N 1E7 Canada, founded 1994, editor Shaun Donnelly.
Magazine Needs: *Writer's Block Magazine* appears biannually and publishes assorted fiction, nonfiction and poetry. They want poetry of any form, length or subject matter. The editor says *WBM* is 48 pgs., digest-sized. They receive about 500 poems a year, accept approximately 12. Press run is 10,000 for 500 subscribers, 2,000 shelf sales; 7,500 distributed free to Edmonton neighborhoods. Single copy: 3.50; subscription: $12/2 years. Sample: $5.
How to Submit: Submit 3 poems at a time. Previously published poems and simultaneous submissions OK. Cover letter preferred. Time between acceptance and publication is 6 months. Always comments on rejections. Send SASE (or SAE and IRC) for guidelines. Reports in 6-8 weeks. Pays $25. Buys first North American serial rights.
Also Offers: Sponsors the biannual Writer's Block Contest for novice poets. Entry deadlines are March 1 and September 1. Awards $75 plus publication to the best poem.

$ Ø ◎ **WRITERS' CENTER PRESS; THE FLYING ISLAND; WRITERS' CENTER OF INDIANAPOLIS (Specialized: regional)**, P.O. Box 88386, Indianapolis IN 46208, phone (317)955-6336, fax (317)955-6450, founded 1979, executive director Jim Powell.
Magazine Needs: Writers' Center Press publishes *The Flying Island*, a biannual of fiction, poetry, reviews and literary commentary by those living in or connected to Indiana. They want poetry of high literary quality; no stylistic or thematic restrictions. They have published poetry by Jared Carter, Alice Friman, Yusef Komunyakaa and Roger Mitchell. *TFI*, a 24-page tabloid, includes artwork, graphics and photography. They receive about 1,000 poems a year, accept approximately 5%. Press run is 1,000 for 500 subscribers. Subscription: $10. Sample: $4.
How to Submit: Submit 2 copies of up to 3 poems. If non-Indiana resident, cover letter must explain Indiana connection. Previously published poems OK, but not encouraged. Simultaneous submissions OK, if so advised.

insider report

Self-publishing: understand the process before taking the plunge

BY ALAN BRITT

In the tradition of Blake, Keats and Whitman, poets everywhere can embrace with dignity the idea of presenting their poetry to the world in the form of a self-published book. Understand that editors, though well intentioned, tend to publish poets of like sensibility. Thus, it becomes imperative for poets themselves to stir the pot of experimentation and diversity by printing their own books. Imagine our world without *Leaves of Grass*. Unthinkable! Although the Academy of his day didn't think much of Whitman's unconventional poems, we're extremely lucky that Whitman believed in himself. The fact of the matter is, truly original poetry usually goes against the grain of fashion. Editors know fashion, but they don't always recognize originality.

You might well have your own reasons for wanting to publish a book or chapbook. In any event, desire is only the first step in a series of decisions you will need to make on your journey to a self-printed book. Because a little planning can eliminate headaches later on, let's start from the beginning.

Perhaps you find that having control over the production of your book is primarily why you've chosen to undertake the challenges of book publishing. Fine. But understand that book publishing is time consuming and requires attention to detail. For example, consider how you'd like to arrange the poems in your manuscript. Do you want your poems to be chronological, or would your prefer your poems arranged according to whether they're lyrical or narrative? Such a decision poses no great stress, but manuscript organization is obviously in order before typesetting your book.

Speaking of typesetting, will you opt to have your poems typeset for letterpress or offset? And what about desktop publishing? If you hire it out, who will do the printing? How many copies should you print? Should you perfect bind or saddle stitch? Do you have a cover design in mind? How will you distribute your wonderful book? These basic questions must be answered before diving head first into a book project that could be fueled more by enthusiasm than by common sense. [For definitions of printing terms, see the Glossary of Listing Terms at the back of this book.]

Decide on the overall number of pages and trim size you want your book to be.

ALAN BRITT *is the editor/publisher of the annual journal* Black Moon: Poetry of Imagination. *He has had two collections of his own poetry published,* Bodies of Lightning *(CypressBooks, 1995) and* Amnesia Tango *(Cedar Hill Publications, 1998), as well as having poems and essays on poetry published in numerous journals and magazines.*

Standard sizes are 6×9 or $5\frac{1}{2} \times 8\frac{1}{2}$. Most printers are equipped for these two sizes without having to undergo costly set-up for a unique format. If you opt for a different size, be sure to inquire about additional production costs.

Let's assume for the moment that you can easily meet the challenges of a modestly produced book. If you use photocopying or a duplication process to print 100 or fewer copies of a 30- to 40-page book, with an $8\frac{1}{2} \times 11$ format, held together by staples along the spine (i.e., saddle-stitched or saddle-stapled), you should be able to accurately predict your production costs. Naturally, you have costs for cover stock, typing or typesetting, paper, printing, and labor (stapling, etc.) to consider. If you intend to hand distribute your modest book, you can gauge how many copies you'll need and simply bypass the challenges of a more elaborate distribution.

On the other hand, the moment you decide to produce a professional looking, perfect-bound, 64-plus-page book, be prepared to devote much more time and money to your book project. Now you must be detail oriented, carefully planning each step in the publishing process. Suddenly you're a designer, cost researcher and marketing expert all rolled up into one inspired poet!

Start by organizing your poems according to your desired presentation. Whether your book will be 64 pages or 100 pages, you might consider dividing it into several sections. There is an advantage to sectioning your book, because this allows the reader a chance to relax a bit without having to undertake the daunting task of reading your 40, 50, or 60 poems from start to finish without a breather somewhere along the way. Check out some books you've enjoyed reading. Do these books have two or more sections to them? Perhaps each section begins with an intriguing quote that helps shed light on the poems. You might find that such a format increases overall reader enjoyment for your highly creative and sometimes obtuse poems. You know best what you'd like the reader to experience, so organize accordingly. By the way, details such as acknowledgment of previously published poems, copyright, printing date, dedications, introduction, inside artwork or photographs all contribute to the reader's experience of your book, so don't overlook a single organizational detail.

It's time to typeset. You can of course pay for professional typesetting, or you can do it yourself on a computer. Either way you'll need to know whether your printer requires typesetting on hard copy or on electronic disk. When printers make their plates from your disk, as opposed to making plates from hard copy, the result is a crisper, cleaner printed page. So why not save time, money and enhance production quality all at the same time? Consult your printer for advice.

Do you have a printer in mind? Well, you'll likely want to canvas your area for printers capable of producing professional books. Give local printers a crack at estimating your project, but don't be too disappointed if their estimates are higher than what you get from nationally advertised printers who specialize in printing short runs for books of your size and format. (Three such printers are Thomson Shore and McNaughton & Gunn, both located near Ann Arbor, Michigan, and BookCrafters, located in Fredericksburg, Virginia.)

It's not unusual for printers to quote prices of around $2 per copy for a 64-page, 6 × 9 or 5½ × 8½ book with a 2-color, laminated cover and a print run of 500 copies. Regardless of who you choose to print your book, make sure to review samples of their work. You might well discover that one printer with a low estimate is planning to use paper masters as opposed to metal plates. For a print run of 500 or less, paper masters might suffice, but it's likely you'll tell the difference between using paper masters instead of higher-quality metal plates.

Printers should walk you through details of the estimate, but be prepared to decide on matters of paper type and weight, cover stock, shrink wrapping, and even some minor differences concerning the perfect binding process. Photographs, or half-tones, are more expensive to print than straight text. Also, some printers estimate according to folios of 32 pages each. Two folios equal 64 pages, while three folios result in a 96-page book. You can still have a 100-page book by adding a 4-page, partial folio at the end, but partial folios cost proportionally more than the standard 32 page ones.

So, what do you think? Having fun yet? Remember, you still must consider a method of distribution. Distribution has a direct bearing on your print run. Finding a commercial distributor for a self-published book is nearly impossible. No need to panic. You simply must become your own publicist and distributor. Consider how many copies you can place on consignment at local bookstores. How many copies can you reasonably sell at poetry readings? Do you need review copies? How many copies will you give to family, friends and acquaintances? Remember, you can print 1,000 copies at a better rate per copy than if you print, say, 500. But if the additional 500 copies merely collect dust in your basement, how much have you really saved? Be realistic in your judgment. You can always print more.

As we enter the new millennium, alternative ways to publish poetry books will be explored. With commercial publishers opting more and more to delete new poets from their trade lists, the opportunity to keep the creative flame alive is being inherited by university presses and many small presses. The quality of poetry being written does not appear to be adversely affected by this current publishing evolution. Though many books produced by the commercial houses these days may appear stale to young poets who are eager to explore and experiment, some university presses and small publishers are rallying by producing books by new poets of great promise. Likewise, we are witnessing alternatives to traditional distribution. Some online bookstores are great places to find otherwise obscure titles. Small press distributors continue to come and go, with some developing catalogues of considerable diversity.

So, take heart. Much of our greatest poetry was self-published, initially ignored by the purveyors of fashion and compliance. But looking back, who do we revere most, Edmund Waller and John Pomfert, who were the fashionable cliché writers of their day, or Blake, Keats and Whitman, who all began by self-publishing? Sometimes true visionaries are hard to see, even when we're standing only two feet away.

[Also read *The Complete Guide to Self-Publishing* by Tom and Marilyn Ross (Writer's Digest Books) or *The Self-Publishing Manual* by Dan Poynter (Para Publishing).]

Brief bio required. Often comments on rejections. Send SASE for guidelines. Reports in 3-6 months. Pays $5 minimum for previously unpublished work. Buys first North American serial rights.
Advice: They advise, "Balance solitary writing time by getting involved in a writing community. We frequently recommend rejected writers join a poetry workshop."

$⊘◎ WRITER'S DIGEST (Specialized: writing, humor); WRITER'S DIGEST WRITING COMPETITION, 1507 Dana Ave., Cincinnati OH 45207, phone (513)531-2690, website http://www.writersdigest.com, founded 1921, managing editor Amanda Boyd.
Magazine Needs: *Writer's Digest* is a monthly magazine for writers—fiction, nonfiction, poetry and drama. "All editorial copy is aimed at helping writers to write better and become more successful. Poetry is included in 'The Writing Life' section of *Writer's Digest* only. Preference is given to short, light verse concerning 'the writing life'—the foibles, frenzies, delights and distractions inherent in being a writer. Serious verse is acceptable; however, no poetry unrelated to writing." Length: 4-12 lines. The magazine has published poetry by Charles Ghigna. They use a maximum of 5 poems/year of the 1,500 submitted. *Writer's Digest* has a circulation of 215,000. Subscription: $27. Sample: $4.
How to Submit: Submit to Amanda Boyd, managing editor, each poem on a separate page, no more than 8/ submission. Editor comments on rejections "when we want to encourage or explain decision." Send SASE for guidelines and/or reply. Reports in 6-8 weeks. Always sends prepublication galleys. Pays $25-50/poem plus 1 copy.
Also Offers: Poetry up to 32 lines on any theme is eligible for the annual Writer's Digest Writing Competition. Watch magazine for information, or send a SASE to Leanna Wesley for a copy of the contest's rules. Deadline: May 31. (Also see Writer's Digest Books under Publications of Interest.)

✓◯ WRITER'S EXCHANGE; R.S.V.P. PRESS; NEW MARKETS, P.O. Box 394, Society Hill SC 29593, e-mail eboone@aol.com, website http://users.aol.com/WriterNet, founded 1983, editor Gene Boone.
Magazine Needs: *Writer's Exchange* published quarterly, "is a small press magazine for writers and poets that covers the small press and its ever-changing array of diverse publications. The editor seeks articles on writing-related topics, particularly those that relate to small press writers and poets, such as how-to techniques for writing various types of poetry (from haiku to sonnets!), personal experiences about writing groups, conferences, writing courses, etc." He wants "poetry in various forms, including free verse, light verse, sonnets, tanka, haiku and other fixed-forms. Length: 3-35 lines. Topics of interest include relationships, personal experience, nature, etc. How-ever, what the editor is most interested in is what interests the poet, the subjects he or she choses to write about, these are the poems that will convey the uniqueness of the poet. What the editor does not want to see: poems that preach or "say" what the poet feels about problems facing our society. Take homelessness, for example. Show what the homeless person sees through his or her eyes and that will show your feelings as well and help to evoke a response, sometimes a deep, emotional reaction in the reader. I like writing that is upbeat or at least positive, enlightening or inspiring, especially humorous poetry about every day life, writing, etc. I will not consider material that is anti-religious, racist or obscene." He has published poetry by Victor Chapman, Najwa Salam Brax, Sarah Jense and Edd McWatters. As a sample he selected these lines by Diane L. Krueger:

> all my hopes and dreams/feel possible once more with/resurgence of dreams . . . hopes/and . . . belief
> in our tomorrows

WE is 36 pgs., digest-sized, saddle-stitched, with a full-color cover. He accepts about half or more of the poetry received. Press run is 250. Subscription: $12. Sample: $3.
How to Submit: Submit no more than 8 poems at a time with SASE. "I prefer typed mss, one poem per page, readable. Poets should always proofread mss before sending them out. Errors can cause rejection." Previously published poetry OK; no simultaneous submissions. E-mail submissions *not* encouraged. "Electronic and disk-based submissions are not being accepted at this time. Please send manuscripts in standard, paper format, with your name and address on every page and a SASE for reply." Cover letter appreciated; list "prior credits, if any, and other details of writing background, such as writing interests." Time between acceptance and publication is 4 months. Send SASE for guidelines, request via e-mail or visit the website. Reports in 2-4 weeks. Pays 1 copy. Acquires one-time rights. Staff reviews books of poetry. Send books for review consideration.
Also Offers: They offer cash awards for quarterly contests sponsored through the magazine. Send SASE for current rules. In 1995 they began publishing *New Markets*, a newsletter featuring information on small press and New Age markets. Send SASE for details. The newsletter may become a column feature in *WE* when a new Paying Small Press Markets column is added to the magazine. *The Best of New Markets*, a compilation of the first six issues, is available for $3.95 postpaid. *Remembrance* has ceased publication. The editor says he comments on rejections, "if I feel it will benefit the poet in the long run, never anything too harsh or overly discouraging." Website features guidelines for *WE* and other small press publications, including paying publications and others.
Advice: His advice to poets: "Support the small press publications you read and enjoy. Without your support these publications will cease to exist. The small press has given many poets their start. In essence, the small press is where poetry lives!"

⊕✓◎ WRITERS FORUM; AND MAGAZINE (Specialized: form), 89A Petherton Rd., London N5 2QT England, phone (0171)226-2657, founded 1963, editors Bob Cobbing and Adrian Clarke.
Magazine Needs: Writers Forum is a small press publisher of experimental work including sound and visual

poetry in cards, leaflets, chapbooks, occasional paperbacks and a magazine. The editors seek "explorations of 'the limits of poetry' including 'graphic' displays, notations for sound and performance, as well as semantic and syntactic developments, not to mention fun." They have published poetry by Pierre Garnier, Ernst Jandl, Arrigo Lora-Totino, Jackson Maclow and Clemente Padin. As a sample the editor selected these lines from "Wingsun-song" by Maggie O'Sullivan:

> voi singey vo hums bellowing bolds gifting sing song/crocko crunkle crinkle crankle camellia//elastic genetics torso leavened voodoo berries rue row ratches/heart singey o boat meat ballet button budded jig jog jarl iris//girlie hooves cloutie span joy stave bluely robin ronic//persimmon tantra lizard inkings cuniform crescent amethyst miraculous

And Magazine is published "irregularly" and uses "very little unsolicited poetry; practically none." Press run "varies."

How to Submit: Submit 6 poems at a time. "We normally don't publish previously published work." Work should generally be submitted camera-ready. Pays 2 copies, additional copies at half price.

Book/Chapbook Needs & How to Submit: Under the imprint Writers Forum they publish 12-18 books a year averaging 28 pgs. Samples and listing: £3. For book publication, query with 6 samples, bio, publications. Pays 12 copies, additional copies at half price.

Advice: The editors say, "We publish only that which surprises and excites us; poets who have a very individual voice and style."

N: ◎ WRITER'S GUIDELINES & NEWS MAGAZINE (Specialized: writing); INDEPENDENT PUBLISHING CO., P.O. Box 18566, Sarasota FL 34276-1566, phone (941)924-3201, fax (941)925-4468, e-mail writersgn@aol.com, founded 1988, editor-in-chief Ned Burke, associate editor Carrillee Collins.

Magazine Needs: *WG&N* is "the friend of the writer. Our quarterly magazine offers regular reviews of small press publications, articles on playwriting, travel writing, overseas markets, pals with pens, hot off the press new items, markets, contests, magazine listings, market news, poetry, fiction and much more." They want "poetry with a writing slant. No erotica." They have published poetry by Joan Stanley and Errol Miller. As a sample the editor selected this poem, "Paper Clip Capes" by Angie Monnens:

> The editor must collect them/I'm sure of this one fact,/For when my work's rejected . . ./He never sends them back.

WG&N is 52 pgs., magazine-sized, offset printed and saddle-stapled with glossy paper cover, includes art/graphics and ads. They receive about 100 poems a year, accept approximately 25%. Press run is 2,500 for 1,000 subscribers, 500 shelf sales. Subscription: $19.95/year. Sample: $5. Make checks payable to Independent Publishing Co.

How to Submit: Submit up to 4 poems at a time. Line length for poetry is 24 lines maximum. No previously published poems or simultaneous submissions. Cover letter preferred. "SASE is a must for reply. Bio info desired." Time between acceptance and publication is 4-6 months. Seldom comments on rejections. Send SASE for guidelines. Reports in 2-4 months. Pays 2 copies. Acquires one-time rights. Reviews books and chapbooks of poetry and other magazines in 500 words, single book format. Open to unsolicited reviews. Poets may also send books for review consideration.

Also Offers: The Independent Publishing Co. offers printing to self-published authors.

Advice: The editor says, "We are always seeking new and innovative writers."

☑ $ ◯ ◙ WRITER'S JOURNAL, P.O. Box 394, Perham MN 56573-0394, phone (218)346-7921, fax (218)346-7924, e-mail writersjournal@wadena.net, website http://www.sowashco.com/writersjournal/, founded 1980, poetry editor Esther M. Leiper.

Magazine Needs: *Writer's Journal* is a bimonthly magazine "for writers and poets that offers advice and guidance, motivation, inspiration, to the more serious and published writers and poets." Esther Leiper has 2 columns: "Esther Comments," which specifically critiques poems sent in by readers, and "Every Day with Poetry," which discusses a wide range of poetry topics, often—but not always—including readers' work. She says, "I enjoy a variety of poetry: free verse, strict forms, concrete, Oriental. But we take nothing vulgar, preachy or sloppily written. Since we appeal to those of different skill levels, some poems are more sophisticated than others, but those accepted must move, intrigue or otherwise positively capture me. 'Esther Comments' is never used as a negative force to put a poem or a poet down. Indeed, I focus on the best part of a given work and seek to suggest means of improvement on weaker aspects." They have published poetry by Lawrence Schug, Diana Sutliff and Eugene E. Grollmes. *Writer's Journal* is 64 pgs. (including paper cover), magazine-sized, profession-ally printed, using 4-5 pgs. of poetry in each issue, including columns. Circulation is 54,000. They receive about 900 submissions a year, use approximately 25 (including those used in Esther's columns). Single copy: $3.99; subscription: $19.97/year (US), $25.97/year (Canadian). Sample: $5.

How to Submit: "Short is best: 25-line limit, though very occasionally we use longer. Three to four poems at a time is just right." No query. Reports in 4-5 months. Pays $5/poem plus 1 copy.

Also Offers: The magazine also has poetry contests for previously unpublished poetry. Submit up to 6 poems on any subject or in any form, 25 line limit. Send SASE for guidelines only. Deadlines: April 30, August 30 and December 30. Reading fee for each contest: $2 first poem, $1 each poem thereafter. Competition receives 1,000 entries a year. Wnner announced in *The Writer's Journal*.

✔ ◯ ◎ **WRITES OF PASSAGE (Specialized: teens/young adult)**, P.O. Box 1935, Livingston NJ 07039, e-mail wopassage@aol.com, website http://www.writes.org, founded 1994, editor/publisher Wendy Mass.
Magazine Needs: *Writes of Passage* is a biannual literary journal for teenagers across the country. They only publish poems by teenagers (12-19). "We accept all topics and forms, but do not want poems longer than three pages." As a sample the editor selected these lines from "We Were Bandits" by Megan McConnel:

> . . . *And one of the saddest things/about being able to drive these days/is that you never really go anywhere—/like across America,/or all those places/you only pretended to go in the car/parked in the garage of your childhood.*

Writes of Passage is 100 pgs., 5½ × 8½, professionally printed and perfect-bound with semiglossy color cover. They receive about 2,500 poems a year, accept approximately 100. Press run is 3,000 for 500 subscribers of which 100 are libraries, 1,500 shelf sales. Subscription: $12. Sample: $6.
How to Submit: Submit up to 5 poems at a time. Previously published poems OK; no simultaneous submissions. Cover letter with brief bio (2-3 lines) preferred. Three editors review poems. Seldom comments on rejections. Send SASE for guidelines or request via e-mail. Reports in 6-8 weeks. Pays 2 copies.
Also Offers: Writes of Passage USA is a nonprofit educational organization dedicated to providing teenagers with a forum for their creative writing. In addition to publishing the literary journal, they also occasionally conduct workshops and organize readings.
Advice: The editor says, "Our motto is: 'your poem may make your parents cringe, your teachers blush, but your best friend will understand it.' We also accept tips and advice on writing poetry by authors and educators."

◎ **WRITING FOR OUR LIVES; RUNNING DEER PRESS (Specialized: women, feminism)**, 647 N. Santa Cruz Ave., The Annex, Los Gatos CA 95030-4350, founded 1991, editor/publisher Janet McEwan.
Magazine Needs: Appearing twice a year, "*Writing For Our Lives* serves as a vessel for poems, short fiction, stories, letters, autobiographies and journal excerpts from the life stories, experiences and spiritual journeys of women." They want poetry that is "personal, women's real life, life-saving, autobiographical, serious—but don't forget humorous, silence-breaking, many styles, many voices. Women writers only, please." They have published poetry by Kathy Abelson, Joyce Brady, Mary Caroline Cummins, Terry Louise Eubanks and Jennifer Crystal Fang-Chien. As a sample the editor selected these lines from "I Was There" by Marilynn Winston:

> *There comes a time/When a woman/Rises/In her prime/Examining more/Than her breasts/Ultimately/ Seeking lost self.*

Writing For Our Lives is 80-92 pgs., 5¼ × 8¼, printed on recycled paper and perfect-bound with matte card cover. They receive about 400 poems a year, accept approximately 5%. Press run is 700. Subscription: $15.50 (CA residents add 8.25% sales tax). Back issues and overseas rates available, send SASE for info. Sample: $8, $11 overseas.
How to Submit: Submit up to 5 typed poems with name and phone number on each page. Previously published poems ("sometimes") and simultaneous submissions OK. Include 2 SASEs; "at least one of them should be sufficient to return manuscripts if you want them returned." Closing dates are February 15 and August 15. Usually reports in 1-3 days, occasionally longer. "As we are now shaping 2-4 issues in advance, we may ask to hold certain poems for later consideration over a period of 18 to 24 months." Seldom comments on rejections. Send SASE for guidelines. Pays 2 copies, discount on additional copies and discount on 1-year subscription. Acquires first world-wide English language serial (or one-time reprint) rights.
Advice: The editor says, "Our contributors and circulation are international. We welcome new writers, but cannot often comment or advise. In 1999 we published only one issue, in September/October. For 2000 and later, please check with us. Subscribe or try a sample copy—gauge the fit of your writing with *WFOL*—support our ability to serve women's life-sustaining writing."

Ⓝ ◎ **WRITING ON THE EDGE (Specialized: writing/teaching writing)**, Campus Writing Center, UC Davis, One Shields Ave., Davis CA 95616, phone (530)752-2147, e-mail jdboe@ucdavis.edu, website http://www.english.ucdavis.edu/compos/woe/default.html, founded 1989, editor John Boe (queries), managing editor Margaret Eldred (submission requirements).
Magazine Needs: *Writing on the Edge* appears 2 times a year. "Our primary audience is college composition teachers but *WOE* is only partly academic in nature. We publish articles, personal essays, interviews, experimental writing, fiction, poetry and cartoons about writing and teaching writing." They want any poetry related to their specialty. Prefer poems under three pages. They have published poetry by Gary Snyder, Robert Grudin and Michael Steinberg. As a sample the editor selected these lines from "His Window" by Rick Kempa:

> *"Here, let me cut down on the glare." Jeremy's head/is bowed above his task, so I steal a glance outside:/The far-off peaks, usually masked, are ablaze with light;/they summon me. But his eyes, wild and pure//with need, call me back:* Mr. Kempa, Now you've/seen it too. Don't cut me off! *He's right/ How can I command what I would have him give?/How can I delete this day from his famished view?*

WOE is about 104 pgs., digest-sized, professionally printed and perfect-bound with matte card cover. They receive about 20 poems a year, accept approximately 20%. Press run is 600 for 350 subscribers of which 50 are libraries; 50 distributed free to editors, contributors. Subscription: $20. Sample: $10. Make checks payable to Regents of the University of California.
How to Submit: Submit up to 3 poems at a time. Previously published poems and simultaneous submissions OK. Cover letter preferred. "Omit name and address from manuscripts. Keep cover letters short. Include SASE."

Time between acceptance and publication is 1-2 years. Poems are circulated to an editorial board. "We send poems to reviewers; if they like the poems or if their reactions are mixed, the editors arrive at a concensus." Often comments on rejections. Publishes theme issues occasionally. Send SASE for guidelines. Reports in 6 months. Pays 2 copies. Authors retain all rights.

Also Offers: Website includes names of editors, writer's guidelines and tables of contents.

XANADU; POETIMES; LONG ISLAND POETRY COLLECTIVE, % LIPC, P.O. Box 773, Huntington NY 11743, founded 1979, editors Lois V. Walker, Mildred Jeffrey, Sue Kain and Weslea Sidon.

Magazine Needs: *Xanadu* is an annual publishing "serious poems including prose poems, and an occasional adventuresome essay on contemporary poetry or critical theory." They want "well-crafted quality poems. Nothing inspirational, obscene or from beginners." They have published poetry by L.L. Harper, Hugh Fox, Hillel Schwartz and Anna Ruth Ediger Baehr. As a sample the editors selected these lines from "Autumn" by EG Burrows:

> First cold slows flies/though the spider weaves/more brilliant mazes/hung with grace notes./Webs
> ornament/the double glass

Xanadu is 64 pgs., 5½×8½, perfect-bound with b&w CS1 cover stock cover. Press run is 300 for 100 subscribers of which 5 are libraries. Sample: $7.

How to Submit: Submit 3-5 poems, typed, with your name and address on each page and #10 SASE. Include a brief bio. No previously published poems; simultaneous submissions OK. Poems must be typed. Seldom comments on rejections. Send #10 SASE for guidelines. Reports in 2-24 weeks. Pays 1 copy. Acquires first North American serial rights.

Also Offers: The Long Island Poetry Collective also publishes *Poetimes*, a bimonthly newsletter edited by Binnie Pasquier that includes an extensive calendar of poetry events on Long Island, contests, market listings and poetry by its members. Subscription: $20/year, includes membership in LIPC and subscription to *Xanadu*.

Advice: They say, "We would be glad to look at more quality post-modernist and formalist poetry."

XCP: CROSS-CULTURAL POETICS (Specialized: anthropology), % College of St. Catherine-Mpls, 601 25th Ave., South Minneapolis MN 55454, website http://www.stkate.edu/xcp/, founded 1997, editor Mark Nowak.

• *Xcp* is a member of the Council of Literary Magazines and Presses.

Magazine Needs: *Xcp: Cross-Cultural Poetics* is published biannually. About *Xcp*, *The Poetry Project Newsletter* is quoted as saying, "Welcome to a writer's manual on how to detonate the Master Axis of Big Brother Narratives." They have published poetry by Amiri Baraka, Diane Glancy, Juan Felipe Herrera and Edwin Torres. *Xcp* is 150 pgs., 6×9, perfect-bound, includes ads. Subscription: $18/2 issues individuals, $40/2 issues institutions (outside US add $4). Sample (including guidelines): $10. Make checks payable to College of St. Catherine.

How to Submit: Submit 6-8 poems at a time. No previously published poems or simultaneous submissions. Cover letter preferred. Time between acceptance and publication is 1-4 months. Seldom comments on rejections. Publishes theme issues. Reports in 2-8 weeks. Always sends prepublication galleys. Pays 2 copies. Acquires first rights. Reviews books of poetry in 1,500-2,000 words, single or multi-book format. Open to unsolicited reviews. Poets may also send books for review consideration.

Advice: The editor says, "We advise all potential contributors to read at least one copy (cover to cover) before submitting work." Sample copies also available from Small Press Distribution, 1-800-869-7553.

YALE UNIVERSITY PRESS; THE YALE SERIES OF YOUNGER POETS COMPETITION, P.O. Box 209040, New Haven CT 06520-9040, phone (203)432-0900, website http://www.yale.edu/yup/, founded 1919, poetry editor (Yale University Press) Richard Miller.

Book/Chapbook Needs & How to Submit: The Yale Series of Younger Poets Competition is open to poets under 40 who have not had a book previously published. Submit ms of 48-64 pgs. in February. Entry fee: $15. Send SASE for rules and guidelines. Poets are not disqualified by previous publication of limited editions of no more than 300 copies or previously published poems in newspapers and periodicals, which may be used in the book ms if so identified. Previous winners include Richard Kenney, Carolyn Forché and Robert Hass.

$ YANKEE MAGAZINE; YANKEE ANNUAL POETRY CONTEST, P.O. Box 520, Dublin NH 03444-0520, phone (603)563-8111, founded in 1935, poetry editor (since 1955) Jean Burden.

Magazine Needs: Though it has a New England emphasis, the poetry is not necessarily about New England or by New Englanders. They want to see "high-quality contemporary poems in either free verse or traditional form. Does not have to be regional in theme. Any subject acceptable, provided it is in good taste. We look for originality in thought, imagery, insight—as well as technical control." They do not want translations or poetry that is "cliché-ridden, banal verse." They have published poetry by Maxine Kumin, Liz Rosenberg, Josephine Jacobsen, Nancy Willard, Linda Pastan, Paul Zimmer and Hayden Carruth. As a sample the editor selected these lines from "Planting the Impatiens on St. Norbert's Day" by Joan Vayo:

> three Saturdays ago/the dogwood foamed//gone green now/I see white shells of it/in the impatiens/I
> rest around its roots

The monthly is 6×9, 144 pgs., professionally printed, saddle-stapled, using full-color and b&w ads and illustrations, with full-color glossy paper cover. They receive over 30,000 submissions a year, accept about 50-60 poems, use 4-5 poems/monthly issue. They have a national distribution of more than 700,000 subscribers. Single copy: $2.99. Subscription: $24.

How to Submit: Submit up to 6 poems at a time, up to 32 lines each, free verse or traditional. No previously published poems or simultaneous submissions. "Cover letters are interesting if they include previous publication information." Submissions without SASE "are tossed." Editor comments on rejections "only if poem has so many good qualities it only needs minor revisions." Reports in 4-6 weeks. Approximately 18-month backlog. Pays $50/poem, all rights; $35, first magazine rights.

Also Offers: Sponsors an annual poetry contest judged by a prominent New England poet and published in the February issue, with awards of $150, $100 and $50 for the best 3 poems in the preceding year.

Advice: Jean Burden advises, "Study previous issues of *Yankee* to determine the kind of poetry we want. Get involved in poetry workshops at home. Read the best contemporary poetry you can find."

◯ YEFIEF, P.O. Box 8505, Santa Fe NM 87504-8505, phone (505)753-3648, fax (505)753-7049, e-mail arr@imagesformedia.com, founded 1993, editor Ann Racuya-Robbins.

Magazine Needs: *Yefief* is an annual designed "to construct a narrative of culture at the end of the century." They want "innovative visionary work of all kinds." They have published poetry by Michael Palmer, Simon Perchik and Carla Harryman. *Yefief* is 176 pgs., 7½ × 10, offset printed and perfect-bound with color coated card cover and b&w photos, art and graphics inside. Press run is 1,000. Single copy: $15.95.

How to Submit: Submit 3-6 poems at a time. Previously published poems and simultaneous submissions OK. Reports in 6-8 weeks. Pays 2-3 copies. Open to unsolicited reviews. Poets may also send books for review consideration.

☑ ◯ YEMASSEE; YEMASSEE AWARDS, Dept. of English, University of South Carolina, Columbia SC 29208, website http://www.cla.sc.edu/ENGL/index.html, founded 1993, editor Melissa Johnson.

Magazine Needs: *Yemassee* appears semiannually and "publishes primarily fiction and poetry, but we are also interested in one-act plays, brief excerpts of novels, essays, reviews and interviews with literary figures. Our essential consideration for acceptance is the quality of the work; we are open to a variety of subjects and writing styles." They accept 10-25 poems/issue. "No poems of such a highly personal nature that their primary relevance is to the author; bad Ginsberg." They have published poetry by Kwame Dawes, Virgil Saurez, Phoebe Davidson, Pamela McClure and Catherine Davidson. *Yemassee* is 60-80 pgs., 5½ × 8½, professionally printed and saddle-stitched, quality uncoated cover stock, one-color cover graphic, no ads. They receive about 400 poems a year, accept approximately 10%. Press run is 750 for 63 subscribers, 10 shelf sales; 275-300 distributed free to English department heads, creative writing chairs, agents and publishers. Subscription: $6 for students, $15 regular. Sample: $4. Make checks payable to Education Foundation/English Literary Magazine Fund.

How to Submit: Submit up to 5 poems at a time. Line length for poetry is fewer than 50, "but poems of exceptional quality are considered regardless of length." No previously published poems. Cover letter required. "Each issue's contents are determined on the basis of blind selections. Therefore we ask that all works be submitted, without the author's name or address anywhere on the typescript. Include this information along with the title(s) of the work(s) in a cover letter. For longer submissions, please include an approximate word count." Reads submissions October 1 through November 15 and March 15 through April 30. Time between acceptance and publication is 2-4 months. "Staff reads and votes on 'blind' submissions." Seldom comments on rejections. Send SASE for guidelines. Reports in 8-10 weeks after submission deadline. Pays 2 copies with the option to purchase additional copies at a reduced rate. Acquires first rights.

Also Offers: Sponsors the *Yemassee* Awards when funding permits. Awards $400/issue, usually $200 each for poetry and fiction. Website includes writer's guidelines, editor's names, sponsor's names, table of contents and cover of most recent issues.

🖼 $ ◎ YES! A JOURNAL OF POSITIVE FUTURES (Specialized), P.O. Box 10818, Bainbridge Island WA 98110, phone (206)842-0216, fax (206)842-5208, e-mail yes@futurenet.org, website http://www.futurenet.org, founded 1996, associate editor Tracy Rysavy.

Magazine Needs: "Published quarterly, *Yes!* supports active citizen engagement in creating a just, sustainable and compassionate world. We help people find, inform and inspire one another to make a difference on issues that count for the long-term future of people and the planet. We're seeking poetry that relates to our overall purpose of creating a just, sustainable and compassionate world. No 'Hallmark' verse." They have reviewed the works of Joy Harjo and Martín Espada. As a sample the editor selected these lines from "Eagle Poem" by Joy Harjo:

> Remember the sky that you were born under/Know each of the star's stories./Remember the moon, know who she is. I met her/in a bar once in Iowa City./Remember the sun's birth at dawn, that is the/ strongest point of time.

The editor says *Yes!* is 64 pgs., magazine-sized, sheet-fed printed, includes b&w photos and illustrations. They receive about 20 poems a year, accept approximately 10%. Press run is 15,000 for about 9,000 subscribers; about 1,500 distributed free to organizations and activists. Subscription: $24. Sample: $6.

How to Submit: Submit up to 5 poems at a time. Previously published poems and simultaneous submissions OK. Cover letter required. E-mail submissions OK. "Send SASE; become familiar with our content before submitting." Time between acceptance and publication is 3-6 months. Seldom comments on rejections. Publishes theme issues. Send SASE for guidelines and upcoming themes or obtain via e-mail or website. Reports in 3 months. Always sends prepublication galleys. Pays $20-30 honorarium plus 2 copies plus subscription. Buys all rights. Reviews books of poetry in 300-1,000 words, single book format. Open to unsolicited reviews. Poets may also send books for review consideration.

Also Offers: Website includes sample articles, guidelines, book reviews, letter to the editor and news of the nonprofit organization/publisher.

YORKSHIRE JOURNAL (Specialized: regional), Ilkley Rd., Otley, West Yorkshire LS2 3JP England, phone (01943)467958, fax (01943)850057, founded 1992, contact Mark Whitley.

Magazine Needs: *Yorkshire Journal* is a quarterly general interest magazine about Yorkshire. They want poetry no longer than 25 lines with some relevance to Yorkshire. They have published poetry by Vernon Scannell, Anna Adams and Simon Armitage. As a sample we selected these lines from "Magnum Opus In Memoriam Jacob Kramer 1892-1962" by Vernon Scannell:

> One night in The Victoria in Leeds/Jacob said to me, "Before I die/I'm going to paint a picture that
> will stun/them all. They think I've lost/whatever talent I once had,/that drink and craziness have
> neutered me./I'll prove them wrong./It's going to be a northern landscape,/forests, mountains, peaks,
> a pitiless sky—/but non-specific, if you follow me—/a landscape of the heart./It's haunted me for years./
> I'll show you . . . look . . ."

Mr. Whitley says *YJ* is 120 pgs., highly illustrated. They receive about 200 poems a year, accept approximately 10%. Press run is 3,000 for 700 subscribers, 2,300 shelf sales. Subscription: £12. Sample: £2.95. Make checks payable to SMITH Settle Ltd.

How to Submit: Submit up to 6 poems at a time. Previously published poems and simultaneous submissions OK. Cover letter required including biographical information. Has a large backlog. Time between acceptance and publication varies. Sometimes comments on rejections. Send SASE (or SAE and IRC) for guidelines. Reports within 1 month maximum. Pays 1 copy.

ZINE ZONE, 47 Retreat Place, London E9 6RH United Kingdom, phone (0181)9857488, fax (0181)5251466, e-mail zine.zone@ndirect.co.uk, founded 1992, contact "editorial."

Magazine Needs: *Zine Zone* appears 8 times a year and publishes "a chaotic mix of illustrative works with poetry, short stories, music reviews, etc." For their poetry wants, they say, "anything goes. Although, we mostly publish obscure unpublished poets and students." As a sample they selected these lines from "Laughing at Nothing" by Steve Andrews (Wales):

> Doing something ordinary is only an act;/There's freedom of expression in the ethers./I was talking to
> a Neanderthal face/And inspecting rooms on a personal pilgrimage,/Running like a child under smiling
> Heavens,/Laughing at nothing is too much for some it seems.

They say *ZZ* is 52 pgs., A4, photocopied and stapled with b&w paper cover, b&w graphics. They receive about 200 poems a year, accept approximately 50-70%. Press run is 500 for 120 subscribers. Single copy: £1.95 ($3 US); subscription: £18/8 copies, £11/4 copies. Sample: £3 ($5 US).

How to Submit: Previously published poems and simultaneous submissions OK. Cover letter preferred. Fax, e-mail and disk submissions (text format) OK. Time between acceptance and publication is 2 months. Reviews books and chapbooks of poetry and other magazines, single book format. Open to unsolicited reviews.

Also Offers: "Poetry nights organized in and around London (UK) where poets read their work to an audience."

$ ☑ ZOLAND BOOKS INC., 384 Huron Ave., Cambridge MA 02138, phone (617)864-6252, founded 1987, publisher Roland Pease.

Book/Chapbook Needs: Zoland is a "literary press: fiction, poetry, photography, gift books, books of literary interest." They want "high-quality" poetry, not sentimental. They have published poetry by Ange Mlinko, Joseph Lease, Michael Franco and Rane Arroyo. They publish 15 books/year, flat-spined, averaging 104 pgs.

How to Submit: Query with 5-10 sample poems, bio, publications and SASE. Sometimes sends prepublication galleys. Pays 5-10% royalties plus 5 copies. Buys all rights.

$ ☑ ZOMBIE LOGIC PRESS, 420 E. Third St., Box 319, Byron IL 61010, e-mail dobe1969@aol.com, founded 1997, publisher Thomas L. Vaultonburg.

Book/Chapbook Needs: Zombie Logic Press seeks "to find and publish the best poetry available, preferably by a younger poet." They publish 1 paperback/year. The publisher "likes surrealism, avant-garde and Beat poetry; originality, daring and intensity impress me." As a sample the editor selected his poem "Doppelganger":

> shadows are men/tearing themselves from darkness/I step into each/and bleed like an amethyst/
> discovering pain.

Books are usually 50-100 pgs., digest-sized, professionally printed, perfect-bound.

How to Submit: Query first, with a few sample poems and a cover letter with brief bio and publication credits. "Send enough to give me an idea of whether or not I'd like to read more. I won't publish work by anyone I don't like or respect. Take the time to become someone who I actually care about." E-mail submissions OK. Previously published poems and simultaneous submissions OK. Cover letter preferred. "Those who have the common courtesy to tell me something about themselves and ask me about my own book before rattling off a list of prior pubs and rambling about how great they are stand the best chance." Time between acceptance and publication is 6 months. Seldom comments on rejections. Replies to queries in 2 weeks; to mss in 1 month. Pays advance or 100 author's copies (out of a press run of 1,000). *Detached Retinas*, by Thomas Vaultonburg, is available for $6 from Zombie Logic Press (make checks payable to Thomas Vaultonburg).

Advice: The publisher says, "I started my own press and published my own book because I love poetry. Nobody wants to receive an endless stream of arrogant cover letters spouting off about how great and unappreciated you are, backed up by weak poetry. I know I don't. Challenge me and I'll do your book."

☑ ▣ ◑ **ZUZU'S PETALS QUARTERLY ONLINE**, P.O. Box 4853, Ithaca NY 14852, phone (607)844-9009, e-mail info@zuzu.com, website http://www.zuzu.com, founded 1992, editor T. Dunn.

Magazine Needs: "We publish high-quality fiction, essays, poetry and reviews on our award-winning website, which was featured in *USA Today Online*, *Entertainment Weekly*, and *Web Magazine*. Becoming an Internet publication allows us to offer thousands of helpful resources and addresses for poets, writers, editors and researchers, as well as to greatly expand our readership. Free verse, blank verse, experimental, visually sensual poetry, etc. are especially welcome here. We're looking for a freshness of language, new ideas and original expression. No 'June, moon and spoon' rhymed poetry. No light verse. I'm open to considering more feminist, ethnic, alternative poetry, as well as poetry of place." They have published poetry by Ruth Daigon, Robert Sward, Laurel Bogen, W.T. Pfefferle and Kate Gale. As a sample the editor selected these lines from "San Francisco Earthquake" by Kathryn Young:

> *Padre Pablo, in the dream I could understand/how the angels of death like wild birds/can be entertained*
> *with kind gestures/like strangers, how white their teeth,/how warm and dark their skin*

ZPQO averages 70-100 pgs., using full-color artwork, and is an electronic publication available free of charge on the Internet. "Many libraries, colleges, and coffeehouses offer access to the Internet for those without home Internet accounts." They receive about 3,000 poems a year, accept approximately 10%. A copy of *Zuzu's Petals Poetry Buffet*, a sample of writing from the past 4 years is available for $5.

How to Submit: Submit up to 4 poems at a time. Previously published poems and simultaneous submissions OK. "Cover letters are not necessary. The work should speak for itself." Submissions via e-mail are welcome, as well as submissions in ASCII (DOS IBM) format on 3½" disks OK. Include e-mail submissions in the body of the message. Seldom comments on rejections. Send SASE for guidelines or request via e-mail. Reports in 2 weeks to 2 months. Acquires one-time electronic rights. Staff reviews books of poetry in approximately 200 words. Send books, galleys or proofs for review consideration.

Also Offers: Website includes full text of *Zuzu's Petals Quarterly*, writer's guidelines, over 10,000 helpful addresses, over 7,000 arts links, online discussion salon, updated literary news, poetry videos.

Advice: The editor says, "Read as much poetry as you can. Support the literary arts: Go to poetry readings, read chapbooks and collections of verse. Eat poetry for breakfast, cultivate a love of language, then write!"

Ⓝ ☒ **$** ◯ ◑ **ZYGOTE MAGAZINE**, 1474 Wall St., Winnipeg, Manitoba R3E 2S4 Canada, e-mail cjlittle@escape.ca, founded 1993, editors Kerry Ryan and Cindy Little.

Magazine Needs: *Zygote* appears quarterly and "publishes the best of new and established poets and short story writers across genres." They want poetry on "any subject matter; free verse; usually lyric, social or even some alternative verse with an edge. No rhyming, high school type." They have published poetry by Joy Hewitt Mann, John B. Lee, Beth Goobie and Alice Major. As a sample the editor selected this poem, "How to piss in the cold and dark," by Victor Jerrett Enns:

> *Check first the direction/of the wind, then/piss off the porch-//your name/under the night light/of the*
> *January moon.//In the morning/your embarrassed roommate/covers your tracks.*

The editor says *Zygote* is 40-60 pgs., magazine-sized, sheet fed printed and saddle-stitched with b&w 60 lb. cover, includes b&w photos and drawings and various writing ads. They receive about 400 poems a year, accept approximately 25%. Press run is 750 for 250 subscribers of which 20 are libraries, 250 shelf sales; 200 distributed free to contributors. Single copy: $3.95; subscription: $16/4 issues. Sample: $5. Make checks payable to *Zygote Magazine*.

How to Submit: Submit up to 5 poems at a time. Line length for poetry is 50 maximum. No previously published poems; simultaneous submissions OK. Cover letter required. E-mail and disk submissions preferred. "You must include a SASE [with regular mail submissions] if you want a reply." Time between acceptance and publication is 3 months." Poems are selected by guest editors. Then, the editorial collective reads and discusses all picks." Seldom comments on rejections. Send SASE for guidelines or obtain via e-mail. Reports in 3 months. Pays $5/poem, $15 for fiction, $15 for reviews; plus 2 copies. Acquires first rights. Reviews books and chapbooks of poetry in 250 words, single and multi-book format. Open to unsolicited reviews. Poets may also send books for review consideration.

Also Offers: Sponsors a theme contest in each issue. Entry fee: $16, includes subscription. Cash prizes offered. Contributors are not required to enter.

Advice: The editors say, "Spend time preparing your work. Proofreading and editing will produce lean, powerful poetry, the kind we like."

Contests & Awards

The opportunities for poets to receive recognition and publish their work are growing via the route of contests and awards. And while this section of *Poet's Market* is considerably smaller than Publishers of Poetry, it contains 37 new entries within its approximately 150 "markets."

Here you will find a wide range of competitions—from contests with modest prizes sponsored by state poetry societies, colleges or even cities to prestigious awards offered by private foundations. Among the various contests and awards included in this section are those that offer publication in addition to their monetary prizes. But even if publication is not included, the publicity generated upon winning some of these contests can make your name more familiar to editors.

SELECTING CONTESTS

Whether you're submitting one poem to a quarterly contest sponsored by a journal or an entire manuscript to an award offered by a book publisher, you should never submit to contests and awards blindly. Because many contests require entry fees, blind submissions will just waste your time. As in the Publishers of Poetry section, each listing here contains one or more Openness to Submissions symbols in its heading. These symbols will not only help you narrow the list of contests and awards to those open to your experience level, but they can also help you evaluate your chances of winning.

The ☐ symbol, for instance, is given to contests that welcome entries from beginning or unpublished poets. While most contests require entry fees, or membership in the sponsoring organization, they typically are not exploitative of poets, beginning or otherwise. Keep in mind, however, that if a contest charges a $5 entry fee and offers $75 in prizes, the organizers only need 15 entries to cover the prizes. Even though fees may also go toward providing a small honorarium for the judge, 100 entries will surely net the organizers a tidy profit—at the expense of the participating poets. Be careful when deciding which contests are worth your money.

The ◪ symbol precedes the name of general literary contests, usually for poets with some experience. This symbol may also precede awards for recently published collections, such as the Colorado Book Awards (new to this edition) and the Pulitzer Prize in Letters, or fellowships designed for poets of "demonstrated ability," such as the Guggenheims. And competitions like the Stan and Tom Wick Poetry Prize, a contest open to poets writing in English who have not yet published a full-length collection, are listed under this symbol. If you're just beginning, start building a reputation by publishing in periodicals, then try your hand at these competitions.

Of all the symbols, perhaps the most useful is ◎, which designates specialized contests and awards. That is, you—or your poetry—must meet certain criteria to be eligible. Some contests are regional, so only poets from a certain area may enter. For example, the Montalvo Biennial Poetry Competition offers $2,000 in prizes to poets residing in California, Nevada, Oregon and Washington. Also, fellowships and grants offered by state and provincial arts councils are only open to residents of the particular state or province. Some of these programs are detailed here. For those not found, see the list of State and Provincial Grants following this section.

Other contests are limited to certain groups, such as women or students. For instance, the Frank O'Hara Award Chapbook Competition offers $500 and publication to gay, lesbian or bisexual poets. Also, the Senior Poet Laureate Poetry Competition offers an annual award to American poets age 50 or older.

A few contests are for translations only. Still others are limited to poets writing in certain forms or on certain subjects. If you write haiku, for example, consider the Penumbra Poetry

Competition. One award limited to a certain subject is The Trewithen Poetry Prize, which only considers work dealing with rural themes. Competitions that primarily consider themselves specialized are often open to both beginning and established poets.

Also noteworthy are several other symbols often found at the beginning of a listing. These symbols are included to convey certain information at a glance. The ∎ symbol identifies new listings, the ⊕ symbol denotes international listings, the ✦ symbol indicates Canadian listings, and the ✓ symbol signifies a change in a listing's address, phone number, e-mail address or contact name.

In addition to the listings in this section, there are contests and awards (particularly those sponsored by journals) mentioned in listings in other sections of this book. For those, you should refer to the list of Additional Contests & Awards at the end of this section and consult the listings noted there for details. (See the General Index for the listings' page numbers.)

Once you've narrowed the contests and awards you want to enter, treat the submission process just as you would if you were submitting to a magazine: Always send a SASE for more information. Many contests want you to submit work along with their specific entry form or application. Others offer guidelines detailing exactly how they want poetry submitted. Also, deadlines for entries are often subject to change and if your work arrives after the deadline date, it will automatically be disqualified. Finally, obtain copies of recent winning entries for any contest you are considering. This will give you a good idea of the kind of work the judges appreciate. However, this may not apply if the judges change each year.

DISCOVER OTHER RESOURCES

Besides this section of *Poet's Market*, there are other sources of information on competitions. In fact, some good places to locate contests are in your own city or town. Many bookstores and libraries post announcements for local contests on their bulletin boards. Calling a nearby college's English department may provide you with the scoop on regional competitions. And, many poetry groups publish newsletters containing information on competitions that are available to nonmembers. Finally, don't forget to check websites and the classified ads of community arts/entertainment papers for those contests currently seeking entries.

For more information on the national level, *Poets & Writers Magazine* (see the listing in the Publications of Interest section) includes calls for entries for numerous contests and awards along the margins of its pages. In addition, the magazine also includes a Grants and Awards section listing recent winners of poetry and fiction prizes of $500 or more and prestigious nonmonetary awards in fiction and poetry. Reading the winners' work is a good way to determine the type of poetry these competitions are seeking.

Other publications containing information on contests and awards include the *Writer's Chronicle* published by Associated Writing Programs (see listing in the Organizations section), *Grants and Awards Available to American Writers* (published by the PEN American Center; see PEN's listing in Organizations), *The Writer* (published by The Writer, Inc., 120 Boylston St., Boston MA 02116), *Writer's Digest* magazine and the annual directory *Writer's Market* (both published by Writer's Digest Books). Check local bookstores for these publications or order copies directly from the publisher.

For detailed information on selecting and submitting to contests, read Chapter Three: Entering Contests in Michael J. Bugeja's *Poet's Guide* (Story Line Press, 1995). The chapter also includes essays from some well-known poets on their experiences with and opinions on competitions.

2000 POET'S MARKET POETRY CONTEST

With the completion of the fourth *Poet's Market* Poetry Contest, we would like to thank all those who entered the competition and say congratulations to our winners: first-place winner Mikal Lofgren of Salt Lake City, Utah; second-place winner Linden Ontjes of Fairbanks, Alaska;

and third-place winner Sharon Helberg of Kelowna, British Columbia, Canada. The winning poems along with information about the winning poets can be found on our Writer's Digest website (www.writersdigest.com/poetsmarket).

◯ ◎ **ADAPTABLES ANNUAL POETRY AWARD (Specialized: poems by persons with all types of disabilities)**, The Adaptables, Inc., P.O. Box 30246, Winston-Salem NC 27130-0246, phone (336)896-0779, fax (336)759-2677, established in 1998, offers annual awards of 1st Prize: $200, 2nd Prize: $100, 3rd Prize: $50. Winners and "poems of merit" will be published in an anthology and will receive free copies. Submissions must be unpublished. Submit poems on any subject or in any form. Entry fee(s): $10/poem. Deadline: September 15. Winner(s) will be notified by letter. "The Adaptables, Inc. is a grassroots organization of persons with disabilities promoting improved attitudes toward people with disabilities. The Winston-Salem Foundation is partially underwriting the expense of the contest. We feel that persons with disabilities have a great deal to contribute to mankind's understanding of himself and his place in the universe. If writing poetry is an outlet for you and if you enjoy reading great poetry—the kind that shocks you into another order of perception and ushers you into an experience so moving that you feel (to quote King Lear) 'cut to the brain,' then send us your work."

◪ **AKRON POETRY PRIZE**, The University of Akron Press, 374B Bierce Library, Akron OH 44325-1703, phone (330)972-5342, fax (330)972-5132, e-mail press@uakron.edu, website http://www.uakron.edu/uapress, award director Elton Glaser, offers annual award of $1,000 plus publication. Submissions must be unpublished and may be entered in other contests (with notification of acceptance elsewhere). Submit 60-100 pages maximum, typed, double-spaced, postmarked between May 15 and June 30, with SASE for results. Mss will not be returned. Do not send mss bound or enclosed in covers. Send SASE for guidelines. Inquiries via fax and e-mail OK. Entry fee: $20. Deadline: entries are accepted May 15 through June 30 only. Competition receives about 500 entries. Judge for the 1999 prize was Yusef Komunyakaa. Winner will be announced in September. Copies of previous winning books may be obtained by contacting UAP or through your local bookstore. The University of Akron Press "is committed to publishing poetry that, as Robert Frost said, 'begins in delight and ends in wisdom.' Books accepted must exhibit three essential qualities: mastery of language, maturity of feeling, and complexity of thought."

◎ **THE AMY AWARD (Specialized: women, form, regional)**, Guild Hall of East Hampton, 158 Main St., East Hampton NY 11937, phone (516)324-0806, fax (516)324-2722, website http://www.thehamptons.com/guild_hall, established in 1996, director of literary programs Robert Long, offers annual honorarium plus a reading with a well-known poet in the *Writers at Guild Hall* series. Submissions may be entered in other contests. Submit 3 lyric poems of no more than 50 lines each, with name, address and phone on each page. Enclose SASE and bio. Entrants must be women 30 years of age or under residing on Long Island or in the New York metropolitan region. Send SASE for guidelines and deadline. Most recent award winner was Prudence Peiffer. Entrants will be notified of winner via their SASE approximately 2 months after contest deadline. Guild Hall is the East End of Long Island's leading cultural center. It hosts, besides major museum, theater, and musical events, the *Writers at Guild Hall* series. Readers have included Tom Wolfe, Kurt Vonnegut, Joseph Brodsky, Maxine Kumin, Allen Ginsberg, Sharon Olds, John Ashbery, E.L. Doctorow, Eileen Myles and Linda Gregg.

🄽 🌐 ◪ ◎ **ANDREAS-GRYPHIUS-PREIS; NIKOLAUS-LENAU-PREIS (Specialized: foreign Language)**, Die Künstlergilde e.V., Hafenmarkt 2, D-73728, Esslingen a.N., Germany, phone 0711/3969 01-0. "The prize is given annually to German-speaking authors who are dealing with the particular problems of the German culture in eastern Europe or to the best published literary works (which may be poems) that promote understanding between Germans and eastern Europeans." Prizes awarded: 1 Grand Prize of DM 25,000; 1 prize of DM 7,000. Submissions judged by a 7-member jury. They also sponsor the Nikolaus-Lenau-Preis for German-speaking poets. The prize is named in honor of Nikolaus Lenau, "a poet who facilitated understanding with the people of eastern Europe." The prize of DM 11,000 is awarded for published poems. Write for details.

✔ ◯ ◪ **ARIZONA STATE POETRY SOCIETY ANNUAL CONTEST**, 10914 Manzanita Dr., Sun City AZ 85373, phone (602)972-9316, e-mail elaine139@juno.com, established in 1967, president Jim Groundwater. Contest for various poetry forms and subjects. Prizes range from $10-100; 1st, 2nd and 3rd place winners are published in the winter edition of *The Sandcutters*, the group's quarterly publication, and names are listed for honorable mention winners. Contest information available for SASE. Inquires via e-mail OK. Fees vary. Deadline: August 31. Competition receives over 1,000 entries a year. "ASPS sponsors a variety of monthly contests for members. Membership is available to anyone anywhere."

◯ **ARKANSAS POETRY DAY CONTEST; POETS' ROUNDTABLE OF ARKANSAS**, over 25 categories, many open to all poets. Brochure available in June; deadline in September; awards given in October. For copy send SASE to Verna Lee Hinegardner, 605 Higdon, Apt. 109, Hot Springs AR 71913.

🄽 ◯ **ART COOP FELLOWSHIP IN POETRY**, % Charli Valdez, 1124 Columbia N.E., Albuquerque NM 87106, e-mail cottonwood@geocities.com, website http://www.geocities.com/~cottonwood, established in

1996, director Charli Buono de Valdez, offers annual fellowship in poetry open to poets everywhere. Awards cash prize (not less than $250) and publication. Include cover sheet, bio and list of publications. Send SASE for guidelines or visit website. Entry fee(s): $5 for first poem, $2 each thereafter. "For flat $10 fee and SASE, feedback on poems provided." Deadline: May 31.

N **$** 🖉 **"ART IN THE AIR" POETRY CONTEST**, Inventing the Invisible/"Art in the Air" Radio Show, 3128 Walton Blvd., Suite 186, Rochester Hills MI 48309, phone (248)693-7344, fax (248)693-7344, e-mail lagapvp@aol.com, website http://www.inventingtheinvisible.com, established in 1991, award director Margo LaGattuta, offers biannual award of 1st Prize: $100; 2nd Prize: $50; and 4 Honorable Mentions. ("All winners read poems on the radio.") Submissions may be entered in other contests. Submit 3 poems maximum in any form, typed, single-spaced, limit 2 pages per poem. Send SASE for guidelines or visit website. Inquiries via fax or e-mail OK. Entry fee(s): $5 for up to 3 poems. Accepts entry fees in foreign currencies. Deadlines: October 30, 1999 and April 30, 2000. Competition receives over 600 entries a year. Most recent contest winners include Simone Muench, Marilyn Krysi, Julie Moulds, Elizabeth Rosner, Bill Rudolph, Jenny Brown and Wyatt Townley (1998). Judges were Mary Jo Firth Gillett and Margo LaGattuta. Winner(s) will be announced 2 months after deadline. Copies of previous winning poems or books may be obtained by sending an SASE to the Inventing the Invisible address. " 'Art in the Air' is an interview radio show on WPON, 1460 AM, in Bloomfield Hills, MI, hosted by Margo LaGattuta. The theme is creativity & the creative process, especially featuring writers both local and national. Send only your best work—well crafted and creative. Judges look for excellence in content and execution."

✓ 🖉 **ARTIST TRUST; ARTIST TRUST GAP GRANTS; ARTIST TRUST FELLOWSHIPS (Specialized: regional)**, 1402 Third Ave., Suite 404, Seattle WA 98101, phone (206)467-8734, fax (206)467-9633, e-mail info@artisttrust.org, program director Heather Dwyer. Artist Trust is a nonprofit arts organization that provides grants to artists (including poets) who are residents of the state. Inquiries via fax and e-mail OK. Competition receives 650 entries a year. Most recent contest winners include Allen Braden, Anita Feng and Pamela Dionne. It also publishes, three times a year, a journal of news about arts opportunities and cultural issues.

✓ 🖉 🖉 **ARTS RECOGNITION AND TALENT SEARCH (ARTS) (Specialized: students)**, National Foundation for Advancement in the Arts, 800 Brickell Ave., Suite 500, Miami FL 33131, phone (800)970-ARTS, fax (305)377-1149, e-mail nfaa@nfaa.org, established in 1981, program coordinator Dena Willman. "ARTS is a national program designed to identify, recognize and encourage young people who demonstrate excellence in Dance, Music, Music/Jazz, Music/Voice, Theater, Visual Arts, Photography and Writing." Offers annual awards of $3,000 (Level 1), $1,500 (Level 2), $1,000 (Level 3), $500 (Level 4) and $100 (Level 5). Submissions may be entered in other contests. Submit up to 6 poems in up to but not more than 10 pgs. Open to high school seniors and young people aged 17 or 18 by or on December 1 of the award year. Send SASE for entry form and guidelines. Inquiries via fax and e-mail OK. Entry fee: $25 (June 1 early application deadline), $35 (October 1 regular application deadline). Competition receives over 8,000 entries a year. Most recent award winners include Kirsten Noelle Anderson, Katherine Ruth Erb and Parker D. Everett. Winners are announced by December 30 by mail. Website includes applications, deadlines and updates.

✓ 🖉 **BAY AREA BOOK REVIEWERS ASSOCIATION AWARDS (BABRA); FRED CODY AWARD (Specialized: regional)**, 1450 Fourth St., #4, Berkeley CA 94710, phone (415)883-2353, fax (415)883-4280, established in 1981, contact Jon Sharp, offers annual awards which recognize "the best of Northern California (from Fresno north) fiction, poetry, nonfiction, and children's literature." Submissions must be previously published. Submit 3 copies of each book entered. Open to Northern California residents. Send SASE for guidelines. Deadline: December 1. BABRA also sponsors the Fred Cody Award for lifetime achievement given to a Northern California writer who also serves the community; and gives, on an irregular basis, awards for outstanding work in translation and publishing. The Cody Award winner for 1998 was Maxine Hong Kingston.

🖉 **GEORGE BENNETT FELLOWSHIP**, Phillips Exeter Academy, 20 Main St., Exeter NH 03833-2460, website http://www.exeter.edu, established in 1968, provides a $6,000 fellowship plus room and board to a writer with a ms in progress. The Fellow's only official duties are to be in residence while the academy is in session and to be available to students interested in writing. The committee favors writers who have not yet published a book-length work with a major publisher. Send SASE for application materials or obtain via website. Deadline: December 1. Competition receives 150 entries. Recent award winners were Gina Apostol (1997-1998) and Lysley Tenorio (1998-1999). Website includes a description of fellowship, an application form and application instructions.

🖉 **BIGGER THAN TEXAS WRITERS CONTEST**, (formerly Texas-Wide Writers Contest), Byliners of Corpus Christi, P.O. Box 6218, Corpus Christi TX 78466-6218, e-mail otter@newton.tamuk.edu, established in 1940, offers annual cash prizes or $50, $20 and $10 in 2 categories, rhymed and unrhymed poems. Submissions must be unpublished and may be entered in other contests. Submit 40 lines on any subject or in any form. Open to all. Submit poems on white paper, one-sided; poems may be single spaced. Send SASE for guidelines only.

Entry fee: $4/poem. Deadline: February 28. Competition receives 300 entries in all categories (poetry, fiction, nonfiction, children's). "Winners are announced at Byliners May luncheon which is held the third Saturday in May. Winners need not be present to win. Winners list available for SASE after May 15. Byliners is a writers support group. We hold monthly meetings with speakers in the writing/editing professions."

BLUE NOSE POETRY POETS-OF-THE-YEAR COMPETITION, Blue Nose Poetry, 61 Athelstan House, Homerton Rd., Hackney, London E9 5PH United Kingdom, established in 1988, offers annual contest. £1,000 in prize money will be distributed at the discretion of the judges (none of the winners will receive less than £100) plus publication in an anthology. Submit up to 6 mss of 10 pages each of no more than 40 lines/page. Include SASE or IRC for winners list. Poems may have been previously published in a magazine or journal, but *not* in a collection or anthology. Pages should be consecutively numbered and stapled together in the top left-hand corner. Send SASE for entry form and guidelines or obtain via website. Entry fee: £6 sterling. Make checks payable to Blue Nose Poets. Postmark deadline: May 10. Competition receives around 1,000 entries. Winners will be announced in September.

BLUESTEM PRESS AWARD, Bluestem Press, Emporia State University, English Dept., Box 4019, website http://www.emporia.edu/bluestem/index.htm, Emporia KS 66801-5087, phone (316)341-5216, fax (316)341-5547, established in 1989, editor/contest coordinator Philip Heldrich, offers annual award of $1,000 and publication for an original book-length collection of poems. Submissions must be unpublished and may be entered in other contests (with notification). Submit a typed ms of at least 48 pages on any subject in any form with a #10 SASE for notification. Send SASE for guidelines. Inquiries via e-mail OK. Entry fee: $15. Deadline: March 1. Competition receives 500-700 entries a year. Recent award winner was Mary Crockett Hill. Judge was Mark Cox. Winner will be announced in May. Copies of previous winning poems or books may be obtained by contacting the Bluestem Press at the above number. Enter early to avoid entering after the deadline. Also, looking at the different winners from past years would help. Manuscripts will *not* be accepted after the deadline and will not be returned. Website includes guidelines, announcements, previous winners and booklist.

THE BOARDMAN TASKER AWARD (Specialized: mountain literature), The Boardman Tasker Charitable Trust, 14 Pine Lodge, Dairyground Rd., Bramhall, Stockport, Cheshire SK7 2HS United Kingdom, fax (0161)439-4624, established in 1983, secretary Dorothy Boardman, offers prize of £2,000 to "the author or authors of the best literary work, whether fiction, nonfiction, drama or poetry, the central theme of which is concerned with the mountain environment. Entries for consideration may have been written by authors of any nationality but the work must be published or distributed in the United Kingdom between November 1, 1999 and October 31, 2000. (If not published in the U.K., please indicate name of distributor.) The work must be written or have been translated into the English language." Submit ms in book format. "In a collection of essays or articles by a single author, the inclusion of some material previously published but now in book form for the first time will be acceptable." Submissions accepted from the publisher only. Four copies of entry must be submitted with application. Inquiries via fax OK. Deadline: August 15, 2000. Competition receives about 20 entries. Most recent winner was *Eric Shipton, Everest and Beyond* by Peter Steele, published by Constable (London).

BP NICHOL CHAPBOOK AWARD (Specialized: regional), 316 Dupont St., Toronto, Ontario M5R 1V9 Canada, phone (416)964-7919, fax (416)964-6941, established in 1985, $1,000 (Canadian) prize for the best poetry chapbook (10-48 pgs.) in English published in Canada in the preceding year. Submit 3 copies (not returnable) and a brief curriculum vitae of the author. Inquiries via fax OK. Deadline: March 31. Competition receives between 40-60 entries on average. Most recent contest winner was Nicole Markotic.

THE BRIDPORT PRIZE, Bridport Arts Centre, South St., Bridport, Dorset DT6 3NR United Kingdom, phone (01308)427183, fax (01308)59166, e-mail arts@bridport.co.uk, established in 1980, offers annual award for an original poem of not more than 42 lines and an original story of not more than 5,000 words. 1st Prize: £2,500, 2nd Prize: £1,000, and 3rd Prize: £500 in each category plus small supplementary prize. Prize winning entries also published in anthology. Submissions must be previously unpublished. Open as to subject or form. Send SASE (or SAE and IRC) for entry form and guidelines. Entry fee: £4 sterling per entry. Deadline: June 30. Competition receives approximately 8,000 entries. Most recent contest winners were Corinna Weyreter and John Greening. Judges for 1999 contest were Peter Benson and Tobias Hill. Winners will be announced at the end of September. Copies of the previous winning anthologies may be obtained by sending £8 sterling (£7 within UK) to Competition Secretary at the above address.

BUCKNELL SEMINAR FOR YOUNGER POETS; STADLER SEMESTER FOR YOUNGER POETS; PHILIP ROTH RESIDENCE IN CREATIVE WRITING (Specialized: students), Bucknell University, Lewisburg PA 17837, phone (570)577-1853 or (570)577-1944, e-mail hogue@bucknell.edu, website http://www.departments.buckhell.edu/stadler_center/, director Cynthia Hogue, includes the Stadler Semester for Younger Poets, the Seminar for Younger Poets and the Roth Residence Series. The Stadler Semester is distinctive in allowing an undergraduate poet almost four months of concentrated work centered in poetry. Guided by practicing poets, the apprentice will write and read poetry and will receive critical response. The Fellow selected will work with Bucknell's writing faculty. The visiting Poet-in-Residence also will participate in the program. The Fellow will earn a semester of academic credit by taking four units of study: a tutorial or individual project with a mentor poet, a poetry-writing workshop, a literature course, and an elective. Undergraduates from four-year colleges with at least one course in poetry writing are eligible to apply; most applicants will be second-semester juniors. Send a 10- to 12-page portfolio and a letter of presentation (a brief autobiography that expresses commitment to writing poetry, cites relevant courses and lists any publications). Also include a transcript, two recommendations (at least one from a poetry-writing instructor), and a letter from the academic dean granting permission for the student to attend Bucknell for a semester. Application deadline for the Stadler Semester is November 1. The student chosen for the fellowship will be notified by November 25. The Bucknell Seminar For Younger Poets is not a contest for poems but for 8 fellowships to the Bucknell Seminar, held for 4 weeks in June every year. Seniors and juniors from American colleges are eligible to compete for the 8 fellowships, which consist of tuition, room, board and spaces for writing. Application deadline for each year's seminar is March 1. Students chosen for fellowships will be notified by April 7. Please send SASE for details. The Philip Roth Residence in Creative Writing, established in 1993, awards a residence in the Fall Semester for poets in even-numbered years and for fiction writers in odd-numbered years. Submit 15 pages of poetry or fiction on any subject, in any form. Open to residents of the US, over 21 years of age, not presently a student in a college or university. Some record of publication is expected. Send SASE for guidelines. Inquiries via fax and e-mail OK. Deadline: March 1. Recent award winner was Adrian Oktenberg. Winner will be notified by letter April 15. Website includes schedule of readings; information and application guidelines; newsletter and a link to Bucknell's English Department.

◎ **CALIFORNIA BOOK AWARDS OF THE COMMONWEALTH CLUB OF CALIFORNIA (Specialized: regional)**, 595 Market St., San Francisco CA 94105, phone (415)597-6700, fax (415)597-6729, website http://www.commonwealthclub.org, established in 1931, senior director Jim Coplan, annual awards "consisting of not more than two gold and eight silver medals" for books of "exceptional literary merit" in poetry, fiction and nonfiction (including work related to California and work for children), plus 2 "outstanding" categories. Submissions must be previously published. Submit at least 3 copies of each book entered with an official entry form. (Books may be submitted by author or publisher.) Open to books, published during the year prior to the contest, whose author "must have been a legal resident of California at the time the manuscript was submitted for publication." Send SASE for entry form and guidelines or obtain via website. Most recent award winner was Amy Gertsler.

☘ ◎ Ø **CANADIAN AUTHORS ASSOCIATION FOR ADULT LITERATURE AWARDS (Specialized: regional); THE AIR CANADA AWARD; CANADIAN AUTHORS ASSOCIATION**, Box 419, Campbellford, Ontario K0L 1L0 Canada, phone (705)653-0323, fax (705)653-0593, e-mail canauth@redden .on.ca, website http://www.canauthors.org/national.html. Canadian Authors Association Awards for Adult Literature provides $2,500 and a silver medal in each of 6 categories (fiction, poetry, short stories, Canadian history, biography, drama) to Canadian writers, for a published book in the year of publication (or, in the case of drama, first produced). Entry fee: $20/title. Deadline: December 15; except for works published after December 1, in which case the postmark deadline is January 15. The Air Canada Award is an annual award of two tickets to any Air Canada destination, to a Canadian author under 30 who shows the most promise. **Nominations are made before March 31 by Canadian Authors Association branches or other writers' organizations, agents or publishers.** The award is given at the CAA banquet in June.

◻ Ø **CAPRICORN POETRY AWARD; OPEN VOICE AWARDS; THE WRITER'S VOICE**, Writer's Voice, 5 W. 63rd St., New York NY 10023, phone (212)875-4124, e-mail wtrsvoice1@aol.com, website http://www.ymcanyc.org. Capricorn Poetry Award, a cash prize of $2,000 and a reading at The Writer's Voice, "given annually in recognition of excellence to an emerging poet over 40." $20 entry fee. Deadline: December 31. Submit a mss of at least 48 pgs., but no more than 68 pgs. No more than 50% of entry may have been previously published. Send SASE for application guidelines. Open Voice Awards, annual awards, $1,000 honorarium and a reading at The Writer's Voice, open to both published and unpublished poets who have not previously read at The Writer's Voice. $15 entry fee. Deadline: December 31. Send SASE for application form. "Write 'Genre' on the envelope." The Writer's Voice is a literary center sponsoring weekly readings, writing workshops, writing awards and other activities.

Ø **CENTER FOR BOOK ARTS' ANNUAL POETRY CHAPBOOK COMPETITION**, 626 Broadway, 5th Floor, New York NY 10012, phone (212)460-9768, e-mail info@centerforbookarts.org, established in 1995, award director Sharon Dolin, offers $500 cash prize, a $500 reading honorarium and publication of winning manuscript in a limited edition letterpress printed and handbound chapbook. Submissions may be entered in other contests. Submit no more than 500 lines on any subject, in any form. Mss must be typed on one side of 8½×11 paper. Send SASE for guidelines. Entry fee: $10/ms. Postmark deadline: December 4. Most recent contest winner was James Haug. Judges were Sharon Dolin and Gerald Stern. Winner will be contacted mid-April by telephone. Each contestant receives a letter announcing the winner. Copies of previous winning books may be obtained by sending $45. Reading fee is credited toward the purchase of the winning chapbook. "Center for Book Arts is a non-profit organization dedicated to the traditional crafts of bookmaking and contemporary interpretations of the book as an art object. Through the Center's Education, Exhibition and Workspace Programs we ensure that the ancient craft of the book remains a viable and vital part of our civilization."

N: ◑ CHICANO/LATINO LITERARY CONTEST, Dept. of Spanish & Portuguese, University of California-Irvine, Irvine CA 92697-5275, e-mail rubyt@uci.edu, website http://www.hnet.uci.edu/spanishandportugu ese/contest/.html, established in 1974, contest director Prof. Alejandro Morales, is an annual contest focusing on 1 of 4 genres each year: short story (2000), poetry (2001), drama (2002), novel (2003). Prizes: 1st, $1,000, publication of work if not under previous contract, and transportation to Irvine to receive the award; 2nd, $500; and 3rd, $250. Work may be in English or Spanish. Only one entry/author. Open to US citizens or permanent residents of the US. Send SASE for guidelines or obtain via e-mail or website. Deadline: May 15. Most recent contest winner was Angelo Parra. Judge was Gary Soto. Winners will be notified by letter in October. Prizes will be awarded during a ceremony in November.

N: ◎ COLORADO BOOK AWARDS (Specialized: regional), Colorado Center for The Book, 2123 Downing, Denver CO 80205, phone (303)839-8320, fax (303)839-8319, e-mail ccftb@compuserve.com, website http://www.aclin.org/~ccftb, executive director Christiane Citron, offers annual award of $500 plus promotion for books published in the year prior to the award. Submissions may be entered in other contests. Submit 6 copies of each book entered. Open to residents of Colorado. Send SASE for entry form and guidelines or obtain via e-mail or website. Entry fee: $30. Deadline: December 1. Competition receives 60 entries a year. Most recent award winner was Carolyn Evans Campbell. Winner will be announced at a ceremony/dinner in the spring. "We are a nonprofit organization affiliated with the Library of Congress Center for The Book. We promote the love of books, reading and literacy. We annually sponsor the Rocky Mountain Book Festival which attracts tens of thousands of people. It's free and includes hundreds of authors from throughout the country. We are located in the home of Thomas Hornsby Ferril, Colorado's late former poet laureate. This historic landmark home is used as a literary center and a tribute to Ferril's life and work."

N: ◎ INA COOLBRITH CIRCLE ANNUAL POETRY CONTEST (Specialized: regional), 2712 Oak Rd., #54, Walnut Creek CA 94596, treasurer Audrey Allison, has prizes of $10-50 in each of several categories for California residents and out-of-state members only. Three poems per contestant, but no more than 1 poem in any one category. Poems submitted in 2 copies, include name, address, phone number and member status on 1 copy only. Enclose a 3×5 card with name, address, phone number, category, title, first line of poem and status as member or nonmember. Members of the Ina Coolbrith Circle pay no fee; others pay $2 for each poem (limit 3). Send SASE for details. Deadline is August.

◑ ◎ CREATIVE WRITING FELLOWSHIPS IN POETRY (Specialized: regional), Arizona Commission on the Arts, 417 W. Roosevelt St., Phoenix AZ 85003, phone (602)255-5882, fax (602)256-0282, e-mail general@arizonaarts.org, website http://az.arts.asu.edu/artscomm, literature director Jill Bernstein, offers biennial prizes of $5,000-7,500. Poetry fellowships awarded in odd-numbered years. Submissions can be previously published or unpublished, and can be entered in other contests. Submit 10 pgs. maximum on any subject. Open to Arizona residents over 18 years old. To request an application form, contact the Literature Director at (602)229-8226 or via e-mail. Entry deadline is in September of the year prior to the award.

◔ ◎ CRUMB ELBOW PUBLISHING POETRY CONTESTS (Specialized: themes), P.O. Box 294, Rhododendron OR 97049, phone (503)622-4798, established in 1996, award director Michael P. Jones, offers annual awards of publication and copies, "for both established poets and beginners to introduce their work to new audiences by having their work published in a collection of poetry." Crumb Elbow sponsors 7 contests all having different themes. They are the Scarecrow Poetry Harvest Contest (deadline August 1), Old Traditions & New Festivities: Winter Holiday Poetry Contest (deadline October 1), Natural Enchantment: Henry David Thoreau Poetry Contest (deadline February 1), Centuries of Journeys: History & Folk Traditions Poetry Contest (deadline April 1), Onward to the New Eden! Oregon Trail Poetry Contest (deadline January 1), Westward! Historic Trails Poetry Contest (deadline November 1), and Beyond the Shadows: Social Justice Poetry Contest (deadline June 1). Submissions may be entered in other contests. Submit at least 3 poems or verses. All submissions should be typed and accompanied by SASE. Send SASE for entry form and guidelines. Entry fees range from $2 for 3 poems to $15 for 22-30 poems. The award director says, "Have fun with your creativity. Explore with your words and don't be afraid of themes or to try something different." Crumb Elbow also publishes *The Final Edition* and *Wy'East Historical Journal*. Write for more information.

◑ DANA AWARD IN POETRY, 7207 Townsend Forest Ct., Browns Summit NC 27214, e-mail danaawards @pipeline.com (for emergency questions only), website http://danaawards.home.pipeline.com, established in 1996, award chair Mary Elizabeth Parker, offers annual award of $500 for the best group of 5 poems. Submissions must be unpublished; may be entered in other contests. Submit 5 poems on any subject, in any form; no light verse. Include SASE for winners list. No mss will be returned. Include a separate cover sheet with name, address, phone and titles of poems. Send SASE for guidelines or obtain via website. "We will not send guidelines via e-mail." Entry fee: $10/5 poems. Postmark deadline: October 31. Competition receives 300-400 poetry entries. Most recent award winner was Melanie Atmeder. Judges were Christine Garren and Eve Shelnutt. Winner will be announced in early spring. Website includes submission information, all competitions, information on winners, judges and the philosophy behind the awards.

◐ DANCING POETRY CONTEST, Artists Embassy International, 704 Brigham Ave., Santa Rosa CA 95404-5245, phone/fax (707)528-0912 (for fax, call first after 5 p.m.), e-mail jhcheung@aol.com, established in 1993, contest chair Judy Cheung. Annual contest awarding three Grand prizes of $100, five 1st Prizes of $50, 10 Second Prizes of $25, 25 3rd Prizes of certificates. The 3 Grand prize winning poems will be danced, choreographed, costumed, premiered and videotaped at the annual Dancing Poetry Festival at Palace of Legion of Honor, San Francisco. Natica Angilly's Poetic Dance Theater Company will perform the 3 Grand Prize-winning poems. Pays winners from other countries in international money orders with US value at the time of the transaction. Submissions must be unpublished or poet must own rights. Submit 2 copies of any number of poems, 40 lines maximum (each), with name, address, phone on one copy only. Foreign language poems must include English translations. Include SASE for winners list. Send SASE for entry form. Inquiries via e-mail OK. Entry fee: $5/poem or $10/3 poems. Does not accept entry fees in foreign currencies. Send international money order in US dollars. Deadline: June 15. Competition receives about 500-800 entries. Most recent contest winners include Alden Dean, Joseph Hunt and Mary Hope Whitehead. Judges for upcoming contest will be members of Artists Embassy International. Artist Embassy International has been a non-profit educational art organization since 1951, "Furthering intercultural understanding and peace through the universal language of the arts."

◯ ◐ THE DOROTHY DANIELS ANNUAL HONORARY WRITING AWARD, The National League of American Pen Women, Inc.—Simi Valley Branch, P.O. Box 1485, Simi Valley CA 93062, established in 1980, award director Diane Reichick. Annual award with 1st Prize of $100 in each category: poetry, fiction, nonfiction. Submissions must be unpublished. Submit any number of poems, 50 lines maximum, on any subject in free verse or traditional. Manuscript must not include name and address. Include cover letter with name, address, phone, title and category of each entry; and line count for each. Poem must be titled and typed on 8½×11 white paper, single- or double-spaced spaced and one poem per page. Send SASE for guidelines. Entry fee: $3/poem. Deadline: July 30. Competition receives 1,500 entries a year. Recent award winner was Eileen Malone. Judges were 3 poets from their Pen Women branch. Send SASE for winners list; announced by mail on or before November 1. The National League of American Pen Women, a non-profit organization head-quartered in Washington, DC, was established in 1897 and has a membership of more than 7,000 professional writers, artists and composers. The Simi Valley Branch, of which noted novelists Dorothy Daniels and Elizabeth Forsythe Hailey are Honorary Members, was founded in 1977. "Request rules and follow them carefully—always include SASE."

◐ BILLEE MURRAY DENNY POETRY AWARD, % Janet Overton, Lincoln College, 300 Keokuk St., Lincoln IL 62656-1699, established in 1981. Annual award with prizes of $1,000, $500 and $250. Open to poets who have not previously published a book of poetry with a commercial or university press (except for chapbooks with a circulation of less than 250). Enter up to 3 poems, 100 lines/poem or less at $10/poem. (Make checks payable to Poetry Contest—Lincoln College.) Poems may be on any subject, using any style, but may not contain "any vulgar, obscene, suggestive or offensive word or phrase." Winning poems are published in *The Denny Poems*, a biennial anthology, available for $5 from Lincoln College. Send SASE for entry form. Postmark deadline: May 31. Most recent award winner was James Fairhall (1998). Winners will be announced on or before September 30.

N ◐ EMILY DICKINSON AWARD IN POETRY, Universities West Press, P.O. Box 22310, Flagstaff AZ 86002-2310, phone (520)213-9877, website http://www.popularpicks.com, contact J.A. Woodman, offers annual award of $1,000 and publication. "All finalists considered for publication in an anthology of poems published by Universities West Press." Submissions must be unpublished. Submit up to 3 poems, total entry not to exceed 6 pgs., on any subject, in any form or style. Include short bio statement. Students and employees of Northern Arizona University may not enter. Send SASE for complete guidelines or visit website. Entry fee(s): $10. Make checks or money orders payable to Universities West Press. Postmark deadline: August 31. Judge for last award was Andrew Hudgins.

N ◯ MILTON DORFMAN NATIONAL POETRY PRIZE, % Rome Art & Community Center, 308 W. Bloomfield St., Rome NY 13440, phone (315)336-1040, fax (315)336-1090, e-mail racc@borg.com, website http://www.borg.com/~racc, contact Maureen Dunn Murphy. Annual award for unpublished poetry. Prizes: $500,

$200 and $100. Entry fee: $5/poem (American funds only; $10 returned check penalty); make checks payable to: Rome Art & Community Center. Contest opens July 1. Deadline: November 1. Include name, address and phone number on each entry. Poems are printed in Center's Newsletter. Competition receives about 1,000 entries a year. Most recent winners were G.R. Holloway, first place; Michael Jennings, second place; and Celia Bland, third place. The judge for the upcoming award will be Sabra Loomis. Winners are notified by December 1. Send SASE for results. Website includes information on upcoming events at the Rome Art & Community Center.

N ⊕ ⦰ T.S. ELIOT PRIZE, The Poetry Book Society, Book House, 45 East Hill, London SW18 2Q2 United Kingdom, phone (0181)870 8403, fax (0181)877 1615, established in 1993, award director Clare Brown, offers annual award for the best poetry collection published in the UK/Republic of Ireland each year. Prize is £5000 (donated by Mrs. Valerie Eliot) and "winning book is bound in Moroccan leather." Submissions must be previously published. **Book/ms must be submitted by publisher** and have been published (or scheduled to be published) the year of the contest. Deadline: end of August. Send SASE for entry form and guidelines. Winners will be announced in January.

N ✓ ⦰ T.S. ELIOT PRIZE FOR POETRY; THOMAS JEFFERSON UNIVERSITY PRESS, 100 E. Normal, Kirksville MO 63501-4221, phone (660)785-7199, fax (660)785-4181, e-mail tjup@truman.edu, website http://www2.truman.edu/tjup/, established in 1996, offers annual award of $2,000, publication, and 10 copies first prize. All entrants will receive a copy of the winning book. Submit 60-100 pages, include 2 title pages, 1 with name, address, phone and ms title; the other with only the title. Individual poems may have been previously published in periodicals or anthologies, but the collection must not have been published as a book. Include SASE if you wish acknowledgement of receipt of your ms. Mss will not be returned. Send SASE for guidelines. Inquiries via fax and e-mail OK. Entry fee: $25. Deadline: October 31. Competition receives 600 entries a year. Most recent contest winners were David Keplinger, 1999; Rhina Espaillat, 1998. Website includes T.S. Eliot Prize guidelines and past winners and judges. Also books and order form. Thomas Jefferson University Press also publishes critical books about poetry or poets.

✓ ◎ EMERGING LESBIAN WRITERS AWARD (Specialized: lesbian), Astraea National Lesbian Action Foundation, 116 E. 16th St., New York NY 10003, phone (212)529-8021, fax (212)982-3321, e-mail grants@astraea.org, website http://www.astraea.org, offers an annual award of $10,000 to "support the work of emerging lesbian writers." Submit 10-15 pgs. of collated poetry. "You may only submit in one category (fiction or poetry) per year." Open to US residents who have published "at least one piece of writing (in any genre) in a newspaper, magazine, journal or anthology; but not more than one book. Your work should include some lesbian content (broadly defined)." Submit 3 copies of ms with completed cover sheet and 1-paragraph bio. Send SASE for entry form and guidelines. Inquiries via fax and e-mail OK. Entry fee: $5. Deadline: March 8. Most recent award winners include Elena Georgiou and Cheryl Whitehead. Applications are judged by a panel of lesbian writers who remain anonymous until after the competition. Applicants are notified by mail after June 30. Website includes general information and grant guidelines.

N $ ⦰ THE WILLIAM FAULKNER CREATIVE WRITING COMPETITION/POETRY CATE-GORY, The Pirate's Alley Faulkner Society, Inc., 632 Pirate's Alley, New Orleans LA 70116, phone (504)586-1612, fax (504)522-9725, e-mail faulkhouse@aol.com, website http://members.aol.com/faulkhouse, established in 1993, award director Rosemary James, offers annual publication, The Double Dealer Redux Cash Prize $750; gold medal; trip to New Orleans from any Continental US city. "Foreign nationals are ineligible unless they reside in the U.S. Winners must be present at annual meeting to receive award." Submissions must be unpublished. Submit 1 poem on any subject in any English language form. US and Canadian citizens, US residents only. Send SASE or visit website for entry form and guidelines. Inquiries via e-mail OK. Entry fee(s): $25 per entry. "We do not accept entries from other countries." Deadline: April 15. Competition receives 1,000 (for 5 categories) entries a year. Most recent contest winner(s) was Katherine Soniat (1998). Judge was James Nolan. Winners will be announced by letter and phone on September 1. "Competition is keen. Send your best work."

⦰ ◎ FLORIDA INDIVIDUAL ARTIST FELLOWSHIPS (Specialized: regional), Florida Division of Cultural Affairs, Dept. of State, The Capitol, Tallahassee FL 32399-0250, phone (850)487-2980, fax (850)922-5259, e-mail vohlsson@mail.dos.state.fl.us, website http://www.dos.state.fl.us, arts consultant Valerie Ohlsson, annually offers an undetermined number of fellowships in the amount of $5,000 each. "The Individual Artist Fellowship Program is designed to recognize practicing professional creative artists residing in Florida through monetary fellowship awards. The program provides support for artists of exceptional talent and demonstrated ability to improve their artistic skills and enhance their careers. Fellowships may be awarded in the following discipline categories: dance, folk arts, interdisciplinary, literature, media arts, music, theatre and visual arts and crafts." Submissions can be previously published or unpublished. Submit 3-5 representative poems, single or double-spaced. "Reproductions of published work may not be submitted in published format. Open to Florida residents of at least 18 years of age who are not enrolled in undergraduate or graduate programs. Eight copies of the work sample must be included with 8 copies of the application form. Write for entry form and guidelines. Inquiries via fax and e-mail OK. Deadline: mid-January. Competitions receive 600 entries. Most recent winners were Richard Grayson, Preston Allen, Sheila Oritiz-Taylor and Lucinda Vickers. They also publish the *Dept. of*

State, Division of Cultural Affairs Informational Memo, a newsletter of "information of concern to writers at state, regional, national and international levels." Website includes general information about the Florida Department of State, Division of Cultural Affairs.

FOSTER CITY INTERNATIONAL WRITERS' CONTEST, Foster City Arts & Culture Committee, 650 Shell Blvd., Foster City CA 94404. Yearly competition for previously unpublished work. $10 entry fee. Awards $250 each first prize for rhymed or blank verse and $125 for each honorable mention. Send SASE for instructions. Deadline: October 31. Awards announced January 15.

FRIENDS OF DOG WATCH OPEN POETRY COMPETITION, 267 Hillbury Rd., Warlingham, Surrey CR6 9TL England, phone 01883-622121, contact Michaela Edridge. Annual competition for poems up to 40 lines. Cash prizes. Entry fees: £2/poem. Contest information available for SASE (or SAE and IRCs). Deadline: September 1.

JOHN GLASSCO TRANSLATION PRIZE (Specialized: translation, regional), Literary Translators' Association of Canada, 3492, avenue Laval, Montreal, Quebec H2X 3C8 Canada, e-mail alterego@rocler.q c.ca. website http://www.geocities.com/Athens/Oracle/9070. $500 awarded annually for a translator's first book-length literary translation into French or English, published in Canada during the previous calendar year. The translator must be a Canadian citizen or landed immigrant. Eligible genres include fiction, creative nonfiction, poetry, published plays and children's books. Write for application form. Inquiries via e-mail OK. Deadline: February 15. Competition receives 15 entries a year. Most recent prize winner was Diego Bastiannti. Website includes membership form, directory of members, model contract and list of events.

GLIMMER TRAIN'S APRIL POETRY OPEN, Glimmer Train Press, 710 SW Madison St., #504, Portland OR 97205, phone (503)221-0836, fax (503)221-0837, website http://www.glimmertrain.com, established in 1998, award director Linda Burmeister Davies, offers annual prizes. 1st Place: $500, publication in *Glimmer Train Stories* and 20 copies of that issue; 2nd Place: $250; 3rd Place: $100. Submissions must be unpublished and may be entered in other contests. Submit up to 3 poems with no subject or form restrictions. "Name, address and phone number need to appear on all submitted poems." Send SASE for guidelines only. Inquiries via fax OK. Entry fee(s): $10 for up to 3 poems (sent together). Postmark deadline: April 30. Competition receives several hundred entries a year. Judged by the editors of Glimmer Train Press. Winners will be contacted by September 1. Glimmer Train Press publishes the quarterly *Glimmer Train Stories*, circulation 13,000.

GLIMMER TRAIN'S OCTOBER POETRY OPEN, Glimmer Train Press, 710 SW Madison St., #504, Portland OR 97205-2900, phone (503)221-0836, fax (503)221-0837, website http://www.glimmertrain.c om, established in 1998, award director Linda Burmeister Davies, offers annual prizes. 1st Place: $500, publication in *Glimmer Train Stories* and 20 copies of that issue; 2nd Place: $250; 3rd Place: $100. Submissions must be unpublished and may be entered in other contests. Submit up to 3 poems with no subject or form restrictions. "Name, address and phone number need to appear on all submitted poems." Send SASE for guidelines only. Inquiries via fax OK. Entry fee(s): $10 for up to 3 poems (sent together). Postmark deadline: October 31. Competition receives "several hundred" entries a year. Judged by the editors of Glimmer Train Press. Winners will be contacted by March 1. Glimmer Train Press publishes the quarterly *Glimmer Train Stories*, circulation 13,000.

GRANDMOTHER EARTH NATIONAL AWARD, Grandmother Earth Creations, P.O. Box 241986, Memphis TN 38124, phone (901)758-0804, fax (901)757-0506 (call first), established in 1994, award director Frances Cowden, offers annual award of $1,000 with varying distributions each year. $1,000 minimum in awards for poetry and prose $200 first, etc., plus publication in anthology; non-winning finalists considered if permission is given. Send published or unpublished work. Submissions may be entered in other contests. Submit at least 3 poems, any subject, in any form. Include SASE for winners list. Send 2 copies with name and address on one copy and on a 3×5 card. Send SASE for guidelines. Entry fee: $10/3 poems, $2 each additional poem. Entry fee includes a copy of the anthology. Deadline: July 15. Most recent award winner was J.C. Hoffman and others. Judge was Tod Marshall, Rhodes College and others. Winner will be announced on October 1 at the Mid-South Poetry Festival in Memphis. Copies of previous winning poems or books may be obtained by writing the above address. "Our contest anthology offers optional publication for non-winning entries. Each year the quality goes up."

THE GREAT BLUE BEACON POETRY CONTEST, The Great Blue Beacon, 1425 Patriot Dr., Melbourne FL 32940, phone (407)253-5869, e-mail ajircc@juno.com, established in 1997, award director A.J. Byers, offers prizes approximately 3 times/year, as announced, of 1st: $30; 2nd: $20; 3rd: $10. "Winning poem to be published in The Great Blue Beacon (amounts will be increased if sufficient entries are received.)" Submissions must be unpublished and may be entered in other contests. Submit up to 3 poems maximum on any subject in any form. "Submit two typed copies of each entry. On one copy, place your name, address and telephone number on the upper left-hand corner of the first page. No name or address on the second copy." Send SASE for guidelines. Inquiries via e-mail OK. Entry fee(s): $5/poem ($4 for subscribers of The Great Blue

Beacon). Does not accept entry fees in foreign currencies. Accepts entry fees from other countries in US dollars. Competition receives 100-150 entries a year. Most recent contest winner was Janet Bruce (1998). Winner(s) will be announced approximately 2 months after deadline date. "Contestants must send SASE with entry to receive notification of results. Submit your best work—no more than 24 lines/poem."

GREAT LAKES COLLEGES ASSOCIATION NEW WRITERS AWARD, GLCA, The Philadelphia Center, North American Bldg., 121 S. Broad St., 7th Floor, Philadelphia PA 19107-4577, phone (215)735-7300, fax (215)735-7373, director Mark Andrew Clark, Ph.D., offers annual award to "the best first book of poetry and the best first book of fiction among those **submitted by publishers**. The winning authors tour several of the Great Lakes Colleges reading, lecturing, visiting classes, doing workshops, and publicizing their books. Each writer receives an honorarium of at least $300 from each college visited, as well as travel expenses, hotel accommodations, and hospitality. Usually, one winner (fiction) tours in the fall, and the other winner (poetry) tours in the spring, following the competition." Submissions must be previously published. Submit 4 copies of galleys or the printed book plus a statement stating author's agreement to commit to the college tour. Send SASE for guidelines. Inquiries via fax OK. Deadline: February 28. Competition receives about 60 entries for poetry, 35 for fiction a year. Most recent award winners were *Rainlight* (fiction) by Alison McGhee (published by Paper-Mache Press) and *Apology for Want* (poetry) by Mary Jo Bang (published by University Press of New England/Middlebury).

GREEN RIVER WRITERS' CONTESTS (Specialized: themes, forms), 1043 Thornfield Lane, Cincinnati OH 45224, e-mail lindafrisa@aol.com, website http://www.pol.com/greenriver, established in 1991, contact contest chairman, offers 9 contests for poetry on various themes and in various forms. Entry fees range from $5-8 for nonmembers, prizes range from $5-200. Send SASE for rules. Deadline: October 31. Competition receives 600 entries. Most recent contest winners include Sandra Lake Lassen and Donna Jean Tennis. Website includes full contest rules and categories, information on Green River Writers organization, list of precious year's winners.

GROLIER POETRY PRIZE; ELLEN LA FORGE MEMORIAL POETRY FOUNDATION, INC., 6 Plympton St., Cambridge MA 02138, phone (617)547-4230, established in 1974, award director Louisa Solano. The Grolier Poetry Prize is open to all poets who have not published either a vanity, small press, trade or chapbook of poetry. Two poets receive an honorarium of $150 each. Up to 4 poems by each winner and 1-2 by each of 4 runners-up are chosen for publication in the *Grolier Poetry Prize Annual*. Opens January 15 of each year; deadline May 1. Submissions must be unpublished and may not be simultaneously submitted. Submit up to 5 poems, not more than 10 double-spaced pages. Submit one ms in duplicate, without name of poet. On a separate sheet give name, address, phone number and titles of poems. Only 1 submission/contestant; mss are not returned. $6 entry fee includes copy of *Annual*, checks payable to the Ellen La Forge Memorial Poetry Foundation, Inc. Enclose self-addressed stamped postcard if acknowledgement of receipt is required. For update of rules, send SASE to Ellen La Forge Memorial Poetry Foundation before submitting mss. Competition receives approximately 500 entries. Most recent award winners include Allen Braden, Julie Carr and Karen D'Amato. The Ellen La Forge Memorial Poetry Foundation sponsors an annual intercollegiate poetry reading and a reading series, generally 10/semester, held on the grounds of Harvard University. These are generally poets who have new collections of poetry available for sale at the Grolier Poetry Book Shop, Inc., which donates money toward costs (such as rental of the auditorium). They pay poets honoraria from $100-400 and occasionally provide overnight accommodations (but not transportation). Such poets as Joshua Beckman, Philip Levine, Laure-Anne Gosselaar, Donald Hall and Susan Wheele have given readings under their auspices. The small foundation depends upon private gifts and support for its activities.

GUGGENHEIM FELLOWSHIPS, John Simon Guggenheim Memorial Foundation, 90 Park Ave., New York NY 10016, phone (212)687-4470, fax (212)697-3248, e-mail fellowships@gf.org, website http://www.gf.o rg. Guggenheims are awarded each year to persons who have already demonstrated exceptional capacity for productive scholarship or exceptional creative ability in the arts. The amounts of the grants vary. The average grant is about $33,800. Most recent award winners were Robin Behn, David Bottoms and B.H. Fairchild (1999). In 1999, there were 179 winners awarded fellowships in the US. Application deadline: October 1.

HACKNEY LITERARY AWARDS; BIRMINGHAM-SOUTHERN COLLEGE WRITER'S CONFERENCE, Birmingham-Southern College, Box 549003, Birmingham AL 35254, phone (205)226-4921, fax (205)226-3072, e-mail dcwilson@bsc.edu, website http://www.bsc.edu. This competition, sponsored by the Cecil Hackney family since 1969, offers $10,000 in prizes for novels, poetry and short stories as part of the annual Birmingham-Southern Writer's Conference. Send SASE for Hackney guidelines. Novels postmarked by September 30. Poems and short stories must be postmarked by December 31.

J.C. AND RUTH HALLS FELLOWSHIP; THE DIANE MIDDLEBROOK FELLOWSHIP IN POETRY (Specialized: MFA or equivalent degree in creative writing), Wisconsin Institute for Creative Writing, English Dept., 600 North Park St., Madison WI 53706, established in 1986, award director Jesse Lee Kercheval. Annual fellowships will pay $22,000 for one academic year. Applicants will teach one creative writing class per semester at U. of Wisconsin and give a public reading at the end of their stay. Submissions may be entered in other contests. Submit 10 poems maximum on any subject in any form. Applicants must have an MFA or equivalent degree in creative writing. Applicants cannot have published a book (chapbooks will not disqualify an applicant). Send SASE for guidelines. Deadline: last day of February. Competitions receive 200 entries a year. Most recent winners were Beth Ann Fennelly and Kathy Whitcomb. Judges were faculty of creative writing program. Results will be sent to applicants by May 1. Winners announced in *Poets & Writers* and *AWP Chronicle*. "The Halls fellowships are administered by the Program in Creative Writing at the University of Wisconsin-Madison. Funding is provided by the Jay C. and Ruth Halls Writing Fund and the Carl Djerassi and Diane Middlebrook Fund through the University of Wisconsin Foundation."

🌐 ◎ **FELICIA HEMANS PRIZE FOR LYRICAL POETRY (Specialized: membership, students)**, The University of Liverpool, P.O. Box 147, Liverpool PR8 2PS England, phone (0151)794 2458, fax (0151)794 3765, e-mail wilderc@liv.ac.uk, established in 1899, contact registrar, University of Liverpool, offers annual award of £30. Submissions may be entered in other contests. Submit 1 poem. Open to past or present members and students of the University of Liverpool. Send SASE for guidelines only. Inquiries via fax and e-mail OK. Deadline: May 1. Competition receives 12-15 entries. Judges were "the two professors of English Literature in the University." The winner and all other competitors will be notified by mail in June.

N $🔵🖊 **ERNEST HEMINGWAY POETRY COMPETITION**, International Hemingway Festival, Sanibel Captiva Review, 2323 Del Prado Blvd., Suite #7, Cape Coral FL 33990, phone (800)916-9727, website http://www.hemingwayfestival.com, established in 1997, award director Anne Hemingway, offers annual $250 cash prize for one grand prize winner, publication in the *Sanibel Captiva Review* and entry to the 2000 Ernest Hemingway Literary Conference on Sanibel Island, Florida. Submissions must be unpublished. Submit any number of poems maximum on any subject, any form. "Must be postmarked by May 1. Must be typed, double-spaced and on 8½×11 paper, no additional artwork. Must have author statement and entry fee included." Send SASE or visit website for entry form and guidelines. Entry fee(s): $10/poem. Postmark deadline: May 1. Competition receives 200 entries a year. Most recent contest winner(s) was Maria Ercilla (1998). Judge(s) for upcoming contest will be Anne Hemingway and Dr. Jack Crocker. Winner(s) will be announced "last day of festival at the end of Literary Conference. Open to public and media." "We offer First Novel Contest, Short Story Contest, Playwriting Contest as well as the Poetry Competition. During the festival, we hold a Literary Conference, Story Telling Contest and Poetry Slam. Please send a SASE first for guidelines. Then submit your best work."

🖊 **THE HODDER FELLOWSHIP**, The Council of the Humanities, 122 E. Pyne, Princeton University, Princeton NJ 08544, phone (609)258-4713, e-mail humcounc@princeton.edu, website http://www.princeton.edu/~humcounc, is awarded to a humanist in the early stages of a career. The recipient has usually written one book and is working on a second. Preference is given to applicants outside academia. "The Fellowship is designed specifically to identify and nurture extraordinary potential rather than to honor distinguished achievement." **Candidates for the Ph.D. are not eligible.** The Hodder Fellow spends an academic year in residence at Princeton working on an independent project in the humanities. Stipend is approximately $44,500. Submit a résumé, sample of previous work (10 pgs. maximum, not returnable), a project proposal of 2 to 3 pgs., and SASE. Guidelines available on website. The announcement of the Hodder Fellow is made in February by the President of Princeton University. Postmark deadline: November 1.

N $🖊 **QUENTIN R. HOWARD POETRY PRIZE**, Wind Publications, P.O. Box 24548, Lexington KY 40524, phone (606)885-5342, e-mail wind@literaryarts.org, website http://www.literaryarts.org/wind, established in 1994, award director Charlie Hughes, offers annual awards of $100 plus publication and 25 copies of published chapbook. Submissions may be entered in other contests. Submit 24-28 pages on any subject in any form, "name on one of two cover sheets." Send SASE for guidelines or visit website. Entry fee(s): $10 per chapbook ms. Does not accept entry fees in foreign currencies. Accepts entry fees from other countries as US money order. Deadline: October 31. Competition receives about 150 entries a year. Most recent contest or award winner(s) was Anne Ohman Youngs (1998). Judge was Robert Morgan. Winner(s) will be announced "via SASE to contest entrants, also announcement in *Wind Magazine* also ad in *Poets & Writers Magazine*." Copies of previous winning chapbooks may be obtained by ordering from the publisher via mail or website. "Wind Publications is a literary small press, and publisher of Wind Magazine. Be familiar with poetry in Wind Magazine—samples on our website."

🖊 **HENRY HOYNS FELLOWSHIPS**, Creative Writing Program, 219 Bryan Hall, University of Virginia, Charlottesville VA 22903, phone (804)924-6675, fax (804)924-1478, e-mail lrs9e@virginia.edu, website http://www.engl.virginia.edu/, are fellowships in poetry and fiction of varying amounts for candidates for the M.F.A. in creative writing. Sample poems/prose required with application. Inquiries via e-mail OK. Deadline: January 1. Competition receives 300-400 entries.

◎ **INDIVIDUAL ARTIST GRANTS (Specialized: regional)**, Cultural Arts Council of Houston/Harris County, 3201 Allen Parkway, Houston TX 77019, phone (713)527-9330, fax (713)630-5210, e-mail grants@cach.org. Offers awards to Houston, Harris County visual artists, writers, choreographers and composers selected through an annual competition. The program offers awards in three categories: Artist Project, General Artist Fellowship and Emerging Artist Fellowships. Fellowship awards for writers are awarded every other year (2000), but encouraged to apply for project grants on off-years. Write for deadline date, application forms and guidelines.

✓ ◎ **THE JAPAN FOUNDATION ARTIST FELLOWSHIP PROGRAM (Specialized: US residents with Japanese affiliations)**, The Japan Foundation New York Office, 152 W. 57th St., 39th Floor, New York NY 10019, phone (212)489-0299, fax (212)489-0409, e-mail chris_watanabe@jfny.org, website http://www.jfny.org, director general Mr. Masaya Usuda, program assistant Chris Watanabe, offers annual fellowships of 2-6 months in Japan (during the Japanese fiscal year of April 1 through March 31) for "accredited professional writers, musicians, painters, sculptors, stage artists, movie directors, etc." Submissions may be entered in other contests. Open to citizens or permanent residents of the US. "Affiliation with a Japanese artist or institution is required. Three letters of reference, including one from the Japanese affiliate must accompany all applications." Inquiries via fax and e-mail OK. Deadline: December 1. Competition receives 20-30 entries a year. Website includes program descriptions and award announcements.

🅽 $ ◎ **JAPANESE LITERARY TRANSLATION PRIZE (Specialized: translation of Japanese classical or modern literature into English)**, Donald Keene Center of Japanese Culture, Columbia University, 507 Kent Hall, New York NY 10027, phone (212)854-5036, fax (212)854-4019, established in 1981, award director Peter Grilli, offers annual $2,500 prize for translation of a work of Japanese classical literature into English and a $2,500 prize for translation of a work of Japanese modern literature into English. "Special attention is given to new or unpublished translators." Submissions may be entered in other contests. Submit 6 copies of book-length ms or published book. Send SASE for entry form and guidelines. Inquiries via fax OK. Deadline: February 15. Competition receives 20-25 entries a year. Most recent award winner(s) was Elaine Gerbert (modern Japanese literature) and Thomas Rima/Jonathan Chaves (classical Japanese literature). Judge(s) were Donald Keene, Hortense Calisher, Howard Hibbett, Bonnie Crown and Robert Gottlieb.

🅽 🌐 ⊘ **JOHANN-HEINRICH-VOSS PRIZE FOR TRANSLATION**, German Academy for Language and Literature, Alexandraweg 23, 64287 Darmstadt, Germany, phone (06151)40920, fax (06151)409299, e-mail deutsche.akademie@t-online.de, president Prof. Dr. Christian Meier, is an annual award of DM 20,000 for outstanding lifetime achievement for translating into German, **by nomination only**.

⊘ **THE CHESTER H. JONES FOUNDATION NATIONAL POETRY COMPETITION**, P.O. Box 498, Chardon OH 44024, an annual competition for persons living, working or studying in the USA, Canadian and American citizens living abroad. Prizes: $1,000, $750, $500, $250, $100, $50 honorable mentions and $10 commendation awards. Winning poems are published in an anthology available for $3.50 from the foundation. Submissions must be unpublished. Submit no more than 10 entries, no more than 32 lines each. Send SASE for latest brochure. Entry fee $2 for the first poem, $1 each for others. Deadline: March 31. Distinguished poets serve as judges. 1999 judges were David Citino, Walt McDonald and Diane Wakoski. Winners will be announced in the fall in either *Poets & Writers* or the American Poetry Review, or both. Competitors may receive results by sending SASE marked "Prizewinners."

⊘ **BARBARA MANDIGO KELLY PEACE POETRY CONTEST**, Nuclear Age Peace Foundation, 1187 Coast Village Rd. #123, Santa Barbara CA 93108, phone (805)965-3443, fax (805)568-0466, e-mail wagingpeace @napf.org, website http://www.wagingpeace.org, established in 1996, offers an annual series of awards "to encourage poets to explore and illuminate positive visions of peace and the human spirit." Awards $500 to adult contestants, $250 to youth (13 to 18), $250 to youth (12 and under) and honorable mentions in each category. Submissions must be unpublished and may be entered in other contests. Submit up to 3 poems on "positive visions of peace and the human spirit" in any form. Send 2 copies; maximum of 40 lines per poem. Put name, address, phone number and age in upper right hand corner of one copy. Send SASE for guidelines or download from website. Entry fee: $5, free for youth. Postmark deadline: July 1. Competition receives over 300 entries. Recent contest winner was Keith Antar Mason. Judged by a committee of poets. Winners will be announced through press release and mail notification by October. The Foundation reserves the right to publish the winning poems. "Nuclear Age Peace Foundation is a nonprofit peace and international security-related organization, focusing on the abolition of nuclear weapons, the establishment of an international criminal court and the development of sustainable living practices." To poets thinking about entering their contest they say, "Be creative and positive."

🌐 ◎ **"GIORGIO LA PIRA" INTERNATIONAL LITERARY PRIZE (Specialized: foreign language)**, Centro Studi "G. Donati", Piazza S. Francesco, Pistoia 60-51100 Italy, phone (0573)367251, fax (0573)33196, contact Secretary, offers prizes of 1.500.000 lire (1st Prize), 1.000.000 lire (2nd Prize) and 500.000 lire (3rd Prize). Submit 6 copies each of 3 poems *in Italian*, not more than 40 lines each. Mss are not returned. Send SASE for guidelines. Entry fee: 25.00 lire. Deadline: May 31. Winners must collect prizes in person.

🍁 ◎ **THE STEPHEN LEACOCK MEDAL FOR HUMOUR (Specialized: humor, regional)**, Stephen Leacock Associates, P.O. Box 854, Orillia, Ontario L3V 3P4 Canada, fax (705)325-9955, contact Marilyn Rum-ball (corresponding secretary), award chairman Judith Rapson, for a book of humor in prose, verse, drama or any book form—by a Canadian citizen. "Book must have been published in the current year and no part of it may have been previously published in book form." Submit 10 copies of book, 8 × 10 b&w photo, bio and $25 entry fee. Prize: Silver Leacock Medal for Humour and Laurentian Bank of Canada cash award of $5,000. Deadline: December 31. Competition receives 40-50 entries. The 1998 winner was *Barney's Version* by Mordecai Richler. The committee also publishes *The Newspacket* 3 times/year.

N ☐ ◎ THE LEAGUE OF MINNESOTA POETS CONTEST (Specialized: students), 432 Tyrol Dr., Brainerd MN 56401, contact Joan Wiesner. Offers 20 different contests in a variety of categories and prizes of $5-100 for poems up to 55 lines, fees of $3 to enter all categories for members and $1/category for nonmembers. There is one category for students in grades 7 through 12 and one category for elementary students through grade 6. Send SASE for details. Deadline: July 31. Winners are not published.

⊕ ✔ ◎ LONDON WRITERS COMPETITION (Specialized: regional), Wandsworth Borough Council, The Arts and Community Services Office, Room 224a, Town Hall, Wandsworth High St., London SW18 2PU United Kingdom, phone (0181)871-7380, fax (0181)871-7630, chairman Martyn Goff OBE, offers annual award of £1,000 each in poetry and short story plus publication. Submissions must be unpublished. Open to residents of Greater London (UK). Submit no more than 50 lines (poetry); 2,000-5,000 words (short story). Send SASE for entry form and guidelines. Entry fee: £2 (poetry), £4 (short story). Deadline is in July. Competition receives 3,000 entries. Most recent contest winners were Mario Petrucci, Eva Salzman and John Murphy. Judges were David Harsent and Ruth Padel. Copies of previous winning poems may be obtained by sending £2.50 to the address above. Make checks payable to The Wandsworth Borough Council.

N $ ◢ A LOVE AFFAIR LITERARY CONTEST, Arts Experiment Station/Abraham Baldwin College, 2802 Moore Hwy., ABAC 45, Tifton GA 31794-2601, phone (912)386-3558, established in 1989, award director Liz Carson Reed, offers annual awards of $500 total. "Entries not accepted from outside USA." Submissions must be unpublished and may be entered in other contests. Submit any number of poems on any subject, in any form, no entry longer than 2 pgs., single-spaced. "No names on submissions. Identify with social security number. Include name, address, phone number and social security number on cover sheet." Send SASE for guidelines. Entry fee(s): $7 for up to 2 poems. Deadline: February 14, 2000. Competition receives 50 entries a year. The judge for upcoming awards will be Liz Carson Reed. "One 1st, 2nd and 3rd place winner announced during A Love Affair Festival events; first week in May." "Affinity Health Group and Arts Experiment Station sponsor numerous artistic activities and artists in a 5-county area. This is a literary contest. High quality poetry of any genre is desired."

◎ MATURE WOMEN'S GRANTS (Specialized: women), National League of American Pen Women, 1300 17th St., Washington DC 20036, established in 1976, award director Shirley Holden Helberg, offers biennial (even-numbered years) award of $1,000 each for the categories of arts, letters and music. Submit 3 poems. Previously published submissions OK. Include SASE for winners list. Open to women over the age of 35 during the calendar year of the award. "Women who enter may never have been a member of the Pen women." Include letter stating age, creative purpose and how you learned of the grant. Send SASE for guidelines during odd-numbered years. Entry fee: $8. Deadline: January 15th of the even-numbered year. Competition receives 160 entries in art, 140 in letters and 7-8 in music a year. Winner will be announced July 15.

◢ MID-LIST PRESS FIRST SERIES AWARD FOR POETRY (II), Mid-List Press, 4324 12th Ave. S., Minneapolis MN 55407-3218, phone (612)822-3733, fax (612)823-8387, e-mail guide@midlist.org, website http://www.midlist.org, established in 1990, senior editor Lane Stiles. "The First Series Award for Poetry is an annual contest we sponsor for poets who have never published a book of poetry. The award includes publication and a $500 advance against royalties." Individual poems within the book ms can be previously published and can be entered in other contests. Submit at least 60 single-spaced pages. "Note: We do not return manuscripts. Other than length we have no restrictions, but poets are encouraged to read previous award winners we have published." Recent award winners include Jennifer O'Grady, Donald Morrill, Dina Ben-Lev, Neva Hacker, Jeff Worley, Neil Shepard, Douglas Gray, Stephen Behrendt, J.E. Sorrell and Mary Logue. Submissions are circulated to an editorial board. Send #10 SASE for guidelines or print from website. "Guidelines for the 2000 award will be available after July 1, 1999." Entry fee: $15. Accepts submissions October 1 through February 1. Competition receives about 300 entries/year. "The First Series Award contest is highly competitive. We are looking for poets who have produced a significant body of work but have never published a book-length collection. (A chapbook is not considered a 'book' of poetry.)" No fax or e-mail inquiries.

◎ MILTON CENTER POETRY FELLOWSHIP (Specialized: religious), The Milton Center, 3100 Mc-Cormick Ave., Wichita KS 67213-2097, phone (316)942-4291 ext. 326, fax (316)942-9658, e-mail miltonc@new manu.edu, established in 1986, award director Essie Sappenfield, offers annual residential fellowship of $11,000 stipend to complete first book-length work while in residence in Wichita, Kansas (September through May). Submissions must be unpublished. Submit 10 poems on any subject or in any form. Open to poets of Christian commitment." Send SASE for entry form and guidelines. Inquiries via fax and e-mail OK. Entry fee: $15.

Deadline: March 1. Competition receives 300 entries. Most recent award winner was Stephen Frech. Winner will be announced in mid March. Notification is by letter. "The Milton Center promotes excellence in Christian writing. Write well and have mature work habits. Don't worry about doctrinal matters, counting Christian symbols, etc. What you believe will automatically show up in your writing."

MONEY FOR WOMEN (Specialized: women/feminism), Barbara Deming Memorial Fund, Inc., P.O. Box 630125, Bronx NY 10463, administrator Susan Pliner, biannually awards small grants of up to $1,000 to feminists in the arts "whose work addresses women's concerns and/or speaks for peace and justice from a feminist perspective." Send SASE for application form. Applicants must be citizens of US or Canada. Application fee: $10. Deadlines: December 31 and June 30. Competition receives 250 entries a year. Most recent award winners were Diana Der-Hovanessian and Pesha Gertler. Winners announced in May and October. Also offers the "Gerty, Gerty, Gerty in the Arts, Arts, Arts" for outstanding work by a lesbian, and the "Fannie Lou Hamer Award" for work which combats racism and celebrates women of color.

MONTALVO BIENNIAL POETRY COMPETITION (Specialized: regional), Villa Montalvo, P.O. Box 158, Saratoga CA 95071-0158, phone (408)961-5818, fax (408)961-5850, e-mail kfunk@villamontalvo.org (artist residencies only), website http://www.villamontalvo.org, director artist residency program Kathryn Funk, offers biennial awards (in odd-numbered years only) "to recognize the talent and efforts of those engaged in the poetic arts, both established and emerging." 1st Prize: $1,000 plus an artist residency at Villa Montalvo, California's historic estate for the arts, 2nd Prize: $500, 3rd Prize: $300, 8 Honorable Mentions: $25 each. Residency provides a furnished, self-sufficient apartment for one month. Submissions must be unpublished. "Open to all forms of poetry in English from residents of California, Nevada, Oregon and Washington." Send SASE for guidelines only. Entry fee: $5 for 3 poems. Postmark deadline: October 1, 1999. Competition receives about 150 entries. Judge for 1999 is Denise Duhamel. Winners will be notified by December 15, 1999, and will be honored in an awards ceremony and reading at Villa Montalvo. Website includes information pertaining to all activities at Montalvo, including artist residencies, the gallery, outreach programs and performing arts series information.

MONTANA ARTS; MARY BRENNEN CLAPP MEMORIAL POETRY CONTEST (Specialized: regional), P.O. Box 1872, Bozeman MT 59771, annual contest. Open to Montana poets or former Montana poets only, for 3 unpublished poems up to 100 lines total. Awards prizes of $50, $40, $30 and $20. Submit 3 poems and cover letter. Send SASE for guidelines.

SAMUEL FRENCH MORSE POETRY PRIZE, English Dept., 406 Holmes, Northeastern University, Boston MA 02115, e-mail grotella@lynx.neu.edu, website http://www.casdu.neu.edu/~english/morse.htm, editor Prof. Guy Rotella, for book publication (ms 50-70 pgs.) by Northeastern University Press and an award of $1,000. Inquiries via e-mail OK. Entry fee: $15. Deadline of August 1 for inquiries, September 15 for single copy of ms. Ms will not be returned. Open to US poets who have published no more than 1 book of poetry. Competition receives approximately 400 entries a year. Most recent award winners include Michelle Boisseau, Charles Webb and Jeffrey Greene. Website includes contest rules.

NASHVILLE NEWSLETTER POETRY CONTEST, P.O. Box 60535, Nashville TN 37206-0535, editor/publisher Roger Dale Miller. Founded 1977. Reporting time 6-10 weeks. Published quarterly. Sample copy: $3. Awards prizes of $50, $25 and $10 plus possible publication in newsletter, and at least 50 Certificates of Merit. Any style or subject up to 40 lines. One unpublished poem to a page with name and address in upper left corner. Send large #10 SASE for more information and/or extra entry forms for future contests. Entry fee: $5 for up to 3 poems. Must be sent all at once. "All other nonwinning poems will be considered for possible publication in future issues." Competition receives over 500 entries a year. Recent contest winners include Jamie Simpson, Melina Vratny and Dale Harris.

NATIONAL BOOK AWARD, National Book Foundation, 260 Fifth Ave., Room 904, New York NY 10001, phone (212)685-0261, e-mail natbkfdn@mindspring.com, website http://www.nationalbook.org, award directors Neil Baldwin and Meg Kearney, offers annual grand prize of $10,000 plus 4 finalist awards of $1,000. Submissions must be previously published and **must be entered by the publisher**. Send SASE for entry form and guidelines. Entry fee: $100/title. Deadline: July 12.

**FOR EXPLANATIONS OF THESE SYMBOLS,
SEE THE INSIDE FRONT AND BACK COVERS OF THIS BOOK.**

NATIONAL POETRY SERIES ANNUAL OPEN COMPETITION, P.O. Box G, Hopewell NJ 08525, established in 1978, between January 1 and February 15 considers book-length mss (approximately 48-64 pgs.). Entry fee: $25. Mss will not be returned. The 5 winners receive $1,000 each and are published by participating small press, university press and trade publishers. Send SASE for complete submissions procedures. Competition receives over 1,500 entries a year. Most recent winners were Rigoberto González, Ed Roberson, Joan Murray, Lee Ann Roripaugh and Harry Humes (1998).

NATIONAL WRITERS UNION ANNUAL NATIONAL POETRY COMPETITION, P.O. Box 2409, Aptos CA 95001, e-mail monkerud@scruznet.com, website http://www.mbay.net/~NWU, chair Don Monkerud. See National Writers Union listing under Organizations. The Santa Cruz/Monterey Local 7 chapter at this address sponsors an annual competition with entry fee: $3/poem; prizes of $200, $100 and $50 plus publication in newsletter, with prominent poets as judges. Send SASE for rules beginning in April. Deadline: November 1. Competition receives 1,000 entries a year. Judge for 1998 was Alicia Ostriker. Website includes information about local and national events, and links for writers.

THE NATIONAL WRITTEN & ILLUSTRATED BY . . . AWARDS CONTEST FOR STUDENTS; LANDMARK EDITIONS (Specialized: students), P.O. Box 270169, Kansas City MO 64127, award director David Melton, is an annual contest for unpublished work for a book written and illustrated by a student. Three books published, one from each of 3 age categories (6-9; 10-13; 14-19). Send #10 SAE with 2 first-class stamps for rules.

NEUSTADT INTERNATIONAL PRIZE FOR LITERATURE; WORLD LITERATURE TODAY, University of Oklahoma, 110 Monnet Hall, Norman OK 73019-4033, phone (405)325-4531, fax (405)325-7495, website http://www.ou.edu/worldlit/, editor Dr. William Riggan. Award of $40,000 given every other year in recognition of life achievement or to a writer whose work is still in progress; **nominations from an international jury only**. Website includes general information on *World Literature Today* and the Neustadt Prize.

NEW MILLENNIUM AWARD FOR POETRY, New Millennium Writings, P.O. Box 2463, Knoxville TN 37901, website http://www.mach2.com/books, contact poetry editor, offers 2 annual awards of $1,000 each. Submissions must be previously unpublished, but may be entered in other contests. Submit up to 3 poems, 5 pages maximum. No restrictions on style or content. Include name, address, phone number and a #10 SASE for notification. Manuscripts are not returned. Send SASE for guidelines. Entry fee: $10. Make checks payable to New Millennium Writing. Deadlines: June 11 and November 15. "Two winners and selected finalists will be published." Most recent award winners include Claire Bateman and Madeline Marcotte. Competition receives 2,000 entries a year. Website includes table of contents, photos of contributors, contest guidelines, cover graphics, how to order past issues, subscription information and much more.

NEW YORK FOUNDATION FOR THE ARTS (Specialized: regional), 155 Avenue of Americas, 14th Floor, New York NY 10013, phone (212)366-6900, ext. 217, e-mail nyfaafp@nyfa.org, website http://www.nyfa.org, established in 1984, offers fellowships of $7,000 every other year for poets who are at least 18 and have resided in New York State for 2 years prior to application. Submit up to 10 pages of poetry (at least 2 poems), 3 copies of a 1-page résumé, and an application form. Call for application form in June or request via e-mail. Postmark deadline is October 4.

NEW YORK UNIVERSITY PRIZE FOR POETRY, New York University Press, 70 Washington Square S., New York NY 10012, phone (212)998-2575, fax (212)995-3833, e-mail nyupress@elmer5.bobst.nyu.edu, website http://www.nyupress.nyu.edu, contact prize coordinator, established in 1990, offers annual award of a $1,000 honorarium, plus book publication. Submit 1 typewritten copy of a book-length ms; a 1-page support letter on letterhead from a qualified reader (teacher, editor, agent, etc.); a cover sheet with name, address and daytime phone; a SASE postcard to acknowledge receipt. Send SASE for guidelines. Inquiries via e-mail OK. Deadline: May 1, 2000. Most recent award winner was Barbara Hamby. Winners will be notified in Fall, 2000. Website includes guidelines and information on previous winners.

NEWBURYPORT ART ASSOCIATION ANNUAL SPRING POETRY CONTEST, 12 Charron Dr., Newburyport MA 01950, e-mail espmosk@juno.com, established in 1990, contest coordinator Rhina P. Espaillat, awards prizes of $200, 1st; $100, 2nd; and $50, 3rd; plus Honorable Mentions. Submit any number of unpublished poems; no restrictions as to length, style or theme. Open to anyone over 16 years old. Send 2 copies of each poem, one without identification, one bearing your name, address and telephone number, typed on 8½ × 11 paper with SASE for notification of contest results. Send SASE for guidelines. Entry fee: $3/poem. Make checks payable to Newburyport Art Association. Postmark deadline: March 13, 1999. "In 1998, we received 487 entries from 19 states. Winners were Alfred Dorn, A.M. Juster and Jennifer White, and the judge was Thomas Carper. The judge for 1999 will be David Berman. Prizes will be awarded at a ceremony on May 16."

FRANK O'HARA AWARD CHAPBOOK COMPETITION; THORNGATE ROAD PRESS (Specialized: gay/lesbian/bisexual), Campus Box 4240, English Dept., Illinois State University,

Normal IL 61790-4240, phone (309)438-7705, fax (309)438-5414, e-mail jmelled@ilstu.edu, website http://www.litline.org/html/thorngate.html, established in 1996, award director Jim Elledge, offers annual award of $500, publication and 25 copies. All entrants receive a copy of winning chapbook. Submissions may be a combination of previously published and unpublished work and may be entered in other contests. Submit 16 pages on any topic, in any form. Another 4 pages for front matter is permitted, making the maximum total of 20 pages. Poets must be gay, lesbian or bisexual (any race, age, background, etc.). One poem/page. Send SASE for guidelines. Inquiries via e-mail OK. Entry fee: $15/submission. Deadline: February 1. Competition receives 200-300 entries. Most recent contest winner was *Amateur Grief* by Ron Mohring. Judge is a nationally-recognized gay, lesbian or bisexual poet. Judge remains anonymous until the winner has been announced. Winners will be announced by April 15 in various media—both lesbigay and "straight" in focus. Copies of previous winning books may be obtained by sending $6 to the above address made out to Thorngate Road. "Thorngate Road publishes at least two chapbooks annually, and they are selected by one of two methods. The first is through the contest. The second, the Berdache Chapbook Series, is by invitation only. "We published chapbooks by Kristy Nielsen, David Trinidad, Reginald Shepherd, Karen Lee Osborne, and Maureen Seaton in the Berdache series." Although the contest is only open to gay, lesbian, bisexual and transgendered authors, the content of submissions does not necessarily have to be gay, lesbian, bisexual or transgendered."

OHIOANA BOOK AWARDS; OHIOANA KROUT MEMORIAL AWARD FOR POETRY; OHIOANA QUARTERLY; OHIOANA LIBRARY ASSOCIATION (Specialized: regional), Ohioana Library Association, 65 S. Front St., Suite 1105, Columbus OH 43215-4163, phone (614)466-3831, fax (614)728-6974, e-mail ohioana@winslo.state.ohio.us, website http://www.oplin.org/ohioana, contact Linda Heugst, established in 1984. Ohioana Book Awards given yearly to outstanding books. Up to 6 awards may be given for books (including books of poetry) by authors born in Ohio or who have lived in Ohio for at least 5 years. The Ohioana Poetry Award of $1,000 (with the same residence requirements), made possible by a bequest of Helen Krout, is given yearly "to an individual whose body of work has made, and continues to make, a significant contribution to the poetry of Ohio, and through whose work as a writer, teacher, administrator, or in community service, interest in poetry has been developed." Nominations to be received by December 31. *Ohioana Quarterly* regularly reviews Ohio magazines and books by Ohio authors. It is available through membership in Ohioana Library Association ($25/year). Website includes information about the Ohioana Library Association, the Ohioana Awards and the Award recipients.

NATALIE ORNISH POETRY AWARD (Specialized: regional); SOEURETTE DIEHL FRA-SER TRANSLATION AWARD (Specialized: translations, regional); TEXAS INSTITUTE OF LET-TERS, % Judy Alter T.I.L., P.O. Box 298300, Ft. Worth TX 76129, phone (817)257-7822, fax (817)257-5075, e-mail j.alter@tcu.edu, website http://www.prs.tcu.edu/prs/til/rules, established in 1947, contact Judy Alter. The Texas Institute of Letters gives annual awards for books by Texas authors in 8 categories, including the Natalie Ornish Poetry Award, a $1,000 award for best volume of poetry. Books must have been first published in the year in question, and entries may be made by authors or by their publishers. Deadline is January 4 of the following year. One copy of each entry must be mailed to each of three judges, with "information showing an author's Texas association . . . if it is not otherwise obvious." Poets must have lived in Texas for at least two consecutive years at some time or their work must reflect a notable concern with matters associated with the state. Soeurette Diehl Fraser Translation Award ($1,000) is given for best translation of a book into English. Same rules as those for Natalie Ornish poetry award. Write during the fall for complete instructions. Inquiries via fax and e-mail OK. Competitions receive 30 entries a year. Most recent award winners include Isabel Nathaniel, Betty Adcock, Jack Myers and Pattiann Rogers. Website includes contest guidelines.

PAUMANOK POETRY AWARD COMPETITION; THE VISITING WRITERS PROGRAM, SUNY Farmingdale, Farmingdale NY 11735, e-mail brownml@farmingdale.edu, website http://www.farmingdale.edu/CampusPages/ArtsSciences/EnglishHumanities/paward.html, established 1990, director Dr. Margery Brown. The Paumanok Poetry Award Competition offers a prize of $1,000 plus an all-expense-paid feature reading in their 2000-2001 series. They will also award two runner-up prizes of $500 plus expenses for a reading in the series. Submit cover letter, 1-paragraph literary bio, up to 5 poems of up to 10 pgs. (published or unpublished), and $12 entry fee postmarked by September 15. Make checks payable to SUNY Farmingdale Visiting Writers Program (VWP). Send SASE for results. Results will be mailed by late December. Send SASE for guidelines or obtain via their website. Inquiries via e-mail OK. Competition receives over 600 entries. Most recent contest winners include Douglas Goetsch (winner) and Tony Gloeggler and Patricia Hooper (runners-up). Poets who have read in their series include Hayden Carruth, Allen Ginsberg, Linda Pastan, Marge Piercy, Joyce Carol Oates, Louis Simpson and David Ignatow. The series changes each year, entries in 1998 for the 1999-2000 series, so entries in the 1999 competition will be considered for the 2000-2001 series, and so on. Website includes Paumanok Poetry Award guidelines and other links to information on the Visiting Writers Program.

JUDITH SIEGEL PEARSON AWARD (Specialized: women), Wayne State University/Family of Judith Siegel Pearson, 51 W. Warren, Detroit MI 48202, phone (313)577-2450, contact Deborah Currie, offers an annual award of up to $250 for "the best creative or scholarly work on a subject concerning women." The type of work accepted rotates each year: poetry, 1999; fiction, 2000; plays and nonfictional prose, 2001. Submissions must be unpublished. Submit 4-10 poems on 20 pgs. maximum. Open to "all interested writers and scholars." Send SASE for guidelines. Deadline: March 1. Competition received 32 entries in 1998. Most recent contest winners were C. Rusch (plays) and Dayana Stetco (nonfictional prose). Winner announced in April.

◎ **PEN CENTER USA WEST LITERARY AWARD IN POETRY (Specialized: regional)**, PEN Center USA West, 672 S. Lafayette Park Place, #41, Los Angeles CA 90057, phone (213)365-8500, fax (213)365-9616, e-mail penwest@tx.netcom.com, website http://www.pen-west-usa.org, awards coordinator Christina Apeles, offers annual $1,000 cash award to a book of poetry published during the previous calendar year. Open to writers living west of the Mississippi. Submit 4 copies of the entry. Send SASE for entry form and guidelines. Inquiries via fax and e-mail OK. Entry fee: $20. Deadline: December 31. Recent award winner was Linda Bierds. Judges were Mark Doty, Eloise Klein Healy and Martha Ronk. Winner will be announced in a spring press release and then honored at a ceremony in Los Angeles. Website includes entry forms, guidelines, press releases, membership info and program info.

PENNSYLVANIA POETRY SOCIETY ANNUAL CONTEST, 801 Spruce St., West Reading PA 19611-1448, phone (610)374-5848, newsletter editor and recording secretary Ann Gasser. The deadline for the society's annual contest, which has 17 categories open to nonmembers and 4 to members only, is January 15. Grand prize category awards 3 prizes of $100, $50, $25 and three poems may be entered at $2 each for members and nonmembers alike. All other categories award three prizes of $25, $15 and $10 and permit one poem in each category. 17 categories are open to all poets; nonmembers pay $1.50 per category 2-12 and 17-21. PPS members pay $2.50 total for entries in categories 2-21. For information about the annual contest send a SASE to Lillian Tweedy, contest chairman, 2488 New Franklin Rd., Chambersburg, PA 17201. Also sponsors the Pegasus Contest for Students. For information write to Anne Pierre Spangler, contest chairman, 1685 Christine Dr., R.D. #2, Lebanon PA 17042. "*Pegasus contest for students is open only to Pennsylvania students!*" Deadline for the Pegasus contest is March 1. The Carlisle Chapter of PPS sponsors the "Kids 'N Critters" contest which has a deadline of October 31. For information send SASE to Jessie Ruhl Miller, 670 West Louther St., Carlisle PA 17013. The Pennsylvania Poetry Society publishes a quarterly newsletter and an annual *Prize Poems* soft cover book, containing prize-winning poems. Prize poems in the Pegasus contest are published in a booklet for the schools which enter. PPS membership dues are $15/year. Make check payable to PPS, Inc. and mail to Richard R. Gasser, Treasurer, at the above address.

◻ ◎ **PENUMBRA POETRY COMPETITION (Specialized: form)**, Tallahassee Writers' Association, P.O. Box 15995, Tallahassee FL 32317-5995, e-mail available via website, website http://www.twaonline.org, established in 1987, editor Carole Timin, offers cash prizes plus publication in and one copy of a chapbook of winners and finalists. Prizes: $100, $30 and $20 for poetry; $50, $20 and $10 for haiku. Submission must be unpublished. No simultaneous submissions. Two categories: (1) poetry of up to 50 lines (shorter poetry is of equal value) and (2) 3-line haiku. Poems must be typed on 8½×11 paper; haiku on 3×5 cards. Please send 2 copies of each entry. On the back of one copy only, write author's name, full address, telephone, e-mail and source of contest information. Send 1-paragraph bio with personal information and publications. Send SASE for complete guidelines or obtain via website. Entry fee: $5/poem, $3/haiku. Deadline: June 30. Competition receives 400-500 entries a year from US, Canada, Japan and others. Most recent winners were Claire Vreel and Helen J. Sherry. Judges change yearly; 1998 judge was Lola Haskins. Sample copy of *Penumbra* chapbook with over 50 pgs. of top winners and finalists available for $7.50. Website includes information on the Tallahassee Writers' Association, guidelines for The Penumbra competition, e-mail contact to editor, articles on Web publishing, links and purchasing information.

◎ **PEW FELLOWSHIP IN THE ARTS (Specialized: regional)**, The University of the Arts, 230 S. Broad St., Suite 1003, Philadelphia PA 19102, phone (215)875-2285, fax (215)875-2276, established in 1991, award director Melissa Franklin. Call or write for application and guidelines (available in mid-September). Must be a Pennsylvania resident of Bucks, Chester, Delaware, Montgomery or Philadelphia county for at least two years; must be 25 or older. Matriculated students, full or part-time, are not eligible. Deadline: December of the preceding year. Most recent judge was a panel of artists and art professionals. Winner will be announced by letter. "The Pew Fellowships in the Arts provides financial support directly to artists so they may have the opportunity to dedicate themselves wholly to the development of their artwork for up to 2 years. Up to 12 fellowships of $50,000 each (in 3 different categories) awarded each year."

◖ **THE RICHARD PHILLIPS POETRY PRIZE**, The Phillips Publishing Co., P.O. Box 121, Watts OK 74964, founded 1993, award director Richard Phillips, Jr. Annual award of $2,000 open to all poets. Submit 40-page ms, published or unpublished poems, any subject, any form. Include $15 reading fee/ms, payable to Richard Phillips Poetry Prize. Mss are not returned. Send SASE for guidelines. Postmark deadline: January 31. "Winner will be announced and check for $1,000 presented by March 31." Publication is the following September. Competition receives approximately 100 entries. Most recent prize winners were: Paul Davidson (1999), Jana Klenburg (1998) and Deborah Vallet (1997). "There are no anthologies to buy, no strings attached. The best manuscript will win the prize."

○ ☑ POETIC POTPOURRI QUARTERLY CONTESTS, P.O. Box 13, Lattimore NC 28089, award director Dennis Norville, offers quarterly awards of $75, $50, $25 and three Honorable Mentions. Submissions may be previously published and may be entered in other contests. Submit any number of poems on any subject in any style. "No porn! Put name and address on each page. No additional guidelines necessary." Entry fee: $2 for the first poem, $1 each additional poem. Postmark deadlines: March 31, June 30, September 30 and December 31. Send SASE with your entry if you want a winners' list. Winners will be announced within one month after contest deadlines.

☑ THE POETRY CENTER BOOK AWARD, 1600 Holloway Ave., San Francisco CA 94132, phone (415)338-3132, e-mail newlit@sfsu.edu, website http://www.sfsu.edu/~newlit/welcome.htm, established in 1980. Method for entering contest is to submit a published book and a $10 entry fee. "Please include cover sheet noting author's name, book title(s), name of person or publisher issuing check and check number." Book must be published and copyrighted during the year of the contest and submitted by December 31. "Beginners may enter but in the past winners have published several previous books." Translations and anthologies are not accepted. Books should be by an individual writer and must be entirely poetry. Prize (only one) is $500 and an invitation to read for the Poetry Center. No entry form is required. Recent winners include Alicia Ostriker and Robert Wrigley. "The Poetry Center and American Poetry Archives at San Francisco State University was founded in 1954. Its archives is the largest circulating tape collection of writers reading their own work in the United States."

[N] ⚏ ○ POETRY FOREVER; MILTON ACORN PRIZE FOR POETRY; ORION PRIZE FOR POETRY; TIDEPOOL PRIZE FOR POETRY, Poetry Forever, P.O. Box 68018, Hamilton, Ontario L8M 3M7 Canada, phone (905)312-1779, fax (905)312-8285, administrator James Deahl. Poetry Forever sponsors 3 annual contests for poets everywhere—the Milton Acorn Prize, the Orion Prize and the Tidepool Prize. Each contest awards 50% of its entry fees in 1st, 2nd and 3rd Place prizes. The top 3 poems also receive broadsheet publication. For all 3 contests, poems may be no longer than 30 lines. "Poems should be typed or neatly printed. Photocopied submissions OK." Send SASE or e-mail address to receive winners' list. Entry fee(s): $3/poem. Make checks payable to Poetry Forever. Deadlines: May 15 (Milton Acorn), June 15 (Orion Prize), July 15 (Tidepool Prize). "The purpose of the contests is to fund the publication of full-size collections by the People's Poet Milton Acorn (1923-1986), Ottawa poet Marty Flomen (1942-1997) and Hamilton poet Herb Barrett (1912-1995)."

[N] ⚏ ◎ POETS' CLUB OF CHICAGO INTERNATIONAL SHAKESPEAREAN/PETRARCHAN SONNET CONTEST; THE INTERNATIONAL NARRATIVE CONTEST (Specialized: form), 130 Windsor Park Dr., C-323, Carol Stream IL 60188, chairman LaVone Holt. The International Shakespearean/Petrarchan Sonnet Contest is open to anyone **except** members of Poets' Club of Chicago. Submit only 1 entry of either a Shakespearean or a Petrarchan sonnet, which must be original and unpublished and must not have won a cash award in any contest sponsored previously by the Club. Write for rules, include SASE, no earlier than March. No entry fee. Prizes of $50, $35 and $15 plus 2 honorable mentions. Postmark deadline: September 1. Most recent contest winners include Linda Bosson, Robert Sheridan and Edith Richey. Winners will be notified by October 15. Send SASE with entry to receive winners' list. Also sponsors The International Narrative Contest, awarding annually a $75 first prize and a $25 second prize. Submissions must be unpublished. Submit 2 copies of 1 narrative poem, any form, any subject, of up to 40 lines to Constance Vogel, Chairman, 1206 Hutchings Ave., Glenview IL 60025. Send SASE for guidelines. Entry must be typed on 8½×11 paper, single-spaced. Put name of contest and title of poem in the upper right-hand corner of both copies, and name and address in the upper left-hand corner on only one copy. No entry fee. Postmark deadline: September 1. Winners will be notified by October 15. The Poets' Club of Chicago meets monthly to critique original poetry, read at and man the Poetry Room in the Harold Washington Library, and read at open-mike coffeehouses. Members also conduct workshops at area high schools by invitation.

◎ POETS' DINNER CONTEST (Specialized: regional), 2214 Derby St., Berkeley CA 94705-1018, phone (510)841-1217, contact Dorothy V. Benson. Since 1927 there has been an annual awards banquet sponsored by the ad hoc Poets' Dinner Committee, usually at Spenger's Fish Grotto (a Berkeley Landmark). Three typed copies of original, unpublished poems in not more than 3 of the 8 categories [Humor, Love, Nature, Beginnings & Endings, Spaces & Places, People, Theme (changed annually) and Poet's Choice] are submitted anonymously without fee, and the winning poems (Grand Prize, 1st, 2nd, 3rd) are read at the banquet and honorable mentions awarded. **Contestant must be present to win.** Cash prizes awarded; Honorable Mention receives books. The event is nonprofit. Send SASE for contest rules. Deadline is in January. Competition receives about 300 entries. Recent contest winners include Mary Rudge (Grand Prize); 1st Prizes, Joyce Odam, James Cardwell, Hodee Edwards, Danyen Powell, Connie Post and Arthur Dawson.

◎ PRESIDIO LA BAHIA AWARD; SUMMERFIELD G. ROBERTS AWARD (Specialized: regional), Sons of the Republic of Texas, 1717 Eighth St., Bay City TX 77414, phone/fax (409)245-6644, e-mail srtexas@tgn.net, website http://www.tgn.net/~srtexas, contact Melinda Williams. Both may be awarded for poetry. The Presidio La Bahia Award is an annual award or awards (depending upon the number and quality of entries) for writing that promotes research into and preservation of the Spanish Colonial influence on Texas culture. $2,000 is available, with a minimum first prize of $1,200. Entries must be in quadruplicate and will not be returned. Deadline: September 30. The Summerfield G. Roberts Award, available to US citizens, is an annual award of $2,500 for a book or manuscript depicting or representing the Republic of Texas (1836-46), written or published during the calendar year for which the award is given. Entries must be submitted in quintuplicate and will not be returned. Deadline: January 15. Inquiries via fax and e-mail OK. Competitions receive 10-20 entries.

● ❍ **PRO DOGS CREATIVE WRITING & PHOTOGRAPHIC COMPETITION**, PRO Dogs National Charity, 267 Hillbury Rd., Warlingham, Surrey CR6 9TL England, phone 01883 622121, award director Michaela Edridge. Annual contest for poems up to 40 lines, any style or theme, with prizes of £200, £150 and £75. Contest information available for SASE (or SAE and IRCs). Fees: £3 for first entry; £1.50 for subsequent entries. Deadline: October 1. Winners announced at the Pro Dogs Awards Luncheon in November.

⬤ **PULITZER PRIZE IN LETTERS**, % The Pulitzer Prize Board, 709 Journalism, Columbia University, New York NY 10027, phone (212)854-3841, e-mail pulitzer-feedback@pulitzer.org, website http://www.pulitzer. org, offers 5 prizes of $5,000 each year, including 1 in poetry, for books published in the calendar year preceding the award. Submit 4 copies of published books (or galley proofs if book is being published after November), photo, bio, entry form and $50 entry fee. July 1 deadline for books published between January 1 and June 30; November 1 deadline for books published between July 1 and December 31. Competition receives 155 entries a year. Recent award winner was Charles Wright for *Black Zodiac* published by Farrar, Straus & Giroux. Website includes downloadable entry form and guidelines, bios and photos of winners from 1995 to present.

N ● **$❍** **PUPPY LIFELINE SHORT STORY & POETRY COMPETITION**, Puppy Lifeline, "Farplace" Sidehead, Westgate, County Durham DL13 1LE United Kingdom, phone +44(0)1388 517397, fax +44(0)1388 517044, e-mail farplace@msn.com, established in 1997, offers annual cash prizes of £60 (sterling) 1st Prize and for poetry, £10 (sterling) runner up competition. Other cash prizes for short story entries. "At present can only award prizes as UK sterling cheque." Submit any number of poems, any subject, in any form. Include SASE (or SAE with IRCs) for notification and receipt. Send SASE for entry form and guidelines. Inquiries via fax or e-mail OK. Entry fee(s): £2 sterling per poem/£3 per story. Make checks payable to Puppy Lifeline. Entry fees from other countries accepted in "sterling only at present." Deadline: July 31. Competition receives approximately 350-400 entries a year. The judge for upcoming contest will be Jan Edwards. Winner(s) will be announced by letter—usually first week of September. Write for details on ordering copies of previous winning poems. "Puppy Lifeline rescues and rehomes abandoned puppies in the UK. Entry fees help pay our vet bills, food bills, etc."

◆ ◎ **QSPELL LITERARY AWARDS; QUEBEC WRITERS' FEDERATION, (Specialized: regional, translations)**, 1200 Atwater Ave., Montreal, Quebec H3Z 1X4 Canada, phone (514)933-0878, fax (514)934-2485, e-mail qspell@total.net, website http://www.qspell.org, contact Award Director, offers annual awards of $2,000 each for poetry, fiction and nonfiction and translation. Also offers a $500 first book award. Submissions must be previously published. Open to authors "who have lived in Quebec for 3 of the past 5 years." Submit a book published between October 1 of the preceding year and September 30 of the current year. "Books should have at least 48 pgs." Write for entry form. Inquiries via fax and e-mail OK. Entry fee: $10/title. Deadline: May 31. Finished proofs: August 15. Competition receives approximately 50 entries. Most recent award winners were Anne Carson (poetry), Mordecai Richler (fiction), David Manicom (nonfiction) and Matthew Friedman (first book). Judges were Antonio d'Alfonso, George Eliot Clarke and Mitsiko Miller. Winners will be announced in November. "QSPELL was formed in 1988 to honor and promote literature written in English by Quebec authors."

N ⬤ **RAINMAKER AWARDS IN POETRY**, *Zone 3*, Austin Peay State University, P.O. Box 4565, Clarksville TN 37044, managing editor Susan Wallace, offers annual awards of 1st Place $500, 2nd Place $300 and 3rd Place $100. Winning poems will also be featured in *Zone 3*. Submissions must be unpublished. Submit no more than 3 poems with SASE. Entry fee is 1 year's subscription (2 issues) to *Zone 3*: $8. "Submitters who prefer not to subscribe will be considered for publications but will not be included in the competition." Postmark deadline: January 1. Winner(s) will be announced in the Fall/Winter 2000 issue of *Zone 3*.

❍ **REDWOOD ACRES FAIR POETRY CONTEST**, P.O. Box 6576, Eureka CA 95502, phone (707)445-3037, fax (707)445-1583, offers an annual contest with various categories for both juniors and seniors with entry fee of 50¢/poem for the junior contests and $1/poem for the senior contests. Deadline: May 27. Competition receives 200 entries.

✔ ◎ **ROANOKE-CHOWAN POETRY AWARD (Specialized: regional)**, North Carolina Literary and Historical Association, 109 E. Jones St., Room 23, Raleigh NC 27601, phone (919)733-9375, contact Jerry C. Caskion, offers annual award for "an original volume of poetry published during the twelve months ending June 30 of the year for which the award is given." Open to "authors who have maintained legal or physical residence, or a combination of both, in North Carolina for the three years preceding the close of the contest period." Submit

3 copies of each entry. Deadline: July 15. Competition receives about 25 entries. Recent award winner was James Seay. Winner will be announced during the annual meeting in November.

N ⊘ MARY ROBERTS RINEHART FOUNDATION AWARD, Mail Stop Number 3E4, The Mary Roberts Rinehart Award, English Dept., George Mason University, Fairfax VA 22030-4444, phone (703)993-1180. Two grants are made annually to writers who need financial assistance "to complete work definitely projected." The amount of the award depends upon income the fund generates; in the past the amount was approximately $1,000 in each category. Work by poets and fiction writers is accepted in odd numbered years, e.g., 1999, 2001. **A writer's work must be nominated in writing by an established author or editor**. Nominations must be accompanied by a sample of the nominee's work, up to 25 pgs. of poetry and 30 pgs. of fiction. Deadline: November 30. Competition receives over 200 entries. Send SASE for guidelines.

◐ ◎ ANNA DAVIDSON ROSENBERG AWARD, FOR POEMS ON THE JEWISH EXPERIENCE (Specialized: ethnic), Judah L. Magnes Museum, 2911 Russell St., Berkeley CA 94705, website http://www.jfed.org/magnes/magnes, established in 1987, offers prizes of $100, $50 and $25, as well as honorable mentions, for up to 8 pgs. of 1-3 unpublished poems (in English) on the Jewish Experience. "This award is open to all poets. You needn't be Jewish to enter." There is also a Youth Commendation for poets under 19, a Senior Award if 65 or over, and a New/Emerging Poet Award. Do not send poems without entry form; write between April 1 and July 15 for form and guidelines (enclose SASE). Deadline: August 31. No electronic entries of any sort. Competition receives 250-450 entries a year. Recent winners include Doren Robbins, Alicia Ostriker, Myra Sklarew and Joan I. Siegel. The Magnes Museum is the third largest Jewish museum in the country and sponsors numerous programs in the arts and literature.

✓ ◐ ◎ THE CONSTANCE SALTONSTALL FOUNDATION FOR THE ARTS GRANTS (Specialized: regional), 120 Brindley St., Ithaca NY 14850, phone/fax (607)277-4933, e-mail artsfound@claritycon nect.com, award director Lee-Ellen Marvin, grants of $5,000 awarded to a limited number of individual painters, writers and photographers. Submit up to 15 pages. Must be 21 years or older and resident of one of 23 counties in New York state. Send SASE for entry form and guidelines. Inquiries via fax and e-mail OK. Deadline: January 15. Recent contest winners were Justine Dougherty, Chris Kennedy, Anthony Piccione and Ellen Samuels. Most recent judge was jury of distinguished writers. Winners will be announced April 30. The foundation was established according to the wishes of Connie Saltonstall, a painter and photographer, who asked that after her death her estate be used to benefit the arts.

◎ SAN FRANCISCO FOUNDATION; JOSEPH HENRY JACKSON AWARD; JAMES D. PHELAN AWARD (Specialized: regional, young adult), ℅ Intersection for the Arts, 446 Valencia St., San Francisco CA 94103, phone (415)626-2787, fax (415)626-1636, e-mail intrsect@wenet.net, website http://www.wenet.net/~intrsect. The Jackson Award ($2,000), established in 1955, will be made to the author of an unpublished work-in-progress in the form of fiction (novel or short stories), nonfictional prose, or poetry. Applicants must be residents of northern California or Nevada for three consecutive years immediately prior to the deadline date of January 31, and must be between the ages of 20 and 35 as of the deadline. The Phelan Award ($2,000), established in 1935, will be made to the author of an unpublished work-in-progress in the form of fiction (novel or short stories), nonfictional prose, poetry or drama. Applicants must be California-born (although they may now reside outside of the state), and must be between the ages of 20 and 35 as of the January 31 deadline. Mss for both awards must be accompanied by an application form, which may be obtained by sending a SASE. Entries accepted November 15 through January 31. Competitions receive 200 entries. Most recent contest writers include Dana Lomax (Joseph Henry Jackson Award) and Amanda Kim (James D. Phelan Award). "Guidelines and application forms are available through the scholarship provider service, http://www.fastweb.com."

◻ SAN MATEO COUNTY FAIR FINE ARTS COMPETITION, P.O. Box 1027, San Mateo CA 94403, phone (650)574-3247 or (800)338-EXPO (outside California), fax (650)574-3985, e-mail info@smexpo.xo.com, website http://www.sanmateoexpo.org, established in 1939, for unpublished poetry. Adult and youth divisions. Write or call for entry form and additional information or request via e-mail. Adult Division awards of $100, $50, and $25; fee $10 for each poem. Youth Division awards of $2, $1.50 and $1; no fee. Limit 2 entries per division. July 10 deadline for poems.

N ◻ ◐ ◎ SARASOTA POETRY THEATRE PRESS; EDDA POETRY CHAPBOOK COMPETITION FOR WOMEN; SARASOTA POETRY THEATRE CHAPBOOK COMPETITION; ANIMALS IN POETRY; SOULSPEAK POETRY COMPETITION (Specialized), P.O. Box 48955, Sarasota FL 34230-6955, phone (941)366-6468, e-mail soultalk@aol.com, website http://augment.sis.pitt.edu/jms/, established in 1994-1998, award director Scylla Liscombe, offers 4 annual contests for poetry with prizes ranging from $25 1st Prize plus publication in an anthology to $50 1st Prize plus 25 published chapbooks. Honorable Mentions also awarded. Pays winners from other countries in copies. Send SASE for guidelines or visit website. Entry fees range from $4/poem to $10/ms. Competition receives an average of 200 entries a year. Judges for contests are the staff of the press and ranking state poets. Winners are notified by mail. "Sarasota Poetry Theatre Press is a division of Soulspeak/Sarasota Poetry Theatre, a non-profit organization dedicated to encouraging poetry in all its forms through the Sarasota Poetry Theatre Press, Therapeutic Soulspeak for at-risk youth and the Soulspeak Performance Center. We are looking for honest, not showy, poetry; use a good readable font. Do not send extraneous materials."

CLAUDIA ANN SEAMAN POETRY AWARD (Specialized: students), The Community Foundation of Dutchess County, 80 Washington St., Suite 201, Poughkeepsie NY 12601, phone (914)452-3077, fax (914)452-3083, established in 1983, offers annual award of $250 (1st Prize) and $100 (2nd Prize). Submissions may be entered in other contests. Submit 1 or 2 poems on any subject or in any form. Open to students in grades 9-12. "Entry must contain student and school names, addresses, and phone numbers and the name of the English or writing teacher." Send SASE for entry form and guidelines. Inquiries via fax OK. Deadline: approximately May 1. Most recent award winner was Emma Straub. Judged by "a panel of judges, including Donna Seaman (Claudia's sister)." Winner announced in September each year at the Barnes & Noble in Manhattan. Copies of previous winning poems may be obtained by contacting The Community Foundation (by phone or in writing). "The Community Foundation is a nonprofit organization serving Dutchess County, NY; it administers numerous grant programs, scholarship funds, and endowment requests. This is an excellent opportunity for young, previously unpublished poets to earn recognition for their work. Since there's no fee, there is little to lose; realize, however, that a national contest will have more entries than a regional competition."

SENIOR POET LAUREATE POETRY COMPETITION (Specialized: senior citizen), Goodin Communications & Penny Peephole Publications, Chapbook Dept., P.O. Box 6003, Springfield MO 65801, e-mail goldenword@aol.com, website http://hometown.aol.com/goldenword/index.html, established in 1993, co-sponsors Wanda Sue Parrott and Vera-Jane Goodin, offers annual award to "American poets age 50 and older. Top winner will receive $60 and the Senior Poet Laureate title. Cash awards will also be given 1st Place winners in nine poetry categories. The top 55 winning poems will be published in *Golden Words* chapbook of poems by leading older American poets." Submit any number of poems; 32 lines or less (unless specified otherwise); 1/page. Categories are haiku, short poem (12 lines or less), nostalgic, long poem (over 32 lines), sonnet, love, inspirational, light verse and western/pioneer/tall tales poem. Send SASE for entry form and guidelines. Inquiries via e-mail OK. Entry fee: $1/poem. Deadline: August 1. Competition receives 1,000 entries a year. Most recent contest winner was Joan Ritty. Winners will be announced in October. The top winning poems from the 9 categories and the new Senior Poet Laureate's poem will also be published in *Hodgepodge* literary magazine.

SKY BLUE WATERS POETRY CONTESTS, Sky Blue Waters Poetry Society, 232 SE 12th Ave., Faribault MN 55021-6406, phone (507)332-2803. The society sponsors monthly contests with prizes of $40, $30, $20, $10 plus 3 honorable mentions. Also sponsors semiannual awards in March and September with 1st Prize of $50, 2nd Prize $40, 3rd Prize $30, 4th through 10th Prizes $10. Simultaneous submissions are permitted. Submit any number of poems on any subject. Guidelines available for SASE. Entry fee: $2 first poem, $1 each additional poem. All winning poems (monthly and semi-annual) automatically entered in The Best of the Best Contest to be judged each January. No fee required. 1st Prize $50, 2nd Prize $30, 3rd Prize $20. Winners will be announced by mail one month following deadline date. "The Sky Blue Waters Poetry Society is a group of Southern Minnesota poets who exist for the sheer 'love of writing.' Most members agree that writing is not just a love but a necessity. Keep writing. Keep submitting. Today's creation will be tomorrow's winner."

SLAPERING HOL PRESS CHAPBOOK COMPETITION, Hudson Valley Writer's Center, 300 Riverside Dr., Sleepy Hollow NY 10591, phone (914)332-5953, e-mail hvwc@aol.com, established in 1990, co-editors Stephanie Strickland and Margo Stever, offers annual award of $500 plus 10 author's copies. Submissions must be from poets who have not previously published a book or chapbook. Submit 24 pages of poems with acknowledgements, any form or style, SASE and $10 reading fee. "Manuscript should be anonymous with second title page containing name, address and phone." Send SASE for guidelines. "See *Poets & Writers* for deadline, usually in the late spring." Competition receives 450-550 entries. Most recent contest winner was Rachel Loden, *The Last Campaign*. Copies of previous winning books may be obtained by requesting order form.

KAY SNOW WRITING AWARDS, Willamette Writers, 9045 SW Barbur Blvd., Suite 5A, Portland OR 97219-4027, phone (503)452-1592, fax (503)452-0372, e-mail wilwrite@teleport.com, website http://www.teleport.com/~wilwrite, established in 1986, award director Liam Cullen, offers annual 1st Prize of $200, 2nd Prize of $100, 3rd Prize of $50 and publication of excerpt only, in January issue of *The Willamette Writer*. Submissions must be unpublished. Submit 1-5 pages on any subject in any style or form, single spaced, one side of paper only. Send SASE for entry form and guidelines. Entry fee: $10 for members of Willamette Writers; $15 for nonmembers. Deadline: May 15. Inquiries via fax and e-mail OK. Competition receives 150 entries. Most recent award winner was Sarah McCandless. Winners will be announced July 31. "Write and send in your very best poem. Read it aloud. If it still sounds like the best poem you've ever heard, send it in."

SOUNDPOST PRESS ANNUAL CHAPBOOK AWARD, Soundpost Press, 632 23rd St. N., La Crosse WI 54601-3825, established in 1993, award directors C. Mikal Oness and Elizabeth Oness, offers annual award of $500 against royalties. Submissions may be entered in other contests. Submit 18 pages on any subject in any form. "Entries submitted close to the deadline do *not* need to use overnight mail." Entry fee: $10. Deadline: May 1. Most recent award winner was Ted Genoways (1998). The judge will be a nationally recognized poet. Winner will be announced September 2000. "The edition will be handsomely designed, with a hand-printed cover of Fabriano Ingles." Copies of previous winning books may be obtained by sending a check for $6.50 ($5 for book and $1.50 postage) to Soundpost Press.

SPAWN POETRY CONTEST, SPAWN (Small Publishers Artists and Writers Network), P.O. Box 2653, Ventura CA 93002-2653, contact Mary Embree, offers annual prizes of $100, $50 and $25 for poetry in rhymed and non-rhyming categories. Entries accepted from October 1 through January 31. Entry fees: $5 for SPAWN members, $10 for nonmembers. Send SASE for guidelines.

SSA WRITER'S CONTEST, The Society of Southwestern Authors, P.O. Box 30355, Tucson AZ 85751, offers annual awards of 1st Prize $100, 2nd Prize $50, 3rd Prize $25 and Honorable Mentions. Submissions must be original and unpublished. Submit no more than 6 pages/entry, "traditional or free verse with a single theme-focus. Title should intrigue reader. Should have feeling, rhythm, consistency, empathy, appropriate imagery, and be understandable with unique use of metaphors and similes. If rhymed, nothing hackneyed, no jingles." Only 1 double-spaced poem/white 8½ × 11 page; 12 point type (courier preferred). Send SASE for entry form and complete guidelines. Entry fee(s): $10/entry. Postmark deadline: May 31. "1st, 2nd, 3rd Place and Honorable Mention winners will be our guests at an awards luncheon in September." The SSA also sponsors a conference, Wrangling with Writing. See the conference's listing in the Conferences & Workshops section of this book. "Entries not complying with Official Rules will be disqualified, not judged, or critiqued. Critiqued manuscripts will be returned only if accompanied by SASE with sufficient postage."

STARVING ROMANTICS POETRY COMPETITION, Starving Romantics, 942 Yonge St., #1216, Toronto, Ontario M4W 3S8 Canada, phone (416)962-7188, fax (416)969-3850, established in 1995, director I.J. Schecter, offers annual awards for work that "hearkens to the style of Romantic poetry." 1st Place: $125 plus recitation at literary venues; 2nd Place: $50 plus recitation; 3rd Place: $25 plus recitation; 4th through 10th: recitation plus free entry for the following year's contest. Submissions must be unpublished and may be entered in other contests. Include separate cover sheet with name and address and SASE for notification. Send SASE (or SAE and IRC) for guidelines. Inquiries via fax OK. Entry fee: $3/poem, maximum 5 poems. Annual deadline: July 31. Competition receives 800 entries a year. Recent award winners include Len Krisak, Simon Moromiewicz and Marlene Meehl. All entrants notified of results by October 30. The director says, "Our continuing mandate is to restore the tradition established by Wordsworth, Shelley and others of the period by seeking the most accomplished Romantic poetry being written today. If entering from the U.S., please remember to send International Reply Coupons or an extra dollar for return postage, rather than U.S. stamps."

WALLACE E. STEGNER FELLOWSHIPS, Creative Writing Program, Stanford University, Stanford CA 94305, phone (650)725-1208, fax (650)723-3679, e-mail gay.pierce@forsythe.stanford.edu, website http://www.stanford.edu/dept/english/cw/, administrator Gay Pierce, 5 in poetry, $15,000 plus tuition of over $5,000, for promising writers who can benefit from 2 years instruction and criticism at the Writing Center. Previous publication not required, though it can strengthen one's application. Deadline: Postmarked by the first working day after December 1. Inquiries via fax and e-mail OK. Competition receives 1,000 entries a year. Most recent winners were Rick Barot, Andrew Feld, Joanie MacKowski, David Yezzi and Monica Yaun.

DONNA J. STONE NATIONAL LITERARY AWARDS (Specialized: membership), American Mothers, Inc., Matthew J. Pascal Foundation, 301 Park Ave., New York NY 10022, phone/fax (212)755-2539, e-mail info@americanmothers.org, website http://www.pascalfoundation.org/donnajstone.html, founded 1996, literature chair (American Mothers, Inc.) Yavonne Bagwell, offers annual prizes of $400, $100 and Honorable Mentions. "Winners are published in the annual Donna J. Stone National Literary Awards Booklet of American Mothers, Inc. Publications." Submissions must be unpublished. Submit any number of poems in any form on family themes, 100 lines or less. "Poet must be a mother and a member of American Mothers, Inc. (membership included with $20 entry fee)." Send SASE for entry form and guidelines. Inquiries via fax and e-mail OK. Entry fee: $20. Does not accept entry fees in foreign currencies. Deadline: January 31, 2000. "Winners will be notified by mail in late March of 2000 and formally announced at the National Convention of American Mothers, Inc. in late April of 2000." Visit website for more information.

DAVID THOMAS CHARITABLE TRUST OPEN POETRY CONTEST, David Thomas Charitable Trust, P.O. Box 6055, Nairn IV12 4YB Scotland, phone +44(1667)454441, fax +44(1667)454401, established in 1994, award director David St. John Thomas, offers annual award of £250 per category plus £250 (4 categories) overall winner. Pays winners from other countries in a bank draft in their currency. Submissions must be unpublished. Submit any number of poems on love, religion, travel and humorous subjects, in any form. Send SASE for entry form and guidelines. Entry fee(s): £2.50/poem. Does not accept entry fees in foreign currencies. Deadline: January 15. Competition receives over 2,000 entries a year. Judges for upcoming contest will be Alison Chisholm and Doris Corti. Winner(s) will be announced "through our own magazine, subscription and newsstand."

N **●** **TLS/BLACKWELL'S POETRY COMPETITION**, The Times Literary Supplement, Admiral House, 66-68 East Smithfield, London E1 9XY England, phone 0171 782 3000, fax 0171 782 3398, website http://www.the-tls.co.uk, established in 1997, award director Sonya Allen, offers annual 1st Prize £2,000, 3 runners-up: £500 each, publication in The Times Literary Supplement. Submissions must be unpublished. Submit 5 poems maximum on any subject, no longer than 40 lines, typed on one sheet of A4 paper. "Entrant's name must not appear anywhere on the poem." Send SASE for entry form. Inquiries via fax or e-mail OK. Entry fee(s): £6 for first entry, £4 for each additional entry. Accepts entry fees in foreign currencies. Deadline: January 5. Competition receives 3,000 entries a year. Judges for upcoming contest will be Mick Imlah, poetry editor, *The Times Literary Supplement*. Winner(s) will be announced in *The Times Literary Supplement*. "The *TLS* is the world's best known weekly literary review publishing new poets work almost every week."

● **◎** **TOWSON UNIVERSITY PRIZE FOR LITERATURE (Specialized: regional)**, Towson University, College of Liberal Arts, Towson MD 21252, phone (410)830-2128, award director Dean of the College of Liberal Arts, offers annual prize of $1,500 "for a single book or book-length manuscript of fiction, poetry, drama or imaginative nonfiction by a young Maryland writer. The prize is granted on the basis of literary and aesthetic excellence as determined by a panel of distinguished judges appointed by the university. The first award, made in the fall of 1980, went to novelist Anne Tyler." The work must have been published within the three years prior to the year of nomination or must be scheduled for publication within the year in which nominated. Open to Maryland residents under 40 years of age. Submit 5 copies of work in bound form or in typewritten, double-spaced ms form. Send SASE for entry form and guidelines. Deadline: May 15. Competition receives 8-10 entries. Most recent contest winners were Ned Balbo and Charles Marsh.

⊕ **●** **●** **◎** **THE TREWITHEN POETRY PRIZE (Specialized: rural)**, Trewithen Poetry, Chy-An-Dour, Treskewes Cottage, Trewithen Moor, Stithians, Truro, Cornwall TR3 7DU England, established in 1995, award secretary D. Atkinson, offers annual award of 1st Prize £300, 2nd Prize £150, 3rd Prize £75, plus 3 runner-up prizes of £25 each and publication in *The Trewithen Chapbook*. Submissions may be entered in other contests, "*but* must *not* previously have won another competition." Submit any number of poems on a rural theme in any form. Send SASE for entry form. Entry fee: £3 for the first poem and £1.75 for each additional poem. Deadline: October 31. Competition receives 1,000-1,500 entries. Most recent contest winners were Ann Drysdale and Roger Elkin. Judged by a panel of 3-4 working poets who remain anonymous. Winners will be announced at the end of December by results sheet and through poetry magazines and organizations. Winning poems published biennially in March/April. Copies of *The Trewithen Chapbook* may be obtained by using order form on entry form or by writing direct to the secretary enclosing a SAE with IRC. "We are seeking good writing with a contemporary approach, reflecting any aspect of nature or rural life in any country."

N **⊕** **$** **●** **VER POETS OPEN COMPETITION**, Ver Poets, Haycroft, 61/63 Chiswell Green Lane, St. Albans, Hertfordshire AL2 3AL United Kingdom, phone (01727)867005, established in 1974, award director May Badman, offers annual prizes of £500, £300, 2 £100 prizes and a free copy of anthology "Vision On" to all winners and 30 selected poems. Submissions must be unpublished. Submit any number of poems on any subject, "open as to style, form, content. Poem must be no more than 30 lines excluding title, typed on white A4 sheets. Entry forms provided, pseudonyms to be used on poems." Send SASE for entry form and guidelines. Entry fee(s): £2.50 per poem. Deadline: April 30. Competition receives approximately 1,000 entries a year. Most recent contest winner(s) were Bill Headdon, Daphne Gloag, John Gallas and Suzanne Burrows (1998). Judge was Peter Scupham. Winner(s) announced at an "Adjudication & Tea" event in June each year. "We have local and postal members, meet regularly in St. Albans, study poetry and the writing of it, try to guide members to reach a good standard, arrange 3 competitions per year with prizes and anthologies for members only. Plus the annual open competition. We do expect a high standard of art and skill."

⊕ **◎** **THE VICTORIAN FELLOWSHIP OF AUSTRALIAN WRITERS; FAW AWARDS (Specialized: regional)**, FAW (Vic) Inc., P.O. Box 1270, Kensington, Victoria 3031, Australia, phone/fax (03)9376 7242, all awards for Australian authors. The FAW Anne Elder Poetry Award (prizes of $1,000 and $500) is for a first published book of poetry. The FAW Christopher Brennan Award is a bronze plaque to honor an Australian poet who has written work of sustained quality and distinction (entries not required; award by committee). The FAW John Shaw Neilson Poetry Award (prizes of $500 and $250) is for an unpublished poem of at least 14 lines. The FAW Colin Thiele Poetry Award ($200 and $100) is for unpublished poems by Australian writers 15-20 years old. The FAW C.J. Dennis Poetry Award (prizes of $125 and $75) is for unpublished poems by Australian writers 10-14 years old.

● **◎** **VISITING FELLOWSHIPS FOR HISTORICAL RESEARCH BY CREATIVE AND PERFORMING ARTISTS AND WRITERS (Specialized: American history and culture)**, American Antiquarian Society, 185 Salisbury St., Worcester MA 01609-1634, phone (508)755-5221, fax (508)754-9069, e-mail jdm@mwa.org, established in 1994, award director James David Moran, offers annual award of "a stipend of $1,200/four-week period of residency in Worcester, MA. Plus an allowance for travel." Submissions may be entered in other contests. "The contest is for a fellowship to do research in a national library of American history and culture. The library is devoted to pre-twentieth century materials." Send SASE for entry form and guidelines.

Inquiries via fax and e-mail OK. Deadline: October 5. Competition receives 60 entries. Most recent award winners were Christopher Cokinos, nonfiction writer; Tom Dunn, playwright; Cornelia Nixon, novelist/short story writer; and Barbara Weisberg, children's writer and producer (1998). Winners will be announced in December. "Founded in 1812, as the country's first national historical organization, the American Antiquarian Society is both a learned society and a major independent research library. The AAS library today houses the largest and most accessible collection of books, pamphlets, broadsides, newspapers, periodicals, sheet music and graphic arts material produced through 1876 in what is now the United States, as well as manuscripts and a substantial collection of secondary works, bibliographies, and other reference works related to all aspects of American history and culture before the twentieth century." To poets thinking about entering the contest the director says, "learn about the collections in the library; consult *Under Its Generous Dome, A Guide to the Collections and Programs of the American Antiquarian Society.*"

◎ **THE W.D. WEATHERFORD AWARD (Specialized: regional)**, Berea College, CPO 2336, Berea KY 40404, contact chairman, for the published work (including poetry) which "best illuminates the problems, personalities, and unique qualities of the Appalachian South." Work is nominated by its publisher, by a member of the award committee or by any reader. The award is for $500 and sometimes there are special awards of $200 each. Deadline: December 31 of the year work was published.

[N] ◎ **WESTERN HERITAGE AWARDS (Specialized)**, National Cowboy Hall of Fame and Western Heritage Center, 1700 NE 63rd St., Oklahoma City OK 73111. Since 1960, this national museum has awarded excellence in western literature, music, television and film. Principal creators of winning entries in 15 categories receive the bronze "Wrangler," an original sculpture by artist John Free, during special awards ceremonies held at the museum each spring. Entry forms are mailed annually in September for works published between January 1 and November 30 of that year. Deadline for entries: November 30. The 1998 award for poetry went to *The Medicine Keepers* by J.B. Allen, published by Grey Horse Press, Lubbock, Texas.

⊠ ◎ **WFNB ANNUAL LITERARY CONTEST; THE ALFRED G. BAILEY AWARD; WRITERS' FEDERATION OF NEW BRUNSWICK (Specialized: regional)**, P.O. Box 37, Station A, Fredericton, New Brunswick E3B 4Y2 Canada, phone/fax (506)459-7228, e-mail aa821@fan.nb.ca, website http://www.sjfn.n b.ca/community_hall/w/writers_federation_NB/index.htm, established in 1985, offers prizes of $150, $75, $50, for unpublished poems of up to 100 lines (typed). Open to New Brunswick residents only. The Alfred G. Bailey Award is a $400 prize given annually for poetry mss of 48 pgs. or more. May include some individual poems that have been published. Entry fee: $10 for members, $15 for nonmembers. Send SASE for guidelines. Inquiries via e-mail OK. Deadline: February 14. Competitions received 140 entries in 1998. Recent award winners include Shane Rhodes for the Bailey Award and Phyllis McKinley WFNB Contest.

[N] ∅ **WHITING WRITERS' AWARDS; MRS. GILES WHITING FOUNDATION**, 1133 Avenue of the Americas, 22nd Floor, New York NY 10036-6710, director Barbara K. Bristol. The Foundation makes awards of $30,000 each to up to 10 writers of fiction, nonfiction, poetry and plays chosen by a selection committee drawn from a list of recognized writers, literary scholars and editors. Recipients of the award are selected from nominations made by writers, educators and editors from communities across the country whose experience and vocations bring them in contact with individuals of unusual talent. The nominators and selectors are appointed by the foundation and serve anonymously. **Direct applications and informal nominations are not accepted by the foundation.**

∅ **STAN AND TOM WICK POETRY PRIZE**, Wick Poetry Program, Kent State University, P.O. Box 5190, Kent OH 44242-0001, phone (330)672-2067 or (330)672-2676, website http://www.kent.edu:80/english/wick/WickPoetry.htm, established in 1994, award director Maggie Anderson, offers annual award of $2,000 and publication by The Kent State University Press. Submissions must be unpublished as a whole and may be entered in other contests. Submit 48-68 pages of poetry. Open to poets writing in English who have not yet published a full-length collection. Entries must include cover sheet with poet's name, address, telephone number and title of ms. Send SASE for guidelines. Entry fee: $15. Deadline: May 1, 2000. Competition receives 700 entries. 1998 contest winner was Karen Kovacik. Judge for 1999 contest was Lucille Clifton.

[N] ◎ **THE RICHARD WILBUR AWARD (Specialized: nationality)**, Dept. of English, University of Evansville, 1800 Lincoln Ave., Evansville IN 47722, phone (812)479-2975, offers an annual award of $1,000 and book publication to "recognize a quality book-length manuscript of poetry." Submissions must be unpublished, original poetry collections ("public domain or permission-secured translations may comprise up to one-third of the manuscript"). Submit ms of 50-100 typed pages, unbound, bound or clipped. Open to all American poets. Mss should be accompanied by 2 title pages: one with collection's title, author's name, address and phone number and one with only the title. Include SASE for contest results. Send SASE for guidelines. Entry fee(s): $20/ms. Postmark deadline: December 1. Judge for last contest was Dana Gioia. The winning ms is published and copyrighted by the University of Evansville Press.

N Ø OSCAR WILLIAMS & GENE DERWOOD AWARD, New York Community Trust, 2 Park Ave., New York NY 10016, is an award given annually to nominees of the selection committee "to help needy or worthy artists or poets." **Selection Committee for the award does not accept nominations.** Amount varies from year to year.

Ø © WISCONSIN ARTS BOARD FELLOWSHIPS (Specialized: regional), Wisconsin Arts Board, 101 E. Wilson St., 1st Floor, Madison WI 53702, phone (608)264-8191, fax (608)267-0380, e-mail mark.fraire@a rts.state.wi.us, website http://www.uwc.arts.state.wi.us, award director Mark Fraire, offers fellowships to "recognize the significant contributions of professional artists." Open to Wisconsin residents who are *not* fulltime students. Write for entry form and guidelines. Inquiries via fax and e-mail OK. Deadline: September ("call for exact date").

Ø © WORLD ORDER OF NARRATIVE AND FORMALIST POETS (Specialized: subscription, form), P.O. Box 580174, Station A, Flushing NY 11358-0174, established in 1980, contest chairman Dr. Alfred Dorn. This organization sponsors contests in at least 15 categories of traditional and contemporary poetic forms, including the sonnet, blank verse, ballade, villanelle, free verse and new forms created by Alfred Dorn. Prizes total at least $5,000 and range from $20 to $300. Only subscribers to *The Formalist* will be eligible for the competition, as explained in the complete guidelines available from the contest chairman. "We look for originality of thought, phrase and image, combined with masterful craftsmanship. Trite, trivial or technically inept work stands no chance." Postmark deadline for entries: December 30, 1999. Recent contest winners include Brian E. Drake, Rachel Hadas, Annie Finch, Len Krisak, Roy Scheele, Melissa Cannon and Rhina P. Espaillat. (For more information on *The Formalist*, see their listing in the Publishers of Poetry section.)

N ⊕ $ ☐ Ø THE WRITERS BUREAU POETRY AND SHORT STORY COMPETITION, The Writers Bureau, Sevendale House, 7 Dale St., Manchester M1 1JB England, phone (0161)228 2362, fax (0161)228 3533, e-mail writersbureau@zen.co.uk, website http://www.writersbureau.com, established in 1994, offers annual prizes of £500, £250, £125, £75, £50, plus publication of the first places in Freelance Market News. Submissions must be unpublished. "Any number of entries may be sent. There is no set theme or form. Entries must be typed, and no longer than 40 lines." Send SASE for entry form. Inquiries via fax or e-mail OK. Accepts entry fees in foreign currencies as bank drafts in US currency. Deadline: July 31, 2000. Judge for last contest was Alison Chisholm. Winner(s) will be announced in September. "The Writers Bureau is a distance learning college offering correspondence courses in Journalism, Creative Writing and Poetry."

Additional Contests & Awards

The following listings also contain information about contests and awards. See the General Index for page numbers, then read the listings and send SASEs (or SAEs and IRCs) for specific details about their offerings.

Full Moon Press
Future Tense Press
Generator
Gerbil
Godine, Publisher, David R.
Golden Isis Magazine
Gotta Write Network Litmag
Gravity Presses
Green Bean Press
Heartlands Today, The
Heaven Bone Magazine
Hellp!
Hey, listen!
High/Coo Press
Hunger Magazine
Implosion Press
Indian Heritage Publishing
Inkwell, The
Insects Are People Two
Inverted-A, Inc.
K.T. Publications
Kawabata Press
Krax
Lapwing Publications
League of Canadian Poets, The
Ledge, The
Lilliput Review
Limited Editions Press
Lone Willow Press
Low-Tech Press
Lucidity
Lummox Press
Luna Bisonte Prods
Luz en Arte y Literatura
Mad River Press
Malafemmina Press
Maryland Poetry Review
Mekler & Deahl, Publishers
Mid-American Review
Minority Literary Expo
(m)öthêr TØñgué Press
Negative Capability
Nerve Cowboy
New Orleans Poetry Journal Press
New Song, A
Northeast
Ohio Review, The

One Trick Pony
Onthebus
Osric Publishing
Outposts Poetry Quarterly
Outrider Press
Oyster Boy Review
Pacific Coast Journal
Painted Bride Quarterly
Palanquin
Paradoxism
Parting Gifts
Pavement Saw
Peaky Hide
Pearl
Pecan Grove Press
Peer Poetry Magazine
Penny Dreadful Press
Pennywhistle Press
Peregrine
Permafrost
Philomel Books
Phoenix
Pirate Writings
Pitchfork
Plowman, The
Poems & Plays
Poetic License Poetry Magazine
Poetic Space
Poetry Forum
Poetry Harbor
Poetry Miscellany, The
Poets at Work
Poets' Roundtable
Potato Eyes
Prairie Journal, The
Pudding House Publications
Qoph
Rag Mag
Raintown Review, The
Rattapallax
Raw Dog Press
Red Dragon Press
Red Moon Press
Riverstone
Ruah
Rustic Rub
Score Magazine

Scroll Publications
Semiquasi Press
Serpent & Eagle Press
Shamal Books
Sheila-Na-Gig
Sixth Chamber
Sky, The
Slipstream
Slugfest, Ltd.
Smoke
Southern Poetry Association
Southfields
Sow's Ear Poetry Review, The
Spuyten Duyvil
Star Rising
Still Waters Press
Stovepipe
sub-Terrain
Symbiotic Oatmeal
Synaesthesia Press
Syncopated City
Tale Spinners
"Teak" Roundup
Temporary Vandalism Recordings
Terrible Work
Thin Coyote
Third Half Literary Magazine, The
Tickled by Thunder
Tightrope
Time of Singing
Touchstone Literary Journal
Understanding Magazine
University of Massachusetts Press, The
Urbanite, The
Water Mark Press
Waterways
Whelks Walk Review
White Eagle Coffee Store Press
Whole Notes
Wind Publications
Wolfsong Publications
Wordwrights!
World-Wide Writers Service, Inc.
WoRM fEASt!
Writers Forum (England)

State & Provincial Grants

Arts councils in the United States and Canada provide assistance to artists (including poets) in the form of fellowships or grants. These grants can be substantial and confer prestige upon recipients; however, **only state or province residents are eligible**. Because deadlines and available support vary annually, query first (with a SASE).

UNITED STATES ARTS AGENCIES

Alabama State Council on the Arts, *201 Monroe St., Montgomery AL 32530-1800. (334)242-4076. E-mail: staff@arts.state.al.us. Website: http://www.arts.state.al.us.*

Alaska State Council on the Arts, *411 W. Fourth Ave., Suite 1-E, Anchorage AK 99501-2343. (907)269-6610. E-mail: info@aksca.org. Website: http://www.aksca.org.*

Arizona Commission on the Arts, *417 W. Roosevelt, Phoenix AZ 85003. (602)255-5882. E-mail: general@arizonaarts.org. Website: http://az.arts.asu.edu/artscomm/.*

Arkansas Arts Council, *1500 Tower Bldg., 323 Center St., Little Rock AR 72201. (501)324-9766. E-mail: info@dah.state.ar.us. Website: http://www.heritage.state.ar.us/acc/index.html.*

California Arts Council, *1300 I St., Suite 930, Sacramento CA 95814. (916)322-6555. E-mail: cac@cwo.com. Website: http://www.cac.ca.gov/.*

Colorado Council on the Arts and Humanities, *750 Pennsylvania St., Denver CO 80203-3699. (303)894-2617. E-mail: coloarts@artswire.org. Website: http://www.state.co.us/gov_dir/arts/.*

Connecticut Commission on the Arts, *1 Financial Plaza, 755 Main St., Hartford CT 06103. (860)566-4770. Website: http://www.cslnet.ctstateu.edu/cca/.*

Delaware State Arts Council, *Carvel State Office Building, 820 N. French St., Wilmington DE 19801. (302)577-8278. E-mail: delarts@artswire.org. Website: http://www.artsdel.org/about/delaware.htm.*

District of Columbia Commission on the Arts & Humanities, *410 Eighth St. NW, 5th Floor, Washington DC 20004. (202)724-5613. E-mail: carrien@tmn.com. Website: http://www.capaccess.org/ane/dccah/.*

Florida Arts Council, *Division of Cultural Affairs, Florida Dept. of State, The Capitol, Tallahassee FL 32399-0250. (850)487-2980. Website: http://www.dos.state.fl.us/dca/general/html.*

Georgia Council for the Arts, *530 Means St. NW, Suite 115, Atlanta GA 30318-5793. (404)651-7920.*

Hawaii State Foundation on Culture & Arts, *44 Merchant St., Honolulu HI 96813. (808)586-0300. E-mail: sfca@sfca.state.hi.us. Website: http://www.state.hi.us/sfca.*

Idaho Commission on the Arts, *P.O. Box 83720, Boise ID 83720-0008. (208)334-2119. E-mail: mcknight@ica.state.id.us. Website: http://www2.state.id.us/arts.*

Illinois Arts Council, *100 W. Randolph, Suite 10-500, Chicago IL 60601. (312)814-6750. E-mail: info@arts.state.il.us. Website: http://www.state.il.us/agency/iac.*

Indiana Arts Commission, *402 W. Washington St., Indianapolis IN 46204-2741. (317)232-1268. Website: http://www.state.in.us/iac/.*

Iowa Arts Council, *600 E. Locust, Capitol Complex, Des Moines IA 50319-0290. (515)281-4451.*

Kansas Arts Commission, *Jay Hawk Tower, SW 700 Jackson, Suite 1004, Topeka KS 66603. (785)296-3335.*

Kentucky Arts Council, *31 Fountain Place, Frankfort KY 40601-1942. (502)564-3757.*

Louisiana State Arts Council, *P.O. Box 44247, Baton Rouge LA 70804-4247. (225)342-8180. E-mail: arts@crt.state.la.us. Website: http://www.crt.state.la.us/arts/.*

Maine State Arts Commission, *55 Capitol St., 25 State House Station, Augusta ME 04333-0025. (207)287-2724. E-mail: jan.poulin@state.me.us. Website: http://www.mainearts.com.*

Maryland State Arts Council, *601 N. Howard St., Baltimore MD 21201. (410)767-6555.*
E-mail: tcolvin@mdbusiness.state.md.us. Website: http://www.msac.org/.

Massachusetts Cultural Council, *120 Boylston St., Boston MA 02116. (617)727-3668.*
Website: http://www.massculturalcouncil.org/.

Michigan Council for Arts & Cultural Affairs, *1200 Sixth St., Executive Plaza, Detroit MI 48226-2461.*
(313)256-3735. E-mail: mcacal@artswire.org. Website: http://www.commerce.state.mi.us/arts/home.htm.

Minnesota State Arts Board, *Park Square Court, 400 Sibley St., Suite 200, St. Paul MN 55101-1928.*
(651)215-1600. E-mail: msab@state.mn.us. Website: http://www.state.mn.us/ebranch/msab.

Mississippi Arts Commission, *239 N. Lamar St., Suite 207, Jackson MS 39201. (601)359-6030.*
E-mail: bradley@arts.state.ms.us. Website: http://www.arts.state.ms.us/.

Missouri Arts Council, *111 N. Seventh St., Suite 105, St. Louis MO 63101-2188.*
(314)340-6845. E-mail: mhunt01@mail.state.mo.us. Website: http://www.missouriartscouncil.org.

Montana Arts Council, *316 N. Park Ave., Room 252, Helena MT 59620-2201. (406)444-6430.*
E-mail: mac@state.mt.us. Website: http://www.art.state.mt.us.

Nebraska Arts Council, *3838 Davenport St., Omaha NE 68131-2329. (402)595-2122.*
E-mail: mskomal@cwis.unomaha.edu. Website: http://www.gps.k12.ne.us/nac_web_site/nac.htm.

Nevada State Council on the Arts, *602 N. Curry, Carson City NV 89703. (702)687-6680.*
Website: http://www.clan.lib.nv.us/docs/ARTS.

New Hampshire State Council on the Arts, *40 N. Main St., Concord NH 03301-4974. (603)271-2789.*
Website: http://www.state.nh.us/nharts.

New Jersey State Council on the Arts, *CN 306, 20 W. State St., Trenton NJ 08625. (609)292-6130.*
Website: http://www.artswire.org/Artswire/njsca/.

New Mexico Arts Division, *228 E. Palace Ave., Santa Fe NM 87501. (505)827-6490.*

New York State Council on the Arts, *915 Broadway, New York NY 10010. (212)387-7000.*
E-mail: pinfo@nysca.org. Website: http://www.nysca.org.

North Carolina Arts Council, *221 E. Lane St., Raleigh NC 27601-2807. (919)733-2111.*
Website: http://www.ncarts.org/home.html.

North Dakota Council on the Arts, *418 E. Broadway, Suite 70, Bismark ND 58501-4086. (701)328-3954.*
E-mail: thompson@pioneer.state.nd.us. Website: http://www.state.nd.us/arts/index.html.

Ohio Arts Council, *727 E. Main St., Columbus OH 43205. (614)466-2613. E-mail: wlawson@mail.oac.ohio.gov.*
Website: http://www.oac.ohio.gov/.

Oklahoma Arts Council, *P.O. Box 52001-2001, Oklahoma City OK 73152-2001. (405)521-2931.*
E-mail: okarts@oklaosf.state.ok.us. Website: http://www.oklaosf.state.ok.us/~arts/.

Oregon Arts Commission, *775 Summer St. NE, Floor 2, Salem OR 97310. (503)986-0088.*
E-mail: oregon.artscomm@state.or.us.

Pennsylvania Council on the Arts, *Room 216, Finance Bldg., Harrisburg PA 17120. (717)787-6883.*
Website: http://artsnet.heinz.cmu.edu/pca/.

Institute of Puerto Rican Culture, *P.O. Box 9024184, San Juan PR 00902-4184. (787)725-5137.*

Rhode Island State Council on the Arts, *95 Cedar St., Suite 103, Providence RI 02903. (401)222-3880.*
E-mail: info@risca.state.ri.us. Website: http://www.risca.state.ri.us/.

South Carolina Arts Commission, *1800 Gervais St., Columbia SC 29201. (803)734-8696.*
Website: http://www.state.sc.us/arts/.

South Dakota Arts Council, *800 Governors Dr., Pierre SD 57501. (605)773-3131. E-mail: sdac@stlib.state.sd.us.*
Website: http://www.state.sd.us/state/executive/deca/sdarts/sdarts.htm.

Tennessee Arts Commission, *401 Charlotte Ave., Nashville TN 37243-0780. (615)741-1701.*
Website: http://www.arts.state.tn.us/index.html.

Texas Commission on the Arts, *P.O. Box 13406, Austin TX 78711-3406. (512)463-5535.*
E-mail: front.desk@arts.state.tx.us. Website: http://www.arts.state.tx.us/.

Utah Arts Council, *617 E. South Temple, Salt Lake City UT 84102-1177. (801)236-7555.*
Website: http://www.ce.ex.state.ut.us/arts/.

Vermont Arts Council, *136 State St., Drawer 33, Montpelier VT 05633-6001. (802)828-3291.*
E-mail: info@arts.vca.state.vt.us. Website: http://www.state.vt.us/vermont-arts/.

Virgin Islands Council on the Arts, *41-42 Norre Gada, P.O. Box 103, St. Thomas VI 00804. (340)774-5984.*
E-mail: vicouncil@islands.vi.

Virginia Commission for the Arts, *Lewis House, 2nd Floor, 223 Governor St., Richmond VA 23219.*
(804)225-3132. E-mail: vacomm@artswire.org. Website: http://www.artswire.org/~vacomm/.

Washington State Arts Commission, *P.O. Box 42675, Olympia WA 98504-2675. (360)753-3860.*
E-mail: wsac@artswire.org.

West Virginia Arts Commission, *Cultural Center, 1900 Kanawha Blvd. E., Charleston WV 25305-0300.*
(304)558-0220. Website: http://www.wvlc.wvnet.edu/culture/arts.html.

Wisconsin Arts Board, *101 E. Wilson St., 1st Floor, Madison WI 53702. (608)266-0190.*
E-mail: artsboard@arts.state.wi.us. Website: http://www.arts.state.wi.us.

Wyoming Arts Council, *2320 Capitol Ave., Cheyenne WY 82002. (307)777-7742.*
Website: http://commerce.state.wy.us/cr/arts/index.htm.

CANADIAN PROVINCES ARTS AGENCIES

Alberta Foundation for the Arts, *901 Standard Life Centre, 10405 Jasper Ave., 9th Floor, Edmonton, Alberta T5J*
4R7. (403)427-9968. E-mail: afa@mcd.gov.ab.ca. Website: http://www.affta.ab.ca.

British Columbia Arts Council, *800 Johnson St., 5th Floor, Victoria, British Columbia V8V 1X4. (250)356-1728.*

Manitoba Arts Council, *525 - 93 Lombard Ave., Winnipeg, Manitoba R3B 3B1. (204)945-0421.*
E-mail: manart1@mb.sympatico.ca. Website: http://www.artscouncil.mb.ca.

New Brunswick Department of Economic Development, Tourism & Culture, *Arts Branch, P.O. Box 6000,*
Fredericton, New Brunswick E3B 5H1. (506)453-2555. Website: http://www.gov.nb.ca/edit/index.htm.

Newfoundland & Labrador Arts Council, *P.O. Box 98, St. John's, Newfoundland A1C 5H5. (709)726-2212.*
E-mail: nlacmail@newcomm.net. Website: http://www.nlac.nf.ca/.

Nova Scotia Arts Council, *1660 Hollis St., Suite 302, P.O. Box 1559, CRO, Halifax, Nova Scotia B3J 2Y3.*
(902)422-1123.

The Canada Council, *350 Albert St., P.O. Box 1047, Ottawa, Ontario K1P 5V8. (613)566-4414.*
Website: http://www.canadacouncil.ca/.

Ontario Arts Council, *151 Bloor St. W., 6th Floor, Toronto, Ontario M5S 1T6. (416)961-1660.*
E-mail: info@arts.on.ca. Website: http://www.arts.on.ca/.

Prince Edward Island Council of the Arts, *115 Richmond, Charlottetown, Prince Edward Island C1A 1H7.*
(902)368-4410. Website: http://www.peisland.com/arts/council.htm.

Saskatchewan Arts Board, *3475 Albert St., Regina, Saskatchewan S4S 6X6. (306)787-4056.*

Yukon Arts Branch, *Box 2703, Whitehorse, Yukon Y1A 2C6. (867)667-8589. Website: http://www.artsyukon.com.*

Resources

Conferences & Workshops

Conferences and workshops are valuable resources for many poets, especially beginners. A conference or workshop serves as an opportunity to learn about specific aspects of the craft, connect with and gather feedback from other poets and writers, listen to submission tips from editors, and revel in a creative atmosphere that may stimulate one's muse.

In this section you'll find listings for more than 60 conferences and workshops—14 of which are new to this edition. All listings contain information indicating to whom the event is open, its general purpose, and areas of concentration. Some, such as the Catskill Poetry Workshop, are specifically geared to poets. Most, however, are more general conferences with offerings for a variety of writers, including poets.

A "typical" conference may have a number of workshop sessions, keynote speakers and perhaps even a panel or two. Topics may include everything from writing fiction, poetry, and books for children to marketing one's work. Often a theme, which may change from year to year, will be the connecting factor.

Other conferences and workshops cover a number of topics but have a primary focus. For example, the Mount Hermon Christian Writers Conference offers sessions on poetry, fiction, article writing and writing for children, but is geared toward authors interested in the Christian writing market. There are also events especially for women writers, Appalachian writers and Jewish writers.

Despite different themes or focuses, each listing in this section details the information poets need to determine which conference suits them best. To provide quick access to that information, we've included subheads with key terms to identify the type of information immediately following the subhead. For example, the subhead **Purpose/Features** contains information on a conference's general purpose, who may attend the event, scheduled themes and panels, offerings specifically available for poets, and speakers who have either attended or are scheduled to attend. The **Costs/Accommodations** subhead precedes information regarding the conference fee as well as any additional costs for food or housing, the availability of transportation to and from the event, and information on overnight accommodations. The subhead **Additional Info** details information on individual critiques, contests sponsored during a conference, and how to obtain brochures and registration forms.

In addition to subheads, you may find symbols at the beginning of a listing. These symbols are intended to provide certain information at a glance. The ▓ symbol signifies listings new to this edition, the ⊕ symbol indicates international listings, the ♥ symbol denotes Canadian listings and the ✓ symbol indicates a change in a listing's address, phone number, e-mail address or contact name.

It is important to note, however, that conference and workshop directors were still in the organizing stages when contacted. Consequently, some listings include information from last year's events simply to provide an idea of what to expect this year. For more up-to-date details, including current costs, send a SASE to the conference and workshop directors a few months before the dates listed.

BENEFITING FROM CONFERENCES

Without a doubt, attending conferences and workshops is beneficial. First, these events provide opportunities to learn more about the poetic craft. Some even feature individual sessions with workshop leaders, allowing you to specifically discuss your work with others. If these one-on-one sessions include critiques (generally for an additional fee), we have included this information, as mentioned above, under **Additional Info**.

Besides learning from workshop leaders, you can also benefit from conversations with other attendees. Writers on all levels often enjoy talking to and sharing insights with others. A conversation over lunch may reveal a new market for your work, or a casual chat while waiting for a session to begin can acquaint you with a new resource.

Also, if a conference or workshop includes time for open readings and you choose to participate, you may gain feedback from workshop leaders and others. For some, however, just the relief from the solitude of writing can make a conference or workshop worthwhile.

Another reason conferences and workshops are valuable is the opportunity they provide to meet editors and publishers who often have tips about marketing work. The availability of these individuals, however, does not necessarily mean they will want to read your latest collection of poems (unless, of course, they are workshop leaders and you have separate meetings scheduled with them).

Although editors and publishers cannot give personal attention to everyone they meet, don't be afraid to approach them. If they weren't interested in speaking to writers, they wouldn't have agreed to attend the conference. However, if the editor or publisher's schedule is too full to allow discussion of your work, ask if you may follow up with a letter after the event. This will give you the benefit of his or her undivided attention and, perhaps, develop into a contact in the poetry field.

SELECTING A CONFERENCE OR WORKSHOP

When selecting a conference or workshop to attend, keep your goals in mind. If you want to learn how to improve your craft, for example, consider one of the events entirely devoted to poetry or locate a more general conference where one-on-one critique sessions are offered. If you're looking for more informal feedback, choose an event that includes open readings. If marketing your work seems like an ominous task, register for a conference that includes a session with editors. And if you also have an interest in other forms of writing, an event with a wide range of workshops is a good bet.

Of course, also take your personal resources into consideration. If both your time and funds are limited, search for a conference or workshop within your area. Many events are held during weekends and may be close enough for you to commute. On the other hand, if you want to combine your family vacation with time spent meeting other writers and working on your craft, consider workshops such as those sponsored by The Writers' Center at Chautauqua. In either case, it is important to at least consider the conference location and learn about other enjoyable activities in the area.

Still other factors may influence your decision. Events sponsoring contests, for instance, may allow you to gain recognition and recoup some of your expenses. Similarly, some conferences and workshops have financial assistance or scholarships available. Finally, many are associated with colleges or universities and offer continuing education credits. When available, these options are included in the listings. Again, send a SASE for more details.

For other conferences and workshops, see *The Guide to Writers Conferences* (by ShawGuides, available at website http://www.shawguides.com or through our website http://www.writersdiges t.com); *Writers Conferences: An Annual Guide to Literary Conferences* (Poets & Writers, Inc., 72 Spring St., New York NY 10012, website http://www.pw.org); or the May issue of *Writer's Digest* magazine (available on newsstands or directly from the publisher at 1507 Dana Ave.,

Cincinnati OH 45207, website http://www.writersdigest.com). You may also want to check the bulletin boards at libraries and bookstores for local events.

AMERICAN CHRISTIAN WRITERS CONFERENCES, P.O. Box 110390, Nashville TN 37222, phone (800)21-WRITE, director Reg Forder. Annual 3-day events founded 1981. 30 conferences/year. Held throughout the year in cities including Houston, Boston, Minneapolis, Chicago, St. Louis, Detroit, Atlanta, Miami, Phoenix and Los Angeles. Usually located at a major hotel chain like Holiday Inn. Average attendance is 100.
Purpose/Features: Open to anyone. Conferences cover fiction, poetry, writing for children.
Costs/Accommodations: Cost is $99-199, participants are responsible for their own meals. Accommodations include special rates at host hotel.
Additional Info: They also sponsor an annual Caribbean Christian Writers Conference Cruise each November. Send SASE for brochures and registration forms.

ANTIOCH WRITERS' WORKSHOP, P.O. Box 494, Yellow Springs OH 45387, phone (937)767-9047, e-mail writersworkshop@yellowsprings.com, director Kim Frazier. Annual 7-day event founded 1986. Usually held in late July or early August at Antioch College in the village of Yellow Springs. "The campus is quiet, shady, relaxed. The village is unusual for its size: a hotbed of artists, writers and creative people." Average attendance is 70.
Purpose/Features: Open to everyone. "We create an intense community of writers and cover fiction, poetry, mystery and nonfiction. Also talks by editors, agents and others in the industry." Offerings specifically available for poets include an introductory class in writing poetry, an intensive seminar, night sessions for participants to share poetry, and critiquing. Speakers for the 1999 conference included Alison Lurie, Michael Bugeja and Ruth L. Schwartz.
Costs/Accommodations: Cost for 1999 conference was $485; scholarships and some work-study fellowships are available (including the Judson Jerome Scholarship sponsored by *Writer's Digest* magazine). Both graduate and undergraduate credit is available for an additional fee. Campus dining room meal ticket is $121 (for 20 meals); must be purchased in advance. Transportation from airport is provided. Information on overnight accommodations is available and includes housing in campus dorms.
Additional Info: Individual critiques available. Submit work for critique in advance with $60 fee for poetry; $60 fee for story, book or script. Send SASE for brochures and registration forms.

ASPEN WRITERS' CONFERENCE, P.O. Drawer 7726, Aspen CO 81612, phone (970)925-3122 or (800)925-2526, fax (970)920-5700, e-mail Aspenwrite@aol.com, executive director Jeanne McGovern. Annual week-long event founded 1975. Usually held the third week of June. Location: The Aspen Institute, Aspen Meadows campus or other site in Aspen. Average attendance is 100.
Purpose/Features: Open to all writers. Conference includes intensive writing workshops in poetry, fiction, nonfiction and children's literature. Offerings specifically available for poets include poetry workshops, craft lectures and readings by faculty and participants. Speakers at last conference were Mary Crow (poetry); Ron Carlson and Janice Eidus (fiction); Bernard Cooper (memoir); and Jan Greenberg (children's writer).
Costs/Accommodations: Cost for conference was $495, does not include meals or lodging. Transportation to and from on-site lodging and event is available. Information on overnight accommodations is available for registrants. Cost of on-site accommodations was $70/person/day double occupancy or $95/person/day single occupancy.
Additional Info: "We accept poetry in advance that will be discussed during workshop." Send SASE for brochures and registration forms or request via e-mail. Include mailing address with all e-mail requests for brochures/registration forms. Inquiries via fax and e-mail OK.

AUSTIN WRITERS' LEAGUE SPRING AND FALL WORKSHOPS, 1501 W. Fifth St., Suite E-2, Austin TX 78703, phone (512)499-8914, fax (512)499-0441, e-mail awl@writersleague.org, website http://www.writersl eague.org, executive director Jim Bob McMillan. Biannual workshops founded 1982. "Workshops are usually three- or six-hour sessions. Intensive classes last from 10-15 weeks and meet for three hours each week." Usually held weekends in March, April, May and September, October, November. Location: Austin Writers' League Resource Center/Library. Registration limited.
Purpose/Features: Open to all writers, beginners and advanced. Workshops cover fiction, poetry, writing for children, nonfiction, screenwriting, book promotion/marketing, working with agents/publishers, journal writing, special interest writing, creativity, grantwriting, copyright law and taxes for writers. Offerings specifically available for poets include at least 2 workshops during each series. Poetry presenters have included Ralph Angel, Rosellen Brown, Reginald Gibbons and Marion Winik. Past speakers have included Sandra Scofield, Sue Grafton, Peter Mehlman, Gregg Levoy, Lee Merrill Byrd and several New York agents and editors. "Occasionally, presenters agree to do private consults with participants. Also, workshops may incorporate hands-on practice and critique."

Costs/Accommodations: Cost is $35-75. Members get discount.

Additional Info: Requirements for critiques are posted in workshop brochure. Send SASE for brochures and registration forms or request via fax or e-mail (include mailing address). The Austin Writers' League publishes *The Austin Writer*, a monthly publication of prose and poetry selected from submissions each month. These poems are eligible for four $25 Word Is Art awards presented in January of each year. Poetry guidelines for other publications, awards and grants programs, and market listings are available through the League library.

✔ **BREAD LOAF WRITERS' CONFERENCE**, Middlebury College, Middlebury VT 05753, phone (802)443-5286, fax (802)443-2087, e-mail blwc@mail.middlebury.edu, website http://www.middlebury.edu/~bl wc, administrative coordinator Carol Knauss. Annual 11-day event founded 1926. Usually held in mid-August. Average attendance is 230.

Purpose/Features: Conference is designed to promote dialogue among writers and provide professional critiques for students. Conference usually covers fiction, nonfiction and poetry.

Costs/Accommodations: Cost for the last conference was $1,690, including tuition, room and board. Fellowships and scholarships for the conference are available. "Candidates for fellowships must have a book published. Candidates for scholarships must have published in major literary periodicals or newspapers. A letter of recommendation, application and supporting materials due by April 1. Awards are announced in June for the conference in August." Taxis to and from the airport or bus station are available.

Additional Info: Individual critiques are also available. Sponsors the Bakeless Literary Publication Prizes, an annual book series competition for new authors of literary works in poetry, fiction and creative nonfiction. Send SASE for details. Send for conference brochures and application forms or obtain via website. Inquiries via fax and e-mail OK.

CAPE COD WRITERS' CENTER SUMMER CONFERENCE, % Cape Cod Writers' Center, P.O. Box 186, Barnstable MA 02630, phone (508)375-0516, fax (508)362-2718, e-mail ccwc@capecod.net, website http://www.capecod.net/writers, contact Don Ellis or Nancy Richard. Annual week-long event founded 1963. Usually held the third week of August at the Craigville Conference Center. Average attendance is 150.

Purpose/Features: Open to everyone. The conference covers poetry, fiction, mystery writing, nonfiction, children's writing, screenwriting plus one-evening Master Class.

Costs/Accommodations: Participants are responsible for their own meals. "It is recommended that participants stay at the Craigville Conference Center (early registration necessary)." Other housing information available from Bed & Breakfast Cape Cod.

Additional Info: Manuscript evaluations and personal conferences are also available. For ms evaluation, submit a few poems, short story, article, or one book chapter by July 1st. Send SASE for cost, brochures and registration forms or obtain via website. Inquiries via fax and e-mail OK. Sponsors workshops and seminars in the fall and spring. Send SASE for details. Website includes event schedules, conference/workshop information, news about members and the World Television Interview Program.

✔ **CATSKILL POETRY WORKSHOP**, Hartwick College, Oneonta NY 13820, phone (607)431-4448, fax (607)431-4457, e-mail frostc@hartwick.edu, website http://www.hartwick.edu/osp, director Carol Frost. Annual week long event. 1999 dates were July 3-10. Location: Hartwick College, a small, private college in the Catskill Mountain area. Average attendance is 25-30.

Purpose/Features: Open to "talented adult writers." Workshops cover poetry only. Offerings specifically available to poets include "traditional meters, free verse lineation and uses of metaphor; individual instruction."

Costs/Accommodations: Cost for 1999 was $750, including meals. Housing available in on-site facilities.

Additional Info: Send SASE for brochures and registration forms. Inquiries via fax and e-mail OK. Website includes information about the workshop, a list of the faculty and information about fees, credits and scholarships.

CHENANGO VALLEY WRITERS' CONFERENCE, Colgate University, Hamilton NY 13346, phone (315)228-7771, fax (315)228-7975, e-mail mleone@mail.colgate.edu, website http://www.colgate.edu, conference director Matthew Leone. Annual week-long event founded 1996. Usually held the last week in June, first week of July. 1999 dates were June 20-26. The conference site, Colgate University, has "an expansive campus, with classrooms, dormitories, libraries and recreational facilities all in close proximity to each other." Average attendance is 75.

Purpose/Features: Open to "all serious writers or aspirants. Our purpose is to work on honing writing skills: fiction, poetry and nonfiction prose are covered." Offerings specifically available to poets have included workshops with Tom Sleigh and Kelly Cherry; readings from Peter Balakian and W.D. Snodgrass.

USE THE GENERAL INDEX, located at the back of this book, to find the page number of a specific publisher. Also, publishers that were listed in last year's edition but not included in this edition are listed in the General Index with a notation explaining why they were omitted.

Costs/Accommodations: Cost for 1999 was $895, including meals; discounts are available through fellowships. "Applicants for fellowships must apply before the May 1 deadline." Transportation to and from the event is provided. "We will pick up airport and train station arrivals with prior notification." Housing available in on-site facilities. Cost is included in the tuition.

Additional Info: Individual critiques are also available. Submit poems in advance to Matthew Leone. Send SASE for brochures and registration forms or obtain via website. Inquiries via fax and e-mail OK.

DESERT WRITERS WORKSHOP, P.O. Box 68, Moab UT 84532, phone (435)259-7750, fax (435)259-2335, contact director of education. Annual 3-day event founded 1985. Usually held the first weekend in November at Pack Creek Ranch in the foothills of the LaSal Mountains. Attendance is a maximum of 33.

Purpose/Features: Open to all. Workshop covers 3 categories—fiction, nonfiction and poetry—and focuses on relationship to natural world.

Costs/Accommodations: Cost is $525, including meals, instruction and lodging. "All participants stay at Pack Creek."

Additional Info: Individual critiques are also available. "Participants will be able to mail some samples to their instructor before the workshop for critique." Send SASE for brochures and registration forms for both workshops.

N DOWN EAST MAINE WRITER'S WORKSHOPS, P.O. Box 446, Stockton Springs ME 04981, phone (207)567-4317, fax (207)567-3023, e-mail redbaron@ime.net, website http://www.maineweb.com/writers, director Janet J. Barron. Annual 3-day events founded 1993. Usually held last part of July and first part of August. 1999 dates were July 16-18 and August 6-8. "The conference/workshop facility is a historic, 200 year-old writer's studio in the heart of a tiny, sleepy village in mid-coastal Maine. It is comfortable, within 100-or-so yards of Penobscot Bay, and handicapped-accessible." Average attendance is 10-12.

Purpose/Features: "Our workshops are small, intimate gatherings, limited to 12 participants. These workshops are actually constructed around each student's needs and writing levels as evidenced by their responses to a comprehensive questionnaire sent them upon their registration. In other words, our enjoyable workshops are truly geared to and for each of the individuals who enroll in the intense, interactive and experiential, hands-on classes. The DownEast Maine Writer's Workshop's main purpose is to help aspiring writers understand the world of writing for publication. Each summer, a conference is held on "How to Get Your Writing Published," and sometimes one or more other subjects are treated in a 3-day workshop. Among these topics are: Poetry, Fiction, Nonfiction, Humor, Scriptwriting, Writing for the Children's Market and a Sampler (a half-day devoted to each of six writing environments)."

Costs/Accommodations: Cost for each 1999 conference was $295. Lunch is included in this cost. However, participants are responsible for their own dinners. "Local B&Bs and Inns provide full breakfasts." Discounts are available: 10% for AARP members, 10% for two people registering together, or 10% for early registration (at least 60 days before workshop). Information on overnight accommodations is available. Accommodations include special rates at area Bed & Breakfasts and Inns.

Additional Info: Individual critiques are also available during and immediately after each day's workshops or after workshops by fax or e-mail. Send SASE for brochures and registration forms or obtain via fax, e-mail or website. Inquiries via fax and e-mail OK. "The DownEast Maine Writer's Workshop's website contains comprehensive information re: the DEMWW's Director, what our three-day workshops are all about, dates and details of the annual conferences, editorial help novice writers can tap into when they need assistance, and the textbook used in the workshops and that also is available to all who have an interest in the writing world. In addition, we treat all participants as the special people that they are. We support them, encourage them, and inspire them. While communicating with them the realities of getting published in today's mega-competitive publishing environment, we motivate them to find the editors who will invite them to submit their work, then show them how to fill those editor's wish-lists."

EASTERN KENTUCKY UNIVERSITY CREATIVE WRITING CONFERENCE, Case Annex 467, Richmond KY 40475-3140, phone (606)622-5861, e-mail engnorto@acs.eku.edu, website http://www.english.eku.edu/conferences, co-directors Dorothy Sutton and Harry Brown. Annual 5-day event founded 1964. Usually held Monday through Friday of the third week in June. Location: Eastern Kentucky University. Average attendance is 15.

Purpose/Features: Open to poetry and fiction. The conference provides lectures, workshops and private conferences with visiting writers to "help writers increase their skills in writing poetry and fiction." A ms of 4-8 poems (8 pgs. maximum) must be submitted by May 15 and accepted before enrollment in conference is allowed. Offerings specifically available for poets include workshop discussions and individual conferences. Visiting writers have included David Citino, George Ella Lyon and Stephen Smith.

Costs/Accommodations: Cost for the last conference was $86 undergraduate and $124 graduate (in-state fees), $236 undergraduate and $344 graduate (out-of-state fees); participants are responsible for their own meals, available on campus. Cost for housing in on-site facilities was $56/week single occupancy, $40/week double occupancy. "Must bring your own sheets, pillow, blanket."

Additional Info: Send SASE for brochure or request via e-mail. Website also includes the brochure which lists the visiting writers and their bios, schedule of events, registration information, cost, etc.

FESTIVAL OF POETRY, Robert Frost Place, Franconia NH 03580, phone (603)823-5510, e-mail donald.sheeh an@dartmouth.edu, executive director Donald Sheehan. Annual week-long event founded 1978. Usually held first week of August at Robert Frost's mountain farm (house and barn), made into a center for poetry and the arts. Average attendance is 50-55.
Purpose/Features: Open to poets only. Faculty has included Galway Kinnell, Grace Paley, Molly Peacock, Martin Espada, Dana Gioia and Ellen Bryant Voigt.
Costs/Accommodations: Cost is $465 tuition, plus a $25 reading fee. "Room and board available locally; information sent upon acceptance to program."
Additional Info: Application should be accompanied by 3 sample pages of your work. Send SASE for brochures and registration forms.

FISHTRAP, P.O. Box 38, Enterprise OR 97828, phone (541)426-3623, director Rich Wandschneider. Holds 3 annual 3- to 4-day events. Founded 1988. 1999 dates were Winter Fishtrap—February 19-21; Summer Workshop—June 28 through July 1; Summer Gathering—July 2-4. Location: "Winter site is a meeting room attached to a motel at Wallowa Lake, Oregon (off season); summer site is an old Methodist church camp." Average attendance is 50 for Winter Fishtrap ("always sold out"); 8 workshops (12 people/workshop) for Summer Workshop; 90 for Summer Gathering.
Purpose/Features: Open to anyone. "Fishtrap's goal is to promote good writing and clear thinking about the West. Also to encourage and promote new writers. There are always craft workshops on fiction, poetry, nonfiction; sometimes in children's writing, playwriting, radio, etc." Offerings specifically available for poets included a poetry workshop. Themes for 1999 are "growing up" and "borders." Instructors for 1999 were Craig Lesley, Luis Irrea, Sue Armitage and Primus St. John..
Costs/Accommodations: Cost for winter Fishtrap was $215-320 includes meals (higher price includes lodging); Summer Workshop was $220, Gathering was $175, meals and lodging available at $32/day at camp. Lodging also available at nearby motels.
Additional Info: Awards 5 fellowships annually. Send SASE for brochures and registration forms. Each year the selected writings of workshop students and workshop instructors is published in an anthology.

THE FLIGHT OF THE MIND, WOMEN'S WRITING WORKSHOPS, 622 SE 29th Ave., Portland OR 97214, phone (503)236-9862, fax (503)233-0774, e-mail soapston@teleport.com, website http://www.teleport.com/~soapston/FLIGHT/, director Judith Barrington. Annual events founded 1983. Usually held at the end of June, beginning of July. Two workshops in summer for 7 days each at "a rustic retreat center on the wild McKenzie River in the foothills of the Oregon Cascades." Average attendance is 70 women/workshop in 5 different classes.
Purpose/Features: Open to women writers. Workshops cover fiction, poetry, essays, memoirs, special-topic classes (e.g., "landscape and memory") with a feminist philosophy. In 1999 workshop leaders included Ursula K. Le Guin, Lucille Clifton, Olga Broumas and Molly Gloss.
Costs/Accommodations: Cost for workshop (including tuition, all meals and room) was $595-785. Scholarships available.
Additional Info: Participants are selected on the basis of work submitted. Peer critique groups form at workshop. Send first-class stamp for brochure and registration forms.

FLORIDA CHRISTIAN WRITERS CONFERENCE, 2600 Park Ave., Titusville FL 32780, phone (407)269-6702 ext. 202, fax (407)383-1741, e-mail writer@digital.net, website http://www.kipertek.com/writer, director Billie Wilson. Annual 4-day event founded 1988. 2000 dates: January 27-31. Location: retreat center setting—conferee housing at motel. Meals, workshops and all general sessions held at retreat center. Average attendance is 200.
Purpose/Features: Open to all writers. "The conference has an instructional and marketing thrust. All genres are usually covered—49 workshops. Publishers and editors from over 35 publishing houses attend. Writers may submit manuscripts to the editors and publishers for critique and sale." Offerings specifically available for poets include 2 workshops plus marketing opportunities. Speakers at last conference were Kay Hall (Cross & Quill), Jim Stafford (Devo'zine), Harold Hostetler (Guideposts), Cindy Bunch Hotaling (Intervarsity Press), Andrew Scheer (Moody Magazine), David Fault (Standard Publishing), Amy Eckert (The Christian Traveler), Dan Elliott (Tyndale House Publishers), Elaine Wright Colvin (Writers Information Network).
Costs/Accommodations: Cost for 1999 was $515 for single occupancy, meals and tuition; $425 for double occupancy, meals and tuition; $300 for meals and tuition only. Discounts are available through early registration and scholarships. Transportation to and from the event is provided. "We provide shuttles from the Orlando International airport. Also, we provide transportation to and from the motel to the retreat center." Airport shuttle cost is $40/person. Information on overnight accommodations is available for registrants. Individual critiques also available.
Additional Info: "Each conferee may submit four manuscripts (five poems constitutes one manuscript) for critique. No fee." Send SASE for brochures and registration forms.

FLORIDA SUNCOAST WRITERS' CONFERENCE, Dept. of English, University of South Florida, Tampa FL 33620, phone (813)974-1711, fax (813)974-5732, e-mail fswc@outreach.usf.edu, directors Steve Rubin and

Edgar Hirshberg. Annual 3-day event founded 1970. 2000 dates: February 3-5. Location: University of South Florida, St. Petersburg campus. Average attendance is 350.

Purpose/Features: "Open to students, teachers, established and aspiring writers. Conference covers all areas—fiction, poetry, nonfiction, children's, mystery/detective, romance, etc." Offerings specifically available for poets included seminars, workshops, poetry readings and ms evaluation. Speakers at past conferences included John Updike, Sonia Sanchez, Nikki Giovanni, Yevgeny Yevtushenko, Maxine Kumin, William Styron, Edward Albee, Marge Piercy, Carolyn Forché, P.D. James, Joyce Carol Oates and Robert Pinsky.

Costs/Accommodations: Cost for 2000 conference is $145; $135 for students and teachers. Information on overnight accommodations is available. Accommodations include special rates at area hotels.

Additional Info: Manuscript evaluation available at extra cost. Write for brochures and registration forms. Inquiries via fax and e-mail OK. They also publish *Sunscripts*, an anthology of writing from Florida Suncoast Writers' Conference. All participants eligible to submit.

FLORIDA SUNCOAST WRITERS' WEEKEND WORKSHOP, Dept. of English, University of South Florida, Tampa FL 33620, phone (813)974-2403, director Rita Ciresi. Annual 3-day event founded 1995. Usually held in October at the University of South Florida, Tampa campus. Average attendance is 75-80.

Purpose/Features: "Open to all writers, beginning and advanced. Workshop covers poetry, fiction, screenwriting and nonfiction." Offerings specifically available for poets include poetry workshop and readings. Speakers at past conferences included Tobias Wolff, Dannie Abse, Peter Meinke, Michael Dennis Browne and Dionisio Martínez. Other special features include intensive small-group seminars, guest speakers and a banquet.

Costs/Accommodations: Cost for conference is approximately $200, additional fee for ms evaluation. Information on overnight accommodations is available for registrants. Accommodations include special rates at area hotels.

Additional Info: Manuscript evaluation available for each participant. Write for brochures and registration forms. They also publish *Sunscripts*, an anthology of writing from Suncoast programs participants.

FOOTHILL WRITERS' CONFERENCE, 12345 El Monte Rd., Los Altos Hills CA 94022-4599, phone (650)949-7316 or 949-7436, e-mail ksw@mercury.fhda.edu, conference director Kim Wolterbeek. Annual 6-day event founded 1975. Usually held the end of June/beginning of July. Location: Foothill College in Los Altos Hills. 1999 dates: June 24-29.

Purpose/Features: Open to everyone. Conference includes panel discussions and manuscript workshops; poetry one-on-one sessions; and poetry and prose readings. Past panels have included publishing on the World Wide Web, translating life experience into story, the use of silence in poetry and memoirs in non-Western society. Offerings specifically available for poets included a one-on-one manuscript workshop. Speaker at the last conference was Tom Jenks.

Costs/Accommodations: Cost for conference was $75, included enrollment fees and admission to faculty afternoon and evening readings, intensive writing workshops, and lectures and panels by faculty (college credit available). Participants are responsible for their own meals.

Additional Info: Individual critiques available on a first come, first serve basis. "Sign up posted on the first day of conference." Send SASE for brochures and registration forms. Inquiries via e-mail OK.

GREEN LAKE WRITERS CONFERENCE, Green Lake Conference Center, W2511 State Highway 23, Green Lake WI 54941-9300, phone (800)558-8898, fax (920)294-3848, e-mail blythean@greenlake.aba.org, website http://www.greenlake-aba.org, vice president of adult program Blythe Ann Cooper. Annual weeklong event founded 1946. 2000 dates: June 25 to July 1. "Attendees stay in a lovely Inn overlooking beautiful Green Lake located 30 miles southwest of Oshkosh. Large private bath, double occupancy rooms, with singles available, extra charge. After class enjoy boating on the lake, tennis courts, biking, exercise trails, a new indoor recreation center and a fully-equipped arts and crafts center. Site includes a 36-hole public golf course listed among the top 75 in the nation. It is located on 1,000 acres and is the national conference center for American Baptists. Alcoholic beverages are not permitted." Average attendance is 80-100.

Purpose/Features: Open to regional and national participants. Conference covers Writiting for Children, Exploring the Writer in You, Essay Writing, Poetry Writing, Article Writing for Fun and Profit, Fiction Writing and Devotional/Inspirational Writing. Speakers at last conference were Jeri McCormick, Ellen Kort, Laura Alden, Bill Nelson, Carol Pierskalla, Barbara Smith and Liz Curtis Higgs.

Costs/Accommodations: Cost for 1998 conference was $85, plus $308-441/person for double occupancy room with meals. Camping available. Shuttle service to and from the airport provided for an additional fee. Information on overnight accommodations is available for registrants.

Additional Info: Individual critiques also available. Send SASE for brochures and registration forms. Inquiries via fax and e-mail OK. Website includes conference and registration information, accommodations, grounds and building descriptions. "A past participant wrote, 'I would recommend this conference to anyone committed to writing and sharing their work in a spiritual atmosphere. What I found to be most incredible was the fact that everyone was friendly, willing to talk, and incredibly generous with their time.' "

HAYSTACK WRITING PROGRAM, Summer Session, School of Extended Studies, Portland State University, P.O. Box 1491, Portland OR 97207, phone (800)547-8887 ext. 4027 or (503)725-4186, fax (503)725-4840,

e-mail herrinm@pdx.edu, website http://www.extended.pdx.edu/summer/haystack.htm, contact Maggie Herrington. Annual summer program founded 1969. One-week courses over the four weeks of the program. 1999 dates were July 12 to August 13. Classes are held in the local school of this small coastal community; some evening lectures and other activities. Average attendance is 10-15/class; 350 total.
Purpose/Features: Open to all writers. One-week workshops cover fiction, poetry, mystery, screenplay and nonfiction.
Costs/Accommodations: Cost for workshops is $125-400; participants pay for their own lodging and meals. Accommodation options range from camping to luxury hotels.
Additional Info: Write for brochures and registration forms. Inquiries via fax and e-mail OK.

HEARTLAND WRITERS CONFERENCE, P.O. Box 652, Kennett MO 63857-0652, phone (573)297-3325, fax (573)297-3352, e-mail hwg@heartlandwriters.org, website http://www.heartlandwriters.org, contact registrar. Biennial 3-day event founded 1989. 2000 dates: June 8-10. Location: Coach House Inn, Sikeston MO. Average attendance is 150.
Purpose/Features: Open to all writers of popular fiction, nonfiction and poetry. Offerings specifically available for poets include critique sessions. Speakers for next conference are 10 agents and editors from prominent New York-based publishing houses/agencies, as well as 12 published authors from the Midwest.
Costs/Accommodations: Cost for the last conference was $175, including meals. Information on overnight accommodations is available for registrants. Accommodations include special rates at area hotels.
Additional Info: Contest sponsored as part of conference. Judges are industry professionals. Send name and address to be included on conference mailing list. Inquiries via e-mail OK. Website includes conference information and updates, also Heartland Writers Guild membership information.

THE HEIGHTS WRITER'S CONFERENCE, Writer's World Press, P.O. Box 24684, Cleveland OH 44124, phone (330)562-6667, fax (330)562-1216, e-mail writersworld@juno.com, conference director Lavern Hall. Annual 1-day event founded 1992. Held the first Saturday in May. "The conference is held at the Marriott hotel in Beachwood, OH. Conference rooms are centrally located and handicapped accessible. Lunch is served in the ballroom." Average attendance is 125.
Purpose/Features: "Open to all writers who are interested in learning about the craft and business of writing and networking with professionals. We cover a variety of genres including poetry, fiction, marketing, getting published, mystery, travel, etc." The workshops have included topics in turning memories into memoirs, playwriting, writing book proposals and writing for children. These intensive workshops are limited to 25 students who must pre-register and are taken on a first come, first-served basis. They say, "Our format is unique. We have four breakout sessions (two in the morning and two in the afternoon) with three concurrent one-hour seminars. In addition, we offer two 2½-hour intensive workshops, 1 in the morning, 1 in the afternoon. The genre teaching workshops vary each year."
Costs/Accommodations: Cost is $85 preregistration; $95 late registration. "All activities are included: continental breakfast, seminars/workshops, lunch with guest speaker program, networking reception and author autographing at conclusion of day. In addition there are many free handouts and The Writer's Book Shop™ offers a selection of writing-related books. We provide accommodation information upon request for those arriving the day before."
Additional Info: Critiques are handled through speakers directly. Send SASE for brochure, map and area hotels or request via fax or e-mail.

INDIANA UNIVERSITY WRITERS' CONFERENCE, Ballantine Hall 464, Indiana University, Bloomington IN 47405, phone (812)855-1877, fax (812)855-9535, e-mail pagodbey@indiana.edu, website http://php.indiana.edu/~iuwc/, director Maura Stanton. Annual week-long event founded 1940. Usually held the last week in June at the university student union. Average attendance is 100.
Purpose/Features: Open to all. Conference covers fiction and poetry. Offerings specifically available for poets included workshops and classes. Speakers at last conference included Amy Gerstler (poetry) and Pinckney Benedict (fiction).
Costs/Accommodations: Cost for the last conference was $200 for conference and classes, $300 for conference, classes and workshop; plus $25 application fee. Information on overnight accommodations is available for registrants. "Rooms available in the student union or in a dorm."
Additional Info: Individual critiques are also available. Submit 10 pgs. of poetry in advance. "All manuscripts are considered for scholarships." Send SASE for brochures and registration forms.

IOWA SUMMER WRITING FESTIVAL, University of Iowa, 116 International Center, Iowa City IA 52242-1802, phone (319)335-2534, fax (319)335-3533, e-mail amy-margolis@uiowa.edu, website http://www.uiowa.edu/~iswfest, coordinators Peggy Houston and Amy Margolis. Annual event founded 1987. Held each summer in June and July for six weeks, includes one-week and weekend workshops at the University of Iowa campus. Average attendance is 125/week.
Purpose/Features: Open to "all adults who have a desire to write." Conference offers courses in nearly all writing forms. In 1999, offerings available for poets included 21 poetry classes for all levels. Speakers were Michael Dennis Browne, Christopher Davis, Jim Heynen, Timothy Liu, James McKean and Kathryn Rhett.

Costs/Accommodations: Cost for 1999 conference was $175 for a weekend course and $375-400 for a one-week course. Participants are responsible for their own meals. Accommodations available at the Iowa House and the Holiday Inn. Housing in residence hall costs about $28/night.
Additional Info: Participants in week-long workshops will have private conference/critique with workshop leader. Send for brochures and registration forms. "Requests for info are accepted via phone, fax or e-mail." Website includes complete catalog of courses, faculty, schedules, etc.

THE IWWG SUMMER CONFERENCE, The International Women's Writing Guild, P.O. Box 810, Gracie Station, New York NY 10028, phone (212)737-7536, fax (212)737-9469, e-mail dirhahn@aol.com, website http://www.iwwg.com, executive director Hannelore Hahn. Annual week-long event founded 1978. Usually held the second Friday in August through the following Friday. Location: Skidmore College in Saratoga Springs, NY. Average attendance is 450.
Purpose/Features: Open to all women. Sixty-five workshops offered. "At least four poetry workshops offered for full week."
Costs/Accommodations: Cost is $750 for conference program and room and board.
Additional Info: "Critiquing available throughout the week." Send SASE for brochures and registration forms or request via e-mail (include mailing address for response). The International Women's Writing Guild's bi-monthly newsletter publishes and features hundreds of outlets for poets. See listing in Organizations.

LIGONIER VALLEY WRITERS CONFERENCE, P.O. Box B, Ligonier PA 15658, phone (724)537-3341, fax (724)537-0482. Annual 3-day event founded 1986. Usually held in July. 1999 dates were July 9-11. "This is a relaxing, educational, inspirational conference in a scenic, small town." Average attendance is 80.
Purpose/Features: Open to anyone interested in writing. Conference covers fiction, creative nonfiction and poetry.
Costs/Accommodations: Cost for conference is approximately $200. Participants are responsible for their own dinner and lodging. Information on overnight accommodations is available for registrants.
Additional Info: Send 9×6 SASE for brochures and registration forms. "We also publish *The Loyalhanna Review*, a literary journal, which is open to participants."

THE LITERARY FESTIVAL AT ST. MARY'S, St. Mary's College of Maryland, St. Mary's City MD 20686, phone (301)862-0239. An annual event held during the last 2 weekends in May. Approximately 18 guest poets and artists participate in and lead workshops, seminars and readings. Concurrent with the festival, St. Mary's College offers 2-week intensive writing workshops in poetry and fiction and a 10-day writer's community retreat.
Purpose/Features: The poetry and fiction workshop engages the participants in structured writing experiences. Intended for anyone with a serious interest in writing. They offer 4 college credits or may be taken as non-credit courses. The retreat, designed for the serious writer, offers individual plans for writing alone or in conjunction with other participants..
Additional Info: For applications or more information on these workshops or the festival, please write to Michael S. Glaser at the above address.

LUCIDITY POETS' OZARK RETREAT, 398 Mundell Rd., Eureka Springs AR 72631-9505, phone (501)253-9351, e-mail tbadget@ipa.net, website http://www.ipa.net/~tbadger, director Ted O. Badger. Annual 3-day event ("always mid-week") founded 1992. 2000 dates: April 11-13 (Tuesday, Wednesday and Thursday). Location: The Best Western Inn of the Ozarks in Eureka Springs. Average attendance is 65.
Purpose/Features: Open to all poets. Retreat features lectures, workshops and read-arounds—all poetry. "No stated theme other than giving opportunity to meet other poets from across the USA, have one's own work critiqued and read poems to the group. If there be a theme, it would be 'The Fellowship of Poets.' " Offerings specifically available to poets include "critiquing of poems done in small groups; lectures by distinguished poets and teachers." Speakers at last retreat were Tom Padgett, college English professor from Bolivar, MO, and Laurence Thomas, international teacher, poet and author from Ypsilanti, MI. Other special features include an "awards banquet on closing night with several hundred dollars given as awards."
Costs/Accommodations: Cost for 2000 is $20; participants are responsible for their own meals. Housing in on-site facilities costs $36 (couple).
Additional Info: Individual critiques are also available. Submit 2 poems with a limit of 36 lines/page in advance to *Lucidity Poetry Journal* at above address. Contest sponsored as part of retreat. Submit 1 poem of 36 lines or less—any form or subject. Send SASE for brochures and registration forms. Inquiries via e-mail OK. "We are loosely affiliated with a dozen State Poetry Societies which offer annual poetry competitions with cash awards, some of which are underwritten by our own *Lucidity Poetry Journal*, which offers publication and cash payments each quarter. (See listing for *Lucidity* in Publishers of Poetry section.) "*Lucidity* has tried since 1985 to promote and publish understandable poetry as opposed to obscure or highly esoteric verse. Nowhere else will you find a poetry conference offering three days of activity for only $20."

MANHATTANVILLE'S WRITERS' WEEK, Manhattanville College, 2900 Purchase St., Purchase NY 10577, phone (914)694-3425, fax (914)694-3488, e-mail rdowd@mville:edu, dean—adult and special programs Ruth Dowd, RSCJ. Annual 5-day event founded 1983. Usually held the last week in June at the Manhattanville

College campus—"suburban surroundings 45 minutes from downtown Manhattan." Average attendance is 90.
Purpose/Features: Open to "published writers, would-be writers and teachers of creative writing. The conference offers workshops in five genres: fiction, short story, creative non-fiction, poetry, children's/young adult literature. There is also a special workshop in The Writers' Craft for beginners." Offerings specifically available for poets include a poetry workshop. "We have had such distinguished poet/workshop leaders as Mark Doty, Stephanie Strickland and Honor Moore. We generally feature a lecture by a distinguished writer."
Costs/Accommodations: Cost for conference is $560. Participants are responsible for their own meals. Information on overnight accommodations is available. "Rooms in the residence halls are available or students may choose to stay at area hotels. Housing in on-site facilities costs $25/night."

✔ ▚ **MARITIME WRITERS' WORKSHOP**, UNB Dept. of Extension, Box 4400, Fredericton, New Brunswick E3B 5A3 Canada, phone/fax (506)474-1144, e-mail extensin@unb.ca or k4jc@unb.ca, website http://www.unb.ca/web/coned/mww, coordinator Rhona Sawlor. Annual 1-week event founded 1976. Usually held the first week in July. Location: University of New Brunswick campus. Average attendance is 50.
Purpose/Features: Open to all writers. Workshop covers fiction, nonfiction, poetry and writing for children. Offerings specifically available for poets include a daily workshop group for poets, limited to 10 participants, and individual conferences arranged with instructors. Instructors at last conference were Kent Thompson and Carol Malyon (fiction); Brian Bartlett (poetry); George Galt (nonfiction); Julie Johnston (writing for children). Other special features included readings.
Costs/Accommodations: Cost was $350 plus $300 for room and board. Scholarships are available.
Additional Info: "All participants must submit a manuscript which is then 'workshopped' during the week." Phone, fax or write for brochures and registration forms.

✔ **MOUNT HERMON CHRISTIAN WRITERS CONFERENCE**, P.O. Box 413, Mount Hermon CA 95041, phone (831)335-4466, fax (831)335-9218, e-mail dtalbott@mhcamps.org, website http://www.mountherm on.org, director of specialized programs David R. Talbott. Annual 5-day event founded 1970. Always held Friday through Tuesday over Palm Sunday weekend. 2000 dates: April 14-18. Location: Full hotel-service-style conference center in the heart of the California redwoods. Average attendance is 200-250.
Purpose/Features: Open to "anyone interested in the Christian writing market." Conference is very broad-based. Always covers poetry, fiction, article writing, writing for children, plus an advanced track for published authors. Offerings specifically available for poets have included several workshops on poetry, plus sessions on the greeting card industry plus individual one-hour workshops on poetry. "We usually have 35-40 teaching faculty. Faculty is made up of publishing reps of leading Christian book and magazine publishers, plus selected freelancers." Other special features have included an advance critique service (no extra fee); residential conference, with meals taken family-style with faculty; private appointments with faculty; and an autograph party. "High spiritual impact."
Costs/Accommodations: Cost for 1999 conference was $730 deluxe; $610 standard; $520 economy; including 13 meals, snacks, on-site housing and $300 tuition fee. No-housing fee: $450. $15 airport, Greyhound or Amtrack shuttle from San Jose, CA.
Additional Info: Send SASE for brochures and registration forms.

✔ **CHRISTOPHER NEWPORT UNIVERSITY WRITERS' CONFERENCE & CONTEST**, 1 University Place, Newport News VA 23606, phone (757)594-7158, fax (757)594-8736. Annual 2-day event founded 1981. Usually held in early April. 1999 dates were April 9-10. Location: the Christopher Newport University Student Center. Average attendance is 110.
Purpose/Features: Open to "all writers, any age, professional or amateur." Covers fiction, nonfiction, poetry, juvenile fiction, mystery, romance, screenplay and sometimes humor. Conference is designed "to educate, entertain, network, support and enrich." The 1999 afternoon workshop was a panel of publishers from a variety of backgrounds. Offerings specifically available to poets included a poetry workshop and contest.
Costs/Accommodations: Cost for 1999 was $70, including lunches; discounts are available to senior citizens and students. Information on overnight accommodations is available.
Additional Info: Contest sponsored for poetry, nonfiction, fiction and juvenile writing as part of conference. Judges are "different each year; authors, professors in each field." Send SASE for brochures and registration forms. Inquiries via fax OK. Also publishes *The Voyager* ($5/year) which "contains information regarding the planning of the conference, other contest information in the region and accomplishments of past presenters."

N **NORTH EAST TEXAS WRITERS' ORGANIZATION'S ANNUAL SPRING WRITERS' CONFERENCE**, % Rt. 1, Box 440, Mt Vernon TX 75457, phone (903)537-4292, conference coordinator Jean

---

MARKETS THAT WERE listed in the 1999 edition of *Poet's Market* but do not appear this year are listed in the General Index with a notation explaining why they were omitted.

Pamplin. Annual 1-day event founded 1986. 1999 date: April 17. Location: Northeast Texas Community College, Mt. Pleasant, Texas. Average attendance is 50.

Purpose/Features: Open to all writers. Conferences is designed to "encourage writing by securing excellent speakers, promoting and selling our local authors' work as well as that of our speakers' work. We cover fiction and nonfiction, including poetry, plays, romance, western, mystery, short stories, childrens' stories, articles, cartoons and young adult books." Offerings specifically available for poets "depends on our speakers. However, there are many award-winning poets in our writers' organizations with whom attendees can network." Other special features include "book tables to sell members' and speakers' books as well as magazines, articles. When we have an agent speak, he/she meets with attendees generally for 10 minutes each if they pre-register before the meeting. We usually have a reception for speakers on Friday evening before the conference on Saturday."

Costs/Accommodations: Cost for 1999 conference was $50; $45 for members of the North East Texas Writers' Organization. Information on overnight accommodations is available.

Additional Info: Send SASE for brochures and registration forms. "Our conference is co-sponsored with the Northeast Texas Community College. We publish poetry in our newsletter and in regional books."

N: NORTHWEST OKLAHOMA WRITERS WORKSHOP, P.O. Box 5994, Enid OK 73702-5994, phone (580)237-6535, fax (580)237-2744, e-mail enidwriters@hotmail.com, website http://welcome.to/EnidWritersClub, orkshop coordinator Bev Walton-Porter. Annual 1-day event (9 AM to 3:30 PM) founded 1991. Usually held in April. Location: Cherokee Strip Conference Center, 123 W. Maine, Enid OK 73701. Average attendance is 40-50.

Purpose/Features: Open to writers of all genres. The workshop provides general writing instruction. Offerings specifically available for poets include a section on poetry. Speaker at last workshop was Annie Jones.

Costs/Accommodations: Cost is $45, including meals, discounts are available for early registration ($40 if registered a week before the workshop).

Additional Info: Send SASE for brochures and registration forms or obtain via website. Inquiries via fax and e-mail OK. The workshop is sponsored by the Enid Writers Club which publishes *Scribe and Quill*, a bimonthly newsletter for writers. Website includes information about writers club, writing samples, information on contests/ workshop and bookstore.

PIMA WRITERS' WORKSHOP, Pima College, 2202 W. Anklam Rd., Tucson AZ 85709, phone (520)206-6974, e-mail mfiles@pimacc.pima.edu, director Meg Files. Annual 3-day event founded 1987. 1999 dates were May 28-30. Location: Pima College's Center for the Arts, "includes a proscenium theater, a black box theater, a recital hall, and conference rooms, as well as a courtyard with amphitheater." Average attendance is 200.

Purpose/Features: Open to all writers, beginning and experienced. "The workshop includes sessions on all genres (nonfiction, fiction, poetry, writing for children and juveniles, screenwriting) and on editing and publishing, as well as manuscript critiques and writing exercises." Faculty included David Citino, Karla Kuban, Victoria Lipman, Nancy Mairs, Howard Meibach, Robert J. Serling, Sherri Szeman, Jacqueline Woodson and others, including 2 agents. Other special features include "the workshop's accessible to writers, agents and editors; and the workshop's atmosphere—friendly and supportive, practical and inspirational."

Costs/Accommodations: Cost for 1998 workshop was $65; participants are responsible for their own meals. Information on overnight accommodations is available.

Additional Info: Individual critiques also available. Submit 3 poems in advance to Meg Files.

POETRY ALIVE! SUMMER RESIDENCY INSTITUTE FOR TEACHERS, 20 Battery Park, Suite 505, Asheville NC 28801, phone (800)476-8172, fax (828)232-1045, e-mail poetry@poetryalive.com, website http://www.poetryalive.com, director Allan Wolf. Annual 6-day event founded 1990. 1999 dates were June 20-26, July 11-17, July 18-24. Location: University of North Carolina at Asheville. Average attendance is 20/session.

Purpose/Features: Open to anyone. Themes or panels for conference have included "creative writing (poetry), reader response techniques, poem performance techniques and teaching." Speakers at last conference were Allan Wolf (performance poetry, writing) and Cheryl Bromley Jones (reader response, writing). Other special features include a trip to Connemara, the Carl Sandburg Home Place.

Costs/Accommodations: Cost for the 1999 conference was $650, including meals and housing in on-site facilities; discounts available to local commuters "who don't pay the cost of food and lodging." Transportation to and from the event is provided. "We provide transportation from the airport."

Additional Info: Send SASE for brochures and registration forms. Inquiries via fax and e-mail OK. "This workshop is designed specifically for teachers or any poets interested in working with students in the schools or as an educational consultant." Website includes photos, descriptions, dates and prices.

PORT TOWNSEND WRITERS' CONFERENCE, c/o Centrum, P.O. Box 1158, Port Townsend WA 98368, phone (360)385-3102, fax (360)385-2470, director Sam Hamill. Annual 10-day event founded 1974. Usually held the second week in July at a 400-acre state park at the entrance to Puget Sound. Average attendance is 160.

Purpose/Features: Open to "all serious writers." Conference usually covers fiction (no genre fiction), poetry and creative nonfiction. Offerings include "three limited-enrollment workshops, private manuscript conference, open-mike readings, faculty readings and technique classes." Speakers at the last conference were Ursula LeGuin, Olga Broumas, Quincy Troupe, Arthur Sze, C.D. Wright, Alan Cheuse and Dorianne Laux.

Costs/Accommodations: Cost for the conference was $425 tuition including workshop, ms conference, classes, readings, lectures; $300 tuition without workshop or ms conference; plus $330 optional for dormitory housing and 3 meals per day. Information on overnight accommodations is available for registrants.

Additional Info: Individual critiques are also available at no extra charge, however "you must be enrolled in a manuscript workshop." Send SASE for brochures and registration forms.

SAGE HILL WRITING FALL POETRY COLLOQUIUM, P.O. Box 1731, Saskatoon, Saskatchewan S7K 3S1 Canada, phone/fax (306)652-7395, e-mail sage.hill@sk.sympatico.ca, website http://www.lights.com/sagehill, executive director Steven Ross Smith. Annual 21-day event founded 1995. Usually held the first 3 weeks in October at "the peaceful milieu of St. Peter's College, adjoining St. Peter's Abbey, in Muenster, 150 kilometers east of Saskatoon."

Purpose/Features: Open to poets, 19 years of age and older, who are working in English. The colloquium offers "an intensive three-week workshop/retreat designed to assist poets with manuscripts-in-progress. Each writer will have established a publishing record in books or periodicals and will wish to develop his/her craft and tune a manuscript. There will be ample time for writing, one-on-one critiques, and group meetings to discuss recent thinking in poetics. Eight writers will be selected. Writers in and outside Saskatchewan are eligible." The instructor for the upcoming workshop is Robert Kroetsch.

Costs/Accommodations: Cost was $875, including tuition, accommodations and meals. "A university registration fee of $25 will be added if taking this course for credit." Transportation from Saskatoon can be arranged as needed. On-site accommodations included in cost.

Additional Info: Send SASE for brochures and registration forms. Website includes program information, scholarship information, tuition, application information and down-loadable application forms.

SAGE HILL WRITING SUMMER EXPERIENCE, P.O. Box 1731, Saskatoon, Saskatchewan S7K 3S1 Canada, phone/fax (306)652-7395, e-mail sage.hill@sk.sympatico.ca, website http://www.lights.com/sagehill, executive director Steven Ross Smith. Annual 7-day and 10-day events founded in 1990. Usually held the end of July through the beginning of August. The Summer Experience is located at St. Michael's Retreat, "a tranquil facility in the beautiful Qu'Appelle Valley just outside the town of Lumsden, 25 kilometers north of Regina." Average attendance is 54.

Purpose/Features: Open to writers, 19 years of age and older, who are working in English. No geographic restrictions. The retreat/workshops are designed to "offer a special working and learning opportunity to writers at different stages of development. Top quality instruction, a low instructor-writer ratio, and the rural Saskatchewan setting offers conditions ideal for the pursuit of excellence in the arts of fiction, poetry, playwriting, and creative nonfiction." Offerings specifically available for poets include a poetry workshop and poetry colloquium. The faculty in 1999 includes Don McKay, Dennis Cooley and Elizabeth Philips.

Costs/Accommodations: Cost for the last conference was $595, includes instruction, accommodations and meals. Limited local transportation to the conference is available. "Van transportation from Regina airport to Lumsden will be arranged for out-of-province travellers." On-site accommodations offer individual rooms with a writing desk and washroom.

Additional Info: Individual critiques offered as part of workshop and colloquium. Writing sample required with application. Application deadline: May 1. Send SASE for brochures and registration forms. Website includes program information, scholarship information, tuition, application information and down-loadable application forms.

SAN DIEGO STATE UNIVERSITY WRITERS CONFERENCE, 5250 Campanile Dr., San Diego CA 92182-1920, phone (619)594-2517, fax (619)594-8566, e-mail jwahl@mail.sdsu.edu, website http://www.ces.sdsu.edu, extension director Jan Wahl. Annual 3-day event founded 1984. 2000 dates: January 21-23. Location: Double Tree Hotel, San Diego Mission Valley, 7450 Hazard Center Dr., San Diego. Average attendance is 350.

Purpose/Features: Open to writers of fiction, nonfiction, children's, poetry and screenwriting. "We have participants from across North America." The conference offers numerous workshops in fiction, nonfiction, general interest, children's, screenwriting, magazine writing and poetry. Speakers at last conference included Paul Breznick (senior editor, William Morrow), Tracy Carns (publishing director, Overlook Press), John Lehman (poet and publisher of *Rosebud Magazine*) and Joe Veltre (associate editor, St. Martins Press). Other special features include networking lunch, editor/agent appointments, book signing for published authors.

Costs/Accommodations: Cost is $225-300, including 1 meal, discounts are available for early registration. Transportation to and from the event is provided by the Doubletree Hotel. Information on overnight accommodations is available. Accommodations include special rates at The Doubletree Hotel.

Additional Info: Individual critiques are also available. See brochure for details. Contest sponsored as part of conference. "Editors and agents give awards for favorite submissions." Send SASE for brochures and registration forms or obtain via website. Inquiries via fax or e-mail OK.

THE SANDHILLS WRITERS CONFERENCE, Augusta State University, Augusta GA 30904, phone (706)737-1500, fax (706)667-4770, e-mail lkellman@aug.edu, website http://www.aug.edu/langlitcom/sand_hills_conference, conference director Anthony Kellman. Annual 3-day event founded 1975. Facilities are handicapped accessible. Usually held the third weekend in March. 2000 dates: March 23-25. Average attendance is 100.

Purpose/Features: Open to all aspiring writers. Conference designed to "hone the creative writing skills of participants and provide networking opportunities. All areas are covered—fiction, poetry, children's literature, playwriting, screenwriting and writing of song lyrics, also nonfiction." Offerings specifically available to poets include craft lectures, ms evaluations and open readings. Speakers for next conference are Pulitzer Prize winner Robert Olen Butler (keynote) and New York literary agent Jane Dystel. Other faculty will give craft sessions and readings in poetry, fiction, nonfiction, children's literature, playwriting and songwriting.
Costs/Accommodations: Cost for 1999 was $156, including lunches; participants are responsible for dinners only. Information on overnight accommodations is available. Accommodations include special rates at area hotels.
Additional Info: Individual critiques are also available. Submit 6 poems with a limit of 15 pages. Contest sponsored as part of conference. "All registrants who submit a manuscript for evaluation are eligible for the contest determined by the visiting authors in each respective genre." Send SASE for brochures and registration forms. Inquiries via fax and e-mail OK.

SANTA BARBARA WRITERS' CONFERENCE, P.O. Box 304, Carpinteria CA 93014, phone (805)684-2250, fax (805)684-7003, conference director Barnaby Conrad. Annual week-long event founded in 1973. Held the last Friday to Friday in June at the Miramar Hotel on the beach in Montecito. Average attendance is 350.
Purpose/Features: Open to everyone. Covers all genres of writing. Workshops in poetry offered. Past speakers have included Ray Bradbury, Phillip Levine, Sol Stein, Dorothy Wall, Gore Vidal and Willian Styron.
Costs/Accommodations: Cost for 1999 conference, including all workshops and lectures, 2 al fresco dinners and room (no board), was $1,340 single, $864 double occupancy, $385 day students.
Additional Info: Individual critiques available. Submit 1 ms of no more than 3,000 words in advance with SASE. Competitions with awards sponsored as part of conference. Send SASE for brochures and registration forms.

☑ **SEWANEE WRITERS' CONFERENCE**, 310 St. Luke's Hall, 735 University Ave., Sewanee TN 37383-1000, phone (931)598-1141, e-mail cpeters@sewanee.edu, website http://www.sewanee.edu/Writers_Conference/home.html, conference administrator Cheri B. Peters. Annual 12-day event founded 1990. Usually held the last 2 weeks in July at The University of the South ("dormitories for housing, Women's Center for public events, classrooms for workshops, Sewanee Inn for dining, etc."). Attendance is about 105.
Purpose/Features: Open to poets, fiction writers and playwrights who submit their work for review in a competitive admissions process. "Genre, rather than thematic, workshops are offered in each of the three areas." In 1999, faculty members included fiction writers Barry Hannah, Amy Hempel, Charles Johnson, Diane Johnson, Margot Livesey, Alice McDermott, Rick Moody, and Padgett Powell; poets Rachell Hadas, John Hollander, Andrew Hudgins, and Dave Smith; and playwrights Romulus Linney and Marsha Norman. Other speakers included editors, agents and additional writers.
Costs/Accommodations: Cost for conference was $1,205, including room and board. Each year scholarships and fellowships based on merit are available on a competitive basis. "We provide free bus transportation from the Nashville airport on the opening day of the conference and back to the airport on the closing day."
Additional Info: Individual critiques are also available. "All writers admitted to the conference will have an individual session with a member of the faculty." A ms should be sent in advance after admission to the conference. Write for brochure and application forms. No SASE necessary. Inquiries via e-mail OK.

[N] **SOUTH FLORIDA WRITERS CONFERENCE**, 3109 Grand Ave, Suite 175, Miami FL 33133, phone/fax (305)285-0283, e-mail mipress@aol.com, conference director Judith Welsh. Annual 3-day event founded 1990. 1999 dates were February 25-27. Average attendance is 150.
Purpose/Features: Open to all writers from emerging to professional. Conference is designed to "enhance writers skills in creating, marketing and publishing from the article, the short story, the essay to the play and the novel, including children's art and fiction and poetry." Panels for 1999 conference include "What Editors & Publishers Want" and "The Changing Marketplace." Offerings specifically available for poets include presentations by six of Miami Master of Fine Arts program professors and accomplished poets. Speakers include nationally published poets, novelists, playwrights, journalists; also editors, publishers and agents. Other special features include networking opportunities at all social events as well as at lectures/workshops.
Costs/Accommodations: Cost is $120, including meals, discounts are available to full-time students (high school and college). Information on overnight accommodations is available. Accommodations include special rates at area hotels.
Additional Info: Individual critiques are also available. Submit 3 poems with a limit of 25 lines/page in advance to SF Writers, National Writers Assoc., P.O. Box 570415, Miami FL 33257-0415 with $25 fee. Send SASE for brochures and registration forms. Inquiries via fax or e-mail OK. South Florida Writers is affiliated with the National Writer's Association. "NWA has a large membership, many of whom are poets."

[N] **SOUTHAMPTON COLLEGE WRITING CONFERENCE**, 239 Montauk Hwy., Southampton NY 11968, phone (516)287-8349, e-mail caglioti@southampton.liu.edu, website http://www.southampton.liunet.edu, summer director Carla Caglioti. Annual 10-day to 2-week events founded 1976. 1999 dates were June 30-July 8. "The Writers Conference is held at Southampton College of Long Island University. The College is located in the heart of the Hamptons, one of the most beautiful and culturally rich resorts in the country. The campus occupies an attractive 110-acre site in the gently sloping Shinnecock Hills with views of the Atlantic Ocean, Shinnecock Bay and Peconic Bay." Average attendance is 45.

Purpose/Features: Open to writers, graduate students and upper-level undergraduate students. Conference covers poetry, fiction, short story and nonfiction. Theme for 1999 conference was "Writers on Writing Reading and Lecture Series: What's Wrong with American Writing." Offerings specifically available for poets include a poetry workshop. Speakers at last conference were George Plimpton, Roger Rosenblatt, Spalding Gray, Walter Bernstein, Kaylie Jones, Billy Collins, Nahid Rachlin, Stephen O'Connor, Kit Hathaway, Robin Hemley and Robert Reeves.

Costs/Accommodations: Cost was $550; participants are responsible for their own meals, discounts are available. "Each additional workshop is at the reduced rate of $330." Information on overnight accommodations is available. Housing in on-site facilities costs $200 to share a room with another participant, $330 for a single.

Additional Info: Send SASE for brochures and registration forms or obtain via website. Inquiries via fax or e-mail OK. "We have a College website which contains information on the Writers Conference under its summer offerings. Visitors should go to to the index and click on 'Summer.' "

SOUTHERN CALIFORNIA WRITERS' CONFERENCE*SAN DIEGO, 3735 India St., San Diego CA 92103, phone (619)291-6805, e-mail wewrite@writersconference.com, website http://www.writersconference.com, executive director Michael Gregory. Annual 4-day event founded 1986. 1999 dates were March 12-15. Usually held at the Ramada Inn Conference Center in San Diego. Average attendance: 300.

Purpose/Features: Open to all aspiring and accomplished writers of fiction, nonfiction, screen and poetry. Conference offers 50 read and critique sessions as well as Q&A workshops.

Costs/Accommodations: Cost for conferences was $250; participants are responsible for their own meals. Information on overnight accommodations is available for registrants. Accommodations include special rates at area hotels. Housing in on-site facilities costs $515 for single room (including cost of conference) and $405 shared double room (including cost of conference).

Additional Info: Individual critiques are also available. Submit poetry in advance to Leroy Quintana at the above address. Contest sponsored as part of conference. Competition receives 50-100 entries. Send SASE or e-mail for brochures and registration forms.

N̄ SOUTHWEST WRITERS WORKSHOP, 8200 Mountain Rd., NE, Albuquerque NM 87110, phone (505)265-9485, fax (505)265-9483, e-mail swriters@aol.com, website http://www.us1.net/sww, executive director Carol Bruce-Fritz. Annual 3- to 4-day event founded 1982. 1999 dates: August 19-22. Location: Hyatt Hotel, downtown Albuquerque. Average attendance is 500.

Purpose/Features: Open to all writers. Workshop covers all genres, focus on getting published—over 20 editors, agents and producers as presenters. "As part of the conference, SWW has an annual writing contest with a category for poetry. Contest judges are editors and agents." Other special features include preconference sessions on first 2 days of conference, appointments with editors, agents, producers and publicists.

Costs/Accommodations: Cost is $245-375, including meals. Early Bird discount if registered by July 15. Information on overnight accommodations is available. Accommodations include special rates at area hotels.

Additional Info: Individual critiques are also available through entry in annual contest. Submit 1 poem with a limit of 50 lines in advance with $18 (member), $23 (nonmember) fee. Send for entry form and rules. Send SASE for brochures and registration forms or obtain via website. Inquiries via fax or e-mail OK. Website includes contest rules and registration forms, conference registration forms and membership information.

N̄ SPLIT ROCK ARTS PROGRAM, University of Minnesota, 335 Nolte Center, 315 Pillsbury Dr., SE, Minneapolis MN 55455-0139, phone (612)624-6800, fax (612)624-5891, e-mail srap@mail.cee.umn.edu, website http://www.cee.umn.edu/splitrockarts/, program associate Vivien Oja. Annual week-long workshop founded 1983. 2000 dates: July 9-August 12. "Workshops are held on the University's Duluth campus overlooking Lake Superior, and some retreat-style workshops are held at the University of Minnesota's Cloquet Forestry Center tucked away in the forests southwest of Duluth which offers a peaceful seclusion of the north woods." Average attendance is 500.

Purpose/Features: Open to "anyone over 18 years old who has an interest in the arts including creative writing, visual arts, fine crafts and creativity enhancement. Split Rock Arts participants are lifelong learners from all walks of life—novices, professionals, passionate hobbyists and advanced amateurs. The purpose of our program is to offer our audience uninterrupted time and space for them to explore their art in an inviting, supportive community that nourishes their spirit and an opportunity to work with renowned practising artists, writers and craftspeople from across the country and around the world. Areas of concentration include poetry, stories, memoirs, novels and personal essays." Instructors for the 1999 program included Paulette Bates Alden, Carol Bly, Michael Dennis Browne, Ellen Cooney, Ray Gonzalez, Susan Hubbard, Craig Lesley, Kent Meyers, Lawrence Sutin, Joyce Sutphen, Sylvia Watanabe, Catherine Watson and Karen Tei Yamashita. Offerings specifically available for poets included Michael Dennis Browne, "Is That a Real Poem or Did You Just Make It Up Yourself?"; Ray Gonzalez, "The Image Behind the Voice: A Poetry Workshop"; and Joyce Sutphen, "The Poetry of Memory." Other special features include over 35 workshops offered each summer in creative writing, visual arts, fine crafts, and creativity enhancement which offer artists and writers a unique opportunity to learn from outstanding artists/writers-in-residence in an inviting, supportive community."

Costs/Accommodations: Cost for each 1999 workshop was $430; participants are responsible for their own meals. "Limited scholarships are available based on artist merit and financial need." Housing in on-site facilities costs $168-258/week.

Additional Info: Write or call for free catalog or visit website. Inquiries via fax or e-mail OK. Website includes catalog with workshop description, instructor bios, registration information, program and housing information, scholarship information and application forms; registration forms are available on the website beginning mid-March of each year.

SQUAW VALLEY COMMUNITY OF WRITERS POETRY WORKSHOP, 10626 Banner Lava Cap, Nevada City CA 95959, phone (530)274-8551 or 583-5200, e-mail svcw@oro.net, website http://www.oro.net/ ~5vcw, executive director Brett Hall Jones. Annual 7-day event founded 1969. 1999 dates were July 24-31. The workshop is held in The Squaw Valley Ski Corporation's Lodge. Squaw Valley is located in the Sierra Nevada near Lake Tahoe. "The workshop takes place in the off-season of the ski area. Participants can find time to enjoy the Squaw Valley landscape; hiking, swimming, river rafting and tennis are available." Average attendance is 64.

Purpose/Features: Open to talented writers of diverse ethnic backgrounds and a wide range of ages. "The Poetry Program differs in concept from other workshops in poetry. Our project's purpose is to help our participants to break through old habits and write something daring and difficult. Workshops are intended to provide a supportive atmosphere in which no one will be embarrassed, and at the same time to challenge the participants to go beyond what they have done before. Admissions are based on quality of the submitted manuscripts." Offerings include regular morning workshops, craft lectures and staff readings. "The participants gather in daily workshops to discuss the work they wrote in the previous 24 hours." 1999 staff poets: Lucille Clifton, Galway Kinnell, Sharon Olds, Cornelius Tady and Brenda Hillman.

Costs/Accommodations: Cost was $580, included regular morning workshops, craft lectures, staff readings and dinners. Scholarships are available. "Requests for financial aid must accompany submission/application, and will be granted on the perceived quality of manuscript submitted and financial need of applicant." Transportation to workshop is available. "We will pick poets up at the Reno/Lake Tahoe Airport if arranged in advance. Also, we arrange housing for participants in local houses and condominiums on the valley. Participants can choose from a single room for $375/week or a double room for $250/week within these shared houses. We do offer inexpensive bunk bed accommodations on a first come, first served basis."

Additional Info: Individual conferences are also available. "Only work-in-progress will be discussed." Send SASE for brochures and registration forms or request via e-mail (include mailing address for response). Website also includes content of brochure. "We also publish an annual newsletter."

N· **STEAMBOAT SPRINGS WRITERS CONFERENCE**, P.O. Box 774284, Steamboat Springs CO 80477, phone (970)879-8079, e-mail freiberger@compuserve.com, director Harriet Freiberger. Annual 1-day event founded 1981. Usually held the third weekend in July. The conference site is a "renovated train station, the Depot is home of the Steamboat Springs Arts Council—friendly, relaxed atmosphere." Average attendance is 35-40 (registration limited).

Purpose/Features: Open to anyone. Conference is "designed for writers who have limited time. Instructors vary from year to year, offering maximum instruction during a weekend at a nominal cost." Speakers for 1999 included fiction writer Robert Greer, editor-in-chief of *High Plains Literary Review*, and Renate Wood, published poet, instructor at University of Colorado and on the faculty of MFA Program for Writers at Warren Wilson College.

Costs/Accommodations: Cost for 1999 was $35 (before May 29), including lunch. "A variety of lodgings available. Special discounts at Steamboat Resorts."

Additional Info: Send SASE for brochures and registration forms. Inquiries via e-mail OK. The conference is affiliated with *Seedhouse*, "a new publication with rapidly expanding circulation encourages submissions from unpublished writers. It is a 'not-for-profit' and 'no advertisement' publication." (See complete listing for *Seedhouse* in the Publishers of Poetry section of this book.)

✓ SUMMER WRITING PROGRAM AT THE UNIVERSITY OF VERMONT, 322 S. Prospect St., Burlington VT 05401, phone (800)639-3210, fax (802)656-0306, e-mail dlusk@ced.uvm.edu, website http:// uvmce.uvm.edu:443/sumwrite.htm, director Daniel Lusk. Annual event founded 1994. Usually held during the month of July on the University of Vermont's campus, located in Burlington and close to Lake Champlain; room and board available on campus." Average attendance is 75-100.

Purpose/Features: Open to all qualified writers. "Workshops designed to provide supportive, non-competitive, demanding environments that focus on constructive criticism and encouragement. Less intensive lecture option offers seminars, small group sessions, and readings intended for new writers and those who prefer to work at their own pace." Workshop and lecture options covers fiction, poetry, autobiographies and nonfiction. The 1999 program featured Stephen Dunn, Gary Margolis, Philip Baruth, Pamela Painter, David Bradley, Joyce Johnson, David Huddle, Bill Roorbach and Leslie Ullman.

Costs/Accommodations: Costs for 1999 were $850 (workshop option), $200 (lecture option); residency fee of $700 includes private room and meals.

Additional Info: Request brochures by phone, fax or e-mail.

SWT SUMMER CREATIVE WRITING CAMP, Dept. of English, Southwest Texas State University, San Marcos TX 78666, phone (512)245-2163, fax (512)245-8546, e-mail swl3@swt.edu, director Steve Wilson. Annual week-long event founded 1989. Usually held the last week in June. "The camp is held on the campus of the 21,000-student Southwest Texas State University, which is also home to a nationally recognized Master of Fine Arts program in creative writing. SWTSU is located in Central Texas, roughly twenty miles from Austin." Attendance is limited to 20 participants.
Purpose/Features: Open to all high school students. "Because the camp is for high school students, we ask that participants take workshops in both fiction and poetry. In addition to our standard workshops in poetry, we offer workshops in revision, and each camper takes part in one-on-one tutorials with the poetry workshop leaders. On the final day of the writing camp, campers present a public reading of their writing for friends, family and people from the local community."
Costs/Accommodations: Cost is $250, including meals. All campers stay in SWT residence halls. Costs included in program fee.
Additional Info: Individual critiques are also available. Submit 3 poems. Send SASE for brochures and registration forms. "Our application deadline is April 15 of each year." Inquiries via fax or e-mail OK. "Our writing camp is quite competitive, so we encourage interested poets to send their best work."

TENNESSEE MOUNTAIN WRITERS CONFERENCE, P.O. Box 4895, Oak Ridge TN 37831-4895, phone/fax (423)482-6567, e-mail tnmtnwrite@aol.com, executive director Patricia Hope. Annual 3½-day event founded 1989. 1999 dates were April 14-17. Location: Garden Plaza Hotel in Oak Ridge. Average attendance is 150-200.
Purpose/Features: Open to "all aspiring writers, including students." Conference covers fiction, poetry, nonfiction and writing for children, plus special classes on romance, mystery, business, etc. Speakers at last conference included David Hunter, A.C. Crispin, Thomas Clark, Gloria Houston, Bettie Sellers, Bobby Taylor, Sheila Kay Adams and Bob Middlemiss. Other special features included a contest in conjunction with conference offering prizes to adults/students and a book fair featuring participants' books.
Costs/Accommodations: Cost for 1999 conference was (if preregistered by April 1st) $175 for full participants, $130 for day-only participants, $45 for students. Information on overnight accommodations is available for registrants. Host hotel provides discount to participants. Cost for 1999 was $66/night lodging.
Additional Info: Individual critiques are also available. Submit up to 10 pgs. prior to conference. Send SASE for brochures and registration forms.

UND WRITERS CONFERENCE, P.O. Box 7209, Grand Forks ND 58202-7209, phone (701)777-2768, e-mail jmckenzi@badlands.nodak.edu, website http://www.und.nodak.edu, director/professor James McKenzie. Annual 4- to 5-day event founded 1970. 1999 dates: March 14-18. "The conference takes place in the UND student Memorial Union, with occasional events at other campus sites, especially the large Chester Fritz Auditorium or the North Dakota Museum of Art." Average attendance is 3,000-5,000. "Some individual events as few as 20, some over 1,000."
Purpose/Features: All events are free and open to the public. "The conference is really more of a festival, though it has been called a conference since its inception. The conference has a history of inviting writers from all genres. The conference's purpose is public education, as well as a kind of bonus curriculum at the University. It is the region's premier intellectual and cultural event." Theme for 2000 conference is "Writing War." Offerings specifically available for poets include several well-known poets included in the roster. "They read, participate in panels and otherwise make themselves available in public and academic venues." Speakers at last conference were Joseph Bruchac, Lucille Clifton, Mark Doty, Galway Kinnell, Ruhama Veltfort and Terry Tempest Williams. Other special features include open-mike student/public readings every morning, informal meetings with writers, autograph sessions and dinners, receptions.
Additional Info: Send SASE for brochures. Inquiries via fax OK. Website includes biographies of visiting writers and complete conference schedule.

UNIVERSITY OF WISCONSIN-MADISON'S SCHOOL OF THE ARTS AT RHINELANDER, 715 Lowell Center, 610 Langdon St., Madison WI 53703-1195, fax (608)265-2475, e-mail kathy.berigan@ccmail.adp.wisc.edu, website http://www.dsc.wisc.edu/art/soa.htm, administrative coordinator Kathy Berigan. Annual 5-day event founded 1964. Usually held the third or fourth week in July. Held at a local junior high school. Average attendance is 300.
Purpose/Features: Open to all levels and ages. Offerings specifically available for poets include poetry workshops and related workshops in creativity.
Costs/Accommodations: Cost for 1999 workshop ranged from $150-300. Information on overnight accommodations is available for registrants.
Additional Info: Write for brochures and registration forms.

VICTORIA SCHOOL OF WRITING, Box 8152, Victoria, British Columbia V8W 3R8 Canada, phone (250)598-5300, fax (250)598-0066, e-mail writeawy@islandnet.com, website http://www.islandnet.com/vicwrite/, registrar Margaret Dyment. Annual 4-day event founded 1996. 1999 dates were July 20-23. Location: "Residential school in natural, parklike setting. Easy parking, access to university, downtown." Average attendance is 100.

Purpose/Features: "A three- to ten-page manuscript is required as part of the registration process, which is open to all. The general purpose of the workshop is to give hands-on assistance with better writing, working closely with established writers/instructors. We have workshops in fiction, poetry and work-in-progress; plus two other workshops which vary." Offerings specifically available for poets include 2 intensive 4-day workshops (12 hours of instruction and one-on-one consultation). In 1999, one workshop was led by Patricia Young; the other was led by Terence Young.

Costs/Accommodations: Cost for 1999 workshop was $475 Canadian; includes 4 lunches and 1 dinner. Other meals and accommodations are available on site. "For people who register with payment in full before May 1, the cost is $435 Canadian."

Additional Info: Contest sponsored as part of conference. Competition receives approximately 100 entries. Send SASE for brochures and registration forms. "We are affiliated with 'Write Away!' a company which offers courses in creative writing in Victoria and publishes a chapbook of poetry 3 times/year." Inquiries via fax and e-mail OK. Website includes bios of instructors, some workshop information and registration form.

WESLEYAN WRITERS CONFERENCE, Wesleyan University, Middletown CT 06457, phone (860)685-3604, fax (860)347-3996, e-mail agreene@wesleyan.edu, website http://www.wesleyan.edu/writing/conferen.ht ml, director Anne Greene. Annual 5-day event founded 1956. Usually held the last week in June on the campus of Wesleyan University. The campus is located "in the hills overlooking the Connecticut River, a brief drive from the Connecticut shore. Wesleyan's outstanding library, poetry reading room, and other university facilities are open to participants." Average attendance is 100.

Purpose/Features: "Open to both experienced and new writers. The participants are an international group. The conference covers the novel, short story, fiction techniques, fiction-and-film, poetry, literary journalism and memoir." Special sessions in 1999 included "Reading of New Fiction," "The Writers Life," "Writing Memoirs," and "Publishing." Offerings specifically for poets included manuscript consultations and daily seminars with Pulitzer Prize-winner William Meredith and Honor Moore and Ha Jin. Other faculty include Madison Smartt Bell, Chris Offutt, Roxana Robinson and Jonathan Schell.

Costs/Accommodations: Cost in 1999, including meals, was $680 (day rate); $795 (boarding rate). "Wesleyan has scholarships for journalists, fiction writers, nonfiction writers and poets. Request brochure for application information." Information on overnight accommodations is available. "Conference participants may stay in university dormitories or off campus in local hotels."

Additional Info: Individual critiques are also available. Registration for critiques must be made before the conference. Send SASE for brochures and registration forms. Inquiries via fax and e-mail OK.

▓N▓ WHIDBEY ISLAND WRITERS' CONFERENCES, 5456 Pleasant View Lane, Freeland WA 98249, phone (360)331-2739, e-mail writers@whidbey.com, website http://www.whidbey.com/writers, director Celeste Mergens. Annual weekend event founded 1997. Usually held the first weekend in March at the South Whidbey High School's state-of-the-art facility, except for our Author Fireside Chats, which are held in private residencies in our community." 2000 dates: March 3-5. Average attendance is 250.

Purpose/Features: Open to writers of every genre and skill level. Conference covers fiction, nonfiction, poetry, children's and screenwriting. Offerings specifically available for poets include workshops, panels and readings. Speakers at last conference included poets Pattiann Rogers, Susan Zwinger, Tim McNulty and Marian Blue. "So far, we have invited Terry Tempest Williams and Lucille Clifton to attend the 2000 conference." Other special features include "Author Fireside Chats which are opportunities to meet and learn from the faculty in personable home settings with groups of 20 or less. Participants spend the day focusing on their chosen genre."

Costs/Accommodations: Cost for 2000 conference is $258, includes 2 meals, volunteer discounts available. "Rideshare board available through our website." Information on overnight accommodations is available. Accommodations include special rates at "local B&B's, as well as roommate share lists and dorm-style accommodations as low as $10/night.

Additional Info: Individual critiques are also available. Submit 8 poems with a limit of 2 lines/page in advance with $35 fee. Send SASE for brochures and registration forms or obtain via website. Inquiries via e-mail OK. The conference is sponsored by the Whidbey Island Writers' Association. Website includes information about the conference, the presenters, accommodations, links to Whidbey Island information, registration forms, how-to best prepare to make the most of agent/editor/publisher meetings and conference opportunities. "This conference has been designed to offer personable interaction and learning opportunities. We consider all presenters and participants to be part of the 'team' here. We emphasize practical application strategies for success as well as workshop opportunities. We try to invite at least one poetry publisher per year (Copper Canyon Press in 1999)."

WINTER POETRY & PROSE GETAWAY IN CAPE MAY, 18 North Richards Ave., Ventnor NJ 08406, phone (609)823-5076, e-mail wintergetaway@hotmail.com, website http://www.geocities.com/soho/atrium/9007, founder/director Peter E. Murphy. Annual 4-day event founded 1994. 2000 dates: January 14-17. "The Conference is held at the Grand Hotel on the Oceanfront in Historic Cape May, New Jersey. Participants stay in comfortable rooms with an ocean view, perfect for thawing out the muse. Hotel facilities include a pool, sauna, and whirlpool, as well as a lounge and disco for late evening dancing for night people." Average attendance is 125.

Purpose/Features: Open to all writers, beginners and experienced, over the age of 18. "The poetry workshop meets for an hour or so each morning before sending you off with an assignment that will encourage and inspire you to produce exciting new work. After lunch, we gather together to read new drafts in feedback sessions led by experienced poet-teachers who help identify the poem's virtues and offer suggestions to strengthen its weaknesses. The groups are small and you receive positive attention to help your poem mature. In late afternoon, you can continue writing or schedule a personal tutorial session with one of the poets on staff." Previous staff included Renee Ashley, Robert Carnevale, Cat Doty, Stephen Dunn, Kathleen Rockwell Lawrence, Charles Lynch, Peter Murphy, Jim Richardson and Robbie Clipper Sethi. There are usually 10 participants in each poetry workshop and 5 in each of the prose workshops. Other special features include extra-supportive sessions for beginners.

Costs/Accommodations: Cost for 1999 conference was $350, includes breakfast and lunch for 3 days, all sessions as well as a double room; participants are responsible for dinner only. Discounts are available. "Early Bard Discount: Deduct $25 if paid in full by November 15, 1999." Single-occupancy rooms are available at additional cost.

Additional Info: Individual critiques also available. "Each poet may have a 20-minute tutorial with one of the poets on staff." Write for brochures and registration forms. "The Winter Getaway is known for its challenging, yet supportive atmosphere that encourages imaginative risk-taking and promotes freedom and transformation in the participants' writing."

☑ **WISCONSIN REGIONAL WRITERS' ASSOCIATION INC.**, 510 W. Sunset Ave., Appleton WI 54911-1139, phone (920)734-3724, fax (920)734-5146, e-mail padubo@aol.com. Founded in 1948. Biannual conferences. Founded in 1948. Held first Saturday in May and last weekend in September at various hotel-conference centers around the state. Average attendance is 100-150.

Purpose/Features: Open to all writers, "aspiring, amateur or professional." All forms of writing/marketing presentations rotated between conferences. "The purpose is to keep writers informed and prepared to express and market their writing in a proper format." Poetry covered formally once a year. A book fair is held at the fall conference where members can sell their published works. A banquet is also held at the fall conference where the Jade Ring writing contest winners from 6 categories receive awards. Winners of two additional writing contests also receive awards at the spring conference.

Costs/Accommodations: Spring conference is approximately $35-40, the 2-day fall conference approximately $40-60. Conferences also include Saturday morning buffet, the fall conference offers a hors d'oeuvres buffet at the Book Fair and entertainment at the Jade Ring Banquet. Meals (Saturday luncheon and dinner) are at an additional cost. Information about overnight accommodations is available for registrants. "Our organization 'blocks' rooms at a reduced rate."

Additional Info: Sponsors 3 writing contests/year. Membership in the WRWA and small fee are required. Send SASE for brochures and registration forms. "We are affiliated with the Wisconsin Fellowship of Poets and the Council of Wisconsin Writers. We also publish a newsletter, *Wisconsin Regional Writer*, four times a year for members." Website includes conference information, including a registration form; membership application; local club network; links to numerous other writers websites; link to upcoming speakers.

☒ **WRANGLING WITH WRITING**, Society of Southwestern Authors, P.O. Box 30355, Tucson AZ 85751-0355, e-mail wporter202@aol.com, website http://www.azstarnet.com/nonprofit/ssa, director Penny Porter. Annual 2-day event founded 1973. 2000 dates: January 21-22. Location: The Inn Suites in Tucson, Arizona. Average attendance is 300.

Purpose/Features: Open to beginning, intermediate and professional writers. Conference's purpose is to "aid all writers in all ways." Offerings specifically available for poets include 2-hour workshops and a contest. Speakers for next conference include Andrew Greeley plus editors, agents and publishers.

Costs/Accommodations: Cost is $175, including meals, discounts available for full-time teachers ($150), full-time students ($100), senior citizens ($150-160) and members of SSA ($150). Information on overnight accommodations is available. Accommodations include special rates at The Holiday Inn.

Additional Info: Individual critiques are also available. Send SASE for brochures and registration forms or obtain via website. Inquiries via e-mail OK. The Society of Southwestern Authors offers professional memberships to "published writers and qualified individuals in related fields" and Associate memberships to "aspiring writers who can demonstrate a sincere desire to become published." Send SASE for details. The Society also sponsors a contest. See the listing for the SSA Writer's Contest in the Contests & Awards section.

THE WRITERS' CENTER AT CHAUTAUQUA, 953 Forest Ave. Ext., Jamestown NY 14701, phone (716)483-0381, fax (716)483-0511, e-mail BLSaid@madbbs.com, director Janette Martin. Annual event founded 1988. Held 9 weeks in summer from late June to late August. Participants may attend for 1 week or more. "We are an independent, cooperative association of writers located on the grounds of Chautauqua Institution." Average attendance is 60 for readings and speeches, 15 for workshops.

Purpose/Features: Readings and speeches are open to anyone; workshops are open to writers (or auditors). The purpose is "to make creative writing one of the serious arts in progress at Chautauqua; to provide a vacation opportunity for skilled artists and their families; and to help learning writers improve their skills and vision." Workshops are available all 9 weeks. Poetry Works meets 2 hours each day. In 1999, leaders included William Heyer, Margaret Gibson, Greg Kuzma, Liz Rosenberg, Edward Hower, Dan Masterson, Alison Lurie, Stephen Corey, Robert Cording, Judith Kitchen and Stan Rubin. Prose Works offers 2 hours a day in fiction and nonfiction, writing for children and Young Writers' Workshops. Poets are welcome to explore other fields. Other special features include 2 speeches a week and 1 reading, usually done by the Writers-In-Residence.

Costs/Accommodations: Cost is $100/week. Participants are responsible for gate fees, housing and meals and "may bring family; sports, concerts, activities for all ages. A week's gate ticket to Chautauqua is $180/ adult (less if ordered early); housing cost varies widely, but is not cheap; meals vary widely depending on accommodations—from fine restaurants to cooking in a shared kitchen." Access is best by car or plane to Jamestown, NY. Contact the center for housing options.

Additional Info: Individual critiques are also available. Information published in spring mailing. Send SAE with 2 first-class stamps for brochures and registration forms. Inquiries via fax or e-mail OK. "We offer retroactive scholarship to one poet per summer. He or she is elected by workshop peers." The center also offers 4 workshops for children. "We now aid in the publication of poetry, creative nonfiction and fiction in two area newspapers (*The Post-Journal* and *The Dunkirk Observer*) via the coordination of two Saturday literature pages for the papers' joint Saturday magazine. The readership is 85,000. We have published poets from the likes of Lewis Turco and Marjorie Agosin to a 'beginning' 97-year-old nursing home resident. We seek excellence, general audience appeal and are limited to publishing regional writers and poets."

WRITERS' FORUM, Extended Learning Dept., Pasadena City College, 1570 E. Colorado, Pasadena CA 91106-2003, phone (626)445-0704, fax (626)585-7910, contact Meredith Brucker. Annual 1-day event founded 1954. Usually held all day Saturday in early March at Pasadena City College. Average attendance is 150.

Purpose/Features: Open to all. Conference covers a wide variety of topics and always includes 1 poet. Speakers have included poet Ron Koertge, *ONTHEBUS* editor Jack Grapes and Dennis Phillips of Littoral Books.

Costs/Accommodations: Cost for the last conference was $85, including lunch.

Additional Info: Write for brochures and registration forms. No SASE necessary. Inquiries via fax OK. No e-mail inquiries.

☑ **YELLOW BAY WRITERS' WORKSHOP**, Center for Continuing Education & Summer Programs, The University of Montana, Missoula MT 59812, phone (406)243-2094, fax (406)243-2047, e-mail hhi@selway.umt.e du, website http://www.umt.edu./ccesp/c&i/yellowba/, program manager Lea Upshaw. Annual week-long event founded 1987. 1999 dates were August 8-14. Location: University of Montana's biological research station located on beautiful Flathead Lake. The facility includes informal educational facilities, and rustic cabin or dorm living. Maximum attendance is 60.

Purpose/Features: Open to all writers. Conference offers two workshops in fiction, one in nonfiction and one in poetry. In 1999, workshop faculty included Denis Johnson (fiction), Pam Houston (fiction), Jane Miller (poetry) and Fred Haefele (nonfiction). "Special guests usually include editors/publishers/agents who engage in a forum of discussion and information dissemination."

Costs/Accommodations: Cost for 1999 workshop was $495, commuter fee; $840, tuition and single-occupancy lodging/meals; $815, tuition and double-occupancy lodging/meals. Round-trip shuttle from Missoula to Yellow Bay (85 miles) is available for $45 and airfare packages are offered.

Additional Info: Applicants must send a 5-page writing sample or 5 poems. Full and partial scholarships are available. Deadline for scholarship applications is June 10. Call or write for brochures and registration forms.

YOSEMITE: ALIVE WITH POETRY, The Yosemite Association, Yosemite Field Seminars, P.O. Box 230, El Portal CA 95318, phone (209)379-2321, fax (209)379-2486, e-mail yose_yosemite_association@nps.gov, website http://www.yosemite.org, seminar coordinator Penny Otwell. Annual 3-day event. 1999 dates: October 8-10. Location: Yosemite Valley in Yosemite National Park. Average attendance is 10-12.

Purpose/Features: Open to "both emerging poets and those who are perhaps already published." Seminar is designed to "explore the exquisite fall scenery of Yosemite Valley through poetry. The seminar combines poetry writing tehniques with interesting, short hikes to areas that offer enticing fall color. Time is planned for free-writing exercises as well as for solitude to reflect and to write personal poems. Each day will feature a hike of no more that two miles, and will end with a friendly, informal group poetry reading and discussion. The instructor, poet-naturalist Kristina Rylands, will be available to help students throughout the seminar. A group anthology will be compiled by the instructor at a later day for mailing to each interested student."

Costs/Accommodations: Cost is $180 ($167 for Yosemite Association members); participants are responsible for their own meals. "Cabins are pre-reserved for students, and run about $54/night. We also offer free camping."

Additional Info: Call for brochures. "The Yosemite Association is a non-profit organization dedicated to educating the public about Yosemite. We publish books, offer 68 field seminars, and give funding to the National Park Service from our book sales. We welcome new members and will honor the member fee for those individuals just joining." Website includes course description for Alive With Poetry and 60 other seminars.

Organizations

The organizations listed in this section offer encouragement and support to poets and other writers through a wide variety of services. They may sponsor contests and awards, hold regular workshops or open-mike readings, or release publications with details about new opportunities and area events. Many of these groups provide a combination of these services to both members and nonmembers.

The PEN American Center, for instance, holds public events, sponsors literary awards, and offers grants and loans to writers in need. Poets seeking financial assistance should contact the arts council in their state or province (see State & Provincial Grants on pages 505-507).

Many organizations provide opportunities to meet and discuss work with others. Those poets with access to the Internet can connect with other poets from around the world through various online writing groups. The National Federation of State Poetry Societies, Inc., the National Writers Association and the Canadian Poetry Association are all national organizations with smaller affiliated groups which may meet in your state or province. And for those seeking gatherings more local or regional in focus, there are organizations such as the Davidson County Writers' Guild, the Ozark Poets and Writers Collective and Writers of Kern.

In addition to local and regional associations, there are organizations that focus on helping certain groups of writers. For instance, the International Women's Writing Guild supports women writers through various national and regional events and services.

For organizations close to home, check for information at a library or bookstore, or contact the English department at a nearby college. Your local branch of the YMCA is also a good source for information on writing groups and programs. In fact, the YMCA National Writer's Voice Project sponsors both open-mike readings and readings by nationally known writers in various YMCAs throughout the country. For more information, contact your local YMCA or the Chicago-based offices of the National Writer's Voice Project at (800)USA-YMCA, ext. 515, website www.YMCA.net.

If you are unable to find a local writer's group, however, start one by placing an ad in your community newspaper or posting a notice on a library or bookstore bulletin board. There are sure to be others in your area who would welcome the support, and the library or bookstore might even have space for your group to meet on a regular basis.

To locate some of the larger organizations (or representative samples of smaller groups), read through the listings that follow. Then send a SASE to those groups that interest you to receive more details about their services and membership fees. Also refer to the list of Additional Organizations at the end of this section, as well as the Publications of Interest section on pages 545-550.

N ⊕ **ACADEMI–YR ACADEMI GYMREIG/THE WELSH ACADEMY**, Mount Stuart House, 3rd Floor, Cardiff, Wales CF10 5FQ United Kingdom, phone 029 2047 2266, fax 029 2049 2930, e-mail academi@dial.pipex .com, website http://www.dspace.dial.pipex.com/academi, chief executive Peter Finch. Founded in 1959 to "promote literature in Wales and to assist in the maintaining of its standard." Open to "the population of Wales and those outside Wales with an interest in Welsh writing." Currently has 1,500 total members. Levels of membership available are associate, full and fellow. Offerings available for poets include promotion of readings, events, conferences, exchanges, tours; employment of literature development workers; publication of a bimonthly events magazine; publication of a literary magazine in Welsh (*Taliesin*) and another (*NWR*) in English. Sponsors conferences/workshops and contests/awards. Publishes *A470: What's On In Literary Wales*, a magazine appearing 6 times a year that contains information on Welsh literary events. Also available to nonmembers for £15 (annual subscription). Members and nationally known writers give readings that are open to the public. Sponsors open-mike readings for members and the public. Membership dues are £15/year. Send SASE for additional information or obtain via website. Inquiries via fax OK.

THE ACADEMY OF AMERICAN POETS; FELLOWSHIP OF THE ACADEMY OF AMERICAN POETS; WALT WHITMAN AWARD; THE JAMES LAUGHLIN AWARD; HAROLD MORTON LANDON TRANSLATION AWARD; THE LENORE MARSHALL POETRY PRIZE; THE ERIC MATHIEU KING FUND; THE RAIZISS/DEPALCHI TRANSLATION AWARD; THE TANNING PRIZE, 584 Broadway, Suite 1208, New York NY 10012-3250, phone (212)274-0343, fax (212)274-9427, e-mail poets@artswire.org, website http://www.poets.org, founded 1934, executive director William Wadsworth. Robert Penn Warren wrote in *Introduction to Fifty Years of American Poetry*, an anthology published in 1984 containing one poem from each of the 126 Chancellors, Fellows and Award Winners of the Academy: "What does the Academy do? According to its certificate of incorporation, its purpose is 'To encourage, stimulate and foster the production of American poetry. . . .' The responsibility for its activities lies with the Board of Directors and the Board of 12 Chancellors, which has included, over the years, such figures as Louise Bogan, W.H. Auden, Witter Bynner, Randall Jarrell, Robert Lowell, Robinson Jeffers, Marianne Moore, James Merrill, Robert Fitzgerald, F.O. Matthiessen and Archibald MacLeish—certainly not members of the same poetic church." They award fellowships, currently of $20,000 each, to distinguished American poets (no applications taken)—64 to date—and other annual awards. The Walt Whitman Award pays $5,000 plus publication of a poet's first book by Louisiana State University Press. Winner also receives a 1-month residency at the Vermont Studio Center. Mss of 50-100 pgs. must be submitted between September 15 and November 15 with a $20 entry fee. Entry form required. Send SASE. The James Laughlin Award, for a poet's second book, is also a prize of $5,000. Submissions must be made by a publisher, in ms form. The Academy distributes 6,000 copies of the Whitman Award and Laughlin Award-winning books to its members. Poets entering either contest must be American citizens. The Harold Morton Landon Translation Award is for translation of a book-length poem, a collection of poems or a verse-drama translated into English from any language. One award of $1,000 each year to a US citizen. Write for guidelines. Most recent award winner was Louis Simpton (1998). The Lenore Marshall Poetry Prize is a $10,000 award for the most outstanding book of poems published in the US in the preceding year. The contest is open to books by living American poets published in a standard edition (40 pgs. or more in length with 500 or more copies). Self-published books are not eligible. Publishers may enter as many books as they wish. Deadline: June 1. Most recent award winner was Mark Jarman (1998). SASE for guidelines. The Eric Mathieu King Fund assists noncommercial publishers of poetry. Send SASE for guidelines. The Raiziss/de Palchi Translation Award is for outstanding translations of modern Italian poetry into English. A $5,000 book prize and a $20,000 fellowship are given in alternate years. Submissions for the book prize are accepted in odd-numbered years from September 1 through November 1. Submissions for the fellowship are accepted in even-numbered years from September 1 through November 1. Most recent fellow was Geoffrey Brock (1998). The Tanning Prize, of $100,000, is given annually for proven mastery in the art of poetry. No applications are accepted. *American Poet* is an informative periodical sent to those who contribute $25 or more/year. Membership: $45/year. The Academy inaugurated the first Annual National Poetry Month in April 1996. It also sponsors a national series of poetry readings and panel discussions and offers for sale select audio tapes from its archive of poetry readings. Call or write for a catalog.

■ **ADIRONDACK LAKES CENTER FOR THE ARTS**, P.O. Box 205, Rte. 28, Blue Mountain Lake NY 12812, phone (518)352-7715, fax (518)352-7333, e-mail alca@netheaven.com, executive director Ellen C. Bütz. An independent, private, nonprofit educational organization founded in 1967 to promote "visual and performing arts through programs and services, to serve established professional and aspiring artists and the region through educational programs and activities of general interest." Open to everyone. Currently has 1,300 members. Levels of membership available are individual, family and business. Offerings available for poets include workshops for adults and children, reading performances, discussions and lectures. Offers a "comfortable, cozy performance space—coffeehouse setting with tables, candles, etc." Computers available for members and artists. Publishes a triannual newsletter/schedule that contains news, articles, photos and a schedule of events. "All members are automatically sent the schedule and others may request a copy." Sponsors a few readings each year. "These are usually given by the instructor of our writing workshops. There is no set fee for membership, a gift of any size makes you a member." Members meet each July. Send SASE for additional information. Inquiries via fax and e-mail OK.

N̲ ALABAMA STATE POETRY SOCIETY; THE SAMPLER; THE MUSE MESSENGER, P.O. Box 230787, Montgomery AL 36123-0787, phone (334)244-8920, e-mail poettennis@aol.com, editor and membership chair Donna Jean Tennis. Founded in 1968 to promote "poetry as a vital cultural medium, improve our skills, share opportunities and support one another, and join with others who enjoy the written and spoken word to delight in good poetry of every form and persuasion." State-wide organization open to anyone engaged in writing poetry, or in furthering the cause of poetry. Currently has 225 total members. Levels of membership available are Regular Membership open to anyone engaged in writing poetry or furthering the cause of poetry. Student Membership available to any person enrolled full-time in a college or university. Affiliated with the National Federation of State Poetry Societies, and payment of dues to Alabama State Poetry Society includes membership with all its privileges into NFSPS. Sponsors conferences, workshops, contests and awards, semi-annual luncheons featuring speakers/workshops and members' poetry. ASPS sponsors spring and fall poetry contests, the fall contest open to non-members. Also sponsors an annual student contest for grades one through five. "Each year we publish *The Sampler*, an annual anthology of members' poems, now in it's 31st year." Publishes *The Muse Messenger*, a quarterly newsletter designed to be a teaching tool, featuring poetry forms, techniques, and terms, as well as publishing poetry by a wide range of poets including members. Members or nationally-known writers give readings that are open to the public. Sponsors open-mike readings. Membership dues are $15 per year for Regular and Associate members and $7 for Student members. Members meet quarterly. Send SASE for additional information. "The Alabama State Poetry Society meets the needs of poets around the country. Our fall contests are open to non-members as well as members, and guidelines are available with an SASE."

☑ ARIZONA AUTHORS ASSOCIATION; ARIZONA LITERARY MAGAZINE; ARIZONA AUTHORS NEWSLETTER, P.O. Box 87857, Phoenix AZ 85080-7857, phone (602)780-0053, fax (602)780-0468, e-mail vijayaschartz@az.rmci.net, president Vijaya Scharts. Founded in 1978 to provide education and referral for writers and others in publishing. State-wide organization. Currently has 250 total members. Levels of memberships available are Published, Unpublished (seeking publication), Professional (printers, agents and publishers) and Student. Sponsors conferences, workshops, contests, awards. Sponsors annual literary contest with 4 categories: poetry, short story, essay and novel. Awards publication in *Arizona Literary Magazine* and $125 1st Prize, $75 2nd Prize, $40 3rd Prize and $10 for honorable mention (6 awarded) for poetry. Submissions must be unpublished and may be entered in other contests. Submit any number of poems on any subject of up to 42 lines. Submissions must be typed on $8\frac{1}{2} \times 11$ paper, single-spaced stanzas and double-spaced between. Include a 3×5 index card for each poem with name, address, phone and title of poem (or first line). Do not put name on submissions. Include SASE for winners list. Send SASE for entry form and guidelines. Entry fee: $7/poem. Submission period: January 1 through July 29. Competition receives 2,000 entries a year. Most recent contest winners include Philip A. Buonpastore, Marlene E. Meehl, Abraham Burickson, Liza Guzman and Stella Pope Duarte. Judges are Arizona authors. Winners will be announced by November 15. Publishes *Arizona Literary Magazine*. Also publishes *Arizona Authors Newsletter*. Members or nationally-known writers give readings that are open to the public. Membership dues are $45. Members meet monthly. Send SASE for additional information. Inquiries via fax and e-mail OK.

☑ ASSOCIATED WRITING PROGRAMS; WRITER'S CHRONICLE; THE AWP AWARD SERIES, Tallwood House, MS 1E3, George Mason University, Fairfax VA 22030, phone (703)993-4301, fax (703)993-4302, e-mail awp@gmu.edu, website http://www.web.gmu.edu/departments/awp, founded 1967. Offers a variety of services to the writing community, including information, job placement assistance, writing contests, literary arts advocacy and forums. Annual individual membership is $57; placement service extra. For $20/6 issues you can subscribe to the *Writer's Chronicle* (formerly *AWP Chronicle*), containing information about grants and awards, publishing opportunities, fellowships, and writing programs. They have a directory, *The AWP Official Guide to Writing Programs*, of over 250 college and university writing programs for $25.95 (includes shipping). Also publishes the *AWP Job List* magazine, approximately 20 pgs., that contains employment opportunity listings for writers in higher education, editing and publishing. Also publishes *The Director*, approximately 600 pgs. that contains information on writers conferences and festivals. The AWP Award Series selects a volume of poetry (48 pg. minimum) each year ($10 entry fee for members; $20 for nonmembers) with an award of $2,000 and publication. Deadline: February 28. Send SASE for submission guidelines. Query after November. Competition receives approximately 1,400 entries. Inquiries via fax and e-mail OK. Most recent contest winners include Bonnie Jo Campbell, Edward Klein Schmidt Mayes and Michael Martone. Their placement service helps writers find jobs in teaching, editing and other related fields. Website includes information on AWP's core services, contest guidelines, conference information and links to other writer's organizations and creative writing programs.

⊕ ☑ ASSOCIATION OF CHRISTIAN WRITERS, 73 Lodge Hill Rd., Farnham, Surrey GU10 3RB England, phone/fax (01252)715746, e-mail christian-writers@dial.pipex.com, website http://dspace.dial.pipex.com/christian-writers/, administrator Warren Crawford. Founded in 1971 "to inspire, train, equip and encourage Christian writers." National charity with regional affiliations open to "anyone who affirms and practises the Christian faith and writes for pleasure or profit." Currently has 750 total members. Levels of membership available are New Writers (exploring), Intermediate (few pieces published) and Experienced Writers (regularly published). Offerings available for poets include "market news in quarterly magazine, two poetry advisers for personal manuscript critiques, postal workshops with other poets and poetry competitions." Sponsors 3 training days/year and annual contests. Publishes *Candle and Keyboard*, a quarterly magazine. Membership dues are £10 sterling/year. Send SASE for additional information. Inquiries via fax OK.

☑ THE AUTHORS GUILD, INC., 330 W. 42nd St., New York NY 10036, phone (212)563-5904, fax (212)563-8363, e-mail staff@authorsguild.org, website http://www.authorsguild.org, executive director Paul Aiken. Founded in 1912, it "is the largest association of published writers in the United States. The Guild focuses its efforts on the legal and business concerns of published authors in the areas of publishing contract terms, copyright, taxation and freedom of expression. The Guild provides free 75-point book and magazine contract reviews to members and makes group health insurance available to its members. "The Guild also sponsors Backinprint.com, a service that allows members to sell their out-of-print books." Writers must be published by a recognized book publisher or periodical of general circulation to be eligible for membership. We do not work in the area of marketing mss to publishers nor do we sponsor or participate in awards or prize selections." Also publishes the *Bulletin*, a quarterly journal for professional writers. Write, call or e-mail for information on membership.

THE BEATLICKS, 1016 Kipling Dr., Nashville TN 37217, phone (615)366-9012, fax (615)366-4117, e-mail beatlick@bellsouth.net, website http://www.geocities.com/SoHo/Studios/9307/beatlick.html, editors Joe Speer and Pamela Hirst. Founded in 1988 to "promote literature and create a place where writers can share their work." International organization open to "anyone interested in literature." Currently has 200 members. "There is no official distinction between members, but there is a core group that does the work, writes reviews, organizes readings, etc." Offerings available for poets include publication of work (they have published poets from Australia, Egypt, India and Holland), reviews of books and venues, readings for local and touring poets and a poetry hotline. "We have also hosted an open mic reading in Nashville since 1988. We have read in bars, bookstores, churches, libraries, festivals, TV and radio. We produce an hour show every Friday on public access TV. Poets submit audio and video tapes from all over. We interview poets about their work and where they are from." Publishes 2 newsletters: *Speer Presents* (bimonthly) and *Beatlick Poetry News* (bimonthly). The *Beatlick Poetry News* is a networking tool, designed to inform poets of local events and to bring awareness of the national scene. "We include poems, short fiction, art, photos, and articles about poets and venues." Submit short pieces, no vulgar language. "We try to elevate the creative spirit. We publish new voices plus well-established talents." Subscription: $10/year. Members meet twice a month. Send SASE for additional information. Inquiries via fax and e-mail OK. "We promote all the arts." Website includes poetry, fiction, articles and Beatlick products.

BURNABY WRITERS' SOCIETY, 6584 Deer Lake Ave., Burnaby, British Columbia V5G 3T7 Canada, contact person Eileen Kernaghan, founded 1967. Corresponding membership in the society, including a newsletter subscription, is open to anyone, anywhere. Yearly dues are $30. Sample newsletter in return for SASE with Canadian stamp. The society holds monthly meetings at The Burnaby Arts Centre (located at 6450 Deer Lake Ave.), with a business meeting at 7:30 followed by a writing workshop or speaker. Members of the society stage regular public readings of their own work. Sponsors a contest for poetry related to British Columbia. Competition receives about 400 entries a year. Recent contest winners include Dan Bar-El, Billie Livingston and Winona Baker. Send SASE for details.

THE WITTER BYNNER FOUNDATION FOR POETRY, INC., P.O. Box 10169, Santa Fe NM 87504, phone (505)988-3251, fax (505)986-8222, e-mail bynner@trail.com, contact Steven Schwartz. The foundation awards grants, ranging from $1,000 to $20,000, exclusively to nonprofit organizations for the support of poetry-related projects in the area of: 1) support of individual poets through existing nonprofit institutions; 2) developing the poetry audience; 3) poetry translation and the process of poetry translation; and 4) uses of poetry. The foundation "may consider the support of other creative and innovative projects in poetry." Letters of intent are accepted annually from September 1 through January 1; requests for application forms should be submitted to Steven Schwartz, executive director, at the address above. Applications if approved must be returned to the Foundation postmarked by February 1. Inquiries via fax and e-mail OK.

THE CANADA COUNCIL FOR THE ARTS; GOVERNOR GENERAL'S LITERARY AWARDS, P.O. Box 1047, 350 Albert St., Ottawa, Ontario K1P 5V8 Canada, phone (613)566-4414, fax (613)566-4410. Established by Parliament in 1957, the Canada Council for the Arts "provides a wide range of grants and services to professional Canadian artists and art organizations in dance, media arts, music, theatre, writing, publishing and the visual arts." The Governor General's Literary Awards, valued at $10,000 (Canadian) each, are given annually for the best English-language and best French-language work in each of seven categories, including poetry. Books must be first-edition trade books written, translated or illustrated by Canadian citizens or permanent residents of Canada and published in Canada or abroad during the previous year (September 1 through the following September 30). Collections of poetry must be at least 48 pgs. long and at least half the book must contain work not published previously in book form. In the case of translation, the original work must also be a Canadian-authored title. Books must be submitted by publishers with a Publisher's Submission Form, which is available from the Writing and Publishing Section. Send SASE for guidelines and current deadlines.

CANADIAN CONFERENCE OF THE ARTS (CCA), 130 Albert St., Suite 804, Ottawa, Ontario K1P 5G4 Canada, phone (613)238-3561, fax (613)238-4849, is a national, nongovernmental, not-for-profit arts service

MARKET CONDITIONS are constantly changing! If you're still using this book and it is 2001 or later, buy the newest edition of *Poet's Market* at your favorite bookstore or order directly from Writer's Digest Books (800)289-0963.

organization dedicated to the growth and vitality of the arts and cultural industries in Canada. The CCA represents all Canadian artists, cultural workers and arts supporters, and works with all levels of government, the corporate sector and voluntary organizations to enhance appreciation for the role of culture in Canadian life. Each year, the CCA presents awards for contribution to the arts. Regular meetings held across the country ensure members' views on urgent and ongoing issues are heard and considered in organizing advocacy efforts and forming Board policies. Members stay informed and up-to-date through *Blizzart*, a newsletter, which is published 4 times a year, and receive discounts on conference fees and on all other publications. Membership is $30 (plus GST) for Canadian individual members, $35 for US members and $45 for international members.

CANADIAN POETRY ASSOCIATION; POEMATA; THE SHAUNT BASMAJIAN CHAP-BOOK AWARD; THE HERB BARRETT AWARD, P.O. Box 22571, St. George PO, Toronto, Ontario M5S 1V0 Canada, phone (905)312-1779, fax (905)312-8285, e-mail ad507@freenet.hamilton.on.ca or cpa@wwdc.com, website http://www.mirror.org/grouips/cpa, national coordinator Wayne Ray. Founded in 1985, "to promote all aspects of the reading, writing, publishing, purchasing and preservation of poetry in Canada. The CPA promotes the creation of local chapters to organize readings, workshops, publishing projects, readings and other poetry-related events in their area." The CPS's bimonthly magazine, *Poemata*, features news articles, chapter reports, poetry by new members, book reviews, markets information, announcements and more. Membership is open to anyone with an interest in poetry, including publishers, schools, libraries, booksellers and other literary organizations, for $30/year. Seniors and students: $20. Send SASE for membership form. Also sponsors The Shaunt Basmajian Chapbook Award, awarding $100 (Canadian) and publication, plus 50 copies. Submissions may be entered in other contests. Submit up to 24 pgs. of poetry, in any style or tradition. Mss must be typed, single-spaced with title on each page. A separate sheet should give the title and the author's name and address. Simultaneous submissions OK. Send SASE for guidelines. Entry fee: $15 (Canadian). All entrants receive a copy of the winning chapbook. Annual deadline: March 31. Sponsors The Herb Barrett Award, with 3 prizes of $75, $50 and $25 (Canadian), and publication in anthology. Submit haiku no more than 4 lines long. Mss must be typed or printed, 1 poem/page, on letter-size paper with no identifying marks. Name, address and phone, with titles or first lines, should be on a separate sheet of paper. Submissions will not be returned. Send SASE for guidelines. Entry fees: $10 (Canadian)/1-2 poems $15 (Canadian)/3 or more poems. Each entrant will receive a copy of the anthology. Deadline: November 30. *Poemata* publishes articles, book reviews and essays related to writing. Sample newsletter: $3. Request information via e-mail. Make checks payable to Canadian Poetry Association.

CANADIAN SOCIETY OF CHILDREN'S AUTHORS, ILLUSTRATORS & PERFORMERS, 35 Spadina Rd., Toronto, Ontario M5R 2S9 Canada, phone (416)515-1559, fax (416)515-7022, e-mail canscaip@interlog.com, website http://www.interlog.com/~canscaip, is a "society of professionals in the field of children's culture. Puts people into contact with publishers, offers advice to beginners, and generally provides a visible profile for members; 365 professional members and over 1,000 associates who are termed 'friends.' An annual conference in Toronto the last week of October provides workshops to people interested in writing, illustrating, and performing for children." Membership is $60 for professional members (and a free copy of the Membership Directory); $25 for associates/year. Both include a subscription to the quarterly *CANSCAIP News*.

COLUMBINE STATE POETRY SOCIETY OF COLORADO, 10751 Routt St., Broomfield CO 80021, phone (303)465-0883, e-mail wagil@aol.com, website http://members.aol.com/wagil, secretary/treasurer Anita Gilbert. Founded in 1978 to promote the writing and appreciation of poetry throughout Colorado. State-wide organization open to anyone interested in poetry. Currently has 86 total members. Levels of membership available are: Members at Large who do not participate in the local chapters, but who belong to the National Federation and the State level; and members who belong to the national, state and local chapter, in Denver, Colorado. Offerings for the Denver Chapter include weekly workshops and monthly critiques. Sponsors contests, awards for students and adults. Sponsors the Annual Poets Fest in Golden, CO, where members and nationally-known writers give readings and workshops that are open to the public. Contests receive 200-300 entries. Also will sponsor a chapbook contest in 1999 under Riverstone Press, to be published in 2000. Send SASE for guidelines. Inquiries via e-mail OK. Most recent winner was Laura Fargas. Membership dues are $10 state and national, $25 local, state and national. Members meet weekly. Send SASE for additional information. Inquiries via e-mail OK. No fax inquiries. Website includes membership information, activities and contact information.

COUNCIL OF LITERARY MAGAZINES AND PRESSES, 154 Christopher St., Suite 3C, New York NY 10014-2839, phone (212)741-9110. Compiles an annual directory useful to writers: The *Directory of Literary Magazines*, which has detailed descriptions of over 600 literary magazines, including type of work published, payment to contributors and submission requirements. The directory is $16 postage paid and may be ordered by sending a check to CLMP.

DAVIDSON COUNTY WRITERS' GUILD, Arts Council for Davidson County, 23 W. Second Ave., Lexington NC 27292, phone (336)248-2551, fax (336)248-2000, e-mail fraziers@infoave.net, president Eric Frazier. Founded in 1972 to "encourage creative writing; to bring together writers and those interested in writing; to share ideas and inspiration and to critique original pieces; to provide resources and programs to help develop writing talents; to provide opportunities to have writing talents recognized; and to promote writing through contests for children, youth and adults." A county-wide organization open to any interested person 16 years of age and older. Currently has 15 active members. Membership benefits include "monthly meetings that offer 6-7 opportunities to read original work and occasional guest speakers conducting workshops—including poetry-related topics. The Guild's monthly meetings are conducted in a conference room above Frazier's Bookstore." Sponsors 3 annual writing contests—Adult, High School and Youth. "Winning and runner-up entries are published for the High School and Youth Contests in a book entitled *Ventures in Writing*." Competition receives over 300 entries a year. Members give readings that are open to the public. Sponsors open-mike readings. Memberships dues are $15/year. Members meet monthly. Send SASE for additional informational. Inquiries via fax and e-mail OK.

GEORGIA POETRY SOCIETY; BYRON HERBERT REECE CONTEST; EDWARD DAVIN VICKERS CONTEST; CHARLES B. DICKSON CHAPBOOK CONTEST; GEORGIA POETRY SOCIETY NEWSLETTER, 6426 Woodstone Terrace, Morrow GA 30260, phone (770)961-5653, president Emily B. Vail. Founded in 1979 to further the purposes of the National Federation of State Poetry Societies, Inc. in securing fuller public recognition of the art of poetry; to stimulate a finer and more intelligent appreciation of poetry; and to provide opportunity for study of and incentive for practice in the writing and reading of poetry. State-wide organization open to any person who is in accord with the objectives listed above. There are no restrictions as to age, race, religion, color, national origin or physical or mental abilities. Currently has 190 total members. Levels of membership available are Active, fully eligible for all aspects of membership; Student, same as Active except they pay lower dues, do not vote or hold office, and must be full-time enrolled students through college level; Lifetime, same as Active but pay a one-time membership fee the equivalent of approximately 15 years dues, receive free anthologies each year, and pay no contest entry fees. Offerings available for poets include affiliation with NFSPS. At least one workshop is held annually, contests are throughout the year, some for members only and some for general submissions. Workshops deal with specific areas of poetry writing, publishing, etc. Contests include the Byron Herbert Reece Contest, Edward Davin Vickers Contest, Charles B. Dickson Chapbook Contest (members only) and many ongoing or one-time contests, with awards ranging from $250 downwards. Entry fees and deadlines vary. Send SASE for complete guidelines. Publishes *Georgia Poetry Society Newsletter*, a quarterly. Also available to nonmembers on request. Readings are held annually to celebrate National Poetry Day (October) and National Poetry Month (April) in public forums such as libraries; some are with specified poets reading their own poetry or works of famous poets, and some are open-mike readings. At each quarterly meeting (open to the public) members have an opportunity to read their own poems. Current annual membership dues are Active: $20; Family: $35; Student: $10; Lifetime: $300. Members meet quarterly. "Our bylaws require rotation in office. We sponsor an active and popular Poetry in the Schools project, conducting workshops or readings in schools throughout the state by invitation. We also sponsor the annual Margery Carlson Youth Awards contest in all Georgia schools and winning poems are submitted to the Manningham Youth Awards contest of NFSPS. Our membership ranges from 9 to 93 years of age."

✔ **GREATER CINCINNATI WRITERS' LEAGUE**, 2735 Rosina Ave., Latonia KY 41015, phone (606)491-2130, e-mail leegeorge@juno.com, president Karen George. Founded in 1930s "to promote and support poetry and those who write poetry in the Cincinnati area and the attainment of excellence in poetry as an art and a craft. We believe in education and discipline, as well as creative freedom, as important components in the development of our own poetry and open, constructive critique as a learning tool." Regional organization open to anyone interested in and actively writing. Currently has 35 total members. Offerings available for poets include a monthly meeting/workshop or critique. Critics are published poets, usually faculty members from local universities, who critique poems submitted by members. The group also joins in the critique. Sponsors workshops, contests, awards with monetary awards, and an anthology published every 2 years. Members give readings that are open to the public or sponsor open-mike readings at bookstores and other locations. Membership dues are $20. Members meet monthly. Send SASE for additional information.

GUILD COMPLEX, 2936 N. Southport, Suite 210, Chicago IL 60657, phone (773)278-2210, fax (773)528-5452, e-mail guild@charlie.cns.iit.edu, website http://www.nupress.nwu.edu/guild, executive director Michael Warr. Founded in 1989 to "serve as a forum for literary cross-cultural expression, discussion and education, in combination with other arts. We believe that the arts are instrumental in defining and exploring human experience, while encouraging participation by artists and audience alike in changing the conditions of our society. Through its culturally inclusive, primarily literary programming, the Guild Complex provides the vital link that connects communities, artists and ideas. Over 10,000 people attend at least one of our events each year." Offerings available for poets include "over 140 literary events each year—workshops, featured readings, open-mikes, youth focused events, contests, multimedia literary festivals and a yearly writers conference. Our twice weekly featured readings range from the solo voice to book release parties to festivals combining poetry with video or music." Events are held at The Chopin Theater in Chicago. Sponsors "a women writers conference (also open to men) each fall, and offers writing workshops with locally and nationally known writers throughout the year. We also sponsor the Gwendolyn Brooks Open Mike Award each spring ($500 prize), and Tia Chucha Press, the publishing wing of Guild Complex, which publishes four full-length manuscripts of poetry per year." (See listing in Publishers of Poetry section.) Also publishes semi-monthly calendar of events sent "to everyone on a mailing list, not just members." Locally or nationally known writers give readings that are open to the public. Sponsors open-mike readings. "We present biweekly events featuring poets, writers, performance poets and storytellers. Our Tuesday night events are youth-focused, and our Wednesday night events are for general audiences. Open-mikes precede most of these events." Basic membership is $25. Send SASE for additional information. Inquiries via fax and e-mail OK.

INDIANA STATE FEDERATION OF POETRY CLUBS; THE POETS RENDEZVOUS CONTEST; THE POETS SUMMER STANZAS CONTEST; THE POETS WINTERS FORUM CONTEST; INDIANA POET, 808 E. 32nd St., Anderson IN 46016, phone (765)642-3611. Founded in 1941 to unite poetry clubs in the state; to educate the public concerning poetry; and to encourage poet members. State-wide organization open to anyone interested in poetry. Currently has 151 total members. Offerings available for poets include 2 conventions each year, and membership in NFSPS. Sponsors conferences, workshops. Sponsors The Poets Rendezvous Contest. Offers $1,000 in prizes for poems in 25 categories. Entry fee: $5. Deadline: August 15. Sponsors the Poets Winters Forum and The Poets Summer Stanzas contests, with prizes of $25, $15 and $10 with 3 honorable mentions. Entry fee: $1/poem. Deadlines: January 15 and June 15 (respectively). Send SASE for details. Competitions receive 150-200 entries. Publishes *Indiana Poet*, a bimonthly newsletter. Members or nationally known writers give readings that are open to the public. Sponsors open-mike readings. Membership dues are $10/year (includes national membership). Members meet monthly in various local clubs. Send SASE for additional information.

☑ **INTERNATIONAL WOMEN'S WRITING GUILD**, P.O. Box 810, Gracie Station, New York NY 10028, phone (212)737-7536, fax (212)737-9469, e-mail dirhahn@aol.com, website http://www.iwwg.com, founded 1976, "a network for the personal and professional empowerment of women through writing." The Guild publishes a bimonthly 32-page newsletter, *Network*, which includes members' needs, achievements, contests, and publishing information. A manuscript referral service introduces members to literary agents. Other activities and benefits are annual national and regional events, including a summer conference at Skidmore College (see listing under Conferences and Workshops); "regional clusters" (independent regional groups); round robin manuscript exchanges; and group health insurance. Membership in the nonprofit Guild costs $35/year in the US and $45/year foreign.

N: IOWA POETRY ASSOCIATION, 2325 61st St., Des Moines IA 50322, phone (515)279-1106, editor Lucille Morgan Wilson. Founded in 1945 "to encourage and improve the quality of poetry written by Iowans of all ages." Statewide organization open to "anyone interested in poetry, with a residence or valid address in the state of Iowa." Currently has over 400 total members. Levels of membership available include Regular and Patron ("same services, but patron members contribute to cost of running the association"). Offerings available for poets include "semiannual workshops to which a poem may be sent in advance for critique; annual contest—also open to nonmembers—with no entry fee; IPA Newsletter, published 5 or 6 times a year, including a quarterly national publication listing of contest opportunities; and a annual poetry anthology, *Lyrical Iowa*, containing prize-winning and high-ranking poems from contest entries, available for purchase at production cost plus postage. No requirement for purchase to insure publication." Membership dues are $6/year (Regular); $10 or more/year (Patron). "Semiannual workshops are the only 'meetings' of the Association." Send SASE for additional information (Iowa residents only).

☑ **JUST BUFFALO LITERARY CENTER**, 2495 Main St., Buffalo NY 14214, phone (716)832-5400, fax (716)832-5710, e-mail justbflo@aol.com, executive director Ed Taylor, founded 1975. It offers readings, workshops, master classes, an annual competition for Western New York writers, Spoken Arts Radio broadcasts on National Public Radio affiliate WBFO, and Writers-in-Education programs for school-age populations. Just Buffalo acts as a clearinghouse for literary events in the Greater Buffalo area and offers diverse services to writers and to the WNY region. "Although we are not accepting submissions for publication, we will review works for possible readings."

THE KENTUCKY STATE POETRY SOCIETY; PEGASUS; KSPS NEWSLETTER, 3289 Hunting Hills Dr., Lexington KY 40515, contact/editor Miriam Woolfolk. Founded in 1966 to promote interest in writing poetry, improve skills in writing poetry, present poetry readings and poetry workshops, and publish poetry. Regional organization open to all. Current membership about 250. Affiliated with The National Federation of State Poetry Societies. Offerings available for poets include association with other poets, information on contests and poetry happenings across the state and nation; annual state and national contests; national and state annual conventions with workshops, selected speakers and open poetry readings. Sponsors workshops, contests, awards. Membership includes the bimonthly *KSPS Newsletter*. Also includes a quarterly newsletter, STROPHES, of the NFSPS; and the KSPS journal, PEGASUS, published 3 times yearly: a spring/summer and fall/winter issue which solicits good poetry for publication, and a Prize Poems issue of 1st Place contest winners in over 40 categories. Members or nationally-known writers give readings that are open to the public. Dues for students $5; adults $15; senior adults $10. Other categories: Life; Patron; Benefactor. The 1999 annual Awards Weekend/Workshop is planned for October at Jenny Wiley State Park, Kentucky. Send SASE for additional information.

■■ THE LEAGUE OF CANADIAN POETS; POETS IN THE CLASSROOM; WHO'S WHO IN THE LEAGUE OF CANADIAN POETS; POETRY MARKETS FOR CANADIANS; LIVING ARCHIVES SERIES; NATIONAL POETRY CONTEST; GERALD LAMPERT MEMORIAL AWARD; PAT LOWTHER MEMORIAL AWARD; CANADIAN YOUTH POETRY COMPETITION, 54 Wolseley, 3rd Floor, Toronto, Ontario M5T 1A5 Canada, phone (416)504-1657, fax (416)504-0096, e-mail league@ican.net, website http://www.poets.ca, contact Edita Petrauskaite, founded 1966. The League's aims are the advancement of poetry in Canada and promotion of the interests of professional, Canadian poets. Information on full, associate student and supporting membership can be obtained via e-mail, website or by sending a SASE for the brochure, League of Canadian Poets: Services and Membership. The League publishes 6 newsletters; *Poets in the Classroom*, on teaching poetry to children; a directory called *Who's Who in The League of Canadian Poets* that contains 1 page of information, including a picture, bio, publications and "what critics say" about each of the members; Living Archives Series, chapbooks of feminist studies in Canada; and *Poetry Markets for Canadians* which covers contracts, markets, agents and more. The League's members go on reading tours, and the League encourages them to speak on any facet of Canadian literature at schools and universities, libraries or organizations. The League has arranged "thousands of readings in every part of Canada"; they are now arranging exchange visits featuring the leading poets of such countries as Great Britain, Germany and the US. The League sponsors a National Poetry Contest with prizes of $1,000, $750 and $500; the best 50 poems published in a book. Deadline: January 31. Entry fee: $6/poem. Poems should be unpublished, under 75 lines and typed. Names and addresses should *not* appear on poems but on a separate covering sheet. Please send SASE for complete rules, info on judges, etc. Open to Canadian citizens or landed immigrants only. The Gerald Lampert Memorial Award of $1,000 is for a first book of poetry written by a Canadian, published professionally. The Pat Lowther Memorial Award of $1,000 is for a book of poetry written by a Canadian woman and published professionally. Write for entry forms. The league also sponsors a Canadian chapbook manuscript competition with prizes of $1,000, $750 and $500. Submit 15-24 pg. ms with $12 entry fee. Deadline: March 1. Also sponsors The Canadian Youth Poetry Competition. Prizes: $250, $350, $500. Deadline: March 1. Contact the League for full guidelines. "The League markets members books through a direct mail flyer."

MAINE WRITERS & PUBLISHERS ALLIANCE, 12 Pleasant St., Brunswick ME 04011-2201, phone (207)729-6333, fax (207)725-1014, founded 1975, program director Jill Shultz. This organization is "a nonprofit organization dedicated to promoting the value of literature and the art of writing by building a community of writers, readers, and publishers within Maine. Our membership currently includes over 1,500 writers, publishers, librarians, teachers, booksellers and readers from across Maine and the nation." For an individual contribution of $35 per year members receive discounts on MWPA programs and books, and *Maine in Print*, a monthly compilation of calendar events, updated markets, book annotations, interviews with Maine authors and publishers, articles about writing and more. The alliance distributes selected books about Maine and by Maine authors and publishers, and it maintains a bookstore and reference library at its office in Brunswick. "We also have extensive writing and publishing workshops and offer an annual fall writing retreat."

■■ **MANITOBA WRITERS' GUILD INC.**, 206-100 Arthur St., Winnipeg, Manitoba R3B 1H3 Canada, phone (204)942-6134, fax (204)942-5754, e-mail mbwriter@escape.ca, website http://www.mbwriter.mb.ca. Founded in 1981 to "promote and advance the art of writing, in all its forms, throughout the province of Manitoba." Regional organization open to "any individual with an interest in the art of writing." Currently has 430-500 members. Levels of membership are Regular and Student/Senior/Fixed income. Programs and services include: the Manitoba Workshop Series, intensive one-day sessions conducted by professional writers; Open Workshops, monthly sessions held in the fall and winter; an Annual Spring Conference, a 1-day event which includes panel discussions, readings, performances and special events; the Mentor Program, a limited number of promising writers selected to work one-on-one with experienced mentors; the Manitoba Literary Awards which include the McNally Robinson Book of the Year Award and the John Hirsch Award for Most Promising Manitoba Writer, all awards are to "recognize and celebrate excellence in Manitoba writing and publishing"; the Café Reading Series, a weekly series showcasing emerging and established local writers; the Writers' Resource Centre, containing information about writing, publishing, markets, as well as Canadian periodicals and books by Manitoba authors; and a studio offering writers comfortable, private work space. Also now sponsors the Winnipeg International Writers Festival in the fall. Published 6 times/year, their newsletter, *WordWrap*, includes feature articles, regular columns, information on current markets and competitions, and profiles of Manitoba writers. They also publish *The Writers' Handbook*, the Guild's "comprehensive resource manual on the business of writing." Membership fees are $40 Regular, $20 Student/Senior/Fixed Income. Send SASE for additional information.

MASSACHUSETTS STATE POETRY SOCIETY, INC.; BAY STATE ECHO; THE NATIONAL POETRY DAY CONTEST; THE GERTRUDE DOLE MEMORIAL CONTEST, 64 Harrison Ave., Lynn MA 01905, president Jeanette C. Maes. Founded in 1959, dedicated to the writing and appreciation of poetry and promoting the art form. State-wide organization open to anyone with an interest in poetry. Currently has 200 total members. Offerings available for poets include critique groups. Sponsors workshops, contests. Sponsors The National Poetry Day Contest, with prizes of $25, $15 and $10 (or higher) for each of 30 categories. Entry fee: $5. Deadline: August 1. Competition receives approximately 1,800 entries a year. Also sponsors The Gertrude Dole Memorial Contest, with prizes of $25, $15 and $10. Entry fee: $3. Deadline: March 1. Also sponsors the

Poet's Choice Contest, with prizes of $50, $25 and $15. Entry fee: $3/poem. Deadline: November 1, 1999. Send SASE for guidelines. Competitions receive 300-500 entries a year. Publishes a yearly anthology of poetry and a yearly publication of student poetry contest winners. Publishes *Bay State Echo*, a newsletter, 5 times/year. Members or nationally-known writers give readings that are open to the public. Sponsors open-mike readings. Membership dues are $10/year. Members meet 5 times/year. Send SASE for additional information.

MOUNTAIN WRITERS SERIES, Mountain Writers Center, 3624 SE Milwaukee Ave., Portland OR 97202, phone (503)236-4854, fax (503)232-4517, e-mail pdxmws@aol.com, website http://www.frii.com/~pdx.mws, associate director Meredith Martin. Founded in 1973/1993, "Mountain writers series is an independent non-profit organization dedicated to supporting writers, audiences and other sponsors by promoting literature and literacy through artistic and educational literary arts events in the Pacific Northwest." The Center is open to both members and nonmembers. Currently has about 200 total members. Levels of membership available are Contributing ($100), Supporting ($500), Patron ($1,000), Basic ($50), Student/Retired ($25) and Family ($75). "Poets have access to our extensive poetry library, resource center and space as well as discounts to most events. Members receive a seasonal newsletter as well. Poets may attend one-day workshops, weekend master classes, five-week and ten-week courses about writing." Authors who participated in 1998-99 season were Sabreay Kinnell, Stephen Dobyns, Marilyn Nelson, Donald Hall, Lucille Clifton and James Tate. "The Mountain Writers Center is an 100-year-old Victorian house with plenty of comfortable gathering space, a reading room, visiting writers room, library, resource center, garden and Mountain Writers Series offices." Sponsors conferences/workshops. Publishes the *Mountain Writers Center Newsletter*. Also available to nonmembers for $12/year. Sponsors readings that are open to the public. "Nationally and internationally known writers are sponsored by the Mountain Writers Series Northwest Regional Residencies Program (reading tours) and the campus readings program (Pulitzer Prize winners, Nobel Prize winners, MacArthur Fellows, etc.). Send SASE for additional information or visit website. Inquiries via fax and e-mail OK.

NATIONAL FEDERATION OF STATE POETRY SOCIETIES, INC.; STEVEN'S MANUSCRIPT COMPETITION, Membership Chairperson: Sy Swann, 2712 Scott Ave., Ft. Worth TX 76103, phone (817)535-7304 or (605)768-2127, fax (817)531-6593, e-mail JFS@flash.net, contest chairperson Claire Van Breeman Downes, 1206 13th Ave. SE, St. Cloud MN 56304. Founded in 1959, "NFSPS is a nonprofit organization exclusively educational and literary. Its purpose is to recognize the importance of poetry with respect to national cultural heritage. It is dedicated solely to the furtherance of poetry on the national level and serves to unite poets in the bonds of fellowship and understanding." Any poetry group located in a state not already affiliated but interested in affiliating with NFSPS may contact the membership chairperson. Canadian groups may also apply. "In a state where no valid group exists, help may also be obtained by individuals interested in organizing a poetry group for affiliation." Most reputable state poetry societies are members of the National Federation and advertise their various poetry contests through the quarterly bulletin, *Strophes*, available for SASE and $1, editor Linda Banks, 2912 Falls Church Lane, Mesquite, TX 75149. Beware of organizations calling themselves state poetry societies (however named) that are not members of NFSPS, as such labels are sometimes used by vanity schemes trying to sound respectable. Others, such as the Oregon State Poetry Association, are quite reputable, but they don't belong to NFSPS. NFSPS holds an annual meeting in a different city each year with a large awards banquet, addressed by a renowned poet and writer. They sponsor 50 national contests in various categories each year, including the NFSPS Prize of $1,500 for 1st Prize; $500, 2nd; $250, 3rd; with entry fees ($3 for the entire contest for members, $5 for NFSPS Award; $1/poem for nonmembers and $5 for NFSPS Award, up to 4 poems/ entry). All poems winning over $15 are published in their anthology *ENCORE*. Rules for all contests are given in a brochure available from Linda Banks at *Strophes* or Claire Van Breeman Downes at the address above; you can also write for the address of your state poetry society. They also sponsor the annual Steven's Manuscript Competition with a 1st Prize of $1,000 and publication, 2nd Prize $500; October 1 deadline; contact Amy Zook, 3520 St. Rd. 56, Mechanicsburg OH 43044. Scholarship information is available from Pj Doyle, 4242 Stevens Ave., Minneapolis MN 55409. Inquiries via fax and e-mail OK.

THE NATIONAL POETRY FOUNDATION; SAGETRIEB; PAIDEUMA, University of Maine, 5752 Neville Hall, Room 302, Orono ME 04469-5752, phone (207)581-3813, e-mail sapiel@maine.edu, website http://www.ume.maine.edu/~npf/, contact publications coordinator. "The NPF is a nonprofit organization concerned with publishing scholarship on the work of 20th century poets, particularly Ezra Pound and those in the Imagist/ Objectivist tradition. We publish *Paideuma*, a journal devoted to Ezra Pound scholarship, and *Sagetrieb*, a journal devoted to poets in the imagist/objectivist tradition, as well as books on and of poetry. NPF occasionally conducts a summer conference." Sample copies: $8.95 for *Paideuma* or *Sagetrieb*. Send SASE for information or obtain via e-mail or website.

☑ **NATIONAL WRITERS ASSOCIATION; AUTHORSHIP**, 3140 S. Peoria, #295, Aurora CO 80014, phone (303)841-0246, fax (303)751-8593, executive director Sandy Whelchel, founded 1937. National organization with regional affiliations open to writers. Currently has 3,000 total members. Levels of membership available are Published Writers and Other Writers. They have an annual Summer Conference where workshops/panels etc. are available to all attendees, including poets. Also offer a yearly poetry writing contest with cash awards of $100, $50 and $25. Entry fee: $10/poem. Deadline: October 1. Send SASE for judging sheet copies. Publishes

Authorship, an annual magazine. Also available to nonmembers for $18. Memberships dues are Professional $85; others $65. Members meet monthly. Send SASE for additional information. Contest forms available on website.

☑ **NATIONAL WRITERS UNION**, 113 University Place, 6th Floor, New York NY 10003, phone (212)254-0279, e-mail nwu@nwu.org, website http://www.nwu.org, contact Corrina Marshall. Offers members such services as a grievance committee, contract guidelines, health insurance, press credentials, car rental discounts, and caucuses and trade groups for exchange of information about special markets. Members receive *The American Writer*, the organization's newsletter. Membership is $90 for those earning less than $5,000/year; $145 for those earning $5,000-25,000; and $195 for those earning more than $25,000.

☑ **NEVADA POETRY SOCIETY; NEVADA NATIONAL POETRY CONTEST**, P.O. Box 7014, Reno NV 89510, phone/fax (702)323-5345, president Gordon Holladay. Founded in 1976 to encourage the writing and critiquing of poetry. State-wide organization. Currently has 30 total members. Levels of membership available are Active and Emeritus. Offerings available for poets include membership in the National Federation of State Poetry Societies, including their publication *Strophes*; monthly challenges followed by critiquing of all new poems; distribution of contest fliers; lessons on types of poetry. Sponsors contests. "We sponsor an annual Nevada National Poetry Contest with $500 in prizes." Competition receives approximately 300 entries. Members of the society are occasionally called upon to read to organizations or in public meetings. Membership dues are $10 (this includes membership in NFSPS). Members meet monthly. "We advise poets to enter their poems in contests before thinking about publication." Inquiries via fax OK.

☑ **NEW ENGLAND POETRY CLUB**, Box 330, Cambridge MA 02140, president Diana Der-Hovanessian, founded in 1915 by Amy Lowell, Robert Frost and Conrad Aiken to "bring the best poets to the area and foster fellowship among writers." National organization open to beginning poets, professional poets and teachers of poetry. Currently has 500 members. Offerings available for poets include a newsletter with poetry information, free admission to readings and contests and free participation in workshops. Nationally known writers regularly give readings that are open to the public. Sponsors open-mike readings for members only. Membership dues are $20. Readings and workshops are held monthly. Of the 12 contests they sponsor, 9 are open to nonmembers for an entry fee of $10/3 poems. Entries must be original, unpublished poems in English. Also sponsors the Daniel Varoujan Award. Submit 2 copies of each poem. Deadline: June 30. Most recent winner was A. Susan Manchester. Judge for the last award was Peter Liotta. Winner is announced in October. Send SASE for details or membership information to Victor Howes, 137 West Newton St., Boston MA 02118. Other recent contest winners include Mary Oliver (Golden Rose Award) and Maria Gillan (May Sarton Award).

☑ **NEW HAMPSHIRE WRITERS' PROJECT**, P.O. Box 2693, Concord NH 03302-2693, phone (603)226-6649, fax (603)226-0035, e-mail nhwp@ultranet.com, website http://orbit.unh.edu/NHWP, executive director Jackie Bonafide. Founded in 1988 "to foster the literary arts community in New Hampshire, to serve as a resource for and about New Hampshire writers, to support the development of individual writers, and to encourage an audience for literature in New Hampshire." State-wide organization open to anyone. Currently has 750 members. Offerings specifically available for poets include workshops, seminars and information about poetry readings held throughout northern New England. Sponsors day-long workshops and 4- to 6-week intensive courses. Also sponsors a biennial award for outstanding literary achievement. Publishes *Ex Libris*, a bimonthly newsletter for members only. Members and nationally known writers give readings that are open to the public. Also sponsors open-mike readings. Membership dues are $35/year; $20/year for Seniors and students. Members meet annually. Send SASE for additional information. Inquiries via fax and e-mail OK. Website includes updated calendar of events, articles of interest to writers, links to author's homepages and information about NHWP.

☑ **THE NORTH CAROLINA POETRY SOCIETY; BROCKMAN/CAMPBELL BOOK AWARD CONTEST**, 555 E. Connecticut Ave., Southern Pines NC 28387, phone/fax (843)527-8669, e-mail bluesue@sc-coast.net, website http://ww2.esn.net/~poetry, president Susan Meyers. Founded in 1932 to "foster the writing of poetry; to bring together in meetings of mutual interest and fellowship the poets of North Carolina; to encourage the study, writing, and publication of poetry; and to develop a public taste for the reading and appreciation of poetry." State-wide organization open to "all interested persons." Levels of membership available are Regular ($20/year) and Student ($5/year). NCPS conducts 3 general meetings and numerous statewide workshops each year, sponsors annual poetry contests with categories for adults and students (open to anyone, with small fee for nonmembers; December/January deadline; cash prizes), publishes the contest-winning poems in the annual book *Award Winning Poems*; publishes a newsletter and supports other poetry activities. They also sponsor the annual Brockman/Campbell Book Award Contest for a book of poetry (over 20 pgs.) by a North Carolina poet (native-born or current resident for 3 years). $100 cash prize and a Revere-style bowl is awarded. $5 entry fee for nonmembers. Deadline: May 1. Competitions receive 300 entries a year. Most recent contest winners include James Applewhite, Kathryn Kirkpatrick and Deborah Pope. For details, send SASE to Sharon A. Sharp, P.O. Box 3345, Boone NC 28607. Inquiries via e-mail OK. For membership information, send SASE or visit website. Website includes information/resources for poets message board; poems; information on meetings, workshops, contests, etc.; poetry links.

NORTH CAROLINA WRITERS' NETWORK; THE NETWORK NEWS; NORTH CAROLINA'S LITERARY RESOURCE GUIDE; RANDALL JARRELL POETRY PRIZE, P.O. Box 954, Carrboro NC 27510, phone (919)967-9540, fax (919)929-0535, e-mail bobbiecp@ncwriters.org, website http://www.ncwriters.org/, program & services director Bobbie Collins-Perry, founded in 1985. Supports the work of writers, writers' organizations, independent bookstores, little magazines and small presses, and literary programming statewide. $35 membership dues annually brings members *The Network News*, a 28-page bimonthly newsletter containing organizational news, national market information and other literary material of interest to writers, and access to the Resource Center, other writers, workshops, conferences, readings and competitions, and a critiquing service. 1,700 members nationwide. They also publish the *North Carolina's Literary Resource Guide*, an annual including information about retreats, fellowships, markets, writers groups, conferences, agents and literary organizations. Available for $8 members/$10 nonmembers. Annual fall conference features nationally-known writers, publishers and editors. It is held in a different North Carolina location each year in November. Sponsors competitions in short fiction, nonfiction essays and chapbooks of poetry for North Carolinians and members. Also sponsors 3 international competitions: Randall Jarrell Poetry Prize, Thomas Wolfe Fiction Prize and Paul Green Playwrights Prize. The Randall Jarrell Poetry Prize annually awards $1,000, reading and reception in Greensboro, NC, and publication in *Parnassus: Poetry in Review*. Submissions must be unpublished. Entry fee: $7. Deadline: November 1. Competitions receive 600-800 entries a year. Most recent poetry contest winner was Lia Purpura (1998). Winner announced in February. Send SASE for guidelines. Website includes complete information about NCWN and all its programs and services.

THE OREGON STATE POETRY ASSOCIATION, % President David Hedges, P.O. Box 602, West Linn OR 97068, phone (503)655-1274; website http://www.peak.org/~ospa, treasurer Marg Petersen, 3284 SW Knollbrook, Corvallis OR 97333, phone (541)753-6310. Founded in 1936 for "the promotion and creation of poetry," the association has over 400 members, $18 dues, publishes a quarterly *OSPA Newsletter*, and sponsors contests twice yearly, October and April, with total cash prizes of $700 each (no entry fee to members, $3/poem for nonmembers; out-of-state entries welcome). Themes and categories vary; special category for New Poets. Competition receives 1,400 entries a year. Most recent contest winners include Elizabeth McLagen, Rita Z. Mazur, June Foye, Linda Elegant, Elissa A.L. Gordon, Susan Claton-Goldner, G.L. Morrison and Amanda Bonds. For details write to OSPA, contest chair Joan Henson, 6071 SW Prosperity Park Rd., Tualatin OR 97062, phone (503)638-7488 after July 1 and January 15 each year. The association, a member of the National Federation of State Poetry Societies, Inc. (NFSPS), sponsors workshops, readings and seminars around the state.

OZARK POETS AND WRITERS COLLECTIVE, P.O. Box 3717, Fayetteville AR 72702, phone (501)443-7575 or 521-0119, e-mail poemedy@aol.com or bjmoossy@aol.com, website http://www.uark.edu/ALADDIN/opwc, co-chairpersons Lisa Martinovic and Brenda J. Moossy. Founded reading series in 1993, incorporated in 1995, "to support and promote community involvement in Ozark literary arts; to encourage an appreciation of local writers by providing access to their work through readings, publications, workshops and other events; to ensure that the experience of writing and reading remain a vital part of life in the Ozarks." Regional organization open to any interested poets and writers. "Most participants come from the Ozarks, which encompasses parts of Arkansas, Missouri and Oklahoma." Offerings available for poets include slams with cash prizes and reading series and open mic. "OPWC also runs a weekly column in the *Northwest Arkansas Times* with space to showcase local and not so local poets, provide information about upcoming readers and events, and invite comment about the feast of poetry and all its flavors. *The Fayetteville Free Weekly* runs a monthly column showcasing the monthly featured reader." Nationally and locally known writers give readings that are open to the public. The readings are held on the last Wednesday of each month and are immediately followed by an open-mike session. "Our slams are held on the second Wednesday of every month. Poets on Tour, the performing arm of the OPWC, is available for performances nationwide. They were recently added to the Arts on Tour Roster of the Arkansas Arts Council, becoming the first performance poetry troupe to do so." Board members meet quarterly; interested poets and writers may attend the meetings. Send SASE for additional information. Inquiries via e-mail OK. Website includes listings of current events and samples of members' poetry.

PEN AMERICAN CENTER; PEN WRITERS FUND; PEN TRANSLATION PRIZE; GRANTS AND AWARDS, 568 Broadway, New York NY 10012, phone (212)334-1660, website http://www.pen.org. PEN American Center "is the largest of more than 100 centers which comprise International PEN, founded in London in 1921 by John Galsworthy to foster understanding among men and women of letters in all countries. Members of PEN work for freedom of expression wherever it has been endangered, and International PEN is the only worldwide organization of writers and the chief voice of the literary community." Its total membership on all continents is approximately 10,000. The 2,700 members of the American Center include poets, play-

---

🍁 🌐 **SENDING TO A COUNTRY** other than your own? Be sure to send International Reply Coupons (IRCs) instead of stamps for replies or return of your manuscript.

wrights, essayists, editors, novelists (for the original letters in the acronym PEN), as well as translators and those editors and agents who have made a substantial contribution to the literary community. Membership in American PEN includes reciprocal privileges in foreign centers for those traveling abroad. Branch offices are located in Cambridge, Chicago, Portland/Seattle, New Orleans and San Francisco. Among PEN's various activities are public events and symposia, literary awards, assistance to writers in prison and to American writers in need (grants and loans up to $1,000 from PEN Writers Fund). Medical insurance for writers is available to members. The quarterly *PEN Newsletter* is sent to all members and is available to nonmembers by subscription. The PEN Translation Prize is sponsored by the Book-of-the-Month Club, 1 prize each year of $3,000 for works published in the current calendar year. They publish *Grants and Awards* biennially, containing guidelines, deadlines, eligibility requirements and other information about hundreds of grants, awards and competitions for poets and other writers: $15. Send SASE for booklet describing their activities and listing their publications, some of them available free.

PITTSBURGH POETRY EXCHANGE, P.O. Box 4279, Pittsburgh PA 15203, phone (412)481-POEM. Founded in 1974 as a community-based organization for local poets, it functions as a service organization and information exchange, conducting ongoing workshops, readings, forums and other special events. No dues or fees. "Any monetary contributions are voluntary, often from outside sources. We've managed not to let our reach exceed our grasp." Their reading programs are primarily committed to local and area poets, with honorariums of $25-75. They sponsor a minimum of three major events each year in addition to a monthly workshop. Some of these have been reading programs in conjunction with community arts festivals, such as the October South Side Poetry Smorgasbord—a series of readings throughout the evening at different shops (galleries, bookstores). Poets from out of town may contact the exchange for assistance in setting up readings at bookstores to help sell their books. Contact Michael Wurster at the above address or phone number.

THE POETRY LIBRARY, South Bank Center, Royal Festival Hall, London SE1 8XX United Kingdom, phone (0171)921 0943/0664, fax (0171)921 0939, e-mail poetrylibrary@rfh.org.uk, website http://www.poetrylib rary.org.uk, poetry librarian Mary Enright. Founded in 1953 as a "free public library of 20-century poetry. It contains a comprehensive collection of all British poetry published since 1912 and an international collection of poetry from all over the world, either written in, or translated into English. As the United Kingdom's national library for poetry, it offers loan and information service and large collections of poetry magazines, tapes, videos, records, poem posters and cards; also press cuttings and photographs of poets." National center with "open access for all visitors. Those wishing to borrow books and other materials must be residents of U.K." Offerings available for poets include "Library and information service; access to all recently published poetry and to full range of national magazines; only source of international poetry, including magazines; and information on all aspects of poetry." Offers browsing facilities and quieter area for study; listening facilities for poetry on tape, video record and CD. Adjacent to "Voice Box" venue for literature readings. Nationally known writers give readings that are open to the public. "Separate administration for readings in 'The Voice Box'—a year-round program of readings, talks and literature events for all writing. Poetry library does not arrange readings." Send SASE for additional information. Inquiries via fax and e-mail OK. "Our focus is more on published poets than unpublished. No unpublished poems or manuscripts kept or accepted. Donations welcome but please write or call in advance."

POETRY SOCIETY OF AMERICA; POETRY SOCIETY OF AMERICA AWARDS, 15 Gramercy Park, New York NY 10003, phone (212)254-9628, fax (212)673-2352, website http://www.poetrysociety.org, managing director Timothy Donnelly, founded in 1910, is a nonprofit cultural organization in support of poetry and poets, member and nonmember, young and established, which sponsors readings, lectures and workshops both in New York City and around the country. Their Peer Group Workshop is open to all members and meets on a weekly basis. They publish the *PSA Journal*, approximately 40 pgs., letter-sized. The following are open to members only: Alice Fay Di Castagnola Award ($1,000); *Writer Magazine*/Emily Dickinson Award ($250); Cecil Hemley Memorial Award ($500); Lucille Medwick Memorial Award ($500); Lyric Poetry Award ($500). Nonmembers may enter as many of the following contests as they wish, no more than 1 entry for each, for a $5 fee: Louise Louis/Emily F. Bourne Student Poetry Award, $250 for students in grades 9-12; George Bogin Memorial Award, $500 for a selection of 4 to 5 poems which take a stand against oppression; Robert H. Winner Memorial Award, $2,500 for a poem written by a poet over 40, still unpublished or with one book. (All have a deadline of December 21; awards are made at a ceremony and banquet in late spring.) The Society also has 2 book contests open to works submitted by publishers only. They must obtain an entry form, and there is a $10 fee for each book entered. Book awards are: Norma Farber Award, $500 for a first book; William Carlos Williams Award, a purchase prize of $500-1,000 for a book of poetry published by a small, nonprofit or university press, by a permanent resident of the US—translations not eligible. The Shelley Memorial Award of $5,000-7,500 and The Frost Medal $2,500 are by nomination only. For necessary rules and guidelines for their various contests send #10 SASE between October 1 and December 21. Inquiries via fax OK. Rules and awards are subject to change. Membership: $40. Website includes information and calendar for awards and seminars; information on journal; postcards to send; discussion groups, etc.

POETRY SOCIETY OF TENNESSEE; TENNESSEE VOICES, P.O. Box 241986, Memphis TN 38124, corresponding secretary Frances Cowden. Founded in 1953 to promote the reading and writing of fine poetry. State-wide organization. Currently has 125 total members. Levels of membership available are Regular, Student (grades 1-12), Associate (non-TN residents). Sponsors monthly contests for members, 2 student contests each year and 2 annual contests open to everyone. Sponsors annual Mid-South Poetry Festival Contest. Deadline in August. Send SASE in May for guidelines. Publishes an annual volume of prize winning poems available to nonmembers for $10. Publishes *Tennessee Voices*, a newsletter published bimonthly. Members or nationally-known writers give readings that are open to the public. Memberships dues are $20/year. Members meet monthly September through May. Send SASE for additional information.

THE POETRY SOCIETY OF TEXAS; THE BULLETIN, 3005 Stanford, Plano TX 75075, membership chairman Alan Birkelbach. Founded in 1921 to secure fuller public recognition of the art of poetry and to encourage the writing of poetry by its members. State-wide organization. Currently has 600 total members. Levels of membership available are active, associate, sustaining, supporting, benefactors, patrons and student. Offerings available for poets include membership with the National Federation of State Poetry Societies, an annual state conference and NFSPS Convention. Sponsors conferences, workshops, contests and awards. Awards winning poems are published annually in A Book of the Year, with $5,000 in prizes. Competition receives over 5,000 entries. Publishes *The Bulletin* a monthly newsletter. Members or nationally-known writers give readings that are open to the public. Chapters participate in many reading activities. Membership dues are $20 for Active and Associates. Members meet monthly December through June, and October. Send SASE for additional information.

THE POETRY SOCIETY OF VIRGINIA, 4712 Old Dominion Dr., Lynchburg VA 24503-2226, phone (804)386-3138, e-mail eonianone@aol.com, president J. Pendleton Campbell. Founded in 1923 to "encourage excellence in the writing, reading, study and appreciation of poetry." State-wide organization open to "anyone who supports the purpose of the society." Currently has 330 total members. Levels of membership available are Single, Family, Sustaining and Life. Offerings available for poets include annual contest, regional meetings with readings and guest poets. "We have collected published works of past and present poets; located at the library in Richmond." Sponsors annual contest. "There are categories for all poets 18 years of age and older, categories restricted to members only, and categories for school students. There are modest entry fees for poets who are not members of the Society. There are no entry fees for elementary and middle school students." Publishes a newsletter 6 times/year. Also available to nonmembers. Members and nationally known writers give readings that are open to the public. Sponsors open-mike readings. Membership dues are $14, $20 and $250 for Life membership. Members meet in March, April, May, September, October and November. Send SASE for additional information.

POETS & WRITERS, INC. See listing under Publications of Interest.

☑ **POETS HOUSE: THE REED FOUNDATION LIBRARY; THE POETRY PUBLICATION SHOWCASE; DIRECTORY OF AMERICAN POETRY BOOKS; POETRY IN THE BRANCHES; NYC POETRY TEACHER OF THE YEAR**, 72 Spring St., New York NY 10012, phone (212)431-7920, e-mail info@poetshouse.org, website http://www.poetshouse.org, founded 1985, executive director Lee Ellen Briccetti. Poets House is a 35,000-volume (noncirculating) poetry library of books, tapes and literary journals, with reading and writing space available. This comfortably furnished literary center is open to the public year-round. Over 30 annual public events include 1) poetic programs of cross-cultural and interdisciplinary exchange, 2) readings in which distinguished poets discuss and share the work of other poets, 3) workshops and seminars on various topics led by visiting poets, and 4) an annual $1,000 award for the designated NYC Poetry Teacher of the Year. In addition, Poets House continues its collaboration with public library systems, Poetry in The Branches, aimed at bringing poetry into NYC neighborhoods—through collection-building, public programs, seminars for librarians, and poetry workshops for young adults (information available upon request). Finally, in April Poets House hosts the Poetry Publication Showcase—a comprehensive exhibit of the year's new poetry releases from commercial, university, and independent presses across the country. Related Showcase events include receptions, panel discussions, and seminars which are open to the public and of special interest to poets, publishers, booksellers, distributers and reviewers. (Note: Poets House is not a publisher.) Following each Showcase, copies of new titles are added to the library collection and an updated edition of the *Directory of American Poetry Books*—edited by Poets House and available by mail is compiled. "Poets House depends, in part, on tax-deductible contributions of its nationwide members." Membership levels begin at $40/year, and along with other graduated benefits each new or renewing member receives a free copy of the most current directory. Website includes general information about their library, programs and resources; also contains a calendar of events.

☑ **POETS THEATRE**, 30 East Lake Rd., Cohocton NY 14826, e-mail bobrien4@juno.com, website http://www.members.tripod.com/~poetstheatre/index.html, director Beatrice Obrien, founded 1981. Sponsors readings and performances with limited funding from Poets & Writers. For a mostly conservative, rural audience. A featured poet, followed by open reading. Sponsors a summer Poetry Festival and an annual Poets Picnic in September. Meets second Thursday frequently as announced on web page.

POETS-IN-THE-SCHOOLS. Most states have PITS programs that send published poets into classrooms to teach students poetry writing. If you have published poetry widely and have a proven commitment to children, contact your state arts council, Arts-in-Education Dept., or other writing programs in your area to see whether you qualify. Three of the biggest programs are Teachers & Writers Collaborative, Inc., 5 Union Square W., Seventh Floor, New York NY 10003-3306, phone (212)691-6590, website http://www.twc.org, which requires poets in its program have some prior teaching experience; California Poets-in-the-Schools, 870 Market St., Suite 1148, San Francisco CA 94102, phone (415)399-1565, website http://www.cpits.org; and Writers & Artists in the Schools, COMPAS, 304 Landmark Center, 75 W. Fifth St., St. Paul MN 55102, phone (651)292-3254, which includes both Minnesota-based writers and artists in their program.

🌐 ✅ **SCOTTISH POETRY LIBRARY; SCHOOL OF POETS; CRITICAL SERVICE**, 5 Crichton's Close, Edinburgh EH8 8DT Scotland, phone (0131)557-2876, director Tessa Ransford, librarian Penny Duce. A reference information source and free lending library, also lends by post and has a travelling van service lending at schools, prisons and community centres. The library has a computerized catalogue allowing subject-based searches and indexes of poetry and poetry magazines. The collection comprises over 18,000 items of Scottish and international poetry. The School of Poets is open to anyone; "at meetings members divide into small groups in which each participant reads a poem which is then analyzed and discussed." Meetings normally take place at 7:30 p.m. on the first Tuesday of each month at the library. They also offer a Critical Service in which groups of up to 6 poems, not exceeding 200 lines in all, are given critical comment by members of the School: £15 for each critique (with SAE). Publishes the *Scottish Poetry Index*, a multi-volume indexing series, photocopied, spiral-bound, that indexes poetry and poetry-related material in selected Scottish literary magazines from 1952 to present.

SMALL PRESS CENTER/THE CENTER FOR INDEPENDENT PUBLISHING, Society of Mechanics & Tradesmen, 20 W. 44th, New York NY 10036, phone (212)764-7021, fax (212)354-5365, e-mail smallpress@aol.com, website http://www.smallpress.org, director Karin Taylor. Founded in 1984, "the Small Press Center is a nonprofit reference center devoted to publishing and membership organization of small press independent publishers, writers and independent press enthusiasts." National organization open to "any person, company or organization that supports the small press." Currently has 1,200 total members—300 Friends, 900 Publisher Members. Offerings available for poets include workshops, readings, publishing reference center and "support of the organization." Offers "a place in which the public may examine and order the books of independent publishers, free from commercial pressures. The Center is open five days a week." Sponsors conferences/workshops and awards. Quarterly publishes a newsletter. Members give readings that are open to the public. Publisher Membership dues are $75. Writer Membership dues start at $50. Send SASE for additional information. Inquiries via fax and e-mail OK. Website includes general information on the center and information on events.

📰 **SMALL PUBLISHERS ASSOCIATION OF NORTH AMERICA (SPAN)**, P.O. Box 1306, Buena Vista CO 81211, phone (719)395-4790, fax (719)395-8374, e-mail span@spannet.org, website http://www.spannet.org, executive director Marilyn Ross. Founded in 1996 to "advance the image and profits of independent publishers and authors through education and marketing opportunities." Open to "authors, small- to medium-sized publishers and the vendors who serve them." Currently has 1,100 total members. Levels of membership available are regular and associate vendor. Offerings available for poets include marketing ideas. Sponsors annual conference. Publishes *SPAN Connection*, "a 24-page monthly newsletter jam-packed with informative, money-making articles. Also available to nonmembers for $8/issue. Membership dues are $95/year (Regular), $120/year (Associate Vendor). Send SASE for additional information or visit website. Inquiries via fax OK.

SONGWRITERS AND POETS CRITIQUE, 2804 Kingston Ave., Grove City OH 43125, e-mail spcmusic@yahoo.com, website http://www.freeyellow.com/members2/spcmusic, founded in 1985 by Ellis Cordle, treasurer Pat Adcock. A nonprofit association whose purpose is to serve songwriters, poets and musicians in their area. The president of the organization says, "We have over 200 members from the U.S. and Canada at several levels of ability from novice to advanced, and try to help and support each other with the craft and the business of poetry and songs. We have published writers and recorded artists. We share information about how to pitch, send and package a demo and who to send it to. We also have a songwriting contest for member writers." Annual dues are $25. For more information send a #10 SASE, e-mail or visit website. Website includes upcoming events, newsletters, membership application, members' winning songs and poems (in Real Audio format), and links.

📰 **SOUTH CAROLINA WRITERS WORKSHOP**, P.O. Box 7104, Columbia SC 29202, phone (803)787-9948, SCWW board member Bonny Millard. Founded in 1990 "to offer writers a wide range of opportunities to improve their writing, network with others, and gain practical 'how to' information about getting published." Statewide organization open to all writers. Currently has 169 total members. Offerings available for poets include "chapter meetings where members give readings and receive critiques; *The Quill*, SCWW's bimonthly newsletter which features writing competitions and publishing opportunities; an annual conference with registration discount for members; two free seminars each year; and an annual anthology featuring members' work." Chapters meet in libraries, bookstores and public buildings. Sponsors 3-day annual conference at Myrtle Beach and literary

Get America's #1 Poetry Resource Delivered to Your Door—and Save!

Completely Updated Each Year

100% UPDATED!

POET'S MARKET

1,800 PLACES TO PUBLISH YOUR POETRY

- 300 new publishing opportunities
- 1,000+ journals & magazines
- 200+ chapbook publishers
- 500 book publishers
- 200+ contests
- 1,200 phone numbers
- 600+ e-mail addresses & websites

FROM THE PUBLISHER OF WRITER'S MARKET

SUBMISSION GUIDELINES, CONTACT NAMES & REPORTING TIMES

Finding the right outlets for your poetry is crucial to publishing success. With constant changes in the industry, it's not always easy to stay informed. That's why every year poets trust the newest edition of *Poet's Market* for the most up-to-date information on the people and places that will get their poetry published (over 1,800 editors and publishers are included). This definitive resource also features insider tips from successful poets and editors that will further increase publishing opportunities.

2001 Poet's Market will be published and ready for shipment in August 2000.

Through this special offer, you can get the *2001 Poet's Market* at the 2000 price—just $23.99. Order today and save!
10665/$23.99/608 pgs/pb

Turn Over for More Great Books to Help Get Your Poems Published!

☐ **Yes!** I want the 2001 edition of *Poet's Market* at the 2000 price—$23.99. (Note the *2001 Poet's Market* will be ready for shipment in August 2000.) #10665

Additional books from the back of this card:

Book	Price
#	$
#	$
#	$
#	$
Subtotal	$

*Add $3.50 postage and handling for one book; $1.50 for each additional book.

Postage & Handling	$

Payment must accompany order. Ohioans add 6% sales tax. Canadians add 7% GST.

Total	$

VISA/MasterCard orders call
TOLL FREE 1-800-289-0963
8:30 to 5:00 Mon.-Fri. Eastern Time
or FAX 1-888-590-4082

☐ Payment enclosed $_____ (or)

Charge my: ☐ Visa ☐ MasterCard Exp._____

Account #_____

Signature_____

Name_____

Address_____

City_____

State/Prov._____ Zip/PC _____

30-Day Money Back Guarantee on every book you buy!

☐ **FREE CATALOG!** Ask your bookstore about other fine Writer's Digest Books, or mail this card today for a complete catalog.

6560

Mail to: Writer's Digest Books • 1507 Dana Avenue • Cincinnati, OH 45207

More Great Books to Help You Write and Sell Your Poetry!

NEW!
Writing Personal Poetry
by Sheila Bender
Using this warm, encouraging instruction, you'll learn how to peel away your inhibitions and get in touch with your deepest feelings, then sculpt rich and meaningful poems. Whether you desire to write first poems, better poems or more poems, this book is designed to help you with a lifelong commitment to poetry.
#10595/$14.99/208 pgs/paperback

NEW!
Word Painting: A Guide to Writing More Descriptively
by Rebecca McClanahan
In this extraordinary guide instruction is combined with engaging word exercises to help elevate your writing to a new level of richness and clarity. You also find 75 creativity exercises and examples from award-winning writers.
#10598/$18.99/256 pgs

You Can Write Poetry
by Jeff Mock
Discover how to express your thoughts and feelings using the rich, descriptive language of poetry. Through dozens of examples and "practice sessions," you'll learn about poetry's styles and structures, then create your own poems filled with texture and emotion.
#10571/$12.99/128 pgs/paperback

The Art & Craft of Poetry
by Michael J. Bugeja
Nurture your poetry-writing skills with inspiration and insight from the masters of the past and present. From idea generation to methods of expression, you'll find everything you need to create well-crafted poetry!
#10392/$19.99/352 pgs

Creating Poetry
by John Drury
Definitions, examples, and hands-on exercises show you how to use language text, subject matter, free and measured verse, imagery, and metaphor to create your own wonderful works!
#10209/$18.99/224 pgs

The Poet's Handbook
by Judson Jerome
With expert instruction, you'll unlock the secrets of using figurative language, symbols, and concrete images. Plus, you'll discover the requirements for lyric, narrative, dramatic, didactic, and satirical poetry!
#01836/$14.99/224 pgs/paperback

The Poetry Dictionary
by John Drury
This comprehensive book uncovers the rich and complex language of poetry with clear, working definitions. Several different poems are used to demonstrate the evolution of the form, making *The Poetry Dictionary* a unique anthology.
It's a guide to the poetry of today and yesterday, with intriguing hints as to what tomorrow holds.
#48007/$18.99/352 pgs

Books are available at your local bookstore, or directly from the publisher using the order card on the reverse.

competitions in poetry, fiction and nonfiction. Membership dues are $50/year. Members meet monthly. Send SASE for additional information.

N SOUTHERN POETRY ASSOCIATION; THE POET'S VOICE, P.O. Box 524, Pass Christian MS 39571, e-mail southpoets@aol.com, website http://www.southernpoetry.com, founded 1986, poetry editor Mildred Klyce. SPA offers networking, publishing, free critique service for members through Round Robin Groups and assistance in publishing chapbooks. $12 annual membership fee includes *The Poet's Voice* quarterly newsletter. The association sponsors a number of contests, including Voices of the South, Yarn Spinner, Poetry in Motion, Special People; some are for members only; some, such as the Voices of the South Contest, are open to all. High-scoring poems are published in an anthology (which the poet is not required to purchase). Send #10 SAE with 64¢ postage for details. *The Poet's Voice* contains poetry book reviews, articles on great poets of the past, current activities, input from SPA members and contest winning poems. "We have been nominated to receive the 1996 Mississippi State Governor's Award for Excellence in the Arts for our work with senior citizens, students and prison inmates. This is the 6th year SPA has been nominated." Also sponsors *The Poet's Voice* Poetry Contest. Send SASE or visit website for guidelines. Also publishes the *SPW Writer's Handbook*, 46 pgs., 5½ × 8½, perfect-bound, $8.95, "This book is filled to the brim with helpful tips and many answers to questions often asked by writers. This basic reference book is a guide to important aspects of writing such as: copyright, pen names, legal rights, query letters, manuscript preparation, and much more." Website includes poetry, contests, book reviews, information about our Student Writing Program and many other interesting features.

THE THURBER HOUSE; JAMES THURBER WRITER-IN-RESIDENCE, 77 Jefferson Ave., Columbus OH 43215, phone (614)464-1032, fax (614)228-7445, officially opened in 1984. Listed on the National Register of Historic Places, The Thurber House is a literary center, bookstore and museum of Thurber materials. Programs include writing classes for children, author readings, Thurber celebrations and an art gallery. The Thurber House sponsors a writer-in-residence program that brings 2 journalists, a playwright, a poet or a fiction writer to spend a season living and writing in The Thurber House while teaching a course at The Ohio State University. Each writer will receive a stipend and housing in the third-floor apartment of Thurber's boyhood home. Please send a letter of interest and a curriculum vitae to Michael J. Rosen, literary director before December 15. Please note that The Thurber House is *not* a publishing house and does not accept unsolicited material. No inquiries via e-mail. Inquiries via fax OK.

✓ UNIVERSITY OF ARIZONA POETRY CENTER, 1216 N. Cherry Ave., Tucson AZ 85721-0410, phone (520)321-7760, fax (520)621-5566, e-mail poetry@u.arizona.edu, website http://www.coh.arizona.edu/poetry/, director Alison Deming. Founded in 1960 "to maintain and cherish the spirit of poetry." Open to the public. The Center is located in 2 historic adobe houses near the main campus and contains a nationally acclaimed poetry collection that includes over 30,000 items. Programs and services include: a library with a noncirculating poetry collection and space for small classes, poetry-related meetings and activities; facilities, research support, and referral information about poetry and poets for local and national communities; the Free Public Reading Series, a series of 12 to 18 readings each year featuring poets, fiction writers, and writers of literary nonfiction; a guest house for residencies of visiting writers and for use by other University departments and community literary activities; a 1-month summer residency at the Center's guest house offered each year to an emerging writer selected by jury; and poetry awards, readings, and special events for undergraduate and graduate students. Publishes a biannual newsletter. Send SASE for additional information. "We do not have members, though one can become a 'Friend' through a contribution to our Friends of the Poetry Center account." Inquiries via fax and e-mail OK.

THE UNTERBERG POETRY CENTER OF THE 92ND STREET Y; "DISCOVERY"/THE NATION POETRY CONTEST, 1395 Lexington Ave., New York NY 10128, phone (212)415-5759. Offers annual series of readings by major literary figures (weekly readings October through May), writing workshops, master classes in fiction and poetry, and lectures and literary seminars. Also co-sponsors the "Discovery"/*The Nation* Poetry Contest. Deadline in January. Competition receives approximately 2,000 entries a year. Most recent contest winners include John Poch, Gabriel Gudding, Yerra Sugarman and Martin Walls. Send SASE for information. "No phone queries, please."

UTAH STATE POETRY SOCIETY; POET TREE, Utah Arts Council & NEA, 7685 Dell Rd., Salt Lake City UT 84121-5221, phone (801)943-4211, e-mail rosieo4@juno.com, website http://www.spectre.com/usps, treasurer Rosalyn Ostler. Founded in 1950 to secure a wider appreciation of the poetry arts and to promote excellence in writing poetry. State-wide organization. Membership is open to all citizens of the State of Utah and to interested people from any other state in the union, without consideration of age, race, regional, religious, educational or other backgrounds. Currently has about 250 members. Sponsors conferences, workshops, contests, awards. USPS publishes, biannually, work of members in a chapbook anthology. Publishes *Poet Tree*, a biannual newsletter. Publishes one winning manuscript annually. Members or nationally-known writers give readings/workshops that are open to the public. Chapters meet at least once a month, with open readings, critiques, lessons. Annual Awards Festival includes open reading. Membership dues are $20/year ($15 for students) including membership in National Federation of State Poetry Societies and their newsletter *Strophes*, copy of the Book of the Year and other publications, and full contesting privileges. Send SASE for information. "We welcome all potential members." Website includes general membership information; information on workshops, contests and activities; and a complete online version of *Poet Tree*.

VIRGINIA WRITERS CLUB, P.O. Box 300, Richmond VA 23218, phone (804)648-0357, fax (804)782-2142, editor/administrator Charlie Finley. Founded in 1918 "to promote the art and craft of writing; to serve writers and writing in Virginia." State-wide organization with 7 local chapters open to "any and all writers." Currently has 350 total members. Offerings available for poets include networking with other poets and writers, discussions on getting published, workshops and a newsletter. Publishes *The Virginia Writer*, a newsletter appearing 5 times/year. Nationally known writers give readings that are open to the public. Membership dues are $25/year. Members meet 5 times/year plus workshops and monthly chapter meetings. Send SASE for additional information. Inquiries via fax OK.

☑ **WISCONSIN FELLOWSHIP OF POETS; MUSELETTER**, 1325 Madison St., Lake Geneva WI 53147, e-mail slocumss@gateway.net, vice president Peter Sherrill, president Sheryl Slocum. Founded in 1950 to secure fuller recognition of poetry as one of the important forces making for a higher civilization and to create a finer appreciation of poetry by the public at large. State-wide organization open to current and past residents of Wisconsin who write poetry acceptable to the Credentials Chairperson. Currently has 360 total members. Levels of memberships available are Associate, Active, Student and Life. Sponsors biannual conferences, workshops, contests and awards. Publishes "Wisconsin Poets' Calendar" poems of Wisconsin (resident) poets. Also publishes *Museletter* a quarterly newsletter. Members or nationally-known writers give readings that are open to the public. Sponsors open-mike readings. Membership dues are Active $15, Associate $10, Student $7.50, Life $100. Members meet biannually. Send SASE for additional information to WFOP Vice President Peter Sherrill, 8605 County Rd. D, Forestville WI 54213. Inquiries via e-mail OK.

☑ **WOMEN WHO WRITE INC.**, P.O. Box 652, Madison NJ 07940, phone (973)540-0591, membership chair Pam Greenwood. Founded in 1990 to assist woman writers, beginners and pros alike, with every phase of the writing process, through writing groups, classes, workshops, lectures and panel discussions. To bring the work of women writers into the community through readings, publications and performances. To provide information, encouragement, assistance and a sense of community to women writers who might otherwise write alone or not at all. State-wide organization open to all women interested in writing. Currently has 140 total members. Offerings available for poets include critique groups (mixed genre as well as poets only), courses through local adult schools (reduced tuition to members). Sponsors 3-5 workshops per year, and offer 3-4 courses through adult schools. Publishes *Writer's Notes*, a quarterly newsletter available to nonmembers for $1.50/issue or $5/year. They also publish a literary journal annually, with work submitted by members, selected by a group of editors. Members give readings that are open to the public. Sponsors open-mike readings. Membership dues are $30/year. Members meet twice a month. Send SASE for additional information.

🌐 ☑ **WOMEN WRITERS NETWORK**, % Cathy Smith, Membership Chair, 23 Prospect Rd., London NW2 2JU United Kingdom. Founded in 1985 "to help women writers of all disciplines and experience make contact with other women writers and editors. We provide a forum for exchanging information and support, and offer an ideal base for networking opportunities. Many members are established in their careers with a wealth of experience to share, others are at the beginning stages. We are not a 'writer's circle' but a group formed to help women writers further their professional development." National organization open to all women writers—all disciplines. Currently has 215 total members. Levels of membership available are full memberships and a "newsletter only" membership for overseas and UK members who cannot attend meetings. Offerings available for poets include people contact and occasional speakers. Sponsors conferences/workshops and contests/awards. Publishes the *WWN Newsletter*, "a monthly newsletter with practical tips on markets and editors, highlights of our monthly meeting, articles sharing the experiences of working writers, and updates on all WWN activities." Members and nationally known writers give readings that are open to the public. Membership dues are £30 for full membership, £25 for overseas members. £20 for newsletter only. Members meet monthly. Send SASE for additional information. "WWN was founded by five freelancers who missed regular contact with other professionals. They had a vision of mutual support among women who write for a living. We have grown considerably, but still see ourselves as a friendly, lively, professional group with members from many different spheres, including journalism, fiction, nonfiction, children's writing, poetry, drama, editing, desktop publishing, photography and illustration."

📰 **WORDTECH COMMUNICATIONS**, P.O Box 1204, Cincinnati OH 45254-1204, e-mail wordtech@fuse .net, website http://home.fuse.net/wordtech/services.html, editor Kevin Walzer. Founded in 1998. "We are a production house specializing in helping poets self-publish. The current system of publishing poetry—competitions charging reading fees—needs reform. Our method allows poets to take charge of their own work and deliver their work to an audience at reasonable prices. Whitman and other great poets self-published. Today's poets should not be ashamed to follow their example. Poets should send entire manuscript with SASE and cover letter outlining their background and publishing needs. We will review the manuscript to determine if we can work with the poet. The poet pays for production costs and receives all copies of the book to market. We charge for design, editing, critiquing if requested, and similar services. We keep our costs low to allow poets to recoup their investments. We request a limited number of books—5% of the press run—for archival purposes." Send SASE for additional information.

☑ **WORLD-WIDE WRITERS SERVICE, INC. (3WS); WRITERS INK; WRITERS INK PRESS; WRITERS UNLIMITED AGENCY, INC.**, 233 Mooney Pond Rd., P.O. Box 2344, Selden NY 11784, phone/fax (516)451-0478, director Dr. David B. Axelrod, founded in 1976, Writers Ink Press founded 1978. "World-Wide Writers Service is a literary and speakers' booking agency. With its not-for-profit affiliate, Writers Unlimited Agency, Inc., it presents literary workshops and performances, conferences and other literary services, and publishes through Writers Ink Press, chapbooks and small flat-spined books as well as arts editions. **We publish only by our specific invitation at this time.**" *Writers Ink* is "a sometimes newsletter of events on Long Island, now including programs of our conferences. We welcome news of other presses and poets' activities. Review books of poetry. We fund raise for nonprofit projects and are associates of Long Island Writers Festival and Jeanne Voege Poetry Awards as well as the Key West Poetry Writing, January Workshops and Writing Therapy Trainings throughout the year in various locations. Arts Editions are profit productions employing hand-made papers, bindings, etc. We have editorial services available at small fees ($50 minimum), but only after inquiry and if appropriate. We are currently concentrating on poetry related to, or derived from healing experiences."

THE WRITER'S CENTER; WRITER'S CAROUSEL; POET LORE, 4508 Walsh St., Bethesda MD 20815, phone (301)654-8664, fax (301)654-8667, e-mail postmaster@writer.org, website http://www.writer.org, founder and artistic director Allan Lefcowitz, executive director Jane Fox, founded 1976. This is an outstanding resource for writers not only in Washington DC but in the wider area ranging from southern Pennsylvania to North Carolina and West Virginia. The Center offers 260 multi-meeting workshops each year in writing, word processing, and graphic arts. It is open 7 days a week, 10 hours a day. Some 2,300 members support the center with $30 annual donations, which allows for 7 paid staff members. There is a book gallery at which publications of small presses are displayed and sold. The center's publication, *Writer's Carousel*, is a 24-page magazine that comes out 6 times a year. They also sponsor 80 annual performance events, which include presentations in poetry, fiction and theater. The Center is publisher of *Poet Lore*—110 years old in 1999 (see listing in the Publishers of Poetry section). Their website has news and information about the Washington metropolitan literary community. Inquiries via e-mail OK. No fax inquiries.

⃞ ⃞ **WRITERS' FEDERATION OF NOVA SCOTIA; ATLANTIC POETRY PRIZE; ATLANTIC WRITING COMPETITION; EASTWORD**, 1113 Marginal Rd., Halifax, Nova Scotia B3H 4P7 Canada, phone (902)423-8116, fax (902)422-0881, e-mail writers1@fox.nstn.ca, website http://www.chebucto.ns.ca/Cult ure/WFNS. Founded in 1975 "to foster creative writing and the profession of writing in Nova Scotia; to provide advice and assistance to writers at all stages of their careers; and to encourage greater public recognition of Nova Scotian writers and their achievements." Regional/national organization open to anybody who writes. Currently has 500 total members. Offerings available for poets include resource library with over 1,200 titles, promotional services, workshop series, annual festivals, manuscript reading service, and contract advice. Sponsors the Atlantic Writing Competition, for unpublished works by beginning writers, and the Atlantic Poetry Prize, for the best book of poetry by an Atlantic Canadian. Publishes *Eastword*, a bimonthly newsletter containing "a plethora of information on who's doing what, markets and contests, and current writing events and issues." Send SASE for additional information or obtain via website. Inquiries via fax and e-mail OK.

WRITERS OF KERN, P.O. Box 6694, Bakersfield CA 93386-6694, phone (805)665-0326, fax (805)665-8092, e-mail jasimel@goldstate.net, president James Imel, founded 1993. Writers of Kern is the Bakersfield Branch of the California Writers' Club and is open to "published writers and any person interested in writing." Currently has 58 members. Levels of membership available are professional, writers with published work; writers working toward publication; and students. Membership benefits include "meetings on the third Saturday of every month, with speakers who are authors, agents, etc., on topics pertaining to writing; several critique groups including fiction genres, nonfiction and poetry; a monthly newsletter with marketing tips; and discount to annual conference." Membership dues are $35/year. Send SASE for additional information.

THE WRITERS ROOM, 10 Astor Place, 6th Floor, New York NY 10003, phone (212)254-6995, fax (212)533-6059, website http://www.writersroom.org. Founded in 1978 to provide a "home away from home" for any writer who needs a place to work. It is open 24 hours a day, 7 days a week, offering desk space, storage and comraderie at the rate of $175/quarter. It is supported by the National Endowment for the Arts, the New York City Department of Cultural Affairs and private sector funding. Call for application or download from website.

⃞ **THE WRITERS' UNION OF CANADA**, 24 Ryerson Ave., Toronto, Ontario M5T 2P3 Canada, phone (416)703-8982, fax (416)703-0826, e-mail twuc@the-wire.com, website http://www.swifty.com/twuc, founded 1973. Dedicated to advancing the status of Canadian writers. The Union is devoted to protecting the rights of published authors, defending the freedom to write and publish, and serving its members. National organization. Open to poets who have had a trade book published by a commercial or university press; must be a Canadian citizen or landed immigrant. Currently has 1,290 total members. Offerings available for poets include contact with peers, contract advice/negotiation, grievance support, electronic communication, random royalty audit and ms evaluation service. Sponsors conferences and workshops. Sponsors Annual General Meeting, usually held in May, where members debate and determine Union policy, elect representatives, attend workshops, socialize, and renew friendships with their colleagues from across the country. Publishes *The Writers' Union of Canada Newsletter* 9 times/year. Membership dues are $180/year. Regional reps meet with members when possible. Send SASE (or SAE and IRC) for additional information. For writers not eligible for membership, the Union offers, for a fee: publications on publishing, contracts, awards and more; a Manuscript Evaluation Service for any level writer; Contract Services, including a Self-Help Package, a Contract Evaluation Service, and a Contract Negotiation Service; and three annual writing competitions for developing writers.

Additional Organizations

The following listings also contain information about organizations. See the General Index for page numbers.

Publications of Interest

The publications in this section are designed to help poets with all aspects of writing and publishing poetry. While few are actual markets, many detail new publishing opportunities in addition to providing information on craft, advice on marketing, or interviews with poets and writers.

Poets & Writers Magazine, in fact, is one of the most useful resources for both poets and fiction writers. In addition to informative articles and interviews, it includes calls for submissions and contests and awards. *Writer's Digest*, on the other hand, covers the entire field of writing and features market listings as well as a monthly poetry column by Michael J. Bugeja, author of *The Art and Craft of Poetry* (Writer's Digest Books, 1994) and *Poet's Guide: How to Publish and Perform Your Work* (Story Line Press, 1995).

Other publications, such as *Taproot Reviews*, *Independent Publisher* and *Rain Taxi Review of Books* (both new to this edition), include reviews of poetry books and chapbooks or reviews of small press magazines. These reviews provide further insight into the different markets.

For poets seeking resources more regional in focus, several of the listings in this section are publications that include, among other items, markets, news and events for specific areas of the United States and Canada. For example, *First Draft* publishes information of interest to Alabama writers and *Word: The Literary Calendar* focuses on literary events in Ontario, Canada.

Finally, for those interested in various publishing opportunities, this section also includes information about other market directories as well as materials on self-publishing. And, in addition to the listings that follow, you will find other useful publications noted in Additional Publications of Interest on page 549.

To determine which of these publications may be most useful to you, read sample issues. Many of these books and periodicals may be found in your local library or located on newsstands or in bookstores. If you are unable to locate a certain magazine, order a copy from the publisher. For books, send a SASE with a request for the publisher's catalog or order information.

R.R. BOWKER; LITERARY MARKET PLACE; BOOKS IN PRINT, 121 Chanlon Rd., New Providence NJ 07974, phone (908)464-6800, fax (908)508-7696, e-mail info@bowker.com, website http://www.bowker.com. *LMP* is the major trade directory of publishers and people involved in publishing books. It is available in most libraries, or individual copies may be purchased (published in September each year). *BIP* is another standard reference available in most libraries and bookstores. Bowker publishes a wide range of reference books pertaining to publishing. Write for their catalog.

CANADIAN POETRY, English Dept., University of Western Ontario, London, Ontario N6A 3K7 Canada, phone (519)661-3403, ext. 3403 or 5834, fax (519)661-3776, website http://www.arts.uwo.ca/canpoetry, editor Prof. D.M.R. Bentley, founded 1977. A biannual journal of critical articles, reviews and historical documents (such as interviews). It is a professionally printed, scholarly edited, flat-spined, 150-page journal which pays contributors in copies. Subscription: $15. Sample: $7.50. **Note that they publish no poetry except as quotations in articles.** Also offer Canadian Poetry Press Scholarly Editions, DocuTech printed, perfect-bound, containing scholarship and criticism of Canadian poetry. Send SASE for details.

DUSTBOOKS; INTERNATIONAL DIRECTORY OF LITTLE MAGAZINES AND SMALL PRESSES; DIRECTORY OF POETRY PUBLISHERS; SMALL PRESS REVIEW; SMALL MAGAZINE REVIEW, P.O. Box 100, Paradise CA 95967, phone (530)877-6110, fax (530)877-0222, e-mail dustbooks @telis.org, website http://www.dustbooks.com. Dustbooks publishes a number of books useful to writers. Send SASE for catalog. Among their regular publications, *International Directory* is an annual directory of small presses and literary magazines, over 6,000 entries, a third being magazines, half being book publishers, and the rest being both. There is very detailed information about what these presses and magazines report to be their policies in regard to payment, copyright, format and publishing schedules. *Directory of Poetry Publishers* has similar information for over 2,000 publishers of poetry. *Small Press Review* is a bimonthly magazine, newsprint, carrying current updating of listings in *ID*, small press needs, news, announcements and reviews—a valuable way to stay abreast of the literary marketplace. *Small Magazine Review*, which began publication in June, 1993, is included within *Small Press Review* and covers small press magazines. Inquiries via fax and e-mail OK.

ESSENTIAL MEDIA DISCOUNT COUNTERCULTURE CATALOG, P.O. Box 661245, Los Angeles CA 90066-1245, phone (310)574-1554, fax (310)574-3060, e-mail underground@essentialmedia.com, website http://www.essentialmedia.com, editor Kevin Segall, founded 1996, is a biannual "catalog and guide to the best of alternative culture—fiction, poetry, cult videos, CDs, comics, small press magazines and assorted oddities." Devotes 5% of its pages to poetry. It is 44 pgs., 8½×11, offset printed and saddle-stitched. Reviews books and chapbooks of poetry and other magazines—"we write reviews for everything we carry." Poets may send books for review consideration. Single copy: $2. Inquiries via fax and e-mail OK. Website includes entire catalog.

FIRST DRAFT: THE JOURNAL OF THE ALABAMA WRITERS' FORUM, The Alabama Writers' Forum, Alabama State Council on the Arts, 201 Monroe St., Montgomery AL 36130-1800, phone (334)242-4076 ext. 233, fax (334)240-3269, e-mail awf1@arts.state.al.us, website http://www.writersforum.org, editor Jeanie Thompson, founded 1992, appears 4 times a year, publishing news, features, book reviews, and interviews relating to Alabama writers. "We do not publish original poetry or fiction." It is 28 pgs., 8½×11, professionally printed on coated paper and saddle-stitched with b&w photos inside and on the cover. Lists markets for poetry, contests/awards and workshops. Sponsored by the Alabama Writers' Forum, "the official literary arts advocacy organization for the state of Alabama." Reviews books of poetry by "Alabama poets or from Alabama presses." Subscription: $25/year. Sample: $3.

FREELANCE MARKET NEWS, Sevendale House, 7 Dale St., Manchester M1 1JB England, phone (+44)0161 228 2362, fax (+44)0161 228 3533, e-mail fmn@writersbureau.com, editor Angela Cox, founded 1968, is "a monthly newsletter providing market information for writers and poets." Regular features are market information and how-to articles. It is 16 pgs., A4. Lists markets for poetry, contests/awards and conferences/workshops. Associated with The Writers College which offers correspondence courses in poetry. Occasionally reviews books or chapbooks of poetry. Subscription: £29. Sample: £2.50. Inquiries via fax OK.

HANDSHAKE; THE EIGHT HAND GANG, 5 Cross Farm Station Rd., Padgate, Warrington, Cheshire WA2 0QG England, contact John Francis Haines, founded 1992, is published irregularly to "encourage the writing of genre poetry, to provide a source of news and information about genre poetry, to encourage the reading of poetry of all types, including genre, and to provide an outlet for a little genre poetry." It is 1 A4 pg., printed on front and back. Lists markets for poetry and contests/awards. Single copy available for SAE and IRC.

INDEPENDENT PUBLISHER; INDEPENDENT PUBLISHER BOOK AWARDS, Jenkins Group Inc., 121 E. Front St., 4th Floor, Traverse City MI 49684, phone (616)933-0445, fax (616)933-0919, e-mail jgsales@northlink.net, website http://www.bookpublishing.com, editor Phil Murphy, founded 1983, is a "bi-monthly trade publication for the independent publishing sector, contains advice, trends, reviews (including poetry)." It is 60 pgs., 8½×11, professionally printed on coated paper and perfect-bound with glossy color cover. Lists markets for poetry, contests/awards and conferences/workshops. Reviews books or chapbooks of poetry or other magazines. Poets may send books for review consideration. Single copy: $5.95; subsciption: $30. Sample: $6.95. Inquiries via fax or e-mail OK. *IP* also sponsors the Independent Publisher Book Awards, an annual award for books published by independent, university and small press publishers in North American. Send SASE to Jim Barnes for details.

LAUGHING BEAR NEWSLETTER; LAUGHING BEAR PRESS, P.O. Box 613322, Dallas TX 75261-3322, phone (817)858-9515, e-mail editor@laughingbear.com, website http://www.LaughingBear.com, editor Tom Person, founded 1976. *LBN* is a monthly publication of small press news, information and inspiration for writers and publishers containing articles, news and reviews. Cost: $15/year. Send SASE for sample copy or request via e-mail. *LBN* uses short (200- to 300-word) articles on self-publishing and small press. Pays copies.

LIGHT'S LIST, 37 The Meadows, Berwick-Upon-Tweed, Northumberland, TD15 1NY England, phone (01289)306523, editor John Light, founded 1986, is an annual publication "listing some 1,200 small press magazines publishing poetry, prose, market information, articles and artwork with address and brief note of

FOR EXPLANATIONS OF THESE SYMBOLS,
SEE THE INSIDE FRONT AND BACK COVERS OF THIS BOOK.

interests. All magazines publish work in English. Listings are from the United Kingdom, Europe, United States, Canada, Australia, New Zealand, South Africa and Asia." It is 54 pgs., A5, photocopied and saddle-stitched with card cover. Lists markets for poetry. Single copy: $4 (air $5).

LITERARY MAGAZINE REVIEW, Dept. of English Language and Literature, The University of Northern Iowa, Cedar Falls IA 50614-0502, phone (319)273-2821, fax (319)273-5807, e-mail grant.tracey@uni.edu, editor Grant Tracey, founded 1981. A quarterly magazine (digest-sized, saddle-stitched, about 48-64 pgs.) that publishes critiques, 2-5 pgs. long, of various literary magazines, plus shorter "reviews" (about ½ page) of new journals during a particular year. Single copies: $5; subscriptions: $13.50/year. Request copies via e-mail.

MINNESOTA LITERATURE, One Nord Circle, St. Paul MN 55127, phone (651)483-3904, fax (651)766-0144, e-mail mnlit@aol.com, editor Mary Bround Smith, founded 1975. *ML* appears 10 times a year (September through June), providing news and announcements for Minnesota writers. Regularly features "Minnesota literary events such as readings, lectures, workshops, conferences and classes; news of publications written by Minnesotans or published in Minnesota; and opportunities for writers, such as grants, awards and want-ads." It is 8½ × 11, 8 pgs. (two 11 × 17 sheets folded), unbound. Subscription: $10 for 10 issues. Sponsors annual reading for creative writing nominees of Minnesota Book Awards. Publish biennial bibliography of Minnesota publishers and literary publications.

OPEN HORIZONS, P.O. Box 205, Fairfield IA 52556-0205, phone (515)472-6130, fax (515)472-1560, e-mail John Kremer@bookmarket.com, website http://www.bookmarket.com, publisher John Kremer, founded 1982. Publishes how-to books about book publishing and self-publishing, such as *1001 Ways to Market Your Books*, *Book Marketing Update*, *Directory of Book Printers*, and *Book Publishing Resource Guide* (also available on IBM PC or Macintosh disk as a database). Send SASE for catalog. Inquiries via fax and e-mail OK. Website provides information and resources on editing, designing and marketing books.

OXFORD UNIVERSITY PRESS, 198 Madison Ave., New York NY 10016, phone (212)726-6000, literature editor T. Susan Chang (NY), founded 1478, is a large university press publishing academic, trade and college books in a wide variety of fields. **Not accepting poetry mss.** "Our list includes editions of English and American poets for classroom use, thematically-oriented anthologies and critical studies of poets and their work for general readers. Unfortunately, we do not publish new poetry by contemporary writers."

PARA PUBLISHING, Box 8206-880, Santa Barbara CA 93118-8206, phone (805)968-7277, orders (800)727-2782, fax (805)968-1379, e-mail danpoynter@parapublishing.com, website http://www.parapublishing.com. Author/publisher Dan Poynter publishes how-to books on book publishing and self-publishing. *Is There a Book Inside You?* shows you how to get your book out. *The Self-Publishing Manual, How to Write, Print and Sell Your Own Book* is all about book promotion. Poynter also publishes *Publishing Contracts on Disk, Book Fairs* and 45 Special Reports on various aspects of book production, promotion, marketing and distribution. *Free* book publishing information kit. Available through Para Publishing is a 24-hour fax service called Fax-On-Demand. This service enables you to obtain free documents on book writing and publishing; and lists of workshops and presentations offered by Dan Poynter. Call (805)968-8947 from your fax machine handset, then follow the voice prompts to hear a list of documents and to order. The fax machine will retrieve the documents and print them instantly. This is a good way to sample Para Publishing's offerings. Inquiries via fax and e-mail OK.

☑ **PERSONAL POEMS**, % Jean Hesse, 56 Arapaho Dr., Pensacola FL 32507, phone (850)492-9828, Jean Hesse started a business in 1980 writing poems for individuals for a fee (for greetings, special occasions, etc.). Others started similar businesses, after she began instructing them in the process, especially through a cassette tape training program and other training materials. Send SASE for free brochure or $30 plus $4.50 p&h (make checks payable to F. Jean Hesse) for training manual, *How to Make Your Poems Pay*.

🌐 **POETRY BOOK SOCIETY**, Book House, 45 East Hill, London SW18 2QZ England, phone 44 0181 870 8403, fax 44 0181 877 1615, founded in 1953 "to promote the best newly published contemporary poetry to as wide an audience as possible." A book club with an annual subscription rate of £40, which covers 4 books of new poetry, the *PBS Bulletin*, and a premium offer (for new members). The selectors also recommend other books of special merit, which are obtainable at a discount of 25%. The Poetry Book Society is subsidized by the Arts Council of England. Please write (Attn: Clare Brown) for details or phone 0181-877-1615 (24-hour fax/answer service).

POETRY CALENDAR, 611 Broadway #905, New York NY 10012, phone (212)260-7097, fax (212)475-7110, editor and publisher Dallas Galvin, founded 1975. "*Poetry Calendar* is a monthly magazine that combines reviews, interviews, excerpts, and essays along with one of the most comprehensive literary listings in New York City. Thirteen-thousand copies are distributed each month, providing a comprehensive schedule of poetry and fiction readings, performances, lectures, exhibits, workshops and related activities." It is 32-40 pgs., 8½ × 11, newsprint, saddle-stitched. Subscription: $20. Sample available for free.

THE POETRY CONNECTION, 13455 SW 16 Court #F-405-PM, Pembroke Pines FL 33027, phone (954)431-3016, editor/publisher Sylvia Shichman. *The Poetry Connection*, a monthly newsletter, provides information in flyer format. Poets, writers and songwriters receive information on how to sell their poetry/books, poetry and musical publications and contests, and obtain assistance in getting poetry published. Plus info on how to win cash for your talent and mailing list rental. *TPC* has information on writing for greeting card companies, poetry and songwriting publications, and greeting card directories. Plus info on a director that lists poetry contests with cash awards. Subscription: $20. Sample (including guidelines): $7. Make checks payable to Sylvia Shichman. Also sponsors The Magic Circle, a poetry reading/musical network service. Send SASE for information.

POETRY FLASH, 1450 Fourth St. #4, Berkeley CA 94710, phone (510)525-5476, fax (510)525-6752, editor Joyce Jenkins, founded 1972, appears 6 times a year. "*Poetry Flash*, a Poetry Review & Literary Calendar for the West, publishes reviews, interviews, essays and information for writers. Poems, as well as announcements about submitting to other publications, appear in each issue." *PF* focuses on poetry, but its literary calendar also includes events celebrating all forms of creative writing in areas across the nation. It is about 46 pgs., printed on newsprint. Lists markets for poetry, contests/awards and workshops. *Poetry Flash* also sponsors a weekly poetry reading series at Cody's Books in Berkeley and sponsors the Bay Area Book Reviewers Association. (Also see listing in Contests and Awards.) Reviews books and chapbooks of poetry. Poets may send books for review consideration. Subscription $16/year. Sample: $2. "We publish at least three poems per issue—sometimes more in a special feature." Even though *Poetry Flash* publishes a limited amount of poetry, work published here has also been selected for inclusion in *The Best American Poetry 1996.*

POETS & WRITERS, INC.; A DIRECTORY OF AMERICAN POETS AND FICTION WRITERS; LITERARY AGENTS; POETS & WRITERS MAGAZINE, 72 Spring St., New York NY 10012, phone (212)226-3586 or (800)666-2268 (California only), website http://www.pw.org, is a major support organization. Its many helpful publications include *Poets & Writers Magazine*, which appears 6 times a year ($19.95 or $3.95 for a single copy), 120 pgs., magazine-sized, offset printed, has been called *The Wall Street Journal* of our profession, and it is there that one most readily finds out about resources, current needs of magazines and presses, contests, awards, jobs and retreats for writers, and discussions of business, legal and other issues affecting writers. *Poets & Writers Magazine* does not accept advertising from vanity/subsidy presses. P&W also publishes a number of valuable directories such as its biennial *A Directory of American Poets and Fiction Writers*, which editors, publishers, agents and sponsors of readings and workshops use to locate over 7,000 active writers in the country. (You may qualify for a listing if you have a number of publications.) They also publish *Literary Agents*; and "Into Print: Guides to the Writing Life," a comprehensive, updated and revised collection of the best articles from *Poets & Writers Magazine*, that includes *Out of the Slush Pile and Into Print*; *Contracts and Royalties: Negotiating Your Own*; *On Cloud Nine: Writers' Colonies, Retreats, Ranches, Residencies, and Sanctuaries*; and *Helping Writers Help Themselves: A National Guide to Writers' Resources.*

PUSHCART PRESS, P.O. Box 380, Wainscott NY 11975. Publishes a number of books useful to writers, including the Pushcart Prize Series—annual anthologies representing the best small press publications, according to the judges; The Editors' Book Award Series, "to encourage the writing of distinguished books of uncertain financial value"; *The Original Publish-It-Yourself Handbook*; and the Literary Companion Series. Send SASE for catalog.

RAIN TAXI REVIEW OF BOOKS, P.O. Box 3840, Minneapolis MN 55403, phone/fax (612)825-1528, e-mail raintaxi@bitstream.net, website http://www.raintaxi.com, editor Eric Lorberer, founded 1996. "*Rain Taxi Review of Books* is a quarterly publication available free in bookstores nationwide. Our circulation is 20,000 copies. We publish reviews of books that are overlooked by mainstream media, and each issue includes several pages of poetry reviews, as well as author interviews and original essays." Devotes 20% of publication to poetry. "We review poetry books in every issue and often feature interviews with poets." *Rain Taxi* is 56 pgs., 8½×11, web offset printed on newsprint and saddle-stitched. Poets may send books for review consideration. Subscription: $10. Sample: $3. Inquiries via e-mail OK. Website includes a selection of the contents of each issue, full table of contents for current and back issues and information about the organization. "We DO NOT publish original poetry. Please don't send poems."

SPRINGBOARD: WRITING TO SUCCEED, 30 Orange Hill Rd., Prestwich M25 1LS England, e-mail leobooks@rammy.com, editor Leo Brooks, is published quarterly to help aspiring writers. It is 32 pgs., A5, desktop-published and saddle-stapled with paper cover, includes clip art. Lists markets for poetry and contests/awards. Sponsors quarterly competitions for subscribers. Subscription: £8/year. Inquiries via e-mail OK. "Subscription to the magazine brings the right to belong to one or more of the folios which it supports. These postal folios are made of groups of six to eight writers who pass their work round the group for mutual encouragement and constructive criticism."

TAPROOT REVIEWS; BURNING PRESS INC., P.O. Box 585, Lakewood OH 44107, phone (216)221-8940, e-mail au462@cleveland.freenet.edu, website http://www.burningpress.org, editor luigibob drake, founded 1980, is an quarterly publication "providing reviews of experimental and alternative poetry, fiction, visual-literature, spoken-word recordings, hypertext, intermedia, etc. We intend to expand readers access to a wide variety of literatures; each issue reviews 200-300 publications. We do not accept submissions of poetry." Devotes 80% of its pages to reviews of poetry publication. *Taproot Reviews* is 40 pgs., A5, tabloid-sized, offset-printed on newsprint and folded. Lists markets for poetry. Reviews books or chapbooks of poetry. Poets may send books for review consideration. Subscription: $10/year. Sample: $5. The editor says, "We accept review submissions, however, potential reviewers must be familiar with our format (i.e., read us before submitting). Strong emphasis on independent publishers and non-mainstream writing. We do not read poetry manuscripts." Inquiries via e-mail OK. No fax inquiries.

WORD: THE LITERARY CALENDAR, Insomniac Press, 393 Shaw St., Toronto, Ontario M6J 2X4 Canada, phone (416)536-4308, fax (416)588-4198, publisher e-mail mike@insomniacpress.com, website http://www.insomniacpress.com, publisher Mike O'Connor, founded 1995, a monthly publication providing an "all-inclusive calendar of literary events, book launches, readings, slams and workshops in Ontario (also lists contests and calls for submissions)." It is 8 pgs., 8½×11, offset printed, unbound, with ads. Subscription: $10/year. Make checks payable to Insomniac Press. "All listings are free. An excellent resource for poets in Ontario."

WORDWRIGHTS CANADA, P.O. Box 456 Station O, Toronto, Ontario M4A 2P1 Canada, e-mail susioan@ican.net, website http://www.home.ican.net/~susioan, director Susan Ioannou, publishes "books on poetics in layman's, not academic terms, such as *Writing Reader-friendly Poems: Over 50 Rules of Thumb for Clearer Communication*; and *The Crafted Poem: A Step-by-Step Guide to Writing and Appreciation* (rev. ed.)." They consider mss of such books for publication, paying $50 advance, 10% royalties and 5% of press run. They also conduct "Manuscript Reading and Editing Services, as well as The Poetry Tutorial correspondence course for writers." Request order form via mail or e-mail to buy samples.

WRITER ONLINE, 190 Mt. Vernon Ave., Rochester NY 14620, phone (716)271-2250, fax (716)271-5602, e-mail wol@novalearn.com, website http://www.novalearn.com, editors Clare Mann and Cindy Mindell-Wong, founded 1998, is a "bimonthly online magazine for writers of all kinds." Devotes 10% of its content to poetry and regularly features columns by Michael Bugeja and associate editor Jeff Hillard. "Poetry selected by editors only." Lists markets for poetry, contests/awards and conferences/workshops. "Entire magazine is at website and all former issues are archived."

WRITERS' BULLETIN, P.O. Box 96, Altrincham, Cheshire WA14 2LN United Kingdom, phone/fax (+44 0161)928 9711, e-mail mcbulletin@aol.com, editor Mrs. Chriss McCallum, founded 1997. "Published bimonthly, *Writers' Bulletin* aims to give writers the most reliable and up-to-date information on markets for fiction, nonfiction, poetry, photographs, artwork, cartoons, plus information on resources, courses and conferences, book reviews (books about writing), editors' moves, publishing news, address changes, advice and tips on writing. All markets are verified with the editors—no guesswork or second-hand information." It is about 28 pgs., desktop-published and photocopied, saddle-stapled with colored paper cover. Lists markets for poetry, contests/awards and conferences/workshops. Reviews informational or instructional books for poets and writers. Single copy: £2.40 Europe, £3 USA sterling only, £2 UK. Inquiries via e-mail OK. "Because we are adding news right up to publication day, *Writers' Bulletin* has the most up-to-date information available in print."

WRITER'S DIGEST BOOKS; WRITER'S DIGEST, 1507 Dana Ave., Cincinnati OH 45207, phone (800)289-0963 or (513)531-2690, website http://www.writersdigest.com. Writer's Digest Books publishes a remarkable array of books useful to all types of writers. In addition to *Poet's Market*, books for poets include *Writing Personal Poetry* by Sheila Bender, *You Can Write Poetry* by Jeff Mock, *The Poet's Handbook* by Judson Jerome, *Creating Poetry* by John Drury, and *The Art and Craft of Poetry* by Michael J. Bugeja. Call or write for a complete catalog. *Writer's Digest* is a monthly magazine about writing with frequent articles and market news about poetry, in addition to a monthly poetry column. See the listing in the Publishers of Poetry section.

Additional Publications of Interest

The following listings also contain information about instructive publications for poets. See the General Index for page numbers.

Connecticut River Review
Council of Literary Magazines and
    Presses
Cyber Oasis
Dandelion Arts Magazine
Frank
Georgia Poetry Society
Great Blue Beacon Poetry Contest,
    The
Guild Complex
Indiana State Federation of Poetry
    Clubs
Interbang
International Women's Writing Guild
Iowa Poetry Association
IWWG Summer Conference, The
Kentucky State Poetry Society, The
Laureate Letter Chapbook, The
Leacock Medal for Humour, The
    Stephen
League of Canadian Poets, The
Ligonier Valley Writers Conference
Mad Poets Review
Maine Writers & Publishers Alliance
Manitoba Writers' Guild Inc.
Massachusetts State Poetry Society,
    Inc.
Nashville Newsletter Poetry Contest
National Federation of State Poetry
    Societies, Inc.
National Poetry Foundation, The
National Writers Association

National Writers Union
Nevada Poetry Society
New Hampshire Writers' Project
New Writer, The
New Writer's Magazine
Newport University Writers' Confer-
    ence & Contest, Christopher
North Carolina Writers' Network
Northeast Arts Magazine
Northwest Oklahoma Writers
    Workshop
Northwoods Press
Oak, The
Ohioana Book Awards
Oregon State Poetry Association, The
Papyrus
PEN American Center
Pequod
Piedmont Literary Review
Pigasus Press
Poet Born Press, A
Poetic Realm
Poetic Space
Poetry Ireland Review
Poetry Salzburg
Poetry Society of America
Poetry Society of Tennessee
Poets House: The Reed Foundation
    Library
Poets' Roundtable
Po'Flye Internationale
Prosetry

Rio Grande Press
Scavenger's Newsletter
Simply Words Magazine
Small Publishers Association of
    North America
Southern Poetry Association
Squaw Valley Community of Writers
    Poetry Workshop
Steamboat Springs Writers Confer-
    ence
Time For Rhyme
University of Arizona Poetry Center
Verse
Virginia Writers Club
Wisconsin Fellowship of Poets
Wisconsin Regional Writers' Associ-
    ation Inc.
Women Who Write Inc.
Women Writers Network
World-Wide Writers Service, Inc.
Writer, The
Writer's Center, The
Writer's Digest
Writer's Exchange
Writers' Federation of Nova Scotia
Writer's Guidelines & News
    Magazine
Writer's Journal
Writers of Kern
Xanadu

Websites of Interest

The Internet can be a useful tool for crafting and publishing poetry. Doing searches for specific forms of poetry will bring up many sites catering to your forms of choice. The following list can be used as a starting point for investigating pertinent websites for poets. We have broken them into four categories: The Business, The Organizations, The Search, and The Craft.

THE BUSINESS
IRS: http://www.irs.ustreas.gov/basic/cover.html
Information, forms and publications, plus comments and help.
U.S. Copyright Office: http://www.loc.gov/copyright
General information and forms you can print.

THE ORGANIZATIONS
The following websites contain information about the organization, list poetry awards and contests, and provide links to other literary resources, conferences and workshops.
The Academy of American Poets: http://www.poets.org
The International Organization of Performing Poets: http://www.slamnews.com/iopp.htm
Poets & Writers: http://www.pw.org
Poetry Society of America: http://www.poetrysociety.org
Teachers & Writers Collaborative: http://www.twc.org
Zuzu's Petals Organizations of Interest: http://www.zuzu.com

THE SEARCH
The following are search directories providing literary links.
Electronic Poetry Center: http://wings.buffalo.edu/epc/
Factsheet Five—Electric 'Zines!: http://www.factsheet5.com
John Hewitt's Writer's Resource: http://www.azstarnet.com/~poewar/writer/writer.html
John Labovitz's e-zine-list: http://www.meer.net/~johnl/e-zine-list
The Poetry Exchange: http://www.w3px.com
The Poetry Forum World Wide Registry: http://www.poetryforum.org/registry.htm
Poetry Today Online: http://www.poetrytodayonline.com
Writer's Resources: http://www.arcana.com/shannon/write/index.html
Writers Write™—The Write Resource™: http://www.writerswrite.com/

THE CRAFT
These sites can serve as a source of inspiration when creating your poetry.
Alan Cooper's Homonym List: http://www.cooper.com/alan/homonym.html
The Albany Poetry Workshop: http://www.sonic.net/poetry/albany/
Richard Lederer's Verbivore Page: http://pw1.netcom.com/~rlederer/index.htm
Rhetorical Figures: http://www.uky.edu/ArtsSciences/Classics/rhetoric.html
Rhyming Dictionary: http://www.cs.cmu.edu/~dougb/rhyme.html
A Word a Day: http://www.wordsmith.org/awad/index.html
The Word Wizard: http://wordwizard.com/

PUBLICATIONS ACCEPTING E-MAIL SUBMISSIONS

The following publications accept e-mail submissions. See the General Index for their page numbers. For e-mail submission instructions, see the publication's listing or obtain a copy of its writer's guidelines.

A Small Garlic Press
Abundance
Acid Angel
Acorn, The
Alden Enterprises
Allison Press
American Tanka
Amherst Review, The
Anaconda Press
Angel News Magazine
Anthology
Appalachian Heritage
Arkansas Review
Artisan
Avocet
Backspace
Backwater Review
Badlands Press
Bangtale International
Bathtub Gin
Bear Deluxe, The
Beauty for Ashes Poetry Review
Bible Advocate
Black Bear Publications
Blue Satellite
Blueline
Bordighera, Inc.
Bugle
Cafe Review, The
Canadian Journal of Contemporary
   Literary Stuff, The
Canadian Woman Studies
Canadian Writer's Journal
Caribbean Writer, The
Carpe Laureate Diem
Cencrastus
Chaff
Challenger International
Children, Churches and Daddies
Claremont Review, The
Community of Poets Press
Companion in Zeor, A
Concrete Abstract
Confluence
Cortland Review
Coteau Books
Crania
Creative Juices
Creativity Unlimited Press
Current Accounts
Curriculum Vitae Literary Supple-
   ment
Cyber Oasis
Dead End Street Publications, LLC
Descanso Literary Journal
Dial 174 Magazine
Dig
Dim Gray Bar Press
Dixie Phoenix
Draigeye
Drinkin' Buddy Magazine, The
Dwan
Edgar: Digested Verse
Edge City Review, The
1812
Emotions

English Journal
Enterzone
Equilibrium [10]
Eratica
Etcetera
Fat Tuesday
Filling Station
Flarestack Publishing
For Poetry.Com
Forklift,Ohio
4*9*1 Neo-Immanentist*Imagina-
   tion
Frogpond
The Funny Paper
G.W. Review
Gargoyle Magazine
Garnet
Gerbil
GLB Publishers
Gleeful Press!, A
Gotta Write Network Litmag
Green Bean Press
Hanover Press, Ltd.
Harpweaver, The
Harvard Advocate, The
Heliotrope
Herb Network, The
Hey, Listen!
Higginsville Reader, The
High/Coo Press
Hunger Magazine
Hunted News, The
Idiot, The
Illuminations
Implosion Press
Improvijazzation Nation
In the Family
In the Spirit of the Buffalo
Inklings
Inner Voices
Innovative Publishing Concepts
Interbang
Interlink BBS
Japanophile
Jewish Affairs
Jones Av.
Journal of Asian Martial Arts
Journal of New Jersey Poets
Joyful Woman, The
Jupiter's Freedom
Key Satch(el)
Kimera
Koja
Kuumba
Lactuca
Laire, Inc., The
Laureate Letter Chapbook, The
Laurels
Leapings Literary Magazine
Lilith
Limestone Circle
Links
Linq
Literal Latte
Literary Focus Poetry Publications
Litrag

Little Magazine, The
Lone Willow Press
Louisiana Review, The
Lowell Review, The
Lummox Press
Lungfull! Magazine
Lynx
Maelstrom
Magma Poetry Magazine
Making Waves
Mandrake Poetry Review
Massage Magazine
Mature Years
Medicinal Purposes Literary Review
Medusa's Hairdo
Mekler & Deahl, Publishers
Mennonite, The
Metropolitan Review
Midwifery Today
Milton Magazine, John
Mind Matters Review
Mind Purge
Minority Literary Expo
Monkey Flower
Murderous Intent
Muse Journal
Muse's Kiss Webzine
Mythic Circle, The
National Forum
Naturally
Negative Capability
New London Writers
New Mirage Quarterly, The
New Song, A
North American Review
North Carolina Literary Review
Northern Centinel, The
Nova Express
O!!Zone
Oasis
Octavo
Office Number One
Ohio Teachers Write
Osric Publishing
Our Family
Our Journey
Oyster Boy Review
P.D.Q. (Poetry Depth Quarterly)
Pacific Enterprise Magazine
Pandaloon
Pannus Index, The
Paperplates
Papyrus
Paris/Atlantic
Parting Gifts
Peoplenet Disability Datenet
Pif Magazine
Plaza, The
Pleiades
Plume Literary Magazine
Pocahontas Press, Inc.
Poet Born Press, A
Poetry & Prose Annual
Poetry Forum
Poetry of the People
Poet's Energy, The

Poet's Haven, The
Poet's Paradise
Porcupine Literary Arts Magazine
Portland Review
Prague Revue, The
Prayerworks
Premiere Generation Ink
Presstheedge
Pride Magazine
Princeton University Press
Prism International
Prosetry
Qoph
Queen's Quarterly
Rattapallax
Rattle
Red Dancefloor
Red Hen Press
Red Moon Press
Red Owl Magazine
Red Rock Review
Renaissance Online Magazine
Renditions
Rio
River King Poetry Supplement
Rocket Press
Ruah
Rural Heritage

Satire
Scavenger's Newsletter
Science Fiction Poetry Association
Scroll Publications
Seedhouse
Seeds Poetry Magazine
Shades of December
Sharing Magazine
Society of American Poets (Soap),
  The
Somniloquy
Soul Fountain
Sour Grapes
South
Southern Indiana Review
Spinning Jenny
Spoonfed
Stone Soup
Stoneflower Press
Sun Poetic Times
Syncopated City
Talus and Scree
Tea Party
Temporary Vandalism Recordings
Textshop
Thirst Magazine
32 Pages
Thunder Rain Publishing Corp.

Timbooktu
Time Of Singing
Touchstone
Tri Lingua
Tyro Publishing
The Ultimate Unknown
Understanding Magazine
Unlikely Stories
Uprising
Urban Graffiti
Urthona Press
Virginia Literary Review
Voiding the Void
War Cry, The
Westerly
Western Digest
Whiskey Island Magazine
Wild Word
Windhover
Wolf Head Quarterly
Word Salad
Worm Feast
Yes!
Zine Zone
Zombie Logic Press
Zuzu's Petals Quarterly Online
Zygote Magazine

U.S. and Canadian Postal Codes

United States

AL	Alabama
AK	Alaska
AZ	Arizona
AR	Arkansas
CA	California
CO	Colorado
CT	Connecticut
DE	Delaware
DC	District of Columbia
FL	Florida
GA	Georgia
GU	Guam
HI	Hawaii
ID	Idaho
IL	Illinois
IN	Indiana
IA	Iowa
KS	Kansas
KY	Kentucky
LA	Louisiana
ME	Maine
MD	Maryland
MA	Massachusetts

MI	Michigan
MN	Minnesota
MS	Mississippi
MO	Missouri
MT	Montana
NE	Nebraska
NV	Nevada
NH	New Hampshire
NJ	New Jersey
NM	New Mexico
NY	New York
NC	North Carolina
ND	North Dakota
OH	Ohio
OK	Oklahoma
OR	Oregon
PA	Pennsylvania
PR	Puerto Rico
RI	Rhode Island
SC	South Carolina
SD	South Dakota
TN	Tennessee
TX	Texas
UT	Utah

VT	Vermont
VI	Virgin Islands
VA	Virginia
WA	Washington
WV	West Virginia
WI	Wisconsin
WY	Wyoming

Canada

AB	Alberta
BC	British Columbia
LB	Labrador
MB	Manitoba
NB	New Brunswick
NF	Newfoundland
NT	Northwest Territories
NS	Nova Scotia
ON	Ontario
PEI	Prince Edward Island
PQ	Quebec
SK	Saskatchewan
YT	Yukon

Glossary of Poetic Forms & Styles

Abstract poem: uses sound, rhythm and rhyme to convey emotion. The words' meanings are secondary to their sound.

Acrostic: the first or last letter in a line, read downward, form a word, phrase or sentence.

Alphabet poem: uses letters of the alphabet as points of departure for lines or whole poems.

Ballad: stories commonly about fatal relationships. Stanzas are quatrains with four beats in lines 1 and 3; and three beats in lines 2 and 4, which also rhyme.

Ballade: three stanzas rhyming *ababbcbC* (capital "C" meaning a refrain) and an envoie (half the number of lines of a stanza) rhyming *bcbC*.

Beat poetry: an anti-academic school of poetry born in the '50s in San Francisco. It is fast-paced free verse resembling jazz. The language is irreverent and slangy.

Blank verse: unrhymed, usually with iambic pentameter.

Calligram: poems whose words on the page form a shape or object related to the poem.

Cento: poem made up of pieces from poems by other authors.

Chant: poem where one or more line is repeated over and over.

Cinquain: five-line stanza; or poem of five lines with 2, 4, 6, 8 and 2 syllables, respectively.

Concrete poem: the words dramatize their meaning by where they appear on the page; make use of space and sound.

Dada: movement based on deliberate irrationality and rejection of traditional artistic values.

Epigram: short, witty, satirical poem or saying written to be easily remembered. Like a punchline.

Free verse: no regular beat or rhyme.

Ghazal: usually five to fifteen lines of long-lined couplets, customarily expressing mystical thoughts. The couplets are not connected, but separate units.

Haibun: a Japanese form where prose is mixed with verse, specifically haiku, often in diary or travel journal form.

Haiku: poem about how nature is linked to human nature. Only three short lines containing 17 syllables, generally arranged 5-7-5. Uses simple words and expression, almost no adjectives.

Language poetry: attempts to detach words from their traditional meanings so something new arises. The poetry tries to break away from what we already know about poetry to experiment.

Limerick: five lines rhyming *aabba*, with a bawdy or scatalogical theme. The stresses in the lines are 3-3-2-2-3.

Lune: three-line poem of 13 syllables (5-3-5).

Lyric: intimate poem where poet speaks in own voice or a monologue, expressing emotion.

Nonsense verse: doesn't make sense, but it's not gibberish. Poem is consistent, but wacky.

Pantoum: poem of any length in four-line stanzas. Lines 2 and 4 are repeated as lines 1 and 3 of the next stanza, and so on. Doesn't have to rhyme. Ideally, in the last stanza, lines 2 and 4 repeat the opening stanza's lines 1 and 3.

Prose poem: looks like prose, but reads like poetry. No rhyme or set rhythm. It's unlike regular prose because of its intense and condensed language.

Quatrain: a four-line stanza.

Renga: long, image-filled in alternating stanzas of three and two lines, customarily created by a big group of poets taking turns.

Rondeau: the repeating lines and rhyme give the poem the quality of a round. It's usually 15 lines that rhyme *aabba aabR aabbaR* ("R" is the refrain).

Senryu: like haiku, but about human nature, often humorous, using direct language.

Sequence: a series of poems, often numbered. The poems must be connected in some way e.g., by theme, subject, stanza form, or ongoing narrative.

Sestina: six unrhymed stanzas of six lines each. The words at the end of the first stanza's lines repeat at ends of other lines. Each subsequent stanza rearranges the previous stanza's end-words as 6, 1, 5, 2, 4, 3. Ends with a three-line stanza using all six end-words, two to a line.

Sijo: a Korean form of poetry, 44 to 46 syllables, usually on three lines.

Skeltonic verse: short lines whose rhymes continue as long as they work, then changes to another rhyme.

Sonnet: often written about love and/or philosophy. It's a 14-line poem in two parts: octave (eight lines) and a sestet (six lines). There are three types: the Petrarchan (or Italian) rhymes *abbaabba* and varies the last six lines (*cdcdcd* or *cdecde* or *cdedce* or *ccdccd* or *cddcdd* or *cddcee*); the Shakespearean rhymes *abab cdcd efef gg*; the Spenserian rhymes *ababbcbccdcdee*.

Surrealism: literary and artistic movement stressing the importance of dreams, the unconscious, irrational thought, free associations and disturbing imagery.

Tanka: frequently about love, seasons, sadness, with strong images and poetic devices haiku avoids. Five lines, with lines 1 and 3 being shorter. Syllables per line are 5-7-5-7-7.

Triolet: eight lines, with two rhymes and two repeating lines. The first line is repeated as lines 4 and 7. Lines 2 and 8 are the same: *ABaAabAB* (capitals indicate repeated lines or refrains).

Villanelle: six stanzas. The first five are three lines long, the sixth is four lines long. The first and last lines of the first stanza repeat as the final line of the next four stanzas and are also the last two lines of the poem. Rhyme scheme of *aba* for first five stanzas.

Visual: a combination of text and graphics usually only reproduced photographically.

Glossary of Listing Terms

A3, A4, A5. Metric equivalents of $11\frac{3}{4} \times 16\frac{1}{2}$, $8\frac{1}{4} \times 11\frac{3}{4}$ and $5\frac{7}{8} \times 8\frac{1}{4}$ respectively.

Anthology. A collection of selected writings by various authors.

b&w. black & white (photo or illustration).

Bio. A short biographical paragraph often requested with a submission.

Camera-ready. Poems that are completely prepared for copy camera platemaking.

Chapbook. A small book of under 50 pages of poetry. Such a book is less expensive to produce than a full-length book collection, though it is seldom noted by reviewers.

Contributor's copy. Copy of an issue of a magazine or published book sent to an author whose work is included.

Cover letter. Letter accompanying a submission; it usually lists titles of poems and gives a brief account of publishing credits and biographical information.

Cover stock. Heavier book or text paper used to cover a publication, often coated on one or both sides.

Digest-sized. Approximately $5\frac{1}{2} \times 8\frac{1}{2}$, the size of a folded sheet of conventional printer paper.

Electronic magazine. Publication circulated solely via the Internet or e-mail.

E-mail. Mail that has been sent electronically using a computer and modem.

Flat-spined. What many publishers call "perfect-bound," glued with a flat edge (usually permitting readable type on the spine).

Font. A particular style or design of type; typeface.

Galleys. Typeset copies of your poem(s). You should proofread and correct any mistakes and return galleys to editors within 48 hours of receipt.

Honorarium. A small, token payment for published work.

IRC. International Reply Coupon, postage for return of submissions from another country. One IRC is sufficient for one ounce by *surface mail*. If you want an airmail return, you need one IRC for each half-ounce. Do not send checks or cash for postage to other countries: The exchange rates are so high it is not worth the inconvenience it causes editors. (Exception: Many Canadian editors do not object to U.S. dollars; use IRCs the first time and inquire.)

Magazine-sized. Approximately $8\frac{1}{2} \times 11$, the size of conventional printer paper unfolded.

ms. manuscript; **mss.** manuscripts.

Multi-book review. Also known as an omnibus or essay review. A review of several books by the same author or by several authors, such as a review of four or five political poetry books.

Multiple submission. Submission of more than one poem at a time; most poetry publishers *prefer* multiple submissions and specify how many poems should be in a packet. Some say a multiple submission means the poet has sent another manuscript to the same publication before receiving word on the first submission. This type of multiple submission is generally discouraged (see Simultaneous submission).

Offset. A printing method in which ink is transferred from an image-bearing plate to a "blanket" and from the blanket to the paper.

p. Abbreviation for pence.

p&h. postage & handling.

Perfect-bound. See Flat-spined.

Publishing credits. A list of magazines having published a poet's work, or a list of a poet's published books.

Query letter. Letter written to a publisher to elicit interest in a manuscript or to determine if submissions are acceptable.

Rights. First North American serial rights means the publisher is acquiring the right to publish your poem first in a U.S. or Canadian periodical. All rights means the publisher is buying the poem outright. Selling all rights usually requires that you obtain permission to reprint your work, even in a book-length collection.

Royalties. A percentage of the retail price paid to an author for each copy of the book that is sold.

Saddle-stapled. What many publishers call "saddle-stitched," folded and stapled along the fold.

SAE. Self-addressed envelope.

SASE. Self-addressed, stamped envelope. *Every* publisher requires, with any submission, query or request for information, a self-addressed, stamped envelope.

Simultaneous submission. Submission of the same manuscript to more than one publisher at a time. Many magazine editors *refuse to accept* simultaneous submissions. Some book and chapbook publishers do not object to simultaneous submissions. In all cases, notify editors that the manuscript is being simultaneously submitted.

Subsidy press. See Vanity press.

Tabloid-sized. 11×15 or larger, the size of an ordinary newspaper folded and turned sideways.

Unsolicited manuscript. A manuscript an editor did not specifically ask to see.

Vanity press. A slang term for a publisher that requires the writer to pay publishing costs, especially one that flatters an author to generate business. These presses often use the term "subsidy" to describe themselves. Some presses, however, derive subsidies from other sources, such as government grants, and do not require author payment. These are not considered vanity presses.

Indexes

Chapbook Publishers

A chapbook is a slim volume of a poet's work, usually under 50 pages (although page requirements vary greatly). Given the high cost of printing, a publisher is more apt to accept a chapbook than an entire book from an unproven poet.

Some chapbooks are published as inserts in magazines. (The winner of The Tennessee Chapbook Prize, for instance, is published as an insert in *Poems & Plays*.) Others are separate volumes. A physical description (binding, method of printing, cover, etc.) is usually included in the market listings, but whenever possible, request submission guidelines and samples to determine the quality of the product.

You'll find many presses, particularly those that sponsor chapbook contests, charge reading fees. Avoid any over $10. (Some folks go as high as $15 for book-length manuscripts, but chapbooks are easier to produce.)

If your chapbook is published, by the way, you may still participate in "first-book" competitions. For more information about both chapbook and book publishing, read The *Poet's Market* Guide to Poetry Submission Etiquette, beginning on page 8.

Following are publishers who consider chapbook manuscripts. See the General Index for the page numbers of their market listings.

Book Publishers Index

The following are magazines and publishers that consider full-length book manuscripts. See the General Index for the page numbers to their market listings.

Openness to Submissions Index

This index ranks all magazines, publishers, contests and awards contained in *Poet's Market* according to their openness to unsolicited submissions. Some markets are listed in more than one category. See the General Index for the page numbers of their corresponding listings.

◻ OPEN TO BEGINNING POETS

Competition; Quadrant Magazine; Quantum Leap; Radiance; RB's Poets' Viewpoint; Red Herring; Red Owl Magazine; Red Rock Review; Redwood Acres Fair Poetry Contest; Reflections of You® Journal; Renaissance Online Magazine; Richmond Communications LLC; River King Poetry Supplement; Rockford Review, The; Ruah; Rural Heritage; Rustic Rub; St. Joseph Messenger and Advocate of the Blind; San Mateo County Fair Fine Arts Competition; Sarasota Poetry Theatre Press; Screaming Ray Review, The; Scroll Publications; Sea Oats; Seaman Poetry Award, Claudia Ann; Seasons of the Muse; Seedhouse; Seeds Poetry Magazine; Senior Poet Laureate Poetry Competition; Sidewalks; Sierra Nevada College Review; Silver Web, The; Simple Vows; Simply Words Magazine; Skald; Skipping Stones; Sky Blue Waters Poetry Contests; Skylark; Slugfest, Ltd.; SMILE; Smiths Knoll; Snow Writing Awards, Kay; So Young!; Society of American Poets (SOAP), The; Somniloquy; Soul Fountain; Sounds of Poetry, The; Southern Indiana Review; SPAWN; spelunker flophouse; SPIN; SpoonFed; SSA Writer's Contest; Star Rising; Starving Romantics Poetry Competition; State Street Review; Stone National Literary Awards, Donna J.; Storyteller, The; Struggle; sub-Terrain; Sun Poetic Times; Superior Poetry News; Suzerain Enterprises; Sweet Annie & Sweet Pea Review; Symbiotic Oatmeal; Syncopated City; Tale Spinners; Taproot Literary Review; "Teak" Roundup; Temporary Vandalism Recordings; Texas Review; Texas Young Writers' Newsletter; Textshop; Thalia; Third Half Literary Magazine, The; 32 Pages; Threshold, The; Thumbprints; Thunder Rain Publishing; Tickled by Thunder; TimBookTu; Time For Rhyme; Time of Singing; Touchstone; Tradition Magazine; Transcendent Visions; Trewithen Poetry Prize, The; Tyro Publishing; Ultimate Unknown, The; Understanding Magazine; Unlikely Stories; Upsouth; Urban Graffiti; Urban Spaghetti; Urthona Press; Voices Israel; Voiding The Void; Waterways; Way Station Magazine; Wellspring; Western Archipelago Review; White Wall Review; Whitecrow Foundation, Tahana; Whole Notes; Wild Word; Windhover; Word Process; Writer, The; Writer's Block Magazine; Writer's Block, The; Writers Bureau Poetry and Short Story Competition, The; Writer's Exchange; Writer's Journal; Zine Zone; Zygote Magazine

◪ OPEN TO BEGINNING & EXPERIENCED POETS

Abbey; Abiko Annual; Abundance; ACM (Another Chicago Magazine); Acorn, The; Acorn Whistle; Acumen Magazine; Adobe Abalone; Adrift; Aethlon; Affair of the Mind; African Voices; Afterthoughts; Aguilar Expression, The; Aim Magazine; Akron Poetry Prize; Akros Publications; Alabama Literary Review; Alaska Quarterly Review; Albatross; Alden Enterprises; Alice James Books; Alligator Juniper; Amaranth; Amelia; America; American Literary Review; American Poets & Poetry; American Voice, The; Amethyst Review, The; Amherst Review, The; Anaconda Press; Anamnesis Press; Andreas-Gryphius-Preis; Anhinga Press; Anthology; Anthology of New England Writers, The; Appalachia; Arc; Arizona State Poetry Society Annual Contest; Arjuna Library Press; Arktos; Arnazella; Arshile; "Art in the Air" Poetry Contest; Art Times; Artful Dodge; Artisan; Arts Recognition and Talent Search; ArtWord Quarterly; Ascent; Asher Publishing, Sherman; Asheville Poetry Review; Atlanta Review; Atlantic Monthly, The; Atom Mind; Aurorean, The; Axe Factory Review; Back Porch, The; Backwater Review; Bad Poetry Quarterly; Baltimore Review, The; Bangtale International; Barbarian Press; Barbaric Yawp; Barrow Street; Bathtub Gin; Baybury Review; Beacon Street Review; Bear Star Press; Beatnik Pachyderm, The; Beauty for Ashes Poetry Review; Behind Bars; Bellingham Review, The; Bellowing Ark; Bell's Letters Poet; Beloit Poetry Journal, The; Beneath the Surface; Bennett Fellowship, George; Bibliophilos; Birmingham Poetry Review; Bitter Oleander, The; BKMK Press; Black Bear Publications; black bough; Black Buzzard Press; Black Dirt; Black Moon; Black Warrior Review; Blaxland Tan; Blood and Fire Review; Blue Collar Review; Blue Ink Press; Blue Light Press; Blue Mesa Review; Blue Nose Poetry Poets-of-the-Year Competition; Blue Unicorn; Blue Violin; Bluestem Press Award; Bogg Publications; Bombay Gin; Borderlands; Borderlines; Bordighera, Inc.; Bottomfish; Boulevard; Brando's Hat; Briar Cliff Review, The; Bridge, The; Bridport Prize, The; Bright Hill Press; Brilliant Corners; Brobdingnagian Times, The; Brownout Laboratories; Brownstone Review, The; Buffalo Bones; Buffalo Spree Magazine; Bugle; Cadence; Camellia; Canadian Journal of Contemporary Literary Stuff, The; Cape Rock, The; Capricorn Poetry Award; Carleton Arts Review; Carolina Quarterly, The; Catamount Press; Catbird Seat, The; Cedar Hill Publications; Cencrastus; Centennial Review, The; Center for Book Arts' Annual Poetry Chapbook Competition; Chachalaca Poetry Review; Challenger international; Chance Magazine; Chariton Review, The; Chattahoochee Review, The; Chicano/Latino Literary Contest; Chiron Review; Christian Century, The; Christian Science Monitor, The; Christianity and the Arts; Chrysalis Reader; Cider Press Review; Cimarron Review; Cincinnati Poets' Collective, The; Clackamas Literary Review; Cleveland State University Poetry Center; Clutch; Coal City Review; Cold Mountain Review; Collages & Bricolages; Colorado Review; Columbia; Community of Poets Press; Comstock Review, The; Concho River Review; Concrete Abstract; Conduit; Confluence; Confluence Press; Confrontation Magazine; Connecticut Poetry Review, The; Connecticut Review; Connecticut River Review; Contemporary Verse 2; Corona; Coteau Books; Cottonwood; Cover Magazine; Coyote Chronicles; Crab Creek Review; Crab Orchard Review; Crania; Cream City Review; Creative Juices; Creative Writing Fellowships in Poetry; Cross-Cultural Communications; Crucible; Cumberland Poetry Review; Curio; Current Accounts; Curriculum Vitae Literary Supplement; Cutbank; Cyber Oasis; Dana Award in Poetry; Dancing Poetry Contest; Daniel and Company, Publisher, John; Daniels Annual Honorary Writing Award, The Dorothy; Dark Regions; Debut Review; Defined Providence; Denny Poetry Award, Billee Murray; Denver Quarterly; Descanso Literary Journal; Descant: Fort Worth's Journal of Poetry and Fiction; Desperate Act; Devil Blossoms; Devil's Millhopper Press, The; Dickinson Award in Poetry, Emily; Didactic, The; dig.; Dirigible; Distillery, The; Dixie Phoenix; Doc(k)s; Dolphin-Moon Press; doublebunny press; Dragon Heart Press; Dry Creek Review, The; Eagle's Flight; Eckerd College Review; ECW Press; Edge City Review, The; 1812; Ekphrasis; Eliot Prize for Poetry, T.S.; Elm; Emotions Literary Magazine; Emrys Journal; English Journal; Enterzone; Epicenter; Eratica; Etcetera; Eternity; Ethereal Green; Event; Ever Dancing Muse, The; Explorations; Fat Tuesday; Faulkner Creative Writing Competition/Poetry Category, The William; Faultline; Fauquier Poetry Journal; Feminist Voices; Fenice Broadsheets; Fiddlehead, The; Field;

filling Station; Fine Madness; Firewater Press Inc.; Firm Noncommittal; First Class; First Step Press; First Time; Fish Drum; 5 AM; Five Points; Flaming Arrows; Flarestack Publishing; Flint Hills Review; Florida Individual Artist Fellowships; Florida Review, The; Flyway; Footprints; For Poetry.Com; Formalist, The; Foster City International Writers' Contest; Fox Cry Review; Frank; Free Lunch; Fugue; Future Tense Press; G.W. Review; Garnet; Gathering of the Tribes, A; George & Mertie's Place; Georgetown Review; Georgia Review, The; Gertrude; Gettysburg Review, The; Ginger Hill; GLB Publishers; Glimmer Train's April Poetry Open; Glimmer Train's October Poetry Open; Gotta Write Network Litmag; Graffiti Rag; Graffito; Grain; Grandmother Earth National Award; Grasslands Review; Gravity Presses; Great Blue Beacon Poetry Contest, The; Great Lakes Colleges Association New Writers Award; Green Hills Literary Lantern; Green Mountains Review; Green's Magazine; Greensboro Review, The; Grolier Poetry Prize; Guggenheim Fellowships; Gulf Stream Magazine; Hackney Literary Awards; Haight Ashbury Literary Journal; Handshake Editions; Hanging Loose Press; Hanover Press, Ltd.; Harpweaver, The; Hawaii Pacific Review; Hawai'i Review; Hayden's Ferry Review; Heartlands Today, The; Heaven Bone Magazine; Heist Magazine; Heliotrope; Hellas; Hellp!; Hemingway Poetry Competition, Ernest; Higginsville Reader, The; Hippopotamus Press; Hiram Poetry Review; Hobo Poetry & Haiku Magazine; Hodder Fellowship, The; Hollins Critic, The; House of Anansi Press; Howard Poetry Prize, Quentin R.; Hoyns Fellowships, Henry; HQ Poetry Magazine; HU; Hunger Magazine; Hunted News, The; Icon; Iconoclast, The; Ideals Magazine; Illuminations; Imago; Implosion Press; In the Grove; Indiana Review; Indigenous Fiction; Inklings; Inkslinger; Inkwell, The; Interbang; Interim; International Poetry Review; International Quarterly; Interpreter's House; Iota; Iowa Review, The; Jack Mackerel Magazine; Jewish Currents; Jones Av.; Jones Foundation National Poetry Competition, The Chester H.; Journal of Contemporary Anglo-Scandinavian Poetry; Journal of New Jersey Poets; Journal of the American Medical Association (JAMA); Junction Press; Jupiter's Freedom; K.T. Publications; Karamu; Kawabata Press; Kerf, The; Kimera; Kiosk; Kit-Cat Review, The; Koja; Konfluence; Krax; Kumquat Meringue; Lactuca; the LAIRE, Inc.; Ledge, The; Libido; Licking River Review, The; Light; Lilliput Review; Limestone Circle; LiNQ; Lintel; Listening Eye, The; Literal Latté; Literary Review, The; Literature and Belief; LitRag; Little Magazine, The; Lochs Magazine; London Magazine; Lone Stars Magazine; Long Islander; Loonfeather; Louisiana Literature; Louisville Review, The; Love Affair Literary Contest, A; Lowell Review, The; Lucid Stone, The; Lucidity; Lummox Press; LUNGFULL! Magazine; Lynx Eye; MacGuffin, The; Mad Poets Review; Madison Review, The; Maelstrom; Magazine, The; Magma Poetry Magazine; Magpie's Nest; Main Street Rag Poetry Journal; Mammoth Books; Mandrake Poetry Review; Mangrove; Manhattan Review, The; Mankato Poetry Review; Manoa; Marlboro Review, The; Maryland Poetry Review; Massachusetts Review, The; Mattoid; Medicinal Purposes Literary Review; Mediphors; Medusa's Hairdo; Mellen Poetry; Messages From the Heart; Metropolitan Review, The; Michigan State University Press; Mid-America Press, Inc., The; Mid-American Review; Mid-List Press First Series Award for Poetry; Midwest Poetry Review; Midwest Quarterly, The; Milkweed Editions; Milton Magazine, John; Mind in Motion; Mind Purge; Minnesota Review, The; Mississippi Review; Missouri Review; MM Review; Möbius; Modern Poetry In Translation; Monkey Flower; Morse Poetry Prize, Samuel French; Mount Olive College Press; Muse Journal; Muse of Fire; Muse Portfolio; Mythic Circle, The; Nada Press; Nanny Fanny; National Book Award; National Enquirer; National Poetry Series Annual Open Competition; Nebraska Review, The; Nedge; Neovictorian/Cochlea, The; Nerve Cowboy; New CollAge Magazine; New Delta Review; New England Review; New Issues Press; New Laurel Review, The; New Letters; New Millennium Award for Poetry; New Orleans Review; New Press Literary Quarterly, The; New Writer, The; New Writer's Magazine; New York Quarterly; New Zoo Poetry Review; Newburyport Art Association Annual Spring Poetry Contest; Nexus; Nightsun; Nimrod; 96 Inc Magazine; Nite-Writer's International Literary Arts Journal; No Exit; Nomad's Choir; Northeast Corridor; Northern Stars Magazine; Northwest Review; Northwoods Press; Northwords; Nostalgia; Notre Dame Review; Oasis; Octavo; Offerings; O'Hara Award Chapbook Competition, Frank; Ohio Review, The; Ohio State University Press/The Journal Award in Poetry; Ohio Teachers Write; One Trick Pony; Onset Review, The; Onthebus; Orange Willow Review; Orbis; Osiris; Other Voices; Outerbridge; Outposts Poetry Quarterly; Outrider Press; Owen Wister Review; Oxford Magazine; Oyster Boy Review; P.D.Q. (Poetry Depth Quarterly); Pacific Coast Journal; Pacific Enterprise Magazine; Paintbrush; Painted Bride Quarterly; Palanquin; Palo Alto Review; PandaLoon; Pannus Index, The; Paperplates; Paris/Atlantic; Parnassus Literary Journal; Parting Gifts; Partisan Review; Passager; Passages North; Paterson Literary Review, The; Paumanok Poetry Award Competition; Pavement Saw; Peaky Hide; Pearl; Pecan Grove Press; Peer Poetry Magazine; Pegasus; Pembroke Magazine; Pemmican; Penmanship; Pennine Ink; Pennine Platform; Pennsylvania English; Penny Dreadful Press; Penwood Review, The; People's Press, The; Peregrine; Permafrost; Perspectives; Perugia Press; Peterloo Poets; Phillips Poetry Prize, The Richard; Philomel; Phoebe (VA); Phoebe (NY); Piedmont Literary Review; Pif Magazine; Pig Iron; Pikeville Review; Pine Island Journal of New England Poetry; Pinyon Poetry; Pirate Writings; Pitchfork; Pitt Poetry Series; Plainsongs; Plastic Tower, The; Plaza, The; Pleiades; Plowman, The; Plume Literary Magazine; Poem; Poem du Jour; Poems & Plays; Poet Lore; Poetic Potpourri Quarterly Contests; Poetry & Prose Annual; Poetry Bone; Poetry Center Book Award, The; Poetry Explosion Newsletter, The; Poetry Forum; Poetry Harbor; Poetry Ireland Review; Poetry Kanto; Poetry Miscellany, The; Poetry Motel; Poetry New York; Poetry Northwest; Poetry Nottingham International; Poetry Review; Poetry Salzburg; Poetry USA; Poetry Wales; Poets at Work; Poets' Club of Chicago International Shakespearean/Petrarchan Sonnet Contest; Poets' Dinner Contest; Poet's Page, The; Poets'Paper; Pointed Circle, The; Polygon; Porcupine Literary Arts Magazine; Portland Review; Potato Eyes; Potomac Review; Potpourri; Pottersfield Portfolio; Prague Revue, The; Prairie Journal, The; Prairie Schooner; Prairie Winds; presstheEDGE; Pride Imprints; Primavera; Prism International; Procreation; Provincetown Arts; Psychopoetica; Puckerbrush Press, The; Pudding House Publications; Puerto Del Sol; Pulitzer Prize in Letters; Pulsar Poetry Magazine; Purdue University Press; QED Press; Qoph; Quadrant Magazine; Quantum Leap; Quarter After Eight; Quarterly Review of Literature Poetry Book Series; Quarterly West; Queen's Quarterly; Rag Mag; Rainmaker Awards in Poetry; Ralph's Review; Rambunctious Press; Rattapallax; Rattle; Raw Dog Press; Raw Seed Review, The; RE:AL;

Reater, The; Red Candle Press, The; Red Cedar Review; Red Deer Press; Red Dragon Press; Red Hen Press; Red Herring; Red Owl Magazine; Red Rock Review; Rejected Quarterly, The; Rhino; Rio; Rio Grande Review; Rivelin Grapheme Press; River King Poetry Supplement; River Oak Review; River Styx Magazine; Riverrun; Riverstone; Rocket Press; Rockford Review, The; Ronsdale Press; Room of One's Own; Rosebud; Rosenberg Award, Anna Davidson; Rustic Rub; Sachem Press; Salt Hill; Saltonstall Foundation for the Arts Grants, The Constance; Sarabande Books, Inc.; Sarasota Poetry Theatre Press; Score Magazine; Scrivener; Seattle Review; Seems; Seneca Review; Senior Poet Laureate Poetry Competition; Sensations Magazine; Shades of December; Shattered Wig Review; Sheila-Na-Gig; Shenandoah; Sidewalks; Sierra Nevada College Review; Silverfish Review; Simple Vows; Sisters Today; Situation; Sixth Chamber; Skipping Stones; Sky, The; Skylark; Slant; Slapering Hol Press Chapbook Competition; Slipstream; Small Pond Magazine of Literature; Smiths Knoll; Smoke; Snowapple Press; Snowy Egret; So To Speak; Society of American Poets (SOAP), The; Somniloquy; Soul Fountain; Soundpost Press Annual Chapbook Award; Sounds of Poetry, The; South; South Carolina Review; Southern Humanities Review; Southern Poetry Review; Southern Review, The; Southfields; Southwest Review; Southwestern American Literature; Sou'wester; Sow's Ear Poetry Review, The; spelunker flophouse; Spillway; Spindrift; Spinning Jenny; Spirit That Moves Us, The; SpoonFed; Spout Magazine; Spunk; Spuyten Duyvil; Star Rising; Starving Romantics Poetry Competition; State Street Review; Stegner Fellowships, Wallace E.; Still Waters Press; Stone Soup Magazine; Stoneflower Press; Story Line Press; Stovepipe; Strain, The; Stride Publications; Struggle; Studio; Sulphur River Literary Review; Summer Stream Press; Summer's Reading, A; Sun Poetic Times; Sun, The; Sunstone; Superior Poetry News; Sweet Annie & Sweet Pea Review; Sycamore Review; Synaesthesia Press; Syncopated City; Takahe; Talking River Review; Taproot Literary Review; Tar River Poetry; Tea Party; Teacup; Tears in the Fence; Temporary Vandalism Recordings; Texas Review; Thema; Thin Coyote; Third Coast; Third Half Literary Magazine, The; Thirst Magazine; 13th Moon; 32 Pages; Thomas Charitable Trust Open Poetry Contest, David; Thorny Locust; 360 Degrees; Threepenny Review, The; Thumbscrew; Tia Chucha Press; Tickled by Thunder; Tightrope; Time of Singing; TLS/Blackwell's Poetry Competition; Tmp Irregular, The; To Topio; Touchstone; Towson University Prize for Literature; Trestle Creek Review; Trewithen Poetry Prize, The; Tri Lingua; TriQuarterly Magazine; Troubadour; True Romance; Tsunami Inc.; Tucumcari Literary Review; Twilight Ending; two girls review; Two Rivers Review; Tyro Publishing; U.S. 1 Worksheets; Ultramarine Publishing Co., Inc.; Understanding Magazine; University of Central Florida Contemporary Poetry Series; University of Georgia Press; University of Massachusetts Press, The; Urbanite, The; Urthona Magazine; Ver Poets Open Competition; Vigil; Virginia Literary Review; Visiting Fellowships for Historical Research; Vol. No. Magazine; War Cry, The; Warthog Press; Wasafiri; Wascana Review; Washington Square; Way Station Magazine; Wellspring; West Branch; West Coast Line; West Wind Review; Westerly; Western Humanities Review; Westview; Weyfarers; Whelks Walk Review; Whetstone; Whiskey Island Magazine; White Eagle Coffee Store Press; White Pine Press; Whole Notes; Wick Poetry Prize, Stan and Tom; William and Mary Review, The; Willow Review; Willow Springs; Wind Publications; Windsor Review; Wings Magazine, Inc.; Wisconsin Arts Board Fellowships; Wisconsin Review; Wolf Head Quarterly; Worcester Review; Word Salad; Word Works, The; Words of Wisdom; Wordwrights!; World Order of Narrative and Formalist Poets; Writer, The; Writer's Block, The; Writers Bureau Poetry and Short Story Competition, The; Writers' Center Press; Writer's Digest; Writer's Journal; Xanadu; Xcp: Cross-Cultural Poetics; Yankee Magazine; Yefief; Yemassee; Zombie Logic Press; Zygote Magazine

◙ OPEN MOSTLY TO EXPERIENCED POETS, FEW BEGINNERS

A Small Garlic Press; Aabye; Abraxas Magazine; Acid Angel; Afterthoughts; Agni; American Poetry Review; American Scholar, The; Amicus Journal, The; Angel Exhaust; Antioch Review, The; ARC Publications; Arjuna Library Press; Bacchae Press; Barbarian Press; Birch Brook Press; Black Belt Press; Black Tie Press; Boa Editions, Ltd.; Boston Phoenix, The; Boston Review; BrickHouse Books, Inc.; Café Review, The; Canadian Dimension; Capilano Review, The; Caveat Lector; Center Press; Chelsea; Chicago Review; City Lights Books; Coffee House Press; Commonweal; Conjunctions; Copper Canyon Press; Cortland Review, The; Debut Review; DeeMar Communications; Descant; Dial Books for Young Readers; Dickey Newsletter, James; Dim Gray Bar Press; Écrits des Forges; Epoch; European Judaism; Evangel; Expedition Press; Fire; First Things; Flambard; Forklift Ohio; Frogmore Papers; Galaxy Press; Gargoyle Magazine; Gecko; Grand Street; Green Bean Press; Green Mountains Review; Habersham Review; Holiday House, Inc.; Horizon; Hubbub; Hudson Review, The; Image; Indigenous Fiction; Iris; Janus; Javelina Press; Journal, The; Joyful Woman, The; Kaimana; La Jolla Poet's Press; Laurel Review; Limited Editions Press; Lips; Lone Willow Press; Long Shot; Loom Press; Los; Lothrop, Lee & Shepard Books; Matriarch's Way; Mekler & Deahl, Publishers; Membrane; Mesechabe; Michigan Quarterly Review; Mind Matters Review; Mississippi Mud; mojo risin' magazine; Nassau Review; Nation, The; National Forum; Negative Capability; New Criterion, The; New Orleans Poetry Journal Press; New Republic, The; New Rivers Press; New Yorker, The; North American Review; North Dakota Quarterly; Northeast; Northeast Arts Magazine; Norton & Company, Inc., W.W.; O!!Zone; Ocean View Books; Open Spaces; Orchises Press; Other Press; Other Side Magazine, The; Papyrus; Paris Review, The; Passeggiata Press; Pavement Saw; Pequod; Philomel Books; Planet; Ploughshares; Poetry; Poetry Life; Po'Flye Internationale; Portals Press; Prairie Publishing Company, The; Prose Poem, The; Pygmy Forest Press; Raintown Review, The; Red Dancefloor Press; Red Moon Press; Salmon Run Press; Santa Barbara Review; Semiquasi Press; Smith Publisher, Gibbs; Smith, The; Soft Skull Press, Inc.; Sono Nis Press; Southern California Anthology, The; Spinning Jenny; Spoon River Poetry Review, The; Stevens Journal, The Wallace; Sticks; Tampa Review; Tebot Bach; 10th Muse; Terrible Work; Timber Creek Review; Touchstone Literary Journal; University of Iowa Press; Utah State University Press; Vehicule Press; Verse; Virginia Quarterly Review, The; Wesleyan University Press; West Anglia Publications; Whelks Walk Review; Wolfsong Publications; Women's Review of Books; Womenwise; World Letter; Yale University Press; Zoland Books Inc.; Zuzu's Petals Quarterly Online

◎ SPECIALIZED—OPEN TO POETS FROM SPECIFIC AREAS OR GROUPS OR POEMS IN SPECIFIC FORMS OR ON SPECIFIC THEMES

Abiko Annual; Aboriginal SF; About Such Things; Above the Bridge Magazine; Acorn, The; Adaptables Annual Poetry Award; Adobe Abalone; Adrift; Aethlon; African Voices; Afro-Hispanic Review; Afterthoughts; Aguilar Expression, The; Ahsahta Press; Aim Magazine; Albatross; Alice James Books; Alive Now; Allegheny Review; Alpha Beat Soup; Amelia; American Cowboy Poet Magazine, The; American Dissident, The; American Tanka; American Writing; Amicus Journal, The; Amy Award, The; Analecta; Ancient Paths; Andreas-Gryphius-Preis; Angel News Magazine; Anna's Journal; Anthology of New England Writers, The; Antietam Review; Antipodes; Apostolic Crusade, The; Appalachia; Appalachian Heritage; Apropos; Arachne, Inc.; Arkansas Review; Artful Dodge; Artist Trust; Arts Recognition and Talent Search; Asian Pacific American Journal; Avocet; Backspace; BadLands Press; Barbarian Press; Barking Dog Books; Bauhan, Publisher, William L.; Bay Area Book Reviewers Association Awards; Bay Windows; Baybury Review; Beacon; Beacon Street Review; Bear Deluxe, The; Bear Star Press; Belhue Press; Bell's Letters Poet; Bennett & Kitchel; Bible Advocate; Bilingual Review Press; Bird Watcher's Digest; Birmingham Poetry Review; Bitter Oleander, The; Black Bear Publications; black bough; Black Diaspora Magazine; Blackwater Press; Blind Beggar Press; Blindskills, Inc.; Blue Collar Review; Blue Mesa Review; Blue Mountain Arts, Inc.; Blue Skunk Companion, The; Blue Unicorn; Blue Violin; Blueline; Bluster; Boardman Tasker Award, The; Bordighera, Inc.; Borealis Press; Bouillabaisse; BP Nichol Chapbook Award; Bread of Life Magazine, The; Briar Cliff Review, The; BrickHouse Books, Inc.; Brilliant Corners; Brilliant Star; Bucknell Seminar for Younger Poets; Buffalo Bones; Bugle, Journal of Elk and the Hunt; Byline Magazine; California Book Awards; Calyx; Canadian Authors Association Literary Awards; Canadian Dimension; Canadian Literature; Canadian Woman Studies; Canadian Writer's Journal; Capper's; Caribbean Writer, The; Carolina Wren Press; Catamount Press; Cayo; CC Motorcycle News Magazine; Challenger international; Chapman; Chelsea; Chicago Review; Chicory Blue Press; Christian Century, The; Christianity and the Arts; Chronicles of Disorder; Chrysalis Reader; Claremont Review, The; Classical Outlook, The; Cleaning Business Magazine; Cleveland State University Poetry Center; Climbing Art, The; Cló Iar-Chonnachta; Clubhouse; Clubhouse Jr.; Cochran's Corner; Collages & Bricolages; Colorado Book Awards; Common Threads; Commonweal; Communities; Community of Poets Press; Companion in Zeor, A; Confluence Press; Coolbrith Circle Annual Poetry Contest, Ina; Cornerstone; Cortland Review, The; Cosmic Trend; Coteau Books; Cottonwood; Country Woman; Coyote Chronicles; Crab Creek Review; Creative With Words Publications (C.W.W.); Creative Writing Fellowships in Poetry; Cricket; Cross & Quill; Cross-Cultural Communications; Crumb Elbow Publishing Poetry Contests; Cumberland Poetry Review; Current Accounts; Curriculum Vitae Literary Supplement; Cycle Press; Dagger of the Mind; Dandelion Arts Magazine; Dark Regions; Dead Fun; Descant; Dial Books for Young Readers; Dirigible; Dissident Editions; Doc(k)s; Dolphin-Moon Press; Draigeye; Dream International Quarterly; Driftwood Review, The; Dry Bones Press; Dwan; Eagle's Flight; Earth's Daughters; Eastern Caribbean Institute; Écrits des Forges; Edgar; Eidos Magazine; Eighth Mountain Press, The; Ekphrasis; Emerging Lesbian Writers Award; Emshock Letter, The; Endemoniada Fanzine; Equilibrium [10]; European Judaism; Evangel; Event; Exit 13; Expedition Press; Feather Books; Feminist Studies; Feminist Voices; Fiddlehead, The; Field, The; Firebrand Books; Fireweed: A Feminist Quarterly; Fireweed: Poetry of Western Oregon; Firm Noncommittal; First Offense; Floating Bridge Press; Florida Individual Artist Fellowships; Formalist, The; 4*9*1 Neo-Immanentist*Imagination; Frank; frisson; Frogpond; Full Moon Press; Futurific; Gairm; Gertrude; Glassco Translation Prize, John; GLB Publishers; Gleeful Press!, A; Golden Isis Magazine; Goose Lane Editions; Gospel Publishing House; Gotta Write Network Litmag; Green River Writers' Contests; Guernica Editions Inc.; Habersham Review; Haight Ashbury Literary Journal; Halls Fellowship, J.C. and Ruth; Handshake; Hanging Loose Press; Hard Row to Hoe; Harvard Advocate, The; Haypenny Press; Heartlands Today, The; Heaven Bone Magazine; Heist Magazine; Hellas; Hemans Prize for Lyrical Poetry, Felicia; Herald Press; Herb Network, The; High Plains Press; High/Coo Press; Highlights for Children; Hilltop Press; Hippopotamus Press; Hodgepodge Short Stories & Poetry; Holiday House, Inc.; Home Times; Hopscotch; House of Anansi Press; HU; Human Quest, The; Hurricane Alice; Idiot, The; Image; Imago; Implosion Press; In the Family; In the Grove; Indian Heritage Publishing; Individual Artist Grants; Inklingsger; Inner Voices; Innovative Publishing Concepts; Insects Are People Two; International Poetry Review; International Quarterly; Interpreter's House; Intertext; Intro; Iris; Italian Americana; Italica Press; Japan Foundation Artist Fellowship Program, The; Japanese Literary Translation Prize; Japanophile; Javelina Press; Jewish Affairs; Jewish Currents; Jewish Spectator; Jewish Women's Literary Annual; Journal of African Travel-Writing; Journal of Asian Martial Arts; Journal of Contemporary Anglo-Scandinavian Poetry; Journal of New Jersey Poets; Journal of the American Medical Association (JAMA); Jupiter's Freedom; Kaimana; Kaleidoscope; Kalliope; Kawabata Press; Kelsey Review; Kerf, The; Key Satch(el); Koja; Koshkovich Press; Krax; Kuumba; La Pira'' International Literary Prize, ''Giorgio; Lactuca; Landfall; Lapwing Publications; Laurels; Leacock Medal for Humour, The Stephen; Leading Edge, The; League of Minnesota Poets Contest, The; Libido; Lilith Magazine; Lilliput Review; Listening Eye, The; Literary Focus Poetry Publications; Literature and Belief; London Writers Competition; Long Island Quarterly; Lonzie's Fried Chicken© Literary Magazine; Loonfeather; Lotus Press, Inc.; Louisiana Literature; Louisiana Review, The; Louisville Review, The; Luna Bisonte Prods; Luz en Arte y Literatura; Lynx, A Journal for Linking Poets; M.I.P. Company; Magazine of Speculative Poetry, The; Mail Call Journal; Main Street Rag Poetry Journal; Making Waves; Malafemmina Press; Mandrake Poetry Review; Manhattan Review, The; Marymark Press; Matriarch's Way; Mature Women's Grants; Mature Years; Meadowbrook Press; Mediphors; Mennonite, The; Merlyn's Pen; Miami University Press; Mid-America Press, Inc., The; Mid-American Review; Middle East Report; Midstream; Midwifery Today; Milton Center Poetry Fellowship; Milton Magazine, John; Minority Literary Expo; Miraculous Medal, The; Mkashef Enterprises; Modern Haiku; Modern Poetry In Translation; Money For Women; Montalvo Biennial Poetry Competition;

Geographical Index

Use this index to locate poetry-related publishers and events in your region. Much of the poetry published today reflects regional interests. In addition, publishers often favor poets (and work) from their own areas. We also include conferences and workshops in this index to help you easily find local happenings. Also, keep your neighboring areas in mind for other opportunities.

Here you will find the names of U.S. publishers, conferences and workshops arranged alphabetically within their state or territory. Following them are lists of publishers in Canada, the United Kingdom, Australia, France, Japan and other countries. See the General Index for the page numbers of their corresponding listings.

ALABAMA
Publishers of Poetry
Alabama Literary Review
Alden Enterprises
Birmingham Poetry Review
Black Belt Press
Black Warrior Review
Catamount Press
Inverted-A, Inc.
Laureate Letter Chapbook, The
Minority Literary Expo
National Forum
Native Tongue
Negative Capability
Poem
Science Fiction Poetry
    Association
Southern Humanities Review
Sticks
TimBookTu
Uprising

ALASKA
Publishers of Poetry
Alaska Quarterly Review
Explorations
Intertext
Permafrost
Salmon Run Press

ARIZONA
Publishers of Poetry
Alligator Juniper
Allison Press
Anthology
Bangtale International
Bilingual Review Press
Coyote Chronicles
Dusty Dog Press
Hayden's Ferry Review
Innovative Publishing Concepts
Javelina Press
Lucid Stone, The
Messages From the Heart
Newsletter Inago

Pannus Index, The
Star Rising
Synaesthesia Press
University of Arizona Press

Conferences & Workshops
Pima Writers' Workshop
Wrangling With Writing

ARKANSAS
Publishers of Poetry
Arkansas Review
Cedar Hill Publications
Lucidity
Nebo: A Literary Journal
Slant
Storyteller, The

Conferences & Workshops
Lucidity Poets' Ozark Retreat

CALIFORNIA
Publishers of Poetry
Acorn, The
Adobe Abalone
Amelia
American Indian Studies Center
Anamnesis Press
Apostolic Crusade, The
Arctos Press
Arshile
Avocet
Bay Area Poets Coalition (BAPC)
Bear Star Press
Blue Satellite
Blue Unicorn
Bottomfish
Caveat Lector
Center Press
Cider Press Review
City Lights Books
Clutch
Concrete Abstract
Crania
Creative With Words
    Publications (C.W.W.)

Creativity Unlimited Press®
Cyber Oasis
Daniel and Company, Publisher,
    John
Dark Regions
Draigeye
Drinkin' Buddy Magazine, The
Dry Bones Press
Ekphrasis
Emotions Literary Magazine
Enterzone
Epicenter
Faultline
For Poetry.Com
Free Lunch
GLB Publishers
Golden Isis Magazine
Haight Ashbury Literary Journal
Harcourt, Inc.
Hard Row to Hoe
Idiot, The
In the Grove
Interbang
Jewish Spectator
Junction Press
Kerf, The
Konocti Books
Kuumba
La Jolla Poet's Press
Leapings Literary Magazine
Left Curve
Libra Publishers, Inc.
Limestone Circle
Los
Lummox Press
Luz en Arte y Literatura
Lynx, A Journal for Linking Poets
Lynx Eye
Mama Yama Magazine
Metropolitan Review, The
Mind in Motion
Mind Matters Review
Mkashef Enterprises
Monkey Flower
Moving Parts Press

New Laurel Review, The
New Orleans Poetry Forum
New Orleans Poetry Journal
  Press
New Orleans Review
Pelican Publishing Company
Piedmont Literary Review
Portals Press
Southern Review, The
Thema
Thunder Rain Publishing
Tri Lingua

MAINE
Publishers of Poetry
Alice James Books
Beloit Poetry Journal, The
Café Review, The
Northeast Arts Magazine
Northwoods Press
Potato Eyes
Puckerbrush Press, The

Conferences & Workshops
DownEast Maine Writer's
  Workshops

MARYLAND
Publishers of Poetry
Abbey
Antietam Review
Baltimore Review, The
Black Moon
BrickHouse Books, Inc.
Cochran's Corner
Dolphin-Moon Press
Feminist Studies
In the Family
Johns Hopkins University Press,
  The
Maryland Poetry Review
Nightsun
Octavo
Open University of America
  Press
Oracle Poetry
Passager
People's Press, The
Plastic Tower, The
Poet Lore
Potomac Review
Satire
Shattered Wig Review
Situation
Vegetarian Journal

Conferences & Workshops
Literary Festival at St. Mary's

MASSACHUSETTS
Publishers of Poetry
Aboriginal SF
Adastra Press
Agni
American Dissident, The

Amherst Review, The
Appalachia
Atlantic Monthly, The
Aurorean, The
Backspace
Bay Windows
Beacon Street Review
Bluster
Boston Phoenix, The
Boston Review
Button Magazine
Christian Science Monitor, The
doublebunny press
Eidos Magazine
Godine, Publisher, David R.
Harvard Advocate, The
Houghton Mifflin Co.
Key Satch(el)
Loom Press
Mad River Press
Massachusetts Review, The
Muse Portfolio
New Renaissance, The
96 Inc Magazine
Onset Review, The
Osiris
Partisan Review
Peregrine
Perugia Press
Pine Island Journal of New
  England Poetry
Ploughshares
Point Judith Light
Provincetown Arts
Sour Grapes
Suzerain Enterprises
Tightrope
University of Massachusetts
  Press, The
Voiding The Void
Women's Review of Books
Womenwise
Worcester Review
Writer, The
Zoland Books Inc.

Conferences & Workshops
Cape Cod Writers' Center
  Summer Conference
Whidbey Island Writers'
  Conferences

MICHIGAN
Publishers of Poetry
Above the Bridge Magazine
Angelflesh
Bennett & Kitchel
Bridge, The
Centennial Review, The
Clubhouse
Dead Fun
Driftwood Review, The
Eratica
Ethereal Green
Expedition Press

Gazelle Publications
Gravity Presses
Japanophile
Lotus Press, Inc.
MacGuffin, The
Michigan Quarterly Review
Michigan State University Press
Nada Press
New Issues Press
Northern Stars Magazine
Osric Publishing
Passages North
Perspectives
Poet's Energy, The
Rarach Press
Red Cedar Review
Riverrun
Sounds of Poetry, The
Struggle
Third Coast
Thumbprints
Touch
Way Station Magazine

MINNESOTA
Publishers of Poetry
ArtWord Quarterly
Ascent
Blue Skunk Companion, The
Cadence
Coffee House Press
Conduit
Gleeful Press!, A
Kumquat Meringue
Liftouts Magazine
Loonfeather
Lutheran Digest, The
M.I.P. Company
Mankato Poetry Review
Meadowbrook Press
Midwest Villages & Voices
Milkweed Editions
New Rivers Press
Poetry Harbor
Poetry Motel
Rag Mag
Sidewalks
Sing Heavenly Muse!
Sisters Today
Sixth Chamber
Spout Magazine
Thin Coyote
Voices From the Well
Writer's Journal
Xcp: Cross-Cultural Poetics

Conferences & Workshops
Split Rock Arts Program

MISSISSIPPI
Publishers of Poetry
Bell's Letters Poet
Doggerel
Georgetown Review
Mississippi Review

Semiquasi Press

MISSOURI
Publishers of Poetry
Afro-Hispanic Review
BKMK Press
Boulevard
Cape Rock, The
Chariton Review, The
Country Folk
Debut Review
Funny Paper, The
Gospel Publishing House
Green Hills Literary Lantern
Hodgepodge Short Stories &
    Poetry
Laurel Review
Lowell Review, The
Mid-America Press, Inc., The
Missouri Review
Nazarene International
    Headquarters
New Letters
Offerings
Paintbrush
Pleiades
River Styx Magazine
Thorny Locust
Timberline Press
Wolf Head Quarterly

Conferences & Workshops
Heartland Writers Conference

MONTANA
Publishers of Poetry
Bugle
Corona
Cutbank
Poem du Jour
Seven Buffaloes Press
Superior Poetry News
Teacup

Conferences & Workshops
Yellow Bay Writers' Workshop

NEBRASKA
Publishers of Poetry
Beggar's Press
In the Spirit of the Buffalo
Lone Willow Press
Nebraska Review, The
Plainsongs
Prairie Schooner

NEVADA
Publishers of Poetry
Interim
Limited Editions Press
Pegasus
Red Rock Review
Sierra Nevada College Review

NEW HAMPSHIRE
Publishers of Poetry
Bauhan, Publisher, William L.
Compass Rose
Northern Centinel, The
Red Owl Magazine
Verse
Yankee Magazine

Conferences & Workshops
Festival of Poetry

NEW JERSEY
Publishers of Poetry
black bough
Companion in Zeor, A
Devil Blossoms
Edgar
Ever Dancing Muse, The
Exit 13
Hellp!
Higginsville Reader, The
Journal of New Jersey Poets
Kelsey Review
Lactuca
Lips
Literary Review, The
Long Shot
Lucid Moon
Maelstrom
Mail Call Journal
Marymark Press
Naturally
Paterson Literary Review, The
Princeton University Press
Quarterly Review of Literature
    Poetry Book Series
Sacred Journey
St. Joseph Messenger and
    Advocate of the Blind
Saturday Press, Inc.
Sensations Magazine
Still Waters Press
Timber Creek Review
U.S. 1 Worksheets
Vista Publishing, Inc.
Warthog Press
Wings Magazine, Inc.
Writes of Passage

Conferences & Workshops
Winter Poetry & Prose Getaway
    in Cape May

NEW MEXICO
Publishers of Poetry
Asher Publishing, Sherman
Atom Mind
Blue Mesa Review
Herb Network, The
Katydid Books
Paradoxism
Pennywhistle Press
Puerto Del Sol
RB's Poets' Viewpoint

Tmp Irregular, The
Whole Notes
Yefief

Conferences & Workshops
Southwest Writers Workshop

NEW YORK
Publishers of Poetry
Aardvark Adventurer, The
Adrift
Advocate
Affair of the Mind
African Voices
Alms House Press
America
American Tanka
Amicus Journal, The
Antipodes
Arachne, Inc.
Art Times
Asian Pacific American Journal
Barbaric Yawp
Barrow Street
Belhue Press
Birch Brook Press
Bitter Oleander, The
Black Diaspora Magazine
Black Spring Press
Black Thistle Press
Blind Beggar Press
Blue Ink Press
Blueline
Boa Editions, Ltd.
Bomb Magazine
Bright Hill Press
Brownout Laboratories
Brownstone Review, The
Buffalo Spree Magazine
Camellia
CC Motorcycle News Magazine
Chelsea
Chronicles of Disorder
Columbia
Commonweal
Comstock Review, The
Confrontation Magazine
Conjunctions
Cover Magazine
Cross-Cultural Communications
Curio
Desperate Act
Dial Books for Young Readers
Dim Gray Bar Press
Earth's Daughters
Edgewise Press, Inc.
1812
Endemoniada Fanzine
Epoch
Firebrand Books
First Things
Fish Drum
Frogpond
Futurific
Gathering of the Tribes, A

Gerbil
Graffiti Rag
Grand Street
Green Bean Press
Hanging Loose Press
Heaven Bone Magazine
Helikon Press
Holiday House, Inc.
Hudson Review, The
Hunger Magazine
Iconoclast, The
Italica Press
Jewish Currents
Jewish Women's Literary Annual
Kiosk
Kit-Cat Review, The
Knopf, Alfred A.
Koja
Ledge, The
Lilith Magazine
Lintel
Literal Latté
Little Magazine, The
Long Island Quarterly
Long Islander
Lothrop, Lee & Shepard Books
Low-Tech Press
LUNGFULL! Magazine
Malafemmina Press
Manhattan Review, The
Matriarch's Way
Medicinal Purposes Literary
   Review
Mellen Poetry
Midstream
Milton Magazine, John
Nassau Review
Nation, The
New Criterion, The
New Press Literary Quarterly
New York Quarterly
New Yorker, The
Nomad's Choir
Norton & Company, Inc., W.W.
Outerbridge
Oxford University Press
Paris Review, The
Pavement Saw
Penny Dreadful
Peoplenet Disability Datenet
Pequod
Philomel Books
Phoebe (NY)
Pipe Smoker's Ephemeris, The
Pirate Writings
Poetry Bone
Poetry New York
Poets on the Line
Poet's Paradise
Queen of All Hearts
Queen's Mystery Magazine,
   Ellery
Ralph's Review
Rattapallax
Review

Richmond Communications LLC
Rocket Press
Sachem Press
Salt Hill
Seneca Review
Serpent & Eagle Press
Shades of December
Shamal Books
Shofar
Slate & Style
Slipstream
Smith, The
Soft Skull Press, Inc.
Soul Fountain
Spinning Jenny
Spirit That Moves Us, The
Spring
Spuyten Duyvil
Stevens Journal, The Wallace
13th Moon
True Romance
Ultramarine Publishing Co.
Washington Square
Water Mark Press
Waterways
Whelks Walk Review
White Pine Press
Xanadu
Zuzu's Petals Quarterly Online

Conferences & Workshops
Catskill Poetry Workshop
Chenango Valley Writers'
   Conference
IWWG Summer Conference
Manhattanville's Writers' Week
Southampton College Writing
   Conference
Writers' Center at Chautauqua

NORTH CAROLINA
Publishers of Poetry
Asheville Poetry Review
Carolina Quarterly, The
Carolina Wren Press
Cold Mountain Review
Communities
Crucible
DeeMar Communications
frisson: disconcerting verse
Greensboro Review, The
International Poetry Review
Journal of African Travel-Writing
Lonzie's Fried Chicken™
   Literary Magazine
Main Street Rag Poetry Journal
Minnesota Review, The
Mount Olive College Press
Muse's Kiss Webzine
New Native Press
North Carolina Literary Review
Oyster Boy Review
Parting Gifts
Pembroke Magazine
Procreation

Southern Poetry Review
Sun, The
Tar River Poetry
Urthona Press
Wake Forest University Press
Wellspring
Word Salad
Words of Wisdom

Conferences & Workshops
Poetry Alive!

NORTH DAKOTA
Publishers of Poetry
North Dakota Quarterly

Conferences & Workshops
UND Writers Conference

OHIO
Publishers of Poetry
Antioch Review, The
Artful Dodge
Bird Watcher's Digest
Cleveland State University
   Poetry Center
Common Threads
Confluence
English Journal
Field
Forklift, Ohio
Generator
Grasslands Review
Heartlands Today, The
Hey, listen!
Hiram Poetry Review
Hopscotch
Icon
Implosion Press
Inkslinger
Journal, The
Kaleidoscope
Koshkovich Press
Lilith
Listening Eye, The
Luna Bisonte Prods
Luna Negra
Miami University Press
Mid-American Review
MM Review
New Song, A
Nexus
Ohio Review, The
Ohio State University Press/The
   Journal Award in Poetry
Ohio Teachers Write
"Over The Back Fence"
   Magazine
Oxford Magazine
Pig Iron
Poet's Haven, The
Pudding House Publications
Quarter After Eight
St. Anthony Messenger
Screaming Ray Review, The

OTHER COUNTRIES
Publishers of Poetry

Subject Index

Use this index to save time in your search for the best markets for your poetry. The categories are listed alphabetically and contain the magazines, publishers, contests and awards that buy or accept poetry dealing with specific subjects. Most of these markets have the ◎ symbol before their listing titles.

Check through the index first to see what subjects are represented. Then look at the listings in the categories you're interested in. For example, if you're seeking a magazine or contest for your poem about "baseball," look at the titles under **Sports/Recreation**. After you've selected a possible market, refer to the General Index for the page number. Then read the listing *carefully* for details on submission requirements.

Under **Themes**, you will find those book and magazine publishers that regularly publish anthologies or issues on announced themes (if interested, send a SASE to these publishers for details on upcoming topics). **Regional** includes those outlets which publish poetry about or by poets from a certain geographic area; and the category **Form/Style** contains those magazines and presses that seek particular poetic forms or styles, such as haiku or sonnets or experimental work. Finally, those publishers listed under **Specialized** are very narrow in their interests—too narrow, in fact, to be listed in one of our other categories.

We do not recommend you use this index exclusively in your search for markets. Most magazines, publishers and contests listed in *Poet's Market* have wide-ranging poetry preferences and don't choose to be listed by category. Also, many of those who specialize in one subject are often open to others as well. Reading *all* the listings is still your best marketing strategy.

Animal: Bugle, Journal of Elk and the Hunt; Wise Woman's Garden, A

Anthology: Arctos Press; Asher Publishing, Sherman; Asian Pacific American Journal; Bay Area Poets Coalition (BAPC); Birch Brook Press; Blind Beggar Press; Catamount Press; Coteau Books; Cross-Cultural Communications; Dial 174 Magazine; Feather Books; Floating Bridge Press; Full Moon Press; Kawabata Press; Kingfisher Publications Plc; Literary Focus Poetry Publications; Meadowbrook Press; Mekler & Deahl, Publishers; Nada Press; New Mirage Quarterly, The; Northwoods Press; Outrider Press; PandaLoon; Papier-Mache Press; Passeggiata Press; Peace & Freedom; Pennywhistle Press; Phoenix; Pigasus Press; Plowman, The; Poet's Fantasy; Polygon; Prairie Journal, The; Pudding House Publications; Red Moon Press; Scroll Publications; Seeds Poetry Magazine; Seven Buffaloes Press; Shamal Books; Society of American Poets (SOAP), The; Southern California Anthology, The; Spirit That Moves Us, The; Sticks; To Topio; Voices Israel; Waterways; West Wind Review; White Eagle Coffee Store Press; Word Works, The

Bilingual/Foreign Language: Andreas-Gryphius-Preis (German); Bilingual Review Press (Spanish); Borderlands; Cló Iar-Chonnachta (Gaelic); Cross-Cultural Communications; Doc(k)s (French); Dwan; Écrits des Forges; Gairm (Scottish Gaelic); Horizontes (Spanish); Italica Press (Italian); La Pira" International Literary Prize, "Giorgio (Italian); Luz en Arte y Literatura (Spanish); M.I.P. Company (Russian); New Renaissance, The; Osiris (French, Italian, Polish, Danish, German); Plaza, The (Japanese); Polygon (Gaelic); Prakalpana Literature (Bengali); Princeton University Press; Rarach Press (Czech); Sachem Press (Spanish); Skipping Stones; To Topio; Trilingua (American, French, Italian); Tsunami Inc. (Chinese, Spanish); Wake Forest University Press (French)

Children/Teen/Young Adult: Alive Now; Blind Beggar Press; Bluster; Brilliant Star; Challenger international; Claremont Review, The; Clubhouse; Clubhouse Jr.; Coteau Books; Creative With Words Publications (C.W.W.); Cricket; Dial Books for Young Readers; Gospel Publishing House; Hanging Loose Press; Herald Press; Highlights for Children; Holiday House, Inc.; Hopscotch; In 2 Print Magazine; Kingfisher Publications Plc; Louisville Review, The; Meadowbrook Press; Merlyn's Pen; Milton Magazine, John; Nazarene International Headquarters; New Era Magazine; Night Roses; Oak, The; Pelican Publishing Company; Shofar; Skipping Stones; Spring Tides; Stone Soup; Straight; Texas Young Writers' Newsletter; Touch; Vegetarian Journal; Waterways; Whole Notes; Wordsong; Writes of Passage

SUBJECT INDEX

Membership/Subscription: Apropos; Bell's Letters Poet; Cochran's Corner; Common Threads; Current Accounts; Dandelion Arts Magazine; Emshock Letter, The; Hemans Prize for Lyrical Poetry, Felicia; Herb Network, The; Hodgepodge Short Stories & Poetry; Inkslinger; Intro; Laurels; Minority Literary Expo; Mystery Time; New Orleans Poetry Forum; Pennsylvania Poetry Society Annual Contest; Poetry Forum; Poetry Life; Poetry Nottingham International; Poets at Work; Poet's Paradise; Poets' Roundtable; Quarterly Review of Literature Poetry Book Series; Sensations Magazine; Society of American Poets (SOAP), The; "Teak" Roundup; Thalia; Tickled by Thunder; Voices Israel; Wishing Well, The; World Order of Narrative and Formalist Poets

Mystery: Murderous Intent; Mystery Time; Oak, The; Outer Darkness; Pirate Writings; Queen's Mystery Magazine, Ellery; Scavenger's Newsletter; Wise Woman's Garden, A

Nature/Rural/Ecology: Albatross; Amicus Journal, The; Appalachia; Arachne, Inc.; Avocet; Bear Deluxe, The; Bird Watcher's Digest; Bugle, Journal of Elk and the Hunt; Capper's; Hard Row to Hoe; Heaven Bone Magazine; Herb Network, The; Houghton Mifflin Co.; Kerf, The; Night Roses; Northern Centinel, The; Open University of America Press; Poetry of the People; Rural Heritage; Seven Buffaloes Press; Skipping Stones; Snowy Egret; Tale Spinners; Trewithen Poetry Prize, The; Wise Woman's Garden, A

Political: Afterthoughts; Aim Magazine; American Dissident, The; Blue Collar Review; Canadian Dimension; Collages & Bricolages; Coyote Chronicles; Human Quest, The; Northern Centinel, The; Other Side Magazine, The; Pudding House Publications; Sojourners; Struggle; Uprising

Psychic/Occult: Draigeye; Endemoniada Fanzine; Mkashef Enterprises; South 666 Bitch, The; Superior Poetry News; Wise Woman's Garden, A

Regional: Above the Bridge Magazine (Michigan's Upper Peninsula); Acorn, The (Western Sierra); Ahsahta Press (ID); Alice James Books (New England); Amy Award, The (NYC, Long Island); Antietam Review (DC, DE, MD, PA, VA, WV); Antipodes (Australia); Appalachian Heritage (Southern Appalachia); Arkansas Review (seven-state Mississippi River Delta); Artist Trust (WA); Bay Area Book Reviewers Association Awards (Northern CA); Baybury Review (Midwest); Beacon (Southwestern Oregon); Bear Star Press (Western and Pacific states); Blackwater Press (UK); Blue Skunk Companion, The (MN); Blueline (Adirondacks); Borderlands (TX, Southwest); BP Nichol Chapbook Award (Canada); Briar Cliff Review, The (Midwest, Siouxland); Buffalo Bones (Western states); California Book Awards of The Commonwealth Club of California; Canadian Authors Association Literary Awards; Canadian Literature; Caribbean Writer, The; Cayo (Florida Keys); Cleveland State University Poetry Center (OH); Colorado Book Awards; Confluence Press (Northwestern US); Coolbrith Circle Annual Poetry Contest, Ina (CA); Coteau Books (Canada); Cottonwood (Midwest); Coyote Chronicles (Southwest); Creative Writing Fellowships in Poetry (AZ); Cycle Press (Florida Keys); Descant (Canada); Dolphin-Moon Press (MD); Driftwood Review, The (MI); Eastern Caribbean Institute; Fiddlehead, The (Atlantic Region); Fireweed: Poetry of Western Oregon; Floating Bridge Press (WA); Florida Individual Artist Fellowships; Glassco Translation Prize, John (Canada); Goose Lane Editions (Canada); Guernica Editions Inc. (Canada, US); Habersham Review (GA); Heartlands Today, The (Midwest); High Plains Press (WY, West); House of Anansi Press (Canada); HU (Ireland); Imago: New Writing (Queensland, Australia); In the Grove (CA, Central Valley); In 2 Print Magazine (Canada); Individual Artist Grants (TX, Houston, Harris County); Interpreter's House (UK); Javelina Press (Southwest US); Journal of New Jersey Poets; Kaimana (Pacific); Kelsey Review (Mercer County, NJ); Landfall (New Zealand); Leacock Medal for Humour, The Stephen (Canada); London Writers Competition; Long Island Quarterly; Lonzie's Fried Chicken® Literary Magazine (South); Loonfeather (MN); Louisiana Literature; Louisiana Review, The; Mid-America Press, Inc., The (AR, IA, IL, KS, MO, NE, OK); Middle East Report; Midwest Villages & Voices; Montalvo Biennial Poetry Competition (CA, NE, OR, WA); Montana Arts; (m)öthêr TØñgué Press (Canada); New Issues Press (US affiliation); New Rivers Press (MN); New York Foundation for the Arts; Ninety-Six Press (Greenville, SC); North Carolina Literary Review; Northeast Corridor; Northwords (Northern Scotland); Now & Then (Appalachia); Ohioana Book Awards; On Spec (Canada); Ornish Poetry Award, Natalie (TX); "Over The Back Fence" Magazine (OH); Paterson Literary Review, The; Pelican Publishing Company (LA); PEN Center USA West Literary Award in Poetry; Permafrost (AK); Pew Fellowship In The Arts (PA); Pine Island Journal of New England Poetry; Poetry Harbor (Upper Midwest); Poetry Ireland Review; Poets' Dinner Contest (CA); Potomac Review (MD); Prairie Journal, The (Canada); Prairie Publishing Company, The (Canada); Presidio La Bahia Award (TX); Puckerbrush Press, The (ME); Puerto Del Sol (Southwest); QSPELL Literary Awards (Quebec, Canada); Queen's Quarterly (Canada); Review (Latin America); Revista/Review Interamericana (Caribbean, Latin America, Puerto Rico); Roanoke-Chowan Poetry Award (NC); Ronsdale Press (Canada); Rossley Literary Awards, Bruce P. (New England); San Francisco Foundation (CA, NV); Seven Buffaloes Press; Southern Indiana Review; Southwestern American Literature; Spoon River Poetry Review, The (IL); Storyboard (Pacific Region); Superior Poetry News; Thistledown Press Ltd. (Canada); Towson University Prize for Literature (MD); Trestle Creek Review (innermountain West); Turnstone Press Limited (Canada); Upsouth (South); Vehicule Press (Canada); Victorian Fellowship of Australian Writers, The; Weatherford Award, The W.D. (Appalachian South); West Coast Line (Canada); Western Archipelago Review (Asia, Pacific); Western Producer Publications (Western Canada); WFNB Annual Literary Contest (New Brunswick, Canada); Wisconsin Academy Review; Wisconsin Arts Board Fellowships; Woodley Memorial Press (KS); Worcester Review (New England); Writers' Center Press (IN); Yorkshire Journal

Religious: About Such Things; Alive Now; Ancient Paths; Angel News Magazine; Bible Advocate; Bread of Life Magazine, The; Brilliant Star; Christian Century, The; Christianity and the Arts; Clubhouse Jr.; Commonweal; Cornerstone; Cross & Quill; European Judaism; Evangel; Expedition Press; Feather Books; Gospel Publishing House; Herald Press; Image: A Journal of Arts & Religion; Jewish Currents; Jewish Spectator; Literature and Belief; Lutheran Digest, The; Mature Years; Mennonite, The; Milton Center Poetry Fellowship; Milton Magazine, John; Miraculous Medal, The; Nazarene International Headquarters; New Era Magazine; Oblates; Open University of America Press; Other Side Magazine, The; Our Family; Outreach; Perspectives; Prayerworks; Presbyterian Record, The; Queen of All Hearts; Sacred Journey; St. Anthony Messenger; St. Joseph Messenger and Advocate of the Blind; Sharing Magazine; Shofar; Silver Wings/Mayflower Pulpit; Society of American Poets (SOAP), The; Sojourners; Straight; Student Leadership Journal; Studio; Time of Singing; Touch; Upsouth; Urthona Magazine; War Cry, The; Windhover

Science Fiction/Fantasy: Aboriginal SF; Adaptables Annual Poetry Award; BadLands Press; Companion in Zeor, A; Dagger of the Mind; Dark Regions; Draigeye; Gotta Write Network Litmag; Handshake; Hilltop Press; Jupiter's Freedom; Koshkovich Press; Leading Edge, The; Magazine of Speculative Poetry, The; Mkashef Enterprises; Mythic Circle, The; Oak, The; Ocean View Books; Of Unicorns and Space Stations; On Spec; Outer Darkness; Pablo Lennis; Pigasus Press; Pirate Writings; Poetry of the People; Poet's Fantasy; Scavenger's Newsletter; Science Fiction Poetry Association; Silver Web, The; Struggle; Suzerain Enterprises; Ultimate Unknown, The; Urbanite, The; Wise Woman's Garden, A; Works Magazine

Senior Citizen: Capper's; Chicory Blue Press; Mature Years; Oak, The; Outreach; Passager; Senior Poet Laureate Poetry Competition; Wise Woman's Garden, A

Social Issues: Afterthoughts; Aguilar Expression, The; Aim Magazine; Black Bear Publications; Blue Collar Review; Carolina Wren Press; Christian Century, The; Collages & Bricolages; Haight Ashbury Literary Journal; Left Curve; Northern Centinel, The; Other Side Magazine, The; Our Family; Pudding House Publications; Skipping Stones; South 666 Bitch, The; Struggle; Wise Woman's Garden, A

Specialized: Adaptables Annual Poetry Award (poets with disabilities); Anna's Journal (childlessness issues); Barking Dog Books (expatriate life and travel in Baja, Mexico and Gen'ly); Beacon Street Review (graduate-level writers); Blindskills, Inc. (blind or visually impaired); Blue Mountain Arts, Inc. (greeting cards); Boardman Tasker Award, The (mountain literature); Brilliant Corners (jazz-related literature); CC Motorcycle News Magazine; Classical Outlook, The (classics, Latin); Cleaning Business Magazine; Communities (intentional community living); Community of Poets Press (community and organizational focus); Dissident Editions (non-anecdotal, dissident, metaphysical verse); Dream International Quarterly; Dry Bones Press (nursing); Ekphrasis (ekphrastic verse); Endemoniada Fanzine (left-hand path/satanic/occult); Equilibrium [10]; Exit 13 (geography/travel); 4*9*1 Neo-Immanentist*Imagination (neo-immanentist/sursymbolist); Futurific (optimistic poems of the future); Golden Isis Magazine (pagan/wiccan); Halls Fellowship, J.C. and Ruth (MFA or equivalent degree in creative writing); Harvard Advocate, The (university affiliation); Heist Magazine (men); Herb Network, The (men); Inner Voices (prisoners); Innovative Publishing Concepts (overcoming adversity); Insects Are People Two; Japan Foundation Artist Fellowship Program, The (US residents with Japanese affiliations); Japanese Literary Translation Prize; Journal of African Travel-Writing; Kaleidoscope (disability themes); Mail Call Journal (American Civil War); Midwifery Today (childbirth); Milton Magazine, John (visual impairment); Minority Literary Expo; Musing Place, The (poets with a history of mental illness); Naturally (family nudism and naturism); Northern Centinel, The; O!!Zone (visual poetry, photography, collage); Ohio Teachers Write; Open University of America Press (distance learning, English pedagogy); Our Family (family/marriage/parenting); Our Journey (recovery issues); Outreach (disabled); Peoplenet Disability Datenet; Pep Publishing ("ethical multiple relationships"); Pipe Smoker's Ephemeris, The; Poet's Energy, The (metaphysical, New Age, holistic perspective); Psychopoetica; Slate & Style (blind writers); Sounds of a Grey Metal Day (prisoners); Spring (e.e. cummings society); Stevens Journal, The Wallace; Transcendent Visions (psychiatric survivors, ex-mental patients); Urthona Magazine (Buddhism); Vegetarian Journal; Visiting Fellowships for Historical Research (American history and cultural); Vista Publishing, Inc. (nurses); Voices From the Well (open mic/spoken word performers in Twin Cities area); Welcome Home (mothers, parenting, families, children); Western Heritage Awards; Xcp: Cross-Cultural Poetics (anthropology)

Spirituality/Inspirational: Adobe Abalone; Alive Now; Angel News Magazine; Avocet; Capper's; Chrysalis Reader; Heaven Bone Magazine; Lutheran Digest, The; New Song, A; Oak, The; Oblates; Our Family; Penwood Review, The; Presbyterian Record, The; Ruah; Science of Mind; Silver Wings/Mayflower Pulpit; Sisters Today; SMILE; Studio; Superior Poetry News; Wise Woman's Garden, A

Sports/Recreation: Aethlon; Bugle, Journal of Elk and the Hunt; CC Motorcycle News Magazine; Climbing Art, The; Journal of Asian Martial Arts; Spitball

Students: Allegheny Review; Analecta; Arts Recognition and Talent Search; Bucknell Seminar for Younger Poets; Common Threads; Fiddlehead, The; Hanging Loose Press; Hemans Prize for Lyrical Poetry, Felicia; Intro; League of Minnesota Poets Contest, The; Merlyn's Pen; Modern Haiku; National Written & Illustrated By . . . Awards Contest for Students, The; Night Roses; Offerings; Pennsylvania Poetry Society Annual Contest; Seaman Poetry Award, Claudia Ann; Student Leadership Journal

Themes: Alive Now; Blue Mesa Review; Chronicles of Disorder; Chrysalis Reader; Collages & Bricolages; Columbia; Cosmic Trend; Crab Creek Review; Creative With Words Publications (C.W.W.); Crumb Elbow Publishing Poetry Contests; Curriculum Vitae Literary Supplement; Earth's Daughters; Event; Gleeful Press!, A; Green River Writers' Contests; Haight Ashbury Literary Journal; Heartlands Today, The; Jewish Currents; Journal of the American Medical Association (JAMA); Kaleidoscope; Kalliope; Middle East Report; Now & Then; Our Family; Paintbrush; Palo Alto Review; Pannus Index, The; Papier-Mache Press; Partisan Review; Passager; Pig Iron; Poetic Realm; Poetry of the People; Poetry Salzburg; Prairie Journal, The; Rosebud; Sensations Magazine; Skylark; Slipstream; South Carolina Review; Thema; Time of Singing; Touch; Urbanite, The; Vol. No. Magazine; Waterways

Translations: Abiko Annual With James Joyce FW Studies; Artful Dodge; Barbarian Press; Birmingham Poetry Review; Black Buzzard Press; Blue Unicorn; Borderlands; Carolina Quarterly, The; Chelsea; Chicago Review; Classical Outlook, The; Collages & Bricolages; Cross-Cultural Communications; Cumberland Poetry Review; Denver Quarterly; Dirigible; Dwan; Eagle's Flight; Field; Formalist, The; Frank; Frogpond; G.W. Review; Glassco Translation Prize, John; Green Mountains Review; Guernica Editions Inc.; Hunger Magazine; International Poetry Review; International Quarterly; Intertext; Iris: A Journal About Women; Japanese Literary Translation Prize; Johann-Heinrich-Voss Prize for Translation; Journal of African Travel-Writing; Journal of Contemporary Anglo-Scandinavian Poetry; Kalliope; Lactuca; Luz en Arte y Literatura; Making Waves; Mandrake Poetry Review; Manhattan Review, The; Mid-American Review; Modern Poetry In Translation; New Laurel Review, The; New Native Press; New Renaissance, The; New Rivers Press; New Yorker, The; Ornish Poetry Award, Natalie; Osiris; Paintbrush; Partisan Review; Passeggiata Press; Poetry New York; Post-Apollo Press, The; Princeton University Press; Puerto Del Sol; Quarterly Review of Literature Poetry Book Series; Quarterly West; Renditions; Review; Rhino; Sachem Press; Seneca Review; Spoon River Poetry Review, The; Superior Poetry News; Tampa Review; Touchstone Literary Journal; Whole Notes; Willow Springs

Women/Feminism: Alice James Books; Amy Award, The; Calyx; Canadian Woman Studies; Carolina Wren Press; Chicory Blue Press; Collages & Bricolages; Country Woman; Earth's Daughters; Écrits des Forges; Eidos Magazine; Eighth Mountain Press, The; Feminist Studies; Feminist Voices; Firebrand Books; Fireweed: A Feminist Quarterly; Hurricane Alice; Implosion Press; Innovative Publishing Concepts; Iris: A Journal About Women; Javelina Press; Jewish Women's Literary Annual; Kalliope; Lilith Magazine; Matriarch's Way; Mature Women's Grants; Money For Women; Night Roses; Other Press; Outrider Press; Papier-Mache Press; Pearson Award, Judith Siegel; Perugia Press; Phoebe (NY); Post-Apollo Press, The; Primavera; Radiance; Room of One's Own; Sing Heavenly Muse!; So To Speak; Still Waters Press; Struggle; 13th Moon; True Romance; Wise Woman's Garden, A; Wishing Well, The; Womenwise; Writing For Our Lives

Writing: Byline Magazine; Canadian Writer's Journal; New Writer's Magazine; Paintbrush; Prosetry; Scavenger's Newsletter; Writer's Digest; Writer's Guidelines & News Magazine; Writing on the Edge

General Index

Markets and resources that appeared in the *1999 Poet's Market* but do not appear in this edition are identified by two-letter codes in parentheses explaining why these entries no longer appear.

The codes are: **(ED)—Editorial Decision; (NR)—No (or late) Response** to Requests for Updated Information; **(NS)—Not Accepting Submissions** (which include publishers who are overstocked as well as those who no longer publish poetry); **(OB)—Out of Business** (or, in the case of contests, cancelled); **(RR)—Removed by Request** (no reason given); and **(UF)— Uncertain Future** (which includes publishers who have suspended publication or are reorganizing their operation).

A

A.L.I. (The Avon Literary Intelligencer) (OB)
A Small Garlic Press (ASGP) 19
Aabye's Baby (see Aabye)
A&C Limerick Prizes, The (see Amelia)
Aardvark Adventurer, The 20
Abbey 20
Abbey Cheapochapbooks (see Abbey)
Abiko Annual with James Joyce FW Studies 20
Aboriginal SF 21
About Such Things 21
Above the Bridge Magazine 21
Abraxas Magazine 22
Abstract Concrete, The (see Concrete Abstract)
Abundance 22
Abundance Press (see Abundance)
Academi-YR Academi Gymreig/ The Welsh Academy 527
Academy of American Poets, The 528
ACM (Another Chicago Magazine) 23
Acorn Poetry Award, Milton (NR)
Acorn Prize for Poetry, Milton (see Poetry Forever)
Acorn, The 23
Acorn, The (see The Oak)
Acorn Whistle 24
Acorn Whistle Press (see Acorn Whistle)
Acorn-Rukeyser Chapbook Contest, The (see Mekler & Deahl Publishers)
Acropolis Books, Inc. (NS)
Acumen Magazine 24
Adaptables Annual Poetry Award 480
Adastra Press 24
Adirondack Lakes Center for the Arts 528

Adobe Abalone 25
Adrift 25
Advocate, PKA's Publication 25
Aegina Press, Inc. (OB)
Aethlon 26
Affair of the Mind 26
African American Review (RR)
African Voices 26
Afro-Hispanic Review 26
After Hours Club Magazine 26
AgD (see A Small Garlic Press)
AGNI 27
Agnieszka's Dowry (AgD) (see A Small Garlic Press)
Aguilar Expression, The 27
AHA Books (see Lynx)
Ahsahta Press 28
Aim Magazine 28
Air Canada Award, The (see Canadian Authors Association Awards for Adult Literature)
Akron Poetry Prize 480
Akros Publications 29
Alabama Literary Review 29
Alabama State Council on the Arts 505
Alabama State Poetry Society 528
Alaska Quarterly Review 29
Alaska State Council on the Arts 505
Albatross 29
Alberta Foundation for the Arts 507
Alden Enterprises 30
Aldine Press, Ltd., The (see Hellas)
Alembic 30
Alembic Annual Poetry Contest (see Alembic)
Alice James Books 31
Alive Now 31
Allegheny Review 32
Alligator Juniper 32
Allison Press 32
Alms House Journal, The (see Alms House Press)
Alms House Press 33

Aloha (OB)
Along the Path (NS)
Alpha Beat Press (see Alpha Beat Soup)
Alpha Beat Soup 33
Alsop Review, The (see Octavo)
Amaranth 33
Amaranth Quarterly (RR)
Ambit (NR)
Amelia 34
Amelia Awards, The (see Amelia)
Amelia Chapbook Award, The (see Amelia)
America 35
American Atheist Press (NR)
American Book Series (see La Jolla Poet's Press)
American Christian Writers Conferences 510
American Cowboy Poet Magazine, The 35
American Dissident, The 35
American Haibun & Haiga (see Red Moon Press)
American Indian Culture and Research Journal (see American Indian Studies Center)
American Indian Studies Center 36
American Literary Review 36
American Poetry Monthly (NR)
American Poetry Review 36
American Poets & Poetry 36
American Scholar, The 37
American Tanka 37
American Tolkien Society (NR)
American Voice, The 37
American Writing 37
Amethyst Review, The 38
Amherst Review, The 38
Amicus Journal, The 38
Amy Award, The 480
Anabiosis Press, The (see Albatross)
Anaconda Press 38
Analecta 39

GENERAL INDEX

GENERAL INDEX

Harmona Press (see The Raintown Review)
Harp-Strings Poetry Journal (NR)
Harpweaver, The 179
Hart Crane Award (see Icon)
Harvard Advocate, The 179
Hathaway Prize, Baxter (see Epoch)
Haunts (NR)
Hawaii Literary Arts Council (see Kaimana)
Hawaii Pacific Review 179
Hawai'i Review 180
Hawaii State Foundation on Culture & Arts 505
Hawley Award, Beatrice (see Alice James Books)
Hayden's Ferry Review 180
Haypenny Press 180
Haystack Writing Program 514
HB Children's Books (see Harcourt, Inc.)
HCE Publications (NR)
Headwaters Literary Competition (see New Rivers Press)
Healing Woman, The (NR)
Healthy Body-Healthy Minds (see Poetry Forum)
Heartland Writers Conference 515
Heartlands Today, The 180
Heaven Bone Magazine 180
Heaven Bone Press (see Heaven Bone Magazine)
Heaven Bone Press International Chapbook Competition (see Heaven Bone Magazine)
Heights Writer's Conference, The 515
Heist Magazine 181
Helicon Nine Editions (NR)
Helikon Press 181
Heliotrope 181
Hellas 181
Hellas Award, The (see Hellas)
HELLP! 182
HELLP! Press (see HELLP!)
Hemans Prize for Lyrical Poetry, Felicia 489
Hemingway Poetry Competition, Ernest 489
Henderson Haiku Award Contest, The Harold G. (see Frogpond)
Herald Press 182
Herb Network, The 183
Heron Quarterly (NR)
Hey, Listen! 183
Hidden Brook Press (see Seeds Poetry Magazine)
Higginsville Reader, The 183
Higginsville Writers, The (see The Higginsville Reader)
High Plains Literary Review (NR)
High Plains Press 184
Highcliff Press (OB)
High/Coo Press 184

Highlights for Children 184
Hill and Holler Anthology Series (see Seven Buffaloes Press)
Hilltop Press 185
Hines Narrative Poetry Award, The Grace (see Amelia)
Hinterland Award for Poetry (see Backwater Review)
Hippopotamus Press 185
Hiram Poetry Review 185
Hobear Publications (see Arctos Press)
Hobo Poetry & Haiku Magazine 185
Hobo Publishers, Inc. (see Hobo Poetry & Haiku Magazine)
Hodder Fellowship, The 489
Hodge Podge Poetry (see The TMP Irregular)
Hodge Podge Press (see The TMP Irregular)
Hodgepodge Short Stories & Poetry 186
Hoepfner Award, Theodore Christian (see Southern Humanities Review)
Hofstra University Summer Writers' Conference (NR)
Hokin Prize, Bess (see Poetry)
Holiday House, Inc. 186
Holiness Today (see Nazarene International Headquarters)
Hollins Critic, The 186
Home Times 186
Honest Ulsterman (see HU)
Hopscotch 187
Horizon 187
Horizontes (see The Paterson Literary Review)
Houghton Mifflin Co. 187
House of Anansi Press 187
Howard and Barbara M.J. Wood Prize, J. (see Poetry)
Howard Poetry Prize, Quentin R. 489
Hoyns Fellowships, Henry 489
HQ Poetry Magazine (The Haiku Quarterly) 188
HU (Honest Ulsterman) 188
Hubbub 188
Hudson Review, The 189
Hugo Memorial Poetry Award, The Richard (see Cutbank)
Hull Poetry Award, Lynda (see Denver Quarterly)
Human Quest, The 189
Hunger Magazine 189
Hunger Press (see Hunger Magazine)
Hunted News, The 189
Huntsville Literary Association (see Poem)
Hurricane Alice 190

I

IBIS Review (RR)
Icon 190
Iconoclast, The 190
Idaho Commission on the Arts 505
Iddings, Kathleen, Insider Report Interview 390
Ideals Magazine 190
Ideals Publications Inc. (see Ideals Magazine)
Idiom 23 (NR)
Idiot, The 190
Illinois Arts Council 505
Illinois State Poetry Society (NR)
Illuminations 191
Illya's Honey (NR)
Image 191
Imagination (NR)
Imago 191
Impetus (see Implosion Press)
Implosion Press 192
Imprimatur Press (see Simple Vows)
Improvijazzation Nation 192
imps in the inkwell (see A Gleeful Press!)
Impulse Magazine, The (OB)
In His Steps Publishing Company (see The Society of American Poets)
In the Family 192
In the Grove 193
In the Spirit of the Buffalo 193
In 2 Print Magzine 193
Inc and the Arts (NR)
Independence Boulevard (see Main Street Rag Poetry Journal)
Independent Press, The (see Lochs Magazine)
Independent Publisher 546
Independent Publisher Book Awards (see Independent Publisher)
Independent Publishing Co. (see Writer's Guidelines & News Magazine)
Indian Heritage Council Quarterly (see Indian Heritage Publishing)
Indian Heritage Publishing 194
Indiana Arts Commission 505
Indiana Poet (see Indiana State Federation of Poetry Clubs)
Indiana Review 194
Indiana State Federation of Poetry Clubs 533
Indiana University Writers' Conference 515
Indigenous Fiction 194
Individual Artist Grants 489
Inez, Colette, Insider Report Interview 412
Infinate Hiway (see Buddha Eyes)
Inklings 195
Inkslinger 195

GENERAL INDEX